ALICE NIELSEN AND THE GAYETY OF NATIONS

Alice Nielsen in her 20s

ALICE NIELSEN AND THE GAYETY OF NATIONS

Biography by
► **DALL WILSON** ◄

2023 Edition. Revised.
Copyright © 2001-2023 by Dall Wilson. All rights reserved.
Music videos of Alice Nielsen and co-stars at
http://youtube.com/@dallwilson
Restored Alice Nielsen recordings from Dall Wilson available from
amazon.com and other vendors.
For a multimedia presentation on Alice Nielsen's career, for any
questions, suggestions, corrections, contributions, remarks:
contact author: dallwilson@yahoo.com

ISBN: 978-0-557-47367-0
LIBRARY OF CONGRESS CONTROL NUMBER: 2010907225

Arts by Dall Wilson:
> **The Symphonic Films:**
>> Grand Canyon & Back
>> Alaska & Back
>> Czech: Prague Bohemia Moravia & Back
>> Raleigh After Rain
>
> *32 Songs 32 Days*
> *The Love Songs:* art songs and opers.
> *Aliss Afire! When Aliss Laughs at Love What Happens Next?*
>> Musical theatre based on the Alice Nielsen story.

PROGRAM

1.—(a) The Spirit Flower ....Campbell-Tipton
   (b) The Weathercock...........Liza Lehmann
   (c) Down in the Forest ....Landon Ronald
   (d) My Lover he Comes on the Skee
                      Clough Leighter

2.—(a) Si mes vers avaient des ailes .Renaldo Hahn
   (b) Pourquoi rester seulette........Saint Saens
   (c) Mandoline ....Claude Debussy
   (d) Ouvre tes yeux bleus........Jules Massenet

3.—(a) Vergebliches Standchen ....Brahms
   (b) Haiden Roslein.................Schubert
   (c) Volksliedchen.................Schumann
   (d) Komm lass uns spielen ....Bleichmann

4.—(a) At Parting................James Rogers
   (b) The Low-Back'd Car.........Samuel Lover
   (c) The Fairy Pipers.............John Brewer
   (d) An Open Secret .....Huntington Woodman

5.—Aria—Un bel di ....Giacomo Puccini
      (From Madam Butterfly)

Alice Nielsen in concert gown with touring program

CONTENTS

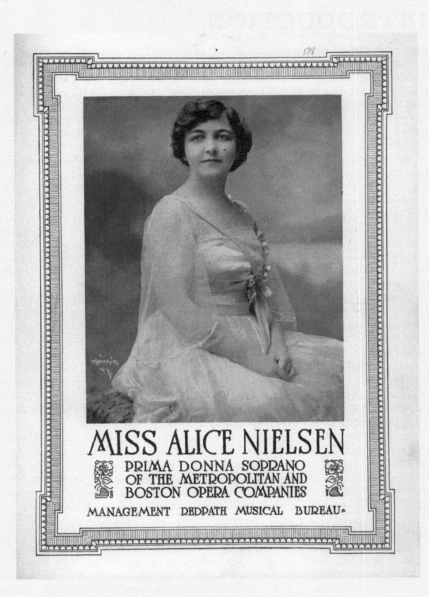

MISS ALICE NIELSEN
PRIMA DONNA SOPRANO
OF THE METROPOLITAN AND
BOSTON OPERA COMPANIES

MANAGEMENT REDPATH MUSICAL BUREAU

INTRODUCTION

Alice Nielsen, American icon of artistic integrity, fascinated countless audiences giving gayety to nations during the golden age of live theatre. In Jefferson's century of no taxes, gold and silver money, small government, few rules, the sovereign citizens left at liberty to live and let live. Theatre was the only night sport, a huge industry, taking all the passion given pro sports today. During days, horseracing. America was a talent hunt; stars began careers as kids when worldly experience is the kingmaker, never spending long years kept as captives in drear cubical classrooms.

Born in Nashville to a Danish troubadour dad and Irish musician mom, barefoot child Alice Nielsen roams 1880s Kansas City streets singing songs learned from home or absorbed from touring shows. She may have spent a few days in a schoolhouse. By sixteen she had sung at the White House and toured a summer season in a professional company.

Popular as skilled church soloist, Alice joins local musicals. Marrying her church organist who beat her unconscious while eight months pregnant, she had their baby then boldly set out on vaudeville's yellow brick road. Despite a frigid 1891 Missouri winter, Alice and colorful pals sing and dance to that magic city in the clouds, San Francisco.

Young virtuoso trombonist Arthur Pryor postpones his Sousa career to join Alice as they tour with Burton Stanley (famed for diva roles in drag) to Salt Lake and San Francisco where Alice Nielsen becomes a St. Patrick's soloist and stars at the vaudeville Wigwam on Union Square. Sends fare to siblings and mom who kidnap th ebaby and reunite.

Alice lucks into just-retired international *bel canto* star Ida Valerga who places her protégé in the Tivoli Opera Company for about ten dozen repertory roles in less than two years. In scarlet tights as Balfe's *Satanella* Alice becomes a San Francisco star. Valerga imparts grand opera roles and arranges Alice's Tivoli debut as Lucia.

At that moment in fall 1895, Alice meets the wonderful wizard of music theatre, Henry Clay Barnabee of "The Famous Original Bostonians" touring in original and repertory shows. Alice debuts in NYC with their *Robin Hood*. Their 1896 Victor Herbert show *The Serenade* makes Alice Nielsen famous across the nation. Two years later, Alice Nielsen Company breaks all the box office records. Recognized as a genius at her craft.

Boston author of 1900's *Famous Prima Donnas*, Louis Strang selects Alice Nielsen "the leading woman star in light opera on the American stage ...who sings as if singing were the best fun in the world; who is so frankly happy when her audience likes her work and applauds her; and who goes soaring up and away on the high notes, sounding clear and pure above chorus and orchestra.... To appear perfectly natural on the stage is the best possible acting, and that is what Alice Nielsen does".

By 1900 Alice has become Americana. Fascinating audiences with magnetic, virtuoso fun, she gaily brings a glory voice to acting, dance and comedy to guarantee hit shows. Her hits are bespoke new shows scored by Victor Herbert. *Fortune Teller* and *Singing Girl* sell out across North America, even during a Chicago blizzard. Theatre critics speculate the super-group Alice Nielsen Company is divinely destined to originate "the great American musical". In 1901 famed Alice Nielsen Company jumps to London and disbands. Corruption conspired by producer and manager kills the project. Yet she is the talk of town.

Double-crossed in musicals, Alice Nielsen has made influential London pals who help her rapidly crossover to opera. Within weeks she auditions for Covent Garden, absorbs French repertory from Pablo Tosti, and reaches Italy to join Enrico Bevignani, vocal coach to the stars Adelina Patti, Christina Nilsson. Rapidly mastering an Italian repertoire "Aliss" Nielsen debuts in Naples. There Henry Higgins, who had sent his sister to spy, casts Nielsen for a 1904 Covent debut in a spring season of Mozart to great success. That fall she returns with Naples' San Carlo Opera for a season of Italian opera with Caruso and Scotti. London critics call their *La Bohème* an ensemble masterpiece. The press back home proclaim, "We love our Nielsen, proud she is an American". Nielsen's intelligently sincere acting, vocal skill, and artistic integrity are praised.

In 1905 after creating a London summer season of drama-and-opera with actress Eleonora Duse, Emma Calvé, and Basque tenor Constantino, Alice Nielsen is lured to NYC by deceitful Florenz Ziegfeld and Lee Shubert. Performing over sabotage meant to shackle her to lucrative Broadway hits, Nielsen meets mixed reviews in NYC. As she tours west, her sparse concert version of *Don Pasquale* steadily gains praise in Chicago, San Francisco, Los Angeles, Dallas, and New Orleans. Sponsors step up for a return. New Orleans will grubstake Alice Nielsen to bring a full grand opera company for the winter. In Jacksonville, she combines forces with famed diva Lillian Nordic. The company (mostly Spanish) is fancifully mislabeled "San Carlo Opera Company". By any name, the Nielsen-Nordica venture created "a fad for grand opera" across North America. Newspaper critics regard the result superior to The Metropolitan Opera tour.

Los Angeles critics, hailing Alice Nielsen's success in the West, declare artistic independence from NYC, "one day we will create our own shows".

Her skill and endurance to sing complex Herbert scores eight times weekly carries over to grand opera. In Chicago, Alice sings two Puccini operas same day. In Boston, nine operas in seven days create a sensation beyond ovations when arts patrons Isabella Gardner and Eben Jordan Jr. initiate the project of Boston Opera House. Jordan reuses his Symphony Hall team to fast-track the construction. Deal done, the Nielsen sisters Alice and Hortense will scour Europe to select scenery, costumes, talent. Alice brings Loie Fuller then Josef Urban into Boston as designers. When arrives her 1909 opening night, Boston critics proclaim Alice Nielsen at last has a stage worthy of her art. She joins the Met the same year.

Manager corruption shortens her success a second time. Termed the Titanic tragedy of American music, this great gift to gayety, the grand palace of Boston lyric culture will be lost by 1917 and demolished in 1970s. Boston Opera House was built entirely by private subscriptions and donors. Beyond the mistake of appointing a manager without Boston roots who loots and leaves as predicted, the tragic loss of Nordica during a 1914 Australian tour, the new US Income Tax, the connived European war, are factors. Entire opera companies vanish into trenches to be obliterated by machine guns, shells, and poison gas. Grand opera tragedy.

If Boston Opera House had endured, Alice Nielsen would be cherished lifelong, never falling into obscurity. This biography corrects subsequent sagas replicating the errors of 1965's *Boston Opera* by ditsy Quaintance Eaton. Reckless Eaton plagiarized by the page; daughter of the disgraced absconding manager was a co-writer. Joan Sutherland spoke truer than she knew of another Eaton effort, "Quaintance's book is dicey". Eaton mindlessly echoes phrases lifted by producer Michael Leavitt in 1912 from the bad guy's press agent: Yes, "Boston Opera House is the centre of the movement which promises to make opera part of the common life of the American people". No, the bad guy who killed it wasn't "responsible for its success" nor "capable of projecting, organizing and putting into execution the scheme...." We will dispel the fogs.

When the titanic Boston Opera tragedy iced her operatic voyage Nielsen was crossing soprano categories, as Bevignani had coached Nilsson. Alice's chance to sing Wagner sank with her mainstage. Blocked by rival divas from Met and Covent, the golden goose Alice Nielsen led sold-out concerts at Carnegie Hall and toured America with art songs, arias, and encores of the popular parlor and Celtic songs she learned from mom who learned from grandma. Art songs in four languages kept audiences spellbound; voice and piano. The touring Chautauqua Festival Week closed with "Alice Nielsen Day". Iconic Alice; her career vindicated the American dream: success by talent, integrity, hard work, genius.

Perhaps the first Broadway cast recording was Alice Nielsen's 1898 *The Fortune Teller*. With Boston Opera she made over sixty recordings 1909-10. Never film, rarely radio. Big hit record *Home, Sweet Home*, that 1823 aria quoted by Dorothy in *Wizard of Oz* whose author Frank Baum was a music theatre veteran and fan. Alice's wintery adventure along the vaudeville road to San Francisco with a few friends was a tale to behold.

Alice Nielsen had a very devoted family—never a devoted husband. The petite pretty singer stood five-foot-three, 102 pounds. Career spans 1890s to 1920s. In 1917, after revisiting Broadway briefly for Belasco, Nielsen marries a plastic surgeon from an artistic NY family and moves to Bedford, NY. Touring dwindles. After a dozen years her marriage is betrayed.

By 1930, divorced Alice Nielsen resides cattycorner from Carnegie Hall at the Osborn, enjoying NYC cultural life, her Maine cottage, her siblings, kid and offspring. About 1940 she packs costumes off to new-founded Kansas City Museum. A few years later the star is called away.

Rapidly her impact obscures. Friendships with famed talents fade. Loss of Boston Opera blocked Alice Nielsen from becoming a cherished living legend honored by galas; loss of Nordica removed her strongest ally. The gayety of nations has been erased from reality by a corrupt 20th Century of connived wars. As many people would suffer.

When Alice Nielsen became lost to us the best of our past went missing. By coincidence the author rediscovered her. Before Victor Herbert died in 1924, told agent Jacoby that his "best score had the worst words". Eighty years later I met the agent to ask about my singing granddad's favorite composer. Herbert's demand "throw away the words" reached my ears.

Crazily I took it up. After all, he had been Chaplin's agent too. In NYC and Reykjavik this crazy congealed as the musical *Aliss Afire*. Bespoke score composed for Alice Nielsen Company spoke to me with a story needs telling. An 1898 Deluxe Souvenir Program inspired with intriguing photos; Alice's tale of an out-of-body experience on opening night starts the new show. Now with meaning. And laugh at love—what happens next?

This biography demanded doing too. Nielsen's candid yet coy memoirs in a defunct 1930s magazine proved a keen music memory, little else. Boston Opera dismissed in a phrase. A trove to discover awaited. Wrongs to right. Truth to speak freely. Fog to dispel. Clarity to deliver.

Rare eras make rare life. Her arts drew many people into unforgettable happiness. She made things happen.

Alice Nielsen created the gayety of nations.

As to get the Cape Hatteras Lighthouse moved, my much labor was fun.

This biography has evolved. Expanded, corrected, condensed, revised; made better. *Mu Phi Epsilon* published my first Nielsen article, sponsored first talk. Met her family; met relatives of her costars and patrons.

Today I better appreciate Alice's alliances: Ida Valerga, Duse, Calvé, Nordica, Loie Fuller, Isadora Duncan, Pavlova. And recognize the family: her son joins stage designer Josef Urban; sister Hortense joins Modjeska before touring in her own Ibsen company; brother Erasmus in Far Rockaway the organist and pianist for musical theatre.

Cherish Alice Nielsen as a great performer with a glory voice who lived for her arts. Magnetized audiences with fire and joy, beauty, fashions, witty virtuoso fun. Unified popular, folk and high art. In the golden age of live performance, she was the star. And to sing gives meaning to the universe.

So it was. Paraphrasing *NY Times'* review of her Broadway debut, we must give praise and thanksgiving for Alice Nielsen who gave gayety to nations; the glorious phrase of delight for creating our shared artistic culture coined by Samuel Johnson at the 1779 passing of theatre legend David Garrick.

Let us entertain you.

BEFORE

Born in Nashville, bred in Missouri, Alice Nielsen inherits the great performance traditions of Ireland and Denmark. Her Danish dad dies before she is ten, mother never remarries. Alice and siblings stay Irish Catholic, not Scandinavian Mormon. Erasmus Nielsen and Sarah Kilroy met in the Midwest after daunting journeys to America by their parents.

From Århus, Denmark, the Nielsen family sailed into 1854 America among many Mormon Scandinavians set for Utah. Abolitionist views of founder Joseph Smith drew violent persecution by plantation terrorists from slavery states such as Missouri; religious intolerance added troubles. Teenager Rasmus arrived in New Orleans for the terrible trek up the Mississippi where cholera took its toll.

From Donegal, Ireland, the Kilroys had sailed to 1840s Boston to escape the Potato Famine killing twelve-percent of inhabitants as two-million fled. Alice knew grandmother was exiled to Tasmania for the wearing of a patriotic green petticoat. Mom Sarah, when the Kilroys docked, was age two, they swiftly transposed the toddler's birthplace as Boston to save trouble.

To glean Alice Nielsen's outlook (as revealed in 1932 *Colliers'* magazine memoir *Born To Sing* fully incorporated herein) we must read between the lines. As a master musician, Nielsen speaks eloquently with silence. Consider her NYC gravestone: no dates, just "Alice Nielsen" carved granite.

What she skips and what tells reveal her true insight: "I was born to sing". Life's choices were directed that way. She repeatedly skips riches and relations of cozy comfort. Alice lived her art's true expression. She sang songs she wished to sing.

An unaffected, gregarious, natural storyteller, Nielsen talks well and writes well. Other divas of the day made worse memoirs. Very few, say her Southern predecessor Clara Kellogg, produced better. Of course, Nielsen leaves fuzzy areas and pulls punches. In a life rich with fans, friends, triumph, tragedy, rivals, and betrayers, she selects to spend her memoir moments with friends. Skips conflicts. Especially skips any mention of men troubles. Among women, Nielsen would only criticize a troublesome Kansas City thorn forty years after. She does make many inside jokes for theatre pals to enjoy, clever woman.

Parents were happy, musical people. Mom a lifelong helper, dad dies when she is eight. Love between parents is keenly felt by the close-knit quintet kids who sing and play and go pro. Among four girls, says Alice, "I had the voice". Look-alike Nielsen siblings replicate mom. Alice sports dad's fair hair and blue eyes, sister Hortense mom's darker features.

Telling her parents' origins, Alice Nielsen dodges controversy. How she handles family secrets reveals her method of hints. Revealing dad's Danish birthplace as Århus, she skips Mormon connections and arduous journey over to Indiana and Sarah Kilroy for the classic Viking-Celt marriage.

Glance at less-controversial Sarah before Rasmus. Sarah, says sly Alice, was born in Boston of Irish parents "in the house where General Warren of Revolutionary renown was shot". Her claim seems plausible until we take her hint. Warren (1741-1775) was not shot in a house, but murdered across town at Bunker Hill. Known for fiery speeches on "the baleful influence of standing armies in times of peace", Warren had sent Paul Revere on his famed ride. Recognized and shot, Warren was thrown into a common grave. Paul Revere identified the dental work. By 1930s, recalls Alice, Warren House had "passed through all the fires and frosts of fortune. Now, rescued by patriots, it has become a museum which you must pay to inspect".

Alice's grandparents had arrived as Roxbury's Irish newcomers builded St. Patrick's Church, gorgeous 1840s monument to woodcraft with superb pipe organ. Only a historical plaque marks the Warren House on Warren Street at Elliot Square. Socialites spirited Warren's statue to Bunker Hill.

And Nielsen knew Boston far too well for error. She had opened there in 1896 with musical superstars The Bostonians. Twelve years later she purchased her first residence atop 117 Hemenway Street near Symphony Hall. Mom, son, sister join. Son will work for stage designer Josef Urban and marry a Boston Opera ballerina. Sister Hortense, actress, joined Curry Institute of Expression (now Curry College) and continued to tour.

Alice could have told more of her extended Irish family in Boston. Early as 1899 Alice told Boston papers her wish to buy Warren House for mom. So the hint is plain Sarah was raised but not born in the house. Alice perhaps liked General Warren's story because he led a rebellion. Tracking down the riddle wasn't simple; several area houses are associated with the Warrens. His brother Dr. John Warren built the house now occupied by Harvard's Celtic Department.

Her first red herring points to a missing fact and sets a pattern.

Alice Nielsen's memoirs bring us many such signs. She knew little American history yet sang for Presidents. Her mom taught the quintet kids Irish culture, singing songs and telling stories bundled in bed cold winter nights. Sarah had Gaelic and a musical education from the French and Irish nuns at St. Mary's College in South Bend, Indiana. Alice's brother will marry an Irish girl. At St. Theresa's Academy in Kansas City, led by French and Irish nuns, young Alice had scant exposure to book learnin' or American history. She absorbed things by speaking with people. She spoke in a torrent as suits anyone never silent in schools for years upon years.

Her spelling resembles the Kit Carson irony: "I was a young boy in the school house when the cry came, Injuns! I jumped for my rifle and threw down my spelling book, and thar it lies". Many memoir names she misspells into obscurity, adding to puzzles we solve.

Sarah Kilroy raises a flock of Irish patriots, "Had she been born in Cork or Limerick my mother could not have been a hotter Irish Nationalist. Instead of Mother Goose or Kate Greenaway, I learned the legends of the Dark Rosaleen, the Blind Rafferty, Finn MacCumhaill, Deirdre, The O'Neill and Art MacMurrough and the bold heroisms of Wolfe Tone, Daniel O'Connell and Robert Emmet. Such lessons would always conclude with the story of Grandmother Brigid—Mother's grandmother—who had been exiled by the British to Van Diemen's Land for wearing a green petticoat, no less".

Nielsen's clever contrast must be made clear as Waterford crystal. In the 1600s, Boston's Mother Goose put kid songs into a book published by son-in-law Thomas Fleet. In 1870s, England's Kate Greenaway drew kid stories. If Goose and Greenaway are rather cute, Irish history hardly.

Casually, Nielsen rattles off an impressive list spanning history from Celtic legends to recent events. Only her musical life rivals the depth of her Irish culture. To appreciate her depths, unpack her hints.

Van Diemen's Land, grandma Brigid's exile, is Tasmania. Brits grabbed it from Dutch East India Company for a penal colony in 1803. Before banning banishment, Brits deported seventy-five thousand Irish. Abel Tasman's exotic island has been targeted by fiction: Swift's Lilliput is northwest, Edgar Allan Poe put A. Gordon Pym there; Tex Avery captured the island's shape for his "Tasmanian Devil", a small loud fierce critter.

The rest of Alice's evocative list darts across time.

Dark Rosaleen, Gaelic's *Roisin Dubh* or "Black Rose" is a 1600s poem urging Donegal's Red Hugh O'Donnell to make a pact with cruel tyrant King Philip of Spanish Inquisition infamy to repel the British crown's invasion. Doubtful if Alice knew the original Irish church had been a joy. English elites invaded Ireland (to suppress orthodox Christianity extending from Greece across Bohemia to Ireland) at demand of Pope Adrian IV who in 1171 sent King Henry to destroy the orthodox and substitute Roman coercive control. The Pope demanded a yearly fee for privilege of enslaving Ireland; Magna Carta will revoke paying the fee. Four sad centuries later, O'Donnell's appeal to Spanish tyranny fails to stop British aristocrats expanding their tax base. The independent Irish church traded away for hierarchy and dogma.

Blind Rafferty (born 1784) wrote the song *Anac Cuan* about nineteen people drowned near Galway. Alice drops into deep history with Finn MacCumhail or "mac Cool" the cave-bred, fair-haired Celt warrior who ate the Salmon of Knowledge to grow great in magic, poetry and wisdom celebrated by poet Dall. Gaelic heroine Deirdre raised by Ulster's King Conchobar was a source of romantic troubles related in Ulster Cycle retold by Yeats, re-retold by his playwright protégé John Synge.

We are halfway down Alice's list. Hugh, Earl of Tyrone, took the Gaelic title "O'Neill" to lead the defense in 1593. In 1607 when he fled Donegal (Alice's focus is mom's birthplace), three centuries' subjugation follow. The rare victor Art MacMurrough (1357-1417), as King of Leinster had successfully confined King Richard II to Dublin.

Alice's final three inhabit 18th Century. Traces of original Irish church obscured, the conflict deceptively acquires the stark, misleading labels of Catholic vs Protestant until Protestants reform to discover they are orthodox and insightful Catholics rejoin. Theobald Wolfe Tone (1763-1798), Protestant leader of 1798 Uprising with thirty-thousand Irish casualties, helps United Irishmen put aside religious differences to focus on freedom. Daniel O'Connell (1775-1847) advocates non-violent ways to freedom. Robert Emmett led an 1803 armed rebellion and is executed.

Nielsen gave her memoirs an Irish history lesson, proving patriotic devotion. Deeply Irish, *sean-nós:* soulfully singing a story, varies slightly each telling; fierce: she proudly sings mom's Irish songs to British royalty.

So it was. Sarah was age two when her young parents arrive 1838 Boston. Troubles met the Irish newcomers fleeing famine and legalized political cruelty. Large numbers created confusion, protests. Arrivals were no Puritans who had seized power, killed a king, and settled the wilderness. In that Roxbury plight, Kilroys sent daughter Sarah "to Juliet, Illinois, to be reared by her Aunt Clary, another militant Irish Republican".

Again, Alice's haphazard spellings create memoir ambiguity. Alice's "Clary" should be spelled Carey. Uncle Daniel Carey lived in Minooka, Illinois. Dozen miles east, the town "Juliet" after 1848 became "Joliet", where Irish built Illinois & Michigan Canal, Rock Island Railroad, sent limestone across Midwest.

The Careys treat Sarah as their own. Sarah Nielsen and Rosann Carey are sent to new-built St. Mary's boarding school at South Bend, Indiana, a hundred miles east. Founded by Sisters of the Holy Cross from Le Mans, France, its "Mother Elizabeth" from family of George Arnold, Queen Elizabeth's organist at Westchester Cathedral, creates the music program whih remains strong. Faculty often visit Dublin, London, Paris. When the cousins enroll, fifty female classmates consist of Kellys, Kilroys, Murphys, Fitspatricks and Inhills.

And the education impressive. John Kovach at St. Mary's provided Sarah Kilroy's 1855-56 school records. In transition from a frontier school, a new school building had opened August 15th 1855 with "large and carefully-selected library", science laboratory and herbarium. French and German "spoken in the Institution as fluently as the English", the women study Latin, Greek, Italian, astronomy, algebra, botany, geometry, physics. Exercise includes swimming, "riding on horseback and thorough calisthenics". Significantly for Alice, young Sarah finds "Great attention is paid to Music. Independent of the private lessons received weekly by the pupils, regular instructions are given, in classes three times a week, in all the principles of vocal and instrumental music".

The school's ledger shows Sarah Kilroy's first year as an adventurous winter of hard snows for thirty staff and pupils within frame-and-shingle houses. September 1855 through June 1856, Sarah studies piano, accordion, astronomy, drawing and painting in oils and watercolors. May 1855, Sarah is busy "cutting a dress".

At nineteen, Sarah's life changes. "Whatever plans mother had dreamed for herself—and you may understand her complex self better when you know that she was torn between entering a convent and taking the lecture platform for Clan-na-Gael to exhort the world's freemen to succor Ireland—whatever plans she may have fondled went a-glimmering when she was nineteen".

Alice blurs time: Irish-American Civil War vets of Fenian Brotherhood had founded Clan-na-Gael in 1867, creating a golden harp flag and coining "Irish Republican Army". They attack British outposts in Canada 1868-1871. A British crackdown in Ireland fractures Fenians, so Dublin's Irish Republican Brotherhood seize Clan-na-Gael and sail to liberate Australia's political prisoners. But you get the point Alice makes.

At nineteen, Sarah met the man she loves.

Ireland's Sarah Hortense Kilroy marries Denmark's Erasmus Ivarius Nielsen in Jolliet, June 14, 1857.

Now the Erasmus saga. Four years senior to Sarah, in Arhus born January 5, 1834, as second son of 29-year-old Rasmus Nielsen and 28-year-old Bolette Dahl, who haughtily Latinize "Rasmus" to "Erasmus". By 1840 Alice's Danish grandparents had four kids. Helping raise the boys is Ane Rasmusdotter age 21. Her surname "daughter of Rasmus" suggests a story long lost to us.

Erasmus grew up in a lively theatre culture. Århus, Viking town on Århus Bay, remains a beautiful farmland of rolling, wooded hills where its Old Town museum preserves seventy-five historic buildings familiar to Alice's young father. 96-meter-tall Domkirke cathedral built 1500. IN 1843 Tivoli Park had opened in Copenhagen, inspiring Disneyland with lagoon and pirate ship. After 1805 Hans Christian Andersen rose from child singer to music theatre, creating vaudevilles, musicals, libretti; famed for fairy tales. Among Czech influence the philosopher Soren Kierkegaard (1813-1855), and 1773's intentional town Christianfeld built by diaspora Czech church, replicated worldwide. Their bishop Jan "Comenius" Komensky advocated world peace, universal science education and spontaneous order. Seventy years later Scandinavians build Mormon intentional communities. 20th Century Copenhagen has Christiania.

Alice calls dad "a solemn child of whatever fortune Heaven sent".

Erasmus solemn! Droll Danish irony from daughter Alice. "He was a poet who left no verses behind him. He was a minstrel who would play the violin if you had one, or a 'cello if he met one; and sing as he played—sing songs that neither you nor he had ever heard before because he made them up without rhyme or meter or theme as he sang".

She inherits spontaneity.

His own father, "Protestant clergyman, sought with fierce punishments to change the nature of a boy who was born to wander and sing and play but not to pray. So as soon as he was able, this boy—my father—stowed away on a brig that eventually gave him to America".

Alice skips an important episode. His parents brought Erasmus to America among seventeen-thousand "Scandinavian Saints" influenced by Erastus Snow's 1850 missionary visit to Denmark. Grandfather had been a singer and teacher in the Lutheran church, not clergy.

In *History of the Danish Missions*, Carolyn Mollinet tells of Magdalene Jensen, granddaughter of Alice Nielsen's clan settling Utah and a first cousin to Alice's dad Erasmus. When Mormon missionaries arrived in Århus about 1852: "Although Grandpa had always been a member of the Lutheran Church and was a deeply religious man, nothing had so burned in his soul as the truths that the Mormon missionaries taught him. This act completely changed their lives. Their old friends they had associated with turned against them, and also some of their relatives". Led by Vermont's Joseph Smith whose revelations created the book of faith, the Mormon group loved theatre, dance, music. Salt Lake City's first theatre formed within two years of pioneering the town.

When her grandfather decided on the Utah trek, four-hundred others join the ordeal. From Århus to Copenhagen, sail to Liverpool in cold

December 1853. On January 22, 1854, leave for New Orleans. They describe the Atlantic voyage as pleasant; food plentiful and good. Church meetings held, nine marriages, eight deaths, two births. They amaze at "Cuba's high mountains that went above the clouds". Fog forces a week's wait at New Orleans before docking on March 22, "amazed at all the strange sights, especially the selling of Negro slaves, some for $25.00".

Disaster strikes on the riverboat route to Kansas City. Cholera kills two-hundred voyagers including Erasmus' parents. His brother Christian Nielsen writes March 28, 1854, "Great sorrow rests on my mind. I am now both father and motherless. My youngest sister is very sick of the same sickness". Survivors leave Westpoint June 15 to settle Sanpete County, Utah, but newly-orphaned Erasmus splits to Illinois where a Mormon group had relocated after a conflict with slave-owning cronies controlling slave-state Missouri.

Twenty years earlier in Palmyra NY, Joseph Smith had published *Book of Mormon*. Smith names Independence Missouri as the "new Zion". Powerful plantation politicians hate the anti-slavery arrivals. Religious innovation and Biblical polygamy is contentious. Pushing people into rebellion has been an old trick for corrupt politicians. After repelling attacks against their farms, Mormon properties are seized by the pro-slavery group controlling the state. Displaced Mormons relocate two-hundred-fifty miles northeast to build a new haven in Quincy, Indiana. Smith's 1844 Presidential campaign advocates Abolition until he is murdered in Carthage, Illinois. No doubt young lawyer Abraham Lincoln was aware of the crime when purchasing his nearby Springfield home. Smith's assassination may have taught Lincoln opposing slavery could incur violent costs. The looming conflict will enrich war profiteers and cotton speculators with London and Paris bankster ties such as George Trenholm and Judah Benjamin but cost Erasmus dearly. Lincoln would warn, "As a result of war, corporations have been enthroned, and an era of corruption will follow and the money power...prolong its reign by working upon the prejudices of the people until wealth is aggregated in a few hands and the republic is destroyed. I feel at this moment more anxiety for the safety of my country than ever before in the midst of the war" (1864). Reformer lost to us, like JFK, or Ron Paul's presidential bid.

In Jensen's recollection, Nielsen family believed in hard work, music, and discipline: "Grandpa Nielsen was a very industrious and hardworking man. He was quite apt at doing carpenter work. He made most of the furniture used in their home, which he also built. He taught his sons the best way to farm, using the tools and machinery to the best advantage. He had his own workshop in which many of these tools were made and the machinery repaired, so as to keep in good running order. Music was important in the home. They had an organ, an accordion and a harmonica eventually. He was a kind husband and father and his family had fond memories of a happy home life. However, he was a strict disciplinarian and allowed no foolishness among his children". Alice Nielsen's great-uncle dies at seventy-nine in 1889 Ephraim, Utah.

Skills his father mastered, Erasmus learns.

Alice skips her Mormon legacy. In 1891 Salt Lake taking the vaudeville trail she sang. Her later concerts were sponsored by Mormon Tabernacle Choir. Alice's career often visits Salt Lake.

When his parents die abruptly in a strange land. Erasmus, about twenty, roams northwest through Quincy toward Chicago. Strong, skilled in carpentry, tool-making, and music with a strong baritone.

The wandering minstrel takes any work, "For a livelihood he was a carpenter, a ditch digger, a contractor's laborer, a nonchalant worker of the world who would take any job you might offer, first offered, first taken, with no thought from him whether he could do the work".

In Indiana, Erasmus becomes a citizen. Reaching South Bend, the tall, lanky fair-haired Dane meets petite dark Irish music student. They fall in love. They do not return to Sarah Kilroy's Boston family, they go to Aunt and Uncle Carey in Minooka, "If he were to be asked how, with all his dreaming and inconstancy, he might expect to provide for an ever-increasing family, he would reply that he was not presumptuous enough to contest with nature and fate".

In 1861 Erasmus joins 500,000 Southerners to enlist in the anti-slavery side of the Civil War racket. Not with LSU founder Sherman, but with the Scandinavian regiment Company K 15th Wisconsin Infantry. Near Atlanta July 20, 1864, Sergeant Erasmus is among 1,710 US and 4,796 Confederates hurt or killed. "The debonair gods, whose child he was, protected him until he sauntered into the battle of Peachtree Creek, one of the last actions of the war. And there he was shot through the lungs and one arm. The arm became paralyzed and it was thus, a cripple, but a light-hearted one, that I knew him".

Clara Kellogg, top diva of generation before Alice, describes the war's impact on gayety of nations. America's big nighttime sport crushed. Just made her debut, "After *Linda* I was rushed on in Bellini's *I Puritani* and had to 'get up in it' in three days. It went very well, and was followed with *La Somnambula* by the same composer and after only one week's rehearsal. I was a busy girl in those weeks; and I should have been still busier if opera in America had not received a sudden and tragic blow. The 'vacillating' Buchanan's reign was over.

"On March 4th Lincoln was inaugurated. A hush of suspense was in the air:—a hush broken on April 12th by the shot fired by South Carolina upon Fort Sumter. On April 14th Sumter capitulated and Abraham Lincoln called for volunteers. The Civil War had begun. At first the tremendous crisis filled everyone with a purely impersonal excitement and concern; but one fine morning we awoke to the fact that our opera season was paralyzed. The American people found the actual dramas of Bull Run, Big Bethel and Harpers Ferry more absorbing than any play or opera ever put upon the boards, and the airs of *Yankee Doodle* and *The Girl I Left Behind Me* more inspiring than the finest operatic arias in the world. They did not want to go to the theatres in the evening. They wanted to read the bulletin boards. Every move in the big game of war that was being played by the ruling powers of our country was of thrilling interest, and as fast as things happened they were 'posted.'"

With peace the Nielsens settle in Nashville.

1870-1880s: CHILD PRODIGY

In Nashville within a decade after the Civil War a third daughter is born to Erasmus and Sarah Nielsen, name of Alice Maude, June 7, the exact year a mystery by family tradition. "I was born in the middle 1870s (I'm not so certain of the date as I might be had fire not destroyed the records) in Nashville, Tennessee, whither Father had wandered to find work that his dying lungs and impotent arm could manage". So her birthdate became a playful lifelong mystery as befits a diva.

Unclear if fire at home or church. Nashville kept no birth records until 1880, nor Tennessee until 1907. Her skill to grow younger became an American folk legend. To push the humor charming. People in her era were not so regimented by age as those born after the World War One racket.

Her principle is sincere: hers is the only undated grave at St. Mary's Star of the Sea cemetery in Far Rockaway, NY.

Pals made sly jokes; David Belasco suggested Alice had returned from 1905 Europe several years younger than she left in 1901. She gives 1876 as her birth in 1910's *Who's Who In Music* but her first press interview tells 1888 *KC Star* she is eighteen. Alice Nielsen is playful with age; signing immigration forms sailing back-and-forth to Europe, she usually puts age "twenty-nine". Five years later, in 1920 she writes "thirty" yet her son ages from eighteen to twenty-three: he's no diva. Her memoirs say "about 1875".

'Twas about. Young-spirited elfin Alice Nielsen; by singerly wisdom age matters nothing: talent counts. After all, she was born to sing. Her triumphs transcend age. Was she fourteen or ten singing at White House? Twenty-six or thirty-two as Mimi in *La Bohème* with Caruso and Scotti at Covent? Thirty-six or thirty-two in grand opera thrilling Boston in March 1907? Only she sang those shows.

Among divas of her day Alice Nielsen seems a tower of candor. Whenever she gets foggy, playfulness has a point. If she says she went to the White House as child, maturity sees teenage self a child. Anything before grand opera she regards immature. Fogs end by 1896 with lifelong press coverage of her fame.

After Nashville the Nielsens move to 1880s Missouri. Alice recalls being "about two" arriving by train sixty miles SE of Kansas City in Warrensburg where ailing, invalid Union veteran dad had work. Alice arrives with three older sisters: Julia, Mary, Hortense born September 1868, and brother Erasmus born March 2, 1873. All kids will take performing arts careers.

Alice had "good times" in Warrensburg. As a loyal Warrensburger, Nielsen prized her pet spaniels. Had not George Vest famously testified in Warrensburg Courthouse "a man's best friend is his dog" (1870)? Settling in Warrensburg, the six Nielsens were poor, happy, musical, gregarious.

Alice cherishes dad, "Small as is my memory of him, he is worth all that I can set down about him". Sarah sings and gives history; Erasmus invents fantasy. His storyline suggests strong disagreements with dad.

"He would tell me lovely stories about the moon, of whom he spoke so familiarly that I asked what the gentleman's name might be. 'Oh, the reason I know him so well', said he, 'is because he is my father. When I die

I shall join him and then there will be two of us up there and it may not be good for the world either, because we will never agree and the heat of our argument may darken the moon, if not set it on fire. Which was why, after his death, I ran in terror to my mother because I could see but one man in the moon—the old familiar face. 'Our father is lost', I wept. 'There is only one man there—the same one—his father.' 'Your father', said Mother, 'was always a great one to wander. It would take him a year to do a day's travel. Don't worry, *acushia*; dear knows he may be there this minute but hiding around on the other side of the moon to be contrary.'"

When Alice's life was art, she repeats dad's tale to Nelle Richmond Eberhart "who wrote so many beautiful lyrics for Charles Wakefield Cadman or if you choose, whose lyrics were set to music by him. At once they collaborated and out of it came one of Cadman's loveliest songs". Cadman and Nielsen had a mutual artistic friend, diva Nordica, credited by William Armstrong as starting a fad for American art song, "Her artistic position was unassailable; she could do as she willed. Above all she was ardently American", searching American composers and "made tireless propaganda" for Cadman "whose great melodic talent she instantly recognized when he was utterly unknown. To her he owes primarily his quick rise to fame" (1920, *Delineator*).

Eberhart, Nebraska back country teacher, had moved to 1900 Pittsburgh where she and Cadman created two-hundred songs plus two operas. Eberhart, says Nielsen, pushed Cadman to use Native American tunes, creating big hit *From the Land of the Sky-Blue Water*. When Alice Nielsen plays Carnegie Hall, Cadman plays piano. For Pittsburgh's big Cadman tribute, loyal Alice sings.

Back in Warrensburg, says Alice, Erasmus "died in 1879 or '80" when she was "about six" leaving wife Sarah "a legacy of five children and a pension of $12 a month". His grave, located for us by the affable Warrensburg Historical Association, records Erasmus died two years earlier: June 20, 1877.

The 1920s Warrensburg paper reports a "check for $100" to the cemetery fund from the star "whose father is buried in the city cemetery. Miss Nielsen visited the grave of her father when she was here a few years ago and since that time has kept up an interest in this city, where she passed several years of her childhood". When Erasmus died, Alice was "about eight. She has been spending the winter in the West Indies and her son, Benjamin T. Nielsen of Boston, sent the check 'with cordial greetings and best wishes.'"

Trouble getting Erasmus' military pension is fast fixed by a family friend, lawyer Thomas Crittenden. Born in 1832 Kentucky, the Union Cavalry colonel relocated to 1865 Warrensburg. Twice elected to Congress, as Governor 1881-1885, his "Dead or Alive" reward on Jesse James resulted in the outlaw's 1882 death in St. Joseph MO.

Crittenden moved to 1885 Kansas City where he merrily recalled bouncing "little Alice Nielsen" on his knee: "I considered Alice Nielsen when a small girl a sweet, beautiful child with a conduct and bearing older than her years, with no especial promise then of developing into the charming songbird of this day, thrilling our people from Maine to California". The retired politician added, "She deserves her reputation. Her life has been that of a true, good woman, into which some 'rain has fallen', yet from it all she has lost none of her old friends yet gained thousands of others. I rejoice at her success. Amidst it all she has not forgotten to provide a home, with its comforts, for her mother".

In 1880 widowed Sarah leaves Warrensburg for Kansas City where the new Missouri River Bridge connects the continent to create a boom town. Oldest daughter Mary went first in 1879, took a domestic job. Next year, Sarah brought "the hungry flock" when "friends told her she could find work there".

Living among steep Kansas City hills, Sarah Kilroy Nielsen will guide her kids into adulthood. Despite poverty Sarah positions her flock for success. Kansas City's talented musical scene makes Alice's future stardom possible. Touring theatre groups thrill young Alice who haunts theatres to memorize songs to sing in the streets.

Her boldness and natural talent begin to flower in Kansas City.

1880s KANSAS CITY: THE SINGING SIDEWALK GIRL

Since 1870 stockyards and the new-built Missouri railroad span had doubled the town size to sixty thousands. Within five years after Sarah and kids arrive, the town again doubles. Sarah labors a year at Troy Steam Laundry on 1309 Main Street before taking her school skills as dressmaker to Woolf Brothers on the fashionable women's shopping street Petticoat Lane, first section for raised wooden sidewalks. Leaving the street mud.

Sarah's $9-weekly pay is supplemented by Erasmus' monthly $12 war pension (under $600 today). Sarah starts a boarding house. To help her kids, she invites musicians for musical evenings. By 1887 composer-conductor Karl Busch arrives, his Danish culture endearing to the Nielsens. Born in Jutland, graduating Copenhagen University, Busch brings masterful musical education from Danish Philharmonic, Brussels Conservatory, and Paris with composer-conductor Charles Gounod. Busch will direct Kansas City's Oratorio Society and create its Philharmonic. Local historian Mickey Coalwell tells us Wilheim Leib brought Busch to town. Busch would meet his future wife at Sarah's and move in. He adds profound value to their musical culture, and a lifelong friend.

Older sisters sing in choirs—a lucrative gig. Meatpackers Armour and Dold are the big employers but boy Erasmus joins Kingan stockyards "supporting his mother and sisters". Young Alice earns coins singing in streets. Later a local poet—name lost to us—recalls "a little girl, barefooted, buoyant, with neglected hair. Eyes full of laughter; what promise then a flame divine was kindling?"

Nielsen sisters attend St. Theresa's Catholic school on Quality Hill and new-built St. Patrick's across town on Cherry Street. Michael Coleman relates that the volunteer-built church in 1880 lacked a furnace and interior finishes. For the eight-hundred parish families, Blake Woodson relates, "After the Civil War a large number of Irish Catholics migrated to town, settling on the east side. We had only board sidewalks and dirt roads for streets. The mud in wet weather was awful and dust when it was dry was choking". And Alice sang in the same sack dress.

Almost yearly, the Nielsens relocate until south of Quality Hill overlooking Kaw River where Saxon-born migrant Jacob Dold built a magnificent mansion on meat-packing profits sent soaring by the recent war: "If It's Dold's It's The Best". Dold's "White Rose Leaf Lard...absolutely pure, prepared with utmost cleanliness...positively no chemicals". His "sugar-cured meats...on sale at all reputable dealers everywhere, have long enjoyed a reputation second to none". (*Evangelist,* Ap 21 1898). Dold and Swift shared the lucrative Army contract for 1.5-million pounds of meat monthly (*Herald of Gospel Liberty,* Jul 13, 1916).

Interestingly, Dold sponsors *Philistine, Periodical of Protest* of Buffalo-based editor Elbert Hubbard: "Jacob Dold of Buffalo is a Pork-Packer. To everybody he is plain Jake Dold, and with those who are close up, the use of the diminutive is allowed thus, 'Jakey' But in the Society Events, it is Mrs. Jacob Rumsey-Dold" (Oct 1901). In heyday of reform failures Hubbard promotes progressive free-trade socialism, founder of arts-and-crafts village Roycroft before an ironic death on JP Morgan's war-bait *Lusitania* that foreign war loan bailout excuse.

Now back in 1880s Kansas City, Dold has big business on his busy mind. Meanwhile, petite feral blue-eyed Alice in pigtails barefoot sings her mama songs outside saloons, theatres, and shops. Vivid glimpse of the girl Alice is given by Boston critic Louis Strang in *American Prima Donnas* (1900) who retells a *Kansas City World* story from an unnamed man of St. Patrick's choir: "I was in a grocery store near 12th and Locust streets with Alice one day when she was about fifteen years old, I should judge. A couple of boys her age were plaguing her. She took it good-naturedly for a while, but finally warned them to let her alone. They persisted. Then becoming exasperated, she picked up an egg and threw it, hitting one of her tormentors squarely in the face. Of course the egg was broken, and the boy's countenance was a sight for the gods. This may be recorded as her first hit!" Gives significant insight into Alice's character.

Lifelong Alice Nielsen would throw—verbal—eggs when peeved.

Siblings and childhood pals, Alice skips mention in recollections. Hortense and Erasmus (wife, child, and Alice's son) are future tour companions. Kansas City pals aid her escape via vaudeville. Decades later, pal chorister "Mrs. Hugh McGowan" presents roses at an Indianapolis concert. In 1930, Alice receives a romantic 1883 portrait of a young Judge William Teasdale "who sang with Alice Nielsen in St. Patrick's choir" from a sentimental daughter Margerit T. Moriarty.

Young Alice sees raw street life. Recalls her lost world. Charmed by touring companies who whistle-stop America's only rail link between San Francisco and New York. Best talent in the world plays Kansas City while she grows. And she absorbs every moment they perform.

Alice gloats of sneaking into the now-vanquished Coates' theatre across from still-delicious Majestic Steak House. Pennsylvania Quaker Kersey Coates built his 1870 Opera House across from his Hotel with bricks from his brickyard. His theatre on Quality Hill at Broadway and 10th was a typical design. Ground floor, wine bar and restaurant; wide stairway up to ticket office and theatre. Frescos adorn the oak-trimmed theatre with 36x76-foot stage and eighteen-hundred scarlet seats lit by gilded gaslights. Pricier competitor Gillis Theatre had walnut trim and chandeliers. Orpheum Theatre stood 12th and Baltimore.

Penniless prodigy, Alice sings for coins outside the shows. Rarely in school, as huge freight wagons called drays arrive to unload the sets and the baggage, Alice often chances to sneak inside, "sequestered my small self somewhere in the jumble of theatrical paraphernalia, hoping thus to become an accepted part of it". Thereby Alice beheld top talents creating the gayety of nations.

A favorite story of hers is sneaking past the alert manager of Coates' Theatre: "Mel Hudson was not beautiful, nor had his voice that sublime quality that gives archangels pause. Yet many years after, when I returned to Kansas City to sing, I went alone one evening to where the old Coates' Opera House had stood and, shivering in the little street where Mel had roared his orders to the dray drivers and me, I heard him bid me, beg me, beseech me to begone. 'Whoa there. Hold them hosses while I chase that Irish brat out from under them wheels, if she ain't there already. Whoa.'"

She hid among scenery or "otherwise I would let go the tail of the dray to which I had been clinging and by skillful dodging—at which I had grown acrobatically adept, thanks to Mr. Hudson and the many others who were forever shooing me homeward—dance nimbly out of his reach".

She lists favorite shows, a hint to explore. Those big wagons were "sagging under the weight of the scenery, props and huge, romantic boxes of a Tom show, or perhaps a *Black Crook* Company or an extravaganza of the *Evangeline* school". Offhand, Nielsen sketches music theatre history.

Nineteenth century theatre was drama, opera, minstrelsy, and circus—plus saloon shows. European hits were often repacked with original twists. Producer James Planché, who profitably debuted Mozart's *Magic Flute* in 1838 England with Dublin composer Michael Balfe as Papagano, reflects: "The increased demand for novelty drives the dramatist to the foreign market, for such materials as may be most speedily converted to the purpose required. If the public are amused, they come — if they are not, they stay away, without caring one farthing whence that which they like or dislike is derived" (1872).

Of course, theatre originates of folk culture: Slavic dances, Bohemian bands, Baltic songs among the song, dance and storytelling which humankind loves eternally to play at. Alice Nielsen musicals by Victor Herbert raise folk rhythms to show-biz intensity. As America generated a critical mass of creative life, originality arrives and new arts emerge. Nielsen and Herbert knew they were.

Regard her list:

"Tom" shows originate in Harriet Beecher Stowe's 1851 *Uncle Tom's Cabin*, a huge bestseller opposing slavery. Stowe wrote the book at forty to protest the Fugitive Slave Law returning runaways to the plantation. Adapted for stage, the 1852 play runs in various versions seventy years with an exciting escape over ice flows and such songs as Foster's insightful *Old Folks At Home* which Nielsen puts into encores lifelong. Quickly arose innumerable parodies, adding to stock characters of American comedy as Frontiersman, Yankee, Plantation Colonel, and Cowboy.

Theatre follows the money. Since about 1844 the Virginia Minstrels—from Boston!—had toured America with skilled singer-comics in blackface, playing England that first year. Blackface became theatre gold; Christie Minstrels began a seven-year NYC run monopolizing Stephen Foster songs. Minstrel companies grew; mostly all-male casts specialized as dancers, musicians. Players took male and female roles. Minstrelsy absorbed many European migrants such as Russia's Al Jolson. Most 19th-century male stars and musicians, even Ireland's Patrick Gilmore, put on blackface. Many actors played drag skits, such Tony Hart's female comedy role with Ned Harrigan. Acting was acting in those days.

Burton Stanley "America's best female impersonator" expertly mimics his era's top divas then dons drag blackface for comedy skits with comic Gus Pixley giving "three hours of continuous hilarity". When Stanley casts young Alice for a tour to 1891 San Francisco, she learns comedy from a master. Popular Stanley plays parody and serious roles. Expert artist, writer, self-producing director, Stanley from London is the 1880's Milton Berle with a virtuoso voice.

Black performers in blackface such as George Callender's Georgia Colored Minstrels also gain profitable tours, reaching beyond Europe. 19th century black stars include Bob Haight, Cole & Johnson, Alra Aldridge, Bohee Brothers, "Black Patti" Matilda Jones, Mme. Flower, Ernest Hogan, and the superb Hyers Sisters who often tour young Alice Nielsen's region in concert and bespoke musicals. "Whiteface" parody remains commercial for films and comedians.

As Edward Rice relates in *Monarchs of Minstrelsy* (1913), this gigantic fad employs thousands of performers for decades. Acts first appear in circus among clowns, spread to variety shows, then fill theatres. Minstrelsy gave black culture a human face, as a satire of slavery. Parody operates across the color lines. The post-Civil War Democratic Party inhibited integrated shows until Republicans restore civil rights. Bondage gone, fad loses parody purpose as did surrealism fad when liberalized oppression removed the necessity of obscurity.

Producer Michael Leavitt (*Fifty Years of Theatrical Management*, 1912), tells the "innocent comicalities" of a "vivid and picturesque" minstrelsy "before the [Civil] war...demanded rare mimic talent. Pathetic and sympathetic ballads were sung admirably by beautiful voices. Wit and humor were keen and telling. This was very different from the so-called minstrelsy of the present day which clad in Punch and Judy costumes evolves stale newspaper jokes...." Minstrelsy skits entered the television era, see *Rowan and Martin's Laugh-In* (1967-73).

Minstrelsy, circuses, and diverse opera styles ruled the 19th-century stage. Diva Clara Kellogg recalls "In my young days the negro minstrels were a great diversion. They were amusing because they were so typical. There are none left, but in the old times they were delightful, and it is a thousand pities that they have passed away. All the essence of slavery, and the efforts of the slaves to amuse themselves, were in their quaint performances". Minstrelsy was protest satire. When conflict began Confederate racketeers banished these troupes.

Beyond 1865, the Dante's *Inferno* musical *Black Crook* and Longfellow poem musical *Evangeline* set profitable patterns for future "grand spectacular drama" touring for decades. Show styles making big money set persistent patterns: we must give thanks to *Crook* for birthing a *Les Misérables*. Michael Leavitt recalls the 1866 opening night of "*Crook* at Niblo's Garden...more than an event, it was an epoch. Really the birth of all the ballets, burlesques, comic operas and musical comedy of the present day. It was the first time in which the feminine form divine had been displayed in all its fullness and beauty, or in plain vernacular it was the initial big leg show...." Pulpit and press switched from Civil War rage to denounce the show—"What a storm it raised!" The public "rendered its own verdict by crowding the enormous auditorium of Niblo's Garden at every performance....

"The ballet was launched [toured] then, and ever since it and its allies, spectacles and burlesques, comic opera and musical comedy has been safely riding upon the high seas of public favor and prosperity".

Opening night lasted five hours. Mark Twain met *Crook* produced by William Wheatley, directed-choreographed by David Costa, book by Charles Barras, music and lyrics George Bickwell, Guiseppe Operti, Theodore Kennick.

Starring ballet dancer Marie Bonfante, "Scenic effects—the waterfalls, cascades, fountains, oceans, fairies, devils, hells, heavens, angels—are gorgeous beyond anything ever witnessed in America.... Then the endless ballets and splendid tableaux, seventy beauties arrayed in dazzling half costumes; displaying all possible compromises between nakedness and decency..., girls hanging in flower baskets; others stretched in groups on great sea shells; others clustered around fluted columns; others in all possible attitudes; girls—nothing but a wilderness of girls—stacked up, pile on pile, away aloft to the dome of the theatre, diminishing in size and clothing, till the last row, mere children, dangle high up from invisible ropes resplendent with columns, scrolls, and a vast ornamental work, wrought in gold, silver and brilliant rayed only in a camisa.

"The whole tableau recolors—all lit up with gorgeous theatrical fires, and witnessed through a great gauzy curtain that counterfeits a soft silver mist! It is the wonders of the Arabian Nights realized. Those girls dance in ballet dressed with a meagerness that would make a parasol blush. And they prance around and expose themselves in a way that is scandalous to me. Moreover, they come trooping on the stage in platoons and battalions, in most princely attire I grant you, but always with more tights in view than anything else. They change their clothes every fifteen minutes for four hours, and their dresses become more beautiful and more rascally all the time". *Crook* made a vividly sensual antidote to Civil War pain.

Imagine as kid. Magic. Meet cast. Absorb songs: "*When you want a kiss or favor, you put on your best behavior. All the while, you know you're trying to deceive, you naughty, naughty men*". This blockbuster employs thousands of theatre-people for decades touring America.

Interestingly, *Crook* ballet star Maria Bonfanti (1847-1921) of Milan's La Scala becomes *prima* at Met, opens a NYC dance school. La Scala dancers train the ballet in Russia, Boston, and young Fred Astaire. *Crook* reaches Washington's National Theatre 1868 with "Parisienne Ballet... M'lle Wesmael, M'lle Christine, M'lle Emily Rigalli, Martino Malino and the Zavistowski sisters".

Crook's dancing women in tights who frequently change costume will thrill young Alice Nielsen whose hits reuse same schemes to great success.

Alice's third show, *Crook*'s rival in success, is a wild musical burlesque of Longfellow's famed 1847 epic poem *Evangeline* wherein Evangeline seeks lost fiancé Gabriel in the 1755-era *le Grand Dérangement* wherein Acadians must abandon Canada for New Orleans and elsewhere.

Taking liberties and coining the phrase "musical comedy", Boston's Edward Rice and Cheever Goodwin debut the show in 1874 New York. *Evangeline* clocks three-thousand performances over decades. Plotted around a picnic-basket, the show sports spectacular sets of exotic locales such as Sahara and Arizona.

Evangeline originates the ever-popular dancing heifer enjoyed by future theatre-goers in many contexts. Dancing heifer's backside belongs to a singing Yankee comic who joins Nielsen's 1898 tours, Richard Golden. Henry Dixey plays the front legs; future Alice friend Lillian Russell labors in the chorus.

Added novelty, *Evangeline's* long-lost lover Gabriel is cross-dressed woman in a "trouser role", Fay Templeton, who began stagework in her parent's theatre group. She tours in a "Juvenile *Mikado*" before forming a company under her own name. Templeton stars in a Harry Smith libretto show in 1884 Chicago, Alice Nielsen stars in a Harry Smith libretto show in 1896 New York. Both stars play guys in pants for comedy.

Note the development timeline of *Crook* and *Evangeline*. *Crook* is based on a 1314 poem set in 1300; *Evangeline*, the 1846 poem of 1755 event.

Loosely indeed the pair derived from the sources. Such is the fun. This playful spirit produced *Houseboat on the Styx* (1895) by John Bangs, and his 1907 *Alice in Wonderland*-ish political satire *Alice in Blunderland*.

Vivid theatre memories for young Alice shape her later hits. 1880s KC offers countless performances by world's best players to absorb. Alice and chums spy on visiting theatre companies. The fatherless child often tries to sneak past Mel Hudson "clumping hither and yon over the cobbles, his wooden leg banging the stones in nervous fury. He would address me, 'Gwan home now like a good child, you imp, and listen to me for the last time. Get away from them hosses and out from under them wheels before you're the death of all of us. G'wan now, your mother wants you, like a good girl.' 'Aw Mr. Hudson—just this once.' 'Just this once', Mr. Hudson would bawl in outraged appeal to the dray driver, 'Just this once. Will you listen to her—the size of her? There isn't a day when she ain't here with her "Just this once". G'wan on home now—you with no shoes or stockings in November. 'Hold them hosses and back in here, while the brat's out there in the middle of the street making her monkey faces.'"

In a rare retort Nielsen corrects Hudson: "It might have been November but I was not without shoes and stockings, poor as we were. Mr. Hudson doubtless was too exasperated to notice that my shoes with their lovely brass toe-plates were slung around my neck, the laces knotted together and my stocking stuffed inside. I was used to weather hot or cold, and my uncommon regard for my mother's lament—'Dear knows where the next pair'll be coming from at this rate'—prompted such conservation".

Mel Hudson; only man Nielsen openly criticizes. Other men could abuse and cheat, only Mel set straight for suggesting street child Alice had no shoes. Wonderfully she adds, "I was to learn after listening to many songs and a thousand singers that the beautiful voice is the one you never cease to hear. I still hear Mel. I still smell his opera house because in spite of him, I soon got into it by the stage door to inhale the reek of its coal-oil lamps and the hard mustiness of its never-swept corners".

She retells this scene various ways.

Point is: the child Alice foresees her future.

At times she eludes Mel who could not always guard the stage door across from Coates' Hotel where "financially embarrassed patrons were forever departing by way of the rope fire escapes". More than once she "dodged into the enchanted hall to hide behind a woebegone pine-and-canvas tree, until all the trappings of the latest extravaganza were inside and the truck had departed.

"The place was gloomy and full of hollow echoes and rustling drafts. In the weak light from two sickly kerosene lamps at the stage lip they might have terrorized me, had I not been armored with an imagination which excluded all but the glorious, the triumphant, the magnificent. The opera house rats, shrill with anger at the disturbance, sped back and forth, occasionally leaping from the stage into the orchestra pit. But what of it? I was eight years old—a tiny squirrel of a gamin who already was achieving a little fame in the streets of Kansas City as 'that Nielsen child.' What did I care for the cold, damp darkness of the littered stage, for the huge ghosts that inhabited it, for the eerie noises of the old programs rustling in the drafts that slithered under the empty seats?

"At last I was on the stage. Alone? By no means. My imagination peopled it with handsome tenors who were to sing lovely appeals to my heart beneath the sad property trees (Fragrant magnolias and cherry boughs to me!). With a flick of my mind I produced an idolatrous chorus; this, you understand, being many years before I was to learn that choruses do not idolize prima donnas.

"And my blue young eyes were dazzled by the brilliant lights my imagination set ablaze, and the jewels and satins and white linen of the vast audience which filled every seat. So, waving a gay thanks to my adoring support which I had assembled in the wings to watch me in my debut, I motioned to the stagehands that I, the great Madame Something-or-other, was ready.

"I advanced to the front of the stage, bowing to the thunderous applause which rolled in upon me from my noble audience and the great orchestra which was proud to play for such superb talent. A few wild leaps of music from my orchestra and I was off on my first stage appearance. With a majestic sweep of my hand I cast off the yoke of shoes and stockings and, my arms outstretched to gather my audience to my heart, I sang".

Of course she recalls the very song, *"Thou Art So Near And Yet So Far"*, the popular 1858 Alexander Reichardt ballad: *"I know an eye so softly bright, That glistens like a star of night; my soul it draws, with glances kind To heav'n blue vault, And there I find..."* Closes *"Beloved eye, beloved star, thou art so near and yet so far"* on a sopranophilic high F.

"I had learned it from an older sister—Mary—who was to be one of the world's most beautiful women. But I had the voice". Mary, if never again mentioned, follows Alice and family to San Francisco, enters a convent.

"Perhaps Mr. Hudson was within earshot. Or maybe a passer-by heard my song and hastened to tell him. Anyway, the listeners whom only I could see, were denied the encore that I was saving for them—*Killarney*—because, with tears in his voice and a dreadful hammering of his wooden leg, he came roaring into his opera house. My debut was over; I don't pretend to remember what he said or what he threatened to do. I recall that in his hand he held a light stick and that in his face there was determination. I scooped my shoes and stockings out of the dust and litter and the glorious diva who but a moment before was simply devastating a royal audience took a running jump at a horizontal pipe, caught it, swung herself monkey-like far out over the orchestra pit, dropped to her feet and ran for her life. And as I ran, I heard Mr. Hudson exhorting me to 'gwan home and stay home' and who did I think I was anyway, Jenny Lind or somebody? Anyway, keep out of his opera house".

Swedish soprano Jenny Lind's 1850s tour for Barnum netted a fortune for both. Next decade the Euro-born, NY-raised Adelina Patti made bigger money; next was America's Clara Kellogg, Sweden's Christine Nilsson; Calvé; Nordica; and then Alice Nielsen.

If indeed eight, theatre adventures became her first delight upon promotion from Warrensburg brass bands. Kansas City was the big theatre town for the region where all national tours perform. Chicago, Kansas City, Denver.... Wonderfully she told yet another version some years earlier.

Or just another episode at Coates? Not as brave: "My first appearance upon the stage was made without the aid of an audience—I was almost going to say, 'without the aid of a net.' It was in Kansas City at Coates Opera House, and I was a little girl of twelve". With sly wit, she continues: "Even at that time I was something of a singer, and had already appeared at a few church concerts. Concert work did not satisfy me, though. My ambition was grand opera. I longed for a chance to appear upon the stage. Mel Hudson, then as now, manager of the Coates Opera House had many a time to shoo me from the stage door, and two or three times I got back upon the stage during the performance, only to be hustled off again as soon as I was noticed. My first appearance was made on a winter afternoon during an engagement of the Carlton Opera Company".

Nielsen singles out respected tenor William Carlton in the usual repertory such as *The Tar and the Tartar*, and *Jupiter* featuring Kansas-born star Trixie O'Callaghan (stage name "Friganza") playing Ganymede. Another Carlton star was Mr. O'Hare "world's greatest boy soprano". The Carlton cast includes singer and cornetist Fanny Rice, who toured with The Boston Ideals who became The Bostonians who hired Alice Nielsen for a national debut; and Carlton had arrived in America with Clara Kellogg's English Opera Company. Small stageworld!

Alice continues naming songs: "While a matinee was in progress I succeeded in reaching, by way of the property room, the mysterious regions back of the footlights. I was very little then and easily hid myself by coiling upon the seat of a big throne chair. Through the interstices of the back of which I witnessed the performance. The music and the glitter fairly charmed me, and when it was all over I still lay snuggled up, in an almost comatose condition until everyone had gone.

"The delicious melodies of Balfe's *Bohemian Girl* were ringing in my ears. I knew them well, and when I saw that the big black stage was utterly deserted I crawled from my hiding place, crept down to the footlights, and taking the centre of the stage, sang *Marble Halls* for all I was worth; at the same time, in imagination, peopling the empty chairs with a grand and demonstrative audience".

Marble Halls, romantic ballad by Dublin-born Balfe takes four complex minutes to belt in E-flat and 3/8 time. Alice is indeed precocious to sing her Coates debut, "*I dreamt I dwelt in marble halls, vassals and serfs at my side. And of all who assembled within those walls, I was the hope and the pride.... I also dreamt, which pleased me most, that you loved me still the same. That you lov'd me, you lov'd me still the same*".

Alice would master much Balfe with such 19th-century tongue-twister lyrics as *Killarney*. Try fast yourself: "*Ev'ry rock that you pass by, Verdure broiders or besprints. Virgin there the green grass grows, Ev'ry morn Spring's natal day; Bright-hued berries daff the snows, Smiling winter's frown away*" until the chorus ends, "*Beauty's home Killarney, Heaven's reflex Killarney*".

Her spooky debut continues: "I gave myself an encore and was bowing my acknowledgements when the solitary bunch-light, which had thus far illuminated the gloom, sputtered and went out. For a moment the darkness overawed me; then, being nerve-strung and excited anyway, the shadows seemed to take form. Ghostly shapes appeared form the black cavities formed by the wings and dismal sounds came from the murky emptiness of the auditorium. I shrieked in terror and rushed to the stage door, which I pounded with my fists until my knuckles bled.

"The man in the ticket office finally heard me and came to my rescue. He took me, nearly fainting, to the office and sent a messenger to my mother, who shortly arrived and vigorously applied where they were most needed restoratives of strictly physical sort—and thus ended my first stage experience".

As Mel Hudson met prodigy Alice, his patience admirable. Her diligence formidable. "I marvel at Mel Hudson's forbearance. Just how he controlled himself and squandered so much of his time saving me from the horses' hoofs and the wheels of the scenery drays is most mysterious. Viewing those days from my present mellow years, I am moved to reach back and bestow a lusty wallop on the pert nose of the brat, Alice".

Before leaving town Alice will take Coates' stage legit for a local show; and returns to town and that stage a star.

Active 1880s child, every "morning I was at it again, singing in the streets of Kansas City—in front of saloons, stores, private houses, livery stables, hotels, anywhere". Never was money tops: "Sometimes they threw pennies at me, not that it mattered. If they didn't pay me it would be quite all right with me as long as they let me sing". Her human connection matters most. She brings the magical unity, "As long as there were places to sing, audiences to applaud, critics to approve, I sang for dollars, for pennies, for love. But whatever the reward, I sang". She recalls singing to a drunk tossed out a saloon, "things like that".

To the gutter drunk, Alice sang *Bonnie Sweet Bessie*, lyrics by Arabella Root, music by J.L Gilbert, *"But sorrow came to her heart one day, And her dear darlin' was taken away, Then oh how sad and lone was she, Poor Bonnie sweet Bessie, the maid o' Dundee...."*

1886: PARLOR TO WHITE HOUSE TO CHOIR

Soon her Kansas City audience grows more interesting when she crosses paths with Jacob Dold. Also in 1880 arrived the Dold family from Buffalo NY, renown for choirs, where the 1883 *Sängerfeste* parade fills main street. Dold Packing's plant at Liberty and 9th used twelve-hundred men to slaughter four-thousand sheep, cattle and hogs daily; consumes two-thousand gallons of milk making butter. Dold and Armours run Kansas City Livestock Exchange. Jacob Dold from Saxony started in Buffalo, sons J.C. and Charles oversee KC operations. The Dolds deal with complexity from industrial innovation to farms, logistics, labor, and pricing. Their reputation is progressive, outlook spiritual, says John Hobbes in *Our Great Meat Kingdom in the West* (1900).

One busy day Dold emerges from Kansas City Club to take his waiting carriage up steep short streets to his Quality Hill mansion. The magnetic voice of a ragged Irish girl raised in song stills him. Spontaneous meeting of tycoon and kid singer is significant for America's future cultural history. Not the last time Alice made people realize what matters more than money.

Jacob Dold had daughters, in say 1885 Clara nine and Florence twelve. "In front of Mr. Dold's club", Alice recalls, "I was ordered off by a doorman whose livery was so romantic that I sang to him from the opposite side of the street after the chase". Dold heard the voice; strode to ask if the kid would like to perform at his daughter's birthday party next afternoon.

She said she would. He promised to send his carriage. She could not paint it grander than it was: "I had my first carriage ride behind proper horses. That, believe me, was a day of days". All her life recalls.

Dold's mansion, site of Alice's drawing room debut, today marks an empty grassy lot on the south crest of Quality Hill overlooking a glorious sunset and the Kaw River, Kansas beyond. Vacant lot, scatterings of Coate's bricks, graced by curved driveway going nowhere sided by elegant trees was where Mrs. Dold "led me upstairs and put a muslin dress on me. Then downstairs again, they huddled around to listen to 'the child who sings in the streets.'"

Soaking up every detail in the "Victorian walnut and horsehair parlor of the home of Jacob Dold the meat packer", young Alice Nielsen, a seasoned *acapella* street singer with surprisingly large repertoire of Irish and parlor songs learned from musical mom, begins: "Mrs. Dold sat at the piano and told me to sing what I knew. Poor lady, she didn't realize. Sing what I knew? Why, I knew a dozen songs, a score perhaps. Happy? Why, here in a mansion they had asked me to sing what I knew. Which meant to me *all* that I knew. I sang until she gently stopped me—*Thou Art So Near And Yet So Far, Killarney, Bonnie Sweet Bessie, Comin' Through The Rye, Home Sweet Home, The Low-Back Car*—and promised to continue indefinitely".

So it was. Alice Nielsen makes her society debut at a child's birthday musicale in Dold mansion. Offers an intriguing set of Celtic, popular parlor and art songs. Lifelong her concerts keep the same program. By 1910 she will have recorded all songs sung at Dold's party. Concert tours offer the same musical mix, pop hits of grandmother's era. Keeps this format for her Carnegie Hall concert, albeit four languages plus aria. Then sings these childhood street songs as encores to the eight-thousand people.

Alice's latest list:

Home, Sweet Home is from 1823's opera *Clari, or the Maid of Milan* by John Payne and Henry Bishop. Nielsen sang, "*'Mid pleasures and palaces, Though we may roam, Be it ever so humble, There's no place like home. Home, home, sweet sweet home, There's no place like home, There's no place like home*".

Adelina Patti had sung this to Lincoln.

Alice's hit record and most-requested encore holds other resonances: actor-playwright born near Syracuse NY whose many failures include a job as South Dakota editor; who relocated to 1891 Chicago's *Evening Post*; in 1896 he heard Alice Nielsen perform with The Bostonians. Next year his *Mother Goose in Prose* illustrated by Maxfield Parrish brought success; sequel *Father Goose His Book*. In 1900 Frank Baum publishes *The Wonderful Wizard of Oz* wherein Dorothy repeats Nielsen's lyric mantra.

Samuel Lover's (1797-1868) *Low-Backed Car* was penned by the Irish poet, singer, novelist whose 1848 American tour of "Irish Evenings" gave a "tribute of gratitude to America for her munificent contribution to Ireland in her distress". In his *Emigrant's Dream or The Land Of Promise*, Lover acted multiple roles, and played *Macarthy Moore* with Darby Sullivan. Mlles. Celeste and St. Clair danced; Mr. Thompson "did a clog hornpipe". Significantly, Lover helps daughter Fanny raise son Victor Herbert, whose father died when the boy seven, near age Alice's father passed. Nielsen sang, "*When first I saw sweet Peggy, 'Twas on a market day; A low-back'd car she drove, and sat Upon a truss of hay; But when that hay was blooming grass, And deck'd with flowers of Spring, No flow'r was there that could compare With the blooming girl I sing*".

Her next-named song again spotlights Ireland's famed singer-composer Michael Balfe (1808-1870) who had blazed a trail from Dublin to Italy to sing for Rossini before creating his twenty-eight popular operas. Balfe combines dialog with song in the comic opera (or Broadway) style. In repertory Nielsen will perform many Balfe shows, first big San Francisco hit being Balfe's *Satanella*.

Nielsen names Scots *Bonnie Sweet Bessie* and popular encore Robert Burns' *Comin' Thro the Rye*. Nielsen sang, "*If a body meet a body, coming thro the rye, if a body kiss a body, need a body cry? Ev'ry lassie has her laddie, nane they say have I!*" Rye helps whisky and romance.

Lastly, Nielsen lists art songs: 1858's *Thou Art So Near And yet So Far*, translated from Alexander Reichardt's *Du Bist Mir Nah und Doch So Fern*.

Quite a list for a kid singer. And the people notice.

When the Dold birthday party ends, the carriage "went far out of its way to deposit me on my own doorstep where out of sheer triumph, I announced myself to my mother by singing a song she hadn't taught me!"

Success with the Dolds instantly raises her celebrity.

His socialite wife promotes Alice: "On the following day we—my mother and I—were called upon by so important and impressive a gentleman as Congressman Dougherty who, after a few well-chosen remarks about Kansas City, its talented sons and daughters and other features of such an unusually meritorious municipality, asked that I be lent to him and his wife for a week or ten days".

Dougherty invites Alice to sing at White House for President Cleveland, whose fashionable young wife fascinates the nation, "Talented juveniles from various states were being escorted to Washington to be exhibited for the edification of the assembled throng and the glory of their native cities".

Working from memory, Alice blurs dates. Attorney John Dougherty (1857-1905), *Liberty Tribune* publisher, joined Congress 1899-1904, long after Nielsen left town. But he ran unsuccessfully for office in the late 1880s. Dold had risen to success in Buffalo where lawyer Grover Cleveland served as Mayor and NY Governor before elected President 1885. He famously refused to annex Hawaii saying it was a racket hijack, and not patriotic. June 1886 Cleveland marries his bride age twenty-one.

Dolds' political clout puts Alice on train to DC. Dougherty and wife deliver Nielsen to Washington. Cleveland was reelected 1893 after a term by Benjamin Harrison. So Alice's first White House concert occurs between 1886 and 1888, she is in San Francisco during Cleveland's second term.

She recalls being "just past nine years old"; perhaps sixteen looks nine.

Mom had mixed feelings. If Sarah "was near to collapse with excitement and misgivings" about Washington, Alice was "quite willing to go anywhere at any time and with anybody merely for the opportunity to sing for somebody". Street-savvy Alice gives a sly hint about schooling, "I hadn't the most remote idea where Washington was or how one got there, but I would gladly have taken Congressman Dougherty's hand and started to walk there had he suggested it".

She focuses on song: "A song was a song, whether for a President or a driver for the Great Western Transfer and Delivery Company. Let us be going and when shall I start singing?" Resistance was futile: Sarah's assent inevitable. The Missouri gang boards for DC, young Alice relishes the long train trip saying significantly: "I have always liked touring".

While traveling Mrs. Dougherty "made me a pink dress with a sash so wide and a bow so enormous that the effect must have been that of a very small child pinned to a vast ribbon exhibit".

Beautiful newly-wed Mrs. Cleveland, the famed White House bride, was an accomplished pianist and singer. Charmed and fascinated Americans.

"Such an egoist was I, that I remember very little of the others except that Mrs. Cleveland herself led us by the hand to the platform and that I, ignoring her and the orchestra (or was it just a piano?), proceeded to sing my songs of the Kansas City streets. And it comes to me too, that I was thoroughly snubbed by another child prodigy who had played the piano— *Silver Fountain polka* or some such tinkle. I asked the little girl how I had done. She turned to me airily, her nose tilted several degrees steeper than nature had set it and shrilled coldly: 'Oh, you're from Kansas City, aren't you?'" Foggy on American politics, geography, dates, or name-spelling, many years later Alice will distinctly recall *Silver Fountain Schottische* (1878) of William Meyer, a popular piano piece as played by a snotty rival kid at her first White House concert.

Alice returns a Kansas City celebrity, the Dold and the White House concerts give showbiz momentum and fan her ambitions.

Kansas City in mid-1880s is hard-working and hard-playing. Perhaps more tame than 1864 when Wild Bill Hickok, Buffalo Bill Cody, Jeremiah Johnson and Frederick Benteen had arrived to seize Union control and launch Union officers as governors of three states.

Horse-drawn trolleys bring people from 12th Street to outlying parks for fashionable picnics. Each has a bandstand. Brass bands play all day. The musical scene is a European migrant club. In 1887 from Denmark arrives master musician Karl Busch to conduct chorales and symphony and marry Sarah Nielsen's boarder the pianist Sallie Smith.

In this universe, free as any minstrel *gamine*, Kansas City is Alice Nielsen's playground from child to woman. Sings at home, around town, in church, in school, at socials, at musicals. Haunts theatres as the great stars parade past. Quality more intense than she suggests or we could readily imagine. This is the golden age of live theatre. That's all there is.

Alice is about fourteen when Mapleson Opera arrives with the world's next Jenny Lind, petite prodigy Adelina Patti; plus Western soprano hit Emma Nevada. Nevada, born in an 1859 California mining camp, attends Mills College before her 1881 Naples *La Somnambula* debut which Verdi describes as "very, very good; extremely good". Not untypical Kansas City fare. *Evening Star* (1885) tells the recipe for success: "Given a sweet, flexible soprano voice, a fair amount of simplicity in acting, and anything like a pretty face and form, and the success of the singer is assured. All these...Miss Nevada possessed in abundance, and of course the audience went mad with enthusiasm. Nevada had the advantage too, of being one of us, an American and more, a daughter of the West".

The pattern is set. Likely young Alice heard their show and during intermission sang outside for coins. Her future vocal coach Ida Valerga would be in the cast as Patti's stand-in. Nielsen never speaks of Patti, of Nevada, of The Bostonians, or of the many great groups who rotated past. Makes instead a blanket promise: she had haunted these touring theatre companies, singing at the stage door and to their audiences outdoors at intermissions.

Busking for pennies, haunting theatres, young Alice candidly observes gritty street life: ladies, actresses, whores. She sees men variously enlightened. "In the days of my extreme youth", Nielsen at sixty regards the 1880s, "when I had acquired a local celebrity as a child who sang in the Kansas City streets, there was a wide social gulf between an actress and a lady". She paints a scene lost to us: "Gentlemen, known among other things as stage-door Johnnies, laid nightly siege to the stage entrances, and considerable literature appeared treating of these dashing males who were popularly pictured as wearing opera cloaks—or at least capes on their shoulders—and opera hats. One beheld them standing simpering in rows in narrow kerosene-lit back streets with cabbage-shaped bouquets in their white-gloved hands. Thus they awaited the star of the show, the toast of the stage, whom they proceeded to bear off to gay midnight suppers where they feted her with champagne salvos for which she did her inimitable dance on the table. Dear me!"

Her keen observations, she says, protect her somewhat. Yet does not find trusting affection. Insufficiently cynical! Had heard *Crook's* women warn, "*And when married how you treat us, and of each fond hope defeat us.... You take us from our mothers, our sisters and our brothers; When you get us flirt with others....*" Yet they fatally forgive: "*But with all your faults, we clearly love you wicked fellows dearly, Oh! you naughty, naughty men*".

After her prestigious debuts at Dolds and White House, Alice says she joins a "Juvenile *Mikado*" tour. Few stars of her era escaped a juvenile *Mikado* and select groups would tour world-wide. Alice describes her showbiz start strictly opportunistic: "Fortunately for me, I wasn't a lady. No lady would have thought of haunting stage doors as I did" or "had my persistency, stamina and controllable gall. Had I been a little lady, my professional stage debut would not have occurred so early".

Alice is a handful: "I have never been one of those polite and self-controlled females who are willing to wait until bidden to demonstrate their talents. I, the minstrel gamine, was all the nuisance that the precocious undisciplined child can be. My mother did her best to teach me restraint, going so far on occasion as to hide my clothes that I might give my favorite haunts (stage doors) and my chronic victims (barnstorming troupes and their managers) a holiday. But when it dawned upon her that it was wholly immaterial to me what I wore and that the neighbors would clothe me rather than see me trotting off with practically nothing on, the poor dear surrendered".

Sarah turned hopefully to the "Sisters at the free parochial school of St Theresa's Academy, to whom I had been given for whatever small education I might absorb, would be able to civilize me". Alike Sarah's school in South Bend, St. Theresa's Academy in Kansas City provides young women with arts, music, and sciences. Sisters of St. Joseph of Carondelet held sway over a three-story brick building; boarding students stay on top floor. In 1880s, daughters of prominent people were the day students, plus "boarders from points as far distant as Mexico City". Spanish, French, Irish, German, and American names filled the rolls. Alas for Sarah, the Sisters only encourage Alice, "They too, seemed to have been the victims of my voice...."

From her schoolyard at 12th Street, Nielsen could hear heavy drays laboring uphill and go meet them to bedevil Mel Hudson who operated only two quick blocks away at Mr. Coat's Opera House.

For her "Juvenile *Mikado*" tour, Alice fancily picks Brno-born producer Jules Grau. Recognized family name, his highly-praised young repertory companies tour North America. Talent-scout Jules reports discoveries to brother Robert, a producer and author. And to his brother Maurice, famed manager at Covent Garden and Metropolitan Opera whose taste and talent, says Henry Krehbiel, bring "prosperity to Mr. Grau and gratification to the lovers of art" by fusing "principles and practices, the matter and manner of Italian, French and German opera into a polyglot institution which satisfied the whims of fashion and also met the demands of art".

Singers admire Maurice Grau. His contract with Nordica a handshake. Calvé recalls "the genius of Maurice Grau" as "one of the most intelligent as well as one of the ablest impresarios".

Grau brothers shaped the vocal life of the era. Four years after the Nielsens arrived, Jules Grau began touring Kansas City. His cast of forty gave the usual fare: *Said Pasha, Bohemian Girl, Brigands, Fra Diavolo*, of course Gilbert & Sullivan. Grau develops new talent among young singers and comics. His 1888 schedule and program typify touring companies at, say, Macon, Georgia: Monday giving *Black Hussar*; Tuesday matinee *Queen's Lace Handkerchief*, and Tuesday night "the musical event of the season, *Erminie*".

Says *Knoxville Journal*, "It was a dollar show for a cheap price to an immense audience. That's the thing in a sentence. Miss Hatcher caught the audience from the start, and Miss Douglass was very acceptable. Miss Read was most comical. Frear was Frear and that's saying enough, for he is one of the funniest comedians on the boards. The chorus was strong and accurate and the whole performance went with a snap and vigor that shows that somewhere there is a capable stage manager and a live conductor". Three years later, "Mr. Grau's people are none of them starred, but an attempt has been successfully made to bring about a strong satisfactory ensemble that is really the essence of success. He has the best chorus...the strongest principles, the most elegant costumes and his own orchestra...."

Strong ensemble at popular prices was Grau's style. Alice's close friend Marie Dressler (1869-1934) at sixteen landed "a job in the chorus of the Grau Grand Opera Company, which was touring the Middle West".

Yet Nielsen and Dressler never mention meeting as teens onstage. Despite Alice's suggestion, Grau never ran a "Juvenile *Mikado*". But we will follow her hint for the moment. Satire of British life set in Japan, the Mikado's son Nanki-Poo flees an arranged marriage. Traveling as a musician he falls for Yum-Yum, the tailor's ward. *Mikado* debuts March of 1885, London. Quick pirated to America where the craze hit hard. Hazy otherwise, Nielsen nails theatre: "On July 6, 1885, two weeks before it appeared in NY, the first American performance of Gilbert and Sullivan's *The Mikado* was heard in the Museum in Chicago". As a national theatre franchise "The Museum" was named—to seem rather than to be— educational. Not just fun and delight, but drudgery of school added.

"The nation went *Mikado* mad. Of what happened before, I have but a misty recollection; but not since then—not even with *Robin Hood, The Merry Widow, Florodora, The Chocolate Soldier* and *The Red Mill*—has there been anything like *The Mikado* epidemic".

Without mentioning her own, Alice Nielsen names the five huge hits of her theatre generation. Selected by a star at the heart of things, let's run her list:

Robin Hood, the Bostonians' 1890 hit was created by Reginald DeKoven and Harry Smith, plus a ballad by Clement Scott. Long stage life. During two years Alice will star in *Robin Hood,* her NY debut. Bostonian star Jessie Davis recalled singing its interpolated hit song *O Promise Me* five-thousand times before 1900.

Merry Widow by Franz Lehár rules 1907-08 Broadway with 416 performances starring Ethel Jackson.

Florodora by Leslie Stuart opens in 1900 with 505 performances, the star Edna Wallace Hopper came from San Francisco theatre, father an usher at the California Theatre where Belasco worked.

Red Mill by Victor Herbert opens 1906 for 274 performances with comedians Fred Stone and David Montgomery; introduces the first electric Broadway sign, a big red windmill turning.

The last show silently opens a curious door into Alice's career.

Chocolate Soldier opens 1909, directed by Stanislaus Stange (1862-1917), who also adapted the book and lyrics to English from the German version of Shaw's anti-war play *Arms and the Man*. Set in Bulgaria, it ran 295 performances at 1300-seat Lyric Theatre on 42nd St. Born in Liverpool with Bavarian roots, Stange arrives in 1881 America. Has talent to act, direct, author. In England, played Shakespeare. Tours America, settles in Kansas City before 1887 when on March 23 Stange plays Coates' Theatre: "the young English tragedian as Richard III supported by the stock company of the Kansas City Delsarte Lyceum and School of Acting...one night only", says *Kansas City Star*. Year later, *Philadelphia Inquirer* reveals Stange as Laertes in *Hamlet* at Chestnut Street Opera House to benefit "Deaf Mute Mission" with "a large and select audience" and Henri de Lussan as Hamlet.

Stange in Kansas City brings Delsarte's influential acting method to look-alike Nielsen sisters Alice and Hortense who absorb skills to create professional stage careers. By 1890 the trio departs oppositely. Stange goes East; tours to DC with Bronson Howard's comedy *The Henrietta*. In 1892 he sells *Man About Town* to Charles Dickson, and tours with Manola-Mason Company acting his 1-act hit romance *Army Surgeon*. Next year he adapts French novel *My Friend Fritz* for Broadway, panned by Alan Dale "tediously pretty". Soon he becomes "that energetic young playwright" whose "little comedy" *Yesterday* is "presented in London", whose burlesque skit on a recent society ball is included by Henry Dixey at the wellspring of American musicals, Casino Theatre. Stange settles into NYC theatre life by 1894, his only flop *Mrs. Dascot* with Kathrine Clemmons and Maurice Barrymore. Next year, says *Kansas City Daily Journal*,

"Stanislaus Stange, formerly of this city, seems to be succeeding well as a playwright and librettist. He wrote the libretto of *The Magic Kiss* which Camilla D'Arville brought out with much success in New York, and for which Julian Edwards wrote the music...." In 1899 Stange supplies Alice Nielsen's libretto for her Victor Herbert hit *Singing Girl*.

Success for two Missouri-based artists!

Stange (1862-1917) uniquely shares Alice Nielsen's progress to world-class theatre. She never mentions him. Must have been great acting coach, Hortense being hired by Modjeska, Alice with Duse. Seasoned young Shakespearian actor, Stanislaus Stange led Delsarte sessions for the Nielsen sisters: designing meaningful patterns of movement and gesture.

François Delsarte (1811-1871), French tenor and actor, sought to clarify "emotional expression". Coached singers and actors to suit word to gesture by applying a vocabulary of gestures drawn from careful observation. His purpose was to reach audiences with or without words. His method—think of silent film actors—swept 1880s America. His daughter Marie spoke in 1892 New York, "My father used to divide orators into 'artists in words and artists in gesture.' Those who are simply artists in words...do not move you. Lamartine said of my father, 'He is art itself.' Théophile Gautier said he 'took possession' of his public. 'The artist', said my father, 'must move, interest and convince.' Gesture is the agent of the heart. Gesture must always precede speech. 'Make me feel in advance', he used to say; 'if it is something frightful, let me read it on your face before you tell me of it.'" This is the key to the method.

Delsarte advised, "Let your attitude, gesture and face foretell what you would make felt. Nothing is more deplorable than a gesture without a motive. Perhaps the best gesture is that which is least apparent. Your inflection must become pantomime to the blind, and your pantomime, inflection to the deaf. No, art is not an imitation of nature: art is nature illuminated".

Delsarte dies 1871, his style is promoted in US by "favorite disciple" James MacKaye. Critic Thomas Brown (*History Of The American Stage* 1903) scorns MacKaye for stilted gestures. His student Genevieve Stebbins' *Delsarte System of Expression* (1885) popularized the "young ladies" gymnastics parodied by *The Music Man* where mayor's wife Eulalie leads a class.

Signify your meaning by gestures: gaze, react, speak. Telling a story by gestures helps Alice Nielsen succeed. Her acting seems natural as only skill can be. So we find Delsarte via Stange shaped Alice's acting style. Delsarte coached artists Alice later knew: Nordica, his final student; others include dancer Isadora Duncan. Incidentally, Delsarte's nephew George Bizet composed *Carmen*.

So mid-1880s, sisters Alice and Hortense attend Stange's Delsarte School of Acting. In 1891, Stange and Nielsens bolt Kansas City in opposite directions. Reaching San Francisco, Alice will speak knowingly of Delsarte; Hortense joins superstar Modjeska onstage. And Stange climbs Broadway heights, adapting *Quo Vadis*, putting words to music by Julian Edwards for 1895 hit *Madeleine: or the Magic Kiss* starring Lillian Russell with Graugrad Marie Dressler. Next year both women became strong friends of Alice

Nielsen. Lillian Russell is the top music theatre star before Alice; Dressler comic relief from beautiful women.

Lillian Russell's career began as Chicago convent-girl coached by Mme. Vaili for grand opera. At seventeen she joins the Rice *Pinafore* company. "At the end of two months she married the musical conductor and retired". Then. Her singing lesson with Mme. Cappiani is overheard by producer Tony Pastor who offers an unrefusable $50 weekly to sing English ballads. Instantly popular, Russell debuts in light opera at John McCaull's Casino Theatre. Stars in America and England, a dozen musicals created for her.

"Conscientious and painstaking...her efforts...placed her in the front rank of her profession". By 1888 Russell will earn an astronomical $20,000 yearly in *The Brigands*. "Miss Russell has formed for us an ideal in her particular roles. Personally she is pretty, vocally she is perfect, and there is an indefinable charm about her acting that compels attention. Her voice is a full, rich soprano, admirably cultivated, and her conception of recitative or aria is worthy the grand roles in which she originally hoped to be heard". At the box office, Russell "has brought more profit to the theatres with which she has been connected than any other woman in her generation" (WSB Matthews, Music In America, 1889). When Alice arrives in 1896 NYC with The Bostonians, Lillian becomes her trusted mentor, connecting her young rival to lawyer and photographers. A strong friend.

If Dressler and Alice were yet unacquainted despite early days with Jules Grau, Stange could link them. Authors the libretto to Alice's third Victor Herbert musical. So after parting 1891 Kansas City, Stange and Nielsen rejoin seven years later for *Singing Girl*. She does not discuss this.

Return to 1885. Teenage Alice becomes a player paid.

Nielsen paints her professional debut a child's game: "Had I been a lady at the age of ten or thereabouts, I should not have captured my first part in comic opera. 'Captured' is the word. They were probably afraid that I would murder any other child given the part, although mine was the advantage of being on the ground when Fate created the opportunity.

"Also I could sing, and by this time I had a considerable following and box-office value in Kansas City. Doubtless there were residents of that lovely municipality who would have fought to the death to assure me the part, if for no other reason than to get me off the streets and out from under their feet.

"Well, at the Gillis Opera House in Kansas City, a juvenile company was taking its toll of the genius of Messrs. Gilbert and Sullivan. This company of children was one of several put out, I think, by Mr. Jules Grau, brother of Maurice, who was one day to have his troubles with the Metropolitan Opera Company's magnificent collection of Aidas, Fausts, Marguerites, Mimis, Carmens and Brunnehildes".

Note her hesitant hint: "I think".

That's a good story and she sticks to it much of the time.

Sets scene of a universal fad: "Hardly an hour, certainly not a day, passed that a brand-new *Mikado* company was not launched". Every baritone "ready at a moment's notice to sing the title role, every tenor—amateur or professional—was rehearsed to a frazzle for Nanki-Poo; and as for the girls—whether they could sing or not, they were doing Yum Yum,

Pitti Sing and Peep Bo. All comedians—parlor, corner, club and stage—were doing The Lord High Executioner, Koko".

As Alice tells it, she has read the poster on the wall.

Savvy stalker of traveling theatre troupes knew Jules Grau (she thinks!) would offer *Mikado*. On the appointed day per usual, she left home to trot across town to the Gillis. At stage door in her only dress singing *Mikado* songs as Grau Company arrives: "Of course I knew my *Mikado*, who didn't? Moreover, I knew all the parts—or the high spots of all—and was as apt to sing Poo Bah's basso contributions (jerking them upward to suit my range of course) as to hold forth in the songs of Katisha, not hesitating even at the duets. My favorite place for thus showing off my *Mikado* was at the stage door of the Gillis; and my favorite time was when the company was going in or coming out".

Nielsen had a keen ear for train whistles, keen eye for theatre placards, and a keen interest in touring companies at adjacent hotels; she had usually a week to entertain the passing entertainers.

Surprisingly, her story goes gothic: "Arriving at the Gillis, hours before the matinee was to be sung, I was among the first to learn that the child—a girl—who sang Nanki-Poo had died that morning". Alice suggests a juvenile *Mikado* with novelty twist: Nanki-Poo sung by a girl.

"With indecent haste I flung myself upon the stage manager—an old man...only member...to pay any visible attention to my competitive singing". Demands audition: "not only did I get the hearing but the director was so impressed with my voice that he confided to the stage manager that he would have me in the company if he had to resort to kidnapping. 'sooner or later', said he (and I would remember this), 'the kid is going to make them break down the doors. I'm going to sign her on first.'"

Takes him home for Sarah's consent.

"Financially, the family's plight was desperate. We weren't starving, but that condition was but one more step downward. And yet mother was hard to win over. Mary was already singing in the churches and Hortense, another sister who has since won distinction as an Ibsen actress and reader, was obviously headed for the stage. Mother, catching at any available protest, announced that my father would not have liked it".

To overcome Sarah, says Producer, an alias preserves propriety: poetic of rosy cheeks "Rose Southern". "Such a nice man", chimes Alice. "'And you, dear little mother, you shall travel with her through the state of Missouri at the company's expense. And for her services, our little Rose shall receive—ah—let us say $40.'"

Sarah made $8 weekly as dressmaker to feed family of five.

"'How often?' asked Mother, who had suddenly turned practical.

"'Why every Saturday night, to be sure. $40 a week is the sum this company pays for a capable Nanki-Poo. You will not do better even in New York.'"

Deal done. "$40 a week! And expenses paid! The shock affected us differently. Mother wept but I merely puffed up with importance. For seven weeks, I sang Nanki-Poo in the great state of Missouri, getting $40 a week, every penny of which Mother saved. Our expenses were paid, you know".

Alice as Nanki-Poo sang, "*A wandering minstrel I—A thing of shreds and patches, Of ballads, songs and snatches, And dreamy lullaby! My catalogue is long, Through every passion ranging, And to your humours changing, I tune my supple song!*"

Mikado craze would repeat the 1879 *Pinafore* craze. *Pinafore* launched many juvenile companies, such as Haverley, and Miles, and (remember this name) Burton Stanley. Juvenile companies were not universally liked. *NY Mirror* (1890) wrote of "genuine pleasure to see children... but the pleasure to be drawn from hearing them deliver lines of which they know not the meaning, and try to sing music of which their immature voices are incapable, is of the same order as that derived from watching dumb animals perform tricks for which their teacher is alone responsible". Juvenile companies, Alice knew, used only child actors. Vintage *Little Rascals* films represent the "juvenile company" tradition.

Alice's tale is pretty but untrue. Follow her hints. As Kansas City child cast in a juvenile Pinafore, her saga would gain plausibility. Few stars of her era escaped juveniles. Another musical prodigy, the celebrated Mrs. Fiske, played Ralph Rickshaw in Hooley's Juvenile *Pinafore* and made a fortune. Alice's childhood escape for onstage pay was not untypical.

Another Victor Herbert star, and future Nielsen neighbor in Bedford NY, the comic Francis Wilson recalls: "I can't remember when first I begat my ambition to act. I know I was nearly ten years of age when my hopes were realized. I was dividing my attention between my school studies and the practice of jig-dancing in our cellar when I chanced to hear that a man known as 'Billy' Wright... had assisted several amateur performers to obtain engagements. I sought him, and ...while he whistled *Essence of Ole Virginny* for me, I jigged away as best I could". Wilson went onstage that same night. "My parents...knew nothing of my employment [age ten!]. But the secret was soon discovered.... I was suspected, watched, and detected.... But a few weeks... back I went to Sanford's. I was again found out, and reprimanded; but I had grown bolder and more determined by this time, and frequently I threw off all restraints, and twice ran away from home to join some strolling company" (*A Player*, 1897). What an age!

Alice claims she was a child player. Wilson was; Alice after her White House gig returned as a young teen talent, not a child. Part of her subtle theatre insider joke herein is that her Bostonian co-star Jessie Davis and librettist Harry Smith had toured as young talents in a Chicago Church Choir *Pinafore* Company—renamed Chicago Church Choir Company. Alice steals the name for memoirs.

Alice weaves us a tall tale. Grau wouldn't hire a girl Nanki-Poo, didn't produce juveniles. His first *Mikado* tour opens Kansas City August 1885; next year in Canada he casts sixteen-year-old future Nielsen pal Marie Dressler $8 weekly plus beer to debut as old woman Katisha in *Mikado*.

Alice claims a player died. *Kansas City Star* (December 1884) reports Grau's production—at Coates—suddenly stopped due to "some little change" in cast due to the "illness of one of the members of the company". Next day, he resumes *Queen's Lace Handkerchief*, 1880 Johann Strauss Jr. musical set in 1570 Portugal based on Cervantes' *Don Quixote*. Grau ran *Handkerchief* in rotation with *La Charbonniere* and *Silver King*. Death of any Grau player touring Kansas City in 1880s didn't hit the tell-all papers. Next season, 1885, Grau begins—at the Gillis—says *Kansas City Star* with "for the first time Gilbert & Sullivan's latest opera, the *Mikado*...each member of the company" playing "his most appropriate part". No gender-bends and if young, not juvenile, cast.

Grau at Gillis Theatre has a summer "repertoire comprising all the comic operas which have been so popular for several years". Town is plastered with "1,500 lithographs". Gillis, a mile east of Coat's, bespeaks quality: higher prices bring best shows, theatre cooled by ton of ice "supplemented by two large fountains on each side of the proscenium. This will doubtless...make the theatre a comfortable place in which to pass an evening". The orchestra promises "best ever heard in this city, being the combined forces of the regular Grau and Gillis companies". To know Grau is to suspect a sly inside joke by Alice to make old theatre pals reading between the lines laugh. What else does a mature diva reasonably do— after Victor Herbert, Covent Garden, Boston Opera, The Met, Carnegie Hall—but call this period a child's play?

So her fabrication puzzle grows curiouser, perhaps a bit posterior. After grand opera divadom, early days bore her sometimes. Other divas of her milieu gloat over affairs and gossip to backstab rivals; Nielsen never so: she skips sordid or backbiting: ever focused on singerly arts.

Grau's actual approach the *Duluth Tribune* (Feb 5, 1886) tells: "In Winnipeg, the Grau company played *The Mikado* six nights and two matinees—the longest run ever known in the city. *The Mikado* being comparatively unknown in the Northwest and having such a reputation...any company giving it here would be sure of a good house...." Amy Gordon is Grau diva: no transsexual antics, never Grau's practice to place sopranos as tenors; no juvenile company.

Yet, touring Missouri many juvenile groups pass. Two wildly popular were Hollywood Juvenile Opera Company, and the Juvenile Mikado Company which hit St. Paul February 1886, papers reporting audience "enthusiasm was almost unbounded. The leading characters are little folks hardly more than three-feet tall, some of them, and the stage setting and costumes are magnificent. The folks have their lines and airs as perfect as any grown-up people, and they were full of little by-plays that are immensely taking. The company is large in numbers, and the members of the chorus hardly as juvenile as the leading characters. The chorus singing is excellent...." Either group could cast Alice for a regional tour. Neither would help her reach San Francisco in the future 1891.

Within her timeframe is Burton Stanley. Who since 1879 produced several Gilbert & Sullivan juvenile companies on-and-off. Stanley, popular across America singing female roles in drag, blends genders. Stanley will first put Alice's name on playbills as a star *prima donna* during his 1891 tour to San Francisco. Alice credits him fondly then drop his name for decades. Stanley, like Stange, embodied the essence of theatre expertise.

Capable of sustaining onstage hilarity for hours, Stanley could give young Alice Nielsen powerful acting and comedy insights. His routines foreshadowed sex-blending plots concocted by Victor Herbert's pilfering librettist, cynically prolific Harry Smith. When the future Alice stars in *The*

Fortune Teller she plays a gypsy, a ballerina and her twin brother. Hats off to Burton Stanley!

Don't we all. Yes indeed! In a fracas mélange young Alice tours, Sarah as chaperone. Not Grau's *Mikado*, possibly Burton Stanley's *Pinafore*.

When summer ends, Alice is "subjected to a thorough inventory by my mother and Father Lillis. Doubtless Mary, my sister, contributed to the symposium". Thomas Lillis (1862-1938) ordained at 23; became Bishop; his County Claire father had married an Irish girl then got railroad rich.

Lillis, mom and Mary squash Alice's lucrative touring career: "I was to return to school, but to soften the blow it was agreed that I be trained for the choir at St. Patrick's". Alice will credit the choir days with teaching her how to read complex music, a critical skill to survive the amazing pace of fast-moving repertory groups. Her ability to read scores like a book then sing from memory is a rare gift noted by many.

First and only, Alice criticizes a woman. At St. Patrick's choir where older sister "Mary was singing, in spite of the unfriendliness of a lady who was not only director of the choir but rather jealous of Mary's undeniably better voice". Alice complains only about sister's treatment, not hers.

Choir member quoted by Lewis Strang (1900), tells us Alice "joined the choir of St. Patrick's...and sang in it about five years, or until she left Kansas City [September 1891] to begin her opera career. A great many persons were jealous of her vocal talents, nor were certain members of the church itself entirely exempt from twinges of envy. Indeed, a no less personage than she who was at that time choir leader manifested symptoms of this kind to a pronounced degree. I remember one Easter service, Alice, then a girl of probably eighteen, was down to sing a solo in Millard's *Mass*". Boston's Harrison Millard (1830-1895) composed his popular *Mass in G* in 1866.

"The leader was angry; she thought the solo should have been assigned to her. Alice knew of the hostility and it worried her, but she rose bravely and started in. Scarcely had she sung the first line when the choir leader turned and gave Alice a hateful look. It had the desired effect.

"The singer's voice trembled, broke, and was mute. She struggled bravely to regain her composure, but it was useless—she could not prevail against that malevolent gaze. This, I believe, was the first and only time Alice ever failed in public".

Skips being chased to marriage by the organist as added friction for a jealous choir leader. Alice's poverty raised risks against success: "It is a wonder in the face of petty jealousy of this kind, coupled with the poverty of her mother which seemed an insurmountable barrier to a musical education, that Alice's talents were not lost to the world. For every influence tending to push her forward, there seemed a dozen counter influences tending to pull her back".

He recalls: "As a child, I have seen her many a time on the street barefooted, clothing poor and scant, running errands for her mother. Later in life when she was almost a young lady, I have known her to sing in public, gowned in the cheapest materials, and she would appear time after time in the same dress. On such occasions she was often wan and haggard, as if from anxiety or overwork.

"But once in a while she received the praise which she so richly merited. One day Father Lillis received a letter from a traveling man [theatrical producer] who was stopping at the Midland [Hotel], in which he asked the name of the young woman who sang soprano in the choir. He had attended church the day before, he said, and had heard her sing. 'It was the most wonderful voice I ever heard. That girl is the coming Florence Nightingale', he wrote. I don't know whether the letter was ever answered or not, but Alice came to know of the incident, and it pleased her".

Alice recalls the praise lifelong.

Successful previous divas to date, Clara Kellogg and Adelina Patti, had enjoyed every advantage. Young Kellogg's parents relocated from Sumter, SC, to NYC by 1856: "I could no more help singing than I could held breathing, or sleeping, or eating; and, one day, Henry Stebbins...of the Academy of Music, was calling on my father and heard me singing to myself in an adjoining room. Then and there he asked to be allowed to have my voice cultivated; and so, when I was fourteen, I began to study singing. The succeeding four years were the hardest worked years of my life". Soaking NYC theatre, Kellogg attributes her stagecraft skills "to the splendid acting that I saw so constantly during my girlhood. And what actors and actresses we had! Those people would be world-famous stars if they were playing to-day; we have no actors or companies like them left. Not even the Comédie Française ever had such a gathering. It may be imagined what an education it was for a young girl with stage aspirations to see such work week after week. For I was taken to see everyone in everything, and some of the impressions I received then were permanent".

Kellogg spent nine months on her debut role! Not so, Nielsen, pushed by necessity. Before debut, Kellogg attended a concert by prodigy Patti. Born in Spain to Italian opera singers, Patti grew up in New York City. George Upton (1908) said "In a remote way she can be affiliated with Jenny Lind, for though but a mere child when she heard the great Swedish singer, she imitated her manner of singing so closely that her parents at once put her under musical instructors". Her parents began ritzy tours; Patti soon a wealthy child. Complete encouragement.

Next-generation Alice overcame obstacles others never faced. Musical mom smartly provided kids with a strong experience, surrounding them with professional musicians. None better than Karl Busch. And Sarah taught her kids the ancient Irish *sean-nós*, traditional *a cappella* singing of sustained song, focused on delivering a sincere story. Alice develops true pitch and lyric memory by this. And the skill informs her lifelong style.

St. Patrick's choir and St. Theresa's give critical training. Vocal scores preserved at Kansas City Public Library show her subtle pencil marks to guide the song. Talent sight-reading complex scores into memory meant she could learn music without aid of piano. Score in hand, Alice visualizes performances note-by-note. Her flawless memory for music will amaze Chicago press, San Francisco, Boston....

At St. Patrick's, Alice "started with fundamentals. I was permitted to spend Sundays in the choir loft with the proviso that I occasionally relieve or help the young fellow who pumped the instrument. I pumped the lighter parts, although being tremendously ambitious, it was sometimes difficult for the lad to pry me away from the bellows handle when in his opinion, a bit of expert pumping was required". Threading up the curved staircase to the choir loft, "my sponge-like mind absorbed the Masses, Mozart's glorious *Twelfth* and Beethoven's dramatic *Second*, and even Brahms' *Deutsches Requiem*, besides Weber's, Berlioz' and Cherubini's. And Handel's oratorio, *The Messiah*, Mendelssohn's *Elijah* and the Bach *Passions*. Rossini's *Sabat Mater* too. It was no trouble for me to retain them, and I took my place in St. Patrick's choir as a matter of course when Mary left to sing in St. John's". Alice skips she also sang at Croatian St. John's.

Weekly services and great oratorios shape her talents. "In St. Patrick's I was drilled honestly and persistently in the serious music of the masters, my receptive ears catching every note, every phrase, every word, and storing them safely in a mind that rebelled at many things but never at music. And there I learned to read the complicated scores".

Kansas City skills performing complex music carry her into repertory and national fame. Delsarte classes with experienced actor, soon-to-be-playwright Stange magnify her stage impact. And she has sung on the streets for rapport. Young Alice works with several local vocal coaches. Lacking the advantages of the previous divas, Alice triumphs thanks to Kansas City. She gains skills to reach the next level.

Alice would be no daughter of the regimentation.

During these 1880 "enchanted years of the stage", March 1886 typifies the Kansas City segue: at Gillis the Boston Ideals, Barnabee's bunch soon to be called "The Bostonians" play a week. Pyke Opera from California follows with *Beggar Student* and a cast of twenty plus chorus and musicians. Both groups will soon hire Alice Nielsen.

December 1889 pulls her decade of Kansas City seasoning to a close.

Joining choir results in romance with a talented twenty-something organist recently migrated from Prussia; her life changes. The region's best instrument is expertly played by Benjamin Nentwig, "an unhappy young man who to me represented the acme of musical power and glory. Child that I was, I think I loved Ben Nentwig the moment I saw his great delicate hands touch the organ console". Nentwig coaches voice, teaches music; plays piano. Migrated as teen with parents from Mittelwalde, Silesia; a lost nation twixt Poland and Czech. Family produced several master organists; Florian Nentwig at Silesia's Pilgrim Church taught Ferdinand Brosswitz and Ignaz Reimann. The father Ben Sr., ex-Prussian Army trumpeter, plays in Carl Bush's orchestra.

From her 1930s viewpoint Alice calls Nentwig "unhappy". In 1889, Sarah and Pastor Lillis spy him as a violent drunk, lost young man warped by cruel Prussian ways. When Sarah warns daughter away from talented Ben Nentwig Jr. the idea of marrying him grows irresistible to Alice.

1889: MARRIAGE AND SON

On May 7, 1889, Benjamin Nentwig Jr. marries Alice Nielsen. She marries Ben in passionate teenage enthusiasm for their music-making connection.

He is a generation older at twenty-four. Highly-visible couple in local music circles, each Sunday they perform together. Beautiful and lively, Alice comes from the wrong side of town, groom's parents believe: "I married him when I was sixteen, Father Lillis performing the ceremony, and both his family and mine taking it rather hard". The cultural clash hinted.

Ceremony over, Nentwig demands a dutiful housewife. The Nentwig family had arrived only three years earlier; Ben one of five kids. Alice's dad had been a playful Dane. Ben demands obedience as taught by his harsh Prussian dad. Coercive societies have obedient roles. If Ben's gregarious, ambitious, street-singing teenage bride challenges Prussian propriety, her performing income hints of possible independence which feeds ambitions.

Talent is a force of nature. Her ambitions are constantly encouraged by experienced theatrical people in the region and touring the region.

Clara Kellog said, "Indeed, there was no illusion nor enchantment to help one in those elementary days. One had to conquer one's public alone and unaided".

Alice regards touring with delight. She admires success.

"Ben lost no time in announcing the program that I was to follow. I was to abandon my stage dreams; I was to be content to sing in the churches of Kansas City or appear occasionally in home-town concerts; I was to establish a home, cook, mend, wash, produce children".

Mormon connections, Irish gregariousness, her delight, theatre talent, genius, ambition, proven prospects for success: she troubles Ben and his parents. Will pugilistic young Alice Nielsen willingly stay in their shadows?

Could her energy be constrained? Stop her force at her age and epoch?

Husband's future seems all-too modest "and Ben—he would continue to play the organ at $25 a month and teach such pupils as he could find at a dollar a lesson". Skips his regional fame as organist and music teacher. His unimaginative plans seem hapless to her. His drinking releases angry demons. Alice does not live in the local world as Ben with steady job. She has already toured to her profit. She has proven herself to seasoned professionals. She has debuted for the President. She has met many great talents. Her local circle held skilled well-traveled Europeans. Karl Busch, Stange, Desci could tell of stagelife in Paris, London, New York, Vienna, Budapest. And Missouri peers shared her theatrical goals.

Her originality could not be squelched: "I had tasted applause. I had smelled grease paint". Her family shares the dream. The talented teenage wife knew her worth: "And I, now graduated from the streets, had already sung upon the professional stage for forty dollars a week!" That "forty dollars had poisoned whatever domesticity there had been in me".

Blandly Alice closes her husband's saga: "Ben Nentwig was one of those men, just as I was one of those women, who would do better not to marry".

She paints a rising conflict of wills and purposes: "We were both selfish, loving nothing nearly so much as our own talents and willing to concede nothing that would not contribute directly and immediately to our professional ambitions".

Hints of clashes of personalities and backgrounds: "Ben was a musician equipped by nature and education to teach and interpret; I was an untrained and undisciplined young voice backed by an aggressive ambition that was no respecter of persons or situations".

Ben had a job to stay put. Her success was a call to go on the road.

As popstars today, theatre money was made by touring.

Alice Nielsen skips the violence her husband inflicted. Stoops to recall that unpleasant woman directing St. Patrick's choir where Alice won its organist in marriage yet skips dreadful episodes with Nentwig. She never publicly rebukes who cross her. Skips speaking freely about double-crossing men trusted unwisely; sought to make peace with fate.

Alice holds a serene philosophy suited to the gift she brings.

Nentwig's plight fatally predictable; as the pastor and mom predicted.

Closed to true cooperation with his genius wife who is far beyond his competence, Nentwig grows disloyal to her talents, thwarts her. In a town filled with her fans and friends. Acquaintances of talent encourage her to drop the pretense and join their profitable play. Against all momentum stands in his mid-20s, staid Ben Nentwig who lustily married an Irish teen prodigy who since childhood had famously haunted city streets singing to every face; toured the countryside to praise for profit. Now regarded one of most beautiful women in town, his bride builds an ever-bigger circle as she sings solo at church, weddings, socials, and shows. Her opportunities soar, and she knows it whets her confidence.

Alice Nielsen is no mousey house-frau to cook, mend and serve."I just hate to cook", she later confesses from her suite at the Met.

No doubt Nentwig enjoys passions of his petite bride. After a year of married life, Alice grows pregnant. Month from giving birth, her husband in a drunken rage beats her unconscious. Stays with him. Yet husband's brutality will not enslave. How she copes with the pain and humiliation of Ben Nentwig's brutality, she never tells but once. Otherwise unmentioned.

After two years of marriage, Nielsen delivers a boy. Immediately she returns to theatre seeking chances to tour. Baby weaned, Alice Nielsen sings in local productions. Interestingly, during this winter 1890, The Bostonians tour Kansas City performing *Robin Hood, Suzette* and *Carmen*.

Early 1891, Alice appears in *Beggar Student* staged by Max Desci at the Music Hall on Broadway Street. Desci, the Hungarian baritone and vocal coach, studied at Budapest National Conservatory and sang in Vienna. He will be in a 1913 silent film *Put to the Test* loosely based on Alice's early saga. After coaching her *Beggar* role, he proves dicey; stalks Alice with lawsuits and fantastical claims meant to lure unwary vocal students.

In Desci's cast, street-singing soprano unironic Alice Nielsen portrays the wealthy Polish aristocrat in Carl Millöcker's 1882 German operetta hit set in Naples. Two poor students pose as wealthy to trick her. Alice's role may have charmed future meetings with the wealthy Polish aristocrat Modjeska. Quickly after *Beggar Student*, Alice stars in a local *Patience*, Gilbert and Sullivan's piece about merely-clever poets. Nielsen plays Patience, simple village milkmaid who cares nothing for poetry so poets adore: which will marry her? She patiently vouchsafed, *"Still brooding on their mad infatuation! I thank thee Love, thou comest not to me! Far happier I, free from thy ministration, Than dukes or duchesses who love can be!"*

Twice starring in local shows with rising visibility and renown, Alice takes her third and most significant show of the year, an ambitious original by two Kansas City men. When her *Patience* ends, Alice starts rehearsals for *Chanticlere* slated to open September 1891.

Alice's first role in an original production ends her marriage. Significantly, plans are afoot to tour regionally if opening night is a success. She agrees to undertake the tour. Her promise creates more friction with husband Nentwig, aware he pianistically coaches his wife for a project which may take her far from his side and out of his control. He senses Alice is praised and encouraged by the touring players and by cheering audiences whose numbers make Nentwig a vanishing fraction. Hapless Nentwig coaches Nielsen for *Chanticlere* hating the piece and his plight. Stars need repertoire. So the couple's big conflict looms: her touring plans and power to turn talent raising the gayety of the town into fame and fortune over a wider region.

Interestingly, the Nielsen-Nentwig marriage ends just a few weeks after local newspapers who labeled her "Mrs. Benjamin Nentwig" are directed to change the billing to "Mrs. Alice Nielsen Nentwig". Wishing to use her own name would trigger further arguments with anti-liberated Prussian hubby. Who may have detected she has made secret plans with touring theatre pals. Such as, say, that genius young trombone virtuoso from St. Joseph.

As Alice Nielsen's first original musical project, *Chanticlere*'s hopes and blunders dole out useful lessons for any diva-to-be. *Chanticlere* opens and closes same night. Nielsen's personal stage success closes her marriage. Six years later she originates new Victor Herbert shows as a national hit.

Her first experience in creation of new musicals is worth a lingering glance. Constructed by duo of Episcopal organist FCF Cramer and the wordsmith James Paddock, the music and text are lost to us. At least the music; the words the reader may anticipate to enjoy. The city's best talent appear in Nielsen's three 1891 shows, her theatre and choir friends a helpful strength willing to take risks. Many players in *Chanticlere* arrive fresh from *Patience*, including McKean Barry. The project had begun at Cramer's house. As he toys at the piano to amuse their wives, Paddock suggests writing an opera. In those days the word "opera" means any form of theatre singing a story.

"In an upper room the two men closeted themselves day after day" to create the piece. Pre-opening publicity praises the lyrics as "excellent" and the music as "admired by all".

Huge hopes held for opening night slated September 7, 1891, at Kansas City Music Hall. Confidence rules the rooster: "There is a strong probability that the opera will, after the brief Kansas City engagement, go out on the road for an initial tour with nearly the same cast", says *Kansas City Times*.

Cramer's *a cappella* rehearsals pressures singers to memorize parts during the summer before joining forces for the very few full rehearsals.

Chanticlere is touted as "strictly legitimate light opera, and the music and libretto are both of a high degree of excellence. Yesterday an orchestra rehearsal indicated pretty clearly that the work will be a success. The chorus is an unusually good one...the costuming will be of the best, and no expense has been spared to make the stage setting worthy of the work".

In an America without aristocrats, royals are a frequent focus of stage satires. Often by migrants embracing the national spontaneity. Arts of the age are usually derived from Europe folk traditions. Kansas City 1880s, the major musical ensemble is led by a Dane, players from central Europe. The passing players tour the same shows to Kansas City as hit Vienna, Paris, London. And of course, almost everyone in town sings and plays in some fashion decades before the radio realm.

Chanticlere, unsubtle plagiarism of profitable Euro-satires by the many successful stage composers over there, is yet another artistic shadow of the genuine plight of people in these old countries. Perhaps best regarded as a kind of Euro-minstrel show. Equal-opportunity satire set remote from Missouri.

As huntsman's daughter Rose, Alice Nielsen pitched as "Mrs. Benjamin Nentwig" is "an exceedingly bright and vivacious little woman, who is the possessor of a clear and melodious soprano voice that has often delighted the people of Kansas City".

In the cast: the experienced players, well-known and well-liked, include Robert Wilson from Leavenworth of "McCall opera company"; tenor Raymond Stephens "who will sing the part of the chef, has just completed his studies in Italy, and has a sweet voice of purest quality". Chancellor is played by basso Addison Madeira; contralto Mrs. Carhart as Duchess.

The "leading comedy role, the Duke" wittily "in the hands of Sylvester Legg" while "J. McKean Harry will create the role of the court jester". George Lillis, huntsman. Rounding cast: GH Moore, Willard Guepner, Bessie Price, Mipple Richart, Elisabeth Russell, Jennie McKeown, Daisy Karnes, and Juli Ollis.

Composer Cramer conducts, aided by HO Wheller. Author Paddock will direct, aided by understudy tenor John Haynes.

With so many cooks, *Chanticlere,* plotted around an errant chef named Louis, has two acts, one after another. Authors put ten songs in Act 1, nineteen Act 2. For Act 1, after opening chorus, Duke rightly sings *I Am The Duke.* Alice Nielsen's seven songs in Act 2 start with her folk song *Spinning;* then ensemble sings *Give Me A Flagon Of Beer* which certainly must resonate with audience. Grand finale is *Haste For The Wedding.*

'Tis Louis finds the chef Louis apprehended whilst "prowling about":

Louis (sings): "*Alas! Alas! Denial of identity can never save me, now that I am known; a noted cook is far from a nonentity; yet in a dungeon deep will I be thrown*".

Duchess: "*Yes, throw him in a dungeon, Chain him to the floor, Never let me see him, Never, never more! Never, never more!*"

Chorus agrees: "*Yes, throw him in a dungeon. Down, down, down!*"

Kansas City Star at dress rehearsal is "well pleased with the orchestration" by Wheeler. Show seems "interesting for several reasons. It is the first effort of Kansas City literary and musical talent...written, composed and presented in ten months. Rehearsals have been conducted without orchestra or piano" except for setting pitch. Soloists had worked separately until full rehearsals began only a week ago. Folly of short rehearsals for full ensemble will soon be obvious and audience-attentive Alice never forgets a flop.

And—most significantly—before opening night the press is strictly told to use only "Mrs. Alice Nielsen Nentwig". "Mrs. B. Nentwig" is never more.

Opening night reviews highly praise her. Rose (as Alice Nielsen as Mrs. B. Nentwig as Mrs. Alice Nielsen Nentwig) has three of the "best numbers in the opera": waltz song, duet with Louis, and quintet.

The show not so. Despite elaborate advance praise, seeing the show soured the press. *Chanticlere's Kansas City Star* review is fair if unflattering: "The libretto is something of a satire upon the divinity of a duke". Plot proves "it is better to marry a cook than a courtier". In the huge hall, after a scant week of full rehearsals the mostly-amateur cast prove shy, mumbling their lines with "treacherous memories". Direction unsure, Paddock had "more success as a writer of lyrics...than as an arranger of scenes and situations". Staging clumsy, "absence of an efficient stage manager was felt at every turn". Cramer "worked hard to hold his large chorus and his principal singers with the orchestra but there were frequent variances". Cuttingly, composer had "greatest success in the less-impassioned numbers" but "smacks too much of the organ chamber".

The orchestra did not always drown out the singers, *Star* continues, calling the chorus large, the stage crowded, the "movement and the flow of the dialogue sluggish".

Among the cast, young basso Madeira "received great applause".

Alice Nielsen's success was clear: "Mrs. Nentwig showed a great deal of intelligence in the direction of stage art, spoke her lines appreciatively, sang her music nicely and seemed altogether much at home. She ought to be allowed to communicate some of her spirit to the chorus".

In her third show that year, Alice Nielsen is highlighted by seasoned Kansas City theatre reporters for her acting, diction, confidence, vivacity and voice. Stange and other coaches worked well. Rose (Nielsen) sang: *"No, my darling, still I love thee, Memory shall keep me true; Hope will ever be above me, And my willing vows renew; Years may come and years may go, love, Yet to thee my heart will cling, Age and sorrow we may know, love, Death alone may solace bring!"*

Her two other songs are folk-ish: *"A rose was floating on the stream, Gently to the west; A maiden standing on the bank, Watched it pensively. The eddies played, the flower swayed, The sun shone bright above, The maiden's thoughts were far away, With her love, her sailor love".*

Increased visibility brings many calls to perform at private events. Brief glimpse of daily artistic life appears three weeks later, September 27 *Star*: "Mrs. Alice Nielsen Nentwig...who has made pronounced hits in several local operatic productions, sang in Trenton, Mo., at the fashionable Leonard-Crowley wedding last week. Her efforts were pronounced the finest heard in that city. Mrs. Nentwig's voice is of melodious, pleasing quality and she always sings with feeling. It is not strange that the people of Trenton were pleased". Interestingly, Trenton is 90-miles north past St. Joseph, the railway portal to San Francisco.

Within two days of his wife's out-of-town wedding gig, Nentwig savagely attacks Alice and her mother Sarah for the last time. Next day, Alice files for divorce through lawyer John O'Grady. Within two weeks after opening and closing night for *Chanticlere*, Alice Nielsen leaves her husband.

She would not be controlled. Does it take an unusual man to wish his wife to star in those days? Some wisely help wifely success. Take Mr. Pyke of Pyke's Opera. Plus future husband of Hortense Nielsen, CA Quintard.

The artistic Nielsen-Nentwig marriage makes the failure big news. The story follows the arc of their lives. Talented teenager who Nentwig beat up soon becomes America's most popular musical star. When dies Nentwig, his passing gets press coverage only because married Alice Nielsen.

Met by local reporter the day files for divorce, the articulate youngster speaks freely to *Kansas City Star*. First and only time she reveals the problems. What triggers Ben Nentwig's final rage, she skips. After two years of abuse, she describes the marriage "a perfect nightmare".

Trusting by nature, Alice Nielsen too slowly learned to distrust.

September 30th, 1891, the brutal story is published. Alice Nielsen, says *Star*, "has long been known as one of the prettiest girls... and lately she has become a local celebrity by her clever acting and singing in the amateur performances of *Patience* and *Chanticleer*". Nentwig, "one of the best organists and all-around musicians in the city", has since age fifteen played for the German Catholic, St. John's and St. Patrick's churches, yet "recently removed from St. Patrick's by the church committee for drinking. He is now with St. John's church".

Three days after her last beating, Alice says "I met Ben at my mother's house when I was but fifteen years old. At first I disliked him heartily and used to hide when he came to see me. My mother encouraged his coming because she wanted me to know musical people". Nentwig joins Karl Busch and other talents at Sarah's place for regular musical evenings. His father, brass player for Busch, belongs to the "German YMCA". Despite their musical fellowship, when Sarah found out Ben drank "she refused to admit him to the house"; and adds Alice candidly, "then I fell in love with him".

Rebellion gave her a son from a talented musician. The Post-Civil War Peace Festivals had advanced the romance. "We had a long courting, and were brought together much during the rehearsals of the Gilmore Festival chorus, which was organized in the spring of 1888. The next year we married. I was but 18".

Union bandmaster Patrick Gilmore created his huge music festivals to celebrate the peace. After a stint in minstrelsy, the Irish-born bandleader had greatly popularized the brass band before Sousa. Gilmore became a bandleader at age nineteen in Salem, Mass. Civil War took him to New Orleans with General Banks. Gilmore organized the first festival with five hundred musicians and chorus of five thousand. His famed Boston Peace Festival held eleven-thousand singers and players with the near-legendary eighty-four trombones, or perhaps seventy-six. When Gilmore passes, Victor Herbert will lead the band.

Significantly, in 1891 Gilmore toured Alice's hometown with a hundred players and half-dozen singers. Young trombone virtuoso Arthur Pryor—after auditioning for Gilmore in KC—will help Alice reach San Francisco in a role, interestingly, she deliberately obscures. Pryor had often worked KC with Alessandro Liberati's Band. Many opportunities to meet.

"I knew Ben drank but had never seen him drunk, so the warnings of my friends received a deaf ear", she continues. After four months married, the paper adds, "Nentwig surprised his pretty little 18-year-old wife by striking her violently on the head with his hand".

Triggers testing Nentwig's temper skipped as Alice unveils woes: "For the first eight months of our married life, we lived with my mother, who practically supported us. Since then, I have had to buy my own clothing with money made at concerts, because Ben would not provide them for me. Although he averaged $75 to $100 per month from his music, he spent it all on himself". Her 1932 memoirs says he earned a quarter that; better to make a point.

Marriage conflicts continue: "When I was making preparations to sing in *Patience*, Ben withheld his permission until he ascertained whether I was to be paid. From the tiring rehearsals of *Patience* he always insisted that I walk home with him from the Music Hall to our home on the corner of 17th and Campbell Streets. One night I refused to walk home with him as it was raining and I had a new dress on. He went home alone and I had to have friends take me home".

The Music Hall on Broadway at Quality Hill was a mile across steep downtown hills, Alice hiking east on Campbell then south on 17th.

For *Chanticleer*, "I earned $46. Ben borrowed $40 of it to buy him a suit of clothes". As a poor child singing for pennies cares about revenue, she regards her undercutting, exploitive husband selfishly cheap as he was.

Heart of her plight, she confides: "My marital troubles really began last spring. Before a Catholic priest of this city he pledged himself not to drink. Two weeks later, he and I attended a church fair in the West bottoms. Leaving me in the fair, Ben wandered into a neighboring saloon and drank excessively".

Church fairs raise funds. Ben Nentwig often played the fund-raisers. *Star* (Ap. 19, 1887) had reported him accompanist at "the Catholic fair and festival" with "Mrs. Kingsberry, Mrs. Watkins, Mrs. Donnelly, Miss Jennie Shannon, Miss Kittie Fitzpatrick and Mr. FC Dahre...on the musical programme..." raising an impressive $1,300.

But now, in the familiar familial church charity setting, Nentwig grows wasted. Leaves pretty wife alone, gets drunk, gets mad. Whatever set him off, "coming up into the fair again he created a sensation by cursing me and ordering me to go home. I was afraid of him and refused to go, but he made me". They walk five long miles taking two hours, Nentwig rages and hits her repeatedly. "Twice on a deserted street he knocked me off a high sidewalk with his fist. That walk home was a perfect nightmare to me".

Despite that attack she stays. Speaking to *Star*, skips others of her circle: siblings, friends, boarders such as Busch; people near around. Skips the change of her name in the press; skips promise to tour if *Chanticleer* had survived opening night.

Relates reporter, Ben Nentwig "was wont to talk back to his mother-in-law and advise her to emigrate to Utah with her daughters". Alice's beloved father's Mormon connection, magnified by local barflies, triggered rage.

To *Star* September 1891, Alice sketches the attacks. Previous March visibly with child, "her husband, in a fit of drunken anger kicked her in the back, with serious results". Next he beats his young pregnant wife unconscious outdoors: she was "just convalescing from this when her husband's ire again became demonstrative and he knocked her down. When she attempted to arise and escape he followed her into the back yard, and there in the presence of the neighbors repeatedly knocked her down, tearing off her clothing. The last blow rendered her unconscious and she had to be carried into the house by the neighbors".

Despite all, Alice stays with Ben until April when Nentwig unleashed "a beating he gave me and my mother. He seized poor momma at the time by her upper lip and tried to tear it off".

Their troubles find Pastor Lillis who by July helps the couple reconcile. They move in with Nentwig's parents. Makes things worse.

"She charges her husband with brutalities difficult to believe could have been inflicted by the fingers that get soulful music out of an organ as Nentwig's do". Drunk, "her husband has applied indecent epithets to her and reflected on her fidelity to him". Insults include "Coliseum dancer" and "Comique woman" referring to racy burlesque places proper women shun—perhaps the choir leader hating Alice.

If Nentwig's scorn has few bounds, father worse: "While the couple was living with Nentwig's father...the father spat upon Mrs. Nentwig, whereupon, she says Ben told him to stop because she was not good enough to be spat upon by the elder Nentwig".

Ben's parents speak German, not English.

Despite attacks, Alice delivers her boy, staying with the Nentwigs over summer tending to baby. By ambitious necessity she joined the three local musicals, takes *Chanticleer's* promised tour to make money, further igniting her husband's fears. After all, "the most beautiful woman in Kansas City" with proven stage appeal could readily coax willing helpers.

In that troubled context she stars onstage restoring her maiden name.

Three weeks after *Chanticleer's* opening (and closing) night arrive the final episodes. Saturday Sept. 26, "he had knocked her down, but his anger only grew overnight". Next day, "he seized her, thrusting his thumb in her mouth and with his hand clasping her face he gave her jaw a wrench that nearly dislocated it. At the same time he cruelly twisted her thumb".

Campaign of cruelty ends. She would not be his whipped slave. Nentwig underestimated his wife, who would not be put down. In her own words, she left him and continued her career. Forty years later, Nielsen skips controversy to bypass departed Nentwig's bigotry and violence. She loves her own father's memory. Prussians like Nentwig prefer plantation politics over Jefferson's framework for mutual independence and cooperation.

Consider the artistic conflict: Prussian-trained Ben Nentwig dutifully plays music as written. He takes and gives orders. Regimented to dullness, coercion; closed. Lively gregarious Alice seeks bold chances, improvises; open. Her horizon expands. Her skills demand the world. She gives things her own style. Alice is original; wins any audience she meets. Talented peers like her; him not so much. She had injured his pride of a fantasy he was important to her.

Monday, September 28 Alice files for divorce and bravely confronts the reigning Nentwigs to reclaim her trunk of possessions. "The family threatened to call a policeman if I entered the house [where they hold her baby]. I told them I had a policeman just around the corner and it scared them, so that they offered me no opposition".

Asks for divorce, alimony, custody of her baby, return of maiden name. Nothing happens: Nentwigs keep her boy, divorce uncompleted, she gets no alimony. Seven years pass before Alice returns to court to restore her legal name and finalize the divorce. Doesn't wait; within a month she splits for San Francisco calling herself a widow. Mom will kidnap the baby and join her. Rest of her life she demands: "Miss Nielsen". She never again speaks publicly of this violence after her interview with *KC Star* that same distraught September 1891 week she filed for divorce just two days after Nentwig's last assault on his young tiny wife, bruises fading from her body.

"My husband and I had parted", she understates in reflections which recall the rude woman choir director at St. Patrick's yet skip the horrid first husband. Tells her grandkids: "My first husband died by a fall, when he climbed up in a tree and sawed off the limb with him on it".

Last-ditch efforts of local clergy to keep the couple together prove thankfully fruitless. She will not need to appear at the final divorce seven years later. Ben Nentwig's last encounter with his wife was the last beating he gave her.

October 1891, after ordeals and a baby, young genius Alice is free by fact if not by law. She has much musical theatre experience. Raised by musical mom, seasoned in complex vocal music, coached by European experts in drama and song, experienced in concerts, praised onstage by theatre-people and press: she is confident. Nielsen has absorbed the world's best companies and stars. She knows touring life, stagecraft. She knows she has a chance. Her problem is only how to live, where to go, who might help. All she owns is voice, talent, magnetism and musical heritage.

Rather than take work in town and fight hostile in-laws, Nielsen follows her inspirations. Husband's family must keep the baby, "Unwillingly I had abided by that, for the time being, because they were financially more capable than I of caring for young Ben".

Her plight "urged me to be on my way. I would go into the world, make much money and return just long enough to get my mother and my boy. Just how I was going to do this was not so definite; but I was never lacking in ambition; and setbacks, momentary or otherwise did not give me pause for long".Of course her antagonists try to thwart. She after all is a young mother and wife desperate to skip out on baby, husband, and town.

Caught in that plight, no passing company instantly hires her: "To my indignation, I did not find managers of visiting troupes eager for my success. There were no jobs to be had". Tosses a few eggs, "Far from being disappointed, however, I dismissed them as incompetents and felt that it was quite as well that I was not to trust my talents to their inept hands".

Determined to make money and tour, cannot go alone. Undeterred, she proceeds with plans put in place with stage pals during *Chanticleer*.

Nielsen makes things happen. Coaxes theatre pals to join her. They form a band and hit the road. The magical "yellow brick road" of her era is the vaudeville circuit over to San Francisco, an Irish haven. Alice becomes the original Dorothy striding toward Oz, big emerald city rising above fog.

Her band has brains, heart, and courage. How Alice Nielsen reaches San Francisco by December 1891 requires a succession of miracles only her natural talent and boldness make possible.

1890s: STAIRWAY TO STARDOM

1891: VAUDEVILLE's YELLOW BRICK ROAD

Touring companies not-so-mysteriously spurn Alice Nielsen in that trying time after her September divorce filing. She is poor in October 1891. Impatient to get going. In a bind. Yet travel could be dangerous, not only from the common Wild West perils but by winter weather which gives rise to such theatre tales as "A harrowing story comes from Michigan. A snowbound Uncle Tom party was reduced to the necessity of eating the trained donkeys" (*Dallas Morning News*, 1886).

Alice knew these tales everybody knew. All newpapers published syndicated theatre news to readers, and gave local stage doings at great detail. Theatre had the intense focus of today's pro sports. Weekly theatre-industry magazines such as *The Musical Courier* tell the insider details; monthlies focus their features on the stars and hit shows. In this era churches are covered for musical hires closely as stage.

Theatre in this golden age of live performance reigns as one of the world's biggest industries. Big-town papers like NY's *Brooklyn Telegraph* specialize in theatre news. Theatre feeds many people: all music is live, the stages live, the only media is print.

October 1891 Alice would be aware: Modjeska is "tired of barnstorming and one-night stands and wants a rest; Henry Irving's pet dramatist Mr. Willis is a Kilkenny man and a fire-eater; Theatre parties are coming into vogue throughout the country and will probably soon develop into a craze; Dora Wiley has been engaged by Robert Grau for an opera company which he is organizing and starts out on the road on March 1, opening at New Haven" with *Bohemian Girl* since "the country has been surfeited with melodrama".

Bitter Missouri winter approaches, Alice Nielsen seeks out. "Nothing prevented me from organizing my own company, and thus was born that quartet of willing and durable singers of which you probably never heard".

Her singers are pals from community theatre. For publicity angle she claims she coined "Chicago Church Choir Company...the 'Chicago' being adopted because, in my estimation, anything coming from that city was necessarily excellent. Big-time singers, you see. None of us had ever been anywhere near Chicago, but there was no reason why we should admit it".

No trace of her claimed named group comes to light. Should have. Didn't because wasn't. Well did once, one night only. As we shall discover.

Her hijacked alliterative name was "Chicago Church Choir Opera Company" with various truncations for various newspaper columns which had since 1879 toured the Midwest performing *Pinafore* and the usual repertory. Alice wasn't in it—her later Bostonian cronies had been. Cast included the librettist Harry Smith and alto Jessie Bartlett Davis. Davis, who sang briefly with Adelina Patti in a tour managed by Mapleson before finding fame in The Bostonians' *Robin Hood*, originated the Alan-a-Dale drag king "trouser role" of Harry Smith's script, a repeated feature for Nielsen shows repeated from *Evangeline*.

Davis' husband, partner of producer JH Haverley, toured minstrelsy and, interestingly, juvenile opera companies. Home base was Haverley's Theatre in Chicago. William Adams in *Our American Cousins* (1883) noticed the group, "a party of ladies and gentlemen who were formerly attached to a religious establishment.... When I visited Milwaukee, large posters on the walls announced that Gilbert & Sullivan's *Patience* would be performed in the theatre on the following Sunday".

Hijacking the name from a litigious Chicago producer would be intolerable, so again we find diva Alice somewhy spreads fog across this sequence of life. Leaves a hinted trail.

No doubt Alice Nielsen's 1891 winter trek from Kansas City to San Francisco was the biggest adventure imaginable. Nearly November when the five Kansas City kids form a band to hit the road. All are about twenty. Alice was joined by tenor Sam Sterrett, contralto Juliette Bothwell, manager "John Haines", and "a bass named Madeiro".

If her comrades seem obscure today, Nielsen lards obscurity by misspelling their names. Indeed, Alice had hijacked the cast of that one-night wonder *Chanticleer* which in pre-opening hubris hoped for a regional tour now realized. After vaudeville adventures, the tenor Sterrett is lost to us, perhaps became judge. And Haines is "John Haynes" *Chanticleer* assistant director and tenor understudy. Otherwise lost, perhaps a lawyer.

Juliet Bothwell settles in Illinois. *Jerseyville Republican* at her 1918 death reports "a wonderful contralto voice and never hesitated to make use of it...for the benefit of charity or friends". Bothwell participated in the musical life of her town and toured the region, "one of the organizers of the well-known Twentieth Century Quartet of young women of Jerseyville. She played a prominent part in the organization and later success of the Monday Musical Club".

Alice's basso "Madeiro" was renown in Kansas City. His thrice-married Presbyterian minister dad introduced Harry Truman to the future Mrs. Truman. Alice's typical phonetic misspelling masks his correct name— Addison Dashiell Madeira, Jr. (1859-1930), a career worth exploring. Born Kentucky, raised KC. After the wintery Alice adventures Madeira will settle in 1892 Minnesota, apparently lured from his understudy gig with The Bostonians by innovative Andrews' Opera Company (whilst also church soloist and in Saint Paul's "Lotus Male Quartette").

Singing bell-ringers in a circus wagon, the Andrews' eleven kids opened for the genuine Chicago Church Choir Company's *Pinafore* in 1882. They liked it to hijack it. After a quick visit to Chicago to spy out The Bostonians and steal a cast they recast themselves an opera company. They offer "opera in English" at low prices. With thirty shows in repertoire they crisscross California and the South to such huge success the Andrews will buy race horses and build resorts.

The Andrews' 1898 tour includes "Dashiell Madeira...fine baritone formerly of the Bostonians". Pennsylvania press say in *Martha* the he "obtained a large part of the applause...a fine and finished singer". The Andrews can well afford to retire after a last 1901 Kansas City show.

In 1899 Madeira joins NYC's branch of Boston's influential Castle Square Opera Company with huge repertory of light and grand "opera in English". By 1901 Madeira is a recording pioneer for Victor and Edison, singing on cylinder hits *Calvary, In the Shadow of the Pines, Little Black Me*, and *Polly and I Were Sweethearts*. Leaving New York by 1903, Madeira ambitiously opens a Minneapolis opera school. His skills supply "a thorough dramatic as well as musical training to his pupils and the course will also include Delsarte physical culture".

Among Madeira coaching credits he links a now-famed Alice Nielsen.

A musical life, Madeira sings fifteen years in Minneapolis at "Metropolitan Opera House". Returns to Kansas City 1919 to run "a large manufacturing plant which he owns". As president of NYC-based National Opera Association, Madeira joins EM Andrews and Boyd White in the "Opera Festival Association of America" giving a week or two of opera in "the larger cities". Clever *Musical Courier* that year reunites Nielsen and Madeira (adjacent pages): his portrait for National Opera Association backs Alice Nielsen's Montreal concert portrait. In 1920 Madeira creates lyrics to *Deep In My Heart, Beloved* by Kansas City songster Charles Johnson, two years later sings a Montana *Mikado* "in lieu of the proposed minstrel show". The basso dies at 71 in 1930.

Youngsters Nielsen, Maderia, Bothwell, Sterrett, Haynes got talent. The Kansas City kids start out on the yellow-brick vaudeville road seeking that great emerald city San Francisco. Via Omaha, Denver, Salt Lake.

Before setting out, Alice says, the quintet hacks together "*Penelope*, a hodge-podge show made up of hits from a dozen operas and musical comedies". Trail goes ninety miles north to St. Joseph, where Alice recently sang a wedding.

By foot, stagecoach and train, they stop at any possible place to raise any possible audience, "always singing between stops and probably sang more and better in the trains and stage-coaches than we did in the performances". Alice says these Kansas City kids were "exceedingly hard to cast down, which was very fortunate with the thermometer out of sight and hotels heated with gas jets and red flannel". Yet they persist.

In luxurious contrast The Bostonians would tour west that March, reaching Aspen's Wheeler opera house "sixty in number, [who] travel in their own private cars on their own special train. The cars are elegantly furnished and the fortunate singers make life one long holiday excursion".

DeWolf Hopper recalls, "Hardship, discomfort and misadventure are inescapable in trouping. Hotels were bad as a rule, train service infrequent and unreliable, theaters individually owned and operated and each stand a law unto itself; companies were usually wildcat enterprises compounded of hope and enthusiasm, the business unorganized and the player with no protection beyond the good faith of the manager. Thanks to Equity, the actor or actress left stranded or unpaid to-day has only himself to blame. Then we accepted conditions as a matter of course, expected them when we set out, muddled through them with as much ingenuity as we could muster and forgot them with the week or the season".

Alice had a fanciful bill as copycat Jenny Lind, Swedish Nightingale: "You can imagine how I felt, a nightingale in such a climate and Swedish at that. I tell you it was hard luck singing in Missouri" where a "local manager, an Irishman, asked us to sing a little piece for him when we arrived. After we had done so, he said he had never heard anything so bad in all his life. As to the Nightingale, he would give her three dollars to sing ballads, but the rest of the troupe were beneath contempt. His language was a dialect blue that was awful".

Alice declines to specify St. Joseph yet has tactfully identified Arthur Pryor's father Samuel, noted for skill cussing and as bandleader at St. Joseph Opera Theatre built 1873, managed by Orson Parker who recurs much later in our wonderland Alice story. Samuel also is house bandleader for St. Joseph *Eden Musee* vaudeville and waxworks chain. Born Missouri 1845, his wife Mary three years later, they live literally in theatre: an apartment inside the theatre. For his three sons, Samuel marks musical mistakes with a slap from a violin bow.

From Samuel, or sons, Nielsen would know about the success of St. Joseph's famed Miss Manfred "charming soprano of the Pyke Opera Company". Samuel's son Arthur its music director. Based in Denver then Los Angeles, Pyke tours as far as Canada. Pyke, unlike Nentwig, was devoted to his wife's career. Charles M. Pyke (1857-1934) had taught school in Kalamazoo, "pleasant off the stage and on, although he wears his hair short when not before the footlights". His director Mr. Martens, "a gentleman of eminent qualifications as a musician and conductor". Cast includes the former dentist Louis Delange. Pyke performs the usual popular repertory, devotes himself to Miss Manfred (Mrs. Pyke in private life) "a charming soprano" from St. Joseph "where her family resides. The young lady adopted the operatic stage" a decade ago 1881. Alice will recognize Pyke as a very good gig, and Pyke will later hire several singing Nielsen sisters. Here fog descends. September-December 1891 as Alice sings toward San Francisco in a rush. By late 1892 she is settled and set.

In Kansas City the Pryors were well-known. Samuel's band toured with his sons who starred on trombone, cornet, drums. Early that year 1891 the Pryor kids toured town with Alessandro Liberati, Italian bandleader and cornetist. Handsome Arthur, Alice's age, conducts at Pyke in Denver.

Alice needs out. Foggily, Alice claims Arthur Pryor was *Eden Musee's* music director in Omaha and sticks with it. He wasn't. Her story is the Kansas City kids discover they need Omaha for a paying gig since St. Joseph locals are baffled by fancy Kansas City songs: "I don't think that in some of the towns we struck they'd ever heard anything newer than the *Maiden's Prayer*, and that was as much as they wanted. But I just sang for all I was worth and I tried to educate them, too".

Maiden's Prayer, 1860's parlor hit, elaborate melody by Thekla Badarzewska given English words by John Adams. Chekov mentions it his 1901 play *Three Sisters*. Nielsen sang: "*Each hour of life to thee I turn; toward thee my inmost soul doth yearn*".

From St. Patrick's repertoire, Alice offers St. Joseph another: "I sang the *Angel's Serenade*, and they didn't like it, because when they tried to whistle it in the auditorium, they couldn't". *Angel's Serenade*, 1880s

Italian art song hit by Gaetano Braga, also complex melody, English by CW Chiplin. Victor Herbert plays cello on a 1910 recording. Nielsen sang: "*What heav'nly sounds are these I hear! Music so sweetly stealing, 'tis the song of the angels wafting hence, Earth's fragile ties revealing*".

When Nielsen's new-fangled songs strike out with St. Joe yokels, the plucky kids jump thirty miles north to Maryville: "Arrived in a snowstorm and, utterly unconcerned over our financial condition which like the weather, was a zero, registered at the hotel and hurried over to the opera house. It was nothing at all for us to arrive in a town a few minutes before we were to sing. Little things like schedules and rehearsals did not concern us. We needed no formal rehearsals anyway; we were always singing".

Starting badly got worse: "A distinctly unsympathetic owner asked us how long our performance lasted. I think our program was to consume two hours, but this was not satisfactory to him. If we couldn't entertain for least two and a half hours we were, he said, cheating the public. Besides, he added, we ought to do something besides sing. I suggested a few dances. No, he said, dancing was sinful. No dancing. Whereat Sam Sterrett inquired about the propriety of magic. Would a few sleight-of-hand tricks do? They would. 'But', said the theatre owner ominously, 'they'd better be good, and don't take no watches from the audience. The last magician tried that and was run out of town afterwards.'"

Maryville sport was to run visitors out of town. An audience appears on cue, "perhaps forty ladies and gentlemen, who sat steaming in the chairs wrapped in overcoats and blankets because the hall was not heated and the storm outside was rapidly becoming a blizzard".

In haste to start, gamines Alice and Juliette err: "There was no dressing room, so we strung a sheet in one corner". They put a lamp on table and began to change. "We were unconsciously treating the audience to a shadow pantomime performance". When they realize, "I held my skirts out while the contralto dressed, and she did the same for me.

"Apparently the men folks in the audience were not offended, but the women were. Juliette and I were clearly a pair of loose hussies who had come to Maryville meaning no good to the male population".

Risqué prelude met disfavor, audience "distinctly hostile, the women refused to encourage such lewd creatures and the men didn't dare. We made a swift shift in our program, and Sam and his parlor tricks went on next. Sam was a fearful failure. It was a coin trick, and before Sam had ceased assuring the audience that the hand was quicker than the eye, the coin hit the stage with a decisive ring. Recovering it, he tried again. This time the coin not only fell out of his hand but vanished through a crack in the floor. And this being the only coin Sam or any of us had, he made the great mistake of asking one of the gentlemen in the audience to lend him a fifty-cent piece.

"That was where the show ended. That satisfied the ladies that Juliette and I were not only birds of prey but that Sam was a crook. Led by a few of the more indignant ladies, the entire audience arose and demanded that we were going to get out of that hall and keep on going. Blizzard or no blizzard, we might not stay in Maryville where, apparently, men were men and not to be trusted.

"They did not demand that we return their money—twenty-five cents each—because they would attend to that themselves. Whereat they went roaring out, headed for the box office. But when they got there they found that somebody had beaten them. Our bass singer [Madeira] had, for one; but even he had been too late. He found only four dollars in the till which, being four dollars more than we had, he took.

"So we left Maryville without argument, stopping at the hotel long enough to be told that we could not have our bags (large canvas carryalls) because we owed the proprietor a dollar apiece for the rooms we hadn't occupied. We huddled together around the red-hot stove in the hotel lobby and sang the *Hallelujah Chorus* for the assembled mob, which included the chief of police and the sheriff. And then we set forth for the next town, whatever it might be and wherein we had no booking. Set forth on foot, of course. How else?

"All that Saturday night, the five of us plunged through the snow, losing the blizzard-blanketed road, tumbling over buried fences. To keep warm we bombarded one another with snowballs, and once we helped a farmer get his storm-shackled wagon out of the ditch.

"We were having the time of our lives.

"The sun was not yet up when we stumbled into the next village, ten or twelve miles from Maryville". In the cold pre-dawn, tiny hamlet Pickering produces a blessing: "We halted in front of a little wooden church, next to which was the parsonage. 'sing', cried Haines, in whose mind an idea had burst. 'sing that *Angels Ever Bright And Fair*. One, two—' And we sang it—Handel's *Angels Ever Bright And Fair*—in front of that parsonage.

"A window went whining upward and the clergyman—an earnest young man with a great shock of black hair—popped forth his head. He listened for a moment, smiled pleasantly and vanished". He invites them inside: "And then, doing the cooking himself, he fed us ham and eggs and coffee. As we ate we surrendered to the weariness that the excitement of the night had fended off. We were just tired children and that parson—whose name, I am ashamed to own, I have forgotten—put us to bed as such".

They "awoke many hours later and I told the clergyman our story—all of it. The truth, I mean. I sang in his choir that evening. Afterward, in the parsonage, he asked us what our plans were. 'so you want to keep on', he said. 'I had hoped you children would want to go home. But I learned a long time ago that it is often wrong to stand in the way of young people who are following a healthy ambition.'"

The practical Methodist parson in 1891 Pickering helps make Alice Nielsen's career possible. Arranges a fund-raiser. "'But you'll need money, won't you? Omaha, you say. Well, that's pretty far away. See here. Our little church is giving a concert tomorrow night. We have some local talent, but I'm sure that if you will sing we shall do better and take in more money. And perhaps there will be enough for you to get to Omaha.'

"We sang in the church concert—until midnight. In the morning the clergyman (I hate myself for forgetting his name) bought us tickets for Omaha and gave us enough cash to keep us from hunger for a few days. He walked with us to the railroad station and gave us his blessing. 'Be good children', was his benediction. 'If the prayers of a village parson can help you—they're yours.'

"On the train we thought it over. A suspicion fixed itself in our minds. That church concert had been organized for two purposes—to buy a new roof and a new carpet for the church and to pay that parson's back salary. Produced enough for both. But the man had given us his back salary".

Omaha train delivers them, she says, to Samuel Pryor's son Arthur, who immediately lets them break a leg. She reflects, the Kansas City kids "got that far or even half that far" thanks only "to the vast musical appetite of the provincial public of that day, to the kindnesses of audiences toward the efforts of children and, to a very large extent, to our own powers of endurance". Consistently, mature diva Alice Nielsen recalls teenage deeds as child-like. Prodigy seems all-too-easy for a genius by given nature.

Alice continues, the Kansas City kids take *Eden Musee's* stage "where for a dime you could enter at any time and remain until you could stand no more". Open from 1-to-10pm, Omaha's *Eden Musee* stood at Eleventh and Farnam, French-owned vaudeville version of wax sculptor Madame Marie Tussaud's galleries had expanded nationwide from New York.

Alice Nielsen lists her fave vaudeville acts.

That Omaha season, she says, "You not only heard the Chicago Church Choir Company sing an amazing variety of comic operas, cantatas, oratorios and popular ballads, but you saw a menagerie of wild animals, stupendous fat ladies riding bicycle races, Siamese twins, sword-swallowers, Jo-Jo The Dog-Faced Boy, a gigantic tragedian doing *Big Moments From Shakespeare* and reciting such classics as *Spartacus To The Gladiators* and *Curfew Shall Not Ring Tonight* (when sober), a four-part stock company in high-society dramas and, of course, all sorts of acrobats and equilibrists".

Let's explore these mainstream acts of Alice's youth. If none actually appear at Omaha's *Eden Musee* when she suggests, that's not her point. These are the acts the child Alice may have seen with mom.

"Jo-Jo the Dog-Faced Boy" was Fedor Jeftichew (1868-1904), a Russian with the "'werewolf" disease, hypertrichosis. Made famous by P.T. Barnum, hairy Jo-Jo would bark and growl on cue. From a French circus, Barnum brought him to America 1884. To Greece Fedor retires rich.

Spartacus to the Gladiators at Capua, 1846 monologue by Maine clergyman Elijah Kellogg (1813-1901) familiar to every American schoolboy forced to recite, "O comrades! warriors! Thracians! If we must fight, let us fight for ourselves! If we must slaughter, let us slaughter our oppressors! If we must die, let it be under the clear sky, by the bright waters, in noble, honorable battle!"

Curfew Shall Not Ring Tonight: 1870 poem by Indiana's Rose Thorpe (1859-1939) of a woman who silences the town's steeple bell to save her beloved, "*I've a lover in the prison, doomed this very night to die, At the ringing of the curfew, and no earthly help is nigh*". She jumps onto the bell's clapper to silence it and stop execution of her man.

In Omaha, Alice claims, her billing morphs from Swede successor to Jenny Lind to the replacement for Adelina Patti. "I was eighteen years old, looked fourteen, and regarded myself as a Patti. Even a trifle better than

Patti. I recall that I was billed as 'The Little American Patti', which may have sounded a bit superlative to the author of that advertisement but did not summon a blush to my cheek. Patti, I told our management, was all right in her time; but what—just what—could she do that I couldn't. I had never heard Patti and don't remember having any great curiosity about the lady". Diva's double irony; prodigy Patti went pro age eleven to make a fast fortune, a petite six inches shorter than five-two Alice, highly unlikely to have missed Patti's Kansas City concerts. And in future Eleonora Duse would make their introductions in Italy.

Now Nielsen's memoirs, mark you, introduce with a flourish: Arthur Pryor. Since age eleven billed for trombone as "Boy Wonder of Missouri", he plays all instruments, plus piano skills from mom and Professor Plato. They would soon become strong forces in American music culture.

In frugal *Eden Musee*, she says, "nobody got anything approximating an adequate salary for the prodigious amount of work he did, not even the piano player, a slight, blond youth who seemed never to stop".

Alice admires Arthur: "If anybody in the *Eden Musee* had talent, this young pianist had. His was the most amazing versatility, commanding an endless repertoire. When, as sometimes happened, singers arrived without scores for what they wanted to give the audience, he would merely nod at the name of the piece or the first few words and play it with utter unconcern and accuracy".

After five decades of her own concerts, diva Nielsen says: "There are accompanists and accompanists. There great ones not only inspire the artist with confidence, but so cover the singer's mistakes that none but the ear trained to music can detect error and rescue. Such was he". These Missouri music geniuses had rapport: "Somehow even his smile restored your slipping assurance".

Starts singing and stops due to lions: "I faced the audience with four apparently hungry lions at my back. An animal act followed me—four lions in whose cage a daring young man sang several songs and turned handsprings". Alice describes the stage, "a series of drops and an intricate arrangement of wings separating lions, tigers, singers, comedians, magicians and acrobats from one another".

Growling lions panic her, skips a "bow to the audience before launching forth upon Rossini. The thing for me to do was to sing poised for instant flight and as near the open wings as possible. It was bad enough to know that they were there, within a short snatch of my legs; but they had to make it worse by snuffling and chop-licking, with a growl tossed in now and then". She has stage bite.

Freezes: "Doubtless that piano player understood. But my voice refused to respond to his introductory phrases, and he repeated them. I gave him a despairing look and then glanced fearfully over my shoulder toward where the lions were apparently getting hungrier by the moment. 'sing', he cried softly. 'Never mind about the lions, they can't reach you. Anyway they haven't teeth enough for anything stronger than bread and milk. Sing.' So I sang, quaveringly at first". Sings Alice Nielsen of magnetic voice and the most beautiful woman in Kansas City just now—widowed—at almost twenty.

Nielsen and Pryor! First duet! Did they foresee they would join forces to San Francisco? Spent a season together. Two seasons. They had time.

These brilliant young concert performers' 1891 duet debut: Domenico Scarlatti's liturgical *Inflammatus et Accensus*, from *Sabat Mater* (1713-1719). Nielsen sang: "*Inflammatus et accensus per te, Virgo sum defensus in die judicii*". In English, "*Inflamed and burning, my I be defended by thee, O Virgin, at the day of judgment*". *Inflammatus* and *accensus* mark a fiery coloratura: the piece Patti sang to golden profit.

Romantically, Alice recalls singing as she looks "straight into his pleasant, amused eyes". She sings when her eyes in his were fastened: "Doubtless I made mistakes which he skillfully covered up. The audience recalled me twice, but it was he they were applauding, not I".

She finishes her anecdote, "You may have heard of him since. His name is Arthur Pryor". This phrase, "you may have heard of" was reserved by Alice for her pride in knowing two peers: Arthur Pryor, and Eleonora Duse.

Today Pryor has been nearly lost to us. Her 1930s readers would recognize Pryor, famed trombone virtuoso, bandleader, composer, ASCAP founder, record producer in the heyday of brass bands. Perhaps you may not have heard of him. No biography of his has been made at this time! This book points the way and hopefully incites interest.

To dispel fog, Nielsen's play at Omaha October 1891 seems open to doubts. Left Kansas City late September, made San Francisco by December. Wraps meeting Arthur Pryor with careful caution. After creating his first composition *Thoughts of Love* around Alice in 1893, two years later in Salt Lake he marries Utah's Maude Russell, child born the next year.

Let us raise the Omaha curtain.

During September at *Eden Musee*, manager Will Lawler offers "Maggle the Midget Mother and her Babe", a Turkish act, Kaston & Quinn in athletic exhibitions, John & Ella McCray, Piquette & Musgraven. Same fare to end of month. No Nielsen in September.

Omaha October, Lawler books talks by Alaskan explorer, Grace Courtland the "Witch of Wall Street", Culhane's Comedy Co., "Zoyarros Arial Artists", musical kings Sharp & Flat, vocalist Giselle Baker, Sundal & Ruthden impressionists, "Seymour the mind healer", "Zeke the Baboon", "The Dancing Bears", Fitzpatrick Family, "the Rowe Purvis Dog Circus", Johnson Trio, "Neal in wax", a sketch of Pinney Farm, "Chittenden the Explorer", Indian scout Joseph Collins, "Donald McGregor the Irish bag-piper", Fitzpatrick Family, bell-ringers Reinhoer's Tyrolean Warblers, and the famed nine-year-old actress Lotte Lodge playing her masterpiece *Editha's Burglar*.

No Nielsen. Unless she plays Lotte Lodge, not untypical vaudeville fraud as she could pass younger. Yet Lotte has played the play four years: doesn't sing.

November's *Musee* offers "Princes Fedora snake charmer", "Tony the dog detective", Panorama of Johnston Flood, "Taylors second-sight artists", baritone Diamond, "Musgrave and Planquette quick-change artists", Retti Ben Dey's impalement art, Jonas Carpenter "149 years old", Grace Courtland, "the Lake sisters highland dancers", "James Thompson the vocalist and dancer", Rogert & O'Brien musical artists, "Powers and Hanson female impersonators".

Lastly, December *Musee* presents Demetrius Kohopiski escaped Nihilist from Siberia, Abdi Ala Rei, Amphion Quartet Co., "Big Missouri Girl" 8-foot tall Ella Swing, comedians Harry Fitzgerald & Donald Lewis plus, "*Fun in a Grocery Store*, the satirical hit of the day".

No Nielsen not neither. Her group never appears in Omaha that season.

Back spring, June 1891 at St. Joseph's *Eden Musee* "St. Joseph's Favorite Trombone Soloist" Arthur Pryor was the top-bill a week, and his hiring offer from the great Gilmore touted on October 12th by the prideful hometown press.

Interestingly, Pryor will postpone Gilmore to music direct Alice Nielsen.

The plot ripens. Nielsen fave "Jo-Jo the Dog-faced Boy" spent a December week at St. Joseph before "Chicago Church Choir Concert Company" appears at *Musee* January 17th 1892 in *Buttons and Beans* starring "Arnold Barrington" as "Beans" with "Miss Camille Atherton", "Jano C. Estlake", and most significantly: "Miss Rose Southern" the already-hinted alias for Alice Nielsen. They play only one night. Their names and show title vanish. Except of course "Rose Southern". Alice had two sisters and a brother with musical theatre skills. Seizing an established group name, easy. She'd do it again.

Beyond Arthur Pryor, two St. Joseph names briefly appear in Alice's future life. Pryor, of course, during the year Alice separates from husband and hits the road, has been repeatedly in Kansas City. During 1891 he plays regional circuits. Transits Kansas City to return home to St. Joseph. Conveniently for Alice's escape, he is in Denver as music director of Pyke Opera that fall. May 1892, Pryor and Nielsen (as "Rose Southern") have aligned with Burton Stanley for a Salt Lake season. Very likely, two lovely Irish prodigies Alice and Arthur met in Kansas City circles and made plans.

Genius loves company. Let nature take its course.

Retracing the scene, 1891 Omaha in October enjoys a well-publicized tour of Great Gilmore Band's hundred players plus vocal quartet including Italian tenor Campanini, soprano Ida Klein, baritone S. Kronberg, "and others to be announced later". Even Sousa plugs Gilmore, "I found no Band equal to Gilmore's organization anywhere" (*Omaha* Oct 24). During his annual cross-country tour, Gilmore reaches St. Louis by October 16, they play Omaha's Coliseum October 26th. In Kansas City, Gilmore auditions Arthur Pryor and offers a job. Pryor delays, Gilmore passes away; Pryor puts off lucrative Sousa until 1893.

Helping Alice Nielsen is more important to him. Arthur Pryor delays joining the best-known bands in the land to spend a season as music director for cross-dressing vocal comic Burton Stanley's burlesque delights. Even so, Alice's pastor story rings true: his help got her to Denver. The author met his granddaughter living across from the church.

Our next hint of anticipation. In St. Joseph, Nielsen tells *Boston Journal* (Oct 29, 1910), she "experienced her first stranding and where she first had a chance to show her marked benevolence—extraordinary benevolence, as some observers of the musical profession describe it—by securing a position in the *Eden Musee* so as to help herself and her associates move West". Directed by Arthur Pryor's dad Samuel. "After brief but breezy experiences with a concert company, she found her first position in opera" with Pyke in Denver, "singing Yum Yum in the *Mikado*".

Which she in fact sang with Burton Stanley, not Pyke.

And Nielsen arrives in San Francisco in early December 1891, she sang at for Christmas at the St. Patrick's.

1891 Kansas City; busy season for talents in transition. Stanislaus Stange goes east. Liberati, tapped by Ringling 1895 to create the first circus band, loses Arthur Pryor who delays lucrative Gilmore. Pryor and brothers (Walter cornet, Sam drums) were with Liberati since mid-1880s.

Pryor and Nielsen head West. Thanks to Alice's colorfully inaccurate tale of progress over the yellow-brick road to California, tales these two tell years later mismatch. When Nielsen speaks vaguely, she hints a story.

Her tales of this season vary. Until this biography, persons telling of Arthur Pryor's passage to join Sousa repeat the claims he somewhy left Liberati until hired in Denver as music director-pianist for Stanley Opera Company; occasionally saying he starts with Pyke before Stanley. Pryor with stark simplicity does say he delayed joining Sousa until fall 1892, without explanation.

If the Pryor brothers met the Nielsen sisters at Kansas City, Arthur is mum. Yet from early 1891 Alice's problems with Nentwig worsen.

Pryor & Nielsen, prodigy performance artists, matchless Missouri couple with great influence upon American music culture. Tracing their lifelong professional contact, two decades later when Pryor's band tours with Redpath Chautauqua, Nielsen is highest-paid performer on the circuit. His assistant Simone Mantia is Met orchestra manager when Nielsen has a suite at the building. Pryor conducts Sousa Band's recordings (Sousa detests newfangled "canned music"). Nielsen sings for Sousa, who states he admires her talent among the world's best. After 1903, Pryor tours and conducts his own band at Asbury Park, NJ. Composer of over three-hundred songs, Pryor joins Victor Herbert and Sousa to create ASCAP. For Victor Talking Machines, Pryor produces about 2,500 recordings. Pryor will conduct the Herbert memorial service in New York, the only reunion of Alice Nielsen Company.

Alice Nielsen, risking her way west, says in Denver she drops the Kansas City kids. She and Pryor combine there with Pyke then jump to Burton Stanley headed back to San Francisco. Stanley is certainly capable of wonderfully singing *Mikado*'s *Yum-Yum* as Nielsen sings tenor, Pryor conducting. Within a decade, Stanley's publicity touts Alice Nielsen sang in his group. As her memoirs hint, Alice temporarily takes alias "Rose Southern" to avoid her meddling husband. In alias, she tours with Stanley and Pyke until safe to resume her own name due to new and very influential San Francisco friends. The durable alias passes to Julia Nielsen, who as the next "Rose Southern" with Pyke gets a nod from 1894 *Sacramento Daily Record-Union*, saying she "is well-known here".

"Rose Southern" was useful to Alice 1891-92 with Burton Stanley.

Popular drag diva, the musical comic Burton Stanley enjoys a long diverse stage career. Deserves a sustained glance. Credibly set Alice Nielsen's career in motion during her vulnerable year on vaudeville road seeking San Francisco. With a glory voice, he's expert at sustained comedy. Few could provide better expertise for effective stagecraft. He performs, produces, directs, authors for every popular musical category: minstrelsy, burlesques, vaudevilles, opera.

Chicago Tribune (1879) bills Stanley "greatest female impersonator". And his soprano voice has no superior. His skits, his burlesques of opera divas, prove persistently popular. His comedy gives audiences "a continuous laugh for three hours". Honed by far-flung tours by 1891, "the famous comedian in his familiar female roles" is a proven showman, skilled impersonator and character actor, praised director trusted by producers. For any music theatre repertory he could sing *prima donna*, his burlesques of reigning divas beautifully sung. As actor-for-hire in skits he could join any ensemble: straight, in cork, in drag, in song.

Stanley's career originates obscurely overseas in Dublin and London, perhaps as a "comic duettist" with Harry Web; age unknown. To counter Stanley's obscurity, we trace his progress over two decades before joined by Alice Nielsen. R. Burton "Burt" Stanley arrives in America during November 1873 for a Southern tour from Thalian Hall in Wilmington, NC, the usual start of Southeastern tours as a major railway hub. His success is immediate and prolonged. November 15th, reports Columbia SC's *Daily Phoenix*, "Burton Stanley is a most admirable personator of female character, and has remarkable vocal adaptabilities for such personations".

In 1874 New York, *Brooklyn Daily Eagle* puts "Greatest impersonator of female characters in the world, Mr. Burton Stanley" onstage at Holley's opera house in a minstrelsy group. Stanley rapidly switches skits as any opportunity to form his own group.

By 1875, "Burton Stanley's Costume Company" is touring from St. Louis; August he joins top flight Haverley's Minstrels. In 1876 Alabama, Mobile *Register* reports "Burton Stanley becomes more inexplicable to us the more we see him. Every movement, look, tone, and gesture are perfect. His make-up is sufficient to deceive the very best judges, and yet make-up is his least merit. In those small trifles, such as arranging his hair, touching his earring and particularly using his needle, we look in vain for the clumsiness of all other female impersonators. His voice in singing is also feminine to the life, being a clear, full and round soprano, with a vibrant ring in the upper register that never once forgets itself in a masculine twang".

From Mobile to Memphis to New Orleans to Dallas, where *Daily Herald* December 19 reports "Burton Stanley as a delineator of female character has won quite a reputation, and we understand is the only man on the stage who has a real soprano voice". In 1878 Baltimore we find Burton Stanley and his son "the boy soprano Clyde Stanley" joining Eddie Stanley and Mabel Stanley in a tour of "their farcical comedy *Flirting*" far as Salt Lake. Same year, the Green Bay *Advocate* announces "The Great London Sensation Burton Stanley".

Interestingly given Alice's hints, Stanley regroups for the *Pinafore* fad, and within a year of *Pinafore's* London debut, 1879 Chicago *Inter Ocean* announces "Burton Stanley's Juvenile *Pinafore*". Reporting "a full house" in April, Oshkosh press say, "Don't forget Burton Stanley's Juvenile

Pinafore". Still going strong in winter, Chicago *Daily Tribune* touts Fielding Theatre's "Burton Stanley's Juvenile Company featuring Twelve first-class and Beautiful Children in Gilbert & Sullivan's *Pinafore*". Before year end, however, Oshkosh *Daily Northwestern* suggests Stanley's "Juvenile Pinafore Company...did not meet expenses".

Disbanding, Stanley moves to minstrelsy with *Oglesby's Troubadors*.

By next year 1879, Stanley again headlines as "greatest of female impersonators" in a vaudeville with "Sam Dearin, the musical man" and "pleasing Serio-Comic artist Trixie Vernon" at Hamlin's theatre. By 1880, papers tell us that "Clement Bros and Forrestor's Concert Company" is "strengthened this year by Mr. Burton Stanley, a male soprano, and an artist of great merit". His ensemble plays Green Bay in June; Helena in November. In 1882, *Chicago Daily Tribune* hails "Burton Stanley, the best of all Burlesque Prima Donnas" in his *Opera Flashes*, as *Philadelphia Times* praises the "finest of any female impersonator" at Arch Theatre before he tours into Wheeling WV with Leavitt's Gigantean Minstrels. "Music and mirth are well combined by this lively company", adds *Philadelphia Inquirer* (Nov. 21).

Resurfacing across America in April 1882 Nevada, he "contributed the usual negro business" before wheeling to Wheeling in Leavitt's Gigantean Minstrels. By January 1883, he starts a long West Coast stay, Sacramento Record-Union praising "especially his imitation of Kate Castleton" the musical comedy star, as player Stanley passes *en route* to Portland and other points. From 1883, again significantly for Alice Nielsen, Burton Stanley grows a very well-established success playing California with Emerson's Minstrels, or solo, or leading his own company. *Daily Alta California* November 4th praises his show at San Francisco's Bush Street theatre, "Burton Stanley's imitation of Kate Castleton was capitally done".

Ranging across America that decade, Stanley in California creates a duo act with Gus Pixley. They join Emerson's Minstrels and tour widely. As Nielsen would sail thirteen years later, Stanley sails from 1885 California for a Pacific tour arriving Australia on *RMS Zealandia* with Gus Pixley and fifteen players of Emerson's Minstrels. Stanley tours also New Zealand, Japan, Hawaii, and such.

Sydney Evening News reports from Gaiety Theatre, "Mr. Burt Stanley again proved himself a very clever female impersonator, and his sketches of Adelina Patti and Maggie Moore were well received". *Melbourne Punch* relates Stanley's "female impersonations are so life-like that nearly all the ladies persist in asserting he is a woman".

As Stanley converges toward Alice, his skill in sustained comedy and song are widely saluted. In 1888 Fort Wayne, he joins "Pixley in *Mrs. Parkington and her son Ike*, at the head of a great Vocal and Comedy cast. A continuous laugh three hours long...the most intensely musical comedy on record". In Lima, Ohio, Stanley and Pixley continue "at the head of a powerful cast of vocal and comedy artists. A continuous roar of laughter for three hours". Stanley and Pixley cover the East and Midwest circuit then return to Kansas with "*A New England Home*" before crossing to Philadelphia and NYC for New Year's 1889.

In 1890 Stanley revisits his long-familiar circuits, plus finds time for New Orleans, Nashville, Minneapolis.

Early 1891, Stanley rejoins his on-and-off potboiler gig (since 1888) playing "Dame Wursa" in sexy extravaganza *The Twelve Temptations*, sequel for *Black Crook* star ballerina Marie Bonfanti, wherein blondes and brunettes dance alternate evenings. After its 1870 debut, the show plays thirty years employing generations of theatre-people. Reviewing it, the *Los Angeles Herald* critic said (1897): "*Twelve Temptations*... affords at least one temptation, which is to compare the popular taste of today with that of thirty years ago. *The Black Crook* was the progenitor of the leg show in this country and in 1867 Fanny Davenport was playing the part of the Fairy Queen in that delectable production".

Changing cultural seasons: *Crook* "caused the greatest sensation, but it was not considered good form for ladies to witness it. It is now bad form to affect prudery...at the up-to-date theatrical 'show.' Other times, other manners. Things that shocked our fathers, not to say our grandfathers, are today strictly permissible. To the pure all things are pure; even a racy extravaganza. *Vive la bagatelle*".

By 1891 Alice's plight is critical. And Stanley works Kansas City before arriving June 14 in Salt Lake, playing San Francisco October 24. They could have met. So now we have Burton Stanley as Alice met him. Working the fading minstrelsy fad, Stanley succeeds in burlesques, vaudevilles, and extravaganza. He picks up the 1880s rising tide of comic or light opera we now call musical theatre.

Before semi-novice Alice hits vaudeville road late 1891, Stanley is a welcome repeat star at every Bay Area venue whose managers will quick-hire the young Nielsen at a critical point in her survival. The great comic, singer, actor, and director is a skilled player perfecting successful characters, costumes, pantomime, stagecraft. He authors his own skits. Alice's future roles will propel her to superstardom in bespoke musicals which rely on her own comedy, dance, acting, and glory voice to carry the show. What better model than Stanley to open doors to theatre success?

Stanley, hailed as a "burlesque prima donna" by George Odell in *Annals of the American Stage*, enjoyed a much larger theatrical life than Alice suggests in her memoirs. Into this theatre context, genius youngsters Alice Nielsen and Arthur Pryor converge with skilled showman Burton Stanley.

They may had met in Kansas City. Certainly in Denver. They organize a tour to San Francisco. Nielsen claims she met Pryor at Omaha's *Eden Musee*, away from Kansas City, St. Joseph, and Denver. Unlikely.

No doubt the couple hit it off: "He left the *Eden Musee* with us". When Alice connects with Arthur Pryor the pair are a producer's dream and Burton Stanley recognizes opportunity. May 1892 the trio of Stanley, Pryor and Nielsen regroup to make more money in the theatre biz at Salt Lake.

Interestingly, she unsticks her story for grand opera. Skips Stanley, tells 1908 *Who's Who on the Stage* she joined Pyke "sang in the chorus...in Oakland, Cal". "Pike Opera House" as she misspells Pyke was in Bay Area after 1886's *Prince Methusalem*, Strauss comic opera. Nielsen repeats this in 1914 *Who's Who of American Women in Music*. In Boston, dear Stanley is dropped from *Who's Who*. But when it really counts, when fog clears for her 1930s lookback, Alice skips Pyke to refocus on colorful critter giving gayety to the world. Restores Stanley somewhat. Taste for genuine always the guiding force. Yet underplays the career of the great musical comedian.

So Alice recalls, "Burton Stanley—whose opera company was not in the best of health—took us into his organization and was overjoyed to get so talented an artist as Pryor. Yet for all of Pryor's genius, the Stanley company refused to be rescued". Stanley's company, she continues, was "not a remarkable outfit in any way except one: Stanley was his own prima donna, singing the soprano roles in a powerful falsetto".

If only we could be there. In fact, Arthur Pryor magically mysteriously reappears as music director, when Stanley in May 1892 directs a praised Salt Lake season of the well-heeled "California Opera Company" in Gilbert & Sullivan and repertory. No drag diva. Stanley is praised for his directing. Talented cast give a "high grade article" at "popular prices within the reach of all". Formula of quality shows at low prices stays a Nielsen mantra.

For Stanley to direct the long-established California Opera Company requires much planning and trust; group being owned and managed by San Francisco's Tivoli Opera House. Tivoli will soon host Alice Nielsen for two years until she joins The Bostonians on national tours. After 1901, her own company's conductor will join Tivoli and help rescue her opera tour after near-disaster in 1905 NYC. And after the successful Salt Lake season for Tivoli managers, Stanley redeploys his own company regionally, occasionally singing diva roles.

Burton Stanley first gives Alice Nielsen star "*prima donna*" billing.

Alice as "Rose Southern" emerges from the chorus in Salt Lake City among the *Mikado* trio. Promoted to *prima donna* under her own name—temptation irresistible—Alice stars as Germaine in *Chimes of Normandy*.

Her Bay Area debut on August 19 1892, says Oakland *Tribune*, has the upscale "Burton Stanley Opera Company" in *Mikado* with cast thirty. In repertory they soon switch to the 1877 hit *Chimes Of Normandy* (Robert Planquette, adapted English, Geoffrey Wilson, 708 London performances).

Nielsen portrays lost heiress, Germaine. In *Legend of The Bells* she sang: "*Yes, that castle old by wizard is enchanted*" &c; the refrain: "*Ding dong, ding dong, ding dong, ding dong, ding dong bell!*" Witnesses say Stanley includes Jacques Offenbach's 1868 *La Perichole* set in Peru. Nielsen plays a pretty street-singer named, well, Périchole.

Nielsen's days with Stanley resemble all-too-closely the second-hand plots hodge-podged by hack wordsmith Harry Smith who for Alice's debut in *Fortune Teller* puts her as gypsy, ballet student, and identical twin brother in uniform. If art imitates life, Smith has none, imitates anybody and happily admits.

So well-liked and connected Stanley delivers Nielsen and Pryor to Oakland. "But there, too", she suggests, "he was short of the success he worked so hard for. Even a male *prima donna* failed to keep the audience interested to the point of paying". Wasn't that way.

With Stanley appears the name Valerga of great significance to Nielsen.

Stanley hired well-liked Bay Area players such as tenor Frank Valerga, who hires Alice for his own projects. Frank tours the gold mining fields and far as Africa. Frank's sister Ida is a famed soprano and vocal coach who brings Alice into grand opera at Tivoli. Eleven Valerga siblings are on the stage. Thanks to Stanley, Alice makes critical contacts for her future.

Burton Stanley starts Alice Nielsen as star. Seasoned tastes and sense of potential at play, he recognizes her magnetism.

San Francisco. If you can make it there, you can make it anywhere.

After August 1892, Alice acquires steady jobs inside San Francisco without touring: Sundays at St. Patrick; during week at vaudeville's capacious Wigwam at Union Square; easy half-mile walk away. So she seemingly settles down in town, as she tells the story.

Stanley revisits Omaha as "Burton Stanley Comedy Company" to perform his own *Razzle Dazzle* and *A Bunch Of Jays*. Brings Bachelor's "school of acting dogs" who do "everything but talk". His company creates "a continual laugh... and with such capable comedians in the cast as Burton Stanley, Lewis Mederic, Harry Barlow, Charley Sully and Jack Raal, there should be no lack of mirth-provoking situations". Action takes place "in the salon of the steamer Bristol" with "special scenery".

Intriguingly, Stanley's Omaha cast has a "Lottie Thorne, the pleasing vocalist and dancer and the greatest of all living child performers" plus "*Le Petit* Freddie, wonderful child phenomenon...exceptionally great musician" who impersonates "celebrated" Patrick Gilmore, plus Carmencita "wonderful Spanish dancer" and minstrel Billy Emerson. "Lottie Thorne" of course is name of character in Margaret Veley's 1878 novel *For Percival*.

"Lottie Lodge" had played Omaha the year before, now "Lottie Thorne"?

Petite Nielsen, child role for cash under alias? Very intriguingly after that Omaha gig, Alice appears a single St. Joseph *Eden Musee* day with trio: two sisters and brother? During 1892 winter, Pryor and Stanley play Omaha's "Wonderland and Bijon" as separate acts. January 1893, Pryor works regional circuit, shares Omaha bill with "Warren children in a perilous trapeze act", Madam Zeondia, Jennie Smyth "character dancer", and Fowler & West "German dialect sketch team".

Back east, Stanley gets an angel: *Wilkes-Barr Times* (PA) reports Mr. Waite providing "a handsome salary and carte blanche to secure the best talent, both stellar and choral, that can be found" for a new production of Stanley Comic Opera Company's *Chimes Of Normandy* in the local "curio hall" (*Eden Musee*). 1894 Stanley returns to San Jose with *La Mascotte* and *Mikado*. His cast also present a skit of "Living Pictures" as riské pantomimes of well-known paintings. Pyke and Stanley often criss-cross: Pyke has "season" in 1895 Salt Lake, Stanley takes over. The Pykes settle down to manage a Fresno opera house, retiring to Los Angeles where a decade later Alice Nielsen performs as a grand opera star. Charles Pyke outlives his dear diva wife until eighty-seven in 1934.

Leaving Stanley and Nielsen after their Salt Lake summer season, Pryor tours with Sousa September to December. Returns to St. Joseph to work the region until 1895, when in Salt Lake meets and marries Maude Russell and Alice Nielsen joins The Bostonians to superstardom.

Nielsen, Pryor and Stanley keep shaping music culture. While minstrelsy pals may believe Stanley retired to run hotels in Rhode Island, in 1897 he returns to juveniles, touring Altoona with "Burton Stanley's

Lilliputian Comedy Company". Told by *Daily Independent,* "A Sensation Everywhere...35-Children in opera *HMS Pinafore*".

When with Sousa in 1900, a Brussels paper dubs Pryor "Paganini of the trombone"; Nielsen is America's highest-grossing musical star; and again at Salt Lake's Wonderland Theatre, *Deseret Evening News* tells us of "the famous comedian Burton Stanley in his well-known female roles. The theatre promises Champagne and oysters" in a double bill "to conclude with the comedy success, *Confusion.* Sunday evening Sacred Concert with full orchestra". Would Stanley burlesque Alice Nielsen?

Fogs surround Burton Stanley afterwards. He appears at a benefit in 1916 Hartford, Connecticut, with another great comic and Alice Nielsen co-star, Joe Cawthorn. 1921 *Philadelphia Inquirer* reflects wistfully, "Not one of the female impersonators, however, of the recent decades ever achieved the artistic success of Burton Stanley".

Whatever happens on vaudeville road, stays.

The young Missouri gang made a way from Kansas City to St. Joseph to Omaha to Denver to Salt Lake City to Oakland to San Francisco where, thanks to Burton Stanley, Alice Nielsen first becomes a star albeit a possible drag-king tenor to a drag-queen soprano. Yet as we see, Stanley is far more than a novelty act. He keeps Alice onstage under his direction in a prestigious Tivoli-sponsored California Opera Company season in Salt Lake. His shows give her a first "prima donna" billing. Stanley is Nielsen's introduction to Bay Area theatre society. Noticed by insider siblings Frank and Ida Valerga, word spreads fast. 1890s a big talent hunt.

So it was. In a few months Alice hurdles from Kansas City crisis to San Francisco plenty. Delivered to 1891 San Francisco by December, Alice joins that town's St. Patrick's choir as Christmas soloist, is a parlor-paid society singer, takes a few jobs with regional touring groups until hired by Stanley pals at The Wigwam on Union Square, an Orpheum theatre. Sends for family. Sarah keeps grandkids, daughters tour, son hired at piano and organ. Critical San Francisco connections made during winter 1891-92.

Stanley, Salt Lake and Oakland cast Lina Crews, Lizzie Daily, Lulu Warde, and "handsome tenor" Frank Valerga whose ten siblings include world-class *bel canto* expert, soprano Ida Valerga sang with Patti in Mapleson's international tours. Valerga parents had arrived from Genoa. By 1900 the Nielsens also live in Oakland, at 560 Sycamore, mile from Ida Valerga's 588 Telegraph Ave. where they have a home theatre.

Ida Valerga is Alice Nielsen's bridge to grand opera. Coaches Alice *bel canto* for Tivoli where Alice becomes a smash *Satanella* and debuts as Lucia. Nielsen claims she first met the Valerga clan at Wigwam; just another stop for Stanley and ensemble; as October 1892 when "proprietor and manager Charles Meyer" proclaims "Burton Stanley Opera Company, largest salaried ensemble now traveling. The list of people comprises twenty-five soloists". Repertory begins with *Bells of Corneville.* But Stanley has played San Francisco years before.

Alice Nielsen's typical path from Kansas City to San Francisco was retold in Louis Strang's *Famous Prima Donnas* (1900). Working from Alice, Boston's Strang skips Stanley and misspells: "Both before and after she joined the choir, Alice appeared in amateur theatricals and in church concerts. She was always applauded and appreciated, but it was in the character of a soubrette in *Chantaclara*, [*Chanticlere*] ... at the Coates Opera House by Professors Maderia and Merrihew [nay, Cramer and Paddock] that she created the most decided sensation. This was but a few weeks before she left Kansas City...with an organization [!] that styled itself the Chicago Concert Company, which planned to tour the small towns of Kansas and Missouri. Miss Nielsen was stranded in St. Joseph, Missouri, before she had been out a week. In St. Joseph, Miss Nielsen was fortunate to secure an engagement to sing in a condensed version of the opera *Penelope* at the *Eden Musee*. She received $75 for her services, and this money paid the railroad fares of herself and [others] to Denver, Colorado. There her singing attracted the attention of the manager of the Pike [Pyke] Opera Company, which she joined and accompanied to Oakland, California". Strang publishes several books of theatrical profiles before he becomes assistant to Mary Baker Eddy.

Vibrant 1891 San Francisco. Alice suspends travel, makes big money at Wigwam. September 1892, Arthur Pryor is back East for first Sousa tour; Stanley tours America, Pyke Opera tours the West before anchoring in Fresno. Vaudeville's yellow brick road has made her a big adventure.

Alice Nielsen's new admirer is the richest heir in California.

1892: SAN FRANCISCO, A STAR SATANELLA

When Alice Nielsen arrives in San Francisco December 1891, theatres bustle. At Tivoli Opera, the Kreilings offer Vasseur's new romantic opera *Madame Cartouche* followed Monday by Varney's *Musketeers*. At "popular prices 25c and 50c". Tivoli's repertory includes Branson as Messmer; Rickertts, Pearson, Cornell and Harris; with Gracie Plaisted, Simone; Tillie Sallinger, Marie; Lena Sallinger, Louise; Kate Marachi as Lady Superior in "a lasting work full of lively music". In town theatre news, Lillian Russell says she will never be satisfied until she sings Marguerite in *Faust*; Baldwin Theatre's "German season" offers Yon Yonson "a character new to the stage"; next week "Mr. Potter of Texas". Big day sport is horse racing; nights belong to theatre, and saloons. During daylight minor sports are polo, cricket, baseball, football—and basketball invented next December.

Quality and intensity of San Francisco's theatre is indicated by this report: "What would not your New York managers give for a summer bright and cool as the month of May with the Standing Room Only sign out at three-fourths of the theatres. Almost a paradox but that is what we are having in this jumping-off place in the world where poor actors seldom care to come on account of the distance and poor condition of the railroad ties". (1889)

Alice Nielsen after three months' touring with Stanley, Pryor, and Pyke, settles down at Langham Hotel, corner of Mason and Ellis Streets three blocks from St. Patrick's and Wigwam. Vivid qualities of town reflect in finances: Irish-founded Hibernia Bank; French Savings Bank; German Savings and Loan. She connects with a strong Irish community by joining St. Patrick's choir as a soloist for Christmas where people notice her voice.

Immediately, as Kansas City, she sings at society gatherings, weddings, musicales; plus stage. Makes money. Quickly sends train tickets to mom and siblings who arrive after snatching Alice's baby. When Sarah, Julia, Hortense, and Erasmus join Alice, Mary remains behind at 304 Maple in KC's Pendleton Heights as domestic.

Four years later, the well-established Alice tells press, "All the members of my family are in the profession, except my mother, who lives with me at the Langham Hotel. I have two sisters, who are now with Pyke's Opera Company, playing the northern circuit, and my only brother, Erasmus Nielsen, is a professional musician at Morosco's theater".

After arrival, Alice takes a quiet period about eight months away from press. Not until August 1892 does Burton Stanley advertise Alice Nielsen in bigger type than "30 People in the Cast". Later, an unnamed man recalls *Chimes of Normandy* who had "witnessed a performance of this popular Planquette score...by the Burton Stanley Opera Company, the prima donna soprano being Alice Nielsen...." Also "enjoyed her work at the beginning of her brilliant career at the Auditorium as it was then called, on 12th Street, Oakland. Needless to add, that Miss Nielsen was a lovely Germaine".

Alice's vaunted Wigwam then Tivoli jobs were partly thanks to Stanley, who brought contacts. Tivoli manager WH Leary recalls, "When I first saw her, she looked like a little girl. I remember that one day when I was in Oakland, Frank Valerga saw me in the street and had me go to Deitz' hall with him. He said they had a little girl in the company that could sing like a bird. That little girl was Alice Nielsen, and I was surprised when I heard her wonderful voice. Shortly after that the company broke up, and she then came to the Wigwam theatre, where they were condensing *The Mikado, Olivette* and other operas into an hours' performance as part of a vaudeville show" by Frank Valerga.

Wigwam, a well-known artistic incubator, pays well, "I had gathered a large following; I was getting $90 a week". She puts timing as early 1892, and perhaps it was; perhaps fall 1893.

"Within a month", she claims, "I was singing for Charlie Meyers, the kindly gentleman who owned and managed the famous Wigwam, a free-and-easy music hall where for ten cents [as *Eden Musee*] one could hear an afternoon or a night of vaudeville and for five cents more purchase an enormous glass of beer. Excellent food was correspondingly cheap. One could entertain a large family party at the Wigwam for two or three dollars, including everything".

The Wigwam, oft described as a "popular opera and vaudeville family resort" held over a thousand people, stage 125-feet wide. A secret staircase was built to escape frantic Stage Door lads. Same as anywhere, Alice says, "There were menageries, Punch and Judy shows, dramatic sketches, condensed opera, ventriloquists, animal acts, acrobats, snake charmers, comedians, beer, all possible sandwiches, cigars and cigarettes—everything". The unnamed witness to her early Bay Area life describes Wigwam as a "somber and inelegant structure that afforded shelter to so many real geniuses, notable among them being, besides Miss Nielsen, the now famous Warfield and others of hardly less ability".

For Alice "struggling with many adverse circumstances, an engagement at the Wigwam...was a thing to be coveted, even if the audiences were so unruly and of such discourteous character that the considerate manager was compelled to place a special stairway from the window in the dressing room of the young vocalist, to enable her to enter and depart from the theatre without encountering the observation and obtruding attentions of the more unruly of the audience". (1896)

Vaudevilles at Wigwam were lively, interactive, and ripe. Alice recalls, "the odor of the place was never to be forgotten and never to be described. I can still see the male portions of our audiences tilted in their chairs, from the backs of which hung their coats, their sleeves rolled up, their hats on the backs of their heads, huge seidels of beer in their hands, roaring their favorite choruses with the singer on the stage".

During her two Wigwam years, Alice gains a rich powerful suitor in Thomas Williams Jr. (1859-1915). Capable of chasing rivals away, ruling-elite Tom controls horse racing in the region. Tom Sr. (1828-1886) had helped create California's 1850 statehood, seventh Attorney General who owned shares of the mother-lode Comstock mine. These Virginians had relocated to Kentucky before settling California. Tom Sr. cultivated visiting theatrepeople, hosting many gaily festive parties. Tom Jr. grew up San Jose. President of Berkley class, graduated instead from Santa Clara. When Alice arrives, Tom Jr. is managing dad's hundred-thousand San Bernardino acres. Toys with land reclamation, dabbles in ballot-machines, Mexican investments, "Shasta Water Company", "Jerome Garage Company". His passion is horses. Tom Jr. began racing 1888, his stables "bred and trained some of the greatest horses claimed by California and he was one of the most influential in contributing to the history of California turf records", says Bailey Millard in *San Francisco Bay*. 1893 *LA Times* reports Williams "secured control" of California Jockey Club, stays president until death, controlling regional race tracks and suppressing competitors. In short, Williams runs tracks and makes book. Despite him, California hoping to stop corruption outlaws betting in 1909 and he sells the stables. Williams belongs to the crony crowd and clubs: Pacific-Union, Olympic, Athenian, Sutter, Yosemite, Press....

Williams has power. No poor Prussian migrant as organist Nentwig, he will prove to share certain traits. Nor a virtuoso prodigy peer as Arthur Pryor. Twice Alice's age, wealthy Williams ruthlessly controls the region's biggest daytime sport. She stars in the biggest nighttime sport. Tall, slender and attractive (as she likes), Williams is the ultimate insider thanks to daddy's money. Offers to share a rich lifestyle before Nielsen grows famous on her own talent. His attentions expose her to savage jealousy from Oakland society dames set on bagging the heir. Alice and family enjoy his ranch. Relationship endures a decade. Creates, destroys.

Williams could play strongman if Alice annoyed by legacy lovers.

Leaving Kansas City, Sarah had grabbed baby Benjamin from the Nentwigs before boarding the train. "I had rescued my mother from her drudgery and she had fetched Ben, my son, with her from Kansas City. Getting Ben was no trivial accomplishment. His father's family had taken him and had notified us that they intended keeping him. There was nothing to do, of course, but capture him by whatever means we might.

"So one morning quite early, Mother loitered around the house until little Ben came out on the porch. Enticing him to the fence with candy, she grabbed him, hustled to the railroad station and arrived in San Francisco with the baby in her arms. He was charmed by the ride, the excitement, and although a bit strange with us for a day or so, was soon quite happy. Anyway, I had him. It may have been altogether illegal, but I had my baby".

Adventurous times bring foggy facts. Appears the Nielsens generated yet another child. Shortly after the family settles in town, *San Francisco Chronicle* January 14, 1892, announces baby Thomas to "wife of Rasmus Nielsen". Did Alice change three-year-old Benjamin's middle name to Tommy? Or is this new child? Alice not the only Nielsen girl. Sarah safely in her fifties has three daughters in theatre. Either way, a Tommy Nielsen appears. For years ahead, Alice speaks to press of son Bennie, never Tommy. Intriguingly, in her 1907 address book both Ben and Tommie live with Sarah. By 1915 a "Tommy Nielsen" shares Alice's Met Opera suite, corresponding with promoters to arrange her concert tours. Letters to mom Alice, however, are from "Bennie". Indeed, a San Francisco name-change to "Benjamin Thomas" would not be an unusual practice; older relatives would often absorb offspring of their kids. Better Alice face the press a young childless widow: grandma Sarah poses grandson as son. Present-day Nielsen family, Alice's grandson, confirmed to this author Benjamin and Tommy were the same "Benjamin Thomas Nielsen". In 1893 San Francisco, no secret that Alice had a child Bennie. Yet Tommy was not Bennie. There's a new kid in the Nielsen household.

However. This fine foggy chase seems a bit complex to solve. The plot stirs when the April 1895 *San Francisco Call* reports "Two Brave Young Girls" who "thwart the bold plans of a would-be kidnapper. Little May Kingsbury, the niece of Alice Nielsen" at age thirteen by "bravery and perseverance" prevents "kidnapping of her three-year-old cousin, Tommy Gavin, by his father, Thomas J. Gavin".

So we have a second Nielsen child, Thomas. Not an Alice child; nephew. After this episode perhaps the ladies slap him as "Nielsen". Like being born in Boston at age two the way Sarah was. Coincidently during the previous October when Alice's faux group of siblings appear at St. Joseph *Eden Musee*, Thomas J. Gavin is on the bill. *Call*'s kidnap story names Hortense as mother, off touring with Pyke Opera. We don't know.

"In her absence" Alice and Sarah "assumed the care of the child, whom they have grown to regard almost as their own". When dad Gavin tries to grab his boy into a waiting transom cab, May Kingsbury and Ettie Robinson (both 13) who had taken the kid outside "for the first time in months", react: "'He's not yours'," cried little Miss Kingsbury. 'He's my grandma's boy.' She ran to her little cousin's aid but was roughly thrown to the sidewalk. Nothing daunted, she sprang to her feet and ran at Gavin ...screaming for help. The other little girl caught the would-be kidnaper's coattails with one hand and beat a lively tattoo on his back with her little fist...." The fast-gathering crowd includes two cops who haul Gavin before Judge Murphy, who previously awarded custody to the mother.

A neighbor, Tivoli star Gracie Plaisted, runs news to Sarah who faints, "prostrated with anxiety and grief". Within two hours, the unchaperoned girls May and Ettie return with the kid. Judge Murphy jails Gavin "under the influence of liquor. Now Baby Gavin is safely domiciled with his grandmother. Brave Little May Kingsbury".

Sarah's family by 1900 lists two grandkids: Benjamin of June 1890, Thomas of September 1892. Both of Missouri to Tennessee moms, fathers German. Decade later in NYC, grandchild "Thomas Gavin" is with Sarah his birthday 1893 and the father from Ohio. "Thomas Nielsen" enjoys life at Alice's Metropolitan Opera suite and Bennie is in Boston at work with Josef Urban. The shape-shifting puzzle stays put. Perhaps another Nielsen was mom. By 1900, Hortense and Charles Quintard will marry, they tour; daughter Anna May will be born Michigan 1904. Never a Thomas.

Another fine foggy chase from Alice. 1890s San Francisco is wild, wild, west with whorehouses regarded superior to even Kansas City; William Chambliss back in 1887 had heard it said, Sacramento and Oakland were better places to live than San Francisco "for married gentlemen who entertained hopes of raising children of their own"

The close-knit brood of talented Nielsen siblings help one another all their lives. Hortense often joins Alice's tours and assists projects. Their brother also serves as travel companion. No further controversy for boys Benjamin and Thomas who stay with grandma Sarah and uncle Erasmus, just as Sarah stayed with the Clarys.

Alice made a miracle wending her way along the yellow-brick vaudeville road between two St. Patrick's. By 1893 the lively arts of San Francisco support the Nielsens, well known and liked. Safely settled, tireless Alice sings for the family supper. Sarah tends the kids, daughters perform, son plays piano, organ, drums, all the usual instruments everybody plays.

Alice and Hortense have artistic affinity. Hortense soon relinquishes the chorus and joins Modjeska's acting company for added artistic affinity.

These intriguing artistic resonances are well worth regarding. Polish superstar Helena Modjeska (1840-1909) had created an 1876 artists' colony near LA; her Arden now a Modjeska Canyon park. Modjeska gave Ernest Legouvé's *Adrienne Lecouvreur* in 1877 San Francisco then toured. In 1883 at Louisville, Kentucky, she debuted Henrik Ibsen's *A Doll's House*. Modjeska played nine Shakespearean heroines. Peer of Duse and Bernhardt, Modjeska beyond women's liberation speaks for all free people. Her 1880 and 1885 Irish tours were "dogged by secret service agents" after she advocated freedom for "a sister oppressed nation" says Edward Pace (1922). At 1893's Chicago World Fair, Modjeska famously speaks about suppressed Poland, and women. In Amy Leslie's 1899 *Some Players: Personal Sketches*, Modjeska says, "Perhaps I shall go to Ireland again, there is always a fervid welcome for me among the Irish".

Within a decade Leslie will profile Alice; then Hortense.

Leslie speaks of Modjeska's *Marie Stuart*, "Her tour through the green island was one triumphal procession...and red-coated guardians kept rigid eyes upon her". She "rises out of the hurry and turmoil of moderninity like a Druid priestess...with vast and active interest in movements, humanity, art and letters. Her fortune is spent in emancipation and amelioration of the down-trodden and helpless. Though she is a repository of all the wisdom of the world...Modjeska likes nothing so well as to laugh, tell witty anecdotes, listen to youth...and pet little children. This gentle, intellectual creature is always looked upon askance as a redeemer of the oppressed, a voice in the wilderness of tyranny, a subtle diplomatist and Joan of Arc".

Leslie compares Modjeska's Camille with Duse as "kindred interpretations". And her Lady Macbeth "a subtle and perfectly crystal interpretation of such gracious symmetry and intellectual force as to be unique...chiefly because Modjeska sinks herself into the thought of things and the depths of characters".

Modjeska will shape Hortense Nielsen's future. By 1897 at Baldwin Theater in San Francisco, Hortense Nielsen acts with Modjeska in *Macbeth*. Hortense plays a boy: Banquo's son Feance. Now Hortense absorbs Modjeska; what she learns she shares with singing sister Alice. These three share artistic, cultural, and political outlooks. After six years around Modjeska, Hortense forms a touring company to perform plays she has learned. Duse would be quoted about Hortense playing Ibsen, "She plays the role with great power. She is a wonderful artist, she is the finest Nora I have ever seen". Amy Leslie adds "Her desirable talent is paving a road for the great master of Norway no other woman has been able to travel" (1911). Hortense would play Nora in *A Doll's House* more than six hundred times, produced most of Ibsen's plays. Her story was unsung.

In San Francisco the Nielsen sisters develop to the next level. Within a decade they will meet Eleonora Duse who tutors Alice's acting and advises Hortense on Ibsen. Here in town as Hortense has Modjeska, Alice has Ida Valerga who shared stages with Adelina Patti and Christine Nilsson, the superstar sopranos whose opera coach and conductor was Italian composer Enrico Bevignani. Within a decade, Bevignani coaches Alice Nielsen as his last student. Valerga knows the world opera elite and those who compose and produce: Arditi, Tosti, Mapleson.

1890s San Francisco is culturally vivid, diverse, genuine. Robert Willson recalled the decade: "Seems sometimes as if San Francisco were about half an Italian city. Grand opera comes along and the music loving population is much excited and interested. You join the throng in the lobby between the acts. If you cannot understand Italian you may expect to hear only about one-fourth of the comments on the performance. After the opera, Polacco, Merola, Gigli, or Martinelli says, 'Come, let us have a bite of supper.' Then if you cannot speak Italian, eat Italian and think Italian, you are as far from home as a Hottentot in Rome". (1923)

NY critic James Huneker recalls in the 1880s "opera from the financial view-point was a fly-by-night affair...still bore the circus stamp of the '70s. Singers were advertised like freaks and managers always a half step from ruin. A perfect flowering was Colonel Mapleson...most successful lion-tamer—vocal lions—I ever encountered. A prima donna, rage in her heart and a horse-whip under her coat, has been seen to leave him placated, hopeful, even smiling. If promises were rejected he applied, and with astonishing results, the unguent of fat praise; he literally smeared his singers". Patti's final American tour was managed by Robert Grau.

World-class soprano Ida Valerga (1851-1944) has sung with the world's best. Toured with Mapleson whose star Patti retired rich to Wales. Valerga remarks of Patti's husband, "Of all the husbands of stage women I have met in this country and Europe, Signor Nicolini was the only man who never seemed to know or see any other woman in the world. He never glanced at or seemed to think of anyone but her. When she made her exits he was always there to place a wrap about her precious shoulders, to take her to her dressing room, and to kiss her hand tenderly as he left her. And he was always on hand to escort her back to the boards".

So Burton Stanley and Frank Valerga "the tenor of San Francisco" deliver Alice Nielsen to expert *bel canto* coach Ida Valerga who also sings at St. Patrick. Ida plucks Alice from vaudeville into quality repertory and coaches her for grand opera. After the Stanley savvy with comedy, Alice gets first-hand accounts of how great opera companies and divas operate. Ida Valerga sang at La Scala at twenty-two, sang for Tsar, Kaiser, Queen Victoria. Her father Bartolomeo Valerga had married Antionette Demonte in Italy; the couple landed in 1850's Boston. He came overland to San Francisco during the 1855 Gold Rush, sent his family by Cape Horn. His kids "dominated local playbills" between 1870 and 1930s: Antonio, Dominic, George, Ida, Riccardo, Madeline, Mary, Tilly, Frank, Katy, Pete, Nina and Tom. His grandkids populated "ranks of the region's composers, vocalists, actresses, screenwriters and artists", says San Francisco's Museum of Performance and Design (2017).

The Valerga siblings knew Pryor from Salt Lake's season. Pryor's recordings should include the cornetist Tom Valerga who also joined Sousa. Alice says when Stanley left the region Frank, Dick, and Kate Valerga seized opportunity to bring "appreciative patrons of the Wigwam *Forty Minutes of Comic Opera*, and it was short a soprano". "Valerga Opera Company" performed in mining camps, saloons; even Africa's diamond camps. Frank Valerga (1854-1904) led Wigwam manager Meyers to Alice in Oakland.

Alice says: "Charlie Meyers at once introduced me to Madame Ida Valerga, one of the best teachers of her day, who had coached Adelina Patti". Ida "listened to me sing. To show her what I could do, I sang my high C and held it until the blood pounded in my ears. Probably my eyes bulged too". Ida's response was revelatory to young Alice who could never resist tossing an egg at Patti. "'Tut, tut, child, what nonsense. Don't throw away your top notes, save them, save them.

"Even the great Patti had to save them. My faith, child, Patti received applause for many high notes that she never uttered. You see, when she could no longer afford to waste them, when she had very few let to give, she resorted to tricks. You too must know the tricks.

"When she was to sing her final top notes, my dear, she would move into the wings and another woman would stand close behind her and sing the note. But that is only one trick.' Valerga knew this because it had been she who had supplied many of the declining Patti's final high C's. 'But you, my child, are young', she said. 'save, save while you are young. You shall sing with my sister and brother and I shall teach you.'"

Ida and Alice shared artistic grounds. After grand opera in Europe, America, and Mexico, Ida Valerga returned to 1889 San Francisco as a grandmaster of the Italian lyric soprano repertoire. Reviews praise her acting and voice. In *Carmen*, "Ida Valerga's personation of the capricious and coquettish gypsy cigargirl is all that is claimed for it in the acting. In the singing her voice...native force and beauty became apparent as she progressed in the role. Valerga's voice is one of those that is always at its best the more it is practiced.... (1891)

Joining the popular Tivoli repertory company meant playing every form of opera—grand, light, comic, frivolous—in fast rotation; same basic program as Grau and Pyke plus grand opera. Located near Union Square on Eddy and Mason, Tivoli held grand opera during winters and lighter fare in summer. The Kreilings manage the place. Joseph dies, wife Mrs. Ernestine Kreiling (1898 phone: "BUsh 9") seizes control. Marries "Doc" Leahy, they run it together. Tivoli runs continuously for "ten-thousand performances" until leveled in 1906 earthquake; they relocate to Denver.

Alice continues, "Art in The Wigwam was long but not serious; but the Tivoli was dignified—relatively, anyway. There a stock company held forth in the more popular Italian, French and German grand operas, digressing now and then to sing *The Bohemian Girl*, for example, and *Fra Diavolo, The Mikado, Patience, The Chimes of Normandy, Erminie* and so on". To reach Tivoli from the Wigwam would be as rare as jumping from Broadway to Covent Garden. Yet in those days art was calling players who sang at Tivoli, Wigwam, church and saloons.

Valerga guides things for her "favorite pupil". Alice suggests, "I'm not at all sure how it happened, but one afternoon Bauer, the Tivoli conductor, came to hear me in *The Queen's Lace Handkerchief* at the Wigwam".

Queen's Lace Handkerchief by Heinrich Bohrmann-Riegen premiered in 1880 Vienna; same show lost a Grau soprano from sudden illness in Kansas City possibly (not really) giving Alice her first professional tour.

Continues coy, "I suspect that Ida Valerga was responsible, although she never admitted it. Poor dear, she couldn't. Hadn't she many singing relatives who looked longingly at the Tivoli?"

In fact, Tillie, Eda, Nina, Kate, Robert, Dick, and Peter Valerga were performing at Tivoli. Ida, the most famous.

Take note, her money is far less. Tivoli offers only a third of her Wigwam pay of $90 weekly. Tivoli offers $30. Slicing salary easy choice. To skip high-paying Wigwam to become a Tivoli soprano and Ida Valerga's understudy, she could not resist: "I leapt at the chance".

Alice emphasizes it: "I did not hesitate".

Her artistic motives ring out: audience quality matters most.

She wishes to sing meaningful songs to a caring audience: "Here was my chance to sing myself into the ears of those who knew music, whose word in the musical world counted for something. Here was my chance to sing The *Barber of Seville, Don Giovanni, Faust* and *Mignon*".

Stories vary. Says Lewis Strang (1901), Tivoli director George Lask (1884-1936) heard Nielsen in *La Perichole* and hired her. San Francisco-born Lask had worked theatre since a child. Nielsen gives him no build-up but he was an famed bicoastal theatre asset. In NYC, Lask works with producer Charles Frohman; returns to Tivoli 1893 to 1900, rejoins Broadway to direct *Florodora*, creating its famed female sextet "The Florodora Girls". In short, George Lask invents the chorus line. The show ran 505 performances, hit song: *Tell Me, Pretty Maiden*. Lask returns to Tivoli 1906; after The Met's *Carmen* at Tivoli he is enjoying late supper with Caruso at Zinkand's when the great earthquake destroys most of the town and entirely his theatre.

Entering Tivoli, Nielsenian fogs clarify for the future. Alice will become famous and soon. Even so, Nielsen never tells she became a San Francisco hit as Satanella in Balfe's *Satanella*, the Tivoli showpiece. Perhaps it seems diva-prudent to speak of tragic *Lucia* instead of bragging on gayety generated for town by Balfe.

So within two years of arriving in town, Alice Nielsen steps away from burlesques and vaudeville to join the musical highlife of opera, comic and grand. Before departing Wigwam forever, we must take note the prettiest girl in Kansas City had the best legs in San Francisco.

Let the woman speak for herself: "I may not have mentioned it, but in addition to a naturally placed voice I had been endowed with legs which seemed to please the hearty audiences at the Wigwam as much as my voice did—possibly more. I think there were two or three occasions when I went on the stage of The Wigwam with my legs partly covered by short skirts.

"Only twice or thrice. The patrons of that very human establishment—the men anyway—protested so vehemently on those occasions that Charlie Meyers all but forbade me to wear skirts at all". Admiration of her womanly form is fine: "All of which was quite agreeable to me".

She would go tights and skip skirts, "inasmuch as I loathed the things anyway". Tivoli she tells "was a bit different. Not, mind you, that pleasing the eyes of the audiences was regarded as unnecessary there; but as Madame Valerga told me, I might not expect to make a hit as Lucia or Marguerite on the strength of my legs".

On this hangs a story. Her last Wigwam season, "I learned to wear skirts, although there were bad moments. Once, forgetting I was clad to the instep, I fell down a whole flight of stairs" thanks to Irish boxer John Sullivan who "had appeared on the same bill with me. That night Mr. Sullivan, although he did not know it, had made me his slave [1890s girlish crush]. And this in spite of his condition: Mr. Sullivan was quite drunk.

"As I remember it, he sang a song—*A Shamrock From My Dear Old Mother's Grave*—in a crashing baritone. There was a riot of applause and Mr. Sullivan seemed pleased—so much so that he dispensed with the monologue he was supposed to give and launched forth upon a eulogy of his mother that dissolved me in tears. Any man, thought I, who loved his mother so fervently was at heart a good man. And it would have been unlike me not to have told him so.

"'Mr. Sullivan', I said, 'you're a good man I—'

"'sure I'm a good man', said Mr. Sullivan. 'I can lick any—'

"'I just wanted to tell you', I went on hurriedly—a little frightened too, 'that I don't care who you fight, you will win. Any man who loves his mother—.' I got no further because John began again to bellow *A Shamrock From My Dear Old Mother's Grave*. They led him away.

"So it was. While I was learning to wear skirts, John fought James Corbett in New Orleans. I was deep in my lesson when the rumor arrived that my mother-worshiping hero had been knocked out. On the ground floor there was a saloon, the head bartender of which had taken a fatherly fancy to me. And I liked him—Tim Boyle. The wardrobe mistress, my instructress in skirt-manipulating, had come up with the rumor and I, dressed for the lesson, announced my disbelief. Forgetting all about the skirt, I ran to the door, opened it, tripped and fell in a bruised heap at the bottom of the stairs. Tim Boyle gathered me up. Was I hurt—badly? I confessed that I wasn't any too pleased, but demanded the truth from New Orleans. Tim wept. Our idol had collapsed".

During summer 1893, Alice Nielsen joins Tivoli on Eddy Street, evolved since 1879 from a German beer garden. Tivoli fills the house with that same gregarious pricing model as Burton Stanley and Jules Grau. Nielsen keeps the popular-price policy in her own future productions.

In a town generating national stars, Tivoli is the classiest music theatre contributing mightily to the gayety of San Francisco. Decade after Alice, *Town Talk* (1903) recalls "Tivoli inspires such tender and fond recollections, fraught with sentiment and emotion, that it seems a profanity to tear down the historic playhouse and thereby efface a picturesque monument to musical triumphs of the long ago.

"To the Tivoli many people in this community owe the development of the love of music. It was in the Tivoli that many of us heard opera for the first time, and within its portals we have witnessed the evolution of talent that first won recognition on the old stage and that subsequently scored triumphs in other climes. Someday the history of the Tivoli will be written, and it will be found to be a chronicle of the development of the musical education of this community".

Opened in 1870s by the Kreiling Brothers as a music and concert hall, for a while it "appealed exclusively to the German colony. In those days there was sawdust on the floor and the auditors sat at round tables with their steins in front of them, and listened to German vocalists. Foreigners were the exclusive patrons of the house".

About 1879, "a good comic opera company was rounded up" using players from the Baldwin stranded on the coast. They created Tivoli's first hit *Satanella* with basso Frederick Bornemann as Mephisto. Interestingly, the soprano-bass voice combination of Alice's shows with Herbert; plus constant costume changes alike *Crook*.

"For years thereafter *Satanella* was the Tivoli's *piece de resistance*. It was revived every time business threatened to be dull". Favorites players included Hattie Moore and husband Harry Gates, Helene Dingeon, Louis Manfred, Harry Norman, Sadi Martinot and husband Max Figman, Emily Soldene, Alice and Francis Gaillard, Alice Vincent, Gracie Plaisted, Tillie Salinger, and "the clever Valergas" including Kate Marchi.

"At the Tivoli...Alice Nielsen developed from a chorus girl into a prima donna. The Tivoli has had many good and many bad singers, but the prices usually silenced criticism. Some of the favorites were vocalists of mediocre ability, but there was always, in the old house, a sort of 'happy family' atmosphere, and crudities and shortcomings were generously overlooked".

Charles Dobie (1939) reflects "Maude Adams began in San Francisco, David Belasco and David Warfield began as ushers at the Bush Street Theatre". Almost predictably, it began a few months after Boston pirated *Pinafore* for Barnabee's group. Tivoli's version of *Pinafore* "started that institution on the road to fame. It was said at one time to be the only comic-opera stock company in existence and it ran seven-days-a-week without interruption for forty years. Most San Franciscans were brought up on the old Tivoli, the cool smell of its beery interior, the hardness of its cushion-less seats. I saw my first performance of *Lohengrin* at the Tivoli for fifty cents, which was top price. The tenor sang in English, the baritone in Italian, the prima donna in German. But it thrilled me.

"I imagined it was good, and good it was". Tivoli "played every opera from *The Geisha* to *Tannhauser*...the training school for such artists as Edwin Stevens, Alice Nielsen, Gracie Plaisted, Helen Merrill. Later, when it had achieved the dignity of a grand opera season, it introduced Luisa Tetrazzini to America and fame. David Belasco, Alice Nielsen and others...all have national reputations".

In *San Francisco Opera* (1997), Joan Chatfield-Taylor calls Tivoli "San Francisco's most successful music theatre" without mentioning the performers who made the success. She focuses weakly on 1922 and after.

Nielsen herself 1890s witness: "Tilly Sallinger was the prima donna— the leading one at any rate, and Grace Plaisted was the soubrette".

At Tivoli, Alice had an astonishing opportunity to play "150 roles in two years" as Valerga polished her talented protégé for bigger better things.

"What a job Ida Valerga had on her hands! I had to unlearn practically everything from walking to breathing".

Tivoli would propel Alice Nielsen at several critical career points. And the affection was entirely mutual.

So from early 1894 until September 1895, Nielsen hones her craft with Ida Valerga whilst singing many roles at big, always-crowded 1,700-seat Tivoli. She is aided by power to sight-read and sing the memorized music, as related by Tivoli's manager WH Leahy: "Alice Nielsen was a wonderful woman in one respect. I never saw her equal. She would read the score of an opera as a man would read a book and she retained it all in her wonderful memory. She memorized her parts quicker than anyone else I have ever seen. She had a great intuition, which enabled her to grasp a score in short order".

Performing nightly in the demanding schedule, Nielsen sang complex scores with verve to a big house. A grueling schedule, her diligent focus on her craft a life discipline: Nielsen always known for tireless, continual work. Only a patient boyfriend, if any, could keep from intruding. In reality, she pushed them all away. She had more important to do.

Steadily Alice and Hortense evolve stage skills in San Francisco.

Soon Alice faces a problem, temporary layoff. Management "decided that the audiences needed a change of musical diet". Opera would pause "and in its place an extravaganza would be put on—all of which suited me perfectly until I was informed that there was no place for me in it. The shock was terrific. That $30 dollars hadn't gone far". After all, she supports her mother and as many as two boys. To save the day she hijacks a show.

Romantically linked to California's wealthiest heir, yet seemingly terrified at the lost income: "I tried to convince the management that I was a superior extravaganza singer, but the reply was always the same—there was no part for me in this piece; be patient, be patient. I had no desire to starve patiently. I had to work—and keep on working".

Alice invents a burlesque: "Now it happened that a few weeks earlier the talented Ada Lewis had played San Francisco—Ada Lewis, 'The Tough Girl.' She did a Bowery dance in a cap pulled askew, a tight short jacket, an abbreviated red skirt and stockings with horizontal white stripes. Her dance had captured San Francisco just as other cities had given her furious approval. She had, in short, started something—a craze, as we called it then".

NYC-born Ada Lewis (1873-1925) grew up in San Francisco. Like Alice, she haunted theatres: working as extra on crowded stages of that day whenever she could skip work at the waterfront's fish-packing plant. Her career is one of those theatre legends: backstage at Alcazar talking tough, Lewis is overheard by Irish vaudeville duo Harrigan and Hart whose shows are thinly-plotted vehicles for songs and comedy arising from minstrelsy; and Hart plays drag roles. Charmed by her talking style, they put Lewis onstage the same day. Moment she hits the stage, magic starts.

"Ada Lewis was a huge overnight sensation in her debut in Harrigan's *Reilly and the 400*", says Mick Malone, NYU's Irish theatre scholar (email 2007). "She played a tough girl from the Lower East Side and when she came on stage in a tight sweater, put her hands on her hips and gave out the line 'Reilly where's me shoes' to the pawnbroker in question she literally stopped the show. Harrigan was forced immediately by the audience reaction to upgrade her part and write her into the final portion of the production. She was a Broadway star from that point on".

Lewis was an expert at physical comedy with her character "Tough Girl Kitty Lynch". A tight jacket shows her figure, short skirt her ankles. Hot stuff in those days. Her gum-chewing slum girl lovably gruff. As with *Evangeline's* dancing heifer, Ada Lewis' "Tough Girl" creation will be widely copied forever. Between 1892-94 Harrigan-Hart with Ada Lewis plays Wigwam and other theatres often proceeded by Burton Stanley Company with ubiquitous Valergii.

San Jose News (1894) reports Stanley producing *The Mascot*, Lina Crews as Bettina and RD Valerga as Pippo, followed by *Mikado* with RO Valerga (Koko), Lina Crews (Yum Yum) and Charles Deane (Nanki-Poo). Two weeks later, *Mercury News* (Aug 25) reports "at the Auditorium" Harrigan in *Reilly and the 400* with Emma Pollock as Maggie Murphy and Ida Lewis as The Tough Girl".

Harrigan, said *News*, had "a little too much of the 'tough' element introduced to suit the theatre-goers of this city". Set in NY, the show is violent. In Act 2's Bowery music hall scene, "a negro girl and a white girl are dancing for a prize. During the contest there were at least a dozen fights in as many minutes. Mr. Harrigan is accredited by the NY critics with holding the mirror up to nature... that is not pleasing".

Seems Nielsen met Lewis in fall 1894, starting at Tivoli.

To grab a salary, Nielsen snatches Ada's role: "on the night the extravaganza opened at the Tivoli, I got into an Ada Lewis costume, adding a few original touches—pigtail braids, shoes far too big for me and worn white gloves".

Herbert's 1899 *Singing Girl* puts Nielsen in pigtail braids and big shoes.

Alice's risqué conspiracy to hijack opening night overturns hiatus. "It took nerve, but I had nothing to lose. In a cloak that hid my costume, I went to the theatre and watched the first act from the wings. I had picked my time rather neatly, because at the dress rehearsal I had noticed a lull just before the first act finale. This lull was taken up by a few bars of fast dance music by the orchestra. That was my chance. I had the idea that I'd do it alone. But when the time came, I saw one of the lesser comedians standing in the wings, his part done, waiting for the finale.

"So I grabbed the startled man and together we ran out on the stage.

"Abandoning him in the middle of the stage, I did an Ada Lewis dance— a tougher, rougher Lewis, dancing for my bed and board, for my $30 a week. I danced as I have never danced before. My imagination went as wild as my legs. In the wings I could see the amazed faces of the assembled company, their cue for the final ensemble held up by the orchestra leader who abandoned the score and had shouted to his musicians to play Ada Lewis' music. And they did it, from memory. I must have danced six or seven minutes before going off.

"The audience, orchestra too, stood as they applauded and demanded more. 'Get on there, get on there, damn you', shouted George Lask, giving me a push stageward. I danced five encores. Things happen like that— sometimes. I brazenly butted my way into a show that had no part for me. I continued my specialty for 20 weeks—the duration of that extravaganza. From *Lucia di Lammermoor* to Maggie Murphy!"

Maggie Murphy and "Tough Girl" are characters in Harrigan & Heart's *Reilly and the 400* (1885) wherein NY lawyer hopes to wed a society girl: "*There's an organ in the parlor, To give the house a tone, And you're welcome ev'ry evening, At Maggie Murphy's home*".

Nielsen puts the jaunty farce soon after shift to Tivoli, so summer 1894. Unlikely that Ada Lewis plays Tivoli; Wigwam or Orpheum more like. More fog. If Alice's schedule seems astounding: will seem much more and soon.

Almost every day she entertains San Francisco singing complex music in theatres or church while constantly learning new shows and training with Ida Valerga for vocal prowess. Steadily Alice absorbs *bel canto* singing style and lyric soprano repertoire including art songs of popular divas.

She never mentions her big hit *Satanella*, never forgotten by those seeing the show. Such reporters shall remind the diva, much later along.

Her stage chrysalis season lasts less than two years.

Ida Valerga spoke of the era: "Alice Nielsen had a beautiful voice. When she came to me in the old Tivoli days I was greatly interested in her. She was studious and worked very hard to acquire her musical education. I am glad she has succeeded so well".

Valerga arranges Alice Nielsen's 1895 opera debut as Lucia in Donizetti's *Lucia di Lammermoor*. Donizetti, born in mountain-top

Bergamo at edge of the old Venetian empire, set *Lucia di Lammermoor* in Scotland. Premiered 1835 at Naples' San Carlo Opera where in time Nielsen would sing and hijack the name.

Alice says, Ida Valerga feigns headache to launch the understudy. "Because she did *Lucia* at the Tivoli, she concentrated on that fine old stand-by for my first important appearance. I suspect that Valerga was eager for someone to take her place—that she had grown tired of singing Lucia and that she preferred to teach, anyway. One morning Valerga was satisfied with me. She was to sing Lucia that night. 'My child', she said, 'my head aches. Run on now and rest. Be sure to rest. Come to see me at four o'clock.' At four o'clock she told me she was too ill to sing that night—that I would sing in her stead.

"Well, I sang Lucia, my first complete grand opera, as a star in a recognized opera organization".

Tivoli's audience includes many first-generation Italians. Nielsen apparently sang in English. Other singers use whatever language they prefer. Her stage fright arose. Visible uncertainty and doubts during such moments will be noted time and again across her career. After fears of rejection pass, she becomes one with the music and audience.

"I sang it and experienced for th first time in my life (but not the last) that ghastly terror that all artists must face at one time or another—stage fright. I appeared to be going well, until the flute and I tackled the Mad Scene. The flute was altogether capable. But I, after a couple of fumbling starts, elected to call it an evening. Somewhere in the midst of that scene, my legs took charge of me. Next thing I knew I was in the wings with George Lask, the stage manager [director], holding me by the shoulders. 'Get back there and finish it', he barked. 'You're doing it beautifully. Get back there and sing. Lord, you look madder than Lucia herself. You look the part—now sing it. Get on, get on.' He literally threw me back to the stage. And I finished—somehow".

Afterwards Alice as *Lucia* never carried a dagger. Years later in Boston, she explains, after the Tivoli fright, a dagger would make her laugh. Among her replicated Tivoli patterns of no dagger, of big shoes, of pigtail braids, Alice would make Victor Herbert compose soprano duets with flute or cello.

Another slant is told by Tivoli manager WH Leahy, who recalls *Lucia* starred "Ida Valerga, a great favorite at that time" alternating with Laura Millard who became intimidated. "When Millard heard Valerga sing, Millard lost confidence and refused to go on. This was Friday afternoon and *Lucia* was to be sung the following Tuesday. We were in a predicament.

"I asked Alice Nielsen whether she could sing Lucia by Tuesday. She had been singing small parts and I was hardly in earnest when I spoke to her, but she replied, 'I can try; I can make a bluff at it.' She didn't know the opera, but she went to work at once with the difficult role. Tuesday night she sang Lucia with wonderful effect. She took the highest notes with the greatest ease and made a great sensation".

Topping it all, the audience held Henry Barnabee and other Bostonians who soon invite her to join their legendary group.

Few years after, from uptown NYC café, an unnamed claret-sipping witness distilled the San Francisco "early struggles of Alice Nielsen": "While

Miss Nielsen is not a native daughter of California, she is regarded by the people as a child of their household. We claim her as our own, and that we are proud of her puts it mildly. She has been a favorite with the music-loving public out there.

"She deserves her success, for no girl ever worked more diligently and faithfully to achieve a laudable ambition. I remember very well when she first came to San Francisco from Kansas City where she had a brief career upon the stage. She married when a wee girl but the union was unhappy, and I see that the court that divorced her from a worthless husband also gave her the custody of her baby boy".

Mom and siblings "came with her, and she began working at the Wigwam Theatre, which is no longer in existence. Of course her struggle was a hard one, but the brother and sister both had industry, courage and talent. Alice's sweet, full, resonant voice soon attracted attention. It obtained her engagements outside of the theatre—in the church choirs and at private concerts.

"I remember she sang the mass at St. Patrick's Church one Christmas morning and made such a hit that she immediately sprung into popularity, and soon after that the old church in Mission Street rang with the sweet melody of her voice. In time she got an engagement at the Orpheum [Oakland], and later she went to the Tivoli, where she sang leads in light opera. Her success from this onward was easy".

Observed diligence. "By her application, tireless energy and splendid voice she became the popular favorite of San Francisco—she had sung her way into the hearts of the people".

She focused by constant training: "She owes her success to hard work, for whatever her natural talents may be she could never have climbed the ladder of fame so rapidly had she not applied herself to study, and this she did in all her waking hours. When not rehearsing or singing before the public she was practicing in her home".

Knew the full family: "And I have to say right here, that her home life has always been beautiful. Several years of her life were passed at the Langham Hotel, where she and her mother and brother and sister had apartments. And her little son was the joy of this family group. I knew them all well".

Sensed genuine gayety: "Alice's mother is one of those rare, delightful souls that Ireland alone produces, for Mrs. Nielsen is a daughter of the old sod. She came to America and went West, where she met and married Alice's father, a man named Nielsen, a Dane, and from whom the young opera singer inherited her musical genius. He is long dead, and since Miss Nielsen's girlhood she had been the chief breadwinner of the family".

Sketches her personality: "She is unselfish, generous and thoughtful of others and makes friends readily".

Closes with a keen insight of durable truth: "One point that is a striking characteristic of Alice Nielsen is that she puts her whole soul into her work. She does not spare herself in the least. And again she is natural—more so probably than any other singer on the American stage today".

Many stars shun the press. Alice, like Modjeska, speaks freely. Future co-star Eugene Cowles never will "grant an interview". Nielsen carefully maintains contact with press by postcard, letters, or dropping by the office.

In 1895 San Francisco, asked to speak about herself, Alice reveals a natural eloquence by tracing her career arc and future hopes: "I early imbibed a love for music, and, I think I must have been stage-struck in my cradle. Later on, when reverses were staring my dear family in the face I thought I would...see what I could do with the gifts that nature had given me and avail myself of the opportunity to do my duty to my family.

"I came to the Pacific Coast. My engagement at the Tivoli began in February, 1894, opening in *Manon*, and since then I have sung in most of the recent popular comic operas. I prefer light comedy or juvenile parts, such as Yum Yum, Patience, Josephine in *Pinafore*, Cora in *Gasparone*, and such like parts. I really devote but little time to study, but of late I have given more attention to it than ever. Singing cannot be taught, but, of course, the voice can be improved, and you can be taught to give the proper expression to your voice".

Applauds her conductor: "My view is that one owes much to the conductor; and here I wish to pay a debt of gratitude to Mr. Hirshbach [at Tivoli]. One who has not taken part in a comic opera or musical play cannot realize how all-important a role is played by the leader of the orchestra, whose duty it is to sustain the voice of the singer. He can either make or mar the song".

Reveals the stage fears, oft-noted awareness of audience reaction: "Like all singers I suffer from stage fright, especially on first nights. No one will ever know what agonies I go through except the leader, not mentioning the possible agonies the audience goes through. I like to watch the audience as I play, and cast my eye row after row to see the effect of the piece. The audience little knows how we are affected by any little inattention and how thankful we are for any consideration paid us by its entire engrossment and attention".

Delight for audience: "Encores are the sweets of a professional life; we must have the appreciation of the audience to sing well. No matter how good the song may be, unless it is applauded we never sing it as well the second time. A cold and cheerless audience can make the brightest gem fall flat. We must have the applause; it strengthens our ambition and generally sends us home happy with our day's or rather night's work".

Daunting tasks: "The road to success is a rugged one and has many pitfalls; it is uphill work, and we are often sidetracked. If a girl is willing to work hard and conscientiously there is no reason why this profession is not as desirable a calling for a lady as any other she may choose. Her success or failure is due entirely to her own exertions.

"'Tis true there are many temptations she has to resist, but in whatever walk of life are we as a sex not assailed by them? If a girl who has a fine voice and has been especially endowed with a graceful figure thinks she can advance into popularity before the footlights she is much mistaken".

Thinking of Ida Valerga: "It must take years of hard work, ups and downs, heart-burnings, disappointments and sacrifices. And even then she may never pass beyond an understudy".

Links success to power over audiences: "It depends much on the manager if a girl is to succeed. If he discovers that she can draw she will be put forward. There are plenty of girls right here in San Francisco with fine flexible voices who have a future before them, but they must await their turn".

Lastly, bouquet to theatre romances: "Kissing on the stage is a mere matter of form to me, much the same as the shake of the hand, and as to kissing off the stage— well we won't speak about it. To use the *Chimmie Fadden* language, it's ten to one off than on". Dialect-rich *Chimmie Fadden* novels by Edward Townsend made silent films about the Bowery Boy.

Obviously Alice found appreciation. Absorbs everything Valerga could impart, seasoned soprano of great skills (Patti's understudy must shine).

When Alice leaves Tivoli, Ida follows for New York for a possible return to the opera stage. Tutor and pupil reunite there and whenever Alice returns to San Francisco. They are friends and family friends.

Alice works as few work and sings daily within a 1500-seat hall. What singer today will perform so much? Focused on chances for progress, in summer 1895 Nielsen sees "America's Greatest Light-Opera Company, The Famous Original Bostonians" would soon return. When they performed in Kansas City the child Alice doubtless gave a serenade from the sidewalk.

Within two years Alice Nielsen would be a national star.

1895: FAME & THE FAMOUS ORIGINAL BOSTONIANS

San Francisco, the saving grace of an adopted hometown where Alice Nielsen develops and seasons skills to star, plays a critical supportive role across her career. She becomes a great pride to the Bay; acclaimed among its best artists. Yet hope to get into the Bostonians is wildly ambitious. The pinnacle of the great American star search.

Far more than touring players, the Bostonians were Americana.

Robert Grau proclaims the Bostonians "a gathering of players and singers that has never been equaled in the history of the American stage".

Louisville (1896), "Concerning these singers dispassionate criticism is an impossibility. Years ago they broke a passage into the people's hearts and from that place they have never been dislodged".

Montreal (1897), "The Bostonians have been together since the beginning of American lyric opera. It is not strange that they should be its best interpreters".

The group had evolved in 1887 from Boston Ideals started by Effie Ober to perform 1879's pirated *Pinafore*. Joining the Bostonians meant a life on trains during winter theatre season. Towns on the circuit got a day or a week of the usual repertory plus their bespoke new American musicals.

Alice explains, "The Bostonians, if you don't know it, were by all means the most famous and most talented singing organization in America. I doubt very much whether any opera company—grand or comic—has ever had more beautiful voices".

She reads Sept. 4th (1895) *San Francisco Call*: "Perley, the manager of the Bostonians, writes that the original famous company that has so long stood at the head of light opera organizations in this country will be the one to play in an extended engagement at the Columbia Theatre". Triggers ambition, "chorus will be made attractive by the substitution of young and fresh voices...."

Interestingly, continues same column for Tivoli, "On Wednesday evening Alice Nielsen will sing the role of Marguerite. The next grand opera production will be Donizetti's Luci de Lammermoor in which role Mlle. Ida Valerga scored her greatest triumphs with the Mapleson Opera Company". Seize the moment.

Bostonian chieftain Henry Barnabee recalls, "Our stay in the city was one round of success and joy...we were prime favorites, and our goings and comings of joy and regret were accentuated by the singing of *Auld Lang Syne* by audience and company". Bass-baritone Barnabee led the group: William MacDonald, Tom Karl, Jessie Bartlett Davis, Marie Stone (Mrs. MacDonald), Eugene Cowles, and George Frothingham were major players in "a company of equals". These stars were stalwarts; many passed by. Nineteen sopranos sang Maid Marian in their biggest hit *Robin Hood*.

Barnabee, legendary one-name icon, played the professional stage a decade before Nielsen born, starting 1864 a late thirty-three. Raised in Portsmouth NH, moved to Boston as a retail clerk. Sang in choirs. Pursued every possible opera performance. If Burton Stanley had decades of theatre savvy and the taste to star Nielsen, Henry Barnabee was the best man at his craft. Tops. Knew the best talents all his life. A Jenny Lind concert, he says, marks "the date when I broke into the unknown enchanted realm of dramatic music filled with suns, moons, planets, stars, falling meteors, and flashing comets of the divine art".

Barnabee met Alice Nielsen after a lifetime's experience with great talents in opera: Kellogg, Lind, Nilsson, Patti, Nevada. His autobiography includes a long long list. Alike Stanley, he is a master of sustained comedy.

More than a show, Bostonians openings are a society event. Many celeb perks for cast such as free entrée to all private clubs. No waiting in lines.

Importantly, the Bostonians commission and produce many new musicals. *Robin Hood* premiers in 1890 Chicago making its creators Reginald DeKoven and Harry Smith (Smith fondly says) rich. DeKoven (1859-1920), born in Connecticut, studied at Oxford, Stuttgart, Italy, Vienna. Worked as a Chicago critic then *NY World*; wife a novelist. Smith (1860-1936), born Buffalo, also a Chicago critic. Cheerfully admits he's fast not good. Nobody disagrees. Cynical without originality, he generates many musical libretti on time and budget.

Illustrated American (1891) of *Robin Hood*, calls creators "wise in their selection of a period which is at once interesting from a historic standpoint and picturesque from a theatric one. We do not forget our affection for bold Robin Hood, who never robbed the poor, just as though the rich were not fatter game.

"The music is light, sweet and refined. At times we fancy Mr. de Koven has been influenced by his musical memories. Someday, perhaps, he will escape his fetters and produce successfully his own thoughts". Librettist Smith "has worked well, but not brilliantly. Every line bears the impress of honest labor and not one flash of genius", the usual slather on Smith's prolific career.

The hit came after three flops.

Barnabee recalls, "Their first joint effort *The Begum*...may be called either failure as a whole or success in spots, as you choose. They tried the Bostonians with a second and more ambitious work, *Don Quixote*.... We liked the music, and decided to take chances on the book. We did so— during one season. The only coastwise defence put up for *Don Quixote* in San Francisco was, 'Well, it will take more than one bad opera to kill the Bostonians.'

"We got another one, entitled *Suzette*, with which to test the friendship of the Golden Gate city. It was thought to be a possibility, but the prefix im soon had to be attached.... A herald ray of sunshine, though, presently struck us at Los Angeles, when we received a peace-offering which Smith and DeKoven had brought us in extenuation of *Don Quixote*".

Robin Hood "was a spontaneous hit from curtain to curtain".

So it was. Savvy observer of the theatrical firmament Alice Nielsen discovers the Bostonians approach. Brags "to several minor members of the Tivolians that I, Alice Nielsen, would not be with them next year. Why? Oh, nothing except I was going with the Bostonians". Reaction—she must be joking.

"Now there wasn't much thought behind the announcement. At that moment there was about as much chance of my being taken on by the Bostonians as there is now, the Bostonians having long ago vanished. But I was not the sort that took such difficulties too seriously.

"But presently it occurred to me that I had better do something about getting acquainted with them. Knowing no better tactics, I fell back upon the method I used to get my first stage job—with *The Mikado*. I modified it, of course; it would scarcely do to return to stage-door singing. But although I did not sing in the street, I began to haunt the Baldwin Theatre where the Bostonians were singing". Classy big Baldwin theatre whose famed stage manager David Belasco had already moved to NYC, if destined to make a bad musical Alice's last.

Nielsen's plan paid: "One day at the stage door, I recognized Henry Clay Barnabee who was then 60 years old or even more". In 1895 a spry 62; almost everybody in North America had seen him perform.

Venerable wit Barnabee recalls: "We were not the first New Englanders who had invaded the land of fairies, fruits and flowers". Even so, the Bostonians "trip to California was memorable in every way—a personally conducted tour in a special train, over prairies, deserts and snow-capped mountains, one continuous picnic of six days' duration, in which real redskins joined with the Indians of our troop in whooping things up".

Nielsen's account is interesting; others later try to hijack credit.

She at stage door: "'Mr. Barnabee?'

"'Yes, yes, m'girl; I'm Mr. Barnabee.'

"'Would you listen to my voice? I want to sing for you—with you.'

"'Tut, tut, tut, m'girl. Where are you from?'"

"'The Tivoli, sir.'

"Perhaps this impressed him a little, although a true Bostonian was not to be impressed by voices from without. But somehow (perhaps because I told him that Ida Valerga had taught me *Lucia*) he took me back into the theatre.

"'Can you sing clear English? Damn few singers can.' Doubtless I assured him that I could. Anyway he caught Macdonald and Marie Stone on their way out and the three of them listened while I sang *Annie Laurie, Comin' Through the Rye* and *Il Bacio*, that lilting song that Arditi wrote for Adelina Patti".

Two street songs learned from mom, plus an Italian waltz learned from the composer's wife Ida Valerga comprise her audition. Alice closes, the Bostonians arise "with vast dignity and in terrible silence left the theatre".

All silent, all calm. Left alone. "Whether I had done well or badly, I didn't know. They said absolutely nothing. I suppose I should have been disconcerted; perhaps I should have taken their silence for disapproval.

"What I actually did (and I know that it's hard to believe) was to return to the Tivoli and announce that I was celebrating my engagement by The Bostonians by giving a supper that night to the chorus!"

Behind scenes, Tivoli's AH Leahy recalls the "Bostonians were in a box that night" for Nielsen's *Lucia* debut "and they were greatly pleased with Alice's work. After the performance Barnabee came to me with a proposition to secure Alice for the Bostonians".

Now Barnabee interrupts: "Here would seem to be the proper place to tell you how the Company recruited its voices. There are a number of requisites for ...success on the operatic stage. In almost every city...we were called upon to help or advise some singers who thought that they had talents that would ensure them a successful stage career. There was not one in a hundred of the voices we heard that could have been utilized outside of the chorus, and that part of the organization was readily filled.

"A person to make other than a bare living in stage work must have temperament; something that is not possessed by everyone; and most of all a strong personality. If a young lady wants to become a singer in opera she must have a good voice, a pretty or attractive face; a good form—not too tall or short; and then she must, in addition to these requirements, be different from the rest. A young man demands the same requirements".

Those who seek the stage "must combine intelligence" with musical talents "to set the musical world on fire". Barnabee scorns "music teachers" who inflate students about their talent; public stage performance by far best school.

"Yes, dear friend, we did make a discovery once in a while. It was like mining. You know a prospector will drudge along for many years searching for gold.... We kept trying voices; we knew they were somewhere, and that we would run across them some day—and we did".

Alice knew the Bostonians would leave town in two weeks, "and day followed day with no word from Barnabee. Wednesday, Thursday and Friday of the second week passed—and no word. On Saturday a messenger arrived asking me to read what he had fetched in the envelope and let him have my reply. It was a contract with the Bostonians! They offered me $50 a week to travel with them and sing ingénue roles and understudy the lyric soprano parts". On the road again, in style. Still makes less than Wigwam.

The date, about October 21, 1895. Without hesitation Alice Nielsen drops mom, children, siblings, coach Ida, Tivoli, and a rich boyfriend. Packs her trunk to join the wide-touring Bostonians.

Casting Alice Nielsen became a brag. "Her fresh young voice, sympathetic face and vivacious personality could not long remain hidden, anywhere", Barnabee recalls.

"We were on the verge of producing Oscar Weil's musical fantasia...*A Wartime Wedding*—and had a first-rate part to offer our new singer. She made good...." Alice "fulfilled her own and our expectations".

Her co-stars were tenor William Philp; soprano Hilda Clark; contraltos Jessie Bartlett Davis, Marcia Van Dresser; bassos Cowles and Merrill; baritones MacDonald and Hanley. Barnabee labels himself, Frothingham, Fitzgerald and Harry Brown comedians, adding "This ensemble, probably, registered the Bostonians' high-tide operatic mark".

The hire needs approval by manager Frank Perley back east, who reports Barnabee and MacDonald wired: "John Nash recommends a girl named Alice Nielsen who is singing at the Tivoli here, for Amelia Stone's place. Kindly wire authority to engage her subject to your approval when you meet company at Minneapolis".

Alice skips Tivoli director John Nash, soon fired by Tivoli owner Mrs. Kreiling "for neglecting his duties with the race track, horseback riding, and the baths". Nash successfully sued for back salary. Mrs. Kreiling, battling for control, married director George Lask, his brother Harry was Tivoli's trustee. John Nash directs in London and New York, and marries actress Lilly Hawthorne.

Amelia Stone? Of vaudeville, plays Princess Soo-Soo on Broadway. Her last musical, *The Gay Musician*, ran twenty-one 1908 performances. Perley tells us "Miss Stone had been engaged for ingénue and soubrette roles second to Helen Bertram, the *prima donna*, and as her sudden withdrawal necessitated filling the place at once, I authorized Miss Nielsen's conditional engagement as requested. At Minneapolis, I heard Miss Nielsen sing the ingénue role" in *War-Time Wedding* by "a noted musician of California...and before leaving, engaged her for the remainder of that and the next season at an increased salary".

Perley had started with circus impresario PT Barnum promoting Jumbo the Elephant and Jenny Lind. Now, the Bostonians, Modjeska and other top stars. Alice's sister Hortense has joined Modjeska, a stage success the Nielsen sisters seek. Modjeska, reveals *LA Times* (1896), "is not dependent on the stage for support. Her beautiful estate in California where she has gone to regain her health, comprises six-hundred acres including a large and prosperous vineyard. Her 16 weeks' tour this season, according to her manager Frank Perley, netted her over $32,000 profit".

Nielsen's "increased salary" was lowest of the group. Timing not so fast. WC Leahy recalls: "Before going with the Bostonians she sang Lucia again, and also Marguerite in *Faust*, but she failed to score as affectively as on that memorable night when she first essayed a grand opera role".

Alice performs a new show with Bostonians after a week's rehearsal. Giving credence to her capability to master new music, Alice Nielsen's debut with the Bostonians had far less rehearsal than Kansas City's *Chanticlere* yet the results same. Singers better than show.

October 27, 1895, Alice Nielsen debuts with the Bostonians in *A War-Time Wedding* at San Francisco's Columbia Theatre. They have rehearsed six days. Don't try this at home.

Music by San Francisco-based Oscar Weil, libretto by Tennessee playwright Charles Dazey, it premiers with a slight success attributed to the fact the Bostonians perform it. Plot pure melodrama: enter band of guerillas. Despite jealous girlfriend, the chief militant woos an orphan heiress in convent secretly nursing wounded American soldier stashed in garden hut. Soldier captured, US Cavalry saves in nick. Hapless chief stabbed by jealous girlfriend. Rescued solider proposes to heiress nurse.

Oscar Weil (1839-1921) composed for Gaston Serpett's *Fanchonette* (1885), Louis Varney's *Musketeers*, Bostonians *Pygmalion and Galalea* (1899). From NY he moved to 1868 San Francisco after Leipzig and Paris. Union Army major, he founded San Francisco Institute of Music, taught Alice B. Toklas. Kentucky-born Dazey (1853-1938) created dozens of plays. Harvard class poet 1881, belongs to The Lambs' theatre club as all the (male) troupe. He founded a North Dakota town; play revenues built Fargo's library. Best-known hit was 1893's novel and play *In Old Kentucky*. Putting his naturalistic heroine in pants helps the show run two decades:

> *Her arms, bare to the elbows and above, might have been the models to drive a sculptor to despair, as their muscles played like pulsing liquid beneath the tinted, velvet skin of wrists and forearms; her short skirt bared her shapely legs above the ankles half-way to the knees; her feet, never pinched by shoes and now quite bare...in strong contrast to the linsey-woolsey of her gown and rough surroundings, were as dainty as a dancing girl's in ancient Athens.*

Opening night reviews for *A War-Time Wedding* ran from bad to worse; even so, the dismal *Wedding* has a year in Bostonian repertory.

San Francisco Chronical (Oct 28): "At the Columbia last evening, the Weil-Dazey opera *A War-Time Wedding: or, Mexico in 1848*, had its premier in the presence of one of the largest audiences of the season". Clumsy title, yet "considering a limited rehearsal and new material to work on, the performance was a successful one. A great many members of the Spanish community were present".

Nielsen, paired with comic star Barnabee, "made a piquant little senorita, with mischief enough in her composition to spoil a whole convent full of girls. What little singing she had to do, concerted and other, was executed very nicely. She will prove an acquisition to the company".

So. October 1895, four years since scuttling Kansas City, Alice Nielsen has joined "America's Greatest Light Opera Company" the Bostonians.

Kansas City jumps for joy.

Kansas City Star (Nov 1): "Miss Alice Nielsen, formerly Mrs. Benjamin Nentwig...has joined The Bostonian Opera company. She made her first appearance with Barnabee & MacDonald's company in *A War Time Wedding* at the Columbia Theatre San Francisco, last Monday evening.

Besides taking principal parts... Miss Nielsen will be understudy to Helen Bertram, who sings in *Robin Hood* and in *Prince Ananias*. The news of Miss Nielsen's 'promotion' will interest many in Kansas City, who know the hard-working little singer".

Star provides Nielsen's bio blurb: "She was driven into professional ranks to earn a livelihood. She made her first operatic appearance as Patience in an amateur production of Gilbert & Sullivan opera in Music Hall of this city. Along with Addison Madeira, she sustained almost the entire performance. So credible was her work that she was given the part of Rose in Cramer & Paddock's opera *Chanticlere*, produced at the Coates theatre for the first time on any stage in September, 1891. Mrs. Nentwig, as she was known then, made a distinct hit and it was her success in these two amateur efforts that eventually led her to the operatic stage. Less than a month after she appeared in *Chanticlere*, Mrs. Nentwig filed for divorce from Benjamin Nentwig, the well-known musician and organist". *Star* fiction: "The desired decree was granted, and early in 1892 Miss Nielsen, accompanied by her child a boy of 2 years, went to San Francisco".

Divorce pending; mom nabbed boy; left fall 1891.

"Since last February she has been signing leading roles with the Tivoli company. Barnabee's eagle eye picked her out last week, and after he and his partner MacDonald had heard her sing one night, they secured her signature to a contract". Alice, *Star* concludes, is "a petite brunette with more than usual claims to good looks".

Star pins Nielsen's Tivoli start as February, 1894. Jumps to Bostonians October 20th 1895. After a single week of rehearsal performs the 27th. Later in life she puts 1896, her NYC debut.

On the road to Denver, Nielsen masters Bostonian repertory plus their bespoke shows like Herbert's *Prince Ananias*, DeKoven's *Robin Hood*. She takes a small *Robin Hood* role then rotates into Maid Marian.

Nielsen looks back with wonder, "In perfectly plain language, I had crashed the Bostonians. Naturally they wouldn't have taken me had I not been able to sing up to their standards; but there were many voices in America capable of maintaining The Bostonians' standards—many voices which never had the chance".

Highlights her outlook: "Proximity of fame and fortune, the presence of greatness, the conceits of genius, the pomp and circumstance of the lordly—all these things went over my head, leaving me as naïve, as heedless (and sometimes headless), as impudent and as rowdy as ever.

"I could have done with a little more diplomacy and a little less of the *gamine*, but then I should not have been Alice Nielsen. I would have crashed the sacred Bostonians had it necessitated smuggling myself into their hearing in their baggage truck or lowering myself from a skylight—singing as I descended".

The Bostonian knew people; everybody knew them: every door opens.

Her life distills to a single word: fame. "Now I had entered the great world—the glittering world where fame dwelt.

"Fortunately I did not realize then that, as a member for the most famous light-opera organization in the world—The Bostonians—I had risen from the streets of Kansas City to a place in the musical world which to ten-thousand excellent singers would have meant the pinnacle of achievement.

"Had such realization come to me, had I been possessed of the seriously adult mentality which takes life solemnly, I might have been impressed by my fine fortune and thereby made humble. And then my second-best talent—my childlike effrontery—would have suffered and I might have become self-conscious. All things considered, the engagement of Alice Nielsen, the singing soubrette, by the staid Bostonians, was in itself remarkable if not sensational".

Only the start.

Impudent, rowdy mother of one, yet upon meeting Barnabee's wife: "Clara Barnabee all but adopted me. I was hardly more than twenty-one years old, and looked less. To her I was a child and her pent-up materialism was lavished upon me, as it was at times upon her kindly, erratic, talented husband. It was one of the oddest friendships a girl ever formed. She was one of the loneliest, unhappiest and most unselfish women I have ever known. Her love for me became oppressive, tyrannical and in time unbearable. And yet is has been the fortune of few women to know such devotion".

Of Barnabee's talent? "I have preserved a clear record in my memory of the innumerable characters which he made his own and which by sheer force of his talent he made into creations which often surpassed the conceptions of either author or composer.... Can one say more of an artist than that he never repeated himself?" (1913)

Alice Nielsen's first Denver performance without a male soprano in drag was November 26, 1895. They give *Robin Hood* two nights, *Prince Ananias* three. *War-Time Wedding* twice Saturday. Denver trip last September had offered only *Robin Hood*, following Pyke Opera's six-week season of six operettas at Elitch's Garden. *War-Time Wedding* takes a beating as Bostonians tour east.

Philadelphia Inquirer: "Third-class melodrama, and the music ...formless, noisy and without appeal, although in some of the choruses it hints of an approach to better things which alas! are never reached". Dazey's Mexican "trite and tawdry" morass, "lyrics are no better than the story". The music: "One thing in favor of Mr. Weil's music is that it is not reminiscent; it has not been heard before, nor is it the kind of music one ardently desired to hear again".

Boston would be a bastion for Alice Nielsen's career after she debuts on May 14, 1896. *War-Time Wedding* gets a brilliantly grim reception

Boston Post: "The wildest melodrama that ever bored an audience.... Not satisfied with becoming responsible for much depression of action and speech, the authors of the story add the torture of music to their crimes". Torture was cloaked, at least at first by the opening chorus, a duet and two other songs: "These exceptions we gladly make. But the rest was excruciating".

Weill's score "made one squirm in one's chair and almost pray for relief in the fall of the curtain...left the word 'contrast' out of his vocabulary. An aria now and then, an aria possessing genuine melody and warmth of expression and feeling, might save an opera from being a total wreck. It would save *A War-Time Wedding* from eternal damnation".

Only the Bostonians' special status kept people from howling with scorn; any other players "would have suffered immensely in loss of artistic reputation" and "cleared the house at the end of the second act". Sadly, the cast had "a grim determination to make it go. After the pastoral simplicity of *Robin Hood* and the careless frivolity of *Prince Ananias*, the acting...seemed astounding. One would have thought they all were in grand opera".

In the cast: Davis "surprisingly effective". Bertram, tellingly, "we fear, never will become an actress". MacDonald and Eugene Cowles "splendid pair... they had studied their parts with intelligence and they acted them with great force". Barnabee "droll...anyone else would have been tiresome. To give comedy relief to this melancholic combination, an impossible New England rustic of no uncertain age is forced to make love to a lisping little ingénue, obviously still in her teens". Playing the lisping little teen, "Miss Nielsen is to be credited with a clever bit of ingénue work".

Herald gives *Wedding* a cannonade: "The situations are without a trace of originality...worn threadbare long ago...the most commonplace of theatrical platitudes". The music, "quite pretentious" and "too persistently noisy". Boston contradicts Philly: the music had been heard before. Weil "judged by this music, does not appear to be strong in invention" and certain composers (gladly listed by the critic) "seem to have obtained so strong a hold on his memory that he could not drive them out". The "well-known air of Delilah, in *Sampson And Delilah* had taken such completed possession of him that he paraphrased it at least three numbers with almost ingenuous frankness".

In the cast: "Alice Nielsen was winsome in piquant in a lively soubrette part, and sang tunefully and brightly". Barnabee's conflicted interpolation of his *Cork Leg* song-and-dance meant "to lighten the dreariness of the story; but the work was already dismal enough without the saddening attempts at humor". *Cork Leg* "came like a lugubrious ghost from a far-away past to chill the blood with its funeral mirthfulness. The wearisomeness of the whole became almost unbearable". Jessie Davis "strong and effective performance", Helen Bertram "sang her exacting music brilliantly" and "the rich and sonorous bass voice of Mr. Cowles was again heard with admirable results".

May 1896 marks Philip Hale's first review of Alice Nielsen's work. His Boston Symphony program notes continue to delight; NY critic James Huneker recalls, "We had a Philip Hale cult then. No wonder".

For *War-Time Wedding*, Hale: "Miss Nielsen displayed a fresh and pleasing voice and an archness that was free from self-consciousness" who "by her quaint freshness won sincere astonishment" contrasts with others.

His contrast of Alice with other cast are matched by others. Hale continues, "Mrs. Davis put a great deal of vitality into the part...but her shading was never fine". Davis "suffered from exaggeration. She does not know the value of repose or suggestion. She is inclined to mouth and blurt in dialogue, and to force her tones in song. When she wishes to make a point, she knows no other means than a strained and tumultuous appeal".

Yet, "Miss Nielsen showed excellent comic force as Anita, and Miss Bertram was an acceptable Marquita".

Hale hates cork: Barnabee's bit "dragged in by the heels. Much time is wasted, the story is well-nigh forgotten while Mr. Barnabee plods through a dreary routine of laborious merry-making which includes a revival of the ditty entitled *The Cork Leg*" Hale despised the first time thirty years ago. Hale notes composer Weil "frequently recalls the thoughts of other composers. There are few sure dramatic touches, there is little genuine, fresh, spontaneous melody".

Despite a difficult property, Nielsen gains praise. She would do so many times for many difficult properties. She could save a show.

They close the Boston season with *Robin Hood.*

Across North America the lone holdout for *War-Time Wedding*? Detroit: "A very noble and impressive piece of musical writing and really should be classed as grand opera. The Mascagni-like story is relieved by scenes of humor in which Mr. Barnabee is the conspicuous figure, though his drolleries are set off and delicately embellished with some dainty and captivating comedy business by Miss Alice Nielsen, a newcomer".

Bostonian Jessie Bartlett remarks, *Wedding* "was no comedy, it was Serious. That opera was indeed, very serious, so serious in fact that the public would have nothing to do with it". (1901)

Alice Nielsen, a hit everywhere with any material (except St. Joseph).

Boston critic Louis Strang awards "best diva" within three years of this debut. Boston critics praise and carefully interpret her artistry. Boston is joined by insightful critics in Los Angeles, Chicago, Dallas, and other centers. These sketch a clear contrast against conflicted old New York. And in the day theatre was on the road. All towns saw all stars. Audiences were equally savvy. Imagine today's Met audience replicated across America.

Young beautiful Alice dances, acts, sings, comic, legs. Gregarious magnetic quality attracts. Impudent Irish upstart stirs ill-will—pretty petite irritates the larger, older competition.

"From the beginning I was not overpopular with all the members of the cast. But a happy-go-lucky heart, a skin thickened by much rubbing against adversity, and a natural love of singing (my own, in particular) that closed out almost everything else, saved me from hurt.

"No female member of the company was in any danger of being popular with the superb Jessie (*O Promise Me*) Davis, but she liked me a little less than the others and the fault was largely my own. Generally speaking, the Bostonians were as magnificent physically as artistically. Large people, deep of chest, wide of hip, inclined to develop chin upon chin.

"But sing? Mother of Heaven, how they could sing! And I was small, petite, the eternal ingénue, a singing soubrette. My legs, my ankles, my feet had won elaborate praise in San Francisco. Just how worthy they were, modesty forbids me even to guess. But this I know: my childish figure was even more pronounced amid Bostonian ruggedness.

"I'm quite sure that Davis' antipathy to me was not founded wholly upon physical envy, because she had ample beauty herself".

Nielsen confides, "Mentally and temperamentally, too, I was far from conventional adulthood.... But she was annoyed by my pertness, my brash disregard for Bostonian dignity and, not the least in importance, by the habit of critics and newspaper paragraphers of comparing my lack of tonnage with my Amazonian associates. All of which was, of course, very unkind". Chicago critics "thought it necessary to allude to me as the mouse brought forth by the labor of the Bostonian mountains".

Audiences spoke freely during shows. In *The Serenade* (1896) "a gentleman in the gallery" clarified the "vast disparity in our sizes. In one scene it was up to me to propose to Davis that she and I exchange clothes that, thus disguised, she might flee her convent and marry her Alvarado. 'Take her up, Jessie', bawled the galleryite. 'I'll go out and get you a shoehorn.' Davis was furious—so furious indeed, that she accused me of having paid the man to make his criticism of her bulk. Alas with all my faults and incivilities, such flank attacks upon my rivals were beyond me. I never thought in such dangerous terms".

The shoehorn shot "deepened Davis' dislike for me". Then with typical fairness, Nielsen adds that Davis "has probably never been excelled on any stage. She died in her forties when she should still have been in the ascendant".

Bostonians were beset by faction before Alice. Under pressure to develop new shows which must feature every ensemble star, authors must showcase each voice. Their repertory, very vintage. Jessie Davis in 1895 had sung *Robin Hood's* interpolated hit *Oh Promise Me* "something like five-thousand times" for 2,041 shows.

Alice continues: "We, the Bostonians, had sung *Robin Hood* and the rest of the company's honorable repertoire until, with all its beauty, it was growing a bit threadbare. We sang Jules Jordan's *A War-Time Wedding* for a few nights, only to find it was a dismal failure". Actually *Wedding* was in their repertory a full year, not "a few nights". Before opening it had been rehearsed "a few nights".

Everybody wants success: composer, writer, performers, producers, and public. Demand outstrips supply of good new musicals. Into this situation arrives Victor Herbert. He realizes Alice creates hits by sheer performance magic to propel his success. In short, a money-maker. Thus begins Bostonians end.

Musical development is complex for *Robin Hood*, *War-Time Wedding*, and Herbert's *Prince Ananias*. Composing showcase music for the Bostonian stars may perhaps be easier than mapping any stage story for the ensemble.

Creators kept trying. Group rehearses a week before play to pay.

Bostonian basso Eugene Cowles tells realities, "They were the first managers to give encouragement to native composers, and always had faith in them; so that while they had two successes, *Robin Hood* by Reginald De Koven, and *The Serenade* by Victor Herbert, they put on a great many pieces by American composers which were absolute failures, and anyone who knows the theatrical business can give you an idea of how much may be lost on a comic opera production, which falls short of success". (1913)

Herbert, when Bostonians fail to turn *Prince Ananias* (1894) into a hit, realizes their limitations. Refuses to supply another until objections are met. His librettist Francis Neilson would introduce Puccini to Belasco's *Madame Butterfly* play from arose opera which famously failed until Puccini "remodeled".

Only right material given right talent properly produced arises success.

In *Ananias*, La Fontaine sings, "*Now here am I, a playwright great, Whom classes high appreciate; Yet I've to please both great and small, Or my receipts soon take a fall. The critics spoil my audience; I cuss the press in self-defense*".

Londoner Neilson then joins Parliament to oppose racket wars.

The Bostonians' invite-only *Prince Ananias* gala in 1896 NYC illustrates their esteem. Packed audience includes best brightest: Wilson Barrett, JH Stoddard, Daniel Frohman, Bessie Tyree, Viola Allen, Frank McKeever, Henry Miller and DeWolf Hopper.

NY Times reports: "Nearly all the players are acquainted, not only with everybody in the house but with everybody on the stage, and between the acts little visiting groups moved from box to box and seat to seat.

"Never did The Bostonians sing or act with more spirit. They were in the house of their friends and they knew it, and the tuneful and merry opera was given with a vim which only such an audience could inspire. Every number" is warmly encored "from Comedian Barnabee to the smallest speaking character.

"After loud cries for 'Herbert!'" the composer is "dragged on the stage by Mr. Barnabee and Mr. Frothingham and blushed to his forehead as he acknowledged the greetings of the audience".

Interestingly two years ago *Times* regarded the show unpolished, Bostonians drab: "no longer the remarkably brilliant assemblage of operetta lights that it was a few seasons ago; it is still the only high-class company engaged in the production of works not built around a 'star.' Their recent ventures...have not had the happiest results, but last night they bravely tried again". *Ananias* will succeed or fail "largely upon the judgment displayed in making the dramatic and musical cuts which are sadly needed".

Music by "popular bandmaster and 'cello player, Victor Herbert" and Francis Neilson's libretto, "shortcoming of the operetta are due to a lack of experience in both men". Book "cheap and obvious". "No novice in the art of composition", Herbert's "long and complicated solo numbers" are too ambitious for Broadway yet "other melodies are bright, clean-cut, full of vim and attractive in rhythm".

In 1896 Irish citizen, Victor Herbert joins the seasoned theatre pros who promote Alice Nielsen's talent: Burton Stanley, Ida Valerga, Henry Barnabee. Herbert, forty-seven (twice Nielsen's age), is fast moving from orchestra pit to limelight to dominate musical theatre in his day.

Born Dublin, educated Stuttgart, trained Vienna, Herbert arrived in 1892 NY as first cellist at The Met whose conductor Anton Seidl had assisted Richard Wagner. Seidl has Herbert compose for the orchestra's summer concerts.

Anton Dvorak hires Herbert for the National Conservatory of Music at 17th and Irving near Union Square, heart of town. Herbert's cello concerto inspires Dvorak to write his. Strollers hear Dvorak on piano with neighbor

Herbert cello. They cultivate new talent, such as singing Catskills waiter Henry Burleigh. James Huneker recalls Herbert, Dvorak, Seidl enjoying "old Vienna Bakery Cafe, next to Grace Church. There the coffee and pastry were the best in town". Seidl and Dvorak "sit for hours without speaking". Huneker recalls a morning stroll with Dvorak, "I left him swallowing his nineteenth cocktail". Huneker had met his match.

Nielsen shares Irish culture and loss of father at same age as Herbert. And a love for art over money. "No sane person will assume", says Robert Grau (1902 *Businessman in the Music World*), "Victor Herbert expects that his efforts with symphony orchestras will financially avail him; his time...would bring tenfold results in the fields wherein Mr. Herbert is known to prosper amazingly [musicals], yet the brilliant Irish maestro has for years allied himself with Pittsburgh's Symphony Orchestra at a great loss and inconvenience to himself". Gregarious Herbert seeks universal art: "I believe that which is not popular is not of much benefit to the world".

Herbert believes Bostonians killed *Ananias* by not rehearsing it sufficiently. Well, hardly any. Well, just about none. Pay to be played to was the Bostonian motto. Yet *Ananias* is staged two years, *Wedding* only one. Assessed by *Philadelphia Inquirer* (1896), the show "by Victor Herbert, the well-known leader of Gilmore's Band, and Francis Neilson, a young journalist of experience. The opera is... laid in France in the sixteenth century, a period fertile in romance....

"Neilson has broken away from the conventional comic opera story in his libretto. It is not necessary to indulge in extravagant praise in behalf of the Bostonians. This organization has long stood for that which is best...." *Ananias* is a "more elaborate production" than previous, a "wealth of pretty music. The comedy element is simply irresistible".

Producer Frank Perley recounts, "When the need of a new opera for the Bostonians presented itself...I approached Victor Herbert and Harry Smith as the ones best equipped to write a suitable vehicle, for both knew the strength as well as the limitations of the company". Herbert declined, "saying that the older members of the Bostonians Company never served an apprenticeship in stagework but had stepped from church and local concert singing into the operatic field through accidental success, and that they could not or would not properly learn an opera before its production but had to 'grow into it' afterwards, which I know was true".

Opera as any story sung. If Barnabee would refute this Herbert-Perley claim of "accidental success" he could not turn back the ensemble clock.

Herbert demands approval over timing of the NYC opening, plus power to approve the cast. "Mr. Herbert cited the failure of his opera *Prince Ananias* as due to the fact that the Bostonians brought it into NY before they had 'grown into' their respective parts". Librettist "Smith coincided and cited *Robin Hood* as another example, for it took several months of playing this delightful score before the Bostonians 'put it over'".

Let us glance at development for *Robin Hood*, a legendary success with a curious creative rush promoted by coincidence. Harry Smith tells he and DeKoven began the show lifted "almost bodily from the old story. The new opera had to be written in a hurry, so DeKoven and I rented a room in an office building in Chicago, where we worked from early in the morning to late at night. *Robin Hood* was written in three weeks, which was a very short time since DeKoven and I had not yet really learned our trade".

Merely-clever Smith candidly is only in it for the money; he's cynical.

Herbert and Nielsen seek the deeper unity with their audiences.

Smith and DeKoven improvise: "As a general rule, in constructing a musical piece the lyrics are written first and the music made to fit, but in this instance a great deal of the music was composed first and the words were written afterwards to fit the music". Of ballads, songs and snatches: in *Tinkers' Chorus*, "DeKoven played two songs and refrains to me and I said, 'Take the verse part of one and the refrain part of the over and put them together and it will make a good number". At first rehearsal Studley "musical director, who had been used to foreign operas and did not care for American music, threw down his baton and exclaimed 'I positively refuse to play such trash!'"

Robin Hood debuts on a hot Chicago July night, Smith in the prompter box "sweltering...and between the murderous assaults the company made on my 'brainchild' and the heat, you may imagine what I suffered. Furthermore, the various members of the company did not know their lines and were not half familiar with the music". Worse, the Bostonians improvised: "compelled to put on the play with any costumes, relevant or irrelevant that they had on hand. We drew on *Il Trovatore* for some of the costumes and also used any scenery that we could dig up—the whole thing being quite a hodge-podge".

When Bostonians and *Robin Hood* appear, *NY Times* darkly suggests "DeKoven and Smith might be forgiven...but it was always good to drown the first litter of puppies".

By the oddest theatre magic, only in Detroit, single town to praise dismal *War-Time Wedding*, would *Robin Hood* become an enduring hit. The Bostonians plan to rotate *Robin Hood* with *Il Trovatore* and *Chimes of Normandy*, but on first night the theatre manager likes *Robin Hood* so much he insists they run it all week. By that slim thread hangs their smash cash cow.

Smith gloats: "It had a fair success. It was played continuously for 21 years". His share provided $225,000 in royalties, huge money in 1890s of gold dollars, no taxes, $300 grand pianos. Not unsurprisingly given the "rescue maiden" story style, Smith assigns the show's success to the men: "It was the male members of the cast—they had several fine, big fellows with fine, big voices—that made the success of *Robin Hood*". Smith's insight Perley confirms, saying *Robin Hood* nearly was "lost to the public" since "'powers that be' too often consider as final the verdict of a New York first night audience".

Perley must give a "personal guarantee" the new Herbert show "should not be brought into NYC" until Herbert and Smith "satisfied with its rendition", and with this agreed they create *The Serenade*. Neglects mention he was dragooned to grant Herbert the right to select the star.

1896: NYC BROADWAY DEBUT, A STAR IS BORN

Alice Nielsen on Sunday February 9 of 1896 hits NYC papers in Bostonian ads for *Robin Hood* and *War-Time Wedding* at Broadway Theatre, "Handsomest and Safest Theatre in the World" managed by TH French. *NY Times'* theatre ads are small blocks of type. Eleonora Duse opens in two weeks; a future Nielsen friend.

"New faces will be seen and new voices heard in the revival of *Robin Hood* by the Bostonians" with "Alice Nielsen, a young Californian to whom is entrusted a minor soprano role", says *Times*. Other new are Helen Bertram Henley, Harold Blake, Charles Hawley. Plus "special scenery" and "well-drilled chorus".

They open Monday for two weeks' repertory with manager Frank Perley's "sumptuous revival" of *Robin Hood*. In the cast: HC Barnabee, Sheriff of Nottingham; WH MacDonald, Little John; Helen Bertram, Maid Marion; Eugene Cowles, Will Scarlet; Jerome Sykes; George Frothingham, Friar Tuck; Harold Blake, Robin Hood; Josephine Bartlett, Dame Durden; Alice Nielsen, Annabel; CE Landie, Guy of Gisborne; and Jessie Davis, Alan-a-Dale.

They sang: Act 1: "*Ever we are gay, Cheerily, merrily, roaming e'er, Living like Kings in the forest fair (never do they worry), Ever they are gay, all the live-long day*". The small part Annabel gives Alice her first Broadway solo (coming forward): "*Surely 'tis an acquisition, to this goodly company, Outlaws of such high position, Gladly at the fair we see. Come and join our dance!* (Alan, Little John, Scarlet join her) A *morris dance must you entrance, Let us dance! Fa la, Trip a morris dance hilarious....*" Such exhilarating lyrics.

Reviews were the usual for *Wedding*. Dazey wrote "in a hackneyed manner. His ideas belonged to the Bowery drama. Indeed...if the aim had been burlesque they could have been made to serve that purpose with little alteration". Scenery cheap, costumes ugly, staging bad. NY critics did not list each Weil plagiarism as Boston, music was merely "commendably ambitious".

"The entertaining value of this musical play is doubtful.... Plainly a surprise and a disappointment...to get a low-grade melodrama from the Bostonians instead of the usual comic opera". Quality voices lent the flop credence, "any other musico-comedy companies would surely have let it drop into ridicule".

Amazingly, Victor Herbert had sent his Viennese-born Metropolitan Opera soprano wife, Therese Forster, to spy out the Bostonians. She enjoyed Nielsen's small part, Nielsen and Barnabee were good foils. Nielsen sang well, danced and moved naturally, expressively.

Mrs. Herbert picked Alice Nielsen as star for her husband's new show.

Nielsen had not met Herbert, "as far as I know, he had never seen or heard of me. But his wife had and, bless her gentle heart, she ran from the theatre to tell Victor that she had found the ideal Yvonne for *The Serenade*. At that time, Victor Herbert had just written *The Serenade* for that company and he was looking for a prima donna".

Of course, Herbert had knew the cast as he created the score they would sing. No doubt he heard praise about the petite young petite Irish soprano: her hiring had been national news. Reviews were republished.

"Well, Mrs. Victor Herbert went home and told her husband that I was the one for the leading lady. Whereat he came to hear me and it was my fortune to be in particularly good voice and spirit that night, and so I was starred in the operetta a year later".

With Nielsen's voice in mind, Herbert completed *The Serenade*. Still a few doubts. "I was in his mind for the role but I was a very frail girl, I only weighed 102 pounds, but now I am up to 134 [1930]. So he thought that the part would be too much responsibility for me".

After the usual short spring season in NYC, Bostonians tour North America until summer. During hiatus Alice returns to San Francisco where sister Hortense, the *Call* announces July 24th: "Aspires to histrionic fame. Hortense Nielsen will begin her career in August". Modjeska's path, "Her ambition is to play the heroines of Shakespeare".

Molasses gets thick when Denmark is invoked, suggesting absurdly "her father played 'Hamlet' with fame in the land where the ghost walked" and Hortense has "a long line of ancestors on the continent famous for histrionic talent". She "aspires to high comedy roles, and with good reason. Her work so far in this line has called forth the most flattering criticism. She has, in fact, been compared even at this early period of her career to Julia Marlowe. There is a marked resemblance...."

Mentioning Danish gold hair and white skin, brunette Hortense "vivacious and winsome and has a fine voice". Hortense, interestingly, "will be assisted by her sister, Alice Nielsen, who has sung with so much success at the Tivoli" and now with Bostonians. Hortense "will also be supported by some of the best talent of San Francisco, the debut to be given either at the Auditorium or at the Metropolitan Temple.

Hortense is quoted in a phrase often familiar of Alice, "I want the people of San Francisco to like me. I have studied long and hard in this City, and I want to make my start here. I shall give probably the balcony scene and the poison scene from Romeo and Juliet. I love Shakespeare, and it is my ambition to play in some of his comedies". She postponed "offers from two good companies, but prefers to wait until she can make her debut in San Francisco". Ink sketches of the two Nielsen sisters illustrate the story.

Tracing the Hortense lost saga: previous June 25th, *Call* has Hortense to Boston, brags San Francisco produces America's greatest theatrical talent: "Miss Hortense Neilson [sic], the sister of Alice Neilson [sic] of the Bostonians, is not the least of this galaxy of theatrical stars near the horizon. She has secured an engagement with the company of Kich and Harris, the Boston Comedy Company".

Hortense, now a California native, "well known here and immensely popular" will take "a prominent part in the comedy, *The Night Clerk*. She has been put through falling, standing, walking and articulating by Fred Belasco. She commences to realize that acting is no longer a thing of butterfly nature. 'Oh, of course', said she, 'I shall not sue Mr. Belasco for compensation, and I do not expect Mr. Belasco to do so either.' A telegram was received by his brother from Dave [David] Belasco last night saying...he would be on this coast within three weeks...will deliver lectures before the actors of this City and the theatrical students".

The proposed fall debut has not been located. Hortense appears in Oakland late as 1901. 1899, she plays *Madame Sans-Gene* with Frawley Company (*LA Herald* Sept. 3rd). Two years earlier, Tuesday 25th 1897, Hortense joined Wilbur Opera Company in Sacramento. She "sang out the chorus for the first time" as Montesque in comic opera *Olivette* "made an excellent impression. She has a sweet and very dainty voice, and she is a very taking figure on the stage". December 29th 1895, *Call* reported "latest theatrical debutantes to abandon the drawing-room are Miss Hortense Neilson, Miss Mabel Hocha and Miss Mayrne Heffron—all well known in local society circles. They will make their first public appearance as one of the local theaters next Friday night in *A Celebrated Case*.

Heffron and Hortense without Hocha are said to "accompany Miss LaFaille" east to DC to play in *Heart of Maryland* "a drama by David Belasco, playwright and actor...well known in this City". Hortense "from Nashville...charming type of the Southern beauty...with large, expressive eyes and a clear, melodious voice.... Fred Belasco has had charge of her training for the past two months and...considers her one of the coming footlight favorites".

How about some jumbo molasses, dearie, to spread some fancy big promotion for daddy Sgt. Erasmus: "She is a niece of General Neilson, who fell fighting for the Southern cause during the rebellion. Miss Neilson's family have resided in Nashville for over a century".

Nielsen sisters knew Belasco brothers in San Francisco where Hortense has absorbed the repertory of Modjeska, who retires 1897. The Ibsen and Shaw plays challenge audiences as Hortense starts her own tours, as late as 1920s playing Modjeska's popular Shakespeare role in *As You Like It* for the good folks at Asheville, NC, in the Blue Ridge near Black Mountain.

Returning to Alice returning to NYC in fall 1896, Bostonians open Murray Hill Theatre on Lexington at 41st, "fine and comfortable...and a fine audience crowded it upon this occasion of its first use". NY Athletic Club take half the seats. Theatre manager Frank Murtha is cheered. Athletic Club prove "vigorous in their enthusiasm for Hilda Clark...sent a great lot of flowers to her across the footlights". Clark's blonde curls appear in 1900s Coca-Cola ads.

Bostonians began to rehearse *Serenade* not knowing Herbert's choice for the star they presume as Clark. Doubting he would exercise power. So the rehearsals star Clark, Nielsen understudy. Bostonians are a national treasure so the new show's development is national news. Herbert is famed himself. Nielsen knows very truly, she now works with the most famous and the greatest. She has obtained the top rank of show biz.

For context consider far-away *LA Times* "About The Theatres" (Dec 13 1896) which reports Henry Irving had celebrated 25th anniversary of *The Bells* with a performance at the Lyceum, Conan Doyle had a new comedy *The Brothers Dawson*, WS Gilbert "completed a new play in the style of his earlier works" and Bostonians "rehearsing a new opera by Victor Herbert and Harry Smith" titled *Queen of the Buccaneers* which never appears by any guise. Frank Perley signs Al Hayman for a month tour with Modjeska tour including two weeks at San Francisco's Baldwin: "Modjeska's physicians say that she is now in perfect health and if she stands the work of this brief tour, a full season will be booked for her by Mr. Perley, commencing next fall". Hortense Nielsen is in the cast.

Rising from their first-ever Southern tour, Bostonians December 1896 reach DC. *Washington Post* on Christmas Eve says, "always pleasant to chronicle the annual engagements of the Bostonians...this favorite light opera company has maintained its excellent standard of work notwithstanding the mutations of time".

The Bostonians' first Southern tour "a succession of triumphs".

Bostonians bring "not only the old favorites, but a coterie of singers who are credited with successes elsewhere and who make their local debut with this organization". To the "old-time spirit of vigor" of familiar favorites arrive "Hilda Clark and Alice Nielsen, two beautiful young sopranos; William Phip, English tenor, and Kelly Cole". SL Studley "veteran director" again welds the baton with stage direction under "competent hands of RH Burnside".

War-Time Wedding oblivion. Monday, Tuesday, Wednesday, Saturday matinee and night is "perennial and ever-popular" *Robin Hood*; Thursday night and Friday (New Year Day) matinee Balfe's "ballad opera" *The Bohemian Girl* "will be rendered". Friday night finds fading *Prince Ananias*.

Meanwhile in California, Alice Nielsen's admirer Tom Williams has inherited everything. The estate is $1.5-million (1896) "chiefly in land of San Joaquin and Sacramento counties" (*LA Times* Dec 27). In this decade a nine-room mansion in downtown San Francisco cost you $13,000; cottages $3,000. Boundless wealth meant Williams could possibly, say, invest in a new Broadway touring company. And he wants to get married someday. If only he could get the rising star to trust him.

What promises could he make?

1897: VICTOR HERBERT: "NIELSEN WILL STAR"

During January the Bostonians feverishly prepare to open *The Serenade*, if blessed by Herbert who joins rehearsals to select a star.

Nielsen recalls: "At dress rehearsal, both Clark and I sang the role for Victor. Quite honestly and without any false modesty, Clark sang it better that afternoon. She sang with that dignity that became her own statuesque presence and all the Bostonian dignity".

Playful Herbert didn't prefer statues doing dignity. Playful Nielsen uses all her cumulative stage savvy, and invents dances: "The eternal gamine in me came to my aid. I sang it well as I could but burlesqued the character. I danced where Clark was still. That which had come to my aid when I bolted upon the Tivoli stage in San Francisco, doing Ada Lewis' dance, came to me now".

Alice Nielsen thrills when she frolics. Hijacks the cliché character away from cliché playwright Harry Smith. Invents herself as Yvonne, an arch young woman with a wink to audience: "I added all my fire, all my nimble clowning...and sang it as well as I knew how. And Victor Herbert was overjoyed".

"'Alice is Yvonne', said Victor, with an air of finality".

"'But', protested Will Macdonald, great baritone of the Bostonians, who shared with Henry Barnabee the last word in Bostonian affairs, 'the part is Hilda Clark's—hers by right of contract. She's our leading prima donna.'

"That's your affair', said Herbert. 'I'm not arguing about Clark's voice. I'm merely telling you that Nielsen's Yvonne.'

"'I must insist', said Macdonald, 'upon Clark.'

"'That's final?' asked Victor.

"'Final', said Macdonald.

"'That's too bad for all of us', snapped Victor. He gathered up the score of *The Serenade* and marched out. For a moment we were all paralyzed. Then Clark, Macdonald, Barnabee and I ran after him.

"'You've said your last word', said Victor, 'and so have I. Nielsen's Yvonne or *The Serenade* goes elsewhere. Good-by.'

"But they detained him while Macdonald and Barnabee consulted, dismissing Clark and me without ceremony. It didn't take long. Victor seemed to know but one sentence—'Nielsen's Yvonne.'

Nielsen's new spotlight irritated Jessie Davis. "Macdonald, who was not only in love with Davis but shared her coldness for me, took me aside and said: 'Very much against my wishes, I have agreed to divide the honors between you and Clark. You may open in one of three cities, New York, Boston or Chicago. Now take your damn' pick!'

"'I'll take all three', I said coolly.

"And I got all three. Victor was still insisting that 'Nielsen's Yvonne.' I should hesitate to tell this, an episode in which I have no pride, had it not been that Hilda Clark came to me that afternoon and, with a generosity that left me ashamed, told me that Victor Herbert was right. 'Alas', said she with her beautiful, rueful smile, 'I have no comedy. I cannot dance. Yvonne must have comedy and must dance. You can do both. Victor is right; you are Yvonne.'"

Clark's candor rings true. Fine voice, never actress. Born Leavenworth, Kansas, grew up Boston, sang NYC's East Village at St. Mark's Place Church before taking the stage. Louis Strang says, "The divine gift of song has placed Hilda Clark, whose ability as an actress is by no means great, in a position of prominence in the theatre world. There will always be a demand for attractive young women with pleasing voices...." Clark will join Sousa in *The Bride Elect*, her best-known role. Even so, Strang says, "her acting was hardly". Clark in 1903 marries a NY banker and continues at profitable church choirs.

Nielsen stars, Herbert profits, Bostonians implode.

Herbert can compose hits. He wants new players who do not thwart. The aging ensemble's baggage is burdensome. Bostonian stalwarts share an ensemble of equals. Now Nielsen gets the press; her pay a fraction.

Mid-February 1897, *Serenade* opens in Cleveland then Chicago.

Perley recalls, "*Serenade* received its premiere at the old Columbia Theatre, Chicago, where it scored an instantaneous success and the excellence of its presentation also won the consent of the authors to take it into NY at once". Neglects to mention Herbert's choice, seeks all credit. Perhaps his praise for Nielsen transcends a bit of the wrongs he cost her.

"Miss Nielsen, whose soul was wrapped up in her art and whose ambition to achieve made her the most willing and conscientious of workers, was then the alternative prima donna of the Bostonians, and it therefore fell to her lot to sing the second night; always a hard and unsatisfactory task because of the natural 'let down' of a company falling the nervous tension incident to a first performance. However, this plucky little singer scored such an emphatic 'hit' that I gave her the opening in NYC, although by contract it really belonged to another". Chasing "Little Nell" again, Perley skips Herbert's choice. Nielsen skips speaking of Perley after 1901. Creates his biggest success; the folly his.

In Chicago "Opera In English by the Bostonians" begins a three-week season on February 22, 1897, at Columbia Theatre. Adopting the publicity slant of Clara Kellogg, they tag themselves "strongest, largest and best English opera organization in the world". The first week is *Robin Hood*.

At Saturday matinee they cautiously perform *Serenade* as "in preparation—first time here—a new comic opera". This matinee may have been performed by Hilda Clark, not Alice Nielsen. The show formally opens next week. Herbert has chosen: Nielsen will star. Bostonian turmoil didn't reliably give her billing. This conflict cost dearly; a frustrated Herbert would generate this pattern of shows for a decade ahead. None for the Bostonian ensemble.

February 28, *Chicago Tribune* (1897): "Bostonians begin their second week's engagement at the Columbia Theatre tomorrow night with the first metropolitan production of a new opera especially written for them". Unlike all-too-serious *War-Time Wedding*, they clown. *The Serenade* "said to be a comic opera, with this element largely in evidence in the personages of a senile Duke, played by Mr. Barnabee; a stage-struck tailor enacted by Mr. Frothingham, and a broken-down tenor played by Mr. Harry Brown". Eugene Cowles "the brigand chief". Alvardo (McDonald) plays a baritone of Royal Opera and Delores (Davis) the ward of Duke "madly infatuated...." "Yvonne, danseuse in love with Alvardo" is "Alice Nielsen or Hilda Clark". Jessie Davis has her usual separate billing.

Cast of twenty-one includes Marcia Van Dresser. Chorus sixty, orchestra twenty-five. Droll sidebar: contra *Robin Hood* debut, *Serenade* sports "special scenery" and "correct costumes".

In Chicago previews March 1st, *Serenade* with Nielsen hailed a great success. Opening NYC on March 16, again Nielsen makes a big hit. Her unique powers with people hailed at this debut generate phrases which follow her career.

Potently, instantly, *NY Times* (Mar 17) focuses on these magnetic qualities applauded by her public: "Miss Nielsen's voice is a soprano of a mellow, sympathetic quality, which addition to other excellences, is round and true and possess that nameless something indefinable but always delightful to hear. When she sings her audiences are unconsciously interested in her personally, and with so auspicious a start she may be expected to go very far in her art".

Predicts her success a sure bet. Starts theatre insiders calculating cash. Advised by wife, Victor Herbert appoints Alice Nielsen star.

She instantly becomes a national celebrity making his show a success.

Less than five years after leaving Kansas City late September 1891, Alice Nielsen April 1896 stars in a major new production created by the best talents in American theatre. Fog dispels, her chronology ever plain to see. She will now be national news all her life. Her impact endures vividly among those fortunate to experience her performances. This fact will be retold repeatedly.

Managing producer Frank Perley praises her constantly-growing artistic progress: "Miss Nielsen did not step from the drawing room to operatic success, nor was her pathway in any sense rose-strewn. On the contrary, she came up from the ranks by hard study and conscientious work in stock and repertoire companies, so that when opportunity knocked at her door, she was equipped by experience to take full advantage of it, and did".

Life-long theatre insider, Perley emphasizes: "Her metropolitan success was little less than sensational, so much so in fact that many said, 'where did you find her', 'where did she come from', etc., and could not understand how they had failed to 'discover' her on the two or three previous NY engagements".

Herbert frees Alice Nielsen to create an unforgettable show.

Her three coaches who detect and shape her potentials had experience commanding audiences. Stanley could sustain comedy onstage for three hours, sang a soprano dream. Barnabee, durable bass-baritone, best singing comic in the nation had created the top musical group. Ida Valerga instills *bel canto* skills and imparts deep insights. All three act superbly.

Perley, his ambivalent situation years after doing Alice wrong, could not directly say she created the role by playing herself, albeit her stage self well-proven at Tivoli, and by so doing, created the hit. He does say she had deeper magic than surface charm: "The explanation was simple; her voice, temperament and personality were just suited to the prima donna role of *The Serenade*, and besides, it gave her opportunity for the full employment of her protean talents".

Rival Hilda Clark made no hit show. Nielsen, an unknown, won the crowds. He recognized: Prestige may draw a good first night attendance and "secure even a generous reception at the hands of the critics, but after then the measure of success is wholly dependent upon the public's point of view; and the public knows". He saw a star is born; yet Nielsen herself had seen success already in Kansas City, Salt Lake, San Francisco: as Satanella and Lucia.

Powering the new Bostonian hit, Alice Nielsen instantly became a hotly contested property for producers who flocked with offers for other projects.

Perley had first access. Sought to sign her to exclusive contract. Made the usual promises. She trusted, she signed.

Nielsen brought outside resources to the deal. Wealthy Tom Williams offers to finance a company of her own. Herbert wants Nielsen without the aging Bostonian baggage. Perley switches over. Not his last trick.

New unproven musicals were a risky business. Nielsen could assure success. Smart investment. Sold out shows.

"Miss Nielsen continued to win new and flattering endorsements in *The Serenade*, and give daily proof of that necessary psychological quality which figuratively reaches over the footlights and gets hold of the heart strings of an audience", Perley relates. "In addition, she always sang just as if nature had so intended and as if she thoroughly enjoyed it, beside being blest with a natural sense of contagious humor which bubbled and sparkled until the people across the footlights became so thoroughly *en rapport* that they seemed to be playing the opera together".

Bring Alice Nielsen, gayety of nations assured. What people pay for.

Onstage and backstage changes challenge the Bostonians with the threat of losing management, backers, and cast to a Nielsen project. She recalls, "I was more unpopular than ever with the Davis-MacDonald faction. What saved me was that Henry Clay Barnabee and his wife, Clara, were on my side. How much they were actuated by their lack of enthusiasm for the Macdonald-Davis faction is not pertinent here".

NY Times reveals the growing rift during a Victor Herbert concert May 3rd casting Jessie Davis and Eugene Cowles as surprise no-shows: "The first special concert of Victor Herbert's 22nd Regiment Band at the Broadway Theatre last night was successful from every point of view, notwithstanding the failure of Mrs. Jessie Bartlett Davis and Eugene Cowles of the Bostonians to appear to sing their numbers on the programme. Both sent word they were indisposed. Announcement of their absence was heard with indignation audibly manifested by the audience, which was a remarkably large one for a damp Sunday Night.

"Miss Alice Nielsen, who sang the waltz song from Herbert's *Serenade*, received an ovation and retired loaded with flowers after being recalled time and again". Other talent took the stage: "William Philip took Mr. Cowles's place, and Teddy Cole...consented to fill Mrs. Davis's place, and sang in a frock coat, having received no warning that he would be called on. He chose *Love's Dream* and sang it so well as to win a double recall. The performance by Victor Herbert and O. Hagedorn of Chopin's *Nocturne* for violin and harp was, however regarded as the gem of the evening".

May 7th *New York Mirror* prints the first Alice Nielsen feature story. Reporter notes her name oft misspelled by "great metropolitan papers". Retells a story: Alice had "a slight cold in the throat the other day and the doctor prescribed a powder". Pocketing the powder she walks absently down 28th then stops to take it then and there. As she swallows it, she hears a voice: "Great heavens! There's a girl trying to commit suicide, she'll keel over in a minute. We must stick close to her, so as to be ready to catch her when she flops". At that instant she sees a friend approaching. "Do you know", Alice says loudly, "I took a powder for my cold and three men thought I was trying to commit suicide. They have been following me ever since". Her would-be saviors vanish.

Noting Nielsen's "round face and big thoughtful eyes", the reporter tells town she sang hymns not long ago. Today "the same girl grown to womanhood" plays Knickerbocker Theatre "prancing nimbly about in boy's clothing and singing with rare charm and overflowing vivacity the sprightly music" of *The Serenade*.

"I began my career by singing hymns in church and here I am in comic opera. And between you and me, I'd rather sing the love songs than the hymns", says Alice. Reporter makes a poetic aside: "Miss Nielsen looks as if she would. A smile becomes her round and dimpled features as the sunshine does a flower garden; her eyes are dancing with merriment most of the time and when she laughs she throws back her head and a free and unrestrained laugh comes rippling out like a robin's note".

"I can remember that when I was very young I used to sing the lullaby with my mother when she rocked me to sleep, and would sing them to my own dolls", Nielsen says. She mentions singing in children's choir at St. Patrick's, then tells *Mirror* she found life's purpose performing Gilbert & Sullivan's *Patience* at Coates Theatre, first starring role 'way back in 1891. Her inspiring reception by the hometown Kansas City audience sent her on her way.

"It was a great night for me. I was horribly nervous at first but after I had become warmed up I began to feel the divine afflatus, don't you know. Then and there I settled in my own mind what my career would be". She will sing "professional opera". No mention of baby, husband.

She had joined Bostonians only eighteen months ago, how did it feel to be now a star? Nielsen's reply is candidly pensive: "Well, I have had my wish and find that there is not so much fun or glory in it after all. There is more hard work than anything else.... You dream of it and keep looking forward to it, but when you really get a little of it you feel about the same as you did before. The bubble's burst. Did you say I am cynical?

"Oh no, I am just philosophical; and now that I consider the matter, I really am happy most of the time, although I am moody. Some days I am in heaven and others I am in—well, I'm down below with Satan".

So speaks our star Satanella. Lifts mood, she grows animated: "I was given the part of Yvonne. Don't you think it suits me? Now be careful with your answer, sir. If I don't like it, why—*Zing Zing!*"

Says *Mirror*, "In mortal fear of that dagger which Yvonne flourishes so recklessly and thrusts so fiercely with that hissing *Zing Zing*, I hastened to assure her that the part suited her to a T".

Nielsen speaks to anxiety and audience connection. "Just before the performance on the first night in New York, I was uncertain of everything—even my legs. So much depended on it that I felt like running away; but I don't believe I could if I had tried. I went on in an automatic sort of way when I got my cue, but before I knew it I had forgotten all about my nervousness and in a very little while felt that I had the audience with me".

Rapport with audiences a hallmark of her onstage presence. If the audience is alertly engaged, she sings her best. Nervous stage fright at the start drew comment across her career, Alice often remarks it.

Skip ahead a moment, pin *NY Mirror*, a decade later Amy Leslie (*Chicago News* Mar 9 1909) will go ask Alice how she copes with stage fear. Amused singer responds: "Do you know what I do when I feel scared blue and tingle all over with stage fright? I just think well, now, this is my party. I am the hostess and what does it matter whether I have the stuff around to mix a cocktail just right or not. My voice is all twisted up in a knot and my hands cold and my feet shaking but it is the best I have got: here goes. You know if a bunch of friends came in and were unawares one day when the cook was gone, the butler drunk, the pantry empty, and the cellar dry, I wouldn't sit around and cry. I'd would just say, 'Come on, boys, there's nothing in the house and nobody to fix it up for you; let's all forage and laugh over it. And do you think they wouldn't have a good time? Well, it would be the best ever!"

Alice has described a Kansas City musical afternoon at Sarah's. Leslie, of course, wrote a Modjeska biography and will interview Alice's sister Hortense.

Returning to 1897's *NY Mirror*, Nielsen speaks of opening night.

"The papers said some nice things about me the next morning, and here I am. There is nothing more to tell, is there? You see, I have no past to speak of; but I do hope I have a future". Saying so, merriment "faded out of Miss Nielsen's eyes". Reporter with insight observes "she became instantly very serious and very earnest, indicating that a solid foundation of determination and purpose in life underlies the vivacity and buoyancy of her character".

This moment is Alice's third session with reporters: the first in bruises filing for divorce, next San Francisco of hopes. Today NYC, Alice Nielsen is caught speaking just as she catches stardom and personal fame. In spring 1897 her artistic life was just beginning; earlier life was child's play.

Six years ago she sang with KC's St. Patrick's choir, determined to join community theatre folk for a few local musicals despite husband's fears and threats. Five years ago she arrived in San Francisco, singing at its St. Patrick choir, making a way with Ida Valerga to Tivoli. Just a year with the Bostonians, now a bankable top box office star, an important talent, an enormous value to audiences, producers, public, and American culture.

Newspapers and rising box-office receipts agreed.

Alice Nielsen isn't satisfied. To *Mirror* makes a startling announcement.

She plans to leave Broadway behind. She wants out. She seeks to sail for Europe to study voice with the top teacher. "I have decided to go to Europe after the production in Providence of the new opera *Rip Van Winkle* which were are now rehearsing" and never plays. Alice identifies a prestigious coach. "I am not going abroad on a pleasure trip—not a bit of it. I am going over to study, probably with Marchesi in Paris. And it is very possible that I won't come back next season".

Mathilda Marchesi (1821-1913), German mezzo based in Paris since 1881, will train many star divas. Marchesi taught the natural voice *bel canto* by repeating short sessions several times daily. Coaches singers to work smart, know all technical issues at play in music, and sing feelingly. Valerga knew Marchesi of course and could introduce. Valerga knew her, and many of Alice's future friends would work with Marchesi or daughter.

"I never had singing lessons except in California under Madame Valerga, who sang with Patti for many years. And while she is an excellent instructor, I am very sure that training by the teacher of Calvé, Melba, Eames, and other great prima donnas would be very beneficial to me".

Interestingly, since sincere, 1896 Nielsen denies ambition for grand opera: "I have no aspirations toward grand opera, however. Light opera and character roles are most suitable to me, I think. To make a little confession, I like to sing coon songs better than almost anything else".

Coon songs, popular 19th-century genre perhaps difficult to appreciate these realigned days, festoon politically-incorrect titles few dare print, except Times Square's Virgin rap section (2007) which seems to consist of covers of these lyrics. Perhaps unknowingly, ignorance mocks bliss. Many 19th-century "coon song" hits were produced by African-American writers such as Bob Cole (1869-1911), vaudeville actor and creator of first black-authored musical, produced by same man who brings Nielsen to London in 1901. Others were by such fellers as Stephen Foster, who as child attended revival meetings with his black maid and liked what he heard people sing. Another popular songwriter was Septimus Winner with aliases any gender and any shade. Alice Nielsen had absorbed music from every ethnicity. Ragtime, her pal Arthur Pryor popularizes, composer and disk producer for Victor Records. Alice is musically and humanly inclusive.

How her hint was taken, that she'd jump hit Broadway shows after a few days as star to go grand opera in Paris, has not been discovered.

Switching tact almost too quickly, *NY Mirror* asks about hobbies. Her answer significant and true; cooking bores her: "Why sing of course. I am afraid I am not a very great reader, nor very domestic". Turns witty, saying she owns a cookbook "but the first time I read any of it was the other night when I had the toothache, and I went to sleep right away".

Deflects questions about the domestic circle. No mention mom Sarah, son, or siblings: "My family consists of myself and Aleck. Who's Aleck? Why he's my little dog, a very cunning little fellow who is pure white except that he has a jet black circle under one eye. They wanted to name him after me, but Alice wouldn't quite be fair to him".

Opera isn't faring well. May 1897 as Nielsen makes her Broadway success, *Peterson Magazine* tells us the grand opera struggles to scrape: "Outlook for grand opera in NY next season is at present rather doubtful. Owing to the heavy losses sustained by the Abbey & Grau company" touring the West (where Alice would succeed!) "these managers are discouraged at the prospects for Franco-Italian opera. Jean and Edouard DeReszke (who have been the backbone of the Metropolitan Company) have announced their intention of singing exclusively in Europe next year, and so has Calvé, while Melba will be heard with Damrosch next season". DeReszke brothers tenor and bass, Calvé famed Carmen, Melba the backstab lording over Covent Garden. All have a part in Nielsen's future.

In contrast Broadway's fiscal prospects: "The Bostonians, famous for so many years as the best light opera organization in this country...have made a long stay in NY this spring, delighting large audiences with the new opera.... *Serenade* must be seen to be appreciated...."

Tellingly, Herbert's music entertains "without aid of the libretto". His "music is delightful—just enough Spanish coloring to lend charm and dash to it and yet maintain the genuine Herbert ring. The orchestration, solos and concerted numbers from overture to finale are all excellent. Every now and then the orchestra breaks for the in droll little suggestive snatches, it is quite laughable without the aid of the libretto. It fact it is all so musically satisfying it is refreshing".

Continues *Petersons*: "Bright, piquant Miss Alice Nielsen is one of the song birds from the South, her home being in Tennessee [*sic*]. She sings and acts the double role in *The Serenade* with all the spirit imaginable; had this part been written for her, both composer and artiste could not have made a happier selection". Nielsen-Herbert gain momentum with every ticket.

In the cast: "other members of the company also seem to be particularly suited to their respective parts and *The Serenade* is wholly satisfying as a genuine comic opera". Hilda Clark, "prima donna for about a year" shows wear, yet "still makes the most beautiful photographs [stage poses] and has gained much in acting and stage presence. Very young when she made the step from a prominent church choir to the stage", but tellingly: "her voice has not been improved..." Clark "had a most beautiful voice and it is a pity she did not give it a less severe strain than inevitable in comic opera".

Munsey Magazine's "The Stage" assesses Serenade: "Comic opera without a spinal column...depends upon the mounting and the music, while the latter depends upon its vernacular. Flabby opera...a concert, pure and simple, is just what it seems to be. It is music from beginning to end, all music— one hundred percent music. It gives certain people what they go to hear, and satisfies them".

There is no story. "Opera that has no force of theme, no plot, no well-defined purpose—nothing but a jumble of brigands and sawdust and time worn absurdities—does not furnish an entirely satisfactory entertainment. It may perhaps contain twenty-five percent of singing to seventy-five percent of rubbish. Let us make ourselves clear. What is rubbish under one condition may be good work under another.

"If everything—the dancing, the scenic effect, the costumes, the jokes, the witticisms, the repartee—if all these tend to the development of the story, and are true to the story, then they are appropriate and effective; but when they come in in a disconnected way, no one thing bearing any relation to any other, then they are tiresome and an injury rather than an aid to the music. A good many of these worthless operatic pretenses are floated by the excellence of the company producing them.

"This was notably true of *The Chieftain*. The opera itself had not enough merit to run a night, but [Francis] Wilson managed to keep it afloat for several months. Hopper and others have had similar experiences—have them, in fact, much too often. There is, perhaps, no organization more capable of floating an indifferent libretto than the Bostonians. They have recently brought out *The Serenade*, an opera that resembles *The Chieftain*. It is scarcely so weak. It has some good work in it, but as a whole it scatters. It is not well knit together".

Fails to let the cast shine, "Barnabee himself has a miserable part, and Jessie Bartlett Davis in trousers is not a delight to the eye. Cowles has no songs in which he could make a reputation, if his reputation were not already made. There is some acceptable music here and there, notably in the monastery scene. Mrs. Davis has a couple of good numbers, but as a whole the opera is floated by the company, conspicuous in which is Alice Nielsen, the new soprano. She is decidedly pretty and sings like a bird. A combination of youth and beauty and a sweet voice is resistless".

"*The Serenade* has apparently made a hit. At this writing it is 'drawing full houses', to use the conventional phrase. It might be more accurate to say that the Bostonians are here again, and are packing the theater. They are prime favorites, and have an assured clientage. Barnabee is a whole company in himself. He has had, moreover, splendid support at one time or another in Whitney, Frothingham, Karl, Macdonald, Miss Beebe, Cowles, Jessie Bartlett Davis, Camille D'Arville, Margaret Reid, and others. Miss Nielsen has brought new strength to the Bostonians, and will add materially to their popularity".

Alice's Euro-longings reappear in June's *Munsey Magazine*, "When the Bostonians were singing in San Francisco, fall of 1895, they found it necessary to revive *Robin Hood*. But just at this time their company lacked a suitable Annabel. Mr. Barnabee decided to look about him for what he wanted, and to this end attended a performance at the Tivoli. Now, the Tivoli is to San Francisco what the Castle Square is to Boston—a theater where a varied repertoire of light and grand opera is presented at really popular prices. And here Mr. Barnabee found just the voice and talent he sought in Alice Nielsen, who had been a member of the Tivoli stock company for two years, and had sung a repertoire of a hundred and fifty parts, extending from Yum Yum on the one hand to Lucia on the other".

For once rarely, *Munsey* highlights Valerga: "Miss Nielsen is a Southerner [who] came to take up her abode in San Francisco, where she studied under Ida Valerga, and finally obtained an engagement at the Tivoli. After joining the Bostonians she sang in *The Bohemian Girl*, was Ninette in *Prince Ananias*, and created Anita in *Mexico*, of unhappy memory. Then, early this spring, came her creation of the rollicking rôle of Yvonne in *The Serenade*, which convinced the public that the Bostonians were in no danger of rusting out from lack of the right sort of new blood. Miss Nielsen is as vivacious off the stage as on it. She loves her work, particularly the bolero in the second act, and there is small likelihood of any one mistaking her for other than an American.

"Her present ambition is to go to Europe to give her voice further cultivation, but it is not improbable that she may soon sing in London with the Bostonians".

For Alice Nielsen, by June 1897 national magazines began spreading buzz. *Frank Leslie's Popular Monthly* (Jun 1897) focused on *Serenade*, listing the cast while pointlessly trying to trace the pointless plot: "The Bostonians well-sustained their reputations. The old favorites... treated their roles, which seemed to be specially made for them, with the intelligence and spirit which have always characterized them...."

Significantly, Nielsen is now listed as the only Yvonne despite forced to share the role with Hilda Clark. Let Bostonians beware, "Newcomer Alice Nielsen, although young and...inexperienced actress, has proved herself worthy of such good company". *Serenade* "achieved an immediate popular success, giving the Bostonians who presented it, a property that will possibly prove as valuable as their *Robin Hood*. The piece is full of wit and humor and charming, captivating melody".

In that era, private lives of pubic people rarely see light. big stars might refuse all interviews. 1897, May 11 (*NY Herald*) reclusive basso Eugene

Cowles, sued for "limited divorce...matter was kept quiet and instead of an open court hearing, Augustus Brown was appointed referee to take testimony" and possibly recommend divorce: "friends of the couple say that incompatibility is the cause of the separation". Cowles, no interviews.

As Nielsen's reputation grows, Bostonians drag. Valuable asset Alice is paid understudy wages. Burden of Bostonian regulars bores a frustrated Herbert who knows his selection of Alice saved the show. Meanwhile behind the scenes, producers and investors are quickly lining up behind Nielsen who weekly proves a very worthy investment. Offers pour in, she speaks to San Francisco pal Tom Williams who offers to invest. Albeit of partly-hidden agenda to curry favor with the young star who has refused to marry him. For his many good promises, Alice declines other offers from the experienced theatrical producers.

This is a risk she takes when trusting Williams. Who pays Perley. Who signs a personal management contract to represent Nielsen and abandons the old-timey Bostonians to coordinate the new venture. Select Bostonian cast join Alice, include the great basso.

By spring 1897 the Alice Nielsen Comic Opera Company is created.

Happens between May 7 (when Nielsen announces Paris plans to study with Marchesi) and June 17 when she assents to stay in America. Within six weeks, Nielsen, Herbert, Perley, Tom Williams make a deal. They will create a new supergroup starring Alice Nielsen. Created, designed, promoted, directed, and performed by the best. They will debut new shows, not descend to repertory. Williams and Nielsen share profits, Perley a slice. Herbert, royalties per show.

The theatre industry—America's biggest nighttime sport—knows the artistic combination of Herbert and Nielsen holds great promise to promote the gayety of nations. Alice Nielsen brings to the stage what Victor Herbert brings to the music: virtuoso fun. She delivers to Herbert popularity and success he seeks.

Frank Perley has managed top drama and music acts, namely Modjeska and the Bostonians. With Nielsen he will peak. Nielsen delivers him the investor Williams. Not theatre pro. Gives Perley more power. For Williams, smart investment. Nielsen is a money-maker, sure hit.

The NY success had unleashed a gold-diggers' rush of producers, many with better taste and track records and as much money. By June she could take her pick of any producers and investors in the theatre biz. Within five years they'd be sending her blank checks. To give Williams and Perley the chance of a lifetime, she turned down the others. Williams and Perley; she knew them; they promised her. Bostonians become old news.

In June's *Dramatic News*, Leander Richardson observes the creative teams for *Serenade* had shaped a production "unexcelled in beauty, richness and elaboration" while onstage "one of the most perfect companies ever organized interprets it". Describes the industry rush for Nielsen, a genuinely artistic hit and producer's dream: "Her success was of that substantial sort that appeals to the mercantile portion of the theatrical profession—the managerial element. Many would-be and already-were impresarios, entrepreneurs and out-and-out speculators made her propositions more or less alluring".

Richardson explainsm Frank Perley, managing "The Bostonians and who consequently was nearer to her in a business way than any one else, succeeded in securing her, and so it is this season that she bursts out in the theatrical firmament as a bright and shining star. Altogether the future looks particularly rosy for her. Alice is an extremely pretty and trim little woman with a fresh, sweet and melodious voice, and a certain modesty of demeanor on the stage that is exceptionally attractive".

Nielsen values cooperation: "What is more, she seems willing to allow herself to be managed [stage directed]—a condition that does not apply to all prima donnas. Many of them, indeed, betray an earnest determination to manage their managers and anchor themselves permanently in the center of the stage to the detriment of the general performance".

June 17, Nielsen's choice not to visit Europe makes national news.

Summer 1897 seals the changes. After The Bostonians' winter season ends, her summer passes in San Francisco completing arrangements with Williams and Perley to begin Alice Nielsen Comic Opera Company. Trusting Williams, Nielsen believed no written contract with her business partner was necessary; as he no doubt often assured her. After all, he hoped she would become his wife in gratitude for his financial favors.

Year earlier, Nielsen was in Bostonian repertory. Now a national star with deep-pockets investor and management. Perley brings the best talent into the project. The great Julian Mitchell is picked to direct. Nielsen and Herbert seem the best possible combination to create the awaited Great American Musical.

August *Life* magazine, theatre columnist Metcalf says: "It must be admitted that Mr. Victor Herbert is easily first among the composers of light opera music for the American stage. He is original, tuneful and musicianly, a combination of qualities which satisfy both the educated and the uneducated ear. He is also a musical humorist". Metcalf senses the witty playfulness.

Bad as was Smith's *Serenade* libretto wasn't his worst.

Certainly not "up to the standard of his *Wizard of the Nile* [largely developed by Daniels, the comic star!] but is a long way ahead of most of the stuff provided for that large section of the NY public which will patronize any balderdash provided it is only labeled 'comic opera.'" With *Serenade* "the Bostonians seem once more to have struck their gait ...always so good—always in the line of clean material and artistic work— that it must please every theatre-goer to see them score a success.

"Miss Alice Nielsen also has a good chance, of which she avails herself and shows very considerable talent, both musically and dramatically".

In the cast, "Jessie Bartlett Davis has a rollicking part with plenty of opportunity for her splendid voice. Mr. Macdonald shares most of his numbers with Miss Davis to the advantage of both. Mr. Cowles's part makes a very slight demand on his powers. The veteran Frothingham show no sign of age either in humor or voice. Mr. H.C. Barnabee—the mention of his name guarantees the nature of his performance.

Stage future soaring, still the star is still legally married to Nentwig. Returning to NYC late August 1897, six years after leaving, Alice reappears in Kansas City to complete the divorce. Brutal husband denies all; she lets him. Hardly matters now: ends here. How different a universe for Alice Nielsen since escaping via vaudeville road!

August 22, *KC Star* reports the diva has landed "from San Francisco to sue her husband for divorce". She is announced to "sing today at the morning mass in St. John's Catholic church on Independence Avenue. Nentwig, the organist at St. Patrick's will make no fight in court against his wife's application for divorce". Nentwig responds "she evidently relishes the notoriety the divorce proceedings have brought her and that she is welcome to it all, he wishes none of it. He denies the allegations of cruelty made in his wife's petition".

Skips mass: "Church was crowded in anticipation, but the prima donna failed to sing. She said this morning that she had not promised to sing and that she was not courting any public attention at present that could be avoided". *Star* asks of rumor Alice is engaged to Tom Williams who wishes she was. Nielsen refutes: "My sole purpose in asking the divorce is to give me absolute control of my boy and restoration of my maiden name. No sir; I've no intention of getting married again" (*KC Star* Aug 23).

Her hometown stopover is a one-night stand. Leaves next night to join Bostonian rehearsals in New York. Plans for her exciting new project are an open secret. Of course frictions increase. Other Bostonians could wish as much: Nielsen has been invested. The press notices: her. Public clamors: her. The underpaid Bostonian newcomer has scaled the blockade. Perhaps inevitable she became a scapegoat for scorn.

By fall 1897, an outstanding creative and business team was tasked to make Alice Nielsen's debut in her own company a success. Nielsen, Herbert, Mitchell, Perley and Williams complete plans for the first show. They schedule to open the project September 1898.

Skipping repertory would be a significant choice. Nielsen has mastered many musicals. Bostonians trot out *Bohemian Girl* and other stuff everybody performs. New star in new shows. Risky. The team was a supergroup who had grown up in theatre. Julian Mitchell would direct and choreograph. South Carolina's Josef Physioc design. George Bowles, business manager. German conductor Paul Steindorf, music director.

Nobody better. Take Paul Steindorf, "a person of appalling energy" (*SF Call* Ap 28 1907). Conducted for Maurice Grau, Lillian Russell and "Smiling Jimmy" Morrissey's Emma Abbott in Europe, NY, Philadelphia. At the moment he runs Society of Musical Art at Waldorf-Astoria. Lively and visible with baton as Alice tours. After Nielsen Company, Steindorf migrates to Tivoli as music director. When Alice returns in grand opera, Steindorf saves her from the NYC saboteurs. Establishes music program at Berkeley College, teaches piano to Antonia Brico. Leads Sunday concerts at Golden Gate Park. In the family, Steindorf's brother-in-law Edouard von Beuchner, conductor coaching Nielsen in *Wedding*, hated *Robin Hood* ("I positively refuse to play such trash!"), and organizes San Francisco Opera Company (*SF Call* Ap 28 1907). Talent to burn.

Costumes designed by Caroline Siedle, sewn by Simpson, Crawford & Simpson; boots and shoes from Cammeyer. Mason & Hamlin, who will build the superb piano for Alice's Maine cottage, supply the show's organ.

Ensemble of stars, Bostonian in style. Players from Bostonians and Lillian Russell are tapped for Nielsen Company. Eugene Cowles, Maria Van Dresser, Richard Ling, Dick Golden (dancing cow's butt *Evangeline*), Joseph Herbert (no relation to Victor), Jack Slavin, Frank Rushworth.

Top comic Joseph Cawthorn freshens the Barnabee role. Onstage in British music halls at age four 1872. Spends twenty-five years on Broadway before Hollywood 1927 as character actor whose fifty-four films include the voice teacher scene in Herbert's *Naughty Marietta*. Showbiz wife, Queenie Vasser. Member of Players Club on Gramercy around corner from Herbert's studio on 17th and Irving.

From this company three women will crossover to grand opera: Nielsen, Sylva, Maria von Dresser. Marguerite Sylva, born Belgium with Spanish-Jewish roots, had played Paris and London. Trained as pianist and singer with Brussels Conservatory. Started as a sister act in England. Possibly maybe not those "Sylva Sisters" who toured Europe and America in blackface as "duettists and dancers". Sylva had arrived in NYC from August Harris's Drury Lane Theatre, debut site of Jean DeReszke, Nordica, Valerga, Calvé. Artists Alice would know well.

Harris and Drury Lane connect many Nielsen strands. Created family fair from novels and fairy tales. Master of stagecraft, mime. Carl Rosa's production of Goring Thomas *Nadeshda* "with Madame Valleria [Valerga] in the principal part, was much admired". Here in 1885, Patti "was indisposed and there was no one to take her place" so her 25th London season postponed; closing crowds "drew her carriage through the streets and escorted her home". Hence the trap for Valerga's career as substitute Patti. Alice's future coach Bevignani conducts, another Valerga link.

When Harris dies, Sylva loses her grand opera stage. Brings her to Alice Nielsen Company after starring in *Princess Chic*. August 1896, *Era* reviewed Sylva as "very handsome, and acts with much self-possession and energy". In another show, "Suzette is played with dash and vivacity by Marguerite Sylva". After Alice, Sylva joins Opéra-Comique for *Carmen*, returning to America 1909. Sylva and Alice will be neighbors in Bedford, NY. Sylva stars in a 1919 French film *Carmen*, 1920's film *The Honey Bee*, then in 1922 sings Carmen at Hollywood Bowl with LA Philharmonic. She has roles in seven 1940s films; and is the focus of TV's *This Is Your Life* on 14th March 1956. Nielsen would not try LA for movies. Little interest in silent films, she was born to sing. 1930 talkies arrive too late for Alice.

Intriguing stage duo, Nielsen and Sylva. Sylva speaks freely to press: "I am not what I seem and it grieves me that the world should regard me as a mere butterfly, instead of a sober-minded woman who aspires to something more tangible and satisfying than the hollow mockery of an artificial public career. I am so tired of it all. I do not like the stage, with its false glamour, shallowness and bitter heartaches. If I could but have a simple little home in the country amid the restful green fields, where I could enjoy the companionship of dogs and birds and a few sober-minded human beings, I would gladly turn my back forever upon the restless excitement of my profession.

"Can you picture me as a purely domestic creature?" she asks.

Reporter wonderfully replies "I gazed at her long and critically, and with admirable candor confessed that I could not".

"But so I am by inclination. Believe me I am honest in what I tell you. Calcium lights, silken stage frippery, flowers, applause—bah, I hate them all. Life would be unendurable but for my little flat uptown. There are days at a time when I never leave it, except when necessity compels".

Sylva manages her career: "I do my own marketing. I keep my own accounts of every penny expended. I supervise every detail of home life from dusting to broiling and bed-making. Believe me it is so".

Back here in 1898, November *Peterson Magazine* has Nielsen's "latest photograph" in costume (feathered hat, patterned dress). Alice, "clever little soprano who bounded so suddenly into favor as a comic opera prima donna last spring through her piquant impersonation of Yvonne in *The Serenade*". The magazine misjudges things: "Wise manager of the famous Bostonians appreciated the fact that they had been rather slow in recognizing the full extent of this animated little southerner's ability; however it did not take them long after she made her New York debut as a prima donna, to make arrangements for her to retain the place".

As the world turns, Bostonians still tour with Nielsen who "now alternates with Miss Guisti" instead of Hilda Clark. Aging Barnabee and MacDonald now lack the usual investors. Talents being to flee. Barnabee's gambling drains him. Inevitably Nielsen's presence is irritating; she is the already-invested future without them.

When the Bostonians reach Chicago in December, critics speak freely about Herbert's high quality music and Harry Smith's low quality words. Smith, after *Robin Hood*, took from the poor and made himself rich.

"The beautiful music that Mr. Victor Herbert has written for the second act in *The Serenade* causes forgetfulness even of the potpourri of stupidity that Mr. Harry B. Smith designates as a libretto", said *Chicago Tribune* (Dec 7). "At the present moment and fresh from the scene, no sincerer commendation is possible. Herbert has a gift...a sense of the humorous, variety in rhythm, and above all a flow of melody that makes, particularly in the second act of last night's opera at McVicker's, a genuine delight".

In the cast: Jessie Davis sang "better than she has done in several seasons" yet Nielsen as a boy upstages the show: "The distinct success with the audience fell to the lot of Miss Alice Nielsen whose charming appearance and manner in boy's costume took immensely".

Keenly aware of the audience, Alice kept in the moment, improvised cleverly. Talk back to audiences. After played Kansas City streets and the Wigwam, she knew how people were. When she improvises Chicago likes it: "It is so seldom that a singer in this guise, or any other, one is tempted to say, does a graceful thing or two not in the stage directions that it is pleasant to chronicle the fact.

"After the love song allotted her in the second act, Miss Nielsen received some flowers across the footlights. She broke off a bud and handed it to Mr. Studley the conductor with an air that reduced her audience to hilarity. This was the beginning of as clever a bit of comedy as she did during the performance, which is saying much, and in consequence she was obliged to give the song three subsequent repetitions". Audience "was a large one, and the principals were recalled on each fall of the curtain".

The world's second Alice Nielsen feature story is published December 19th by *Chicago Tribune*: "She knows one hundred operas, from comic to grand, by heart—that fact would be enough to mark little Alice Nielsen, the new soprano of the Bostonians, who has been at McVicker's Theatre for the last fortnight" who "spent a year at the Tivoli Theatre in San Francisco, where a fresh opera goes on every week". Nielsen sight-read music and had perfect pitch, "but there are other reasons why she should be made a note of. One is that she learns her parts without the aid of a musical instrument of any kind, in just the same way an actress commits words and sentences to memory. Competent judges say she is to succeed Lillian Russell in the favor of the public which likes light opera".

Lastly, says Tribune, Herbert and Smith "write an opera for her".

Chicago keenly appreciates Nielsen from the start. Mutual affection of singer and town follow her into grand opera.

Now for first time since 1891, Alice Nielsen returns Christmas Eve 1897 to Kansas City as star of *The Serenade* in the nation's best musical troupe. Her welcome was overwhelming at Coates' theatre: All Sold Out.

KC Star (Dec 24) details debut: "Last night the Coates theatre was filled from roof to orchestra. It is probable that in all of its history, which covers over twenty years of music and the drama, ranging from the Hoytian farce to the Maplesonean grand opera, the Coates Opera house walls have never resounded to more enthusiastic applause than was bestowed in the welcoming of the Bostonians last night when they presented *The Serenade* for the first time here".

Bringing to life the interactive quality of 1890s theatre, *Star* perfectly describes that marvelous tango of audience and performers: "There was generous applause for the opening chorus, and a quadruple encore for Eugene Cowles in the first solo. After that, Mr. MacDonald was next to appear. He was followed in short order by Mr. Barnabee and Jessie Bartlett Davis, and when the curtain had fallen after the enthusiastic audience had cheered all of these, as well as George Frothingham, Harry Brown, Alice Nielsen and WE Philip, who followed them, the Bostonians must have felt they had fallen among friends. Enthusiasm continued during the entire performance and at the end of the Second Act curtain calls were so numerous that a truly veracious chronicler would be apt to place their number anywhere between seven and ten".

The many encores extend the length. *Star* gives Herbert praise for success: "To the composer...credit for *Serenade* belongs and Mr. Victor Herbert's score is a brilliant achievement along the lines of pure comic opera". Herbert gave complexity, not pop tunes: "few of his airs will be whistled but the entire work has value...and in the performance by full orchestra and chorus there is a continuous succession of new beauties revealed, not a few of them being due to the masterful orchestration".

Scant mention hits wordsmith Harry Smith "who writes most of the words for comic opera in this country...is not hampered by probability...."

Bostonian stars "all stand together" yet Nielsen as Yvonne, ballet dancer in love with Alvarado [Cowles] is most-applauded, "for Kansas City was once her home, and she has only developed in her absence the promise she showed when a member of local musical circles".

Her appearance literally stops the show. When "Alice Nielsen tripped lightly on the stage in a gauzy ballet costume, she had to wait several minutes for the applause to die away. The sweet face was as full and rosy as seven years ago; the stage presence was much better and the voice, too. The audience realized that the amateur prima donna of seven years ago had become the prima donna of a famous opera company, and applauded again and again.

"Miss Nielsen has youth, beauty and a soprano voice of clearness, flexibility and strength besides showing an appreciation of comedy which is a rare accompaniment of soprano voices. Her musical accomplishments are shown in a particularly difficult aria with flute obbligato, while all of her work is carried out with a dash and certainly which easily accounts for her recent fame".

The toll on touring singers is darkly hinted by faint praise for Jessie Davis, "none like her, and she is this season as handsome, as graceful and as magnetic as always with her magnificent voice as smooth and sympathetic as if she had not devoted it to the severe usage of comic opera for several seasons".

Serenade ran three nights. Christmas gave *Robin Hood.*

During the stay Nielsen schedules her final divorce hearing for January. Nentwig wishes to dodge a trial. *Star* (Dec 24) reveals Nentwig "changed his mind and would not contest the case" in Judge Henry's court where "Miss Nielsen herself, and half a dozen witnesses will appear to testify to his cruelly to her". Nentwig comments, "The sooner it is over the better it will suit me. I am just as anxious for the divorce now as she is. If she doesn't get the divorce, I will". His grounds "simply desertion". He did not see the show, "No, I was busy last night and didn't have time. I should like to though. I'm sorry I won't have time". Nentwig "lived with his father at 3028 Cherry Street, and had not seen his wife in years".

In Coates Hotel parlor that same day, *Star* finds Nielsen "stunningly dressed in black velvet". She says, "Took hard work, and if I had taken the advice of some of my Kansas City friends, I would still have been singing in church choirs. Now tell me, did I sing well? Well, I'm glad you think so. You know I've had a cold and I was afraid I wouldn't do as well as usual".

Now first time is recorded the oft-repeated and sincere Nielsen proverb, "And of course I wanted to do my best in..." your town name. "Kansas City; I was awfully pleased at the way I was received last night. I didn't know just how it might be, you know I have had so much trouble and so much has been said about me. But I hope it's nearly over now", referring to the divorce. Quickly refocuses on her performance, "But my work is so delightful. I only have to sing five times a week, but of course, I'll sing at every performance here".

Nielsen reveals her close affinity with audiences: "The audience last night was the most appreciative we have sung to for a long time. Every bright saying was noticed. There's a great difference in audiences. Sometimes the witticisms fall perfectly flat. It's rather discouraging". An egg for Harry Smith....

Each audience at each theatre she keeps in memory. Has spent seven years performing to big houses; two years' touring in the nation's top outfit. Knew the acoustics of each theatre, adjusting her voice. From stage she studies each town's reactions. Has met every North American region.

"Was I glad to get back to Kansas City? Yes, but I was a little afraid to sing last night. I told [conductor] Mr. Studley so, and he laughed at me, but I was. The only reason I don't like to come to Kansas City is because my friends don't give me time to sleep. Why, I told the fifteenth bellboy that brought a card to my room this morning, that if he brought up any more I'd throw a pitcher of ice water on his head. He laughed".

"And she laughed, a merry laugh full of happiness", relates the reporter.

He reveals "Miss Nielsen is puzzled. She wants to know who sent her a magnificent silver toilet and manicure set yesterday. It came in a big morocco leather box, a score of pieces, but there was no card or anything to indicate who the sender was".

Nielsen notices his bafflement and reacts, "You look like you thought I was trying to fool you, but I'm not. I really don't know who sent it; or the American Beauties [roses] last night. I wish I did". Bellboy appears with someone's calling card. "Oh it's my lawyer. You'll excuse me, won't you? I must talk with him". And she makes final divorce plans.

Within two weeks her arrangements to leave the Bostonians would become public knowledge. Leaving the Bostonians would not be graceful. How could it be so, in the clinches?

1898: THE ALICE NIELSEN COMPANY

By mid-January, the national press learn Alice Nielsen is starting her own company, leaving Bostonians behind. In Kansas City she told a few people so the news appeared; confided in confidants who of course tattled.

Initial announcement appears in an odd way. January 5th *Star* reports "Mrs. Hollenbach, the wife of BT Hollenbach, Kansas City teacher of music, has been offered the place of Alice Nielsen, who will not appear with the Bostonians next year". Hollenbach "has not decided whether she will accept the offer, which comes to her from Mr. McDonald...who recommended her going to Europe to study". She had auditioned during a previous visit, studied with Fraulein Brandt in Vienna. Performed three years with Francis Wilson (1854-1935), the musical star of 1899's *Cyrano* by Herbert and Smith, which ran twenty-eight performances before touring. Wilson in 1913 was first president of actor's union Equity, co-founded with Nielsen pals Lillian Russell, Ethel Barrymore, Marie Dressler. Decades later, Wilson is a Bedford NY neighbor of Alice and Sylva.

Oddly, the notice links Hollenbach and Nielsen as "pupils of Max Desci in this city at about the same time and it is a curious fact that it was in *The Beggar Student* at the Coates theatre that Miss Nielsen and Mrs. Hollenbach made their operatic debuts. The two were close rivals for first honors". Desci, odd lame duck. Hollenbach, née "Clena Wright" was unmentioned by past press as any past rival for Nielsen's "first honors". Never joins the Bostonians. Likely source of stupid story, Desci trolls for publicity, stalks Nielsen years in press and courts, plants false stories to take credit for her vocal prowess.

January 7th *Star* reports Nielsen notified her lawyer O'Grady she is ready to return to finish a divorce. Nielsen "at the Planters' hotel in St. Louis...reports her health and spirits 'tip top.'" Nentwig will settle, claiming she deserted him after the beatings he gave her. O'Grady to end it agrees; deal done. She need not appear. Sadly, seizing legal freedom has unintended terrible consequences if being free distresses the backer seeking to pin her into a next marriage.

By January 1898, famous American diva Nielsen receives top theatre news coverage as any major star. On 16th, nationally-syndicated "Some People of the Stage" spreads from *KC Star* the rumor: "Alice Nielsen is to emerge next season at the head of an opera company of her own and the same rumor has it that a gentleman prominent in the turf affairs of the Pacific coast [Tom Williams] is to be the financial backer of the venture".

Tight linkages between the era's two big sports, theatre and horse-racing, continue closely over the arc of Alice Nielsen's career during the free era before 1910s when war banksters bribe politics to suppress the gayety of nations. In 1898 where are divas during day? Racetrack.

Tracks embrace risk-takers who invest at any chance. She's a sure bet.

By January 23, *LA Times* repeats news of Nielsen's new company amid reports Ethel Barrymore, playing in *Peter the Great* with Henry Irving's Lyceum group, got engaged to Irving's son the playwright Laurence; the young author taking the star role "during the indisposition of Sir Henry". Laurence in future plays an important London role when Alice Nielsen switches to grand opera.

At last on January 31, 1898, says *Star*, Nielsen divorce is decided. Nentwig's counter-suit for desertion granted. Nentwig explains: "She wanted to go on the stage". Her lawyer O'Grady declines to cross-examine the two Nentwig pals who "testified to...the desertion, to Nentwig's good character, and also that he had treated Miss Nielsen as a good husband should during the two years they lived together. The entire proceeding did not take five minutes".

Ironically now, investor wealthy Williams wants to marry her.

She has placed her finances in his hands. Managing producer Perley holds the balance of power, traveling with the group as Williams occupied in Oakland. If she could trust these men, great future wealth assured.

To keep Williams at bay, she would have to trust Perley.

When her last Bostonian tour reaches Los Angeles, welcome is joyous.

Alice Nielsen adds life-long fans. They arrive February 6th for a shore week. The national furor over Nielsen's new project intrudes.

LA theatre pundits ponder why. *Los Angeles Times* reports: "That far-famed and ever-popular organization the Bostonians is to be with us" with a "sparkling comic opera *The Serenade*, which will be sung here for the first time. No opera in recent years has aroused more enthusiasm and called out more encomiums than this. It was in *The Serenade* that Mr. Barnabee, Mr. McDonald, Mr. Cowles and Jessie Bartlett Davis added new laurels to their many triumphs and Alice Nielsen, the new soprano, scored so prettily with audiences and critics".

Like Boston, LA plays a strong role in Alice Nielsen's career as she impacts its artistic culture. Almost incredibly, *LA Times* lingers on the scenery. First and third scenes were "views of mountain scenes in Spain, with the haunted castle in the foreground". Second Act "a beautiful bit of painting by Burridge & Albert, representing the garden of the monastery of St. Benedict". We receive (spoiler alert) a glance across the pointless plot: "All ends happily".

In the cast: HC Barnabee, WH MacDonald, Jessie Davis, Eugene Cowles, Alice Nielsen, George Frothingham, Josephine Bartlett, William Philip, Harry Brown, Nellie Guisti, Grafton Baker, Helena Fredericks, Jennie Hawley, Charles Hawley, WH Fitzgerald, conductor SL Studley, "and others".

That same day *Kansas City Star* (Feb 6) confirms Nielsen's divorce. Delivers confirmation direct from Victor Herbert about future plans, who says he agreed last fall to create a new show for Alice Nielsen.

Star notes dual divorce: Nielsen "divorced from Benjamin Nentwig by a decree issued in Judge Henry's court last week, is to star next season in an opera to be written for her" by hit-makers Herbert and librettist Smith.

Star breaks the national news: Nielsen leaves her Bostonian family to go her own way. Breakup of America's most popular cast running the years' biggest hit hits the wire services across the nation next day.

"Rumors that Miss Nielsen intended to star have been current since last December. Doubt and denial, however, were cast abroad from certain authoritative [Bostonian] sources, and it was not until Victor Herbert was heard from yesterday that the truth was established".

Herbert simply replied: "It is true that Mr. Harry B. Smith and I have signed a contract to write an opera for Miss Alice Nielsen, now of the Bostonians". He signals his confidence in Nielsen and frustration with Bostonians: "Miss Nielsen is to star in a company which no doubt will turn out to be the finest ensemble we have yet seen in this country. Mr. Frank Perley will have charge of the business direction of this new company. I cannot give further facts regarding the plot and the cast until later".

Pressure now falls on the Bostonian leaders. Their counter-offers cannot hold her. Too late. Certain Pundits commend Perley for taking Alice Nielsen; others wisely wonder why she would choose Perley over others.

Of course, Perley is clever. Nielsen may not have seen the other offers.

Kansas City Star believes "if anyone is prepared to successfully start a new star", Perley could; and reasonably speculates "his interest in the future of Miss Nielsen, in opposition to The Bostonians with whom he has been associated many years" might cause a falling-out: as did. *Star* accurately guesses the deal's timing: "Presumably, the plans of Mr. Perley as regards Miss Nielsen reached a practically definite stage last fall".

Herbert, seeking a star capable of building profitable shows, likes quality cooperation, not bad attitudes. Doesn't forgive resistance. Shows in pipeline for Bostonians became Nielsen Company projects. Herbert and Smith agreed to furnish a draft plot by December 1897.

Reveals tell-tale *Kansas City Star*, "While the Bostonians were in Chicago in December, Miss Nielsen and Mr. Perley were then expecting the first draft of the book of the proposed new opera from Harry B. Smith, who today has the American field of libretto writing in his vest pocket".

"My success in *The Serenade*", Alice says, "has been in a dual role, and so I'm to have a dual part in my new opera. What is the plot? I haven't the least idea, but my part will be that of a singing comedienne, in which I think I am best. Of course, I am to be the star, but it's to be an all-round company just the same, one of the best to be had. Mr. Perley guarantees that". Asked who backs her venture, Nielsen coyly replies she has pals with money eager to place a sure bet: "Oh, I've friends with plenty of means, and they do not seem to be the least in doubt as to my success".

Star reveals Bostonian efforts to keep her: "When the intentions of Miss Nielsen reached the ears of Messrs. Barnabee and MacDonald, they made haste to try and retain Miss Nielsen for another season or two. Prima donnas are scarce, and the offers to Miss Nielsen were tempting indeed".

They had climbed a tree and sawed off the branch with them on it.

Now comes "a likelihood" of Jessie Davis and Eugene Cowles "leaving the Bostonians next year. Both Mrs. Davis and Mr. Cowles had the starring fever, Mr. Perley said as much. Perhaps Mr. Cowles will become a member of the company which Mr. Perley will organize for Miss Nielsen. Mr. Herbert's letter indicates that Mr. Perley already has made his choice of principal singers".

Bostonians realize they are losing not just Nielsen. Basso Eugene Cowles among other star singers, jump ship. The long-lived group is shattered. Their business proposition becomes unpromising; imagine the aging Barnabee and MacDonald belching *Robin Hood* without Cowles, Davis, and Nielsen!

And on that note despite ominous backstage politics, Monday February 7th the Bostonians open Los Angeles Theatre to huge critical and popular success. *Serenade* three nights, *Robin Hood* matinee and Thursday. Town turns out in fine attire for a welcome. Bostonians are pure Americana, national pride, fun. Los Angeles is coming into its own; Alice Nielsen a kindred spirit will soon inspire LA to declare artistic independence.

Insightful *LA Times* (Feb 8) highlights the spirit: "Whenever the Bostonians come to town, and the town agrees that their visits are entirely too few and far between, the population awakes and wants to go to the show in numbers that makes Los Angeles look like a metropolis with a big M. Such was the case last night as usual; the house was filled to the doors with an audience composed of the city's pink, and flower of youth, loveliness and other qualities more substantial perhaps, but harder to get, if nature had not granted the one or has grown too individually for the other. Anyway, it was an audience delightful in its personnel, and delightfully was it entertained".

Gathers for a great good cause: "The Bostonians hold a place in the American operatic world peerless and unapproachable. Whatever that superb organization attempts is done to the very queen's taste; sumptuously, lavishly, generously, and whenever it puts the stamp of its approval upon a new opera we may be reasonably certain that it will be something worth hearing. And of such is *The Serenade*".

Costumer and scene-painter had a "lavish hand"; score "from the facile pen of Victor Herbert...who has already won his spurs. The new piece riots in melody—melodies not of the tinkling evanescent sort, but big, strong rich harmonies that in some of the concerted numbers, border upon the majestic". His score "was not mere 'tunes', and that prince of baton-wielders Samuel L. Studley" conducts the orchestra.

LA enjoys gayety with delight: "The clever and engaging people who gave to Los Angeles a night that was filled with music" were "that great sextet of artists" Barnabee, McDonald, Cowles, Davis, Bartlett and Frothingham "whose coming is like a visit of royal good fellows and old friends. The years seem to lay not the touch of a finger upon any of them".

Davis "young and fair and dimpled as she was years ago", Barnabee "still the droll wag who makes puns that sound as if spontaneous and who cracks those brittle, crisp, fetching little jokes that catch an audience in the ribs and tickles it until it screams. Cowles, virile, handsome and debonair, is in the very prime of life, and his great voice has that organ tone quality which makes it one that once heard is never forgotten". Frothingham, "unctuous, captivatingly ludicrous...rollicks. The juveniles are up to the Bostonian standard, which is a guarantee of quality in itself". WE Philip, "fresh pure tenor.... Chorus is young, fresh and copious of voice and trained to the limit". Ensembles had "a swing and spirit that were delightful...."

When Nielsen plays a town, nobody forgets. "Alice Nielsen, who was here once before with this company, has developed out of all recollection. Her voice has a superb quality. It is round, full and exquisitely true, and it was put to a trying test in the number with flute obbligato and came out with flying colors. Miss Nielsen has a dainty, winsome presence, and her appearance in the role of Yvonne last evening was one of the big hits of the performance".

Opening night, ladies received "a handsomely-illuminated souvenir... containing portraits of the leading members of the Bostonian company". Closing night was to remember always. The scene received a phrase typical of future Alice Nielsen tours: one of the largest audiences ever....

"One of the largest audiences ever gathered within the walls of the Los Angeles Theatre assembled last night to bid the Bostonians 'farewell until we meet again', and the delightful music and delicious fooling of *Robin Hood* was given with the same vim, spirit and joyousness as ever" (*LA Times* Feb 11).

Barnabee "received a royal ovation as he came upon the scene". Alice Nielsen "appeared as Maid Marian and achieved a great success. Miss Davis and Mr. Cowles came in for the usual repeated recalls for their famous numbers.... The Bostonians' engagement this season breaks the record and the management assures us that upon their next visit they will remain for a week and give everyone a chance to hear them". The company sings in San Diego next day, "where the advance sale is pronounced something phenomenal".

How bittersweet for Bostonians in the know. Nielsen's success in *Serenade* strongly helps the bottom line. These had lost the gold goose.

San Francisco got a bit odd. *New York Times* (Feb 26) from San Francisco: "The Bostonians continue to draw crowded houses, but Marie Wainwright, although well-boomed in *She We Forgive Her*, is more to be pitied than forgiven".

Two jealous women linked with Tom Williams try to disrupt Nielsen by yelling and catcalls. Disturbance stopped, show went on despite rudeness of two rowdy Oakland debutants.

"Talking about the Bostonians, a queer incident occurred at Baldwin's Theatre on Tuesday night during the performance of *The Serenade*. While Alice Nielsen was rendering one of the arias of the opera, it became evident that somebody was trying to disconcert her. The audience first learned that something was unusual was taking place when the singer riveted her gaze upon one of the upper boxes. Her face wore a profound sneer and it was apparent that her mind was not upon the music. When the leader discovered that she was not watching his baton, he too looked toward the box. Soon the entire orchestra and half the audience were glancing in the same direction.

"The box was occupied by two women who had attracted Miss Nielsen's attention by hisses and signs betokening their dislike. The affair caused considerable commotion, and resulted in the members of the orchestra putting down their instruments and hissing back at the disturbers, who were finally suppressed by attachés of the theatre.

"The unpleasant affair, while it aroused sympathy for the prima donna, occasioned considerable speculation as to why she had been made the victim of such an attack. It was surmised by some that jealousy inspired by rivalry in an affair of the heart was at the bottom of it. The women are said to be friends of Thomas H. Williams, a well-known racehorse owner, who it is reported is engaged to Miss Nielsen". In any case, Williams "will be the backer of a company with which she will star" after this season.

In this fateful way, Nielsen's relation to Williams, investor of her new venture, is announced and linked to romance. She flatly and fiercely denies being engaged. Williams insists she is. Her stance is protected by manager Perley, who points to a contract clause stating the star will not marry. Yet Perley also works for investor Williams.

Foiled, Williams reconsiders his options to pressure Alice. Perley is the key. If loyal to Alice, the suitor will be kept at a discrete distance. If Williams, born rich into the political elite of a powerful California family, race-track kingpin who controls bets at his tracks, gets frustrated, Nielsen is vulnerable to the integrity of Williams and Perley.

In this plight, Bostonians tour to Chicago where Herbert and Smith meet with Nielsen on the new project. They attend their *Serenade*. On March 20, *Spirit of the Times* says *Serenade* "performed at the Knickerbocker last evening before a large and very fashionable audience, the performance was a success".

Composer and writer called out after Second Act. Harry Smith wittily addresses the audience, "the purpose of a dramatist was to be clear, so the people could understand the play, while the purpose of a librettist was to be obscure, so that people could listen to the music".

Merely-clever and charming, Smith illuminates a core conflict twixt him and Herbert and Alice. Smith is cynical. They are genuinely. Smith is mere words, they perform (cello and voice).

They connect with audiences. They perform. Smith does not.

Cynical Smith scorns meaning; does not want to start making sense. Smith's program notes say, "To prevent the possibility of the audience understanding the plot, the following synopsis is given...." With a legion of bad reviews, Smith laughs all the way to the gold depository.

As commonly observed, he candidly admits he is unoriginal: "Mr. Smith has taken no chances with *The Serenade*. All of his ideas have been used before and have their popularity established. The notion of a serenade that everybody sings is borrowed from *Manon*. Even the 'Royal Brigandage Association' might be claimed by those wicked foreigners who always produce our plays before we do.

Significantly: "But no matter...the music is bright and tuneful".

The familial respect enjoyed by the doomed Bostonians is conveyed by the March *Theatre Magazine* (1898): they occupy "a unique position among musical companies" as "jolly, whole-souled sort of family. Shortcomings are viewed less seriously with these performers, who some years stepped from the modest organ-loft to the blaze of the footlights, and there is somehow between them and their audiences, a feeling of friendship if not of proprietary interest".

Chicago's confrontation with heft keeps heckling. *Theatre* notes, in Act 2 when Delores had to change clothes with Yvonne, "the audience roared when plump Jessie Bartlett Davis proposed to get into the jacket and trousers of slender Alice Nielsen, but the exchange was safely effected...."

Nielsen tries to ease tensions. "A surprise is the Yvonne of Alice Nielsen, a recruit. She has a pretty face and figure, and a high clear soprano, and her song with flute obbligato was encored [re-sung] half a dozen times. But most of the music was repeatedly encored, and all of the members of the company were cordially welcomed and applauded".

And of course, "Scenery by Ernest Albert and Walter Burridge is so picturesque that their names should have been put in the playbill. The costumes by Van Horn deserve a word of praise". Interestingly, "Victor Herbert conducted the orchestra with exquisite skill".

When Alice returns to NYC, they work together on new songs. Music is crafted to showcase each singer's voice. High soprano, low basso, others as suit the strong singers, or easy songs for the musical comedians. Curiously, Alice Nielsen later would complain about "always fussed over by composer and librettist" as an obstacle to return to Broadway.

Expert Perley discusses plans for Nielsen with *LA Times* April 10th, touted "a press agent of extensive experience and varied resources, so the newspapers will doubtless contain a good many stories of the novel features to be introduced...." *Times* gets it wrong: "The latest is that the chorus of the Nielsen company is to be made up entirely of people who have appeared as principals with other companies. He may change his mind, but if he does not, well-informed observers of the habits and dispositions of singers predict serious trouble when the aggregation of chorus singers takes to the road". Chorus will consist of women Alice's petite height; the other principles have starred in other companies.

Strong national focus on Nielsen's next show, forecast for certain success, her presence onstage gives profits and publicity galore. Bostonians left behind grew unhappy. Petty political schemes backfired badly. Losing her would cost.

As the Spanish-American war warms the Pacific, giving rise to the US Anti-Imperialism League reform attempt, the nation is equally concerned by the Bostonian rift with Alice Nielsen. One day backstage backbiting went too far: press issues editorial. If rift temporary among troupers, seems serious at time. Before May, onstage at Wallack's NYC, Nielsen walks out after a silly Barnabee gesture, and never returns.

1898 TROUBLE IN THE CHOIR *NY Daily Tribune, Apr 27 1898*

Differences in two opera companies due to jealousy and bad luck.

Two disagreements in two opera companies came to light yesterday. A disagreement in an opera company is remarkable enough, anyway, but two in one day are believed to establish a new record.... And these two disagreements occurred in just the most unlikely two places that could have been picked out. One of them was in the Bostonians.

Oh, only think of it! The Bostonians! A company whose whole existence has been one grand, sweet song! Shakespeare says the man that hath no music in himself is as bad as a Spaniard.

But singers and musicians, on the contrary, being full of music, are also full of harmony and kindliness of soul, a quarrel among them is almost unknown, and they are mild of temper, forgiving and loving to a degree that is all but grotesque.

And the quarrel among the Bostonians is incomprehensible. A jealousy between two men or two women, of like age and pursuits, might be understood. But why should there be jealousy between a simple girl like Miss Alice Nielsen and a kind old gentleman like Mr. Barnabee? And why should a woman like Jessie Bartlett Davis, who draws around her form an awful circle of devoted admirers, be jealous of anybody or afraid of anybody?

And then, again, Miss Nielsen was soon to leave the company and be a star, and one would think that the prospect of losing her would have drawn the heartstrings of all more closely around her, and that their eyes would have brimmed over at the thought: "Years hence, when others admire her, we can say to them: 'We knew her when she was in our own company; we watched the bud opening; you see only the full-blown rose.'"

But it was not that way at all. They got jealous all around. Miss Nielsen stood it a good while, and at last, one fatal night, she wore a flag on her gown. Mrs. Davis had a flag, too, and thought that hers ought to be the only one; Mr. Barnabee held a big flag so that it obscured the audience's view of Miss Nielsen, and Miss Nielsen resigned.

Other disagreement in national theatrical news? DeWolf Hopper and manager BD Stevens part after thirteen years.

Morning after *Tribune* publishes its opinion, Nielsen in *NY Mirror* (Apr 28) responds with candor and tact: "My association with The Bostonians had not been comfortable for some time—not since I made something of a hit in *The Serenade*; and from the time of the announcement of my forthcoming starring tour my position was made very uncomfortable by those who have often made others unhappy in the same company, the management going so far as to insist that I should agree not to be interviewed by newspapers this season.

"Similar things meant to annoy me were constantly being done, until the matter reached a climax at Wallack's Theatre on April 23, when Mr. Barnabee offered a very pointed and obvious affront on the stage [held a flag in front of her face], and I promptly and very emphatically resigned".

Tosses trademark verbal egg: "I shall rest until rehearsals begin for my stellar debut in *The Fortune Teller*, the new comic opera written for me by Victor Herbert and Harry Smith, which they believe to be their best work".

Day later the heartland's *KC Star* (Apr 29): "Latest news from the seat of war paled into insignificance yesterday in theatrical circles at least, in the face of the reports that flew up and down Broadway to the effect that Miss Alice M. Nielsen, the prima donna of the Bostonians, had broken off diplomatic relations with her associates and demanded her passports from the company.... The report that there had been serious trouble in the Bostonians aroused special interest in theatrical circles, because it used to be understood that the amity that existed among the members of that organization was little short of Arcadian. 'We're like one big family', Barnabee used to say before Miss Nielsen recently announced her intention of going a-starring".

To her hometown Nielsen speaks freely, "Since that announcement was made, they've done all they could to annoy me. It culminated Saturday night. It had been decided to close the performance of *Robin Hood* with *The Star-Spangled Banner*, and all the chorus girls had flags on for the scene.

"Someone gave me one and I tucked it in my corsage. Mr. Barnabee saw me at once ordered me to take it off and called me a fool. Then he told the stage manager not to allow any flags on the stage. I took mine off and put it in my pocket, but when Mrs. Jessie Bartlett Davis came on she had a flag at her side, and when I saw that I took mine out too and put it back in my corsage.

"Then we sang *The Star-Spangled Banner* and Mr. Barnabee brought a big flag out of the wings and deliberately planted it in front of me, waved it and it struck me in the face. That was just a little too much, and I resigned. I can't begin to tell you all they've done to worry me. Why, they wouldn't put *The Serenade* on this week, just because I had a good part in it. Mr. MacDonald, I understand, was going to fine me $25 for wearing the flag, but he remitted it when heard Mrs. Davis had one".

And Barnabee "denied positively...insulted Miss Nielsen" while MacDonald "denied positively he suggested a fine for wearing a flag". Lamely: "Miss Fredericks replaced Nielsen in *Robin Hood* last night".

Alice Nielsen divorces the Bostonians (both celebrated as pure Americana) after being struck—by an American flag. The Bostonians become hindsight.

She had joined the greatest group on North America's musical stage for three years from September 1895 till April 1898.

Jumps from obscurity to fame. They the reverse.

1898 begins with Alice Nielsen an uncontested major prima donna.

Since 1897 she had rewarded Victor Herbert with a hit, proven box-office cash appeal, delighted the nation with gayety; eclipsed the big stars.

Later away from the action past her career, Alice regards the old Bostonians with clarity. Street-singing girl took life lessons with candor. She had seen the raw tumult at stage doors. She had seen "the gamblers who preyed upon Henry Barnabee". She saw the internal squabbles and audiences they thrilled.

She learned tours, how to create new shows. After all was said and done, the Bostonians were the greatest musical company of the time who led her to a national audience. Her memoirs gently recall Barnabee, her last word on leaving the Bostonians. They tour by train, stay in hotels. Not everything perfectly.

Alice recalls 1889 premier of "Reginald De Koven's finest" with Harry Smith words. Before *Robin Hood*, before she joins. After *The Begum*, his first Bostonian project is a forgotten opera "*Don Quixote*. The piece was hoodooed from the beginning. It opened in Utica, NY, with Barnabee in the title role. The curtain raised on the first act with Jessie Bartlett Davis singing a serenade to somebody and Don Quixote in nightshirt and nightcap peering from a window of an inn.

"Barnabee was standing on a stepladder and for realism's sake leaned out of the window, thereby resting his weight against the flat that represented the front of the inn. The curtain had scarcely reached the arch when the flat gave away under Barnabee's weight and down it came, fetching Barnabee, nightshirt, nightcap and stepladder with it. And there lay Barnabee, cursing horribly, the audience and the rest of the cast weak with laughter.

"The curtain was rung down, Barnabee dusted off and the opera begun afresh. These and other absurdities were enough for The Bostonians. *Don Quixote* was stowed away in the camphor chest. Doubtless it might have been rescued therefrom had somewhat different methods been adopted in presenting it; but there was one Bostonian formula and only one; things were done that way or not done at all—by The Bostonians".

In fact, *Quixote* had sixty performances. The role exhausted and bruised Barnaby, unable to meet its physical demands. Yet he told fine stories, Nielsen well knew. Her point: the star sextet required a complex story to showcase these lead players. Simmering jealousies outweigh sense as perquisites of players put a high penalty on advantageous changes.

She connects the *Quixote* fiasco with hers: "Nor could they see after I had been with them for a year that, whatever my talent as an artist, I was a valuable drawing card. They headlined me. They starred me. I was becoming famous". Touring to ever-growing acclaim, aware of her worth.

Perley had raised her pay only once. Still made less than at Wigwam.

"Yet they would not pay me more than $50 dollars a week. I asked for a $150—little enough; but even Barnabee was against me there. I was lucky to be a Bostonian, they said. There were other girls who would be glad to take my place for $50". Davis took $600 per week, Clark $250. Nielsen works for a fraction when picked as star by Herbert over their objections. My answer was as prompt as it was characteristic: 'Very well, pick one. I'm through'," Nielsen tells.

Timing of the cash conflict is a year before the flag abuse, during period she expresses desire for Europe's top voice coach. Her wish for Europe probably triggers fiancé hopeful Williams to invest, serving his wish to keep her touring Oakland. Faced with losing Alice Nielsen overseas, Williams places money on a sure bet.

The Bostonians' old-timey leaders had made themselves irrelevant.

Outcome obvious: "Perhaps it is a bit unbecoming of me to say it, yet it is true that soon after I departed The Bostonians began to disintegrate. And their collapse was swift. In releasing me they indicated what so many within the theatre already knew—that they lacked the new progressive spirit that was then entering stage methods and presentations".

Of course Barnabee, nearly seventy, had had his seasons.

Performance was a rigorously demanding environ before technology.

And she knew his wife Clara, "within her breast there raged a never-ending battle between love for him and resentment against an early affair he had had with a young singer. After that episode, which I was never able to believe was half as serious as she imagined, she was never more to him than—well a nurse or even an ever-fretting mother. If he was suffering the remorse that came of his little, weak earnings, she comforted him. If he fell ill, she doctored and nursed him. She was his valet, his dresser, his secretary. Without her he would have been as lost...no longer her husband, but something for which she was responsible, for which one day she would have to give an account".

Bostonians faded into "the last stages of disintegration, driven now into the dim background by new music, new singers, new ideas, new methods". Leaders "MacDonald and Barnabee, wakening to their plight but not comprehending it, turned hither and yon for money with which to stave off the inevitable. The response from the bankers and the managers was emphatic. Although Macdonald and Barnabee could not understand, their erstwhile backers made it clear that the day of The Bostonians was closing, its vogue finished".

Wife Clara gave savings to sustain the run, as "vanished like a handful of clouds in a great wind. Whether it helped prolong the life of the dying company, I don't know. Whether any part of it went to the gamblers who preyed upon Henry Barnabee, I don't know. But when it was gone and the Bostonians had become sweet history, they took gentle, sacrificing Clara Barnabee to a hospital where she lived her few remaining days, talking of the glories she had seen".

Alice had returned to America with grand opera before Clara Barnabee died in 1909, Henry Barnabee 1917, year of Nielsen's last Broadway show. His autobiography is a delight.

Bostonians were touring in 1904 when *New York Sun* (April 17) confirmed the analysis: "Bostonians struggled along without any great success until that lucky autumn in 1891 when they produced the best of American comic operas *Robin Hood,* which brought them a greater degree of prosperity than they had ever known before. *Serenade...*did more than anything else to restore the favor of the public to the Bostonians in other operas than *Robin Hood.* To this day there are certain to be large houses whenever it is sung, although it is not sufficient to furnish the repertoire for an entire season".

After Alice, era ends: "Very difficult for the company to find a successor to this work. Mainly for that reason, the company has during the past two seasons been accounted what is called a 'one night stand show.'"

James Huneker recalls the good old days of the Bostonians: "Victor Herbert and his sparkling Gallic music" maliciously never mentioning Alice Nielsen as he describes "old Sam Studley in the conductor's chair. *Robin Hood* in its pristine glory: Henry Clay Barnabee, Tom Karl, McDonald, George Frothingham, one of the best low comedians in the country, Eugene Cowles, Jessie Bartlett Davis, Will Holmes, Marie Stone-McDonald.

"Comic opera has in any case all but disappeared from the stage, and the Bostonians were too staid to take musical farce. So they practically had only *Robin Hood* to depend on. Last year the organization converted to a stock company. It is a fairly safe prophecy that the Bostonians, if they would again revive *Robin Hood* before the old company was altogether disbanded, could draw large audiences for some weeks". New players would shock, each role "always associated with certain singers and have never been sung by any others".

Long before April 1898 when Nielsen makes her break, her new company is complete. Barnabee's impulsive insult, mischievously masks Nielsen from the audience with an American flag to appease Jessie Davis, does not hurt.

Alice joins song sessions with Herbert, fusses with costumes and sets, leaves with the new songs for San Francisco and a long vacation across the Pacific. Her journey has lasting impact. *San Francisco Call* reports March 1. 1898, she "will summer in Japan. The first stops in the preparation of Alice Nielsen's new opera will be tinctured with sea salt and the ocean air.... A great portion of her time will be spent in familiarizing herself with the music of the new opera, of which she will be the bright, particular star of all the firmament.

"With Miss Nielsen will be Eugene Cowles, Tom Williams, Miss Cleary, Miss Hortense Nielsen and the prima donna's son.... Cowles, who is to be Nielsen's leading support" has "several duets in the opera which Tom Williams will float.... After a sojourn in the Mikado's empire for a month or more the party will return to this city and then proceed to New York. There Nielsen and Cowles will join their company" for an early season opening.

She sang along the voyage for the Hawaiian Queen, Lydia Liliuokalani (1838-1917), songwriter of popular hit *Aloha Oe.*

Barnum-protégé Perley pushes the press as "stellar debut" approaches, Kentucky's *Lexington Morning Herald* (Oct. 2) puts the inevitable headline

"A New Star Appears In The Theatrical Firmament" (quoted by MGM 1952 Technicolor hodge-podge *Singing In The Rain*), saying "The realm of light opera has not in many years welcomed an aspirant so well equipped for lyric honors as Alice Nielsen...." Her company "will be the most important American musical organization this year, and it is expected to tour the principal cities at the close of the New York engagement".

By 1897 Alice Nielsen's career problems were those of a star. By 1898 her stellar plans were well underway with the combined talents of the best on Broadway. Their success would be unmatched. Herbert and Nielsen bring their folk arts to high art, obliterate barriers between high and low culture, and unify pop art with classical skills creating the gayety of nations. Nielsen's audience rapport grew from folk traditions absorbed as daughter of Irish player and Danish troubadour. She sang from the heart to every human face. She acquired backstage and onstage skills from experts Burton Stanley, Ida Valerga, the Bostonians. Seen how to make successful theatre at the highest levels. Across North America for two years, Alice Nielsen has absorbed adulation from standing-room crowds. Boldness and skill made her a Bostonian star, famous, pure Americana. Best musical theatre troupe the nation produced.

Stepping out as artists, Herbert and Nielsen consciously intend to transform American theatre with "new music, new singers, new ideas, new methods". Now comes Alice Nielsen Comic Opera Company.

HAWAII, GEISHA GIRLS & TEA

Alice Nielsen Company grows into being. Frank Perley recalls: "For her summer vacation prior to the production...it was deemed advisable to have Miss Nielsen do something of real news value but dignified in character, as I was opposed to diamond robberies, scandals, and milk baths, however beneficial the latter might be to the complexion". Refers to Florenz Ziegfeld's publicity ploys to lure the press to wifely paycheck Anna Held.

When Nielsen departs on steamer *Doric*, Spanish-American war in progress, America busily if unconstitutionally establishing a provisional government in the Philippines. Despite risks she did not stay safe: "she decided to take a trip there and afterwards continue to Japan".

Hawaii and a month in Japan change her life. Returns with kimonos, sings Japanese songs, practices the tea ceremony lifelong. In Philippines she buys big wooden clogs soon used onstage. Kimonos wend their way into her grand opera.

Perley makes every effort: "Letters of introduction were secured to important officials and dignitaries" for the many "receptions, entertainments and concerts given in her honor, as well as other social and diplomatic happenings" he does not specify. On NYC return "extensive interviews were published and the rare curious and trophies secured by her were exhibited in the windows of prominent Broadway stores". He keeps her in the papers all summer.

So. Soon after flouncing off the Bostonians' stage, Alice Nielsen in May hops the transcontinental to San Francisco with Herbert's new songs, sails west on *SS Doric*, first cruise ship with swimming pool (canvas, upper deck, twelve by fifteen feet). Photograph in *Leslie's Weekly* (1902). *Doric* holds the world record for a long-distance steamer: Liverpool by Cape Horn to San Francisco.

Thomas Edison's filmmakers Frederick Blechynden and James White made *Afternoon Tea On Board SS Doric* that summer. Four short silents include "jolly little tea party on saloon deck" and "game of shovel-board".

Nielsen's voyage develops art and attitudes. June 8 from Honolulu, "This trip is doing me so much good, it seems as if my voice were ten times stronger than when I started, and if I continue to gain strength and health, I will be quite equal to any work that Messrs. Herbert and Smith have laid out for me in their new opera. I have some of the music with me and have learned it, so that when I reach NY the middle of August, I shall know my part thoroughly".

Ships in those days—until 1930s—without stabilizers, rolled heavily side-to-side. Alice laughs, "first few days I was so terribly seasick I am sure my high C will be in great shape for next season (laughter—joke). It ought to anyhow especially in NY, for I have said New York several times on this journey, and have tried my top note quite often".

She took "seat of honor at the Captain's table" for mischief: coaxing the officers join her prancing a cakewalk. "We had a concert Decoration Day, and as I was suffering a cold and couldn't sing, I made an offer to Mr. Conger, the new Minister to China, and who is a most charming gentleman, to do the cakewalk with me as our contribution to the program, but I fear he was afraid it might ruffle his official dignity, or that cakewalks were not *en regle* away out in mid-ocean". Edwin Conger, and author wife Sarah Pike who befriends China's Empress, arrive in Beijing for the Boxer Rebellion.

"Captain Smith of the steamship, however, felt that he could afford to do a 'walk', whether he got the cake or not, and you should have seen us walk up and down the deck! After the Captain and I had finished, I made Mr. Hennessey, the purser, try his hand walking for the cake, and you should have heard the roars of laughter, as he is so dignified. My! What fun we had, and we made up the 'bos' cake walk for the finale to the concert".

The cakewalk may not seem familiar today, relegated to the marching bands, a "high-stepping strut". In 1898 the cakewalk was a newish fad of an old game. Dancers move in a square to syncopated music. Couples linked at elbows eliminated one after another, "musical chairs" style. Winners get cake, or slice. Hops and high kicks favored. Irish would give a sweetcake to the day's best jig dancer. Any peoples dance. Cakewalks are regarded a folk hodgepodge, perhaps a plantation parody of European ballroom dance. The fad reached minstrelsy, always promoting black culture, and spread north. By the 1890s, cakewalk contests are popular at Coney Island. Tunes arrive from all corners. Debussy, Arthur Pryor, Sousa pen cakewalks. In 1901 Alice Nielsen will deliver the cakewalk to London. Comedy troupe Monty Python will revive the skit sixty-eight years later with "Ministry of Funny Walks".

Doric ports of call are San Francisco, Honolulu, Yokohama, Kobe, Nagasaki, Shanghai, Hong Kong. US troop ships appear as Alice arrives Honolulu, target Manila, the takeover opposed by Anti-Imperialist League.

"In these days the sight of the dear old flag, even at home, stirs one more than ever, and when you are traveling in a foreign land, even in times of peace, it makes the tears come into your eyes and brings a lump into your throat to see the dear old Stars and Stripes when you are away from home. Can you imagine, then, how we felt here, in far away Honolulu, when we met not only the flag but saw on the crowded decks of the transports our own brave soldiers on their way to distant Manila?

"We felt as I cannot describe—as though we could laugh and cry and hurrah and sob all at the same time, and if ever hearts went out with cheers ours did to the brave fellows whom we met here. They sent ringing cheers back to us, and waved their hats and laughed and tossed their caps and seemed as happy and jolly as though—poor lads!—they would all come back to us soon. How we did cheer them! How we did cry for them—for, to tell you the truth, we didn't keep back our tears. Perhaps it may sound silly, but I'm not ashamed of the tears that came into my eyes. I can tell you, were glad to see those boys. They all looked bronzed and well and ready to 'do' the Spaniards the moment they get at them".

Beyond the Philippines hijack, soldiers annex Hawaii under Nielsen's watch, the final ceremony July, "Arrival of the American expedition woke up this sleepy old tropical town as no other arrival had since Captain Cook looked in here a few years ago; and the officers and soldiers of Uncle Sam's army took the place by storm".

Sam's army unconstitutionally abolishes the Hawaiian monarchy and ends independence. An 1893 corporate coup d'état had put the islands under control of Dole plantation managers who evade pineapple tariffs with annexation. President Cleveland had refused, calling the racket un-American, dishonest.

"Everybody and everything was absorbed by the military, and if the conquest of Manila is half as complete and half as peaceful as their conquest of Honolulu, the 'boys in blue' will have one long picnic.... The Spanish Consul here objected to the wild public demonstration and was...informed that this country was not neutral, but American". Nielsen sings for the troops who give her the last Hawaiian flag raised before annexation. The Queen's niece Ka'iulani tells *San Francisco Chronicle*, "Bad enough to lose the throne, but infinitely worse to have the flag. Few Hawaiians attend that ceremony.

Bob Hope's USO tours followed in Alice Nielsen's footsteps. She without a hint of iron *Star Spangled Banner* (celebrating US independence from foreign hijack) for the soldiers at the occupied "Queen's palace (that used to be) ...and a number of other patriotic airs, which were received by such wild and enthusiastic cheering that it almost frightened me. I have heard applause in theatres, but never such an outburst of enthusiasm as these patriotic soldier boys displayed". Kindness appears: "I wonder, how many of them will return again?"

Decoration Day (May 29th now Memorial Day), "we had fireworks on the deck of the ship and most interesting speeches—one from a Catholic priest who is going to join Admiral Dewey and his forces at Manila".

Beyond politics, "Last night we were serenaded by native Hawaiians who sang only native songs. They were in a large rowboat alongside the *Doric*. I was struck by the sweetness of their melody and the quaintness with which they rendered their songs".

In the countryside, she is charmed by local undress: "One meets with many surprises here...but the traveler who expects to see naked savages in the streets of Honolulu will be like the Englishman who wanted to shoot buffaloes and Indians in Central Park. Through the native quarters there is a supreme disregard of conventionality that is wonderful".

Nielsen meets Queen Lydia and other prominent Hawaiians. Lydia is a talented songwriter of *Aloha Oe*, world's most-recorded song. Nielsen sings for all, of course. Her first royal performance is for Lydia. Alice's report to America reveals familiarity with Delsarte techniques, attributes the annexation to corporate shenanigans. With an Irish sensibility she confirms that the native Hawaiians unanimously prefer not being annexed.

HAWAII by ALICE NIELSEN (1898)

Over 200 years prior to the landing of Capt. Cook on the Island of Kanai, a storm-tossed wreck was cast ashore on the southern coast of Hawaii, and the mother of Kings in the person of the daughter of a Spanish officer commanding one of the ill-fated vessels of Cortez's Pacific fleet first set foot on the land of eternal holiday. This daughter of the gods, as the natives called her, was worshipped for a time then wedded to the reigning monarch. Thus began the mingling of the white and brown races, which has continued until at the present time the native Hawaiians are probably as unlike the original Polynesians as the great luscious grafted peach is unlike the stunted wild fruit of the forest.

From the days of Kamehameha, the landing of runaway sailors, the location here of island traders, and the invasion of white settlers have increased, and the loves of white men and brown women have been the theme of many poetic legends through which the history of this half-way house of the Pacific may be traced with considerably accuracy. Dame Nature evidently created these islands in her sternest mood, and then as if to make amends for a fit of ill-temper to have opened the flood gates of her bounty and given the dusky daughters of the Pacific a bright little Eden where, mounted on their ponies, they can gallop about merrily over the green hills or white sands or else disport themselves heedlessly in the still whiter yeast of the surging billows.

No less charming than the seashore is the scenery further inland, where between densely wooded hills the purling streams often flow invisibly in their deep rocky channels, where the gigantic trees spread their rich leafy branches in all directions, where the banana, guava, bread fruit and cocoanut offer such an overflow of delicious drink and substantial savory food as to exempt them from the common doom, "In the sweat of thy face shalt thou eat bread".

The Hawaiian woman of today and the immediate past is a splendid creature in every sense of the word. She is tall, with a full, rounded figure, regular features, rich complexion, showing the high color welling up under the soft dark skin as though trying to break through the cheeks and lips, great black liquid eyes full of fire and passion or of the languor of love, graceful as a fawn, and as laughter-loving as a child. She is an agreeable companion, good mother, or tender nurse.

On horseback (they all ride with the divided skirt, on a man's saddle), in the water (they swim like fishes), or on the sands, the movements of a Hawaiian girl are lessons in graceful carriage beyond anything ever conceived by Delsarte.

It is indeed to be deplored that this magnificent type of woman is rapidly disappearing. Even now one must visit the interior in order to see in their original forms the seductive dances of the native women gayly decked with flowers, which never fail to challenge the admiration of foreigners. This will soon vanish altogether with the people themselves, who are decreasing with alarming rapidity under the influences of civilization and alcohol.

The idyllic scenes of former days have already mostly disappeared, the missions having caused the short and very picturesque national garb to be lengthened and rendered unsightly. The Sunday songs and dances have been prohibited, the laughter and poetry banished; and intemperance indulged in as a substitute for the dance, song and varied harmless amusements, so injudiciously prohibited by the missionaries, has caused epidemics which have claimed thousands of victims.

The native woman's domestic duties were few and her labors light; the preparations of poi from the taro or water turnip, caching and cooking of fish, beating *tappa* or bark cloth, and keeping the cool grass houses clean left them plenty of time to seek amusement or lie under the shade of the trees and listen to the booming of the surf on the coral reefs or the song and traditions of the wars and loves of the first and greatest people of their land.

The Hawaiian women have countless arts by which they heighten their natural beautify of form and features. They are fond of ornaments, and contrive to make them out of the crudest and simplest materials. Their feather work is the finest in the world, and their *tappa* cloth of beaten bark is soft and silk-like in texture. They have a childlike and almost savage fondness for red, and the lover who would win his sweetheart's kindest smile may do so by offering present of the scarlet feathers of the beautiful forest birds found in the interior. Their taste in color is good to an artistic degree, and although they use the brightest and almost clashing contrasts in colors they do so with much admirable taste that they do not look gaudy or even obtrusive. The fashions of wearing the hair are somewhat various; the natural color is a glossy black, but it is sometimes stained a reddish hue by the use of lime. It is nearly always of great length and worn loose down the back, adding materially to the beauty of the wearer.

The women are tenderly fond of children and pet animals and love the usual afternoon gathering under the shade of trees to chat, laugh and sing, as do our own society ladies the five o'clock tea or the evening call. Hawaiian hospitality is proverbial. Should a stranger call at the house of a native, the wife is sure to greet him and ask him if he is hungry. Should he answer in the affirmative, she or one of the girls will run to the fish pond and in a short time some baked fish, taro and fruit is spread out on the plantain leaves and before the guest. The taro patch and the fish pond are the constant pride of the Hawaiian housewife. They represent the kitchen garden and poultry yard of the American woman, and their size and condition is invariably an indication of the rank and prosperity of the owner.

The semi-amphibious nature of the Sandwich Island woman undoubtedly accounts for her graceful deportment and splendidly developed figure. The younger women spend many hours each day in the water. They are fond of fishing and the care and stocking of the ponds is a pleasure, not a task. The fish pond is usually made by walling in a small cover or the mouth of a creek with coral rock, through which the tide runs but the fish cannot escape, and the merry talk and laughter of those engaged in the care of them is proof of the lightness of the labor.

Under a thatched roof, with a fish pond and taro patch well cared for, a native woman can be happy, comfortable and well fed, while with some garlands of wild flowers, a few yards of *tappa*, and some shell, feather, and shark teeth ornaments, she can be as fashionable as any of her neighbors. The commercial future of these islands may have demanded annexation, but the Hawaiian woman certainly did not and will not be benefited by it, as the enforcements of the creeds and customs suited to more northern climes and higher civilization will only hasten the departure of the most interesting of nature's children and result in her total disappearance from the face of the earth.

Bold mischievous young Alice has adventures with lasting influence on her art. These accounts comprise her primary prose legacy until the memoir; as the later novel in Italy went unpublished—manuscript missing.

San Francisco Argonaut reports July 4th Alice "arrived safely in Yokohama" on her vacation to "China and Japan".

GEISHA GIRLS by ALICE NIELSEN (1898)

After a solid week of the daily grind of sight-seeing, visiting the palace of his Royal Highness the Mikado, the ruler of the island

Empire of the Rising Sun, the great lord of the land of the chrysanthemum; curious old temples, tea-gardens, the grand theatre at Tokio; taking a trip to the giant statue of Diuputsu, the bronze god of wisdom, and doing the curio shops, until satiated with far Eastern lore, I conceived the idea of visiting the Oriental prima donna at home, and communicated it to the obliging little Japanese guide, who had been our constant companion and adviser since our arrival at Yokohama.

I was informed that there was no Japanese prima donna, and could hardly bring myself to believe it. Think of a land of painting, poetry and song, without a prima donna! But such is really the case. Japan has no music of her own, so why have any great singers? There is no denying the fact that, with a decided love for music, the Japanese are sadly unsuccessful in their efforts to make it. They easily learn the airs of other lands and become proficient in the use of foreign musical instruments, and enjoy them, but their national music is intolerable.

The Japanese opera is a reality, however. Bands of professional singers and musicians travel about, with only a stand to hold the libretto, from which they give declamatory readings, accompanied by the music of the samisen and other instruments; and those who understand them insist that these operatic productions are artistic and really worth hearing.

To me, however, in the only tea-garden performance of opera I ever had an opportunity of hearing, the sole charm lay in the surroundings, the gayly dressed audience, the paper lanterns shedding a soft, mellow light among the trees, and gentle sighing of a summer wind and the low, moaning swish and swirl of the tide on the beach. The tea-garden is the favorite Japanese pleasure resort, about which many volumes have been written, but there are gardens and gardens, ranging from those frequented by the aristocratic families to the real "dive" variety, and one must be sure of the guide to avoid being found where the performance would shock even the most broad-minded traveler.

Fully determined to visit a native operatic artist, either in her home or in her dressing-room at the tea-garden, I bribed our guide to arrange for the interview without informing any of the other members of our party, and awaited results. My patience was rewarded by being informed that Ito (not the Marquis) had arranged for me to go the following evening to the quarters of a troop of geisha girls, who were living in a large house across the river from our hotel, just at the foot of the bluffs or range of hills back of the city of Yokohama.

When the time arrived I managed to get away from the hotel on the plea of a slight headache, and after my friends had started for the theatre to hear an English company, I slipped out of the house, entered a jinrikisha, and away we went through the streets to the river, over a long, narrow bridge and through crooked lanes, to an old house, where I found at least a dozen pretty Japanese girls huddled into a small outer hall or room, evidently awaiting my arrival.

They crowded around me, all talking at once, and were quieted only when a middle-aged woman entered and spoke to them; then turning to me she said in excellent English, "We are pleased to see you, miss. Your servant has explained that you are a public performer in your own land, and we were as anxious to meet you as you can possibly be to see us, for although we see many foreign women in this country, we seldom meet with one who takes part in public entertainments".

I was conducted to an inner room and requested to lay aside my wrap and hat and join the party at dinner, and although I had struggled through the *table d'hote* at the "Grand" hardly an hour before, I was delighted to accept, and we were soon seated on a large mat of rice straw, and served with boiled rice, dried fish, poultry, and several kinds of vegetables, nearly everything being eaten with a delicious, highly spiced sauce called soy.

A spoon and fork were furnished for my use; the others used their cups and small bits of white wood to help themselves from the dish or bowl in which the food was served. Cakes, confectionery, preserved fruits, and finally tea, and rice brandy, called sake, were served; and then a stand with a box containing the requisites for smoking was brought in, and we were all supplied with dainty little silver-tipped pipes. One of the girls, who had made a professional trip to Hong Kong, and who had learned English, chatted with me, while the hostess directed the repast and conversed with me in English and the girls in Japanese, explaining things generally. Occasionally some speech would cause a great deal of laughter, in which I would join without understanding the cause. The general mirth was contagious.

I was shown the rooms of the girls, who sleep on soft mattresses spread on the mat-covered floor. Their clothing is hung on a sort of curtain pole. Each girl has a lacquered box with many drawers or compartments for holding toilet articles, and each is provided with a highly polished metal mirror. A paper screen is found in each apartment, but not a chair or table did I see in the house. The rooms are formed by thin movable partitions, which can be taken down at any time to make one large room.

I was instructed in the art of make-up, and at the suggestion of the English-speaking girl, disrobed and changed costumes with her, while the other girls assisted us, laughing and chattering all the time like caged magpies. Laughter is the natural stimulant of the Japanese girl; she thrives on it, and indulges in it on the slightest provocation.

The girls closely examined each article of my clothing as it was explained by Mina, and put on by Komura, whose identity rapidly began to vanish under the quantity of clothing she was assuming.

She was about my height, and the garments fitted her tolerably well. Her small, prettily shaped head crowned a slight but elegant figure, which might have been graceful if left to itself. Her pouting lips were radiant with agreeable smiles, and her white neck lost itself in a young, shapely bust; in repose she was a dream, but once in motion the charm of the picture was lost, as she had the awkward waddle caused by the absurd national costume, which is the most artistic and picturesque dress in the world for a woman in repose, but in which graceful action is an impossibility.

I was soon encased in a dainty jacket, linen stockings and sandals, with an elaborately embroidered overdress (or kimona), with huge flowing sleeves, and a beautifully wrought obi or scarf tied around the waist, with a great bow at the back held in place by a strong cord of red silk. My hair was then done in Japanese fashion, and with a liberal use of the make-up box I was transformed into a fair imitation of a geisha, while Komura wore my clothing with more grace than I expected.

My entertainers danced and sang songs, and did everything to make my visit both pleasant and instructive; in return I sang for them. The hour for departure arrived all too soon. My friends entirely failed to recognize me in the Japanese costume which I wore back to the hotel through the consent of the owner, and which she called for the following day.

The geisha, like the prima donna, has her troubles, being under contract for a number of years with a manager. Oh, that manager! He is in Japan, as in America, a necessary evil.

The geishas appear wherever there is an occasion for merry-making, and are very agreeable persons in their own land, but as unlike the geishas of the stage as can possibly be imagined. They have attracted much more attention, in Europe and America, since Sir Edwin Arnold's selection of one of these daughters of the stage for a wife. A great proportion of these girls are the daughters of the samurai, the soldiers or knights who were attracted to the households of the great lords under the feudal system, until the present government left them nothing but a knowledge of fighting and a disposition to do it, without either fortune or occupation.

These soldiers' daughters are proud of their ancestry, and a number of them wear on their costumes the coats-of-arms of their houses. The majority of them marry well, many with the wealthiest of merchants or most prominent officials in Japan. Their movements are given as much prominence in Japanese periodicals as are the doings of the brightest operatic and dramatic stars in this country, and the engagement of a geisha to a prominent individual is made as much of there as is the wedding of an actress to a European nobleman or an American millionaire. There is another order of geisha, called the *hatta* or *etta* girl, who is of another caste.

The recitation of the geishas are usually native poems, love stories and romances; while their dances represent the four seasons. One very popular figure is called *The Dance Of The Moon*.

HOW TO BREW A PERFECT CUP OF JAPANESE TEA
by ALICE NIELSEN (1898)

Between hot weather and a tiresome sea voyage to and from Japan, I feel amply repaid for my trip, because I have at least learned how to make tea. It is really astounding that none of our writers have taken the trouble to explain the intricacies and inner secrets of the art of tea making. They have given all their time and space to the women, the flowers, the odd life of the people and the gay colors, utterly ignoring what to most American women is of great importance, and incidentally, great comfort.

Americans appear to have been content with visiting the tea gardens or the *O'Chaya*, as one would say in Japanese, and with drinking the delightful tea as it was made by the dainty tea girls. But I felt that I ought to know how to make it all by myself.

So when I arrived at Nagasaki I secured the services of a little Japanese girl who was regarded as one of the best tea makers in all Japan. She came to my room and brought her tea kit with her. She spoke a little English, and when I made my wants known and informed her that I desired to know every trick in the art, she squatted herself on the mat in a bay window and the lesson began.

First she lighted an alcohol lamp, although a charcoal brazier is just as good, and placed upon the flame a quart of fresh, clear water, which in about five minutes came to a boil. While the water was heating she placed in another kettle a portion of green tea, such as would fill a demi-tasse.

She carefully shook the kettle until the tea was spread evenly over the bottom, and when the water in the first kettle began to boil she removed it from the alcohol lamp and set it on the tray until it ceased to bubble. When it stopped seething she poured a sufficient quantity of the hot water over the tea to fill a small tea cup and then as quickly as possible poured it out, without letting it steep at all. Right there was the trick.

She explained to me that the tannin in tea is poisonous, and that the first contact with hot water takes from the leaves all that is worth drinking. The steeping process, common with Americans, is fatal to perfect tea. When her brew came from the spout it was a color between pale green and amber, such a color as I have never seen in American-made tea.

She passed the cup to me without sugar or milk and I tasted it expectantly. It was simply perfect. There was hardly more than two or three swallows, but I supped it for about five minutes, during which time every draught seemed rich with a strong perfume. Like Oliver Twist, I asked for more, whereupon she removed all the tea grounds from the second kettle and began all over again.

I was informed that there was sufficient strength in the remaining tea grounds to make another cup if necessary, but the first perfect aroma was gone. No Japanese who understands the art will permit a second cup to be made out of grounds which have once been wet. It is to them as absurd as pouring more water into a glass that once contained a cocktail.

The tea should be drunk immediately. And a fresh cup should be made whenever more is required. Two people can sit around a tea tray with a single service and spend an hour or two of the most delightful comfort. Eight or ten cups is the average for an afternoon, and the simplicity of the art of making the drink relieves one of giving all one's attention to the work.

I called on several of the leading Japanese families and on each visit the tea tray was brought out immediately on my arrival. The Nagasaki girl had taught me all there was to learn, and I saw that her system was generally in vogue among the best people. After each pot is made and the grounds are emptied again for the next brew, the pot should be allowed to dry from the heat it has gathered during the process of making the tea.

This precaution will be found wise, as it enables one to keep the tea dry until the hot water is ready to be applied. In no case should the water be boiling, as its action on the leaves will be too rapid and the tannic acid will indicate its presence to the tongue, creating a taste that is not pleasant when one becomes a regular tea drinker.

There can be no harmful effects from tea drinking if the recipe I have given is carefully followed. It can be drunk at any and all times and at any hour. It will make your sleep peaceful, your hours of wakefulness pleasant, and your digestion regular. Never use sugar or milk, and above all things, do not steep it for a second.

The girls, who pick and dry the tea on copper trays are obliged to stir it in the sun for several hours a day. The fumes of the tea and the tannic acid, combined with the copper odors, wrinkle the women at twenty years of age so that they look to be forty. That is one of the distressing incidents, and is part of the price that humanity must pay for its comforts.

Nielsen visits Nagasaki, Kobe, Yokohama then British colonies Hong Kong, and Amoy (now Xiamen, China). Returning via Honolulu, her party disembarks at San Francisco July 13th.

Her four-month ocean cruise has cost $316.25.

She has embraced Japan; returns with kimonos, tea, warbles geisha songs, acquired a spaniel and gives another puppy to friend Lillian Russell.

"THE NIELSEN": STANDING ROOM ONLY

July 31, 1898, *Chicago Tribune's* "Dramatic Notes" notes "Alice Nielsen...will go to NY to begin rehearsals for her new opera *The Fortune Teller*" by Herbert and Smith. Regarding Harry Smith, comic Richard Golden (butt of *Evangeline* dancing cow) slyly if wonderfully assures *Tribune*, "The book of the new opera was the greatest libretto he had ever read". Big laugh for theatre-people. Wit and humor of the Alice Nielsen Company is a legend.

Monday August 8 at noon the Nielsen chorus reports to Wallack's Theatre for rehearsals with director-choreographer Julian Mitchell. Week later the principals are "on call". Cast contains twenty-four characters, plus chorus and orchestra. Stage crowded during ensemble numbers.

The plot as such. Opens in courtyard of Opera House adjacent to the ballet school, moves to château Garden of Count Berezowski, closes at Camp of the Hungarian Army near Buda-Pest. Third act is a throw-away to comics with a brief reprise of the finale march.

Supporting cast: Richard Golden, Joseph Herbert, Eugene Cowles, Frank Rushworth, Joseph Cawthorn, Marcia Van Dresser, Jennie Hawley, Paul Nicholson, Fanny Briscoe, May Roley, Frances Sears, William Brown, E. Percy Parsons, Jennie Hawley, Annie Clay, Fanny Briscoe, Neely Marsh, PJ Worthington, John T. Gray, Wm. C. Deusing, JB Henrichs, WH Grimke and J. Smith. At least three women cast as men: Hawley, May, March; play Lieutenants, tradesmen. Nielsen of course switches sex as usual.

Orchestra grows in big towns, shrinks to dozen or less in small. Herbert's score puts A-flat cornets in orchestra, B-flat trumpets and side-drums onstage for the huge 2nd-act finale march.

Completed are the costumes crafted by Simpson, Crawford & Simpson from designs by Caroline Siedle; wigs by C.L. Leitzl; boots and shoes by I. Miller; armor and swords by Siegman & Weil.

Caroline (Carolyn) Siedle (1867-1907), top theatrical designer from London who crafts fifty-eight productions. Husband Edward was property manager at the Met. Her big hits: *Belle of New York, Wizard of Oz, Babes in Toyland, Piff! Paff!! Pouf!!!, Red Mill, Faust*. After thirteen shows together, director Julian Mitchell tells *NY Times* that Mrs. Siedle "enabled me to make my reputation. Without her assistance I should never have been able to carry out the musical comedy color schemes which have made beautiful stage pictures. Her...ability to design amounted to genius".

Joseph (or Josef) Physioc (1866-1951) born Richmond VA, raised Columbia SC, was a boyhood friend of Woodrow Wilson and a child actor. He began at set design for many small Southern theatres. Paints scenes at Met Opera before designing on Broadway for many shows from DeKoven's *Rob Roy* (1894) to *Dracula* (1927), and first Bernard Shaw play produced in America, *Arms and the Man*. He continues acting and paints murals (Hicksville, NY).

Director-choreographer Julian Mitchell (1854-1926). He could hear beats with his ear atop the piano. One day in rehearsals a storm came up and after a thunderclap he asked, "Who is out of step?"

His handicap helps, says critic George Jean Nathan (1917): "Beyond question, the best stage producer of the music show amongst us is Mr. Julian Mitchell.... And why is Mr. Mitchell the best and the most successful artistically and commercially? Simply because Mr. Mitchell is deaf as a post and so being constitutionally unable to hear the lines or lyrics at rehearsals, pays utterly no attention to them and devotes his entire eye to the physical elements of the business in hand".

"An excellent comedian with a lengthy career", adds Robert Grau (1910), Mitchell "began to demonstrate extraordinary ability as a producer of musical plays and burlesque. He can get more out of a stage situation which combines music, action and pretty girls, than any man in the world in his line of endeavor". Mitchell's shows include a sad hodgepodge *Wizard of Oz*, hit *Babes in Toyland*, and *Ziegfeld Follies*. Active from 1890s in a theatrical family, marries Bessie Clayton *NY Times* calls "the nation's first-born prima ballerina". Says Camille Hardy (2006), Clayton perfected "an unusual type of character dancing". Popular across Atlantic she would dance a "toe-tap" atop a drum.

Mitchell, Siedle, Physioc innovate stage designs to huge success.

On the business and technical side, George Crager is Acting Manager; AR Loudon as Representative; William Rochester, Stage Director [manager]; John Timoney, Master Carpenter; George Vail, Assistant Carpenter; Garrie Davidson, Master Of Properties; Sarah Bolwell, Wardrobe Mistress; and the Master of Transportation Sidney Spandauer.

For *Fortune Teller* Alice Nielsen changes costumes constantly. She flaunts military costumes in red, white, black, plus ballet and gypsy outfits. She is a fashion diva onstage and in the street. City Museum of NY describes Nielsen's "*Fortune Teller* Hussar Uniform" as a "Black satin waist-length jacket covered in gold paillettes" with a "false front of white taffeta covered with white chiffon simulating shirt" and lace jabot. Jacket opens to waist: "wide lapels, pointed cuffs and back side pockets in 18th Century manner. Trimmed with heavy machine embroidery in gold thread. Pointed yellow broadcloth cap ending with tassel has wide band of black fur at bottom trimmed with gilt sunburst and gold braid on fur border". Another outfit is "black wool broadcloth military coat with long skirt, trimmed in gold military braid" to her knees. Gold cord shoulder boards, small attached hood. Lined in yellow satin, closes center-front with frogs and gold metallic buttons. Plus "black satin knee breeches trimmed in gold embroidery with faked drop front".

Most unforgettable in the memories of audiences, Alice Nielsen wears the short jackets with dark red tights, thigh-high black leather boots with wide boot tops, buckle trim, and squared scalloped edge, closed with lacing inside. Curved heels on boots and shoes become the "Alice Nielsen heel".

Decades later, young men grown old recall Alice's red tights "very tight".

Postcards of Alice in costume, wildly popular. Her premier is a press riot. *NY Times* prints Nielsen and Cowles in gypsy outfits. *Sunday Telegraph* makes the front page exclusively her own with a center portrait surrounded by Alice striking poses in the long coat.

Press hail the superstar cast: "Alice Nielsen, Marcia Van Dresser, Jennie Hawley, Marguerite Sylva, Richard Golden, Joseph Herbert, Joseph Cawthorn, a quartet of singing comedians—Eugene Cowles, Frank Rushworth, William Rochester and Franklyn Wallace—a chorus of 60 voices, six trumpeters, a prismatic ballet and a large orchestra under the direction of Paul Steindorf".

The cast includes Salt Lake's Jennie Hawley, praised in 1894 with Burton Stanley. Hawley will play all Nielsen shows.

Basso superstar Eugene Cowles deserves elaboration. His presence is key. For years critics had warned Bostonians, "It is a matter for speculation as to what this organization would amount to without Eugene Cowles". Stage impact? *San Francisco Chronical* (1895) wrote, "Interesting to notice the audience when this basso has work on the stage. Each one apparently settles himself, as if for more than usual enjoyment, and the singer's number finished each turns slightly to the other with a commendatory nod".

Cowles has a giant voice, slightest lisp detectable in recordings. Spent his life in music theatre. His hometown Darby Line straddles Quebec and Vermont. His father owned the bank. He joined Bostonians from a bank in Chicago. First National staff took three-hundred seats to greet his onstage debut. Reclusive Cowles never gave interviews. When he speaks from *NY Dramatic News* (1897), it is one of only two public utterances he gave.

MY PAINFUL RECOLLECTION by EUGENE COWLES

When I was about 21, a clerk in a large Chicago bank, with few friends and less spending money, an amateur band was organized in the swell First Regiment Illinois National Guard, and as I was known to have played upon nearly every instrument that 'blew, scraped or pounded', I was asked to become a member of this select organization. When I was introduced to the instructor, he looked me over a few minutes, evidently making a rapid mental calculation as to my lung power (so many pounds pressure to the square inch, I presume), and assigned me to the biggest brass horn that was ever operated upon.

I don't think I exaggerate, for it seems that several promising young men had endeavored to extract some kind of a sound out of this monster, and had failed ignominiously. I survived the test, and rehearsals began. We played at bazaars, etc, in the armory during the winter, every day becoming more proficient, and more pleased with ourselves, until the 30th of May approached— Decoration Day, with its big parade and our chance! Just before this, I had a two weeks' vacation...I spent at home [Darby Line VT/Stanstead QE], returning upon the morning of the fateful day.

During my absence, the boys had learned a lot of new marches, and had been put through various evolutions by a drum major, leaving me somewhat outclassed, but still full of confidence and youthful ambition. The process was to form upon Michigan avenue, march north to Adams street, where the Governor of the State was to review it, then wheel...and march west on Adams street. A platoon of policemen in front, then—then our band—the First Regiment Band!

Imagine if you please, a proud young man marching in the right flank in the front row...in gorgeous uniform, the feathers of his shako falling gracefully over his eyes, said eyes intently fixed upon the music, said young man blowing his heart and soul into that immense instrument...of the shape called 'helicon', encircling his manly form three times, and extending its enormous 'bell' slightly in advance of his left shoulder. *That was I!*

Not to prolong the agony of this recital, I will explain briefly that the big 'bell' of the horn and the feather before my face, shut out the surrounding objects of my sight completely, and as luck would have it, as we were about to wheel by the Governor's reviewing stand, I encountered a bass solo which was...a new one on me.

Well! ...I struck some intricacy of 'fingering' in my solo and marched off on a tangent down the avenue! I was blowing so fiercely that I couldn't hear the rest of the band even when with them so...I did not notice any difference. As I was on the point of colliding with some large object, I forget what, I became aware of a small newsboy, who ran against my proudly marching nether limbs and said: 'Where are you going, sir?' (He didn't use those exact words, but I prefer not to quote literally).

In one awful moment I realized what I had done! My solo ceased—unfinished! I could find nothing to drop into or hide behind, so amid the jeers and laughter of the populace I ran ruefully back to my comrades who, in their endeavor to read their notes and at the same time follow my mad career, were playing all kinds of queer music on their instruments. At the end of that dreadful parade I resigned, leaving the giant 'helicon'...together with my pride and haughty spirit, and that is my painful recollection".

Other men in Fortune Teller were a fair tenor, bass-baritone, singing comedians and a chorus with eight-part harmony and high B-flats.

Nielsen Company could have been named "The Young Bostonians". Herbert and Smith create "topical songs for comedians, characters songs, descriptive and sentimental numbers", ensemble songs performed by a chorus of sixty with six trumpets onstage, a "quartet of singing comedians" and "a prismatic ballet".

Prismatic ballet! Obscurely intriguing: a colorful pantomime dance. Later examples would be in the Gene Kelly films.

"An elaborate scenic production will be furnished by Joseph Physioc and assistants who have been at work on it all summer, while Mme. Siedle has designed the costumes. Julian Mitchell is staging *The Fortune Teller*, being assisted by suggestions from the composer and author, and manager Perley".

So it was. *The Fortune Teller*, a fancy-dress musical revue to showcase the prettiest girl in Kansas City with the best legs in San Francisco having a glory voice who dances and improvises comedy with the best.

Onstage for almost the entire three hours, Nielsen parades onstage in tights and tall boots, or dresses and shoes, or tutus and slippers. Plays the ballet girl in tights for a dance rehearsal, plays her twin brother in uniform and tights for marches, plays a gypsy in skirts for a vocal showpiece, the ever-popular czardas with a cadenza reminding us of Alice's aside about stage doors, champagne and showgirls: "for which she did her inimitable dance on the table. Dear me!"

Her roles require constant costume changes, one of seventeen-seconds.

The plot is nothing. The play is the thing. Herbert and Nielsen, grounded in folk song and dance, raise energy onstage.

Nielsen eggs the Bostonians, "With me went their business manager Frank Perley, and Eugene Cowles their superb basso. Tom Williams…was the financial backer". Looking back three decades later, she tosses the stunning remark, "one of the finest characters I was ever to know".

Such a bitter irony in it.

Williams and Nielsen, close friends since 1892. The Nielsen family used his ranch and had relocated from downtown San Francisco to Oakland near Ida Valerga's family and near Williams. As a star Alice could anticipate vast wealth, hasn't Maude Adams made millions? Nordica? Lillian Russell? Tom Williams by inheritance knows power in politics and finance. He has hidden trouble. Suffers from tuberculosis, contagious with prolonged exposure to shared air.

On with the show. In the late 1890s, two composers begin to merge opera forms. Only Alice Nielsen will star for Herbert and Puccini.

Puccini remarks he does not make opera, he makes music theatre. Herbert's scores tell a story with complex vocals and incidental music.

Vocals and acting at Nielsen Company will be clear and natural.

Fortune Teller wasn't a fixed show. Songs came in and out. Cast improvised dialog. We don't really know what they did onstage. Librettist Smith gave the cast comics complete freedom to adlib. Next show they demand credit. When we see the Bob Hope, Bing Crosby "Road" films—same style in new tech. Stars with absurd plot adlib to audience.

Perley recalls, "I had the principal artists sing for Mr. Herbert so that he might know the strong as well as the weak points of their vocal registers, and Mr. Smith knew Miss Nielsen's personality and the character of work in which she could score most effectively, so that these skillful authors were enabled to do their part with unusually satisfactory results".

Julian Mitchell tells a story in physical action and parallel layers beyond the words. Players morph from one stage-picture to the next.

Mitchell, Perley continues, "not only realized the stage effects and created the song productions, but coached Miss Nielsen in every detail which could contribute to her personal success. Add to this, a most sumptuous costume and scenic setting and careful managerial direction, and the reader will have the important elements which contributed to Miss Nielsen's rise to stardom".

Near Union Square at Irving and 17th, Herbert and Nielsen build her songs, "It was fun working with Victor Herbert. I remember how he'd stop all of a sudden and say, 'Alice, we've got to put another high note right here.' And I'd look stern and answer, 'But you've already put in nine—how many high notes do you expect me to give them for their money?' Then we'd have a fierce fight over it—and end by adding two more high notes instead of one".

Herbert seeks success. Nielsen brings success. To be sure, he had other star clients. Tours his own orchestra, conducts Pittsburgh. He admits to composing four shows simultaneously, sipping wines from each story region. Herbert 1898 teaches at Dvorak's music school, leads Gilmore's Band, conducts Pittsburg Symphony, plays cello in string quartets, leads his own orchestra in tours as he creates a simultaneous string of musicals.

Librettists thwart him. His shows may fail.

Herbert suffered over the Bostonian's 1894 *Prince Ananias*. His 1895 hit *Wizard of the Nile* for comic Frank Daniel as Kabosh who plants into pop culture the iconic: "Am I a wiz?" Next year, Herbert joins Henry MacDonough for *The Gold Bug* debut of black comic Bert Williams. Runs a week. Nassau-born Williams creates a new NY show popularizing the cakewalk with George Walker, his costar in San Francisco's minstrelsy "Two Real Coons". In 1897 Herbert makes two hits, *Serenade* and Daniels' *Idol's Eye* as five Herbert musicals and his band tour. October 23, *Lexington Morning Herald* (*KY*) reports Herbert's (Gilmore's) "Famous 22nd Regiment Band of NY in grand concert". He "lays all opera records in the shade" with five touring shows and "his *Wizard of the Nile* had a famous run in Europe last season".

Socially Herbert likes food, wine, beer, song. For a while chorus girls. No evidence he chases divas, "he had too much sense for that", biographer Neil Gould told the author (2005). Nielsen lists wife Theresa as a close friend, who Huneker recalls as "a handsome Viennese woman, who sang with a sumptuous voice in Goldmark's *Queen of Sheba*". Nielsen's 1932 list of men friends includes Herbert, Pryor, Tom Williams. She only speaks of Herbert professionally.

Fortune Teller has patter songs for comics, showpieces for star singers, plus ever-changing, song-within-song ensemble delights which intoxicate.

Nielsen had learned from mom the songs created by Herbert's grandfather. Now she sings music made for her personal success, "fussed-over by composer and librettist". Pop diva Kate Bush (2002) describes the contrast between development and touring: "Touring is physically tiring, but most of the other things are mentally exhausting. Concentration is the main thing, having to do things all day and just keep up. It teaches you to draw on energies that maybe you didn't think you had and you have to sustain. Because it's so important to keep in control and keep cool".

Onstage almost three hours with cast of seventy, small wonder Nielsen endorses brewer's yeast in 1898. *Fortune Teller*, staged around petite Nielsen and big Cowles, showcases her high soprano and his rolling bass, a four-octive spread. Eight-part harmony closes each act.

Rehearsals continue, opening nears.

Words not so fine. Frivolous, cynical librettist Harry Smith is scorned by all. Winning as a person, his scripts are confections of baffling babble rehashed, distilled from Euro-retta libretti reaching his hands. Misses the local satires illuminating that art form. Knotty lyrics obscure rhythms. Beware verse two!

"To be frank I don't take this work seriously at all. I regard it as a commercial proposition", Smith tells *American Magazine* (Sept 1915). "Like all men who wrote light comedy, I have a notion that I should like to do something better, that is, write a good play dealing with some subject that is in the air; that is identified with modern thought".

Candidly, "I have a personal preference for the one that brings in the highest royalties". His cliché-shuffling made him rich. He likes the result.

Fortune Teller plots, like this: After the women and a comedian play through a long mock-operetta dance rehearsal, Nielsen opens with *Always Do As People Say You Should*. Her song crosses styles from mock-opera to mock-operetta diving into a very Irish melody for two verses until ending with a beautiful Broadway ensemble sound. The men make a satiric march with tenor solo before focus goes to awaited bass Eugene Cowles in *Ho! Ye Townsmen*. His song is bold. Nielsen's lovely, yet less original in form. Then Nielsen wows the crowd with wild Hungarian czardas *Romany Life*, B-flat trills, coloratura and high E-flat tightly woven to a bouncing rhythm.

Few strictly solo songs; the ensemble harmony active across the show.

Act One closes in eight-part harmony for ensemble which rises and falls, soars, has a stinging moment by basso, and fades gorgeously away.

Act Two brings Nielsen and women to play their way through *Serenades of Many Nations* with six musical styles from Irish to ragtime, ending with a cakewalk. Cowles sings a pretty ballad, *Gypsy Love Song*, and Marguerite Sylva belts a playful tune with the tenor. The full ensemble ends the Act with a huge Herbert march with many twists and changes. Herbert puts players from his Gilmore Band onstage while the women's chorus (in orange tights) pound away at side-drums. Big production; during opening night Nielsen will say she "was possessed" and almost threw herself into the cheering crowd. Act Three is an afterthought reprising the march briefly with a few novelty songs added to let the comedians end the show. If today you seek a libretto and score, you find what was not. The Nielsen company improvised dialog, lyrics, and entire songs came and went over the run. There is no genuine *Fortune Teller* capturing the genuine event. That's the beauty. That's why I created *Aliss Afire* as the new show Herbert demanded for his music.

To further horsewhip Harry Smith, despite Perley's sweet dreams that the wordsmith focus only on *Fortune Teller*, all summer Smith wrestled with comic Francis Wilson over poor quality work on Wilson's project.

Unsurprisingly, at the *Fortune Teller* debut *Harpers* said Smith's story dated "from the sandstone stratum of libretto geology". Again, what Alice Nielsen Company actually said or did onstage is unknown. Free to improvise, they did. They had to. They connected with the audience by writing their own lines while playing parts in an extravaganza of fanciful scenes punctuated by many costume changes for leading lady. Show was a framework for spontaneous fun.

The burden of Harry Smith's crazy story, trite dialog, and clumsy lyrics is replaced over three years. Each comedian develops his own lines.

Comedian Joseph Herbert (no relation to Victor) gave major re-writes for the cast without credit. His long Broadway career as performer, director, or writer for forty-seven shows starts with 1888's *Pearl of Pekin* set in 1861 China, adapted from the French. He ends well with 1927's *Yes, Yes, Yvette* set in Palm Beach, Florida, Jeanette MacDonald as Yvette who will star with Nelson Eddy in 1930s operetta films as Nielsen visits Hollywood. The MacDonald-Eddy 1935 debut *Naughty Marietta* loses what Hebert and Rida Young had created. MGM rewrote the New Orleans story.

Eddy gets the alto's songs. Still, fun. Twenty years later, Patrice Munsel and Alfred Drake make a live-for-TV version which is much superior, and Munsel sings clearly, as Barnabee had insisted.

As Alice spouts silly Harry Smith lyrics in a sillier story, Hortense acts with Modjeska's 1898 company touring in *Macbeth, Frou-Frou, Andrienne Lecouvreur* and *As You Like It.* Nielsen sisters will play the same towns that year. When the lively sisters again meet their candor will discuss this.

The hollowness of Harry Smith was indeed strange. Consider the setting of the star and composer. In NYC Nielsen occupied a residence hotel near the theatres. Nearby to the southeast, Union Square and Herbert's house at 17th across from Washington Irving House and Manhattan School of Music. Also on the corner was James Huneker at the "small family hotel at the northeast corner of Irving Place and 17th St. kept by an elderly couple" noted for "cooking and cheerfulness. An artistic rendezvous, its table-d'hote dinner saw many celebrities. It was one of those houses where at any time before midnight the sound of pianos, violins, violoncellos, even the elegiac flute might be heard, and usually played by skilled professionals. There was also much vocal squawking.

"From the vine-covered entrance of Werle's I often heard string music made by Victor Herbert, Max Bendix—then concert-master of the Thomas Orchestra, and a Philadelphian—and others". Also present was "Red Countess, Madame Von Shevitch. Her husband, a pleasant Russian nobleman, was editor of a radical newspaper". Portrayed by George Meredith in fiction as "Clotilde Rudiger" this woman "opposite me at table, who ate suet dumplings as she discoursed art, philosophy, fiction and politics, was the direct cause of the death of Ferdinand Lassalle, of whom Bismarck said, 'When he goes into the field I'll shut up shop.' Lassalle, the one great force of the Social Democrats, one apparently born to lead the German people from the jungle of absolutism—Heinrich Heine proclaimed this—was killed. She married his killer, a Rumanian Prince, then an actor, then a Russian aristocrat. Her recollections of Lassalle fell into the hands of George Meredith". The novel followed. Huneker recalls "in 1890 she returned to Munich, suicide in 1911". Imagine Europe without the torture of absurd 20th Century wars added.

Art springs from life. In this neighborhood among these people, Alice's show took frivolous form. And her desire for deeper arts would grow.

"The rare genius of Victor Herbert", Nielsen recalls, "had us doing things that seemed impossible. He was never at a loss. For example, there was the scene where I was to leave the stage singing, change my costume still singing and reappear in a huzzar's red uniform to join Richard Ling in a duet. But there just wasn't time for the change. Try as I might, there wasn't time. My maid did everything but yank me out of my skirts and into tights—but there wasn't time. Then, at the dress rehearsal I rebelled. I made my appearance on the stage fully garbed with the exception of one shining boot, which I carried in my hand.

"'see here, Victor', I cried, 'I've reduced my time ten seconds—down to one boot. I can't do it any quicker. I've tried until my hips are out of joint. I've got to have time to get this boot on.'

"'For heaven's sake go on with the rehearsal', roared Victor. 'Why bother with such trivial details? Here', he addressed Steindorf, 'hand me that score. There. There's your damned boot.'

"Almost as swiftly as I tell it, he had written fourteen extra bars in the score of *The Fortune Teller*. That gave me time to get the boot on".

Toronto was selected for the debut, then a quick tour down to NYC.

Alice Nielsen Company opens *The Fortune Teller* in Toronto's Grand Opera House on Wednesday, September 14, 1898. Next day, *Kansas City Star* reprints *New York Herald*'s: "Alice Nielsen As A Star"

She has "made her first appearance as a star tonight.... A trial performance, preparatory to Miss Nielsen's metropolitan debut within a few days, but it went with smoothness and spirit, and whatever NY may think of it, the Toronto audience said tonight that they liked it exceedingly, applauded the new star with Torontian fervor, laughed at Harry Smith's book and encored...Victor Herbert's score. Altogether it was a very jolly evening, and Miss Nielsen looked like a very happy young woman when she came out in front of the curtain to answer several hearty recalls. There were numerous calls for the leading members of the company as well. The music...is catchy, bright and tuneful and several of the concerted numbers have a stirring swing to them that caught the house at once. That's what we think of the new score up here".

Next day, Washington State's *Tacoma Daily News* compares America's two top actresses: "When Alice Nielsen created the role of Yvonne in Herbert & Smith's tuneful opera *The Serenade* in NY a year ago last March, the prophecy was made that there were two young ladies destined for stellar honors", Maude Adams in Barrie's *Little Minister*, and "unless all signs fail, Alice Nielsen will accomplish a companion hit in Herbert & Smith's new opera *The Fortune Teller*".

Los Angeles Times agrees (Sep 18): "Every now and then a new star twinkles in the theatrical firmament and the public intuitively begins to speculate on the newcomer's chances of success. The season just commencing is no exception to the rule, except for the fact that the realm of light opera has not in many years welcomed an aspirant so well equipped for lyric honors as Alice Nielsen, who makes her debut at Wallack's Theatre, NY, on the 26th.

"The company, which promises to be the best and most important operatic organization to tour the country this season, has been formed by Frank L. Perley, whose successful direction [production] of various important theatrical enterprises is well known". *Times* approves comic trio Richard Golden, Joseph Herbert, Joseph Cawthorn, plus "chorus of sixty voices, six trumpeters and a [female] drum corps trained by the instructor of the [Gilmore now Herbert] 22nd Regiment Band, a prismatic ballet and a large orchestra under the direction of Paul Steindorf".

Perley suggests libretto and music "received more than ordinary attention" by Herbert and Smith "for their exclusive work...until after this opera was delivered and accepted". Ain't necessarily so. Yet, Physioc had labored on scenery "greater part of the summer". Costumes, "unusually expensive in material and beautiful in design".

We know Alice Nielsen never mentions—*Satanella*—nor this Rochester night which "well-known theatrical man" Warren Ferguson at the New Willard told *Washington Post* (1904): "Ever since the Iroquois Theatre fire [many died] all playhouses" have water tanks of water high above the stage to douse fires. "In this connection I saw an amusing thing.... Alice Nielsen was performing *Fortune Teller*. This tank contrivance could be put in operation merely by pressing a button and one of the stagehands, ignorantly or unconsciously, gave the pressure at the time the lady was doing her best to entertain her audience. All of a sudden there fell upon her a drenching volume of water, which for time put an end to further dramatic action. Very luckily she had the stage all to herself or else the whole chorus would have been baptized. She was undaunted by the mishap however, and finished her set in street costume".

NYC ads for Nielsen begin September 21: "First Metropolitan Presentation of Victor Herbert and Harry B. Smith's new 3-act light opera *The Fortune Teller*, sung by Alice Nielsen" with "Eugene Cowles, Dick Golden, Jos. Herbert, Frank Rushworth, Marguerite Sylva, Marcia Van Dresser, Jennie Hawley, Paul Nicholson, Jr. and 20 others.... Platoon of trumpeters, chorus of 80 voices, drum corps... augmented orchestra under the direction of Paul Steindorf". The show "presented by Frank Perley" skips investor Tom Williams.

Monday, September 26, 1898 Alice Nielsen opens Wallacks at 34th and Broadway. "Soda and mineral water" served during the 3-hour performance.

All Sold Out.

Excitedly waking at dawn, she rings for reviews.

Herald: "Alice Nielsen's Star Debut". "Acted and sang with delightful freedom throughout. If she was in the least nervous over her NY stellar debut, she didn't show it. She entered right into the spirit of the opera— and the music was snappy, and the action full of fun—and went through her role with lots of dash, and now and then a smile to the audience, as if to let them know how much she was enjoying herself". Her "best bit of singing" was *Romany Life* "which she sang at a breakneck pace and with plenty of spirit".

In the cast: "Excellent company". Steindorf "conducted very well. The production was beautifully staged". At the finale "there were numerous curtain calls and demands for Mr. Herbert" and Nielsen spoke, "I can't make a speech and if I tried to you'd know it". Looking over at Herbert, "Come along, Victor", she laughs and beckons over the footlights. At length he "rose and bowed". Onstage they make another bow, and another, and another until Herbert takes Steindorf's baton and conducts the finale march all over again.

Times: "The problem set before the makers of this musical play was to provide a vehicle for the exhibition of the abilities of Miss Alice Nielsen, a young soprano, who has ascended to the position of a star with something of the rapidity of rocket, but who is so agreeable that it is to be hoped she will not come down as fast as one". Nielsen plays three parts, "Musette a gypsy girl, and Irma a pupil of a ballet master. These two girls cannot be told apart, and the latter has a twin brother who is her image". She has "the invaluable faculty of always looking pretty and always being refined, while she sings her music excellently with a small but pure and true voice. Her personal success with the audience was beyond question.

"Victor Herbert, the composer of the music of the operetta, shared the honors of the evening with her. At the end of the second act he was called for with tremendous enthusiasm and in response to shouted demands, took the baton from Paul Steindorf and conducted his own stirring march which brings the curtain down. Herbert fully deserved the warm applause which he received. He has written a score which is rich in all varieties of delightful music. There are numbers grave and gay, light and serious, catchy in the most popular manner and musicianly in a thoroughly praiseworthy style...the finale of the first act is one most admirable pieces of writing ever heard here. In brief, this is a work in which the music is distinctly good, and it ought to prove very attractive".

At very end *Times* put a bare sentence about Harry Smith whose libretto "not always quite clear and somewhat weak in the middle of the second act".

Nobody disagrees the Smith script fatally flawed, not even Detroit. The cast begins re-writes instantly. Smith did not care if they did.

Harper's, scorning Smith "of the Sandstone stratum of libretto geology" says "Alice Nielsen has not merely beauty, piquancy, and a great deal of *gaminerie*, but a fresh and trained voice". Alice has the Irish Midwest voice, "doubtless the provincialisms of accent will pass away in time".

Saucy Alan Dale of Hearst papers: "In *The Fortune Teller* the astonishing Harry B. Smith, who must have gone about all summer perspiring librettos and dripping them into the laps of all the stars, has woven a role for Miss Nielsen that is stellar but difficult to comprehend.

"Miss Nielsen appeared as three people who are always changing their clothes. Just as the poor little woman has got through all her vocal exercises as Irma, Mr. Smith insists that she shall be Musette in other garbs. And no sooner than she appeared as Musette and sang something else than Mr. Smith rushes her off and claps her into another garb as Fedor.

"You don't know who she intends to be from one minute to another, and I am quite sure that she herself doesn't. The variety of dresses, tights, wraps, jackets, and hats sported by this ambitious and earnest little girl is simply astonishing. It must be very difficult to accomplish these chameleon-like changes without getting rattled. Miss Nielsen seemed to enjoy herself, however; and as for getting rattled, she coquetted with her audience as archly after the twelfth change as she did after the first".

New York critics speculate on her power and talent: "Artistic and attractive a woman as can be found on the stage, she sings all her numbers with a freshness and life that are simply irresistible. She really seems to like to sing, and she gives encores with a grace that cannot but make one think that she has not yet found the limit to her powers. And, added to her voice, Miss Nielsen is a charming actress and a better laugh-maker than any of her supporting comedians". She enjoys the stage, the audience.

Picture November night when The Electric Club books the theatre, arriving in newfangled electric cars then carry cast to Waldorf for an Electric Banquet.

Morning Telegraph, thankfully, asks Nielsen how it felt to become a star last night. The young woman speaks freely.

HOW IT FEELS TO BE A STAR by ALICE NIELSEN

While I feel greatly flattered at your kind request for my views of 'How it feels to be a star', I must confess that I reply to it with some misgivings. It would have been much more easy to have told you how it feels trying to be a star, for, thanks to those whose admiration and friendly kindness brought about the existing conditions on the stage at Wallack's at the present time, I find myself, while young in years and in stage experience, confronted with the fatigues, worries, hopes and fears of a star. Manager Perley...completed the preliminary arrangements required for my invasion of the carefully guarded and almost inaccessible operatic stellar solar system.

Now that the kindly welcome given me, here on my first appearance at the head of an organization of which any prima donna whose position is firmly established might justly feel proud, has in a great measure relived this apprehension, but my desire to remain in the planetary world long enough to become one of the fixed stars, and not to comet-like, flit across public vision for a season and then disappear from view forever, causes me quite as much anxiety as I felt before the first New York production of *The Fortune Teller*, and is a great incentive to the hard work and study necessary to retain the place marked out for me, and if possible advance beyond it.

Now, as to how I went through the performance the opening night, I must confess the describing of my sensations on that occasion is a very difficult matter. During the first act, I am satisfied that my heart was so near my teeth that it was in danger of leaving me altogether, and I am quite sure that my nervousness must have been painfully apparent to everyone in the audience. The warm reception given the company and the kindly welcome accorded me did much to dissipate this nervousness, and I entered in to the work of the second act with much more confidence than I did the first. I was painfully self-conscious, embarrassingly mindful of the audience and its applause, and it was not until the beginning of the finale of the second act that I became so interested in the opera as to utterly disregard the manner of its reception.

When all the characters were singing at the top of their voices and the trumpeters emerging from the wing blew their very souls into the instruments and the fanfare of the horns mingled with the martial rattle of the drums behind me, the limelight and footlights glared in my eyes, while through this burst of light I saw a sea of upturned faces. A quick glance around the crowded auditorium revealed the fact that the house was pleased, and the tumultuous applause that greeted Mr. Herbert's music roared up from the orchestra seats and down from the gallery through the strains of the orchestra, affecting me in a most peculiar manner.

While conscious that I was singing with all my might and strength, I was doing so without any physical effort. The blood tingled through my veins, little cold shivers crept up and down my back, my temples throbbed and my heart beat like a trip-hammer stroke that seemed likely to cause serious results. It seemed as though my costume was too small for me, and I was possessed of a desire to do something, to shout, to almost leap into the audience, and I am satisfied that had it not been for the relief gained by singing I should not have been able to finish the act. When it was all over and the curtain went up and down, up and down, again and again, in response to the vociferous demands of the people, and Mr. Herbert came forward and conducted the march once more, I retired to my dressing room in a condition closely bordering on collapse.

The long wait necessary for the changing of costumes and setting of scenes revived me enough to get through with the third act, and I reached my hotel after the performance more dead than alive. After retiring sleep was an impossibility.

I was flattered and delighted with the reception given *The Fortune Teller*, and one would naturally suppose that all anxiety had departed, but such was not the case. I could not help thinking of that critic who, while suffering from an attack of indigestion, had gone down to his office, poured a spoonful or two of Tabasco sauce and a half pinto of vitriol into his inkstand, jabbed his pen clear down through the bottom of it and written, 'what right has she to star; what excuse is there for this great and fashionable gathering at Wallack's; her voice is not as good as Patti's and the book does not compare with the libretto of *Faust*, and I seemed to see these things in cold type, in big black lines, and reasoned with myself, if this view is taken of my humble efforts by everyone there will soon be no new stars, no new companies, and although I went to sleep with the full determination of not rising until noon the sun had not made his appearance over the roofs of the houses on the opposite side of the street before I found myself pulling aside the curtains and ringing vigorously for the morning papers.

I got them and so did you, and you know the result.

Very thankfully yours, Alice Nielsen.

The Stage, a monthly, produced a pithy overview of the theatrical world: "In the last week of September *The Fortune Teller* pitched her tent at Wallack's, and it was speedily discovered that there would be naught but good luck for her sponsors, librettist Smith and composer Victor Herbert. Alice Nielsen, in swinging out into space as a star, was careful to surround herself with capable support. There was a trio of comedians who were really funny, Joe Herbert, Richard Golden, and Joseph Cawthorn. There was also the bass of the many admirers, carried off bodily from the Bostonians, Eugene Cowles. And in the modest part of *Vaninka*, the gipsy girl, there was a player who was to write her name high in no less a house than Daly's before the trees budded—Marcia Van Dresser, the *Countess Charkoff* of *The Great Ruby*".

NY Times (Se 27) columnist "LAJ" waxes ironic: "What the Bostonians think of Frank Perley's success. It must please them. They must be as tickled to death as a man who drops into a cistern with his dress suit on. Perley did a good deal more for the Bostonians than the Bostonians ever did for Perley, and I have a faint suspicion that Mr. Henry Clay Barnabee and his fellow singers are finding this out to their sorrow".

Week past opening, October 2, *Times* publishes a photo of the female leads, Nielsen and Sylva: "The old adage that nothing succeeds like success was never more forcibly confirmed than...last week when the star, the opera, and the company were greeted with such rounds of applause as to leave room for a suspicion that old conventional first night methods were being used and the European claque system worked. This evidently was not the case, as the business of the rest of the week was regulated by the capacity of the theatre at all the performances...."

Except Tuesday nights and the matinee, Wallacks stays All Sold Out.

Chicago Tribune (Oct 2) agrees "Miss Alice Nielsen in the leading role, was a great success when presented last Monday at Wallack's".

At this point the oddity Max Desci resumes his peculiar publicity ploy, suing Nielsen over supposed $720 fees for "music lessons given between February 1890 and July 1891". He takes credit for her voice, giving address for potential students as "10 W. 26th".

Nielsen responds, "I suppose it's the custom for everyone who becomes an operatic star to be sued. I call this very unjust on the part of Mr. Desci, and I'll tell you how it happened. Some seven years ago I was in Kansas City. Mr. Desci was getting up a production of an opera [1891's *Beggar Student*] which he had written himself [confuses with *Chanticlere*], and I, with a number of others, was engaged to appear in it. Mr. Desci instructed us to sing his score, and that was all the instruction I ever got from him.

"Anyhow, I was engaged to receive that instruction at so much per week, and I may add that I have never been paid by Desci for appearing in his work. If I do not bother him for money that he owes me, why should he bother me for money I do not owe him? Now there's a question in law for you. I suppose Desci thinks that because I am successful as a star it will be an easy thing for him to get some money. Well, I'm not as foolish as all that. He seems to make a point of the fact that I was married to Mr. Nentwig. All the world knows that, and I am not denying it".

Desci claims he taught a child of Denmark and Donegal, precocious minstrel gamine of streets, student of St. Theresa's, soloist of dual St. Patricks, tutored by grand opera star Valerga: how to sing.

Desci wife sues after he leaves her penniless in Manhattan. Desci (Fargo ND) "noted baritone and teacher of music in Kansas City...alleges cruelty and cites names and instances where his wife is said to have treated both himself and his pupils in a cruel and unbecoming manner.

Mrs. Desci puts an entirely different light on this. She alleges Desci broke into her trunk, relieving her of all her money while in NY and left her penniless, she being obliged to secure a position as a servant girl and that by this menial labor" returned to Missouri.

Alice more happily is stalked by endorsement offers. She appears in ads for coconut hair oil and brewer's yeast. Soon she endorses pianos, electric cars. A Nielsen cigarette card may exist, traded like today's baseball cards.

Now she is often interviewed. October 23, *Telegraph's* drama reporter visits Nielsen at hotel Gilsey House, 29th and Broadway, a choice residence of Mark Twain, Diamond Jim Brady, Oscar Wilde and others. Wallack's was a block north. The feature reveals her personality. Nielsen turns tables on the journalist asking him many questions. He tells readers, she "came here from Japan, devoted six weeks to rehearsals and then took a warming-up canter through the provinces for two weeks, returned to the city and...scored a success instantaneous and pronounced".

"That success causes success, and that nothing succeeds like it, has caused Miss Nielsen to be inundated with applications to endorse tooth powders, nerve strengtheners, sealskin sacks, hoopskirts and last but not least, a patent back action automatic teething ring and baby rattle combined, and an electric motor powered baby carriage...."

Nielsen interrupts. "I'm not being interviewed here, you're being interviewed. When I received your card I saw a capital opportunity to gratify the curiosity that every member of my sex undoubtedly has by asking you a lot of questions.

"Now confidentially, which of my costumes do you like the best?" When her victim confesses admiration for "the dark green train dress in the third act was unbounded, the little prima donna uncoiled herself, slid out of the armchair and actually doubled up with laughter". She replies, "Why I don't wear even a green ribbon, feather or button. My costumes are all of the other colors, but no green. Mind you, I don't object to the color. There's a little national sentiment connected with it I can't forget. I wear a shamrock instead of a clover leaf for good luck—it's in the blood you know".

Alice resumes, "Now, how on earth do you manage to find out all the theatre news you print from day to day?" Reporter tells. Then, "Oh well, how about the racing news?" Giving up, reporter "seized his hat and slowly but surely worked his way toward the door...diplomatically waited for a pause in the volley of questions and when it came...managed to get in a 'Thank you very much, good afternoon', and departed".

Tables turned by mischievous diva. Her cultural import goes national.

Los Angeles starts; Chicago picks it up: this new Nielsen-Herbert duo must create The Great America Musical. October 9, *LA Times* unveils the great national artistic anticipation. Regarding her show "upon its initial performance in the metropolis last week" *LA* approvingly quotes America's oldest paper (founded by Daniel Webster), *New York Commercial Advertiser* soon renamed *The Sun*: "A new opera by Victor Herbert and Harry B. Smith is something to be looked forward to with mingled certainty and suspense—certainty that it will be at least worth hearing, and suspense because of a lurking suspicion that the new piece may prove 'the' American comic opera. The audience had come last night with the evident intention of being pleased. It was evidently more than pleased, and before the evening was half over the performance had become an ovation".

Wordsmith Smith slapped with faint praise, "contributed a very fair book, not strikingly original or fresh, nor up to the standard of Mr. Herbert's music...."

Herbert "first of all a sound musician; but he is more than that: he has versatility and he has humor. And he has been learning gradually to catch the popular ear, and that without sacrificing the more musicianly side of his work. The rhythms are bright and taking. The orchestration is rich and highly colored, yet never bizarre. There are number of delicate pretty songs, several stirring military marches, and some stunning concerted pieces. Mr. Herbert's versatility appears in the imitation of various styles, imitations serious and satirical". Wit peaks in Act Two's *Serenades Of Many Nations'* "imitations of Irish, Spanish, French and Chinese serenades". Give Herbert a star talent, and "Alice Nielsen as a star...was naturally very nervous during the first act, perhaps because Mr. Herbert was sitting directly in front of her; but her nervousness wore off as the performance went on, and she was able to do herself justice. Miss Nielsen's chief charm lies in her singing. She is besides, very comely to look upon but she cannot act yet".

Others praise Nielsen's acting: note the naturalness of her technique.

Under the Bostonians, Nielsen sang five shows a week. Now eight. Her endurance legendary. Valerga's *bel canto* plus native energy, only perfect technique survives heavy use.

They leaves NYC to meet the pre-arranged bookings. October 29 they close after forty performances. Theatre managers nationwide plead for longer stays. Why so short? DeWolf Hopper's *Once a Clown, Always a Clown* (1927) looks back. NYC wasn't the center: "Hundreds of actors of the first rank did not play New York at all, or for no longer than a week or two in a season. The road was the theater and the theater the road until about 1910".

The NY cast is 120, seventy tour. They book 38,000 miles in trains September to May. Orchestra of thirty shrinks to dozen in small towns.

November 7th *Fortune Teller* opens Philadelphia at Chestnut Street. In cast and crew: J. Lawless joins crew, Paul Nicholson the players.

Philadelphia Inquirer (Nov 8) "A new comic opera and a new comic opera company were introduced to Philadelphians last night. There was a new prima donna, too—Miss Alice Nielsen—but she was so different from the average stars that her brilliancy was somewhat enshrouded. Instead of the dignified, self-important behavior which one naturally expected, there was the madcap, boisterous sort of a girl that is only noticeable in the soubrette of a few years ago. Last season she was, for a long time, prima donna of the Bostonians, but while the company was playing here Miss Nielsen was ill, and did not appear.

"Her local debut last night must have been gratifying to herself and her manager, for the audience was kindly disposed and at the close of the first act insisted upon having the regulation speech. Miss Nielsen murmured sweetly her thanks and the performance went on.

"First honors...must be given to Mr. Victor Herbert...he has eclipsed all former endeavors. The encores last night prolonged the performance until quite a late hour". Ensemble shares rare glory: "seldom that the chorus and ensemble numbers are rewarded with two and three encores".

Words place last. "Mr. Smith's libretto is scarcely in keeping with the score. His story is confusing and incoherent, dealing with banal personages that are not sufficiently differentiated to appear quite clear to the audience without deep study. His [sic] lines however are bright and the humor flows easily...to keep up a constant ripple of laughter". So soon after New York, the text had been recreated by the three comedians, also lacing into the show vaudeville bits they had liked and perhaps originated, going contemporary with wit.

In the cast: Richard Golden "plenty to do"; "Cawthorn, with his concertina, fresh from the vaudevilles". Comics join Nielsen and Sylva to "devote a goodly portion of act second to the introduction of vaudeville turns, not forgetting the cakewalk. This took the house by storm, and was really one of the greatest hits of the evening". Eugene Cowles "not called upon to do much, though what little he did do was in polished style. Frank Rushworth [tenor] and Marguerite Sylva did excellently, the chorus...composed of unusually pretty young women, the costumes were pretty and the staging beautiful".

Contra New York, acting is her best: "Miss Nielsen herself is perhaps more clever in acting than she is gifted in vocal accomplishments. Her voice is not of extraordinary range nor is it of great volume, but she makes up for this by her chic and vivacious mannerisms".

Inevitably, a grand reunion. In Philly when Alice arrive the Bostonians are at Broad Street five miles away. Past disputes? Cordiality resumes; they invite themselves to Nielsen's suite to party. Happily for us, Frank Perley recalls, "One of the most startling and weird incidents I have ever witnessed, and which was received as the very antithesis of the invocation of good luck intended, took place in the Walton Hotel, Philadelphia...."

Bostonians join Alice for "a congratulatory supper on the great success she had scored". As you may recall, Bostonian's Alice substitute was Helen Bertram whose husband EJ Henly "one of our most gifted actors" had recently died. Cremated. His wife Helen "as a testimony of her devotion... enclosed his ashes in a chamois bag and wore them in her bosom".

Stage set, continues Perley, "a more congenial circle of friends, too, never put their feet under the mahogany than gathered round the elaborately-set table in Miss Nielsen's suite about midnight after the opening performance, and good fellowship and conviviality held high carnival until well into the 'wee sma' hours', the last of which was marked by that mellowness which unmasks formality—and, in current slang, encourages those present to 'tell their real names.' Effervescing with that spirit of prodigality...as well as responding to an irresistible impulse to make some supreme expression of the sincerity of her protestations of friendship, Miss Bertram halted the festivities and dramatically pulled poor Henley's unsuspecting remains from her bosom".

Holding the pouch aloft, Helen says "Alice, Ted always liked you. And I'm giving you some of his ashes for luck".

From the chamois casket spills "some portion of Ted's incinerated anatomy on the carpeted floor of Miss Nielsen's room. It was then the hour spooks walk, Banshees wail and graveyards yawn, and as Miss Nielsen came from fine old Irish stock on her mother's side and inherited the temperamental attributes of the Danes from her father, superstitious reverence was hers by divine right, and what she did not receive that way she had had opportunity to annex after becoming a thespian. Miss Bertram's mortuary contribution therefore was about all that was needed to add zest to the occasion, and surely none of Macbeth's famous witches could have cast a more uncanny spell. Hilarity was hushed into oppressive silence and the expressions of horror and surprise on the faces of some of those present baffled description. It was necessary to change Miss Nielsen's rooms, notwithstanding the lateness of the hour, but even then the 'Goddess of Sleep' was not easy to woo, for when ghosts of the departed feel like taking a 'constitutional', they laugh at bolted doors.... Miss Nielsen deeply appreciated the sacrifice involved in her friend's unusual effort to propitiate for her the fairies of fortune, but sober reflection the following day left no doubt of its having been 'Love's labor lost.'"

Returning to earth and Washington, a great success awaits Nielsen troupers at Lafayette Square. "Best in town turned out" to find the gayety of nations. Washington records an Alice moment retold across the nation many times.

Appears Nov. 22nd *Washington Post*: "Alice Nielsen... achieved a triumph in a sense beyond the conventional meaning of that hackneyed phrase. The audience she faced last night was not of a sort to accept any second-hand dictum...the highest-grade audience the little woman has yet shone before, for the best in town turned out to see *The Fortune Teller* and to take note whether little Alice Nielsen, who used to sing small parts with the Bostonians in a very sweet, bell-like voice, had really taken on the radiance the metropolitan critics have been ascribing to her".

Alice Nielsen, talent genius.

"Miss Nielsen had been on the stage last evening for fully three minutes before the whisper went round that she was possessed of talent. Before the descent of the curtain of the first act the audience had arrived at the conviction that she is endowed with genius. And after that it was all very easy for her, and enthusiasm and occasion waited upon her every tone and movement—even when she kicked a strapping hussar on the shins". *Post* compares Nielsen favorably to famed Lotta Crabtree, another California arrival.

Music "rollicking, melodious, tender, snappy, descriptive and—especially at the climaxes preceding the curtains—even inspiring. Herbert seems to betray more musical ambition in each of his successive operas, and his work is liable to lose its ephemeral character as his power grows upon him. Certainly there are in the comic opera under consideration, many themes that would not seem out of place in more serious music.

In the "very large" cast: "there is not an unsatisfactory performer on the bill. Chorus is particularly worthy of mention. The opera is tastefully and sumptuously staged, and the orchestra is thoroughly capable".

Others list notables attending. *Washington Times*: "For nearly three hours and a half last night an audience which filled the Lafayette literally to suffocation watched dainty Alice Nielsen and her excellent company pirouette.... In this audience were such celebrities as [British ambassador] Sir Julian Pauncefote, Secretary of State Hay, Secretary of Agriculture [James] Wilson, Secretary of the Navy Long, Postmaster General Smith, Attorney General Griggs, Solicitor General Richards, Comptroller of the Treasury Dawes, Asst. Secretary of the Navy Allen, Asst. Secretary of War Meiklejohn, [Chinese] Minister Wu Ting-fang, Gen. Miles, Gen. Corbin, Gen. Townsend, [Secretary] John Addison Porter, Henry Clay Evans and many others".

More than soda water, "During the long duration of the opera several persons in the house developed strong thirsts and went out, but all returned in due time, and by increased enthusiasm signified that nothing in the production had caused their apparent dryness".

Knock Harry Smith: "There seems to have been no more reason for calling Mr. Smith's story *The Fortune Teller* than knighting a canary bird, but this little matter occasions no comment.... The author has not written anything newer than usual in his libretto and many of his jokes sound too ancient to be considered even original...." Even plagiarizes himself: "Mr. Smith has not only the habit of constantly repeating his books, as Mr. DeKoven does his music, but in addition he seems to improve with every effort. The result is that he has in the present entertainment episodes out of a line of prior presentations ranging from *Robin Hood* to *Idol's Eye*".

Herbert by contrast, inspired, playful virtuoso who recalls the best Donizetti and Verdi while taking aim at Sousa. "But the music! In this score Mr. Herbert has not only outdone himself by nearly everyone else who ever established a standard to be surpassed. He has composed catchy airs and dainty ballads and glorious ensembles, together with...a choral climax that reminds one of the school in which Donizetti died and Verdi was born; a closing march that has all the swing of a Sousa masterpiece; and a combination of melodies that permits of one leaving the theatre with a completely new stock of whistling material. He has produced military quick-steps for the brass instruments; quaint waltzes for the stringed ones and topical songs for the reeds".

Serenades of Many Nations appreciated. "This wonderful man has shown at once his versatility and depth by using a strange knowledge of color in national music to bring out a collection of the most characteristic gems in the world—Italian, French, Spanish, Ethiopian and even Chinese, finally throwing all into insignificance with a Hungarian 'czardas' in which are combined the wild weird movements of a barbarous race with something of what empowered refinement notable in two or three of Liszt's rhapsodies. There has never been heard in this city a score that comes within sight of that in *The Fortune Teller*. The music is full of charm and grace, of novelty and originality. It is inspired and inspiring".

Toss egg? Fuddy-duddy Bostonians: "Nielsen herself does not appear to have lost anything by leaving that organization of musical antiquities, The Bostonians".

Washington Star: "Audience of such large proportions and containing so many men and women prominent and distinguished in official and social circles as that which gathered in the Lafayette Opera House last night has seldom assembled, even in this city of such things". To the above list add "Captain Dickins of the Navy, Major Hiestand of the Army, all accompanied by parties, while the Metropolitan Club seemed to have been temporarily deserted to judge by its well-known members present".

Nielsen's declaration of artistic liberty hailed, eggs at Bostonians: "There was more in her, however, than the antiquated Bostonians could see, or rather she was too handsome, too bright, too good a singer and too magnetic to be allowed to remain in that organization, and Manager Perley with his usually keen perceptions realized that if he got the proper vehicle for the little woman there was money in her. The result has shown the correctness of his judgment. Miss Nielsen has won her way in to popular favor in every city in which she has appeared. She has an attractive personality and seemingly enjoys her own performance as much as her audience does".

Acts, dances, sings: "She throws her whole soul into her work—likewise her sole, for she is a lively dancer—and there is every evidence of her sincerity. She has not a big voice [perforce *bel canto*], but it is fresh, with remarkable carrying power, and has been highly cultivated. She is a great 'go' and deserves all the success that has come to her".

In the cast: Cowles, rare mixed note, his "popularity was demonstrated by...applause which followed his every song. He stands unique as the possessor of the most noble natural organ ever put in a man's throat, but with little knowledge of how to intelligently use it". Chorus petite, shapely, "sings as good as it looks, and that is saying a good deal".

Alice sings at White House again, decade after first.

Guided by First Lady, Nov. 24 (*Washington Post*), "The bright particular star of the Alice Nielsen company...invited by Mrs. McKinley to call at the White House, which invitation she accepted. After the introductions to several ladies present, Miss Nielsen was shown through the private apartments. On their return to the sitting room, Mrs. McKinley asked Miss Nielsen to sing".

Alice chose *Annie Laurie.* President McKinley and "several members of the Cabinet" appear in the doorway. *Swanee River* next. McKinley and wife attend *Fortune Teller* that night.

In 1898 Washington, Nielsen Company cut an original cast recording with Emil Berliner's new machine, arguably the first. They record *Opening Chorus, Always Do as People Say You Should, Finale to Second Act* with Paul Steindorf on the piano. Only Nielsen recordings of Victor Herbert songs! Nielsen's next recordings are 1908 with Victor Label and Boston Symphony players.

Nov. 26 *NY Telegram* offers Nielsen portraits in costumes and street gear, "most magnificent sealskin coat in America". *Outing* monthly, Alice "fortunate in starting her starring with...*Fortune Teller.* Very dapper Miss Nielsen looked in the second finale [grand march] brandishing her sword in the uniform of the Red Hussars".

Nielsen Company tours to Chicago where Bostonians *Serenade* with Helen Bertram at Powers' New Theatre. Dec. 13, *Chicago Tribune* contrasts stars and shows. Nielsen can make anything interesting. Chicago salutes her acting.

"Miss Bertram has a voice much above the average usually reached in comic opera and she knows how to use it. As an actress she cannot fill Miss Alice Nielsen's place because she has no notion of the soubrette style, and the part of Yvonne distinctly leans in that direction.... Story is of no account anyhow and the audience simply goes to hear the music which is exceedingly bright.... The performance is at best half-an-hour too long, which is almost inexcusable for an opera in its third season". Worse, the text. Harry Smith and the Bostonians make "for a serious form of comic opera in which merriment is rather frowned upon. It is a pity that so much time is wasted in trying not to be funny". *Fortune Teller* was saved by improvising lines and skits.

Amid success storm clouds appear. When Alice Nielsen appears at Chicago January 1899, Tom Williams meets her with marriage on his Oakland mind.

Only manager Perley can protect her. Can he be trusted?

1899: TOURING NORTH AMERICA

Metropolitan Magazine for January publishes an Alice Nielsen pictorial by Jacob Schloss at 23rd Street NYC. That Alice sang *Serenade* in Chicago is civic pride.

The process of announcing the Nielsen event in Chicago was typical.

January 8th *Tribune* announces "There will be a new comic opera at the Columbia tomorrow night when Miss Alice Nielsen makes her first appearance in Chicago as a star. It hardly requires the fertile imaginations of the advance agent [publicity] to arouse interest in the appearance of Miss Nielsen.... everyone will remember the occasion when she made her Chicago debut two years ago at the Columbia with the Bostonians".

Tribune cannot resist egging San Francisco: "She came almost direct from the Tivoli in San Francisco, which in itself was hardly a great recommendation, yet she almost immediately asserted her claims to recognition among the foremost comic opera prime donne of the American stage, and when a week or two later [year or two] she took the principal part in *The Serenade* her position was secured".

Tribune relates she created a sensation among European opera celebrities with *Serenade* which "coincided with the grand opera season at the Auditorium. Boxes at the Columbia were occupied by many of the great operatic stars who were off-duty. Lassalle was there and Plançon, not to speak of Ancona and Mancincilli, and when Miss Nielsen came to the end of the waltz song in *The Serenade*, they absolutely refused to let her leave the stage until she had repeated the air some half a dozen times".

Baritone Jean Lassalle and basso Pol Plançon were top Grau stars at the Met Opera which annually toured Chicago.

Nielsen inspires Lassalle: "Next day it was announced that Lassalle had purchased the French rights of *The Serenade*. Without doing the composer an injustice, it may be assumed that Miss Nielsen's singing had as much to do with the purchase as Mr. Herbert's music".

Egg for Smith: "Possibly Mr. Smith may have been inspired by the advent of a new star to get out of the rut into which he some time ago subsided".

Chicago confirms Alice Nielsen as the top musical star. Without hesitation, "Lillian Russell, glorious beauty that she has been, is now and doubtless will be for many years to come, must hand the palm to this slight young actress with a voice of velvet such as Lillian never had and never can have. Jessie Davis must admit the superiority now, even more plainly than... when they sang together in the Bostonians".

The reason freely stated is profound: "Why? Because Miss Nielsen can both sing and act, a combination rarely found in a musical comedy star. All her humorous scenes are done in a delicate, manner that accentuates the wit of the lines and added to the effectiveness of the situation".

Lillian Russell's daughter avoids naming names: "Young female performers now tended to be petite, thin and dark-haired with a zest and vitality that radiated strongly from the stage". Lillian, an Alice friend, skips to lucrative vaudeville scenes. Deal struck at—Belmont racetrack—near her Far Rockaway summer house, Russell joins Weber and Fields to headline at $3,000 weekly (1898!), belting four pop songs twice a night.

By Chicago superlatives, Nielsen leads the best show ever produced.

Chicago Tribune: "*Fortune Teller* is the by far the best comic opera...in the last three years. Indeed, if *The Belle of New York* which really belongs to a different category, is excepted, there has been no combination of music and farce in the last few years which can compare with this bright medley either for its musical qualities or the cleverness of the presentation".

Tribune sifts creative team and performers: "*Serenade* comes nearest to the present work, and it is rather curious that Mr. Smith, Mr. Herbert and Miss Nielsen were jointly responsible for the success of that one, as they are for this one. The only difference is that *The Serenade* was written for the good Bostonians and the comic element was of necessity mottled; moreover the composer remembered that he was writing for ...ballad singers and made few attempts in the direction of operatic music".

With Nielsen on the boards, Herbert bests Sullivan: "Herbert has let himself go, and the result is that he has achieved by far the best results of his career. Not only is the score full of tuneful melodies which cannot fail to be popular, but the orchestration and ensemble writing are worthy of the best school of comic opera writing. Sir Arthur Sullivan himself never did anything better than the finale of the first act, and it might even be whispered, few things as good. The choruses are also exceptionally profuse in number and full of swing" giving "as good opportunities to the chorus as to the soloists".

Herbert was "not overburdened with originality...finale of the second act with the brass band on the stage and the flags all flying is nothing but undiluted Sousa, yet the audience howled with delight, and then of course there was the inevitable cake walk, which had to be repeated until Miss Nielsen was out of breath. But what else can a composer do when the public insists on going crazy at the suggestion of a cakewalk?

"And so, leaving the imitations out of the question, Mr. Herbert's work may be set down as praiseworthy in every direction. It abounds in good tunes, the ensembles are clever, musicianly and always inspiring".

Tribune realized libretto shreds and patches, cast-improvised: "Of the book it would be rash to speak too highly, because it has been cut to pieces in the most remarkable way since the opera was produced, and it is difficult to say now how much should be credited to Mr. Harry B. Smith and how much to the comedians of the company".

Telling the plot "would be unnecessary even if it were possible...no one could understand it". Significantly *Tribune* adds, "and it has nothing to do with the success of the piece".

Skip plot: "It is more important to relate that Miss Nielsen appears first in a French gray costume, neatly made; next in gypsy guise over which she wears, later on, a tea gown. In the second act she comes in richly attired, as to the trailing skirt, in white satin, with a pink dressing jacket in place of a bodice. She then dons a hussar uniform and appears in dazzling, cherry-colored array, which gives an added effect to the Sousa march that closes the second act".

Chicago highlights Alice: "Of her voice it is hard to speak too highly. Her voice is as fresh as ever in spite of the fact that she uses it unsparingly, and it is to beautifully flexible that she can attack almost anything from an operatic air to a coon song. Her singing, in fact, is the most charming part of the whole performance. And that is to say a good deal. One would like to say as much of her acting, because she herself is so young and full of life and enjoys everything she does so much that the audience cannot fail to enter into her good spirits".

Tribune makes the superb gesture: Nielsen's gayety brings the show a feeling only matched by the very best grand opera gala, "She reminds one strongly in fact, of Sig. Carbone and Sig. Campanari in *The Barber Of Seville* when these two artists enjoyed their own work so much that they literally compelled the audience to laugh with them. For that reason, the voice of cold criticism is apt to be silenced in the presence of Miss Nielsen, otherwise one would be inclined to say that her manners are a trifle aggressive and she evidently has not forgotten the old days at the Tivoli in San Francisco".

Egg the Bostonians: "But it must be such a relief for this buoyant young woman to be free from the fetters of the Bostonians and away from the cold gray eye of Barnabee, that her romping may be to some measure excused".

Alice: "not, perhaps, a finished comedienne but she has an amount of spirit which is quite indescribable and at times almost awe-inspiring".

Profoundly *Chicago Tribune*: Alice is youth itself, "terrible to think of anyone being so young".

In the cast: comedians and the tenor sing not well. If Golden adorns as comic "pity he cannot sing". Cawthorn funny, "sadly marred by his persistent inability to sing in tune...at times absolutely excruciating.

Possibly he had the grip [a cold] and will improve as the week goes on". Of tenor "even the grip hardly would excuse...indifferent as any comic opera singer could be". "Pleasing on the other hand, to find in Miss Marguerite Sylva a French soubrette with an exceedingly good voice and a vivacious manner. The chorus was young, good-looking and well trained and the costumes were all that could be desired".

Passing the four gates (New York, Philly, DC, Chicago), Nielsen Company continues its 1898-99 North American Tour as Perley arranges their next new show. January 19 (*NY Times*), he "closed arrangements with George W. Lederer" at NY's Casino theatre. Lederer, casting a company with Marie Dressler and closing *La Belle Helene*, is "the man who invented Broadway". Lederer had sent huge hit *Belle of New York* to George Musgrove at London's Shaftesbury....

Harry Smith, relegated to lyrics. Stanislaus Stange will create "the speaking libretto. As each gentleman is a specialist in his line, one may reasonably anticipate a book worthy of the music...something that unfortunately could not be said of *The Fortune Teller*". For the star Alice, "Possessed of an undeniably attractive personality, endowed with lyric soprano voice of lovely quality, and being without doubt the best singer among comic opera prima donni of the day, her triumph in any role that she assumes is pretty much a foregone conclusion. When we consider that several years ago she was unknown in opera, her success has been marvelous, and as someone said: 'As a star, they rather fancy Miss Nielsen has come to stay.'"

In *Fortune Teller*, "As the gypsy she was effeminate and youthful, as the heiress ballet girl full of good humor, frolic and refinement; as her own brother...neat a little tin soldier as ever wore shapely red tights".

"Given free reign, the comics create a skit poking fun at librettist Smith writing a clichéd "comique opera". Richard Golden as ballet-master "very entertaining... feet as well as his tongue are exceedingly active in a movement which, if it was his tongue, would be called stuttering. Marguerite Sylva played a diva professing love for every man she meets"— sly satire on Lillian Russell.

Yet "Marcia van Dresser has a part less than her talent". Dresser (1880-1937) deserves a glance. From Memphis, Tennessee. Studies voice with NYC's Mrs. Sarah Robinson-Duff, trained by Marchesi. Robinson-Duff will coach Mary Garden, Hermine Bosetti, Jean DeReszke, and Alice Nielsen. Dresser also drops Bostonians for Nielsen Company, joining the Met Opera 1903 with European concerts 1908-1914 then Chicago Opera then London. Dresser and Nielsen, two Tennessee singers, cross to grand opera.

Scant months from September debut, the big critics ponder What Next.

For *Dramatic Magazine* (Jan 1899), Will Davis attended Nielsen at Chicago's Columbia Theatre. Plainly, "no theatrical entertainment recently produced has met with more praise or prosperity than *The Fortune Teller* as interpreted by Alice Nielsen and her superb Company". Audience pack her theatres, she sells more tickets than Lillian Russell, a new milestone in American theatre.

Pundits grapple with the mystery. What makes a great musical?

Consider the quandary, as guided by *Chicago Tribune* (Jan 15). Nielsen's present success is "one of the events of American theatrical history". Ask yourself, "Why does *The Fortune Teller*, which only played six weeks in NY, get such good notices, when other comic operas which have run for months in the East get nothing but perfunctory praise?

"Moreover, when you have been clamoring for years for certain things on the stage and they are suddenly produced... you feel inclined to expatiate upon the same. Mr. Perley began the season with a new star, a new company and a new opera; consequently when he booked his route he thought he was rash in setting aside six weeks for New York". The big fat hit show could stay almost indefinitely in any town. Toronto proved it a winner, "but it was too late then to make the change". Chicago "would gladly shelve everything if the present engagement could be lengthened. So long runs in NY have little to do with the question of merit".

Tribune assesses the show as "the third great comic opera ever to appear. It must be remembered that good comic operas are about as rare as roses in wintertime. In the whole history of the American stage there have been about three...which really came up to the requirements. Easy enough to say that a good composer and a good comedian can secure success for any comic opera. The trouble lies exactly in finding the composer and the comedian".

Significantly, Victor Herbert "not only writes good music in every sense of the word, but his score has the bright, scintillating freshness which is the peculiar hallmark of this style of composition. His powers of mimicry for instance, are most unusual. Mr. Herbert does not merely make use of a French chanson, a Hungarian czardas, an Irish melody or a coon song, but he actually composes them himself, and each is as characteristic as if had been lifted bodily out of its supposed environment". If he borrows, "he rarely fails to embellish it".

"Good music...requires good singers". Alice Nielsen Company is not quite "perfect...but...where the voices are inadequate [tenor, comics] there is a laughable attempt to sing the music instead of butchering it. A company which has Miss Nielsen, Miss Sylva and Mr. Cowles among the principals, to say nothing of good voices in minor parts, is far about average". Singing songs was not sufficient: "The player must have the comic opera spirit, which is almost indefinable for it does not necessarily imply the ordinary powers of the comedian to raise a laugh".

Chicago's *Tribune* "Nielsen is not a comedienne in the usual sense of the word, because she has never yet learned to act. She does not in fact need to act, as long as she can be so entirely herself on the stage. But she has the comic opera habit developed in the highest degree. Apart from her voice, which is almost perfect for its purpose, she has abundance of dash, abandon and good humor". At dance she "does not appear to have studied the art of dancing much, yet she is so nimble and so light on her feet that she almost gives one the impression that she is a skilled dancer.

To sing her part "is far more difficult and more arduous than a great many parts which fall to stars in grand opera. Compared to it, the title part in *Martha* or in *Bohemian Girl* is mere child's play; yet besides singing, Miss Nielsen is on the stage during three-fourths of the performance and is working hard all the time". Simply put, she does what nobody else can do. Without appearing to act.

"Her fascination of course lies in the fact that she is abnormally young, and not merely in years but in temperament—and to keep up the mock heroic, fairylike atmosphere of comic opera you must be young and irresponsible". In other words, her wonderful acting carries the show.

She will sing "a long time, if she will only give her voice a chance. No grand opera singer would dare to undertake a part like Miss Nielsen's in *The Fortune-Teller* seven times a week".

Subsequently, perhaps Ida Valerga as touring companion, Nielsen begins to resist singing matinees.

Chicago's briefing on the Great American Musical closes: "Lastly comes the confessedly comic element. That there is no more of it in *Fortune Teller* is entirely the fault of Mr. Harry Smith". Cawthorn, Herbert, Golden, "any one of whom" would be tops at comedy. "In *The Bride-Elect*...there was no one so good; in... *The Idol's Eye* or *El Capitan* there is one comedian who has to carry the whole performance...and his work naturally gets hard and metallic before the evening is over". And here, director Mitchell has the comic trio "subordinated to the general effect...." This trio has done "what Mr. Smith should have done, but didn't. It was easy enough to recognize the difference between Mr. Smith's dialog and Mr. Golden's or Mr. Cawthorn's and if the truth must be told, there is still just a little too much of Mr. Smith's. Leave the dialogue entirely to the comedians".

Of course, the Smith "lyrics are not nearly so bad as they might be. Even Mr. Smith cannot make men like Mr. Golden and Mr. Cawthorn entirely dull". This continual chorus of critical discourse proves why no revival of *The Fortune Teller* means anything, proves why Herbert demanded toss away the words, as your author did and discovered this Alice Nielsen saga when his aged agent offered the hint.

Chicago Tribune muses: "Nearly all the requirements are found in *Fortune Teller* as they have seldom been found in any comic opera, outside of the Savoy pieces which have made Gilbert and Sullivan famous. Even the popular *Robin Hood* was more one-sided, for there the music was everything and the comedy nothing". Let Victor Herbert join WS Gilbert for a new Alice Nielsen show.

Perley has plans for London with Lederer and Musgrove. America's best composer needs Gilbert "the only real librettist". Nielsen's London run will "make a bridge between Herbert and Gilbert". *Chicago Tribune* concludes, "If there ever was an American production which should succeed in London it is *The Fortune Teller*. Miss Nielsen could not fail to make a hit, especially at this moment, when everything American is greeted with applause".

Nielsen reaches St. Louis (Jan 24) to make a statement about racial equality which rockets into front page news for weeks. After opening night, Planters' Hotel denies elevator access for Nielsen's black aide Geraldina White. Alice protests. Thirty-five years ago the Civil War had ended after many deaths including Alice's father. Unable to change hotel policy, tired from her three-hour hit show, Alice insists to relocate to the Southern.

New York Times reports Nielsen's stance, saying the Southern Hotel "would make an exception in this case" to let Geraldina White share the elevator. *Grand Forks Herald* (ND Fe 17) gives details: "Alice Nielsen... quit the Planters' hotel, St. Louis, abruptly the other morning, or rather late at night, because her maid, Geraldina White (colored) was not allowed to ride in the passenger elevator. No negroes are employed at this hotel and under no circumstances is one permitted to ride in the passenger elevators. The opera singer evidently was not aware of this when she took apartments there, for when she entered the elevator she beckoned to her maid to follow. There were other guests in the car. The conductor refused to allow the negress to enter.

"Miss Nielsen was angry. She went straight to Manager Weaver, who informed her that the conductor was right. The young woman stormed about awhile, then walked up to the desk, paid her bill and went over to the Southern".

Clara Kellogg had a similar scene in 1870s, "I shall never forget the battle royal I once had with a hotel manager on the road in regard to my coloured maid, Eliza. She was a very nice and entirely presentable girl and he would not let her have even a cup of tea in the dining-room. We had had a long, hard journey, and she was quite as tired as the rest of us. So, when I found her still waiting after I had lunched, I made a few pertinent remarks to the effect that her presence at the table was much to be preferred to the men who had eaten there without table manners, uncouth, feeding themselves with their knives. 'And what else did we have the war for!' I finally cried. How the others laughed at me. But Eliza was fed, and well fed, too". Eliza "was a good traveler and a good maid". Overseas, "She was also very popular in that part of the world. Negroes had no particular stigma attached to them on the Continent. So, wherever we went, my good, dark-skinned Eliza was a real belle".

Similar divas, similar regards.

Nielsen opens Omaha. *World Herald* (Feb. 9) marks "first engagement here of the dainty, delightful prima donna" who "demonstrated the possibilities of the operatic stage when sought and zealously labored for by genius, supplemented by great personal attractiveness. Never has any songstress stepped so easily and so happily ...to that of an operatic star of the first magnitude, and do so with a new opera, of which she has made an unconditional success. There has been a very heavy advance sale of seats and two unusually large audiences are assured".

When she plays South Bend, Indiana, *Chicago Tribune* (Feb 19) relates "a number of parties" will travel ninety miles including "Solomon Sturges, John Jenks, William Thompson, Messrs. Babock, May, [author George] Ade, Davis, Dupree, McCree...and several others" of Chicago's "aristocratic lineage and high social connections". Fable-fabricator George Ade mentions Alice Nielsen in his popular tales as a woman whose shows make every young man fall in love.

After darting the Midwest, Kansas City.

Kansas City World (Jan 25), how do you feel about homecoming?

"I can truly say that every emotion caused by the prospect is one of extreme pleasure. The happiest days of my life were spent in Kansas City as were many sad ones, but the joy of returning to old faces and old familiar places is unmixed and zest is given to it by a little pride which I think is natural. The fact that my homecoming as a stellar prima donna is a triumphant accomplishment of an ambition which was created and nurtured in Kansas City".

World waxes poetic: "*She was bred in Kansas City, where the Kaw and Muddy meet; 'Midst the hills and limestone ledges, where the air is pure and sweet. She was bred in Kansas City, and, My boy it is a pity, If you fail to reach the box office In time to get a seat.*

Town greets child street singer made great. Alice Nielsen has returned home, "heading her own company in an opera which is the great musical success of the year". She "set so high a standard that there is no competition. With her youth, beauty and marvelous voice, she has a brilliant future before her, and may a cloud never darken it". The town's ovations will "come from those who knew her, who are proud of her and have a personal interest in her future".

Star quotes *St. Louis Dispatch*, Alice "Alice Nielsen is the apotheosis of temperamental adolescence. She is young, younger, youngest. She is aggressively, excessively, insistently, persistently youthful. She may have lived for twenty-eight or thirty years, but she is sixteen and she never will be a day older. She skips about the stage like a school girl and when she sings she simply opens her mouth and the silvery notes pour out".

Coates' Theatre is All Sold Out.

Star backstage: "A child in a red hussar uniform rushed breathlessly into the star dressing room of the Coates' opera house last night. She had been caught in the arms of her maid in the wings, but struggled free and ran, sobbing and laughing, into the dressing room. It was her dressing room. She, in her red hussar uniform, was the star". This audience has given Alice Nielsen seven curtain calls. Now they demand she sing: *Home, Sweet Home*. It was impossible, no one could do it, and the little star had lost her voice.

"'Miss Nielsen—" began the manager.

"'Give me your hat!' cried the star, imperiously. The manager was bewildered. 'Give me your hat!' repeated the star, stamping upon the floor of the dressing room with her little red hussar boot. Placing the opera [top] hat of the astonished manager upon her head, the star whirled in a wild pirouette. The hat came down upon her ears. Red hussar uniform and the manager's high hat were a strange incongruity. The manager laughed in spite of himself. Then the star peeped out from under the engulfing hat and laughed, too. It was a child's way to recover composure. That was the star's homecoming".

Her nerves noted: "When Miss Nielsen made her entrée in the first act, she was nervous and shrank from applause. Her opening song gave her confidence" and came "half-challenging, half-entreating, charmingly whimsical, plaintive and saucy Nielsen smile, which had so many variations, one lovelier than the other". She made her gala full of gayety. "The star and the audience just laughed back and forth...then began an era of good feeling".

The big march went over "with a dash and a crash. Thenceforth the big company and the big audience let joy reign unconfined. Welcoming home a Kansas City star was really delightful".

Clever local reviewers weigh in: "*Fortune Teller* unfolded with lavishness of color and costumes and wealth of sound. Among all that mass of operatic splendor the little star, who acts as a beautiful spoiled child, was the jewel amid the gold". Alice Nielsen's art: artlessly perfect. "The artlessness of the singer won the audience. It rippled in contentment over her little mannerisms and funny little gestures; it beamed under her most sunny smile".

Fooled the hometown audience. "Well—there were chorus costumes fit for leading ladies and deep, changing colors; the audience was warming up; the first act was over—four curtain calls—then a gypsy girl dashed to the footlight and the audience was chagrined that it failed to recognize the star as Musette.

"The star was radiant and happy and the audience was delighted because it could not scare her to death with its applause. The finale brought down the house. Fancy the star doing a cakewalk in white bridal satin, her smiling little face surmounted with fleecy pink laces. Then fancy her as a red hussar. Nielsen as the red hussar was a beautiful spoiled child. She doesn't have to act. All she needs to is sing and smile. Her smiles are worth the acting of ten prima donnas. And then that grand drum corps finale! The audience turned loose its enthusiasm".

Final encores: "A little red hussar bobbed in and out before the curtain—bobbed in and out—and the house thundered on. Would it never rest? At the fifth call, Paul Steindorf, the director [conductor], signaled the orchestra to play *Home Sweet Home* in a minor key. At the seventh call, the full measure of the melody burst out, the audience was hushed and the little red hussar tried to sing. Twice she tried to sing as she used to do in Kansas City years ago, and she couldn't". She gently spoke, "You know I wish to thank you, but I can't find, I can't express the words. From the bottom of my heart, I thank you".

A lifelong night's memory.

Star's elegant critic reflects, "Victor Herbert's music is admirable. He has composed a series of solos, part songs and choruses of infinite variety, beautiful melody and marked originality...with the ingenuity of the true musician".

Noting Harry Smith wrote "about all the comic operas now extant", nothing of story is worth saving. "In *The Fortune Teller* nothing pertaining to the highest class of light opera is lacking, save a thread of a story on which to hang the incidents and to give the characters some relation to one another".

Arts of director Julian Mitchell and the players praised: "But strangely these characters are played so cleverly that they had places for themselves and preserve their own distinctness of outline".

These had reshaped the show to give the music its meaning.

"Without a credible story...the singing and acting...of the company is shown. Miss Nielsen plays three roles, none of which is very clearly defined, and as she had little of the finesse of the art of acting she is not of very much assistance to the lame librettist, but she looks continuously pretty in her many costumes and sings with the freedom of a bird, so who shall deny the potency of the prima donna? The demands upon her voice are numerous and all are met admirably, while Miss Nielsen's personality is so charming that no art is necessary to enhance it. It will be a week of great prosperity if the demand for places continues at its present stress".

Touring the familiar 'yellow brick vaudeville trail' to Denver and Salt Lake. Denver paper (undated Harvard clipping) breezily analyzes Nielsen's past and present: "In Kansas City, she was about as poor as a girl could be. Someone wrote a parody in her honor, *She Was Bred in Kansas City*, and when she was shown the verses she said, seriously, 'Yes, and many a time I've been without bread in Kansas City.'"

Denver suggests "Miss Nielsen's greatest attraction is for the young. She has never received a note from a masher and has never been molested by presumptuous men. Her child-like face, her sweet-young presence, seem to forbid such profanation, but everywhere she is the favorite of children, school girls, old ladies, mothers who feel they would like to take her up and pet her as they would a pretty child".

The canard Nielsen never sang chorus repeats. "Every mail bears her scores of requests for autographs...many from struggling chorus singers asking her how success might be attained.... Of course, it is already understood that she never sang in the chorus".

A view of California life, a ranch sited "on the McLeod River" Alice "has a handsome residence, a small army of servants and there she lives with her mother, her instructor [Valerga] and her horses. She is passionately fond of horses". McLeod River, now McCloud River, runs between mountains near Mt. Shasta, a region then controlled by San Francisco founding families 250 miles north of Sacramento.

Chatty: "Some time ago she purchased a tiny dog which might find shelter in a teacup, in NYC. The dog died. The announcement of its death in the newspapers brought to the hotel hundreds of sympathizing owners of canines with dogs to offer, and for a month she saw nothing and heard nothing but dogs, dogs, dogs! One dog, given her by John Sterling of Buffalo, was left at Suspension bridge when she got to Toronto, with a hope it might lose itself. When she passed through on her return to the States, the customs official was there with dog and a bill for $5 for board".

Spring 1899. March 11th, *Brooklyn Eagle* notes Nielsen will perform a week followed by "George Lederer Opera Co. headed by the peerless queen of song Lillian Russell" in *La Belle Helene* with Edna Hopper.

The Bostonians drop Perley as manager March 12th and embrace the theatre syndicate of Klaw & Erlanger. Plans to produce a new opera by Victor Herbert are announced; never happens. Four days later, Perley announces a concert tour for Herbert's brass band.

From Brooklyn, Boston two weeks. *Boston Sunday Globe* (Mar 12), "Alice Nielsen Opera Company in the season's great lyric success *The Fortune Teller*, original NY Cast, Ensemble and Production. Complete drum corps! Band of Trumpeters! Greatly increased orchestra! The most perfect light opera organization in the world". Highly praised; place packed.

"The reception" *Boston Globe* (March 19) reports "very cordial". This is "tuneful, amusing and sumptuously staged comic opera entertainment. The music is in Mr. Herbert's best vein in rhythmic melodies, rich choral effects and stirring finales and the fun is provided by three of the cleverest comedians of the comic opera stage".

Alice Nielsen is deeply appreciated. "The bright little star who names the company, has quickly bounded into high success. She is delightfully pretty and piquant, she has a light but deliciously sweet soprano voice, as clear as a bell. Miss Nielsen is a vivacious little actress, and carries out her impersonation of a ballet girl, a gypsy fortune teller and a young lieutenant of huzzars with abundant verve".

In the cast: "The noble basso of Eugene Cowles has never been heard to finer advantage... a splendid vocal triumph". "Dashing soprano soubrette, Marguerite Sylva, has made a success.... Very charming performances are also given by Jennie Hawley and Billie Norton. Stage management [director Julian Mitchell] is excellent and...alive with action and almost dazzling in its variety of colors".

More talk of London hits the press and Oakland's Tom Williams.

HJ Whigam from London to *Chicago Tribune* April 11th: "Was first decided to bring the Alice Nielsen company over to inaugurate the new regime at the Prince Of Wales Theatre... dates could not be arranged.... Has certainly been nothing in the way of comic opera in London of recent years half so good as *The Fortune Teller*". Interestingly, a few days later April 16th *LA Times* syndicated "Music and Musicians" reveals Nielsen to Europe "in the summer to rest much and to study a little". Instead, returns to Hawaii with usual party.

LA Times quotes *Boston Post* quoting Nielsen's business guy George Bowles on new theatre terms: "Old-time advance agents? They are all 'business managers'.... Take Frank Perley; he used to be about the liveliest circus agent in the business. What is he doing now? Why, 'presenting' Alice Nielsen in the new opera by Herbert and Smith, *The Fortune Teller*. I am the 'business manager' of the show, you know".

Nielsen returns to Washington; April 28th *Washington Post* runs photograph titled "Men Of Alice Nielsen Opera Company at Baseball".

May, Nielsen Company enters Chicago three weeks.

"Return of Alice Nielsen to the Columbia next week is sure to be welcome to the devotees of light opera", says *Chicago Tribune* (May 3). "*Fortune Teller*... has established itself as one of the most important musical productions of the present season. Perhaps more credit for its success belongs to Alice Nielsen and Eugene Cowles than to...the composer and librettist".

Opening May 9th festive, "If the size of the audience and the quantities of American Beauty roses and applause showered upon her and her associates may be taken as indicative of popular favor, the prospects for an extension of the engagement beyond the three weeks originally planned are bright", reports *Chicago Tribune*. "Miss Nielsen acts with as astonishing an amount of inexhaustible vitality as of yore, looks as charming and sings with as admirable ease and skill...."

In the cast: Cowles "acts as well as ever, sings with as good effect, and breathes just as loud and hard while so doing as he ever has done. Cawthorn tells his little bird story with as irresistible funniness as before; Richard Golden is clever...Joseph Herbert is adequate...Marguerite Sylva effervescent"; tenor Rushworth sufficient, "his singing has not improved".

May 18, Alice Nielsen joins the vocalists Weber Quartet for the sixth annual Associated Press banquet.

Herbert is composing three musicals, *NY Times* reports May 24th, he remains "in NYC during the entire Summer" to finish new operas for comedian Francis Wilson, Alice Nielsen and Frank Daniels". Interestingly, Wilson with Harry Smith "had some disagreement regarding the book for this new work which almost resulted in the abandonment of the opera, but within the last week these differences have been satisfactorily arranged...."

Same day, *Chicago Tribune* asks Alice Nielsen and May Irwin, Is Hamlet fat? "Of course he was thin", Alice replies. "Sarah Bernhardt has played him with success, and she is not fat! Bernhardt, I believe, however, would make a success of anything!" Irwin, buxom vaudeville star of Edison's 1896 film "The Kiss" disagrees: "Hamlet should be fat. It would relieve the gloom". Irwin earns a fortune in silents, minstrelsy, and her song *All Coons Look Alike to Me*.

In May the spring tour closes. Insider trouble arises. After her divorce finalized the previous fall, Alice has been pressured by Tom Williams to marry. She resists. Her manager Perley must keep the peace: contract stipulates she will not marry five years. Not his contract for managing Alice Nielsen Company.

Out of Chicago this crisis appears suspiciously. Tom Williams hires a press agent to claim he and Alice are engaged. *Kansas City Star* picks up the story, June 2nd reports Alice engaged to "Tom Williams of San Francisco, financial backer of *The Fortune Teller*...a love match dating back several years".

From Chicago "comes the rumor that she is engaged to wed wealthy Tom Williams of San Francisco, a clubman, horse breeder, friend of the stage and all round good fellow. Mr. Williams has been Miss Nielsen's financial backer in her starring venture. They met when Miss Nielsen went to San Francisco from Kansas City to join the Tivoli stock company".

Skips four years between.

Nielsen disagrees, "Of course the rumor is denied".

So elite publicity-shy Tom Williams, never mentioned directly with the show, has been convinced to approach the Chicago press to announce romance? This puff piece paints Alice as unambitious and a widow at that, while lauding Williams as rich benevolent sportsman.

Chicago News reports "Tom Williams is a figure of worthy note in Golden Gate affairs, social, commercial and sportive. His attachment for Miss Nielsen has dated from the time that piquant singer made her appearance at the old Frisco Tivoli, when Alice was a shy, small widow of a dozen moons or more [etching of Nielsen in *Singing Girl* on balcony, limb outstretched], and who was little ambitious further than necessity urging work for the support of her infant son, took to comic opera and easily found success.

"That young Tom Williams is the son of his picturesque father is enough to insure him something of a reputation on the Pacific coast, and when he was the veriest boy the youthful Tom mad himself popular and influential in many directions. He inherited enormous wealth from his father and likewise his father's spectacular generosity in its expenditure".

Williams Sr. beat a muckraking journalist almost to death. The story lists a few flings: "His father was a patron of the theatre and a devotee at the shrine of Jenreys Lews and that of the beautiful Maud Granger and Eleanor Carey. He was persistent in this amiable social attention to any of the group of charming women and entertaining men.... The theatre, when Louis James, Tom Keene, Jim Herne, Effie Wilton, James O'Neil and that happy crew of talented players throve, was very close to the gold-digging, extravagant community of San Francisco, and except in Boston no place in America supported such brilliant companies and kept in such warm touch with the lives of its actor citizens".

Williams Sr. was so boring he spent money "with whosoever interested him among the visiting stock companies, and his lavish expenditures in courtesies to all actors were among the delightful anticipations of coast renown".

Jr. Williams is portrayed in glowing terms only money can buy, "When the father left his money to young Tom, that scion of a true Westerner [Virginia] devoted to horses and sport launched out as a horseman...he is practically owner and director of the Frisco Jockey club and his wise investments, acute intuitions in stock dealings and widely distributed betting upon fluctuating commercial events have doubled the wealth he inherited. He is still called 'Young Tom', though he is not a boy by any means and is exceedingly shrewd, level of head and steady of hand in speculation".

Tom Williams indeed shrewd; his small investment in Nielsen's certain success put the strongest theatre company into business as a national project raking in the cash. Nielsen most popular and profitable diva. Now the mare has won her race, Williams wants to pasture and breed her.

"He fell in love in the oldest fashion, tumultuous way when he saw her at the Tivoli, and frankly asked her to marry him then".

Ever since, she has said no. "That was several years ago; but the pretty actress would not listen to any court, as she had tasted the sweets of applause and was bent upon an ultimate triumph in her chosen work".

Nielsen, as kind as she is, focuses on her arts. "She was quite as fond of Mr. Williams as he professed to be of her, but she sedately fought shy of the matrimonial offer to assist in spending the Williams wealth and enjoying the idleness of dower in a million".

After finalizing her divorce: "I will never marry".

"When the time came for her to approach the public in a larger way, she allowed the still-devoted Tom to become a shareholder in her starring tour, and together with the astute Perley, Mr. Williams helps count the earnings of the fascinating Alice".

Williams and Perley control finances, box office receipts, contracts, hiring, schedules. What if Williams corrupts Perley? To bully Nielsen would be childish, but Williams is the local elite.

Came to count cash and court star, "that is why Mr. Williams happened to be in Chicago at the close of Miss Nielsen's successful season. It was not a thrilling situation in a romance which of course has not ended, but it is all there is at present".

The story continues, "Nielsen signed in her Perley contract not to marry anybody for five years and while that enthusiastic clause in a prima donna's contract does not hold good when she is sentimentally inclined, the small childish Nielsen...will not wed—not she". Childish indeed.

Her chaperone has been brother Erasmus, "a staid and serious Hamlet with the mark of Denmark strong upon him, always travels with his sister. He is a drummer and assumes the responsibility of the tenor and bass rataplans of the orchestra, and attends his sister as she needs him".

The rest puffs Williams, "not only rich and energetic, but has social qualities most enjoyable and notable. He is a great teller of stories and is something of a club mimic in his way and a fellow of royal extravagance in the matter of entertainment". Curiously, entertains many San Francisco men in a charming manner: "His bachelor quarters in Frisco are the delightful rendezvous for all sorts of amusing and interesting men and the sumptuous hospitalities are presided over by a small army of Chinese servants, who silently purvey with much independence".

Next arrives serious, dangerous news. Health problems confided to public. Williams recovered from life-threatening "phthisis" in a "modern medical miracle" apparently helped by lymph massage. "Phthisis" is Greek for tuberculosis, contagious after about six months of prolonged contact.

Happily, he and Nielsen never spent so much time together.

Williams, tall and vigorous, has "heavy jaws of firmness and aggressive brows" who "divides his time between making money easily and spending it handsomely". Defends turf and demands obedience. General's son.

Despite temptation to marry rich and move to Oakland as housewife, Alice's "friends in KC do not believe she will marry now. She is too much enamored of the stage to leave it, or even share its interest with married life". She really hates to cook.

Terrible complications arise from rejection of Tom Williams in marriage.

His proposal absurd, stop her career? The contrast in their lives.... Nielsen diligently performs seven times weekly to crowds adoring her.

Williams makes his proposal public in Chicago. His investment in Nielsen Company is a small stake small compared with other ventures.

Nielsen and siblings are skilled performers, not party-hound club-kids.

Her peers, pals are the reigning stars of theatre: Lillian Russell, Eugene Cowles, Victor Herbert. She has opera ambitions in Europe.

For a few month these issues submerge. Behind scenes, trouble brews. As Williams decides what kind of man he is.

Banter about the title of their next new show appears in *Kansas City Star* on July 7, "Alice Nielsen's new opera, in which she will open in New York in October, has not yet been named". Possible titles "The Street Singer"—art follows life—or, "The Little Minstrel", or "The Singing Girl". Eugene Cowles "has been re-engaged...as has Joseph Herbert, the comedian" who largely re-wrote *The Fortune Teller* on the fly as it toured. Rehearsals begin late August.

With reasonable optimism Nielsen signs a new artist management contract with Perley which sends her to Europe. As Williams fears. *LA Times* July 23rd reports a five-year Nielsen contract with Perley which "includes appearances in London and Paris, beginning in London on Easter Monday, 1901".

Her true intentions are public now.

"Miss Nielsen's next American appearance" is slated for NY's Casino Theatre.

Related theatre news notes the grand opera star Jeans DeReszke's favorite amusement is "imitation of music-hall singers of ragtime melodies, and he is credited with being an expert mimic". So is Alice Nielsen.

July 26th (*KC Star Jul 22*) Alice Nielsen and party leave San Francisco on the steamer *Yucatan* for a month in Honolulu and Waikiki. *NY Times* reports Herbert has completed his new score July 28.

August goes smoothly. Perley announces other new Nielsen projects, an Elmer Gradin play. Pleased with Victor Herbert composing Stanislaus Stange libretti with Harry Smith lyrics, Perley asks producer George Lederer to shop French farces to adapt.

Williams pressures the *prima*; early August he speaks to California press about plans to marry her. Perley—protecting his star—announces again that any marriage forbid by Nielsen's five-year contract. *NY Times* reports August 6, "Alice Nielsen denies emphatically that she is to be married. Her manager, Frank L. Perley, says that her contract with him expressly states that she is not to wed for five years". Bi-coastal game gets stranger as Perley must issue regular press releases responding to Williams. Denied, Williams wants revenge.

Tom Williams realizes he must corrupt Perley's integrity to vex Alice.

Casting has almost completed in August when Victor Herbert deploys the title, "*The Singing Girl*". Contralto Lucille Saunders joins. John Slavin "in the role of a girl" will swap clothes will Alice who plays her own brother.

Tuesday August 8, Herbert in Manhattan delivered his new score "to the various members of the company". In San Francisco August 9, Nielsen raises money for Red Cross, first many benefits for the group. For the "California regiment" returning from Philippines, she sings a charity auction (Aug 10, *LA Times*) at Orpheum featuring Mayor James Phelan, DeWolf Hopper, Alexandria Dagmar. For this "monster entertainment" theatre boxes sold for $1000, socialite Mrs. Townsend took two.

Nielsen departs for NYC rehearsals late August.

Perley puts national focus on her legs.

LA Times (Aug 27) says, In NYC, "about the first thing she did" was visit Perley in the Knickerbocker. "Miss Nielsen is very impetuous in manner and speech, a fact which Mr. Perley had previous cognizance, so that he need not have been surprised at anything she might have said. As a fact, he blushed so deep a crimson that for the moment he closely resembled a deep and glittering sunset. This was Miss Nielsen's speech, as nearly as the persons to whom she afterward haltingly repeated it, remembered: 'Oh Mr. Perley, I've had such a perfectly glorious vacation. It has done me lots and lots of good. I've gained nine pounds, which is a good deal for a little girl like me. You just ought to see my legs!'" Turn-of-century risqué fun the national press retold.

Big wooden shoes and pigtails, her new show. Recall her Dutch clogs from the Philippines 1898? Visiting the Herberts she playfully danced in the big shoes, "wouldn't it be fun!" So August 27, *NY Times* reports "Miss Nielsen's Wooden Shoes. In the first act of this opera, Miss Nielsen will appear as an Austrian peasant girl, and as such she will wear the wooden shows of the peasantry of that country throughout the entire act. In order to be thoroughly at ease with this peculiar footwear, Miss Nielsen since her return to this city from California has been practicing daily with the clumsy shoes, which she says make pedestrianism to a novice like herself about as difficult as does the snowshoe of the North American Indian of the ski of the native of Norway".

Monday August 28th rehearsals start. Design and direction is same merry band who created *Fortune Teller*: Mitchell, Steindorff, Siedle, Physioc, Simpson, Crawford, Lietz, Hepner, shoes by Cammeyer.

September 7th *New York Times* sketches Physioc's scenery: "vista of the Danube is shown, with the boat landing and quaint old bridge over the river. One side is the celebrated rococo church in Linz [Austria] and on the other the town hall, while in the distance are the Salzburg Alps".

For Nielsen Company, Perley and George Bowles (Sept. 10, *NY Times*) buy rights to Elmer Grandin's melodrama about $2-million robbery of Great Northampton Bank, loot hidden in belfry of Church of the Redeemer in Astoria, Long Island NY.

End of September rehearsals wrap. They board for Canada.

SINGING GIRL: TOP BOX OFFICE FROM MONTREAL

Out-of-town tryouts begin in Montreal. Monday Oct 2nd *Singing Girl* opens at Her Majesty's theatre on Guy Street seating 1,750. Managers are Mr. and Mrs. Frank Murphy. Quebec's Eugene Cowles is co-star.

NY Times reviews the Canadian opening in all its gayety. "The house was crowded. There were seven curtain calls at the end of the first act. In fact, encores were the rule of the evening. Miss Nielsen scored a great hit and her principal number *The Legend of Danube*, a more pretentious effort than is usually found in comic opera, received a great reception".

In the cast, "Eugene Cowles ran the star a close race for honors, Miss Lucille Saunders also made a hit, while a clever trio, Herbert, Cawthorn and Slaven, furnished the comedy element and received great applause for their work".

After a week, they shuffle off to Buffalo. Then special night train to NYC Octobert 19. Three days later, Sunday night preview at Casino Theatre.

NY Times theatre section is packed with one-inch ads: at the Palace Marie Dressler; Mrs. Fiske in *Becky Sharp*; Weber & Fields' *Whirl-i-gig*; grand opera at Met managed by Maurice Grau; Boston Symphony; English superstar Henry Irving with Ellen Terry in *Robespierre, Waterloo, The Amber Heart, The Bells* and *Nance Oldfield*: Henry Irving's son Laurence prestigiously in town as the *Robespierre* playwright acting in their plays.

Monday *October* 23rd *The Singing Girl* opens 8:15pm, ends 10:55. Set in 1820 Linz, Austria: Nielsen is Gretl; Eugene Cowles, Duke Rodolph; Joe Herbert, Prince Pumpernickel; Richie Ling, Count Otto; Aufpassen, Joe Cawthorn.

Cast of thirty: George Tennery, John Slavin, Edward Metcalfe, Louis Kelso, Albert McGourin, George Mason, W. Thompson, C.G. Westcott, William Bechtel, E. Wallace, Albert Busby, M.H. Lawrenz, Lucille Saunders, Jennie Hawley, Barnetta Mueller, Cara Isham, Nan Bewins, Louise Hilliard, Edna Bronson, Lillie Swift, May Boley, Winifred Williams, Louise Lawton, sisters Lillie and May Devere and Rub Capen.

In the chorus: Katherine Sears, Edna Bronson, Geraldine Stevens, Nan Hewins, Lillie Swift, Grace Gordon, Ninette Thullen, Annie Clay, Grace Stewart, May Willard, Nellie Chapman, Alma Bauer, Bessie Miller, Daisy Leighton, Isabel Allison, Jessie Van Hart, George Hall, Harold Reibling, TH Barton, EA Randall, Charles Fiedling, Carl Hartberg, Fred Barton, PH Worthington and ED Baker.

Singing Girl women are women and men men mostly. In Stange's libretto, after Nielsen as brother in *Fortune Teller*, her brother appears as sister in *Singing Girl*, a fun joke.

Act 1 Nielsen sings *Song of the Danube*. Her big hit, Act 2's *Love Is a Tyrant (So I Bid You Beware)*. Once again, throw-away Act 3 ends with trio funny-men; Pumpernickel, Aufpassen and Stephan, *Just Suppose That I Am Going to Arrest You*. What Stange did isn't clear. *Singing Girl* plot must only be explained by professionals. Boston critics excel at clarifying mysteries. People pay for players at spectacle, and music. *Black Crook* extravaganza evolved four decades with distilled cast, hour shorter.

Now our key phrase appears for all time: "A good new operetta", writes *New York Times*, "is not only an important piece of property for a star in search of a repertoire, but it is a considerable contribution to the gayety of nations, and therefore to be received with praise and thanksgiving. It can be said that *The Singing Girl* is good, and it was received with kindness last night by the audience. The story is very slight and quite fanciful. The plot is extravagant, and in one or two of its minor details verges closely on what used to be described on the playbills as 'extravaganza.' But this has been the case with so many operettas from *Apajune* to *The Merry Monarch* that it would be idle to cavil at it.

"The book serves its purpose which is to give the piquant little star a pleasing and effective role and to enable her to surround herself with competent performers not without opportunities for individual distinction".

Dialog, "not without humor". Comedy bits prove "that the Greek dramatists thoroughly understood theatrical effects". And with further faint praise, "Mr. Smith's lyrics are quite as good as any he has given us of late...." Stage business carefully choreographed start to finish: "Plenty of movement in the work...due to the admirable stage management [direction] of Julian Mitchell".

"Greatest merit of the operetta is to be found in the score of Mr. Herbert. This gentleman possess an apparently inexhaustible fund of pretty melody and his thorough musicianship, combined with rare taste and fruitful fancy, enables him to dress it in the most attractive orchestral and vocal garb ...it is music to which a real music lover can listen with constant interest".

If Nielsen's art seems artless, she was that good. "Attended by a large audience which treated some of Mr. Herbert's best numbers with scant consideration and others with warm applause, but reserved its highest enthusiasms for the testimony of its regard for Miss Nielsen. The performance was excellent. Miss Nielsen achieved another personal success with her dainty figure, her pretty ways, and her fresh voice. Her personality is charming, and she has the methods of a genuine comedian".

NY Times restates the star better than her show.

Herbert casts a net for better librettists.

In the cast: "Lucille Saunders displayed her fine contralto voice...Cowles sang in his customary robust style...Joseph Herbert, Joseph Cawthorn and John Slavin made the fun and made it very well". Tenor "Richie Ling looked well and acted satisfactorily but he did not always sing in tune".

New York ponders why Alice Nielsen is great. "There is something about this Nielsen girl that gets to the public unerringly", writes "LR" in *Telegraph*. "The people cannot escape. I sat last night through the opera called *The Singing Girl* and tried vainly to analyze its central figure.

"Alice Nielsen is a pretty little sprite, who sings charmingly and who has at all times about her the indefinable charm of youth. But these things do not account for the fact that she moves the multitude to an ecstasy of acclaim, for we have had countless young women who have sung delightfully, and they have drifted past and out of sight, and have been lost in the eddies miles downstream. This girl comes along, and the surface indications are simply that she has youth and a delightful voice. Yet she winds her audience around her little-finger as it were, till its members are her adoring subjects, and without power to evade her unmistakable and potential influence".

LR gives up, "There is no accounting for it all, excepting upon the general and not technically satisfying proposition that Miss Nielsen is 'a winner.'"

NY Telegraph (Oct) publishes a sidebar about the "real" Alice Nielsen. Pyke (spelled Pike) gets credit for her first San Francisco gig. Nielsen, said to be twenty-four, has gone Japanese. Says *Telegraph*: "Regarding "Johnnies", those men who went with flowers to the stage door, Nielsen has "a clever negro maid [Geraldina White] to whom she says, 'Grace, shoo them off!' Grace shoos! Believes the mole on her cheek brings her good luck. Fad: affects Japanese customs. Sings Japanese music. Wears a beautiful blue hand-painted kimono. Pets: likes tiny dogs. Religion: Roman Catholic...of St. Patrick's Church KC".

She "finds the public more than ready to welcome her. Miss Nielsen has made a decidedly favorable impression... and hereafter will take her place with the rest of the stars in light opera and there are not too many of them. Miss Nielsen...is proof that talent counts for something on the stage, as everywhere else". Broadway at her feet, Alice Nielsen has become legend, hero to women, national artistic treasure. Properties built around her will prosper.

By association, company make news. When George Bowles "advance man" divorces Marie Bowles "known to the theatrical world as Babette Rodney", the actor Edward Frayne is named correspondent. Bowles gets custody of daughter five, Marie "restrained from using the name Bowles". Married fourteen years, divorce makes *NY Times* (Nov 9, 1899).

Singing Girl enters second month at "Casino Theatre and Roof Garden", *NY World* (Nov 12) quotes Alice in "My First Appearance on the Stage". She claims born 1874, dad died when three, plus her usual pilgrim progress.

New York's so-clever critics include stinging Alan Dale, a pseudonym lifted from The Bostonians' *Robin Hood*. London-born Alfred Cohen wrote as Dale for Hearst papers. Visits *Singing Girl* with wit: "Away to land of gay impossible comic opera...when girls are boys and boys are girls, and everyone wants to marry everybody else, and lovely gentlemen in satin trousers sing lordly ballads surrounded by dizzy troops of chorus girls.

"The gay, impossibly comic opera on the occasion was *The Singing Girl*... introducing the cunning little singing soubrette who in *The Fortune Teller* last season proved to us that a comic opera 'star' need not necessarily be fat, forty and frisky. Sang just as blithely, looked just as youthful, and wore her trousers with the same familiar grace as last year".

Show suffers "flabby book" by Stanislaus Stange and lyrics by the "comic opera Rockefeller known as Harry B. Smith. Mr. Stange to be sure, gave Miss Nielsen the chance to be her own brother (the little lady is very fond of supplying herself with male relatives), but there was a deadly lack of comedy that at times became quite oppressive". Star who "busied herself incessantly with the 'plot' could not be expected to supply comedy".

Cast cross-dress both ways, "Already told you that Miss Nielsen appears as her own brother and perhaps I better add that her own brother appears as Miss Nielsen, on the principle I presume, of exchange is no robbery".

Dale believes Herbert's score "vastly inferior to his Cyrano strains" due to overwork: "no man—except Harry B. Smith—can work all the time". Best song went to Eugene Cowles who "with his huge cathedral voice did his small duties nobly. When he was singing, you sat back and gloated. There is only one Cowles in comic opera and Miss Nielsen has him".

In the cast: Richie Ling "took himself very seriously" and "sang fondly" while "John Slavin as his own sister was mildly funny. I never think this trans-sexual humor overweeningly funny. But Mr. Slavin captured all the possibilities of the part, such as they were".

Dale's focuses on star onstage. "Always pleasant to watch little Miss Nielsen. Her personal success was unequivocal. She is such a very earnest little lady, such a comic opera novelty. There are no airs about her (she gave them all to her tenor) and she is so very brave. Her bravery was shown by the chorus, which was distinctly young and pretty". Instead of "a set of old crows" she "surrounded herself by young, pretty girls, who wore their pink tights with Amazonian [*Black Crook*] fervor and flaunted their prettiness...."

To *Criterion's* Rupert Hughes, Nielsen's growth the past year is clear. Titles his review "Alice Nightingale" She is "the most fetching thing in town...in the most stunning suit of white silk and silvered doublet and hose ever worn by a girlish boy. When you have said that the company is so fine it that it reaches the standard of a stock company, that the music is the music of Victor Hubert at his best, and that the costumes are gorgeous, you have said all you can say".

Words awful. Chef Stange let the story flee back to Europe. *Singing Girl* "seems a certain failure unless the libretto is—not patched-up, but re-made. It is bad in toto. The plot is the frailest, the most stupid, the most implausible (even by comic opera standards) seen in NY in many a year. Its spinal column has all the qualities of spaghetti except its palatability. An immediate and complete rewriting may save a structure that has many rights to exist".

Hughes recognized Nielsen has flowered. Only she has had the experience of singing all her shows. She created, and recreated her roles.

Alice may have found Laurence Irving's father Henry helpful: "the actor who combines the electric force of a strong personality with a mastery of the resources of his art will have a greater power of his audiences...." Irving quotes Shakespeare: "Suit the action to the word, the word to the action, with this special observance that you overstep not the modesty of nature" (1882). William Winter (*NY Tribune* 1883) says Irving "always seems to be alive...the soul that is within the man has suffused his art and made it victorious". So Alice Nielsen.

Hughes notices confidence: "She has waxed very brilliant. She has some authority now, and her voice, without losing its singularly pure crystal, has gained body. Her singing was superb".

In the cast: "magnificent organ-tone of Miss Lucille Saunders...she sings wonderfully well". Cowles, "one of the noblest voices this country has ever produced, intercepted on its way to grand opera". Comedians Cawthorn, Joseph Herbert and Slaven "wander aimlessly about longing for such opportunities as they had last year" when they had spontaneously re-authored the show.

Herbert's score "dignifies the American stage, it reaches the highest level of Europeana comic opera, particularly in the very elaborate entrance song for Miss Nielsen. Then too, it is learnedly humorous". Virtuoso fun.

NY Dramatic News prints photo of the quartet: Nielsen, Cowles, Lucille Saunders, Richie Ling.

In this golden age of live entertainment people went to theatre often; saw best and worst. Strong tastes, savvy. Take a displeased NYC audience in 1900: the show was "beautifully dressed, faultlessly rehearsed...a crowd of popular people in the cast...played by an admirable orchestra, admirably conducted. But there its virtues ended. Among many nights of boredom and distress, that night stands out in my remembrance". Dialog pointless, no plot, music bad. People react: "Hisses were heard in the pit and cat-calls in the gallery before the curtain had been up ten minutes, and they grew in a steady crescendo till at the final chorus, the parrot house at the Zoo would have seemed a home of dull tranquility".

Nielsen's projects never faced a horrid fate. As she told us, don't expect to win the crowd on the strength of your legs. However.

Singing Girl crowds Casino nightly through December. On 7th, comic Frank Daniels opened Herbert's *The Ameer* with Helen Redmond, Kate Uart, Norma Kip and George Devoll, plus "Will Rochester of Alice Nielsen's forces". Large cast, chorus sixty. Victor Herbert shows provide hundreds of jobs to theatre-people for decades; which binds his reputation and legend highly on Broadway.

New York ends three months of *Singing Girl* first week January. *NY Times* (Dec 31) reports "Miss Nielsen's travels will extend only as far West as Chicago, and she will appear in but a few of the larger cities, including Philadelphia, Baltimore, Washington, Brooklyn, Pittsburg, Chicago, Detroit and Boston". Interestingly, nothing is scheduled in California where Tom Williams lives. Conflict between diva and backer escalating behind scenes. London opening on the schedule.

Turn of a century.

Alice Nielsen delivers a new era to Broadway and creates unforgettable memories in many many people. Two decades later, Carl Van Vetchen writes (*Old Days and New*, 1918), "Wall Street broker, poet, greengrocer, soldier, banker, lawyer, whatever you are, confess the facts to yourself: you were once as I. You have suffered the same feelings that I suffered. How many times did you go to see Marie Tempest in *The Fencing Master* or Alice Nielsen in *The Serenade*" and fall in love?

1900: FAMOUS PRIMA DONNA

By 1900 Alice Nielsen is the top box-office draw in North America. Her lavishly-produced Company avoids California this year. Public and critics praise the ensemble's success. Actors had overturned an indifferent book by putting themselves into their roles and improvising the show. The director put a story of his own into the stage action: after all, he was deaf to words. The composer did the same, making a riot of fun with witty music. The combination works wonderfully well to create a great audience experience, and critics clamor for a definitive Great American Musical.

For his book *Famous Prima Donnas,* Boston critic Louis Strang (1869-1935) must choose the best woman on the American musical stage. Since 1894 a theatre critic for *Boston Journal*, his theatre books are popular: *Famous Actors of the Day* (1899/1901), *Famous Actresses* (1899/1901) *Players And Plays* (1902), *Famous Stars Of Light Opera* (1900), *Celebrated Comedians* (1900), *Prima Donnas And Soubrettes of Light Opera* (1900).

Now he releases *Famous Prima Donnas* (1901). Interestingly, Strang has keen interest in human energy. Two decades later his spiritual *Freedom Through Right Thinking* (1924) will be dedicated to "All truth seekers, all apostles of freedom, all guardians of enlightenment". Keenly aware of the magnetism of people, he would leave journalism to work with Mary Baker Eddy for Christian Science. Thoughtful and sensitive Strang reasons carefully, strongly feels the social force when humanity joins into live theatre, energy of a crowd in rapture.

He attends all shows, sees every performer, conducts in-depth interviews for his comprehensive books. Given his depth in theatrical happenings, his critical appreciation of Alice Nielsen is one of the great tribute received in her lifetime. He does not like her shows: he likes the artist. He understands the naturalness of her acting proves she has the greatest possible artistry. In *Famous Prima Donnas*, Strang shrinks not from selecting the best. Skips over a few historical facts in those times of Nielsenian fogs, of course:

FAMOUS PRIMA DONNAS by LOUIS STRANG
Chapter 1, Alice Nielsen

Five years ago Alice Nielsen was an obscure church singer in Kansas City; today she is the leading woman star in light opera on the American stage. One feels an instinctive hesitation in putting her in the first place, however sure he may be that she is justly entitled to it. He anxiously seeks the country over for a possible rival. He feels that Alice Nielsen has hardly been tested as yet, for she has been only two seasons at the head of her own company, and she has not appeared in an opera which is of itself artistically worthy of serious consideration.

Moreover, she is such a little thing—a child, it would seem— and is it safe to take seriously a child, even a child of so many and so potent fascinations? This feeling of doubt, caused by Miss Nielsen's stage youthfulness, is, it appears to me, the pith of the whole difficulty, and therein lurks a curious paradox.

Alice Nielsen's great charms are her youth, her spontaneity, and her ingenuousness; but these very qualities are the ones that make one pause and consider before giving her the artistic rank that she has honestly earned.

Alice Nielsen seems almost too human to be really great. She is too natural, too democratic, too free from conceit. She is never disdainful of her public, and she is never bored by her work.

One cannot help being charmed by this little woman, who sings as if singing were the best fun in the world; who is so frankly happy when her audience likes her work and applauds her; and who goes soaring up and away on the high notes, sounding clear and pure above chorus and orchestra, without the slightest apparent effort and without a trace of affectation or of artificial striving for effect. Everybody who has ever written anything about Alice Nielsen has declared that she sings like a bird, freely, naturally, and easily, and this metaphor described exactly the impression that she creates.

Her voice one appreciates at once,—its volume and its colorful brilliancy, its great range, and its rich, sympathetic, and musical qualities; what he misses in her are the conventionalities of the prima donna,—the awe-inspiring stage presence, the impressive posings and contortious vocalizations.

The world is very apt to take one at his own estimate until it gets very well acquainted with him. Alice Nielsen has never proclaimed herself a wonder, and the world has not yet fully made up its mind regarding her as an artist. It acknowledges her great personal charm, her delightful music, but it is not just sure whether she can act. I regard Miss Nielsen as a thoroughly competent actress in a limited field. She is fitted neither physically nor temperamentally for heroics, but she is fully equal to the requirements of operatic light comedy.

She acts as she sings, simply and naturally, and her appeal to her audience is sure and straightforward. As an instance of this, take her striking first entrance in *The Singing Girl*. She appears on a little bridge, which extends across the back of the stage. She runs quickly to the centre, then stops, stoops over with her hands on her knees in Gretchen fashion, and smiles with all her might. The action is quaint and attractive, and she wins the house at once. Alice Nielsen's smile is really a wonderful thing, and it is proof that she knows something about acting. It never seems forced. Yet, when one stops to think, he must see that a girl cannot smile at the same time, night after night, without bringing to her aid a little art.

To appear perfectly natural on the stage is the best possible acting, and that is just what Alice Nielsen does with her smile.

Praising Alice, Strang dislikes *Fortune Teller*, "in which Miss Nielsen made her debut as a star during the season of 1898-99, was from any standpoint except the purely spectacular a pretty poor sort of an opera. There was a great deal to attract the eye. The costuming was sumptuous, the groupings and color effects novel and entrancing, and the action throughout mechanically spirited. Mr. Herbert's music, which was plainly written to catch the public fancy, fulfilled its purpose, though that was about all that could be said in its favor. It waltzed and it marched, and it broke continually into crashing and commonplace refrains. It was strictly theatrical music, with more color than melody, showy and pretentious, but without backbone".

Along with the Chicago critics, Strang focuses on a song Nielsen carries with her acting to create the best moment of the show: "There was really only one song...that stuck to the memory and that was Miss Nielsen's solo, *So I Bid You Beware*. Possibly even in this case I am giving Mr. Herbert more credit than belongs to him, for Miss Nielsen's interpretation of the ditty was nothing short of exquisite. She found a world of meaning in the simple words, coquetted and flirted with a fascinating girlishness that was entrancing, and flashed her merry blue eyes with an invitation so purely personal that for a moment the footlights disappeared".

The libretto was so "woefully weak" into its gaps "a trio of comedians were thrust with a recklessness born of desperation".

Fortune Teller succeeded only by keeping Alice Nielsen onstage "practically all the time that she was not occupied with taking off petticoats and putting on trousers—or else reversing the process".

Strang's crown increases Nielsen's value and raises her self-esteem. Industry consensus: she carries the shows. As her experience grows, also confidence. It is obvious; astute critics diligently remark on her artistic progression throughout life. Only she faces her audiences night after night. Each night, she learns. Each season she progresses. Alice Nielsen sang an astonishing schedule of very challenging material and made it look natural and effortless. She was "all about her work".

Touring from NYC, January 14th Nielsen takes Philadelphia's Chestnut Street. *Philadelphia Inquirer* writes of *Singing Girl*, "the engagement so far has been in several senses a record breaker. Alice Nielsen has sung at every performance to audiences that have completely filled the large auditorium ... and no attraction in recent years has been received with greater appreciation by lovers of genuine comedy, good music and perfect vocalization than Miss Nielsen's splendid supporting company".

Her place in hearts is secure: "The personal success of the youthful prima donna in Philadelphia has been indisputable. Her musical numbers are enthusiastically encored and Miss Nielsen, who only became known to us a year ago as a comic opera star, may now feel safely assured of the affection and permanent fealty of the Philadelphia public".

Her artistic progress obvious: "The vast improvement in Miss Nielsen's acting ability since she was here last season is very noticeable".

Ensemble: "Her supporting company this year is stronger than ever".

January 30, in DC (*Washington Post*), Nielsen "received an enthusiastic reception from an overflowing audience. *Singing Girl* has met with even more favor than *The Fortune Teller*. Miss Nielsen...has been the principal factor in both pieces...."

How possible to star in these complex scores nightly? Valerga's splendid *bel canto* training contributes greatly to Alice Nielsen's Broadway success. Singing such shows on that schedule dangerous or impossible otherwise. Of course, her first vocal coach an Irish mom, Sarah.

Vocals suffer without perfect technique. Patti could not have coped.

Says *Post*, "Distinct night of triumph for Miss Nielsen, the dainty, piquant, girlish, ingénue-sort of a prima donna, with a magnificent voice out of all proportion to her own diminutive measurements. Miss Nielsen's personal attractions, her naïve simplicity, her clear soprano voice, controlled and projected without an effort, her odd ideas of humor, all conspire to make her a prima donna of an entirely novel conception.

"She took her honors with a queer little bow and an artless manner which established her even more firmly as a local favorite with those who saw her".

In the cast: Cowles "shared honors with Miss Nielsen. That strong bass voice of his was given full sway in a couple of solos for which encores were much in demand". Tenor finally a good word: "Richie Lang as Count Otto made a manly lover and sang splendidly". Lucille Saunders "magnificent contralto... received well-earned applause for her solo...and for her subsequent good work". Lovely women's chorus, "small in stature...match their star very well, and produce a dainty and novel background".

The 1900 Nielsen phenomenon opens in Chicago during a blizzard. Same as east coast, all shows Standing Room Only. March 24 (*NY Times*) Alice "closed tonight in one of the most remarkable engagements ever played in Chicago. For three weeks every performance, matinee and night, the standing-room sign has been displayed. Considering the unreliability of March weather the business is nearly, if not quite beyond precedent".

Nielsen Company tours back to Boston.

April 8, *NY Times* reports Nielsen "will take her company to London next season to produce her cycle of Herbert operas". During Easter, April 16-21, Nielsen occupies *Boston Museum*. If admired for *Serenade*, she becomes famed for *Fortune Teller* and *Singing Girl*. "At the Museum last night" says *Boston Herald* (Apr 17), "there was another audience that taxed both the seating and standing capacity of the house to enjoy Alice Nielsen and her company...."

Men in the company play baseball. Earlier photographed by Washington press, April 26 they challenge Francis Wilson's cast "At the South End grounds today there will be a game between...Alice Nielsen and Francis Wilson companies. The rivalry has been intense...." *Boston Globe* adds, "Alice Nielsen will say farewell to Boston Museum audiences next Saturday night...." Her stay "very successful, and the only regret is that it is limited to the present week".

Impossible to include every review every town. *Boston Herald*'s critical assessment typifies 1900 Nielsen tours across North America. Theatres were "packed with enthusiastic admirers—Victor Herbert's music by far the best he has written in some time". Success "wherever it has been played insured a splendid engagement here and certainly the management could not be in the least disappointed by the attendance".

Everybody realizes the stories silly. *Singing Girl*'s book "as is generally the case with modern comic operas, has very little to recommend it. The plot is scant, simply acting as a frame for a number of more or less amusing complications. The story turns on a ridiculous law, adopted by the ruler who has not been fortunate in love, that provides that any couple found kissing must be immediately married or else be imprisoned. As might be expected, the lovers get mixed up and their complications are made to fill out the three acts.

For Boston, "lyrics are decidedly better than the libretto, in fact this seems to be Mr. Smith's best".

For Herbert "of late he has done so much...jangling rubbish in his operas" that it is "gratifying to find that in *The Singing Girl* he has gone back to his old standards and has really written music of value. Unquestionably...he strove to win the popular fancy but his marches and waltzes...are tuneful and catchy, and a number of the songs have real artistic merit. It can fairly be said that *The Singing Girl* is by all odds the best music Herbert has given us in some time".

Star has outdone herself; smart, witty, better than last seen. "Miss Nielsen herself is as artistic and attractive little woman as can be found on the stage. Her voice and method have decidedly improved since she was last heard in Boston. In her dual character she finds a part exactly suited to her dainty personality. As a boy she is winning, graceful and good to look at, while as a maid she is simply fascinating.

"She sings all her numbers with a freshness and life that are simply irresistible. She really seems to like to sing, and she gives encores with a grace that cannot but make one think that she has not yet found the limit to her powers. And added to her voice, Miss Nielsen is a charming actress and a better laugh maker than any of her supporting comedians. One would have to go quite a way back in the annals of comic opera to find anything as taking as her song *So I Bid You Beware*. Lillian Russell in *Girofle-Girofla* is the only thing in recent years that the writer can remember as equaling it in comic opera".

In the cast: "exceptionally strong. Eugene Cowles came in for his full share of the applause. In fact, he shared with Miss Nielsen in being favorites of the evening". Lucille Saunders, "good as anything she has done in the past;" tenor George Tennery "quite satisfactory; comedians "Cawthorn, Herbert and Slavin...made the most of their caprices, though the writer...has a prejudice in favor of Mr. Slavin's style. The ingenious trio for a topical song in the last act is a very clever piece of work.... Chorus "enters into the spirit of the music splendidly...really pretty girls". Julian Mitchell's direction and choreography, costumes, scenery all "excellent, the groupings being very effective". Lastly, Steindorf's "enlarged orchestra helped to make the production a success.

"*The Singing Girl* is one of the most enjoyable comic operas that has been seen here for some time and by all odds the best of the year, and one risks nothing in predicting that the Museum will be literally packed at every performance during its stay, which is limited to two weeks".

That report plays consistently across North America.

They dominate the musical theatre world.

Cast and crew change. August, Viola Gillette is new alto. For business Perley adds WG Smyth, a name almost lost to us. In 1902 Smyth produces *A Rose O'Plymouth-town* by Beulah Dix for twenty-one performances with Douglas Fairbanks; Dix authors novels, plays, children books, silent films. Smyth with Channing Pollock will start the Press Agent's Association which births Friars' Club, Pollock president.

Touring *Serenade*, Alice's wooden shoes a literal hit at least once. She spoke to Zoe Buckley (1936) about her Herbert seasons. Alice had, Buckley tells us, "long nursed a secret desire to do a Dutch dance" with wooden clogs. And of Ada Lewis six years earlier. "Herbert obliged, fashioning the operetta so that the shoes came prominently to the fore". Dancing Alice kicks off a shoe in Chicago, "It flew straight into a proscenium box, and almost into the eye of a dignified dowager. Miss Nielsen screamed, the orchestra stopped, the audience gazed and gasped, the dowager jumped. But nothing ever daunted madcap Alice and when she saw the lady still lived, she hopped up to the box and made a little speech of apology. 'It's quite all right, my dear. I'll forgive you on one condition—that you let me keep the wooden shoe!'"

Buckley closes, "The rest of the number was done in one silk stocking and one pine slipper—and the show went on.

July 7th, *Texas Morning Register* (Fort Worth) publishes a picture of "the dainty prima donna. No woman connected with the lighter forms of amusement in the United States...has in the same period of time won a warmer place in the affections of the theatre-going public than this little woman with the undefinable charm that seems to enable her to captivate the 'coldest' audience imaginable". Same day, Texas arbitrarily in focus, her upcoming European tour is heralded by *Ft. Worth Register*: "and many good judges are of the opinion that she will become as great a favorite there as she is here".

The tour is postponed. Tom Williams prefers Nielsen corralled in America. Finding Perley barrier to his schemes, Williams begins to bait the producer with tempting offers. Racetrack-hard Williams could cajole, threaten, bribe, and whip. His investment binds his target. Gatekeeper Perley has promised to protect her interests by keeping Williams at bay. No alliance between Williams & Perley would be in her favor.

Meanwhile, American audiences highly anticipate a third Nielsen-Herbert show. And her two running shows steadily evolve. Songs come and go, dialog changes, the cast play with it, the music remains the strength.

Chaperoned by brother Erasmus (doubles on drums), Nielsen and Company cover 38,536 miles this year. Nielsen siblings travel "with a sumptuous private car, a maid, a porter and a steward" while Sarah raises Alice's son. Seventy theatre-people travel the eight months crisscrossing North America.

Touring has pratfalls and wit. Joe Cawthorn "clad in gold trousers" gets accidently stranded in Peru IL while talking to a Mr. Epperson as the Nielsen Special pulls away. Caught without a ticket but knowing both trains would stop in St. Louis, Cawthorn has the conductor telegraph to confirm the mistake.

Nielsen Company wires back, "The man who claims to be Cawthorn is an imposter!" Despite their prank, Cawthorn arrives in St. Louis at 7pm to join the others over at Southern Hotel for a good laugh on him.

And people in this group grow inherently newsworthy. August 29th *Columbus Enquirer* (GA) reports "Daisy Leighton, a pretty member of the Alice Nielsen Opera Company...attained some celebrity by publishing a rather erratic novel entitled *Passions Past*", and tours again this season.

Nielsen's taste evolves with experience. September 27th Nielsen writes Harry Smith in her big round script of eight lines per page, seeking new lyrics (UT-Austin Library). She'd asked Herbert for music alike his "Cyrano duet...I know he will let me have it if he can".

With Francis Wilson, Herbert's *Cyrano* had opened NYC September 18th. Lyrics by Smith, book Stuart Reed.

From Chicago, Nielsen asks for yet more, and knows what will suit: "I have just written to Mr. Herbert to write me a 'serenade' for the second act of *The Fortune Teller* with 'cello accompaniment and now I want you to please be so kind & write me some lyrics for same". Significantly she tells Smith, "I want a song where I won't have to depend on the acting of it. A song that I can sing straight. As it will be different from anything I have in the opera". This will wow her pals in San Francisco: "Please Mr. Smith, write to Mr. Herbert if you have any suggestions to make. I want to make an 'individual song' success especially if I am going to 'Frisco. Don't you think my idea a good one write and let me know. Thank you so much for your kind wire, always sincerely, Alice Nielsen".

Herbert and Smith oblige each request with new songs.

Changes continue after two years of *Fortune Teller*. Nielsen writes Smith about the recent revisions: "I like the third act of *Fortune Teller* very much and think it is a great improvement. My songs especially (the last act one) are fine and I think they will be a 'go.' With my thanks & my best regards, believe me to be yours most sincerely, Alice Nielsen".

Across Pacific, debut cover of November *Philippine Magazine* is Furman Hodden woodcut of Alice Nielsen. Influential magazine decades ahead.

In this moment, unheralded by press agents, Williams has proposed again. It is an offer Nielsen can refuse. Again.

When he callously reminds of his money in the show, Alice replies it was a good bet he made, but does not obligate her to marry.

The wealthy heir is displeased. Ire grows at her Europe hopes. Greedy lady pals in Oakland encourage his hate. Williams turns enemy.

The alliance comes to crisis. In the trying days of 1892 San Francisco, fresh from Kansas City arrived a young, abused wife, mother of toddler. Her talent kept poverty away. Now a national star building limitless fortunes, people meet her on that basis; old acquaintances must adjust to her new powers and status. Alice knows what all know, she is only at the start of her artistic career. In San Francisco she had diligently built the performance skills she brandishes so well.

Williams is regional, but Nielsen world-class. Standing in her way would be impossible, any reasonable person would realize. As star, as superstar, she has met many new people who admire her greatly. She has offers, resources. Her art is the talk of the nation, wildly applauded by packed houses; vibrantly onstage twenty-one hours each week of touring season. Revisited the White House. The media call her Americana, a national treasure, a key force to create the fabled Great American Musical. She has made a million fans.

Williams wants her to settle down in Oakland playing house. Her nay tests him sorely, exposes his powerlessness. Money does not buy love. His Bay Area status, the land, race tracks, stables, mansions, servants and the parties mean nothing. Certain Oakland women care greatly about his wealth, stoke his hate.

Perley had kept him at bay several years barking about contracts. Unable to stop Alice from her European plans, Williams seeks revenge.

With offers of money, stock, and future theatrical investment Williams lures Perley to rig the race. Sadly stupid, Perley agrees. Turns disloyal to the star who gives his career's greatest achievements.

Williams & Perley make a deal. They secretly conspire against her. As Nielsen sings onstage a heavy schedule: blindsided, cheated, harassed.

November 6, revisits Kansas City. She has become "the Nielsen".

Homecoming cordial always. *Kansas City Star* notes "the genial personality of the little star. A great audience was present—standing room only—and gave Miss Nielsen greeting both cordial and sincere. It was a sort of mutual exchange. She hasn't changed a bit in two years, the Nielsen, as they speak of her in the East, unless it be that she sings with more surety, force and care than before and is a bit heavier in avoirdupois.

"Otherwise she is the same dainty package of natural, buoyant life as her friends remember her. Nor has she lost that occasional touch of the hoyden [saucy] which gave sparkle to her parts in *The Serenade* and *The*

Fortune Teller. In a word, she's still just Alice Nielsen, and there's no other quite like her".

As expected she plays boy and girl. In the cast: "Eugene Cowles, ponderous basso; Joe Cawthorn and Joseph Herbert, comedians with JC Slavin as a third star in the crescent of comedy. Slavin has succeeded Richard Golden, and shared with Cawthorn the burden of the honors which fall to the funmakers". Slavin plays Nielsen's brother. When he "masquerades...as his sister the masculinity of this false Greta causes convulsions of laughter. Twice...the three comedians take the stage unto themselves and put forward trios very amusing in words, music and treatment. There is a tenor of course—Richie Ling this season, and the other folk are merely incidental to the plot".

Singing Girl rotates with *Fortune Teller*. Matinee days, Nielsen sings two shows. With Bostonians only five times a week. By any measure, Nielsen's vocal endurance was amazing. Her schedule takes toll. She wants relief. Valerga is along and advises her to skip matinees. So do others.

Now-bribed Perley picks a fight after Kansas City.

Dastardly duo Williams & Perley backstab from the shadows. The full story emerges a decade hence. The damage is now. Perley absurdly tries to schedule even more performances, insists she sing all. He abuses his powers and artist manager and show manager. Subverted against the star.

Adds insult to injury with scorn calculated to reduce her reputation. And his long career allows this to happen. To a point.

Stop London, Williams demands. Perley cannot break contracts with the London producers. That fact is the only restraint.

While that storm mounts, Nielsen's winter holiday plans are revealed by *Chicago Tribune* (Nov 7). Back to Pacific ranch and return to Honolulu. In other national theatre news, "Modjeska already has sought her California ranch home near San Diego. An enthusiastic farmer...early riser, and out among her cattle and bees till breakfast. In the morning she rests and in the afternoon rides in the surrounding mountains". Maude Adams rests at "her Long Island estate".

To press and public, plans for London seem secure. Kansas City *Star* quotes "Prof. Johnstone, the palmist" who predicted young Alice "shall sing in foreign lands!" She had replied, 'Now isn't that just splendid! And make lots of money—and—and marry rich, too? Just when shall I go abroad?' 'I believe in 1901' intones seer. 'Glory—goody'. This reading actually took place—a long time ago; long before Alice Nielsen ever thought of 'singing in foreign lands.' It would now appear that Paul Alexander Johnstone's predictions will come to pass...Miss Nielsen will sing in Europe this coming year. Of course there were many other things said during the reading, that cannot be printed...."

Her first KC return fetched a divorce; now judge returns her maiden name (Nov 12) so she may sign contracts Nielsen not Nentwig.

Returning to San Francisco, Nov. 24 (*SF Call*) Nielsen opens "following Frank Daniels" with a cast, "strongest vocally and in the comic elements that has ever appeared in comic opera in America, not even excepting the Bostonians".

Artistic evolution noted. She has skipped a year and her shows sport new, made-to-impress songs. Her acting appreciated. *SF Call*'s L. DuPont Style (Nov. 27): "judging by her performance last night in *The Singing Girl*, she has improved much. Her voice is truer, though hardly stronger than before, her acting shows an intelligent appreciation of character and situation not common in either comic or grand opera prima donnas".

Style continues, "A large and enthusiastic house greeted Miss Nielsen when she appeared at the Columbia Theatre last night. Her record at the Tivoli has not been forgotten and her many friends were strongly in evidence. Her first entrance called forth a burst of friendly applause and her first song received a triple encore. Floral offerings were so numerous that it was impossible to present more than one or two across the footlights; they were therefore packed into the foyer where they lined the entire east wall. They were subsequently sent to the Children's Hospital".

On her way to San Jose, *Fortune Teller* ran December 26th then *Singing Girl*. Nielsen surpasses Bostonians, critics agree. New queen of comic opera, reports *SJ Mercury News* "secured many new subjects at the Victory last evening. There was a large audience. Heralded as a rival of the Bostonians. No one was disappointed, and the Bostonians were relegated to second place. She sang *I Do as I Am Told* [*Fortune Teller*] quite daintily and demurely".

In the cast: Cowles "in excellent voice...an old favorite.... Ling has a pleasing tenor voice and is a good actor". Comic trio: Cawthorn "not a stranger; and has few equals as a Dutch (German-dialect) comedian, and he, Joseph Herbert and Slavin were "all excellent".

Petite choruswomen praised; they were not the usual "stately ladies who seemed out of place and bored". Over a score...they could sing, were tastefully and becomingly attired and could look pleasant. Much of the success of the production was due to the deportment of the chorus, vocally and otherwise. The men's chorus was equally effective. They gave their first number with a dash and vigor that secured immediate recognition".

San Jose sketches conductor Paul Steindorf: "Dash and vigor with which the chorus work was rendered was due to the magnetism of Paul Steindorf, the conductor. He stood up in the orchestra...when the chorus was onstage and the vigorous manner in which he waved the baton was suggestive of Sousa".

San Jose schools San Francisco, where Steindorff "criticized by some of the San Francisco papers for being too much in evidence, it being suggested that he keep his seat and not be so prominent. However, Mr. Steindorff gets results that are seldom secured by musical conductors, even if he has to stand up to do it. The audience was quite enthusiastic...."

Los Angles greets her madly when Nielsen arrives at HC Watt's Los Angeles Theatre a week December 30, 1900 (*LA Times*). And Jules Grau Company is at Burbank Theatre giving *Isle of Champagne*" music by William Furst.

Nielsen opens New Year's Eve "before a large and highly appreciative audience in *The Singing Girl*, a bright and sparkling comic opera, light as thistledown in its motive and decidedly clever in its execution. There are many tuneful airs, and some of the musical effects are unique. The production, as a whole, is excellent. The costumes are rich and beautiful".

In few words, *LA Times* captures the moment. "The story is a mere nothing, not worth the telling. If the piece were called a musical extravaganza, the classification would be nearer the truth" yet "full of life, of action and of melody ...well worth the hearing and seeing. Alice Nielsen's delightful voice adapts itself well to the role of Greta, *The Singing Girl*. While Miss Nielsen's voice is not of extreme range, it is of very sweet quality and good volume. It is noticeably clear in the higher tones, while its mezzo-tones are gentle and caressing. The audience was generous in its appreciation and called Miss Nielsen several times before the curtain".

In the cast: Cowles "several deserved recalls". Cawthorn "as funny as ever". Ling, "there are better tenors...but they are not found in every comic opera company. His tones are clear and confident" acts with "ease and naturalness".

At next night's *Fortune Teller* (*LA Times* Jan 3), for "this talented company of singers and comedians...appreciation of the large audience was manifested in frequent applause and laughter". Show "drops to style of the extravaganza and again approaches the better comic opera.... Orchestra... rather prominently in evidence, was kept well in hand by Mr. Steindorf's decisive direction".

Nielsen's songs "well-suited vocally; she assumes them unaffectedly, and in the various attires donned makes as many attractive appearances".

In the cast: Cowles under weather "a slight huskiness"; "jolly trio" of John Shaw plus Herbert and Cawthorn "furnished a rich fund of amusement". The chorus "young women did admirable work in the terpsichorean evolutions". Thanks director-choreographer Julian Mitchell.

So the year 1900 wraps.

Chicago's George Ade portrays Alice Nielsen in his popular fictional fables as the dream of all young men and impossible to meet. Of course, rather busy onstage. We know her entourage consists of brother Erasmus, at times sister Hortense and Ida Valerga. Nielsen siblings and kids spent summers at ranch with mom Sarah.

During December, George Lederer finalized plans for Alice's April 1st London debut which will replace durable hit *Belle of NY* slated to tour the Continent. Despite what was about to unfold backstage, the show goes on.

1901: DASTARDLY DOUBLE-CROSS

Alice Nielsen's Los Angeles closing January 3rd was the usual SRO party at the biggest theatre of any town they played. "So insistent were...encores that it was 11:30 o'clock before last curtain", reports *LA Times*. "Company is thoroughly up-to-date...amply deserving of the appreciation and patronage which it received".

Before leaving, Alice endorses Chickering Pianos",beauty of tone and delicacy of touch is to my mind unequalled. You are certainly to be congratulated upon having the agency of this noble instrument". Next visit, Baker electric cars.

Returning to San Francisco, she breaks with Williams. Relocates the family to Chicago. Company crosses to New Orleans where Alice makes significant friends for the near future.

They will toward the London crossing. Alice Nielsen's gamble on Williams isn't repaid. Trusted his promises, integrity, business sense. Making big money with the best show onstage as star creates unforgettable happiness in many many people packing the theatres meant nothing to Tom Williams. Her London freedom the last straw. Nielsen insisted to go.

His revenge shows his worst side. Williams, after all, was a rich-kid crony and bookie. Rejected, he reacts viciously. Immediately she departs he announces engagement to that odd Oakland lass from society circles, the jealous shouting skank who disrupted *Serenade*.

Perhaps erstwhile fiancé Alice had sensed his dark side. Decades later, Alice Nielsen put it this way: as her group prepares to sail for London April, "it was a somewhat changed company. In the minds of everyone there was a growing apprehension: Tom Williams, our backer, had withdrawn".

Alice would not be owned: "Tom had made a point of demanding that I quit and return to California with him. I couldn't. I was born to sing. Tom wanted me to marry him, quit the stage, and call it a career".

"What else can you have, Alice?" Williams said. "There is the Alice Nielsen shoe, with its wide tie and colored heel. There is the Alice Nielsen coiffure that everybody is trying to affect. You have sung to audiences which had to buy their tickets 12 weeks in advance. Horses, gowns, babies and theatres have been named after you. Yes, I have seen jockeys swapping ten cigarette picture cards of other celebrities for one Alice Nielsen". With fine-spun Irish irony (plus Danish scorn), Alice tells of he pressed his proposal: "You can't have more than that". Camp in Oakland, drop Europe: "Come on to California with me and enjoy life at home".

Meant nothing to her; abandon career? Skips how Williams & Perley cruelly conspire to cheat her serenity, reputation, and rob her of a fortune.

Nielsen, not yet thirty, cares not about such superficiality as playing house for the Oakland millionaire with tuberculosis she had entrusted to underwrite her career. Many credible offers had pressed her.

Williams goes Nentwig: the woman does not commands take. She does not care to abandon career and share future with him.

Ss she chooses to record they spoke, like this: "I'm sorry Tom, maybe I'll regret it. But I can't quit now. I'd feel cheated, the time would come when I'd regret it. I want to sing".

"Very well Alice. If you can't quit now, I can. Good-by".

She moves on. Truly breathtaking. No mention double-cross. Nielsen's late-life serenity admirable. Let wrongs go by. Vile dead men are buried in every sense. Nentwig, Williams.... Alice gives not the facts she well knew. His violent temper, ruthlessly ran the big horse-racing racket.

"Dear Tom Williams. The time was to come when I had to choose between him and my career as a singer and the choosing was to be my first great sorrow. I simply could not compel myself to retire. I went on singing". Paints him kind, in her version retelling. Such a curious deceit.

"Tom Williams, telling me gently that he hoped I would never regret my decision, sauntered out of my life. He had wealth, he was kind, considerate, and he loved me. Yet—I could not have done otherwise. I was born to sing".

Malicious, not love. Made sure Nielsen had cause to regret her decision. Not gently. Pays Perley to backstab star. Swift vengeance secretive at first. Blame fool Perley who places the wrong bet.

Yet ties that bind Williams and Nielsen many. Couple a decade acquainted in some fashion, despite her intense working life and long winter tours. A son Benjamin grows to a young man in California. Now the trust Williams gained is shattered. Never a paper contract.

North America's greatest musical touring company has floated three years on a verbal agreement between star and investor. Upon that fragile legality, the top theatre professionals combined to create these hits.

Nielsen Company running two shows in rotation on national tour pays about $6,000 gold dollars in weekly expenses. No Federal income taxes exist, so no intrusive reports made, no standardized bookkeeping. Private deals, cash. Essential to Nielsen's prosperity is the honest goodwill. Her success uniquely her own. Trust a weapon used against her.

Perley's judgement makes all the difference. As Williams grows hostile to his ex-fiancé, Perley resists attacking the star. When he succumbs the golden goose soon departs forever. Over a year Perley kept the couple apart. Points repeatedly to a contract clause stops Nielsen marrying.

Williams bribes Perley. Prickly Perley agrees to undercut and harass the star for specific promises of cash, stock and future theatrical investment. They conspire to kill Nielsen's success, distress her mind, defraud. Hide the scheme from the busy, naïve never stupid young star as she entertains America.

Diabolically, Williams & Perley attempt to kill what her performances built; what they invested to create. During this period her happiness and finances are completely compromised. Try to overturn her success; cannot.

Their betrayal could never destroy the fact: the star is on the stage. Loss of Alice Nielsen Company at its height is a major tragedy of theatre history. Stops the nation's strongest diva from making Herbert shows a success. We may only speculate at the future projects lost to us.

After leaving San Francisco, it gets ugly backstage. Yet Alice is contracted into London by April and Williams cannot cancel the contracts.

And the star is onstage nightly.

By March, although Williams has married the disruptive Oakland debutant, he surreptitiously dictates Perley to harass and cheat Nielsen. Perley trades on crony industry connections. Lies blandly. Uses his old-boy publicity network.

America was four decades past the old plantation legal codes of personal control over others. Golden dream of Jefferson's framework for spontaneous order was hanging by a thread. So were gold coins. To speak freely and enjoy with great festival of life with all people, as Epictetus advised, was at risk. Nation founded for pursuit of happiness faced hijack, Lincoln had warned.

The gayety of nations would face attacks. Perley knew how to make trouble. Williams seems a good husband to avoid. The Virginia plantation rhetoric of scorn appears in Perley's press to undercut. Make her seem crazy, rob her. Severe stalking. Yet indeed theatre will have its revenge on villians. With the tall lanky Williams was his short henchmn Perley with handlebar mustache. Perfect icons of theatre villainy. Little Nell forced to marry—dastardly him?

Despite the Williams' hubris, Alice has strong friends among peers.

The managerial assault confuses the press. Why silly fight, pundits wonder. Two corrupt men ended the Alice Nielsen Company.

Squandered their greatest success. She had made them. Without her, the dastardly duo Williams & Perley fade to shadow.

Perley abandoned the winning thoroughbred.

Nielsen skips speaking freely about Williams. She sails past Perley without any mention. Producer of her Broadway success, not a word. Before 1901 ends she refuses to ever speak to him. Or about him.

In this ethical breakdown of spoiled rich boy and corruptible producer the great musical hope of America was lost.

Many women, Nielsen often observed, want a cozy life. Trinkets concern her not very much. Cooperative artists and appreciative audiences matter.

So it was. Behind scenes, Williams turns Perley against the star yet soon his hubris met Nielsen's reality. The shadowy rich kid never listed on the program was nothing to nobody.

Nielsen is performing in LA when Williams wires Perley to contact the producer Lederer "at once, saying star positively refuses and is unmanageable. And besides is in such a state that you feel she will not make good. Say almost anything that occurs to you".

Lederer ain't taking the bait. Insists Perley honor the contract. Bring Nielsen Company to London. Lederer has the power. Perley bends. Only that fact kept the Nielsen show on the road. The one guy in Oakland seeks to scuttle; versus all the others in the biz. Her scorn for Perley grows. Cast caught in-between.

The full betrayal only becomes known after a decade. Sad melodrama worthy of a silent film villain, Williams of Oakland instructs Perley by telegraph and letter. Cloak and especially dagger, Williams uses code for Nielsen: "Jones".

Tells Perley (Jan 12), "We surely want to prevent Jones having any chance to produce the opera [*Fortune Teller, Singing Girl*] in any country". In the later court case, Tom Williams confirms "that referred to Miss Nielsen". Orders Perley to fire Nielsen from her own company: "Think you will find you cannot manage star. The sooner you discharge her, the better". Perley dodges doing so. He has unbreakable contracts with producers who can enforce. Public outrage if to fire Alice from her own show. To please Williams, Perley picks public fights to discredit Alice who is kept unaware that Williams dictates the attacks.

Discontent of producer abuse is simmering. Equity Actors' Union will be created a decade hence by Nielsen pals Lillian Russell, Marie Dressler, Ethel Barrymore, Francis Wilson. Williams of Oakland is a remote regional rube; Alice Nielsen matters to the NY theatricals.

Onstage, Alice Nielsen has left LA for the long tour eastward. Sarah Comstock interviews the star for *San Francisco Call* (Jan 27) with a novelist's eye for nuance. Backstage at Tivoli, "Alice Nielsen, who had once been obliged to line her gowns with rattle-ine [ratline: cheap Indian hemp]...came back with new ones lined with the real thing.... She headed her own company".

Chorus girls asks, "How did you accomplish it all?"

"Oh it wasn't my doing, dear; all the credit is due to my mole. This little brown spot is my mascot; it lifted me from the chorus to the stars".

"There! I always said there was something back of it I didn't understand. I could not explain how a voice like the bird whistle of a Kearny-street fakir ever came to be starred".

Nielsen "jumped from her stool so excitedly that she tipped over the ginger ale bottle. 'Do you suppose that a little brown mole could make me out of a chorus girl? It's talent and voice and hard work that makes a successful star. Dog in the manger!' Alice replies, and "walked tartly away".

End of week, as mentioned, Nielsen picks up her pieces. Brings mom and son to Chicago at 3337 Wabash Avenue, now parking for Chicago Institute of Technology, the Armour Institute of a meatpacker behind Chicago Opera.

February 1st, Musgrove completes arrangements for "Nielsen Company to open at London's Shaftesbury Theatre on April 8 (*Chicago Tribune*)".

Scowling villain Williams of Oakland has been thwarted. Foiled again!

Alice Nielsen will set shoe with curved heel upon London March 20.

Under contrived clouds Alice Nielsen's 1901 North American tour continues, popular demand for tickets soars past Standing Room Only. On February 2nd, *Chicago Tribune* lists the major stories: "Civil War In Abyssinia; Boers Nearing Cape Colony; French Legion Of Honor Given American in Paris; Desperate Battle In Arabia; Wolves Terrify Town of New Buffalo, Mich".

Not last and not least: "Alice Nielsen Has A Sore Foot". The nation cares to know that in Louisville KY, Nielsen got a sore foot from those pesky wood shoes. Grew worse in Terre Haute, she "limped through *The Fortune Teller* before a packed house and appeared only because she was told that there had been so much interest in her first visit to the city that applications were made for twice the capacity of the house".

NY Times amplifies toe troubles: "Singer is suffering severely from a sore in her foot caused by wearing a wooden shoe...the foot became infected with the coloring matter from her stocking at Louisville. Before coming here the foot was lanced. There is fear of blood poisoning".

Sore footed Alice hit Chicago a week Monday, February 4 (*Chicago Tribune*), playing both shows in rotation at Illinois Theatre. They had supplanted the drama *La Tosca* with Sarah Bernhardt and Coquelin. Bernhardt "fascinated her audience, and in spell-bound silence its members watched her wonderful display of anguish". Coincidentally, that weeks' *Tribune* publishes a dramatic letter from Eleanor Duse: "To save the theatre, the theatre must be destroyed. We should return to the Greeks and play in the open air. Boxes, stalls, evening dress and late dinners kill the drama. Ibsen? Ibsen is like a room with all its furniture. What do I care for chairs and tables?"

Unlike affected (or stylish) Bernhardt, Duse has a natural approach to acting; refused stage makeup: "I want beauty and fire. I adore Maeterlinck, but he gives me only shadows, children, mists and spirits. So I am condemned to play Sardou and Pinero. Someday, however a woman will come—a young, beautiful woman, all fire and flame—and will do what I once dreamed to do, but failed. I am too tired now, and cannot begin my life again".

And on her arrival Nielsen had a warm All Sold Out reception: "An audience that tested the capacity of the house welcomed the gifted little woman who occupies first place among the light opera stars...and received not only her work but that of associates with an enthusiastic approval which compelled the repetition of every solo and nearly every ensemble Smith and Herbert's *Fortune Teller* contains" (*Chicago Tribune* Fe 4).

Aware of Perley's chosen dispute with Nielsen over singing at matinees, Chicago focuses on the risks: "Miss Nielsen, although her acting at times shows the effects that frequent and mechanical repetitions of the same part invariably produce, is still winsome in manner and dainty and graceful in appearance, while her singing is at all times a source of pleasure. Her voice is small, but of much natural sweetness, and the thoroughness and correctness of its schooling make it unique among the sopranos heard in light opera today".

In the cast: Cowles "his great bass voice was almost overpowering in the small spaces of the Illinois".

London plans flip-flop in these risky days due to evil machinations. At first—early February—three shows by Herbert were expected: *Serenade*, "Miss Nielsen will employ that opera in conjunction with the two she now has, *The Singing Girl* and *The Fortune Teller*". And Herbert had a project for her, not to mention a possible Gilbert-Herbert collaboration.

Arrival of "The Nielsen" in London is American pride. She symbolizes the magical combination of success by talent and hard work. Spitting in the face of the nation, Williams pursues evil schemes. February arrives, still no public disclosure.

Nielsen Company hops along Mississippi to New Orleans. Brewing conflicts now reach the press. Williams escalates the attempts to shut down Nielsen's career by exhaustion. Perley orders her to sing matinees. Predictably, she refuses. Perley gives out she is "unmanageable" and "difficult".

At the time, Nielsen seems blasé. Egg toss, "New backers line up at every stage door. I met several new men just last night". Indeed she had. New Orleans plays a critical role in future.

Williams dictates Perley to fire Nielsen allies: wardrobe mistress Sarah Bolwell, Gracie Buchell, conductor Paul Steindorf: "I wish you would discharge him at earliest possible moment. Please keep me posted". Pointing at the contract, Herbert and London producer Musgrove demand Steindorf stay.

Years later in court, Perley's counsel Lee read a letter from Williams dated Feb 2 1901: "My dear Frank, There is one thing however, I am firm upon and that is this, that neither Musgrove, Herbert nor anyone else has the slightest right to say to us who shall be our musical director. I would never consent to any such dictation, and I furthermore wish you would discharge Steindorf just as soon as you can. I do not want him to finish the current season with us.

"I do not care even if we have to take a second-rate director and even if the performances go badly. Conditions have greatly changed, so I do not wish you to spend one dollar of our money in any way or to strengthen the cost at all. In fact, under the existing circumstances, I only wish that the London engagement proves a failure".

Caving, Perley fires Steindorf to vex the star. Interestingly, Steindorf moves immediately into San Francisco as music director at Tivoli. *San Francisco Call* (July 1) says, "Of the many good things that the Tivoli has done for music in San Francisco none has probably been of more value than the importation of the present conductor of its orchestra. Mr. Steindorf is a thoroughly cultured musician, a pianist of eminence and of a long and honorable experience as a conductor". Tivoli duties include "drilling his chorus in the grand opera repertoire at the rate of two operas a week" and orchestrating Wagner "with 16 instead of 60 parts so you won't know the difference". Steindorf will be a strong asset to the Bay Area music scene for decades.

Gloating Williams escalates Feb 7th, "Mighty glad you discharged director Saturday. Do same with Jones [Nielsen] if he does not comply with your rules".

Distressed and outraged, Alice cloaks underlying business issues and keeps the press focused on her career, and the roar of the crowd. After all, the star is on the stage. Soon the London stage.

Financial injury adds to insults. Williams orders Perley, "I want all the profits sent to me. I do not intend to put out another cent for the ultimate benefit of the star". If Nielsen objects, "Discharge star if necessary".

Soon Williams wires, "Just received the letter in which you say you wired Hale to refuse to make any advances to her. Awfully glad you did— just to keep up that policy". Hale was Perley's man traveling with the show.

Williams brags, "When I told her our relationship ceased" absurdly claims he had lost $40,000 to $80,000 on the shows. The entire theatre industry knew better. Expanding fraud, Williams prevailed to persuade her to state he "was sole proprietor" of the Alice Nielsen Company, to spare her any financial loss. Yet by all means "Be very firm Frank in this matter of our business and render no statement [accounting] to her. She is certainly showing a very mean and ungrateful spirit in taking such a course" to skip marriage and seek her profits.

Of the Williams & Perley con game of harassment, embezzlement and fraud, Alice's friends will take note. Corrupt producers lying about revenues were a common concern. Lillian Russell pursued many claims against the Shuberts who doctored accounts to show a loss. Examining attendance reports, she discovers her shows profit. They owe half. Russell's determination to make Equity a working force was to protect actors and keep things honest.

Williams & Perley hide the accounts to stop proof of fraud.

As part of the scheme Perley rants to press about Nielsen being "difficult" as he harps on the "personal manager" contract. Blocking her access to profits, Perley gloats publically about the big profitability of her company. Williams & Perley steal the organization Nielsen built. Their corruption obvious to some.

Honest producer could negotiate a settlement and let Nielsen Company continue. Perley conspires to cheat and suppress the star. During a 1909 court cast the truth emerges. Perley sues Williams to fully pay the promised bribes.

Nielsen's emotional distress in late summer 1901 can be traced to the two unscrupulous men who elaborately conspire to defraud and slander.

At that point in 1901—tracing the 1909 case "Williams vs Perley"—*LA Times* says "Here is the unkindest cut". Williams orders Perley to change the company name: "better call it the Williams-Perley Opera Company" and hire rival Helen Bertram. Changing name proves impossible, but Bertram hired. Williams wires Perley: "Good scheme to engage Bertram. Jones [Nielsen] certainly will have a dozen fits, and that is the place we want to put him in now".

Silent films will popularize the Nielsen plight: rejecting an unwanted offer of marriage by a wealthy jerk who retaliates by threatening the heroine with financial disaster. Who will save "Little Nell"? Under this attack by dastardly Williams, little Nielsen elects not to fight. Yet she has powerful lawyers recommended by Lillian Russell.

Talk money. In 1909 Perley's attorney give as evidence a February 1898 contract stating Perley would manage the company and get 25% profits. The rest went to the owners, Nielsen and Williams. In event of Williams' death, everything to Nielsen. Also put into evidence was Perley's contract to manage Nielsen five years starting May 24, 1899. So Perley is managing producer of the Alice Nielsen Company and personal manager of Alice Nielsen. Taking bribes to harm either is a severe conflict of interest.

For Williams, Perley amazes the press. He will drop the nation's star yet keep her shows. Perley plans to fire Alice Nielsen from The Alice Nielsen Company. She seems uppity, demands seeing the books and divas dime a dozen. Of course seems crazy to the entire nation and entire press corps.

A shocked Herbert foresees future projects and profits melting, melting.

Across summer 1901 Perley undercuts. Proclaims void their vaunted personal management contract. Buzzword-wise Perley (twirls mustache and smiles) could never manage an "unreliable" star who "cannot stand success".

When Williams next year fails to pay off the promised bribes, Perley absurdly reverses and attempts to regain control over Alice's career. The theatre industry laughs him to scorn. Nielsen deploys the theatre lawyers suggested by Lillian Russell. Perley slinks away. Curses foiled again!

Why does Alice Nielsen skip out on Victor Herbert? Nobody knew at the time it was Williams & Perley at fault. Until the personal management contract expires in 1905 the golden Alice goose remains in Europe. Outside Perley's zone of influence.

Meanwhile, press celebrates her upcoming London season.

LA Times' (Feb 17) notes Sousa's arrival with soloists "Arthur Pryor, trombone and Herbert Clark, cornet". Readers are reminded "Alice Nielsen and her entire opera company will sail for England" in four weeks. "Considerable curiosity is felt regarding the manner in which this ideal

American company will be received by our British cousins, but as *Serenade* will be rendered along with *Fortune Teller* and *Singing Girl*, the best results are expected. Viola Pratt Gillette will sail with the company".

Glancing at the syndicated report, Nielsen would discover Melba had been "singing small parts in Covent Garden where no one knew her, and where she received the conventional applause. One evening the Prince attended" and asks to hookup. Melba joins the royal playboy privately. "After that she was given better roles and an opportunity to display her voice to a better advantage".

And Perley publicly demands more matinees while cheating her profits!

Consider Lillian Russell's telegram to (Shubert archives NY Belasco Theatre), "Sam Shubert distinctly understood I would play no matinees on one-night-stands. Will not play matinee Hartford. I will positively not play the Hartford matinee. I am no slave for Shuberts or anyone else".

Perhaps Nielsen lacks the mighty force of friend Lillian. Perhaps does not wish to battle Williams. Perhaps henchman Perley does his dirty work via coded messages and Alice doesn't yet realize the complete perfidy of Williams. For a while the press attempted to comprehend what had stopped making sense. The Williams & Perley racket was hid.

February *LA Times* tried solve the mystery: "Miss Nielsen vigorously objected to playing Weds matinees on the ground that they were too trying on her voice. Perley seemed to think this objection was not well founded… this led to considerable argument in which the members of the company took sides". Without access to the Williams coded telegrams, the story lacks coherence.

Over singing more matinees, in New Orleans Nielsen "declared herself in no uncertain terms" and "threatened to leave the company without further ado". So she is blamed for the Williams-dictated trip by Perley to sign Elenoir Guisti and "the difficulties were patched up". Guisti had joined Bostonians three years earler and left for a clone "Boston Serenaders in their own farcical operetta *Davy Jones* by Fred Miller Jr". Cast of ten croons *Venetian Serenade* in "the hoodoo palace" (*Phil. Inquirer* Se 10 1899). Perley schemes to enrage star.

Nielsen has cause for strong feelings. Her hit company built by three years is being hijacked by two conspiring malicious men.

America is for Nielsen; she is on the stage.

Nielsen hangs amazingly tough. Sings and dances to great applause.

Perley seems a master of misinformation playing the media. His press releases become shreds and patches of biz clichés smearing Alice Nielsen as ungrateful and unreliable. After he "made her a star" she crazily refuses to obey. The Nielsen causing the trouble, you see.

Williams in March announces that Nielsen is no longer in his will to inherit, as he brags his wedding to Miss Steele the shouting slut. This doesn't interest anyplace beyond California. "December last, Williams drew up his will, leaving his entire fortune to the operatic singer. Recently this will was destroyed and another drawn. This was the first intimation of a coldness between the turfman and the singer, and it was followed by the announcement of his engagement to Miss Steele, the daughter of the well-known merchant and clubman.

"Mr. Williams and Miss Steele were playmates, and several years ago when the turfman's health was so poor [tuberculosis] that his recovery was deemed impossible, the Steeles did much to make his lot happier. The forthcoming wedding is to be in the nature of a Bohemian affair, following a quiet marriage in Oakland. Mr. and Mrs. Williams and a few friends will come to this city for a dinner at Marchand's and then the party will take in the vaudeville show at the Orpheum".

Williams claims he "has withdrawn from the management" of Nielsen Company after supplying "the funds which made a starring venture possible for Miss Nielsen". Claims "a new partnership to produce comic operas" with Perley in which "Miss Nielsen does not figure". (*LA Times* Mar 17). Happily, dastardly duo Williams & Perley prove equally insincere with each other. The crisis of course demoralizes the cast. Word gets out.

Happily, powerful producers line up now Perley has sidelined himself.

Klaw & Erlanger offer to manage Alice who apparently still holds false hopes and amazingly replies her agreement remains in force with Perley.

Whatever happens, she stars. March 3rd they play Washington to Standing Room Only. *Singing Girl* three nights then *Fortune Teller* on Thursday, Friday and Saturday matinee and evening. "Washington is particularly fond of comic opera, and it especially likes Alice Nielsen", said the *Post* (Mar 3).

"Even before that young lady became a star, and when she was only soprano of the Bostonians, Washingtonians picked her out as a coming diva, and events have proved that their judgment was correct".

At National Theatre, "both operas have been given new settings of scenery and costumes, and to all intents and purposes are said to be as spick and span as on the first nights of their production".

Fortune Teller attracted "the largest audience of the week. Standing room was at a premium" *Post* said March 8. Nielsen "still the very refreshing ingénue, with the magnificent voice and a chic manner of doing things which has made her very popular. She is unconventional and breezy, but not too much so".

Nielsen lives to improvise: "When some students in the upper gallery gave her a college cheer after the first act, she turned like a flash and yelled 'Hello, yourself!' Such is the privilege of a prima donna star".

Post significantly reveals: "It is just the style of impromptu stage business which has made Miss Nielsen so popular". This is key to her stage presence!

In the cast: Joe Cawthorn, "deep-voiced, stalwart popular Eugene Cowles". In her home town, May Boley took the role of Viola Gillete.

March 7th when *NY Times* asks Nielsen about a change in producers, she seems blind-sided. Probably was. "Asked this afternoon if she had made an engagement with Klaw & Erlanger" she "manifested surprise and said it was a subject she did not care to discuss—in fact, she had not heard anything about it". Continues, amazingly, she "had an incompleted contract with Mr. Perley and Mr. Williams and had no present intention of changing her connection with them". She states, "But really, you must not ask me to talk about the matter, as I have no definite information to give.'"

Perley blandly states, from his office within the National Theatre: "Miss Nielsen will cease to sing under my management.... On April 8th we shall take the entire company to the other side, and our stay and Miss Nielsen's engagement will depend altogether upon the degree of success met with by us in London". Then "Miss Nielsen is free to do as she likes, and meantime she is at liberty to contract any engagement she sees fit".

Perley oozes cliché spin: "Miss Nielsen began starring two years ago. She had a friend in Col. Thomas Williams, a wealthy Californian, and his capital made it possible for her to realize her desire to appear as a star. She has met with great success, and is a valuable property, but she cannot stand success. I do not mind her having something to say about how things shall be done, but I also like to have something to say about them myself". He tells other producers take his star, please: "Mr. Erlanger came to see me last week, and asked me if he was at liberty to talk with Miss Nielsen about making an engagement with her at the close of my engagement, and I assured him that I had no objection or obstacle to his consulting her".

Continues corny: "When Miss Nielsen's engagement with me ceases, a firm will be formed under the style of Perley & Williams, Miss Nielsen's benefactor having reached the same conclusion about her that I have. The new firm will continue the organization as it is now, to produce operas. We hope to find a singer who will prove that our present prima donna is not the last of her race. I do not care to mention the one we have in sight".

Claims the shows as property: "We retain the rights to all the operas in which Miss Nielsen has been successful, and we also will have the organization that we believe has been largely responsible for her success as a prima donna".

Perley's attack receives dutiful reporting only at first. March 9, *Washington Post* speculates on "Alice Nielsen's Future". Curious conflict, "exact cause of the strained relations is not perfectly clear, though close friends of prima donna and manager have known for some days that the separation was impending.... The supporting company headed by Eugene Cowles and another prima donna whose name has not yet been divulged, will continue under the management", adding Perley's tagline, he "first made Miss Nielsen a paying star".

Perley terms Nielsen "dictatorial and unreasonable" repeating clichés she is "dazed by the unusual success" to adopt "frills and eccentricities".

Imagine Perley wringing his hands tearfully in tortured fashion, pushed past the edge by a nearly-crazy diva he robbed, while twirling his mustache. Despite his forbearance, he would "simply get a new prima donna who will consent to let the manager"—significantly—"attend to business matters". Stay out the books, pretty little lady!

"Perley... who has managed many prominent stars in the last twenty years, stated that Miss Nielsen has exhibited too strong a desire to interfere with the business management...." Dictatorial, unreasonable, "dazed by the unusual success which has attended her efforts as a star, and has adopted so many frills and eccentricities that it is impossible to further continue as her manager. There are other prima donnas".

Post marks both sides of the dispute. Nielsen "on the other hand states that it is she who is displeased with Mr. Perley: 'I shall no longer be under his management after our London season, which opens next month.'"

Did Williams & Perley make her a star? "I have very little to say, except that I believe I am responsible for my own success and that I have won a place for myself which will permit me to stand alone".

Uncooperative? "I have no wish to defend myself against anything that may said of me personally, for I think the public knows me well enough to know that I require no defense".

Aligned with a robust philosophy, Nielsen takes the high road against her adversaries: "Mr. Perley and I disagreed, and so we part. A number of managers have made offers but I have accepted none. I have not signed with Klaw & Erlanger, as reported. I shall star, however, under the direction of an eminent manager, appearing in a new opera. I really cannot tell you any more of my plans, for there is nothing to say. I am undecided".

Alice Nielsen now expresses the underlying conflict: two 19th-century men try to control the modern self-made woman: "Mr. Perley says I have the 'swelled head.' That is absurd. It is simply a new name for a woman who has worked hard—and I have worked hard—to win success, and now is simply standing up for her rights".

Same day as *Washington Post*, *NY Times* details the split, "Perley and Nielsen part" and "Williams withdraws from the venture". Outside Perley's turf, *Times* corrects *Washington Post*, "just what Williams' grievance is does not appear clearly. It was Miss Nielsen who discovered the backer and who introduced him to Perley. Therefore, she seems to feel she should be considered in whatever new arrangement is made". Contacted for comment, Williams slyly expresses "pride concerning his opera company" saying he "wishes to continue" with a new star. Of course this is to entrap Perley to harm Alice.

Absurdity of Alice Nielsen Company without her is lost on nobody.

Emotional toll on the singer gives Williams of Oakland his revenge.

Shock to Williams & Perley, *Times* relates that Nielsen felt "safe in her present position, inasmuch as she has the promise of future backing". She "will not disclose the name of the man".

First mention of huge help to Alice Nielsen's career by New Orleans.

Dixieland bands built a style from Louis Moreau Gottschalk's syncopations and brass bands. Arthur Pryor's trombone with Sousa! The song *Dixie* arose in minstrelsy during Gottschalk's life (1829-69).

New Orleans' French Opera House was famed. Alice's promised backer was the wealthy Theodore Grunewald, owner of Grunewald Hotel. When Alice returns from Europe in grand opera six years hence, Grunewald helps sponsor a full season for her company at French Opera House.

Perley does damage he could, liar he was: "There is nothing to this trouble except Miss Nielsen got beyond our control...remaining under my management is an impossibility".

Given the truth later in court, Perley clichés make painful reading. He brags of firing Steindoff. "Miss Nielsen has not looked upon the change in musical directors with any special favor". When Alice returns from Europe, Perley is the likely suspect in bribing the orchestra to play badly.

Nielsen had refused to go to Europe without Steindorf. Yet she does; and the Herbert music loses quality. The rich vocal harmony appears to have been lost, London critics complain. Among other factors sabotaging success. The titanic Nielsen Company begins to sink. The band plays.

So it is. Petty jealous Tom Williams the despot of Oakland destroys Alice Nielsen Company, aided and abetted by henchman Frank Perley.

Years later she serenely looks back on her flawed fiancé without mentioning bitter betrayal of her trust.

Los Angeles would reveal the truth in due time.

In 1909 court, Williams seeks from Perley $20,000 for expenses (*LA Times* Jun 1909). Perley responds he was no partner, only "employed at $100 a week to manage her tour". Perley exhibits contracts, telegrams and letters detailing Williams' nefarious plot, saying "the turfman [Williams] told him that he was willing to back other theatrical ventures, but would require him to sever his connection with Miss Nielsen, in consideration for which Perley was to receive 100 shares of stock in the New California Jockey Club and about $15,000 worth of stock in Mexican enterprises...." Related documents reveal "circumstances attending the withdrawal of Williams from Miss Nielsen's financial support. This event took place at the close of the first season".

So. Perley dodged Williams almost a year to protect Nielsen Company before he took bribes and changed course. When Williams welched, Perley attempted to reverse course as only a liar could. Too bad too late.

Wonderfully, Perley counter-sues Williams for unpaid bribes: "100 shares of the stock of the New California Jockey Club, $5,000 worth of stock in the La Puerta Mining Company of Mexico, and $10,000 worth of stock in an abattoir" in Mexico were offered Perley "on certain conditions" to wreck Nielsen's peace, hopes, and finances. Big 1900s fortune Tom Williams willing to spend to squash Nielsen's success after she rejects his offer of a loving marriage in Oakland.

Williams & Perley add to embezzlement, slander. Perley hireling Mose Gunst admits sending a letter to theatrical producers stating that Nielsen's success had "completely turned her head" (and other clichés Perley repeats nauseously to reporters). Gunst expresses regret for his actions.

Fortunately telling, the George Musgrove deal for London was signed before the conspiracy went down. He would not tolerate a double-cross.

March 10th *Washington Post* continues to term the dispute "personal", no hint Williams & Perley were stealing the proceeds. Her "affairs have been marked by storm clouds for some months" and "Miss Nielsen would sever her connection...at the end of the London season, which commences on April 8". Perley claims "Miss Nielsen has been 'dropped' because she has such an exaggerated idea of her own importance that she has become unmanageable".

When Perley signed Nielsen press opined, better for him than her. She made him a star's manager. *Post* blandly takes his word, "the gentlemen [sic] who... expended a small fortune to develop her into the most profitable light opera star of today, will derive no further profit from their labors. It would seem that both sides have only cause for thankfulness that the temporary breach will expand into a permanent one".

Perley re-announces a new company taking the Nielsen players and shows, and named after himself until Williams demands a change to Williams & Perley. He claims rights to the Herbert shows, "I own the rights to both of the operas in which Miss Nielsen appeared.... I shall continue in business partnership with Mr. Tom Williams, of San Francisco.... We will fulfill our contracts with Miss Nielsen and the London managers, but after our season ends our relations will terminate absolutely". Perley had already broken contract obligations to her.

He would sail just to make things unpleasant for her. Perley spins, "I don't mind a prima donna having her say about things, but I wish to have a little something to say myself. The young lady has been made a star under the most favorable circumstances, with a magnificent company, two splendid operas have been written especially for her, and she has had the benefit of such experience as I possess".

As the public love the star, Perley is in a bind. As lackey for Williams, he must undercut the most popular woman on the stage. And he is after all, a creature of the stage. Who senses the rising contempt.

Perley backpedals a fraction: "I do not take credit for her success by a long shot, yet I think those who are familiar with all the details will credit me with some share of it, even if the public does not. When I took Miss Nielsen in hand it was necessary to place her in the care of an experienced stage manager [director Mitchell], who taught her every movement, every inflection, how to speak every line". One wonders how Mitchell, famously deaf, heard her speak.

Perley paints Nielsen a windup worthy Offenbach's *Tales Of Hoffman*: "We drilled her and drilled her, and this, in conjunction with her unquestioned talent and liberal gifts of nature, made her a very pleasing prima donna".

Apparently Perley did everything to make everything. So he suggests.

Beats his dancing strawhorse: "Miss Nielsen scored a tremendous hit in the opera, but it is absurd to suppose that the company, chorus and opera had no share in this success. You can take the most brilliant gem, give it a poor setting, and its luster is lost. Yet Miss Nielsen is not disposed to concede any credit to anyone excepting herself. Miss Nielsen has risen from a minor position to the prominence of one of the best paying stars now on the stage, and she cannot understand how it happened. After my experience I am willing to permit anyone else who wishes to undertake the task of managing her". Perley viciously twists the dagger of "best paying stars" as he defrauds her.

When Tom Williams shoots San Francisco *News-Letter* editor in cold blood, *LA Times* does the best objective reporting. When thieves Williams & Perley fall into lawsuits revealing the lie, *LA Times* reports.

Perley's hoax adds a mad flourish: "Williams, who knew many theatrical managers, first saw that Miss Nielsen's musical education was completed, and was then instrumental in securing her an engagement with the Bostonians".

Henry Barnabee, who should know, tells Alice won audition suggested by Tivoli's manager, and hired her for skill and talent.

Perley claims he (not Mrs. Herbert, then Herbert) "was struck with her voice and talents, and gave her first opportunity in *The Serenade*".

Cheating Nielsen's pay in private, he brags on her earnings in public: "The starring career of Miss Nielsen has not had one interruption and the receipts are generally understood to have been the largest recorded for any operatic star in recent years. Certainly at the present moment, after a little more than two years of endeavor, Miss Nielsen is the most prosperous operatic prima donna in the field".

Perley's memoirs did not repeat such lies. Surrendering to the courtship of Williams, he erased himself. When he killed Alice Nielsen Company, he was.

Whilst pompous Perley preens in press, Nielsen Company rehearses for a London production. New cast members: John Slavin "does not care to make the trip" so Alexander Clarke, "clever comedian" replaces. From her first tour, Frank Rushworth as Ladislas, Paul Nicholson, comedian, and stagemanager Herbert Cripps rejoin for the London trip, "and a dozen new chorus girls were added to the ensemble". The production "one of the most elaborate and complete ever sent from this country".

Perley goes to London, "twenty years or more since Frank Perley left his Washington home to 'go on the road.'"

"One of the best-known and most universally respected managers in the theatrical world", Frank Perley of 32 Bates St., Washington DC, was born Apr. 21, 1856. His reputation diminishes fast after the 1909 court case airs nasty facts. His deeds leave few friends.

Alice only tosses an egg: Perley's supposed project without her will be titled "Le Toupee", double pun combines a recent flop—*Le Poupee* starring Anna Held (1872-1918) which ran fourteen shows—with Perley was bald.

March 10 (*SF Call*), Williams confirms date of the final rift, speaking foggy phrases of man-world jibber-jabber masking sheer malice.

Touring on, final American appearance of Alice Nielsen Company will be by coincidence Philadelphia at Chestnut Street, March 11th, 1901. The *Singing Girl* three nights and *Fortune Teller* two nights plus Saturday matinee. *Inquirer* says, "Philadelphia is particularly fond of comic opera and it especially delights in Alice Nielsen". *Serenade* is "received with much acclaim. When the youthful prima donna returned here last year with another opera, *The Singing Girl*, she found local theatergoers ready to receive her with open arms and she went away from here with a grateful heart and a fat pocketbook. Miss Nielsen will close her American tour in this city on March 16...."

Opening night's review: "This is one of the most attractive and meritorious performances". New contralto Viola Gillette and "a new comedian Harry Dale, late of the Bostonians" noted in the cast. *Inquirer* reveals their London arrival date anticipated as Easter Monday, April 8th.

Unimaginable to people that Nielsen never sings another Herbert show.

Victor Herbert is said to be joining London (Mar 21 *NY Times*) although busy preparing Pittsburgh Orchestra for spring tour starting April 22 in NYC. So if he went a very quick roundtrip and no press mention in London!

Curses, says Williams, foiled again. Before the company depart Williams tries several last-ditch efforts to stop the London visit, albeit without success.

Perley dares not cross the powerful Musgrove and Lederer.

Williams realizes—after all—Alice sails, he drops Oakland and honeymoons over to London to pursue harassment on a personal level. After all, his Oakland bride is known to heckle star performers. Williams will discover his regional charms unappreciated in London; he has no clout, the clod. So it was.

Top-ranked Alice Nielsen Company leaves American shores for the last time, the corrupt pair have oppressed the beleaguered star two years.

Suddenly the London gig is off. Days from departing, Perley proclaims he cancelled "all plans for London" due to "the season of mourning for royalty...." After the death of Queen Victoria (three months ago, Jan 21, 1901): "Londoners, in Perley's judgment, are in no mood to appreciate the winsome Alice. This revision of the schedule was duly announced to Miss Nielsen and she was instructed to be prepared to conclude her present arrangements at the close of the Washington season".

Alice Nielsen Company sails as scheduled. No elaboration.

London is a new ball game. Lederer and Musgrove exercised the power to get the show as promised. They booked a hit; they got clout. Perley folds.

Williams hates Perley now, any deal worthless Williams' integrity.

Even so, *Serenade* drops from the package.

Fortune Teller will debut Europe for Nielsen Company. The stolen French plots filtered by American irony with baffling absurdity, how does it run? *Singing Girl* is planned for the following season.

Overseas, Williams & Perley cannot hide the money.

Alice's yellow brick road has come to a bridge. Nielsen sets sail, her first voyage, Wednesday March 20th, 1901. She does not realize America will not be revisited five years. Things change when the steamer leaves dock to join the great swells of the open sea. For one thing, she finds society congenial. During the voyage, people mix. The players entertain.

Alice Nielsen Company of seventy seasoned theatre pros who have toured North America three years are highly talented wits giving gayety to nations.

On shipboard Nielsen meets several New Orleans friends with London connections who immediately guide her into the most helpful circles of highest society essential to her future. Sooner than later.

LONDON SUCCESS, A NEW BEAU

London as Nielsen sails is bigger than NYC. Has doubled in last forty years to 6.5-millions. Her name is known. First mention in London October 1898 by *The Era* weekly for Toronto *Fortune Teller* debut, saying "formerly of the Bostonians" Alice Nielsen stars in a show written for her. *Era's* "American Amusements" section henceforth covers her progress. December 17th, *Era* reports Alice's debut season of five weeks at Wallack's "averaged $10,000 per week". Next year October 14th, *Era* reports Alice's *Singing Girl* debuted in Montreal on 2nd "to an enthusiastic and crowded house". In 1900, *Stage* notes the Nielsen Company trip to London delayed a year. News they open Shaftesbury April 1901 spreads widely. *Globe* in March tells readers "Alice Nielsen will resume her original role and it appears the cast shall be wholly American". *Sketch* prints the Schloss scene of Alice in drag with Marguerite Sylva, saying Alice "the young comic-opera star...is a delightful actress and singer who had made big successes".

Nielsen's cruise across the Atlantic proves quite socially productive to say the least. Travels with brother Erasmus and her helper from elevator days. Onboard she meets old and new friends from New Orleans such as John Lister-Kaye, brother-in-law of New Orleans-born Consuelo Yznaga (1859-1909), closely related to the Vanderbilts. Consuelo is also the present Duchess of Manchester. Dukes and Duchesses answer only to Kings and Queens. Lister-Kaye introduces Nielsen to Consuelo who helps the singer meet top London society, easily buffers Alice from the fast-fading dreary chains of bumpkin villains Williams & Perley, and encourages a move to grand opera. Life becomes art: Consuelo is portrayed in fiction by Edith Wharton as Conchita Closson, "bohemian" heiress although dad was Cuban, not of Czech Bohemia. Consuelo and her sister enjoy crooning coon songs same as Alice.

The new London producer is a great and good man. George Lederer runs elegant Shaftesbury with 1,270 seats, destined destroyed WWII.

Born in Wilkes-Barre PA, Lederer at thirteen was a boy soprano in a touring juvenile company. Maturity wasn't postponed by a dozen drear schooling years back then. At seventeen he leases NY's Casino theatre through 1903. Lederer has seen Nielsen onstage with Bostonians. His contempt for Williams & Perley may be inferred. Unlike the dastardly duo he is genuinely a theatre-person; no bookie nor circus publicist. Tops at his craft, Lederer had produced Broadway's first musical revue, 1894's *The Passing Show*; first American musical to go to London, 1897's *Belle Of New York*; and the first (NY and London) all-black musical *In Dahomey* (1903) authored by a well-known coon-song composer who had debuted in a Victor Herbert project for the week it was staged.

Nielsen replaces Lederer's great success *Belle of New York* which starred Edna May as Violet Gray. Her 1916 silent film, *Salvation Joan* directed by Wilfrid North, retold the *Belle* story: society woman secretly works at Salvation Army.... After sixty-four NY performances Lederer sailed his Casino troupe to London April 1898. The London show scored 697 performances before starting its European tour at Nielsen's approach.

The 1901 stars were petite: Alice Nielsen, Edna May, Anna Held each weigh about a hundred pounds. May, born 1870s same as Nielsen, had performed a juvenile production of Gilbert & Sullivan while in Syracuse before attending NY Music Conservatory where taught Herbert, Dvorak and Huneker. Her 1895 debut was with Oscar Hammerstein. Interestingly for irony, Edna May retires in 1907 to marry Oscar Lewisohn, millionaire by inheritance who frequents the horse-racing tracks such as Belmont. His 1817 death leaves $5-million to wife. Nielsen rejects rich Tom Williams, who dies 1915 after robbing her of a fortune.

As Nielsen nears London docks, ever-sapient *Los Angeles Times* (Mar 31) publishes "Wanted—an 'Angel' saying "Alice Nielsen, having disagreed with her manager and her financial supporter, departs for Europe to finish her contract there with no definite idea of the future beyond. She will present *The Singing Girl* and *The Fortune Teller* in London, opening the week after Easter".

Dastardly Williams & Perley stalk Nielsen with a vengeance. With the cast "upon the same steamer were Mr. and Mrs. Frank Perley...." He describes this "a vacation. But he and the financier of the Nielsen Company have both withdrawn their support from the little prima donna...." And feeds *LA Times* lies such as "Victor Herbert, though he had contracted to write an opera for Miss Nielsen, has cast his lot with Mr. Perley and the financier".

Herbert suffers no fool gladly; never lets Perley touch another show.

Pittsburg Dispatch relates that Herbert will create "two new operas during the coming summer". One is "a new opera for Alice Nielsen, though that prima donna's season in London will give him time to delay until the success of the Herbert operas is repeated or denied in the English capital". Hedging his bets at least to the press, Herbert, "also to write an opera for Perley", is waiting until "Perley decides upon a star next season".

Perley firing Steindorf won't be forgiven. Losing Alice Nielsen, Herbert withdraws three years from Broadway. His comedy *The Viceroy* had opened 1900. Not until 1903 will *Babes in Toyland* extravaganza reunite the erstwhile Nielsen Company creative team of Julian Mitchell and Caroline Siedle; words by Glen MacDonough. *Babes* features "cast of one hundred, mostly girls". The show murders Santa Clause early in Act One.

Upon return to NY hapless Perley will find Williams has abandoned him, retracting promised funds and bribes.

Nielsen meets the new London audience, well-marinated with publicity.

Within a week she has conquered completely.

9th April, *The Fortune Teller* opens, billed "First appearance in England. Miss Alice Nielsen, supported by her Company of American Artistes".

10th, Alice takes the cover of *The Sketch* as "The new American star who produces the *Fortune-Teller* at the Shaftesbury...." For regional press she is the star "whose fame has preceded her".

11th *Morning Post*, "Alice Nielsen is to be congratulated on her success".

13th *Illustrated Sporting and Dramatic News* sports a double set of stage photos from the show.

17th *The Sketch*, "What an exuberantly active and gay little songstress Miss Alice Nielsen is. She came, sang, and conquered. She bore on her bonny shoulders the full weight of the new American comic opera". Just week the first.

19th Cambridge, "At the Shaftesbury Miss Alice Nielsen has made a big hit with *The Fortune Teller*, a comic opera from America, of a higher class and different style to the ones...." *The Sphere* agrees, "Alice Nielsen, by the rare gift of personality, was to prove a mascot for the Shaftesbury, which has had bad luck...." Alice news appears across the isles. In Dundee, Scotland, "Far away in Kansas City, Missouri, Miss Alice Nielsen, who has made a hit in the *Fortune-Teller*, made her first appearance when she was exactly an eight old mischievous slip of a girl...."

Within a week Alice is iconic. America is overjoyed.

Stanley Jones cabled *NY Telegraph*: "First presentation of the *Fortune Teller* in England was made tonight ....Miss Alice Nielsen...made a big hit, and I judge from the manner in which her support was received the piece will enjoy a long run in London". She starts jittery, "The actress was noticeably nervous when she stepped on the stage, but she seemed to appeal to her audience and before the play was half finished she had worked herself into the graces of almost everyone who came to witness her. The only mistake was on the part of the management—that of allowing too many encores. The gallery and the pit became annoyed at the successive calls for the star, and after a while the urchins there began to hiss".

In the cast: "Eugene Cowles and Joseph Cawthorn made individual hits and received several curtain calls. In the audience: "Among Americans...Phyllis Rankin, Madge Lessing, Marie George, Queenie Vassar [wife of Joe Cawthorn], Richard Carle, and George McLellan".

Pathetic Perley seems caught up by the success: "Audience was one of the biggest that has assembled at the Shaftesbury in a long time...and caused Manager Perley [not managing the star] to remark that he would continue Miss Nielsen's season for two years, at least". Yet it is Perley cannot stand success.

Nielsen has refused to speak to Perley since America. Foiled again.

EA Dithrams reports in *NY Times* (April 14) "At the Shaftesbury the piquancy of Alice Nielsen and the melody of Victor Herbert have secured some sort of popularity for *The Fortune Teller*, though the peculiarities of Harry E. Smith as a dramatist are viewed with polite amazement".

May 9th, fleeting hints of the ugly internals appear. *The Stage* claims "Alice Nielsen Company at the Shaftesbury, is to star Miss Fauchon Thomson in America next season as a successor to Miss Alice Nielsen. It was Mr. Perley's intention, by the bye, to sail yesterday on a flying trip to New York...." Yet the scoundrel lurks longer. By mid-May he will be banished from the theatre.

The star's fame soars. London scorns the show and savors the star.

May 11th, Alice graces the cover of *Sporting and Dramatic News* whose "Captious Critic" praises cast. The show itself does not seem "to be quite worth the trouble either of the players or the audience. It is to be regretted that we do not see Miss Alice Nielsen in work more worthy of her brightness as an actress and her skill and gifts as a singer".

Change is nigh. The curse of Harry Smith's hodgepodge pseudo-Euro plot. London critics join North America in disliking the text. Suprisingly, the music as present does not please. Loss of Herbert's conductor Steindorf could be the culprit.

NY Times reports "London gave an enthusiastic welcome to *The Fortune Teller* last evening.... Unless all signs fail, the piece is in for a run at least as long as that of *The Belle of New York*". Good marks to Nielsen, Cowles, and to Cawthorn's comedy who grew up in London theatre and writes his own lines.

Marking the hit, London society flocks backstage to praise the players. And among this flock are appreciative theatre insiders who recognize Nielsen as an artist very admirable, and provide a ready untouchable defense against any further assaults by the soon-fleeing rustic farce called Williams & Perley.

London Times: text bad, music fair. Depends "for its success entirely upon Miss Nielsen". For besieged Alice Nielsen, if any have any doubts, *London Times* makes the strongest possible case for her artistic and box office value:

> If the expressions of approval which greeted parts of *The Fortune Teller*...produced at the Shaftesbury Theatre last night, were genuine, much cannot be said for the English taste in comic opera. *The Fortune Teller* has none of the charm which should be found in comic opera...it might however, be saved if it had any of the humour that justified the old burlesque. The dialogue has however, not a sparkle of wit in it from beginning to end, the plot is particularly incomprehensible and quite uninteresting, and there is no one amusing situation in the play.

> The comedians with one exception, though they work hard, do not meet with any particular success; and the humour of Mr. Joseph Herbert and Mr. Alexander Clark who play the parts of a Polish pianist and of a ballet-master, is crude and primitive. The exception is Joseph Cawthorn, who plays the part irrevocably connected in American farce with an elderly German. In *The Fortune Teller*, it is true the character is that of a gypsy, but it is intrinsically the same as that of the Polite Lunatic in *The Belle of New York*. Mr. Cawthorn is a comedian of some originality, and he is decidedly entertaining. His scenes were the best in the piece.

> Miss Alice Nielsen, who plays the double role of a fortune teller and a ballet dancer, possess a good voice, which she knows how to use. She is not however provided with very good songs, either in the matter of words or of music. If she could infuse rather more originality into her acting a certain success might be predicted for her. As it is Miss Nielsen does but little more than many other actresses have done before her, and her style has no great measure of individuality. Of the other actors, Mr. Eugene Cowles, who plays the part of Sandor a gypsy musician, has a really remarkably fine bass voice, and he uses it well. Miss Viola Gillette, Miss Winifred Williams, and Mr. Frank Rushworth may also be mentioned as actors who worked hard, though without very much distinction.

> Of the plot nothing need be said; it is intricate, inconsequent, and totally unimportant. The music is bright and catchy but one would like to see a little more musicianship displayed. Part-writing is conspicuous by its absence, and the choruses are for the most part in unison.

[Odd statement; Herbert wrote eight-part harmony in the superb choral parts, perhaps lost with Steindorff's firing. But the cast had been singing them harmony three years!]

Assessing strengths of star and show, *London Times* swings strong toward the singer's side: "*Fortune Teller*...depends for its success entirely upon Miss Nielsen and if she succeeds in hitting the public taste it will very possibly have a long run. Were it to depend upon its merits as a play, its life would probably be extremely short". This review has deep impact across the Atlantic.

This reviewer's flip that the score lacks part-writing is strangely suggestive of the quality lost after Williams forced out Steindorf. If Herbert was indeed present in London, choral textures would have been sung and he would have conducted the show or some encores. This is not so. And if his music was being wrongly presented Herbert would have taken angry action to prevent it.

Despite *London Times, NY Herald's* London correspondent cables New York that these "critics all sing praises. The play is a success. It is just what the English audience loves—comic opera full of wheezes, songs, bright costumes, pretty girls and lively music. Miss Nielsen scored just as American audiences said she would. She has a voice much as we rarely hear—small, but every elastic, the high notes without a fault. She was voted a sweet little woman, with an immense amount of 'go.'"

As expected, Nielsen hits with her *I Do Just As I Am Told* opening song.

Also, the "pretty girls in the chorus were really pretty ones, in all kinds of baby pinks, baby blues and baby mauves; all tempting looking—very tempting".

The cakewalk makes London rave: "The cakewalk song and its incidental action were appreciated in an unexpectedly enthusiastic manner by the English audience, few of whose individual members could have seen such a performance. Recall came upon recall till Miss Nielsen fairly had to cry quarter".

London Daily Telegraph: "The newcomer had to fight for it, but won her way. Miss Alice Nielsen is to be congratulated on her success. *The Fortune Teller* is to be welcomed. Circumstances have put comic opera somewhat under a cloud of late years. The inadequate supply of capable performers has been the chief cause. The sooner the full tide turns is the better".

Without exception every London review says Alice Nielsen carries the show. Stewed crow served at meals for Williams & Perley.

And the show plays on. And the star is on the stage.

In May, the star is interviewed at her hotel the grand Cecil Hotel, largest in London, at 80 Strand near Charing Cross.

Poignant hint for Alice: only a mile's pleasant stroll to crossover from the Shaftesbury Theatre to the Covent Garden Opera House.

The press are no fool. Writer "CAM" crafting prose beautifully precise with a novelists' eye for detail, deflects lingering shadows and touches on her earlier career for *The Era* 15th June when her 75th performance is a week away.

A CHAT WITH MISS NIELSEN by CAM

Picture, if you can, a characteristically pale American woman, apparently twenty-three years of age, with fair hair drawn tightly back from the forehead, robed in a fetching gown of baby blue plentifully showered with heavy cream lace opening over an elaborate underskirt of ivory satin. So I found Miss Alice Nielsen when I had the pleasure of calling upon her one morning, recently at her apartments in the Hotel Cecil. Seated at the breakfast table coaxing the steaming coffee to reluctantly leave its well in the silver urn for the gaping hungry cups ready to receive it, Miss Nielsen captivated me as completely as she had previously done from the stage of the Shaftesbury Theatre.

In her home she is thoroughly natural, entertaining and sympathetic, a gracious hostess and a delightful companion. Her successes, and they have been innumerable, have in no way spoilt her; extremely modest, almost shy, she receives the homage paid to her like a blushing schoolgirl. This unaffectedness of manner is her chief charm. Miss Nielsen is particularly gratified with her reception in this country. For weeks before the opening performance she suffered from nervousness, and was so fearful that she might not please an English audience that sleep was almost unknown.

Now she is quite at home; she has had a warm welcome and is immensely pleased at the spontaneous appreciation of her work which the English people have shown. One thing has agreeably surprised her, and that is the quickness with which the meaning of so much that is purely American has been grasped by her audiences; she imagined that a great many of the humorous saying in *The Fortune Teller* might be like an untranslated book for Londoners; but their instant response has proved a wonderful stimulant to her and to the other members of her company.

Everyone who has seen this latest success at the Shaftesbury will recollect the charming waltz song *Cupid and I* which Miss Nielsen sings in the second act with a flute obbligato.

This she tells me, is a selection from an opera [*Serenade*] by Victor Herbert, in which she made such a tremendous success in America, and it has been introduced by her here to serve as a mascot. It is a beautiful song, beautifully rendered, and as a talisman should never fail.

Miss Nielsen was not trained for a professional career but adopted it from force of circumstances. Her success has been phenomenal.

She tells an amusing incident of her first engagement with The Bostonians. In addition to a small part, she was to understudy the prima donna. This lady becoming suddenly ill, Miss Nielsen was in consequence promoted temporarily to the leading role.

She says, "I played this character for such a lengthy period that I quite forgot I was every anything but the prima donna. One day the manager said to me, 'Miss Nielsen, after tomorrow you will return to your own part. Miss ... has recovered and is coming back.' My indignation was intense and I protested violently, but to no purpose. I was informed that I was 'not engaged as the star.' However, I mentally resolved that I would be next year—and I was".

That was nearly four years ago, and Miss Nielsen has been successfully "starring" ever since. The role in *The Fortune Teller* is a heavy one and rather a severe tax upon Miss Nielsen's strength. For the first few weeks she struggled bravely with the London climate; fortunately it did not affect her voice, but weakened her considerably physically. Now she is better and hopes to remain with us a very long time, and present to the English public some other of her numerous triumphs.

It is in the summer, away at a quiet country place, that this young artist prefers to study; each part is a distinct creation of her own, for she receives instruction from no one; she devotes a portion of each day to vocal practice, and this she considers absolutely essential, whether she be filling an engagement or enjoying a holiday. Riding is her pleasantest recreation. She has neither hobbies nor pets, but likes cats—"a long way off". To my request for a story, Miss Nielsen replied that she "would have to make one up".

"Do", I answered, "but exaggerate sufficiently to give it the appearance of truth—that is the secret of interesting writing".

"Yes", she said, "and so it is on the stage. Our costumes are made from the same material as our house and street gowns, but on the stage we must have spangles".

And with this bright rejoinder I had perforce to content myself, and regretfully took my leave of the fair *Fortune Teller* with the coveted story untold. CAM.

The place Nielsen travels to develop new characters is Harrison, Maine, where before leaving for London she took property and arranged a large summer cottage to be built around a central room having a concert-hall ceiling height of sixty feet. A small singer's colony develops there in her wake. Eventually in Harrison, Met diva Enrica Dillon builds wood-crafted Deertrees Theatre (1933), stage same size as that day's Metropolitan Opera, set within the Maine woods.

From London, *Philadelphia Inquirer* (April 15) reports "Alice Nielsen Eclipses Edna May's Success" when the show "took in more cash at Saturday night's London performance than ever before at the Shaftesbury", topping Edna May's best *Belle* box-office take "by several pounds".

Alice Nielsen's improvisations again highlighted, *Inquirer* relates an opening night momentkl when she saves "an awkward stage hitch". Her character has to write a note. Sitting down at the table to do so, Alice discovers the pen is missing. She "fumbled over the table, lifting inkstand and blotter, but failed to find any pen. In this emergency, her stage lover, leaning over the chair ready to dictate the letter, grew painfully nervous, but the little lady's quick wit saved the situation. Tearing off a slip from the blotter, she twisted it into a quill, which she dipped in the ink and proceeded to write a moment later, throwing away the extemporized pen to pick up one thrown from the wing. The incident evoked a ripple of applause but it certainly betokened anything but nervousness".

London audiences? Loud: "I saw Miss Nielsen yesterday at the Savoy, when she discussed freely her ideas of her reception", *New York Herald* says in the *Los Angeles Times* April 28th, "Alice Nielsen's enthusiastic reception... has quite fulfilled the hopes raised by American notices of this piece".

Nielsen: "Did you ever see anything like a London gallery? It nearly scared me to death the first night. When I heard the shouting I couldn't for the life of me make out what the row was about. I felt so nervous I could scarcely see". Chorus leapt to her aid. "Friends behind, seeing my nervousness, whispered not to be afraid, but all through the first act I was simply bewildered with their bravos. But when we found out what they meant—well, it did make everybody feel good. Next night I was ready for them, I thought, but when somebody up in the gallery shouted "Bravo, Alice!" it simply took my breath away. It seems to me a London gallery gets familiar mighty quick. I had been told that people over here were chilly, but if this is a sample of their chilliness, I am afraid they will get pretty warm when they thaw out".

Meanwhile in American provinces, opera without Alice a losing proposition as Maurice Grau tours his Metropolitan Opera: "Trials and tribulation...in Boston would make a comical story if the results as affecting the season's financial budget were not tragic. The invalid list has taken in the practically the entire company. Even little Fritzi Scheff and Dippel, the most trustworthy of singers, have been victims of the climate. The audiences have been small. Altogether the venture has been disastrous".

Second London month continues success as *NY Times* reports (May 4), "Mrs. Langtry, Edna May, Alice Nielsen and *Sweet and Twenty* at the Vaudeville are doing the best business in town". *Sweet and Twenty* by Basil Hood becomes a 1919 film. Next day *LA Times* reports Herbert "to write a comic opera for Alice Nielsen". Story continues that "Jean Gerardy, the famous 'cellist, who is now entering on a concert tour through Australia, will return to this country in November" and the Sousa band "gave its final concert in this country in Boston, previous to another tour in Europe". In the near future, Gerardy tours with Alice Nielsen, who also will sing concerts with Sousa.

Before scorned Perley slinks, Musgrove grabs "provincial and colonial rights" of both Nielsen Company shows plus *Serenade*. May 13th he announces a "tour with *The Fortune Teller*" starting in Manchester. His tour of *Belle of New York* to Paris and Berlin is a very likely possibility for Alice's projects.

Daily life in London appears in May 13th *Washington Post*, the season "about to begin. Never were the theatres, concert halls, music halls, restaurants more crowded. The churches, the parks, the religious meetings attract huge throngs. The [Boer] war is an unfashionable topic.

The affair drags along so beastly slow, you know". Says *Post,* "the art of gastronomy has made much progress in this town of late years. The number of foreign restaurants has increased immensely. The foreign chefs are certainly pushing the old-fashioned cooks to the rear".

Previous week at Joe Cawthorn and George Schiller's "Bohemian party, if you happened to be a guest...you met pretty well every theatrical man and woman of prominence from the States now in London: Edna May's company, Alice Nielsen's company, George Lederer's company were all represented along those long, hospitable boards.

"Marie George, Queenie Vassar, Madge Lessing, Lillio Hawthorne, Virginia Earle, Emmie Lennox, Margaret Gordon, Rose Kerker, Phyllis Rankin, Floye Redledge, Lou Middleton, Eva Kelly, Trixie Friganza, Mabel Russell, Winifred Johnson, Sylvia Thorne were among the ladies present. "Richard Carle, David Lewis, George McClellan, Gustave Kerker, Norman Norman, Cris Bruno, Frank Perley, Eugene Stratton, RG Knowles, Harry Connor, Skeets Martin, Harry Davenport, Joseph Coyne, Paul Nicholson, George Bowles, Frank Lawton, Herbert Harndin, Pony Moore and AL Southerland among the men".

Of course, "Vesta Tilley, Marie Dainton, Bessie Bonehill, Laurence Irving and Harold Ellis were notable guests" from the London theatre.

Laurence Irving's presence matters to Alice, the pair are engaged. Despite her busy London schedule, she takes time for romance. Despite protestations of work, work, work: she is not always at home when offstage. Curses foiled again Williams.

Laurence Irving, brilliant actor-playwright son of the world's best-known actor Henry Irving, opens every London theatrical and social door. Henry Irving (1838-1905), famed "actor-manager" produces his own plays. His handyman, stage manager, and secretary is Ireland's Bram Stoker, author of *Dracula,* story inspired by Irving's stagework as Macbeth. The Irving group is at the heart of London theatre. During Nielsen's first Bostonian season the famed Irving theatrical family was onstage in NY. Not until June will news reach America.

Within two weeks the evil duo William & Perley slink away. Williams leaves unheralded, banished from the theatre. Alice has not spoken to Perley since NY, London theatre prohibits his access to the star. Interaction with the rascals is an undocumented by-play. Nielsen never speaks in public about them.

When her hometown paper finally breaks the romantic scoop June 1st, *Kansas City Star* reveals "the American theatrical colony in London couples the names of Alice Nielsen and Laurence Irving". Reminiscent of her shyness with Arthur Pryor, Alice will not say she met Laurence Irving in New York. Her story is they met at London: "Ever since Miss Nielsen opened...young Irving has been her devoted attendant. It is the current and generally believed rumor that Miss Nielsen and Laurence Irving are engaged to be married and that the wedding will take place as soon as Miss Nielsen's engagement here is concluded". Adds the report, "Although Laurence Irving does not possess the talent of his father, he is looked upon as a good actor". And his father unrivaled in the world.

So in a single opening night, Alice connects with Britain's strongest theatre family the Irvings. Virtually the Valergas of London. Times have changed indeed with the ocean voyage.

This is not her arrival with Stanley into San Francisco seeking a Wigwam. Alice Nielsen arrives in London a proven star. Famous across North America she has met many significant people. Now a new nation opens new doors. London greets Alice, not as a rising sidewalk singer—that becomes a fun story—but as a proven world-class artist, the diva star. Her early life vanishes as irrelevant. Only her talent matters now. Fame shapes future opportunity. People clamor to meet her.

April, May, now Nielsen's London status as star is forever secure.

She can handle success—can Perley handle failure?

Setting sail from America, Alice Nielsen instantly connects with England's royalty. Theatrical royalty of the Irvings, literal royalty of the Duchess of Manchester, Conseulo who hosts many elite parties for, say, the King wherein the patrons of culture gather and the singers rewarded.

London, 1901 May, dry warm month. The 25th *Washington Post* prints Baker Art Gallery's photo as gypsy *Fortune Teller,* "Alice Nielsen, way ahead of any American singer or actress seen in London in a generation". With Alice "making a big reputation" and her London producers "getting big money", Herbert hopes to resume the collaboration soon.

Same paper next day, Lew Rosen sketches London cultural life.

"King Edward drives about, often without escort, in spite of the recent attacks on his person and his morals. He is rotund, smiling, well dressed and bald. Charles Frohman governs the theatrical world from his rooms in the Carlton. Edna May is still featured at the Duke of York's. Her play has been manicured, pedicured, bathed, sprayed, stage managed, curry-combed, polished, powdered by a conclave of managers, agents, critics, stage sages, librettists, musicians and men about town, and now presents quite an attractive and well-groomed appearance".

Rosen oddly suggests, "Alice Nielsen is not doing wildly well at the Shaftesbury, I'm told [or mistold]. Frank Perley and George Bowles are doing what they can for the clever little lady, but I'm afraid she is not a great draw".

Same day in May, *LA Times* reports Edna May's producer Charles Frohman will star Alice in a musical of *Mme. San Gene* wherein French noblewoman outwits Napoleon. The drama starred Ellen Terry, produced by Nielsen's fiancé dad Henry Irving whose pal JM Barrie—author *Peter Pan*—also was cheated by his manager, who dies by suicide, widow returns money. Perley alas obtains obscurity unreformed. George Edwards at Shaftesbury revealed that Frohman, via Charles Dillingham, asked Nielsen to view *Sans Gene*. News spreads fast.

Frohman is manager Nielsen needs. Believes in star system, "a play requires a star artist, man or woman—woman for choice". Seeks plays for specific stars. George Jean Nathan in *The Magic Mirror* remarks, "As a producer, Mr. Belasco has produced not one fifteenth so many worthy plays as the late Charles Frohman...." William Phelps recalls Frohman's first hit was 1889's *Shenandoah* "complete with an actor playing General Sheridan atop a live horse".

Nielsen-Frohman? Great choice, certain success, strong business proposition. Unlike pikers Williams & Perley, Frohman owns a theatre chain: five in London, six NYC, two hundred across America. Manages twenty-eight stars, pays "more than $35-million a year in salaries to the 10,000 people on his payroll". With quirks, "an amiable frog in a starched collar" so painfully shy "he would dart down a side street to avoid meeting one of his great actors in public".

Big Frohman hit is Maude Adams (1872-1953) in Barrie's *The Little Minister*, superb example of his methods. Born in Salt Lake, raised San Francisco, Adams began NY theatre 1888. "She interprets the subtle, charming and profound character-studies of JM Barrie with consummate skill". Thanks to Frohman, "Audiences know in going to the theatre where she appears, they will see not only a fascinating woman, but the best play of the year". Louis Strang regards Adams, "slight and girlish; her face elfishly bewitching in its very plainness; her eyes large, blue and roguish, her hair ashen brown and delicately rippling, unusually gifted intellectually and with a personality of the most persuasive magnetism... today the most popular woman on the American stage".

Nielsen's musical success equals Maude Adams' success in dramas. Unlike Williams & Perley, Frohman is honest. Charles Frohman a great choice. Honest, has resources, theatres, develops stars in strong shows suited to talents: a great combination. If she had chosen him in 1898, Alice would be wealthy indeed.

Until June, wicked Williams "San Francisco racetrack man" had continued to pose as "Mr. Perley's financial sponsor". Henchman Perley gets a shock when Williams now reneges on paying promised bribes. Played for a fool, Perley is in a trap. He cannot lash out to the press. The thieves of a feather fall out.

Alice Nielsen has triumphed over obstacles extreme. Imagine Nielsen arrival in London with Steindorf conducting, liberated by financial success under an honest and competent management team. She'd be independently wealthy for life. The Victor Herbert collaboration would thrive as they evolve new shows having the genuine impact this duo wished. The right words the right music.

London, June 1901 was cool and wet. Foreign racket wars to steal mineral rights, a banksters' delight, caused turmoil in the gayety of nations. The Eugene Cowles divorce case gives the publicity-shy basso good cause to stay longer in London. By June 3rd, Alice Nielsen's brother Erasmus sails home to join the family in NYC. Her reliable chaperone was homesick, sister sent him packing.

Now comes the strange case of the Perley backpedal.

Nielsen's alliance with Frohman, plus the Williams double-cross, has Perley playing a new tune. He wants "what was due him".

American reporters observe the bizarre twist with amazed scorn.

Perley meets Herbert (*NY Times* June 8) for "a long conference" then to an incredulous press claims he is "preparing a genuine surprise upon her return from London". *NY Times* scoffs, "In view of the report that Charles Frohman had secured Miss Nielsen, Perley's attitude is most astonishing".

Depths of villainy. Strangling Nielsen's career and fortunes as dictated by rich rabid rascally Williams, Perley claims his five-year contract signed April 28, 1898, "binds Miss Nielsen for an indefinite time" if "Alice Nielsen Company" is kept active. Omitting his frauds. As Nielsen is from Missouri, he longs to "show her...to meet her at the wharf upon her arrival, contract in hand. Meanwhile, I am signing people for the Alice Nielsen Opera Company for next season, which will make the usual appearance as in the past three seasons". Unbelievable. Nobody believes.

Herbert tells press he has completed a new Alice Nielsen musical, "whoever the producers might be". Never suggests he'd let Perley touch it.

Asked to comment, Frohman's attorney Alf Hayman is diplomatic: "I believe I would take Mr. Perley's statement for anything regarding his relations with Miss Nielsen. He ought to know what he is talking about, and if he says he has her bound by contract, I presume he has. I don't know that Mr. Frohman has placed her under contract. I have no definite information on the subject".

June 9th *Chicago Tribune*, Perley claims he "found" his "lost" contract with Nielsen, which "binds her to appear as the star of the Alice Nielsen Opera Company as long as he cares to continue in the organization in existence". The lawsuit with Williams proves Perley a hireling, never owner.

How much did Williams & Perley steal? Bostonians' *Robin Hood* had a similar cast, running cost, and popularity about a decade earlier. In 1890 they grossed $1,000 per performance, $8,000 per week. Cost under $5,000 weekly to produce. Profits ran $3,000-week in 1890 gold dollars, enriching authors and Bostonians. Split between Williams and Nielsen as agreed, ten times her weekly pay. Over the six-month season share, perhaps $39,000 (over $1-million 2027). 1901 zero taxes; large houses cost $5000 in downtown San Francisco. Plus the shows a lucrative property for future productions, royalties, value of Nielsen Company as a brand, the star's career momentum, the cultural legacy. The future shows that were never.

Corruption wrecks the future. Pushes Alice Nielsen off Broadway.

Her emotional crisis is suggested by a June 9 story. She meets the reporter in a kimono from Yokohama: "Alice Nielsen has a pleasant suite of rooms at St. Ermins' Hotel, where Edna May lived when she first came to London".

She "is singing just as brilliantly and acting just as brightly as ever, but she is anything but well. She suffers terribly from insomnia and sometimes is unable to sleep during an entire night". Business anxieties. "With the hard strain that a difficult and exacting part must bring upon her and the constant business anxieties she declares that are hers, it is no wonder that Miss Nielsen feels absolutely prostrated; the wonder is that she is able to give as faultless a performance as she does".

Her brother has sailed, "so now the little American singer is quite alone in London, and she evidently is feeling a certain amount of homesickness and depression". No plans to return. "She means...to stay here through the summer and everybody hopes that she will appear in *The Singing Girl*".

London theatre is in a "ruinous slump that seems to have attacked dramatic productions", even the Shaftesbury. "That Miss Nielsen, however, has made a real personal success cannot be denied....

"As I looked at her, a quaint little figure in her white satin gold-embroidered kimono, it seemed impossible that so great a fund of energy and real talent could be concealed within that slim, nervous little frame".

Popular star painted as recluse. "Most members of Miss Nielsen's company went to the Derby run... she finds it absolutely impossible to do anything except work and try to sleep. She sees very few people, does not go out at all, and lives absolutely the most quiet existence that she can manage to while out of the theatre". Her lively life with Laurence Irving and Duchess of Manchester in her new London circle gains surprising silence.

Following Erasmus and family, from Chicago he moves Sarah, Bennie, Tommy to Harlem at 519 W 124th Street. By 1903, he lives in Far Rockaway as organist at St. Mary's Star of the Sea. Also music director for local shows, he marries Irish-born Mary Brennen to produce a daughter Alice. Sarah settles into Brooklyn. Erasmus's home, near Lillian Russell's forty-six room summer place, near Belmont Race Track. Russell often took the Nielsens. Her winter home 57th Street NYC. When Marie Dressler files bankruptcy she moves in.

Lillian Russell, Marie Dressler, Alice Nielsen, Nordica are friends. Stories they could tell. Supper and songs with Caruso and Kreisler! Practical advice shared. Astonishing talent and savvy. In those days sovereign Americans were seriously.

Lillian Russell rejects a command performance, "I am an American and not obliged to obey any royal orders in Germany or anywhere else". Poker-skilled Russell likes antiques; JP Morgan declares her trading skills "astonishing for a woman". Russell and Diamond Jim Brady, Golden Age icons, ate well. Brady put a pound of caviar in his baked potato to start feasts, drinks fresh orange juice by gallon as he enjoys six large lobsters, dozens of oysters, clams and crabs, two ducks, plus steak and dessert at a single sitting. To restaurateur George Rector, Brady was "the best 25 customers I ever had". When doctors tell him stop, Brady gloriously replies, "Hell, I gotta have some fun; I ain't got much longer to live". Born in Irish New York, Brady grew rich innovating the analysis of business planning in the railroads. He caused the first NYC traffic jam in 1895 with the first auto in town.

Returning focus to London, superstar friendships extend across Europe. If here, Lillian Russell stays at Nordica's house, 11 Clarence Terrace in Regent Park. Maine's Nordica, first American in Wagner at Bayreuth, had debuted 1894 as Elsa in *Lohengrin*. Of her Isolde, said NY critic Krehbiel, "Nordica rose to the opportunity which Wagner's drama opened to her. The greater the demand the larger her capacity. In the climaxes of the first act in which Isolde rages like a tempest, her voice rang out with thrilling clearness, power and brilliancy...." As Brunhilde more.

Alas, "all is not lovely in London theatre", says June 13th *Chicago Daily News* (1901). "Nearly every manager and actor-manager in London has been losing money heavily this spring". Mrs. Langtry "has not been successful in her new theatre...soon to be closed. Irving has had a bad frost", *Coriolanus* closes after a few weeks; failure attributed to author's W. Shakespeare's bad writing. Mrs. Patrick Campbell fails "to draw". Two bright spots, "Alice Nielsen is holding on by the heel of her boot and Edna

May…doing only fairly. Charles Frohman has discovered she must have a vacation, no matter what the cost in box office receipts". Without May in June Frohman will dark for two months hiatus.

Nielsen "makes no announcement, the plan seemingly being to hold on if possible". The murderous London bankster attack on the Boers would continue until May 1902. Crisis and summer heat eroded the gayety of London. Alice Nielsen Company held out longest. *Fortune Teller* would go on hiatus before August. McLellan's *Belle of NY* after Budapest, Vienna, Berlin stranded. Cast "forced to work their way back…best they could".

In the cast: failed romances. Eugene Cowles had not paid ex-wife Lizzie the weekly $50 alimony. He must post $5,000 to perform again in NYC. Lizzie opposed a bond reduction, saying Cowles had remarried against a court order.

In such a context during summer Alice contacts clever Alan Dale for a chat. "Little Miss Alice Nielsen has not selected an American nest for her London habitation", Dale says June 12th. "She is not twittering among the temporary expatriates who come to England to yearn for ice water, steam heat and underground trolleys. I found her at St. Ermin's hotel Westminster, in the picturesquest kind of neighborhood, miles away from the flannel-voiced tourists". Lovely half-hour walk to Shaftesbury Theatre.

"I say 'found her' as though I had been hunting London for her. As a matter of fact, she scrawled her address to me and I dashed up to Westminster in real good style". She is closely guarded: "Hall boys, half a dozen clerks, key office officials and a selected number of other dignitaries carefully read my pasteboard before it was sent Nielsenwards. Evidently I passed my exam successfully, even with honors, for the elevator boy showed me up most politely". She was glorious.

"Solomon in all his glory was simply two penn'orth of coppers compared with Miss Alice". From her Yokohama trip, garbed with "a Japanese tea gown of white satin, all plastered over with gold. She looked very pale and un-made-up, and her hair was peeled away from her face, as though she didn't care a hang what became of it".

Said Nielsen, "I'm not at all well today, Mr. Dale. I'm feeling dull, and I don't mind telling you [Mr. Famed National-syndicated Hearst Columnist] in confidence that I'm homesick. Of course I want you to know that I'm immensely elated at being a success in two countries, and all that sort of thing, but I feel lonely. My brother went back to America the other day. He simply couldn't stand it here. He kept saying 'Gee-whiz! Alice, I'm going home.' Finally I said to him, 'stop gee-whizzing and go, if you must.' So he took me at my word".

Dale waxes unsympathetic: "Poor little American Alice alone in London, isn't it sad". Perhaps well-connected critic senses star Alice foggy of her ongoing social whirls with the Duchess and the fiancé Laurence Irving.

Nielsen blithely continues, "Personally I like London immensely. There is a quiet in the atmosphere that is positively restful. The hateful clanging of bells that we get all the time in New York is lacking. It is a very nice lack. Then they treat you well. In the London theatre you rely for applause upon the pit and the gallery, and it is such hearty applause".

Big time popularity: "I think I really go better here than I do in NY".

Takes full credit. Above her material: "They like me better than they do *The Fortune Teller*, and they've said the loveliest things about my voice. I'm glad I came here. It is an experience and I thought I should fail. I was in fear and trembling, for you know how terribly loyal they are in London and how suspiciously they look at all newcomers".

Contrasts London with NY where "they are not loyal and anybody has a chance. I'm thinking of myself. You remember my first appearance with the Bostonians in *The Serenade*. I was a novelty among all those national favorites. Yet that is where I made my hit, you all said so. I suppose that both systems have their good points. Old artists like the loyalty of London. Young ones are thankful for the progressive spirit of NY".

Alice Nielsen says a slightly mysterious thing. "I wish I could tell you that I'd been dining with dukes and duchesses, but I really haven't been 'taken up' as the saying is. I don't invite that kind of thing, because I am heart and soul in my work. That is the only thing I am interested in. And when I am through, I simply come back to my apartments, rest my voice and take life as easily as I can. There's nothing in anything else".

Certainly say nothing of any Duchess, any fiancé. Yet her performances superhuman. As we will see, she develops a rigorous hour-by-hour artistic discipline during performance seasons. Except lunch when she enjoys having people. And after shows, backstage happens.

Reveals backstage negotiations in London. Expects to play *Fortune Teller* in Europe through 1902. Shaftesbury contract runs another year. "By the bye, the statement that Mr. Frohman is to manage me is not correct. My contract with Musgrove does not expire until next July.'" Zero Williams & Perley.

With Herbert's new musical awaiting her in NYC, "The story that I have secured the *Sans Gene* comic opera is also inaccurate. I have nothing. I feel desperate about a new opera".

For Dale's benefit, Nielsen lobs three eggs: Herbert, Smith and Stange.

Overlooking cheat of her company, she complains "I wish I could get one that was not expressly written for me. It is so dreadful to be buzzed around by librettist and composer".

Basket of eggs: "'My comic opera idea is to get something that I could build up and engage a company for. It is so absurd to be fitted on and to have one's company considered. In *The Singing Girl* all my principals had to have entrance songs. Imagine six entrance songs! It grew positively nauseous. You see, I have ideas of my own, haven't I, Mr. Dale".

Dale cannot disagree: "There was no doubt at all about it. For a sensible person with a long level head, commend me to Miss Alice Nielsen of NY and London".

Who else starred as Alice in her performances last four years? Her study of audience reaction across many many theatres was unmatched.

So Alice foggily tells Dale she is home alone. He dutifully favors the diva by reporting this iffy suggestion across America in the Hearst syndicate papers. Dale, who grew up in Britain, neglects to mention her new fiancé Laurence Irving, whose father Henry produced the *Sans Gene*.

London papers don't delay: Alice and Laurence "are constantly together and the theatrical world believes they will be married as soon as Miss

Nielsen" can escape *Fortune Teller*. Indeed as the new star in town, "She has a host of other admirers, many of them with wealth and titles, but she has been cold to all but the young actor". Since she had docked, London was at her unaffected petite feet. Always a big party at the Shaftesbury meet-and-greet after the show.

Alice's new fiancé is all she could wish. Not decades older, talented, cultured. With all the theatrical connections in the world. All doors open to Laurence. Tall, slender, Laurence is "gentle and solemn with streaks of glad", an "eccentric, slightly uncouth yet evidently brilliant young man wearing a little bashfully his heart on his sleeve... Handsome and well-built, his pince-nez and pipe-smoking only adding to the charm of his dreamy intellectuality" of "an earnest Tolstoyan given to melancholy introspection and passionate avowal of his ideals, and with his head in the clouds through which now and again broke rays of mischievous fun he stood out sharply from the genteel and conventional young actors of his day". Writer Count Tolstoy (1828-1910) pushes passion, peace, veggie diet, influences Gandhi. War or peace is key concern of the age tottering between chaos or progress. Will the banksters invest war or peace?

Laurence attended Oxford, fluent in Russian, knows Tolstoy whose views he shares. His family are to drama as The Bostonians to musicals.

George Bernard Shaw regards Laurence's plays as "written with immense vivacity and courage in frank, contemporary, vernacular English". Laurence had collaborated with Tolstoy to write *Peter The Great* (1898) whereat his fiancé—Ethyl Barrymore—broke their engagement, whereat Laurence is free for Alice Nielsen. In September, Frohman will put Laurence's drama *Richard Lovelace* with EH Southern on Broadway for forty performances. Laurance had earlier toured the show discovering "audience distaste for a romance that ended badly".

His *Godfroi and Yolande* (1898) starts with a speech:

> *What a night! What snow! What a wind! The tapestries flap and flutter; the flames of the torches stream all one way. The snow—the snow—the wind—the snow—the wind! How say you, is the snow enwrapping the wind, is the wind enwrapping the snow", said Nimue with wide-staring eyes and slightly parted lips...gazing out of window, a bundle of rushes on her arm.*

Stars Ellen Terry as a leper. Outrages dad and Shaw "who, finding the theme of the play distasteful were for the first and last time in agreement". Shaw gave Laurence "a penetrating diagnosis of his shortcomings as an actor", says the family historian's three-volume biography never mentioning Alice Nielsen.

Shaw hated *Madame Sans-Gene* (1895), "Sardou's Napoleon is rather better than Madame Tussaud's and that is all that can be said for it", creating *The Man of Destiny* in response. "I was asked to do an English *Madame Sans-Gene* as an opera...I said I'd do it if I had time, which I never...will" he wrote Terry.

Alice left a tiny glimpse of Laurence: "If you are interested in those who did not love me, I might name the talented Mrs. Pat Campbell. I met her at a supper given to me by Laurence Irving, son of the great Sir Henry. Laurence Irving and I were engaged to be married at the time. Nothing came of that but after all, the story is about Mrs. Patricia Campbell. She was at the dinner, and after I had sung several arias at her request I asked her to recite. 'My dear young woman', she drawled, 'perhaps you don't know that when I recite I receive sixty guineas.' She was playing P*elleas and Melisande*, and I asked Laurence to take me to see her. The house was less than a quarter full.

"'Come backstage', urged Laurence. 'she's really quite decent when you know her.' 'No', I said. 'But you go—and take her a message from me. Just ask her where she is going to get her sixty guineas today.'"

Alice misspells fiancé "Lawrence". Life leads art, Laurence later weds actress Mabel Hackney; after playing Montreal they take *Empress of Ireland* which sinks May 28, 1914; they vanish into the cold Atlantic.

Resuming 1901, June 16th *Washington Post* reports stranded American players with *Belle Of New York* "finally have reached London, but that city is worshiping newer dramatic idols...few have sufficient car fare to carry them to the pier to look for a boat". Producer Lederer "received a cable message 'collect' from two of the leading women imploring him to forward money enough to secure their baggage and pay passage to New York". Lederer wires funds they can repay cast in his next show. Same day *LA Times* reports Joe Cawthorn fell onstage, leg now "encased in a plaster cast". And Perley fishes for a bribe to release any claim on Alice Nielsen Company whose star "is reported as being under contract with Charles Frohman to appear in...*Madame San Gene*".

Next day, hearing of her plight the former manager of St. Joseph Opera House, now a Texas oil millionaire Orson Parker, cables Nielsen an offer of aid "which was accepted". Foggy relations: "Eight or ten years ago Miss Nielsen did a favor for him when he was in trying circumstances".

During June Perley preens, twisting handlebar mustache and snarling, gives screenwriters perfect portrayal of a villain for the decades ahead.

Morning Telegraph revises his claims, Perley "notified Miss Nielsen's lawyers that he will continue to exercise his rights...not indefinitely, but for the 3-year contract term remaining". Perley, cheated of his bribes by Williams, demands the star he crossed must repay him for cheating her.

Telegraph defends Nielsen who has "had no tantrums, no wrangles with her associates and no objectionable features to any of those surrounding her, excepting she did persist in making a bosom friend of her colored maid—a proceeding which led to complications in some hotels, the proprietors of which resented the idea of black servants being treated as guests within their doors".

In London, Cawthorn upstages her and Cowles has a noisy new song. Alice "suddenly notified Mr. Cawthorn...he must not appear" in her solo songs. "As he had been cutting something of a figure...confusion ensued and Mr. Cawthorn himself resigned". In fact he stays until broke a leg.

Stars together four years, "Cowles too, came in for some curtailment at the hands of Miss Nielsen...he subsequently left the company". Herbert's score exploited the contrast of Cowles' bass and Nielsen's soprano.

For *Telegraph*, Alice's assertive powers are a good sign: "Nielsen has emerged from the chrysalis stage of development and has become a full-fledged double-action prima donna, fitted with the very latest devices in the kicking line". Perley's spin falls splat.

Prosperous Eugene Cowles had made "heavy investments in a number of business ventures, among which is a third interest in a bank in a small town in Iowa". Owns stock in "a mining company in San Diego", plus property in Portland, Oregon. "Of his many holdings, however, he is most deeply interested in a farm" purchased in hometown Darby Line, VT. "He has gone extensively into the cultivation of maple trees, and is one of the biggest producers of sugar in the State of Vermont. In addition he has a dairy farm from which the output of milk, cream and butter is one of the largest in New England, the separating being done by an electrical appliance invented by Mr. Cowles himself".

Cowles sings concerts until he returns to NYC as Major Gordon in *The Boys and Betty* with Marie Cahill at Garrick. Says the role allows him to do business correspondence during the day. *San Antonio Press* reports Cowles had offers to tour England, Australia, South Africa. "After a tour of the principal American cities he would consider an offer abroad". His son will emigrate to South Africa. Cowles creates a concert company with Miss Blamere, pianist Walter Pyck, and violinist Clara Farrington. Teaches voice in Carnegie Hall studio and creates popular songs: *Forgotten, Crossing the Bar, Beneath The Pines, The First Kiss, To Her, When Stars Are In Quiet Skies, A Song Of Black and White,* and *Rienzi's Invocation To Mars.* Happily remarried, Cowles will relocate to Boston.

For Alice Nielsen this 1901 June, Chicago's hope to join Herbert with Gilbert comes very close: "Mr. Gilbert, of Gilbert & Sullivan, is nearly ready with an opera libretto he can give her, but the composer has not yet been selected". Pixies swipe the possible moment perhaps.

Scorn for Perley rises: "According to a report which Frank Perley has set in circulation", says *Chicago Tribune* Jun 18th, "he and the California millionaire Tom Williams are going to" do stuff they never.

Two days later *Tribune* reports "Nielsen and her company will leave London for the United States in a fortnight. When Miss Nielsen went to London, the plan was *The Fortune Teller, The Singing Girl* and *The Serenade* should be produced in turn. Only *The Fortune Teller* has been used. Miss Nielsen was accorded an exceedingly favorable reception, being hailed by a number of newspapers as the most gifted signer and comedienne on the comic opera stage. Of the reality of her triumph there can be no doubt, and it is certain also that the public as well as the newspapers helped to swell it. By all the evidence she became a London favorite, and the prophecy that she would play at the Shaftesbury Theatre for a year did not seem based on hopefulness alone".

Tribune blames where belongs: "The quarrel between Miss Nielsen and Manger Frank Perley hardly was the best of preparation for a London season. The bitterness... increased in volume after they went abroad. Then the month of May proved to be unusually hot, and the audiences fell off at the Shaftesbury as they did at all the theatres". Canard, May rather cool; June cooler.

"Almost at the same time Joseph Cawthorn was the victim of a bad accident, falling and injuring himself in such a way that one leg had to be encased in a plaster cast. He was told he could not leave his bed for five or six weeks, and if he is out of the hospital yet no mention of the fact has been cabled to this country". Corrects Perley lie that Cawthorn quit.

America ponders the tragic puzzle of Alice Nielsen Company a decade until details of the dastardly Williams & Perley conspiracy are uncloaked.

Returning to the star onstage, June 20th a reporter interviews Alice Nielsen. "Miss Nielsen is herself" the headline.

"Nothing could be daintier or more graceful than the figure this lively little actress cuts whether she is a boy or a girl in the play. If there is one actress who makes up scarcely at all, it is Miss Nielsen. Just as she appears, with of course the slightest colouring to get the right stage effect and because of heavy lighting, Miss Nielsen is herself. Youthful, charming and vivacious—full of life, full of go and with a smile and laugh that are irresistible—the clever prima-donna of the Shaftesbury Theatre and *Fortune Teller* captivates one at once".

Work hard for her position? "Struggle? Why yes, I did struggle", she replies. "When I began there were more downs than ups, I can tell you. I think I had as bad a time as any actress in trying to get recognition. I know people did not believe in me. I had to make them. I had to prove I could do something. Have I succeeded? Ah!"

Alice speaks gorgeously of her audiences: "Here in London I have had the kindest reception. And I like your London and I like your London playgoer. He is so enthusiastic and not only sees the points, but recognizes them. He is not afraid to applaud if your efforts please him. Applause is the breath of our souls. Rightly given it makes us new people and stirs us to higher and greater things".

She reveals her desire to act with song. "All this time though, I wanted to be an actress. I wanted to work and do something. There were reasons, you understand". Her thoughts sail to Kansas City; first letter of praise sent to the pastor: "One day a traveling manager, who heard me sing in the church, asked after me, and Father Lillis introduced me to him. I had been playing in amateur theatricals, and in a piece called *Chantaclara* [*Chanticlere*] I had my first part that I consider suited me". Gilbert & Sullivan and Balfe didn't suit!

To London she gives a vaudeville pilgrimage version: "Somewhere out in far Missouri...I did my utmost with my heart in my throat and I don't know exactly how I got on. One or two of the songs went all right—some didn't. You know how it is. Sometimes I felt ready to cry. We all worked so hard. In the 'smalls' as you call them in England, we had just the same lack of accommodation in America as you have this side in the minor places. But we had some fun too".

Trots out the Kansas City kids' shadow-show, "I held out my skirts while the contralto dressed, and she did the same for me. These little things make one laugh now but there was a more pathetic touch in those days, especially as it happened once or twice we had to walk from one town to another. Oh! I know it did me good in a sense".

Follows with her *Penelope* story, rightly set to St. Joseph *Eden Musee*. No mention of Britain's Burton Stanley, no mention of San Francisco's hit *Satanella* by Balfe.

Delivers credo: "Work is the best for all. Nobody ought to live without it. You can't appreciate things—you can't appreciate the goodness and glory of being alive. I hope I do. I love to be alive and to play and to sing. If I please the people in front, they please me, and so God bless us all".

Reporter feels her passion, "Miss Nielsen is emotional. She is at the same time full of fire and life, and the experiences she has had enabled her the better to value the utility of real hard labour and endeavour".

Of *Fortune Teller* she rose above its flaws. In London "great expectations did not exist in regard to it; but Miss Nielsen scored, and all the anxiety of the past years faded into oblivion". Plainly, "Miss Nielsen is certainly the best light opera prima donna that America has sent us".

From the Shaftesbury Theatre a short cross to Covent Garden.

Appears in London during last week of June 1901, unsigned article telling Alice Nielsen try grand opera. The audience, author advices, better would appreciate her arts. Refuse the flatteries of popular theatre, and go really work.

Note her "slight and girlish figure, an unaffected manner and a voice of sympathetic quality and flexibility. If her head is not turned by the lavish compliments bestowed upon her, and she determines to study diligently, she may, one of these days, graduate to the grand opera stage".

Time is now: "The only difficulty in the way of the greater success of gifted young women on the comic opera stage is that they are satisfied with the applause of the hardly critical audiences that gather at performances of that kind and for the triumphs of the moment barter a higher career that they might have enjoyed had they taken are more seriously".

Secret advisor tells a sidewalk singer to try grand opera.

A probable author is fiancé Laurence Irving.

Broadway will send blank checks to return. What does Alice do?

Five days later, 28th June *Fortune Teller's* final curtain is scheduled for the American holiday July 4th. Shaftesbury Theatre managers post a notice Nielsen will certainly re-open in the fall. Nielsen issues a statement that the Company's weekly expenses $5,750 were unmeet for the first time since September 1898, so "receipts did not warrant the persistence of the venture. The termination of my English engagement is an especial disappointment". In less than a dozen words she drops discussion of Alice Nielsen Company.

Same day appears the best-ever glimpse of Alice Nielsen in action during a show. Reported by Clement Scott for July 1st *Broadway Magazine*. He has no doubts about Nielsen. And he has seen everything everybody. Picks the best. Calls attention to her Valerga-trained *bel canto*, her roots in Irish song, her comedy, and to dance singing E-flats.

Alice Nielsen is a genius who rises above her material.

> I said when I saw her at the Casino NY, that Alice Nielsen, if she ever came to London would take the town by storm. She was bound to do it, for pocket geniuses do not turn up every day of the week, and here is one more to add to my not-yet exhausted list.
>
> Let me tell you what to expect when you all go to the Shaftesbury Theatre to see *The Fortune Teller*. You will find a

singer rare in any country, with a voice rich and sweet at the same time, and of marvelous flexibility—a voice heard...with greater advantage at the Shaftesbury than at the Casino—a singer with a method quite unusual in despised comic opera. You will find an actress whose skill in comedy no good judge could dispute. There is not a movement that is not graceful, not an action that does not come natural, whether she be enacting a willful gypsy girl or indulging in the best and most fantastic "cake walk" London has ever seen, or as the dear little neat, taut and trim Red Hussar in which character she is...even better than Janne Granier in *Le Petit Duc*. Think of that, then a singer, an actress, a humorist!

One thing more she has, and that is a power of work that is little less than extraordinary. I never saw such a worker. Alice Nielsen is on the stage from eight to eleven, but she never tires. She changes her dress, I should say, nearly a dozen times, and yet all the pulse of the opera and the success of the finales are due mainly to her.

I think I have a right to speak on this point. I have seen them all, the pick of the basket, from Dejazet, who played burlesque boys until she was nearly eighty. Ah! How clever they were according to their distinct and different temperaments. Schneider, with her opulent charms and her splendid insolence; Jane Hading, when she was a comic singer; the ox-eyed Judic; the delightful Granier; Chaumont, Theo, and all the rest of them, but to that great company of artists Alice Nielsen shall be added, and if they were all here, alive and before us, the gifted little America would be very high up in the class.

True to the excellent American system, the 'pocket genius' is surrounded by more than competent artists. Where shall you find such a grand melodious basso and such a splendid picture of a man as Eugene Cowles, actor and singer, who has already begun to touch the heart of the 'matinee girl.' The critic was right who compared him to Edouard DeReszke [grand opera's star basso].

As for the humour of the play, I doubt not that the serious critics would have turned up their noses at me as I roared with laughter over the comic business of those typical American comedians, Alexander Clark, a ballet master; Joseph Herbert, a musical Count; and Joseph Cawthorn, the comedian with the German accent.

Why may we not be permitted to laugh at the theatre? I cannot help myself. I laughed over Cawthorn and Joseph Herbert till I nearly cried. I think others will do the same.

One word before we leave them on a career that is bound to be triumphant, for London knows a good thing when it sees it and never neglects to patronize it. Criticism of the serious kind may sneer but the public planks down its money. It is too often urged that these American comedians "take the bread' out of the mouths of our actors and actresses. It cannot be helped. If we get better American boots than those made at home, we buy them. When an

Alice Nielsen and a Eugene Cowles appear on the stage, art-loving London certainly has no idea of giving them the cold shoulder.

In the cast as the passing show plays out, romance. *Washington Post* (Jul 2) reports Violet Gillette engaged to "The Hon. Cecil Craven" and Capt. Frederick Nicholson, "a British army officer... betrothed to May Boley". Even "Sir Robert Peel, who has shed something far from luster on his great name, has been devoted to Winifred Williams of Miss Nielsen's support, and it is said that wedding bells may soon ring for both. *Fortune Teller*...will likely go on record as one of the biggest match-making theatrical organizations that ever came to this country from the United States".

Laurence Irving is her Arthur Pryor of London. "There seems little doubt that Laurence Irving, son of Sir Henry Irving and Miss Nielsen will soon be married. Young Irving has never been absent from the theatre during a performance and Alice Nielsen has seldom been seen in public without him. There has been persistent denials of their engagement, however. Laurence Irving seems to have a penchant for getting engaged to American actresses, by the way. His name has been connected with several, but the only formal announcement with the consent of both parties was of his betrothal to Miss Ethel Barrymore at the time that the clever young American was acting with Sir Henry at the Lyceum.

"The engagement was broken off by Miss Barrymore, and it was said to be caused by the moody disposition of Mr. Irving. He is subject to prolonged fits of melancholia and is considered rather eccentric". A "fairly good actor and a rather clever playwright, though his subjects in the later line are nearly always of a gloomy kind...his first play of note had leprosy for its theme. It was originally produced in Chicago with Ellen Terry in the principal part".

Nielsen's theatrical reality has a brilliant report by Curtis Brown. During *The Fortune Teller* between numbers she speaks freely. This widely reprinted piece is published by *Kansas City Star* July 7th, "Edna May and Alice Nielsen Compare America and England". Alice "confided to her visitor with the cheery enthusiasm of the typical American girl". While the show rages around her, she speaks of audiences, health, cost of living, and theatre salaries.

The "romping gypsy girl of Smith and Herbert's opera" speaks candidly "about her English experiences in such odd moments she could spare from her audience and her dresser. The interview was held at Miss Nielsen's dressing room, and punctuated by the melodies that came from the stage and frequent bursts of applause from 'in front.' Dressed in a fetching red Hussar's uniform and attractive as ever with her merry blue eyes and curly light hair, the little San Francisco girl perched herself on a stool and delivered her opinions with much earnestness and many animated gestures".

Nielsen confides, "I'm spending my days in London now doing two things, sleeping at my hotel and singing here. We are very successful, but I am terribly tired. You see, I've never in my life before acted after May 1st and my present part is a particularly exacting one. So I am seeing no one during the day".

Twixt England and America: "I think it costs a lot more to live over here than in America. In fact about the only thing I've discovered isn't dearer than at home is cabs. Well perhaps some parts of women's dress, too—silk and brocades and gloves!"

Detailed analysis how to earn a living. "Salaries are not nearly so high as they are at home, take it right through the profession. I'll tell you, here you get big pay or you get nothing. There doesn't, speaking roughly, seem to be any middle ground. Stars are paid nearly as well as in America but the rank and file get mighty little. Why, in America a chorus man gets from $35 to $50 a week; here you can get all you like at two guineas. And the rates paid to people on the road are even worse.

"I was talking only yesterday to an American girl who had been playing the leading part in a *Belle of New York* company through the provinces and who has been getting on $40 a week. Think of that for a 'lead.' The girls in their chorus had a pound a week.

"But just get to be a popular favorite here, and your fortune is made. The salaries that such people as Dan Leno and Vesta Tilley get are wonderful. Why, there is Lil Hawthorne who was three or four years ago a chorus girl in America. She came over here and was so successful in pantomime that they say she is the most popular 'principal boy' in the country. She is paid at the rate of $300 for six performances, besides getting half the total receipts at matinees, and a benefit at the end of the run".

English audiences? "I enjoy playing to them. They don't care for noisy stage business, but they make a lot of noise themselves. Our people are generally content with applauding, but here they cry 'Bravo! Bravo!' And I tell you, it just pushes you along".

For her, British like Herbert's music: "Make no mistake, they like good music and they know what good music is every time. I get most applause every evening for my song, *Cupid and I* and that is one of the most beautiful things that Victor Herbert has written, and one of those that takes the most art to write.

And the seasoned diva turns to audience analysis.

"Now you're going to ask me if they are more or less demonstrative than our people, aren't you? That's a pretty hard question to answer and I'll tell you why. You must remember that we have three-thousand miles of home, and the audiences you meet in traveling about are as different as those in NY and London. Of all the American audiences I've acted to, I should say that those of Philadelphia are most like Londoners at the theatre. They are very enthusiastic. NY audiences are, I think, less demonstrative than those of London. And of all the places where you are actually frozen stiff the worst, according to my notion, is my own town of San Francisco".

English critics: nice for her, rude for Harry Smith, mixed for Herbert.

"Oh they're delightful. They spoke disrespectfully of our libretto and commented on the noisiness of some of the music but there was not one but spoke nicely of me and my work. I've got all the clippings, and feel very grateful for the kind things that have been said of me. One writer, however, in speaking of my work remarked that my father was killed in the American Civil War. I wonder how old that man thinks I am, anyway!"

Nielsen "made a delightful little face", said Brown. During their entire conversation she has been popping on and off stage: "Some half dozen times, a voice sounded from without and the trim little figure in red hastily smoothed down her curls, made a military clutch at her sword and scampered up the winding stairway out of sight, and a moment afterward her voice could be heard lilting out on the stage".

Nielsen demands of Brown, "Now, what are you going to write?"

"Everything that you have said", he replies.

"Be sure about one thing. Don't you give America a back seat. I've been treated beautifully here, but America is my home and I'll be jolly, jolly glad to get back there. You can say that", says Alice Nielsen before returning to perform her many nightly encores.

She wants home, sweet home. Stays in Europe four more years.

July 5th 1901, Alice Nielsen Company gives the final performance.

1901-1911: GRAND OPERA & CONCERTS

JULY 1901: GRAND OPERA BEGINS

On July 3rd, "brilliantly versatile" Alice Nielsen is hailed by *Sketch* and *Tatler*, which praises the star "made a name for herself instantly at the Shaftesbury for she possess the supreme secret of a magnetic...." On July 5th, London closes *The Fortune Teller*.

Alice herself is why, not ticket sales.

London Times (Jul 5) reports Shaftesbury's George Musgrove "regrets that in consequence of Miss Alice Nielsen requiring absolute rest, *The Fortune Teller* is temporarily withdrawn. This successful piece will be reproduced in a few weeks with Miss Nielsen and augmented cast, of which due notice will be given".

July 8th, *Sportsman* reports "Alice Nielsen, who has been singing continuously the title role in The Fortune Teller for three years past, has suffered extremely from the recent hot weather and by her doctor's orders, will take a rest". She has found the means to break her contract.

On the 10th, *Tatler* features Nielsen on the cover with a huge feature story including a page of photographs.

She has every right to be exhausted. She should be rich and resting.

Now she must create a new career. She cannot rest.

Free from starring; free from Williams & Perley.

Advice to try grand opera fascinates.

Leveraging fame and talent she moves very very fast. And within two weeks of a temporary summer hiatus, Alice Nielsen has crossed over to grand opera. Imagine, say, present country star Reba McIntyre at height of "Grand Ol' Opry" fame vanishing to Italy and after a London debut opening at the Met.

Ida Valerga's young protégé Alice heard many stories of the European grand opera life. With the Bostonians, Nielsen nearly jumps to Paris for Marchesi. Nielsen's voice has survived her rigorous schedule. Risky decisions. Shortly after closing night Alice Nielsen enters Covent Garden to audition for Henry Higgins. Sings her Valerga-coached Tivoli arias.

Does the American street singer impress Covent Garden? Instantly.

Higgins tells my fair lady to learn the opera repertoire in the native language and return. Duchess Consuelo arranges musicales for her protégé to sing for Rothschild, King Edward, Lady de Grey the patroness of Covent Garden. Alice is heard and promoted by Paolo Tosti. Nielsen has told Musgrave her vocal health demands hiatus. *Fortune Teller* closes.

Within two weeks, Alice Nielsen has committed to grand opera concerts in the spring. She tells Musgrave she will not return to the show. He is forced to dismiss the Nielsen Company. Two weeks into July the players return to NYC on steamer *Mesaba*, which in later days warns *Titanic* of icebergs dead ahead.

Eventually Nielsen praises Herbert and cast: "London conceded the beauty of Victor Herbert's *The Fortune Teller*. The British newspapers were almost enthusiastic about our singing. They agreed that Joe Cawthorn's humor was spontaneous and hilarious, that Eugene Cowles as a superb basso and that I was pleasing to the eye and ear". Knowing better the realities of life, Alice fogs: "*Fortune Teller* lasted only three months which, when you consider that it was a national furor in America and that audiences were less petulant and sophisticated in 1901, was a flop".

Then an intriguing diva's practical wisdom: "A musical comedy or light opera survived or perished chiefly on its music. Much more was left to the audience's imagination. Sex was taken for granted; people went to the theatre for other sorts of amusement. If you could sing well enough and your composer had written 'whistleable' tunes (there was much more whistling in those shiny days), your legs could be of any formation nature had decided upon for you—from Duncan Phyeor Chippendale to honest Ionic—and nobody need be the wiser, because even an actress was permitted, early in the century, to wear full-blown skirts. Of course, if you had exhibition legs it was quite all right. But you probably get the picture".

Of *Fortune Teller's* score, Nielsen skips fired conductor Steindorff and other subtleties: "The signs were clear in the first reviews the critics gave us. I asked one of these gentlemen to explain his coolness. 'The whole thing's too infernally noisy', he said. 'Couldn't you, now, bawl it a little less—let's say muscularly, now and then? Ease off with the brasses, I mean. Stop trying to be heard back in the States.' This being my first time in London, my first appearance outside the United States with the exception of a few nights in Canada, I had no ready answer for the man. Presently however, I ventured the fact that *The Fortune Teller* had been an electrical riot in America where, I added, it had been sung just as robustly. 'Oh quite all right for the States I fancy', he replied. 'But everybody roars everything there, they tell me, and one has to sing and play furiously to be heard at all.'"

Nielsen fades to black on that. Like that.

July 1901: Victor Herbert lost Alice Nielsen as a star.

July 1901: Alice Nielsen crosses to opera as a star.

America bewails her loss. Herbert turns from Broadway three years; keeping shows created for Nielsen on ice until the break seems final.

The lost collaboration. The quality of the shared. The gayety of nations.

They could steer pop culture into a rich new terrain.

From 1901 forward Nielsen and Herbert operate only in parallel. Fritzi Scheff leads his Alice shows, *Mlle. Modiste* (1905) and *The Prima Donna*—its famed song satires Nielsen. *Naughty Marietta* (1911) set in New Orleans after American Revolution enjoys a libretto by Rida Johnson Young, and stars Emma Trentini with 136 performances. When Herbert crosses over to opera for *Natoma* (1911) with its *Dagger Dance* rhythms seized by Bugs Bunny cartoons for Wild West scenes, Mary Garden stars with Irish tenor John McCormack who will join Nielsen at Carnegie Hall: All Sold Out. Would Alice advise Herbert not to pick libretti from theatre-accursed *War-*

Time Wedding's era? "Not even Miss Garden's unequalled genius for characterization could transform this cigar-store figure into a breathing, suffering, loving human being", says George Rogers of *Philadelphia Inquirer* (26 Feb 1911). Alice at Boston Opera the same year debuts the same era set to worse score, Frederick Converse's *The Sacrifice*.

Natoma, The Sacrifice, War-Time Wedding: three flops on a theme.

Herbert complains he has "not written a first-rate grand opera because he is unable to get a libretto even third-rate". He is offered "Pilgrim Fathers or the Redman. And there is 'punch' in neither. Most of the things that are wrong with the United States trace to the Puritan tradition; and we should be a great nation of the arts today had the Mayflower gone down with all hands on board before she sighted Plymouth Rock! As to the Indian, I've tried him once and am off him for life! Who cares what happens to one of them, man or maid?" (1918)

Perley grapples with his fatal flaws in unpublished papers fifteen years after London: "It is now theatrical history that the Alice Nielsen Opera Company set a 'high water mark' for organizations of its kind that has never been eclipsed...."

With trademark handlebar mustache Perley is enshrined in theatre's rouge's gallery of stock melodrama villains. A lesser antagonist for Nielsen and Herbert, Bostonian Barnabee supplies the name of the *Babes in Toyland* evildoer.

After *Fortune Teller* closes, Frederick Ward tells *NY Times* (July 6), that Nielsen's "future...grows more and more uncertain. Everyone appears to want the little woman who has made such a hit in *The Fortune Teller* and who is now looked upon as one of the regular London stars. London claims her in at least two theatres [Shaftesbury, Frohman]. New York also claims her for the coming season. If the small prima donna can keep her terrestrial body in one city and project her astral body in another, she may be able to satisfy a portion of at least of the claims of both".

Ward names Alice's attorney, "I interviewed AH Hummel..." supplied by Lillian Russell. Howe & Hummel "without a doubt, the most famous firm in the city" enjoy a reputation for bribery, perjury, and worse (Drehle, 2005) which even Williams & Perley dare not provoke. Naturally, Hummel says Perley is no problem: "Not withstanding the claims of Perley...Miss Nielsen will work under the management of Frank McKee in American next season".

McKee is tops. Produces eighty-one Broadway shows over the decade 1898-1908. Just closed *Hodge, Podge & Co.* Produces Herbert's *Algeria* (1908, text Glen McDonough) running 48 times at 1700-seat Broadway Theatre, reworked as *Rose Of Algeria*, hit song *Love is Like a Cigarette*. Then *Waltz Dream* (1908) by Oscar Strauss, 111 performances, English lyrics by comic Joseph Herbert who largely rewrote *Fortune Teller*. Strauss returns with anti-war *Chocolate Soldier*, libretto by Nielsen's ex-Delsarte coach Stanislaus Strang. Made into film 1941 with Nelson Eddy, Jeanette MacDonald who starred in MGM's 1935 *Naughty Marietta* with Joe Cawthorn.

Nielsen's return, continues Ward, "will be pleasant news but meanwhile, bills are posted outside the Shaftesbury Theatre announcing that the theatre will open in August with Miss Nielsen in *The Fortune Teller*. The fact is that no one seems to know exactly what Miss Nielsen will do.

"The situation is interesting but slightly exasperating to the gentlemen who have money invested in the tuneful young woman, and who are hoping she will help them to realize the proper profits on it".

July 14th to divert America from Nielsen's absence, *LA Times* relates a rare anecdote by erstwhile co-star Eugene Cowles of sailing from London to NYC.

DUET WITH FOGHORN by EUGENE COWLES

I was booked for a number on the programme of the Germanic on the trip from London and scored my first failure since I left the Chicago church choir to go on the stage [Nielsen's co-stars really belonged to a Chicago church choir company]. The ocean had been as smooth as a bowling alley for two days, and not a cloud as big as your hat, but when it came time for the concert we ran into the thickest fog you ever saw, and they had to start the fog horn.

The salon was crowded and everybody ahead of me on the bill had made a hit. Mr. Parsons, who was one of the party of American millionaires that called on Edward VII, was master of ceremonies. He gave me an introduction that made me blush.

I had selected that beautiful French solo *Le Cor* by Flegier, one of those showy pieces for a bass voice that is sure to make a killing. It starts: "I love the sounding horn, At even in forest far—". I was in excellent voice and the song starts forte with all the stops open.

I began: "I love the sounding horn"—just at that point the fog horn let out a blast that fairly shivered the ship's timbers. 'Boor-rr-r-r-r-oor', it roared right above me. Had a yearling heifer stuck her head in the door and bellowed it would not have made a bigger hit. Still I struggled on hoping to hurry through before another blast. The horn was about a half pitch off the key in which I was singing, and this threw me off my trolley for a couple of bars. The passengers smothered their smiles and gazed at me in pity, but I plunged right on as if nothing had happened.

That line occurs four times in the song, and the next time it went like this: "I love the sounding horn—". "Boor-rr-r-r-r-oor" went that fog horn again before I could get a note further. This time there was a spattering of giggles from the women and guttural chuckles from the men. It was certainly comical, but I kept a straight face and resentfully rolled my eyes upward toward the deck. I was in a terrible 'pers-pee-ra-shun', as the comic opera comedian sings, and felt my collar collapse like a concertina out of breath.

The situation was worse than the first night at the Shaftesbury when the "booh-ers club" let loose on *The Fortune Teller* [objecting at too-many encores]. The next line went like this: "I love the sounding horn—". It was no use. The fog horn didn't forget its cue, and this time everybody roared.

"I was done for completely and decided to give it up. When they could hear me, I said, "Ladies and gentlemen, please excuse me. I find my pipes are out of tune". Then I bolted for the door.

Cowles and Nielsen have glory voices nobody could forget.

Art is calling for her. So are blank checks for Broadway. Seven years after Alice left Wigwam for one-third salary at the Tivoli.

Ida Valerga has London contacts, such as Luigi Arditi (1802-1903) conducts at Her Majesty's Theatre and for Mapelson, composer of "Goodbye". And Paolo Tosti (1846-1916), "his graceful, original and expressive harmonies are familiar all the world over" writes Helen Zimmern (*Italy of the Italians* 1906). And Pablo Tosti, voice coach to Royal Family, professor at London Academy of Music, plays society circuit, creates popular songs, promotes Italian folk airs. Conducted Patti's tours for Mapelson.

Duchess of Manchester Consuelo Yznaga has contacts.

Laurence Irving has.

Alice has contacts. Only big talent gets big attention. Complete rest is given a peculiar twist when within three weeks Nielsen has made plans to sing Marguerite in Naples and concerts in London. Concert commitments not ticket sales vanquish Alice Nielsen Company. At gala gatherings Nielsen sings sidewalk songs for London society and gains attention. Via Conseulo to Gladys deGrey (1859-1917) among others of the realm.

Grey, nee Herbert, hosts hot parties with performing artists and literati. Oscar Wilde (1854-1900) dedicates to Grey a play satirizing her parties. "Through her influence", we are told by Royal Opera House (2017), Covent Garden was revived from decline, and she has "influence over all major decisions" including talent. EF Benson (*As We Were, A Victorian Peep-Show* 1930) recalls "this handsome lady, six feet tall and tremendously energetic, had been an important factor in the rejuvenation of Grand Opera in London...not a musical nature, but she had few interests and chafed at inactivity. Grand Opera needed attention...and a year of her industrious interest left its mark.... Nothing that could contribute to improvement escaped her eyes".

So it is. Within three weeks of the last show, *Chicago Tribute* (Jul 26) can report "Miss Nielsen has appeared at various drawing rooms, notably at Lady deGrey's, where her singing of *The Swannee River, Home Sweet Home* and other ballads simply caught society. The result has been several offers [theatrical]. She has however, decided to refuse all....

"Alice Nielsen is abandoning comic for grand opera. The story goes that she recently sang at a reception given by Lady deGrey, who is a noted patroness of the grand opera at Covent Garden. Lady deGrey was captivated by Miss Nielsen's singing and told her that she was wasting her talent and that she would have a brilliant future in operatic roles". Nielsen "will take a short course of instruction from an Italian master [Tosti], with the view to fulfilling engagements already made to sing in *Romeo and Juliet* and *Faust*".

Nielsen's serpentine route toward Naples passes several gates. Grey arranges an audition with Covent's conductor Luigi Mancinelli (1848-1921), who alike Victor Herbert is cellist, composer, conductor. Created four operas; conducts Covent, Madrid, Buenos Aires, and the Metropolitan NYC—theatres Alice will someday sing.

Nielsen sings, Mancinelli approves. We may assume Henry Higgins is present. Stated in negatives so beloved in that era, Mancinelli reports to Grey there is "no reason" Alice "should not follow the career she had planned for herself". Mancinelli packs Alice off to Tosti "with whom she is completing her study of the roles she intends to sing".

Tosti will soon send Alice to Naples for close friend Enrico Bevignani; six years later Tosti selects singers for the touring opera company Nielsen creates with Nordica which debuts in New Orleans. Tosti continues what Ida started until his pupil relocates to Naples for intense sessions with maestro Bevignani.

"Future plans of Alice Nielsen", July 25th *NY Times* reports, "besieged with lucrative offers both in London and NY, have been finally arranged. Miss Nielsen has decided to devote the next two months to close study of music under Signor Tosti in order to fit herself for her debut in grand opera next season". Tosti coaches Alice the French for two Gounod operas, "Juliet in *Romeo and Juliet* and of Marguerite in *Faust*, in which she expects to make her debut".

So it is. All arranged within three weeks between July 5th and 25th.

Consuelo, Grey, Higgins, Mancinelli, Tosti, Bevignani. Italian debut, London debut. Alice realizes what her gift is worth.

Before she leaves London, hopefuls hop to beguile Alice to Broadway. Whatever plans Major Braslan of San Jose made soon surrender. *Mercury News* (July 25) reports he "will not be Alice Nielsen's manager...the comic opera artist who appeared at the Victor Theatre some time ago" will "essay grand opera". And notes the absurd Max Desci has a swell lawyer Ignatious Welner ask $2000 for supposed voice lessons.

July 28th *Washington Post* puzzles: "Papers are full of Alice Nielsen. She will do this, she will not do that. Now she has gone here, now she goes somewhere else. What do we care? Why worry our heads about Alice and her voice? The weather is hot, the new season is almost here and there are many other things to worry about. Autocratic Alice may do as she pleases without any injunction from us. But perhaps you would like to hear of her latest feats? Very well—here goes. She is in London. Last week she was going to Australia. Now she is preparing for grand opera. She thinks she can completely obliterate memories of Melba. She will try Juliet and Elsa.

"No more comic opera for her. It is too undignified, and if there is anything in Alice Nielsen's career that she is fond of, it is her ever-present dignity. Behold then, Alice studying for grand opera and disdainfully dismissing half a dozen managers who implore her to sign contracts and return to the States to be a very demure little comic opera prima donna".

Post urges profit: "This is the proper thing for Alice to do—return to America and profit by her present popularity. (Pardon—we had almost committed the audacity of giving her advice)".

August brings the first public hint of a new name in Alice's career, "She has a new manager now—her seventh. His name is Russell and he is unknown in America", says *Post*. He is an odd choice. And proves worse.

Nielsen had met Russell (no relation to Lillian Russell) in June. Henry Russell, Jr. (1871-1937), taught *bel canto* by a lesson plan lifted whole from Mathilde Marchesi whose daughter Blanche will coach Nielsen later in London.

Enter from backstage a Henry Russell Jr., fringe player on the arty scene. Well-regarded brother Landon Ronald conducts and composes. In future Alice Nielsen will sing a Ronald song at many many concerts. Both brothers are associated with conniving soprano rival Melba who dominates at Covent. Russell Jr. exploits buzz from his same-named father: singer and songwriter who warbled for Rossini, Donizetti, Balfe, studied with Bellini, befriended Paganini the fast-fingered violinist—and guitarist—who had inspired the child Victor Hebert thanks to grandfather Samuel Lover. Russell Sr., related to London rabbi, had mined American cash as organist at First Presbyterian, Rochester NY, reusing hymn-tunes played fast to compose popular songs with words by Charles McKaye. Returned to 1841 England, abandons wife and five kids to live in Paris with Henry Jr.'s mom, petite Portuguese daughter of painter Lirolon deLara. Boy is twelve before parents marry. Russell Jr. uses, well, anything, including dad's fame, name, and connections to coach voice to society babes. The method "based on a study of the art of breathing and physiology of the throat, became the object of considerable jest in the press and indeed suffered ribald interpretation behind proper Bostonian hands as 'horizontal breathing'" suggested gossipy Quaintance Eton (1970).

Just the usual Valerga, Marchesi method standard at Paris Opera since 1880s, books owned by Alice Nielsen prove. Russell in 1890s marries Nina da Costa, a Portuguese singer, son Henry Tosti born 1896. Russell Jr. will marry thrice. The women won't wish him back, help him leave. During summer 1901 in London, removing to Rome at winter to teach at Santa Cecilia Music Conservatory "of which Sgambati is director". At the school, founded 1585, dance is prominent; a permanent symphony and choir established 1895. Today its "Eleonora Duse Drama School" occupies the 1200-seat theatre. The staff included Donizetti, List, and Rossini.

Alice Nielsen becomes Henry Russell Jr's livelihood the next fourteen years. She seems hypnotized to do so. She's proven. He has no resources, nor theatres, nor relevant experience, nor credibility. He's glib. As Alice has said of Mrs. Barnabee, it was one of the strangest relationships. At his insistence she promotes him madly. Russell cannily connives a chance to manage Broadway's big profit-maker. Promises to provide contacts in exchange for percentages of future revenues.

Meeting the golden goose, Russell suggests a fattening job for himself.

Well, choice made. Three weeks after *Fortune Teller* closes to mixed excuses, Russell has an addictively intoxicating dose of big-time publicity, named as Nielsen's manager by *Washington Post* which recounts the passing parade of potential candidtes: Perley "still claims her legally but says he doesn't care if she never comes back; Tom Williams, of California [*sic*]; Major Brashears, a seed contractor; E. Dundas Slater, of London; Charles Frohman of NY; Klaw & Erlanger of NY; George Musgrove of London, and now Mr. Russell. Frohman and the others say they have no contract with Miss Nielsen. Klaw & Erlanger have gone to the trouble of issuing a special bulletin and open letter declaring that Miss Nielsen's attorney AH Hummel some months ago desired them to take the management of his client which they declined to do".

Post advises stay in Europe, interestingly. "Considering the refusal of the most prominent members of the [Theatrical] Syndicate—Frohman, Klaw & Erlanger—to manage Miss Nielsen's affairs after her unfortunate quarrel with Perley, who stands very close to the Syndicate managers, it may be wise for Miss Nielsen to remain abroad and study for grand opera.

"But her admirers will be sorry. In light opera Miss Nielsen has no competitor. Her temper may cause trouble in her company [!] but it cannot keep away the dollars when she appears in a congenial opera".

With unintentional humor, "Why she should seek grand opera honors is not quite clear". Nielsen never no backside of Evangeline's cow: "She hasn't the massive physique which is the first requisite of the grand opera soprano". And acquire repertoire, "She must lose several years in study, and she is already—well, past thirty [about thirty]".

Stay Broadway for money. "Best thing for Alice to do would be to come quietly home and seek to profit by her present popularity before it fades away. Theatrical tastes change quickly, and if she stays abroad even a year Miss Nielsen will find herself only a memory. But really; why should we discuss Miss Nielsen and her movements with such wealth of detail".

Obviously oblivious, *Post* omits Perley cheated Nielsen of a fortune.

Whatever role Russell acquires for his profit, two women painted by John Singer Sargent will help Alice make the shift to a new career.

"When the end came and the rest of the company packed their bags and boxes for the return to America, I found that my old talent for making friends had been hard at work. Two important ladies had heard me sing, had invited me to their homes to entertain them and their guests and had listened to my simple story of my ambition".

Not Lady Grey. Consuelo Yznaga and Mrs. Lionell Phillips.

Dutchess Yznaga, sister-in-law to John Lister-Kaye, met Nielsen that April. Daughter of Cuban-born Don Antonio Yznaga Del Valle of New Orleans, she had married her fortune-hunting Duke in 1876. Romance that turns out badly. Friend Alva Smith of Mobile marries William Vanderbilt then Oliver Belmont, and names her daughter Yznaga. American heiresses trapped by aristocrats are "dollar princesses".

Phillips' husband Lionell had started the cruel war against the Boers to grab commodities; bankster Britain resumes sacrificing the citizens for foreign regime change. He helps Cecil Rhodes dominate diamond mines. Born in South Africa, Florence Ortlepp Phillips (1863-1940) was living in London to avoid Lionell's death sentence for deadly Jameson raid. They live on Grosvenor Square 1898-1906. Florence Phillips collects art and sings; her voice coach: Henry Russell. Phillips herself scorned wars.

Russell's account differs. Claims John Lister-Kaye brought Nielsen to see him and he to Yznaga. Yet Lister-Kaye had introduced Alice to Yznaga much earlier, in April. Russell could not admit that the chorus in Nielsen's cast, who had paid him for lessons, arranged her meeting him; and a Spanish tenor visiting Nielsen's show also urged this. In any case, Alice had been doing the London show seven month when Russell sensed stress in her voice (or more likely life) and strongly urged she quit. Which suited.

Buoys her agenda to quit the conflicted scene by any scheme.

An anecdote each tell illumes their divergence.

Yznaga arranges Alice sing for the King. That much is certain.

Russell tells thus: "King Edward in those days was a friend and frequent guest of Consuelo, Duchess of Manchester, whose sense of humor pleased and amused him. She was extraordinarily handsome, in many ways quite unconventional, and delighted in surrounding herself with vivacious and sparkling people. She and her sister, Miss Emily Yznaga [Mrs. John Lister-Kaye], were frankly and agreeably American and neither of them abandoned their transatlantic accent for the aristocratic drawl assumed by many of their fellow country-women". Interestingly, "The Duchess was quite a good musician and sang negro melodies delightfully". Alice Nielsen sang, "was in good form, and I saw at once that she made a good impression, and the Duchess asked her there and then whether she would like to sing before King Edward.

"I can still remember the expression of surprise and amazement which came into Alice's face. Although she had enjoyed unparalled success in comic opera she was really quite unspoilt. She assumed none of the airs and graces which distinguish certain successful stars, and the prospect of singing for a king seemed to appeal to her much as a fairy story appeals to a child.

"The Duchess, who was always kind to young artists, took her by the hand and told her not to be shy or nervous. 'But', said little Nielsen, obviously trembling in her shoes, 'I shall have to curtsey, walk backwards and do all sorts of funny things!' 'Don't worry', said the Duchess, 'I will give you some lessons myself and by the time the night arrives, you will not be the least bit afraid.'"

Nielsen next confesses to Russell, "I wish I had not to bring off that King stunt in a few days". He replies, "Our King had none of the pomposity or arrogance which she disliked in steel kings, sugar kings, sausage kings and all the other commercial kings of her acquaintance". Russell knew nothing of such men.

In Nielsen's version, Yznaga is candid: "And now, my dear, the King will be here and I want to warn you. He is King of England but his manners are those of a bush chieftain. The man hasn't any to speak of. But he's the King and—well, he's the King. He invariably talks to his companion when there's singing or a piano. There is nothing we can do about it. So don't mind, will you? For heaven's sake, don't do what Melba did last year".

"Not unless it's by accident. I don't know what she did".

"Well, you know Nellie Melba. She marched in and, as usual, removed her pearls from her neck and laid them on the piano. The King began to speak while she was singing and she stopped dead in the middle of a phrase. He went right on talking, so Melba snatched up her pearls and marched right out again".

"Madame, I have no pearls". Nielsen continues, Yznaga "enjoyed the distinction of having been the only woman in England of whom Queen Victoria was afraid". Intriguingly, "She, like so many men I met, seemed determined that I should quit the stage and settle down to something or other. "'One would think', I cried, 'that I had no voice; that I could not sing, the way you urge me to retire before I am nearly thirty!'"

About fifty, Yznaga in a practice not uncommon in those freer days of gayety offers to adopt Alice, and give her a wealthy life: "The light opera didn't go in London, so I accepted an invitation…to go on a trip with her".

Curious phrase choice: "the light opera didn't go". But we get the point.

"There was something on her mind. I knew that she had lost two beautiful daughters, who had suddenly faded like flowers and she often said that I reminded her of them. On that trip she proposed that she adopt me, that I throw my whole energy into her social life. But I preferred my career, and so the duchess lost interest in me. A wayward American waved aside the fairy godmother", says Nielsen of skipping a life of luxury, just as she skipped a meaningless marriage to Tom Williams for mere money.

To consider what fortune Nielsen again skips, Yznaga's father had died in March that year leaving daughter $4-million 1901 gold taxfree dollars; of course a fraction of the fortune Williams had received—his offer rejected.

Nielsen does not mention if Yznaga knew of her son Bennie. She does not specify where, or how long they travel. Yet time is moving fast. July has ended; she is soon in Napoli. Ireland makes a likely location, Yznaga owns Tandragee Castle in northern Ireland where Alice has family roots. Besides London, the Duchess occupies Kimbolton Castle near Cambridge. Yznaga, born in NYC, raised in Louisiana, became fiction as a character in *The Buccaneers* by Edith Wharton (1937) which begins "It was the height of the racing-season at Saratoga". Yes, horse tracks bind the era's society.

During August, Yznaga presents Nielsen to King Edward (1841-1910), whose father will reprimand him for affair with actress. Not Nielsen.

Alice is coached to bow and protocol. "No stage rehearsal was more arduous than the training I went through in my efforts to master the correct way to bow to royalty, and the 'first performance' didn't go off any too successfully, for I almost bowed myself to the floor and was saved from a spill only by the gracious way in which the king himself lifted me up. It was this kind of graciousness, I believe, that endeared him to his people".

Nielsen reuses the phrase of her first carriage ride to Jacob Dold's party: "It was quite an evening". Pianist of the evening is her prestigious coach: "My accompanist was no less than Paolo Tosti, who played his famous *Farewell* for me. For a few bars the King was silent. And then his harsh German gutturals were heard. He had turned to his companion and was telling her of something that had happened a few days back. If the man had to talk, he could not have selected a better moment for me. I was just about to sing—'Hush, a voice from the far-away'—and the chance was huge and golden. 'Hu-u-u-ussssh-h-h', I sang, holding the note and looking straight at His Majesty.

"Tosti, his hands limp at his side, was staring at me half amused, half startled. The Duchess of Manchester and several other women seemed to go rigid. And suddenly Edward stopped speaking. I continued the song and he did not open his mouth until I had ended. And then he came to me, took my hand and laughed. 'Please sing it again', he asked. 'I will show you that I can be polite.' Of course I did. And he kept quiet.

"Mother's audacious child from Missouri had called down royalty!" She adds, "These were exciting days for a girl reared in a democracy". Her account makes American papers preen when the story hits.

Russell recalls Edward good-naturedly saying, "Miss Nielsen, I really deserved that 'hush!' from you and I hope you will forgive me for talking.'"

Nielsen continues, "I remember that he insisted on changing from French to English when I was near him. Tosti, who wrote the famous *Good-Bye* song, was standing near. 'Let us speak English', the king suggested.

"But I can't speak English well', said the composer, who had lived in London for thirty years. I held this over him later when he taught me the role of Juliet in French, and complained that I was slow in learning it".

Without the intriguing details, "I hobnobbed on many occasions with the prince, who seemed to me to be wearing out his usefulness waiting for Queen Victoria to relinquish the reins of power. Then she died and the coronation day was set, when the new king was suddenly taken ill". What did the confirmed Irish patriot Alice tell the notoriously flirtatious King?

Yet her account strangely fuzzy for timing implied. Victoria had died in January 1901, months before Nielsen arrived in London. Prince Edward became King that day, coronation delayed until August 9, 1902. Nielsen simply did not know Edward when "wearing out his usefulness". Due to illness, "there was a postponement of festivities and it was during the interim I was 'commanded' to sing at Buckingham Palace", Nielsen says.

With tragic overtones almost a decade later December 1909 at home of Mrs. Phillips, Nielsen sings to Edward literally the last. Nordica, Fritz Kreisler, and Allessandro Bonci join her. After Nordica's *Ride of the Valkyries*, Nielsen gives "an aria from *Don Pasquale*. The king collapsed from his chair. They picked him up. It wasn't a pretty sight. His face was purple, his mouth agape and slobbering, his soft bulk inert. I continued singing until the end of the aria and the concert went on while the doctors struggled with His Majesty in a bedroom above our heads. He died six months later" in May of 1910.

Alice must keep mom Sara and never-mentioned son Benjamin afloat in NY plus pay for opera progress. Coaches and Italian debuts cost. Lady Grey and Consuelo Yznaga don't make her memoirs. Florence Phillips does. Their critical meetings is left foggy. Nielsen contradicts Henry Russell; the Phillips estate in South African could not confirm things. Russell has the ethics of Perley.

Russell says he arranged. Phillips takes voice from him. By his account, Florence Phillips "waiting one day for her lesson, she overheard a girl with a beautiful voice singing in my studio. She asked me later about the girl, and as I explained that this was a young American anxious to study for opera, but who was forced to accept exhausting engagements [Broadway] in order to support her mother and family. These efforts...would probably ruin her voice. Mrs. Philips, a strangely attractive little woman, with the merriest eyes I have ever seen, always became shy and a trifle self-conscious whenever she made an offer of help.

"She asked me for a few more details, and at her request I arranged that she should meet the girl [Nielsen] that day. The interview was short, but I saw that my protégé had made a favorable impression.

"Then Mrs. Phillips whispered, 'I will see what can be done.' The next day a letter came with a cheque for £1,000 [about $100k today]. She hoped the money would enable the girl to realize her ambitions and would relieve all financial worries in connection with herself and her family".

Alice Nielsen reverses roles: "Mrs. Lionel Phillips, proud of her celebrity as the patroness of so many young artists, took me to Henry Russell, then the foremost [blatant puffery by Alice] voice coach and diva-maker in London, and placing £5,000 in his narrow tapering hands, commissioned him to prepare me for grand opera". Russell "tucked the £5,000 (about $600k today) into his pocket and took me to Italy". He certainly had made no divas in London. He simply had Alice on the hook. Pocketing the £5,000. "Vocal professor" Russell lived with wife and kid at 1901 Egham in Surrey, thirty miles from London. Bad eyesight halted medical ambition.

Their conflicting accounts foretell the future. Russell scorns the women he suggests he dominated and brags exploiting. Likely pockets the £5,000, gives Alice £1000. But let the upcoming Perleyesque revelations about Russell surprise you, gentle reader. Either way, Nielsen's cash relieves his pressing financial worries—for him and family. Nielsen ships a stipend to Sarah and scapes by with pittance in Italy and (foggy) Spain.

Netting Nielsen pays off for Russell first and last. Ironically, NYC theatrical producers throw big legit offers and literal blank checks to play America. Russell, useful to close the Williams & Perley racket by claiming a voice vacation, realizes he has no future aside form Alice. To protect his percents he affects to scorn American musical theatre. His incessant voice and hands-on touch mayhaps hypnotic over Alice Nielsen.

Scorning NY—her lawyers could crush Perley—and huge cash, Alice Nielsen takes the big risk: "I burned my comic opera bridges behind me. I turned down a contract for five seasons at $3,000 [$75,000 today] a week. Oh I'd forgotten what poverty was like. But it came back I tell you!"

£5,000 would have deflected poverty for several years.

Blind trust for Russell—"I don't know what I should have done but for Mr. Russell"—becomes a mantra she repeats a decade until disaster. She mentions the lesser amount, still contradicting Russell: "Mrs. Lionel Phillips sent a check for a £1,000 and the message that there was more when I needed it. Thanks to that, I was able to look after my mother and continue studying".

Nielsen speaks of pressure to perform rapidly to generate revenue. Gives a foggy hint of some severe poverty subsisting in Madrid, Spain. The opera house there furnished many of her future cast who have links to Tosti. Decades later Russell would reveal his 1901 motives by telling his kids he had latched onto Nielsen to exploit her money; after all, he said, she had proved a gold mine for Williams & Perley. Yet Nielsen was no fool about finance. Took his flattery for what it was worth and paid far far more than it was worth. Russell deploys his charms to entangle the the fortunes of the rising opera star assured success for a percent and then some.

In any case, Nielsen credits Florence Phillips who "financed my next move. With her help, I decided to desert the light opera stage for a while and prepare for grand opera". Depending on the timing, she suggests abandoning the Shaftsbury was a scheme.

Being "taken up" meant "seeing great places and meeting the famous. I made many friends and some enemies, and all so swiftly and easily. I too was becoming famous". To Alice Nielsen, fame is only a tool for artistic opportunity, "I had come to the place where Hans Richter was pleased to direct me, where the incomparable Enrico Caruso insisted that I open the Covent Garden season with him in *La Bohème*".

And so it is. All settled during July 1901. Or prearranged June.

America will be in Alice's past for the next four years. Yet anything touching her is nationally famous. August 4, her cast romances are news as *Washington Post, Chicago Tribune* and *NY Times* report "May Blossom Boley...playing small parts in the Alice Nielsen Opera Company, was married Friday in NY to an English admirer who followed her across the seas. Lt. Frederick Lindsley Nicholson saw Boley in "*Fortune Teller*... and proved to be a case of love at first sight". He follows her to NY, "a wedding was consented to" by her mom; his own mom "very much against the attachment...in ignorance of her son's marriage".

Alice's success with Henry Higgins hits America August 11th as *Washington Post* reports she will join "Covent Garden Grand Opera Company". Sidebar on pest Perley opening *Chaperons* September 30th at Hartford going nowhere fast, NY run June 1902. Not Herbert score, Witmark and book by Ranken.

Of summer 1901, Alice recalls "the papers made a great deal of fuss over the American light opera singer who thus suddenly disappeared. They thought it was a madcap idea of mine to desert the merry compositions in which I had won for myself an acknowledged place. One by one the managers ranged themselves in a row, beckoning me back with offers that would have tempted many another, and that would have meant every possible comfort for me".

She drops a bombshell. "Frohman said that he would see that eventually I should have an opera with no other libretto than Barrie's *Peter Pan*", the producer's big success. "But the die was cast and I hurried to Naples, where I put myself under the care of one of Europe's greatest teachers, Bevignani".

Note the careful "I put myself". Five weeks gone since she vaporized Alice Nielsen Company. Napoli! Victor Herbert's *Naughty Marietta* heroine sings praises of Napoli where Alice has spent two years, and never he.

In this critical moment, Alice gives the most significant statement of her artistic purpose and style. She has arrived with seventy-something Enrico Bevignani (1841-1903) who composed 1863's *Caterina Blum*. The conductor-composer is the best possible coach. Nurtures stars. Coached and conducted Adelina Patti and Christine Nilsson. Teaching *Faust* to Alice, "the old man would often turn around and describe the wonderful powers of Christine Nilsson, 'whose voice was soprano, legaro, lyrico and dramatic all in one. Her acting was spontaneous, and came from her heart, and she cast a magnetic spell on her audience which never ceased until the end of her performance.'" Such an artistic challenge Alice Nielsen cannot refuse. She seeks the quality of *legaro*, *lyrico*, dramatic "all in one".

Already she cast a magnetic spell over audiences. Much better soon.

True to her goals, Nielsen within the decade travels to Sweden for Nilsson clutching an introduction from their instructor. Nilsson was, says *A Society Woman On Two Continents* (1897), "the only singer who has left the stage at the zenith of her glory, and who has never made but one farewell tour". Her first American tour had netted a fortune of $380,000 ($9+ million today), relates Thomas Handford in *Pleasant Hours* (1885). His book includes the diva Nilsson with peers in fame: Abraham Lincoln, Henry Irving, Mrs. Langtry, Robert Burns, Mozart, Adelina Patti, Charles Dickens, Lord Byron, and David Livingston. Alikeness of Nielsen and Nilsson comes across as George Upton recalls: "My pleasantest memory of Christine Nilsson is connected with her birthday celebration at the Sherman House in Chicago in 1871. She was in the gayest of moods that evening, waived all the conventionalities, and showed herself a Bohemian of the most rollicking, sunshiny kind.

"Verger sang musical caricatures of the leading barytones on the stage. Vieuxtemps sacrificed his high art ideas to the humor of *The Arkansas Traveller* and the fascinations of *Money Musk*; Brignoli played his *Battle March*, which he thought was an inspiration, and was inclined to be offended when he looked round and saw the company, with Nilsson in the lead, doing an extraordinary cake walk to its rhythm, for Brignoli took that march very seriously.

"Nilsson gave some ludicrous imitations of the trombone, double-bass, tympani, and bassoon, and sang humorous songs.

"The closing act of the revelry, which lasted far into the small hours, was a travesty on the Garden Scene in *Faust* by Nilsson and Brignoli, in which the big tenor's gravity of mien and awkwardness of love-making was admirably set off by Nilsson's volatile foolery. It was a night of hilarity and fun-making long to be remembered.

"And now I read that the once famous singer spent her sixty-fourth birthday in the Swedish village of Gardsby and delighted an enthusiastic audience with the song, *I think I am just fourteen*. I should not be surprised if she honestly believes it, for she is one of the elect who can never grow old in spirit" (1908).

Thus the shared diva spirits who make gayety in the nations.

Bevignani shapes Alice Nielsen's operatic style. No society vocal coach; he conducts and composes. His techniques teach Alice Nielsen. Spends the last two years of life coaching her to top competence. "Under the guidance of the maestro I soon learned the roles which I was to enter my new career", Nielsen simply says. "With kindness, patience and assiduity he enabled me to master the almost incredible difficulties of the *Traviata*, *Rigoletto*, *Faust*, *Figlia del Reggimento*, etc.

"Difficulties there were for one who had never heard a word of a foreign language and who, in a comparatively short space of time, was expected to satisfy the exigencies of the inhabitants of Naples". Dad spoke Danish, mom Gaelic, Alice grew up in polyglot Kansas City schooled as such with French nuns, marries a Prussian whose parents speak German, sings in polyglot San Francisco coached by polyglot Ida Valerga. Tosti had taught her the French roles. She sang songs in Hawaiian and Japanese.

The great influencer Bevignani imparts Alice Nielsen's opera style.

In the backwater provincial, Perley fails to snare a next victim, *LA Times* (Aug 18) reports "Williams & Perley Opera Company, formerly the Alice Nielsen Opera Company, will not open its tour" till later. Perley, "found myself with a Company on my hands, a tour booked and no prima donna, I went to Paris to secure Mary Garden...and offered to star her in Miss Nielsen's stead". The *Opera Comique* star, Scots-born, Chicago-bred Garden does not succumb. She is quite formidable, her own manager, and will manage Chicago Opera Company. Alike Nielsen, she moves, dances, and is memorable in tights.

August fades into September. Nielsen acquires the complex repertoire.

She has traveled London to Rome to Naples. Henry Russell who pocketed her cash, shows her the towns. Hiatus?

November 14th Alice returns to London for musicales to raise cash. Her progress impresses Covent's Henry Higgins: "She will make her debut in grand opera in at Covent Garden in April". *The Stage* on December 5th confirms, Alice Nielsen "has returned to town from Italy where she has been studying, and is being heard in drawing-rooms". Related theatre news has Nielsen's erstwhile co-star Marguerite Sylva starring in "*Princess Chic* under Kirke La Shell" and on the 24th Barnabee "celebrated his 68th birthday in Philadelphia (*Wash. Post*)".

As 1901 closes, remora Russell appears associated with the star in a first mention by press. *The Era*, Dec. 21st, has Nielsen "studying in London under Mr. Henry Russell, son of the great Henry Russell".

Dec. 28th *London and Provential Entr'acte* report "Alice Nielsen is to appear on the concert stage shortly, and it is said, has designs upon the grand opera stage". Her first concert, February at Robert Newman's Queen's Hall orchestra. So by 1902 her crossover is complete and pays.

This year 1901 when Alice loses her company, Hortense creates hers. Sarah's bunch is in Chicago. Actress sisters Hortense and Mary (Maria) stay through 1920 long after the rest relocate to NYC. After Modjeska, Hortense joins western repertory groups then relocates to Washington DC with the Lafayette Theatre Company. *San Francisco Mascot* (Aug 1) reports "Hortense Nielsen, a sister of Alice Nielsen...met with great success in the South and West this season. She is said to bear a striking resembles to the light opera star, with the exception that she is a decided brunette".

In November Hortense leaves Perley-connected Lafayette to start a company of her own, managed by husband Charles Arthur Quintard (b1862). Quintard, who managed Amesbury Opera House until its 1899 fire, in the press goes by CA Arthur or CA Quintard. They tour from Chicago to Shreveport to good reviews in *Under Two Flags*, a Frohman-Belasco show adapted by Paul Potter from Ouida's (Maria Louise Ramé) novel of a heroine in French North Africa who rides a horse Cochise among sandstorms. They tour Texas (*Fort Worth Register* Dec 21) then with cast of sixteen produce the drama *Carmen*.

Adventures of Hortense and husband evoke the lost era. Let's look.

When *LA Times* says "Miss Nielsen is a wisp of a woman with an astounding intellect" it is Hortense. Her 1901 season closes at Greenwall's where she "made such a hit with theatre-goers of Washington DC last winter...pretty, young, of most pleasing personality and a great favorite with both old and young. The critics all mentioned particularly her knowledge of stage technique and her resemblance of her famous sister.

"Her expression has been considerable and varied, as is amply shown by the variety of the roles which she has successfully essayed. While she probably excels in light ingénues, yet her work in pathetic parts is certainly most pleasing. She has played in what are probably of the two representative stock companies of America—Frawley, the acknowledged leader of the West, and Lafayette, the recognized head in Eastern stock. She is thoroughly versed in dramatic art and has much talent which is supplemented by hard work as was shown by her continued success in a line different roles while in Washington, DC. She is sure to prove a favorite wherever she may go". And from Chicago she goes touring the South and West arranged by Fritz Boone with stage manager James H. Lewis.

Hortense has a remarkable husband of constant cooperation. Playing the boonies, they will face difficulties. April 1902, *Iola Register* finds (husband) manager A.C. Arthur "arrested yesterday afternoon and lodged in jail for a while. The arrest was made on a warrant issued in Coffeyville which town the manager left without paying a $20 board bill, probably the bill for the company. The sheriff telegraphed to the police here to hold Arthur and he was arrested, the Montgomery county officer coming after him last-night. Arthur was surely in hard circumstances for he tried to get out of paying several bills here, fearing he would go broke before he got his show to Chanute". Leaving Iola on schedule despite the snag they play Sedalia and Macon—Missouri—two days each and proceed: "one of the most dramatic performances of the season". In one Missouri town they are "Hortense and Maria Nielsen Company", next night "Hortense Nielsen Company". Hortense will tour Midwest for decades with plays by Ibsen and Shaw. Later she retires to a Wilton CT farm thirty miles from Bedford NY where Alice locates in 1920.

Alice and Hortense connect lifelong.

Nashville-born, Kansas City raised, the prodigy Alice has blessed natural gifts—amazing musical memory. She sings with Irish mom; learns to read complex scores in a Kansas City choir; decade of sidewalk songs before San Francisco; gains comic stagecraft from Stanley Burton; receives Ida Valerga's *bel canto*; stars in *Satanella* and *Lucia*; finds far-flung fame with Bostonians. Experience. Success. Audience. Skill.

Reaching London, yes, her homeward path seems blocked, money stolen. Spurning the obstacles of corrupt men, she spurs toward yonder golden dream only she could achieve. She anoints some total novice as manager. Flattery gets him somewhere. Fiancé to the rescue Laurence Irving had a big part in her liberation before he gracefully bows out after sending Alice to Naples to pursue her career.

1901 ends with Alice Nielsen five months beyond Broadway. She will divide time between Italy, England, and France with a mysterious short stopover in Madrid poverty with her loyal maid, foggy crisis untold. In Italy she befriends Eleonora Duse who Laurence would know well.

1902: ELEONORA DUSE PROTÉGÉ

Eleonora Duse is to Italy as Irvings to Britain. She played 1896 NYC the week Nielsen arrived. Since 1893 Duse has toured America regularly. Sensing artistic affinity Nielsen seeks the actress. James Huneker tells how Duse "awed rather than astonished...her skill taking on new meanings, new colours. Her art was a unique something that closely bordered on the clairvoyant. Her helpless silences were actually terrifying; her poses most pathetic".

Century editor Robert Johnson (*Remembered Yesterdays* 1923): "With Duse, one simply was absorbed in the play, not only in her own part but in those of her company to whom she succeeded in imparting the importance of *ensemble*". Equally comedy, "I should hesitate to say whether Signora Duse is greater in tragedy or comedy. I have never seen anything in comedy that compared with her acting...." Alike Alice.

Modjeska of Duse, "To whatever school she belongs, she is a great actress. The intensity with which she abandons herself to the feelings of the characters she personates makes you forget all surroundings...you cease analyzing; you only feel that you are in the presence of terrible pain, despair and agony".

Recalls Alice, "I learned Italian during that time, helped by the interest of Eleonora Duse who prepared me for *Traviata*". Context suggests the duo met in Rome late 1901 as Duse produces and acts in D'Annunzio's *Francesca da Rimini*. In winter Henry Russell taught at the Roman music school his is friendly with D'Annunzio who at sixteen published an erotic poetry book *Primo Vere*.

Duse and poet since 1897 lived "in rural splendor, wearing outlandish clothes, staging wild parties" and fascinating "jealous onlookers". Such as, he swims nude at sunset as she holds his purple robe. Michael Leeden (*D'Annunzio, the First Duce*, 2001) describes D'Annunzio raising eccentricities to an art form, affecting a quill pen, going mystic by 'reading' Tarot, hobnobs with witches and fortune tellers for numerology and oriental occult fad. Alsso pertinent to Russell's affections for him, D'Annunzio had "a totally captivating personality...whose charm and charisma extended to both men and women. He cultivated conversation, always seeming to know the right words to win over an opponent or reinforce a wavering will". Puppeteer he was "with other men, D'Annunzio had a rare ability to convince his acquaintances that he was immensely concerned with their problems, fascinated by their stories, and involved in their lives. In reality, his egotism was so great that his real feeling was invariably almost total indifference to other people.... Direct contact with D'Annunzio was hypnotic".

Tell-tale point. Don't be distracted or the trick will be obvious.

During 1901-05 Nielsen spends time with Duse. Resourceful stars, they combine to present a series of drama-opera tours to Italy and London. Alice is with Duse in 1902 when the actress drops poet and retreats 80km to her "villa in Caponi for fifteen years", relates *Theatre Magazine* (1931).

When Duse's voice freezes, Russell supposedly spends autumn 1903 as her guest at London's Savoy Hotel, "staying another year when she would not hear of my leaving her". Russell will never mentions wife (wives) or children. For the vocal therapy in London of all places, Alice claims Duse insisted, "She would give him every dollar if he would go to London. He went—of course not for the money, for he is an artist".

Yet what did the arty lad make except disaster by backstabbing artists. None ever so silly of hypno-Russell as "The Nielsen" before the disas.

Merely-arty with exploitation added. Artists make art, exploiters cash.

Lee Strasberg observed Duse act in NYC where her "voice was rather high; when she was young she had to train her voice for strength and fullness but it remained the high Italian kind of voice. In fact, when I heard her in 1923 in the big Century Theatre, I thought her voice was a little too big". Strasberg speaks of Duse in ways often applied to Nielsen: the "voice had a strange quality which I have never heard in any other voice. You were never aware of expenditure of effort. The voice came out easily. It was somehow on a stream of breath. It seemed to float. It simply left her and went on. It traveled, and yet you had the sense that it was the same easy voice wherever you might hear it in the theatre. It was a voice that had no difficulty, perhaps of her uncanny ability to relax".

Alice Nielsen says she sought Eleonora Duse "the greatest artist I have ever seen", does not specify where and when. First opportunity was her NY debut, yet quite possible paths crossed earlier in San Francisco. And Mrs. Grover Cleveland in 1898 honored Duse at the White House.

As you may anticipate the Nielsen-Duse meeting has versions.

The pet name for Alice becomes *piccolo*, 'little-one.' Nielsen relates that "a very rare woman had come into my life—Eleonora Duse, the spirit with the beautiful hands and with a face upon which eternal sadness had set its mark! I am thankful for the association I had with her. It was an intimacy [trust] of many years, at a time when the whole of passion [for D'Annunzio] had the grip of her, and afterward when D'Annunzio had turned from her, and all her love for him had turned to ashes".

In most Nielsenian versions rascally Russell goes unmentioned. Alice seeks help for her acting; seeks the sincerity. When in Rome, she gives the actresses' name a buildup, as only Arthur Pryor. "There was but one artist in Italy at that moment. Before I took on airs, I should go to her, observe her, study her and hope that she would let me stay near her. She was not a singer and yet her voice was lovely music. Her name was Eleonora Duse.

"A shock was in store for me. Try as I might, I could not meet her in the conventional way. I managed to have myself invited to houses where she too was invited. She was never there when I was. And presently one of the most popular hostesses in Rome took me aside and explained, 'You know Gabriele D'Annunzio, don't you?' she said. 'No', I replied. 'Do you mean to tell me', she cried, 'that you haven't heard the gossip?' 'What gossip?' 'That you are the new woman.' 'What nonsense', I protested. 'I wouldn't know the man if I saw him.' 'At any rate', she said, 'that's the story. I know it isn't so. But you have been talked of a great deal and Duse is certain it is you. She will not therefore meet you.'"

Duse and D'Annunzio: entourage-ridden self-conscious celebrities.

Poet, novelist, playwright D'Annunzio (1863-1938) is married with Maria di Gallese (three sons) when he beds Duse 1894 helpful to his career. The star produces and acts his plays: 1898's *Dead City*, 1901's

Francesca da Rimini. Some say they separate after his tell-all novel *Flame Of Life* (1900), but the author tells you they toy a decade more until his exploitation expends itself wasted like (supply erotic metaphor here).

Jules Huret (1908) knows D'Annunzio as "medium height, slender, not to say frail, with short, reddish hair which is growing thin...he has the air of one of those aristocratic beings who have begun life too soon. His ruddy mustache is trimmed close to the lip, and the points are turned up sharply at the corners, while the chin ends in a little pointed beard". Tommaso Antongini (1938), D'Annunzio's biographer, tells us the affair "owed its beginning to a prosaic meeting, not only brought about by third parties, but resembling those matrimonial alliances which are desired rather by the families than by the contracting parties". Pushed together by plotting pals. Duse would say "He was never sincere; he lied, he was always lying", relates Francis Winmar in *Winged Victory* (2008). Duse promotes D'Annunzio; Nielsen promotes Russell.

These men had hypnotic words to captivate unwary people. D'Annunzio veered in to fascism and the war folly. Remora Russell lacked the courage.

Huneker in *Iconoclasts* (1908) devotes a chapter: the poet "has chosen to depict decadent men and women and all bristling with vitality is his personal idiosyncrasy". Huneker, never fooled by painted veils, says "his chief defect is an absolute lack of humour, and this, coupled with the tropical quality of his art, causes a certain monotony—we breathe a dense, languorous atmosphere. Human interest in the daily sense of the phrase is often absent". For all his arty pretention, *Francesca da Rimini* is mere "glorified melodrama...an interesting rather than great play, though full of inspiring poetry". Yet "his men and women are genuinely alive and given their various temperaments, they act as they inevitably would in the world of the living". For Duse "the wisdom of her choice in selecting only D'Annunzio dramas is not altogether apparent. She will listen to no advice...." His "plays are not of the kind that appeal to the larger public".

When Duse and D'Annunzio are living at Anzio, between Naples and Rome, Alice unannounced arrives at the door. Duse's maid "would not admit me". Alice discovers the actress was taking the train to Rome that day and waits. "I gave the conductor twenty lire, telling him that I must go to her compartment and the man led me there, bowing thanks.

"Duse was sitting in a corner, her eyes closed, her hands—the hands that her poet-lover had immortalized—flat on her thighs. And then she awoke with a start, demanding to know why I had intruded and who I was.

"'I am an American', I said. 'I have come to Italy to learn the operas. My name is Nielsen.' She understood my atrocious Italian. Never on any stage had she shown such passion as when she rose and ordered me to go". Nielsen ignores Duse's tempest, "'Even if I do not achieve your friendship, I shall not go until I tell you that I am not the woman whom you suspect.'"

Alice does not name Mary Garden.

"'You are worse than unwelcome', she cried, 'You are impudent. Why should you assume that Duse would fear you or be commonly jealous of you?'

"'I may be making a great mistake, signora', I said. 'However, I want you to know that I do not know D'Annunzio and never saw the man.'

"'Of course you lie but your impudence amuses me. After all, what does it matter whether you lie or not? Every woman does—and every man. You must be very much moved however, to burst in on me like this.'

"Whereat I told her that my reason for intruding was to talk to her, to try to make her my friend, to study her great art. I told her frankly that any success I might achieve would be delayed, perhaps for years, unless she was willing to let me be near her. And then she softened".

Nielsen reveals herself: impudent and bold. "I am not a very adroit person and was less so then. Perhaps she recognized my simple directness, my naiveté, my sincerity. Perhaps she was flattered by my obvious idolatry.

"Whatever it was, she melted. Before we had reached Rome she vowed that she would teach me Italian, that she would arrange that I should travel with her through Italy and even that I should stay with her—and D'Annunzio—in Rome, where at the time I was singing". Alice does not elaborate on her singing itinerary nor timing. "Her change of attitude toward me was as swift as, before, her dislike for me had been violent. There was no way of predicting her moods. In no time she had presented me to the man of whom, a little while ago, she had been madly, unreasoningly jealous. My sense of humor reassured her".

So it was. "I went with her to Rome and spent a week with her". At Duse's villa Nielsen meets D'Annunzio: "He had a wonderful singing voice and at a spinet used to intone some of his poetry. I sang for the two of them—some of Mozart—the song, *Oh Leave Me to Weep Alone*".

Inevitably D'Annunzio flirts. "When it was time for to return to my hotel, he walked with me through the beautiful grounds to the gate. 'signorina', he said, "were you ever in love?' "'A thousand times', I exclaimed with a laugh. I could see out of the corner of my eye that this was not the answer he expected. I told the incident to Duse afterward and she laughed until she cried".

Nielsen told that tale variously. Here's another: "With Russell I went to the Borghese Palace in Rome, where they lived. After dinner, D'Annunzio and I followed Russell and Duse into the garden. It was a night made for sentimental reflections and observations—no doubt of that; but I was hardly prepared to have the great D'Annunzio put his arm around me as we went down the stone steps and ask me in curious English whether I had ever loved.

"'Loved? Good Lord, man, I've never been out of love. Why?' 'But I should teach you such love as you have never so much as guessed', he assured me. 'The sort I am familiar with has caused me all the trouble I have any use for. It is another kind of education that I crave. Outside of that, don't be an ass.'"

In this take the actress reacts humorlessly, "He liked me even less when I repeated the incident to Duse who hasted to assure me that I had done wrong in speaking thus to 'the master.' What a pair they were!"

Returning to Napoli, Bevignani keeps her busy. An Italian tutor. At intervals, Nielsen spends time with Duse in London, Paris, Italy.

Time (July 30, 1923) said of Duse and D'Annunzio, "The poet tired of her. In 1900 he deserted, soon to publish a novel [*Flame*] revealing to the world their secrets in intimate detail. It later came to light that through it all he had been playing her simply for literary material. The shock nearly brought about Duse's death. For two decades they were estranged". Alice Nielsen resets *Time*. Duse-D'Annunzio estrangement was highly flexible. *Time* absurdly melodramatic; the famed coupling were realists of mutual convenience. Yet Duse's abuse at his hands well-known; her romantic pains as well.

Nielsen recalls touring Italy with Duse, playing small theatres during 1902-1904. Duse could produce such a tour readily. Switching nights, Nielsen sings or Duse acts. "With her I traveled through Italy.... For example, one night she would play *Camille* and the next I would sing the same story, *Traviata*".

During these days, "I saw Duse with the two men who were the whole of her emotional life. She at one time ardently loved Arrigo Boito, or rather it might be said that he adored her. He was the composer of the opera *Mefistofele* [1868]. On this tour I met her first love—the man she had given up for D'Annunzio...."

Boito "still adored her and would have then taken her back; but after her final break with D'Annunzio—after D'Annunzio had betrayed her once too often—he had his revenge: he refused to receive her. One could mark in his face the adoration and the worship. But when D'Annunzio came, she gave Boito up. And so I cannot but feel that a part of Duse's tragedy was a visitation, the compensating balance, for she had wounded just as much as she was hurt".

Composer and poet Arrigo Boito (1842-1918) wrote libretti for Verdi and for Ponchielli's *La Gioconda*. When he conducts his own *Mefistofele* (based on Goethe's *Faust*), the opera provokes riots and duels, closed by police after two performances. Father an Italian painter, mother a Polish countess, he fought under Garibaldi to unite Italy as a republic. Romance aside, "In spite of the fact that her break with Boito had been so recent, she wanted me to sing in Boito's new opera, the part of Nylia, the blind girl, and arranged an audition".

Alice Nielsen makes a gloriously obscure opera joke: "But I never sang the part, having to fill an engagement elsewhere". You see, Boito would finish only one opera, *Mefistofele. Ero e Leandro*, scrapped. *Nerone* was incomplete when he dies in 1918; six years later Arturo Toscanini completed it for *Il Teatro alla Scala*. She definitely had to fill engagements elsewhere before she could sing Boito's new opera! Her best joke!

Duse and Boito bring Alice Nielsen to "the great Adelina Patti, who they assured me was an extraordinarily stingy woman and otherwise curious; but that under no circumstances was I to laugh or offer any typical American comment at the villa.

"Alas, over the gate of Patti's villa there was the legend, 'Never Give Up', in Italian, of course—and instantly her lack of spendthrift heart popped into my mind. But I could not make Duse and Boito understand why I was laughing". Never give up a dime.

Patti "was holding one of her odd receptions. We were ushered into a room where we stood facing a curtain. Presently there was music and a troupe of little girls came in singing and strewing the place with flowers. Then the curtain was snatched aside and there sat Patti—tiny, wizened, waspish and looking more like a porcelain figurine than a real woman. She sat on a throne.

"One approached on steps and kissed her hand, a tiny, blue-veined claw burdened with great diamonds, emeralds and sapphires. She was the center of adoration. I suppose she expectantly waited for me to kiss her hand, but the American in me somehow rebelled at such hollowness.

"My sense of humor held me back. I did not go up. I did not have the courage. I was afraid I would laugh. I'm afraid I lacked reverence. Or perhaps it was simple ignorance. Precedent meant nothing whatever to me". Difficult to imagine Nielsen meets Patti without dialog. The pair know too many people in common: Arditi, Tosti, Bevignani, Valerga. Alice skips saying more. Tosses egg.

"To return to the beloved Duse. I can see her now in her home at Florence —Settignani [Settignano]. She had known the great Wagner, and had lived in his family circle whenever she played near enough to visit them. One day she brought in one of the rare death masks of Wagner for me to see. Impulsively I put out my hand to take it. 'No, no', she cried, drawing back. And then with that grace which was poetry to her, she played her hands lightly above the still features of the master, as a breath might cool the face without touching it".

Nielsen sees the bouts of romantic misery, "She wept most of the time those days for the break with D'Annunzio had come. I remember how she pleaded with him to leave her his plays, and he refused. In early days of our friendship, Duse had sent me a locket. On it she had engraved the motto, *Alto in Speranza*—'Keep your hopes high.' So easy to do when all goes well, but in Settignani so difficult when the heart was dead. It was after this that Duse went into retirement from which she was to emerge an old woman".

Duse "was his inspiration. Therefore it was necessary, when he was moved to write, that she go to his rooms and throw herself upon a narrow divan and lie there rigid while he filled page after page with phrases. And all this time (it sometimes was three hours) she dared not move a hair's breadth, no matter how great her agony might be. There she lay, cramped, aching, not daring to move one of her beautiful fingers or open her mouth. If she did, he would scream that she had broken the spell, that everything was ruined. Then he would sweep all that he had written off the table and rush at her, threatening to strike her". Italians in romantic arguments grand to behold.

Nielsen scorns, "After these absurd exhibitions I frequently massaged her paralyzed arms and legs back to life".

She matches wits with poet one night in Florence, "While the three of us were dining, he held forth about women—he was always doing that anyway. Let me see—how did it go? Oh, yes—that no girl should remain a virgin after sixteen. 'Aren't you talking shop?' I inquired. Duse frowned— and cringed a little, I thought. But D'Annunzio ignored me and went on to say that all women should be chloroformed at forty. 'But, master', I asked, 'what would the world have done without you?' D'Annunzio's mother was more than forty when he was born. Duse arose, stamped her foot and bade me keep my tongue. 'You are impudent', she cried. 'you may listen to but do not mock the master's thoughts".

Nielsen says, she was included in their "Ceremony of the Dawn" featuring the poet naked on horseback at beach. Duse "insisted that I come with her to her Villa Vignola at Port d'Anzio". Gorgeously set on the Adriatic shore across Italy opposite Naples and Rome. And there, one morning, she aroused me before dawn. 'Get dressed', she whispered. 'Go down to the shore and you shall behold.' I beheld.

"I wrapped myself in a warm cloak and picked out a comfortable sand dune well down toward the water and just overlooking the broad hard beach. And just as the sun nipped above the low, blunt hills I saw three figures emerge from the early dawn. They appeared far up the dunes, very shadowy. First Duse, in a single, sweeping garment, her head thrown back, her eyes fixed on the sea. She was leading a huge white horse on which sat little D'Annunzio. The horse carried no saddle but a simple bridle was fastened to its head.

"D'Annunzio, looking smaller and a little more absurd than ever, on his mighty charger, set pompously erect, his arms folded on his chest, his head reared. He wore a great cloak or cape that covered him from his nose to his feet.

"Gradually the group took shape and in slow majesty they passed me, Duse leading the great animal as if in a trance. As they passed I saw D'Annunzio's lips move and heard him reciting his newest verses. Presently they were on the flat beach—a wide plateau of silver sand. And there Duse released the horse's bridle and fell to her knees. D'Annunzio with a tremendous flourish, with the swaggering gesture of a great cavalier, flung his cloak from him, leaving him naked. Then, with the flat of his hand, he smote the horse and the Ride of the Rising Sun began.

"Furiously he galloped up and down the strand, losing himself in the soft gloom of the dawn and then emerging—his arms still folded on his chest, his voice rising higher and higher as he changed his lines. Presently the dawn was whole, the sun was full and soft in the morning heavens. And Duse arose as the horse sped toward her. She handed the rider his robe which he threw around himself with a great, round flourish. She took the bridle and led the horse and her master up the dunes in the same measured tread.

"It was wonderful. But a horrid sacrilegious thought darted through my mind: 'suppose Joe Cawthorn had seen this. What a riot he would make of it in his next show!' And of course, I giggled. "Thank God, they didn't hear me. I was not artist enough to catch the symbolism of it all—whatever it was.

"All that I knew was that I adored Duse and loathed D'Annunzio because he was unbelievably cruel to her—as cruel as though he were a truck driver and she a paramour of whom he had tired. And there were other things I could not understand. She ate enormously and even more so after one of her terrible spells of weeping for his barbarities. She explained her grief-given appetite: 'That I may have the strength, *piccola*, to bear it.'

"'But how can you love a man who is so cruel?' I protested.

"'You would not understand perhaps. Above all else I see his genius.'

"'But your own—your own genius, Eleonora?' I insisted.

"'I love you, *piccola*, for that. You are simplicity. You are yourself—real. You tell the truth. And you amuse me.'"

Despite *naughty, naughty men* Nielsen and Duse make things happen. Alice focuses 1902, when Duse "taught me the Italian for my *Traviata*. 'Ah, Piccola', she exclaimed once to me—that was her pet name for me—'you have talent.' We were in her villa at Florence [Settignano], and she had risen from her chair and advanced slowly toward me. The quietness of her motion, in intentness of her gaze, had frightened me.

"'You have talent', she repeated. 'You have turned pale with no artifice.'

"'That's not talent', I exclaimed. 'You scared me.'"

Duse at times sends train fare to the apparently scraping singer, and Alice does not reveal detail of their 1901-05 visits in Italy, London, France.

Nielsen jumps to 1905, "She now proposed that we give a series of alternate performances at a London theatre; one evening she would play *Camille*, the next night I would sing *Traviata*". Their actual program includes soprano Emma Calvé; the rising Basque tenor recommended by a monopolized Enrico Caruso, Florencio Constantino; and other stars.

Her 1905 contains more confusion than 1901 if possible. Melee of wannabe producers, tricks, treats, plans for American return. Lee, the honest Shubert, arranges with Duse and Nielsen to debut their unique drama-opera showcase in London at his new Waldorf Theatre. Doing so, he skips over Herbert's *Babes in Toyland* hit extravaganza. Alice recalls Duse at Waldorf, "After her evenings at the theatre, she would return to our hotel and array herself in a soft gray gown with a chiffon scarf around her head, looking more like a nun than an actress, and before a little supper spread on a bench she would eat like a child, never speaking.

"Then when she had finished she would excuse herself in tones that tugged at your heart. 'The more troubles I have', she would explain, with a half-smile of sorrow, 'the more I eat.'" Nielsen—her son in NYC with grandma—tells us Duse "had one daughter living in London, who was a designer and painted exquisite figures on chiffon. She did not use her mother's name, nor did there seem to be any love lost between the two".

At piano, Alice accompanies stagework: "Only once did I go with Duse to the theatre when she was playing at this time [in London]. She wanted me to play the music off-stage when Hedda Gabler goes into the room to shoot herself. As I saw her approach me from the center stage, there crept over me a feeling almost of fright, so marvelous was her expression. It was all I could do to keep my hands in motion on the piano. Such was her art that she gripped one, this art she expected every one to aspire to attain. She possessed a mystic approach that awed. The blessed Duse!"

Nielsen scorns D'Annunzio. "I could not understand her unearthly love for him. My personal inclination was to slap him; and I wonder just why I didn't. To me he was a good bit of a cad and rather shallow flirt". D'Annunzio, poet fascist, hates the woman who inspires yet takes her time for the publicity as if he had gone to Yale. Alice penetrates fog with wit. He "was nothing more than an exceptionally gifted sophomore whose poses were always conscious and carefully rehearsed". Duse "accepted each cruelty as a mark of the master's genius. Presently I was to be convinced that Duse was something of a masochist; the woman seemed to enjoy being tortured by him".

After going broke D'Annunzio snags Romaine Brooks, rich American painter in France who stylishly supports him and his other lovers. Mary Garden rather likes him. In 1928 Paris she is seen by *LA Examiner*'s Harold Horan, "wearing a gold and platinum anklet given her by Gabriele D'Annunzio after her first performance in *Pelleas et Melisande*" at Paris 1902. Horan asked why. Garden replies, "That is a man who possesses sex appeal to the fullest degree. I am going to show them up in my memoirs— but they will only be published after my death". Oddly bashful; Mary Garden hardly coy: prefers to brag.

Francis Waterhouse in *Random Studies in the Romantic Chaos* (1923) said, "To rank Debussy...above Mozart or Beethoven would be about as sensible as to place Swinburne...above Shakespeare or D'Annunzio above Dante".

Duse will be the first woman featured on the cover of *Time* magazine.

ZING ZING ZIZZY ZIZZY JOY COMPLETE: NAPOLI

After Duse divergence, we should recount the latter half of 1901. Climbing the ladder of opera Alice Nielsen all–too-rapidly recovers from vocal distress due to the abuses of Williams & Perley. Lost profits vex. Patron appears in nick. Travels to Italy, money runs low as she speeds to *Faust* and *Traviata*. London gigs join any stipends from Mrs. Phillips, slice to Henry Russell the rascal. She returns Naples to debut. "Only three or four months passed in preparation before I was ready for my debut at the Teatro Bellini. I learned Italian during that time, helped by the interest of Eleonora Duse who prepared me for *Traviata*", Nielsen claims. However *Traviata* will be later at the big San Carlo, not the Bellini. Announces Naples debut as December 1902 to U.S. press; any debut in Italy during fall 1901 is crickets, *silenzio*.

1902 continues London concerts and Italy pursuits. Scrapes by. Every step of trek tred is now tracked by international press. The petty nonsense continues back at the States only given space due to Alice's star status.

January 5th, *NY Times* rehashes Desci's cash claims. Her lawyer invokes the statute of limitations to dismiss it all. Same day, *Washington Post*, "Those who have been laughing at Alice Nielsen for her determination to keep persistently away from comic opera in favor of the concert hall stage may find their merriment was not timely. She has been spending the last few months in taking daily singing lessons for the purpose of strengthening her voice, and has finally arranged to make her debut in the last mentioned field of endeavor at Queen's Hall, London, on February 11. She has come to an agreement with Robert Newman, the director of that establishment, to be a soloist at symphony orchestra concerts for at least a year. After that, Miss Nielsen is hopeful of singing at Covent Garden". The tide has turned, the Nielsen ark rises.

January 26, *LA Times* confirms. Nielsen, "to devote herself in the future to grand opera and concerts, will be heard first since her year of study at an orchestral concert in London on February 11. She has been engaged for the Newman symphony concerts and will make her first appearance in grand opera in French at Convent Garden next spring as Juliette".

Robert Newman created the first permanent orchestra in London, promising to "make a public" for symphonic music. This evolves into London Symphony. Queen's Hall, a gayety destroyed in WWII, is "blue and silver" with "a towering organ...a place of warmth and life and light and color", says Susan Foreman, *London: A Musical Gazetteer* (2005).

Duets are organized with Victor Maurel (1848-1923), one of first singers to record his voice, and admired for acting skills. Huneker describes Maurel: "tall, handsome, athletic, a boxer of skill, his voice could take on any dramatic colouring desired. His characterization parallels in *Iago*, Henry Irving and Edwin Booth". Maurel is "economical in gesture". Alice recalls, Maurel lingers backstage to "let me take the applause".

Decade later Maurel makes his farewell tour with Nielsen's company.

Landon Ronald, Russell's brother, conducts the London concerts. He toured America 1894 as accompanist for conniving Nellie Melba, saying Ronald had "a considerable part in my career". By first wife, Russell Sr. child, William, born 1844 in NY's Carlton Hotel, created popular sea novels *Frozen Pirate* (1877) and *His Island Princess* (1905). Father perhaps set a pattern for bastard kid Henry.

As scheduled February 11, Nielsen appears with Robert Newman Orchestra at Queen's Hall covered by *London Times, NY Times, Kansas City Journal, The Scotsman, Globe, Pall Mall Gazette*, and across America.

Alice "made her debut at Queen's hall tonight as a concert singer. Her programme included selections from *Faust* and *Elijah* plus Mozart airs". Within a decade Harvard will honor Nielsen for matchless Mozart skills. Heartily encored. Critics comment on the fine quality of her voice and superb execution; some "intimated her vocal breadth is inadequate to do fullest justice to the heaviest selections".

Tatler confirms, "Alice Nielsen made a great success of her first concert last week, for in addition to a voice she has the rare qualification of temperament", and columnist *Jottings of a Journalist* will "note that the very capable musical critic of the Times congratulates Miss Alice Nielsen on her abandonment of musical comedy for the concert-room".

Busy schedule for paying gigs, "Miss Nielsen has already sung before King Edward. She will sing next Friday before Queen Alexandra and the princesses at Marlborough house" says *London Times*.

Winter in London. Nielsen returns to Italy, briefly Spain.

During this same season, Laurence Irving tours America in drama.

Reporters ask about Alice; he is protective: "Laurence Irving, Sir Henry's son and heir, is an extremely interesting young fellow" begins *LA Times* (Jan 12). "It was rumored that young Irving was engaged to Alice Nielsen, Kansas City's light-opera star, and when a reporter recently put the question point-blank, Mr. Irving smiled broadly, 'Yes, I know there was a great deal said regarding my engagement to Miss Nielsen, but you fellows were responsible for that. I mean, you newspaper men.'"

During the difficult summer 1901, Irving pushed her into opera. "I was with Miss Nielsen during her London engagement because I found her most interesting company. She has a remarkably fine voice, too good for light opera, and I urged her to study for the heavier roles. She is doing that now, and I think there is a grand future in store for her". Irving generated that helpful newspaper encouragement her crossover.

"I admire her very much, but an engagement—pshaw! One can admire a woman without being engaged to her, can't he?" Nielsen's brave escort defeated Williams & Perley with little Nielsen tied to the tracks and only Laurence in the nick of time could save her!

Meanwhile, perpetual pest Perley spins wicked plots to a rapidly diminishing interest before he melts away in scandal. An amazing proclamation floats up (*NY Times* Jan 31) continuing charade that pristine Perley "had trouble" with Nielsen who did not "live up to her contract". Toxic fog needs logician pierce.

Meanwhile, Alice Nielsen loses herself in champagne of new cultures and new languages: "Those early days of training in Rome, Naples and Florence were dazzling and wholly bewildering. Today, when I look back at them, they are still kaleidoscopic, formless, crashing one upon another".

She reflects, "I have often wondered whether any of those little boys whose aspiration it was one day to be policemen ever achieved their ambition, and whether, having realized their dream, they were good policemen. Or whether the achievement came as a great surprise. Perhaps they in their moment of realization were as I was, entirely too englamored for lasting impressions. But great incidents and experiences stand out clearly, sharply, beautifully".

Days pass. Perley's stonewalling cracks. *NY Times* reports (Mar 1), he hijacked "a stack of mail addressed to Miss Nielsen" kept "heaped up in his office". Whistle-blower is "a pale young man who wore turned-out trousers and long hair of a lyric poet, desperately braved" villainous Perley to retrieve a libretto sent Alice in care of. "Waded through a pile of letters, books and other debris" addressed to her. Nielsen lost far more.

Still, producers pursue. She could name her own terms. She doesn't.

The Shubert overtures are typical. March 7, Lee Shubert writes Alice Nielsen at Russell's 49A Curzon Street Studio, near Hyde Park a block off Piccadilly: "Dear Miss Nielsen: This would be an excellent time to consider plans for next season, if you have any idea of coming to this country. The outlook from day to day becomes more favorable and I do not hesitate to stay that much benefit would be derived financially if you would accept a proposition. We would be very glad to hear from you acquainting us with your ideas at this time". Lee skips that Perley lies in wait within the Shubert swamp. No reply from Alice in Shubert archives.

March 24th, Alice's many concerts continue although "in the course of the afternoon Miss Alice Nielsen, who was hardly in her best voice, was heard in couple of operatic airs" reports *London Daily News*. She soon recovers. Among other events, April 5th Nielsen is again featured with the orchestra at Queen's Hall, giving Mendelssohn's *Hear ye Israel* and Gounod's *Ave Maria*. By April 9th, *Sketch* praises "Alice Nielsen, who has, as I said last week, now definitely put away the things of the stage, and is rapidly blossoming...."

Over the deep blue sea and purple plains, Nielsen romances take press.

Printed by *LA Times* datelined NY (April 18), the snippet says "From Chicago comes the story that Laurence Irving, son of Sir Henry, is to wed Alice Nielsen. Just why the story should have reached Broadway via Chicago is a matter which—well, it is a matter of little importance. The name of Laurence Irving has been coupled with that of Ethel Barrymore". Of course, irrelevantly mentioned is said Nielsen was a "fiancé of Thomas Williams, the California racing magnate" now happily married to the screaming Oakland debutant of his angry dreams.

Erstwhile Nielsen cast, tell press "the prima donna was requested to remain in London by the talented son of Sir Henry Irving". With lively wry irony they add, "While Laurence Irving is quite attractive and might enjoy the company of the singer immensely...his father does not favor the young man's attention to any stage women". Laurence's father Henry ever-involved many stage women.

The hopeful next Nielsen Broadway project is George Edwardes' production of *Country Girl* featuring Lionel Monckton's (1861-1924) first musical score. The team creates a string of hits. James Tanner the book; lyrics Adrian Ross. Alice rejects: "prefers doing London concerts". Without Alice, *Country Girl* opens in January 1902 London for 709 performances at Augustin Daly's Theatre. Daly (1838-1899), producer, writer, director born in Plymouth NC, owns theatres in London and NY; dies Paris. "Augustin Daly Musical Company" opens *Country Girl* September at Daly's NYC (Broadway at 30th) for 112 shows before touring.

Alice's London 1902 concert season continues in May with *Pall Mall* reporting The London Music Festival orchestra, Nielsen singing the waltz from *Romeo and Juliet* "with certain brilliance".

This month Nielsen loses an early enemy to time. Benjamin Nentwig Sr. (*KC Star* May 14). The spitter, "one of the oldest and best-known musicians in KC", dies of typhoid at his Cherry Street home. Trumpeter in the Prussian Army, he and family came to 1881 America. Member of the Musicians' Union, he played with John Behr, Carl Busch, Orpheum theatre, and others. Three sons include Frank, Fred, wife-beater Ben Jr.

By May 10th Alice voyages away until September.

June 17th Stanislaus Stange re-appears with offers starring Alice in *NY Times* reports she gave "the nod to *Dolly Varden*"; first and the last mention. Dolly, flirty girl in Dickens' *Barnaby Rudge* is created by librettist Stange, music Julian Edwards, costumes Caroline Siedle. Opens at Hammerstein's 42nd St. Theatre, Lulu Glasser as Dolly, 163 performances.

During this foggy season when Nielsen labors to join diva elite, intriguing to discover during that same period Metropolitan Opera of Maurice Grau runs a touring company in Italy to give young American singers experience. Indirectly Nielsen is reported in the group by a later article on singer Rosemary Glosz (*SF Call* Jul 2 1906). Grau left 1903. Current manager Conried had "asked Miss Glosz to go with the company of young singers he takes touring in opera every year through Italy and Southern Europe. Mostly, pupils of the Metropolitan Opera House.... Marcia Van Dresser [*Fortune Teller*] was one of them, Alice Nielsen another, Josephine Jacoby another. For the experience, he puts them against the ruthless Italian and even Paris at the *Opera Comique*". Glosz declines, fearing seasickness. Yet as a hint, Alice has revealed singing opera in many small towns across Italy. Does not thank the Met. Joining the juveniles on a Grau tour across Italy and France could be the riddle answered.

On July 12, vaudeville sends the struggling artist a blank check: "Weber & Fields offered Alice Nielsen, who is now in London, a contract in which they left a space for her to write her own salary (*NY Times)*". Nielsen "however, sent word in reply that she was quite satisfied with her present condition as she is receiving sixty guineas [about £5,000 in 2007] every time she appears [in London]. "This closed negotiations...trifle high even for Weber & Fields".

Five days later on 17th producer George Tyler (1868-1946) turns up in London "determined not to return to the US without securing Alice Nielsen's signature to a contract" (*NY Times* Jul 17). Tyler between 1902 and 1935 would produce over fifty Broadway dramas and musicals. He has high hopes. He has cash: $100,000 (about $3-million today). "A letter from Miss Nielsen to her business representative...stated that Tyler had offered to deposit a $100,000 guarantee in order to induce the comic opera star to enlist with Liebler & Co". Representative unnamed; NYC attorney Hummel handled her business.

Given "a very general demand for Miss Nielsen throughout the country... unquestionably her return to the comic opera stage would be both a surprising dramatic and a financial success". Despite rosy gold prospects, Nielsen in penury refuses.

Gesture resonates across America. Celebrated for artistic integrity.

Skips projects with trustworthy people who are theatre legends.

"She will not enter into any contracts until the expiration of her present concert agreement with Robert Newman of the Covent Garden Opera House [London Symphony] in February. She is making a splendid income singing at concerts and at society functions". Press agentry is added: "Studying with the best instructor daily, Miss Nielsen has improved her technique without losing any of the natural grace and melody of phrasing which is her greatest charm".

And the next week amazingly Alice is said Broadway-bound for a Herbert-and-Smith show produced by Klaw & Erlanger, major rivals of Perley-associated Shuberts. *NY Times* reports (Jul 22), "Yesterday closed a contract by cable by which she agreed to make a tour of America during the season of 1903-04". The star "has been besought by letters, cables and personal interviews to ally herself with several theatrical firms, and gossip had it last week that she had already signed". More amazingly, the deal is confirmed by Klaw & Erlanger, who "said last evening that they would star her in a new opera to be written for her by" Smith and Herbert. Contrary-wise Nielsen replies she "will not return home this summer but remain abroad until the beginning of her American season". Within a week Klaw & Erlanger announce Nielsen "closed a contract" to appear that fall. (*KC Star* Jul 27). Herbert and Smith out, *Madame Sans Gene*, text and music by Ivan Carroll and Harry Hamilton: in. Nix. Neither project ain't gonna.

Marcus Klaw (1858-1936) and Abraham Lincoln Erlanger (1860-1930) had operated Theatrical Syndicate's 700 theatres since 1896. They produce Herbert's *Little Nemo* (1908), and Ziegfeld's *Follies* (1907-1931).

Interestingly, a 1919 strike by Equity actors led by Lillian Russell and other Nielsen pals breaks the partnership.

Alice Nielsen projects, these proposals remind, were a rarity: originals.

So what if librettist Harry Smith lifted a hodge here and a podge there.

Even today the merely-clever pattern of adapting a play or photo-play (film) to the musical form appeals to risk-abating producers and their lawyers who corporations pay. They fear creating orginals.

Alice Nielsen Company was better than that.

Composer Victor Herbert evolved Broadway's musical format to please his sense of gayety. Energy to burn. Scope from folk song to the most modern orchestra piece. Composes to orchestra, not tap-tap-tap tunes on piano for arrangers to fix. That game went to less competent: the Berlin, Hammerstein, Gershwin, Sondheim. Unlike Puccini, Herbert does not seek Belasco for storylines. Romantic gayety was Herbert's best.

Nielsen is in Europe. Her performances have entered American folklore.

Ceaseless public clamor serenades producers.

In the cast: Eugene Cowles drops opera hopes (*Washington Post* Aug 3) and "made up his mind to remain in vaudeville indefinitely".

During summer 1902 Nielsen scrimps. We don't know if she sang at Teatro Real, Madrid. Only *Washington Post* (August 17) carries a sliver of Spain: "Alice Nielsen, always lucky, is at present according to her own testimony, in a particularly enviable situation. The little songstress has transferred the scene of her studies from Italy to San Sebastian in Spain whence, she writes she is being pursued by letters from theatrical managers without number, all of them eager to gain her services". Which San Sebastian? Basque coast, lovely *belle epoch* resort? Sebastián de los Reyes, eighteen km north of Madrid's Teatro Real?

"There is hardly a prominent manager either in the United States or London, that has not made me from sort of offer", she tells the KC paper, "her desire to go in for grand opera has not abated, and this is probably the sort of work she will take up".

Her summer of poverty goes otherwise unmentioned.

Passing moment continue to vanish; August the cussing man who hired the touring teenager as "Swedish Nightingale" in St. Joseph, "Samuel Pryor, noted bandmaster and father of Arthur Pryor" dies. "A band played lively airs at his request" says *Telluride Daily Journal,* CO (Aug 22).

Tom Williams shoots an unarmed journalist in September. "Fred Marriott, publisher of the *San Francisco News Letter,* was shot three times tonight and seriously wounded", reports *LA Times* (Sep 3). "His assailants were Thomas H. Williams, Jr., president of the California Jockey Club and Truxton Beale, a former US Minister to Persia and Greece and a well-known clubman of this city". California press rally to cover the story, concerned the pair might try to buy their way out. Williams brags, "Yes, Beale and myself did the shooting. We considered it our duty to punish Marriott for the publication of an article last week in reflecting on the reputation of a young lady [slut Marie Oge]".

The deceptively-friendly pair visit the editor at home where unarmed Marriott is suddenly pistol-whipped by Beale then shot by Williams who also fires at Marriott's wife. After the shooting, they "went to the Pacific

Union Club, where they were placed under arrest and released from custody on $10,000 bail each". Atop Nob Hill, the Club's massive 19th-century brownstone built for silver magnate James Flood hosts wealthy men who meddle in plantation politics.

Six weeks later, Beale gets engaged to stupid slut Oge: "Both are prominent in San Francisco society, and the formal announcement caused surprise to all except a few personal friends" (*LA Times* Oct 22). Cowardly Beal rats slut Oge out, saying she had "appealed to him to defend her against the malicious attacks of Marriott". Before being provoked by that sleazy skank to conspire with Williams to shoot the unarmed man, Beal graduated from Harvard then Columbia law school, source of his ethics.

In music news October 23, Victor Herbert sues *Musical Courier* for saying he plagiarized. In court Herbert is represented by Arthur Palmer. Perley testifies "he had seen the composer composing and saw the music written. He said Herbert sometimes played the air first then wrote the notes, but at other times he wrote first and played afterwards". *Courier* is defended by Nielsen's firm A.H. Hummel as many guilty parties are. Herbert wins.

During October Nielsen appears in a series of British concerts at Manchester with composer-conductor Edgar Elgar (1857-1934), who within two years will be knighted, famed, feted with a three-day Covent Garden festival of his works. Elgar puts Nielsen within circle of violinist Fritz Kreisler, and had in debuted *Enigma Variations* with conductor Hans Richter, yet another Nielsen contact.

November 9th, Williams and Beale begin trial "for an alleged assault with intent to kill, on Frederick Marriott, editor of the *News Letter*".

Significantly, this November 1902 (time is fleeting) Alice has secured her formal Italian debut. She returns to London in April. Bevignani has arranged her debut.

American press now grow cautious about any plans to return her to Broadway. Alice "evidently has not given up her grand opera aspiration, even if she has pledged herself to come to this country next year in that of the comic variety. Word has come from London that the young American singer is to make her debut in classic opera in Naples on December 10, singing the role of Marguerite. If she is successful she will remain in Italy, appearing at the principal opera houses during the entire winter" (*LA Times* Nov. 23 1902).

Within sixteen months from July 1901 to December 1902, Alice has made ready. Vivid lifelong, the Italian audiences taught her well.

Dec 12, Nielsen writes lawyer Hummel in NYC that she would make her debut next week in *Faust* at Theatre Bellini, Naples: "I am also to sing in *Rigoletto*, *Fra Diavolo* and *Le Filie du Regiment*, am engaged for three months and am to be the leading soprano of the company".

Simultaneously she is reported Broadway-bound. Such reports leak into the press frequently 1901-1908. None pan out. Courted with top projects, top talent, top pay. In penury rebuffs. Could choose: show, director, composer, librettist, cast. Select repertory or develop new.

America's top diva has switched sides. Instead of helping Broadway create new arts, she will promote opera in Italian and French, not English.

Her life between fall 1901 and September 1905 stays foggy for many details. Struggling to learn much, she recalls the period with indifference, a time of necessary work same as getting established in San Francisco. A few amusing or impressive anecdotes for the gayety, and closes chapter.

December 20 Alice Nielsen sings *Faust* in Naples at the Bellini Theatre.

Notices are in Naples' *Il Mattino*: "*Questa sera al Bellini è previsto un evento di arte e mondano. E' la serata di onore di quella avvenente e valorosa americana miss Aliss Nielsen, che e' l'idolo del pubblico, per le sue rare qualità artistiche, che tanto sono state apprezzate in questa stagione lirica, che si è svolta così splendidamente e che ora volge al suo termine. La simpatica sala del Bellini raccoglierà questa sera tutto il pubblico eletto e i buongustai. La celebre artista cantera la Traviata, nella quale opera essa è semplicemente grande e deliziosa. La Nielsen indossera magnifiche toilettes. Convegno, adunque, elegantissimi questa sera al Bellini*".

Translated by Bergamo's Paolo Sergi (2006), *Il Mattino* says: "This evening is going to be an artistic and public performance at Bellini Theatre. It is a benefit for that charming and richly talented American singer Alice Nielsen, the idol of the audience for her rare artistic qualities so much appreciated in this lyrical season that has been carried out so well and now is near to the end. The Bellini will welcome this evening all the elected public and the thrilled people. The famous artist will sing *Traviata*, in which she is simply great and delicious. La Nielsen will wear magnificent clothes. See you this evening, very elegantly dressed at the Bellini".

"La Aliss Nielsen" gives two dozen Bellini shows in rapid succession.

Kansas City's "La Nielsen" attains rank of rootin' tootin' diva. Her "great and fashionable gathering" attracts elites. Thankfully an American eye-witness, Mrs. AD Giannin (Mollie Faust) has married and moved to Naples.

Giannin tells *KC Star* about Nielsen's debut (Apr 20 '03): "Alice Nielsen's name appears here in big type on the billboards (Alice being spelled 'Aliss' for the reason that the correct way is the name of some sort of a fish in Italian). She has been singing in Naples since December 20, when she made her debut in *Faust* at the Bellini Theatre. She made an instantaneous success, singing the same opera 24 successive times".

"The next opera she appeared in was Verdi's *Traviata*, in which I heard her April 19. The Crown Prince of Germany with his brother Prince Fritz, occupied one of the boxes incognito, and joined the enthusiasm of the audience in giving our American girl an ovation. The Princes remained to hear the entire opera, which is saying a great deal for members of the royal family, especially when one considers the late hours of Italy, all evening performances beginning at 9:30 o'clock. Miss Nielsen sent for me between acts, and a few days later she called on us at our hotel".

"She is now rehearsing *Lucia* and *Rigoletto* with the Italian maestro Bevignani, the man who trained Patti and Christine Nilsson". He had conducted most of Patti's opera performances at Covent Garden, Russia, NY, and Italy from 1871-1884, according to Hermann Klein in *The Reign of Patti* (1920). To put Alice Nielsen quality in perspective consider her diva rivals—Melba, Garden, and Farrar—never dared sing in Italy. According to Mollie Giannin, Henry Russell utterly confused in her account with his father, "comes twice a week from there to give Miss Nielsen lessons". Bevignani teaches daily; twice weekly Russell advises.

Giannin confirms, "Nielsen has had several enticing offers by cable from America for light opera, but she has decided to continue her studies two years longer in the land of song and music". More importantly for her future "she has signed a contract for next season with the San Carlo theatre". Napoli! Gorgeous royal opera of Naples remains legendary.

Molly Giannin perceives the gains in voice and heft. "Her voice has improved wonderfully, especially in her high notes, which are clear and strong. She sings with great ease. Her appearance has also improved, as she has gained in flesh". After Alice always in tights, Giannin reassures Kansas City that "long-trained dresses have added greatly to her dignity".

Nielsen suggests she rushed the debut for the money. Yet Bellini carries her onward to prestigious San Carlo. Helps her reach Covent Garden, whose manager Higgins had sent sister to spy. And very much recalls Mrs. Herbert's visit to spy out *War-Time Wedding*.

Nielsen recalls, "the sister of Henry V. Higgins, director of the Covent Garden Royal Opera in London, heard me sing and wrote her brother about me, with the results that I soon had a contract to appear in Mozart operas the following year". Thereat Nielsen takes the Mozart away from Melba who never forgot nor forgave. Her rush to Bellini results in *Don Giovanni* at Covent Garden next spring. If the opera encounter of Henry Higgins and Kansas City street singer Alice Nielsen did not result in a musical about the fair lady, should have. Decade later, Bernard Shaw creates 1913's *Pygmalion* destined to become 1956's *My Fair Lady*.

At Bellini that night, Nielsen recalls a Kansas City couple who put her life into perspective. Does not say who. Apparently Molly Giannin was not the only hometown presence in Naples. "When I was leaving the Bellini that night, not quite certain whether I had triumphed or defaulted, two women and a man stopped me. The man, in beautiful Middle-Western English, demanded information. "Are you the Nielsen child who used to sing on the streets of Kansas City or is my wife wrong as usual?"

"I am Alice Nielsen of Kansas City, yes".

"Well I'll be darned. Do you remember me, or my wife here?"

"No—I'm afraid I don't".'

"Well anyway we threw you a dime one afternoon for singing *Annie Laurie*, although I didn't think you'd remember".

"And then it struck me. That night I did not sleep. It was not because the excitement of my debut in grand opera was still raging. Nor was it because I had sung well—so well that the great Enrico Bevignani, the conductor who was famous at La Scala, in Covent Garden, in St. Petersburg, in NY, had kissed me and proclaimed me another Bellicioni, the greatest of all Italian Violettas".

Significant praise! Misspells Gemma Bellincioni (1864-1950) who had made her 1879 debut in Naples, whose "stage presence, acting and interpretation... drew considerable attention...ideally suited for the newer operas developed in the versimo style", reports historicopera.com (2007).

To bring home the Nielsen effect suggested by Bevignani consider the Bellincioni audience impact. An American eye-witness, David Bispham shared stage with Bellincioni and Nielsen-friend Emma Calvé in *Cavalleria Rusticana* (*A Quaker Singer's Recollections* 1920). Bellincioni "possessed that indefinable personality and magnetism which excited the deepest emotion in the minds of her auditors". Bispham traces "the difference in their handling of the role of Santuzza" contrasting the two singers with "the great Italian actress Eleonora Duse who had frequently performed the same part on the London stage. Duse was all intelligence, Calvé was all fire, and Bellincioni was all superbly controlled emotion". Significant how Bellincioni's coach reacts from his direct experience to compare the two.

Meeting that hometown couple brings a revelation, "My eyes suddenly pierced the dazzle, and beyond I saw the street singer of Kansas City, the Nielsen child who sang to the butcher, the baker, the doctor and old Mel Hudson—who had stood barefoot on street corners, thankful for pennies tossed by passers-by". The child whose potentials include this night.

Career blossoming, December 19th Nielsen signs to sing a year of occasional Symphony concerts at Queen's Hall in London. Newman's Promenade Series, called The Proms are continued by the BBC today. During 1903, Nielsen swaps Italy and England, expands repertoire, keeps company with Duse. Gains confidence by many performances.

As Bevignani has forecast, Italy responds to her magnetism with fervor.

At this point fog lifts about the itinerary.

Valentine's Day in Naples (Fe 14) Nielsen sings Violetta in *Traviata*. As *NY Morning Telegraph* (Fe 21) reports, "The loveliest Valentine received by any stage divinity was that which gladdened the heart of Miss Alice Nielsen on the day devoted to the most sentimental old saint in the calendar. It was a shower of praise bestowed by the Italian critics on her debut in a new and difficult role... the brilliant young singer whom Mr. Hummel hails as the coming Patti, appeared on St. Valentine's eve as Violetta in *La Traviata*. Judging from the raptures of the Neapolitan critics which appeared in the newspapers, Miss Nielsen's success fully justified Mr. Hummel's enthusiasm—in which pleasing prophecy, by the way, he is joined by the maestro Bevignani—who declares that she is bound to become one of the great prima donnas of the early future".

Italian critics make "rhapsodical reading and Miss Nielsen with becoming modesty says that she is afraid that the press of that country has been too kind to her. If it has been the dream of her life to become distinguished on the grand opera stage as distinct from comic opera, where she simply coined money with *The Singing Girl* and *The Fortune Teller*, and the question that presents itself is: will she wake up and wish to return to the States and begin to make money as well as fame all over again".

Ironic; as her money was cheated. Now new career. Alice pens "lengthy letters to her friends in NY" about her *Traviata*.

By March, her British publicity permeates the realm; *Dundee Courier* in Scotland repeats a syndicated blurb that "It will not come as a surprise to anyone to that Miss Alice Nielsen has had great success in grand opera".

She will spend the remaining year in Italy.

At Naples March 1903 Alice Nielsen publishes her artistic manifesto.

From her harbor pad on *Via Francesco Caracciolo* near Santa Lucia, Nielsen writes *Kansas City World*. In 1898 *NY Telegraph* had asked how it felt to become a star last night now, "You ask me what it feels like to be a grand opera singer. This is a difficult question to answer, for things look so different according as they are viewed—objectively or subjectively. I assure you of one thing, it is no easy matter to change one's career and for me it has proved especially difficult, as my health was quite broken down when I wound up my company in London in July 1901.

"While appreciating fully the advantages of the position which America had generously awarded me in comic opera, it was obvious to me that my strength had completely come to an end. It was absolutely essential that I should rest myself from the dancing and seven weekly performances which were ruining both my voice and my nervous system".

Far from resting she sought auditions with Covent and began lessons with Tosti for future concerts. Encouraged, turned hiatus to shutdown.

Appealing to her health would be an unbreakable argument against any legal suit seeking to keep her onstage, her attorney may have suggested. She evades the finances. In early 1901, Williams & Perley had been causing trouble all they could of course. Try to make her crazy, kill her career, oppress by overwork. Alice cleverly turns tables; quits show blaming overwork hurts health. To the press, she usually parrots Henry Russell's claim he told her to stop. Deflects inquiry from the realities. From this point she fogs the blarney, skips genuinely significant talents who had acted for her benefit imparting repertory. Pet remora plucked from obscurity talks. Scorns. Her fame will line his pockets for years. Could he stand success? Aping GB Shaw, Russell affects to hate the new musical theatre whereat people sing and dance as Nietzsche wishes us.

Do people naturally talk, burst into song and dance? They do.

Broadway celebrates folk arts: village dances.

Never innovative, never onstage, remora Russell steals Shaw's scorn for song-and-dance theatre as "hybrid". Scolds star to seize pocketbook by sleight. Opportunistic as pal D'Annunzio; yet merely arty not artist. Suits his purposes to resist the new-fangled American art form while promoting to moneymaker Alice his daddy-inherited 19th-century Italian opera lore.

Nielsen parrots his phrases. Appears to be helpful when it suites his purposes to do so. Brags on it. Attitude alike Ziegfeld; flattery pliable women they scorn. Yet Ziegfeld—impresario. Russell nothing. No experience producing results. Russell realizes Alice Nielsen will be his meal ticket only if he keeps her away from those Broadway producers who have no need for his advice. No, Henry Russell is not adding value beyond his flutter of presence. Nielsen, artist genuine fails to detect fraud in others.

From 1901 to 1908, Russell spends more time with Nielsen than anyone else excluding her family circle and maid. Nielsen's interlude with Laurence Irving fades by 1906. She carries him along. He does her wrong.

No fine romance this is. By 1908 Nielsen will find future husband LeRoy Stoddard to summer together. Consider, Russell married with kids all the while, and Nielsen scorns affairs with married men.

Nielsen's open letter contains a calendar conundrum. "As a very little girl, I was always full of dreams of grand opera". Perhaps from the concerts of Patti in Kansas City. "Indeed, you may not know that at the age of eighteen I made my debut in *Lucia di Lammermoor* with considerable success, subsequently singing Marguerite in *Faust*, both of course in English". *Satanella*? Her calendar incoherent. If eighteen at Tivoli in 1896, she married at ten, birthed baby Bennie at twelve. KC readers would know her little joke. Puzzling purpose.

Says of her start a decade previous, "I was like a great many of my sister artists—poor in my childhood and without the necessary means of studying in Europe for the career for which I longed. An English grand opera career does not exist, so there was no alternative for me but to turn my attention to less lofty branches of the art from which I had to derive bread both for myself and my dear mother". Son Bennie, raised by Sarah goes unmentioned.

"This little history will serve to explain to you the reason why, today at the very moment in which my efforts have been crowned with success by the most exacting public in the world—the Neapolitans—, I do not feel any of the astonishment or surprise that you might naturally expect, for little as you may believe it, I assure you that while I danced and sang nightly to the dear, enthusiastic, warm-hearted American public, I always hoped secretly that the day would come when they would hear and applaud me in a high form of art".

Nielsen owns what librettist Harry Smith only dreamt. Now the blarney to pitch a needy pal: "Suddenly, and in the most unexpected way, a road was opened to the practical realization of my hopes and the person who opened it was Henry Russell, a son of America's songwriter, who sixty years ago, gave *Cheer Boys Cheer, Three Cheers for the Red White and Blue*, and 900 other popular songs to the world". Nielsen knew Russell Sr. (1812-1900) was British. Ballad hit, *Woodman, Spare That Tree*, lyrics by Leslie Nelson-Burns: "*Woodman, spare that tree! Touch not a single bough! In youth it sheltered me, And I'll protect it now. 'Twas my forefather's hand That placed it near his cot: There, woodman, let it stand, Thy axe shall harm it not!*" A sheet music best seller in 1837 for Firth and Hall. Stephan Foster set higher marks with 1851's *Old Folks At Home*. Russell Sr is described as "rather stout, but not tall. His face...of the Hebrew cast, dark and heavy whiskers and curly hair. He was an expert at wheedling audiences out of applause" playing "brilliant pianoforte accompaniment". Onstage since three, sang as child to George IV. At fourteen left to Italy "then a sort of cheap paradise where you had breakfast for a penny, and dined and wined variously well for a shilling". At Bologna studied with Rossini; met Balfe, Bellini, Donizetti. Back to London as chorus-master at Her Majesty's Theatre. 1833 took a one-man show to North America. As organist in a Presbyterian church in Rochester, NY, he made music for popular songs with lyrics by Eliza Cook or Charles Mackay. Returns 1842 to British Isles touring his "heavy baritone voice of small compass" until retiring as "opulent money-lender and bill-broker" (*Musical Times* 1901, *Appletons Cyclopaedia* 1900). Of his memoir *Cheer, Boys, Cheer*, said *Speaker* (Jan 18 1896), "Easy to talk evil of this book, it stories 'chestnuts', its moral maxims trite and trivial, its style palpably shoddy, and, though it be very short, much is padding". Like father like son.

In a passing version-of-the-moment, Nielsen tells of meeting Russell Jr. "induced by a friend to go to the Shaftsbury Theatre to hear me sing. His only feeling was one of surprise and annoyance to hear me sing and then see me dance. I remember very well his introductory words when he was first presented to me behind the stage. 'How dare you dance, with that beautiful voice in your throat', he said, almost rudely".

Never sing and dance, seems so Irish.

Nielsen appears impressed with his attack on the lively arts of which she the greatest star. Throws egg, "I was used to the flattery of singing masters and as a body had little or no faith in their sincerity. But here was a man whose time was being sought after at the rate of $16 an hour [$400 today]...." His 20-minute lessons include throat massage of sweet distraction for rich Victorian ladies around London.

"And who deliberately offered to teach me for nothing". Untrue. Offers to spend her money to "undertake the whole responsibility of seeing me floated in grand opera". In short, offers to manage her career for a percent of future revenue calculated large. Which he has zero experience to do. As he brags later. Nielsen skips speaking of the £1000 to £5000 by Mrs. Phillips which he pockets a big percent on the spot. Never states she gave him the role for exaggerated claims of social networking. Often claims Russell is artily above caring for money. Good lie for Russell. He owes her everything. Repays badly. He ploys with opportunity. Her distortions make many misunderstandings downstream. Quaintance Eton suggested what Grove Music Encylopedia replicated, that Nielsen had depended on his favors for her Boston Opera presence. Utterly without merit. He lived on her percentages to get there, got the job due to her influence. Eton put the the ass before the dancing singing mare.

The singer is on the stage.

In any case, he seemed helpful to escape the Williams & Perley trap if overpaid for escort service. Obscure voice coach as manager of biggest American singing star—already cheated out of one fortune—now stranded nearly broke. Eats supper within Nielsen's entourage. His brother actually conducts an orchestra and arranges concerts. Tosti sets things up.

"This was not an offer to pass over lightly", Nielsen claims. "I therefore went off to Italy to study with him" ignoring Tosti and Bevignani. She absorbs Italian, the complex scores, and Bevignani's lessons. Russell appears in Naples twice a week for breathing practices Nielsen had acquired from Ida Valerga who acquired from Marchesi. Yet Alice claims, "For many long months I dedicated myself, under his guidance, to a careful and scientific placing of my voice, the result of which America alone can judge when once more I sing before her great public". For a few months. Russell focuses singing with relaxed throat same as Valerga and Tosti.

Masterpiece of misplaced emphasis: "When he considered me fairly perfect he [that is, Tosti] presented me to Maestro Bevignani whose fame at our Metropolitan in NY and Covent Garden, London, is known to all".

For debut credits both. "When only the other night I debuted in *Traviata* and heard the great '*bis*' of the Latin throats summon me again and again before the curtain, I would like to have stood between Henry Russell and Maestro Bevignani and laid my hands on both their heads and called to the public to cheer them as well as me". Remora Russell was no Bevignani.

Tosses a flirtatious glance homeward: "When I have had a little more experience in Europe, I shall set sail for the land of my birth. I await with beating heart the supreme moment of my life in which I shall hope to convince America that her 'singing girl' who loved her and was, I believe, by her beloved, has returned a woman, humble in spirit, but oh! so anxious to have her success here in Europe crowned and approved by her motherland. Sincerely yours, Alice Nielsen".

During April for Hearst papers, Alan Dale visits Nielsen in Naples.

"Miss Alice Nielsen, who once bade fair to be the leading comic opera soubrette in America..." is now in Naples "and there she is likely to remain indefinitely. In the shadow of the smoky Vesuvius, Miss Nielsen finds the lazy *lazzaroni* picturesque, the Chiaja gardens beautiful and her occasional appearance in grand opera most elevating—and this is all well, for Messrs. Klaw & Erlanger have quite abandoned the project of bringing Miss Nielsen back to this country to head one of their big companies".

Columnist coy, "There is a little story in connection with Miss Nielsen's departure from Britain's capital where many fashionable drawing rooms had been opened to her that never saw print in America and which, as our English friend Hubert Druce would say, is whispered only in the inner circle on the other side of the broad, expansive wet".

As we all know, Druce wrote a best-selling "philosophical story of a carefully-planned murder told from the viewpoint of the murderer, culminating in a trial, not of himself", says Robert Temple Booksellers (2006). Actor noted for light comedy in Nielsen's period at NY and London.

Details of Dale's hinted "little story" in 1900s London did not come to light. If Nielsen made a murder she was never convicted, so presumed innocent. If guilty, Hummel would get her off. Yet dastardly Tom Williams shot a man three times: acquitted, loses civil case, sets California tradition of paying fees to shoot or stab the innocent.

Usual problem regarded too scandalous to print was to reject or accept any horny royal. Nielsen's comment she spent time with King Edward is foggy. Later she will suggest another woman intervened. Her politics could factor. What might Alice (whose dad died to end slavery, mom a staunch Irish republican) say to a flirty English King?

As for his tidbit the "little story...possibly that incident had something to do with Klaw & Erlanger's change of heart" Dale misleads. Klaw & Erlanger will prove ever-eager to promote Alice Nielsen. And will do so.

Coy rumors hint at a Perley influence on NY-based Dale, who stoops to rehash a tattered Perley claim "Miss Nielsen had developed a most decided tendency toward erratic behavior during the latter days of the sponsorship of Frank Perley and Tom Williams". Perhaps she most decidedly objected to the crimes of these scoundrels. Dale airily closes, "so her visit among the foreigners will be continued at her own sweet pleasure. Meanwhile little Miss Nielsen displays a delightful *sang froid* about the matter".

Despite Dale-debris, by April 27th *Sketch* reports Nielsen signed by Covent Garden for next season, grandly realizing her grand opera dreams.

The triumph has been won.

Alice Nielsen has threaded a tightrope from Shaftesbury to Covent.

In the cast: news of Nielsen's opera successes sweep America as the sadly diminished Bostonians tour. *San Jose Mercury News* (May 17) stings, "No singer is so greatly missed from the ranks of The Bostonians as dainty

Alice Nielsen, and the visit of that famous organization has started the inquiry, where has America's most popular light opera artist disappeared to, and when will she return? The truth is, Miss Nielsen is a light opera artist no longer and when she does reappear in her native country it will be in the role of grand opera". In Naples, "famed Italian stronghold of grand opera", her debut as Marguerite in *Faust* [1902] "made one of the biggest hits of the season before the most critical of Italian audiences".

Moving from Bellini, Alice Nielsen joins the grand San Carlo Opera. As her Victor Herbert debut, an out-of-body experience. "I sang Violetta Valery in *La Traviata*. Nervous? Not at all. Excited? Well, all but out of control. Such was my emotional state that I was wholly incapable of understanding until afterward that the mounds of flowers tossed upon the stage after such noble arias as *Pura siccome un angelo* and the famous duets with the tenor (how that man wheezed!) were purchased unwillingly by the chorus—an old Italian custom which visited the enduring hatred of all choruses upon all new prima donnas".

She somewhat shares unfortunate fate of Caruso who vowed never to sing again in his hometown: "But worse, how was I to know that my failure to pay fifty lire to the newspaper critics should cause them to forgather into a compact huddle at the final curtain and hiss in horrible unison?"

First time hissed since St. Joseph. Later she will claim El Paso was the only bad audience, and that due to evil Lee Shubert henchmen. Nielsen says grace. "I had a conference with the journalists later and although I resisted their demand that I retain them for my personal claque, I gave a dinner which as I recall it, was featured by magnum after magnum of red wine and several wagonloads, apparently, of salami.

"Nothing a new diva could do about the flowers extorted by the management from the chorus. The chorus always hated the prima donna and that was all there could be to it. It was a tradition. It was part of one's test to survive the chorus' dislike".

Unattributed clipping at Harvard (April 12, '03) gives her achievement perspective. As she sings in Italy, Big Apple deadly dull: "Here in NY the experience of a season of opera at the Metropolitan has yielded bitter Dead Sea...." No gayety. "Considering the value of Miss Nielsen's Neapolitan success, it must be taken into consideration that it has been won in a city where the traditions of Italian grand opera are most jealously guarded... presented with almost religious reverence. It is in the midst of the altars of song therefore, that Miss Nielsen has won acclaim on being entitled to wear the laurels of Italy's dearest prima donnas in the operas of Italy's dearest composers. There was much for the plucky little singer to forget; there was everything for her to learn and the chance of failure was much stronger than her hope of success".

This Boston story suggests that in Naples, after Marguerite in *Faust*, Nielsen plays Gilda in *Rigoletto*, Mimi in *Bohème*. Despite her acclaimed 1905 London *Bohème* debut, Nielsen at times refers to an earlier chance for Mimi on a day's notice for Caruso. Claims declined; perhaps accepted with results not reasonably worth mentioning. Newspaper accounts may err; yet Nielsen sent many postcards to many people, friends and press, as she makes prima progress. As experience grows she will compress a complex story to help make things comprehensible.

Now Nielsen and Herbert move by parallel paths never to rejoin. Fritzi Scheff steps into Alice's shoes (curved heel) to fetch a fortune. Of all rivals recreating the Nielsen roles, Scheff (1879-1954) most closely re-creates the Alice Nielsen fad. From Vienna, sings opera at Maurice Grau's Met. After Puccini, Wagner, Mozart, Scheff moves to 1903's Herbert-scored *Babbett*, then 1905's *Mlle. Modeste*, then 1908's *The Prima Donna*, then 1913's vaudeville for cash; then 1915's silent film; then talkies, nightclubs; episode of TV's *This Is Your Life*. Both singers wed Prussian first husbands and divorce. Scheff is her own manager, reports *LA Times* (Jul 6), "brilliant soprano who made a distinct hit this season, is organizing a comic opera company...she has engaged Eugene Cowles.... Scheff is in her proper sphere when she enters comic opera. She seems especially made for it, in voice, temperament and personal appearance, being petite and slight without being angular, and vivacious to a degree".

In June, Washington finds *Fortune Teller* with many original players revived by Chase Summer Opera Co. Alice's understudy Edna Bronson stars... How the show is staged when original cast improvised and rewrote, songs flying in and out, is more than difficult to say. (*Post*, Jun 7 '03).

And Alice has her year of Italian theatres.

That fall, Tom Williams returns to news. Avoids jail by "arranging" an acquittal, but faces a $100,000 civil suit by editor he shot. Facts are not in dispute. *LA Times* (Sep 18) states the case will determine "whether the bully even if he be worth $1,000,000 may go to a man's house and shoot him with...a gun—also impunity". When the guilty Williams and Beal go to court (Dec 31 *LA Times*), Marriot testifies the deadly duo "courteous and pleasant when they first called. No angry words passed before the assault". Invited to Marriot's parlor, Beale suddenly pistol-whips him then Williams shoots him three times in front of his wife. The attack, the pair claim, was motivated by an article slighting the character of Beal's now-fiancé, ugly slut Marie Oge. Marriot proved to have had no personal knowledge of article or its publication. Awarded $17,000, set the price of attempted murder for members of swank San Francisco clubs.

Alice's crossover plight is hinted after-the-fact by *Bellingham Herald* (Dec 8 WA) via Associated Press. "The American singer left the Shaftesbury Theatre where she had a tempestuous time two years ago". Details of that tempest caused by those *nasty, nasty men* Williams & Perley are left foggy. "She has been residing in Italy. 'Residing' is perhaps a rose-colored way of putting it. 'Battling for existence' is a more graphic description. It is said that at times she and her maid have lived on as little as a dollar a day (about $25 today) in order to have the wherewithal to pay for a musical education". Nielsen "will return to America only as a grand opera prima donna. It is learned that Miss Nielsen has made arrangements to appear in grand opera at Milan next autumn". Her appearance at Milano's *La Scala* are unconfirmed yet highly possible. Her opera costumes were made by the *La Scala* costumers.

Ends 1903. Alice's helpful genius departs life in Naples, August 29.

Enrico Bevignani lived long enough to see his last student star.

1904: COVENT GARDEN, MOZART & PUCCINI

Two years after giving her regards to Broadway, Alice Nielsen is chosen by Higgins at Covent to star in a season of Mozart. Established divas fall to the upstart. Henry Higgins manages Covent, Hans Richter conducts.

NY Times from London: "All the girls in our set are giving themselves haughty lyric airs over the fact that, with all the divas in the world to choose from, the management of Covent Garden opera season in London has selected two American girls for the principal roles in the great Mozart cycle of revivals which are to be the star features of the current season in the English metropolis. To Suzanne Adams and Alice Nielsen has fallen this coveted honor, which was sought by both Sembrich and Melba".

Massachusetts-born Adams (1872-1953) began grand opera when Alice played Wigwam. Adams, not Alice, studied with Marchesi in Paris who arranged an 1894 Paris Opera debut. After a brief NYC 1907 stint in vaudeville only for the money, Adams remains in London.

Covent Garden's spring season is covered closely in America. April 3, 1904, *Chicago Tribune* says *NY Herald* says Neil Forsyth says that the "manager of the royal opera at Covent Garden" had received "a letter from the king and queen renewing their royal box subscription". And "no falling off in the American contingent" headed by Mrs. Ronalds, Mrs. Adari, Mrs. Newhouse, Mrs. Arthur Paget, Mrs. Ralph Vivian, Mrs. Mackay, Mrs. L.V. Harcourt, Mrs. George Haig and Mrs. H.V. Higgins "whose husband is taking as great an interest as ever in the directorate".

"Miss Nielsen's debut in London on the operatic stage is looked forward to with great interest". Exchanged places with her Herbert substitute: roles "assigned to her in the coming seasons are those in which Fraulein Fritzi Scheff hitherto scored her greatest successes".

Alice Nielsen arrives in London for Covent opera, orchestra concerts, and her per-usual many musicales in the aristocratic parlors. Patti lingers in Alice's competitive mind, "I hate to think of what Patti's rage might have been had she heard me, some months later, after I had returned to England to sing in Covent Garden, sing Arditi's song, *Il Bacio*, in the Rothschild house in Seymour Place".

Alice does not mention Patti's understudy Ida Valerga taught her the song: "Written for Patti, who had sung it first at the Rothschilds'. Thereafter it was the unwritten law that none but Patti should sing it there. But how was I to know that? Landon Ronald, brother of Henry Russell, was at the piano and when he asked me what I would sing for an encore, I said '*Il Bacio*.' He looked at me curiously for a moment, wondering, perhaps, whether I knew what I was doing. But he resolved to go through with it. So I sang *Il Bacio* where only Patti was supposed to. There was a queer hush as I concluded and then great applause, led by the baron, who trotted over to me and gave me a diamond and sapphire horseshoe.

"'A horseshoe for luck', said Rothschild, 'but not that you need luck. You will go very far, my dear, on your talents.'"

Well now. Most soprano guests sang the song for the baron; possibly without horseshoe gifts. And Alice would interpolate *Il Bacio* into every performance possible. HL Mencken ventured a wry crack about the sopranos of the world, referencing the song, in one of his essays.

Nielsen continues, "I suppose my freshness, ingenuousness; simple-mindedness—or whatever it was—amused them. Also I could sing. I was not given to temperamental outbursts [snarling snatch at Melba], I just sang whenever and wherever opportunity offered".

Americans read of their Nielsen proudly in May 1904. The American society set turns out proudly for her debut at Covent Garden. London's season is of course "a social as well as a musical event, as it is in New York". The house had been "remodeled and a particularly successful season is expected". Widespread press coverage; three Alice interviews.

With irony for erstwhile hopes of a collaborative Herbert-Gilbert show becoming the Great American Musical, Alice Nielsen debuts at Covent on the same day WS Gilbert's *Fairy's Dilemma* opens at Garrick Theatre (*NY Herald*). *London Times* finds Gilbert "a quasi-classic in his own lifetime" at peak powers, the show a "most excellent fooling", "verbage is magnificently sesquipedalian", "comedietta...inextricably tangled with this ironic parody of a pantomime". Opportunity lost of a possible future only imagined.

Fort Worth Telegram (May 2) reports of London, "American colony will be much in evidence". For the four-month season, subscribers include "J. Pierpont Morgan, Mrs. Adair, Mrs. Arthur Paget, Mrs. Ralph Vivia, Mrs. Newhouse...."

As Alice realized upon joining the Bostonians, at Covent she has arrived in that lofty place were fame dwelt: "chief among the interpreters this season are Calvé, Terninia, Suzanne Adams, Melba, Caruso, Van Dyke, Salza, Plancon, Van Rooy, Gilbert, Journet and Scotti. The newcomers include Alice Nielsen and Miss Parkins".

NY Herald heralds the glitterati: "Although the King and Queen were in Ireland", present were Duchess of Fife "all in black with silver embroidery and glittering wings in her hair". Lady deGrey's box "next to the stage on the grand tier" embraced American socialites Lady de Trafford, Mrs. Jack Leslie and Mrs. George Cornwallis West. Noted in the house were Mrs. Astor, Lord Rosyln with Mrs. Frank Mackey, Mrs. Chauncy and Lady Charles Beresford. Mrs. Dudley Leigh, Mrs. Parkinson Sharpe and Mrs. Leggett with her daughter Miss Sturgis were seen. Craig Wadsworth of the US Embassy represented the diplomats".

To a full house Alice Nielsen sings Zerlina in *Don Giovanni* at Covent Garden May 3, 1904. Richter conducts. In the cast: Donna Elvira, Suzanne Adams; Renaud, the Don; Gilibert, the Masetto; Destinn, Donna Anna.

Critics strongly positive: "Certainly no such careful or artistic performance of the work which some people consider to be the greatest opera in the world has taken place at Covent Garden in many a year", says *London Times*.

As Broadway well knew, Alice Nielsen is petite, pretty, and moves (even dances!) plus a glory voice. The critic, surprised by Nielsen's quality, seems confused by her zest: "Zerlina was taken by Miss Alice Nielsen, a clever young lady, who manages to sing with less than was to be expected of the manner associated with musical comedy, a genre in which she hitherto won success. Still in manner and style her performance suggests that Miss Edna May rather than Mme. Patti has been her model".

And Alice Nielsen would very much have it be so.

Others are glad for the gayety.

London Daily Mail: Nielsen's "Zerlina was captivatingly fresh, not only socially but histrionically. She has a steady voice. In *Batti-batti* the young artist phrased with remarkable grace and there was more than mere technique in what she did". Significantly, when Nielsen sings "a riveting magnetism existed. It was unmistakable".

Morning Post: "Miss Alice Nielsen impersonated Zerlina with great success and with due restraint; her best vocal effort was the *Batti, Batti*".

Scotsman: "Delightful too, was Miss Alice Nielsen, who by her vivacious acting and charming singing quite justify her appearance on the grand opera stage".

NY Herald (May 7) quotes *London Daily Express*, "Alice Nielsen acted with charm and vivacity as Zerlina, singing with ease and finish and altogether justifying her adoption of an operatic career".

May 17th, *Globe* visits *Figaro*: "Miss Alice Nielsen made a Susanna who might have stepped straight out of a modern musical comedy".

Nielsen scored success in her London opera debut in difficult material mastered. From the Dold parlor to Covent Garden.

Fame secures, visibility soars, contacts widen.

Covent is not her home stage. *Daily Mail* is very quick to add "her chaperone is Lady deGrey". DeGrey is partial to Melba's monopoly and can restrict Alice's access to the mainstage. DeGrey's absence from Nielesen's memoir reflects the breakdown of cordiality. Melba the likely culprit.

May 9th, *NY Sun* publishes an unusually insightful article by a writer well-acquainted with the star's daunting plight: "Alice Nielsen attained one goal of her ambition last Monday night when she sang at Covent Garden in London in *Don Giovanni*. For the sake of making a name for herself in grand opera she has for the last four seasons deliberately thrown away more than $30,000 a year which she might have earned in comic opera".

Sun reveals Maurice Grau has been advising Alice. Suggests possibility she had joined the "juvenile" Italian tour with his singers. Grau, who hired Caruso the previous year, sadly retires for health before hiring Alice for the Met. Maurice Grau's influence on American culture cannot be exaggerated. His brother Robert recalls Maurice touring from Chicago back to NY. Their train crosses Catskills: "Eames, Calvé, Nordica, Plancon, the DeReszkes all gazing on the scenery. Maurice approached his singers and remarked, 'Gaze on, my children, and gaze long at this wondrous spectacle, for it is the last time any of you will very view it at my expense', for the Chicago season had lost money". Per usual.

Continues *Sun*, Grau "only the year before his retirement, asked Miss Nielsen how she could reconcile herself to the financial loss that her ambitions entailed". Unaware of her stolen revenues, Grau continues, "You cannot look forward to earning very much money. Even in Naples and the other large Italian cities, the compensation for young singers is small in comparison with what you could earn in comic opera at home. So it seems to me that you are not likely to make money whatever happens".

Nielsen wonderfully replies, "I don't care about the money now. I am going to stick to my career. My ambition is to be a Sembrich and I shall succeed". Their conversation took place in Europe; Grau would retire February 1903 and relocate to Paris until his March 1907 death.

Left the Met slightly too soon to let Alice Nielsen secure a main-stage presence on subscription nights. Moravian-born Grau operated the Met from 1890-1903 (hiatus 1897-98). Within the hugely-influential Grau family, his uncle Jacob had operated the French Theatre in NY since the 1840s. Maurice produced opera, drama, and music theatre across America and Europe and beyond. His first opera season was at Teatro Solis in Uruguay. His Nielsen-associated stars include Modjeska, Henry Irving, Christina Nilsson, Nordica, Calvé, Adelina Patti, Ida Valerga, and Sarah Bernhardt. Grau's early projects involved a curious banker named Henry F. Gillig of the *American Exchange* whose spectacular shady failure fetched a bitter reproach from investor Mark Twain.

Jacques Offenbach describes Maurice in 1877, "quite a young man, scarcely twenty-eight years old, but looking forty. Incessant work, care of all sort, an extraordinary activity, and continual preoccupations have made him look prematurely old. He has led a busy life... more consuming in America than anywhere else. He has already made and lost five or six fortunes. One day he is worth millions, and the next he has not a penny. Nor is this very strange, for Maurice Grau often manages five theatres at one and the same time; an Italian opera in New York, a French theatre in Chicago, a music-hall in San Francisco, an English dramatic theatre in Havana, and a Spanish comic opera in Mexico".

Offenbach, cellist, composer, and conductor, pens with penchant for diverse detail the witty travelogue *Offenbach in America* (1877). Shaping American musical culture, Maurice profitably toured Offenbach and singer Marie Aimée across America popularizing French *opéra bouffe*—a comic opera—characters drawn from life with dialog recitative: the wellspring of American musicals. His brothers popularized comic opera in America.

Clara Kellogg, who sang at Paris Opera Comique, delineates these styles, "We have some delicate differentiations to make when we go investigating in the fields of light dramatic music. To most persons *opéra comique* means simply... 'high-class comic opera.' Opéra bouffe even is many degrees below opéra comique. Yet *opéra bouffe* is, to my mind, infinitely superior [to] modern comic opera. In Paris at the Comique for the most part these Paris managers choose operas that are light. I use the word advisedly. By light I mean, literally, not heavy. Light music, light drama, does not necessarily mean humorous.

"The only restriction is that it shall not be expressed in the stentorian orchestration of a Meyerbeer, nor in the heart-rending tragedy of a Wagner. In theme and in treatment, in melodies and in text, it must be of delicate fiber, something easily seized and swiftly assimilated, something intimate, perfumed, and agreeable, with *opéra comique*. A careful differentiation discovers that humour, a happy ending, and many rollicking melodies do not at all make an *opéra comique*. These qualities all belong abundantly to *Die Meistersinger* and to Verdi's *Falstaff*, yet these great operas are no nearer being examples of genuine *comique* than *Les Huguenots* is or *Götterdämmerung*".

Of Alice, *Sun* continues, "Now she has sung Zerlina at Covent Garden and has thus advanced another step toward accomplishing what she set out to do". Even so, "probably at Covent Garden she receives less than $100 a night now". Alice Nielsen tosses an entire basket of eggs at Broadway: "She prefers that modest compensation for singing Mozart, Gounod and Donizetti to $1,000 a week which any American firm of managers would pay her for singing Herbert, Kerker, De Koven and other composers who supply music for American comic operas".

Three eggs in one toss: Herbert, Kerker, DeKoven "supply music".

Plus the managerial egg perhaps egged-on by her relentless remora Russell. Yet if she punts the point, so counters Herbert: he is now, Mozart dead. In the Moravian saying, "If you like this place, do the work".

Sun guesstimates her age, "still young, certainly under 30, and it may be that she will ultimately be able to come to the Metropolitan and earn the thousands she has lost through her artistic aspirations".

Analysis turns profound to assess the cultural moment. Her challenges are greater than mastering repertoire. Coloratura is done. Dramatics rule.

Facing artistic realities, "She would have a better chance of doing this were she a Wagnerian soprano. Her repertoire must necessarily be that of the light soprano, whom composers of the day neglect almost entirely. Puccini in *La Bohème* considered her claims, although he forgot her again in *Tosca* and then in *Mme. Butterfly*.

"Sembrich, the most noted light soprano of her time, recently wrote that it was fortunate for her that she was not at the beginning of her career. It takes all her genius now to make Rosina, Violetta, Marie and the rest of the old-fashioned repertoire interesting. The future is for the dramatic soprano".

Only Herbert actively composes for lyrical voice. Unfashionably lyrical, Nielsen should face the future. On Broadway, she is heart of fashionable. Her stage clones enjoy lucrative success. "Miss Nielsen may follow the example of Fritzi Scheff and go into comic opera once more after having made a reputation for herself as a grand opera singer. Miss Scheff frankly admitted that she had taken this step merely to earn more money than was possible in grand opera". Scheff only in it for the money, as Harry Smith. The loser is the public.

Victor Herbert delivers quality gayety. Nielsen & Herbert could drive musical theatre, and make "opera in English" their own. Producers will provide whatever suppprt they wish. Shape theatre's future.

Scheff takes the money and runs. Never her purpose to help Herbert create America's new theatrical arts. "She has been engaged for the Vienna Opera House, and with $30,000 in the bank as the result of her one year in *Babette*, she may be able to make terms with managers that would be impossible if she had not sacrificed a little of her artistic dignity".

Sun revisits the faux quarrel about matinees. Ernestine Schumann-Heink, eminent alto gone Broadway, realizes the strain of singing daily. And she must talk, act—dance! "She is moving heaven and earth to get out of this contract. Her voice has of course been wrecked by this strain, but her popularity with the public is as great as ever. She would, if it were possible to withdraw from her contract, prefer to sing in concert for another year rather than go into comic opera where in addition to singing she will be more compelled to talk and act, which is more wearisome than more concert singing". Broadway needs skill and strength.

Alice Nielsen, an army of one.

Covent Garden season continues, London sings Nielsen's praises. Even the fierce chill of *Times* (London and NY) punctures to a point. Nielsen popularizes; she can make even grand opera interesting. Melba could not.

Complexity of Nielsen's triumph is noticed by *London Chic* (May 16). "Miss Alice Nielsen, the Zerlina of the cast, turned to account all those gifts and graces which have won her renown in other and simpler paths, and she completely won the hearts of the most seasoned of Covent Garden's habitués, many of whom recalled Patti in the same part".

On May 19, Nielsen sings in *Rigoletto* to equal success.

On May 24, her attorney Hummel provides talk for a piece on Nielsen in *NY Times* by William McConnell. "My adroit legal friend AH Hummel is very much and very naturally elated...the American prima donna has scored a distinct hit in London in *Figaro*. Mr. Hummel is not alone the adviser and American representative of Miss Nielsen, but is about the only one of her early friends who didn't shake his head in solemn depreciation when she concluded to quit comic opera gold and devote herself to the higher branch of singing".

"I always knew", says Hummel, "Alice Nielsen would make good for she possesses, in addition to the necessary artistic qualification, an indomitable determination to accomplish anything she may undertake". Adds a curious puffery, "And when I saw that she had placed herself in the training of the eminent [obscure] Russell, my reassurance was doubly sure. She is coming to America in the autumn and I know beforehand that she will greatly astonish even the most ardent of her admirers with the progress she has made".

Any return to America will be postponed a year.

During this 1904 spring success, Alice Nielsen finds rapport with Irish journalist Thomas (TP) O'Connor, who publishes the *Sun* and the weekly *M.A.P.* (*Mainly About People*) magazine, forerunner of today's *People*.

O'Connor, Irish Party member of Parliament, was a founder of the 1879 Land League. Hauled before Parnell Commission and asked if British rule in Ireland was without legal and moral sanction: "Certainly. British rule in Ireland being against the wishes of the Irish people, was without moral sanction; it might be legal because every Government was *de facto* legal".

Cordial O'Connor and Nielsen wax congenial. Articulates her artistic values as she sketches her pilgrim progress, slightly compressed. "My father was a Danish singer and painter, who went to America to make his fortune. He married a lovely, dowerless Irish girl and they had a large family of children. The fortune was never realized except in dreams, but the eight children were a reality, and those of us who could help were obliged to do so at a very early age. I cannot remember when I could not sing. Two things I was born with—a strong throat and a correct and quick musical ear".

Returns to the childhood tour: "At eight years old I was playing Nanki-Poo in a juvenile company in Gilbert and Sullivan's *Mikado*, and if a child goes on the stage she really has no youth". If Nielsen was eight when *Mikado* hits 1885 Kansas City, she was born 1877, married 12, birthing her baby next year. Yet arrived Kansas City 1880 about eight; so at least thirteen.

After shuffling dates she gets back on track Since street-singing days she has felt her future. Any stage child is "always longing to be older; at eighteen she says 'I wish I was twenty-five, then I shall have what I am working for now.' Even now I want five years to fly by, hoping then to have a better position in my new work". Her perspective intrigues. Five years ago she was the top American musical star. Within five years Opera Boston House built for her. Few will ever receive such gifts.

Entrusts O'Connor with her artistic manifesto: "I have given up much to take up art; and whether great success attends me or not, I have had the courage of my convictions".

Prodigy dislikes prodigies: "Because I sang as a child is perhaps the reason I cannot bear to hear a child sing in public; precocious performing children seem to me more pathetic than either astonishing or interesting, and very often the voice is strained by beginning too soon, and does not develop properly". Speaking of her voice puts conscious focus on her throat, "My throat and my good health, however, stood me in good stead, for I have been singing steadily since an early age, and I still feel that much is to be accomplished before I attain my ambition".

Ambition to Alice Nielsen is "not fortune but fame through art in its widest definition". She defines fame as the artistic achievements which provide access to increasingly worthy collaborators.

Difficult to unravel the highly condensed skewed schedule: "My first distinct success was at 15 when I made my debut as a prima donna, singing the part of Yum-Yum in *The Mikado*. Then came a year of hard work and hard traveling in a stock company, which finally fulfilled an engagement in San Francisco". Marriage and son are vanished.

Praises Herbert: "While there, we competed with the old Bostonians, a fine English [language] opera company. Their manager [Barnabee] heard me sing and engaged me at once for a tour with him. Not very long after that, I was starring in operas composed by Victor Herbert—who is our American Arthur Sullivan and writes charming and delightful music, some of his best operas being *The Serenade, The Fortune Teller,* and *The Singing Girl.* My success in America was phenomenal, both my audiences and the press vying with each other in giving me praise and encouragement".

Arriving in London "the opinion of the older world would perhaps be more critical, and it was a nervous and anxious moment when I made my first appearance in London—and when I opened the newspapers the next morning the letters swam before my eyes. But all had gone well.

"Many of my critics indeed suggested that I should go into grand opera and those suggestions I hugged to my heart, for they divined and voiced my real ambition. The dream of my life was taking shape at last...."

Her oft-repeated refrain credits remora Russell. Supposedly her opera ambition was "vague until Mr. Henry Russell [no, Covent Garden, Tosti and Bevignani] told me that my voice and my youth would justify me in taking up a more arduous career". More arduous. Try the experiment.

"I decided at once, although he begged me to wait and consider it seriously. But it required no further consideration on my part, for I had been thinking it over since my childhood". Bespoke musicals composed for her voice by maestro Victor Herbert are set aside to sing repertoire made for others. Skips stinging betrayals by Williams & Perley.

As her sister Hortense would agree, Alice must sing genuinely, "Light opera, musical comedy, even musical burlesques, are all delightful in their way, but they are inadequate for the expression of heartfelt emotion".

Reechoes her hireling, "And they are all unjust to the voice. It is impossible to dance violently and sing perfectly". Recalls the woman with best legs in San Francisco, if not all America: "when I put my whole soul into my singing very often my audience preferred the cakewalk".

Her ideal is meaningful song.

Alice Nielsen proclaims her artistic manifesto: "I had attained in this branch of dramatic art—success, popularity and money. I put all of them aside without one pang to try and attain my ideal; for Italian grand opera is the mother of all opera. In this divine language through this divine music all emotions of the human soul and voice are expressed—love, joy, pain, despair, hatred, longing, death. The supreme moments of life are all conveyed in strains of song".

Beyond frivolous flirt and frolics: "I know what was highest and best in music and I felt it in me to do something more worthy than musical comedy—and yet, if I had known what was before me, would I have had the courage to begin my new career? I fear not. Hard work, disappointment, doubt, anxiety were all before me—but I regret nothing".

Certainly these were behind her and drove her.

And of course, "Very expensive to become an opera singer. You must have the best tuition for the language, for the voice, for diction, for dramatic acting, for repertoire. Maestro Bevignani, the finest teacher in Italy for repertoire, was my teacher in that branch of the art—he is dead now, but he prophesized success for me. Mr. Russell directed my voice production, and I had teachers for Italian and diction. Besides tuition, a girl who studies must have good food, perfect ease of mind, and youth and money enough not to hurry her career".

Nielsen speaks of singing across Italy without mentioning Grau's Met tour of "juveniles": "All to the good if she can sing a couple of years in the small towns in Italy, where the audiences hiss one moment and cry 'Bravo!' the next, in this way she gets a lesson of the greatest value every night.

"Of course, the Italian prima donna has an advantage over every other, temperamentally and through the language. All Italians sing with an open throat; it is almost a natural result of a proper pronunciation of the language. In the beginning I found Italian opera very difficult and was painfully nervous when I first appeared in it; and after all my great successes in America, people said what a bad actress I was.

"The truth is, I was simply paralyzed just as I am when I try to speak a language. I am timid; a charming quality, no doubt, in moderation—but I am too nervous, and find it sometimes very detrimental".

Situation similar to the opening in NYC. Nielsen could be shy

Discusses her speedy debut, "When I made my first appearance at Covent Garden I had only appeared twice before in grand opera". Two roles over many nights. Yet "I felt that it was too soon and I was ill prepared for the ordeal. It is impossible to overrate the importance of singing a role many times in theatres of minor importance before making a debut in the principal theatre of a great city. For instance, up to the very last night I sang in *Don Pasquale* I found I was able to make several important and advantageous changes in the role which enabled me to score a greater success each time".

Art costs cash, "If I had not many calls on my purse, my appearance in London would have been deferred until this coming spring".

Arises an American icon of artistic independence: "In spite of mistakes and disappointments, I am going steadily on with my more exacting career. It is hard sometimes, but perhaps the pursuit of my ambition is less difficult, knowing that at any moment I can still choose between art and fortune". The nation marks her stance, proud she is an American. Lost to Broadway at any price: "Lately an American manager has offered to 'star' me at a salary of $1,600 a week for a long season of comic opera, but I will be true to my present aim unless stern necessity forces my hand".

Concludes her values: "Jewels, fine clothes, the material things of life, appeal to me less than to many women, and the satisfaction of singing in company with great artists and the happiness of interpreting the works of great masters is sufficient compensation for all I have given up".

Two years later O'Connor drops his Irish wife for a Greek girl.

In NYC June as "Signor Caruso" returns to the Met, *NY Sun* reveals a revival of "another of Alice Nielsen's, a stupendous production of *The Singing Girl*" with sixty artists, none named. Dreaming to repeat their three-year success, Julian Mitchell lobbies hard. June 13th Will McConnell reports, "If Julian Mitchell gets his way, and I have seen enough correspondence to lead me to believe that he will, when Alice Nielsen returns to the American stage it will be under the management of Hamlin, Mitchell & Fields, and she will be seen in opera comique, which is near grand opera". Not no mere musical whatsoever. Correspondence between Nielsen and Mitchell has not come to light. Mitchell offers $1,500 per week ($36,500 today); about $200 per show or twice her Covent Garden fee.

Nielsen declines to deal.

McConnell gives careful analysis to Nielsen's choices. Speaks with theatre insider Marcus Mayer who had visited Nielsen's Covent debut. "Bright, dapper and debonair" Mayer (1840-1918) worked with Mapleson, Edwardes, Henry Abbey, and Grau. Assisted at the Metropolitan and with tours for Patti, Bernhardt, Booth, Lily Langtry, Calvé, Henry Irving, Christine Nilsson. Raised in San Francisco, Mayer drove a stagecoach for Pony Express before joining big-time touring. "He has witnessed many go through that most terrible of all ordeals to the operatic artist", McConnell adds. Mayer praises the Nielsen debut at Covent, "Never have I seen any one go through the fire as did Miss Nielsen on Monday night when she appeared as Zerlina in *Don Giovanni* and scored a hit".

Continues McConnell, Mayer "ought to know, as he has been with all the grand opera artistes for the last thirty years. I only hope that Messrs.

Hamlin, Mitchell & Fields can induce Miss Nielsen to head her own company in America next season...just so the public can see her".

Interestingly, McConnell advises Nielsen to avoid the Met where "she would sing only once or twice a week, and she would virtually be lost in the shuffle". Smart and strong, she surmounts any obstacle: "Alice Nielsen deserves to succeed...a case of natural talent allied to real intelligence".

McConnell recaps: "One of the best-paying attractions on the road. Then she went to London at Shaftesbury Theatre and achieved instant and unanimous recognition. Then came the turning point in her career.

"She received numerous offers to appear in musical comedy in London which to her really meant nothing...she could make four times as much money in America. Julian Mitchell, when with Weber & Fields, offered her $1,500 per week. 'Nay, Nay', said Alice, 'when next I appear in America it will be in something above the musical comedy line.'"

Mitchell makes diverse offers. Nielsen declines.

McConnell sknows her artistic values. Significantly, almost tragically, McConnell expresses the hope Nielsen would return to help develop the emerging new Broadway arts. Why promote the aging Italian repertoire? Appreciates her Herbert alliance. Two national treasures.

"We have composers like Victor Herbert, who would be able to turn out a *Bohemian Girl* or *Grand Duchess* that would give Miss Nielsen all the scope she desires and that she would then come over to head her own company". Of course, Mitchell directing Nielsen would be great again. "The time is ripe for real comic opera. Miss Nielsen has every confidence in Julian Mitchell. She says she owes a whole lot to him".

McConnell concludes, "Alice Nielsen is now a good, substantial, full-fledged, real, first-class prima donna" who needs a first-class production.

This great opportunity is lost to us. Such is corrosion of corruption on the gayety of nations. Two weeks before her return, McConnell has died.

Nielsen reveals she holds fourteen grand operas in repertoire. On July 9th (*London Times*), she wraps opera season with a benefit concert for the British Court. At some July point, the candid diva is interviewed in London by Elsie Lathrop for *Broadway Magazine* (November). Lathrop had married a Buffalo Bill Cody Show cowboy. A Cody staffer will join the stampede to handle Alice's American return. Lathrop helping that happen seems likely.

Lathrop, amazed at Nielsen's true grit, "From comic opera to Mozart in less than three years! This is what our little prima donna has accomplished, with the true American girl's pluck and perseverance".

Alice Nielsen, American heroine. Again.

"As Miss Nielsen sat chatting in her sunny little drawing-room in London, in her natural, unaffected manner, she looked younger than ever, fresh and dainty, in spite of the unusual heat. 'Of course, I am delighted with my success'," Nielsen says, "'but I am sorry that now, just when Americans are coming to London in such numbers, I am no longer singing in opera, as the Mozart performances for which I was engaged are over. I should have liked them to hear me. You know everyone in America thought me mad to attempt grand opera, and the letters of remonstrance I received on the subject! It was disheartening then, I assure you. It has been a struggle.'"

Illness of 1901 summer now expands across the year. Sick of Williams & Perley, blame climate change: "In the first place, the climate never agreed with me. I was ill the entire first year, and on the verge of nervous prostration I undertook the plunge and began studying for grand opera. The foreign languages, after having always sung in English, were no easy matter, added to my American friends' dismal forebodings".

Hints at financial struggles past and present. "Now the struggle is to resist the offers, very tempting from a financial point of view, to return to America in my former line of work. I suppose I like money as well as anyone, but nevertheless I shall not return until I return in grand opera".

With Grau removed from Met her options reduce drastically for a stage in grand opera in New York. Yet she rebuffs Julian Mitchell. Irony karma. Mitchell offers top quality new shows with the best producers.

Nielsen has harnessed her dancing horse to the nobody backside.

"Are you not very gratified to think that your London success has been made in Mozart's operas, acknowledged to be the most difficult to sing well?"

"Yes indeed, of course I am. And I will say that I was a great success at Convent Garden. They wanted me to sing Juliette, but it must be in French and I have no French repertoire yet. All my work has been in Italian, and my repertoire in that language includes fourteen operas, so you must see I have worked. Now I must acquire the French".

Lathrop points out, a year earlier Nielsen "sang the waltz song from *Romeo and Juliette* in Queen's Hall, conducted by Hans Richter and made her first London success".

At that point Nielsen trots out her pet Russell with a calculated spiel like she was selling another player piano: "I assure you my voice was nothing then to what it is now. I had only been studying a short time with my maestro, whom I want you to meet. He can tell you more about my work than I should like to do. I must not be too egotistical, you know. I owe everything that I have accomplished to him—everything".

Everything accomplished, sure. If you say so.

Lathrop instantly contradicts, "But I remember how well you sang before you left America!" Nielsen retorts, "Oh, I assure you that was nothing then to what it is now. I knew nothing".

Russell Jr. skulks into the room "not at all English in appearance, due to Spanish ancestry". According to Darryl Lyman's *Jewish Singers in American Popular Music* (2007) his British dad was great-nephew of British Chief Rabbi Solomon Hirschel who tried to suppress the reform movement.

Tells a new version of meeting Nielsen: "An Italian tenor, a friend of mine, begged me to go and hear her sing…but I would not go. Then several members of her company came to study with me, and they all told me of her fine voice and urged me to hear her, so at last I went resignedly. I was amazed. The voice I heard was thin, worn to a thread, for Miss Nielsen was quite ill from overwork and strain, but I recognized a voice of wonderful timbre in spite of all this".

He rages with affected antipathy for the robust new arts developing on Broadway having no use for him whatsoever: "Can you imagine my feelings seeing the owner of such a voice dancing and appearing in comic opera, a kind of music for which I have no use? It was arranged we should meet and Miss Nielsen sang for me".

Nielsen comments, "Yes, the *King of Thule* from *Faust*, in English".

Told her what she wants to hear, stop the show: "I said to her at once, 'You must give up this work you are doing. If you will do so, my services are at your disposal; I will train you for the operatic career you should have. I will give you a week to come to a decision.'"

Now she has a legal out.

Nielsen interjects, "But I said at once, 'I accept.' I decided instantly".

Skip hefty percentage pocketed, spread across pals such as actually useful brother; skips the twice-weekly presence for brief breathing lessons. Skips his financial distress. Skips wife and kids. Artcash was calling him, all about that pose ne'er mere money, as Russell himself cleverly suggested pocketing Alice's £1,000 (or £5,000?) with "long, thin fingers". He proceeds speaking faux-impresario: "After only eight months of lessons she made her debut in the Bellini Theatre Naples, a small theatre, singing Marguerite in *Faust*, where she had just the success I wished and expected".

Arrived mid-April, free July 4th, opens five months later at Bellini. Tosti and Bevignani the why. Her success a certitude.

Spinning hypnotic threads oh her success "not overwhelming—I did not desire that, for I have observed that those who make one of these overwhelming successes at a debut come down like rockets afterwards".

Phrase from Alice's 1898 *NY Times* review celebrating her stardom.

Continues to spin, "She was not yet ready to bring down the house but her success was good and genuine. I was satisfied, although I told her I reserved my real decision... until I heard her in a large theatre".

Broke vocal coach for society dames poses faux impresario: "We went back to work again after the Naples performances—these were in the spring of 1903 [winter 1901—spring 1903]; then last January Miss Nielsen sang in the San Carlo Theater in Naples and had an ovation. The audience rose to applaud her. She was encored and cheered. Then I knew that she was capable of the highest attainment" to enrich his purse.

"She sang Violette in *La Traviata* and sang with a breadth of phrasing and fullness of tone of which a year before she was absolutely incapable.

"You may state" after raising your hand? "that [Duse pal] Boito, after hearing her sing, said that hers was the only voice trained in pure Italian method, without a trace of Anglo-Saxon constriction—such as all we Anglo-Saxons must fight against to attain the freedom inborn in the Italian—that he had heard since Patti".

Rustling autumn leaves as rustler Russell roams from room.

Nielsen speaks of the future. Plans "not definitely settled. At present, my vacation; next spring I shall probably sing here at Covent Garden, and in the winter in Italy. I love Italy and life there but alas, one cannot make much money singing there. Some day I hope to come back to America, but not yet".

July 6th *Tatler* interview along the same lines.

July 20th, mentions Alice "sang very charmingly *Voi che sapete* and Tosti's *Good-bye*, accompanied at pianoforte by Mr. Henry Russell" at the previous week's benefit for Infants' Hospital. Alice has left for Italy. Only on October 5th will her pending return for the London fall opera season appear in *Morning Post*.

Nielsen's Covent debut in Mozart only a prelude to her fantastic fall season. Puccini and Caruso join Nielsen at Covent with San Carlo Opera.

San Carlo since 1735 has interrupted its home season only once, that due to an unruly 1874 French tourist. *Teatro di San Carlo*'s states is "oldest working theatre in Europe". Ballet taught since 1812, design 1816.

London thrills. *Graphic* signals star status, "Familiar names include those of Miss Alice Nielsen and Signor Dani, while Signor Campanini, brother of the famous tenor, will be the principal conductor".

All arranged by San Carlo manager Roberto De Sanna. The London season at Covent Garden benefits Puccini, Scotti, Caruso and Caruso relatives. Formidable cast. Puccini is present. Voices include Nielsen, Caruso, Scotti; Eleonora De Cisneros (1878-1934) the American alto née Eleonora Broadfoot; tenor Francesco Vignas, Pasquale Amato; baritone Mario Ancona and Mario Sammarco. Also Caruso's sister-in-laws Rina Giachetti and Ada who by relation to Enrico someday reappear fictionized.

After her spring Mozart season, Nielsen returns. They create autumn performances hailed as masterpieces of ensemble theatre.

Caruso biographer Bruno Zirato (1922), tell us this event is intensely important to Caruso who must "surpass himself" to chastise Naples 1902 mistreatment—behavior Nielsen related at her debut. As Herbert and Higgins had promoted Nielsen over others, Caruso promotes her as Mimi in *Bohème*. He had performed the show with Melba earlier that year and had a decided preference. Irish tenor John McCormack heard Caruso this same year, "Such smoothness and purity of tone, and such quality; it was like a stream of liquid gold. That voice still rings in my ears, the memory of it will never die (1934)". Caruso and Nielsen have commonalities. About her age, poor child, church singer. Nielsen began recording 1898; Caruso 1902. In London alas Alice doesn't record with FW Gaisbert or others on record. Alice relates that Caruso had already asked her to sing the Mimi role in Italy; apparently refused, not knowing the part. Possibly sang anyway as she had Lucia at the Tivoli. As our credulity permits.

Fatefully, Roberto De Sanna must stay in Napoli. He sends Russell along to report on the faithfulness of a lady in the cast. What the manager has organized, cast, and produced is done deal. Upon arrivel the debble descends to possess the remora spy who lures *Sketch* into a puff piece "Henry Russell, the Director of the San Carlo Opera Company, is probably the youngest impresario who has ever controlled a Company at Covent Garden, almost to vanishing point. Among his other pupils have been Mr. Ben Davies, Mr. Kennerley Rumford..." and of course "Miss Alice Nielsen".

Out of sight over in Naples, of course De Sanna cannot comment except by later action. He would not in future include Russell in anything.

As for "his other pupils" they ignore the name the same. Welsh tenor Ben Davies credits as teachers Alberto Randegger and Signor Fiori, took his 1881 debut in Balfe's *Bohemian Girl*. Baritone Rumford (married to a Nielsen concert co-star the six-foot-two alto Clara Butt) credits as teachers

Giovanni Sbriglia, Jacques Bouhy, George Henschel. Neither speak of Russell as significant. Perhaps a pattern emerges.

La Bohème. World's most popular opera. Art follows life; adapted from Henri Murger's (1822-1861) autobiographical novel *Scènes de la Vie de Bohème* (1853). Murger had lived in a Parisian attic. His pals the "water drinkers" lack money for wine. Murger's novel became basis for two operas, an operetta, and a Broadway musical *Rent*.

To unravel fiction, unravel life. Montparnasse was settled by Czechs fleeing tyranny after losing freedom in their homeland at the Thirty Years' War. To speak freely and enslave none is a Bohemian value which Prague's Jan Hus statue celebrates Bohemians' quarter is where people love music, art, poetry, and money ain't everything. Enjoy the great festival of life with all. World's most popular symphony is Czech, Dvorak's *New World*. Such values best suit the human ecology. What goes in 1776 still goes. Prague is capital of Bohemia, Moravia the highlands around Brno. Czech spirit: let things spontaneously flow without violence, inspires artists.

Unravel fiction: Murger is Rodolphe; Schaunard, Alexandre Schuanne; Marcel is composed of two artists, Lazare and Tabar; Colline a blend of Jean Wallon and Trapadoux; Barbemuch, Charles Barbara. Musette is the mix of painter's model Mariette and Lise, "wife of Pierre Dupont". Mimi a hybrid of three: Murger's cousin Angele's friend Marie, a Parisian Lucile, and blonde Juliette. Original setting is Café de la Rotonde; poverty and events all too real; a person slept in a tree. Art follows life.

Back to art and life. Caruso had clout to put Nielsen in Melba's stead: good art is good business. Beyond San Carlo Company within the Covent regime, the royals Grey and King assure Melba will sing. Box office appeal of Caruso is great, Nielsen popular, Melba so-so. Not toast. Yet consider *English Illustrated Magazine* (1903): "Opera is run on commercial principles and it is recognized that Caruso is the winning card in the pack. Nowadays the announcement that Madame Melba is to sing Juliette has little effect upon attendance; directly Caruso is 'billed', the box office is besieged by a crowd...." For Caruso, Melba strictly commerce. Big Melba stands and sings. Caruso pranks; replaces gum she chews between acts with chewing tobacco. While she sings he presses into her hand a warm meat, quietly saying, "Nice English lady, you like sausage?"

With Nielsen, no practical jokes. "Caruso was more than an angel. He stood with his back to the audience quietly instructing me in the stage business of the part, for I was not very familiar with Mimi, and he put me forward for all the applause. A big artist like that can be the biggest fellow in the world when he wants to".

August 25, *Broadway Weekly* interviews: "I must admit it is a long stride from comic opera to Covent Garden. Perhaps I might put it in another way and say it is only a shilling cab fare from the stage of the Shaftesbury where I made my first London appearance to that of the Grand Opera House. Up to now it has been an expensive cab fare for me, for when I resolved to become a grand opera singer I gave up the offer of an engagement of £300 a week for five years certain [Julian Mitchell]. Do I regret it? Not for a single instant. I would give all the money I could have earned in that time for one night's success in grand opera".

She has won. Unlike Lillian Russell, Nielsen sings *Faust*.

Speaks of challenges mastered, "You must remember it is something of an ordeal to come before the public as Zerlina in *Don Giovanni* and Suzanne in *Le Nozze di Figaro*. Both Mozart roles which have been always associated with the names of the greatest singers". And hired before leaving for Naples, "True, I was specially engaged...by the directors to whom I sang before I went to Italy to study for the undertaking on which I may consider myself now thoroughly embarked. The directors were pleased...but I had naturally no repertoire and they could not engage me". Before tasking herself with Russell.

"The training I had had in comic opera was at the time ill-suited to the exigencies of grand opera. Singing seven times a week as I was doing with dancing too, was simply ruining my voice. Even I could detect a certain roughness, the result of over-use and imperfect knowledge of voice production".

Blarney plug: "I really owe all my success to Mr. Henry Russell". Be a pal. Strictly business. He needs the money. Because he's with her, he gets inroads and attention and cash.

Briefly rehashes her pilgrim progress. "When I was a child I was always singing. I had a phenomenally high voice. When I grew too big for child opera, I went to San Francisco where I stayed as a member of a stock company [Tivoli] for fifteen months, playing all sorts of singing parts and gaining a wide range of experience". Too complex to tell of Stanley, Wigwam, Tivoli, Valerga, Bostonians.

Declines short-notice *Bohème*, "After my debut in Milan [Naples] at the Teatro Bellini I was offered an engagement at the San Carlo to sing Mimi in *La Bohème* the next night. I did not know the role so I refused the offer. In the old days I should have accepted it, learned the part somehow in 24 hours, and got through somehow".

Alice's blessed assurance confirms what Chicago told. Blessed with perfect musical memory. Tivoli's "manager before the fire" WH Leahy recalls, "Never saw her equal. She would read the score of an opera as a man would read a book and she retained it all in her wonderful memory. She had a great intuition, which enabled her to grasp a score in short order" (SF Call, 6 May 1909).

Alice continues, twice a week "three lessons a day, not long lessons, for he limits his instruction to twenty minutes at a time", Marchesi method.

"When I first went to Naples, a report got about that 'a comic opera artist who had lost her voice' had come with the intention of getting an engagement at the Teatro Bellini. 'Ah', said the people, 'wait till she debuts; we'll fix her—we'll kill her.' Of course, they expected to hear an awful old cracked tin pan".

Bevignani reset expectations. "Signor Bevignani, however...had heard [taught] me, and it was through his kindness that some of this feeling was allayed before I did make my first appearance as Marguerite in *Faust*".

Nielsen's magnetism, stage presence and skill achieves the rest. "The joke of the thing is that I became a favorite; indeed I found myself being put up to sing rather more frequently than I anticipated. I noticed that the announcements were invariably headed '*serota d'Onore.*' I had no idea then what 'serota d'Onore' meant [sera in onore di—evening in honor of]. One day I asked one of the artists and learned to my surprise that it was the equivalent of a 'benefit', and every artist is entitled to one during the season. I cannot tell you how many benefits I had, but though they drew crowded houses, the most I ever got for one of those special performances was fifty francs".

Nielsen really owes all her success to Bevignani. Inspired her, coached her, gave her the story of his stars before her. Very alike Valerga.

October 1904, Nielsen returns to London for opera in Italian.

Famed and busy Caruso in in great demand, new son born recently. Tours Europe slated to return soon to the Met. Biographer Pierre Key (1922) reports, after *Rigoletto* and *Traviata* at Berlin's *Des Westens Theatre*, Caruso had "departed for London where he had been engaged to appear in an autumn season to be given at Covent Garden by the San Carlo Opera Company, brought from Naples by its impresario, Roberto De Sanna. It must have been balm to Caruso's heart to have been the choice of the San Carlo Theatre manager to appear in this pretentious London season as leading tenor". Correctly no Russell.

Caruso "wanted his fellow Neapolitans to feel his absence and to yearn for his presence among them in the opera. It became apparent to him that the severest punishment he could administer would be surpass himself and this he undertook to do on October 17th of that year when he reappeared before a London audience in *Manon Lescaut*".

Caruso and baritone Scotti are Napoli natives. Antonio Scotti (1866-1936), principle baritone at the Met twenty-five years.

October 4th *London Times* reports San Carlo Company expected at Covent Garden: famed company, famed venue, top stars. Meanwhile back in America, petite Nielsen leads *Lincoln County Range Ledger* (IL Oct 13) list: "Small People Are Popular. There are many advantages, especially to a woman who follows the musical comedy or operatic lines. It is the 'little girl' who always forges to the front. For instance, there are Alice Nielsen, Edna Wallace Hopper, Madge Lessing, Della Fox and Katie Barry...."

Celofonte Campanini conducts.

Caruso sings eight times: *La Bohème, Pasquale, Carmen*, and *Pagliacci*. Significantly, Alice Nielsen sings in each. Combination so successful Henry Higgins invites her to sign a contract for next year: the greatest possible opportunity—a miraculous offer.

October 22, *London Times* reviews *Carmen*, "the least distinguished of the five performances given by the Neapolitans...and if this means only a little, that is because the other performances have been of such exceptional excellence". Still chilly on Nielsen, "A word of praise is due to Miss Alice Nielsen for her attempt to rise to the heights of Micala's part; she did not attain them but she worked hard".

By *Rigoletto, London Times* softens, "It is a far cry from the luridness of *La Tosca* to the comparatively mild and sedate tragedy of *Rigoletto*, which was played on Thursday evening before another large house. M. Sammarco, the Rigoletto of the occasion, seemed to feel this; for though he sang and acted as magnificently as before save, perhaps, for a slight and perfectly natural tiredness, he failed to carry quite the same sense of conviction as when representing the sinister Scarpia. Miss Alice Nielsen made a very acceptable Gilda everywhere but in the moments which demanded a deeper emotional feeling than is aroused by prettiness and freshness". Is Gilda deep?

Others—joining Henry Higgins—are warm to the upstart American.

Philadelphia Inquirer reports, "Judging from the audiences, the season of Italian opera this autumn at Covent Garden Theatre promises to be a financial as well as an artistic success. Signor Caruso has been a wonderful drawing card. On the nights when he appeared a good proportion of the seats could have been booked twice over. Signor Giachetti also scored a great success".

Key point: "Miss Alice Nielsen has pleased the critics, although it was recognized that in essaying Mimi in *La Bohème* she was courting comparison with Mme. Melba". She means to do so. Has won the contest, judged by the amazing offer of Higgins for next season.

Challenging Grey-connected, King-cordial Melba is risky business.

Other papers detect the hinted contest. *London Times* subtly says of Nielsen, "Not perhaps very high praise to say that her Italian pronunciation and acting are quite as good as those of a more eminent singer, but it is only right to say that her execution of the music reached a good deal nearer to Mme. Melba's level than was to be expected, and of course, her charming freshness of voice made a great effect".

October 30, acting on Nielsen's direction Russell sends cables lauding her work to Hummel and others he has never met. Amazingly, claims credit for what only Roberto De Sanna arranged. He adds spin, "Mr. Russell assured the financial success of his [sic] venture by securing Signor Caruso and he has given added prestige to Miss Nielsen's presentation by getting Signor Puccini to go to London to lead the performances". At the end this kind of grandstanding gets him kicked from Australia by Melba.

De Sanna, of course has managed everything.

During this season, seeking another revenue stream, Russell seeks to sign Caruso who refuses and wisely chooses Naples-born NYC banker Pasquale Simonelli who can afford the impresario role. Russell is broke.

Puccini, who in 1897 called Caruso "my gift from God", is pleased with Nielsen's art. His biographers do not detail this. Her *La Bohème* success helps the composer who appreciates the importance of stars. Unmentioned in any Puccini biography due to her interval of obscurity before this book, Puccini solicits her comments on his *Butterfly* score.

San Carlo Opera Company season at Covent Garden is highly praised.

Within this ensemble Alice Nielsen tames fierce critical lions.

London Times covers *Rigoletto* (Nov 7), Sammarco "once more acted with extraordinary force and conviction, and sang with finished art and vigour. In his hands the melodrama seemed to have the qualities of a real play.... Miss Alice Nielsen acted quite acceptably and sang the music with the required brilliance and purity of tone".

Lively petite Alice is so widely preferred to big stolid Melba that *London Times* suggests "It is absurd to compare her with Mme. Melba, as is being done in certain quarters; for such a comparison must injure the younger singer's position with all who have ears to distinguish between her praiseworthy execution of the passages and the incomparable ease with which Mme. Melba utters them". Decade older, pounds heftier, Melba (1861-1931) had stood singing onstage in Europe since 1886. Migrating from Australia to London, Melba failed at operetta, left for Paris coaching by Marchesi who changed her name to "Melba" and placed her opera debut. Returning to London, she gained a leading Covent role into the 1920s, secured by Grey and King. Melba works viciously to defeat competitors and hates rivals. Soprano Emma Eames portrays Melba as an unnamed "wicked force who frustrated opportunity after opportunity" for the singer. Titta Ruffo, Rosa Ponselle, John McCormack, Luisa Tetrazzini, Frances Alda and others relate their bad Melba backstabs. Nielsen, the most severe threat to Melba at Covent, encounters ceaseless plots. Melba has skills, she makes mistakes. Her Wagnerian foray against Alice's friend Nordica fails badly. Significantly, Melba will not sing in Italy.

Nielsen's *Bohème* success challenges the politically-connected Melba who "sang in almost all subsequent performances during her extended tenure at the theatre, resisting suggestions that she share a role she had studied under Puccini's personal supervision and regarded as her personal property", says Arthur Groos in *Giacomo Puccini: La Bohème* (1986). Groos does not mention Nielsen's acclaimed performance, typical lapse of authors after 1920. Typical of Melba-dominated authors fearing excommunication prior to 1920. Melba will monopolizes *Bohème* at Covent Garden from 1899 to 1928.

Few if any others receive the opportunity Nielsen obtained from De Sanna and Caruso. Nielsen deliberately challenges Melba partly by pride, partly for revenge against Melba's earliest schemes to frustrate her success by political deceits. Told in a new chapter. Turning down Henry Higgins' amazing offer of next years' season with Covent Garden, Alice leaves the battlefield uncontested

London Times praises Nielsen's progress: "Miss Nielsen's Italian, though no doubt quite good enough for the fashionable season, will not pass muster in her present surrounds; so popular a young lady can surely find someone to teach her the proper value of Italian vowels, and the marked improvement in her style since she first essayed grand opera shows that she is quite clever enough to learn".

October 28th, *Manchester Courier* in *Our London Letters* says, "evidently the songs are an integral part of the drama, and not merely mediums for personal display. The last night was Miss Alice Nielsen, who is now rapidly winning her way into the favour of the public. Her voice is certainly of charming quality...."

London Daily News, "Nielsen was able to make triumph Mimi. She looked the part; she acted with naturalness which appeared to have traffic with art..."

Tatler, "We have had the opportunity of hearing Miss Alice Nielsen again in new roles. She brings a dainty sense of acting to bear..."

Sportsman, Nielsen "repeated her performance of Mimi, and many of her notes recalled the voice of Madame Melba".

Nov. 5th, *London Evening Standard* praises "a remarkably good performance of Signor Puccini's opera...Mlle. Alice Nielsen has benefited greatly by better experience with the theatre, and sang last evening as if determined to contradict".

Graphic, "Alice Nielsen is still only on the threshold of her career, but if she lives up to the standard which she set herself as Gilda in Rigoletto..."

Grand opera hopes have survived the climactic test in London.

November 7th San Carlo closes with *Rigoletto*. Caruso leaves for his second Met season, Nielsen many more English concerts. Soon returns to Italy to ponder Covent's offer of a second season. Displace Melba?

Of course, Nielsen has her own opera house built in Boston 1909, a gift of artistic appreciation neither Melba nor Farrar receive.

Punch magazine (Oct-Nov) recalls the Nielsen season: for *Carmen* (Oct 26), Nielsen as Gilda "like *eau sucree*, was sweet but not powerful... House crowded for *Carmen*. Enthusiastic calls for Mlle. Alice Nielsen". All involved "are to be congratulated upon a genuine success that augurs well for the short season". For *Rigoletto* with Victor Maurel (Nov 14), "to a well-filled house, provoked extraordinary enthusiasm". And "Miss Alice Nielsen sang like a bird; not a nightingale, but some other kind of bird more detached in the matter of sentiment". In *Carmen* (Nov 21), Mlle. Alice Nielsen was "sweet and low" a bit too low sometimes. Chorus good. Campanini and orchestra doing their best. House well filled; smart set conspicuous by absence and audience generally lacking enthusiasm". For Gilda in *Rigoletto*, Nielsen "was quite at her very best; sweet, as on the previous night, but never low; tonight sweet and clear. House well filled". On Friday the king and queen of Portugal had a Covent gala, and Nielsen sang the "saddest Act of *La Bohème*".

After closing Covent, Nielsen sings in a benefit for Woman's Hospital on the 17th, five days later for Princess of Wales.

In California news, Tom Williams loses his appeal in the civil trial (*LA Times* Nov 22). He is ordered to pay damages to journalist Marriott he had repeatedly shot at home before the man's wife.

Alice joins other theatre-women to host a high-society charity reception at St. James Theatre, where they "played to perfection the part of hostesses to a multitude of guests among whom ladies predominated".

Friday the 25th, King and Queen of Portugal receive a special-request concert with patches of *Bohème*, *Tosca*, and *Otello* features Nielsen and other San Carlo cast. Alice, "in the role of the unhappy Mimi, sang in quite her brilliant fashion", reports *Daily Telegraph*. The royals' arrival and departure was cheered by a large crowd waiting outside.

With this success onstage, Nielsen's concert career picks up.

December 12 (*London Times*), she gives a joint concert with Victor Maurel at St. James Hall. Tosti accompanies Nielsen on his songs. Russell's brother Landon Ronald acts as primary pianist; each artist sings a set, then joins in Mozart's *La ci darem* duet. *Times* tells us, "the whole of the scene was easily brought before the hearers' imaginations; in this Miss Alice Nielsen sung in a style very far removed from that of her companion, whose voice, intonation and diction were irreproachable throughout". Nielsen's "best impression was made in Tosti's *Good-bye*, although her vocalization in *Ah! Fors' a lui* was excellent". Famed Maurel, seasoned dramatic baritone "purely lyrical, warmly emotional and exquisitely artistic" in French and Italian songs. This event attracted wide attention. "Signor Tosti accompanied three of his own songs. Miss Alice Nielsen sang in a very delightful fashion, and when she can control her tendency to exaggerate her pianos she will be altogether charming", said *Scotsman.*

So it was. 1904 closes as Alice Nielsen triumphs. She has taken honors at Naples and London. Boldly challenged politically-secure Melba with pals in high places; capable, clever, rich, connected, thwarting.

Intriguingly, at this point Nielsen plans to drop Russell. Then taking a zag of a different direction, signs with Florenz Ziegfeld and Sam Shubert to return to America. Promises an opera debut at the Met with Victor Herbert conducting, plus a national concert tour under her banner.

Several credible managerial candidates crop up.

A trio of women stars: Nielsen, Duse, and Calvé will open the Shuberts' new Waldorf theatre with alternating nights of opera and drama in the spring. The Shuberts chose the Nielsen with Duse and Calvé over Herbert's new extravaganza *Babes in Toyland.* For winter Alice jumps back to Italy.

1905: "A FROLIC FROM THE BEGINNING"

Alice Nielsen's praised Covent Garden success resonates to her American fan base. She's a rootin' tootin' grand opera diva. The girl who scampered stage in boy's clothes delighting people with comedy, song and dance has reinvented. Bassano's photograph of Nielsen as Mimi brings her new look to the American papers during first week of January.

Fireworks in the New Year sky. Alice announces her triumphant return, an autumn concert tour of forty cities. Since March 1901 away from mom and son. Clamor to put Nielsen on the Metropolitan Opera stage begins in earnest; loss of Grau turns stage control to another manager, Conried.

First hop on the Nielsen bandwagon is South Carolina's *Columbia State* January 3rd: "The American Girl in Grand Opera". Mentions Indiana's Theo Dora "now the best Carmen in Spain"; Jane Noria "the St. Louis girl…last year's hit at the Grand Opera in Paris". And "Alice Nielsen; last season her sweet voice captured Italy and she has now taken London. Nothing as yet has been done toward engaging Miss Nielsen…. Mr. Conried has been watching the success of the singer most carefully, and it will not be surprising if the little singer is heard next season in grand opera in the roles she sang at Covent Garden".

Columbia expects the Met to do the right thing.

Alice Nielsen's publicity mill begins in earnest January 21st, *NY Times* reporting she returns October for forty opera concerts in major towns.

George Crager "who is expected to reach New York shortly" is Alice's new manager. Buffalo Bill connection; worked with Alice Nielsen Company. Astonishing life. Runaway at thirteen, lived with Lakoda Sioux and served with US Cavalry. For NY World he visited the Wounded Knee massacre site. By 1892 an interpreter in Buffalo Bill's Wild West Show which spent winters in Scotland during European tours.

Publicity for the concert tour: "At Covent Garden, in London, she sang with great success the prima donna roles in *La Bohème, Traviata, Rigoletto* and the *Barber of Seville*. Miss Nielsen in these operas sang opposite Enrico Caruso, now leading tenor of the Metropolitan".

Producer George Edwardes, in London for *Duchess of Dantzic* at Daly's, "considers Miss Nielsen one of the greatest of the younger prima donnas of the present day, and that her success abroad cannot be overestimated here by those who have heard her in less important [Broadway] roles".

And now the zig-zag. Despite the offer from Covent Garden, Alice's next project directly competes. Sam Shubert wants to open his new Waldorf Theatre. Over Herbert's first project since Nielsen departed, Sam chooses Duse, Calvé and Nielsen with a rising new tenor Constantino. Alternative nights of drama and opera versus a Mother Goose extravaganza with cast of 100 "mostly girls". Shubert brothers, born Lithuania, came to America kids, grew up as the boys from Syracuse. Sam and Levi (Lee) opened Harold Square Theatre in NY in 1900 to challenge Klaw & Erlanger.

Intriguing French diva Calvé lives in an eleventh-century French castle near Aveyron with occult connotations related to Knights Templar. Said Huneker of Calvé, "What a night was that first *Carmen* of hers! She chucked tradition to the winds, also her lingerie. Some of the elder critics are still blushing".

Despite the new manager Crager poised to book Alice's US opera tour, Nielsen in May zigs fatefully by signing the Florenz Ziegfeld for the Shubert Bros. For specific revenue and quality guarantees agrees to an American tour. Fatefully, the novice Russell tags along for a percentage and promises to cast a cast of quality. Ziegfeld and Russell pocket a briberly payoff for her signature. Not in blood but you get the point. Trustworthy Sam Shubert dies a week earlier in a train wreck. Lee Shubert grabs the deal.

May 18, Alice Nielsen of 77 Bedford Court Mansions, London, signs with Florenz Ziegfeld of 86 Fauborg St. Honore, Paris, acting on behalf of the Shuberts. Henry Russell of 118 Long Acre, London, signs. On paper the deal is for US tour "to begin in October or November...for the production of at least fifty concerts" by Nielsen with "five other Artistes to be selected" by Russell. Lee Shubert will manage the tour. Sweetening the payoff for Russell, promise of his own opera concert with top billing as impresario. Plus cash advance bribe. Percentage.

Ziegfeld is a high-risk gambler, Lee Shubert a low-risk producer. Both keep promises badly if at all. Russell is no scruples needs cash now.

Nielsen has enormous theatre experience; Russell nothing.

Nielsen knows the American theatre industry; Russell nothing.

Nielsen valuable to the nation; Russell nothing.

If the situation seems familiar...yes, a small bald man with handlebar mustache awaits in wings for entrance.

For this deal Alice declines a second year on the Covent Garden stage.

Perhaps flattery by the bribed guys guided her choice.

Ziegfeld, that is Lee Shubert, agrees to provide concerts "of a first class order and consistent with the dignity and recognized position" of the star. All cooperation rendered. No ambiguity about matinees: Alice agrees to give "at least three concerts per week", perhaps one more "if her voice is equal to giving a fourth concert". Only Alice decides. Artistic control: choice of the concert material only hers.

Revenue spelled out. Twenty-week tour gives her 20% gross receipts with a guaranteed £66 per show. "Proper vouchers shall be produced" to prove actual theatre receipts. Nielsen is paid nightly. Russell gets 10%, guarantee £33 per show. In exchange, "at his own expense" Russell must pay salaries of five supporting artists plus provide their costumes.

Ziegfeld [Lee Shubert] promises to "pay all expenses" to pay any music royalties and supply "first class orchestra". Will seem ironic. Soon.

Ziegfeld books round-trip passages for the Nielsen ensemble. Ziegfeld grabs unspecified bonus for Nielsen's signature and snakes Russell £1000 ($150,000 today) as an advance bribe. Added to his previous take.

Ziegfeld advances Nielsen only £600 ($92,000 today). Frugality ends if it has continued past the Covent debut. Foggy finances since July 1901.

Day after signing, news reaches America making only a small splash after many false reports. The AP story restates she will skip Broadway this concert tour, "principally because she steadfastly declines all overtures for a comic opera career". At Nielsen's request, Ziegfeld will "secure the services of a prominent violinist as an added feature". She consistently prefers a virtuoso joining her pianist on concerts.

Sailing set for September. Deed done.

Opera-drama season opens Waldorf theatre in May. As they had in Italy, on certain nights Duse acts the drama then next night Nielsen sings the opera arising from it.

Drama starts. As Mirandolina in *La Locandiera,* Duse thrills. "The supreme delight of her whole repertory...the actress has never...played the part better and her hearty enjoyment of it seemed to infect and inspirit the rest of the company".

Opera opens. With *Il Barbiere*, gayety of the nation reaches a peak with spirited Nielsen in motion. Even stodgy *London Times* admits: "frolic from beginning to end. Miss Alice Nielsen has advanced so far on the long journey from musical comedy to comedy in music that her Rosina is quite acceptable; she is at last free from all suggestions of what she formerly thought was comic acting, and though she has not the mischievous charm of a Patti, she realizes most of the business of the part. Her execution of florid passages is not as certain as that of some singers, but the quality of her voice is so agreeable and her training so good that her success is assured. Her pronunciation of Italian and her way of singing recitative have improved very greatly.

"The vocal waltz [inevitably *il Baccio*] which she introduced into the lesson scene was much better sung than *Una voce poco fa*, but on the whole it is many years since the spirit of the work was so fully conveyed".

Nielsen brings antiques to life. Not new American musicals.

In the cast: Signor Ancona "recognized as one of the best Figaro's...and last night he was better than ever, joining with the rest in making the whole opera one frolic from beginning to end".

Next, Mascagni's *L'Amico Fritz*: Nielsen, De Lucia, Ancona, Lucca, Folia, De Cisneros, Sillingardi. *NY Morning Telegraph* (Jun 30) reports: "The real opening attraction of the Shuberts' Waldorf Theatre at Aldwych proved to be Alice Nielsen, who appeared tonight in *L'Amico Frits*. The American singer achieved a genuine triumph. She was enthusiastically greeted by an immense audience, including one member of the royal family, who occupied the royal box".

Chicago Tribune (Jun 4): "Young American soprano, Alice Nielsen, who made her debut most successful in this country some years ago in comic opera. Her embodiment of the artless maiden is described by London critics as refined and artistic. She gets a big share of the applause, one of the successes of the evening being her duet with Sig. de Lucia as Fritz in the cherry tree scene". In passing, *Tribune* reveals Alice's friend Maxine Elliott attracts big crowds "at the Savoy".

London Times has warm praise. *L'Amico Fritz*, "revived last night at the Waldorf Theatre with an extreme good cast, who gave a wholly admirable performance of it. Miss Alice Nielsen, a capital Suzel, whose voice seems fuller and riper than before, but who still requires too much prompting, made a splendid effect with the best part of the opera—the opening of the second act".

Stage management: "Evening was dragged out unduly by waits between the acts which are far too long".

By *Don Pasquale, London Times* (Jun 5) is won over: "Mlle. Alice Nielsen sang wonderfully well". Opera fun wins. Nielsen brings gayety to the heart of a once-chill critic: "There is no doubt...such an opera as this goes with far more real fun on a smaller stage than that of Covent Garden". The Act 2 quartet repeated "in answer to uproarious applause". And *Pall Mall* opines of Alice, "Interesting to mark the career of the singer, who has steadily improved...."

London Times praises *La Somnambula*, "As too often presented, even when stars are in the cast, the older operas strike the unprejudiced hearer not only as lacking all dramatic cohesion, but as failing to amuse or interest even those who take part in them. At the Waldorf Theatre, where *La Somnambula* was revived on Saturday night, not only did the principals perform their parts with conviction as well as with vocal skill, but every member of the chorus behaved as if the piece meant something to each one.... It was no longer difficult to realize the enthusiasm which these works must have created at the time of their first production, when there was a good deal beside the mellifluous singing to interest the spectators".

Times mentions "old Italian operas" are fun again with the Nielsen ensemble and perhaps if this continues, "the public will, we fear, turn from the narrow way of Wagnerian drama into the primrose path of the bel canto, and all the reforms will have to be done over again...."

Saturday June 10, *London Times:* "the immense superiority of a good operatic ensemble over what used to be called a 'star' performance was amply proved, if proof were wanted, in the representation of *Il Barbiere* last night". Once again, "The opera was one frolic from beginning to end".

Ensemble has the gala feel: "The greatest success of the whole, where all was good, was the irresistibly comic acting of Signori Pini-Corsi and Arimondi as a diminutive Bartolo and a gigantic Basillo respectively. Those parts can surely never have been better played, although a constant tremolo spoils the former's singing of sustained passages, and the latter has hardly enough power for the famous *Calunnia* song".

Nielsen-Duse at Waldorf gather keen praise. Calvé, who must drop out with a cold but will join Alice on the voyage with coaching, speaks in her memoirs of shyly stalking Duse; wishes to be near yet not speak. Brought near her idol by Nielsen, Calvé says nothing or of Alice.

Foster Hirsch claims in biography *Boys From Syracuse* (1998), "Sam signed a contract with British manager [no mention of key Ziegfeld] Henry Russell for what may well have been the most illustrious of all Shubert openings: a season of split weeks of grand opera...." Hirsch skips the competent women entirely organizing and performing this and absurdly pimps pittance-poor, zero-experienced remora as faux impresario, "a man after Sam's own heart" who "had challenged Covent Garden's monopoly in opera by securing the exclusive rights to a few operas and opera divas".

We must emphasize how badly the later decades distort things. Hirsch badly overstates what society throat masseuse Russell accomplished. And Hirsh notes Nielsen's critical role yet omits her name. Hirsch and Eaton, typical of their decades, omit or belittle.

Hirsch continues, "Sam was concerned...powerful Covent Garden management would undermine Russell, and they may well have done so since neither grand opera nor Duse turned a profit for the Shuberts".

Of course, Sam has died before Waldorf opens. Reviewers recount a full house. Lee Shubert notorious for hiding profits. Yet sponsor *Daily Mail* withdrew support within four days "after complaints from Henry Higgins' Covent Garden of competition. "Duse was half empty" and opera sales "fell to zero" suggests Russell. Reviews contradict sparse attendance. *Daily Mail*'s owner would fire a critic for Melba. Duse created the event.

Duse strongly influences Nielsen and Calvé as artists. Calvé (1858-1942) in *My Life* (1922) speaks of Duse's "wisdom and grace. I cannot see her upon the stage without being profoundly moved. Hers was the spark that set my fires alight. Her art, simple, human, passionately sincere, was a revelation to me. It broke down the false and conventional standards of lyric expression to which I had become accustomed. She taught me to appreciate sincerity in art, a sincerity which in her case went to the length of being unwilling to make up for the stage". Calvé had trailed Duse "through Italy one summer, going from town to town where she was playing, attending each performance and sometimes watching for her at the stage door or in the lobby of her hotel. I never wished to approach my divinity. I wanted her to remain exalted, remote, inaccessible".

Oddly silent on the Waldorf season or Nielsen, Calvé adds that "years later...when we were both touring in America, I learned to know her well and to appreciate deeply her great qualities of mind and heart". An evening with Oscar Wilde and Paul Verlaine at Grey's house years earlier is told in detail. Like Alice, Calvé struggled with poverty in youth. Alice later speaks freely of Duse, skips Calvé. Biographers of Duse ignore Nielsen.

During 1901-05 Duse brings Nielsen to Paris from Milan, writing to Russell, "Please invite the little one in my name, because I want to hear her beautiful voice. It is a force which helps one to dream and protects from life's daily realities". Recognizing poor finances, Duse adds, "I enclose first-class train fare from Milan to Paris. I wish I could send her more".

Duse a decade later writes, "I render my thanks to you for having given me the opportunity of knowing N [Alice Nielsen]. No woman is as pure as N—no one so loyal, no one so faithful. To have been able to understand and know so complete a woman, I thank you and I beg you to like me also, not as much as N, but together with N. I am neither as pure, nor as loyal, nor as faithful as N, but I possess a small part of that light—this is if my soul has properly understood it—always yours. Eleanor Duse, Hotel Bristol, Rome" (Apr '14).

July 22nd after parties, recitals and galas, Alice leaves London to prepare for her US tour. Absence will result in glimpses: 1907, "Lady Vocalist Averts Panic" in Chicago theatre; 1908, "Alice Nielsen "received a bouquet from an unknown admirer with a tiny Japanese spaniel nestled within". In 1910 she returns to Promenade Concerts, and to Covent 1913.

During summer, California's Malcom Frank interviews Alice Nielsen for Southern Pacific railroad's *Sunset Magazine*. Nielsen has lived in private trains during many national tours. Hearing Frank has arrived from San Francisco, Nielsen sends for him. Frank met "Mlle. Alice Nielsen (for so she is featured in the Waldorf theatre program) in her charming apartment in Bedford Court Mansions" located in the fashionable Bloomsbury section.

With keen eyes, the 'Frisco man describes clothes and setting. "A magenta suit, with a wicked little bolero jacket, the reveres trimmed in embroidered white silk, was lying on the divan. In the room were a grand an upright piano; scores of *Bohème, Don Pasquale* and *Il Barbiere* were lying open on chairs and table; and to complete the confusion, a rakish-looking little hat of leghorn set off by a wreath of Royal Anne cherries, set roguishly on an open score of *La Fille del Regimente* on the piano. The little diva sat where the twilight played upon her expressive face. She had written me a characteristic little note, saying she had news for me", Frank says of a meditative Nielsen who had followed her usual pattern of contacting the press directly.

Nielsen: "California! It seems a dream. How often during the three years of striving which have passed since seeing its beautiful landscapes, have I tried to conjure it before me! It has been only while in Italy that I've fairly succeeded, for that is the only country on earth comparable with California. You see, I had always the idea that success awaited me in grand opera, and when I received the hallmark of London approbation in comic opera, I felt I had reached the crossroads".

Graceful diva skips Williams & Perley evermore as irrelevant.

"It meant work and the loss of a large sum of money than most people earn in a lifetime; but I quickly made up my mind and left for Italy, where I was buried for years. Nothing but study and exercise, eating and sleeping". Far change from studing the score sailing to Japan.

"And", Frank gently corrects her, "every detail of your two years' work and sacrifice shows".

"Yes. I have made a success".

Frank observes, "She sighed her profound satisfaction. It was even more forcible though not more honest than her words had been, for Alice Nielsen has silenced the critics by the perfection of her singing and acting, both at Covent Garden and at the Waldorf theatre in the Strand, where she is one English-speaking artiste in an all-Italian cast in modern Italian opera which alternates with the great Italian tragedienne Eleonora Duse in delighting the London playgoer".

Alice reveals she was persuaded to abandon Covent Garden by Russell the poser. Alice provides her clinging vine a fig leaf: "Miss Nielsen was offered a renewal of her last year's contract in the present season of royal opera at Covent Garden, but the Waldorf had just been completed and she wisely chose making her reappearance here during its opening season".

Abandoned Covent prowess as favor for a false friend. Instead of singing at Covent with Caruso, surrenders the stage to Melba. Higgins is a proven manager with talent and resources at Covent. Novice Russell has none. If Nielsen had rejoined Covent she would have spared herself what happens next in New York. Yet Russell pocketed his Lee Shubert bribes....

Waldorf performances were acclaimed, "As Rosina in *Il Barbiere de Siviglia* and Norina in *Don Pasquale*, Miss Nielsen is beyond praise", says Frank. "And this speaks volumes for her art, for in the cast appear the names of De Lucia and Aneona, who created the roles of Canio and Tonio on the occasion of the first performance of Leoncavallo's *Il Pagliacci*. Pini-Corsi, the greatest of Italian bassos comico, is also in the aggregation".

Alice tells Frank, "And now for the news. I cannot give you the minutest details today, as things are not fully settled, but I am going to America in November". She suggests, or hopes, "We open in New York, under Ziegfeld's management with Henry Russell as Impresario".

Starts the swift slide to dismay within a decade. Ziegfeld's fatal flaws are no secret to her set. Busily beds and promotes Anna Held's flirty musicals. Lillian Russell pal Diamond Jim had loaned Ziegfeld loot to sign Held. When Ziegfeld abandons Held, Lillian helps her. When Held dies, Lillian buries her.

And Alice Nielsen gazes westward to a great San Francisco opening; she realizes the thrill for Tivoli audiences. She has been promised, "It will be my own company. And will include Pini-Corsi and the best Italian talent obtainable. We hope to be in San Francisco in the spring of 1906. I anticipate that my opening night in the home city will be the happiest in my stage career".

Frank replies, "You will have to make a speech and order a van to remove the flowers". Nielsen thrills, "This excited the risibilities of the prima donna".

Her June hope is a triumphant 1905 North American tour. Promised a repertory group with "stars such as this very Pini-Corsi offering *La Bohème, Don Pasquale, Il Barbiere de Siviglia* and *La Fille Del Regimente*".

San Francisco's Tivoli would help, music director Paul Steindorf (fired from the Alice Nielsen Company in 1901 by Williams & Perley). Frank returns to California with this news.

The Waldorf season has connected Alice Nielsen onstage with the Basque tenor recommended by Caruso, Florencio Constantino, making a Covent Garden debut as Caruso's alternate. Joins Alice for *Pagliacci* and *Cavalleria Rusticana*. He recorded disks for Edison's National Phonograph Company in London summer 1905, Nielsen alas did not.

Constantino inherits a vibrant folk music culture from Basque country, at twenty relocating to Argentina to avoid a Spanish draft. His Argentine home, Bragado, reports "Florencio did not know Conservatories, nor masters of music" (2008). Worked in mines as child, factories at twelve, locomotive mechanic at fifteen; three years in Spain's navy until 1889, deserting with fiancé Luisa Arrigorriag to Argentina where he joins the Radical Civic Union in the 1890 Revolution. With four children, he sings in church and around. Quick witted, Constantino was famed for a song-and-guitar duel with "legendary *payador* Gabino Ezeiza". *Payadors* cleverly improvise lyrics to songs to compete. "He went from running a threshing machine on the pampa to being launched in 1895 as a tenor by a leading Italian voice teacher", relates John Rosselli (1990). Strong vocal and acting skill swiftly lift the singer from Buenos Aires to the great opera houses across Europe from Madrid to Russia.

Constantino's first biographer Aguado wrongly equates Henry Russell with Hammerstein as "two of the great impresarios". When the smoke gets in your eyes. Difficult to dismiss the toxic fog. Boston Opera his peak of notoriety failed by his frauds.

Duse and Nielsen created the Waldorf event. They gave Russell a job as poseur. Duse produced her own projects. The program ends in June. Just after the Waldorf and Covent season close, Nielsen and Caruso sing at the Foreign Press Club benefit. They coordinate galas.

Whatever happens around her, by fall 1905 Alice Nielsen is determined to return to America and sing her way to San Francisco where certain success awaits. Unless Chicago gets there first. The star who gave up stardom to sing what she really wanted hopes to weave a new career.

In America her challenges become a series of almost-devastating surprises. So it all depends on her. Her art again will create success over many obstacles. Only she could overturn what happens next.

Only she could sing her way out. Makes Alice Nielsen great.

RETURN TO AMERICA: AMBUSH

Sponsored by Lee Shubert, guided by Ziegfeld, accompanied by Russell, Alice Nielsen sails back to America in September, sanguine expectations of superb debut with Herbert conducting at the Metropolitan. After all, she has a contract saying so. Steaming across the Atlantic, Nielsen had not yet reached NYC when Ziegfeld gambles away the entire budget at a French casino. Or at least that's his story. Things get stranger. Omens bad. Ziegfeld often acts as agent for Lee Shubert who also paid to snare Anna Held whose concept for *Follies* makes Ziegfeld a fortune; she gets dumped. Lee wants Nielsen working in the gold mine of profitable Broadway never grand opera. Last not least, dastardly Perley works with Lee. These men share an opportunistic outlook unscrupulous to women as does Ziegfeld, Russell. Might say as we say, if they think they can get away with it.

Arty poses of vain managers be damned, artists do the artwork.

Alice's failure to pick trustable aides hampers her career. Yet each had some moments of usefulness until the success corrupted.

Alice Nielsen in Europe co-stars with Duse. A merry-go-round of press reports appear. Lee Shubert repeatedly assigns Nielsen to the 9th rung of *Crook* and she repeatedly says she ain't gonna.

She sails because San Francisco awaits her.

This year starting, London's society voice masseuse held no place in the future of Alice Nielsen's career. He isn't mentioned when *NY Times* reports June 3: Ziegfeld, "the husband of Anna Held, is in London where he has secured Alice Nielsen". Contract signed two weeks earlier May 18.

Upon signature the Lee Shubert bait-and-switch begins.

June 24, *NY Times* reports Alice returns "not as one of the prima donnas of the [non-existent] Henry Russell Grand Opera Company...but at the head of an organization bearing her name". To "show you Perley" Alice plans to open in his hometown Washington and tour with "one and two-act standard operas as *Cavalleria Rusticana*".

Aye, tear that tattered Herbert down, Alice. She will promote Pietro Mascagni's 1890's short, small-cast opera opening at dawn in a Sicilian village Easter Sunday 1880. Tragedy follows seventy-five minutes for cast of five plus village chorus. *NY Times* confirms Lee Shubert has baited Henry Russell with a self-named "Grand Opera Company" coming 'round the Manhattan when it comes to the 1,260-seat Lyric Theatre at West 42nd constructed by Reginald DeKoven with *Robin Hood* cash leased to Lee.

That Nielsen drops Russell is confirmed July 2nd by *San Francisco Call*, saying Alice returns, not with "Henry Russell Grand Opera Company...but at the head of an organization bearing her name". Recounts her pilgrim progress: "today she is a sensational success of the grand opera season in London".

Within days, Nielsen's program reverses to Broadway and back again.

Ziegfeld "has abandoned the idea of presenting Miss Nielsen in concerts and has persuaded the prima donna that considerable glory and more money await her in opera comique" says *NY Morning Telegraph* (Jul 7). Her rebuttal: "Prominent among the musical attractions this coming season will be Miss Alice Nielsen the American soprano..". who "has decided to devote her time to the higher class of work".

Pronouncements and denials volley across the Atlantic all summer.

Battle lines drawn. Rumors fly. Alice must suspect any promises of a first-class New York debut and national tour are at serious risk. When the diva's resolve does not falter, Lee Shubert realizes Ziegfeld has failed. Bribe of this "Russell Opera Company" concert won't happen.

Alice Nielsen has been Russell's livelihood—and a kind of fame—the last four years. When Lee Shubert declines to puff him as impresario for a day, he has nowhere to go except obscurity. Shubert controls budgets and bookings. If he does not wish Nielsen to succeed in less-profitable operas, he knows how to vex her at every turn. Russell has no profit potential: only an annoyance, not two percent a Ziegfeld.

Press releases from Shubert (Perley is staging a musical for Shubert) drastically downsize Alice's reception. Slated repertoire of operas dwindle to "operatic concerts, assisted by a quartet of eminent vocalists and other artists. The first half of the program will be of the standard concert style, but part second will consist of grand or English opera excerpts or acts with or without costumes and scenery, as desired".

Nielsen relies on San Francisco. Just follow the yellow brick concert road winding toward the magic city rising above the fog.

Telegraph reports, "In addition to singing with her company, Miss Nielsen is to do regular concert work with the various clubs, orchestras and societies and in private musicales, the arrangements for both being made by HG Snow of NYC". Snow, great choice. Robert Grau's *Business Man in the Entertainment World* (1910) lists Snow among "musical agents who control many attractions and are influential" with "vast experience in the routing of musical stars, his most recent activity being in behalf of Oscar Hammerstein in the conduct of the Tetrazzini concert tour".

Given competence, within three years Alice's Snow-arranged concert tours will far outpace her opera revenues. Americans love her art songs.

Each time Shubert announces her going to Broadway, Nielsen rebukes.

July 7th Will McConnell of *NY Morning Telegraph* writes from London of "Alice Nielsen's Real Plans. So much that is grossly inaccurate has been written about Alice Nielsen's forthcoming visit, and so much more that is willfully false has been issued concerning the prima donna's plans, that the public at large has absolutely no means of knowing whether she will appear in grand opera, comic opera or on the lecture platform. So let us set the matter straight once and for all: Miss Nielsen will come to NY in October under the personal management of Henry Russell. F. Ziegfeld Jr. and Messrs. Shubert will also have a substantial interest in her contract".

McConnell reconfirms Russell has definitely lost his promised opera company debut in NYC. Outs as impresario, relegated to agent; again living on percent of Nielsen's income (since four years) plus that hefty advance.

Downsized cast too. No Waldorf stars who bring gayety to the nation, Russell hires cheap "a company of six or eight" with "short scenes from several English and grand operas...but nothing approaching a regular production will be attempted at the outset". Even so, concerts are planned for NY and Philadelphia "in conjunction with one of the big symphony orchestras". "Meanwhile", Russell, totally unknown in America, "will devote himself to a series of lectures on the subject of grand opera and vocal culture". Does not. Before July ends, Nielsen is again slated "for a few weeks in a revival of an English opera...." Does not.

Into this burlesque, apparition Max Desci finds an idiot at *NY Times* and tells a tale (Jul 25) that his supposed bill—now $2000—from days of yore "when she was a struggling and aspiring tot in the Abattoir City. She used to visit his voice-cultivating parlor in a gingham gown. He would close all the doors and windows to keep from being dispossessed for teaching her to sing". Desci claims vocal training was "a necessity in her life" and the law allows a person to provide such necessities "and bring a just bill when the child matured". *Times* seems doubtful but gives coverage: "While it is extremely unique that a music teacher should maintain in the Supreme Court that his lessons to a child...were acts of 'necessity', this is the contention of Prof. Desci and he has served papers on Miss Nielsen in a suit for $2000. He is represented by Ignatius Welter, and the singer's affairs are looked after by Howe and Hummel. The papers were served upon her before she left...and the moment she puts her foot on American soil the complaint will be pressed to the end by Mr. Weltner".

Desci reappears, demon disappears. Ex-husband Ben Nentwig dies August 20th, reports *KC Star*. Pictured in tuxedo with pince-nez and handlebar mustache, "not only a master of the organ, but he played nearly all string instruments and understood the theory of music and thorough harmony far better than the average man in his profession". Funeral at St. Patrick's. Violence against his wife are details of his obit which receives national press due only to her success. *Chanticlere* had tested "the temper of Nentwig and his wife and caused a quarrel". No mention of her intent to tour with the show, or Pryor; yet "he never afterward could be induced to talk about the opera. He hated it.

Of Nielsen he had told friends, "'that is a closed chapter. I helped her, and she left me. I shall never see her again.' Father James Phelan of St. John's...tried again and again to reunite the parted husband and wife, without avail". *Washington Post* reports, "unruly tempers led to a separation. When the singer visited Kansas City at the head of her own opera troupe...the choir of St. Patrick's...turned out to welcome their old colleague, but Nentwig refused to hear her sing".

Nielsen vs. Shubert publicity ping-pong crazily continues. September 8th (*NY Times*), Shubert press agent Channing Pollock wittily announces "advertising for the tour of Alice Nielsen will not begin until November". He brilliantly sends Alice's name across the nation with news he cannot announce her tour yet. Pollock suggests he cannot do because he lacks a summer picture of the singer and "no dramatic editor sweltering through the month of August will consent to print the picture of a lady in furs...".

Pollack (1880-1946), a strong Nielsen fan since 1896, brags on his lies in *Footlights Fore And Aft* (1911) sporting a chapter *People I've Lied About*. He had invented a quote "no brunette could be beautiful" which got play for decades. He likes that kind of thing. Two days after Pollock tells the press, yes we got no press release, he solemnly pitches Alice Nielsen into a drama *The Secret Orchard* based on a novel by Vernon and Irene Castle (adapted for stage by Channing Pollock). In *Orchard* an ignoble nobleman is shot by the American naval officer who forgives the heroine's shameful past. *Orchard*, never mentioned again with Nielsen, got produced for 32 Broadway performances and becomes a 1915 Cecil DeMille film directed by Frank Reicher who acted in *King Kong*. Nielsen would not go from stage to silent screen; she prefers concerts. Coincidently, a novel by Vernon and Irene Castle adapted by Belasco became Nielsen's final musical.

September, Jules Grau dies—Alice's first theatre job which he never was. *Charlotte Observer* describes Jules as "first in this country to bring out the original [pirated] production of *The Mikado*". Siblings Maurice and Robert have been "interested in the promotion of opera houses for the last 20 years" (Se 11).

Signaling confusion, Alice Nielsen postpones American arrival from September to November. Her "coming American tour will be managed by Lee Shubert...under the direction of Samuel F. Kingston, Jr". who works for Ziegfeld and will manage *Ziegfeld Follies*. Kingston in 1923 produces a musical *Kid Boots* about Palm Springs golf, music by Harry Tierney (1891-

1965) which runs 489 performances with Eddie Cantor, joined in the 1926 silent film by Clara Bow dated by the author's grandfather. *Kid Boots* features the song *Let's Do and Say We Didn't.*

Late September, Alice Nielsen announces her intent to sail for New York October 13th on White Star *Celtic*. Despite Ziegfeld-Shubert disasters, she announces her US opera debut as Washington, November 1. In the mix of the moment the re-attached Russell grabs a few cheap singers from Milano and they join the tour. He at least plays piano.

Docking in NYC, he describes his plight, "I had just enough left to pay my debts and provide the fares for the company's return to Milan. My personal position was not amusing as I sat alone in my office signing cheques the day after the last performance". Far after the fact, he reveals that by June "I had scarcely enough left to maintain my family for two months. Although I had no hesitation in asking my friends for financial help for an artistic scheme, I was horrified at the thought of having to borrow to keep body and soul together. To return to teaching was out of the question as far as I was concerned".

Taking cash from Ziegfeld to betray Nielsen, he has met wrath of Lee Shubert when Alice refuses the Broadway scheme. Now Nielsen is again vital to any hopes to evade the dreaded "return to teaching". As he spins it, "There is a peculiar fascination in theatrical management which only those who have experienced it can understand. In spite of the setback I had received, I felt instinctively that my theatrical career had not come to an end". So slithers his flattering.

Two decades later, remora Russell speaks about the star who saved him repeatedly from ruin, brought him to America, promoted him beyond sense, help himself to her money: "One of the singers who had taken part in the Waldorf experiment was Alice Nielsen, a young American with a pretty voice and an attractive stage presence. She had made a reputation in the United States that entitled her to be called 'The Queen of Comic Opera.' She had courageously abandoned this lucrative métier in the hope of gaining recognition in more serious work...."

Russell's sly memoir is queerly titled *The Passing Show* (1926) as if he dind't hate music theatre. By the way, George Lederer's 1894 *The Passing Show* ran 145 times performances at Casino Theatre. Set in the Gardens of Howkumyeso, Dawdle Club, Herald Square, and a Palace of Justice, the Ludwig Englander score features *Round the Operas in 20 Minutes* which give Mascagni, Verdi, Bizet, and Gounod a spin. Lederer's next show *Belle of NY* had occupied Shaftesbury before *Fortune Teller*. Lederer's "passing" success is recycled as *The Passing Show* series 1912-1921, music mostly by Sigmund Romberg with songs *Bohemian Rag* and *Good Ol' Levee Days*.

Russell's claim to memoir rises, like Perley, from his connection with the star he betrayed. Adding insult to injuries, he claims she "made a favorable impression on the London public without in any way causing a sensation". Oh, Nielsen caused quite a sensation. Read the reviews.

And we know Convent Garden cast Alice over Melba for Mozart; and manager Higgins had offered a second year's contract. Practical proof of causing a sensation. Doubtless Alice had abandoned Covent, and a certain remora would benefit by her lost opportunity. Truly, Nielsen had a sensational year singing Mozart and Puccini at Covent Garden. Crazily, Alice Nielsen gave up Covent; and also San Carlo in likelihood.

"The Shuberts were anxious to get her back in America, as she was what was known in theatrical slang as 'a money maker. The Shuberts knew she had signed a contract with me and that they could only get her for musical comedy with my permission". Rather like the use of Perley to block the marriage offer from Williams. And like Perley, taking cash and promises Russell agrees to be bribed. This year Alice has protected herself. Shubert's contract for her return states that any performances must be mutually agreed. Furthermore, she is not limited from making other contracts. Russell is a very constrained faux impresario; he cannot dictate.

Accuracy was not his puffery. Agent's fee from Alice is only financial lifeline. Flings "hybrid" at the rising Broadway arts: "They [Lee Shubert] were also aware of my aversion to this hybrid form of recreation and for this reason asked me whether I knew of an opera which would be suitable to Alice's talent and not too expensive to mount and cast". Writes her out of story. Hides plan to drop him. Hides the lure Lee let dangle and drop.

Claims he "proposed Rossini's masterpiece *The Barber of Seville*. This, they feared, would be too costly on account of the large cast it called for. As a last hope I substituted Donizetti's *Don Pasquale*, and they reluctantly accepted this charming little work". Brazenly blames Shubert for his cheap cast: "They offered me [Alice Nielsen!] a contract for the United States, but the amount they agreed to pay was so small [he hides his £1000 ($150,000 today)] that I was obliged to engage the cheapest singers I could find in Italy, which of course, meant that the company was both inexperienced and immature". Ziegfeld is spun as afterthought, "When the contracts were completed, I was informed that Mr. Flo Ziegfeld was to be a partner in the undertaking". In truth Russell signs Ziegfeld's contract, no other exists in the Shubert Archives. Closes his bizarre Waldorf chapter, "I accepted Shuberts' proposal to go to America". And beyond bizrre, "Thus ended my attempt to make London a great operatic center. Oh! how the warnings of Don Prospero and Lord Northcliffe came back in my hours of discouragement and depression!"

Obscure voice coach ingratiates a first-class star. Since 1901 she has been his paycheck. In 1905 plans to abandon her Eurotrash. Setting the scene in fall 1905: Nielsen famous and set for San Francisco, remora broke, Ziegfeld gambling heavily, Lee Shubert at the NYC helm.

Out of the blue of the western sky, *Chicago Tribune* September 24th reports "from NY comes the statement that Alice Nielsen will begin her concert tour of the country here in Chicago, October 14 is mentioned as the date". Not October, not Chicago, *NY Times* corrects (Se 27): "Alice Nielsen sails from England on October 18 and will begin her American season in Washington November 1st. Her present tour which is under the direction of the Shuberts, will cover the large cities of the country".

Specifics: "Miss Nielsen's repertoire will include *Don Pasquale, Crispino e la Comare, Il Barbiere di Siviglia, L'Elsire d'Amore* and acts from *Carmen, Faust, Lucia, Martha* and *Cavalleria Rusticana*".

Times' straight scoop comes from Ziegfeld's own Samuel Kingston, who the *Telegraph's* Renold Wolf saw arrive "yesterday from Paris on the steamer Der Grosse Kurfurst" to start a season of grand opera with Alice Nielsen now "all by herself". Concert versions, cast of six, nix chorus, shall render principal numbers from *Don Pasquale, Barber of Seville* and *L'Elsire d'Amore*. Nielsen will "indulge in snatches from *Carmen, Faust, Lucia, Martha, La Somnambula* and perhaps *I Pagliacci* and *Cavalleria Rusticana*. The big scenic and ensemble effects sought by grand opera producers are not to be attempted. Like the play in dramatic productions, the music is the thing in this project". A barren stage with a few faded property trees.

No Met gala with Herbert.

"Henry Russell has undertaken the task of developing a supporting sextet of principals whose vocal qualifications will leave no cause for regrets at the absence of the generally cumbersome chorus". Cause for regrets. Later liar liar blames Shubert for sorry cast the swine cast.

Near departure Alice selects a single simple show, *Pasquale*. The plan to go separate ways has been lost in Lee Shubert's reshuffle. Russell needs her utterly, she needs him slightly. Pact of mutual convenience. People will notice, Alice knows, she left 1901 NYC starring in the best production possible with original music with a hundred people in the company. Now her return debut will be cheaply bad at best. Hints her bravery.

"If Miss Nielsen but knew it, she is about to undergo the supreme test of her career. She left America the most popular comic opera soprano in the country. General lamentation followed her across the Atlantic to Italy. The majority of her admirers thought her quest for the coy and reluctant glory of grand opera, when she was already the acknowledged queen of opera comique, to be rank folly. Miss Nielsen persevered...still some were skeptical. There came another and yet another appearance, and on each occasion tributes of praise poured in with convincing regularity".

Nielsen's status is American hero: "Patriotic Americans have come to regard the former star of *The Fortune Teller* and *The Singing Girl* as the equal of any of the imported songbirds. The plane of comparison has been set high, and at her metropolitan debut she will face as critical a crowd of Missourians as ever gathered along Broadway". Bad as it is gets worse.

By contract, Alice could anticipate orchestra concerts in Philadelphia and NYC. Expects the quality of London. In that scenario her relations with Herbert would be restored. His ambition to conduct the Met's NY Philharmonic promoted. Reliable HG Snow will book her national tour. Independent of Shubert—and Western independence is a crucial element of Nielsen's impact—she knows San Francisco prepares a grand reunion for her at Tivoli with trustworthy Steindorf.

Alice also has important friends with plans for her in New Orleans.

Despite Ziegfeld-Shubert obstacles, Nielsen knows American success is within reach. Success at Covent and in Italy has confidently proved her merit. Three months after the Waldorf season, Alice Nielsen leaves Europe for America. Calvé joins her voyage. Alice boards *Celtic* expecting great things. Whatever else, her opening debut conceret at the Met Opera reuniting her with Victor Herbert will be a American cultural milestone.

While her ship is out to sea NY papers report Nielsen will give two NY performances at the Shubert's Casino Theatre and one orchestra concert "with Victor Herbert" at some unspecified location, not the Met. During the voyage, Ziegfeld in France has lost her budget gambling.

Victor Herbert sends a Marconigram of welcome home. Mom, son and siblings await. Nielsen's 1905 summer ends. Her first husband has died, ex-fiancé Williams convicted of shooting an unarmed journalist. America's singing star survived a spell of poverty to master Italian grand opera with a patron or two. Got engaged a bit. Triumphed in Italy and England. Spent time with Duse, met aristocrats, theatre and musical talents. Performed at many concerts, parties, events. Absorbed Italian, French, and a complex new vocal repertoire. Alice Nielsen has changed. America's beloved singing star voyages home after four years away.

TROUBLED NYC DEBUT

Sunday October 22, 1905, Alice Nielsen reaches NYC on the White Star *Celtic*. Calvé travels with her; a star known for flirting with girls. Waiting at the dock are Victor Herbert, Enrico Caruso, and the press. Scheduled to attend Herbert's Sunday Concert that very night; however with the loss of his gala concert at the Met, Alice declines to sing. She takes apartments in Hotel Astor on Times Square and immediately starts for Harlem to meet Sarah and Bennie, a young man of fifteen after four years apart. Siblings Hortense, Erasmus, Julia have moved to NYC area.

"Her enthusiasm over getting back home is a joy to the beholder", says *NY Times* meeting Nielsen that night (Oct 22).

"I cannot begin to say how glad I am to return. I am happier than I can say over my success abroad, but after all I am an American girl and when I drove to Harlem today to see my mother, whom I had not seen since my departure, I was fairly bubbling over with happiness".

NY Times reports the star is "billed for a five months' operatic concert tour of the United States, which will give her old friends an opportunity to hear her in new roles". Nielsen continues with optimism, "I have high hopes of my coming tour. From what I am told, the outlook is very encouraging". Promoting her new-learned repertoire, she advocates opera in native language libretti. "Before I went to London I had sung a few grand opera roles in English. Singing in the Italian language is ever so much better. Italian is really the language of music. It helps the voice to be natural. There are no jarring consonants. It is all liquid melody".

Tosses egg at Broadway: "I am wholly devoted to grand opera. Of course it is a harder mistress than comic opera...." Well, perhaps.

Broadway's sing-and-dance star speaks: "For when I was singing here before, if my voice was a little out of gear, I could gloss it over. In grand opera, the voice is everything".

Recounts her pilgrim's progress. The NYC paper, free of London obligations, sees fit to print the Melba jab. At Covent Garden, "Miss Nielsen took Melba's place and sang all her roles". Such statements reach London, inevitably motivate Melba to ever-greater efforts to squash the upstart.

Times reminds readers that Calvé and Nielsen alternated at Waldorf with "Miss Nielsen singing all the principal roles of the lighter operas". Her last British appearance is revealed as a concert with Edgar Elgar and "the Liverpool Philharmonic society about two weeks ago". Losing no time over loss of her proper NYC debut with Herbert at Met Opera, or the rest of the Ziegfeld follies, Alice Nielsen plans to tour hop-skip by train "for San Francisco next week".

Along the way the remora shall "lecture on voice production in the cities where Miss Nielsen sings. His lectures will be under the direction of the Shuberts". He never gives the lectures; has Nielsen announce in each town he will hear singers as audition for cash. As her ambitious fans flock to emulate her skill, he solicits spare change.

No major promises Nielsen had signed for were kept. Ziegfeld had lost her budget at roulette what he had of it; sued for his season's $20,000 gambling debts by "Biarritz, gaming house proprietor" (*NY Times,* May 27 1909). Gambling house Biarritz, named for the Basque town, had opened 1901. Continues today; resort with casino. Ziegfeld's losses challenge his wife Anna Held; under French law Biarritz could seize her property to pay husband's debt. To keep Biarritz at bay, Held pleads for mercy in open letters about hubby's "unfortunate gambling experiences...at your place where he lost millions of francs...practically forced into bankruptcy. He is doing the best he can...can't get blood out of a stone...." And Biarritz blandly publishes Ziegfeld's letters promising to pay.

If Alice had hopes, Ziegfeld's embezzlement of her budget is fatal. Of course, Lee Shubert only wishes to trap her into musicals.

NY Times isn't alone waiting to meet her. *Philadelphia Inquirer* reports: "Alice Nielsen back covered with honor. She returns a full-fledged grand opera prima donna, bringing the record of successes won in England and on the Continent, some of her greatest triumphs having been attained in Mme. Melba's roles at Covent Garden. With the assistance of a group of capable Italian artists, she is to make a long concert tour this season, the programs consisting of complete scenes from the operas in her repertoire.

"When seen, Miss Nielsen appeared as pretty and sprightly as ever".

"It seems so good to get back, and to feel prepared for bigger things than I have ever done at home before", Nielsen tells Philadelphia fans. She touts time with stars: Mimi to Caruso's Rodolfo in *Bohème*, Micaela to his Don Jose in *Carmen*, and of course of as Gilda in *Rigoletto* with Maurel.

Instead of departing instantly for San Francisco for success, Nielsen's concert tour starts in Washington DC "first week in November".

Calvé had, as we say, sailed along. *NY World's* Paul West arrives Oct 28th for an interview to find Calvé coaching Alice in French repertoire. La Duse, La Nielsen, Calvé: formidable talents who know many many people.

Artists shape artists. Nielsen and Calvé have costarred with "singing actor" Victor Maurel. Calvé—student of Marchesi—recalls that Maurel's "lessons in lyric declamation... greatly influenced my artistic career.... His dramatic gift was so extraordinary that it dominated the minds of those who saw him". His voice "unusual quality, full of colour and exceptionally expressive". Maurel's best role was Mozart's *Don Giovanni, Deh vieni alla fenestra,* "a marvel of lightness and grace. His diction was always exquisite and enchanting". Not unrelated, Maurel in Paris also directed *Theatre des Italiens.* Of course, Calvé knew Franz List: "He alone, with his incredible force, was as mighty as a whole orchestra". During a musical evening at Marchesi's place in Paris she heard List accompany Madame Krauss in the *Erlkönig*: magnetic. Calvé says of Duse, "Her art, simple, human, passionately sincere, was a revelation to me. It broke down the false and conventional standards of lyric expression to which I had become accustomed. She taught me to appreciate sincerity in art...."

For the singers, Duse defends high fees, "Have you ever considered the heritage that goes to the making of so marvelous and delicate an instrument...." Convinces Calvé to start this 1906 tour, "welcomed everywhere with a joyful cordiality by a public which is the most eclectic, the most enthusiastic, that I have ever known. One of the dreams of my childhood was realized. I had always longed to live in a gypsy van, to be able to come and go at will, like a true Bohemian, with my house on my back. I had this experience ...in a private car in the United States. What fun it was to come back after an evening performance to this little house on wheels, with its comfortable bedrooms, its kitchen, dining room and bath! Everything that the heart could desire" plus three Pullman servants to do these everythings.

So Paul West, visiting Nielsen's suite Saturday night, goes into raptures finding "Calvé—the great Calvé—was in the room. I got there just too late to hear her sing—she had been humming a little something for Miss Nielsen they told me—but I had heard the Nielsen sing for the older artist and heard the latter's outburst of praise: "'C'est la plus belle mediume que j'ai jamais entendue! Le diction est vraiment exceptional!" said Calvé. ["That is the most beautiful middle register I've ever heard. The diction is really exceptional!"]

"Oh, I am so proud", replies Nielsen who has gained much fluency in French. West observes her "blushing like a school girl".

Seeing the reporter has entered, "Calvé swept from the room. She was afraid I was going to try to interview her maybe", says West.

Before she left, she did speak a word of Nielsen to West, who reveals being "told...by no less an authority than the great Emma Calvé that Alice Nielsen had accomplished all she set out to do".

"Isn't that kind of her?" Nielsen responds.

They had spent the better part of a year. Strong people with much to discuss; careers overlap; as late as May 1, 1922, parallel NYC concerts.

Paul West tries to get Nielsen to say an American girl need not go abroad to make a success in grand opera. "As soon as I broached the subject, her eyes flashed contradiction...."

"Impossible! Utterly impossible!" Nielsen stops him. "And I ought to know it. I tried, I had the ambition, the 'nerve' if you wish and tried to get the best teachers [Valerga]. But I saw from the first that they were not bringing out what was in me—that I would never get very far ahead. That was why I threw everything over and went abroad to study [with Valerga's ex-husband]".

"But Miss Nielsen, do you not think...."

"I do not, I know".

"I knew that she spoke whereof she was familiar", West says.

Nielsen eggs a rival, Calvé's compliment was "quite different from the treatment I got from" Melba who "would scarcely give me the honor of an interview in London and when she did she tried in every possible way to discourage me. But she couldn't". Details difficult to detect.

Apparently Alice rashly tells Melba her goals to switch to opera, Melba squelches a patron, puts Alice in a hard plight. Nielsen triumphs with the Covent roles: "And later I followed her at Covent Garden singing some of the roles she had sung, and I made a success of them, too!" West observers, "Her eyes sparkled with the satisfaction of revenge!"

Hovering Henry interjects. "Success! Why Miss Nielsen got twice the praise...she deserved it". Returning fire, Melba kills Waldorf attendance by persuading *Daily Mail* (or had it persuaded) to drop sponsorship, major setback. Melba uses politics, Nielsen performs. Melba stands and sings; Alice moves, acts and sings. Melba big as any Bostonian; petite Nielsen. Yet Nielsen has given away Covent Garden to croon at Waldorf with Duse, Calvé being for the benefit of Mr. Russell pretentious.

Why must an American girl go abroad for voice, West asks.

"Well for many reasons. In the first place, the average American girl with a fine voice has little money with which to pursue her studies. There are so many great masters of instruction...in England, Paris, Italy—who for sheer love the art, if they discover a pupil has a voice worth cultivating, will educate it without the least charge. I know of scores of cases. Mine was almost one of them, for I did not have enough money to have obtained the instruction I have had, unless there had been some charity on the part of my instructor".

West said, "Why, everyone thought"—she must be rich.

"Yes, I know. When I was starring at the head of my own company in the operas *The Fortune Teller* and *The Singing Girl* I made money, plenty of it". Skips Williams & Perley stealing her fortune.

"Everybody said I was a fool to throw over my career on the comic opera stage as I did and go abroad to study for grand opera. I went to London first, it may be remembered, and there essayed a little season in *The Fortune Teller* to see if London would receive me as a comic-opera singer.

"I wanted to find out first of all if I was good enough in that line even before trying the more ambitious field. Well, while I made what they call an artistic success—and you know what a deadly thing that lost money, and I had very little left at the end". Confirms poverty without self-pity.

"That's the way it is with them over there. It's art for art's sake. That is one of the differences between them and the Americans. And I believe it is the principal point that makes a year's study abroad worth five here. I don't know how I did it—I seemed to save money on nothing".

Recital skips maestro Bevignani, Tosti, Valerga, blarneying a decade till denouement same phrases repeat: "But I followed Mr. Russell's advice and went to Italy, where in Rome [Naples] I took up the first serious study I had ever undergone. Mr. Russell was my instructor, and a very careful one. As Italian is the language of the grand opera stage above all others, it was necessary to learn it. Mr. Russell did not teach me merely a lot of Italian words or simply the words of some songs, parrot-wise". He did not teach at all: "He put me at work with an Italian teacher of languages, and for almost a year [four months] I studied Italian and nothing [!] else.

"Singing? Hardly a note. My daily practice consisted of the simplest exercises. It was the language first. Well a year [four months] passed and I was little further ahead it seemed to me, in my music that when I had begun". She debuted at Bellini within four months, London orchestra concerts within six months. "But that was a wrong idea. I had absorbed the locale, the temperament, the nameless something that made me *en rapport* with music. It is what cannot be obtained in America for love or money, and it means everything.

"A very little musical study—but very hard—now followed, and in a few months Mr. Russell [Tosti, Bevignani] gave me the glad news that he thought I was ready to make my debut—not in opera, but in concert. So we returned to London, where he obtained engagements for me at Queen's Hall, and later for the music festival under Arthur Nikisch". Nikisch (1855-1922), from Hungary, conducts Berlin, London, Boston orchestras. Leads London Symphony to America 1912, first European orchestra to tour.

"Salary? Oh very small; but I tell you I had long since forgotten how to think about money. I would have sung for nothing".

Skips ahead. "In the spring of 1904, Mr. Russell [Bevignani] obtained an engagement for me that seemed then the grandest thing in the world. If was a chance to sing in grand opera in Italy. I went there in *Faust* at the Bellini theatre, a little house but of magnificent standing. I sang several parts, and for the first time in my life I felt that I had achieved something really worth while". And the NYC out-of-body opening night or her own company's Kansas City debut? Only time will bring her back to reality.

Reporter has garbled or Nielsen has compressed: "At the end of the first week, during which I learned that I had been very successful, I was given my salary. It was forty-five francs, and a little over a year before, I had been getting one-hundred times as many dollars weekly in comic opera with prospects of more. But I didn't care".

Nielsen absurdly puffs the remora: "Mr. Russell was so encouraged by my showing that he conceived the idea of an autumn season at Covent Garden, London". Of course, San Carlo's manager Roberto De Sanna was responsible. Sent Russell who confessed De Sanna had women troubles and needed a spy. Then Alice pushes a patriotic ploy about Covent Garden.

"I had made an effort for an engagement there previously, but was refused by the management on the score that I was an American and lacking in temperament. They hadn't heard me, but thought I must be barren of temperament because I was a Yankee girl!"

London-famous Alice got a hearing by Covent within days of stopping her American show. Told to acquire repertoire. Prestigiously, miraculously hired by Higgins for Covent's spring Mozart season.

Gratitude to Caruso for sharing the stage. "The Autumn season at Covent Garden...became a reality. Caruso appeared with me and to him I owe a great deal of the success that was mine".

Turns to the new tour. "Now...to see if my own people will accept me. I hope they will, for a good many of them laughed when I abandoned my comic opera career and went abroad. I suppose if I was real smart, I would say that an American girl ought to study here even if I didn't; but I'm honest above all else, and I've said what I really truly believe. I hope it won't hurt me with the American public".

The singer is on the stage.

West closes with a vote of confidence: "Those who have heard Miss Nielsen's voice do not believe that it will". She sings for him, as she often does for press. Thrilling to hear a big voice inflame a room. Changes in voice placement and power he notices; as vocals recorded in 1898 and in 1909 prove. Closes, "She will be a revelation to the people who remember her as the singer of light roles in comic opera".

Relive Alice's first American day since 1901: off the gangplank to greet fans, friends, press, and colleagues such as Herbert at the dock. Leaps to her family in Harlem. By late afternoon back at her midtown hotel with Calvé and meets the press. That night her group go to Herbert's orchestra in concert. She chose not to sing. "Almost the first person I met on my return was Victor Herbert. Impulsively I rushed up to him. But Victor was cold, scowling. 'But, Victor', I protested, 'aren't you glad to see me?' 'Glad?' roared Victor. 'Good Lord, think of the money you and I have lost because you would sing grand opera and not stick to me.'"

Herbert opens five Broadway shows that season. Month earlier, October 16th Herbert's *Miss Dolly Dollars* debuts. His *Wonderland* based on a Brothers' Grimm tale, October 24 at Majestic Theatre, esteemed Julian Mitchell directs. Herbert's *It Happened in Nordland* with comic Lew Fields and Marie Cahill (1870-1933) re-opens November with waltzes, marches, ballads, coon songs. Cahill insists on adding songs from other shows and Herbert refuses to conduct. Cahill is replaced. December 12, *Mlle. Modiste* made for Nielsen opens for Scheff.

Herbert took time to meet Nielsen's ship at the dock. His best diva, glorious Alice Nielsen, would open as her next NYC show a cheap 1840s Donizetti small-cast *opéra bouffe*, not *Mlle. Modiste*. Ziegfeld despite all produces a new show for wife Anna Held. During *Follies of 1920*, Ziegfeld writes Herbert, "nobody in the world appreciates your work more than I do, for my greatest ambition is to do a piece where you have entirely written the music" (Dec. 14 1920).

Despite double-cross by Ziegfeld and Shubert, Nielsen's fame brings national bookings. Broadway success has paved a way for her tour. Diva clout. Theatre managers know her name, pay in advance. Critical contacts such as Consuelo Yznaga's family among other "principle box-holders of the New Orleans Opera house" have invited her to swing down to New Orleans to close a deal. In faithful San Francisco, Leahy and Steindorf hold Tivoli ready. Alice foresees future success near at hand. Beyond New York.

Everything depends on her. She must sing her way to San Francsico.

Arrangements for the quality of her NYC debut were left to Russell. Despite his huge payoff for betraying her signature, he arrives in NY broke. To make ends meet, his only collateral is Nielsen. He never clarifies how he used the Shubert-Zeigfeld advance; or any monies. For Russell's £1000 ($150,000 today) he acquires five Italians: Prati, tenor; Fratodi, baritone; Artucci, basso; Cassini, mezzo-soprano; Biscassia the accompanist and pianist, "all recognized artists in the great opera houses of Rome, Naples and Milan". Later confessed, cheapest.

He recalls: "I sailed for America, arriving in NY with the proverbial half-crown in my pocket. It was one of the Shuberts' representatives who met me at the boat and much to my relief, without asking me whether I needed them or not, pulled out a bundle of 'greenbacks.' I gladly accepted the proffered loan and allowed myself to be driven off to the Knickerbocker Hotel" at Times' Square.

Significantly not Alice Nielsen's hotel, nor visiting her family.

Seasick, "Ill effects of a rough passage made it impossible for me to enjoy any of those amazing 'first impressions' as I was lonely, distinctly unhappy and regarded the New World with a jaundiced eye. My first breakfast remains a vivid memory. I was confronted with a grapefruit the size of a small cart-wheel, steaming porridge and cream, fish-cakes, eggs, pancakes and syrup and at least a gallon of coffee to wash it down—this at nine o'clock in the morning. Serious doubts arose in my mind as to the sensibilities of a nation who, so early in the day could master such a quantity of food. However in a short time I realized that the very air of America is hungry and demands an extraordinary amount of vitality, and although I was never able to put away a five-course breakfast, I ate twice as much as I did in Europe".

Next day, "Sam Kingston, Shuberts' [Ziegfeld's] white-haired and good-looking assistant tried to be sympathetic, but was obviously so amused at my bewilderment and what he called my English drawl, that he could not conceal his mirth. He proceeded to imitate me, but I failed to understand half he said, and was far too frightened to admit the fact. Pity overcame him at last, and he leant across the table in the most kindly way, 'say, Russell, I guess you are up against it now. Don't get cold feet. Though New York can be pretty tough on strangers—you'll soon be OK.'

"I admit that I was stupid, but this sentiment conveyed absolutely nothing to my mind. American phrases had not at that time percolated into England. I failed to understand what I was up against and why I should 'get cold feet' on a hot day; and as to soon becoming 'OK' apart from the fact that I had heard of Otto Kahn, the letters conveyed nothing". Soon he would realize "the force and value of slang, which seemed the chief medium of expression".

Meanwhile, Nielsen's first meeting with Lee Shubert has left no doubt that he was hostile to her opera success. Perhaps he was rude or frisky; she later mentions a "personal" affront. Like Ziegfeld, Shubert's style is to own a wife and hire chorus girls for sex. Marie Dressler mentions a set fee.

Nielsen will not submit. And why keep San Francisco waiting?

Shubert seems to comprise. Let the tour proceed. Cheap. Terms of her agreement gone with the wind. No first-class production. In the forced situation Alice Nielsen makes a choice. Needs a pianist. Fails to draft her brother who has duties in Far Rockaway. So the London lad Russell will suffice. His European webs have no utility here. How he has re-attached to Nielsen's tour after being dropping in London he remains forever silent.

In this troubling context Alice, who has arrived after all to present American audiences her singing voice, decides to play New Haven.

NY Herald: "the real provincial premier of the season is at New Haven tonight when Alice Nielsen makes her first American appearance in grand opera at the Hyperion Theatre. *Don Pasquale* is the bill. The event is one of tremendous import to the little prima donna, who rollicked her way from a church choir to the head of the best light opera organization in America and then, not content, sailed away to Italy in search of grand opera honors. Many music lovers and critics will be on hand to pass judgment tonight".

Thursday November 2, first reviews find an expectant nation. Her acting and vocals celebrated. Critics note contrasts between her Broadway days and today's diva. Stage and costumes, spendthrift. From Covent Garden and Napoli's San Carlo Alice descends to New Haven.

The Leader (New Haven): "The American stage has a new and bigger and better prima donna in Miss Nielsen than a few years ago".

Sunday Register (New Haven): "Miss Nielsen shows a remarkable gain in voice volume. Four years abroad have given her a polish she did not possess in old days of light opera. She adds grace of the finished actress to the part of Norina and her rendition of it is ideal in tone and feature".

The audience, reserved at first, soon demands many encores.

NY Herald: "A large and fashionable, as well as musically capable and critical audience, who remembered her as a comic opera prima donna, heard her dispassionately enough until the close of the second act when they gave expression to their pleasure in prolonged applause. This generous welcome continued, although Miss Nielsen reappeared and bowed acknowledgements. The closing duet was therefore resung".

Herald analyzes: "Maturer singer...than in old days. Whereas in former years she was unable to sing in the legato style, this is now a strong point. Her whole voice is equal and is evenly stronger. Her articulation was very clear, and her phrasing was particularly warm compared to other high soprano voices".

In the cast: "Mr. Praer made his first appearance before an American public. He was 'discovered' singing in a small theatre in Milan. His remarkable tenor with phenomenally high notes was...talk of the foyer between acts. Mr. Alfonso Rosa, buffo; Mr. Fratoli, baritone and Mr. Artucci supported Miss Nielsen admirably".

After New Haven's one-night-stand, her show slated November 5th at DC's Belasco Theatre postponed then canceled without explanation.

November 8th, Philadelphia for an afternoon between running shows.

North American (Nov 9): "At a special Lyric Theatre matinee yesterday afternoon, Miss Nielsen amply vindicated her claims to lyric primacy and the flattering encomiums of European critics. Her Norina in *Don Pasquale* was admirably acted and delightfully sung, with a graceful abandon and rare vocal charm that took the audience captive at once. Miss Nielsen sings with wondrous fluency and purity of tone, great range and absolutely even quality throughout all registers, and the indefinable dramatic fire that betokens an artistic temperament. She should go far in her new career as an operatic star.

"After four years of hard study under great masters in Europe, pretty Alice Nielsen, a one-time comic opera favorite, has returned full-fledged prima donna in Italian grand opera, with an Italian company and orchestra to accompany her on a tour of the West".

Philadelphia Inquirer (Nov 9) praises her evolved arts. Alice Nielsen, "well remembered" in *Singing Girl* and *Fortune Teller*, returns "in a bright and enjoyable performance of Donizetti's melodious and amusing... *Don Pasquale*. The advance she has made during the period of her absence in the mastery of her art is very manifest.

"She always was a sprightly and intelligent, if somewhat self-conscious actress, but her voice has gained greatly in quality, range and volume, and her vocalization has become excellent. Her tones still have a tendency to shrillness if they are at all forced, but they are for the most part admirably controlled, and in the breadth and smoothness of her delivery, the effectiveness of her phrasing and the even brilliancy of her scale passages. Miss Nielsen has now acquired a method which suggests plenty of hard work under the best of instruction.

"Her impersonation of Donizetti's captivating but petulant and tantalizing heroine was a distinct success both from a musical and dramatic point of view and the hearty applause which it elicited from the large audience present was richly merited. It would be an improvement if Miss Nielsen could infuse a little more humor into the famous scene of the second act and make it more clear that she is enjoying the fun of badgering the old Don as much as any one and not be quite so serious about it, but that is a subtlety which is easily missed and Miss Nielsen may be expected to exhibit it more clearly as her familiarity with the role increases".

In the cast: "Ably supported by Signor Alfonso Rosa, whose unctuous performance of Don Pasquale is one of the fine things of the operatic stage, and by Filippo Fratoli, who delivered the music of Dr. Malatesta in a well-cultivated baritone.... Isidoro Prati was rather a wooden Ernesto...."

Next stop next day, NYC. Here Shubert rules the result.

November 9th, Broadway busy as ever when Nielsen arrives. Projects on the boards by producers she had declined to help are doing famously. This week finds Maude Adams, Edna May, Maxine Elliot, Joseph Cawthorn, Eddie Foy, and a new musical from a child's book series *The Wizard Of Oz* directed by Julian Mitchell who fashions a hodge-podge despite the author's own script. Leaving NYC at top of Broadway's most successful musical troupe bearing her name, singing songs written for her voice with a cast of a hundred, Alice returns for a one-shot "special matinee" in a cheap concert version and troupe a handful.

One wit calls her the "American girl who bravely gave up a lucrative career in comic opera...and studied for grand opera, with 95% of her friends cheerfully prognosticating disaster. But she didn't disast and she didn't desist".

Nielsen's matinee concert of *Don Pasquale* is at the Shubert-operated Casino Theatre, "in those days was what Radio City is today", recalls Dorothy Russell, Lillian's daughter (no relation to Henry).

Occupying the theatre since November 4th was *Bandit and the Girl* "under the personal direction of Frank L. Perley" who sabotage of Nielsen had not yet come into the light of court and press. Her nemesis makes his longest Broadway run with *Bandit*. He produced six musicals in NY (1898-

1906) after the Bostonians. *Singing Girl* ran 80, *Fortune Teller* 40, *Venetian Romance* by Frederic Wright & Cornelia Tyler 28, *Chaperons* by Isidore Witmark & Frederic Ranken 49, *Billionaire* by Gustav Kerker & Harry Smith 112. *Bandit* ran 148, a silly 'podge which sports songs by eight writers including Jerome Kern. Star Eddie Foy plays Jim Cheese, a dog trainer. As producer of a running show Perley would have full access to the theatre, the musicians, the conductor, the stage. Bodes poorly.

Not at the Met with Victor Herbert conducting, but on November 9th 1905, Alice Nielsen debuts in grand opera in NYC. He revisits the Casino stage to sing Donizetti's antique comic opera *Don Pasquale* with a cheaply cast sextet, an inexperienced or worse conductor, and musicians bribed to play bad. So the worst possible situation. Worse, the performance is closely covered by critics of the nation; pity for her. Yet among many friends.

Alice meets the challenge bravely. The singer sings.

By last act the stage is covered in bouquets thrown from the house. Honest witnesses will tell the true story. The place packed with opera and theatre elites. Critical response decidedly mixed. Of course as connived.

"She has acquired that facility of vocalization and that power to indulge in a brilliant display of vocal fireworks", said *Telegraph*'s St. John-Brenon, who notes her chief claques are the opera stars Caruso and Scotti. The Met should "stop chasing Tetrazzini". Hire Alice Nielsen, he advises.

Dramatic news from *Dramatic News*. Any singer who could succeed despite this horrible production would "set everyone wild" at the Met. "I don't know what you think of last Thursday's audience at Alice Nielsen's performance of *Don Pasquale*, but I feel sure that a little prima donna who could conquer such a house would set every one wild in the lyric roles at the Metropolitan. The house was one wild desert of critical disbelief, with here and there an oasis of friendliness".

Her friends noteworthy. In the boxes "Caruso and Scotti on one side rubbed elbows with AH Hummel and his bright-eyed sympathetic sisters, and...Lillian Russell accompanied by her two sisters and Irene Perry applauded the primavera interpolation. DeWolf Hopper coiffed like an operatic hero; Melville Ellis, quite gorgeous in brand new white spats; Georgia Caine, sabled and stunning, Raymond Hitchcock, who used to sing Malatesta...when the Castle Square people sang *Pasquale* and who could certainly tie double rows of knots around the fearful dago in the Shubert production; and Eddie Foy, who looked as if a dip into grand opera would afford him large gratification...all followed the little singer with inspiring knowledge and appreciation".

Irish comedian Eddie Foy (1856-1928) began as boy dancer and comic, at times in drag, touring NYC to the Wild West and back. Stars in nine musicals 1901-1912. Narrowly escapes death at Chicago's Iroquois Theatre fire. Deep-voiced DeWolf Hopper (1858-1935) is famed for popularizing *Casey at the Bat*; six wives—two more than Foy. Both will die in Kansas City. Intelligent, genuine, fun, Hopper's autobiography is one of very best from his era.

Orchestra and conductor: abominable. Stage setting: cheapest. And yet, demands are made to put Alice Nielsen on the Met stage right now.

"The rest of us simply sat like cold lumps of adamant and dared her to melt us. The orchestra, abominably led by Jose van den Burg, who evidently believes Donizetti belongs to the Black Hand and ought to be murdered; did its worst to suppress the star, but caring not a fig for coldness or carelessness, the great little Norina sang herself straight into triumph. And the delight of Caruso and the Hummel family was simply lovely to see when the adamant gave up and fairly rose at the singer at the end of the third act and of the scene in the final act. It was a great homecoming for Miss Nielsen".

They spoke backstage. "Her voice was full of tears an hour after the curtain fell, when she told me how deeply she felt the cordial affection that came out to her from the whole audience when it finally made up its mind that here was an artist to be taken to its heart and cherished. Yes, indeed; it was the most triumphant of all triumphs, a reluctant but complete surrender which she won". He concludes significantly, "And if Maestro Conried can read the writing on the wall, he will send Bella Alten back to the woods and give a real American singer a chance".

Conried (Grau retired) leads the Met where Bella Alten-Deri (1877-1962) performs, the Polish soprano "who sang with more nature than art, but carried her message home", recalls *Opera Annals*.

NY Dramatic News announces a success: "Miss Nielsen is now a prima donna and grand opera is her vocation. The house was crowded with her friends who filled the stage with flowers. Bouquets of all description were thrown at her after every act, and quite a number were passed behind the scenes and adorned the setting at the finale of the second act. Miss Nielsen retains all her charm, both in looks and voice; her vocalization was perfect.

"She has improved wonderfully since she appeared in comic opera.

"With a clear soprano voice and a high range she sang some of the difficult numbers with exquisite ease and grace, which call forth many encores. It is some years since we have heard this opera, possibly because most of our prima donnas are...overburdened with too much voice. That is why it appeals to us in its present form.

"To some Miss Nielsen was a revelation. She ought to be a fad for the reason that she demonstrates how much chance there is for a clever singer to improve her talents. Miss Nielsen captured NY...Europe with its masters has made her a grand opera singer worthy of the best operas at the Metropolitan".

In the cast: "Her support was only fair. Alfredo Rosa sang the title role in an effective manner, but the balance of the company acted harder than they sang.

Dramatic Mirror: "Upon her entrance as Norina the audience gave her a welcome that resounded with patriotism and pride. She looked daintily pretty and artistic. Her acting, as was expected, was clever, naïve and full of charm. She is so far above the average in personal beauty and attractiveness. Her voice reveals thoughtful study, having increased in volume, brilliancy and artistic control. She should not be judged by the Norina of Nordica and Sembrich, who have had so many years' experience, but as an ambitious young singer who has made a brave fight and who is winning the position that courage, ability and serious study ultimately command. Many beautiful floral pieces were passed to Miss Nielsen over the footlights, and she was called before the curtain at the close of the opera. A speech was demanded, but she modestly declined. The performance was a veritable triumph for Miss Nielsen".

In the cast: "Alfreda Rosa as Don Pasquale was intensely humorous and better dramatically than vocally. Fillippi Fratoli as Dr. Malatesta revealed a voice rich and voluminous but had an unhappy method. The Ernesto of Francesco Prati was spirited... his tenor clear and pure though none too strong. Signor Artucci played the Notary".

NYC critics split. The bad conductor and bad musicians offended Alice, whose memory of the event stays sour. Two critics despise the cast, the Shubert-Perley sabotage of deliberately bad playing. Others focus on her success and demand her transfer to the Met stage. When Alice reaches California, Western critics school New York.

NY Times departs from the revelations of London and other NY critics about Alice's vocal skills. Bad orchestra playing has alienated the critic: "Alice Nielsen, who left America as a singer of operetta, returns from England after an absence of four years as an aspiring prima donna in Italian opera. She appeared in this capacity yesterday afternoon at the Casino in Donizetti's *Don Pasquale*, a higher and subtler form of comic opera that has engaged the talents of some of the greatest coloratura singers, and that has given much delight in the great opera house across the way.

"Miss Nielsen's undertaking is a praiseworthy one, and the purpose of making a popular appeal through a revival of the delightful genre that was represented in yesterday's performance would have most beneficial results if it could succeed. It may be seriously questioned however, whether such a performance as this will accomplish that purpose".

"*Don Pasquale* demands some of the most skillful of singing, and a special style of comic acting that is all too rare upon the operatic stage. Miss Nielsen possesses neither in large measure. She has a graceful and piquant stage presence but Norina must have more distinction, a more wayward caprice, a more sparkling gayety than Miss Nielsen was able to impart". Facing these many obstacles maliciously placed in her path to distress her performance. Persons knowing her plight sympathy for success she achieved under stress.

Compare comments with the *Evening Telegram* coming up next. The *Times* critic alone in all the world claims: "Her voice is a clear light soprano, though it is not of great beauty or quality, and much of the music she sang well, but she has not the technical facility nor the certainty that the more flowery passages demanded".

In the cast: Rose as Pasquale "showed a certain talent in comic expression...only other member of the company who made any approach to fulfilling the requirements that the opera makes". Fratodi and Prato "showed a zeal that was by no means matched by their accomplishment. Vandenberg conducted laboriously and inflexibly a small and strident orchestra".

Now we discover. Nielsen's move from modern Victor Herbert to 1840s Donizetti is remarked by *Evening Telegram's* "Miss Nielsen in a Musical

Antique". *Pasquale* "now a very old-fashioned work, and it is to be regretted that Miss Nielsen's management saw fit to introduce her again to a NY audience in this bit of musical antiquity. Although many cuts were made and a fine waltz introduced instead of the regular finale, the entire performance was far from satisfactory".

Focus on the bad orchestra and conductor: "The orchestra was not only poor in itself, but conducted in a hard and unsympathetic manner…"

In short: "the orchestra was deplorable".

In the cast: "Decidedly mediocre, and the leading tenor had a throat that was in evidence in every note he sang".

Despite extreme shortcomings, "It must be conceded that Miss Nielsen achieved a personal triumph by her excellent singing and acting. Her voice is as mellow and beautiful as before, and the singer has gained in experience and refinement during her study abroad. Her coloratura is almost faultless. She acted with much freedom and vivacity, and presented a picture of much charm. The future will show whether or not the experiment of her managers is a wise one. The audience yesterday afternoon took kindly to it, perhaps because of their personal liking for Miss Nielsen".

More than one NYC critic took offense when they recalled her last outing. Most severe is Richard Aldrich at *NY Tribune*. The cast "invited general condemnation…stage settings were of slipshod character". He trumps *NY Times* by praising her voice.

"Lovers of old-time comic opera. Italian and French—opera buffa and opera comique…long for a proper housing of the amiable old form of entertainment, and a belief that were it to return…in a really artistic garb, it would find many devotees among true lovers of music who, with all their devotion are not consumed with the desire to feed always on tragic things either of the ponderous German kind or the modern Italian, which though volatile are 'hot i' th' mouth.'

An experiment made at the Casino yesterday afternoon gave these well-meaning and well-desiring persons something to think about. *Don Pasquale* had been awakened from a long slumber by Mme. Sembrich at the Metropolitan Opera House and its old witcheries had made themselves felt but the cavernous spaces of the Metropolitan had swallowed up much of the charm inherent in comedy and music". Here at Casino, "five minutes …served to demonstrate that a proper theatre only created the need of a proper performance".

Nielsen "five years ago was a Broadway favorite" who "challenged the attentions and interest of the judicious by exhibiting a voice of fine natural quality and more than usual skill in its use". In *Singing Girl*, "there was a romantic element in the play which invited celebration in romantic song and Mr. Herbert fitted her out with a piece of music which enlisted the best that was in her". Aldrich recounts a version of London move, naïvely removes credit from De Sanni for San Carlo's Covent season wherein Nielsen "sang Mimi to Signor Caruso's Rodolfo in Puccini's *Bohème* and to judge by the newspapers, made an extreme favorable impression. Now she is back in her native land and yesterday she gave her admirers a taste of her quality in the higher form of entertainment".

Alice had anticipated the stars from her Waldorf season would be here at New York.

Aldrich condemns cast: "*Don Pasquale* calls for only a small company— a prima buffa, tenor, baritone and a buffo. Their names do not signify for they invited general condemnation rather than special mention.....

Condemns musicians: "The stage settings were of the slipshod character which were to have been expected and so was the orchestra, under the direction of Jose Vandenberg, erstwhile oboist in the Metropolitan Opera orchestra".

Cast and conductor, "mainly disillusioning".

Alice Nielsen's exalted career "and curiosity to note the results of her European training made it possible to listen to her with more patience".

Aldrich dislikes her comedy, honed as twas by Duse and Calvé: "Still, it did not take long to see how ill her conception of comedy acting, developed in Broadway farce, comported with the character of Norina as it stands in the opera and lives in the memories of those who have seen and heard Patti, Di Murada, Gerater and Sembrich in the part".

Interestingly, Valerga, Tosti, and Bevignani had often seen these singers play the part. Recall their Nielsen praise.

Aldrich continues, "The vocal art of such artists must not be brought into comparison with her singing but something was to have been expected from her familiarity with the stage and her dramatic intelligence. The atmosphere which she carried into the comedy was more foreign to it than the style of her singing—and that is saying much". The innovations of her acting stray from formula.

Praise for Alice's voice: "Her vocal metal has lost none of its brilliant beauty. Her voice is still fresh, true and ringing; her instinct and capacities in cantabile praiseworthy. But she is a novice in much that goes to make up style in bel canto".

So it is. Alice's stressed, sabotaged NYC debut is panned most strongly by Aldrich (1863-1937), Harvard grad linked to critic Henry Krehbiel a Melba friend therefore never a Nielsen fan; and *NY Times*.

Unhappy reviews reference poor sets, bad cast, horrid musicians. Yet all will praise Alice's voice. In contrast to Aldrich and *NY Times*, just two jokers among the newspaper pack in those days, is the strongly theatre-focused *NY Telegraph*. Algernon St. John-Brenon will successfully predict Alice Nielsen's future. Provides her strongest praise.

Familiar with Italy and opera, Algernon regards her Broadway past as a unique asset, never a liability: "Her NY debut in grand opera reveals all her old charm with added arts". She is seen "with deep interest and warm appreciation by a large audience which contained a strong professional element including Signor Caruso and his wife, who occupied a box". The Monday matinee, of course, allows theatre professionals to attend.

Opera has a Nielsen niche. "I do not mean that in a season or two Miss Nielsen will be a Brunnhilde...but Miss Nielsen did prove yesterday afternoon that to the freshness and charm of her earlier self she had added many of the accomplishments necessary to a trained and capable operatic artist".

Alice's acting is superb. "Needless to say, in the purely dramatic work of such a role, Miss Nielsen could not fail to be more than captivating". He significantly adds, "Indeed, had her singing been inferior to what it was her personality would have concealed many vocal deficiencies. She has acquired that facility of vocalization and that power to indulge in a brilliant display of vocal fireworks.... To this must be added that her high notes while not great in volume, are fresh in quality and sweet in tone and that she has a due conception of the nature of her work".

St. John-Brenon advises the "managers of the Metropolitan, who are by no means overloaded with competent coloratura sopranos" and chase "Tetrazzini around the continent" to hire Alice Nielsen. "In any case, Miss Nielsen has already done much toward fulfilling a worthy ambition".

Her last NYC grand opera debut hurdles are Alan Dale of Hearst's *NY American* and the *Daily Telegraph*; neither nice.

Dale not unexpectedly finds the cheap antique-y not his taste. She could do better on Broadway. After all, his pseudonym is taken from The Bostonians' *Robin Hood*; Jessie Bartlett plays the guy Alan O'Dale.

"On Thursday...five tedious people sang for all they were worth. Little Miss Alice Nielsen of whom we are all awfully proud because she charmed us in *The Serenade* and *The Singing Girl* and *The Fortune Teller*, had nothing more to offer us that day upon her return 'fresh from European triumphs' than Donizetti's *Don Pasquale*—with the accent on the 'squal.'

"There is no chorus in this opera, there is no other feminine voice than that of Norina. Miss Nielsen has not changed much in appearance. She is perhaps three or four years younger but prima donnas cannot help growing young—and it is rather foolish to mention the fact.

"She came on in a large poke bonnet and a long silk dress, and bowed as seriously as though she were at the San Carlo Opera House in Naples [where she recently bowed] instead of on the stage where Mr. Eddie Foy holds forth nightly". His satire continues: "Miss Nielsen has adopted the Italian method of clutching occasionally at an imaginary mustard-plaster on the chest. This always seems to help a great deal. Patti loved it...it is less popular than it used to be. But it is very nice.

"It must at once be said that Miss Nielsen's frosty, fragile, well-educated voice scarcely seems to coincide with grand opera aspirations. It is still essentially light opera though she can assuredly do more with it now than she could a few years ago. It is not limped, some of the notes are a bit shrill. It does not send its music to the soul but gets to the ear solely. But Miss Nielsen had learned many valuable tricks.... Her appeal was not an impassioned one.... The Metropolitan...did not shake on its foundations".

In the cast: tenor "frightened"; others just "splendid mediocrities".

Dale advises Nielsen to leave Italian antiquities in Rome; after all, any new New York novelties are vastly superior to the aged foreign shows.

After she "left us after various highly-successful bouts in comic-opera, it seemed tragic to be sitting there today listening to her efforts to place herself in a position that will not suit her. It is nice to be 'fresh from European triumphs', but nicer surely to be unbudgingly ensconced among the shows of American make".

Dale laughingly scents "a faint odor of garlic...one could clairvoyantly perceive lops of spaghetti in the very air. Men with busy hair and oily skins prowled about. It is rumored that...there was a great desertion from the ranks of the show-stands and the banana vendors". In addition to the Italian people, "scores of Miss Nielsen's old comic opera associates were on hand, clapping with their hands in the air in the genial actor's way".

Lastly list, *NY Telegraph* gives a slap to the show and its uppity singer. She clearly must not be blamed for the cast hired by another.

"Miss Nielsen's company—it is not quite fair to saddle her with the responsibility of such a vocally irresponsible lot—may be dismissed with curt verbal nods". In the cast: "a basso who is almost base, of a baritone who cultivated the vibration method; of a tenor who has a cupola voice and of a prompter who has a magnificent voice of virile and carrying qualities, magnificently resonant in all registers and who boasts a clearness of enunciation that is unmistakable".

Worse the orchestra, "a collection of men of different political opinions" deliberately out of tune. Perley, the bribery devotee, was in the house.

Even so, Nielsen has "poured midnight oil upon her vocal chords. She has studied much, evidently, and has added floridness to her singing speech. It has gained in metallic hardness. It is not a pleasing voice now, nor a wonderful one. For a singer of comic opera it would be magnificent but for a singer of grand opera there are many qualities and virtues lacking". Lashes for effrontery: "To pitch her tent right across from the Metropolitan Opera House and give a make-shift performance of *Don Pasquale* just to further her own ambitious ends is hardly excusable".

So it goes. Alice Nielsen chooses to sing to her peers, despite the scuttled first-class debut and the cheap 'podge substitute sabotaged.

By grace of charm and artistry, Alice Nielsen conquers. Despite all, by popular demand a repeat performance was made Monday. If she had gone direct to San Francisco, spared this ordeal. Or was it her triumph?

Notwithstanding bad reports on Met oboist-turned-conductor Jose Vandenburg, he conducts Nielsen's group across the tour. Vandenburg will continue in this field until karma strikes.

How different from Europe for her. Covent Garden, San Carlo, Bellini, the London orchestras. Virtuoso singer with long experience, artist Alice is unsinkable. NYC so be it. Sets sights on Chicago then San Francisco, Los Angeles, Dallas, and New Orleans. Her sister Hortense, now a seasoned actress and producer, joins for the familiar tour over the circuit of that long and winding yellow-brick vaudeville road to home sweet home.

SUCCESS IN SWEET CHICAGO, WEST AND SOUTH

The NY reception is watched with great interest by the rest of the country.

As she tours Alice recalls NYC's three snarky reviews, skips the many of praise demanding she must sing at the Met. Does not drop Donizetti's farce, nor whine about cast. Simply says, some critics did not like her.

Alice's faux impresario after switiching Alice from Covent and delivering her to Lee Shubert for a few pieces of silver, passively passes the buck for the Casino near-fiasco: "Two weeks after my arrival, rehearsals began". In fact, Nielsen docked eleven days before New Haven, allowing ten rehearsal days. DC dropped. Six days prep for Philly. On the seventh day, Alice made NYC. Perhaps she should have rested.

Omitting his responsibilities, Russell continues, "The orchestra was not adequate in any sense and only a quarter the size required for Donizetti's music which, Heaven knows, is simple enough". Of course the praise and push for the Met to hire her without delay, he cannot confess. He spins himself as a hapless bystander. Which he was. "I felt certain that failure was in store for our production and I was not mistaken. The opening was disastrous, the critics merciless, but fair. Now I realize how ridiculous and almost impertinent it was to expect New Yorkers to accept such a ragged performance for they have always demanded the best and do not tolerate the second-rate". Those who don't know better might misbelieve that Alice's "veritable triumph" wasn't a virtuoso egg she tossed at the corrupt regime who schemed to suppress her.

Pathetically passing the buck, he blames Lee Shubert, "As I see it now, the Shuberts must have anticipated that so inferior a production would be doomed in a city like NY and suspect that they hoped, with this for an initial experience, Alice Nielsen and I would no longer scorn the lucrative musical comedy". As if he had anything to do with it.

Reversing his spin, he admits she created success: "Alice had too much Irish blood in her veins to accept defeat without a struggle and in spite of many flattering offers [Broadway], was determined to show America that she would not be beaten".

She led a concert shoehorned into a major Broadway theatre running a first-class production. And created demand for a second performance!

He skips signing the Ziegfeld-Shubert contract, skips Alice had been promised a concert with Herbert at the Met and first-class productions as a lure. Although he knew an immediate western tour was the plan, Russell spins the situation: "So poor *Don Pasquale* was unceremoniously put out of NY and sent on the road on what is known as 'one night stands'".

NY Times' Richard Aldrich (Nov 12) meditated a week before reflecting on failings of cast and orchestra. Skips blame of Shubert and Russell. In his measure, the star produced the situation: "How dangerous the wrong way is, was shown by the production which Miss Alice Nielsen made last week of *Don Pasquale*. Even without the last degree of skill in singing which the opera gives opportunity for, it could be made acceptable by intelligence, grace and comic spirit in the acting and finish in the orchestra, to conduct which needs also refinement and a certain touch. Most of these things were absent".

Touring toward Chicago, as with the Kansas City kids hiking through the Missouri snowdrifts to their next show, she knew success awaits.

Alice has vivid memories of Covent Garden and Napoli.

She was departing town when mad Max Desci pounced: "Miss Nielsen was staying at the Hotel Astor, where an attempt to deliver the court order in a bouquet of chrysanthemums failed. She spurned the floral tribute and went off in a cab at a breakneck pace for the Grand Central Station. By a ruse the process server passed in hot pursuit through the gate to the train and served the order for appearance. Miss Nielsen nevertheless left the city but upon her return will be amenable for contempt of court. The case is an echo from an action begun in 1898 by Professor Max Desci, who has a musical studio in Carnegie Hall, for $701.50" (*NY Tribune* Nov 16).

November 16th in Toledo, Alice Nielsen begins her 1905-06 American Concert Tour. Theatre of the pre-War era was on the road, DeWolf Hopper explains, "We played the road..., one week stands in the larger towns and one-night jumps in between. This was routing in the theatre from the time when the railroads first pushed West to the Missouri River [at Kansas City] until labor and transportation costs and the movies virtually destroyed the legitimate stage in all save a handful of the greater cities. Hundreds of actors of the first rank did not play New York at all, or for no longer than a week or two in a season. The road was the theatre and the theatre was the road until about 1910. Plays customarily were financed and cast in New York and launched there, because the boast that a play had come from a run at such and such a theatre on Broadway was worth money at the box offices in the hinterlands. A twelve weeks' run on Broadway was once considered phenomenal, but whatever the run, the production went on tour as a matter of course" (*Once A Clown Always a Clown*, 1915).

As was St. Joseph, the Ohio rubes ain't gonna like it.

Toledo News Press: "Alice Nielsen, whose memorable performances in comic opera are fragrant annals of the Toledo stage, never appeared to greater disadvantage... when she reappeared at the Valentine as Norina in *Don Pasquale*, an Italian comic opera" (Nov 16).

For Toledo, the vintage Italian comic opera plot seems as superficial as any Harry Smith 'podge; which it isn't but why argue the point sober.

Worse, "impossible not to contrast the penuriousness of Miss Nielsen's present...with the generous and opulent productions provided for her by Frank Perley. One could not help thinking of the superb human and mechanical equipment of the charming singer's series of comic opera successes, and contrast it with the stiff and shabby showing made by her present managers. As they sang in Italian, and as the audience was impatient to see Miss Nielsen, the greater part of the first act was a bore. Miss Nielsen first came on in an alleged garden scene..."

Then magic happens: "Miss Nielsen at once launched into her opening number, and the results of her four years absence abroad were soon apparent in the ease and assurance with which she poured forth the splendid melodies of Donizetti. All through the three acts Miss Nielsen's singing was a revelation of improved vocal artistry".

The Toledo writer embodies a lifetime's theatrical experience to express.

From dancing with wooden shoes to singing with wooden Italians.

"Miss Nielsen's acting, too was improved. She was no longer a stranger to natural dramatic expression. And the grace of her carriage was admirably in contrast to the exaggerated and cumbersome movements and gesture of her wooden associates".

Notices she ain't singing no English. "Nobody not familiar with Italian could understand what she was singing. But music knows no language, and the enjoyment of the singer's personal performance was little less pronounced that had she used the vernacular of the Anglo-Saxon".

In four years Nielsen has "physically matured. She is now a sedate young woman and not the naturally vivacious girl she was in comic opera".

Prophesy: "Her own talents may make a success of this comic opera...."

As Herbert, so Donizetti: Alice Nielsen will make anything interesting.

Lee Shubert's racism intrudes: Alice insists on equality with her maid, and Shubert attorney William Klien objects Nov. 20th to "the maid of Miss Nielsen being transported in drawing-rooms and sleeping cars".

Alice continues without change to Chicago.

Studebaker Theatre. Second City long advised Nielsen to be ambitious, now the turning point. Shallow NYC's disparaging reviews receive rebuke.

Tuesday, Novermber 21st brings universal acclaim.

"At all times an arch, winsome little actress, Miss Nielsen charmed with her comedy", reports *Chicago News'* Mollie Moriss (Nov 22).

"The applause was expressive of the keen enjoyment her hearers found in her interpretation of the role of Norina and in the glory of a fine, true, flexible soprano voice used with an art painstakingly acquired. In the scene prior to the signing of the marriage contract, she was the bashful young girl without a trace of the shrewishness to follow. There was intelligence in her acting and a repression of her natural delight in roguery. The role affords scope for just such talents as this gifted young woman possess, and it must be said she realized many of its possibilities".

The concert "was not designed to impress with its lavishness; costumes were lavish and beautiful but the scenery was of the simplest character. Choral numbers were omitted entirely, there being only four members of the company besides Miss Nielsen. Miss Nielsen's beauty was well set off in the pretty costumes she wore. The first glimpse of her was given in a lavender gown in the Empire style, a silk scarf draped over her arms and a large bonnet framing her face and her brown curls".

Gotham critics who panned Nielsen are panned. How dare New York dictate to Chicago? The Alice Nielsen-inspired independence movement arises which peaks in Los Angeles.

Chicago Evening Post winds up and pitches the first egg: "While it may be perhaps stretching the point to call this production grand opera, it is certainly far above the standard of compositions she has previously been associated with in this country".

Alice's Norina "revealed a certain grasp of the personality of the part in a finished and most artistic vocal ability. In beauty of face, grace of figure, charm of manner and technical perfection this artist is admirably fitted for such roles. Her voice is a brilliant light soprano of extreme flexibility and lightness, but at the same time rich and resonant and perfectly placed".

Chicago Inter-Ocean: "All must admire the ambition of Miss Nielsen. She sacrificed four of the best years of her life and an individual fortune in order to study...for a better class of work than that which she was doing. Singing Norina yesterday, she proved herself equal to the demands made upon the best light sopranos".

Chicago Herald hurls its NYC egg: Broadway frivolity meets genuine artistry. "We beheld a new Alice Nielsen: not a novice in frivolous comedy with a musical accompaniment. We saw a genuine artist in legitimate opera, indicating that here for the first time in years was a singer who had not only the dramatic qualities and the vocal gifts suited to the interpretation of the younger heroines of opera, but an artist who still had the appearance, the industry and the enthusiasm of youth coupled with the grace, the beauty, the years and the spirit of youth itself".

Life magazine runs a Nielsen as Norina photo for a Metcalf article about Heinrich Conried, post-Grau Met manager. Metcalf, like Alan Dale, urges Alice to help the new Broadway arts, not promote ye olde Italian repertoire. Makes a credible case that Broadway, America's original art form, needs her most. "Miss Alice Nielsen's ambition to become a grand opera artist is creditable to her from the point of view of self-improvement, but it is perhaps better...to be the head of a mouse than the tail of a lion".

Shoddy Shubert's tour taints things: "To anyone who heard her recent performance in a bobtailed version of *Don Pasquale*, it is evident that she can never attain anything like the position in grand opera that she held in light opera". Metcalf, of course, has sadly missed Napoli and London when she eternally attained her leading position. "It is also evident that, if she cares to go back to her old love, she possess an ample equipment for it in looks, voice and comedy-acting". Returns to the loss of the star to American shows: "Irrespective of her own wishes, the comic opera stage has greater need of her charms and abilities than the other".

Traveling with Alice and living in Chicago, Hortense has produced her own dramatic tours as far as New Orleans, California, and New England. The sisters craft the business side as Alice progresses. They know how things work. This pays off in Chicago when Alice gains the sponsor for next winter, Bryn Mawr alumnae association. Fund-raiser for the Philadelphia woman's college. With their guarantee, Alice Nielsen can hire a quality cast to produce a proper impression.

Roaming unchaperoned, Russell uses his foggy situation to huff and puff at the press. Dec 6th in *Chicago Herald* Dec 6th he takes crazily untrue credit for discovering Caruso in Milan, and stupidly for Calvé who Chicago knows as a Marchesi student who, after child's death, met her 'Hindoo' guru here.

An Alice egg tossed six years ago has imprinted a writer's memory. As her tour builds momentum *NY Mirror* pokes fun at Perley: "Warbling arias, Alice Nielsen looks as demure as when she was the soubrette in comic opera, not a day older and as near pretty as ever. One wonders if she was same vicious little rogue as when after her quarrel with a bald-headed manager she advised him to get a new star, and if he was at a loss for an opera, to put on 'La Toupee.'" (Dec 3).

December 4, Alice Nielsen returns to Kansas City. No place like home to build the independent spirit. Old friend Karl Busch conducts the orchestra. Alice stays ten days. Rises stronger with the affection.

Dead ex-husband.

Now, Alice Nielsen pushes back at Shubert, who makes concessions.

NY's *Morning Telegram* (Dec 4) proclaims "'square Deal' for Alice Nielsen". Instead of a skeleton team, Lee Shubert has agreed to provide her a "full chorus and full orchestra in San Francisco".

Realizing he was less-than-useless to Lee Shubert, remora Russell has switched sides to his only remaining revenue source. Stops undercutting and starts bad-mouthing: "It is almost brutal to watch the attempts of the management [not his!] to defeat her after her many sacrifices. In spite of this, Miss Nielsen's tour is a success".

Day or two later: "The management [Lee Shubert] is trying to drive Miss Nielsen back to comic opera. At the end of her five months' tour in America they hope to have defeated her ambition, but they will not succeed. Miss Nielsen is triumphing in spite of them". He suggests "They do not properly advertise her" and bizarrely, "It is Shubert's first venture in the field and I predict it will be their last". Helluva spin since Shubert had bribed him for a Broadway baby. The opera venture was Sam. Lee had no intent of fulfilling the conditions; perhaps sessions in a steam room with Perley were a factor, we don't know. In any case, as a faux manager nicely bribed, enforcing contract terms were the remora's duty he did not. If it derailed, how'd he let that happen? Notoriously unreliable Lee Shubert financials suggest the tour broke even until Alice broke the chain.

Since 1896 Alice Nielsen had toured by rail. This trip wasn't cozy with private car, bath, bed, dining room. Russell recalls, "'One night stands' in America...were not exactly an amusing way of gaining one's livelihood. Distances appalling, hotels filthy, food uneatable".

Recoils at "hardship and privations of bad accommodations in small towns. Visitors from abroad were rare birds and the idea they should be pampered had only developed on the fringes of the country. We were regarded as 'greenhorns.' Our party, which consisted mostly of Latins, was often treated with contempt by suspicious hotel-keepers who considered us 'a heap of good-for-nothing peanut-eating dagos who chattered like monkeys in a cage.'"

They traverse the Midwest in winter: "We often traveled from town to town without sleeping in a bed for six or seven nights. After a performance we would hurry off to a railway station in a broken-down carriage drawn by wretched horses that continually slipped on the ice-covered roads, only to find that a snowstorm had delayed our train for several hours.

"The waiting-rooms of the small towns of the Middle West were scarcely as comfortable as cattle sheds in England, but anything was better than exposing ourselves to the wind-driven snow. So we carried our own suitcases (as often there were no porters in the railway stations) and had to pick our weary way through sleeping negroes to find a corner where we could huddle together until the arrival of the train.

"We journeyed through the Middle West, arriving early in the morning at a town called Meridian, in Kansas. We were advertised to perform that night, and anxious to make up for several hours delay. As the train crept slowly into the station we saw what might have been a scene from the day of judgment—houses torn in half, trees uprooted, pavements twisted and dazed inhabitants frantically poking about the ruins. 'Guess it ain't no good unpacking that there scenery today, Govenor', a rough-looking person called out as I walked towards the van; 'you won't be able to give no darn show in this town, there ain't a brick house left standing.'

"The chaos, we discovered, was the result of a cyclone that had come whirling from the prairie with such terrific force that buildings in a thorough-fare as long and broad as Regent Street had been complete destroyed. Fortunately for us, a few houses built on a hill outside the town were still intact. One of them was occupied by a lover of music who, hearing of our plight, offered us refuge".

Skips the pocketed Ziegfeld-Shubert cash "advances", he often repeats how Lee Shubert had "twice urged her to accept a contract to return to comic opera. I came to America to prevent this, and I am going to do it".

Paints himself Alice's "patron" when penniless except for a percenage of her revenue. When gullible Chicago suggests "It has been hinted that, were Miss Nielsen without the influence of her tutor and patron [!], she might be persuaded to return to comic opera", Lee Shubert coyly responds "I have something to say, but I shan't say it".

As this wayward gossip spins webs, people who do stuff are leading the way. Puccini and Herbert compose a unified musical score. Herbert blends high and pop art with folk art. Loss of this unified approach leaves the variety hodge-podge of pop confections: *Singing in the Rain (1952), Good Vibrations* (2005), *Spring Awakening* (2007), *Mama Mia* (2001).

Before Christmas, Nielsen sings in Denver, nearing San Francisco.

San Francisco Call reports Dec 14th, "Alice Nielsen is coming with own company" bypassing Salt Lake and "direct from Denver" December 26. She will join the Tivioli orchestra conducted by Steindorf. One Night Only. Next day, San Jose's Victory Theatre then Oakland's MacDonough.

Chicago Tribune publishes on December 17th Alice's *How to Become Prima Donna*. In an aside she reveals her extensive sense of the acoustic properties of various theatres with insight on her artistic life. At this point, she gives a reasoned view of her hovering remora: vocal coach. Nothing more. Of course, she leaves his financial dependence untold. No mention of the money pocketed since 1901; fed him a decade until he found his mediocrity. 1970's Quaintance Eaton wrongly painted Nielsen as an impresario's gal; well, Russell ain't no impresario nohow. Alice Nielsen was singing onstage for the paying audiences. Eaton got it backwards. Before this biography, canards carried the day by default. Facts fix fog. Her deal with the remora was business, bad business, an unfair trade agreement.

For Chicago, Nielsen claims she trained in Rome. Was Naples. At no point will Alice clarify time split among England, Italy, France, and Spain between 1901-1905. Only to local press in America will she pitch the name of her remora to help his purse with coins from young Americans who pay for brief auditions with no job pending. Bevignani's importance to her success she omits. And Valerga, always a friend whenever they have time.

ADVICE TO SINGERS: HOW TO BECOME A PRIMA DONNA
by Alice Nielsen

It is an easy matter to talk of being a grand opera prima donna, but the difficulties which beset the path of an ambitious and aspiring student are incredible. In saying this, I am naturally influenced by my own personal experiences, but I believe that the difficulties I have had to contend with are nothing as compared to those which have been experienced by hundreds of others.

A girl born in this country is told by her family and her friends that she possesses an exceptionally good voice. She, herself, is conscious of possessing this heaven-born gift, and she decides to cultivate her voice for the purpose of singing in public. Following on this decision, she is at one brought face to face with the vital question of where and with whom she shall study. Is she going to aim at grand opera, the concert platform, or the comic opera stage? Should she choose grand opera as her career I am afraid she has no alternative but to sail for Europe with as little delay as possible.

Should she not have been brought into contact with the more cultured and exclusive musical set of America, she may be surprised to find that in the home of opera the word "grand" is seldom used.

Here and in England there is a sharp line of demarcation drawn between grand opera and comic opera, but in Europe the term 'opera comic' includes such masterpieces as *Carmen, Mignon, Manon, Il Barbiere* etc, whereas what we call comic opera is known as "opera bouffe" or "operetta" and has little or no claim on the favor of the Latin races.

America abounds with good teachers, and when I say that it is necessary to go to Europe to study, it is not meant as a reflection on their abilities. I wager that I am as good and as loyal an American as will be found in the States, but this is an English-speaking country, and its great force is commerce, and as a center for operatic study it lacks both languages, artistic atmosphere and the opportunity of gaining practical experience. The latter is the really insurmountable obstacle which presents itself to the would-be home student for an operatic career; and, admitting that she can acquire her languages, train her voice and get her style within a car ride of her home, where is she to debut? Where is she to witness the various interpretations of her roles by other artists, and where is she to gain that finish and abandon which alone comes from the actual experience of the footlights? My answer is, Italy. And I name this beautiful country in preference to any other because, apart from its climatic and artistic advantages, it possesses more opera houses within a limited area than any other place in the world.

A village of 3,000 inhabitants has its dear little theatre which is always a miniature opera house with its tiers of boxes, its open auditorium to sing into, with no balconies and galleries butting into the center and cutting one's voice in half. Even the stage is constructed so that the public shall get the full benefit of the vocal efforts of the singer, and those who know the country will remember the protruding semi-circle, which protects the singer's voice from being lost in the wings and paraphernalia of the stage settings.

The Italian public is in itself a teacher. If you sing musically, if you invest a bar of melody with the true note of pathos, or if you sustain a tone until it dies into the distance, a murmur of approval rewards your efforts and encourages you to do better things without having to wait until the end of the act to know whether you have satisfied the exigencies of your listeners. On the other hand, that same public is merciless. A faulty intonation, a careless scale—even a word incorrectly pronounced—will be deliberately hissed; and if an artist attempts to go through a performance accentuating these defects, it may be necessary for the impresario to lower the curtain and close the theatre: hence the value of studying in Italy—for no matter how much encouragement you may have from you teacher and how sincerely he may believe in your talents, it is from the public and the public only, that you can get the final verdict which justifies you in continuing the fight for supremacy.

It is generally known that I pursued my studies with Henry Russell, who occupied a prominent position amongst London teachers when I visited that city in *The Fortune Teller*, nearly five years ago. He was asked to hear me sing, and when at the end of the performance he was introduced to me behind the stage, he told me bluntly and in few words that if I did not stop dancing and singing high E-flats seven times a week, I would not have a shred of voice left in two years.

His frank disapproval of my methods was rather a surprise, after the many encomiums I had received from other members of his profession. The conviction of his sincerity made me anxious to induce him to continue his criticism. Here I would venture to advise every student to beware of a teacher who immediately flatters her into the belief that she is a future Patti, who will take the world by storm after a year or two of study.

Mr. Russell carefully examined my voice and pronounced it to be an instrument worthy of a higher form of art than that to which I was devoting my energies. He warned me that to make the necessary change it would take two to three years hard study, during which time I should be unable to earn a cent. Fortunately for me, Mr. Russell had just been offered an important position as teacher in Italy, and I made up my mind to follow him to Rome, in which city I acquired the school of singing to which I attribute a large portion of the successes which I have scored in my new career.

For the benefit of those who may need a guiding hand I will summarize as briefly as possible the nature of the tuition I received. For six months I was made to study breath control and tone formation—never separately but in their relation to each other—which, to students, is an important point of distinction. To learn to articulate clearly was my next occupation and I went through a course of interesting and special exercises to enable me to overcome defects of enunciations, which are the birth inheritance of English speaking races. Finally equality, freedom and the art of singing legato occupied the second year of my studies, and how far I was successful in acquiring these qualities I must leave to my public to judge.

I remembered Mr. Russell's warnings and I think I derived almost as much benefit from them as I did from his tuition, "Never aim at making your voice bigger than its natural capacity", he would say, if I attempted to force any of my tones. "Never try to impersonate a role which is not within the natural resources of your temperament or your voice; never pine over your natural limitations, but let your knowledge of those limitations be so complete that the public never sees you striving for that which it feels you cannot attain".

These and other words of wisdom helped me to avoid some of the snares into which my students often fall. Space prevents me from dealing as largely as I should like to with the subject, but in conclusion I would like to say that in selecting a teacher be sure that he has, in addition to a technical knowledge of the voice, a practical knowledge of the requirements which fit a woman to make a successful operatic career. I was fortunate in having a teacher who is at the head of great operatic enterprises [Oddly implies Russell by omitting Bevignani's name], but there is often danger of a student being innocently misled by enthusiastic vocal faddists, who imagine that when their pupils acquire a special method of so-called voice production this is a sufficient equipment to stir large audiences to enthusiasm. Mr. Russell always used to tell me that no teacher can make an artist, but that more often— an artist makes the teacher. [Literally his cash in this case]

The gifts of magnetism, sympathy and personal charm enter so largely into an artists success that it is absurd for teachers to ignore the importance of the presence of these factors, and I think it is quite as injurious for students to depend entirely upon their instructors for their future success as it is absurd for conceited novices to imagine they can jump into fame without the assistance of experience and able masters.

Nielsen's bogus implication that Russell stood ever "at the head of great operatic enterprises" suggests the fine-spun Irish irony of an inside joke. After all, *Pasquale* cast miserable; Waldorf by Duse aided by Tosti as talent scout; San Carlo at Covent arranged by the actual manager in Napoli.

Bevignani actually headed great operatic enterprises: he taught Alice's repertoire, conducted and coached Patti and Nilsson.

December 19th, stopping along her old vaudeville route Nielsen plays Denver's Central Presbyterian for a "grand operatic concert". The London handiman is amazed: "After every variety of trail and tribulation we arrived in Denver, that strange city sprung up in the mountains of Colorado—an extraordinary conglomeration of wonderful new houses and primitive shacks that sing of vast wealth wrested suddenly from the surrounding hills". Schooled in Chicago about "Pork Kings", Alice's wanna-be sycophant no longer speaks scornfully of America's newly-rich.

Denver is "a city of great contrast, both physical and hum; a city of pride, confidence and amazing vitality; where riches were made almost overnight, and lost sometimes as quickly; where the gambler, the miner and the western businessman rubbed shoulders.... Never have I seen a place more typical of what I take to be the American characteristics of impatience, affluence, generosity, youthfulness and unquestioning confidence in the future. Here, at least we found a good hotel".

Most important is the reunion with bosom pal Grimthorpe: "The first evening I was sitting alone in the dining room, immersed in gloom, thinking of the old days of luxury in Curzon Street, of Tosti and the scintillating group I had left in London—and for what?—when suddenly I felt a hand on my shoulder. 'Hen, what the devil are you doing here?'

"Could I be dreaming? No, it was not a vision, but actually my old friend Grimthorpe. His surprise was almost as great as mine, and the excitement of finding ourselves together in the wilderness reduced us to a state of incoherency. Finally I gathered that he had been taking a cure for his rheumatism, and was on his way back to NY.

"I outlined my past adventures and the programme I had undertaken for the next few months. The idea of my sheparding such a company through the wilds of the West so intrigued and amused him that he decided to change his plans and to accompany us as far as the coast".

Shearing more like. Newbie Russell the supernumerary shepherd; droll.

"The fact that a member of the House of Lords was traveling in an ordinary day coach with a small Italian opera company gave the reporters of the prairie towns unlimited scope which they used to their own ends, indirectly benefiting us". Slap at Nielsen by hubris, "Not the presence of the greatest singer in the world could have lent us more publicity, and thanks to this our progress became triumphant".

Top idiocy by the roving remora. Grimthorpe didn't sing a note. Flatters his banker lad, never the star who kept and fed him. In reality, Grimthorpe got little or no press at all. The star has been big national news a decade.

With or without the duo of intimate old pals Russell and Grimthorpe, Alice Nielsen would return to San Francisco by Christmas Eve. If she could make it there.... Momentum gained in Chicago explodes in California.

San Francisco changes everything. Partly, her ensemble has jelled. Partly, Tivoli unleashes a quality show. Partly, Lee Shubert dropped as producer. Excitement grows a frenzy as Nielsen nears the Golden City.

Two days before her concert *SF Call* gives Alice Nielsen a feature (Dec 24) with the revealing revelation of *Satanella!*

"Long time we have been hearing of Alice Nielsen in grand opera, little Alice Nielsen who used to do 'bits' at the Tivoli and finally emerged to fame as a charming Satanella".

Cheating us, Alice skips the big *Satanella* fun. More the pity pomposity; could we ever miss Alice Nielsen in her first big hit: playing devilish Satanella in Balfe's *Satanella*? His opera, also titled *The Power of Love*, a 19th-century hit with very Broadway-style dialog and songs. That hybrid art form hated by Shaw and Russell. In Balfe's shows people speak, sing and dance: pure Broadway, or life as it is lived. Satanella is a she-devil in an occult story. Count Rupert of Brockenberg had wealth. He lost a fortune gaming then sold his soul to the devil like anybody would do. Like Ziegfeld did. Satanella, sent to ensnare Rupert, sends fiancé Stella into slavery and puts herself in the bride's dress on wedding night. We skip the fun part.

At the end, Satanella rescues fiancé and is herself saved by a rosary given by forgiving, grateful Stella. The cast: "Nobles, Peasants, Pirates, Demons &c". Nielsen's Satanella began with recitative, *"Myself once more...all woman now..."* then gorgeously sings, *"There's a power whose sway, Angel souls adore, And the lost obey, Weeping evermore. Doubtful mortals prize, Smiles from it above, Bliss that never dies, Such thy power—oh, love!"*

Satanella's *Power of Love* showcases the beauty and skill of Nielsen's voice to great advantage. Only *San Francisco Call*—working from memory—will link Alice Nielsen's career with Balfe's *Satanella*. Alice never mentions the spirited show to press. Sticks to Gilbert & Sullivan, Donizetti, Herbert, Puccini. Like that.

"After that...the Bostonians got hold of the young Californian, who made a stir all through comic opera land.... Rumors, at first incredulously received, came along as to the little singer's intention to adventure into grand opera". With rare accuracy, *Call* continues "Mancinelli himself [at request of Lady DeGrey] was said to have advised her to the step". Then side-steps Tosti and Bevignani who taught her to sing the operas, and absurdly promotes the remora's agenda of pathetic self-aggrandizement: "One heard of her then at Rome, her voice in charge of Henry Russell" now a "famous maestro of singing" he wasn't.

Call confirms a suggestion that Alice Nielsen sang in Milan's *La Scala*: "In Naples one heard of again...like word came from Milan. Then London. Miss Nielsen's success in London, in particular as Zerlina in *Don Giovanni*, seems to have been unquestioned. The freshness and purity of the voice, its easy production, the charm and piquancy of the little singer's acting, all were subjects of the most favorable comment".

Call pins NYC's minority of resistant critics: "Her home tour beginning in NY has not occasioned any great furor so far, the American critic...not being disposed to take very seriously her grand opera aspirations, and jealous possibly of the undoubted loss to comic opera".

Standing Room Only the pride of San Francisco performs: "Tuesday evening Miss Nielsen appears at the Tivoli and a house already practically sold out will be there to hear her. She will be singing against the note, still brilliantly fluting through the Tivoli, of Tetrazzini. But also, the little singer will be singing against her own comic opera memories and to an audience proud of her and widely prejudiced in her favor—which perhaps squares the critical situation". Wonderfully, "Miss Nielsen's company is said to be good.... Importantly, the opera will be again sung" Sunday for those "unable to get seats on Tuesday".

So it was. The former Tivoli understudy brought her miracle of progress to a packed San Francisco audience who knew her long before.

She leaves no doubt. "Miss Nielsen's Triumph" headlines *Musical America* Dec 27th. "Alice Nielsen scored a triumph in her first appearance in grand opera in this her native city, last night. Miss Nielsen caused much favorable comment by the admirable manner in which she essayed the role of Norina in *Don Pasquale*".

Blanche Partington agrees, "Alice Nielsen Triumphant in *Don Pasquale*" in *Call* (Dec 27). Partington, keen observer of the literary scene, is a close friend of Ambrose Bierce and Jack London. Her siblings include painter

Richard and opera singer Phyllis (Francis Peralta). Eventually Blanche will join Christian Science. Never marries. Interestingly, Nielsen's most subtle appreciations arise from two critics associated with Christian Science: Partington and Strang.

Partington's poetic tale of Nielsen's triumph deserves preservation: "Brava, little Nielsen! Brava! Alice Nielsen came home last night to show what she could do in grand opera. She came as Norina...Tivoli the place and Pacific Avenue, Telegraph Hill and everything between for audience. We have heard here of Milan approving, of Naples admiring, of Miss Nielsen's London triumphs—but she 'had to show us', as they say at the Orpheum. She 'showed us' last night, and the local incredulity as to its own was neatly shattered, and those who believed that the fetching little singer had simply dimpled her way into grand opera were fairly confuted. For Miss Nielsen has distinctly 'arrived.'

"The poetic fitness would have been better served had it been the old Tivoli where Alice Nielsen sang last night. It was there that the silvery little voice was first heard and that fascinating little mole first seen. But she did not look a day different last night. She is just the same round-eyed, dimpled, dainty little thing as ever, and the voice, though larger, is still fresh and pure. But the Nielsen of last night is a very different person from the little singer that used to do 'bits' at the old Tivoli".

Insightful Partington recognizes Nielsen's artistic progress: "Perhaps she has not yet the full sweep of grand opera. A year will make a tremendous difference in the singer. She is now on the operatic fence".

If two or so NYC holdouts had said Nielsen went too far; Partington sees her not going far enough: "Palpably she is a little afraid of the comic opera suggestion, and as *Don Pasquale* happens to be that kind of opera, one misses therein the natural merriment that she fears to bring to the role. But give Miss Nielsen the aplomb that comes from full recognition, and the operatic stage will gain one of the most charming of the lighter lyric singers. She sang a charming Norina last night that in time should be as brilliant as it is now exquisite. That means, of course, that Miss Nielsen, always a good student, has been hard at work since she left here.

"Her coloratura work in particular has gained and the voice has gained both in volume and quality. The trill is still not good, but the scales pearl out delightfully and she has one of the prettiest of staccatos. She is still true as a lark in the intonation and the purity and freshness of the voice surprise anew each time one thinks of them. And as easily as a lark she sings, phrasing with charming taste—except perhaps for an exaggerated pianissimo. Miss Nielsen is not the fair Luisa but from her work last night one sees ample room both for her and Tetrazzini on the grand opera stage. Even Telegraph Hill shouted 'Bis!' for her, and the rest of the house heartily added its quota of appreciation".

Alice Nielsen, best legs in town, prettiest girl in grand opera.

"As to acting—in spite of the aforesaid fear of being wholly her very comical self—Miss Nielsen was most piquantly satisfying, and as to picture she was prettiest that grand opera has to give".

Nielsen's gift *Good-Bye* pricks Partington as too proud. "That was why, perhaps, one forgave the last curtain being rung up while she sang Tosti's

Good-Bye that had been 'requested' by some good but inartistic souls. Not that she did not sing it well but that kind of things should be left to the Melbas and Pattis. Miss Nielsen is much too pretty so to offend". And Alice had learned this air by Tosti from Valerga and of course from Tosti.

In the cast: "A little jewel of a tenor, a pocket Guille, who matches Miss Nielsen's canary note with a little vocal silver of his own, Signor Pratti...is pure tenor, lyric in the fullest sense...not a powerful voice but so delicately shaded, so nicely used, that all the effect of volume is given. He smiles as prettily as he sings, which makes up for acting that is somewhat naïve. Barytone Fratodi might be better if he remembered to bring the rest of his voice along—and Signor Rosa is almost a voiceless basso".

At Tivoli the show is fully cast: "Tivoli chorus, so rejoiced to get into grand opera again that it came in a scene ahead, did well".

After this triumph, confidence rises. A flurry of West Coast press focus on "the Nielsen" as hero. Within days, Nielsen cuts Shubert and joins his rivals. Leaves the biz dialog to remora Russell who with forked tongue claims the Shuberts [Lee] were "trying to drive Miss Nielsen back to comic opera. At the end of her five months' tour in America they hope to have defeated her. This kind of thing will not succeed".

Shubert wittily responds he has "the greatest respect for Alice Nielsen's talent especially in the comic opera field".

Day after her Tivoli gala, Nielsen gives two major interviews. First is *LA Times'* Ashton Stevens, who reveals Alice traveling with Hortense. "It is Alice Nielsen's morning-after and I am waiting for her in the lounge of the St. Francis hotel. Surely this morning after will be a joyous one, for Miss Nielsen, coming home a prima donna in Italian and triumphing in her little Tivoli presentation of *Don Pasquale*, almost as did the American singer of Mr. Fitch's *Captain Jinks*, is a subject for celebration".

Clyde Fitche's *Captain Jinks of the Horse Marines* (1902), popular play with Ethel Barrymore as Aurelia, was a popular song by William Lingard before it was a musical by Sheldon Harnick then a satiric novel by Ernest Cosby: "*I'm Captain Jinks of the Horse Marines, I feed my horse on corn and beans, And sport young ladies in their teens, Tho' a Captain in the Army. I teach the ladies how to dance, how to dance, how to dance, For I'm the pet of the Army*".

Says Stevens, "I am wondering if any in that clamorous cheering gallery of the night before were Wigwam patrons of the other days when Alice Nielsen the girl sang 'side by each' with Tommy Leary, the Irish low comedian and fastidious Wigwam firstnighters paid ten cents at the door and five cents within for much foam and a little red, and as much again for an Havana-plated cigar".

Russell arrives with his usual chatty spin, "Very happy. He feels like thanking somebody, indeed he thanks me wherefore I feel like one of the trustees of the Voice of the People". Although not onstage, he "pours out enthusiastically: 'Ah that welcome last night! I cannot tell you what it meant to Miss Nielsen and to me.

"When I met you at the Tivoli I did not tell you what Miss Nielsen had suffered in NY; I did not want to arouse your sympathy. I wanted the critics' unbiased opinion of Miss Nielsen's voice. But now that she has sung and the verdict has been given, I can tell you what she has suffered".

Confesses the NY orchestra out of tune: "It is terrible to think what the Shuberts did to ruin her performance of *Don Pasquale* in NY. Six, yes, six instruments in the orchestra provided were vilely out of tune. Such a conspiracy!'" Yes very odd Russell had permitted that to happen.

"'But I was about to say that Miss Nielsen will be down in a minute— Oh, here she is now!'

"Unwittingly I looked around for a woman of prima donna appearance— and shake hands with a casually clad girl that looks not unlike one I used to see as a boy when the Tivoli chorus would come chattering down the old Eddy-street steps after rehearsal. I tell her so.

"'The same girl! If you are looking for ancient history, don't forget the Wigwam. I must', she says, 'come into the café and bite some breakfast.'

"And it matters not at all that I have already bitten my breakfast, I must meet sister Hortense who is there. So we bolt".

They take a table, "to the apparent consternation of twenty waiters and the delighted amazement of twice as many guests; and Miss Nielsen's sister, like enough to be her twin, hastily approaches from a far table".

Russell fails to direct attention to his companion Gilmore: "Mr. Russell joins, but he's too nervous to sit. He hovers about, talking eagerly. 'Lord Gilmore wanted you at luncheon', he says to Miss Nielsen". Ignoring Russell, spurning Gilmore, Alice disappears to sing to a blind doorman.

Russell spoke "swiftly" of the London smart set. Compared Nielsen's London opera performances with Melba, "the idol of the English public, though I could never understand why". Oft repeats the phrase: could never understand why. His brother Landon Ronald conducts and accompanies Melba, yet get no mention for creating Alice's concerts with Victor Morel: "I said to Morel: 'London has not heard you for ten years. Come sing in this production of *Rigoletto* and it will be the making of her!' He sang, and after the big duet he retired to let her take the applause".

"'Yes', chimes Miss Alice, "'after he had first put his arm around my waist and almost carried me to the footlights.'"

Russell continues, "'I wish her San Francisco admirers could hear Alice in these operas. *Don Pasquale* is only a little of the story. I wish you could hear her sing Mozart, hear her sing Cherubina's *voi che aspete*; I am very proud of the way she sings that". Dropping many names he departs.

Nielsen now "Opens fire. 'Don't think because he mentioned the dollars I might have saved that he thinks of money, for Mr. Russell is an artist if there ever was one'". Yes, diva. He has pocketed how much from your patrons, and Ziegfeld and Shubert. Thoughtlessly, perhaps. Not thinking of the money, he mindlessly puts the money in his purse and forgets you.

Alice the artist earns the money. Her choices have financial results. Her arty remora clings doggedly since London so as not to teach anymore. £1,000 from Ziegfeld to deliver Alice to the NYC ordeal. His fee from her receipts. Does not perform nor create. Strictly backstage. Doesn't care about money, he says, picking her pocket.

Alice the claque spins the teaching he said he hated: "He gave up the best sort of position in London to go to Rome and teach; and you know that very little money is to be made in Rome. In London he had everything and everybody; members of the royal family were his pupils". So the very little money in Rome, he doesn't think of. The more money in London, he doesn't think of neither. Giving this paradox thought seems unprofitable, yet long before Nielsen had arrived in London, Russell spent each winter teaching at the Roman music school, a key point of his marketing pitch in America. In Rome he could be intimate with bosom buddies D'Annunzio and Grimthorpe while leaving wife and kids in Britain. Alice has given up fortunes to pursue her art. Russell has spent her patron's money.

Further finishing the fog, Alice inflates him as a pianist who plays Wagner "and not a drop of German in him!—for his father was English and his mother Spanish [Jewish]. He sits and plays Wagner by ear, in any key— he transposes anything at sight or without music. One night at a concert I lost my music and he accompanied me even in songs he had never heard". This skill wasn't uncommon, as a decade earlier Alice bragged on the young Arthur Pryor who didn't need her to blarney him. After Tosti, Bevignani, Alice gushes: "He knows more about the voice than any other man; he knows absolutely how to place it and how to build it". She didn't say more than any woman, as Valerga.

Of course her purpose is to lure local singers into paying him a peck of pocket change to let the "impresario" listen to them sing a song.

Alice spins a new view of meeting Duse via Russell's intimate relations with D'Annunzio, portrayed by Lucy Hughes-Hallet's 2014 biography as a sexual predator using cocaine, petite as Russell, thinning hair and terrible teeth. D'Annunzio lives on Duse's money. Alice recasts the Duse meeting as a favor via the playwright. Contradicts her London account. "It was through his restoring Duse's voice that she became my instructor in acting. I'll tell you how it came about. He met Duse through D'Annunzio, and I was present when he gave her the first lesson in breathing. At once her voice improved. And she said she'd give him every dollar she made...."

Whatever Alice says serves to promote her attaché to paying locals.

Duse pushes Nielsen to be onstage natural and strong. "The idea of trying to act before Duse scared the life out of me. But that first lesson wasn't all compliments. When I was doing my bravest gesticulation, Duse commented, "Pugilistico!" That's exactly like a pugilist! You'd love Duse, she's such a dear and so beautiful. And don't blame me if I look proud when I mention her. I'm her only pupil. D'Annunzio told us that she had never before given a lesson".

Nielsen closes her pandering, "But you must remember that Duse didn't do this for me, but for Mr. Russell to whom she was grateful". That's not what Duse said about Alice as she dealt with the hovering go-between.

Joy at reaching San Francisco: "And so am I grateful—and happy! I'm the happiest woman in the world today.

Interestingly, "S-s-sh! He's coming back", Alice says.

Hortense intones the ironic: Russell "is a dear".

"Oho", said Alice, "Oho just listen to Hortense! On Christmas she tried to get him under the mistletoe". Hortense fails, Russell closer to guys.

Appears, "Alice be good enough to put down that cup of coffee and cream. That's the second, and one too many. I'm surprised, Hortense, that you let her have it". Disappears. Alice winks at Stevens, "Since he told me to put it down and isn't here to see how that's done, I'll proceed to obey", thereat drains cup. Let the talker talk, the artist is on the stage.

Stevens asks Nielsen how she got the courage to quit comic opera and the fortune it provided her. His question suggests he did not know she was robbed by Williams & Perley. In near future *LA Times* reports in detail when the two thieves fall out in a San Francisco court of law.

Nielsen reacts "in a burst of feeling. All my life I wanted to study music but poverty stood in the way, and poverty is a terrible obstacle. My mother fought poverty". Speaks of eight children, herself youngest. A few children too many for Sarah; and Alice wasn't youngest.

For this once, Alice confirms the timing of her first professional tour and does not pretend to be eight years old. At sixteen, she "'was able to earn a little. Soon as you know, I was earning more, but by that time [San Francisco 1892] I had become the family breadwinner. What I saved during the winter was eaten up by the idle summer months [only after 1895, the Bostonian hiatus]. The calls on my purse became heavier, and from year to year I put off studying".

Does not admit going broke in London, just "Oh I'd forgotten what poverty was like. But it came back, I tell you! I've been hard pressed during the last four years. I don't know what I should have done, but for Mr. Russell. He was nearly as poor as I, but he had influence, friends". And sold his influence for a percentage, parking money to his friends.

Yet she the famed star. Alice confirms Mrs. Philips sent a £1000 check, not cash. "He told only the briefest part of my story to Mrs. Lionel Philips, and she sent a check for a £1000 with the message there was more if I needed it. Thanks to that, I was able to look after my mother [no mention of son] and continue studying. And after the reception by last night's audience, I don't feel that the money and time have been wasted. I'm the happiest woman in the world". Steindorf and manager Leahy gave the Tivoli success. Leahy "laying off the regular company two nights to give her a chance to sing in the city". This gift she omits from the discourse.

Deemphasizing the NYC critical majority who strongly advised the Metropolitan Opera to hire her on the spot, Alice contrasts her Western welcome to the cavalier Gotham cavilling. Sets in motion her influential call for artistic independence by the West. And the West is history.

Of her NYC reception, "NY critics [three]—not the audience, the audience was everything that is kind—nearly broke my heart. If the critics here had been of the same opinion, you wouldn't have seen me today—nobody would. But I'll yet win those NY critics; and as it is, I'm the happiest woman in the world. And why?"

Her outpouring devolves a poor choice: "Sift it all and you will find that it is because of Mr. Russell. Everything has come through him. He has been to me like—like a knight—like Lohengrin?" To be fair, he had already cost her a second year at Covent, a Met debut with Herbert, a large chunk of patron cash, lured her to Lee Shubert, taken cash from Ziegfeld, and primps to the press if they don't know better.

To be fair to Russell, he has already cost her a year starring at Covent Garden, debut at the Met with Herbert, ongoing undercuts by Lee Shubert, and a large chunk of patron cash. To be fair to Russell, he has hired cheap supporting cast, dealt abysmally with Ziegfeld and Shubert for payoffs, and puffs himself to press if they don't know better. Yes, diva. Only Alice Nielsen could pull success out of that hat he had concatenated.

"My life today looks to me like a beautiful fairy tale".

These well-crafted, fully-cast San Francisco performances with Steindorf could very well compare to what Herbert would have delivered for Alice Nielsen at the Met in NYC if the projects had been staged.

Thwarted in NYC, praised in California.

December in San Francisco saves Alice Nielsen again, as in 1891.

Los Angeles waits expectantly.

In this glorious success, Nielsen speaks also with Blanche Partington in a piece published on New Years' Eve in *San Francisco Call*. Most savvy of any feature on the singer since London's *Mostly About People*, Partington knows much, observes closely, feels keenly, writes well:

It was the morning after. The very air seemed full of it. The big Christmas tree towering and glittering in the St. Francis lobby seemed only a part of it, of Alice Nielsen's triumph of the night before. Even his sophisticated majesty, the bellboy, seemed impressed, tweaking a discreet thumb over his shoulder in the direction of the bit of a girl coming to meet me from the elevator. "It's Alice Nielsen", the man next me whispered to the man next him. "Alice Nielsen", the ermined woman passed off to her friend in mink, sisterly rejoicing in her smile. The bored person at the counter even had taken time to say, as I handed in my card, "Awful glad the little woman has made good. She's a sweet little thing".

Then a soft, small: "How d'ye do?" and a friendly little hand tucked into mine, and I met Alice Nielsen. Where should we talk? Not there, in the hall, for all the keen, clean, sweet and spice of the tree alluring. Nor in the library—where there were more folk to whisper "Alice Nielsen".

Upstairs we went, fourth floor. "Haven't a drawing-room—yet", the little singer laughed, but there was nothing to quarrel with the spacious quarters into which we turned.

It was when my hostess dragged up the next coziest seat that I found that "little" Alice Nielsen's eyes were level with mine. Honorably I had given her more than our noble five feet five, yet I defy anyone to call her aught but "little" [Nielsen stood five feet two (158 cm)]. She is that kind, a slim dimpled demure nestling thing that you want to stroke. Her round, hazel eyes look up at you with trustful appeal, her round childlike cheek is another appeal. Her baby mouth seems to pout "Please be good to me", and you would think him a villain indeed who should bring a frown to that smooth, child brow.

Yet life has meant hard things to Alice Nielsen. That was what we began with—some of the hard things. Whimpering? No. Anything else I heard from Alice Nielsen. Of the NY critics who would appear to have been manifestly unjust to her, she simply said: "I suppose they just didn't like me"—then beamed—"but I'll make them like me some day".

She did not say "it was hard to come home to be so treated". She did not suggest cabals, critical Mafias, critical ignorance or stupidity. Simply she "supposed that the critics did not like her". There was the same fine tolerance in her viewpoints throughout.

There is in fact, all kinds of curious strength and wisdom behind Alice Nielsen's baby make-up. Here we have all known that behind her demure deviltry lay a large ambition.

We have not known, most of us, of the long faithfulness to an artistic ideal that has governed the little singer's life. Nor have we known of her reverent studentship, of the long stern sacrifice that has placed her where she is. Perhaps the Nielsen dimples have helped—why not—since singers must be seen as well as heard. And I found in Miss Nielsen a fine grace of gratitude, a most wholesome modesty, a large courage, and above all the sweet reasonableness, before mentioned, that must have gone far to contribute to her success.

In a word then she disposed of the NY critics and added blithely: "But San Francisco made up last night". Afraid?—to my query. "I should think I was afraid! Never was more nervous in my life! I'd had such a big success in comic opera here and I was afraid you would think I didn't belong in grand opera. But the minute after my first song, I knew you were with me—oh, but I was happy". So were we, I told her.

And how did she like our new Tivoli? [Tivoli steadily reincarnates until destroyed by earthquake].

"It's lovely. But honestly I missed the old house. It was such a dear, homely, comfy old hole—wasn't it? But this new place is beautiful, like an Italian theatre".

But it was at the old Tivoli you began.

"That I really began", Nielsen replied.

Partington recalls Nielsen at Oakland, "Penitently she whispered then that she was not a Californian, and I spared her any further confession here. It was as Yum-Yum that her California career began, and of all places at the Oakland Theatre. Before that—well, she told it this way".

Nielsen tells Partington of singing in that paid tour at age eight—not the sixteen she had told Stevens earlier the same day.

Nielsen: "We were very poor, you know, mother couldn't do anything to help me. I was the youngest of eight [four], and the only one of them that helped mother—the only one that could help her [all the kids worked]. Wasn't it nice I could. But I was in a juvenile company when I was eight years old, and—well, I fell I have been pretty much grown-up all my life".

Partington: "Then came the Oakland days, where those who remember things remember a round-eyed, pigtailed girl going to and from the theatre. Then came Wigwam days in San Francisco".

Nielsen: "I'm proud of that time. Imagine, I got $90 a week for singing ballads and doing condensed opera. And what do you think? I gave that up for $30 a week at the Tivoli and the chance to sing 'real' things!"

Partington: "She did not say she was proud of that. The page in *Nanon* [Zell and Genée, Vienna, 1877] was her first part at the Tivoli, she remembered. Then 'everything.' She understudied everybody. She sang all sorts of parts.

"*Satanella* [!!!] was her first real chance.

"Seventeen months of this, the Wigwam dangling its $90 a week meanwhile before her, and then the Bostonians heard her [Sept. 1905].

Nielsen: "You don't need to tell, but it was *Lucia* in English that I was singing—God forgive me!" She laughs; relates the pilgrim progress whereat diva praises the way of the remora lifted from Marchesi as Velerga would well know. Tall tale told, Partington relays readers a fable that the faux impresario without portfolio or purse deigned to attend the most popular musical in London and "heard her and The Chance came. There was big, beautiful gratitude in Miss Nielsen's voice as she said the name. There was gratitude in her hazel eyes, there was all gratitude in her next quick words". Alice acts very well, as many observers observe. And down the sluce go the dregs, "Oh, I simply cannot tell you what Mr. Russell has done for me. He has done everything. He has taught me everything; he has given me every opportunity. It is only right I should say this, that you should understand it, that you should tell the people about it". So to pay him the coins he thinks about constantly. She steps out, speaking Italian, returns: "Mr. Russell is out. I talk Italian like a Chinese, don't I?"

Partington. "I thought it went pretty good last night".

Nielsen: "Caruso says it is good, but then he is very kind. He is most kind. What do you think? He came to meet me at the steamer at NY and told the reporters how good I was. Did it just to help me, I understand—"

Partington: "Back to London...."

Nielsen: "It was the queerest way I went to Mr. Russell. One of my chorus girls went to study with him. She annoyed me to death about this wonderful teacher of hers. I suppose she annoyed him to death about me.

"Then there was a man that kept asking Mr. Russell to go hear me— Fernando Valero, another singer".

Valero's interest in Alice is artistically significant. The great Spanish tenor [1854-1914] and noted actor with exceptional breath support, had made his 1878 début at Madrid's *Teatro Real*. Perhaps he is the missing link to Nielsen's stay in Spain. They met spring 1901. He was Don Jose in *Carmen* and *Rigoletto*'s Duke at Covent during the season she auditions for Higgins. Valero joined the Met 1901-02, retiring to teach voice at St. Petersburg, Russia (*Grandi Tenori*, J. Anthonisen, 2005).

Nielsen continues, "He told him—Mr. Russell did—that he was sure I had 'a voice like a cat!' I guess it was to get rid of them that he did come to hear me at last.'"

Partington: "And went into raptures—"

Nielsen: "Not so that you could notice it. In fact he said he didn't know what kind of a voice it was; that it was tremolo in the middle; that it was perhaps good in spots; that he couldn't tell because I wasn't singing anything, only that pitter-patter!"

Alice again misleads about her hit show: "They didn't like *The Fortune Teller* in London anyway. They like the more delicate opera. But I had a personal success in it. In fact all the critics were picking out parts that I ought to sing. They were perfectly horrified at my flopping up in the air and dancing a cakewalk!" The most popular part of the show which became legendary since.

In this version Russell meets Nielsen at his studio. She sings *The King of Thule*: "Then he told me that I ought to give up comic opera, told me what he thought I could perhaps do and', her hands clasped themselves, 'and—oh Lord! I thought, perhaps here's the man who can help me". The only way out was stop the show. Health complaint. Yes, help is here.

"All my life I had wanted this thing. But no one, not one person had wished to elevate me". No one person. Except Ida Valerga, Laurence Irving, Arditi, Tosti, Grey, Consuelo Yznaga, Mrs. Phillips, Henry Higgins, Bevignani, Puccini, Caruso, the Graus.... Only the top musical star in North America and London with open doors anyplace she wants.

Vaguely, "They all thought I was good enough as I was but all the time I was wanting, wanting this". This antique Bellini comic opera.

Alice hides everything of the severe financial and emotional abuses by Williams & Perley when she candidly confesses her plight: "I wasn't well then, in London. And I had about given up my ambition. And I had no money, was tired out, was ill, remember. Then this man took me—you can imagine that I am grateful". This man pocketed her patron's gift, a huge sum in those days. Associated himself with proven stars Nielsen and Duse and develops nobody. Laurence Irving and Duchess Consuelo arrange contacts. Mrs. Phillips donates a fortune (£1,000) to start Alice to Italy. As the remora so well said: a star as student makes the teacher's career. And now touted as impresario without portfolio. After all, he has the massive accomplishment of his several seasons in Rome at the music school and a playmate libertine pal D'Annunzio with the penis-shaped shoes.

Birds of a feather flock. And brag to exploit. And beg for favors.

By Nielsen's present fancy, Russell took her to Mancinelli at Covent so the maestro could hear her "'voice in the raw.' Yet it was Lady Grey made that happen. Trots out the canard he "himself gave a fall season of grand opera at Covent Garden with Caruso and Maurel". Yet he only took, never gave. Perhaps not yet undeceived about the actual San Carlo arrangement until reading the man's confession two decades later: manager Robert De Sanni sent him to keep an eye on Sanni's girlfriend. Puccini and San Carlo staff handle the shows. Likewise was dodging his cheap cast and collusion with Ziegfeld and Shubert. Meanwhile, blarney paints a false competence.

Partington: "And that was the end of Alice Nielsen's comic opera career. She entered then upon a course of study with Mr. Russell, of which she speaks as a priest of his rites. High breathing 'like Melba's and Sembrich's' is the basis of his method and for eight weeks she did nothing else". Given her literal schedule with Bevignini the eight weeks seems iffy.

Polish dramatic coloratura soprano, Sembrich (1858-1935) sang for Liszt at sixteen, studied voice with the Lamperti son and father, debuted at Covent 1880 and Met 1883 where she set the record for debut roles, retiring 1909 to teach voice at Curtis and Julliard before retiring to Lake Placid; her museum is in Bolton Landing, NY. Melba of course had started with Piertro Cecchi; then had success under Marchesi in Paris.

Nielsen: "'After that', she opened her button of a mouth to show as many of the pearly teeth as it would, 'he asked me to do that and sing. Ah! There wasn't a sound! I'd never used the proper vocal muscles.'"

Alice, who can read a score to memory and perform it, also will visualize her roles: "And she sat there like little Miss Muffet and talked of the psychological side of the Russell [let us say, Nielsen] method. How she studied all her roles without singing a note, or rather...."

Nielsen: "'singing them with my brain. I used to hate to be alone, but now every moment some new feeling or thought of song is with me. It's funny, isn't it? I'm not talking like a lunatic, am I?'"

Partington: "I'm listening like one if you are".

At Waldorf Theatre, stars Duse, Calvé and Nielsen rotated nights until Calvé's cold left it to Duse and Nielsen. "An artistic success, this financially not so much so, Miss Nielsen told me" Partington relates. The Sam Shubert guarantees for the stars to appear was never revealed in their anecdotes.

Inevitably after pitching her remora madly to the press, Nielsen asked the reporter to tell the public he "would be glad to hear the San Francisco girls' voices and say that they might come to him at the St. Francis, and that he was here on a voyage of discovery". Alice's blarney be glib.

Partington blandly, "What does he think of the American voice?"

Nielsen: "That it is the finest in the world". Russell does not speak that way. Before abandoning the States he infamously ignores American voices to search across Soviet Russia, or as a cover appear so.

Encore show in NYC, encore show in San Francisco December 31st.

More than a tossed egg, Lee Shubert is axed: spokesman Russell tells press (*SF Telegraph* De 31), "He had severed all connection with the Shuberts". Shubert henceforth "would have nothing to do with Miss Nielsen's tour". Russell claims "interesting facts" are behind the separation, no details.

Lee Shuberts' denial: "Mr. Russell could not 'sever connections' with me for the good and sufficient reasons that we have had no dealings with him. We are not and have not been Miss Nielsen's principals". Ziegfeld "is her manager and he is in Europe. We represent him simply for the purpose of booking, that is all". None of the promised contract terms had been met.

Klaw & Erlanger complete Nielsen's tour. Happy to oblige. Alice tells Russell to wire Klaw at New Amsterdam Theatre, "Have completely severed with Shuberts. Alice Nielsen Company now reorganized. Opened brilliantly at Tivoli. Will positively not play another Shubert theatre. Wish to book your houses exclusively". Klaw, "man of culture and distinction who takes a genuine interest in the artistic side of the theatre, while Mr. Erlanger's corpulent figure and expensive jewelry are products of his shrewd commercial ability", Russell would recall.

Now *NY Telegraph* hears of the unpleasant NYC surprises: "On May 18 a contract was drawn between Florenz Ziegfeld, Miss Nielsen and me for operatic concerts. Well, after many changes, Ziegfeld saw me in October and guaranteed a great debut November 1st for Miss Nielsen with Victor Herbert's Orchestra". Admits cash came from Shubert; Ziegfeld was the modest go-between who baited Russell to lure Alice.

"We arrived in New York October 22. Nothing had been done, and there were no bookings. The Shuberts, having advanced money on the contract, took up the tour themselves and were wholly responsible for the bad orchestra and bad scenery. After the matinee in NY at the Casino, we were sent on the road with five inferior musicians", Russell suggests, dodging any managerial impresario role in the realm where he knows nothing.

Enter competence, November 2nd Alice's lawyer Hummel tells Shubert the contract will be canceled "unless they carried it out properly. Nothing was done about this. Miss Nielsen's success at the Tivoli Opera House in San Francisco was enormous. The local management gave a fine orchestra, chorus and scenery. We have organized a large and improved company and are doing good business everywhere". In fact the tour is completed by same cast same size.

Shubert corrects Russell: "Nielsen was never under our management. Mr. Ziegfeld had her fortunes in charge with Russell, and Ziegfeld's contract with us was purely for bookings. Miss Nielsen has never yet played to business large enough to pay half the guarantee that we required of Mr. Ziegfeld before we would contract to book her". Review of account books from the 1905-06 opera concert tour suggests Shubert lies; Alice Nielsen broke even despite Shubert's abysmal tour management.

Telegraph: "Every expert manager in America, while conceding Miss Nielsen's talents, shook his head when a concert tour was proposed by the ambitious Russell". The experienced Snow pre-booked the tour; and Alice had not planned a place for the grasping unambitious remora in the tour.

When George Edwards offered Nielsen a "forty-week contract" at "$500 weekly" in London and "$1,000 weekly" America, Edwards "spoke feelingly of *Veronique, The Little Michus* and musical plays of that class".

Not inferior to Donizette's 1840 antique pony Alice saddled, André Messanger's *Veronique,* the 3-act French comic opera set in—1840—opens 1898; Lady Grey produces it 1903 London; Edwards in 1905 NYC. Cast of seventeen plus chorus.

Interestingly, Edwards "did arrange, as a balm to Russell's [!] wounded aspirations, a single performance of *La Bohème*" for Alice Nielsen at Met under Conried. Obviously Russell prefers the cold cash in slight-of-hand to anything promoting Alice Nielsen. Edwards' reliable offer of a Met debut declined. Because of course if Alice joins Edwards the remora must detach from her revenues. "Russell remained obdurate and ignorant to the judgment of men who know every intricacy and ramification of the theatre situation, so Russell brought his star to American by arrangement with Ziegfeld" because bribes. During 1905 he had cost Nielsen a season at Covent, a Met debut in *Bohème* no doubt with Caruso, a Victor Herbert-conducted NYC gala, and wealth. Instead he joins Ziegfeld and Shubert for foggy reasons called cash, frantic to exploit the famed star who agreeably and glibly promotes him beyond sense and sincerity.

Only Nielsen could make her American plight a success.

1906: MIRACLE FROM DISASTER; FRIENDS IN DEED

Alice Nielsen spends New Year 1906 in San Francisco. In four months the city loses three-thousand people in the earthquake and fire. Tivoli will be obliterated. Hortense had placed her theatre gear in storage, all is lost.

Gold and silver paid to box offices by Alice's audiences will mesmerize the remora, keenly aware the Nielsen sisters signed a Chicago sponsor for the coming year. With hints of funds from New Orleans by summer's end.

January 1st, *SF Call* reports that remora Russell "in connection with Florenz Ziegfeld, husband of Anna Held, signed up with Miss Nielsen to give operatic concerts". Fails to mention Ziegfeld slipped him £1000 of Shuberts' money to sign her and paid the voyage. No, he "came to this country at considerable expense". Not his!

Russell's motives for lying lie obscure. "He adds Ziegfeld changed his mind [gambled the promised budget away] and when he arrived he found that an inferior orchestra had been engaged for Miss Nielsen and no arrangements made for her debut in NY". He claims "bad management and bad handling by the bookers were encountered all the time".

Next lie: "According to Russell, Miss Nielsen never had a contract with the Shuberts. She simply went under their wing to get clear of Ziegfeld".

Since Ziegfeld lost the budget gambling (if he ever meant to produce Nielsen), no hurdle to clear. Operating as Lee Shubert's agent, Ziegfeld may have pocketed a payoff and left. Or embezzled budget as inspiration to Russell. In near future when Shubert and Ziegfeld have legal intercourse a hint of the scam emerges. Yet Russell admits the deal in other interviews. Never explains why Nielsen seems to reject credible producers over Shubert, Ziegfeld. Contradicting claims he had kept Alice from Broadway, he suggests the star "intended to go back" to Klaw & Erlanger "as soon as she entered comic opera again".

Returning focus to Alice, a week later with *San Jose Mercury News* (Jan 7) she recites usual pilgrim progress. Perhaps to make things interesting she keeps changing it: "Although I have been before the public all my life, strangely enough I still shrink from publicity [yes, diva] and only an earnest request such as yours would induce me to speak of the days of my youth, which are still mine—but if youth means to be careless and happy and free from all responsibility, then indeed I have never known it".

Reporters of rapport receive Alice's best; others get boilerplate. Early poverty difficult, sings for coins. Big talented family, Alice sings for supper. Reporter, inspired by Luther Burbank's new botanical science, grafts branches of previous interviews into the piece: "I cannot remember when I could not sing. Two things I was born with—a strong throat and a correct and quick musical ear" and claims "Nanki-Poo in a juvenile company in Gilbert and Sullivan' *Mikado*" at eight despite the show being unwritten when eight. Of course, "always wishing to be older". At eighteen sought twenty-seven and "even now I want five years to fly by, hoping then to have a better position in my new work". Nielsen claims an unlikely Yum-Yum at fifteen in early 1892 Oakland; tells of "hard work and hard traveling in a stock company which finally fulfilled an engagement in San Francisco" without naming the well-known Burton Stanley.

Then Tivoli until the Bostonians. Skips to Italy, claims "When I made my first appearance at Covent Garden, London, I had only twice appeared before in grand opera. I felt that it was too soon and I was ill-prepared for the ordeal. If I had not had many calls on my purse my appearance in London would not have occurred until the coming spring". Appeared in two Napoli theatres many times each. As Kansas City, as Bostonians, so grand opera: "It is impossible to overrate the importance of singing a role many times in theatres of minor importance before making a debut in the principal theatres of a great city".

Her performances evolve: "For instance, up to the very last night I sang in *Don Pasquale* I found I was able to make several important and advantageous changes in the role which enabled me to score a greater success each time".

After her mixed NY success under duress, since Chicago praise has soared. San Francisco produced a prime performance with a cooperative theatre in a quality production. This proves all.

Developing new arts within American theatre has less appeal. Beyond the Chicago gift of a sponsored season, another trick is up Alice's ruffled sleeve. She has New Orleans friends with an opera house straight ahead.

When in San Jose, Alice omits Ziegfeld, Shubert and subtly suggests she holds wily Russell to blame after all for the tribulations, "In spite of mistakes and disappointments, I am going right on with my more exacting career. It is hard sometimes, but perhaps the pursuit of my ambition is less difficult, knowing that any moment I can still choose between art and fortune". Transfers her girlhood from Missouri to California, "I have given up much to take up art, and whether great success attends me or not, I have had the courage of my convictions. I look forward to much pleasure to your beautiful city of San Jose, where I am to sing *Don Pasquale* next Tuesday night, for I feel sure it will recall some joyful memories of girlhood days spent among the cities of my California. Here in San Francisco I am perfectly happy and cannot forget the old Tivoli days on Eddy street".

Years later, the remora's recollections skip the tour's successes to focus on buddy time traveling with Grimthorpe, who absurdly complains, "Damn the American newspapers, and damn you and your Italian company too, and damn the vulgar publicity of this country! Here's a letter from my dearest friend, threatening never to speak to me again because some ass of a reporter cabled the London newspapers that I had eloped with your prima donna!" Soon, says Russell, "his sense of humor conquered and...we were both able to laugh at the situation". Indeed.

Intriguingly, says Russell, Grimthorpe suggests finding "an important city where opera could be given, and moreover to count on him for a substantial sum. Considering how generous he had been in helping my London experiment [Waldorf], it was delightful to find that he was willing to assist me again". So enjoined, he and Grimthorpe share the sleeper on the cross-country train as Nielsen company is comin' into Los Angeles.

Among rarest of gifts, Alice Nielsen tells *LA Times* January 1906 her daily schedule during the tour. On less than five hours' sleep, Nielsen grabs a cold bath late and rises early. "From the time I appeared in grand opera in Italy I have done little else but work, and work hard. My maid calls me every day, weekday, Sunday or holiday, at 7:15am, and from that time on until I retire at 2:30am, I do not get a moment's rest".

Rises at 7:15am, breakfasts until 8, vocalizes until 10. Music studies continue until 11:30 "when she dresses for lunch". At 12:30 she prepares her wardrobe until 3, then music studies until 4. Again she vocalizes until 5:30; relaxes until 6:30. Performance evenings she heads to the theatre at 6:45 for makeup. At the 8:15 performance, "acts and sings until 11:15. Leaves theatre at midnight and dines until 1". Reads until 2am, taking a cold bath at 2:15 and "retires at 2:30" sleeping until of course 7:15 the arising time to repeat until done.

"I spend very little time in dressing in the morning and only the required few moments of my breakfast, because at 8am the maestro [conductor] comes with the score of the role in which I am to appear".

Nielsen knows she is superwoman: "I vocalize until 10am, and that is in itself an ordinary day's labor which would wear out the average woman in a month. From 10am to 11:30am I study harmony and read works and reference books on opera. At 11:30 my maid dresses me for lunch, which I usually take in the public dining room in the hotel in which I am staying".

Energy of people around strongly helps: "to see the different faces gather there, relieves the strain under which I have to labor.

"Immediately after lunch I return to my apartment, and with the assistance of my maid lay out my wardrobe for the evening performance. Supervision of every detail of the garments occupies my time until 3pm, as often there is hurried sewing to be done, and in this work I do my share to hurry matters along. At 3pm my French teacher appears and I pass an hour with him in studying grammar and literature. Time between 4 and 5:30pm is again devoted to singing practice. At this time I have my vocal chords in perfect condition and then my task is to preserve them so that nothing goes wrong with them before I 'go on.' Therefore, I take light nourishment in my apartments and drive in a closed carriage to the theatre.

"I generally arrive at 6:45 and the time until the curtain goes up is occupied in 'making up', dressing my hair, looking after the different costumes and endeavoring to attain the 'local color and atmosphere' of the opera. Everyone who has seen grand opera knows what my duties are behind the footlights. The performance is usually over at 11:15, but it is always midnight before I can leave the theatre.

"The dinner which the day laborer takes at noon I take at midnight. I feel that my body needs nourishment. In plain language I am hungry and I need food. I drive back to my hotel with my maid who takes off my wraps and I enter the public dining room with my companions and enjoy a hearty meal. At 1am I return to my rooms, read some current literature, newspapers and musical periodicals until 2am, when I take a cold bath which seems to quiet my nerves and invigorates my body, and I retire feeling that I have done a good day's work".

Schedule continues the decades of a working life. Alice Nielsen never lets up. Born to sing, labor of a lifetime to sing her best. Life disciplined. Endurance strong. Tours well over rough terrain in tough conditions.

Obviously Alice does not have much time to manage her opportunistic manager; and the capable Snow has orchestrated the tour. The company has become skilled by repetition.

Alice arrives at LA's Mason Theatre confronted with a petty farce, as *LA Times* reports: "She's furious, not engaged. Sweet singer's blue eyes almost seen by telephone as she tells why 'tisn't so". Asked if engaged to "a leading member of the English peerage who is touring Southern California" replies "I am perfectly furious about it. I am really not pleased a bit".

"Are you engaged to him, Miss Nielsen?" reiterates the reporter by newfangled telephone, saying "the scorn that came back over the wire might have caused electric complication, and though pictures are not yet transmitted with the messages at the current rates in the local telephone system, it took little imagination to see those big blue eyes of the noted prima donna catch fire. It was more than the transformation of the demure little convent girl in her favorite role in *Don Pasquale*.

"Came that compelling voice. Nielsen replied, 'It is simply disgraceful. That British lord is a married man with two grown daughters. How could I be engaged to him? He is a great friend of mine but', and the indignation gave way to an amused note, a little rippling laugh like low music came over the wire melting all unpleasantness, 'Why he is married, I needn't say any more.'" Russell also left second wife with two kids in London.

"The rumor came from Santa Barbara where Miss Nielsen gave one performance of *Don Pasquale* and also appeared in concert, and where the notable English lord has been for a short time". Grimthorpe is of zero interest to the press. His only two mentions were planted by Russell.

The reporter speaks of gayety: "So simple, so unaffected, so sure that other people have done things too", Nielsen is "made for the lighter moods of grand opera and she has such a joy in it all".

"Yes, I have always had the grand opera bee in my bonnet. Oh, it is great to sing when one is in good voice", she realistically replies.

For some reason difficult to fathom, Alice suggests Russell "gave up his season in London to come to America with his brilliant pupil". As if he had any seasons to give up. Only she had offers of a second season in London.

Russell in future brags of his manipulations of her gullibility.

Primed by Alice Nielsen's Tivoli success and her artistic presence in the past, Los Angeles is delighted when she opens the night of January 17th.

Her performance is the evidence. Thereby creates a strong sense of superiority over New York. The year is early 1906, of course. LA critics feel Nielsen's force in the theatre. And speak freely the facts they are given to know. They scorn the inferior judgments of the Eastern establishment.

Alice Nielsen ignites a 1906 Declaration of Artistic Independence.

"Alice Nielsen's *Don Pasquale* was the operatic event of the season" writes *LA Times* Jan 18th. "If you were there, you heard one of the purest soprano voices in the world, trained to its ultimate point of placement and clear intonation".

Cast and conductor work passably well "and not very much behind... came the little tenor, Prati". Rosa "made good in every respect....

Orchestra of twenty-five with Kraw and Erlinger, not five from Shubert.

Amazingly, "orchestra under Jose Vandenberg played mightily". Rare compliment for Vandenberg. The oboist-turned-conductor has learned.

Nielsen works with him never after.

Next year however, Vandenberg fields his own opera company. Well-liked by his cast. Perhaps tainted by association with Russell, in future he faces scandal when his "manager and promoter" Will J. Block "vanished" with "the available funds of the opera troupe" bearing the name of former oboist Jose Vandenberg (*NY Times* Jul 5 1911).

LA Times continues of Nielsen's show: "That's the summing up. No chorus; scenery taken from the Mason sets and but little change of costuming—save as might be expected, on the prima donna. But 'that's all' is covering a good deal of ground, for a soprano voice that is pure silver and a tenor of equal beauty are not to be considered as trifles.

"Miss Nielsen's voice...has improved wonderfully...to have perfected its placement and increased its size. It's not physical strength...but poise and certain establishment where for every atom of breath the singer gets an equivalent atom of brilliant sound".

Judgement: "From a mere comic-opera prima donna Alice Nielsen has broadened to operatic dignity and strength".

As Chicago and San Francisco, she makes practical plans to return next year by obtaining financial guarantees for her venture.

"As Mimi in *La Bohème* she would be more than interesting. If certain embryonic plans are carried to consummation LA may see her as Mimi ere another twelvemonth has gone 'round".

Nielsen's magic has turned a fuddy into a worthy: "*Don Pasquale* is such a ridiculously formal opera, with trills and arpeggios for the most common subjects of conversation, that in Italian with poor singers it would be deadly drear. Nevertheless, with Nielsen, Prati and Rosa it is intensely interesting. Each of these three possesses a jovial magnetism in addition to other talents. Last night's audience was extremely hearty in its appreciation".

Turning east on the southerly route, Nielsen tours.

Two weeks after leaving LA she approaches Texas. Dallas delivers the deepest praise of her debut opera season's tour. Critic dares what *London Times* feared. Contrasts Nielsen to Melba and to Sembrich. Goes right to the point about about Nielsen's Broadway shows. Not just the bad text, the insincere story.

Dallas Morning News (Feb 11): "There is no doubt that the audience will greet the same vivacious and charming Alice Nielsen that received the applause of thousands when she headed the best comic opera company possible in America.... She has merely chosen to develop her voice and to devote herself to the more melodious, spontaneous and sincerely sentimental comic opera of Italy".

Insight of "sincerely" cuts into Herbert's libretti by cynical, money-mongering Harry Smith. The deep-feeling composer has a story problem.

Same cast is now promoted as from "Covent Garden and the Waldorf and from Italy. The tenor Prati is regarded as a phenomenal 'find' and the basso buffo, Rosa and the baritone Fratodi, are artists of high reputation".

Dallas Morning News (Feb 17), Nielsen's concert brings a revelation to Texans. The singer scores a hit. The discerning *Dallas News* critic has the gumption to directly contrast her with the day's leading divas how have recently toured the town, Melba and Sembrich. As Boston's Lewis Strang had in 1899, *Dallas News* in 1906 names the best woman singing.

"For the first time in its history Dallas has heard a really great singer in real opera and the event will not soon pass from memory. After years spent in persistent study and conscientious work abroad, Miss Alice Nielsen came back to us and again sang her way into our hearts—a place where she is likely to remain. She came back with a voice developed and rounded out until its notes are clear as those of a flute and powerful and thrilling as the call from a bugle.

"Furthermore she is graceful, modest and a talented actress. As her glorious voice soared up and down with all the ease and grace of that of a nightingale, the attention was breathless. But when the last note died away, the applause began and did not end until she had sung again and again. At last, at the end of two hours and a half, the performance came to a close".

Alice Nielsen invokes the amazing turn-of-century phrase linked with "gaiety of nations" which is: "the most remarkable demonstration which has ever been witnessed..." in an audience. Repeats across her life.

Brilliant journalist witnesses the rarest theatre magic: "It was then that occurred what is probably the most remarkable demonstration which has ever been witnessed in a Dallas theatre. Not a soul moved to depart, but the applause, at first very enthusiastic, grew in volume as the realization spread that there was to be no more. Finally the curtain went up and Miss Nielsen sang in English Tosti's famous *Good-Bye*. It was sung with the same artistic fervor which imbued the composer when he wrote it. The gamut of emotions was depicted by the inflections of Miss Nielsen's voice.

"When she finished the people simply would not leave. Even the ushers forgot to throw open the side exits. The curtain rose again and Miss Nielsen smiled and bowed her acknowledgements, but it was not smiles and bows that the people wanted; it was another song; and at last, as the orchestra began the accompaniment of *Comin' Thro' The Rye*, the crowd burst into a cheer which was joined by even the occupants of the boxes.

"Then there were flowers and more applause and the curtain went down finally on what was at once the most remarkable and the most satisfactory performance of the kind ever given in this city.

"Not only one of the world's greatest singers, but a very beautiful woman as well—one who has made a plucky uphill fight to win and has at least reached the top. Her voice is absolutely flawless and as full of Nature's music—real music—as the voice of a mockingbird on a moonlight night in midsummer. After hearing that voice one is prepared to accept without reservation even the enthusiastic statements made in the advance notices; even the assertion of the world's greatest critics that she is as great as Melba or Sembrich".

The Dallas critic prefers Alice Nielsen and is capable of telling why. He begins with a too-modest disclaimer, "In fact, to a mind untutored musically she is the superior of these". Vocal gymnastics and piercing high notes never truly satisfy. This unsigned Dallas critic proclaims Nielsen as best in grand opera, an accolade arriving only six years after Boston's Strang proclaimed her as best in the Broadway musicals.

"Sembrich came to Dallas and gave a magnificent exhibition of vocal gymnastics—but was it real music? Melba came and our eardrums vibrated painfully when she touched the high notes in the 'mad scene' from *Lucia di Lammermoor*. Then Miss Nielsen came. She opened her mouth and simply let the music pure and undefiled roll out, as it were.

"We have heard back in New York a few critical complaints that Nielsen lacks piercing high notes. She has better style. There was no visible effort, no facial contortion, no spasmodic jerking of the arms".

Born to sing; kindred spirit of Herbert, Duse, Modjeska; a child grown of Denmark, Ireland, Kansas City, 'Frisco; a woman cultivated by three master Italian musicians: Valerga, Tosti, Bevignani. God bless Texas.

Dallas News describes the contrasting audience experience provided by these three divas with confident sensitivity. Few others dared try.

"She sang as if she really loved to sing and not because it was her means of earning a livelihood. Miss Nielsen's voice is perfect. It is a pure soprano. Last night at the Dallas Opera House she exhibited all its beauties in Donizetti's *Don Pasquale*, a three-act comedy opera.

"It there is any music which seems to have been specially designed for the purpose of tripping up the partially-trained signer or one who has natural limitations, it is that which was composed by Donizetti. But Miss Nielsen rendered it without leaving grounds for anything but the most enthusiastic praise. Sometimes you were certain that it was a human voice making all the music and then again you were almost persuaded that it was the plaintive strains of a violin in the hands of a master".

He detects Nielsen's technique: "Her pianissimo notes were marvelous. Soft and low, almost, as a whisper, they were yet distinctly heard in every part of the house—a house, it should be remembered which is not famed for its acoustic properties".

The inevitable realm of attendant puffery materializes with assertions repeated that "Melba and other famous singers owe much of their success to Mr. Russell but his favorite of them all is Miss Nielsen". The amazing canard that he brought her "to this country for a tour..." appears.

In the cast: Alfonso Rosa "cannot be said to really sing", yet acts well.

Dallas News speaks of staging. "Nielsen and her company give opera without frills. There are no spectacular effects. The man who handles the limelight remains idle. The stage manager has little to do. All the scenery used last night belonged to the opera house. The costumes are a mere detail and not a feature. There is no chorus. There is nothing but music—music of the kind which is worth going miles to hear. Four singers and an orchestra present a comedy opera in three acts in a manner which makes the audience forget the passing of time, and be convinced until the end that they have only just come.

"To illustrate the spell cast by the music, it is only necessary to relate the conditions which existed here last night at the opening of the performance.

"Miss Nielsen came heralded as a very great singer who was supported by a wonderfully capable company. There have been other singers who have come here similarly heralded and proved disappointing. Therefore, while there was a large audience the house was not filled and the occupants of the seats were coldly critical. When the curtain went up it was found that nothing was English. Every word uttered was Italian. This was resented, there being a prejudice here against anything except an English production. This resentment did not last five minutes. In ten minutes it was forgotten and in 15 minutes the spectators did not care whether the words were in Sanskrit or Portuguese. Fratodi's baritone aroused interest. Prati appeared and sang a few words until it was near akin to enthusiasm. In the next act Miss Nielsen was heard and from that minute until the end the enthusiasm waxed greater and greater".

They sing again "tonight and they are deserving of the largest audience which can be crowded into that theatre". Musical directors are noted as Jose Vandenberg and Mari Bisacei.

Alice crashes a chair: "There was one very amusing incident during the evening. Miss Nielsen was seated in a chair, she attempted to push it back and the legs gave way, precipitating her to the floor. Her mishap caused much merriment".

"Singing *Swannee River* and Tosti's *Good-Bye* in response to the insistent demands of the audience...brought her engagement in this city to a close last night at Dallas Opera House. Miss Nielsen seemed to be in even better voice than on the night before and no such rendition of *Swannee River* had ever been heard here. She sang it with feeling and the flute-like yet languorous tones gave to the words a sentiment such as until then they had never seemed to possess. Tosti's *Good-Bye* was rendered in a manner equally as admirable. If anything the audience was even more demonstrative than on the opening night and Miss Nielsen can have only pleasant recollections of the reception...she received in Dallas" (*Morning News* Feb 18).

February 17th Nielsen leaves Dallas in triumph as she has left Chicago, San Francisco, Los Angeles. Now she closes on New Orleans. Old friends await her with an offer that changes American music history.

Alice has more than survived this tour, she triumphs. Italy beckons for spring and summer. Made many miracles by surviving the NYC gauntlet.

From Dallas, quick rail to New Orleans where Consuelo Yznaga's family and other old friends happen to have a fine historic opera house available for the perfect opportunity. Of course Nielsen makes something happen.

Although anticipated, the deal takes time. Her concert is scheduled a very long three weeks after arrival. Plenty of opportunity to socialize.

New Orleans opera has a prideful history. Opera Association archivist Jack Belsom tells us Alice Nielsen appeared at "Tulane Theatre on 11 March 1906 as Norina in Donizetti's *Don Pasquale. Daily Picayune* noted that she 'has not been here since her great successes in Victor Herbert's light operas, *The Serenade, The Singing Girl* and *The Fortune Teller.*' On March 12, *Picayune* reviewed the sole performance of *Pasquale*, 'Alice Nielsen in good form—she has gained much in volume. Tone quality is silvery. She closed the performance with Tosti's *Goodbye* and *Comin' Thru the Rye.*'"

Behind scenes, Nielsen closes her ambitious deal with the New Orleans Opera board to bring a new grand opera company from Europe for the coming winter season. Despite rich traditions New Orleans at the moment lacks a resident company. Opera houses are maintained by shareholders who set policy for the cultural institution without government funds. For Alice Nielsen, French Opera House proposes to offer shows in the native libretto language. The innovation, taken in stride by shareholders making the Nielsen contract, is regarded an affront to regional pride by certain persons among the Louisiana press who only desire an opera given in French.

New Orleans changes everything for Alice Nielsen.

With French Opera's up-front money, financial guarantees, and surety of a contract, Alice and Hortense ambitiously plan on putting together a new opera company in Europe to debut November in New Orleans for the winter season then touring North America.

Star power makes things happen. After almost a month in New Orleans to close that deal, Alice proceeds touring across the Southeast.

Florida begins the great collaboration of her career. Yet another miracle only Alice could create. By coincidence, Lillian Russell's friend Nordica performs in Jacksonville, Florida. Nielsen pitches Nordica to join forces.

Nordica learns that in Los Angeles, "Alice Nielsen had cleared $7,000 in four nights". She decides to collaborate.

Nordica (1857-1914), from Farmington, Maine, graduated New England Conservatory at 18. Like Nielsen, her opera debut was Italy, 1879. Nordica sang at London's Drury Lane with Valerga in 1887. Joined Mapleson's "provincial tours" to Ireland and Scotland. In Dublin her "Violetta was a delightful impersonation. Her vocalism was of a high order of excellence, and her acting was full of power..." (*Era* 1886). In Scotland, "Nordica made her debut in Scotland as Violetta, and created a most favorable impression. Her voice is pure soprano of extensive compass...." Returning to London, "this clever young lady was heartily applauded for the beauty of her voice and the excellence of her singing". Only as *Carmen* was she "in no way fitted for the character". By next year, "constantly advancing in public estimation. Her pure voice, expressive style, and natural acting...." And the next, "Nordica by her most brilliant vocalization, created a furor.... In *Traviata* she has gained a splendid success. The critics are unanimous...." An 1891 "revival of *Aide* again introduced Madame Nordica, who proved herself once more one of the finest living vocalists, and a capital actress".

When Nielsen meets Nordica she encounters a celebrated star who has thrilled Russia, France, Italy, England, Germany. First American to sing Wagner at Beyreuth. Debut at Covent 1887, Grau's Met 1891. Nordica has been active on the concert, musicale, and oratorio circuit, moving readily from Chopin to Wagner "in splendid voice, and her singing was exquisite".

Lives on sixth floor of Waldorf-Astoria NYC. Last of the three marriages, present husband runs Bank of New York. Nordica and Nielsen share friends: Lillian Russell, Valerga, Maurice Grau, many others. Nordica was last student of François Delsarte, her vocal coach Mathilde Marchesi. Nordica's contest with Melba for Brunnhilde happily ends with disaster when Melba fails singing the role. Upstart Alice would like that.

Nordica, of course, has been a top star thirty years. "I saw Mme. Nordica at Jacksonville in her private car, and I shall never forget the kindly encouragement she gave me in regard to my present and future. Lillian Nordica is one woman in a million, and it is certainly the proudest thought in my life to realize that I am about to be associated with her in an important opera venture", Nielsen said. She will give Nordica all credit for organizing the company they grace the next two years. Nordica's husband handles finances.

During these proceedings, Henry Russell intrudes to divert the group from being named the "Nordica-Nielsen Grand Opera Company". The ruse succeeds. After all, the stars have roles to sing. They need helpers. He offers his. The name announced is "San Carlo Opera Company of San Francisco".

Only the most scrupulous journalists could keep this cumbersome alias accurate. Not consulted was De Sanna, the manager for San Carlo Opera in Napoli. And allows soaring pretensions by the spokesman faux impresario.

Jacksonville Times-Union later recalled (FL Se 10): "The forming of the San Carlo opera company [of San Francisco], in so far as the joint appearance of Nordica and Nielsen is concerned, had its beginnings in Jacksonville...."

Upon arrival, Alice attends Nordica's concert at the skating auditorium. Afterwards for *Times-Union,* she pens "a beautiful little tribute beginning, 'I am proud, when I hear Nordica sing, that I am an American'.

The paper comments, "The spontaneous tribute was that of one great artist to another, and it was widely commented upon throughout the entire country. From this beginning the two singers came closer together.... And this [winter] season New Orleans will have them.

"For the first time in the history of the city they will enjoy opera both in French and Italian, and an interesting feature is that Madame Nordica has never sung in opera in New Orleans".

When Nielsen recounts how she initiated the Nordica partnership, she puts Nordica firmly in charge. Contract details have not surfaced. Nordica supplies additional financing, her banker husband manages accounts.

Mr. Snow continues to arrange bookings. Restoring Alice's original hopes, the cast assembled at Waldorf reassembles: Conductor Conte will manage singers, orchestra and chorus. Hortense will join Alice in Italy to select sets, costumes. Tosti will cast singers. Superb tenor Constantino will make his American debut. Russell's role foggy as figurehead and spokesman.

Following her victory in New Orleans, creating the formidable Nielsen-Nordica alliance, Alice tours toward Manhattan, port of departure for Italy.

Even attending her concert is news, as March 16 *Weekly True Democrat* of Tallahassee reports Mary Whitfeld departing for Jacksonville "to partake of the three big attractions, Bernhardt, Nordica, and Alice Nielsen".

March 19, *Macon Telegraph* (GA) reports Alice Nielsen "at the Grand tonight". Russell, "eminent singing master" fluffed as "impresario and director".

Nielsen has hodge-podged a new opera company thanks to Chicago, San Francisco, Los Angeles, New Orleans. And she knows she has.

The diva he later refuses to name, praise, or thank—allows a quiet promotion to faux impresario for the remora. Wildest dream trued.

Four days later, *Columbia State* (SC) speaks to Alice Nielsen. *State* quotes much of that rapport-rich London piece by TP O'Connor in *Mostly*

About People published during Alice's season at Covent singing Mozart. No attribution. Layering atop the O'Connor text, *State's* reporter has a painterly eye: "Alice Nielsen like Ellen Terry...is the possessor of a charming personality both on and off the stage. There is doubt whatever about her femininity; she...is purely womanly. Perhaps the strongest trait of her character is that of modesty. She is modest of her attainments, of her voice, of her opinions, and of her success and her manner has a pretty deference that at once wins all hearts both masculine and feminine. It is not the deference of the studied woman of the world who wishes to be agreeable, but of the woman with a childlike heart and a childlike nature who is always a little doubtful of herself and dependent upon the interest and the affection of others to make her happiness.

"The moment you look into the sweet, appealing eyes of Alice Nielsen you feel sympathetically drawn towards her. She has no pose of any kind whatever and is as natural as a lovable child. Miss Nielsen is petite in form and has a quantity of thick light brown hair which she wears parted in the middle like a little Madonna and arranged round her well-shaped head in coronet form. Her skin is pale, and though her features are not regular she is a most charmingly pretty person with a delightful laugh and beautiful white teeth. Her figure is slender, round and exquisitely graceful, and she has small, childlike hands and feet. Dressed in a little blue cotton frock, with a long string of coral beads and a while straw hat, she looks a girl of about 20, with somewhat severe taste in dress. In truth she is not very much more, and the future lies before her".

Strong regional accent noticed in 1896 NYC has now succumbed: "When she left musical comedy she was the acknowledged queen of that branch of art; she was a beautiful singer, an exquisite dancer, and she spoke pure and charming cosmopolitan English without any trace of an American accent".

As a top comedienne "she had a strong sense of humor, and she made her audience adore her. America has clamored for her ever since she left, and now she returns to her native country for fresh triumphs".

Alice performs at Charleston whose *News and Courier* says of *Pasquale*, "The audience was not the largest of the season—more the pity—but it was one of the most critical, and the verdict was unanimous and favorable. Miss Nielsen's art is fascinating, her voice remarkable. She sings with the greatest ease, almost abandon. The slightest whisper is musical and true; the highest, strongest notes fairly on key, resonant, true and clear until allowed to die away. An actress of consummate skill, the beauties of her vocal powers were intensified by the play of emotions as revealed with eyes and lips, movement and gesture. From her first appearance Miss Nielsen was followed with the greatest interest and every number was received with enthusiastic applause.

"Charleston has not her equal since Nordica sang here four or five years ago. Her voice is simply delicious".

Delsarte-trained Nielsen, tempered by Duse, spoke in clear gestures. "If she had to sing in Italian, what could be more acceptable to her audience than *Don Pasquale*? Last night was one of the few times when one felt that he had a decided grudge against the English language" in favor of the "limpid, liquid, lyrical music of Italian writers. And yet Alice Nielsen and her company were not at a loss to convey the idea of the composer, although the words were in a language unfamiliar".

"At first the audience...of the usual diminutive proportions when anything artistic is offered, felt that it would be difficult to get into the spirit of this piece. But the clever acting of Alfredo Rosa and the singing of Miss Nielsen and of Francesco Prati made the performance enjoyable. Miss Nielsen really has very little to do in some of the acts, but the two songs permitted her brought the audience to her feet. Her comedy work was surprisingly vivacious.

"It is her wonderful voice, after all, which makes the music capable of being understood or felt. Such flexibility, such tone, such range is wonderful. Her reputation as a comedienne was already established, but her classical efforts of this season have given her a new place among American singers.

In the cast: "Mr. Francesco Prati, while hardly of the size to give the little play a romantic effect, has a very remarkable tenor and received encore after encore" while Alfreda Rosa "presented almost daintily a part which any other than an artist would have made horseplay. And plain old American lingo would have been inadequate to express the emotions which Donizetti has pictured in such a masterful way in this bright, breezy little opera".

For Charleston, "the orchestra also was far above what is usually afforded in the South...under the direction of Jose Vandenberg".

After the sixth curtain call at end of Act Two, it is announced Nielsen will sing "some familiar old songs at the close of the regular performance". With *Home, Sweet Home* "she had the audience at her feet and *Swannee River* was followed by a great ovation". She sang *Swannee River*, "not Italian, not English, but plain old Southern negro dialect". Her song was "received at first with tumultuous applause, and the house was in perfect quite as she sang in notes of birdlike sweetness and purity...." Last she "sang another dialect [Scots] song *Comin' Thro' the Rye*. A treat it was and a treat thoroughly enjoyed".

From Charleston she returns to Columbia. March 28th the *Columbia State* reports "Alice Nielsen...the South's very own sweet singer...is now heralded as the second Patti". A long way from 1891's vaudeville *Eden Musee* when she posed as a second Patti with Arthur Pryor playing piano.

Nielsen Company register at Wright's Hotel. No trouble with her maid.

She is touted "a true Southern woman. It was to the South she turned [last] after her return from continental Europe...and the South up to now has given the little songbird such a welcome that it has been a triumphant homecoming. Everywhere she has received an ovation".

For his bystander part, Russell loftily claims to be "touring America on a pleasure tour as well as for business reasons...he has never seen audiences feel the spell of music more than some Southern audiences...." For the moment skips posing as impresario. As in San Francisco, Russell lures young singers for cash, "and has heard many in the South. He arrived in the city last night from Charleston and will spend the entire day in the city".

After Columbia, the region hails Alice Nielsen as "greatest prima donna of the South". *Columbia State* initiates the slogan, "In the South the audience has arisen *en masse* and has demanded...Southern airs. She has always complied cheerfully. It is hoped the greatest prima donna of the South will be given a good house tonight and those who do not go may be sure that they are indeed keeping Lent and are denying themselves something very, very enjoyable".

Nielsen acquires the title from South Carolina's Clara Kellogg (1842-1915) who had sung the same Southern airs. Her saga deserves attention; she knew Nordica well, met Alice in Napoli. Kellogg sang *Swannee River, Last Rose of Summer*, and *Comin' Thro' The Rye* as encores, saying Swedish diva Christine Nilsson "having heard the Goodwin girls sing *Way Down upon the Swanee River* first introduced it on the concert stage as an encore". Kellogg succeeds in business and marriage, a flawless model for diva success. Spent winters in Rome when Nielsen was in Italy. Social gravity of meeting seems inescapable. Kept the same circles for decades: Maurice Grau, Henry Irving, Coquelin, Nilsson.

Alice never discusses Kellogg, who recalls, "Once I heard *Faust* in the Segundo Teatro of Naples with Alice Nielsen [misspelled Neilson!], and thought she gave a charming performance. She was greatly helped by not having to wear a wig. A wig, however becoming, and no matter how well put on, does certainly do something strange to the expression of a woman's face". Kellogg knew Gounod, "I found it very difficult ...when I tried to sing what at that time seemed to me the remarkable intervals of this strange, new, operatic heroine, Marguerite.

"In *Faust* the musical intelligence had an entirely new task and was exercised quite differently from in anything that had gone before. This sequence of notes was a new and unlearned language to me, which I had to master before I could find freedom or ease. But when once mastered, how the music enchanted me; how it satisfied a thirst that had never been satisfied by Donizetti or Bellini!

"Musically, I loved the part of Marguerite—and I still love it. Dramatically, I confess to some impatience over the imbecility of the girl. Stupidity is really the keynote of Marguerite's character. Marguerite was an easy dupe. She was dull, and sweet, and open to flattery. Most of the Marguerites whom I have seen make her too sophisticated, too but anything original or daring in connection with Marguerite is a little like mixing red pepper with vanilla blanc mange.

"Nilsson was much the most attractive of all the Marguerites I have ever seen, yet she was altogether too sophisticated for the character and for the period, although to-day I suppose she would be considered quite mild. Lucca was an absolute little devil in the part. She was, also, one of the Marguerites who wore black hair. As for Patti—I have a picture of Adelina as Marguerite in which she looks like Satan's own daughter, a young and feminine Mephistopheles to the life".

Kellogg met Lilian Nordica in 1877 Paris, "after she had returned from making a tour of Europe with Patrick Gilmore's band. A few years later she and I sang together in Russia; and we have always been good friends. Her breathing and tone production are about as nearly perfect as anyone's can be, and, if I wanted any young student to learn by imitation, I could say to her, 'Go and hear Nordica and do as nearly like her as you can!'"

Kellogg took Nordica's advice for a Paris vocal coach, "Sbriglia's method was the old Italian method known to teachers as *diaphragmatic*, of all forms of vocal training the one most productive of endurance and stability in a voice". In Russia "when I first knew her, she had no dramatic quality above G sharp. She could not hope for leading rôles in grand opera until she had perfect control of the upper notes needed to complete her vocal equipment. She went to Sbriglia in Paris and worked with him until she could sing a high C that thrilled the soul. That C of hers in the *Inflammatus* in Rossini's *Sabat Mater* was something superb. Her voice, while increasing in register, never suffered the least detriment in tone nor timbre. It was Nordica who first told me of Sbriglia, giving him honest credit for the help he had been to her. Like all truly big natures she has always been ready to acknowledge assistance wherever she has received it. When I was in Paris, I took advantage of being near the great teacher, Sbriglia, to consult him". Her sessions followed Plançon "who had begun to sing out of tune so badly that he resolved to come to Paris to see if he could find someone who might help him. He was quite frank in saying that Sbriglia had 'made him.'"

Kellogg retired 1887 to New Hartford CN, her estate Elpstone is near the Hortense Nielsen farm and Alice's future Bedford home. "I have never sung in either Spain or Italy principally because of my dread of the hissing habit" Kellogg recalled. (1907).

Vintage divas: Patti, Kellogg, Nielsen: 4'-10", 5'-4", 5'-3".

Introducing Kellogg's *Memoirs*, Isabel More says, "So fundamentally is she a musician that her knowledge of life itself is as much a matter of harmony as her music. She lives her melody; applying the basic principle that Carlyle has expressed so admirably when he says, 'see deeply enough and you see musically". As artists, Kellogg and Nielsen much alike.

Switching Carolinas, Nielsen progresses to Charlotte's Academy of Music. March 30, *Charlotte Observer* (NC) waxes poetic as it notes that Alice is not singing in English.

The audience "showed its appreciation by liberal applause. The play has a pretty plot, which was easily followed notwithstanding the fact that Italian instead of English was used. But it was not the play, the mere pretty plot, that made the audience glad it was there. It was the singing.

"Anyone who hears Alice Nielsen sing once will have the desire to hear her sing again. Her voice has wonderful sweetness and range and is so thoroughly under control that no effort is apparent in her singing. And what if the winsome little woman does sing in Italian, as she sings, it is the notes, the sweetness, the singing that enters the soul. It matters not if the words are English or Italian, so she sings".

In the cast: "artists of a high class" who "acted as well as they sang.

"After the last act, after two or three curtain calls Miss Nielsen sang in English, *Way Down Upon the Swannee River* and again, *Home, Sweet Home*. And here is where she got very near the audience. All the tenderness, the longing, the sweet memories of the songs were brought out in the voice of the singer, while the audience breathed softly for fear of missing one sighing note".

In Kentucky she and Hortense are well-known.

April 4, *Lexington Herald* (KY) heralds Alice, "delightful comedienne will always be remembered gratefully by theatre-goers who witnessed" *Singing*

Girl and *Fortune Teller*". *Herald* rightly emphasizes London and drops NY: "Just a few months ago, she repeated that success in London as prima donna in grand opera associated with such stars as Calvé and Caruso. And now she is with us again... there can be no doubt of Miss Nielsen's reception here. She has proved herself a credit to her birthright, her country and her profession".

In old Kentucky a detail of Nielsen's daily life reaches the press. Prank by Emma White, identified by the Shubert lawyer as a person who need not travel first class but Nielsen insists she do. The two women had experienced much of life touring together. "On April 6 after attending a funeral, White said she had met her next husband and had to resign to get married". Quoted by the day's press in thick Southern dialectese, White says "I gotta resign, Miss Allus". "Resign? Why Emma, this is worse than an earthquake. What ever shall I do if you resign?" The joke on Nielsen. Emma had met the best possible husband: the funeral's corpse. She would marry: only a dead man.

Nielsen has descended into Chattanooga when Shubert stirs trouble (*Morning Telegraph* NY Apr 10). The Shubert-Nielsen skirmish concerns rivals Klaw & Erlanger. Shubert "attached the scenery and costumes of the company and also the box office receipts, claiming that several sums of money were due that firm by Miss Nielsen and her personal manager, Henry Russell. A long and stubbornly contested battle will follow, for Miss Nielsen and Mr. Russell determined to compel an accounting and a readjustment on the part of the Shuberts".

Klaw & Erlanger's lawyer Nat Roth replies, "The matter in dispute is but one of many disagreements between the singer and the Shuberts" who had booked her original tour until "after many bitter disputes and much dissatisfaction on both sides" she "withdrew...with their complete accord".

Her Klaw & Erlanger tour "has been a very successful one, and she has made a lot of money...and she believes the present proceedings" indicate a desire of Shubert to harass her which is only true. *Telegraph* said Nielsen's intent is signaled by "her suggestion that *Don Pasquale* must give place to *The Daughter of the Regiment*".

Lee Shubert replies he had relinquished management of Nielsen's tour "some months ago with a dull and sickening thud".

April 18th occurs the San Francisco earthquake. Hortense Nielsen loses everything theatrical in storage. In shock she "became invalid". Alice invites Hortense join her for Italy. The disaster relocates a destroyed Tivoli to Denver to resume repertory of *Bohemian Girl, Fra Diavolo, Mikado, Satanella,* plus *Fortune Teller* and *Singing Girl.*

Alice tours over to Ohio. As in Dallas, a regional critic becomes profoundly inspired. In 1905-06 under trying circumstances from NY to Chicago to San Francisco, LA to Dallas, New Orleans to Carolina, Nielsen has secured impressive critical accolades. Pulls a miracle of herself.

NYC left mixed reviews. Revival began in Chicago. Success secure by San Francisco. Los Angeles and Dallas heap praise on the artist. Yet Cleveland says it best: Alice Nielsen has "genius and art". Attendance sparse. Numbers count nothing of taste.

April 20th *Cleveland Leader.* "By actual count there were not enough men and women in the audience at the Opera House yesterday afternoon to go upon the stage and make up the chorus which Alice Nielsen had omitted from the version of *Don Pasquale* she presented. Well, what of it?

"What am I going to do about it? Nothing. I had a delightful afternoon in the presence of genius and art, as represented by Donizetti and Miss Nielsen and with the joyous Easter spirit still unevaporated I am sorry you were not there to share my pleasure. But that's your affair. I am not your artistic keeper. I don't propose to dragoon you into liking things for which you do not care or to browbeat and bully and slangwhang you just because we pull in different directions. Appreciation, when it isn't intuitive is a matter of education, not of fisticuffs. You cannot be fought into a liking for Italian opera, even in so light and frolicsome a manifestation of Donizetti's masterpiece of comedy. You have got to climb up to it yourself.

"Now let's talk of pleasanter matters; of Miss Nielsen. You remember her, of course, as the most vivacious of singers in light opera. A girl with a voice and a superimposed talent. She could act as well as sing. When she got as high as she could go in that fluffy kind of work, save in the matter of salary which would have been anything she asked, she chucked it all and went in for grand opera. About a year ago she made her debut in the artwork she loved and had sacrificed so much for. She made a big hit in England and then, womanlike and like an actress, which multiplies femininity, she wanted to come back to American and 'show 'em'—the croakers...."

Encore songs a San Francisco reporter scorned, signal her success. "I'd say I know she is a prima donna because she sang *Swannee River* and *Home, Sweet Home* in English at the close of the opera which was given in Italian. Either one of these ballads is the song manual of the great singer. Both make assurance doubly sure. The simple truth, due both to Miss Nielsen and myself, is that she went away a comic opera singer and has returned an artist. That's all and that's enough.

"Most sopranos with a voice of her quality—liquid, limpid, sweet and bird-like—would have made a heroic organ out of it; have tried to broaden or deepen and put somber tragedy in it. Nature intended Miss Nielsen to be a coloratura singer and that is what she has made herself. Her voice has grown somewhat stronger, but not disastrously so. It has still the notes of the skylark in it".

He expertly paints her voice: "Her gain has been in technic, in the mechanics of her profession and in the finer artistry...her execution was always fluent; now it is facile in an extraordinary way. Her runs are clear; her trills even, and thanks to a marvelous management of the breath, she uses the *messa voce* as beautifully as any singer I have heard for years. The old Italian teachers use to tell their pupils to 'spin the voice.' That is just what she does, into the most gossamery of tones' notes that sound like 'horns of elfland softly blowing.' This beautiful *messa voce* was displayed throughout the entire opera".

In the cast: "effective support". Rosa "unusually good buffo singer and clever actor"; Francesco Prati "tenor in the embryonic stage...his schooling has been insufficient". Baritone Fratodi, fair. "The orchestra though small, played nicely".

Cleveland Leader. "Went away a comic opera singer...returned an arist".

April 28, Nielsen arrives Rochester, postponing San Francisco earthquake benefit at Star Theatre due to a throat illness. Despite the illness she plays Rochester's Lyceum next day.

Rochester Post (April 29): "Miss Nielsen is at home in the music of the florid Donizettian school; she sings it as a young woman of sprightly temper and happy gift might be expected to do". Rochester contrasts Donizetti to Victor Herbert. Herbert scores with harmony and orchestration, fails due to bad librettists. His 1898 shows had plots set in 1840 Europe festooned with contemporary comedy; *Don Pasquale* composed 1840 is set that same year.

"Society owes her thanks for reviving *Don Pasquale*, if only in order to remind the present generation of composers of so-called light opera—your Herberts and your Englanders—that they are far below the standard of Donizetti, though he was a far poorer harmonist than they and knew surprisingly little of orchestration, in comparison".

Herbert has a different standard, not below.

People will always recall "with pleasure her attractive presence, her sprightly manners and her fluent gift of song, so full of charm". Rochester asks the big question: "In Europe Miss Nielsen played Marguerite and Mimi; why should she not play the same roles here?"

Message to the Metropolitan crystal clear.

April 30th from Ithaca arises first mention of Nielsen's new Americano "San Carlo Opera Company [of San Francisco]". *NY Herald* reports she has secured agreements to return with a full grand opera company booked into a winter season in New Orleans, short season for Bryn Mawr in Chicago, and a tour from LA to Boston. Name a false banner. Silly scheme hijacking the name benefits but Russell; bestows a credibility he lacks, floats fallacy he had "managed" San Carlo at Covent.

Perhaps Nielsen and Nordica had early hopes that Robert De Sanni at San Carlo Opera would join; or they were promised such by the remora who had repeatedly denied De Sanni the manager credit since leaving London.

The "San Carlo Opera Company of San Francisco" moniker for Nielsen's new project recalls the quasi-mythical "Chicago Church Choir Company" quartet. In this guise the phony brand carries forth. No direct connection claimed, none exists. Singers in group refer to "Nielsen-Nordica company".

Alice's own concert tours with pianist booked around the opera tour.

To *NY Herald*, Alice speaks of Nordica "a majestic being, as towering, as massive as the Brunhilde of Wagner's opera. Oh I am so glad to think the American will hear me in such surroundings and then imagine my pride at finding my name side by side with America's—nay the world's greatest dramatic singer, Mme. Nordica. She is a lovely woman...and she had nothing but sweet words of encouragement and praise for me. She told me to work on, never to give in, never to stop. How little then did I think that I was destined to find my name linked with hers, and that too in my own country".

"I am doubly happy because after many years of work abroad, my natural ambition is to make a debut in my own country such as I made in the old. Thus far I have not had the opportunity, for reasons that I need not go into now". And Nielsen foggily suggests, "not Mr. Russell's fault by any means".

In genuine Alice Nielsen fashion she has created her own best opportunity: "But now I shall have a real operatic debut in my native land".

Alice, perhaps still hopeful of Napoli participation, tells of her connection to the genuine San Carlo managed by De Sanni, "I had the honor of being one of the stars of the San Carlo Opera Company the first time the company appeared in Covent Garden. I sang with Mr. Caruso in *Bohème, Rigoletto* and other operas. Oh! You should hear that ensemble. It's wonderful, the best chorus and the best orchestra that was ever heard". With glimmering hopes actual San Carlo will join, "I know Madame Nordica will be delighted".

By May 1st, 1906., the rough and risky business of Nielsen's American first grand opera season has ended. Her season of cheap concerts with poor talent closes. Italy beckons for summer, Hortense joins. Busy time ahead for the sisters picking the components of a misbranded new opera company.

Anticipates against all odds the thrill of a quality season in New Orleans with a seasoned company and a national tour. After the awful NYC start, Alice's artistic miracle has come true in America. As she had planned.

May 7 preparing to depart for Italy, Alice speaks from Park Avenue Hotel to the friendly *Telegraph*. No further chase by the squelched Desci.

In her last talk to the American press that season, Nielsen's business savvy receives a rare display; not since her discussion of theatre salaries in London 1901 has such analysis by this brilliant diva received print. Pertinent to recall here that both Nielsen sisters are strong theatre pros who have seen, done, and been there. Hortense runs her own touring company, helped by doting husband. These sisters are expert with tours, producing, and revenue. They are productive and practical. They have made things happen. They possess magnetic talent.

Alice says "I have met with the most remarkable success in my tour. In Los Angeles and in San Francisco we played night after night to $2,000 houses in Donizetti's *Don Pasquale*".

Takes full responsibility for what is now "my own" company; gives remora Russell a fresh start for any not in the know. "I was supported by my own Italian company. We had trouble at the beginning of the tour, but I don't want to talk about that or those who were responsible for it.

"Everybody in my profession knows them and those who don't—well—the truth is only a question of time. But I do want to say this—both Mr. Klaw and Mr. Erlanger have shown me every kindness and consideration".

Shubert shares with Ziegfeld a sordid reputation.

Nielsen says, "You know as well as I do that managers are always glad to take advantage of a woman...."

Praises the play-nice Syndicate, "Klaw & Erlanger have protected me in every way and without any motive of personal interest, present or future". And then, as assiduously as she has pitched Russell to local singers with a bit of cash to spend on him, she promotes her help: "But apart from personalities, the only way to tour this country in comfort is with the Syndicate. They don't make promises and break them; they don't pose to the public as the protectors of art, but they are good to their artists. They are business people with an astounding organization".

Tosses a parting Shubert egg, "And as far as I'm concerned, I would not advise performing animals, let alone humans, to sing with anyone else".

Dropping a portion of the pretense for the remora, Alice tells *Telegraph* "Henry Russell who brought over my company [sic], is no longer its proprietor". Never held more than an agent's role. Erases herself from making the New Orleans deal: "He has, as has been so generally announced, decided to bring over the San Carlo Opera Company [sic] to this country next Winter. About six weeks ago, Mr. Russell sold his interests in my company so as to be free for the handling of his [!] San Carlo venture". He has no role with the genuine San Carlo Opera. No resources to do anything. Strange shift from the "Nordica-Nielsen Company" which would highlight the stars' alliance. In a business sense, false advertising. What has he falsely promised? Later admits deceptions.

If money is made, Nordica and Nielsen will take. If losses, Nordica and Nielsen will pay. Nordica is the financial power and will receive top billing.

Deed largely done by this moment, the famed San Carlo name is hijacked for the duration and pitched to public. The two diva headliners have been coaxed to collusion, ownership stake in shadows. Later each admits the fact.

Of Alice's tour from NY, Shubert's contract replicated by Klaw & Erlanger allowed Russell a guaranteed percentage. Not a stake. Unsupervised he has posed as manager for reporters, and drafted as pianist and prompter while "on vacation in America" selling his elixir to locals willing to pay him to listen. If the notorious "$5 for 5 minutes" we don't know.

De Sanni-managed San Carlo Opera of Naples declines the tour. In later years his San Carlo tours America, confusion with the false flag group arises.

Nielsen-Nordica group uses various variations: "San Carlo Opera Company of San Francisco" or "San Carlo" or "San Carlo Opera Company". If certain editors balk applying the pirated label with its bogus implications, others innocently link the aggregation falsely with Napoli. Newspapers don't have space for correct version. Truncated, misleading version substituted.

Alice actually sang with San Carlo. Her remora babysat.

To Alice's credit, her new company proves sensational.

The false name will have future costs. Although he dares not thank her later, Russell has hit paydirt to plant wild pretensions. Arriving penniless and obscure in NYC, after touring with Nielsen six months he returns to London with intoxicated hopes. Not only has Alice acquired the Chicago, LA, and San Francisco return agreements, the French Opera Association puts a hefty $70,000 guarantee for her winter season. And she brings bonus of Nordica, with sufficient wealth to organize such a tour; and a NY banker husband.

The duo hire Constantino; this trio will create a sensation.

Down in New Orleans, an opera season not in French shocks Cajun press and makes national news. Upstart Alice rides again. NY Telegraph reports "For upwards of fifty years New Orleans has always had an exclusively French Opera Company". To Telegraph, Alice Nielsen relates how she and Nordica combined forces in Tampa to create the project. Ambitious to bring a quality company with genuine talent ashore to make magic across North America. In any case, "I will pass the summer in Italy".

What a year Alice Nielsen made! Faced down disaster to create a tidal wave of success by doing what only she could do.

Returns to Naples with Hortense mid-May.

May 13th, Los Angeles Herald's At the Theatre: "New Opera Company. Nordica, Nielsen, and a thoroughly adequate Italian opera company: this is the promise held out for next season". Conried at Met lost too much money in the San Francisco quake disaster to tour. "Thus it is gratifying to hear that there will be a company on tour...a cordial hearing is assured it".

Nordica relays the design of her new venture, "During my frequent trips across the United States, through big cities as well as small, where grand opera has never been heard, I have met every-where the most earnest desire" for opera "at prices which make it possible for all to attend". Her solution is this tour, "only a few very high priced singers in a splendid and artistically rounded out ensemble" to transform opera "from a luxury for a favored few to an educational factor in the musical lives of the masses of the great American public".

Nielsen adds, "Oh I am glad to think the Americans will hear me in such surroundings, and then, imagine my pride at finding my name side by side with America's—nay, the world's greatest dramatic singer—Mme. Nordica. She is a lovely woman. I met her in Jacksonville, Fla, and she had nothing but sweet words of encouragement and praise for me. She told me to work on, never to give in, never to stop. How little then did I think that I was destined to find my name linked with hers, and that too, in my own country. I am doubly happy because after many years of work abroad my natural ambition is to make a debut in my own country such as I made in the old. Thus far I have not had the opportunity...."

New Orleans will be her chose American grand opera debut.

"Hortense Nielsen, accompanied by her sister Alice, sailed last week for Italy where she will spend the summer", says *Washington Times* May 20th.

Alice Nielsen has accomplished something great. Again. Successor to her famed musical company is her grand opera company. As they visit Paris, London, Berlin, and Italy they of course meet Tosti, Duse, Bernhardt and others. The sisters cannot suspect they will take another shopping spree within three years to furnish a new Boston Opera House.

MAY: RETURNS TO EUROPE WITH A PLAN

Alice Nielsen sails to Italy to organize the new company, aided by the ever-resourceful Hortense. Both have toured widely; Alice has big fame and four European years. Gregarious and deeply alive, they travel happily. Any children and Hortense's husband remain unmentioned.

Business arrangements for the Nordica-Nielsen company remain foggy, Nordica's husband is involved. Never mentioning wife and kids in London, Henry Russell leaves this sketch of his activity after New Orleans, "At the end of May I returned to Paris and at once got into touch with Grimthorpe, who...invited me to dine with him at the Chateau de Madrid. Grimthorpe uncharacteristically ignored the food and wine".

He "suddenly blurted out, 'My Dear Hen, you will be sorry to hear that I have lost a lot of money. After I left you in Los Angeles I went to San Francisco, where a friend of mine persuaded me to invest in a new scheme of surface cars [trollys]'" just before the great quake. "'Just my luck, the damned earthquake upset everything and I am afraid my money is lost.' He also told me something about his uncle's will being thrown into Chancery. I don't remember the details, but do remember him saying, 'I am so hard up for the moment that I really don't know which way to turn, and until my lawyers have straightened out my affairs I shall not know where I am.' This coming from a man who I believe had once enjoyed one of the largest incomes in London, was a serious statement.

"It shocked me all the more because I knew how generous he had been to his friends. It is impossible to conceive a more trusting, open-hearted and unselfish friend that Ernest Grimthorpe. Few people know how much he gave away. With him there was no ostentation or newspaper notoriety..." such as Russell had striven and failed to obtain in America. "Even so, Grimthorpe asked about New Orleans and said, "Listen, I have never broken a promise in my life, and I am not going to begin now. If you can wait a couple of months I will let you have the amount I promised. So you can go ahead with your arrangements as though nothing had happened. I will see that you have all the money you need."' Grimthorpe soon advances funds from a bank he controls. In some way of course this if true would coordinate with Nordica's financial plans. Details not known.

Meanwhile, news spreads fast that Nielsen plans to attack New Orleans.

June 10 *Washington Post* provides the setting: "French Opera House is for the first time in its history to abandon the opera with which its history has been connected. Sometimes there has been no season of opera at all. At others there has been opera bouffe or a dramatic company brought over from France, but whenever there was opera...it was in French. Next season there is to be a season of opera in Italian. The weeks have been granted by the French Opera Association to an impresario who promises performances in Italian. Alice Nielsen is to be the light soprano of the company" and Nordica the dramatic. Actually the duo sing the same repertoire, except Wagner which Alice has not yet attempted.

"Various causes have led to this radical change. The companies at the French Opera House have not been up to the standard in recent seasons. Critical disapproval was expressed so strongly in some quarters last winter that the impresario retorted with libel suits. Although the Grau company [that is, the Met] which brought the leading singers of the world to New Orleans played to enormous business, the press was not disposed to consider the performances superior to those given by their own company. That was mere loyalty to a home institution however and the public saw the superiority of the NY organization to a degree that created deep dissatisfaction".

New Orleans' opera began 1791 with Louis Tabary's troupe. In 1837 Julie Calvé arrives at age twenty-two, graduate of Paris Conservatoire thanks to Rossini. Marries opera house director Charles Boudourquie. "A beloved singer...best in the light soprano roles", she dies 1898. JG de Broncelle's records say a third balcony added 1845 to seat slaves "who accompanied their masters.... Present French Opera House replaced Theatre d'Orleans in 1859". Impudent Nielsen ends a century of French-only performances.

Post writes "French Opera Association makes liberal enough terms" for a ten week season, "a guarantee of something like $70,000 [$2-million today]. In addition to this sum, there is the assurance of liberal patronage [ticket sales] if the performances are good".

From nothing Alice has generated this guarantee and not even Ziegfeld could gamble it away. Now she shall sing what she wants. Selects *Bohème*.

By mid-summer "San Carlo" moniker sticks to the ensemble. Convenient shorthand for a fictional "Celebrated San Carlo of San Francisco Opera Company which ranks with the Metropolitan of NY" which in newsprint clips to a misleading "San Carlo".

An Italian equal would be forming "The Celebrated Metropolitan Opera Company of Bergamo Which Ranks with La Scala" and playing Torino as "The Metropolitan Opera" before touring Europe.

The canard keeps Nordica and Nielsen off the ownership marquee, beyond implying a false continuity to that vaunted San Carlo season at Covent Garden season where Alice sang. In practice Nordica takes top billing. She does not share Nielsen's quirk for indulging Russell's hubris. And Nielsen will later give Nordica full credit for organizing the group.

After her conflicted NYC debut, Alice Nielsen has been hailed a genius by every region visited: Midwest, West, South. Surmounting great odds, she has acquired a power base beyond Big Apple. Rebel with a cause, her patriotic alliance with Nordica is national news. Theatre managers rapidly book their winter 1906-07 North American Tour.

July 1st, *Washington Times*: "Nordica, for years an important member of the Conried forces [at Met], has joined not 'the opposition' which is Hammerstein but 'an opposition' which is the San Carlo opera company [etc "of San Francisco"].... It does not hope to invade NY just yet, but it will be heard in most of the large cities in the country, opening October 29 in Pittsburg and playing a ten-week season at the famous old French Opera House in New Orleans beginning November 26".

Repertory has been set: *Giaconda, Aida, Trovatore, Tosca, Faust, L'Africain, Daughter of the Regiment* and *La Bohème*.

Doubles size of Alice Nielsen's previous tours, "The company will number one-hundred-sixty-five people and is said to be better equipped for a long road tour than any company which has gone out for many years".

By August preparations complete. Sets, costumes, music, players and singers are signed. The company embarks on the voyage to New Orleans.

August 14th *NY Times* reports national theatre news. Architect Stanford White shot by outraged husband Harry Thaw; North German Lloyd liner *Kaiser Wilhelm* arrives with Ziegfeld and wife Anna Held; Herbert's diva Fritzi Scheff soon to open at Knickerbocker in "her last season's success *Mlle. Modiste*"; Alice Nielsen due back mid-September.

South Carolina clamors for her return. Alice attracts repeat business, a booking-agent's dream. August 16th *Columbia State* (SC): "Manager Brown is receiving letters from all parts of SC asking him to hold seats for Alice Nielsen's concert here Thursday night of Fair Week" in September. "Miss Nielsen was here last season in *Don Pasquale* and all hearts were laid at her feet. It is believed that she will please the audience even more than Nordica would have done". Briefly sketches her pilgrim progress, then "Nielsen will be supported by a quartette from Henry Russell's Celebrated San Carlo of San Francisco Opera Company Which Ranks Along With the Metropolitan of NY [caps added—fast work for a non-existent company]".

Honest *Columbia State* prints the full company title, few papers do. The genuine San Carlo remains silent about these name-rustlers stealing its brand. No posse appears over the horizon to do justice to the rascals.

Columbia State Aug 22nd prints as a feature story, "Nielsen's memoir, the Southern Queen of Song Tells Her Life Story". This hijacks the San Jose tale which hijacks the London *Mostly About People* article wherein "many of my critics indeed suggested that I should go into grand opera, and these suggestions I hugged to my heart, for they divined and voiced my real ambition..." and the usual pilgrim progress.

September 8, *Musical America* continues the misleading fable that Nielsen was "not received with any undue amount of favor during her last appearance in NY" and paraphrases the singer's response. She "will return this season with a determination to compel the NY critics to like her and write kind things about her work". A minority of three NY critics (actually two, Alan Dale being a columnist) had recoiled at the five out-of-tune bribed musicians, bad cast, nervous former Met-oboist conductor, shabby production. Bemoaning how she done Broadway wrong to sing weary old Donizetti. Majority of NYC critics praised her and pushed the Met to hire her without delay.

Fanning the Nielsen-sparked flame of Western independence, *Musical America* reminds readers, "Whatever disappointments this singer may have had as a result of the lack of favor extended by NY...were overcome in large measure by the ovations she received during her last Western appearances. In Chicago, St. Louis, Cincinnati, Indianapolis, Denver and San Francisco her work was accepted with enthusiasm".

The new opera company gets the attention. Concert tours, Nielsen's greatest future revenue source, accompany the opera plans.

September 10th, *Jacksonville Times-Union* (FL) reports Nielsen would "en route to New Orleans" revisit sixteen southern cities with a vocal quartet, "and Jacksonville—Manager Burbridge offering a very heavy guarantee—is fortunate enough to be one of the sixteen".

The Nielsen sisters return to NYC from Italy late September.

Alice's winter 1906 North American Tour had sparked a Great Awakening for grand opera. Before she leaves in spring 1907, movements will begin to build permanent companies in Chicago, Los Angeles, Boston, and Montreal.

AMERICAN OPERA REVELATION

September 20, 1906 (*NY Times*), White Star's *Cretic* docks in NYC, kept in quarantine overnight as Dr. Doty investigates a suspected typhoid case; the ship's surgeon must warrant passengers free of infection. The ship had arrived from Naples and Genoa. Among 338 cabin and 858 steerage passengers the press mention only the president of Catholic University DJ O'Connell, and Alice Nielsen who signs her age as twenty-three a very snarky joke indeed. Her sister Hortense N. Nielsen signs as single, age twenty-five. Alice takes a short NYC stay with mom Sarah and son Ben. She visits Nordica at the Waldorf, much to discuss.

Alice proceeds toward New Orleans without any New York performances; she does not "give the critics a new chance to like her". Their new-formed opera company sails direct from Italy to New Orleans. Alice joins to rehearse for a month before taking time away to start her Southern concert series.

From this point it becomes her practice to return from Europe ahead of opera season for a concert tour.

Her concert career starts in South Carolina. And as prelude October 22, *Columbia State* (SC) reprints "Nielsen's Autobiography, the Southern Queen of Song tells her life story". Three days later her group arrives from New Orleans—without booking rooms in advance. "Finding all of the hotels and boarding houses crowded, they were considerably disturbed, but were entertained as the guests of Mr. Asher P. Brown". The gracious Asher Brown and his brother Fitz Hugh Brown manage the 1,500-seat Columbia Theatre.

"Inimitable Alice Nielsen has charmed Columbia", says *State*. Rested, she sounds even better. *Pasquale* eight months ago "was so remarkable it seemed as if no singer could ever surpass the qualities she then displayed, both as a vocalist and actress, and yet as one listened to her yesterday she appeared to surpass all memories of herself and the voice of liquid gold seemed more golden than ever—the velvet tones seemed even more velvety and the wondrous art has gained in depth during these eight months' absence" instead of her singing at the near end of an exhausting, stressful if triumphant American tour.

Opera, concert, Broadway: the triple-threat cross-over artist.

Her artistry is profoundly felt in Columbia that night. Few opera singers could match Nielsen in concert. Caruso refused to sing with McCormack in a concert Nielsen sought to produce. Nielsen could do it all.

And can sing and dance.

Columbia State: "In concert and not in opera...Alice Nielsen appeared at the Columbia theatre. Her triumph was the greater on this account because she was not assisted by the thousand opportunities which her talent as an actress gives her.... It was just her singing, just her voice, just the woman which the public had to criticize.

"The verdict was unanimous, instantaneous and unhesitating. It was gratifying to watch the pleased expression on the faces of cultured people as the prima donna attacked the difficult coloratura in...the famous aria, *Ah forse lui* from the *Traviata*. Each individual note was as a chime of bells—true, clean and telling and when finally she reached the brilliant trill which brings the number to an end, a great storm of applause greeted the youthful artist who has risen by sheer force of gift and work...to the giddy heights of the world's great singers".

She gave encores "call after call, and gracefully she bowed and happily she smiled, but an encore had to be given. With touching pathos and clear enunciation she sang Tosti's *Good-Bye* and the public not yet contented, demanded more. Then followed *Comin' Thro' The Rye*, *Annie Laurie* and a host of others all sung so faultlessly, so perfectly and yet with so much appropriateness of feeling that the applause only subsided when the footlights were lowered as an intimation that the gifted singer could give no more. Bright and brilliant star—*au revoir*".

In the cast: "admirable" tenor Riccardo Martin and mezzo Elfrida. De Fonteynes, "although not up to the average of the other artists, gave a more-or-less satisfactory rendition of his two songs".

Faux impresario must earn his keep, "the pianist on the program was 'sig. Angslini.' This must have been an error of printing for surely it was... Henry Russell". Not for the first time outed.

Speaking to *State*, Nielsen thanks "Manager Brown" who induced his friends the Sloans to help house her group. "We arrived believing rooms were engaged for us and then we found there was not a room free in the town, but for those dear kind people we should have been in the street—oh! I'm so grateful to them!" Brown hopes to bring "this wonderful ensemble to pay a visit here next spring". Nielsen sang evening and matinee at a cost "not less than $250" (about $6000 today).

Travels to the historic harbor town of mischief in bygone 1860s.

October 26, Charleston SC provides one of the great accounts of Nielsen's art. *News and Courier* (SC) captures the vanished moment: "Then came dainty, pretty, laughing Alice—little Alice Nielsen, who sang her way into thousands and thousands of hearts while in comic opera and then brought as many more to love her with her more serious roles in grand opera...her entry was a signal for a demonstration...." When she sang "not a program fluttered, fans poised in the air and silence absolute and deferential prevailed. Clear, pure, limpid as a mountain stream, the melody flowed along.

"Without effort, trick or evasion the notes came true to the score and shaded as delicately as the miniaturist lays the colors upon the ivory panel. Miss Nielsen's voice seems to know only the steps between the notes and upward or downward the interval is perfectly made, and the flute-like tone is held, seemingly at will.

"Flexible, resonant, sweet, it charms to stillness any assemblage and fills the air with quivering, pulsating music. There is no affectation, no artificial demonstration of technical drudgery; she sings like a canary or better still a Southern mocking bird, and her pretty throat swells and throbs as the score suggests a crescendo or fortissimo.

"Her second triumph was complete as her first, and those who recalled *Don Pasquale* were right glad to be within the sound of her voice again. Miss Nielsen's first number was an aria from *La Traviata* and it was sung delightfully. An enthusiastic recall brought her out again, and she sang Tosti's beautiful *Good-Bye* with feeling and exquisite taste".

Tours three weeks toward New Orleans where her grand opera company is poised to occupy French Opera House from November 20 until 2 February. In January, Nordica joins. Afterwards they tour "far west as San Francisco, Portland, Vancouver and Seattle and places in eastern Canada and New England", reports *San Jose Mercury News* (Nov 20).

At New Orleans, Alice Nielsen has many old friends dating from Bostonian days who made the deal happen. Despite these facts, Russell obliterates Nielsen from the equation in typical pose as bogus impresario: "I arrived in New Orleans in October 1906". No, he had arrived the previous March. "I was introduced to several of the principal box-holders of the famous French Opera House" by Nielsen as she inspired them to bet the season on her. As a bonus, she delivers Nordica and Constantino. The reliable Tosti and Constantino pull talent from Italy and Madrid.

Alice has her stage, patrons, and fans. She makes things happen.

At New Orleans the Nielsen party with remora is met by Alice's old friends: "Mr. and Mrs. Harry Howard, Mrs. Yznaga mother of Consuelo, Lady Lister-Kaye [sister of Conseulo], and Miss Emily Yznaga. They were anxious to revive the glories of their operatic past, and said that if I could find enough backing to bring a good company [Nielsen] to New Orleans the following winter, they would guarantee a good subscription for the season.

Makes understatement of his life, "Here indeed was an opening I had not expected" entirely thanks to the uncredited Nielsen. "Remembering the generous offer of Grimthorpe [loan on the guarantee], I signed a contract with them for the following year". Later, he admits the two women stars own and opera the company. In New Orleans, the contract was given Alice.

Spanish basso Andreas DeSegurola (1873-1953) in *Through My Monocle* (1991) recalls Paolo Tosti cast the singers such as Fely Dereyne, who sang *Carmen* with DeSegurola: "My genuine Spanish interpretation of that colorful role took the public by storm, and since that first performance my name figured among those of the Company's most favored singers. That performance also marked the beginning of an ardent romance between Fely Dereyne and me. A romance that left in my heart recollection of mutual happiness". He recalls the group "was rich in artists of great standing and reputation: Lillian Nordica, the celebrated dramatic soprano, the popular American singer Alice Nielsen, Victor Maurel the king of baritones, and Guiseppe Campanari of Metropolitan fame".

Campanari (1855-1927) had detoured as cellist at La Scala and Boston Symphony until regaining his voice in 1893; at Met 1894-1912.

French Opera House stockholders sponsored Alice Nielsen's winter return: 167 box subscribers plus eleven of *avan scene* include AJ Cassard, Mrs. Leon Godchaux, FJ Gasquet, Mrs. DA Milliken, Henry Beer, Walter Denegre, Walter Stauffer, DA Cahffraix. Mrs. CA Whitney, H Laroussini, Geo. Denegre.

General subscribers include Theodore Grunewald of Grunewald Hotel. Since 1852 the Grunewald family had operated a music store at 310 Main Street; Theodore Grunewald had met Nielsen in Bostonian days. He offered practical help in 1901 when Alice was at odds with Tom Williams. He and wife appear in Nielsen's 1907 address book beside French Opera manager Thomas Brulatour and wife.

She plans to sing frequently. Show America what she could do. Good health or bad, Alice Nielsen sang a grueling schedule to astonishing acclaim.

American musical press converges on New Orleans for Nielsen's grand opera debut. Countering past controversy with an egg at Lee Shubert, Alice Nielsen opens with *Daughter of the Regiment.*

New Orleans Opera's Jack Belsom lists Alice Nielsen's appearances during this 1906-07 season. Suggests she sang over illness, "she did cancel a few scheduled performances during the run". Singers in New Orleans frequently wrestled with bronchitis and grippe. Winter weather damp. And Nielsen had supplanted the region's French, certain local critics seem scalded cats. Italian operas sung in Italian so outrageous.

November 24 Marie, *La Figlia del Reggimento;* 25 Nov Concert with *Good-bye*, J. Strauss's *Primavera Waltz*, other English and American songs; 29 Nov Gilda, *Rigoletto;* 1 Dec Gilda, *Rigoletto;* 4 Dec Mimi, *La Bohème;* 5 Dec (mat)

Gilda, *Rigoletto;* 11 Dec Mimi, *La Bohème;* 13 Dec Violetta, *La Traviata;* 18 Dec Rosina, *Barbiere di Siviglia;* 20 Dec Mimi, *La Bohème;* 22 Dec Mimi, *La Bohème;* 27 Dec Lucia, *Lucia di Lammermoor;* 30 Dec (mat) Mimi in *La Bohème.*

Starting New Year 1907: 2 Jan benefit performance, balcony scene from *Roméo et Juliette* and Act 3 of *Bohème;* 6 Jan Mimi, *La Bohème;* 10 Jan Violetta, *La Traviata;* 13 Jan (mat) Lucia, *Lucia di Lammermoor;* 15 Jan Rosina, *Barbiere di Siviglia;* Jan 19 and 24, Norina, *Don Pasquale;* 27 Jan Mimi, *La Bohème;* 1 Feb Marguerite de Valois, *Les Huguenots;* 2 Feb Mimi, *La Bohème.*

New Orleans Picayune reviews opening night. Local memory still sharp for Nielsen's preceding performances. *Picayune* curiously seems pleased to plagiarize Louis Strang:

> *New Orleans Picayune,* Nov 25 1906
> New Orleans has awaited with a great deal of interest the appearance of Miss Alice Nielsen as Maria, in Donizetti's opera, *The Daughter of the Regiment.* Years ago, when this charming singer was a member of the Bostonians, and more recently, when she was at the head of her own company, she sang in this city.
>
> Her birdlike voice and winsome personality won her a host of friends here then, and many of them turned out last night to see how she would stand the ordeal of grand opera. *The Daughter of the Regiment* belongs to a school which has practically lost its hold on the public. Puccini, Leoncavallo and Mascagni have taken the place of Donizetti, and it is not likely that the furor which the latter's works made some 60 years ago will ever be repeated. In spite of the thinness of the orchestration, however, *The Daughter of the Regiment* contains many pretty airs, some of whom like the *Rataplan,* the *Salute to France,* and the delightful *Quando il Destino,* are known the world over.
>
> The role of the heroine, small as it is, has always been a favorite with great artists. Jenny Lind, Sontag, Patti, Alhani, and in this country Miss Kellogg and Mrs. Richings-Bernard have sung it with success. It was, therefore, quite natural that Miss Nielsen should elect to make her bow to New Orleans as a singer of grand opera in the role of Maria in a composition hallowed by association with so many famous names.
>
> Her work throughout the evening was very enjoyable, and toward the close of the third act there were moments of genuine enthusiasm, when the audience applauded cordially, insisting upon encores, and when great sheaves of flowers and large floral designs were borne triumphantly across the stage and heaped at the feet of the singer.
>
> ["]Indeed, it is impossible not to be charmed by this little woman, who sings as if singing where the best fun in the world, who is so frankly gratified when her audience likes her work and commends her, and who goes soaring up and away on the high notes sounding clear and pure above chorus and orchestra,

without the slightest apparent effort and without a trace of affection or of artificial striving ["].

"Like a bird" is the phrase which, in the old days of the Bostonians, was invariable used to describe her vocal efforts, and the words still apply. She still has the grace, the ease and the simplicity which inspired the metaphor five years ago.

Miss Nielsen's voice is appreciated at once. In spite of the vastness of the auditorium which she had to fill, its colorful brilliancy, its range and its rich, sympathetic and musical qualities make themselves promptly felt. From the opening song, *The Camp is My Birthplace*, in which Maria tells the story of her life among the soldiers; to the *Salute to France* and *When Destiny In The Midst Of War*, the frequent encores and curtain calls showed that her success in grand opera is assured.

In the third act, where the comedy approximates in dash and sparkle the merry little plays in which the public first learned to love Alice Nielsen, her acting was delightful. She was the "daughter of the regiment", untamed in spite of her laces and satins, and trailing robes, and the saucy little kick with which she disengaged her embarrassing skirts never failed to elicit a prompt response of laughter.

The rehearsal scene was delightfully done and the duet with Sulpizio was sung with a vigor and elation that were infectious. Senor Perello de Segurolea as Sulpizio...was capable and conscientious artist with a fine voice used to excellent advantage. Umberio Sachetti made a capital Tonio. He has a light tenor with a good range. The voice is much richer and fuller than is usually the case with singers of his class. His phrasing was excellent, and the simplicity and clearness of his pronunciation, which enabled practically every word he uttered to be...understood were...a great improvement [over other light tenors]. As an actor Sig. Sachetti showed a good deal of intelligence and skill. His parting with Maria at the end of the second act was done with genuine feeling, and the gesture of impotent rage with which he dashed his hat to the ground as he watched his sweetheart being led away....

The work of the chorus deserves a word of commendation in passing.... Orchestra improves from night to night under Sg. Conti's competent direction. Altogether, last night's performance was a very agreeable one free from anything which could jar upon the sensitive nerves of the most exacting critic, and giving further earnest, if such were necessary, of the many congenial evenings which the San Carlo Opera Company [of San Francisco etc] engagement still has in store for the opera-going public of this city.

Although as Louis Strang had said, "impossible not to be charmed by this little woman" the contrarian *Times-Democrat* (November 25) writes of *Figlia del Reggimento* her "voice has many flaws but charmed the audience and after a nervous start she recovered composure in Act 2 and won applause".

Basque tenor Constantino causes a sensation at his American debut in New Orleans as *Don Jose* in *Carmen*. After six years in Argentina where he was a renowned *payador* (sings improvises lyrics on a competitive dare) and sang at *Teatro Odeon* in Buenos Aires, he was an 1899 success at *Teatro Real Madrid* then Portugal and Poland before five years in Russia, joining Covent Garden for his 1905 debut. Caruso had promoted the rival tenor to Alice for two Waldorf performances. In New Orleans, Nielsen and Constantino share eleven operas with huge success

Their *neplusultra* is *La Bohème*.

December 6th, *Musical Courier's* Zeno says of *Rigoletto*, "heretofore always given in French with a great many cuts and changes which robbed the score of much of its beauty", the Nielsen company has "presented the entire opera with elaborate stage settings and beautiful costumes, both the orchestra and chorus again scoring a complete triumph.

"Alice Nielsen's singing of Gilda was a revelation even to her greatest admirers, and apart from her admirable vocalization of the famous *Caro Nome*, her acting in the third act displayed a dramatic fervor and histrionic ability which came as a surprise to many who had heretofore maintained that her art was more adapted to such operas as *Don Pasquale* and *The Daughter Of The Regiment*. It was the unanimous verdict of the New Orleans public that Nielsen's Gilda was one of the finest interpretations of the part ever heard in the French Opera House".

Adds Zeno tartly, "It would require an experience of over forty years to decide whether this is really high praise for the young prima donna".

In the cast: the company "so infinitely superior both in individual artists and ensemble to anything ever experienced in New Orleans that even the local critic's standard of comparison can only have a limited value".

New Orleans egg to NYC: "That Alice Nielsen has the makings of a great singer is beyond dispute, and that New York will one day endorse this verdict is a prophecy which is bound to be fulfilled".

As the Duke "Signor Constantino was superb".

Erstwhile conductor and oboist Jose Vanderberg has surrendered the baton to the renowned Arnaldo Conti, who led the Waldorf sessions. Conti (1855-1919) conducted Patti, Calvé, Scotti, de Reszkes. In Madrid he had conducted many of the ensemble's singers.

Conti's attempt to stop encores fails. Louisiana demands encores not to be denied: "Angelini Fornari's interpretation of the title role elicited the hearty approval of the audience...a fine actor and a good singer, his powerful baritone voice together with Miss Nielsen's dramatic action, at the end of the third act caused the public literally to rise from their seats and although strong effects have been made on the part of the management not to encourage the encore system, the last part of the third act had to be repeated, otherwise order would not have been restored in the upper parts of the theatre".

New Orleans strongly likes, or dislikes: "This public is in no way to be compared with the Eastern audiences, and its noisy demonstrations of approval or disapproval (as the case may be) remind one of the scenes which are everyday occurrences in the Southern part of France and the smaller theatres of Italy". Gayety is rampant: "It is no exaggeration to state that the one topic of conversation in New Orleans is the success of the company".

Even so, December 14th *Daily States* finds *Traviata* "artistically a very ordinary production...Nielsen found Violetta too much for her". Perhaps this reaction accounts for these many wry sly remarks from Zeno about past quality of New Orleans opera. Jus' don't know nuttin'.

New Orleans' season is closely observed by the nation. *Chicago Tribune* (Dec 16) recaps her career, tosses egg at Bostonian troupe for mistreatment of protégé, "Alice Nielsen, the former light opera favorite who is now singing with a grand opera company in New Orleans, probably is the most successful understudy that ever understudied on the light opera stage in this country. She was with the Bostonians for many weeks before she was given a chance".

Untrue: *War-Time Wedding* was a leading role day one; soon stars in *Robin Hood*. After a year, stars in *Serenade* only thanks to Herbert.

"Even after she had won the right to be considered a clever comedienne and a good singer, she was held back in order that older members of the organization might be kept in the foreground. Which is what frequently happens to understudies". As only true, consider Ida Valerga's Patti plight.

Back New Orleans where the good tunes roll.

December 21, *Musical Courier's* Zeno reports the company "continues to improve its prestige from week to week. Every new production has new qualities of excellence, and it is impossible to overrate the artistic work which is now being done by this magnificent ensemble of talent". Yet "the path of success...has been far from easy in New Orleans. Considering that the French language is spoken here almost as generally as in Paris itself, it was with very divided feelings that the public anticipated the innovation of hearing opera sung in Italian".

Zeno attempts halfheartedly to clarify the phony brand name. "Although the San Carlo [of San Francisco] opera company is not, as its title would indicate, a purely Italian organization [mostly Madrid], it very rightly insists upon presenting all the Italian operas in Italian and all French operas in French. The company is in reality formed of international talent, which included singers of all nations" mostly Spain.

Nielsen and Constantino prove sensational.

As Richard Aldrich has once said, "Soprano and the tenor were the chief ornaments of the cast and the whole justification of the production".

New Orleans and *Music Courier's* Zeno first witness the duo's stellar magic. Soon to amaze Los Angeles, Chicago, Boston.

Ensemble masterpiece *La Bohème* "easily surpassed every other effort of the company. Every artist was perfectly adapted to his or her respective parts, and one almost hesitates to criticize lest one accentuate the merits of any individual at the expense of the whole. Miss Nielsen's Mimi, which rose gradually from the first scene to the last scene, was exquisitely done and worthy to rank among the finest presentations of Murger's heroine. The public was electrified by the beauty of the high C which she and Constantino sang together at the end of the first act as they both exited from the first scene on which the curtain was gradually lowered".

Zeno knew Bonci and Caruso. Prefers Constantino whose "Rodolfo is one of his finest creations. I remember when Bonci first sang in London in this role and I have heard Caruso sing it on numerous occasions, but anything more perfect than the rendition of the great Spanish tenor cannot be imagined, and I doubt whether it has ever been equaled".

In the cast: Musetta "adequately filled by Madame Dereyne. Signor Fornari's Marcello was excellent. Segurola's colline was full of dignity and warm emotion". Chorus gains special mention as the nation's best, thanks to conductor Conti. "The exhilarating scene of the Café Momus... (which was the storm signal of great applause) was handsomely staged and the singing of the chorus was a testimonial to the modest chorusmaster who unknown to the public, has played so important a part in the opera, perfecting the best chorus that has ever been heard in the United States".

After twelve curtain calls, encore-resistant conductor Conti surrenders.

"At the close of the Third Act...enthusiasm reached the fever point and notwithstanding the long resistance of Maestro Conti, the public succeeded in forcing him to repeat the famous quartet.

"Before he did so however, the public made one of the liveliest demonstrations of insistence which has ever been seen in this or in any other opera house. After the curtain had been raised at least twelve times, Signor Conti was dragged forcibly onto the platform".

As 1898 Honolulu, again appears the US Navy for Alice Nielsen.

December 22 with battleship Louisiana in port, crew and officers attend a performance of La Traviata given in their honor. Afterwards, as in Hawaii, Nielsen sings Star Spangled Banner with the Navy and Marine voices.

December 23, Musical America reports "a brilliant audience attended last week's performance of La Bohème...and heard a performance which could not have been any better. Charming as Mimi was Miss Nielsen, whose admirable interpretation of the role won her repeated recalls. The audience was delighted with her artistry, not only vocal, but histrionic".

Sadly, illness strikes Alice after Christmas. For Lucia, on December 28th Daily Picayune notes, "Nielsen not at her best...sang with perceptible effort".

Mischievous Daily States claims "Nielsen's Lucia was the poorest heard on the French Opera House stage in many years. One wonders what she will attempt to sing next? In the Mad scene her high notes were untrue and her vocalization not worthy of a student". Obviously ill of the vile local miasma.

Success in New Orleans is hailed by the American press as a sign. Alice's rare artistic courage gives the world a moral about money and art.

December 30 Chicago Tribune writes, "While it is true that [Henry] Irving was right when he said that to succeed as an art the theatre must first succeed as a business, it is not true that the money should smother the art. Sothern and Marlow get the money and they nurture art. But players are few who will follow Alice Nielsen's example and forsake big sure money in order to develop their talents for a better, higher purpose, as Nielsen did when she quit profitable light opera and went abroad at the height of her career to become a humble student in schools for grand opera singers".

For second time, America praises Alice Nielsen as icon of artistic integrity.

She left Shaftesbury theatre early July 1901.

December 1907 she is for legends to be made of. Twice over.

1907: GRAND OPERA TOUR: STANDING ROOM ONLY

During New Orleans the fledgling company is hailed better than the Met. Soon arises this same praise (and so say all of us!) wherever Nielsen follows the Metropolitan tour: Los Angeles, Chicago, Boston.

1907 January's *Current Literature*: "No less than four grand opera companies are competing for the approval of the American public this winter". The Met; Hammerstein's Manhattan "opened brilliantly during the first week in December"; Henry Savage Company has "large audiences in many cities with a vivid and effective presentation in English of Puccini's *Madam Butterfly*"; and a new—nameless—company including "among its prima donnas such distinguished singers as Lillian Nordica and Alice Nielsen, is helping to maintain and perpetuate in New Orleans operatic traditions that date back eighty-three years".

Current Literature is far too clever to slap the San Carlo's great name on the new-made touring company of Nielsen, Nordica, and Constantino.

Story continues that Oscar Hammerstein "already built some ten theatres and music-halls in NY" and "made and lost several fortunes". In December '06 of course, Met met or Met meets, rival Hammerstein opening a competing opera venture. Charles Meltzer *Pearson's Magazine* (Dec 1907) reports that Hammerstein came to 1860s America with a few dollars and grew rich in tobacco. Lives in Harlem, "his round, ruddy face with its adornment of black beard, mustache and whiskers, his thick-set form, his smile and his eccentric hats grew to be as familiar as the goats which a quarter of a century ago abounded in the neighborhood".

Nielsen's flu begins to abate. And on January 3 *Daily States* says of the gala concert, she "showed much improvement in the beginning... but weakened considerably at the end. Her Juliette was very poor".

Ticket demand unprecedented and nearly precipitate a January riot.

Musical Courier's Zeno (Jan 4) experiences the event: "Last week's operatic doings of the San Carlo opera company ended with the first matinee performance of the *Bohème* which has been given this season, and some very remarkable scenes occurred outside the French Opera House. The Sunday matinee here is generally attended exclusively by the Creole inhabitants....

"There was an extraordinary demand for seats from the moment the first announcements was made and by Friday at 10 o'clock the whole theatre had been secured. When Sunday afternoon arrived it was necessary to put out the sign of 'standing Room Only' which to the American populace is conveyed by the letters SRO.

"Such a proceeding had never been known in the history of the French Opera House, and when the public saw the announcement very few, in fact none of the French portion, understood what it meant. About half an hour before the curtain was timed to go up, a crowd of 200 or 300 people collected outside the opera house and demanded to be admitted. It was in vain that the men in the box office told them that no more tickets or standing room could be sold... They could not believe the theatre was sold out. In forty years, they said, this had never come to pass.... As the crowd grew denser a rumor spread that the management had some motive for not letting the public in. Ridiculous as was this suggestion...it had the effect of exciting the already excited French people and but for the timely interference of the police, the men in the box office might have been rudely handled.

"The matinee performance proved a gigantic success, and never in the recollection of the oldest inhabitants of the city has such a house been witnessed as was gathered together for last Sunday afternoon".

January 11, Zeno (*Musical Courier*): the "company gave a remarkably fine performance of *Lucia di Lammermoor* last week. This somewhat antiquated opera, although it contains delightful melodies and one or two great ensembles, is nevertheless mostly dependent for its success on the artists who are singing the principal roles. It was a fresh occasion for the public to tender an enthusiastic ovation to Nielsen and Constantino who may be truthfully said to have shared honors in the singing of their respective roles.

"Miss Nielsen has Lucia had every opportunity to make a display of vocal gymnastics, a display which is the inevitable concomitant of a famous prima donna. If Nielsen's claim to priority in her profession depended solely upon vocal fireworks she would easily take a first prize, for certainly her remarkable singing of the mad scene brought us back to the palmy days of Madame Melba when that golden-voiced singer was first heard in Covent Garden about sixteen years ago".

For Zeno, Nielsen compares very favorably with Melba. "It has been frequently and very rightly asserted that comparisons between one great singer and another are both odious and futile, but as the entire press of this city seemed to take it for granted that Nielsen's singing of the mad scene had to be measured by the standard created by her famous rival, it is only fair to the more youthful prima donna to state that she did not disappoint the most ardent admirers of Madame Melba. Miss Nielsen was obviously suffering from a severe cold, doubtless due to the sudden changes of climate which are so frequent in New Orleans, and which often prove so disastrous to the singers who come here. This did not prevent her, however, from doing justice to the difficult music which she had to sing".

Nielsen's fortunes soar with a stage and co-star equal.

"Constantino proved himself one of the greatest Edgardos who has ever been heard on the lyric stage. His acting was as remarkable as his singing. There are no encomiums which are too high for his exquisite singing of the last act and for the dramatic fervor he displayed in the famous third act. The resources both vocal and histrionic of this great Spanish [Basque] tenor are truly astounding...."

Music made to match. "Maestro Conti held his orchestra and chorus in perfect unison, and such is the personal magnetism of this truly remarkable conductor that he seems to control the public with the same power as he does his orchestra". Faddish war on encores continues, "On three occasions during the opera the public endeavored to force a 'bis....' Conti was obdurate and looked around defiantly at the public which is gradually beginning to understand that the day has passed when noisy interruptions...will be encouraged by an intelligent conductor or truly artistic singers".

January 11, *L'Abeille de la Nouvelle Orleans* says of *Traviata*, "Alice Nielsen was apparently tired because at times only those close to the stage could hear her".

At last by January 20th Alice Nielsen's winter illness passes completely.

Daily Picayune tells us in *Don Pasquale*, "Norina suits Alice Nielsen's voice exactly and she sang it with charm and ease".

Daily States remains contrarian: "Nielsen's artistic interpretation left much to be desired while her dramatic interpretation... was exceedingly poor. She showed a lack of 'finesse de jeu' and in many parts was even vulgar".

In daily life of the town, even vulgar Alice Nielsen acts to save a stranger. *St. Louis Star* reports (Jan 27), "a most pleasing bit of romantic interest was added to what nearly became a tragedy on Canal Street the other day in New Orleans. A nicely-dressed young man, attempting to board a car, was run down by another. Hundreds of persons rushed to the scene.

"A passing carriage stopped at the curb, and a richly-attired little woman with a childish face alighted and made her way through the mob. The woman was not prompted by curiosity. She astounded the crowd by demanding that the unfortunate individual be placed in her carriage and removed to a hospital. 'Is he alive?' was her question. 'Yes.' 'Well, place the poor fellow in my carriage and take him to a doctor quickly!' Street railway employees and the blue-coated brass-buttoned officers said: 'No.' And evidently they meant it, for instead of the carriage they proceeded to hoist the injured man into the car that had run him down.

"'shame! Shame!' cried the little woman in a tearful and scornful voice. But the officers paid no heed to her. The clang of the ambulance was heard as it dashed up, and the disappointed little angel of mercy slipped through the wondering and questioning throng. There is only one thing that will distract man's attention from a scene of horror and that is a picture of beauty. 'Who is she?' was the query.

"But there was no answer until she had gathered up her skirts and disappeared in the carriage. As the coachman closed the door and mounted the box, a gentleman removed his hat and saved the shop girl at his elbow from being transformed into a question mark by answering the query she was flinging into the faces of everyone.

"'Madam', said the big man, 'that is Miss Alice Nielsen.'"

Nordica joins Nielsen down in New Orleans. Alice's 1907 address book gives a cordial glimpse, January 31 "Madame Nordica dressed my hair said insisted to me I makeup myself to look pretty as I was pretty". And a bit more; Alice notes her measurements. (inches): bust 32, waist 21, hips 33, at 5-feet 2½ inches without shoes. For the sewing of how many costumes?

Illness fated of both. After singing in NYC for Hammerstein and concerts across January, Nordica falls quickly in New Orleans. Even so, she sang *La Gioconda*, Marguerite in *Faust* and Valentine in an "apparently disastrous *Huguenots*" according to testy Jack Belsom, who explains, "*Huguenots* was one of the most popular operas in the New Orleans' French Opera repertoire, season after season, and audiences knew it by heart. This staging took great cuts and Nordica sidestepped all the difficult moments".

His view confirmed by *Daily States* (Feb 2): "Most unsuccessful *Huguenots*. It was a real, a genuine massacre of *Les Huguenots*. Many of the finest parts of the score were eliminated". Distaste includes Nielsen, "unattractive in appearance" whose "attempt to sing the part was a failure".

No explanation discovered for cuts.

February 3, so-called "San Carlo Company of SF" packs for the American tour. *Chicago Daily Tribune*'s WL Hubbard prepares the town, "Grand opera is only a fortnight distant. It is not the Metropolitan galaxy of stars from NY that is approaching, but it nevertheless promises to be a company of good capabilities. Reports received from the southern city have been unqualifiedly enthusiastic and the conclusion seems to be general that as good grand opera performances have not been offered there in many years".

Chicago knows three well: Nordica, Campanari "long-popular baritone", and Nielsen "deservedly the idol of the light opera lovers of this broad land of ours" who "rose to grand operahood two seasons ago and now comes to us as one of the leading prime donne of the present company".

Nordica and Nielsen will sing thrice each.

"Of singers new to Chicago...first and foremost is the leading tenor, Florencio Constantino. He is a Spaniard by birth and by training, and scored his first success in his native country [Basque by birth, Argentinean by choice, success in Buenos Aires and Madrid]. Later he journeyed to France, to Russia and ...everywhere praises for the exceptional beauty of his voice and his complete mastery of the art of singing have been his portion. He has carried everything before him in New Orleans and many who have heard both him and Caruso declare that the Spaniard is the equal as regards voice beauty of the Italian and that as regards taste and musicianship in singing, he is his superior".

Tenor Ricardo Martin "excellent"; baritone Angelini Fornari and basso, Andre de Segurola "of uncommon merits". Soprano Fely Dereyne from Paris. Orchestra of sixty-five, "said to be competent" plus "chorus of fifty singers whose voices are fresh and whose singing has been hailed by the New Orleans patrons as the finest ever heard in that city". Conti, a "director of worth...on the high road".

Significantly, Hubbard suggests the new Nielsen gang take a permanent Chicago home. After this second Chicago appearance in grand opera, her regular return is a forgone conclusion. If public support liberal "several weeks of grand opera here next year is reasonably certain". After all, he adds, Nielsen had signed a 2-year contract at New Orleans and has a grand opera company second to none. Nowhere better than Chicago for this grand opera company to be based. Let music history take note: reacting to the New Orleans season's success, Hubbard and *Tribune* begin to lobby for a Chicago opera company. Thanks, Alice Nielsen. To be celebrated.

Leaving Louisiana, troupe trots up the Mississippi to St. Louis, Cincinnati toward Chicago. Looking back, Nielsen will make clear who underwrote the tour and organized the company. Nordica "had organized the San Carlo Opera Company [of San Francisco] and we were touring the country with it", says Nielsen, giving no credit where none is deserved. And the faux, inessential impresario will later confirm this in a backhanded way.

Nordica has wealth. Until the company morphs into Boston Opera her banker husband handles the finances. What happened with the supposed loan from Grimthorpe after transfer to his Pullman pal, we don't know.

We don't know why the company foisted a flat tenor on St. Louis.

Thursday February 8th the *St. Louis Star* reports the company "has every reason to be grateful for the treatment received at the hands of the St. Louis public and press, and in whatever desperate predicament it may have found itself Thursday night in staging Verdi's beautiful *Trovatore*, it is hardly fair treatment when they foisted an untried tenor on the audience. The very entrance of Sig. Bussetti was fraught with a voice so markedly off (almost a whole note flat) that nearly all present stirred in wonderment of what was to come. It may be he was not given the right pitch or was laboring under excitement and strange surroundings, but they had no excuse for it". Worse was his acting, as a relief from the vocal insult.

Noticeably annoyed, Nordica and Mme. Conti-Borlinetto, save the show: "Nordica in the role of Leonore of course compensated for any defects; she is so strong in her art with her clear, beautiful voice. Mme. Conti-Borlinetto as Ascucena was decidedly better placed than in *La Giaconda*, in fact it is hard to conceive how or by whom her role could be improved. Orchestra and chorus, too, did their work excellently". Before leaving St. Louis, Constantino and Nielsen sing *Lucia*.

Touring up the Mississippi, Nielsen recalls Nordica literally playing with fire. "A humorous quirk in Nordica's mood became apparent, she felt she was not getting enough publicity and wanted a newspaper headline. Our chorus watched her and came to the conclusion that she eagerly desired a fire scare in the theatre during a performance". In *Gioconda* she "had a scene with a lighted lamp, she tried her best to upset it; and once she succeeded. Aghast we saw her soak her scarf in the oil in hope the flames would spread. Instead she succeeded in wiping the fire out".

Reaching Chicago (*Chicago Trib.*), Alice gives a "popular concert at popular prices" for *Tribune's* Emergency Lodging House" with "old time songs" joined by Constantino. With "stars of the company" they perform segments of *Aida's* 3rd, *Barbiere's* 2nd, *Trovatore's* 4th and *Lucia's* 2nd.

Ticket prices undercut the Met. Box seats $1.50 ($34 in 2007), house seats $1 or less ($22 today). Perhaps to overturn fallout from the previous *Pasquale* tour, ads proclaim "All-Star Cast". Clara Kellogg recalls the rise of all-star casts. Fifty years earlier "Mapleson was planning as a *tour de force* with which to stun London a series of operas in which he could present all of us. 'All-star casts' were rare in those days. Most managers saved their singers and doled them out judiciously, one at a time, in a very conservative fashion. But Mapleson had other notions. Our 'all-star' Mozart casts were the wonder of all London. These were casts unequalled in all Europe—almost, I believe, in all time! Gye, of Covent Garden, declared that we were killing the goose that laid the golden egg by putting all our prime donne into one opera. He said that this made it not only impossible for rival houses to draw any audiences, but...nobody wanted to go on ordinary nights...."

All-star casts make money to shape next shows.

Nielsen's modesty makes national news Feb. 13th via *NY Telegraph*, "I don't wonder that Klaw and Erlanger leaped eagerly to rescue pretty Alice Nielsen from the hands of the Philistines [Shubert] a few months ago! The shrewdest of American managers recognized doubtless, in the most ambitious of American singers, something besides vocal chords and a big bright brain. They perceived the quality of heart that makes so loud a call upon the public and recognized the generosity that wins.

"Ever since Mme. Nordica added her wealth of talent and voice to the San Carlo Opera Company [of San Francisco etc], Miss Nielsen has been sending me notices of the Nordica appearances with joyous regularity. Each 'good notice' for the established American singer seems to give a certain personal joy to the younger diva, who is struggling for the recognition that is already accorded to Nordica. Not a single paper containing notices of Miss Nielsen's own triumphs at New Orleans and St. Louis came my way until yesterday, when a big batch of clippings reached me. They all breathed boundless praise for little Alice and all predicted great achievements for her in the future and, if you please, this paragraph is written because they were all sent me by Madame Nordica herself".

Monday February 18, they open in Chicago. From the start they are acknowledged as equals of the Metropolitan of NY. Soon they are preferred.

Chicago Tribune (Feb 18): "Grand Opera Opens Tonight. Advance sale of seats indicates that the season...will be a great success from the financial as well as the social standpoint. Public interest...fully equal to... Metropolitan Opera company".

First week: Monday: *Giaconda,* Nordica and Constantino; Tuesday: *Rigoletto,* Nielsen; Wednesday afternoon *Trovatore*; Weds evening: *Carmen,* Dereyne; Thursday *Les Huguenots,* Nordica; Friday: *Barber of Seville,* Nielsen and Constantino; Saturday afternoon: *Faust,* Nordica; Saturday evening: *La Bohème* with Nielsen and Constantino.

Second week: Monday: *Lohengrin* with Nora and Constantino. Tuesday: *Don Pasquale* with Nielsen and Fornari. Wednesday: matinee, *Trovatore*; evening: *Carmen* with Noria and Constantino. Thursday: *Traviata* with Nielsen and Blanchert. Friday, a benefit. Saturday: matinee, *Aida*; evening *Lucia* with Nielsen and Constantino.

Chicago Examiner (Feb 20) gives a full page feature to Nielsen and Bryn Mawr's week of grand opera. The singer's pilgrim progress recounted. Then: "The fifty or more Chicago women who comprise the Bryn Mawr Club—all graduates of the famous girls' school—are enthusiastic over the success of their venture in bringing the San Carlo opera company to Chicago. $5,000 worth of seats were sold today', said one, 'Chicago is appreciative and Bryn Mawr is a sure winner.' The patronage of the French and Italian elements in Chicago society is particularly noticeable", reports *Tribune.*

Alice's Japanese-acquired habits surface with tea onstage between shows Wednesday afternoon, a society mixer with "members of the company and many Chicago people eminent in music" (*Chicago Trib.* Fe 21). Bryn Mawr Alumnae (between *Il Trovatore* and *Carmen*) take tea with Miss Alice Nielsen and Mlle. Luisa Milesa assisted by Mme. Nordica and Mlle. Fely Dereyn".

Frederic Griswold writes of *Rigoletto* (*Chicago Record* Fe 21), "owing to Miss Nielsen's long identification with lighter works, there was much interest in her work on the Auditorium stage for her auditors were not certain in advance regarding the result of her new venture. Her vocal abilities are familiar but her standards have not hitherto been of as severe at type as those surrounding her present appearance".

Once again, "she began somewhat nervously but quickly gained confidence and there was certainty thereafter in all that she did.

"Miss Nielsen's singing proved even better than had been anticipated. Her voice is a clear, flexible soprano that lends itself well to dramatic purposes. Steady work on the operatic stage has made no inroads, for there are no appreciable signs of wear. The tone is fresh and pure, the upper notes being unusually effective". And the acting, "her enactment of the part of the old jester's daughter was true to the demands of composer and librettist".

Inevitably Chicago notices and remarks on her petite size. Continues to contrast to other diva: "her figure is of normal proportions and, not being of traditional prima donna dimensions, she does not look ridiculous in a girlish role. The audience responded to her efforts with much cordiality".

Chicago joins Dallas to applaud her quality. In Chicago, as New Orleans, remain memories of "best performances" and "remarkable demonstrations".

Glenn Dillard Gunn (*Chicago Inter*-Ocean Fe 21): "Two performances ...suffice to demonstrate that the organization is animated by a different spirit from that to which we have so long been accustomed. Earnest purpose and artistic sincerity are the motives back of each production. Even the accidents of the opening night did not detract from this impression and it was materially strengthened last night by one of the best performances of *Rigoletto* it has ever been my privilege to hear".

Friendly rivalry: "Chicagoans again showed their appreciation for the worthy efforts of the company by turning out another good audience. There were a few vacant rows on the main floor and many boxes were empty but the lower priced seats were all taken. In orchestra chorus or gallery, the auditors were all enthusiastic.

"The Italians above applauded Signors Constantino and Campari. The Americans downstairs... showed a marked tendency to value Miss Nielsen's efforts quite as highly. This in turn did not meet with Latin approval and after that charming singer had four recalls in the second act, hisses and catcalls were mingled with the hand clapping".

Of repertory, Gunn agrees the appeal of these operatic antiques is due mainly to the talent of the singers. "Seems strange to ears and minds attuned to the logical, unified art of Wagner that the old Italian opera should still possess the power to charm us. But there is such a wealth of melody in the score of *Rigoletto* and the climaxes...that we are still moved to enthusiasm even against our better judgment. *Rigoletto* is therefore still a grateful opera, especially with three such admirable singers as Miss Alice Nielsen, Sig. Constantino and Sig. Campanari in the principal roles.

"Miss Nielsen is a most charming Gilda. She is not, and probably never will be, a queen of tragedy—even of Italian grand opera tragedy. But she is sweet and fair to look upon, and her voice is fully equal to the demands of the part. Sweet, fresh, youthful voices are so rarely heard in grand opera that Miss Nielsen's singing never ceases to be a surprise as well as a source of keenest pleasure. Her voice is not large. But it has carrying power, which enables her to sing with ease about Verdi's light orchestration and to hold her own in the concerted numbers even when she had to sing against the robust tenor of Sig. Constantino, Companari's powerful baritone, and the bass choir of the orchestra".

Gunn assesses Nielsen's progress and future: "She still has much to learn both as singer and actress. But she is young. Maturity will bring added volume to the voice. Experience will make her portrayals of deep feeling more convincing. She has already sung herself into the hearts of the American public, and her career will be followed with interest by a host of friends and admirers".

Constantino's voice is "truly one of great natural beauty. He again scored a great success with the audience, being obliged to repeat the last verse of *La Doanna e Mobile*—singing it much better, it should be said".

In the cast: "Campanari too was in fine voice and mood and gave a splendidly convincing portrayal of the title role. Sig. Pulcini pronounced the curse of Monterone in the first act with fine effect and Sig. Perini was an adequate Sperafulle. Moni-Baldini contributed the contralto part of the quartet...finest moment of the evening—not unpleasantly. For the rest of her performance...has a rival in...Galberli, who bids fair to surpass her in giving disagreeable prominence to unimportant parts". Chorus as in New Orleans "again called for heartiest commendation".

Nielsen's *Barber Of Seville* (Feb 22), Gunn recalls, "for inimitable grace, humor and vocal excellence it would be difficult to surpass the performance which Miss Nielsen put forward; a performance so good that it became possible to pardon even her introduction of Arditi's vulgar waltz song, *Il Bacio*, in the lesson scene".

Chicago season big success. Bryn Mawr does well. Acclaim soars.

Alice arranges to return next year.

Insightful WL Hubbard places Nielsen in perspective (*Chicago Tribune* Feb 23), "The brief but brilliant engagement...at the Auditorium... has been significant with surprises and gratifying with success. While powerful influences awakened interest in its behalf as beneficial to the Bryn Mawr club, it has fulfilled all the promises made for it, its ministry has never been oppressive, and it has pleased the people". Bryn Mawr "worked tirelessly at the disposal of tickets for the first night and they accomplished satisfactory results not only for that night but for the remainder of the week".

In Nielsen's first direct competition with the Met, Hubbard regards the success with amazement. They overshadow the Met's recent Chicago tour in quality and cash. The eight performances "breaks the record for financial receipts and creates a stir in general amusement-seeking circles greater than...the Metropolitan opera company from NY".

Changes the theatre equation. Hubbard proclaims "the outcome of such a procedure is nothing less than startling. It upsets all previously established standards and knocks over a lot of supposedly proved facts". Bryn Mawr could not "have made the week the success it proved, had not the organization 'made good' in more than average fashion.... Behind and beyond all, there stands the fact of the company's having given the public something of worth and something that was wanted by that public".

Until now, grand opera was "burdensome in its exactions and extravagant in all the caprices of its coadjutors".

Chicago eggs GB Shaw: Hubbard revels in hybrid, relishes gayety: "Great names have grown to be potential attractions, sensations in the matter of exploitation and even in productions have been called into play to quicken the jaded senses, so that the mission of music as exemplified in *the hybrid art of grand opera* [emphasis added] has grown so elaborate and involved in its organization that expenses have multiplied out of all proportion to merit, as far as it concerns the satisfaction of the general public—that pays the cost.

"In the present instance, Lillian Nordica the alleged mistress of her art, after years of coquetting with the voice-wrecking heroines of Wagner, returns to the field of melody...." Nielsen's "music of Gilda was sung with excellent taste and thorough musical intelligence, even the trying *Caro Nome*" was given "with fine under-standing and good effect".

Hubbard concurs with the Dallas critic: Alice Nielsen's artistry in sustained song unique, her acting peerless. "There was not the dazzling brilliancy lent the difficult aria which certain eminent sopranos can give it, but there was something equally good and even more desirable—artistic intelligence and appreciation of the dramatic significance of the music. And it may be said right here, that Miss Nielsen acted Gilda better than it ever has been acted before in Chicago".

Audiences respond to artful gifts. "Her slight, girlish figure and youthful face made her an ideal embodiment of the fair daughter of *Rigoletto*. It was a distinct success for Miss Nielsen and the audience was not slow in telling her so". Since 1896 Hubbard has observed this artist: "Alice Nielsen has not exactly 'bobbed up.' On the contrary, she has come up slowly and with much hard work. At times it looked as though she would be submerged entirely. But her indomitable pluck and belief in herself won out, as it always will".

Hubbard knows all theatre-people. Tells a story on Nielsen: "About four years ago a certain NY milliner, much patronized by women of the stage, made a run from Paris to Florence where Nielsen was staying [with Duse] and studying hard. She had given up her fine salary as a light opera singer and the goal seemed far ahead, and the man brought back word to NY that she seemed rather discouraged. Immediately Joe Weber cabled over to her offering a fabulous salary if she would sing at the Weber & Field music hall, but the little American stuck it out and declined, and now she has come to her reward".

Hubbard is influential. His insight carries powerfully to New York and LA.

February 23, press flurry of Nielsen coverage.

Toledo Blade: "This week Chicago is having opera, 'grand opera' as WL Hubbard expresses it, 'such as we need in this great country of ours—grand opera in which the opera itself and not the personality of the singers is the prime factor...." *Musical America* stated the eight performances "drew $30,000 at popular prices which, all things considered, is really remarkable".

Bryn Mawr as promoter pocketed thirty percent for scholarships.

Chicago Tribune interviews Henry Russell, "Our success in Chicago has been unprecedented. Indeed, I was nervous about coming here. But the cordiality with which we have been received surpassed all my expectations. The Auditorium is an enormous hall, one of the biggest in which I have seen in my life—but it was filled to capacity four times, and nearly so for other times. Chicago audiences are not wildly demonstrative like some, but they appreciated our efforts and seemed to like everything we did. There were a few shortcomings in our company which we hope to remedy, they have been kindly overlooked. A great many people say Chicago has dirty streets and all that, but the warmth with which we have been received makes me quite in love with the city". He suggests moving to Chicago permanently.

As a direct result of the Nielsen week, *Chicago Tribune* reports, "Plans are being made to subscribe a guarantee fund to ensure the permanency of the San Carlo company [of San Francisco etc] in Chicago. New Orleans offered a fund of $75,000, but only $40,000 was actually subscribed. It is believed that an adequate sum will be subscribed to insure an opera season in Chicago next year of at least four weeks. Once the financial foundation is secured— we are to hear such novelties [new operas] such as NY never heard". Next year's program proposes to add Boito, Debussy, Weber and Wagner.

Closing night, Alice Nielsen became an international heroine due to fire in a crowded theatre. Headlines around world. She calms the crowd. Chicago had been the site of the world's worst single-building fire disaster two years earlier when the Iroquois Theatre fire killed 602 people. Eddie Foy, who we recall taking a box for Alice's conflicted NY debut, was hailed a hero trying to calm crowd; escapes through a sewer. The fatalities occurred within fifteen minutes. Within thirty minutes firemen had suppressed the flames. Political corruption blamed for the horror. And Chicago theatres closed a week.

LA Times (Fe 24), "Panic Is Averted. Nielsen Stops Fire-Frenzied Crowd". Subhead: "Nielsen Alone Stands Firm. When All Quail Prima Donna Springs In Front And Stills Fear By Song". When suddenly smoke pours out from under the stage: crowd and cast panic. To stop chaos Nielsen sings *Star-Spangled Banner* "in a calm voice wholly devoid of nervousness" and "checked a fire panic among the thousands who attended the final performance of the grand opera season and prevented what might have proved a repetition of the Iroquois disaster. All the principals in the cast with the exception of Miss Nielsen, fled from the stage as did also the big chorus".

The fire? Arson to cover theft.

During the panic "thieves were at work" in "the dressing rooms, the boxes and parquet, making away with sealskin wraps, fur pieces and a medal set in diamonds, the gift of Alfonso King of Spain to Constantino".

Chicago Inter-Ocean (Fe 24): "Startled by the cry of 'Fire' and by the clouds of smoke that filled the stage of the great Auditorium, hundreds of men and women...were thrown into a frenzied panic between the first and second acts of *Lucia di Lammermoor* last evening when Miss Nielsen, Mme. Maria Golfieri and Signori Perini and Ghidini were singing the quartet before the second act finale". They sing (if in Italian): *Ah these words when doubts confound me; All seems mystery around me; Now distrust and fear enthrall me, And dark clouds of fate appall me.* "At that moment, smoke poured up from the stage floor.

Someone cries "Fire! Four thousand people started to their feet...fighting for the exits when Miss Alice Nielsen...ducked under the falling fire curtain [steel!] and advanced to the footlights.... Screams of the women and the hoarse shouts of the men as they fought their way toward the doors were the only sound audible in the theatre.

"'There is no danger', said Miss Nielsen, coming to the edge of the stage, 'Keep your seats. It will be all right.' Above all the din of the fighting, panic-stricken mob" she started the anthem. "And in a moment the audience, forgetting its fear and panic, had joined in the words. Men in the boxes stood up and waved their handkerchiefs, women...join. They were still singing when the police and the fire department arrived...and the panic ended".

Nielsen's heroism contrasts to others. "At the cry of 'Fire', Constantino and the women of the chorus rushed off the stage, the signor in his hurry losing a $2,000 diamond pin from his cravat. Sig. Constantino, who according to the score of the opera was able to contemplate death with a fair degree of equanimity, did not appear to regard the real thing in the same dispassionate manner, and it was not until all danger was passed that he returned to the stage". He had rushed to save his wife in the dressing rooms.

"Rather peculiar", Alice said, "for I am usually nervous, but I did not have the least fear this evening. I did what I thought was the best thing under the circumstances and the idea of personal danger never entered my head. To show I was not nervous, I took the high notes in my score just as easily as I could have done it before the scare took place".

When the panic quells, Nielsen is hoisted onto the shoulders of the stagehands in a celebratory procession around the theatre. The fire is news for several weeks. *Chicago Examiner's* Miller Ular (Fe 25) reports Alice Nielsen pitched to Andrew Carnegie for a Carnegie Hero Medal. Ular's source HC Williams, assistant to Russell, hints at a press push. Huge story, even Irish papers report the event.

Nielsen answers *Musical America,* "I? A heroine? Oh, no. I'm only what I am. What can anybody do except what's to be done? That isn't heroism?" Reporter observes, "with this and a deprecatory wave of her hand, Alice Nielsen apparently dismissed all thoughts of such a thing from her mind. As she talked, seated at her writing desk in her private car, she tossed into a corner a bundle of telegrams from all over the country congratulating her on her presence of mind in averting a panic.... 'A medal? For me? Why, no; why should I have a medal? Why, I only did what anybody would have done. Why, actually I was scared myself. They all told me how calm and self-possessed I was. The stagehands actually carried me off the stage on their shoulders and they told me I ought to be a fireman. But really I was scared. I wasn't scared for myself but for the others, for the audience. A theatre panic is a dreadful thing. When I heard that terrible cry of 'Fire' my heart sank.

"I remembered the terrible loss of life in the Iroquois Theatre and I thought of the women who would be crushed to death or maimed in the stampede that I knew must follow unless the audience was restrained. I trembled all over. Scarcely knowing what I was doing I rushed to the front of the stage, though it seemed my feet were of lead and almost without thinking I screamed above the din to Signor Conti to play *Star-Spangled Banner*. The first note calmed me, and with all the power I could command I began to sing the stirring words". No, she sang first. Conti does not know 'the air.'

"Before I realized it the audience had stopped the rush and in a few moments we resumed the opera—*Lucia di Lammermoor*".

While Nielsen's heroics receive worldwide praise, links between horse-racing and opera ripen. Active in Chicago before Capone is Joe Ullman, the well-known bookie. Divas visit tracks. Alice jots in her 1907 address book, "Joe Ullman won $100 for me at the races". Ullman is a multi-millionaire gambler so her winnings seem amusing in the context. Betting is big in Chicago where Alice had relocated mom and son in 1901 after ditching the turfman Tom. Hortense lives in Chicago. Well-heeled Ullman joins the tour. Makes news: "Once he backed the ponies. Now he is backing grand opera. Surely there is nothing more material than a betting ring. Certainly there is nothing more altruistic than a grand opera stage. Yes, extremes meet" exclaims the startled *Chicago Tribune* (Fe 21).

Of this wondrous epiphany between turf and aria, oddly odd Russell in them shifty memories claims, "After a disastrous week in Chicago, Joe Ullman began to support...San Carlo Opera Company [of San Francisco etc]". In fact, the week in Chicago was such a success the financial details make the papers. Remora must have conflated this with his own disasters.

Not the typical multi-millionaire gambler, Ullman authored *What's the Odds—Stories of the Turf* (1903). Ran the largest gambling houses in NY, Chicago, Long Branch, Minneapolis, and Saratoga. He and partner Kid Weller famously refused no bets, big or little. Rich men bet big, like Jess Lewisohn who married *Belle of New York*'s star of the long-running London musical Nielsen supplanted at Shaftesbury; or "Bet-A-Million" Gates. Who knows what dangers lurk; Ullman established the "Bridge Whist Club" on Saratoga's Philadelphia Street in 1905 and received letter-bombs which don't detonate. Intriguingly, Ullman competed directly with Tom Williams.

Back in 1885 Ullman encroached on Williams' California horse-racing monopoly by combining with Edward Corrigan to build Ingleside racetrack and forming Pacific Coast Jockey Club to build "the most sumptuous racing course in the West" with bandstand, clubhouse, and stables for three-hundred horses. Opens to a crowd of eight-thousand. Prosperity had continued until 1905 when California restricted horse betting; the year Williams sold his stables. The amenable Corrigan conducted stockholder meetings using a loaded revolver as gavel, stating things would run his way or not at all. Corrigan used Pinkerton's detective agency of thugs to control Chicago bookies.

So Joe Ullman lived at the heart of big-time betting and racing. Nielsen, now allied with Williams' chief competitor, tours toward California.

Chicago Tribune continues, "There was a day when Mr. Ullman was a bookmaker. St. Louis, especially, knew him well. So did Chicago when there was racing here. So did NY. So did Saratoga. So did Hot Springs. So did other racing towns, for that matter. Many and many a time did Mr. Ullman spy out the ponies with his big glass as they started to the post. Many and many a bet Mr. Ullman and his gentlemanly assistants chalk up at odds of 'steen to one as the game went merrily on".

To the complete delight of the Chicago press, Ullman hops on the Nielsen opera train. Riding along the tracks. Springfield for a one-nighter.

Then three nights in Kansas City, turning point of her scrappy national tour last year. Convention Hall is packed to the limit.

KC Evening News (Fe 26) tries to be candid about the company name, "A large advance sale of seats indicate a financial success for the Kansas City engagement of the San Carlo Opera company of New Orleans [SF!].... The company is to give four performances of grand opera with Nordica, Nielsen, Constantino and Campanari heading the list of principals. Many music lovers are here from various points in Missouri and Kansas to attend the opening".

After Missouri, Alice Nielsen tours Texas. In ambush lay the Lee Shubert gang. In El Paso on March 3rd at Crawford's Theatre, the tenor Campanari is substituted by a lesser talent; they shorten show to catch train. They cut Act 2, cut 3rd Scene and close with 5th Scene. This artistic outrage allows the manager of the rival Shubert theatre (lyin' low) to stampede the audience and storm the box office.

LA Times: "El Paso Hoots Sweet Singer. Inspired by stockholder in rival theatre, crowd demands return of admission money or complete performance of *Barber of Seville*. Alice Nielsen collapses in tears. Standing on a deserted stage without scenery of any sort, she sang *Swannee River, Comin' Thru' the Rye* and *Annie Laurie* in an effort to satisfy the crowd, in which she was only partly successful". The story suggests the recently heroic Alice "broke down in her dressing-room, collapsing completely, declaring amid tears: 'I never was hissed in my life before. This treatment is awful. I will never again sing in El Paso if it gets to have half a million population [about ninety years].'"

Sidewinder Shubert sabotage: "Many were satisfied and stayed until the close of the performance as given, while others left after the songs of Miss Nielsen. Several hundred however, led by Robert Silverberg, a leading stockholder in the rival theatre leased by the Shuberts, remained around the box office and following the arrival of the police, Joe Ullman, a noted NY bookmaker financing the tour of the company, was forcibly detained until he had sent for the treasurer of the company, who had already gone to the depot, and agreed to return the money".

Louisville Herald (KY) reveals El Paso jeweler AN Richards had "jumped up a chair and called on people to remain and demand the entire show. There were cries of 'money back or give us the whole show' and howls and feet-stamping from all parts of the house".

Starts the ruckus Silverberg escalates, "offered to bet $1000 to $50 that the opera had been cut and declared that he knew more about Rossini's music than the whole San Carlo Company [of SF etc]". Alice argues, perhaps pointing at the quivering faux impresario to say his daddy sang with Rossini and knows stuff. Remora fails to step forward. Silverberg argues, grabs Alice by shoulder, says she don't know nuttin'. At that point Alice, revealing her roots (Nashville, Missouri, Viking, Celt), sincerely asserts "She would shoot him if she was a man".

El Pasoans detain the wily coyote Russell and Chicago gangster Ullman, "financial backer of the company, under the charge of a policeman behind the cigar counter in the lobby, until the Treasurer brought back the money, amounting to $1,200". Despite this raucous interlude, and after a Mexican supper, promptly at 6 o'clock "their special train continued to Los Angeles".

Press pundits react. "High Art Riot" essays Amy Leslie in *Chicago News* Mar 9th. Nielsen, Leslie asserts, would be inspiring even in "sliced Rossini. Nielsen could stop...in the middle of Rossini cadenza and go over to the comic opera enemy to clean up a hundred thousand a year without half trying. But she has abandoned the delectable cakewalk and the topical ditty for sliced Rossini, Gounod and Verdi...."

"She sings divinely. She is a chic embodiment of spirit, actual dramatic art and comedy that is quite novel in lyrical or classical opera and she has been put to terrific tests during her brief carousel with grand opera in her own country. The high art riot in El Paso [did not] crush her faith.

"She is a saucy, exquisite creature who takes her work solemnly but herself with modest equanimity. She has mastered the Italian language, has captivated two countries other than her own and it only remains for Texas to come up and sweep its sombrero to the ground in apology...."

In the cast: basso Andreas DeSegurola recalls the El Paso theatre as "simply a simple wooden shack, large but unattractive, the outside painted in stark white and the inside in drab green. That El Paso audience was the noisiest and most vociferous one I had ever heard. Cowboys' 'Yippees!', babies crying and explosive laughter stopped our performance several times.

"Because of a sudden indisposition of Giuseppe Campanari, the role of Figaro had to be assumed at the last moment by Angelo Fornari, our experienced utility Italian Baritone. The performance finished to the enjoyment of our large public, but much to our surprise the audience continued to remain seated, waiting for something else in spite of the fact that the musicians of the orchestra were seen leaving the theatre with their instruments.

"Suddenly, a group of voices...yelled in unison 'Geeee Cam-pa-ni-ri!' Apparently very few people had read, before the curtain rose, the posted bulletins announcing the last minutes' change of baritones. The news spread among the spectators little by little during the performance, and a few 'smart alecks' conceived the splendid idea of putting on a demonstration after the opera". In response, the theatre manager suggests Nielsen sing *Il Bacio* "which the people rewarded enthusiastically, applauding, whistling, yelling and stamping their feet. Alice gave an encore. But as soon as she left the stage and the applause for our Star faded out, the audience, led by those few rabble-rousers, began to shout again...".

And the rest of this merry melody of a stalled show as a sideshow.

Apparently the cast took this escapade well in stride, because DeSegurola says very simply" "After a heavy, spicy Mexican dinner, our Special train steamed west for Los Angeles". Leaving nadir El Paso, LA awaits.

"The California sun was glorious, the skies were blue, the ocean near, the flowers abundant, the people kind; so it appeared to most observers a propitious place for a beautiful town", DeSegurola recalls. "Our two weeks engagement in LA was fully enjoyed by all the members of our Company, and the public was appreciative indeed. The local Manager LE Behyer was a real character and an exceptional promoter.

"I don't know if this first US tour of the San Carlo yielded any great profit to the bank accounts of Alice Nielsen and Henry Russell, but at the end of the 16th week, the last of our artistic pilgrimage, all the singers of the organization as well as the music staff were offered a contract renewal for the following Winter of 1907-08. Very courageous and generous of Alice and Henry". DeSegurola was not privy to the ownership of Nielsen-Nordica, who had hired Russell to manage backstage.

Meanwhile in Chicago, the prospect of a permanent company grows increasingly practical. March 3, *Musical America* writes, "Although it is a full week since the San Carlo grand opera company [of NO, of SF] was here there is still opera talk in the air because the engagement was so successful beyond expectation". Chicago had been promised "a return visit every year".

Nielsen's group "may decide to make Chicago its headquarters. That will be pleasing news to local music lovers as the company is a very capable one and something that Chicago would be proud of".

Nielsen and Nordica, patriotic symbols of American pride.

March 5th (*LA Examiner*), the special train "delayed by a severe rain and thunderstorm on the desert", arrives "at the opera house that Manager Snow and Impresario Behyer have constructed out of the Los Angeles Rink" to accommodate 3,000 seats. Public response exceeds last year.

After the March 6th opening, *LA Examiner's* Charlotte Voorsanger reports "Miss Nielsen's Gilda is rich and brilliant" and notes "the unusually large audience that assembled...." Again Alice Nielsen inspires: in Los Angeles as New Orleans as Chicago as Dallas as Kansas City, "one of the finest tributes ever". This profound shared human experience is sensed by the press.

Robert H. Willson (*LA Examiner*) first raises the freedom flag. Willson pens the region's Artistic Declaration of Independence. Nielsen's conflicted reception in New York triggers his stance. Signifies her cultural impact.

Facts of experience inspired him to describe Alice Nielsen in grateful tears "because an audience gave her one of the finest tributes ever paid a singer in Los Angeles". Willson sees it happen in Rigoletto: "The scene that followed the quartet in the third act has seldom been witnessed in a calm American audience and is not outdone by the tempestuous burst of feeling that distinguished the warm-blooded Latins. 'Bravo!' 'Nielsen!' 'Encore!' 'Vive la Nielsen!' And with it all, a long steady roar of applause.

"In Constantino, who took the famous tenor role in *Rigoletto* last night, and in Alice Nielsen whose *Caro Nome* has all but obliterated some of the fondest impressions of opera devotees, Mr. Russell has twin stars whose present ascendancy is almost unquestionable".

"It was Nielsen's night. *The Singing Girl* who had pattered her way into tunes with the pulse-beats of heyday fun and frolic in her wooden shoes, came back with the girlish charm ripened into fascination and swaying power of blossoming womanhood".

Confirming Chicago, Willson vividly senses Nielsen's quality.

"The world has been waiting for an Alice Nielsen whom it might love as well as admire. With the hearts of her audience stolen away she has little to fear from the judgment. Her voice is as fresh and untrammeled as if it had never been to school".

Confirming Dallas, Willson has met her rest. "Her grace and beauty are almost a revelation to patrons of grand opera. To see a prima donna, 'fat and forty', and a corpulent tenor struggling vainly against the manifest incongruities of a love scene between an innocent maiden and her student sweetheart is almost sufficient to overcome the sublime, romantic achievements of a Verdi".

Confirming Boston, Willson bestows the highest compliment. "It is safe to say that no more harmonious and beautiful love scene has been produced on an opera stage than the picture of Gilda and the Duke of Mantua as the roles are essayed by Nielsen and Constantino".

Confirming Cincinnati, Willson carefully observes the artist's craft. "*Caro Nome*, for instance, has been given much more brilliant renditions than Nielsen's. Stronger voices and more dramatic interpretations are familiar in the quartet.... But rarely have sweetness, purity and appeal been given a vocal expression to equal the note that Nielsen struck as she inclined her graceful figure against the balustrade, pillowed her head upon her arms and sang her love for Gualtino Malde.

In the cast: "Constantino did not sing as well as on the opening night but his triumph was none-the-less marked. He was obliged to repeat *La Donna Mobile* and his part in the quartet was largely responsible for the ovation that followed and the repetition, after much reluctance, on the part of director Conti and the other singers. Monti-Baldini as Magdalene and Galperni as Rigoletto completed as fine a quartet as could be desired for the magnificent score. Campanini and Fornari, successively scheduled to appear in the title role of the opera, were both indisposed and the burden fell upon Galperni, who like Constantino, had sustained a leading part in *La Gioconda*.

"Alice Nielsen in the second act of *Rigoletto* is deserving of a place in some picture that might be painted to typify all the beauty and art of grand opera. She bursts upon the scene, among the gay courtiers of Mantua, in filmy robes of white with an effect that almost takes the breath away. The folds of the gown sway about her figure with an effect that is too perfect to be unconscious and too artistic to be studied".

Who could be unmoved by such an audience response to a performer?

After a night at the opera, Willson snaps a few choice words to NYC: "Gotham, they say, overlooked Nielsen and Constantino. So be it".

Willson declares independence: "The West is evidently determined to set its own standards, as they do in Naples or Milan.

"A cosmopolitan New Yorker will tell you there is no place in America more provincial in many respects than NY. The magnificent testimonial that was given the singers of the San Carlo [of SF etc] company last night reflects credit little less than it carries it".

Independence is the ecological best practice.

Profound night; past is prelude when Nielsen and Constantino follow with *Bohème*, a night "that will never be forgotten by those fortunate to be there". Profound phrase celebrating the quality of the shared; the magical mystery.

LA Examiner's Otheman Steens tells the magic story (Mar 9): "Every act of *La Bohème* last night was a draught of intoxicating beauty. The gems of this delicious music-drama of youth, love and joy, and sorrow found their fitting setting in the auditorium, and all details conspired to produce a performance that will never be forgotten by those fortunate to be there.

In the cast: "Orchestra, singers, scenery, appointments, chorus, gave no point for fault-finding".

Then *Faust.* "A well-nigh perfect production" matches the Met's best, reports *LA Times* (Mar 14): "the most magnificent performance of grand opera that Los Angeles has seen since [Maurice] Grau's great all-star cast in *Huguenots.* An almost incomparable cast delivered to an immense audience a well-nigh perfect production of *Faust,* a production fully equal in chorals, scenery and orchestral addition to the fine offering of last Saturday, and with the added wealth of Nielsen's tones and dramatic art, and Constantino's perfect voice and great stage presence. More than three thousand people sat listening and watching. Constantino, Nielsen, Segurola and Fornari—here is a superb quartette of singers and to their effects must be added the exquisite personality and experienced acting of Mme. Monti-Baldini".

Nielsen and Constantino are magnificent singing actors. "Constantino's success was probably the most sensational...his inspired *Salve dimora* has never been surpassed here—probably never equaled. It demonstrated not only his wonderful vocal technique, and the rich and flawless voice that is his, but the acme of acting art in an operatic singer. His phrasing, his enunciation, his intonation, his emotional conception of this immortal love-song—all seemed impossible of betterment. His high C in the finale was a veritable tour de force, for as his tone rose into its loftiest register, it was not with a fortissimo volume, or even in forte, but in thrilling, crystalline, ringing mezzo-voce, as light and gentle as a breath.

Nielsen "qualified herself an ideal Margaret. Her mere vocal achievements were as easy and delightful as was her attainments in *Lucia*, but with the added value of extraordinary acting. Looking the part completely, the young singer put all the enthusiasm of her vigorous little person into its complete portrayal".

Los Angles notices Alice sings more often than anyone imagines possible.

"Miss Nielsen is startlingly near being a freak in point of endurance", Otheman Stevens remarks (*LA Examiner* Mar 16). "On Tuesday night she sang *Lucia*, which is enough work for one week alone. On Wednesday evening she sang *Marguerite* for the first time and sang it with ineffable charm and perfect technique. On Thursday evening she was Mimi, giving a portrait in harmony that will endure as long as the memories of those who heard and saw her".

Nielsen's innovations in acting once deprecated by stodgy lads of London and NYC are deeply appreciated: "Last night she gaily skipped over the demarcation-line of tragic grand opera into the land of high comic opera and produced a Norina which, while strictly-classical, was marked with all the alluring grace, the ingenious coquetry and archness that in former years gave her renown in the modern things which are called comic operas.

"Norina is one of the most thoroughly feminine roles in opera, merging all the divergent traits of young womanhood, from the scratchy feline to the wholly lovely phases. It is a trial of versatility and fully as difficult and exacting to play and sing as Lucia herself.

"But this charming little woman sang and acted as if she had been resting for a week, her voice was redolent of spontaneity and freshness, attacking and conquering without an apparent effort, all the floriture and the succession of arias and complicated recitative peculiar to this pretty but old-fashioned opera. In her singing Miss Nielsen extracted every possible whit of beauty that Donizetti gave to the score, but it was in her acting that she gleamed about the stage like a fitting ray of sunshine, illuminating the harmonies and warming our emotions".

In the cast: Adding color to onstage events, French mezzo Fely Dereyne (1884-?) is interviewed by cartoonist Harry Carr, future author of *Los Angeles: City Of Dreams*. Two of cast translate. Dereyne remarks she didn't study *Carmen* as a character, "Just natural. I am just like that myself".

"Gee", says Carr, "have you really got a temper like that?"

"Sometimes", she replies.

"Well then I hope you like this picture", showing his cartoon of Dereyne.

"Oh, sometimes I am ver—how do you call it? Ver' nice".

"Like the little girl that had the little curl?"

Dereyne looks troubled. "I don' know zee ladee; who is she, please?" It pleases Carr to relate how two newspapermen, the theatre manager, and a tenor divert themselves to tell lovely Dereyne the tragedy of the little girl with a curl.

Dereyne "one of the best Carmens...with her vigor and vivacity she never loses sight of the vocal demands.... At all times, she sings. Her stage work and byplay are constantly assertive", relates *LA Times*. Joins Covent Garden 1906, the Met 1907, plus Boston Opera, Montreal Opera, and across South America, joining Constantino and Nielsen in Buenos Aires, to inaugurate Teatro Colón "se presentó *La Bohème* el 16 de Julio de 1909". 1911-1913 Dereyne records for Columbia *Gaily I March on My Way* from *Manon* and the *Musetta Waltz Song*. She and Nielsen share stages several years ahead.

When the Los Angeles season ends, Nielsen and party tour toward San Francisco, then Seattle, Vancouver, Spokane, Salt Lake, Denver, Kansas City, Chicago, St. Louis, Milwaukee, Toledo, Cincinnati, Indianapolis, Philadelphia, Baltimore, Washington, Troy, Ottawa, Toronto, finally reaching Montreal, their port of departure for Europe. First year of Alice Nielsen's North American Opera Tour. Boston is not scheduled this year.

March news; Alice's brother Erasmus adds baby boy in Far Rockaway.

Poignant Perley news: he had sued Shubert for contract fraud, "the jury agreeing that the bookings had not been furnished as specified" awards $25,000 to Perley. Typical Shubert scam as Alice can attest. Even more happily, peeved Perley starts two additional suits against Shubert, claiming "accounts were falsified so as to show a loss on really profitable productions and thus defraud him"; the very technique he used to cheat Nielsen who never sues Perley before swine.

Nielsen and Nordica obtain a full-page spread by James Crawford in *Call* the 17th. Matching portraits, Nordica in profile on left looking across the page at Alice gazing straight ahead. Insets of costars Constantino and Companari.

Crawford analyses the opera business back to Grau; wrongly credits another with the policies set by Nordica and Nielsen. San Francisco had recently seen Henry Savage's Castle Square company debut Butterfly at $3 without stars of note and "comparative lack of vocal strength" yet "musically and pictorially" superb. Last year before the quake, the post-Grau Met of Conried profitably staged Caruso and Parsifal at $7. This season Conreid "is apparently depending upon *Salome* to entice $7 patrons to overlook his shortage of really great artists. San Francisco is not in his itinerary".

And here comes "this week on both sides of the bay" a new group at $3 with "principle singers whose value is known here" being "Nordica, Nielsen and Campanari". Nordica and Campanari were Met stars. "Nielsen—well, we heard her in grand opera about a year ago at the Tivoli, when she had no such artistic aids". Plus Constantino and Mll. Deyrene "whose Carmen is said to be one of the notable features of the season".

Crawford points out the group plays "only the most capacious theatres obtainable" and fills them. They are reaching a new audience. Tossing playful eggs at publicity agent Marcus Mayer, he lists theatres and shows scheduled: Liberty Playhouse for *Giaconda, Boheme, Faust and Carmen*; then moving to Chutes Theatre for same plus *Barber, Pagliacci, Lecouvreur, Trovatore, Rigoletto, Traviata, Huguenots, Rusticana* and *Daughter of the Regement.*

Giving play to critical praise by Chicago, Crawford states "stellar quality of Nordica, Nielsen, and Campanari cannot be questioned. And in addition we are promised a tenor, Constantino by name...fine as Caruso. Orchestra, choral and scenic accessories are worthy of such great singers".

Most significant: "If all this turns out to be true we may hail a revolution in grand opera production in the United States".

March 19, Nielsen's new gang of lyric outlaws add to the gayety of San Francisco (*SF Chronical, Oakland Tribune*).

March 24th, Constantino obtains a full-page *Call* feature by witty James Crawford in *Chats and Poses* "as we sat in the lounging room of his private car sidetracked in Oakland" attended by his "English-mangling secretary" and "his handsome wife frequently dropping in". With good humor, Crawford seems amazed the tenor had never heard of Tivoli. "For longer than a quarter of a century, San Francisco's Tivoli was the only open-all-year-round home of opera in America". Tenor shows little interest, till told "Mascagni directed a production of his *Cavalleria* in the Tivoli". Constantino responds "with unbridled enthusiasm...Mascagni is his warm personal friend. When he had exhausted laudation of Mascagni he took up Puccini, and treated him in similar vein. He created a role in each of Puccini's great works...and when his Rodolofo in *La Boheme* won encomiums from the New Orleans critics he was cabled a nice message by Puccini, then in Italy". Constantino has not yet heard *Butterfly*, "but he had read the score.... Puccini had chided him for not studying the tenor part in *Madam Butterfly*, but since coming to this country he had found little time to devote to study". His favorite operas are *Huguenots* and *Lohengrin.* Crawford tries to provoke, "some of the Eastern critics have pronounced you a greater artist than Caruso. We think he has a beautiful voice that is imperfectly educated, and some of us say he is lacking in dramatic force". Constantino "responded '*sí?*' with a non-committal smile".

We learn he was born in Bilabao, learned the marine engineer trade and worked a steamship to Buenos Aires, abandoning the sea to sing. Sang Lazzaro in Bretor's *Delores* in Montevideo, then on to Buenos Aires, then to Milano with four operas in repertoire. "He studied by himself because his small hoard did not permit him to indulge in the extravagance of engaging a teacher". In time he "was booked for Cremona, then Acqui, and his artistic future was assured". Constantino sang in Holland, Russia. Composer Boito (who Alice met with Duse) had hired him at Rimini. Spurning Scala he went to Madrid, Lisbon, sang French at Nice. The Queen of Spain, after attending a concert, restored his citizenship.

The group appears in Seattle at The Grand three nights Thursday, Friday and Saturday with Matinee, starting April 4th. Now the big typeface in the display ad is shared three ways: Nordica, Nielsen, Constantino. They present *Giocanda, Boheme, Traviata, Don Pasquale, Pagliacci.*

April 12th, gambler Ullman goes crazy: "Joe Ullman Loses Mind. Troubles of Opera Company the Cause" claims *Chicago Tribune*, spinning a story, "Broken in health by worries caused by the troubles of the San Carlo opera company [of SF, of NO] of which he was the 'angel', Joe Ullman, the famous horseman and bookmaker, will be taken east tomorrow and placed in a sanitarium for the insane. His case is considered almost hopeless. When Ullman reached here with the company two weeks ago, he was placed in a room at the hotel and a trained nurse was put in charge of him. He grew more violent and a few days later was transferred to a sanitarium in Oakland where he has remained since".

What Ullman actually contributed to the tour beyond his presence was never revealed and is not known. The tour was doing fine financially.

"The company had had a prosperous season, and after an extremely successful stay in Chicago...came west to round out the season. Everything went well until the company reached Kansas, when several of the chorus girls were put off a Burlington train in the snow, owing to a misunderstanding over their tickets. This greatly excited Ullman, who had been acting queerly for several days. Then at El Paso a great crowd hissed Miss Nielsen and threatened to do bodily harm to members of the company.... Ullman was wildly excited by the actions of the crowd and on the train from El Paso to LA he never slept. He feared the train would be held up and often would start up in his berth, shouting: 'They are going to rob me.' He secreted his diamonds and remained awake every night. When the opera company reached LA, Ullman was a nervous wreck, but he insisted on coming north with the troupe and arrived in San Francisco in a complete state of collapse".

As done those lazy days, the paper retells his full life story. For his greater glory in supporting the flowering of American opera culture: Now fifty-five, Ullman was for twenty years "among the leading racetrack bookmakers operating in this country ...owner of several gambling establishments in NY and a rival of Richard Canfield at Saratoga". Reared in an "orphan asylum... since he became wealthy his charities to similar institutions have been heavy". With Barney "Kid" Weller and John Gates, Ullman made book at Saratoga since 1902. His game was called the "big store" because $75,000 wagers were accepted freely as a $5 bet. Ullman came to NYC from St. Louis where he had been a newsboy. He was a heavy gambler, betting as $50,000 in a single day. Familiar figure at the Waldorf-Astoria (perhaps not coincidently where Nordica lives), Delmonico's and Rector's, in 1904 he married Mrs. JN Gallatin who had divorced her previous husband after three months' honeymoon. Ullman of course knows Lillian Russell's Diamond Jim; same crowd. After his stroke, Ullman vanishes from notice.

No impact on the tour. No known contribution. Nordica's husband has an accountant riding along. By train continues the theatrical cargo of sets, costumes, baggage, instruments, and the many people of the cast.

Touring Alice knows; many of the cast get their first American glimpse.

They barnstorm one-nighters or short weeks going cross-country toward Montreal. Early April, Nielsen and Nordica return to Denver at Broadway Theatre three days. Nordica gives *La Gioconda* and *La Traviata*. Nielsen gives *La Bohème*, *The Barber of Seville* (two acts), and *I Pagliacci*.

Hortense, the other Nielsen headliner, stars this season in drama. She tours *Mrs. Dane's Defense*" by Henry Jones. On April 12th she reaches Oswego's Empire Theatre (*Washington Herald* Ap 14). Hortense works under direction of husband Charles A. Quintard. No interviews surfaced with Quintard, fine modernistic man. Truly helps his wife. Alice never knew his equal. The Quintard's family historian, asked to comment for this book replied: "Quintards don't marry actresses". Affection of Charles and Hortense is durably strong. They follow their arts, share good times and bad, raise kids.... They tour from Canada to Louisiana and across to New England. Hortense produces Ibsen, Shaw, as *Billboard* reports, "Ibsen's *A Doll's House* was at Music Hall Saturday evening December 7 by Miss Hortense Nielsen and her company. After filling ready engagements the Nielsen company will return December 2 for a run of several weeks" with "*A Doll's House, Ghosts, Hedda Gabblcr,* and other Ibsen dramas". Hortense masters the Ibsen canon and tours. If a gig doesn't pay her husband stays captive until the company earns cash.

With Alice by Salt Lake, the typeface hierarchy reveals Nordica's primary role financing and organizing the company. Decode status by type size. *Salt Lake City Herald's* theatre ad (April 15) lists Nordica in the biggest type, Nielsen and Constantino a third smaller. San Carlo Opera Company [of SF, of NO] very small type. Chorus 55, ballet 20, orchestra 50 tiny type. No mention for remora Russell whatsoever. In Alice Nielsen Company ads, the manager Perley's name had top billing. Russell nominal, not integral.

Monday in Salt Lake, Nielsen and Constantino give *La Bohème*, Tuesday Nordica in *Faust*. Prices $1 to $5. Nielsen given a big portrait.

Long tour nearly over. Nielsen's merry band plans to close in Canada. Three weeks of whistle-stops remain:: Toledo, Cincinnati, Indianapolis, Philadelphia, Baltimore, Washington, Troy, Ottawa and Toronto. Not all the dates could be confirmed in fading records. At last the phenomenon ends.

Closing Toronto, Nordica departs for home in Farmington, Maine. The rest continue to Montreal, departure port for Europe.

Suddenly in Boston, Charles Frohman's Park Theatre offers Alice a short season. Otherwise a dark week (nothing scheduled). Will she sing?

Nielsen races to Boston. Frohman, of course, had attempted to sign her to a musical contract in 1901 London. News from New Orleans, Chicago, and Los Angeles has excited Boston press and public. Importantly, Nielsen knows Boston likes her. Despite the rigors of this very long season which had opened November with her Carolina concerts, she decides to go. Pulls Company out of Montreal over to Boston. Lost only few of musicians and chorus; Nordica otherwise occupied cannot join.

Ever-ready Alice agrees to host an impromptu opera marathon. For Boston, and at the end of this long tour, Nielsen promises to sing an opera every night for a week plus two matinees.

Nine operas in seven days.

La Bohème four times starting Monday, *Pasquale* twice, a gala *Faust* and *Trovatore* on Thursday night. Wednesday and Saturday she will sing *Pasquale* matinee, *Bohème* at night. As if doing Herbert again.

So it is. With three days' notice, a new Boston grand opera season is slated at Park Theatre on Washington Street. Built by San Francisco's wealthy actress Lotta Crabtree in 1879, today called State Theatre.

What happens next?

Press notices begin the very same day she gives consent.

Three days ahead of opening, anticipating Nielsen, critic Philip Hale vividly recalls 1896 when the singer was Annabel in *Robin Hood* at Tremont Theatre April 27; Anita in *Wartime Wedding* May 14; next year in *Serenade* September 20; 1899's *Fortune Teller* and 1900's *Singing Girl.*

Frohman's small Park Theatre brings Alice Nielsen's big triumph. She follows the Castle Square's tour of *Robin Hood*. Castle Square, we recall, absorbed young Alice's Kansas City cohort the basso Addison Madeira!

May 4, Park Theatre ads appear (*Boston Daily Globe*) touting grand opera "6 nights...beginning Next Monday Eve. at 8" with "Alice Nielsen, Sig. Constantino, Chorus 50, Augmented Orchestra, Sig. Conti, conductor". Popular-priced tickets are $2.50 top to $0.50.

Two days later, *MIT Tech* proclaims "Boston is to have a week of grand opera with Italian celebrities at the Park Theatre" featuring "Alice Nielsen, the American prima donna", Constantino, and Martin.

Musical Courier (1917) tells the tale: after touring America they had closed shop in Canada: "The chorus had already departed for Montreal en route for Europe when it was proposed to engage the Park Theatre, then vacant for a fortnight, for a few performances of opera, provided Miss Nielsen agree to sing. She consented, the chorus was telegraphed to return, and 14 performances were given in 11 days".

Nielsen's music theatre connections created the opportunity. At this key point, Alice Nielsen credibly credits Nordica with running everything, "When Nordica disbanded her company, I caught hold of the remnants of the chorus and took them to the Boston's Park Theatre for an engagement, making a great success with *La Bohème*". Nordica, her company.

The Met had just left town after giving hometown diva Geraldine Farrar a Boston debut. As in Chicago and LA, the comparison favors Nielsen. This resets errors by Met author Eaton evaluating Farrar versus Nielsen. Farrar plays Boston with the full weight of the Met's support and does not get Nielsen's praise—much less an opera house built. Seals the artistic fact.

Sunday May 5 *Boston Globe*: "Boston's second grand opera season of the year will begin at the Park theatre tomorrow evening, when a galaxy of operatic stars new to the Boston stage but famous in Europe, will appear".

The company "just returned from a tour to the Pacific coast" after a "winter in New Orleans, supplanting the resident French Company. The success there was highly gratifying and when the company went on tour, cordial praises were won in every city visited.

"Star of the organization is Alice Nielsen, the American prima donna who is pleasantly remembered here for her excellent work in light opera. She went to Italy a few years ago to study grand opera, and in a short time became famous as one of the most promising young prima donnas of the day. Later she achieved remarkable success in London. She will appear in each performance...at the Park theatre".

Co-star Constantino "newcomer to America this year. His Boston debut will be awaited with interest, for much has been heard about his art".

In the cast: "singers of special note in Italy" and we must add, Spain.

Fely Dereyne "appeared at Nice and Marseilles; Anita Perego, the Bellini in Naples;" Mlle. Targuini, Palermo's Massimo opera. Among men: Riccardo Martin, Milan; Giocone, the Met; Sacchetti, Torino's Teatro

Vittorio Emanuele; Fornari, Covent Garden and La Scala; Barocchi, Rome's Teatro Costanzi; and basso De Segurola from the Royal at Madrid.

On Nielsen's opening May 6th, interviews appear. *Globe* focuses on her pricing model and intent to return, "Miss Nielsen Here, Singer in town after seven-year absence. Regards Boston as good field for grand opera at popular prices". Nielsen applies the pricing model of Burton Stanley, Jules Grau, Tivoli, and Wigwam. Hers is a popular art by a popular artist.

Nielsen gives *Globe* a statement they print in paraphrase. "Who among Boston theatergoers does not remember with pleasure the ingenuous smile of Alice Nielsen, its charm always accented by a perfect little dimple on once cheek and on the other, prettiest little chocolate brown mole in America? Well, those ever-popular personal attractions are with us once more, for Miss Nielsen... arrived in Boston yesterday...."

Encouraged by Dallas, Chicago, and LA, Nielsen eggs Melba: "The sweet singer, who left here the leading light of the light opera world and after a course of training in Europe and of conspicuous success in roles of the Melba repertory, in which she sang heroines in company with Caruso, now comes back to us the particular star of the San Carlo opera company [of SF, of NO etc] singing...French and Italian".

Reiterates her faith in popular-priced opera. "Miss Nielsen, who is in private life the most frank, unassuming, democratic and winning little woman in the realm of grand opera, in a chat last evening...spoke with animation of her aim to give Boston grand opera at prices less than half of those charged for the Metropolitan opera variety".

Globe eggs Bostonian troupe: "Miss Nielsen regards Boston...so partial to her in the days when she was the best leading soprano the Bostonians ever had, as a most encouraging field in which to start a grand opera venture with first-class European singers, best works and popular prices".

Despite its grand love of music, Boston has no opera house. Nielsen regards grand opera a popular art form. For gregarious virtuosos, grand opera must be popular. *Globe* confirms, Nielsen defines high art as popular art. Her outlook unites the singer with composer Victor Herbert.

Before the Park season begins, Nielsen had already made plans to play Boston next fall. She has established the great American opera company. With mostly persons from Europe: "She says she intends to begin a season here next October, with just that object in view, believing that in every large city throughout the United States are thousands of people ready to give support to an enterprise so greatly in the interest of musical art and culture and popular amusement.

"As proof of her contention, she cites receipts of $50,000 for her one week recently in Chicago...." Alice's marketing skill would appeal to the merchandizing savvy of Eben Jordan, Jr., the music patron who built Symphony Hall. His father founded the Jordan-Marsh department store.

Globe turns to her lifestyle, traveling in a private train car now parked at a North Station siding. With white Maltese puppy she has just traversed Canada, "Miss Nielsen has a cozy little home on board her private car at the North station. She has lived in it exclusively during her tour of the Pacific coast and Canada, just ended. She was delighted with the northwest of our own country and Canada, both as to climate and patronage, and says she believes it is to prove a fine operatic field if catered to on right principles".

Thereby hangs a tale on a dog. "Miss Nielsen has not a mania for pets, as so many great artists have, yet she harbors one in spite of herself, at present a most extraordinary little Maltese terrier, a bunch of soft, silky fluff of pure white with three little shiny jet black spots corresponding to the situation of the eyes and the tip of its little nose. She calls it Pinky, because it was given to her recently by William Pinkerton of the detective world". Given by Chicago detective William Pinkerton (1846-1923), son of Pinkerton National Detective Agency founder. William worked closely with lost-but-not-forgotten-if-now-forever-obscure turfman Ullman of the sad fate. The private eye is listed in Alice's address book. Any professional efforts on her behalf have not come to light. Pinkerton was unscrupulous.

Nielsen speaks to *Post* of her Boston roots, saying she was "born in Nashville of a Danish father and Bostonian mother" before she grew up in KC and San Francisco. Here in 1905 Boston, Nielsen claims her stage debut was "amateur *Chimes of Normandy* [1876] when she was 9 years old". Playing Gertrude with half-a-dozen lines. Possible; deserves a place alongside her other tales. Leaves her free for a professional tour at sixteen. One group touring *Chimes* in 1880s Kansas City was CD Hess who didn't produce juveniles but may have cast a child in a child's part.

Possible local play of course: "I learned the part perfectly and rehearsed it right, but on the opening night when the time came for me to sing, I tried to remember my part, gave a look of horror at the audience, clapped my hands over my mouth, cried out 'I've lost my voice' and vanished into the wings. The affair so broke up both audience and chorus that the curtain had to be rung down and act started all over again".

After Boston, Alice anticipates sailing to Paris to shop "for costumes for two new operatic roles for next season, and then to her villa in Rome for the summer". Interestingly, Duse has plans to leave for Rio by June, returning from South America in September, her Rome villa available.

Globe speaks to Constantino "really a joint star with Miss Nielsen...a most agreeably modest and amiable as well as a very handsome young man". He tells *Globe* "in the most unaffected manner, his admiration for the American patrons of opera, declaring that nowhere in the world has he ever seen a public so considerate of the singers and so manifestly appreciative of their work". In Europe, he tells Boston, the occupants of boxes talk during performances.

Globe confirms "Miss Nielsen will appear at every performance".

Monday night May 6th, 1907, Alice Nielsen opens at Park Theatre.

As a result by winter 1909 Boston Opera House is built.

La Bohème: Mimi: Alice Nielsen; Musetta: Feley Dereyne; Rodolfo: Florencio Constantino; Marcello: Sig. Fornari; Colline: de Segurola; Schaunard: Attilio Pulcini; Benoit: Raffaelle Barochi; Alcindoro: Sig. Bironi; Parpignol: Sig. Ghidini; Sergento: Sig. Fille.

Success from the start. Four extra performances added.

Boston Globe (May 7): "A performance of real grand opera in an auditorium the size of the Park theatre is a novelty that had not been offered Bostonians until last evening when the San Carlo Opera company [of SF, of NO] made its first appearance here and gave a performance of Puccini's *La Bohème* that proved delightful beyond expectations.

"The coming of this company was unexpected and almost unheralded, for the engagement was not contemplated until three days ago. Under these circumstances, the audience last evening was surprisingly large, and the demonstrations of approval were so enthusiastic that crowded audiences seem assured for the remaining performances".

In Boston immediately after Farrar, Melba, Sembrich: Alice Nielsen triumphs. The Metropolitan had just left town. Geraldine Farrar had sung *Faust* and *Madama Butterfly* without making any great impression.

Alice Nielsen offers Boston "an ensemble of much greater artistic excellence than has been given here...by far more pretentious companies whose admission charges have been twice as large", that is, the NY Met.

Sophisticated Boston critics capture the contrast.

Boston Globe: "Perhaps this week of grand opera will not appeal very strongly to 'society' for there are no world-famous names in the cast of principals, but to the real lover of music it will be gratefully welcome.

"Two of the singers heard last evening ought to be world-famous and they probably soon will be. Sig. Constantino is a genuinely great tenor. He is entitled to rank among the greatest who have been heard here in recent years. In some respects his voice is not equal to that of Caruso's but in other respects it is quite as wonderful, and he is a much better actor.

"Alice Nielsen is the other member of the company who deserves recognition as an artist of brilliant promise. This charming young woman so pleasantly remembered in light opera returns to us with her vocal powers greatly strengthened and with her artistic resources sufficiently developed to make her cordially welcome on the grand opera stage, where the charm of youth and beauty is not too often in evidence".

La Bohème "was a happy selection" since it "has been frequently sung here both by the...Metropolitan opera house and by the modest but thoroughly meritorious Castle Square company.... The book is perhaps trivial and frivolous, but it is all very delightful, this story of sunshine and shadow in the gay Quartier Latin of Paris".

Alike London, Boston dares not speak freely: "Mme. Melba and Mme. Sembrich have both sung the Mimi role here and of course they are beyond compare, but the tenor role has never been sung so well in Boston as by Sig. Constantino. The minor roles were also admirably interpreted last evening, and the superb septet of the second act was so grandly sung that a repetition was insisted upon. There were also demands for repetition of the no-less-beautiful quartet of the third act".

Singers labor under a musical cloud. Strangely, the orchestra was described as "rather rough and noisy" and unfamiliar with the score.

Nielsen's intelligent acting is deeply appreciated. Her "impersonation of Mimi was charming in its sincerity, appealing sentiment and tender pathos. Perhaps the earlier scenes should have been played more lightly, but the closing scenes were acted with exquisite art and impressive effect.

"Vocally she more than realized expectations. Her voice is delicious in quality, rather light, but of good carrying power and her technique shows the results of intelligent schooling. Occasionally when she forced her tones in the upper register there was a rather unpleasant suggestion of metallic harshness, but otherwise she sang with purity of intonation and delicious sweetness.

"Constantino won an absolute and overwhelming triumph as Rodolfo. He has a glorious voice, big and virile and of splendid quality. More than once during the evening the audience shouted its approval—conventional hand-clapping was too mild an expression of appreciation. He sang every aria, every concerted number superbly, with general trueness of intonation and with smoothness of execution and beauty of color quite extraordinary for a tenor of such virile type. It is reported that both Conried and Hammerstein are bidding for his services next season. It will be a lucky manager who secures him".

In the cast: "a memorable artistic success...Mlle. Dereyne, who gave a captivatingly vivacious performance of the Musetta role both as a singer and as an actress". Fornari's Marcello "a performance of splendid merit....

After repeating *Bohème* Tuesday, on Wednesday Nielsen sings *Pasquale*, an opera antique less attended.

Globe (May 9) eruditely and uniquely notes *Pasquale* derived from an earlier work "by Pavesi called *Marc Antonio*.

"Nielsen wins success as the vivacious heroine Norina. Donizetti's quartet opera *Don Pasquale*...is characteristic of a style in vogue some 60 years ago" performed by "many prominent coloratura sopranos...a brilliant trifle...heard effectively only in small auditoriums". Opera in small theatres is not "favorable to managerial opulence". Despite "inadequacy" of tenor Sacchetti, "Nielsen's Norina was surprisingly artistic and to the dainty charm of her personality was added a dramatic vivacity and sweet voice...as witching as was her Mimi earlier in the week".

With Nielsen onstage nightly in *Bohème* or *Pasquale*, perceptive *Globe* grows alert to her subtlety: "The young American artist can express humor in her vocalism as well as in her acting. Her skill as a comedienne and her vocal art adequately presented the clever little mock-bride in a delightfully appealing guise. She sang with admirable purity of tone as a rule, and the more florid passages of the score were given with commendable fluency of execution. And Miss Nielsen skillfully avoided all vulgarity, even in the scene that follows the marriage.... Enthusiastically applauded through the evening, but the audience was not so large as it should have been".

In the cast: Barocci as Pasquale and Rodolfo Angelini-Fornari as Malatesta "fairly shared with Miss Nielsen in the honors of the evening".

May 10 *Boston Transcript* affirms "Nielsen has surpassed those who recalled her in her days of operetta by the quality of her voice, the art of her singing, the emotional color she brings to it on occasion and the pleasing conception of her acting".

Park Theatre is visited by *Musical Courier* (May 11): "Late as it is in the season, grand opera was literally 'sprung' upon us the past week in the way of a most unexpected announcement in the local papers.... Little obsequious Park Theatre" previously associated "with theatrical events only" and a "stage of most limited proportions..." caused the town to "flutter with curiosity as to its questionable success".

The publicity hook of that hijacked "San Carlo" name helped little. "Even the name...San Carlo Opera Company [of SF, of NO etc] with its unimpeachable prestige [as hijacked!] did not cause any allaying of this pardonable curiosity. It grew apace and the box office receipts likewise grew apace, at least after the dreaded first night, for Boston's anxiety proved the fabled 'straw', and the result is that the San Carlo Opera Company [of SF, of NO etc] has scored such a positive success here during the past week, the engagement has to be prolonged".

Four additional shows are added through May 12th.

"The repertory has been of engrossing interest...Puccini's *La Bohème* with Alice Nielsen, Dereyne, Constantino, Fornari, Glacan and Segurola; Donizetti's *Don Pasquale*, Garden Scene from *Faust* and the two final acts of *Il Trovatore*". For the gala, "*La Traviata*, second act, *The Barber of Seville*, third act, and *Rigoletto*, fourth act".

Nielsen "has re-established herself in the music lover's heart. She has shown her climb in the art of singing while Mr. Constantino, one of the most interesting tenors to be heard, has shown broad artistry".

Musical Courier predicts future success; not anticipating the scope. Nielsen's production bodes well for next season, "the introduction bids fair for a very triumph...when the autumn arrives".

HT Parker reviews *Pasquale*, brilliant analysis. Agrees with Chicago versus GB Shaw. Parker does not fear "hybrid" arts.

Pasquale's gayety is nourishing fun: "We all crave entertainment and many of us crave also the zest, the fineness and the lightness that music adds to it. The theatres proffer it to weariness in musical plays that run up or down a narrow scale of prettiness and 'tunefulness' of humor and sentiment. Many of them are cheap and common, clownish and gaudy. They want lightness and brightness and their mechanical animation is often no more than a clicking sham. In NY, in London, in Paris, the world over almost in recent years, it has discovered anew the pleasure in the lighter operas of Donizetti, Rossini and Mozart and it has delighted in them...thus these operas live again as much for their winning selves as for their opportunities for eminent singers.

"*Don Pasquale* makes such entertainment almost to perfection. True, it was Donizetti's 60th opera...written only a few years before he ceased composing... and designed frankly for the voices and acting resources for Grisi, Mario, Temburini and LaBlache".

Donizetti advocated "opera in Italian" with contemporary settings: "Was even a 'modern-dress' opera—a very bold experiment to try in the [18]40s though it seems an easy venture today".

Norina sings "her light epilogue, but the real moral is gayety and felicity itself, music that has been charm, freshness, lightness, brightness, gaiety and felicity itself, music that has turned melody, harmony, rhythm and all its other means into a speech that has made comedy doubly comedy as for graver ends it can make tragedy doubly tragedy".

Celebrate Nielsen's gayety, O Boston town. "And most of us had nearly forgotten that music can wear this comic mask too, when Rossini or Donizetti or Mozart adjusts it". Alice, as London, generates this rare gala sensibility. "Often the performance was almost as grateful as the opera itself. Italian vivacity of temperament, freedom from self-consciousness and quick sense of simple humor...served the singing actors well.

"It is good again to see in Miss Nielsen a Norina of youthful aspect and youthful pliancy, a Norina who was spontaneously and thoughtfully sprightly. Her archness was pleasant to watch in her action and to hear in her tones; her caprice was as gaily impulsive as Donizetti's music; and she filled her action as full of bright, quick, easy details. Her sentiment in turn was pleasantly simple, and in her Norina often was the very spirit of Donizetti's music, text and character".

Parker carefully catalogues her vocals: "Her singing, too, shared this brightness and lightness. Her tones were warmer, fuller and more supple than they had been on Monday. The bare and the dull spots in them were fewer, and their sparkle was seldom hard. She is capable of the ornaments and of the smoothness of song".

Summarizes the virtuoso fun of Boston's electrical riot: "Throughout, opera was light entertainment again, and for some of us the art of music has not yet found a pastime to match it in fine pleasure".

Within three days of Alice's opera debut her honors are secure.

Many Boston music lovers flock to see her, onstage and backstage. The son of music patron Eben Jordan Jr., Robert Jordan introduces himself.

Losing no time, Nielsen pitches her proposal for a permanent opera house. Robert brings Eben to the deal. Before Alice Nielsen leaves Boston spring 1907, the Boston Opera House has been made practical. The miracle of a permanent stage home is in progress. Her season of constant triumphs in New Orleans, Los Angeles, and Chicago are capped when Boston agrees to build a new opera house for this Alice Nielsen company.

During this avalanche of appreciation Alice Nielsen connects with another Boston patron, Isabella Stewart Gardner (1840-1924). She had completed Fenway Court 1903, now the Gardner Museum. Lived on the top floor, opened the building twenty days each year for the public to appreciate the art. Her husband's fortune was inherited from pepper imports. She absorbed the spice. Gardner is a steadfast Nielsen advocate.

Jordan Jr. inherits retail money from women shoppers. Dad in 1861 joined Benjamin Marsh to create department store, Jordan-Marsh. Began as wholesalers importing European linens, silks, and woolens. Retail geniuses Marsh and Jordan Sr., pioneer new business methods; mix art and music with the shopping experience. 1890s Jordan-Marsh mail-order catalog has 100,000 names. Jordan Sr. in 1872 founded *Boston Globe* with Charles Taylor, editor.

Jordan Sr. coined the phrase ""Satisfaction or your money back".

Interestingly, no biography appeared for Eben Jordan Jr. who built the town's magnificent music spaces. Born in 1857, after a few months at the community college Harvard, in 1883 he married May Sheppard. After a severe 1900 illness, Jordan regained health. Lives at 46 Beacon St. with the two kids, Dorothy and Robert. In 1904 Jordan's first car, French-built with "dark green body and red interior, reportedly costing ten thousand dollars". Building structures to provide music his passion. His father's business demands kept him away from performing. So he gave great gifts to the music world by building places to play. Musical by nature, too busy to sing, Jordan Jr. put his money into music.

Prior to Alice's arrival he had financed Symphony Hall 1900, and New England Conservatory's Jordan Hall 1903. Both renowned for acoustics designed by Edmund Wheelwright. Cellist Yo-Yo Ma has said, "I love Jordan Hall...for the unbelievable acoustics. And for its warmth and intimacy. But most of all for the sense of event when you go there" (NE Conservatory 2006). According to *Men Of Boston* (1919), "Eben Jordan Jr was a man of many facets—an enigma—a man who loved music, but business gave him no time to sing; who built an English country estate in a Yankee village, but his family wanted the real thing. He left a legacy of the enjoyment of music to others, a thriving hospital, good roads, and a legend never to be forgotten". Jordan "had a fine singing voice", according to *Pilgrim Society Notes* (1978).

Spring 1907, Alice Nielsen needs a theatre home. Eben Jordan Jr. needs to complete his legacy. Her appearance makes his wish practical; he makes hers possible. Sets things in motion. Boston Opera is a genuinely *Titanic* achievement: biggest, best, fastest.

Nielsen recalls, "At that time Boston had no opera house and there was a civic feeling of shame about the want. Robert Jordan, the son of Boston's financier Eben Jordan, came to hear me". Backstage they speak. She boldly pitches the project. She may mention New Orleans, LA and Chicago await with similar ideas. Act now. Robert "sent a hurried message to his father Eben, 'If you want to start an opera company', he said, 'here is the beginning.'" Due to Nielsen's bash boldness.

"Our Park Theatre venture was the forerunner of the Boston Opera House. My blood is in its foundations, and music records by Nordica, Louise Homer, Caruso and myself are in its foundation stone. It was here that I sang *Madame Butterfly*", she recalls proudly.

Nielsen's account is confirmed by Philip Hale (1917), "When the San Carlo Opera Company [of SF, of NO etc] first visited Boston in 1907, the leading soprano was Alice Nielsen and the leading tenor Florencio Constantino. People spoke less of hearing the San Carlo Company [of SF, of NO] than of hearing Nielsen and Constantino. It was largely due to the excellent work of these artists, supported by a good company, that the idea of permanent opera in Boston assumed definite shape and when the project was formed, the principals filled their time in other places and were ready as soon as the opera-house opened".

Dicey scribe Quaintance Eaton agrees: "Few of the Metropolitan's annual spring visits had been as brilliant, Jordan believed" (1965).

Continues Hale, Constantino was "not remarkable as an actor, but as a singer he constantly challenged comparison with Caruso. His voice was of a more lyric quality and his singing smooth and graceful".

Hale errs of memory: "The idea of establishing grand opera on a permanent basis in Boston germinated with the previous 1907 season of the Nielsen Company at the Majestic Theatre". No, her Park season in May of that year. Deal was done and in progress when she returned six months later to the Majestic in December. Nielsen's overtures to Eben Jordan were at Park Theatre. Deal done, she returns fall. To Boston, not New Orleans.

Jordan's business background means he knows how to get things done. He has built the two music buildings in Boston. His family operates the most popular shopping store. Jordan recognizes Nielsen as a bankable popular brand. The Jordan-Nielsen combination makes Boston Opera a fast-track reality. Branding is key. Alice is a star. Constantino is a star.

Jordan knows Nielsen's artistry and track record prove her reliability. Realizes her fame with the Bostonians and the earlier Alice Nielsen Company will anchor the project.

Just as he finds the best architect, Jordan finds the best diva. She creates great shows, he creates great music halls. Her deep theatre experience brilliantly combines with Jordan's who built Symphony Hall and New England Conservatory. Who else has created so much?

Nielsen's role founding Boston Opera is crystal clear in May 1907.

Yet Jordan wasn't the first Bostonian to act. According to contemporary accounts, Mrs. Gardner gave first backing. And her art-filled Venetian palace in Boston will host Alice's voice for years ahead.

Jordon reignites the trusted team who had built his two matchless music buildings. Design begins with construction due complete fall 1909.

Who should be the chief of Boston Opera House? Boston has legions of qualified. Nordica and Nielsen represent vast practical opera experience; and Gardner, consider what deGrey did for Covent Garden.

Boston triumph closes Nielsen's unforgettable 1906-07 season.

Kicking off in New Orleans last fall, it went something like this:

Alice Nielsen, North American Tour 1906-07, grand opera: New Orleans Nov 20-Feb 1; St Louis Feb 5-9; Cincinnati Feb 11-16; Kansas City Convention Hall Feb 26-27; El Paso March 1; Los Angeles Palm Gardens March 5-8; LA Auditorium March 12-16; Oakland Liberty Playhouse March 18-19; San Francisco Chutes Theatre March 21-31; Portland Heilig Theatre April 2-3; Seattle Grand Theatre April 5-7; Spokane, Spokane Theatre April 4; Helena, Helena Theatre Apr 11; Butte Broadway Theatre April 12; Salt Lake City April 15; Denver Broadway Theatre April 18-20; Clinton Theatre Clinton April; Toronto Massey Hall April 26; Ottawa Russell Theatre Apr 29; Montreal Theatre Francais Apr 30; Portland ME's Jefferson Theatre May 3; Boston Park Theatre April 6-15.

When Alice had arrived in NYC she skipped any public performances, yet during her visit with Nordica at the Waldorf-Astoria she had consented to sing for Victor Talking Machines where old friend Arthur Pryor is a producer. Her first recordings since 1898's *Fortune Teller* will be slated for release on the Victrola Red Seal label.

Nordica's husband George Young will keep the company bankroll in his Windsor Trust Bank. In future Nordica and Young become fiction. Willa Cather's serialized short novel *The Diamond Mine* (1916) paints Young as unscrupulous Jerome Brown; Nordica as Cressida Garnet who supports accompanist, relatives, son, husbands.

Alice Nielsen had arrived by plan in New York. Leaves by coincidence from Boston. Her next North American tour will begin in Boston.

Just after she sails, her success is summarized by *Boston Post's* John Royal on May 17th, 1907. Boston's own opera company is almost a reality,

Mrs. John Gardner the prime backer. Although for the fall no theatre has yet been selected: "The company will have its own in a few years".

Crowns Alice Nielsen's 1906-07 season.

BOSTON OPERA HOUSE; CONCRETE PLANS

Between November 1905 and May 1907, Alice Nielsen has transformed her situation. She anticipates construction of a brand-new Boston Opera House as a lifelong stage. Boston's *Titanic* new enterprise proudly promises an enduring legacy. Eben Jordan Jr. builds his greatest gift. Her European summer passes in artistic pursuits and preparations. Nielsen gives the usual recitals as she studies and masters new materials. Meets artistic equals among European theatre-people.

July 1907, Victor Talking Machines releases solos and duets by Nielsen and Constantino with orchestra. Complex technical task in those days. Victor's display ads feature Arthur Pryor's band along with "Five Nielsen-Constantino records". Nielsen's release is *Una voce poco fa*. Constantino sings *La donna e mobile* and *Ecco ridente*. Their duets are *Traviata* (*Parigi o cara*) and *Faust* (*Dammi ancor*). Victor's marketing campaign continues for the next decade. Constantino eventually makes about two-hundred records, Nielsen seventy.

Let's glance into Alice Nielsen's 1907 circle of close acquaintances. Alice and Hortense are unpretentious. Of Alice "it is difficult to persuade Miss Nielsen to speak of herself. She...bubbles over with genuine and generous praise for any other singer you may mention" (*Boston Herald* (Se 1908).

Her audiences have included how many tens of thousands of persons?

Nielsen the superstar is socially well-connected after a decade of international fame. She knows milliners, maids, kings, presidents, artists, journalists, politicians, gamblers, dressmakers, critics, composers, theatre pros, producers, patrons, aristocrats, the wealthy, and society dames.

Among these, Alice's address book lists over a hundred.

Names in her address book are divided by country and town; America, Spain, Italy, France, England. People close to Nielsen exchange many letters, few missives have been located. She also has long-term correspondents from trips to Japan, Philippines, Hawaii.

America: Boston: Char. Pierpont Phelps; Charlotte, Kate Bonnollay, 701 Independence Ave.; Chicago: J. Kern, 70 Clark St.; Wm. Pinkerton 281 5th Ave; Jessie Davis, 4740 Grand Blvd; Amy Leslie Buck, 265 Crescent Ave., Norwood Park; Denver: Gussie Anderson (Fay), 460 S. Tremont St.; Kansas City: Gov NT Crittenden 514 Mass Blvd.; Nashville: Mrs. Mary Morris Perdue, 1808 State St.; Mr. Pat Morris, 1311 Hameiers St.; New Orleans [French Opera House]: Theo. Grunewald, Grunewald Hotel; Thos. Brulatour, Boston Club; Philadelphia: James Potter, Mgr. *Evening Telegraph.* San Francisco: Ida Valerga, 488 38th St. Oakland; Madame Uznay, 824 Waller St.; Paul Steindorf, Tivoli Theatre.; Mrs. Mamie Emerson 401 Baker St.

NYC: Mr. & Mrs. HC Barnabee, 225 Riverside Dr.; Dr. GH Wynkop, 12 Madison Ave.; Mrs. George Whellock, 43 5th Avenue, atty.; Mrs. Chas. H.

Truax, 667 Madison Ave.; Melville E. Stone, Assoc Press.; Mrs. Clement Scott, 15 Woodburn St.; Dr. Sullivan, 43 East 25th; Nat Roth, Empire Theatre 40th & Broadway; Lillian Russell, 161 W 57th; Dr. Rice, 128 E 19th St.; Jack Pernquin, Lambs Club; Mrs. MacDonald, 479 West 146th St.; PJ McQuade, Utica.; Sara, Bennie, Tommie Nielsen, 265 W 153rd; Mrs Krehbiel, *NY Tribune*; Charles Joseph (Milliner) 3 W 29th St; Jennie Harley, Hotel Cadillac; AH Hummel, 346 B'way; Rosa Epstein, 8 E 32 St.; Alice Freus; Doctor Curtis, 118 Madison Ave.; Grover Cleveland, President; Marc Blumberg, St. James *Musical Courier*.

London: Jose Arana, 24 Saville Row W.; Arthur Boyd, *NY Telegraph*; Buckstone Browne, 80 Wimpole St. Cavendish Sq.; Mrs. Gracie Mackenzie Wood, 15 York Place, Baker St W.; Mrs. Randegger, 5 Nottingham Pl. [Alberto R. 1822-1911]; Milson Rees,18 Upper Walpole St.; Henry Russell, 6 Norwik Rd, Mad Hill W.; Alfred de Rothschild, 1 Seymore Place, Park Lane; Landon Ronald, 117 West Bourne Terrace; Mrs Ronalds, 7 Cadogan Place; Dr. Han Richter, "the First" Bordon, Chester; Kate Phillips 1 Carlisle Place, Victoria St. SW; Mrs. Lionel Phillips, 33 Grosvenor Sq; Rosea Oditzka, 270 Gloucester Terrace Hyde Park; Lady Merry Theobalds Park, Watham Cross; Duchess of Manchester 45 Portman Sq.; Blanche Marchesi, 16 Greville Pl, Kilburn; Walter Kingsley *London Daily Express*; Lady Lister-Kaye, 26 Manchester Sq; Laurence Irving 10 Gilston Rd, 'The Bottoms' SW; Mr./Mrs HB Irving, 2 Russell Marins Southbury Rd.; Countess deGrey, Coombe New Kingston on Thames; Madame deGresac, England; Mrs. Lena Gilbot Ford, 14 Warrington Cresent; Elfie Mackenzie Evans, 4 Carlyle Mansure; Doctor Croll, 14 Lower Berkley St W; Lady Cunard, Nevill Hole Market Harbor; Mrs Cazalet 19 Grosvenor Sq.; Cavendish Bentick, Richmond Terrace, Whitehall. Mrs Forward Delfield Aigberth, Liverpool.

Paris: Mildred Aldrich, 23 Rue Boissonade; Renard, hairdresser, 14 Rue des Pyramids; Mrs. Theo Byard, 64 Ave Malakoff; Martri Newhouse, 3 Ave du Bois de Boulogne.

Italy: Naples: Doctor Sorge, 36 via Giovanni Bassai; Signora de Luca, Monte ti dio 15. Milano: Tito Ricardi, via Omenonil; Sig. Finzi, Galleria Milano; Franco Fano, via pietro verri 14; Sig. Colombati, 8 Antonio 21.

Last listed was Mlle. Duse, 62 Cadogan Place, so famous a person no town name is needed.

Madrid: Names taking mail at Theatre Royal hint Alice visited during foggy frugal 1901-1905. She skips speaking of Madrid so detail lost to us: Fernandez Arbós; Luis Carmena, and Jose Bilbas. Arbós (1863-1939), the violin virtuoso, composer, conductor worked London, Berlin, Boston. In 1896 he wrote a Spanish comic opera, *El Centro de la Tierra*.

Late September, Nielsen sends postcards: "I have just got a postal card from Alice Nielsen, showing that fortunate young holiday-maker floating in an enchanted felucca 'far away on a Vesuvian bay' with the Grotto of Nero in the background. A line on the side of the card tells me that Miss Nielsen is leaving Italy for the Bronx by way of Paris and that she will arrive on the East River shore of 179th street on the 7th of October". The writer wryly notes Naples a prettier scene than the long line of "ice wharves and gas tanks" found on arrival at College Point (Harvard clipping, Sep 23).

Over October the Victor adverts feature Nielsen's *Don Pasquale* and Constantino in *Traviata, Mefistofele, L'Africaine.*

Week later than anticipated, on October 12 Alice Nielsen returns to America via Genoa on steamship *Canopic.* Moves into the one-year-old, fifteen-story 556-room Hotel Knickerbocker in Times Square at 42nd and Broadway. She docks to discover financial troubles.

Seemed secure last spring when Nordica's George Young put the tour's profits into his Windsor Trust, now Bank of NY. Under what business name has not been discovered.

Windsor Trust had gone broke in last month's October's Copper Panic. Culprit was, according to Federal Reserve Bank of Minneapolis (2007), a power struggle between old-line bankers and newly-rich young financiers such as Augustus Heinze. A conspiracy (proved, no theory) by rivals trigged a run on the bank owned by Heinze, the Knickerbocker Trust. Its president Charles Baryney shoots himself when the bank cannot raise adequate fast cash for withdrawals and closes to cause a wider panic which engulfs Windsor Trust. "Financial fires...quickly roared out of control and the Panic of 1907 became a...catastrophe for the nation".

Companies and banks crash as the stock market drops 50% from its 1906 peak. Heinze, acquitted of wrongdoing, returns to Butte a broken man, dying seven years later. The Panic results in various regulations used to promote a questionable racket of a private Federal Reserve Corporation with Treasury access, a monopoly priviledge opposed by progressives such as Congressman Lindbergh, who responds with his trenchant "Articles of Impeachment...."

Yet back to the gayety of nations albeit in turmoil.

Young's bank had a liquidity crisis created by competitors. Like a wildfire set by arson, the crisis spread; his bank went down with the others. Nielsen's funds lost. Recalls the crisis created by gambling Ziegfeld.

The so-called "San Carlo" company of seventy-six "needed $20,000 in forty-eight hours", Henry Russell recalled. The fix is obvious and only possible because, before Alice had left Boston, Eben Jordan had agreed to underwrite her return. Located on vacation in Hot Springs, Virginia, Jordan readily provides a check for $20,000 (about $364,000 today).

Specifics foggy; Jordan, alike the situation with the French Opera House last year, had already made a financial guarantee to bring the group into Boston. Becomes an advance deposit.

To help things happen, Jordan provides New England Conservatory for rehearsals. Bigger Boston theatre: The Majestic.

Due to obfuscations about origins of the project made after the fact, we must emphasize that the project was a done deal that spring before Alice Nielsen left town. Months before the winter's Majestic season starts, the project of a new opera house in Boston has been promised. Planning was in process. Deal was done. Cornerstone of the building was Park Theatre.

The practicality of the project has been set in stone.

And after all this time on Alice's dime, the prospect of a possible job as a manager of the Boston project became irresistible to remora Russell. His suppressed pretentions inflate. Avails himself of access to the Boston men's clubs to brag to the Jordans of many supposed achievements. Eben

Jordan is an honorable man who gives trust in good faith. He distrusts too little. Jordan joins Nielsen in this regard. The prospects of salary, expense account, hiring powers, lure the remora to detach for a new prospect.

This leads to such later assertions by wily Russell that the emergency funds were produced because Jordan "had been so enthusiastic about my performances in Boston the year before". The stars were on the stage.

Bystander to the stars. Envy in the wings possessed by hubris.

Jordan skips local talent, trustworthy and true. Lards Russell, nominal manager of Nordica's group, with the job. Into the grasp of an obscure, unproven voice coach falls Boston's lyric palace. Russell loses loyalty to those who know him better; he anticipates an office and access to the rich. Future prospects ballooning, his actual past becomes a thing of shreds and patches, rapidly recast into a wizard's garb. Jordan needs credibility and legacy; so Russell manufactures a similitude and promises anything, insisting as a point of honor on unquestioned control without oversight.

Jordan is swayed. After all, he has seen the stars on the stage.

Nielsen, born to sing, does not wish to administer an opera company; yet excluding her, Nordica, and Gardner from the Board proves folly. The Boston Opera was inspired by the stars and invested for the stars. It would seem reasonable to guarantee them a voice in management.

So it is. Not this Fall season at the Majestic, the Spring season at the Park, was Boston Opera House decided. At Majestic, only the undecided details were discussed.

The error will be widely propagated during the Russell regime.

For example, ignoring Alice Nielsen's choice to appear at Boston and her pitch to the Jordans, DeSegurola recalls, "During one of those Don Giovanni performances that Eben D. Jordan, a wealthy philanthropist and music patron came backstage to congratulate Russell and to meet the principals. Russell told me afterwards that Jordan had invited him to a men's [only] luncheon the next day....

"During that luncheon that Russell and I (but especially me) planted in Mr. Jordan's mind the original idea for the construction of Boston's own Civic Opera House. And how well I remember the enthusiasm with which, on our returning by taxi to the Lenox Hotel, Russell complimented me for bringing that suggestion to the benevolent consideration of good Mr. Jordan!! That seed, thrown by me to the hazard of winds, dropped into fertile soil....the magnificent Boston Opera House, second to none in the United States". Of course Nielsen would suggest that Jordan discuss with the nominal manager. Of course Russell would opportune.

All would be disambiguated within a decade.

Winter 1907, the Boston Opera deal done last spring, the ambiguity to be decided was who would manage the new undertaking. When Eben Jordan tosses Russell the nod, the Boston Opera *Titanic* receives its captain: unproven, unknown, and racing ahead to scrounge whatever he could chisel and loot. Jordan would live to regret, not live past it. In any case, Jordan saves Nielsen's winter season by keeping his word and making good an advance for expenses when the Bank Panic occurs.

Yet. From this moment forward Alice has forever lost the loyalty of Russell, financially linked to another host for the first time since 1901—

six years—to another host. Excluding the Ziegfeld-Shubert cash he took to sign her name into that nasty bait-and-switch.

Jordan sets him up with a generous salary, staff, expense account for first-class travel with entourage. Not to American towns where kids paid coins to let him hear them sing. Across Europe to brag and preen, scorning Boston. At first he will recite the phrases Jordan and Boston expect to hear. Boston Opera salary makes him seem wealthy. Unrestricted access to the budget for schemes. Could spend other people's money on whatever he wants with whoever he wished with any side deals he chooses without being questioned: as long as he has Jordan's trust—difficult for gentleman Jordan to revoke. Glib sycophant has hijacked the role of a Robert de Sanna, Henry Higgins, Maurice Grau, or Oscar Hammerstein. Lacks their experience, talent, financial savvy, honesty, intelligence. Significantly, Russell gains access to Boston elites; consorts with the Met's director, financier Otto Kahn who quickly forms alliances with Jordan and joins the Boston Opera Board.

Russell, charged to create a lasting legacy equal to Boston Symphony, first hires a publicist to spin his worse-than-weak theatrical management experience into a passably pleasing pose. These hot-air blurbs, the shallow author Quaintance Eaton repeats. And others. Realizes he can spend other people's money. Women have supported him six years. His loyalty is never to women. Prefers men, men with wealth. Begins to rapidly undercut the great singers who made him. Begins to heap scorn on the "star system".

To Jordan, women are welcome shoppers; business authority closed. Loses the insight and experience of these brilliant self-made women of American theatre Nielsen and Nordica. And Gardner. Perhaps Jordan's views cursed the project, dangerous as coal-bunker fire when a new-launched steamer races through icy waters.

So it is. Alice has surmounted a national financial racket. Same as last year, Nordica sings for Hammerstein in NYC; joins afterwards. The winter program is unchanged from the spring tour.

Nielsen's gift of a new Boston opera house anchors her fall success.

Chicago, New Orleans, Dallas, Los Angeles, Cincinnati sense this.

Los Angeles critic Julian Johnson realizes Alice Nielsen is a cultural disruptor, that rarest of artists who inspires others to act.

After her stunning LA performances make such strong contrast to the sprinkling of NYC critics crazily cold to her, Johnson proclaims California must be artistically independent.

Overland Monthly publishes his declaration of artistic independence. Other writers for the prestigious California magazine (1868-1935) include Willa Cather and Bret Harte. Los Angeles adored Nielsen's opera gamble as she gamboled through the heartland of American pop culture. Her modest origins in Nashville and Kansas City, her tireless work in San Francisco, her Broadway fame, her valiant transition to grand opera in a dramatic showdown with the Shubert gang's attempt to rustle her career, all play a part in Johnson's declaration. Nielsen's Western success versus the scorn of a few well-placed NYC critics has made him aware of the rift. Johnson wants to deepen the rift. He realizes LA does not need dictation from New York. The West has its own opinions.

Julian Johnson's 1907 vision foreshadows the future movie and music industry. He predicts the West Coast is "destined soon to become a new and attention-compelling center of dramatic life. Within the next ten years this great West, the mightiest and most resourceful part of America after all, will be writing a great part of its own plays, raising and training its own actors, composing its own music and even sending its productions abroad". Catalyst of change was Nielsen's 1906 opera experiment.

That "splendid organization" came West "to the biggest business of its whole season" including "New Orleans to Chicago and from LA to Boston". Johnson suggests New England affects to love music, yet its Puritan heart never dances to the pulse; the West puts money where its heart beats.

Johnson applies pragmatic science: "A single matinee in San Francisco to a gross of $7,000 as against two performances in Portland ME to a gross of $500, speaks in factful figures of the comparative love of real music. The San Carlo Company [of SF etc] containing the great tenor Constantino, Mme. Lillian Nordica, Alice Nielsen and numerous other celebrities, was very loath to leave the pleasant Pacific breezes".

Attending her opera successes, Johnson spoke to Alice Nielsen and Steindorff. Knows that the West critically boosted her career. From *Satanella* to *Lucia*, from *Singing Girl* to *Bohème*, it is in California Alice Nielsen has reached each stage of her artistic progress. Alice Nielsen has invented her onstage success. Her only requirement has been a quality ensemble equal to her own talent and dedication.

Even the outlander Russell sensed it, "The most wonderful musical development of the coming...artistic America will be upon the Pacific Slope. There is a spontaneous response from the West, a call of kin as it were, that the artists do not feel elsewhere. Believe me, the West is soon going to create for herself, some of the great singing organizations of the world".

Old NYC favorites will no more get deference out West. It is Nielsen who sets the modern style: the new art must be a truly unified art, not those fat ladies standing still selected to sing tralala because they flirted with lazy overseas aristocrats commanding the coveted opera stage.

LA must declare independence from NYC now: "In the not distant future I believe we will be making our own plays". Our own plays.

Let the cliché Western, Johnson demands, "be relegated to Broadway".

The real West, "where hearts are human and where minds rise to creative originality unhampered by narrowness of bound or the stifling confines of formal environment" will be the basis of our new art. California will produce the doors.

Julian Johnson prophesizes Los Angeles as "the future battleground of America. Here will be the struggles of industrial and intellectual freedom. The future political arena is here. The bright day of our intellectual drama is approaching, for more than any other locality or even any other country, our West is the New World of the play".

Perhaps ironically, Alice has based herself in Boston.

Arriving in New York, on October 24 Nielsen sings at the Waldorf where Nordica lives, as benefit for Californian Society. The prima pair have ample time to plan their tour and discuss the project of a new opera house. Nordica intends to endow an opera institution for the lyric arts in Boston.

The complete company begins Boston rehearsals at New England Conservatory for the 2nd season, now set for Majestic Theatre. Due to the necessary preparations for the new opera house project, the American tour will be short. Boston Opera needs costumes, sets, lighting, and creative talents. Nielsen knew just what to do and where to go. Preparations to put permanent grand opera into Boston will consume a good portion of her attention over the year ahead. Helped by Hortense.

November 5, NYC's opera season begins. Keeping contract obligations, Nordica opens at Hammerstein's NYC opera house, giving *La Gioconda* to an overflow house. Nielsen's friend and patron Consuelo Yznaga, Duchess of Marlborough, shares the Mackay box. They "had dined at Sherry's and arrived late". Mary Garden with father and sister are in audience.

Boston Globe (Nov 17) announces, "San Carlo grand opera company [of SF, of NO etc] will return to Boston for a two weeks' engagement at the Majestic theatre" on their "second transatlantic tour". The stars come out: Nielsen; Constantino the "eminent Spanish tenor who will be remembered for his fine voice and acting last year at the Park Theatre"; the "celebrated baritone" Victor Maurel; basso Andres De Segurola "a favorite at the Spanish Court"; soprano Jane Noria "former Josie Ludwig of St. Louis"; mezzo Rosa Olitzka; alto Mari Claessens "from La Scala and Buenos Aires". Many in the "Italian opera company" are Spanish or Argentinean.

Onstage, Nielsen is surrounded with familiar faces.

Victor Maurel is a master class in opera technique. DeSegurola recalls, "each one of the many performances I sang with him were invaluable lessons for me! And a good share of the ensuing successes...all over Europe I really owed to the fact that I had sung it opposite him. I firmly believe it. Triumphs and excellent criticism our San Carlo Opera were reaped in abundance".

For that year, "and I don't know for what reason, business was lower than in the previous season". After aristocrat politically praises Russell, DeSegurola credits Nordica and Nielsen with financing the company.

The winter's tour "gouged a deep indentation in Alice Nielsen's savings, as well as in those of Lillian Nordica.... However on several occasions years later, Alice Nielsen told me... 'segurola, I don't regret the loss at all. I enjoyed my work, and I am sure we made friends all over America for ourselves and for grand opera.'"

With his bridge loan Jordan saves disaster. Tour seems abruptly short.

Nielsen will shop overseas for Boston Opera properties and talent. She does not bring her Broadway directors and designers to Boston, despite the success of designer Joseph Physioc at Metropolitan. She takes new talent met in Paris: Loie Fuller, and at Debussy's place Josef Urban.

Ralph Flanders, New England Conservatory's business manager, takes charge of the rehearsal coordination. Flanders would be the ideal Boston Opera manager for a sustained legacy. Serves in the business role until pushed out by Russell who fears competent oversight could interfere with plans to vamoose with the cash to Europe. The Jordans allow this.

November 28th, Boston rehearsals begin for chorus, orchestra, and the newly-added ballet "selected and rehearsed by Sig. Albertieri". Italy's Luigi Albertieri (1860-1930) is legendary. He was discovered in a juvenile opera company singing Figaro. During Nielsen's first two years in London, he was principal dancer for Empire Ballet and Covent Garden choreographer. Author of *Art of Terpsichore* (1923, serves sixteen years as ballet master at Met. His NYC dance school trained young Fred Astaire. Choreographs five Broadway shows and countless operas in Italy, Russia, London. Starts dancing at ten, adopted by Cecchetti, the ballet master at La Scala Opera which furnished the stars of Broadway's biggest 19th-century hit *The Black Crook* to fascinatenKansas City child Alice Nielsen. Gets better. Albertieri's teacher Enrico Cecchetti, considered best male dancer of his day, moved to St. Petersburg to teach Imperial Russian Ballet. Hired by Diaghilev to tour Ballets Russes. Ever-inspired, Cecchetti works with modern artists: Picasso, Matisse, Debussy, Ravel, Prokofiev. Cecchetti student Anna Pavlova will join Boston Opera for joint concerts with Alice Nielsen.

Albertieri says, "Everywhere there is dancing; everybody dances.... All may say that poetry, music, and dancing were born with the primitive language; as music reaches the ear, so gesture reaches the eye, and together they form one language. Dancing and singing must have begun with the existence of man. The arts of singing and dancing, once known, remain in the life of man as natural ways of expressing his feelings, and therefore represent an absolute necessity of the human organism, in whatever sphere man puts forth his moral and material energy. Dancing is, in fact, a very difficult art, one which cannot be appreciated by every body...." Explains how ballet fell from unified theatre: by arbitrary politics.

Albertieri embraces theatre unity, not separate songs from dance.

Alice Nielsen invites artistic peers. She's invaluable for insight.

December 9th, The Majestic's opera season opens. Previous spring Alice Nielsen became a Boston revelation; winter makes her an institution.

Fact of Nielsen and Constantino as the talented basis of a permanent Boston opera company sells investors. Fund-raising for building the Boston Opera House hits unimaginable peaks. The project is subscribed with demand is so great seating capacity must be expanded. Twice.

Majestic Theatre, on Tremont near Boston Commons, seats 850, about half capacity Boston Opera will accommodate. Unlike the Park, Majestic has box seats. *Boston Globe* December 8th reports "opening of the grand opera season by the San Carlo [of SF, of NO, not Italy] company...gives promise of being a decidedly brilliant event both musically and socially".

Sixteen boxholders are "representative of Boston's aristocracy".

Constantino and St. Louis soprano Jane Noria open with *La Gioconda* featuring "the glory of Constantino's voice".

Noria divorced husband Charles Becker in July 1906 after leaving St. Louis with mom for opera studies in Italy where she remarries and co-authors songs with composer CP Cintanini now in NYC on Met's executive staff; she was known in Savage's English Grand Opera Company under her real name Josephine Ludwig. Savage produced the Broadway hit by Alice's Delsarte coach and librettist Stanislaus Stange, *Chocolate Soldier*.

Alice Nielsen opens Tuesday with *Rigoletto*, joining Victor Maurel in the title role "universally conceded to be his greatest creation".

Friday night *Faust*: Nielsen, Marguerite; Milly Bramonia, Siebel; Annita Perego, Marta; Victor Maurel, Mephistophele; Carlo Dani, Faust; Ramon

Blanchart, Attilo; Franzini, Wagner. Saturday night *Traviata*: Nielsen, Violetta; Marchi, Amina; Perego, Flora; Dani, Alfredo; Blanchard, Germont; Villani, Dottore; Pulcini, Barone; Franzini, Marchese.

Tuesday 10th, Nielsen has "a severe cold" and does not sing. Four days later, she "fully recovered" to repeat *Rigoletto*.

Due to popular demand the Majestic season is extended another week.

Musical Courier reports December 14th, the first "brilliant and splendid performance set the pace...the company has a hold now on Boston to the extent that...the final curtain will fall on December 28".

Boston Globe (Dec 14) says of *Aida* (Constantino, Blanchard, Noria), "Much less artistic productions of this opera have been given here by organizations that demanded double the admission charges of last evening", the Met. *Aida* was created "thirty-five years ago by imperial request for the opening of Ismail Pacha's new opera house in Cairo".

In the cast: "Constantino's singing fairly set the house aflame. He sang with charm and fervor, he delighted in every scene...and in the finale his voice rang out with thrilling effect. His was a magnificent performance, one that has rarely been excelled". Ramon Blanchart "sang with authority and power and his dramatic acting added much...." Noria "sang and acted with splendid spirit, possibly at times with over-enthusiasm but always with telling effect".

Between Nielsen's arrival October 12th and her departure, final details for Boston Opera House are hammered out. The complex project requires detailed plans: fund-raising, architects, and theatre services must be completed on a rapid schedule to build, furnish and staff the prestigious new theatre. Jordan plans to open Boston Opera House within 18 months, an incredible complement to the team's design-build competence. Eben Jordan and son will tour European opera houses. Trusted Bostonians handle the necessary funds pouring in.

December 18th *NY Times* reports "a projected new opera house in this city is a certainty" and Jordan tagged "one of the leading moving forces in the enterprise". Jordan donates the property, "The new home of grand opera will be on Huntington Avenue opposite Symphony Hall". Sited between Symphony Hall and Museum of Fine Arts, Boston Opera House will rise directly across from New England Conservatory's Jordan Hall. His architects Wheelwright and Haven created Boston Public Library, Jordan Hall, and Horticultural Hall. Wheelwright founded *Harvard Lampoon*.

Jordan's pick for post of director has the least track record.

Russell's first public statement on Jordan's payroll blends his agenda with Jordan's: "American composers will be encouraged and new operas will be sung. The ensemble is to be strong" yet fires an instant warning shot to the stars "there will be no attempt to feature this or that particular singer" since he only promotes Henry Russell. Its cultural goal clear, "I hope to give the opera house the same serious and dignified standing now enjoyed by the Boston Symphony Orchestra". Grand opera at "popular prices" of $2.50 and less.

Boston Opera adopts Nielsen's values; not invited to join the Board.

The players proceed. December 25th for *La Traviata* (*Boston Globe*), "Alice Nielsen as Violetta wins another triumph". *Traviata* "may be old-fashioned, but there are several arias that probably will last as long as any other of their kind...." Electricity of the Park Theatre remains vivid to *Globe*, which reminds Boston "in May of this year, one act of the opera was given...in a composite bill at the Park Theatre, Miss Nielsen singing the Violetta role. Many great voices have warbled Verdi's tuneful score even when the artists were long past the supposed age of the unfortunate heroine. And youth is one of the charms in Miss Nielsen's effective delineation of the delicate character, for the young woman looks as if she might be in years just about the age of Verdi's Violetta".

Globe describes the thrill: "Does not require any stretch of imagination to realize the prototype and...there is a voice that is admirably suited to the role and an exhibition of histrionic art coupled with expressive and melodious singing which makes the character particularly appealing".

Joins Chicago's praise: Nielsen "last evening...equaled her former successes of this season by the vitalized tone, suggestive and mellow, that indicated the frailty of that pathetic human from created by Dumas as Camille". Vocal endurance: "Two nights in succession Miss Nielsen had been called upon to sing difficult roles, yet last evening she seldom gave evidence of an attempt to hold her voice in unnecessary reserve. Throughout the whole range of her vocal register there was discernible only slight deviations from the true pitch".

Acting skill and vocal dramatics: "On the histrionic side, the young prima donna was very satisfactory in a quiet suggestive way, as if the poor girl lacked the vitality to enjoy life, excepting when influenced by excitement. It was a very touching character study and free from exaggerated symptoms of a fatal disease. Her vocal color was very skillfully shaded to suit the action, and the whole impersonation was one highly enjoyable and deserving the applause bestowed upon the artist".

Quality: "The flori passages of the score were generally executed with the required flexibility and clarity. The well-known 'big' numbers went all right with the audience. *Ah, fors elui* was sung with exquisite tenderness. *Sempre Libera*, the splendid finale of the first act, was given with fine fervor, and the duet with Germont in the second act was also excellent in its varying expressions of hope, fear and resignation to fate. The closing death scene on Miss Nielsen's part was highly effective and won unstinted appreciation".

With Nordica in the house, "applause was liberally and judiciously bestowed and the audience evidently enjoyed the presentation".

Commendation was not, however, evenly distributed.

In the cast: "ponderous voice" of Blanchart "quite tuneful", Giaccone's Alfredo "more to be commended for intention than realization", Annita Parego and Mme. Marchi "adequate". Others, mere "participants in the performance". Liberal cuts to score, Conti "again directed his orchestra with commendable skill. The chorus work...was uniformly smooth and harmonious".

Boston Globe ignores the Keystone Cop scene by Hammerstein who sent police to arrest tenor Carlos Albani during the show for alleged contract violations. Boston constable follows Albani onstage throughout, and is roundly hissed. Hammerstein's abuse of singers often reaches the news. Gloats when mistreating: Nordica, Constantino, Sylva. Nielsen never works for Hammerstein. Too smart for that.

Winter in Boston, illness again affects Nielsen yet she perseveres as in New Orleans. Struggles (*Boston Transcript* Dec 25) "resourcefully and ingeniously with a touch of bronchitis when she undertook Violetta in *La Traviata*...Tuesday evening". It spread; Alfredo with hoarse throat replaced just before 8pm. "In spite of these difficulties, Verdi's opera proceeded...."

Boston critics, deeply-felt, knowledgeable, ever-competitive with NYC, respond to subtleties. America's greatest singer of sustained song has found the setting she could best develop sustained work. After all, Boston's own Louis Strang had selected Nielsen as 1900's best musical theatre diva.

Boston Transcript on Christmas Day 1907: "It is the custom on both sides of the footlights to believe that *La Traviata* is sure to sound hackneyed unless a Melba and a Caruso, a Sembrich and a Bonci strew the cast" yet "all four merely add their voices and their artistry to the accepted conventions". Nielsen, Blanchart and Conti on Tuesday in Boston "departed intelligently, imaginatively and illusively" from convention. The magical ensemble innovates.

As London had observed, Nielsen seeks sympathetic ensembles.

"The average operatic conductor... takes the orchestral part of *La Traviata* as so much accompaniment. He lets it run, merely adjusting its pace and flow to the requirements of the singers..." to get home earlier.

"Yet if the conductor is alive...played as it was by Mr. Conti and his men, it weaves its little web of atmosphere. Once clear of the 'drum and trumpet" music of the supper scene of the First Act and of the dance in the Third, the orchestra time and time again speaks with significant phrase and heightening emotion accent.... Mr. Conti caught this speech unobtrusively, but in a fashion that gave the orchestral part new meaning and vitality".

Boston Transcript sagely ties Nielsen's Violetta to Duse's Margherita. Nielsen gives sincerity to roles, never a cliché singer pardon Melba.

"Intelligently and imaginatively, Miss Nielsen escaped the conventions of Violetta. She may not use the part for a display of opulent or delicate voice and of spontaneous or subtle artistry as the custom is with more exalted primi donne. She could make Violetta an operatic character and make it such in the new fashion of Marguerite Gautliers. The old Camilles, flaunting their changeful emotions at highest pitch through the five Acts of the play or the three Acts of the opera are fast vanishing. Duse long ago set the custom of softening, refining and idealizing the girl" which Nielsen continues. The beginning *Ah! For a ae fui* was tender musing and not a prima donna's showpiece, and *Sempre Libera* was the voice of momentary caprice and not a cascade of vocal floritora. Delicacy and poignancy of feeling were in her tones in the scene with Germont, and in the last act from *addio del Passato* to the end, her singing was of a very gentle, toughing, and idealizing beauty.

"So sung, Verdi's music sounded new and strange and became the voice of this new, idealized and touching Marguerite Gautier that has come to be the Camille of our taste and time. And Miss Nielsen has had the intelligence and the imagination to put her into *La Traviata* and make the music disclose her".

Nielsen's greatest performance at Majestic: *Traviata*. "In all her parts here, the singer has done nothing so interesting, so individual, so clearly designed and persuasively accomplished".

Blanchart as well, Phillip Hale remarks the role of Germont is "one of the most conspicuous figures in the bleak and dreary gallery of operatic bores and Mr. Blanchart made this boresome lay figure a man of flesh and blood and sympathies".

December 29th the Boston season closes with *La Gioconda*, "the theatre was crowded to the doors and enthusiasm ran wild".

Overall, "if at times...disappointments, either in changes in the schedule of operas...or in the cast, they were entirely made up for by the exceptionally artistic performances..."Jordan faces the future with optimism. He foresees the setting only he could provide must quickly be realized. The Majestic's season confirms that last spring's Park Theatre excitement was no fluke. Papers to create Boston Opera's first three seasons are signed before the group tours. Contracts details by Nielsen, Constantino, and Conte are not know.

Publicity focuses on who controls publicity: Russell "signed a contract for his services as director for a period of three years". His first full-time theatre job is to manage the great new Boston Opera; his given mission to create a permanent American legacy in the style of Harvard College and Boston Orchestra. His life's biggest chance, a fine gift harvested from Nielsen's wake which anyone must appreciate with undying gratitude.

Now Nielsen will have a permanent stage to develop her craft.

Romantic American hero Alice Nielsen.

Immediately after Christmas, the company with bogus name San Carlo (of SF etc) leaves Boston for Philadelphia's Lyric Theatre. Also in town that week at Academy of Music is the Metropolitan Opera tour. Mostly Spanish men sing in this so-called Italian company of two American divas,

Philadelphia Inquirer accurately points out (De 29). Madrid's Royal Opera has provided Ramon Blanchart, de Segurola and Constantino; plus the featured Frenchman Victor Maurel.

Philadelphia ads for the faux "San Carlo Grand Opera Co". at Shubert's Lyric Theatre now give Henry Russell billing: "First appearance this season of Mlle. Alice Nielsen" and "farewell tour" of Victor Maurel.

Nordica's ownership is confirmed: "Madame Nordica has a business interest in the San Carlo...and lately left Mr. Hammerstein's company in NY", says *Philadelphia Inquirer* (Dec 27). Victor Maurel "eminent singing actor" who "made his American debut at the Academy of Music" makes "last American tour" with Nielsen as Gilda "particularly grateful for her lyric soprano voice and simple direct style of acting".

The week-long Philadelphia season starts December 30. Philadelphia reviews shed no new light. Frank Hamilton's research revealed the typical one-week seasons in the towns they toured that spring.

December 30: *La gioconda*: *La gioconda* Lillian Nordica, *Laura Adorno* Maria Claessens, *Alvise Badoero* Andrés de Segurola, *La cieca* Rosa

Olitzka, *Enzo Grimaldo* Florencio Constantino, *Barnaba* Ramon Blanchart, *Zuàne* Attilio Pulcini, *Isèpo* Giovanni Ghidini, maestro Arnaldo Conti.

December 31: Competing with The Met's *Il barbiere di Siviglia* by Sembrich, Chaliapin and Campanari, *Rigoletto*: *Il duca di Mantova* Florencio Constantino, *Rigoletto* Victor Maurel, *Gilda* Alice Nielsen, *Sparafucile* Giulio Rossi, *Maddalena* Guglielmina Marchi, *Il conte di Monterone* Attilio Pulcini, *Matteo Borsa* Ernesto Giaccone, *Giovanna* Anita Perego, *Il cavaliere Marullo* Attilio Franzini, maestro Arnaldo Conti.

1908: NORTH AMERICA, EUROPE, OPERA & CONCERTS

January 1: Philadelphia, matinee: *Il trovatore*: *Il conte di Luna* Rodolfo Fornari, *Leonora* Tina Desana, *Azucena* Rosa Olitzka, *Manrico* Giuseppe Opezzo, *Ferrando* Oreste Villani, *Ruiz* Ernesto Giaccone and maestro Shavalgia Giaccone.

Night: *Carmen*: *Carmen* Jane Noria, *Don José* Carlo Albani, *Escamillo* Andrés de Segurola, *Micaëla* Milly Bramonia, *Fr asquita* Anita Perigo, *Mercédès* Guglielmina Marchi, *Zuniga* Oreste Villani, *Moralès* Attilio Pulcini, *Le Dancaïre* Attilio Franzini, *Le Remendado* Ernesto Giaccone, maestro Arnaldo Conti.

January 2: *Aida*: *Il re d'Egitto* Oreste Villani, *Amneris* Maria Claessens, *Aida* Jane Noria, *Radamès* Florencio Constantino, *Ramfis* Andrés de Segurola, *Amonasro* Ramon Blanchart, *Un messaggero* Ernesto Giaccone, maestro Arnaldo Conti.

January 3: *Rigoletto*: *Il duca di Mantova* Florencio Constantino, *Rigoletto* Victor Maurel, *Gilda* Alice Nielsen, *Sparafucile* Giulio Rossi, *Maddalena* Guglielmina Marchi, *Il conte di Monterone* Attilio Pulcini, *Matteo Borsa* Ernesto Giaccone, *Giovanna* Anita Perego, *Il cavaliere Marullo* Attilio Franzini, maestro Arnaldo Conti.

January 4 matinee: two works, *Cavalleria rusticana*: *Santuzza* Tina Desana, *Lola* Milly Bramonia, *Turiddu* Carlo Dani, *Alfio* Rodolfo Fornari, *Lucia* Anita Perego; followed by *Pa gliacci*: *Canio* Giuseppe Opezzo, *Nedda* Jane Noria, *Tonio* Ramon Blanchart, *Beppe* Ernesto Giaccone, *Silvio* Carlo Albani, maestro Arnaldo Conti.

January 4 night concert: *Il barbiere di Siviglia* (Acts II, III) with *Il conte d'Almaviva* Florencio Constantino, *Il dottore Bartolo* M. Te vecchia, *Rosina* Alice Neilson, *Figaro* Rodolfo Fornari, *Don Basilio* Andrés de Segurola, *Berta* Anita Perego. La traviata (Act III), *Violetta Valéry* Lillian Nordica, *Alfredo Germont* Carlo Cani, *Giorgio Germont* Ramon Blanchart, *Flora Bervoix* Anita Perego. Lucia di Lammermoor (Act II), *Miss Lucia* Alice Nielsen, *Sir Edgardo di Ravenswood* Florencio Constantino, *Lord Enrico Asthon* Rodolfo Fornari, *Raimondo Bidebent* Giulio Rossi, *Lord Arturo Buclaw* Ernesto Giaccone, *Alisa* Anita Perego, maestro Arnaldo Conti.

Alice Nielsen's costumes for *Barber of Seville's* Rosina have been preserved by City Museum of NY, a "yellow satin soubrette dress cut princess style, sleeveless with square décolletage in front and lower pointed-back neck line, trimmed in Spanish floral embroidery in full color and gilt thread. Trimmed at hem with yellow ball fringe and taffeta dust ruffle, it closed center back with lacing". Her next costume is a "gold silk velvet bolero jacket with short sleeves, laced together with gold thread, at the bottom finished with a ball fringe of yellow silk & gold sequins".

Philadelphia Inquirer (Mar 31) remarks the stay "was not remunerative, largely through a lack of good business management...." Foreshadows on the wall. Ensemble continues same program remaining towns.

"Grand opera or comic, the incidents were just as hilarious", Alice recalls. "We sang small towns and cities, villages and hamlets, sometimes in theatres, sometimes in halls, but always to good houses and fine applause. "For example, Jeska Schwartz, Riccardo Martin, Mardones and I sang one night in Tombstone, Arizona. That night we opened with the *Rigoletto* quartette. An awful silence followed the final notes. Not a hand smote a hand; not a foot tapped the floor. What was the matter?

"Then I sang, and the oppressive silence continued. No suggestion of applause. Schwartz came offstage in tears, calling the audience names that I shan't repeat. 'Well by heaven, I'll wake them up', snarled Martin. But he didn't. That audience might have been dead for all the demonstration he got. And Mardones too failed.

"'What's the matter with this crowd?'" they asked the manager. "'Nothing at all', was the reply. 'They enjoyed it thoroughly. But, you see, we had to hold the concert in this hall, which is also used as a church. And they feel sort of queer about applauding in church.'"

As Alice tours in opera, Hortense Nielsen tours in drama.

January 6, (*St. Paul Dispatch*, MN), Hortense plays Nora in Ibsen's *A Doll's House*. MKB said, "Hortense Nielsen gave an intelligent and deeply-felt interpretation of the role of Nora.... "The actress has a face that is an unusual combination of piquancy and power—a face of many surprises and therefore a charming face. Its plasticity in the final scene, in which the character of Nora reaches its full stature, was remarkable. With body tense throughout Thorvald's long speech of forgiveness, her face changed gradually, but startlingly from that of the 'doll' to that of the honest, courageous woman, strong in the consciousness of her own weaknesses. It was such a portrayal as the audience might well be grateful for".

In the cast: Bennett Kilpack's Dr. Rank, "full of intelligent restraint...." Others "not so satisfactory"; Lawrence Lee as Thorvald, "frozen".

Hortense takes *Doll's House* to Chicago in February when Alice arrives to sing grand opera.

Chicago Tribune's WL Hubbard (Jan 12) still hopes Alice Nielsen will be based in Chicago, the town now "likely to have permanent grand opera". People are "awakening to the fact that this big city by the lake is about ready for the largest form of all musical entertainment".

Hubbard gladly gives vaudeville the boot. "One week from tomorrow night, the Auditorium will return to its own once more. Vaudeville, which for three months has desecrated the finest opera house in America, will retire from that stage, it is to be hoped forever, and...Mme. Nordica and Miss Nielsen as prime donne will begin...grand opera for about three weeks". Pleads for a long season soon, "Perhaps next year will find us with...several weeks or months of grand opera in the Auditorium".He notes the big orchestra plus ballet corps.

On the 16th, four days before opening (*Chicago Record*), Nielsen and others sing at a 3am Mass for Father O'Callaghan at St. Mary's Church on Wabash and Eldridge. All her life, Alice Nielsen sings in churches.

Monday January 20 has *Gioconda* by Nordica and Constantino; Tuesday *Rigoletto*, Maurel and Nielsen; Wednesday matinee *Faust*, Nordica and Blanchart; evening *Aida*, Noria and Constantino; Thursday *Rusticana* and *Pagliacci*; Friday Nordica's *Traviata* with Blanchart, then *Trovatore* Saturday afternoon. They close with *Lucia* by Nielsen and Constantino.

January 21, when Nielsen sings *Rigoletto* the audience gives flowers, plus a new puppy. Alice has attracted puppies all her career.

Chicago Tribune's review states the star sang despite illness to save show and season, with gorgeous photo of Nielsen in concert dress, a low-cut black beaded gown by Seattle's James Bushness.

"Alice Nielsen deserved the basket of roses she received last evening at the close of the second act of *Rigoletto*. She deserved it, and also the pretty little Japanese spaniel that was stowed away in the center of the floral tribute", says WL Hubbard. "For she, by sheer grit, had saved the management from having to make a change of bill on the second night of the opera season—a procedure which is bad not only in its immediate effects but in the influence it has upon the public confidence....

He explains, "Yesterday morning Miss. Nielsen awoke to find herself so hoarse that she could only with the greatest difficulty speak above a whisper. The day was spent in doctoring and striving to overcome the hampering condition, but at 5 o'clock it seemed inevitable that the opera for the evening would have to be changed". By her "insistent" demand, the show went on.

"*Cavalleria* and *Pagliacci* were put in readiness, but it was found that Miss Nielsen's voice still was clear so far as singing was concerned, although when used in speaking it remained almost completely veiled. She was insistent upon appearing as Gilda, and finally it was decided that appear she should".

Her voice "rang out wonderfully clear, fresh and pure throughout her first scene, and although it was noticed that she seemed struggling against a slight cold or hoarseness that left her throat not comfortable, there was no trace whatsoever in the tone of the voice itself...."

Her "self-will and self-control, coupled with an excellent method of singing, made such a feat possible and successful. Few in the audience knew of the state of affairs—had all realized it, the approval bestowed on the singer would have been even greater than it was. She scored a success, did this plucky little countrywoman of ours".

Appreciates Nielsen's artistic evolution: "She has grown and developed in her art since she was heard here last season; and the promise then found in her work is now knowing happy fulfillment. Her voice is larger and stronger than it then was and her employment of it now is authoritative and certain. It is a voice of distinct beauty—exceptionally pure, exceptionally pure to accurate pitch, and beautifully free and exact in emission. Its schooling has been of the best, and while it may not rank as one of the 'great' voices in the world, it is a voice of rare charm, beauty and worth.

"Delightful last evening was the steadfastness with which integrity of pitch values was maintained by the singer. Even where certain of her associates were wandering...she, singing close beside them, adhered with astonishing persistency and success to accuracy of tone, and saved many a phrase from downfall and ended by leading her companions back to purity and right".

Chicago cannot refrain from weighing divas. "In appearance Miss Nielsen makes an ideal Gilda—slight, winsomely girlish and delicate, light in movement as a sprite and captivatingly natural and graceful". In the brawny town of stockyards, the reviewer contrasts the heifers' weights. "It is such a relief to find a Miss *Rigoletto* who does not weigh 200 pounds and look and walk it!"

Focus moves from stage-picture to quality of work. "Vocally, the music...was sung with complete understanding and with a beauty and finish that made it uncommonly satisfying. The *Caro nome* was an achievement of which any coloratura artist of note might have been proud, the impassioned duet in the second act was given with tonal beauty and yet with a feeling that rang true, and the top line of the famous quartet was sung in a manner thoroughly effective. The performance in its entirety, so far as Miss Nielsen is concerned, was one highly creditable and satisfactory, and one which demonstrated clearly her wisdom in fighting for a place for herself in grand opera", he concludes.

Singing-actors Nielsen and Victor Maurel, superb paired. *Chicago News* attends same, Chicago's best-ever *Rigoletto*: "Perhaps this unwearied spirit of self-sacrifice animated the entire performance, for not withstanding conditions were not favorable for inspiring the best efforts of the singers, one of the best performances of *Rigoletto* witnessed in years on the local stage marked the memory of last night's performance...."

For Maurel, "the art was so fine, so telling and decisive...every phrase was freighted with dramatic significance... so rich, so meaningful and so potential, every detail of the vengeful jester's progress toward the final tragedy were delicately differentiated and potentially marked. Work of this character is worth a multitude of roaring, rushing, bawling baritones, who don the motley—but never wear the mantle of the art, where temperament is subtle in every detail of splendid histrionism. The welcome of Victor Maurel was worthy the return of this great artist to the stage that he has graced so significantly and so long.

"The caprice of climate played pranks with the tender throat of Alice Nielsen yesterday...when the proverbial pluck of the Missouri linnet asserted itself as superior to minor matters of personal comfort and she disobeyed the stern mandate of the attending physician and dared her season's debut despite depressing conditions".

Alice's puppy is invited (*Chicago Tribune* Ja 24) to "annual exhibition of the American Toy Dog Club combined with the Beresford Cat Club".

Of *Pasquale* the *Chicago News* (Feb 4) says, "Few works of the opera bouffe class...have survived half a century and they can all be named on the fingers of one hand...*Don Pasquale* with all of its gayety, scintillating sentiment and lovemaking...lingers superfluous on the stage and is simply tolerated because it advances a charming cantatrice in fascinating fashion.

Happily the performance of last evening had so much to commend it in admirable action and in charm of musical ensemble that it was tolerated and approved".

Interestingly, *Pasquale* survives by realism; Harry Smith fails by surrealism. "Compared with the current styles of comic opera, it would appear that the old school had some distinct advantage in holding, as it were, a mirror up to nature.... The audience of last night keenly enjoyed the delightful fooling.

"Miss Nielsen was a delightful embodiment of the svelte, girlish and captivating Norina through the power of her personality, grace of action and witchery of song. The beauty of her voice finds its highest state in this class of music, and she is mistress of every phrase with distinction and authority. She had an excellent foil for her vixenish masquerading in...[Luigi] Tavecchia, who gave the title role a really rare creative value...."

How wildly would Chicago have admired Alice Nielsen's *Satanella!*

February 5: afternoon *Il Trovatore*, evening *Carmen*.

Constantino, De Segurola and Maurel "made this season notable" for their acting. The chorus looked well and sang better.

Next morning as if playing *Robin Hood*, a sheriff met Nielsen at her hotel with a warrant to collect a small bill including, "a pair of 50-cent leggings and ...50-cent gloves (*Trib* Fe 6)". The shocked diva wept "two tears which her press agent Lederer claimed were worth the amount of the entire bill". Russell calls those responsible "blackguards, pirates, worms...his hands clenched in rage". Nielsen's maid "Daisy Williams" had charged these things in NYC, singer never saw the bill.

Triggers a chain of melodrama. *Chicago News* (Feb 8) dips into 1901-era gossip to regurgitate relations with Tom Williams. Tale ties to pathetic Frank Perley's attempt to pump publicity. Concerns three singers: Nielsen, Marie Doro and Mabel Hite, supposedly from KC. Doro and Hite play Perley. Doro (1882-1956), Pennsylvania; Hite (?-1912), Kentucky. Hite's home told as Kansas City where daddy lives. Tours now in *Girl And The Bandit* for "Frank Perley Opera Company" and Doro debuted in Perley's 1902 *The Billionaire. News* graciously says, "Nielsen is older than the other two stage favorites but she looks younger than either of them. She is fragile, with shining blue eyes and pretty teeth, delicate profile and a throat too handsome and vigorous for the rest of her torso. In that throat lies the golden glory of Missouri".

News retells Alice's career in style of novelist George Ade's *Fables in Slang*. Ade works *News*. Dabbles theatre. His light opera *Sultan of Sulu* (1902) produced by Castle Square at Chicago's Studebaker theatre ran on Broadway. Dingbat sings *"From the land of the cerebellum, where clubs abound and books are plenty, where people know before you tell 'em....*

Ade (1866-1944) reveals that Lillian Russell vetted scores Nielsen sang. "Little Nielsen with her large and flaming ambition was a pretty sort of toy widow when years ago she came enveloped in black to the old Tivoli in San Francisco, where they gave nice comic opera and allowed the service of beer and other cheering hospitalities. Alice sung like a bobolink and was so lovely, so apt and so merry a widow that she and her little boy became the greatest personages of that small but popular company at the Tivoli.

"And then there came a rich and powerful young gentleman, one of the richest young men on the coast, with his millions, and paid court to Alice, but she dimpled up her chic visage, made eyes at his pocketbook and sternly refused to do anything but sing and gave him the option of building her a theatre or providing her an opera company instead of a wedding ring.

"The young man brooded lonesomely and smothered the hard-working little diva with flowers and jewels and beautiful expressions of big undying devotion. Meantime along came Papa Barnaby and Jessie Bartlett Davis and Nielsen was caught up within the musical arms of the Bostonians and made famous enough to excite the wildest jealousies of all the busy prima donnas in the land. She held firmly to her friendship with Jessie Davis and mourned that singer tearfully when all too early she was snatched away.

"And for Lillian Russell too, Nielsen has the most faithful friendship, for Russell used to 'pass' the score of any part Nielsen happened to be playing in her earlier, less-polished days when they came across each other on the road. For Nielsen, though her lovely waltz has left Lillian's far behind in the dust for top notes, was always modest and believed anybody could teach her something. They all loved to hear the Nielsen voice and suggest an easier way to make it even more beautiful.

"Then along came the billionaire of the coast again, still passing his suit before the dimpling and singing Alice. And he gave her the opera company and the opera and everything to make her into a celebrity".

And Ade ends his fable to pocket the beer money from Perley.

Reading Ade, we fill with sympathy for Williams who bribed Perley in a secret conspiracy to defraud Nielsen and destroy her career a few years before he shot an unarmed journalist several times in the man's parlor with the horrified wife watching.

Those facts no fairy tale.

January 30, at Nielsen's invites *Chicago Tribune* to arrange a charity concert for Chicago's needy as the regular performances continue.

Barber of Seville: "This merry work was given virtually in its entirety— a treatment it has not received in Chicago in a considerable number of seasons—and the performance was in high degree meritorious, but unfortunately it was listened to by an audience of small proportions. The boxes were well filled for it was 'university night', but the other portions of the house displayed gaping spaces of unoccupied chairs".

Tribune emphasizes the absolute value of stars. The founding singers of Boston Opera had not been protected by the Board. And the rascally manager given a three-year contract had instantly begun attacks on what was termed the star system, threatening the talents who got him the post.

"Chicago's interest in the *Barber* clearly is not of a keen kind, and Mr. Russell is discovering slowly but expensively that the old operas will not attract save when the glory of some star singer's nature is lent them. Our public in general knows nothing about grand opera itself—it has had no chance to learn, thanks to the conditions that have obtained for many years" so they must perforce follow celebrity.

Nielsen, a gala feast: "The performance was delightfully neat, crisp and gay. The musical taste of today is different from that time when Rossini in some three weeks' time wrote his merry comedy, and slightly slow moving unless the recitative is handled with unusual animation....

"Fortunately, last evening they were so treated and the performance was accordingly effective. Every singer in the cast, Miss Nielsen included—was admirably at ease with the long stretches of conversational singing and rattled off the Italian with a smoothness and rapidity that prevented all suggestion of monotony and heaviness. Rosina is a role which fits Miss Nielsen's capabilities and natural talents excellently. Her clear, birdlike voice is heard at the best possible advantage in the flowing and the florid melodies of Rossini, and the archness of her manner and the neat comedy of her acting make her embodiment of the part charming and amusing".

February 1st. The stars came out. Chicago peaks.

"The inevitable has happened: *The Huguenots* was presented with an all-star cast—the house was crowded, enthusiasm unbounded, everybody happy, including management", observes *Chicago Tribune* (Fe 1).

"Like all the works...newly and attractively costumed, and the chorus looked quite human, plumed in feathers and bedecked in brocades and satins, while the stalwart old one-gesture choristers, who line up and sing in unison with flashing swords uplifted to emphasize their vocal flights, were the brave gallants of the day when the symphony of life was song.

"Papa Conti had a large orchestra under admirable discipline, managed to play over the bald spots in the Meyerbeerian score with enough precision to make it appear quite luxuriant, and with tireless activity kept the accompanists close to the singers—in fact, the ensemble was excellent in all departments under his direction".

Nielsen "as Marguerite de Valois had her brief reign where the white light beats upon the throne, and again indicated her gain in poise and advance in artistry. She was in good voice with purity of tone and accuracy of phrasing, threading the perilous pathway of coloratura with prescience and brilliancy, and in the duet with Raoul based upon one of the most flowing melodies, the round and silvery qualities of her voice were charmingly apparent".

Constantino, "a dashing and delightful Raoul, carrying conviction with meaningful grace of action and graceful gift of studied song...he sang the big duets splendidly; one beauty of this artist's work is that he is ever musical; he rises to the high places easily and naturally; his art like that of the perfect actor, conceals its art.

"Mme. Lillian Nordica was warmly welcomed as Valentine...while the effects of the recent cold were somewhat noticeable, her admirable art and glorious Yankee pluck overcame the weakness and despite the disadvantage conquered completely".

DeSegurola "bluff and breezy St. Bris, and M. Blanchart an imposing impersonator of Comte de Nevers, and Sig. Rossi gave telling value to the sonorous music of the stalwart Marcel".

Nordica is "so familiar with the role that every moment is fraught with meaning and every phrase has musical value...her curtain calls during the evening were veritable ovations. She carried the tremendous last act with its tour de force in the duet with Raoul, in finished and fiery fashion that aroused the audience to great enthusiasm".

February 1st. Matinee: *Carmen*, Jane Noria. Evening *Rigoletto* Nielsen and Maurel. Next city on the tour St. Louis. Near Valentine's Day, St. Louis makes the surprise announcement that Alice Nielsen will soon be engaged.

Always after leaving Chicago.

Post Dispatch (Fe 14) predicts Nielsen "will announce her engagement to a St. Louisian while in this city...." Her voice "exquisite a year ago... improved remarkably since", and hometown diva Jane Noria "well-known locally as Josephine Von Ludwig", with Rosa Olitzka, mezzo-soprano and Carlo Dani, lyric tenor. Usual program of *Aida, Il Trovatore, Rigoletto, Lohengrin, Faust, Carmen* and *Les Huguenots* "with an all-star cast, probably including Nordica". They "came here a year ago unheralded but left very dear to the heart of the music-loving public".

Not neither Nielsen's fiancé nor none engagement surfaces notime.

Company hits Duluth's Lyceum Theatre February 17, 18 and 19.

Then touring to Minnesota, not in good health, good shape, or good-looking. *Musical Leader* does not mince words. "*Cavalleria Rusticana* and *I Pagliacci* was...unspeakably bad. The cast was so changed from the one advertised that it could not be recognized. After hearing the substitutes, one wished that he had not gone at all. It was a deplorable anticlimax to an otherwise splendid engagement. Wednesday was unspeakably poor. Literally I will not use up space to tell about it".

Better night, Monday's *Aida* with Tina Desana "altogether satisfactory" and Constantino "admirable". The chorus does "such good work that one did not mind...hard on the eyes to look at them. The costuming and the mounting in general was not all that might be desired".

Tuesday's *Rigoletto* with Nielsen and Blanchart, "audience was most enthusiastic and rightly so...to call forth the hearty applause and shouts of 'bravo' that were given the singers. We had a treat. All that had been heralded to us of the powers of this American was verified. Clear, full, sweet, liquid tones, dramatic ability, beauty and grace, all were there to charm the audience and they did not fail in their mission. She first made her powers felt in the passionate love song, *Caro Nome*, in the second scene of the first act. In the duet with Rigoletto, at the end of the second act, she was superb. Blanchard as Rigoletto was all that could be desired. He is no less an actor than a singer, and that is saying much".

Conductor Conti, "who held the success of the performance in his hands, inspired the admiration of every careful listener. Calm, quiet, with, it seemed, boundless reserve, he was always alert and had the attention of very singer and every member of the orchestra".

Joining St. Paul (*St. Paul Dispatch* Fe 19), ANielsen pairs with La Scala star Rossi, who "sings such magnificent bass roles as Leperello in *Don Giovanni* with much fire and distinction".

And Alice Nielsen announced plans to visit Buenos Aires in May for the re-opening of *Teatro Colón*. Constantino began his career there. Nielsen, only American singer invited; Melba and Tetrazzini also appear. Proud opera tradition in Buenos Aires, theatre has 2,478 seats, standing room five hundred. Nielsen slated to sing Zerlina in *Don Giovanni*. She made an impact; fan mail from Buenos Aires continues the rest of her life.

In St. Paul, Nielsen and Segurola (*Chicago Trib.* Feb. 22): "so excellent were these two, so artistic in all minor details was the production and withal so exquisite is Mozart's music that the audience experienced wholly justifiable delight". Gayety to Minnesota, "Its humor has never been matched and its characters, instead of singing arias in conscious vocal grandeur, sing them because song is per force the only adequate vent for such absurdly comic, intensely sad or sentimental and exquisitely subtle situations. Miss Nielsen and Mr. Segurola realized this ideal of the opera last evening, and whenever either was on the stage the action took on spirit and the singing became faultless.

"There is no longer occasion for surprise that the little American comic opera star should have pleased the critical audiences at Covent Garden. Her voice is fresh and beautiful, with sufficient volume and flexibility to open every flower in the garden of Mozart's music, and with a lovely mezzo voce, employed and so much to display its own perfect beauty as to give the last significant touch of color to the meaning the composer has so miraculously wedded to the music.

Segurola "brought to his Leporello a voice of splendid range and robustness and rich timbre, and a mind capable of conceiving and reproducing the wealth of jolly satire in this unique role. He gave a masterly interpretation of a masterpiece in comedy, filling it with telling and original action, and yet observing that restraint without which there is no artistic performance".

In the cast: "not much to be said. The inadequacy of certain individuals marred the perfection of some of Mozart's finest ensembles". Chorus and orchestra were "something for which to be grateful. The audience did not nearly fill the house, which is of course a discouragingly large one".

March 4th Nielsen responds to a sudden request from St. Louis' "Relief and Prevention of Tuberculosis" by auctioning theatre box seats for performances Friday and Saturday at Odeon Theatre. She takes the Midnight Special to St. Louis to sing *Lucia*. Meets the charity chaired by Mrs. Edward Goltra, Mrs. Kate Howard, Mrs. David Francis, Mrs. Rolla Wells, Mrs. JDL Morrison. Conducts the auction. Jumps the Midnight Special back in time to sing *Martha*.

"It takes an American woman to do this", Russell quips.

March 7th, Alice Nielsen returns to "opera in English" for the first time since 1901 by reviving 1847's *Martha*. March 7; She first sang *Last Rose Of Summer* as student at St. Theresa's Kansas City.

Chicago News reports "a large and enthusiastic audience approved the revival.... The masterpiece of the English line came last; but after all was not least in public esteem. Alice Nielsen again demonstrated her emphatic charm and capability in the lighter lyric line by her delightful impersonation of the dashing and venturesome Lady Henrietta. She sang and resang *The Last Rose Of Summer* in English; in fact, the audience could hardly get enough of it, and she was easily the dominating spirit of the night".

In the cast: Carlo Dani "made his best impression", Roso Raisa "vivacious Nancy", Fornari "the telling local favorite", Luigi Tavecchia "pleasing as usual".

Nielsen onstage charms Chicago.

Jordan backstage completes plans to build Boston Opera House. "After months of speculation", reports *NY Times* (Mar 21), "Boston has been assured that it is to have a new Opera House... Jordan will not only erect the building but will guarantee the expenses of opera performances in it for three years".

Boston Opera expects revenues of $98,000 from box subscriptions and $150,000 from selling stock. Building and land cost $700,000. Original directors are Boston boys: Eben Jordan Jr, George Freaing Jr, Charles Hayden, Francis Peabody Jr, BJ Lang, George Chadwick, Ralph Flanders, Camual Care, Gardiner Lane, Robert Jordan, Charles Loeffler, Thomas Perkins and Frank Converse. No intrusion of NYC banksters yet.

Public response to be shareholders in a company featuring Nielsen and Constantino overwhelm all expectations. More seats! Jordan demands architects increase the house capacity, despite delay. Twice.

Note there is no appeal to taxes, no political money at all. Arts arise from the people cooperating. This is the age of the sovereign citizen.

Olin Downes (*Boston Post* Mar 21) notifies readers Boston Opera has been duly incorporated. Jordan, "with an open-handedness that has seldom been equaled in the history of such affairs, agreed to provide a site for an opera house, to erect this house at his own expense, to let it to the company at a nominal rental and furthermore to donate a substantial sum to meet any deficit in the working expenses after performances had begun". Jordan instructs the design-build team: "Get it done, get it done on time, make it the best theatre of the kind that can be made". He knew people who could be trusted to do so and had proved it. Not the manager.

Downes details business specifics: for three years, forty-six boxholders will pay $2,000 annually to cover the company's rent, leaving $45,000 for expenses. For equipment and salaries, subscribers purchased $150,000 of stock, $100 per share, qualifying to get advance ticket offers.

"The unheard-of alacrity with which the public of New England, and indeed of the United States, responded to this offer is now a matter of history. The house was originally intended to seat between 2300 and 2400". Demand has been so great "seating capacity was extended as far as the ideas—ideals—of the architect and directors would permit. Thirty boxes became forty-six and the house now seats 2,751".

"Originally calculated to cost $700,000, when entirely completed... $1,200,000. This has not deterred Mr. Jordan. It has simply strengthened his original mandate". In today's dollars, Eben's fast-track opera project cost $28 million raised entirely by citizen participation.

With this announcement of concrete going into the ground for a new building designed for lyric performance, the choice of a manager looms large. The manager role assumes backstage powers over schedule, shows, budgets, contracts, hiring of staff, hiring of artists. And dictates what the press agent will publish. Needless to say, Jordan's choice of an overseas unknown surprises many who know Boston has several highly qualified candidates who have well-proved their worth in the town's beloved musical institutions. Of course the Park Theatre season was inspiring thanks to the stars, the onstage talent, and the Park manager. What realistically was the role of the faux impresario in Nordica's company by contract, we cannot be certain. We do know Jordan and the Board had a choice. We do know the choice was a curious contrast to the persons who managed Boston Symphony, New England Conservatory, and, say, Harvard. We do know that the stars who inspired this were not included in the Board.

The choice was doomed.

So the manager contract gives a prestigious three-year appointment, lofting the chosen one into the realm of Bostonian elite; salaried, yet to be powerfully defended and loyally obeyed. Irregardless. "Full power" is given a man who has never spent more than two or three weeks in Boston, and resides overseas where he has spent his entire life except touring with Alice Nielsen twice because he lived from her purse.

We do know that a competent business manager from the Conservatory was engaged to oversee the Boston Opera finances who was rapidly pushed out due to his disruptive desire to see Boston Opera competently managed.

Jordan has given his word. Russell rules on Jordan's good faith.

Henceforth all official publicity puffs Russell to absurdity, as an intrepid reporter will detect and expose. And some of the people will not be fooled all of the time. In the first Boston Opera press release the town is told the new manager first visited "US with a company of some forty [nay, five] members and made [accompanied] a long tour [thanks to Snow, Nielsen's booking agent] which covered most of the principal cities. He [Nielsen-Nordica] returned again...a season of fourteen weeks' opera...in New Orleans, in addition to other engagements in St. Louis, San Francisco, Chicago and other big cities of the West". Along for ride with Grimthorpe.

Russell would lief be cast as peer of Grau, Mapleson, Higgins. Or Ziegfeld. Grau put the stars onstage; Russell prefers Ziegfeld, the manager as star with cash advances for a suitable sycophant. And raises his voice against the "star system", hardly an idle threat against their revenue.

Nielsen's Park Theatre triumph is suppressed, swept away by a flood of Boston Opera molasses when Russell controls the press agent. Stars are airbrushed out of the picture: "San Carlo company [of SF, of NO etc] visited Boston in the spring of 1907. It [not Nielsen and Constantino] opened at the Park Theatre with a performance of Puccini's La Bohème which fairly took the city by storm". No mention that Nielsen dealt directly with Mrs. Gardner and Jordan to generate "whispers afloat of a scheme for permanent opera in Boston".

Concrete soon will be poured into the prideful ground.

History is rewritten after March 1908 as Boston Opera press releases put Russell's name in front of "San Carlo Opera Company [of SF, of NO etc]". Ownership by Nielsen and Nordica vanishes. Russell provokes disputes with Constantino, arguing over money! Gratitude! A perfect model of the modern arty bureaucrat. And the plans put in place during Alice's season at the Park are lost among fog, Post obediently suggests the fall season at Majestic "confirmed" the first season and "from that time on [sic], the operatic project moved swiftly".

The creators of Boston Opera consciously crafted a cultural legacy for the ages in their best traditions: Harvard, Symphony Hall, Bunker Hill.

"More than an opera house...it is a thing of romance and youth and beauty and it is 'of the people, for the people, by the people", brags *Boston Post*. As Jordan's team makes plans to pour concrete into the ground, the talented Nielsen-Nordica company tours North America its second year.

Moments of Alice Nielsen's life: March 22 in Columbus Ohio, *Columbus Citizen* discovers Alice "sitting in the lobby of the Southern Theatre reading a letter". She "made room on the settee and said, 'sit down', and an interview was on—or was it merely a conversation? Miss Nielsen was charmingly informal, quite American. She talked modestly of her voice, hopefully of her 'artistic development' and laudingly of the vocal abilities of the foreigners who surrounded her".

Alice gestures at letter, "This is from a girl who believes she has a voice". She receives "a wonderful lot of them. When I was playing in *The Singing Girl*, I wrote a long letter asking the advice of one of the biggest grand opera stars in the country. I never received a reply, and it stung me; you don't know how it stung me. So I know how much a little encouragement is appreciated, and how much it hurts to be ignored". Skips who spurned.

"If a girl has a voice, I advise her to go on the stage. She should first find out by going to some honest man who knows and will tell her the truth. The truth may hurt, but false praise will hurt her worse in the end. I always had ambition, from the time I first sang a wee bit in the *Mikado* at the age of eight [impossible] until I starred in *The Singing Girl* and *The Fortune Teller*".

Reflects on stardom with understatement: "Then I sang with the voice of a child. It must have been good, for lots of people liked it. But an untrained voice [two years with Valerga!] does not last a lifetime, and I did so want to sing grand opera. Then I went to London and met Mr. Russell and he induced me to study, and I'm studying yet.

"My mother has never heard me sing grand opera except through a talking machine. She has a phonograph and the records of all my roles at home in NY. Dear old mother is Irish full-blooded, so you see I'm half Irish but American-born. Recently a newspaper had a long story about my Danish father who is dead, saying that I inherited my voice from him— which is true—and my mother wrote me and jokingly wanted to know why something wasn't said about my 'poor old Irish mother.'"

At that moment Constantino is heard singing within. Instantly Nielsen focuses on her co-star: "Oh you must meet Constantino. He is a great tenor, not yet very well known in America. We think he is the equal of Caruso". Thereat she runs reporter up spiral stairs to the dressing room, introducing Constantino and wife in Italian, not Spanish. "You lika ma singing? You speaka Italiana?" asks the Basque star with worldwide fame.

Nielsen sings *Faust* at Southern Theatre that night.

March 26, *Indianapolis News* reports "a pitifully small audience at the matinee" of *Carmen* "but the few witnessed a performance not soon to be forgotten, with its gorgeous color in music and stage setting and with a richness of song...."

The evening, Nielsen packs the place. "Last night's attendance...that filled the opera house" shows "there is a clientele for opera in Indianapolis and the vicinity, especially when so great a favorite as Alice Nielsen sings Marguerite in *Faust*". *News* makes a patriotic appeal.

"Faith in her own powers and a willingness to work...was shown last night in her artistic singing and acting...she was the ideal of girlish purity and grace and nothing more charming and poetic can be recalled than the scene of the famous 'Jewel' song. Her beautiful voice, admirably cultivated, is adequate to the varied demands upon it, from the gentle delicacy of the love song to the stars, to the shriek of insanity at the close of the last scene...thoroughly consistent from beginning to end".

In the cast: Rossie "a great Mephistopheles, and his big bass voice, his acting and his makeup combined were in fine contrast to the gentle Marguerite". Tenor Carlo Dani (Faust) "not of the robusto quality" but had "power and a wide range of expression". Annita Parego "took the small part of Marta very acceptably...her by-play with Mephisto being one of the few comedy bits in the opera". Blanchart as Valentine "fine baritone voice".

As Broadway, grand opera blends genders. The cross-dresser in *Faust*, Milly Bramonia, sings Siebel, "this part of a man assumed by a young woman and calling for a woman's voice...causes one to speculate what would have been the effect of having Marguerite under the protection of a manly man instead of a womanly one". Stage direction poor, much "singing was done to the audience" not as characters onstage. Chorus, "merely as a costumed mass of singers" sang "splendidly". Company tours onward.

The merry month of March ends at Cincinnati.

Montgomery Phister adds to the profound praise Alice Nielsen has gathered since 1905 in Chicago, Los Angeles, Dallas, Boston. Ohio, one of the greats. Phister (1851-1917) is a Kentucky-born, Yale-educated war correspondent, diplomat, playwright with essays in national magazines. Phister knows gayety; comedienne Fanny Brice starred for him. He refuses offers by NYC. Loves Cincinnati where he reviews touring shows.

In *Cincinnati Commercial Tribune* (Mar 29), Phister portrays Nielsen as "determined in ambition, prolific in talent, untiring in zeal and triumphant in most of her undertakings".

As did the NYC critic reflecting on the mysteries and meaning of the sabotaged Casino *Pasquale*, Phister waits a pensive week until for eternity he concisely summarizes: Alice Nielsen is "an artist in the best sense of the word". Thenn asks, "What is art?" Phister speaks movingly of the present living world, of Nielsen's place in history.

"Art has had her votaries in all ages. She always has and always will demand sacrifices. Fables have been told of the self-sacrifices of the artists of the beautiful. We seldom believe that in our very midst and in the everyday of our humdrum lives we stand should-to-shoulder, bumping elbows in the familiarity of contact with scores of these struggling restless...mortals who in the glory of their achievements are to be exalted in the future...sanctified in romance, or done with halos and wreaths in stained glass as myths of the past, real beings ...who aided by the gods have found immortality sacred and secure.

"Alice Nielsen has not been fixed in saintly solitude upon any alter prepared by the Muses; her achievements have not been commemorated in tablets of brass; nor does the light shine down upon her lifted countenance, reassuring her in her ambitions or making joyous the pathway of hope...nor has her likeness 'done in little' been hung from gilded chains of the worshipers of song. Even Bim 'the button man' has overlooked her".

As every child knows, Myer "Bim" Bimberg (d1908) invented the campaign button in 1896 at a St. Louis political convention; got national fame with buttons for Teddy Roosevelt. His profits built five theatres.

Phister as oracle: "The time is indeed far distant when her votaries will proclaim days for her celebration, when her 'farewells' will bring suffocating throngs to her adoration or create furors in the capitals of the kingdoms of the world. Miss Nielsen is a remarkable young woman, marvelous indeed as an evidence of what energy, ambition, self-abnegation and the greatest of industry may accomplish....

"She is too much of this day, too much of the woman to be hallowed as a saint, too practical, too substantial of flesh and too warm of blood to inspire the romanticist; too successful to permit any belief in her own great sacrifices or that severe renunciation that has marked the lives generally of the great teachers, the real geniuses who ruled in the world of art or the realms of sublime thought".

Even Michelangelo needed the Sistine Chapel to paint his ceiling.

"Yet Alice Nielsen is an artist in the best sense of the word; she is devoted to her art. None of the lyric queens who at different times have shone resplendent upon the stage, none especially who have been nurtured exclusively on American soil, have ever excelled her in this respect. Her own fame, and what to a woman is more, her own appearance are always made secondary to the interests of music.

"She frequently sings a part as in *Martha* for example, for which she has no liking, if it is not manifestly unsuited to her or for the display of her best ability, simply because if she refused the public would be denied the privilege of hearing a work that it has always held dear".

Of *Martha*, "while her admirers were not prevented the pleasure of extolling her work, still a great sacrifice was asked of so young a devotee, and her marvelous singing of *The Last Rose Of Summer* unavoidably invited comparisons with the greatest lyric stars of the past and present.... Because of her conscious desire to please, she undertook this as she has done even less satisfying tasks. Because of this sincerity, again, she has never failed to score a triumph, as she did in her beautiful and appealing rendition of this song.

"Nor has Miss Nielsen's gauge been accurately taken. Her position, even in her brief operatic career, has been somewhat firmly secured, and as was manifested last week, her great ability thoroughly well appreciated, yet she risks much in reality.... Today she is accepted as one of the most successful singers among the reigning great. And her few appearances at the Lyric last week showed conclusively that in spite of all prejudices, in the face of all discouragements, she must go on until even great fame rewards her for the sacrifices and renunciations of the past".

Phister quotes Nielsen: "Yes, I have had tempting offers to return to comic opera, some that you might call fabulous, so great that my sincerest friends might doubt their truth. It is another sacrifice, I suppose, but I shall never accept any of them". As Alice glancingly refers to the poverty bringing her back to America in 1905, her thoughts turn to another star.

"It is the one thing for which I can never forgive Schuman-Heink [taking Broadway]. She is a genius. Oh, a singer with a voice beyond compare. And to think of her going back to sing in a work so trivial that but for her worthy interpolations might be considered a sacrilege. She no doubt needed the money, as I and all of us have, as I really did when I left Europe to sing in America, when I should still be abroad further perfecting myself. I am firm however, in the resistance of all unworthy temptations and mean to hold out in defiance of all 'greed of gold.'"

She had left Herbert's career before they could do their best.

Continues Phister, "It is this one characteristic, this religious sincerity in ambition that has made Miss Nielsen what she is, has given her the position she now occupies and promises her still other honors in the not misty future".

Phister summarizes Nielsen's place in American culture and what she must symbolize to all the people of the future of the world: "This remarkable young woman has done wonders for the encouragement of American art and native singers. She has shown us that it may be made the object of a lifetime, and that its professors may be pure and lovely and of good report; that they may, through their own exertions, be people of education and taste and breeding. She exemplifies the refining and exalting influence the prosecution of such studies should have. She makes us recognize the legitimate object and effect of art. She realizes the desire and belief of many writers and thinkers who ascribe to art an influence over life, a real and tangible influence, extending beyond emotions to purposes and deeds".

Phister reveals the respect Alice Nielsen has obtained.

With a home stage in Boston for her artistic progress, things seem bright for a long lifetime of galas and honors.

Alice Nielsen brings her life to art, now her art to life.

Cincinnati season ends. To Indianapolis. March 31st, Nielsen attends Toledo at the Valentine for two days. And has a night on Broadway.

For One Night Only! Alice Nielsen joins the *Wizard of Oz* cast in a vaudeville for Toledo Press Club. Reports *Toledo Blade* (Apr 1): "There was nothing but standing room left when the annual entertainment of the Toledo Press club opened at the Valentine. Even the balcony was filled, and many who were unable to secure desirable seats were turned away".

"When Alice Nielsen sang grand opera, the big audience at the Press Club show Wednesday afternoon was enthralled; but when Miss Nielsen chucked her accompanist under the chin, smiled and coquetted and sang *Comin' Through The Rye*, the house went wild. The people out in the audience knew the grand opera star was singing to them for the pure joy of it. An artist who demands $1,000 for a single night is a rare attraction when she sings for nothing at all".

Again she "sang her way into the hearts of the people". Big frolic.

Broadway's touring *Wizard* was a 'podge nobody knows nothing like the MGM movie because the director Julian Mitchell obliterated the script provided by the author of the novel. Even so, holy Toledo, the cast included

Dorothy (Hatty Sims McCarty), Tinman (Charles Wilkins), Scarecrow (George Stone) and "many pretty girls" of the chorus playing three scenes including *Sitting Bull* (tried to warn you). Worthy of any *Eden Musee*, they are followed by baritone George Dunston and Nielsen who share the stage with Van Doren's band; Mrs. EH Turner on vocals with player piano; Al Reeves "banjo player"; Miss Charlotte Townsend; M'lle Titenia the "world's greatest toe dancer"; the singer Devoy; and the Dayton sisters "eccentric dancers of class". One regrets missing these vintage evenings.

Next night Nielsen crosses back to grand opera.

The very skilled reviewer at *Toledo Blade* (Ap 3) reports that Nielsen's *Faust* "distinguished herself by her realistic acting and skill in singing. Her voice was as fresh and sweet as a summer morning after a shower. It had in it the lilt of the lark, and yet it did not fail to convey intense emotion where intensity was required".

"Miss Nielsen made an ideal Marguerite in appearance. She was charming in the garden scene, where she sits at her spinning wheel and sing a ballad called *The King of Thule*. It is a sad little song, but the sadness changes to joyousness, when Marguerite discovers the jewel box placed at her door by Mephisto. In the delight awakened by its contents, she starts to trilling like a bird. The low trill glides into the ascending scale which begins the brilliant theme of the famous *Jewel Song*, an aria that is as difficult as it is beautiful. Miss Nielsen sang its intricacies without apparent effort and with a vocal grace deserving of high praise. "She was again charming in the love duet, *It Groweth Late*, a composition considered in musical literature as the ideal love music. The church scene brought into prominence Miss Nielsen's power of emotional acting, but it was in the last act where Marguerite is in prison that one glimpsed the heights of sublimity and thrilled with the wonder of the music. The theme is magnificent and as it unfolds it grows in grandeur. The theme is thrice repeated, and each time its key is higher until the soprano tones soar to their last, clear, supernal note. Miss Nielsen sang the prayer superbly and after it was ended, with its beauty still vibrating in the air, Faust's few words of lamentation which close the opera, mattered little".

In the cast: basso Guillio Rossi obviously ill sang anyway, making "a heroic effort...was by no means a failure". Valentine "excellently sung and acted" by Blanchart.

A second Toledo writer notes of Nielsen: "The clarity and sweetness of her voice and the ease with which it maintains itself in the upper registers, also its increase in volume and expression since the days of her comic opera career". Even so, "her eyes seem still to have the old mischievous smile of Anita and Musetta lurking in them".

When *Toledo Blade* meets Russell the paper properly ponders why he was entrusted with running a Boston Opera in a masterpiece of misplaced emphasis: "When a comparative unknown can impress the musical world of his greatness to such an extent that wealthy men...support...a permanent opera house, there must be something extraordinary in the unlimited possibilities of this man and the class of grand opera he is capable of producing".

Blade did not do its duty of speaking freely. If intelligent people believe reflected glory is glory earned, heaven help Boston.

Cleveland links Alice Nielsen's career to painter Charles Dana Gibson. The unsigned article (Harvard clipping undated) references Foster's theatre and the singer's return to America "two years ago" saying "in this money-mad land of ours" two artists have turned their backs "upon easily-won success in the very moment of its flood-tide of adulation and fortune...one of these heroic souls is Charles Dana Gibson, who gave up an income of $60,000 a year that he made by drawing Gibson Girls and clean-shaven young men, to go to Paris to study. The other who sacrificed at the shrine of art is Alice Nielsen".

The writer defines Nielsen's status: "Four years ago, pretty little Alice Nielsen was the undisputed queen of comic opera in this country. She had a voice like a lark, with unexpected deep, high, true notes of piercing sweetness in it. She was lithe, and slim and graceful. She could act as well as sing. She had a temperament that bubbled over and effervesced like a bottle of champagne and went to the heads of the audience and intoxicated it. Managers fought with each other for her services and offered her salaries that almost staggered belief, for the craze for light operas and musical comedies was just beginning to sweep over the country and comic opera stars were worth their weight in gold.

"And there was no other to compare with Alice Nielsen. She was the one who in one person united all the requisites and hence her value on the stage in merry-go-round music was above rubies".

Nielsen responds, "It was only a success postponed. I know what I can do and I know what I am going to do. That sounds conceited, but I don't mean it that way. Anyone who isn't a fool knows their own abilities and limitations. I know mine, and I know that some day I am going to make a bigger success in grand opera than I ever did in comic opera. I have really gotten along much faster than I expected, but I have never had any doubt that I would arrive at the goal of my ambitions sooner or later.

"You see...I am the child of luck. Really although I have had a pretty hard time of it in many ways and have always had heavy burdens to carry, for since I was fifteen years old [true age of regional tour], I have supported my family and been the breadwinner of it ...still the good fairies have always had me in their keeping. I have always had luck. You know, I am a sort of adopted daughter of the south, as I was born in Nashville, Tenn. My parents though, were foreigners".

Again she expresses the fact Sarah was Irish-born, "My mother was an Irish woman and my father was a Danish artist". Her pilgrim progress to London skips Williams & Perley; *Fortune Teller*'s demise is foggy. Despite doing better box office than *Belle of New York*, the hit it replaced, Nielsen claims it was "a failure, as I had predicted it would be in England".

Never predicted that. And never was. Skips the corruption trauma.

"However, I had personal success vocally in it, and all the leading London critics said that I should study grand opera and had even gone so far as to pick out the roles in which they predicted success for me. It had been the dream of my life to be a grand opera *prima donna* and I felt that the opportunity had come for me to try to realize it. All my friends tried to dissuade me and told me how foolish I was to give up the good thing I had for something I might never attain, but I had provided for my family [sent patron's funds to mom and son and I felt I had a right to do what I desired".

For about the last time in her life, Alice again skips Valerga, Tosti, Grey, and Bevignani to promote her avaricious aide who has abandoned his take from her purse to attach to the Jordan salary and expense account.

"So I went to Henry Russell...most fashionable high-priced teacher of singing and acting in London and began to study with him". Yes, diva. He never taught acting and hated his teaching gig. Real singers not society dames seemed to prefer the famed Marchesi in Paris as you and your pals.

Nielsen skips her key collaboration with Nordica to pawn Russell as an organizer of foggy San Carlo [of SF, of NO, never Naples]. She dismisses now at last the fake name, suggesting it was "in honor of the theatre where I had made my debut [Bellini] and because many of the artists engaged for his [sic] company had sung there".

Russell is about the bite the diva who fed him. She is more candid later.

To Alice in her pride of having Boston Opera built as a home stage to evolve her operatic arts, beseems polite to promote her remora, perhaps counting on his relentless promises of gratitude.

That's her story she sticks to Cleveland.

In the very merry month of May the Nielsen winter tour 1907-08 wraps without visiting the profitable big towns out West. Cuts revenue, raises setup and overseas travel costs. Her North American Tour 1909-10 lasted from Boston on November 8th to New Haven on April 2nd.

Preparations for Boston Opera await her in Europe.

Until Boston Opera opens, Alice will focus on society gigs and concert tours. The concert career, always strong, rapidly builds into her major profit center. She picks songs she wishes to sing, adds a pianist and string virtuoso; and makes big money touring to many audiences glad she is.

Her opera is for art more than money; she knows money makes art.

She's no salary flunky who gets paid whether or not.

NYC before boarding, Nielsen greets columnist *Mlle. Manhattan*, who poetically remarks that the path to lyric success is "haunted with broken melodies...." Over lunch Nielsen speaks her artistic principles.

Corruption has cost dearly. Yet she has made a miracle. What drove her to deny Broadway? Insistence on singing meaningful songs.

"Something of that struggle which Miss Nielsen endured...crept into her voice yesterday as she spoke of her art". Nordica had just endowed Boston Opera's vocalist school at New England Conservancy. And wasn't invited to join the Boston Opera Board of Directors.

Nielsen: "When I think of Madame Nordica's wonderful gift to the future of American prima donnas in the school she hopes to establish for opera singers, there's a big lump in my throat and a big prayer for her work in my heart.

"When I look back at the difficulties and hardships that I encountered on the uphill path between the place destiny seemed to have marked for me and the one pointed out by ambition and a longing for the higher expression of soul in song, my heart aches for the other girls who struggle on the same difficult road". Stay focused on "stars overhead, rather than on the difficulties underfoot.

"When I determined to study for grand opera, I thought I understood thoroughly all the sacrifices, all the work, all the hardships entailed in the change. I was prepared, blithely enough, to give up a career that promised great reward, to put aside a very large income, to leave home and friends to learn a new art in a new language in a strange country. But I realized after less than a year's work at the foot of the difficult ladder I meant to mount, that all these things were only incidents in the life of toil and self-renunciation that Art really demands".

She confesses doubts. "Sometimes I wonder if it is worth what it costs, the few moments of success a singer sometimes wins, for all the sacrifice and self-denial she gave in exchange for a career".

Mlle. Manhattan: "Miss Nielsen's large blue eyes...are those of the idealist and of the stargazer, and heaven has spared some of its celestial blue and some of the star shine to light them—Miss Nielsen's eyes grew sad and took on a faraway look as she munched a bit of boiled chop. Did I tell you I was lunching with the...prima donna?"

Mlle. breaks the long silence, "'And what do you think sustained the artist who doesn't sink by the wayside?' Miss Nielsen brightened, and laid her fork neatly on the side of her plate".

From the heart: "Truth. Very simply, truth. Of course, there are those to whom the path to success is not difficult, but they are too few to be counted and the many who have kept courage and held out have been sustained by the one first loyalty—to be true to what their own heart felt was the true thing, the right thing, the big thing in life. You'll go hungry for that. You'll wear shabby clothes for that. You'll give up what the world calls success and popularity and wealth for that. And when you get it—"

Mlle. Manhattan: "The big blue eyes were shining like stars now, and there was a bright glow on Miss Nielsen's pretty cheek".

"—when you get it, you know that poverty doesn't count, that sorrow and discouragement only help you along; that discouragement is only the voice of the Tempter, and that the one thing life means is the bright shining truth that you are trying to translate into song".

Mlle. Manhattan cherishes the moment. "And do you know, at this point I rose softly and tiptoed out into the gray October morning. I didn't want to hear anything that would make me forget that here was a little woman who had paid a big price for her success, but had won it well and would wear it wisely because she had been true to her ideal—true to the voice that said, 'Come higher.'"

Leaving Manhattan, Nielsen returns to Boston. She arranges to buy her first home, the top floor of a building on Hemenway Avenue overlooking the park, equidistant from Symphony Hall and the arising Boston Opera House. She is joined by Hortense, mom Sarah, son Benjamin.

May 17th Alice Nielsen sails to Italy with Hortense. Shopping to do. They will furnish Boston Opera with sets, costumes, and properties for the first year and forever. Renew connections with creative people. The new project has made music industry headlines. Welcome is warm for the upstart.

Nielsen to *Boston Globe* (May 17) confirms her mission, saying she "sails on the *Canopic* today for Europe, where she will remain until the fall. Miss Nielsen, who was with—" the grand opera company formerly known as San Carlo of San Francisco etc "—last season, will attend to the selection of the costumes and properties for the company which Mr. Russell will organize for the Boston grand opera house".

Indeed organize the pre-organized Nielsen cast.

Mary E. Toye, "confidential secretary to Mr. Russell...will remain with her until her return. Miss Nielsen and Miss Toye will attend the principal debuts of the season and will be on the watch for promising material for the Boston company...." Toye and family become close friends to Alice.

Alice makes a rare political statement departure. Boarding *Canopic* she sees SC Senator Benjamin Tillman speaking to press, "The senator was introduced to Miss Nielsen, who carried a Teddy bear, wore a profusion of flowers and was radiant with smiles". Nielsen says, "Oh senator, this is a great pleasure, for I've often heard of you as a wonderful statesman". Tillman "fairly blushed with pleasure, his huge shoulders towering above the head of the little singer as they stood together on the boat deck".

Suddenly he spies her Teddy bear and recoils. Bryan, Taft or Teddy where the choices for President. Tillman dislikes Teddy, he wants a Progressive to fight monopoly and banksters, keep things safe, keep US out of foreign wars.

"What are you doing with that thing in your arms? I'm out for Bryan".

"Oh senator, I was going to present it to you".

"If I had a pitchfork I'd run it through the animal, for I have no use for Teddy bears". His emphasis on 'Teddy' set the group in an uproar. Fun furious as Tillman refuses to take the toy in his arms. He proves right.

June 30 (*LA Times*), Victor Records lists new releases, "All vocal selections have accompaniments by the Victor Orchestra" usually conducted by Arthur Pryor whose band is featured on many Victor Red Seal records. Vocal stars include Enrico Caruso, Emma Calvé, Louise Homer, Pol Plancon, Florencio Constantino and Alice Nielsen, who offers *Il Bacio*. Constantino and Nielsen have given Victor a duet from *Romeo and Juliet*, *Ange Adorable*. The Victor disk player is "a perfect musical instrument. It is every instrument and every voice in one. There is a Victor for every purse", says Victor Talking Machine Company of Camden, NJ.

EUROPE: DEBUSSY, LOIE FULLER

During summer 1908, Alice sends reports to Boston papers similar to her superb articles during the 1898 Hawaii and Japan trip. Her fame again peaks, reminiscent of the summer buildup to *Fortune Teller*.

July 11 Nielsen advises *Boston Sunday Herald*, "Once again I find myself in gay Paris! In the Bois de Boulogne one sees nothing but celebrities. Almost daily in a smart automobile, Mr. Debussy, the famous composer of *Pelleas et Melisande*, and his attractive wife may be seen taking their regular afternoon drive". Nielsen meets Loie Fuller and Debussy's designer Josef Urban, the new design stars in Paris. American dance pioneer Fuller has created costume and lighting effects; innovates techniques Urban elaborates with skill in America. And Vienna's Urban is an architect and illustrator become stage designer.

"Apropos of Debussy, he is a remarkable personality...and is often the recipient of extraordinary ovations from the musical students who collect in the Latin quarter of Paris and march to the composer's beautiful villa to tender their expressions of admiration and respect".

Apropos of Debussy, gossipy Quaintance Eton claims Russell's wife Nina put Debussy's pal Andre Caplet as a Boston Opera music director for romance; and disinterested Russell hires Andre to please and occupy Nina. Caplet (1878-1925) had performed since age twelve. Born Normandy, he composes, conducts, and for Debussy orchestrates. Savaged by poison gas during World War One, dies young; ends badly.

Nielsen continues, "I was invited to tea at the Elysee Palace Hotel and was introduced to some of the younger artists of the Opera Comique. The conversation soon turned to the latest novelty to be given in the National Theatre, *Le Clown*. The book by Victor Caponi and music by A. Camondo, were being criticized both favorably and unfavorably". The composer, a "well-known millionaire of Paris, and this proved very unfortunate for him" due to "strong feeling of prejudice against him". Attending *Le Clown*, "imagine my surprise at the end of the first act when I heard vigorous cries, not only from the gallery, "Down with the music of the millionaire!"

Alice observes rival Geraldine Farrar in a "somewhat ungrateful role of Zephirine", saying "I have always been an admirer of my talented compatriot". Perhaps a sly egg: "Miss Farrar's career is another brilliant example of the perseverance and determination of the American woman". Alice does not say talent or skill.

Herald observes, "See how neatly Miss Nielsen sticks her hatpin into Madame Melba. She first characterizes her as 'golden-voiced.' Then, 'last night, Melba showed the public that she still possess some of those qualities which have made her famous.' Some!"

Both Melba and Farrar assiduously block rival sopranos.

Alice up late: "Surprising to us American to see how late the theatres remain open in Paris". Opera lasts till after midnight "and there is no attempt to prepare supper until about 12:30. About 2am in the morning, Paris is gayer than most other cities are at 10 in the evening. I was invited to join some artistic celebrities at Durands after the opera".

Notices men dress badly. "Beautifully gowned women, accompanied by badly dressed men (even Frenchmen who have their clothes made in England are always badly dressed)".

August 20 Alice writes from Breslau, Germany, "After leaving Paris I went straight to Frankfort. This was my first visit to Germany and naturally, the journey up the Rhine was a necessity not to be avoided...it is not for my pen to attempt a description of the famous banks of this famous river. It suffices to affirm that its traditional castles and traditional fables are just what Badeker says they are".

Leipzig's Baedeker Company publishes the 1900's popular travel series *Rhine From Rotterdam To Constance*, and *London and its Environs*, &c.

Red-bound, gilt-lettered travel guides by Karl Baedeker (1801-1859) first give detailed routes, lodging, prices.

Nielsen gaily notices saucy bits of daily life. "There are sights, however, which are to be seen on the Rhine's still banks which Baedeker for some unknown reason seems to entirely ignore. Enamored Germans may be seen by the dozens encircling, not always successfully, the waists of their excellent fraus, who more oft than not, surprised American sensibility by kissing their male counterparts in so cozy and conspicuous a fashion as to actually divert the attention of the devout tourist from the all-inspiring castles on the hills.

"I could not resist speculating on what the exact result would be if this curious form of entertainment ever took place on Broadway NY or Boylston Street, Boston. Remembering that Mrs. Campbell was requested not to smoke cigarettes in public and that certain diligent protectors of the public's morals have protested from time to time some very fine works of art in the name of decency and respectability, I wonder...."

Alice Nielsen, self-described best legs in San Francisco, who toured with Burton Stanley, the woman whose tight red leggings in Herbert shows would be vividly recalled by male spectators later in life as "very tight", continues to travel Germany along the Polish border to Denmark.

Her thoughts on D'Annunzio are mild. Reacting to the countryside, she quotes the poet's criticism of Wagner who lacks "'the magic touch of the olive.' However much one may admire the classic beauty of the German master, one cannot resist a sigh of longing for more joy-giving song which springs from the heart of the vine-covered valleys and olive-crested hills".

Her host in Germany is beautiful English actress Daisy West (1873-1943) who in 1891 had married Prince Henry XV of Pless. Quite a story and Nielsen says nothing of it. Daisy grew up in India. Henry, dismissed from diplomatic corps by Chancellor von Caprivi for marrying a foreigner, is by his wife now related to the Duke of Westminster. He is restored to London's German consulate in time for WWI. With great joy, the author has discovered Henry eventually appealed to the Pope to dissolve his marriage to Daisy on grounds his wife's father had "forced him in 1891 to marry her at the point of a revolver" (*Time*, Feb 02 1925). Henry at 63 divorces Daisy to marry the 26-year-old Senorita Candamo.

Daisy and Alice are born same month about same year. Edgar Elgar is a mutual friend. Other guests present include "India's princess Maralah of Koochpahap [Maharini of Cooch-Behar], Sheila [Shelagh, Daisy's sister] West and her fiancé Lord Belgrave, naturally Count of Turin with Berlin Opera's Count Hochberg, and not unexpectedly Mrs. Lawrence Townsend, "an American woman of great beauty who is well-known in NY".

Mysteriously, Alice with subtle 1900s wit suggests Mrs. Townsend "was most kind to me on a certain occasion when I had the privilege of singing for the King of England whose friendship and esteem she enjoyed in common with most of the American women who have homes in Europe".

The womanizer King. Mary Scott Townsend inherited a railroad and coal fortune; her husband died 1902; fell from horse. The couple had loaned their DC mansion to the President as the White House refurbished.

These companions are the "up-to-date aristocratic pleasure-seekers" who seem "strangely out of tune with the massive stone walls and gloomy aspect of the Fürstenstein castle", the greatest palace of Silesia which borders on Moravia; Alice sleeps near the Nentwig ancestral home.

She seeks the soprano she most admires.

Into Denmark, visiting Copenhagen and we hope Århus, Alice Nielsen arrives in Stockholm with a "letter of introduction to the great Christine Nilsson. What a magic name that is to the young singers of today! I can scarcely believe that I am really going to shake hands with the great singer whose voice and genius are comparatively unknown to us of the present generation".

Bevignani, teaching *Faust*, "the old man would often turn around and describe the wonderful powers of Christine Nilsson, 'whose voice was soprano, legaro, lyrico and dramatic all in one. Her acting was spontaneous, and came from her heart, and she cast a magnetic spell on her audience which never ceased until the end of her performance.'"

Obviously Nilsson inspired Nielsen, Bevignani as catalyst. Their great teacher shared techniques with the two stars. Bevignani became available to Alice at a critical time, just retired to Italy after conducting over four hundred performances at the Met between 1883 and 1900. Sadly, Alice Nielsen's time with Christine Nilsson is unshared. Their teacher guides their vocal and stage techniques. Nielsen asked Bevignani who compares with Nilsson: "Nobody! There world has known but one Christine Nilsson and the advent of another will mean a new era in a lost art".

Clara Kellogg knew Nilsson and Patti, saying: "I have been often asked my opinion of Patti's voice. She had a beautiful voice that, in her early days, was very high. But her voice...has changed, changed in pitch and register. It is no longer a soprano; it is a mezzo and must be judged by quite different standards". Hence the high Cs provided by Valerga.

To Alice's performance prowess, Kellogg paints a strong contrast when describing Patti: "Always a light voice. She was always desperately afraid of overstraining it. She never could sing more than three times in a week and, of those three, one rôle at least had to be very light. Such a life! Everything divided off carefully according to régime:—so much to eat, so far to walk, so long to sleep, just such and such things to do and no others! And, above all, she has allowed herself few emotions. Every singer knows that emotions are what exhaust and injure the voice".

Intriguingly, "She never acted; and she never, never felt. As Violetta she did express some slight emotion, to be sure. Her *Gran Dio* in the last act was sung with something like passion, at least with more passion than she ever sang anything else. Yes: in *La Traviata*, after she had run away with [tenor] Nicolini, she did succeed in putting an unusual amount of warmth into the rôle of Violetta. But her great success was always due to her wonderful voice. Her acting was essentially mechanical.

Tellingly, "As an intelligent actress, a creator of parts, or even as an interesting personality, she could never approach Christine Nilsson. Nilsson had both originality and magnetism, a combination irresistibly captivating. Her singing was the embodiment of dramatic expression".

When the author played Alice Nielsen's restored recordings to a group of NYC opera singers (2006) of *Un bel di*, the raction was, "She gives a master class in a lost art. Singers are taught today that it is impossible to sing that way". Alice Nielsen jumps in and out of chest resonance to emphasize feelings of her character; to tell a better story. Learned her craft from Valerga, Bevignani. And chest tones have risks.

Kellogg recalls Christine Nilsson, "I was present on the night when she practically murdered the high register of her voice.... The second aria in *The Magic Flute* is more famous and less difficult than the first aria and, also, more effective. Nilsson knew well the ineffectiveness of the ending of the first aria in the two weakest notes of a soprano's voice, A natural and B flat. I never could understand why a master like Mozart should have chosen to use them as he did. There is no climax to the song. One has to climb up hard and fast and then stop short in the middle.

"It is an appalling thing to do: and that night Nilsson took those two notes at the last in chest tones! 'Great heavens!' I gasped, 'what is she doing? What is the woman thinking of!' Of course I knew she was doing it to get volume and vibration and to give that trying climax some character.

"But to say that it was a fatal attempt is to put it mildly. She absolutely killed a certain quality in her voice there and then and she never recovered it. Even that night she had to cut out the second great aria. Her beautiful high notes were gone forever. After that she began to be dramatic to make up for what she had lost. She, the classical and cold artist, became full of expression and animation. But the later Nilsson was very different from the Nilsson whom I first heard in Paris during the winter of 1868".

BOSTON: ALICE OPERA, HORTENSE DRAMA

In September when Alice Nielsen returns to Boston, Jordan is poised to complete the opera house construction and well-pleased with progress. Boston prepares for the grand opening next winter. New England Conservatory, also used for rehearsals, is training the women's chorus who establish a chapter of *Mu Phi Epsilon* now lost at present. The male chorus continues to consist mostly of Italian, Spanish, and French men to chaperone the American women.

Now-salaried, manager Russell directs staff. His publicity man fluffs stuff: obey or highway. Russell has an American tycoon as chairman, big budget to spend, Board of Directors to fog, and business manager to dodge. Could make promises others will pay. Shielded from scrutiny yet highly visible in Boston society. In Europe the peacock may better preen. Far more chance for grift than he ever knew. Pocketing Alice's patron money or Ziegfeld cash or coins from young US singers for a listen was nothing compared to this. He was, as many said at the time, a very unlikely choice.

Construction of the best, most modern opera house began at Jordan's order without "formality or proclamation". When Boston City Hall hints the new street may be named for Jordan, he modestly chooses the simple "Opera Place" instead.

Strong public response had delayed plans as architects twice enlarge the theatre. "To increase the seating capacity and...retain promising lines of sight...asked time and work of the architect". Then with "plans finally settled, the making of estimates and contracts followed. Mr. Jordan and his followers sought the best of work at the most reasonable terms. Thus...actual construction did not begin until nearly the end of August".

Boston Opera goals are revealed in the 1908 prospectus. To buy a hundred-dollar share meant guaranteed seats would be available before any public ticket sales. Potential shareholders are told the Opera will "engage the best artists available but with a view to achieve perfection of ensemble rather than to exploit the individual". The sly attack on the stars who delivered the ingrate here begins.

First season is fifteen weeks, plus five weeks' touring. Repertory "about fifteen operas chosen from standard Italian, French, German and English works...sung in its original language". Chorus "will be usually large, number about 100" and the orchestra "will likewise be large...from 60 to 90 players". Boston Opera will maintain "the best standards".

Focus on American talent promised: "American singers and composers will be given every encouragement; native talent will be sought in all parts of the country and systematically trained in the Opera School. Students who are now obliged to go abroad for practical training and experience will be enabled to receive it here".

Frequent interchange of "artists and works" with the Met are planned. Met chairman Otto Kahn joins the Boston board, puts Jordan on his.

Boston Opera Board: President Eben Jordan, Frank Converse VP, Eben's son Robert Jordan, Secretary, Charles Hayden treasurer. Others are George Fearing Jr., Francis Peabody Jr., SJ Lang, Samuel Carr, Gardiner Lane, Thomas Perkins, NL Amster, Charles Loeffler, Ralph Flanders, and George Chadwick.

Converse composes and teaches at Harvard. Loeffler operates Boston Symphony. Flanders is business manager for New England Conservatory and Chadwick (1854-1931) is its director, an organist and teacher who composes over a hundred songs plus operas.

Boston Opera staff is from the Nielsen tour. Northern Italy's Arnaldo Conti conducted in Padova at sixteen, Rome, Paris' *Theatre des Italiens*, Buenos Aires where Constantino and others often sing. *Regisseur* (stage manager) is Menotti Delfino, Italian baritone out of Odessa. The Boston hire is conductor Wallace Goodrich, dean of New England Conservatory, born Newton (MA) and trained Europe.

The attempt to "star" Russell to justify his elevation to the Boston role will suffer the press agent when debunked later. Concocts a patented parasitical progress retold without a wink over the sadly limited lifetime of the project. Truly a tragic grand opera experience for Boston Opera House.

He is spun "a singing teacher of unusual ability" after teaching London society babes to relax hands-on; as a lad who went to Rome on Alice's purse and returned to England 1904 to spy on the girlfriend of San Carlo manager; who installed the season at Waldorf then brought "a company to America and gave performances of Donizetti's *Don Pasquale*". A company, yet. He gave performances. Gave a disaster only Nielsen could overcome; as the theatre industry was aware. And asserts to have brought the San Carlo company [of SF, of NO] to America.

Stars obscured entirely. No Nordica, no Nielsen, no Duse.

Yet not to worry, his "scientific attainments as vocal teacher" together with huge "practical experience in operatic management peculiarly" fit Russell for running Boston Opera" the Prospectus assures investors. His experience with graft was strangely omitted. Wildly weak logic and foggy facts goes not unnoticed by local and distant spectators.

We divert to happy Hortense Nielsen, based in Boston now and finding friends at Curry Institute of Expression. Nielsen sisters have vision, masters of practical theatre. No doubt financial success a topic of their talks. Hortense could not expect to produce Ibsen plays to these regions with huge financial rewards.

August 30th Hortense tours to Tennessee. "The accomplished artiste... striving to achieve the pinnacle of her ambition as an emotional actress", says *Knoxville Journal*. "Instead of confining herself for the exploitation of her extraordinary talent to a single play as is customary with American stars, Miss Nielsen will follow the European method of producing a collection of great dramas all varied in style of construction, depicting a variety of emotions and situations of striking difference in conception". Her repertoire "collected from the greatest examples of modern German, French, English and Norwegian literature...*Magda, Monna Vanna, Mrs. Dane's Defence* and *A Doll's House*".

Rare glimpse of Hortense occurs a week later in Louisville (*Louisville Courier-Journal*, KY Se 7). In Seelbach Hotel she grants a rare interview. Louisville 1908 is devoted to baseball; reporter asks if she enjoyed attending the ballgame that day: "Stopping to talk, she gently stroked the wavy hair of her little daughter at her side and smilingly replied".

Hortense: "No, I did not attend the baseball game this afternoon but I want to say that I admire an enthusiast in anything. I understand that the people of Louisville now have the fever at a high pitch, and I am for them. The winning of the pennant will be a sure cure for all of them, and to that end I am heart and soul for them.

"I was actually too busy today to go to the game or anywhere else. I have been hard at work. In fact, the only rest has just been experienced as I partook of dinner with my husband and little daughter. Let's go up to the parlor, for the glare of a hotel lobby is always more depressing to me than even stage fright. However, do not think for a minute that I am susceptible to stage fright. I have long since become proof against that".

Within the parlor, Hortense, "Mrs. Quintard in private life, turned the conversation to the little daughter who was playing at her side. It was easily apparent she is a great lover of the home life and that all of her spare moments are spent with her family. She even alluded to her mother who is back in NY, saying that she wished she could see her and that her home was always where her mother was.

"Miss Nielsen was dressed in a plain white lounging gown, indicative of an easy working dress. Her manners were those of a kind mother in her home. There was nothing stagy in her actions".

Hortense: "I am always delighted to get South. I think the people are simply charming in their nature and action. They are not so intensely critical as Easterners, yet they possess the highest degree of refinement.

This is my second trip to Louisville. I must say that I greatly appreciated the reception accorded me last season when I appeared in *The Doll's House*. We have only been out a week this season but we were pleased with the success that has attended us. In fact, I did not think that *Magda* would take half as well as it has. I feel satisfied that the people of Louisville will like the play".

In Sudermann's *Magda* a free-spirited daughter asserts independence to her conservative father. She returns home as a star after long absence, with her child from an early affair with a man in the town. Magda says: "Gag us, stupefy us, shut us up in harems or in cloisters—but if you give us our freedom do not wonder if we take advantage of it".

Hortense is "a splendid conversationalist and there is no topic that she does not show familiarity with. She positively declined to talk politics because it is a presidential year. She admitted though, that she was a great admirer of the personality of Mr. Bryan and casually remarked that Mr. Taft was showing some signs of speed [untrustworthy, slick]".

The sisters share a deep-seated reluctance to self-promote. Hortense remarks "I will talk about anybody in the world but myself. I can't bear to talk about myself. That has to be done by somebody else".

Both sisters have strong energy: "The vivacity of this little actress, for she is of a petite figure, is something wonderful. She looks as if she never tires, although she declared that she did at times but was loath to admit it on all occasions". Hortense spent a week at Macauley's Theatre playing *Magda* and Arthur Jones' *Mrs. Dane's Defense* before leaving for Paris, KY.

September 11 (*Bourbon News*), Hortense opens at the Paris Grand. The local paper says Hortense "who has for years striven worthily to present the best plays, deserves the patronage of the lovers of the theatre and it is to be hoped that the artiste will be greeted by an audience of such large and intelligent proportions as to be an encouragement to an actress of her great talent".

Hortense opens Nashville by Sept 17th in *Magda* and *A Doll's House*.

Her touring season takes these challenging modern plays into the heartland. She had ended the previous April 1907 in Mansfield, Ohio. She resumes by December in Chicago, then touring Illinois, Wisconsin, Minnesota—the Metropolitan in Minneapolis Jan 5-10; Nebraska, Kansas, Missouri—of course Kansas City, Kentucky, Arkansas, Tennessee—Nashville at Vendome; Alabama, Mississippi—at Jackson, Vicksburg, Natchez; Texas, Alabama, Georgia—at the Grand in Atlanta—, looping and crossing back along her routes as demand calls. From Michigan to Mississippi to Vermont, and over into California.

Much later Hortense has several theatrical weeks in Asheville, NC before her career seems to halt in 1938 Illinois. She gave Shaw's anti-war *Arms and the Man* and Drinkwater's *Abraham Lincoln* frequently during the 20s, mainly in Midwest with jaunts East. Not in California after 1910.

By mid-October Hortense is in Paris KY, Alice in Paris FR. And new-minted Boston Opera manager Russell leaves Italy for Boston where he remains until mid-January, busy with "organization of the chorus and the orchestra of the house and the school that in time...will feed these forces".

Program set, trust given, power taken. "He will have authority to act and he will return to Europe to complete the engagement of the company. No one knows better than he or than do the directors how much depends for the future on the first year of the new house" inheriting the Nielsen-Nordica program and personnel. Swamp literal, not literary, discovered underneath Boston Opera increases the cost for underpinning.

During November, skatterlings of Alice Nielsen rumors arise. *Musical American* (Nov 14) announces her "engaged by the Shuberts to head an all-star cast in a revival of Balfe's *Bohemian Girl*". Nothing follows; nor any Nielsen *Satanella* appear for the greater glory of the theatrical firmament.

Within two weeks, *Musical Leader* (Nov 26) announces "Alice Nielsen is to be the star of the new opera season in Mexico" playing *La Bohème* and *Don Pasquale*. Such beauty of art and seriousness of voice are wasted upon anything less than grand opera performances". Her presence has not been confirmed, yet as Boston Opera was a-building, *Christian Science Monitor* (Boston 1909) reports Mexico City opening the "largest opera house on the continent" and gives access "to companies practically free of charge". Both Mexico City and Buenos Aires plan 1910 centennials. Many of Nielsen's circle had South American careers; Constantino builds a beautiful opera house of his own in his adopted hometown Bragado.

In New England, *Musical Leader* (November) has great hopes: "This city is eager to see the completion of the Boston opera house on Huntington Avenue. Citizens have shown their interest and confidence.... Viewed on every side, aesthetic, educational, commercial, permanent opera should be of great benefit to Boston and its citizens".

Nielsen's views are its founding principles: low prices, lots of opera: "The time is ripe for long operatic seasons at reasonable prices".

Boston pride: "A city that has prided itself on being the dwelling house of culture and the favorite abode of the muses, will at least have both a building dedicated to opera and a company identified with the town. Hitherto Boston has been only a convenience to the purposes of managers who have given it what they could afford to give and given it as they pleased".

Now the eyes of the world watch Boston: "Singers of international reputation, musicians of high degree, all interested in art are watching with approval....the plan".

Boston Opera will change how American singers train. Two stars (Nordica for one) have given "scholarships that students of talent may be... trained for the stage". Boston will become a haven for "musically dramatic talent" of American hitherto "thwarted and crushed" by "foreign prejudice".

Ironically, the manager hiring talent is foreign with prejudice. Despite Boston Opera's promise to seek native talent, Russell does the opposite. Tours first-class "into remotest Russia" during dramatic days of the Russian revolution in 1905, a time of plots and spies. Between1905-1912 many conflicts arise between Lenin, Trotsky, Martov, Plekhanov, Labor Bund and others at conferences in Russell's familiar haunts in London. As conferences switch to Paris, Russell relocates. So the foreign prejudice is builded into the start, and like Trotsky paid by Jacob Schiff, the Boston manager takes to Revolutionary Russia.

Once hired, the foreign manager drops any promise to pursue American singers. Serves the migrant banksters who took a safe haven in NYC before making massive murder across Europe. As he travels Russia, Russell reports back to Boston directors weekly whatever he wants them to hear. Stays away from Boston unless absolutely essential.

The Board has deeply loyal Boston roots. Their hirling Russell spends Boston Opera money like a Czar in the cookie jar.

Yet as the building rises *Musical Leader* has hopes that opera shall lift pop culture and permeate daily life: "No observer of arts that entertain and at the same time cultivate taste and develop artistic understanding will deny the mighty influence of opera, when it is part of the daily life of a people". This optimism is widely held. And if the hopes are dashed, the morale supporting the project may be difficult to muster—if the facts prove to challenges such noble Puritan faith.

Musical Leader believes opera shall make daily life righteous; a logical and fascinating hope for the Puritan haven built on Plymouth Rock. This is a decade before Boston's Comstock gang bans James Branch Cabell's witty, monstrous clever novel *Jurgen* (1919). "No doubt your notion is sensible", says Jurgen, "But mine is prettier". And so on. Cabell also says, "The song was no masterpiece, and would not be bettered by repetition".

Boston hopes: that a large group of Italian and French wandering minstrels will nicely mingle with young American women to create a fine moral example during the opera season. Star singers, management, a Russian ballet shall set an example of propriety all admire.

To help this fine expectation, Jordan tosses leadership to a dilettante manager soon thrice married; who hobnobs with boy-pals; who cultivates young sopranos; who hates Boston; who longs to settle in Paris on the payroll; and operates in a decidedly Bolshevik manner: that is, corruptly.

Jordan bypasses virtuous New England talents who prove their worth.

Russell has fibbed about promoting the American singers.

Yet be as it may, *Musical Leader* believes grand opera in Boston will be or become: "righteous". The hope: "Boston opera is designed to enter into the daily life of Bostonians, to attract others to the city, to encourage young singers of talent and composers of stage instincts, to make for general musical righteousness.

"Nor need anyone fear that the establishment of opera will be injurious to other musical organization of which Boston is justly proud". Opera is synergistic: "The success of the opera will, on the contrary, awaken addition interest in music as an art". And this was only true; and possible.

With such pearls cast before town and Russell cast up, the time arrives to cornerstone and build a building and try the plan.

Cornerstone is dedicated November 30, 1908 (*Boston Herald*), proudly packed with programs, newspapers, scores, yearbooks, phonograph needles and recordings by singers none being Alice Nielsen the woman chiefly responsible for starting this. She is in concerts out West.

With Eben Jordan "in charge of the exercise", Governor Curtis Guild Jr., Mayor Hibbard and others speak. Henry Russell "who is to be the manager" reads well-wishing telegrams.

Skipping to the other Nielsen, as Alice works West, Amy Leslie (*Chicago News* Dec 7) reviews Hortense Nielsen's production of Ibsen's *Doll's House*. Leslie befriends both sisters. Alice instantly memorizes scores, Hortense dramas; they share artistic tastes, styles, and a common focus on performance arts. They do not combine forces in professional life; their familial reluctance to brag may constrain them from replicating Alice's duo with Duse. Artistic connect between the Nielsen sisters is hinted by Leslie's perceptive analysis of the actress:

"Hortense Nielsen, one of the cleverest stock actresses of the West, has been appearing in Ibsen plays anywhere a door would open intelligently to receive her admirable work, and at Music Hall last night before a grave and interested audience, Miss Nielsen gave her charming portrayal of Nora Helmer in *A Doll's House*. She is a pretty, emotional and sincere young artist, with a kind of stateliness of technique something like Mrs. Fiske's. Miss Nielsen is a sister of Alice Nielsen, although she does not care to add that distinction to her own many reasons for ultimate hope of celebrity.

"Her Nora has moments of splendid tone and grace...severely handicapped by...narrow production and other inadequacies. Miss Nielsen was a figure of eloquence and depth unexpected in an actress so hidden from general acquaintance. She has been a star and has played the most ardent dramas of symbolism and philosophy for more than a year, but her effort to enter the metropolitan reserves has not been attended with the success she deserves.

"The way of the Ibsenite is thorny and discouraging...but Miss Nielsen's intrepid determination and her undeniable talent are paving a road for the great master of Norway no woman has quite been able to travel. She is a brainy, indefatigable artist and so much younger than the average devotee to the mysticisms of D'Annunzio and Maeterlinck as well as Ibsen, that her Music Hall venture is fairly at the beginning of a career which promises vast achievements.

"Her Nora is replete with spontaneity, charm and dramatic power. The great test act, in which Barrymore fell down...and which overpowered Blance Bates, seemed to have no mental or artistic terrors for Miss Nielsen, even when stringent law denied Nora the exquisite scene with her babies for the curtain, a clever substitute did not mar Miss Nielsen's performance as a whole, though the beauty of that one motherly, childlike and willful scene was destroyed. The three Helmer children were not in the Ibsen play at all last night and still it went on vividly without them. Much enthusiastic applause followed her Nora through her doll's growth and a round after the final curtain was for her alone, though her company in the main was adequate".

Hortense plays the regional towns, touring widely. She and husband Charles Quintard hope and plan to open their own repertory theatre; Los Angeles seems promising. Second big hope after the world tour collapsed.

The Nielsen sisters have met many European creatives in the parlors of the arty. Paris parties with Debussy and Maeterlinck brought Josef Urban and the Belgian playwright back to Boston. When Maeterlinck tours America, Hortense acts scenes from his plays and gives his talk for him when his English proves poor. Urban, soon designer and director at Boston

Opera, gives style to Ziegfeld Follies after 1914, artistic director for the Met after 1917; dies 1933. Urban, like both Nielsens, brings to the stage "a heightened sense of life" (*Theatres* 1929).

Fallout from Lee Shubert triggers Alice Nielsen's surprise bankruptcy filing. Despite upcoming debuts at Boston Opera and The Met, before year's end many persons are shocked as she files bankruptcy. While Henry Russell gains power and salary in Boston, his erstwhile patroness in NYC December 16th files bankruptcy No. 11,783.

NY Times reports, "a sensation has been created in theatrical circles in this city of the announcement that Alice Nielsen the comic opera star has petitioned the Federal Court to be adjudged bankrupt" (Dec 17). Lee Shubert has sued Ziegfeld to recover costs related to the producers-sabotaged 1905 Nielsen tour and a grubstake lost gambling. Shubert pulls Alice into the dispute who responds by filing bankruptcy. Interestingly, he ignores any recovery from Henry Russell confirming the remora had no legal management responsibility for the tour as he touted. Shubert and Ziegfeld often go back-and-forth in court for trivial amounts overshadowed by legal fees. Alice claims assets $25 "consisting of wearing apparel" exempt by law, apparently forgetting to list valuable property such as several real estate holdings. Creditors are given as Sam and Lee Shubert for $1,900, milliner Charles Joseph $2,200, and no surprise Max Desci $1,450. The subsequent judgment formally closes Desci's tedious pursuit.

Alice's bankruptcy proceedings draw many Broadway booking offers, which she declines. Next decade will be her most profitable.

Ever the proper Bostonian, Eben Jordan does not like "his people" in lawsuits. Ironically after hiring Russell, Jordan seems careful to shun impropriety as he sells yarn and dry goods. Boston Opera would become a revelation for the retail heir; many Boston singers will be dogged by the usual flurry of harassing Hammerstein lawsuits.

Five days after filing bankrupt (Dec 21) Nielsen joins St. Paul Orchestra in a joint concert with cellist Rosario Bourdon. The program is Mozart, Sibelius' *Swan Of Tuonela* and three orchestra pieces by Grieg. Nielsen "sang with captivating charm". Bourdon played Saint-Saëns *Concerto 1*, not the Herbert or Dvorak concertos for cello. Waiting for Boston Opera to open November, Nielsen sings society events and ever more of her far-flung American concert tours with a pianist plus violinist or cellist.

By year's end, thanks to a miracle only she could create at Park Theatre, the Boston Opera House arises. Alice has achieved strong critical and popular acclaim by returning to America at New Orleans with a Spanish-laden company with Italian operas outshining the Met. She sings amazing schedules to overjoyed audiences. She stacks up critical praise worthy of eternal fame. She survives tragic losses during the Copper Panic; files bankruptcy after a trivial suit by Lee Shubert aimed at Ziegfeld.

The winter opera tour was short; but after all, she must shop for Boston Opera in Europe. Until her stage opens, ever-busy Nielsen focuses on concerts and musicales in Europe and America.

Next year Alice Nielsen opens her Boston Opera and debuts at the Met.

1909: THE ARTIST ON HER STAGE

Alice Nielsen incessantly tours; only during her Bostonian and Herbert years will she skip concertizing. Singing to people is her career, her hobby.

The Sarah Nielsen tribe has settled around NYC, first in Harlem then nearer the sea. Sarah moves to downtown Brooklyn. Brother Erasmus is in Far Rockaway by 1903 the organist for Rev. Herbert Farrer at St. Mary's Star of the Sea, the 1,700 congregation doubling during summers. By the ocean north of NYC, Irish people tend to work wealthy homes in adjacent Lawrence, Italian-speaking people in the fisheries. When Erasmus arrives "dramatics flourished in the parish with the staging of numerous new productions including" of course the fabled *Mikado* and *Pinafore*, reports the Star of the Sea parish history (2006).

January's *Green Book* magazine publishes Alice Nielsen's second version of her *Singing Girl* memoir which first appeared in Columbia SC *State*. Steadily grows over time to a three-issue Colliers' 1932 *Born To Sing*.

Her oft-told tale solidifies. Nielsen speaks of creating "Chicago Concert Company" (not church choir) to launch the teenage barnstorming tour of Kansas and Missouri. As we recall, the only potential group given this style name appears only once over a weekend at St. Joseph Eden Musee.

To previously-listed repertoire, she adds two more songs. "We struck a lot of towns where they had never heard anything later than *Monastery Bells* or *The Sailor's Dream*, and the reception we usually got would have frozen an Esquimo. They didn't like our program because they couldn't whistle the tunes. We sang in town-halls and 'opery houses' where there was no scenery...."

Nielsen sang Lefebure-Wely's *Monastery Bells*. Popular piano piece Arthur Pryor could play easy. Franz Abt's sailor song has English lyrics, however. Alice sang, "*Our ship rides on a stormy sea; Farewell the picture bright and fair, Which fancy fondly drew for me! It was a dream!*"

She retells her shadow-dressing story, now set before St. Joseph's *Eden Musee* where she claims earning $75 to bring the gang to Denver. In 1907, she makes no mention of Omaha, nor the pastor who saves them after a snowy night and gives his salary. Our prima saves that for later.

Early January, *Toledo Blade* (Jan 4) reports Nielsen "although she was financially broken" for purposes of coaxing a bankruptcy court, prepares to sing in South America and "spurned several offers to return to comic opera". She may have if invited by fellow singers, specifics lost to us.

If during much of the year Alice uncharacteristically falls out of the news, this lapse is likely due to her face lift and mole-removal by future partner Stoddard who at the time was married to his first wife. The couple sponsor the Cotillion Society and join theatricals at NY Theatregoers' Club. Such societies often hire Nielsen to sing. Apparently Nielsen met Stoddard at his surgery. Recovery takes her out of the public view a few months.

Reacting to her supposed financial plight, *Chicago News* (Jan 16) gives Nielsen strong advice to do Broadway, get rich, then do what she wants.

Her help is critically needed by new composers to create hit shows. "Here she is, the one and only creature all like herself. A butterfly with the song of a nightingale in her heart and throat, a delicious comedienne, a dainty person of gifts delicate and wonderful, somebody the world wants badly, but she is hitched to a distant hazy star and traveling with kneeboots and hobbles, with her eyes fixed upon the dazzling ultimate.

"There is nothing to it, Alice. Fritzi Scheff has corralled a lot of your money while you have been waltzing with Queen Mab. Come out of it awhile and then you can take your hallucinations carefully packed in bank notes down into the Riviera and build a castle of gold and crystal, and give your own opera to kings and queens and twospots if you like, but stay here and reap your own harvest now. It is still waiting for you, likely".

The unnamed *News* writer had met Nielsen recently. "Alice looks sad and ethereal and has a palpitating, wounded note in her speaking voice but she is obstinate as a little Berkshire and has ambitions immeasurable and glorified by years of inspired study".

She deserves creative support, advises *News*. And others need hers. As she needs new music, new composers need her voice. Critically, she needs quality new operas in English to perform. As in Russia, as in Italy, the opera season for America must have new works.

"She sings beautifully enough to have grand operas written for her, but they have all been written, and poor armies of loving, hoping, glowing songsters who live in the holy clouds of unfulfilled promises grow grander, more angelic and less able to pay their bills every day in the cycle of years".

News advises Nielsen help herself, help new composers, get busy with new works and make money. "It is a measly, scampish, low-down way to look at it, beautiful diva, but...a bird in the comic opera is better than two in a trance".

Chicago's heartfelt advice arises from a practical, innovative town.

Suspicious Boston—left on its own hook—might make opera of Greek fairies and Mexico wars while importing Bolshevik ballet companies for suspicious purpose overseas. Alice needs original American opera.

In short, Chicago warns, no Great American Musical will be created by Boston. Lacks the spirit. What propelled Nielsen to top of Broadway is calling. The old stuff has been done already, Alice: now help make more of the new. Nielsen and Herbert are ideal allies to create the new Great American Musical. Rejected as usual.

February 7, her bankruptcy is discharged (*NY Times*). Debt-free; of those supposed debts wherein the supposed manager wasn't named.

The first and truest account of dealing with Henry Russell is by Loie Fuller (1868-1928) the famed designer and dancer. On Broadway and in the art world since 1891, Fuller is a dance pioneer, the original American in Paris. Her autobiography *Fifteen Years of My Life* (1908), preface by Anatole France. Fuller candidly tells of her successes and problems producing and touring worldwide. Robert Grau tells us, in art-dance "let it not be said that there was ever a real rival to Loie Fuller... ever regarded as an artistic genius" (*Business Man In The Amusement World*, 1910).

Fuller's move to Boston Opera made international news.

Her Russell conflict typifies how the arty conniver treats artists. Her assessment of his character stands the test of time.

NY Times (Fe 14) reports Fuller, "the American woman who invented the color dance" would travel from Paris to "have charge of the light effects and the ballet at the new Boston Opera House". Fuller designs *Rigoletto,*

Faust, Lohengrin and other works the first year. A creative pioneer, in Paris she had developed "an invention which illustrates orchestral music in color", also exhibited in Berlin.

Loie Fuller created the famed Boston Opera design innovations Josef Urban continued to develop; he often receives solitary credit.

Times notes "although Isadora Duncan's dancing class is famous, little is known about Loie Fuller's class. Only a few of her dancers have as yet appeared in public". In Paris, Fuller's ballet on Mendelssohn's *Midsummer Night's Dream* at Theatre Marigny, "elves and fairies and all sorts of strange creatures and Miss Fuller herself will appear for a few moments as a great white bird" (*NY Times* Fe 21).

Fuller and Nielsen met in Paris. Nielsen shops for costumes, sets and creative talent, and convinces Fuller to join Boston Opera. Once there, she must deal with unreliable Russell.

Arriving Boston, Fuller is inspired, "I am glad at last to have full scope for my ideas and an opportunity to put them into practice. Stage lighting as I used it in my dances only half brought out what I wanted to bring out. My latest idea...is the amplification of music in color and this is something which will assist me very much in my work at the Boston Opera House. As a matter of fact, my eyes are so sensitive to light and color that I can't go to the theatre any more with pleasure".

Fuller's designs become the basis of Josef Urban's famed experiments in theatre combining color and music—the standard practice today. Disney's *Fantasia* (1940) uses Fuller's techniques in the opening segment narrated by NYC critic Deems Taylor. Urban was impressed by her work in Paris and Boston, follows her lead. His maleness a bonus dealing with the all-male Boston Opera board and quite obviously, with Russell.

Fuller is first and foremost a choreographer: "I am training my dancers along entirely new lines. I am training them to think and feel and to express their thoughts and feeling in dancing. I don't teach them the steps, but only suggest the ideas to them. I find that gradually they carry these ideas out. I believe that this was the origin of the Greek dance. It was free, spontaneous and full of feeling. If one copies Greek vases one only has succeeded in copying Greek vases, not Greek dances. To get the spirit of the Greek dance, one must feel the dance one's self.

"My idea is eventually to give sacred dances in the churches, and I have an idea of carrying out Tissot's Biblical pictures in dances. In connection with the recent Salome craze, you will perhaps remember that Tissot represents Salome dancing on her hands, with jeweled feet in the air. Curiously enough, I have a Salome dancer of exactly that type. She can do that dance at present, and do it wonderfully. Another little girl I have crawls marvelously. She does all her dancing on the ground. Still a third dances only with her hands. These dances of the hands are a new idea of mine, which I shall make public very soon".

Given Fuller's genius, Isadora Duncan seeks her out. Nielsen's catalytic role is revealed by Duncan's *My Life* (1924): "One night the Western nightingale [Nielsen] brought Loie Fuller to my studio. Naturally I danced for her and explained to her all my theories". Duncan continues, "No imitator of Loie Fuller has ever been able to hint at her genius! She transformed herself into a thousand colorful images before the eyes of her audiences. Unbelievable. She was one of the first original inspirations of light and changing color".

As artistic gatherings continue, American press presses on.

January 19, columnist *Mlle. Manhattan* wildly claims Nielsen would star in *Dollar Princess* at Empire Theatre with "rumors of a fabulous salary proposition go with this pretty report...." Other rumors put Nielsen at Hammerstein's NYC opera. He and Mary Garden were arguing via lawyers over his attempt to share out her "exclusive roles". Garden's solution is to stop rehearsals of *Salome* until he relents.

Obvious answer arrives from *Chicago Tribune* (Jan 21). Nielsen "laughingly disclaims all intention of succeeding to Mary Garden's roles at the Manhattan [Hammerstein], and she says she will not create the title part in *The Dollar Princess*".

Princess, adapted from German by Fall and Ross, ran well in London before opening Broadway September 1909 for 288 shows.

Wealthy parlors were calling for her. "As many concert dates as Miss Nielsen cares to fill have been offered her, and she will be heard at Palm Beach and St. Augustine during the height of the Florida season. Otherwise she will spend the remainder of the season in study and rest" likely from face-lift by future husband Stoddard.

Alice is in Chicago when Pinkie dies, puppy gifted from Pinkerton. She "arrived in Chicago yesterday to fill an engagement for a recital to be given at the home of Mrs. JT Harahan, wife of the president of the Illinois Central Railroad. When she stepped up to the desk at the Auditorium Annex, she found a small envelope containing a cablegram waiting for her. 'Pinkie is dead; earthquake', it read. Miss Nielsen immediately retired to her room. There she shut herself up nearly all day. She had her meals served to her there. Last night, however, she had recovered sufficiently to give expression of her sorrow". Suggests how Nielsen suffered in 1901's abuse aimed to destroy her and her career. By Detroit, grief has dissolved.

Gives her usual pilgrim progress to *Detroit News* (Jan 24), adding the untold tale of why she never holds a dagger in *Lucia*, a performance detail never mentioned before or since. Lucia usually clutches a dagger in the mad scene after she kills who thwarts her as Alice never. And danger lurked, the *Fortune Teller* and *Singing Girl* roles put Alice onstage with real swords and daggers in hand—risky stage business. In such a stage fight, Constantino had accidently wounded a singer seriously.

Playing Lucia at Tivoli, "I was substituted for Ida Valerga, the prima donna who had trained me for the role, and I was frightened to death. When the third act arrived and I knew I had that terrible mad scene ahead of me, I simply went crazy with terror. I begged George Lask, the stage manager [director], to go on and tell the public something—anything—but not to make me go out on that stage. I clung to him and cried hysterically while he pulled me toward the wings. 'Don't! I can't!' I wailed, and I fell in a heap. Mr. Lask lifted me up bodily and literally threw me on the stage".

She makes a joke not uncommon in those days: "That entrance was an enormous hit. Two critics prophesied great things for me". Diva cleverness on critics continues, "I was singing—I don't know what—when I suddenly noticed the dagger Mr. Lask had put in my hand. It was wooden, and there was a splinter loose. Of course, I was hysterical, and that wooden dagger finished me. I went into peals of laughter. That too was a hit. The critics spoke about my mad laughter chilling the marrow of their bones. That is why I never carry a dagger now [in *Lucia*]. I couldn't. I'd roar with laughter".

Whilst Nielsen cracks wise, January 29 Mary Garden gives *Salome* at Hammerstein's. Creates notorious sensation due to veils. Garden dances barefoot, under last veil sports a flesh-colored skimpy for the thrills.

As Hammerstein builds a new opera house in Philadelphia and threatens to expand into Chicago, Otto Kahn of Met officially joins Boston's board and puts Jordan on his (NY Times Feb 27), "It is understood that the two houses will be closely allied". Interlocked boards facilitate interchange of singers and productions, put pressure on Hammerstein.

This Boston-Met alliance was badly confused by writer Quaintance Eaton's *Miracle of The Met* (1984). She claims "the exchange with Boston had turned out rather one-sided: Gatti sent many more hostages than he received. Little lasting impression had been made on NY by Alice Nielsen, George Baklanoff, Lydia Lipkowska, Florencio Constantino, Maria Claessens, Elvira Leveroni, Giovanni Polese and Lankow, no matter what their importance to the Hub". Eaton misleads.

To prove the contrary, consider 1916 *Theatre Magazine*'s story: *Alice Nielsen, the American Patti*. Revealing anecdote about her NYC importance: "Two men at a recent concert [Nielsen at Carnegie]...were discussing the singer. 'There's no denying it', the first one was heard to exclaim enthusiastically, 'she's the American Patti. I wonder why she's not singing at the Metropolitan Opera House.' 'she's engaged to sing there for two performances this season. But it's not enough. An artist of her talent ought to be a regular member of The Metropolitan Company.'"

Musical Courier (Ja 18, 1911) attends Alice Nielsen's Met debut: "special interest was manifested in the performance because...Miss Nielsen is one of the prime favorites of the Boston Opera Company and she is equally admired by a large following in NY. This American prima donna's advancement has been a source of genuine pride to her country-people and opera subscribers, too, have expressed delight over her lovely voice and histrionic ability".

As in LA, her NYC Mimi is a great success: "As the fragile heroine in Puccini's best-loved opera [*Bohème*], Miss Nielsen achieved on this occasion a notable triumph. She invested her impersonation with captivating charm. In the last Act, Miss Nielsen made a most inviting entrance and the big aria was exquisitely sung, and later...the third act emotions were once more stirred by the real pathos of Miss Nielsen's portrayal. Above all, she was thoroughly natural and simple as a girl in Mimi's station should be. Miss Nielsen was born to be loved and cared for by those who learned to value her fine qualities of heart".

Nielsen makes things meaningful; Farrar merely-clever. As Eaton well knew, the causes of Nielsen's absence from the Met's main stage during subscription nights were in fear of her popularity. Boston's own Geraldine Farrar never motivated her hometown to build what Nielsen had inspired, yet had a Met contract giving a monopoly on certain roles on those nights;

and an affair with the conductor. In fact, Nielsen has a large NYC following and national focus. Boston Opera arose from her voice.

At Nielsen's Met debut, critical praise was not evenly distributed.

In the cast: Sharing praise are bassos Andrea de Segurola "one of the moving operatic portraits" and Adamo Didur "of rare value". Yet tenor Dimitri Smirnoff "no more successful than in his recent appearance of Romeo"; and "the Musetta of Bella Alten was a trifle exaggerated". As Marcello, "Antonio Scotti was not 'at home' in the part... his attempts at humor were far from successful"; and "nothing acceptable in the leading of Mr. Podesti".

During February (*NY Times* Feb 28), the foreign prejudice strikes as the Boston manager has hired "former Italian pupil" Cavaliere Sarmiento "a prominent member of Roman society noted for his handsome appearance" with "a fortune of several millions" to appear at Boston Opera. Russell has had a long relationship with Sarmiento. The baritone was with him for studies six years. After singing in Buenos Ayres, he returned to Rome where "serious efforts were made to prevent his accepting any further engagements and it is only due to his friendly relations with Mr. Russell that the Boston public will have the privilege of hearing him". Sarmiento "and his beautiful wife...prominent member of the Roman nobility" by the way, choose to motor "in the Corso every afternoon. Queen Margherita, who is noted for her love of music, takes a personal interest in the Cavalier" singing at Court. With this deed, the Boston manager, indeed, returns to his Paris "apartment in the Rue Spontini" on March 14th before sailing for America March 21st", said *Times*. He keeps his Roman studio in Palazzo Roccagiovino at Trajan's Forum "with a view to returning eventually...." Soon as possible using Boston money. Doesn't live in Boston. No focus on developing Boston culture; plans to return to Europe rich quick. Recall how archly advised Alice to skip Broadway cash to keep him around.

Meanwhile the world watches as Boston Opera grows from the ground as the great gift to world gayety.

During March, LA's resident prophet Julian Johnson sees Christine Nielsen (no relation) sing Alice Nielsen's role in *Fortune Teller* at Grand Opera House produced by Ferris Hartman. Her voice "eminently suited to the demands of the more than ordinarily difficult music of this role".

Boston Opera is bombed March 29 (*Boston Post*). The noise "awakened and alarmed the entire population of the Back Bay, but caused only slight damage to the structure upon which the interest of musical Boston is centered". The motive seems a construction dispute. Although anarchists Nicola Sacco and Bartolomeo Vanzetti go to trial for murder 1921 their connection to the blast and Italian chorus of Boston Opera was never clearly established only because Pinkereton never asked to fabricate it.

April 1909, the truth finally emerges about destruction of Nielsen's Broadway company by Williams & Perley. Where Perley lives and works, Washington and NYC, the papers suppress the story. Western press who hate Williams for shooting an editor in cold blood before the man's wife and in his parlor, cover it.

"A San Francisco legal battle between Williams and Perley revealed the behind-the-scenes tragedy of the Alice Nielsen Company's demise", reports

LA Times (Apr 22). Case continues a year. Slowly a picture of the corruption Nielsen faced in 1901 emerges vicious and cruel.

Meanwhile, 1909's debut Boston Opera has very few changes from the original company Nielsen delivered Park Theatre in spring 1907. Keep in mind, the shareholders who financed Boston Opera House expect Nielsen and Constantino. The stars made the investment attractive.

The new foreign manager is a complete unknown nobody cares of. Yet he attacks the stars who created his job. First target Constantino, almost losing the tenor for Boston's first season! Unknown to Alice, the remora in New Orleans when Constantino arrived, borrowed money or connived a kickback. When the tenor demands repayment, Russell embezzles Boston Opera funds to settle the debt or refund the kickback. Then he hatches a scheme to remove Constantino with deniability. He contacts Hammerstein saying the tenor will refuse a too-low offer from Boston. Constantino signs with the untrustworthy impresario (Hammerstein) who will deliberately insult the singer who recommits to the too-low offer from untrustworthy Russell, securely salaried by Jordan for three years. This scheme is played against Nielsen next. Called a gentleman's agreement; anything but.

Discussing the problem, *NY Times* (Ap 28) explains that when Boston Opera "was originally planned, it was understood that Mr. Constantino would be its leading tenor, but when last December Oscar Hammerstein offered him a contract, he at once accepted it...the contract was for five years". All-too-strangely Hammerstein fails to honor the terms he troubled to sign with the popular profitable tenor star and then goes out of his way to insult Constantino personally. This puts the tenor in a strange plight— a season with no place to sing. Now, all-too-conveniently, the low Boston offer from malicious Russell has appeal.

Constantino's manager Theodore Bauer explains, "It is true that Mr. Constantino will not sing next season at the Manhattan. When he called on Mr. Hammerstein last week at his hotel in Paris, Mr. Hammerstein sent down word that he could not see him". Tenor was insulted as Hammerstein intended. Constantino "sent up word" to speak "a few moments but Mr. Hammerstein's reply was that he did not wish to see him at all".

The tenor then "cabled Mr. Russell of the Boston Opera House that he would accept the contract...Boston...offered him". Hammerstein of course will harass Constantino several years in court over this farce.

Accepting Boston, Constantino tenor returns to Argentina for summer. September 5th he gives *Bohème* in Buenos Aires, Teatro Colón debut.

May 4, Nielsen formally joins the Met, signing with Kahn's new manager Gatti-Casazzi of Milan whose wife is New Zealand singer Frances Alda. Phillip Hale notes, "Where Gatti goes, there goes she. Generous are the operatic fates that watch over her". At the Met until 1929 Alda's "red hair, resonant voice and startling figure dominating the halls wherein she trod as the boss's wife". She overhears Kahn say "as the director's wife it is much better that Alda should not sing here next season". Thinking of Farrar's affair with Toscanini, and others, Alda retorts "I suppose it would be all right if I were his mistress instead of his wife. I resign right now!"

Conflicts mark Russell's management from the start.

After Constantino, he troubles Alice's friend Loie Fuller. Promising in Paris to bring Fuller's company to America as the Boston Opera ballet troupe. After they arrive, Russell returns to Boston for April. He somehow rejects the deal and returns to Paris after planting a false story in the news as if Perley had learned him something.

Fuller of course is in turmoil. Russell has lured her company to Boston then switcharoo pulls a Lee Shubert.

May 1, Russell writes Fuller on Boston Opera stationary, "I much regret that I had to leave NY without seeing you or telephoning to Mr. Cantor".

Sailed Tuesday on *Kaiser Wilhelm II.*

On margins of his note, furious Fuller writes her daughter in Paris: "This is all I have heard or seen or Mr. Russell since he came & told me a week ago that I need not count on any more money from the Boston Opera Co, that—they wouldn't give me a cent!"

Yet Fuller has influential friends: "I and the Senator [Jacob Cantor] wrote to Mr. Flanders [Boston Opera business manager] and we are now waiting answer! This is 10am Tuesday and the *K. Wilhelm SS* has sailed. I presume Mr. Russell is on it as I have not seen him".

Russell deliberately left Fuller stranded without funds. Of course, his words cannot be trusted. Maliciously, he suggested to Fuller that Jordan objects to hiring people involved with lawsuits. If true, naïve Jordan would be strangely unaware of Shubert and Hammerstein; both men sue Boston Opera stars. So seems a canard of many canards.

Fuller tells her daughter Russell snatched "that *Herald* article...about being sued for 50,000...and kept & never gave it back always promising to...so I could not have it to show what he had got me into. Please get his copies, send one to the Senator and keep the other".

The manager manipulates Jordan and demands others obey: "Russell said not to speak of it that Mr. Jordan had said he didn't want to have anybody in the Boston business who had lawsuits. Fancy R. telling me that when it was he who got me into it! And he used it of course, so I wouldn't let other people turn it against him, not the lawsuit but because having done that, there is no excuse to justify his leaving me here like this.

"For any fool in reading [the] article would believe I had not come here without that money being made good to me.

"So when he arrives go see him...ask him what he meant by pretending to us in Paris...and which letter was false, the one he showed us there from Flanders, or the one that Flanders showed to the Senator saying we will not give an advance the 5,000 to Miss Fuller!

"Well, they have left me here and I do not know how to pay my board as the Senator cannot raise a cent. He is overpowered now with things. No, all Russell wanted—jook a crook—was to get the ballet—and once he got me here I was in their hands. He also has only given me December and March 24 performances! & I can hustle for the rest—who on earth would bring 25 people here for 24 performances at their own expense, but it was 'take it or leave it.'"

Russell deliberately insults top creative talents to exploit financially.

Fuller created the "flame dance" which put dancers on panels of illuminated glass. Another Fuller creation, the twirling serpentine dance caught on film. In Boston as a designer she has problems getting designs implemented, "And the lights they had clever people there & they refused to engage the lights unless their electrical engineer accepted them! & then refused them, saying when I came with the ballet, I could light an opera a little at a time & if they liked it, they would install the theatre".

"Ah! God, Russell is all & more than Eva Fairfax said. No wonder she said his methods are known in England [details unrevealed yet hinted by Nielsen's 1905 NYC plight] & he won't come back there for a while". So the American travel on Nielsen's ticket was to escape a London posse.

Eva Fairfax is known as "Rodin's muse". Joseph Jongen dedicates music to her. Rodin's country place which hosts Isadora Duncan and others very likely includes as a guest Alice Nielsen.

Fuller describes Russell, Boston be warned: "He can do things at a minimum, and he doesn't care either how he does it".

Character: "He lies without lying. He deceives without deceiving. He is like an eel. He deceived all the artists too, and they are there in Boston in despair". Talks so cleverly, "When you talk to him he will convince you against all facts and against yourself even".

Nothing in Russell's career contradicts Fuller's accuracy. Her sketch of the sad situation only suggests the number of people impacted.

"One girl is going back because R. said he even promised to keep her in the summer. He only offers her 100 francs a week after they open (without date) to sing small parts!!! Some friends have made up a purse to send her back to Italy to study her roles there, as the conservatory has no one capable of teaching *mise en scene*.

"Well, Mr. Russell has left me here without even saying 'goodbye.' Clarence Markey is going on this ship & Mr. Russell told me last week he was trying to get $200,000 dollars out of him. As Mr. Jordan only gives the theatre and there is not enough capital". Not true.

Russell left lying. Fuller distrusts Russell too little. Boston Opera has exceedingly much capital, more than enough. Even she cannot fathom the depth of Russell's deceits. He has motives to solicit donations: skimming.

"So I suppose that is why R is sailing off on this ship. He is occupied for money for himself & he doesn't care about me".

Correctly states Russell was "occupied for money for himself".

"See Russell—believe nothing except by facts", Loie Fuller closes the handwritten note to her daughter (NYC Library of Performing Arts).

Loie Fuller and Constantino expose the pattern played against many persons and the entire organization. Rascally Russell creates deliberate trouble to manipulate the money for himself. The foreign manager has foreign principles. Without Nielsen he is nothing; without Jordan he has nothing; yet he betrays. Nielsen he cannot confront directly.

Despite betrayals shading the quality Boston Opera hoped to obtain, the dance stars appear onstage. Alice arranges joint concerts with Fuller, Isadora Duncan, and Pavlova. Duncan (1877-1927) began dancing in San Francisco when Alice at Tivoli and when the Nielsens lived in Oakland, gave dance clsess. As with many connections, stories are lost to us.

Dance stars Fuller, Duncan, Pavlova profoundly shape American pop culture. Flowing bodies move minds.

Krehbiel in *More Chapters Of Opera* (1919) captures their influence: "The world has been dance-mad for several years…. Our foxtrotting and tangoing had little to do with the revival of pantomimic dancing by Loie Fuller, Isadora Duncan and the Russian Ballet, but a good deal to do with that popular frame of mind which refuses to demand seriousness in the theatre and is content with a stimulation of the senses".

Fuller, Duncan, Pavlova promote the gayety of nations.

In London May 28 (*NY Times*), Nielsen sings at a benefit for royals, two days later for friend Yznaga who has husband trouble: "Society rallies to American Duchess, even Marlborough's family take side of wife, who is separated from him". After dinner, the band "which had been playing in the hall moved to the gallery in the new ballroom, where four hundred guests assembled for a concert. The Duchess of Marlborough wore a dress of white satin, veiled with white tulle and beautifully embroidered, and the famous Vanderbilt pearls". John McCormack, Destinn, Kreisler, Gillibert, and Alice Nielsen contribute to the night's music program.

On the other shore of the Nielsen sisters, news of a world tour for Hortense surfaces this month. She has a supportive husband, Charles Arthur Quintard who nurtures her career. The Quintards have Huguenot descent; Charles' father from Stamford CN became an Episcopal Bishop and Civil War chaplain in Tennessee on the slavery side. Charles goes by CA Quintard and by CA Arthur. Operates a theatre in New England among a host of Quintards. How he meets and marries Hortense is lost to us. They will live in St. Louis, Connecticut, Chicago, and Los Angeles before resettling near New Haven where Hortense retires. With Alice at Boston, Hortense joins Curry Institute of Expression (now Curry College), performs the Chautauqua circuit and is a well-known theatrical reader (performing all parts solo). This supports her after peak years.

Hortense announces plans to launch her repertory company across the Pacific. Stops are Australia and China, crossing Russia to Europe.

Chicago Tribune (May 30) reports, "When Hortense Nielsen first conceived the idea of making a tour of the world she little knew how big the undertaking would prove". For two years Hortense has prepared her itinerary "which includes the larger cities on every continent in the world except South America". She will "open in Honolulu, Hawaii, in the middle of August, and after playing there for three weeks will proceed to Yokohama for an engagement of equal length, and after that there will be a week or two in Kobe.

"From Kobe the company will proceed to Shanghai for a stay of a month, and the next stopping place will be Hong Kong" for a month. To Manila and six weeks in the Pacific before "sailing to Singapore for a short engagement, and thence to Colombo for a one or two night stand, depending on the sailing of the next streamer". She continues to India for six weeks' in Bombay, then Calcutta, then Cape Town, then "tour the east coast" Africa, stops at Port Elizabeth, Durban, Mombass, Johannesburg, Aden and "other cities where there are a sufficient number of English-speaking inhabitants to make it profitable.

"From Aden they will go to Cairo and Alexandria". Lastly, Europe "from St. Petersburg to Paris, playing in all the larger cities of Germany, Austria, Italy, France, Holland and Belgium and then on to London for a long stay".

Hortense plans to take eighteen people on 36,000 mile trek, including "leading man...John Maurice Sullivan". Sullivan [1875-1949] keeps active on Broadway and made 30 films whilst sisters Hortense and Alice none.

The scope of her undertaking bold. Yet did it happen?

Unlike Alice's opera antiques, Hortense keeps things modern: new drama in English. She selects sixty plays, "standard classical dramas and comedies..., plays of modern dramatists...practically all the plays which have proven successful in America and England for the last two years...."

Astonishing plan proves she and Alice are ambitiously competent.

Hortense speaks freely to *Chicago Tribune*, "I want to give the people what they want, and I have no intention on forcing on them the plays of my choice. My purpose is to entertain the strangers in a foreign land with something that will make them lose sight of their exile for a few hours and permit them to indulge the thought that they are once more back in their native country". Her project carries "60 tons of scenery" plus "personal and costume trunks for the members of the company". Last-minute discovery that only Europe could print flyers for advertising adds ten tons of printing equipment and paper to the cargo. "Canvas billboards will be taken for use in Japan and China, where no billboards exist". Passage has been booked from Minneapolis to Sydney, and all reservations and hotels far as Australia.... And with this announcement the trail runs cold. And by the 21st of September, 1909, Hortense headlines in Doll's House at Sault-Ste-Marie, Michigan. What happens with her World Tour remains unclear.

Lost project or not, astonishing plan. Nielsen sisters are business-savvy artists with big plans who connect many people over active careers.

Grinding along at Boston Opera, Jordan (if ever had doubts attributed to him) has relented about hiring folk with pending litigation. Fuller has influential friends. And as she says, nothing Russell stands scrutiny.

Helped by the Met, Loie Fuller on June 5 (*NY Times*) announces hiring Paul Jones Chute, "one of the most graceful dancers she ever saw" as "premier male dancer of the Boston Opera House for three years".

Chute, "noted in Boston, Newport, and NY for dancing at social functions", opposes pants: "I most certainly believe in knickerbockers as the coming garment for men. Knickerbockers are a logical form of dress. They are comfortable and always neat. They are more easily donned and they permit a greater freedom of movement". Trousers were "a detestable invention of a prosaic age". Knickers, traditional boy garb, are the knee-length pants still seen in baseball games.

More good news for Loie Fuller two weeks later (*NY Times* Jun 19). The Met will sponsor Fuller to appear onstage with fifty pupils. Her contract is "practically a duplicate of that signed with the Boston Opera". Among the "constellation of star dancers selected by *La Louie*" is German-born Rita Sacchetto. The Met also commissions a new Fuller ballet "at the instigation of Andreas Dippel [tenor and Met manager]...for the season of 1909-10". Thereafter the popular Fuller's "Terpsichorean band will tour the country with a symphony orchestra" reports *Putnam's Magazine* (Oct 1909).

In London, Alice Nielsen performs many private concerts. Her American schedule is packed with concert bookings prior to opening Boston Opera.

Musical Courier (Jun 26) illumes her popularity, "If anyone believes that Alice Nielsen...is taking a vacation in London or leading a purely social life prior to beginning what promises to be a busy and eventful season in America next Autumn" her engagements prove otherwise. "A concert here, a reception to sing at, a musicale, appointments with an operatic coach, a costumer, a rehearsal, and so the list goes".

And yet "Miss Nielsen lives quietly in the attractive little apartment which she has taken for the season". Regarding the Met debut, she is "naturally pleased that at last her NY friends will have a chance to hear her in opera under proper auspices". Of Mimi and *Bohème*: "That is perhaps my favorite role. The music, the character—everything about it seems to appeal specially to me. I feel the part when I am playing it".

Musical Courier reminds us that in London "with the waltz song from *Romeo and Juliette* sung with orchestra under Nikisch that Miss Nielsen first appeared as a singer of grand opera...at a concert at St. James' Hall five years ago. Rapid has been the little prima donna's advancement".

In London Nielsen returns to Tosti for coaching. *Courier* tells us they work on her Nedda, Mrs. Ford, Mme. Butterfly.

At the moment she has power to bring Boston an elaborate production of her squashed NYC debut. For *Pasquale*, "Pini-Corsi, engaged for both NY and Boston" has the title role. "The two artists appeared a number of times together in this opera in London four years ago during the excellent season of Italian opera given at the Waldorf Theatre....

Alice adds, "Pini-Corsi is simply delightful in the role. His singing and acting are both wonderful" At Waldorf they posed for photos, "And the faces he makes are, as you can see from the photographs, droll beyond words. I think the pictures are very good, and it is no wonder. He made us all laugh at the photographer's while they were being taken, so it is not strange that I look smiling. They were taken at the time we were singing here together, but have never been published in America".

These players define gayety.

Nielsen speaks graciously of her Met audition. "Gatti-Casazza was very kind when I sang for him before signing my contract. I sang Mimi's aria, the aria from *Don Pasquale* and several other numbers. How nervous I was!"

Disquiet with Russell (scouring deepest Russia for Bolshevik vocalists instead of building the promised American cast for Boston) emerges. He has cast a toxic shadow over the opening.

Alice carefully praises homeland talent: "There is no doubt, surely, that the best women voices in the world are American, and I think that our audiences are the most critical in the world. When they are pleased they know exactly why. The days are gone when anything was good enough musically for America.

"I think the success of two opera houses in NY has been an amazement to Europeans, and I believe too that the building of the new Boston opera house is a marvelous object lesson to European opera-goers".

Almost inadvertently admitting ownership, she possessively states _her_ San Carlo [of SF etc] "disbanded" when Boston Opera became a reality. In America, outside opera she has "devoted herself to concert work and...recitals throughout the country" with three events at Palm Beach alone. Her repertoire holds "old Italian classics as well as the most modern French and German songs".

After London, Alice "will go for a short rest to Salso Maggiore, Italy, that great resort for singers and whose waters she finds most beneficial". The Northern Italian town of Salsomaggiore Terme became an artesian healing resort during the reign of Marie Louise (1791-1847), fashionable since.

As summer progresses, the Boston Opera patron Eben Jordan and son dock back in Boston July 19 (*NY Times*), "returned from a two months' trip abroad... enthusiastic over the new singers engaged". The capitalist heir has been charmed by Russell-approved Bolshevik singers in Paris where communists hold planning meetings to guide a foreign-paid conspiracy of "propaganda and coercion" to hijack Russia into grim decades of Bolshevik tyranny. Ends badly.

Says Jordan, "The great thing in an operatic way in Paris...is the fuss of the Russians. The Russian season has been a tremendous success. Boston will hear some of these Russian stars". Lydia Lipkowski "pronounced the find of the operatic season. Impresarios were after her. I am glad to say" she will sing *Lakme* at Boston. In Paris, the wealthy merchandizing heir had sensed "a lively interest...in what we are doing" in Boston. "Of course our reciprocal relations with the Met...are valuable to us both here and over there", Jordan adds diplomatically, as his *Titanic* Boston Opera builds toward its maiden voyage. American singers?

Soon life would become alike a very grand opera.

CONCERT TOURS GALORE

During winter 1909-10 Alice Nielsen debuts at the Met, opens Boston Opera House, opens Montreal Opera, makes most of seventy recordings by singing up to six discs a day for Columbia, and completes a North American concert tour. Busy winter for the soprano star. John Phillip Sousa recognizes her fame and appeal. Invited to his Sunday concerts at NYC's Hippodrome are "Nellie Melba, Alice Nielsen, John McCormack...." Gatti-Casazza in *Memories of the Opera* (1941) recalls 1909 as the year "of Lillian Nordica's and Melba's return to the Metropolitan" when "important newcomers included...Alice Nielsen".

Alice Nielsen in NYC is deeply enjoyed for the identical reasons stated with critical clarity in LA, Chicago, Boston, Dallas, New Orleans, San Francisco, Napoli, Columbia, Cincinnati, Montreal, Toronto, London. The Met gig gives Nielsen access to a suite she keeps as residence for a decade; a non-Alice Nielsen child we met among foggy circumstances tags along, the Thomas Nielsen who will act as aide and start a promotion agency.

In America she tours in concert over the winter. If summer is taken in the States she uses her huge Maine pagoda or fiancé Stoddard's place at Glen Falls.

For the Met Alice gives only sixteen appearances, five on the mainstage. Others occur during out-of-town tours: Chicago, Baltimore, Philadelphia, Boston, Brooklyn. Her 1910 peak is eight: Caruso twice: *La Bohème* April 6, 1910 at Chicago and *Pagliacci* at Boston April 17, 1912. Alice's last Met concert is a sudden 1915 *Il Barbiere di Siviglia* to replace ailing Hempel.

And this for a singer of such popularity. Her own company was hailed superior to the Met. Nielsen's access to the Met main stage is blocked by internal schemes. The Met wasn't built for her. Boston is. At Boston Opera's grand opening, she sings in a superb new theatre built by her own spark, outfitted to her taste and intended to last as legacy forever.

The moment's real meaning must be imagined for an artist of Alice's sensibilities, arising busker kid in Kansas City.The stars are onstage albeit the manager a scheming swamp. Loses legacy.

Power corrupts only those who are corruptible.

Yet Jordan is an honest trader who adds value. His trade caters to respectable Boston housewives who shop on hubby's money. Nielsen is independent, outspoken, a self-made star, a praised artist, an American cultural icon. She is divorced, has had lawsuits, filed bankruptcy, enjoys Irish-Catholic and Danish-Mormon connections. Has gambling pals, knows Diamond Jim and his girl Lillian Russell. Associates with the most-talented performers. Works intensely at making herself great. Has a child. Starred Broadway, singing and dancing in very tights. Seasoned theatre pro who sang on Kansas City streets as a child. She has seen very kindly both nude Hawaiians and kissing Germans. Not a Puritan shocked and afraid. She has that positive humor of the artist set.

Alice Nielsen had not stayed at home leading a quiet life. She absorbs song: *Traviata, Butterfly, Faust, Carmen, Satanella*. To Jordan, Nielsen could be formidable. She may boost Jordan's kids to careers in the arts and to marry who they really wanted. Does not invite her to the Board. No woman informs Jordan's board. Nordica has compelling experience and financial purse. Nordica and Nielsen are theatre experts. Mrs. Gardner would have made Boston Opera more secure. Covent Garden has Gladys Grey, Mrs. Gardner was lost to Boston Opera.

Nielsen and Constantino created Jordan's opera brand. Knowing this, Russell targeted the tenor. The stars who put him in his place. And could stop him Nielsen speaks truly, her blood is the building foundation. She guarantees quality productions. Made possible the business and creative case for Boston Opera. Her talent and fame justify the investment to Jordan, justify the sponsoring shareholders who crowd-sourced Boston Opera House, justify the audience buying tickets to see...her.

And Alice brings her address book of contacts. Merchandiser Eben Jordan recognizes her value proposition. When she meets the Jordans during her Park Theatre gig and pitches the Boston Opera she wishes to create, she advocates her project just as she had suggested Tom Williams invest the Alice Nielsen Company. The lackey on her payroll last seven years hates truth be told. For Jordan, as for Williams, Nielsen is obviously the right wave to catch. Do they do her justice? She wants to sing. Jordan foresaw the newest fashion trend, an opera fad hinted by Alice Nielsen's touring triumphs. Acts fast to beat Chicago and New Orleans.

Character counts. Jordan ignored prudent advice by others. Pick people with local roots and observable talent. That's the essence of competent political ecology. Much as Nielsen wishes an American home, Russell wishes a return to Europe. That is the downfall. He uses Boston to feather his Paris nest. From the start, Russell's actions contradict claims to build the Boston opera institution. Russell deploys deceit described accurately by Loie Fuller.

Jordan pays a costly lesson by the rah-rah loyalty to the boys' club.

Stockholders believe they invest Nielsen, Nordica, Constantino. They welcome the offerings of Boston Opera promising to popularize, promising to cultivate American talent. "Native talent would be fostered through an opera school" at New England Conservatory which Nordica endows.

Bait-and-switch.

Foreign manager never seeks American singers. Spends costly months sifting Russia and Paris for hires who agree to kickbacks. Russell taunts the talent who got him the job, advocates destroying the star system.

Excluded from the oversight board, the priceless stars lack contractual guarantees to continue within the opera house they inspired.

Nielsen made miracles by cooperation and competence. Who could create a West Coast success from NYC disaster yet finish with a big contract from New Orleans Opera? In 1909 Alice Nielsen believes she will be set for life on Hemenway street.

Managerial expectations? Consider Alice's friend Maurice Grau. Calvé describes "the genius...one of the most intelligent as well as one of the ablest impresarios I have ever known. He was more than a capable business man. He was an artist and an enthusiast as well. If he considered an opera about the average, a true work of art, he would produce it without regard to its money-making possibilities". Grau "was always a thoughtful and considerate manager in his relations with his artists, interested first and foremost in achieving artistic success. That practical and financial success should follow was not distasteful to him, but at least it did not blind him to other issues!"

Russell except for the required weeks in a Boston hotel, lives in Europe.

So it is. From the start of Russell as salaryman, the story is faked.

Here's his official press release: "Two men shared the responsibility for the daring Boston venture.... Henry Russell, a bold impresario from London who had piloted a troupe named after the Naples San Carlo company thru the US for several seasons, enlisted the hearty support of Boston's department-store prince, Eben D. Jordan of Jordan-Marsh, who guaranteed a roof for Russell's coterie". Rather false by far.

Nielsen, Nordica, Constantino reduced to "a troupe".

August 18, *Musical Courier* reports Alice returns soon "from Switzerland where she is just now spending a few weeks. She and her mother have been living in NY, but will remove to Boston this fall and live somewhere in the Fenway district" within a block of the opera house.

August 29 (*NY Times*), Russell "returning home, successful beyond all hopes". The season has thirty standard works and one novelty, *Auton* by Cesare Galeotti. Few famous singers, "aside from Nordica, Nielsen and Lipkowska". As he had Nielsen's NYC debut, Russell packs the place with cheap. Even so, its chorus "Scotti of the Metropolitan helped to form will include 125 singers", orchestra ninety.

Ballet and lighting directed by Loie Fuller.

September Nielsen sails. Short NYC stay. Does not rest for her double debuts at Boston and Met. Embarks on ambitious concert tour crossing Canada and States on a schedule so busy her debuts seem anticlimactic.

Her plans precipitate publicity. *New York Times* (Se 20) produces a full-page feature: "Alice Nielsen Tells of Opera Triumphs" As usual, Nielsen speaks of another singer first, reminding *Times* that she and Marguerite Sylva sang in the same comic opera company: Alice's own. Sylva, now a renowned Carmen, works with Hammerstein. Nielsen reveals her first *Bohème* had been "without even an orchestra rehearsal. Mr. Caruso was so kind to me on this occasion, all the time that he wasn't singing he was giving me stage direction". She implies this was Covent Garden, but the tale arose in fog-shrouded Napoli.

September 25th, *Musical America* meets Alice at the dock. "Looking a little more mature than when she charmed NY seven years ago in *The Singing Girl*, Alice Nielsen the prima donna soprano of the Metropolitan and Boston opera companies, arrives in NY on the steamship *Cretic* of the White Star Line". Nielsen intriguingly states she will sing at the Met Elsa in *Lohengrin*, Marguerite in *Faust*, and Mistress Page in *Falstaff*. That is her expectation.

"Am I glad to be back in NY again? Well, what would you think when after years of hard work with one aim, I have at least attained my ambition—to sing in leading roles at the Metropolitan Opera House?"

She paraphrases that 1901 hint of Laurence Irving (*London Times*) to chase grand opera, "I will go before the most critical audience in the world at the Metropolitan confident that I shall please". Speaks with authority: "I have had success abroad in roles that I will sing here, and since my appearances abroad I have been perfecting myself in my art".

Musical America remarks on Henry Russell's factual, not fanciful, pedigree by saying that two years ago Nielsen "was a member of the San Carlo Opera Company [of SF] of which Mme. Lillian Nordica was the head, and toured the Middle and Far West...but she was not heard in this city".

And so it was.

Reporters take the hint about Sylva and Alice, the pair at "rival opera houses, the Manhattan and the Metropolitan, were at one time members of the same comic opera organization" (*NY Times* Se 29). "I am so very glad that she has made a success. I have always considered her a remarkable personality, and she is one of the dearest little women in the world. As for me, I am just about as happy as I can be, because I am realizing the ambition of my life, to sing opera in the Metropolitan", said Alice, adding ambiguously "I don't know yet in what part nor when, but I am a member of the company and I am to sing there. I could not want anything more. I am also to sing at the Boston Opera House, but the details have not as yet been arranged".

Speaking from her "apartments in the Hotel Willard", Nielsen recounts her pilgrim progress, emphasizing without naming Ida Valerga's coaching. Skips the Williams & Perley gang: "All the time that I had been singing in light opera I had remembered the trills of *Lucia* and the jewel song from *Faust* and I was always waiting for a chance to sing them again. The London critics said such nice things about my voice that I thought this might be a good time to leave the comic opera stage". Yes, diva.

Delivers accurate details: "I made my debut in *Faust* at Theatre Bellini in Naples. I sang Marguerite eighteen times and *Traviata* twenty-eight times that season. The following season I was engaged for the San Carlo Opera Company of Naples, where I sang fourteen performances of *Traviata*. Then Mr. Higgins engaged me for the grand opera season at Covent Garden in the Spring of 1905. I sang Zerlina in *Don Giovanni* and Suzanne in *Le Nozze de Figaro*. Hans Richter conducted".

Careful to qualify genuine San Carlo "of Naples" before she misleads: "In the fall of 1905 Henry Russell brought the San Carlo Company of Naples to Covent Garden and I sang in this season *Rigoletto, La Traviata, Barbiere, Don Pasquale* and Micaëla in *Carmen*". San Carlo's manager De Sanni sent his company to London. If Alice is not yet undeceived, much later Russell admits he was excess baggage.

October 3, Loie Fuller brings Boston "a ballet of fifty young girls from Paris, all her pupils and many of them members of well-to-do families". Her French studio was "a round building, a copy of an ancient Pompeian house. She sits on a raised dais, while imparting her rules. The girls learn to pose, skip, run and play. Each girl, on coming under the guidance of Miss Fuller, gets a fanciful name and no girl is allowed to divulge her identity".

Abandoning Boston, Nielsen leaves NYC for a long North American concert tour. Typical example, October 4th in Des Moines "the evening of grand opera in Central Congregational church last evening was a musical event of an exceedingly high order. Not only were the leading singers of the first rank, but the supporting company was of unusual excellence.

{Alice Nielsen's singing was a constant delight. Her beautiful voice is probably most appealing in music that is not very dramatic but she has a temperament that makes her impassioned signing exceedingly effective. She enters into the spirit of everything she sings, and her facial expressions emphasize the impression made by the feeling that she voices in song. One listens to her with eyes as well as ears, for she has a very fascinating appearance. Her vocal technique is so good that she gets her great variety of effects without apparent effort. In songs like *The Moon Drops Low* by Wakefield Cadman, songs of a subdued character, she displays the great beauty of her voice to advantage. In the selections from *Madame Butterfly* she shows great ability in the higher part of the scale and in music demanding powerful utterance. In fact she is an all-round artist, about equally pleasing in whatever she sings".

Minneapolis, Fargo, Grand Forks; Nielsen reaches Winnipeg October 5th, a "rare treat for Winnipeggers". The coloratura singer "lives and her art is glorified in Alice Nielsen. Alice Nielsen has lived and has let her voice live".

Meanwhile *Boston Globe* (Oct 23) assures readers she'll be back, "Alice Nielsen, prima donna soprano of the Boston and Metropolitan opera houses" will go to Indianapolis, St. Louis, Denver and Chicago and return

November 1st "for the opening of the new Boston Opera House, of which she is to be a prominent feature" says ever-faithful albeit wishful *Globe*.

October 24, *Indianapolis Star* calls to Nielsen over at Claypool hotel using a newfangled "telephone". At 8pm her maid says, "You can't possible see Miss Nielsen" who "has retired and I can't disturb her now".

Alice overhears and takes the phone, "I've just had my bath and my dinner and had gone to bed. I know you must have heard me hit the floor. And if I have a cold tomorrow I shall blame you for it", she laughs. She claims to stand "on tiptoe to reach a telephone that must have been built for a woman six feet tall. Perhaps you have seen that famous painting 'Ambition' —a woman standing tiptoe with her arms extended toward the sky? I feel just so about my work. I am ambitious to accomplish just as great things as possible. If you haven't seen that painting, just imagine me tiptoeing to speak into this six-foot telephone".

Star reveals Nielsen is to sing at Caleb Mills Hall "inaugurating the People's Concerts' series". She is "worrying little about her debut this winter with the Metropolitan. She is thinking about it of course, and waiting for it anxiously, but she is confident of herself and believes in herself. It is no little distinction to her to be chosen successor to Mme. Marcella Sembrich.... Still the charming and delightfully sparkling and hopeful woman of the days when she sang the melodies of Victor Herbert and was hoping then for the successes that now have come".

Her concerts keep the familiar pattern.

Indiana is Standing Room Only. People are seated onstage. Typical of reactions to Nielsen's concert programs that year will be the *Star* review.

Indianapolis Star Oct 25th: Alice Nielsen, Nordica's Romayne Simmons at piano, provided "an evening of rare enjoyment for about 1,800 people, this exceeding by nearly two hundred the usual seating capacity of the hall. About one hundred seats were placed on the platform, and whenever Miss Nielsen came on the stage it was through an aisle of delighted auditors". She sang twenty-six songs "of great variety and so arranged that gay followed grave and all were full of poetry and music combined, words having some meaning when delivered with such clearness. The songs without exception were choice, and each one was sung with such a perfection that it seemed a jewel of purest type".

Nielsen compels attention, as 1894 SF realized by *Satanella*.

"Her personality is magnetic. She is gracious and dignified in manner and at the same time full of spirit, as shown in the little way in which she let action suit the song".

And a glory voice: "Her voice is of a beautiful quality, rich and pure, every tone perfectly emitted, every word enunciated with distinctness and also with distinction. Whenever a song was finished one felt that it had been sung with a completeness that left nothing to be desired.

"No less artistic...accompanist, Mr. Simmons, for voice and instrument were in absolute harmony. The accompaniment was not for an instant subservient; it was a part of the song". Of arias *Un bel di* and *Ah fors e lui*, "seldom in a whole lifetime is it heard sung so artistically and so brilliantly as by Miss Nielsen".

Encored Loomis' *In A Little Dutch Garden* before starting the Richard Strauss group *Night, Morning* and *Serenade*, "and then riches piled on riches" with *Si Mes Vers* (Hahn), *Mis Piocirella* (Gomez), *Im Kahn* (Grieg), *Who Knows?* (Clough Leighter), Leoncavallo's *Mattinata* plus two by Hammond.

Nielsen's ambition "to become a great singer is being realized, and the friends that thought she was foolish to waste her years in further study for grand opera admit that she has won". After Tosti's *Good-bye*, Nielsen takes "a bouquet of Killarney roses from Mrs. Hugh McGowan, who knew her when they were girls together in Kansas City" in St. Patrick's choir.

Denver on October 28, joined onstage by the Met's famous Scotti, her skill at concert singing "without a net" dominates the baritone.

Twas a great and fashionable gathering.

Musical America reports, "Nielsen captures favor of Denver, overshadows Scotti in their joint concert. The audience at the Nielsen-Scotti concert resembled a gathering at the Metropolitan during grand opera season. Practically every seat in the great Auditorium Theatre was occupied, and as the [Robert] Slick concerts have the approval of Dame Fashion, this great audience was remarkably well dressed".

Barefoot in Kansas City, or starring *Fortune Teller*, or starring grand opera, so with art songs: "The audience was predisposed in Scotti's favor since he bears the greater reputation in the operatic world, but as the evening wore on, Miss Nielsen's joyous personality and the exquisite delicacy of her art won first place in the audience's favor".

Romayne Simmons accompanies the singers.

Nielsen "revealed great versatility in her offerings, singing the *Madama Butterfly* second act aria and the *Traviata's Ah Fors e Lui* in Italian, a group of Strauss songs and one by Grieg in German, Bemberg's *A Toi* in French and Tosti's *Goodby* and Strauss's *Serende* in English. Her encore numbers, all in English, included one or two piquant things which brought out the playful Nielsen of light opera days".

Scotti's Italian songs: "cloying, artificial, sentimental... Incidentally, Scotti's diction even in his native tongue, was far from pure".

Another haunting Halloween: Shubert collects from Ziegfeld on the "financially unsuccessful concert tour made by Miss Alice Nielsen in 1905". Court appointed referee to resolve conflicting financial accounts. The decision follows the unfollowed contract. Alike Williams & Perley, a secret is exposed: Russell had surrendered Nielsen over to Ziegfeld and Shuberts for a few pieces of silver.

Ziegfeld, "it appears, secured Miss Nielsen through Henry Russell...an impresario, under the agreement that she was to receive twenty percent of the receipts and Russell ten". Pretty big cut for himself. Half her take. No discussion of the cash advances put into the remora's hands. Ziegfeld guaranteed $500 per performance and made a contract with Shubert, "who agreed to take an equal share in the remaining seventy percent". Tour ended September 1905 showing, says Shubert, a loss of $17,331. Shubert sues Ziegfeld for $5,000. And the fog gathers over the wreckage.

November 1st (*Boston Globe* Nov 2), Nielsen returns to Boston. Nordica and Constantino arrive; Boston Opera tenor Christian Hansen visits NYC for *Otello* at the Met "in accordance with the working agreement existing between the two organizations".

NY Times touts Boston Opera's Monday opening "one of the most important events in Boston's musical circles...Boston now stands on a par with other great cities of the world" and "bids fair to outrival many of the older houses (Nov 6)".

Richard Aldrich, severest critic of Nielsen's Casino trials, heralds her approach to the Met in *NY Times* Nov 7th: "Alice Nielsen is well known here for her appearances in Victor Herbert operettas. She has sung in higher forms of opera with the San Carlo Company [of SF etc] but she makes her NY debut in grand opera at the Metropolitan". Skips sad *Pasquale* fiasco.

At Hammerstein's "young Irish tenor" John McCormack will make his American debut in *La Traviata*. McCormack makes millions by recordings, never joins for a Nielsen duet. She records with Constantino.

November 6, new-formed Chicago Grand Opera announces "its 20-weeks' season", aligned with Met and Boston to bring Caruso, Melba, Louise Homer, Constantino, Nielsen to town. City of Boston has "after much discussion and dissension" completed a short street named Opera Place to connect the stage door with Huntington Avenue.

All is ready.

BOSTON OPERA HOUSE OPENS & MET DEBUT

Boston Opera opens its doors November 8, 1909. The fifteen-week season offers fifteen Italian, four French, one German opera. Construction of the White Star's *Titanic* had begun the previous March. Alice Nielsen gives her world premier as Butterfly and sings *Bohème*, *Pasquale*, and others from her repertoire.

Monograph of the Boston Opera House by Frank Jackson (1909) gives elaborate detail on a building now lost to us.

Printed for the ages, provides photographs of participants. Speed and quality of construction marvelous to behold.

Cornerstone states: "This stone was laid by Eben D. Jordan, 1 December, 1908". Jackson tells us, "In the earlier stages of this huge undertaking, Mr. Parkman B. Haven of the firm of Messrs. Wheelwright & Haven, well known architects, was called in. He formed his general idea of stage plan and equipment and made disposition of galleries, circles, boxes &c, after a careful study of the most up-to-date European Opera Houses— a plan such as would enable one of the largest Boston audiences to hear and see without the slightest impediment". Contractor George W. Harvey.

The building, "unique effort in theatrical architecture...in which neither money nor talent has been spared", was built in a year. "The most perfectly equipped building of its class seen in America. In the multitudes who pass through Huntington Avenue every hour of the day, many will now become conscious of the beauty of this new building among the other fine buildings which have been and are being erected in its vicinity.

"For the facades...red brick and cream-white terra-cotta facings were selected" to harmonize with surroundings. "The elevation on the main street is 132 feet; western return end is 220 feet. The façade is divided into three parts—the center...three windows divided by four renaissance columns and surmounted by a pediment, and two ends or staircased towers completing the whole. Under the main cornice and recesses are emblematical statuary bas-reliefs by Bela Pratt". East elevation same design. Bela Pratt (1867-1917) had sculpted "Personifications of Art and Science" gracing Boston Public Library; designs several famed US coins.

Hall interior pearl-gray and gold. Traditional red seats, boxes and carpets. Crescent of boxes about parquet trimmed with pale gold Carrara marble. The foyer "the customary neutral gray". Over the proscenium arch are carved the names of Gounod, Gluck, Wagner, Verdi, Mozart.

We voyage into cold murky depths to view the tragic glory of Boston Opera House. "Let us approach the theatre through the main entrance in the front façade. This is rectangular and treated in the severe Doric order with engaged columns and simple-beamed ceilings. Appropriate box-office windows and the manager's office are adjacent. The Carriage Entrance is on the east side of the building and is approached through five spacious doorways, giving easy ingress and egress.

"From the broad elliptical promenade following the line of the box tiers, two spacious staircases give access to the upper tiers and the Foyer. The boxes on these tiers are made private by mahogany doors bearing the owners' names on them. The Foyer is a fine room of ample dimensions with a barrel-vaulted ceiling pierced by three arched windows. The walls are treated in classic relief and tinted to the soft tones of the grays generally used in the theatre".

Interior design, twice expanded due to demand: "2,750 seats in the house. 634 in the orchestra stalls, 150 in the first tier of boxes, 174 in the second tier of boxes, and the balance in the side tiers of boxes; 644 in the first circle; 754 in the second circle, and there is some standing room".

Eighty-four boxes "are arranged in two grand tiers and in triplicate bays on either side of the proscenium. Each is carpeted and furnished with appropriate gold chairs covered in tapestry. A small mirror and clothes-pole are the useful finishing touches".

Colors are "grays, ivory and antique dull gold...relieved by the Burgundian red used in the box hangings and proscenium curtains and valences. It will be noticed there is no gold in the draperies, the relief being obtained by embroideries and trimmings... the contrast of materials giving the desire effect".

Innovative interior has clear sight lines thanks to the brilliant designers and engineers. "It will be noticed too, that the view of the stage from the back rows in unimpeded by columns. All the tiers of the new Opera House are supported by immense steel cantilevers ...being introduced into modern architecture by this and kindred uses of strong light material such as steel. Theatre-goers will no doubt prefer the upward curve of the galleries and circle rows to the old-fashioned level rigid line. It is more pleasing and lighter in every way. Although the interior of the new Opera House presents a combination of form and color that for simplicity, taste and skill are perhaps unique.

"The opening to the stage is based on a true ellipse, and has a gradual recessed line, consisting of well-defined members, to about twelve feet. The ornament is in Italian Renaissance and is treated in antique gold with slight embellishment of color. The dimensions of the theatre opening are 39 feet high and 48 feet wide. The stage is "one of the highest and deepest in any theatre, and without doubt the most perfectly equipped in the world...the construction and arrangement of the stage are absolutely unique. The whole admirable system has been devised by Mr. Castle-Bert, theatrical mechanist".

The building's "electric switches and telephones" send "orders, messages of all sorts to actors, managers, scene-shifters and everybody in fact employed in the theatre, are transmitted in a moment". Fire safe with sprinklers "like so many shower-baths".

Walter Sabine [1868-1919], Harvard professor of physics, rendered the architectural acoustics. He designed Symphony Hall. The scientific unit of sound absorption is named the sabin, founder of the science.

Construction team: Architects: Wheelwright & Haven; Builders: Geo. Harvey & Co.; Consulting Engineers: Hollis French & Allen Hubbard; Interior Decorator: Frank H. Jackson; Draperies and Furnishings: Jordan Marsh Co.; Painting and Gilding: Max Phillip; Terra Cotta: Atlantic Terra Cotta Col; Steel: New England Structural Co.; Electric Lighting: Foster Electric Co.; Electric Fixtures: Caldwell & Col; Heating: Bradlee & Chapman; Elevators: Otis Elevator Col.; Plumbing: Pierce & Cox; Ornamental Iron: Winslow Bros; Stage Steelwork: AB Robins Iron Co., Cummings Machine Works and George T. McLaughlin Co; Glass: Pittsburgh Plate Glass Co.; Floors: De Paoli Mosaic Association; Soda Fountains: American Soda Fountain Co.

The Company: Eben Jordan, President; Frederick Converse, Vice-president; Charles Hayden, Treasurer; Robert Jordan, Secretary; Edwin Westby, Assistant Secretary. The Board: N.L. Amster, Samuel Carr, George Chadwick, Frederick Converse, George Fearing Jr., Ralph Flanders, Charles Hayden, Eben Jordan, Robert Jordan, Otto Kahn, Gardiner Lane, Charles Loeffler, Francis Peabody Jr., Thomas Perkins, Eugene Thayer Jr.

The Foreign Advisory Committee: Russell's traveling pal Lord Grimthorpe, London; Alice's ever-helpful F. Paolo Tosti, London; Max Lyon, Paris; James Hazen Hyde, Paris; Isidore Braggiotti, Florence.

The Staff: Henry Russell, managing director; William MacDonald, business manager; musical conductors Arnaldo Conti, Wallace Goodrich; assistant musical conductors, A. Luzatti, Oscar Spirescu; regisseur general, Delfino Menotti; Chorus master, Oreste Sbavaglia; assistant chorus master Ralph Lyford; prompter, E. Lombardi; Ass't Treasurer, William Hall; general press representative Theodore Bauer; NY Press representative, Willard Coxey; Russell's scheming bagman and private secretary Randolofo Barocchi; Master of transportation, Walter Hearn; Box Office, Fred Pond; Program publisher, Joseph Woodhead; Stage managers, Antonio Muschietto, Raymond Roze, C. Urban; Scenic artists, Pietro Stroppa and Hugh Logan Reid; Costumer, Antonio Favretto, Ass't Martha Pellegrini; Ballet mistress, Baubl Muschietto.

Designer Loie Fuller was denied the staff list.

To founders, investors, and subscribers, Boston Opera House symbolizes hope and unity—and a decided focus on America and Americans: "An opera house of beautiful proportions and unlimited resources; a company of gifted and eminent singers; a chorus a proportion of which are American singers; a ballet of American dancers; an opportunity to enjoy grand opera at lower rates than was ever known before; and best of all, the definite launching of a movement which will make grand opera in America what it is in Europe—an institution adapted to the native sprit and temperament and calculated to develop the formant American musical instinct—all of these things are realized with the inauguration of the Boston Opera House".

Public support: "doubtful whether in the musical history of the world there is to be found a more remarkable instance of unity of purpose that that which has been manifested by the Boston public in its willingness to support this splendid Opera House of its own".

Amazing achievement in two years is "not due to any supernatural power but to the resistless energy of a man [Eben Jordan Jr.] who believes in his life's work, and to the enterprise and patriotism of the music-loving people of not only Boston but of the entire New England states. And let us hope this influence, begun so quietly and bearing fruit so rapidly, is destined to be felt eventually in every part of the United States".

As democratic as the region: "Boston Opera House is the centre of the movement which promises to make opera part of the common life of the American people; not something whose enjoyment is restricted comparatively, as heretofore, to the wealthy few, but something that will be acceptable to the masses and that will tend to awaken them to an appreciate of the great masterpieces of music".

Since Nielsen's arrival, the demand for opera greatly increased. "A movement like this had to come. The widespread interest in opera which has manifested in this country during the past few years made it inevitable. Year after year [since 1907 Park Theatre] the demand for opera increased until...it had to find expression in just such a movement as Boston has given birth to.

Civic pride: "It was natural that Boston should be its birthplace. It is in line with the undisputed reputation of general culture which the city has long held. Boston has also been for years the center of musical culture in America. Its orchestra and chamber concerts are famous all over the world. Its Symphony Hall is without parallel, and choral music is cultivated here as in no other American city. "In one thing however was Boston lacking...it was without an opera house. The only opera it heard came every spring when the NY companies, exhausted by the hard winter's work, made their visit, staying only a week or two, with their chief singers returned to Europe and thus offering uneven performance which only half satisfied the hungry music-lovers who always craved for more. And every spring Boston music-lovers felt a keen desire to free themselves from dependence upon other cities for their opera".

Eben Jordan and his investors and his builders have much to be proud.

Three years' promoised salary Russell grabs credit as "the one man who was capable of...the scheme". Ironic very as we shall see soon.

Press agent is his hireling. Park Theatre season drops from view: "December 1907, the success of a brief season of the San Carlo Opera Company [of SF etc] at a local theatre [by context the Majestic] aroused an enthusiasm which amounted to a sensation".

The fabulous foreign manager on the lam from London, "who brought the San Carlo Opera Company [of SF etc, of Nielsen and Nordica, never of Naples' San Carlo] to Boston, the man who organized it and who was responsible for its success, was the one man who was capable of projecting, organizing and putting into execution the scheme to give Boston what it had so long desired".

One imagines he sings songs, dances ballet, conducts orchestra, plays instruments, applauds himself. Inspired the *American in Paris* scene. In his own publicity Russell claims to be "a remarkable man, perhaps the most remarkable in the operatic world today". Age thirty-seven "he has crowded into those years an immense amount of activity of a rare sort..." teaching by hour and playing piano at aristocratic parlors. Puffing his pathetic past, Russell cleverly pushes the regional education button. His "set purpose" now is to give "opera a wider scope as an educational and ennobling influence by placing it within the reach of a constituency which embraces all walks of life, he sensed the psychological moment in Boston and proceeded to take advantage of it". And remotely do so from Europe.

Many know him better.

Of course, Jordan made the Boston Opera project happen. He "fulfilled a long-cherished ambition and desire by offering to provide the city with an opera house and give an ample guarantee of the expenses...for the first three years".

Frederick Converse, "eminent American composer...made a personal appeal to Boston society leaders and music-lovers, and with the cooperation of Mr. Robert Jordan and his secretary Mr. Edwin Westby, the fifty-four boxes were subscribed for almost immediately".

Thanks to Alice Nielsen's success with her co-stars at Park Theatre.

Exposing Russell's lies to Loie Fuller, all money to equip the theatre was raised by selling $100 shares to public subscribers enthused by the Nielsen performances.

And "much credit is due" Ralph Flanders for "able assistance he rendered Mr. Russell in the organization..." while absent in Paris of lurking in revolutionary Russia most of that year with a luxury expense account beyond reckoning. Now enjoying a three-year salary, staff, office, expense account, and contract powers, Russell does not share the wealth. Singers must sing for their suppers without secure multi-year contracts and if they are new hires, pay bribes. Flanders won't last long; too competent.

Touching on Nielsen's mission to shop sets and costumes, scenery is "painted by P. Stroppa of Milan and Oliver Bernard of London. Costumes are "designed and made by Mr. A Faveretto and Mme. Marta Pellegrini", the "foreign costumes by C. Chiappa of Milan and E Ascoli of Venice". Wigmaster is Vittore Miglietti. Properties and furniture by RF Brunton of London, foreign properties by E Rancati of Milan.

The manager-approved official Boston Opera history by Jackson gives no credit Nielsen. An invoice for Boston Opera Costumes preserved in

Columba's Joseph Urban reveals *Satoria Teatrale Chiappa* in Milan, costumers for *La Scala*, created the fashions Nielsen selects for the Boston cast of *Mefistofele, Faust, Manon, "Guiletta e Romeo"* and other productions. The invoice has a section, "Costumi la Sig. Nielsen" which details pieces for *La Bohème, Don Pasquale, Fritz,* and *"cappelli a Bohème"*.

Talks between Alice Nielsen, Loie Fuller and Josef Urban seem lost to us. Details of planning stage design, costumes, and lighting at Boston Opera would be fascinating to discover. The Boston Opera stage design is admired from the start, two years before Urban appears and gathers his laurels. Nielsen and Fuller put things in motion.

Contradicting promises to shareholders to promote American talent, "artists of the Company have been engaged from almost every nation of the world. No particular country has been favored by the Director" who never seeks Americans in America. Denying reality, "yet American singers figure largely in the list of prima donnas. It is his firm belief that in the years to come the great international and cosmopolitan blood of America will supply us with all the operatic talent we need". Confusing by plan.

Nations are protected cultural ecologies. The great international? As Bakunin warned against in his 1880s critique of pal Marx? Sure.

Russell wants Alice out. She knows his truth. He cannot suppress her.

And she knows what she wants and why. She has art. On her stage.

So it is. Boston Opera begins its maiden voyage, "brave and beautiful... more than an opera house. It is a thing of romance and youth and beauty, and it is 'of the people, for the people, by the people".

Three days before opening workmen ordered out. Stage prepped.

Nordica gives *La Gioconda* . Two days later, Nielsen gives *La Bohème*, the show that started it all. Priceless tenor Constantino sings with both.

NY Times (November 8th), "Boston's new opera house was opened tonight with a production of Ponchielli's famous opera *La Gioconda* with Lillian Nordica as Gioconda, Louise Homer as Luara, Anna Meitschick as Gioconda's mother, Constantino as Enzo, Nivette as Alvise and Baklanoff as Barnaba.

"There had been small opportunity to rehearse...the house was not fairly out of the hands of the workman until Saturday, but the performance began punctually and went off more smoothly than had been expected".

In the theatre: "Acoustically the house is perfect...the first notes of the orchestra and later the first vocal utterances from the stage were distinctly heard in the remotest corner of the third balcony".

In the audience: "filled the house...thoroughly representative of the wealth and culture of the city, and its manifestations of pleasure were without stint.

In the cast: "Chorus, orchestra and ballet are Boston's own and it may be said that more pleasing and shapely ballet never danced in *La Gioconda*" thanks to Loie Fuller. "Mmes. Nordica and Homer too, are Bostonians, and the greeting they got therefore was not entirely in reward for their singing".

November 12, Nielsen sings in her new theatre. Puccini, *La Bohème*.

Cast: Mimi: Alice Nielsen; Musetta: Matilde Lewiska; Rodolpho: Florencio Constantino with Raymond Boulogne, Jose Mardones, Attilo Pulcini, John Morgan, Luigi Tavecchin, George Dustan, and C. Stroesco.

Boston Herald: "Miss Nielsen triumphs in Puccini's *La Bohème*, first extra production at the Boston Opera a brilliant affair. Surpassing in balance of cast and general excellence of ensemble the performances of *La Gioconda* on Monday and of *Aida* on Wednesday, the Boston Opera Company gave *La Bohème* superbly last evening for the third performance in the new theatre and for the first of the 'extra' subscription nights".

Loie Fuller's lights, sets, dancers, "added another to the succession of masterpieces. No opera which has visited Boston, certainly at any recent date and even at $5, has ever surrounded its singers with the illusion of so beautiful and sumptuous a pictorial environment. Beautiful as was the mounting of the opera, the singing was worthy of the setting".

Boston Globe's Arthur Wilson captures the moment. "At last Miss Nielsen has come into her own. Despite the persistent and often, because of circumstances, the well-nigh overpowering inducements to return to light opera, whose managers and public still clamored for her, this artist has persevered to her goal. Last night she reached it and proved herself abundantly worthy of it and its dearest reward.

"At last she has the accompaniment and environment of supporting cast, orchestra, conductor, stage management and possibilities of two of the world's principal lyric theatres. In them she will find her justly earned opportunity, both as she sings to this public and to that of the Metropolitan company in NY as this present season progresses".

After Act Two, flowers blanket the stage. Towering above all "an immense basket of chrysanthemums for Miss Nielsen".

And she sings gloriously; "If Italian singers who come to America demanding recognition, or who induce others to demand it for them, would sing with as clear a fidelity to the traditions of their own school, in the emission of a musical tone, and in a series of tones which are meant to be woven smoothly into a musical phrase, as Miss Nielsen observed throughout the evening, criticism would be a joyful pastime".

"Not once...was a tone to be heard, not even in the long and treacherous *mezzo voce* passages in the last act, where Mimi sinks deeper in weakness and the voice refines and refines into a mere silver thread—yet not once was there a tone to be heard which had lost its velvet lining.

"More completely than any other soprano voice now upon our stage or concert platform, which approaches the brilliance of Miss Nielsen's tone, has this artist found the happy alloy of glowing and broadening resonance to mellow and enrich its beauty.

"To the eye, and to the senses through the power of action, here was a Mimi who, first by quaint simplicity of her costume—and Miss Nielsen had the good taste not to overdress the part—and by the same simple directness of appeal, both in gesture, face and manner was always in the character. This portrayal was logical, cumulative and in the heart-gripping moments of 'goodby' to the lass of ardent Rudolf in the third act and in her reassurance of her love for him before death takes her it was keen in poignant pathos.

"In the duets with Mr. Constantino, Miss Nielsen's voice combined with happiest effect. Mr. Constantino himself, now quite at home upon this stage, gave a superb... Rodolfo, both in voice and characterization. Free of the nervousness of opening night, Mr. Constantino threw himself with much abandon into the part and revealed...the added breadth of tone and ripened surety of his artistry".

Conductor Conti "brought out the rare beauty of Puccini's music... ensembles went with animation and the whole performance was vital with the power both to charm and to impress".

Boston Opera House 1909. Seamless progression of artistry evolving on the newest American stage. People knew themselves blessed to be there.

BOSTON OPERA'S FIRST SEASON: A STAGE WORTHY

Boston Herald: "Miss Nielsen as Mimi...looked the part and identified herself with it fully by every device of song, action and by-play. Not only Miss Nielsen, but most of her associates, succeeded by the spontaneity of sincerity of their action, in creating an illusion that was rare in an opera house, although common enough in theatre".

Boston Post, Olin Downes: "Mimi was surely conceived for a soprano with the voice and temperament and the personality of Miss Nielsen. There have been passionate Mimi's, simpering and sophisticated Mimis, but we do not know of a Mimi more truly the impersonation of [Henri] Murger's character than Miss Nielsen. That is Mimi's voice, those are her innocent ways. She has never sung better in this city, her voice seemed to gain more freshness and beauty with every act".

Tellingly, "Boston has never seen a Mimi equal to Miss Nielsen's. Her delicacy of touch is marvelous. Miss Nielsen is not only a great actress, but her vocal artistry is beyond words of praise".

Philip Hale knew every role Nielsen had ever performed in Boston.

Hale: "Miss Alice Nielsen, welcomed heartily when she entered, played the part of Mimi with sympathetic intelligence. Her Mimi was of Mimi's world, a simple, trustful, loving creature. She was not a prima donna who stopped or condescended by the request of the librettist to play the grisette.

"Never for a moment did Miss Nielsen forget the character in the desire to shine as a singer, but her singing of Puccini's music was the natural expression of Mimi's happiness and woe.

"Her happiness was that of the grisette adoring her man, not understanding his poetry, but believing that he was great and some day would be famous. Her woe was not that of a professional heroine; it was that of hundreds who die quietly, unobtrusively, as Mimi died, and as Mimi dies today. The tragedy is none the less.

"Miss Nielsen has had the inestimable advantage of experience in operetta, which she graced for some years by her singing and acting. In this school she learned fleetness and naturalness in recitative; lightness in movement, ease in action and in repose, variety of facial and bodily expression.

"Mimi is more than a soubrette part; but in Mimi there are characteristics that are associated with the soubrette. Miss Nielsen did not make the mistake of idealizing the character, nor did she play the part with the realism that does not pass over the footlights. There were charming bits of detail in the performance; they enhanced the beauty of the impersonation by the quite dexterity with which they were introduced".

Nielsen joins the Met in Philadelphia November 14th at the Academy Of Music (*Philadelphia Inquirer*): "Alice Nielsen of *Singing Girl* fame will be heard in grand opera for the first time in Philadelphia [untrue]...when she is to sustain the role of Mimi in Puccini's popular opera". Bonci, Rodolfo; Bella Alten, "saucy and tempestive but charming Musetta". Cast "promises an adequate, satisfying and even brilliant performance".

Mary Garden's *Pelleas and Melisande* competes at Hammerstein's new opera house. Garden gets a big press feature the day Nielsen debuts.

Reacting to the barrage of Russell-fog, the Boston press makes things perfectly clear there is no doubt who gets credit for Boston Opera: "Gala Performance Of *La Bohème*; Production Which Aroused Music Lovers To Be Presented At Boston Opera House Tomorrow Evening".

Constantino and Nielsen anchor *Globe's* story, "gala performance at the new Boston opera house tomorrow evening...with Miss Alice Nielsen as Mimi and Sig. Florencio Constantino as Rudolfo" with portraits.

Plain fact once and for all time: "It was the performance of *La Bohème* given with the same principals at the Park theatre in the spring of 1907...which aroused Boston music lovers to such tremendous enthusiasm that the movement for the organization of a permanent opera company in Boston was started" rightly asserts *Boston Globe* (Nov 10).

Reentering the wicked woods, the hireling Russell claims (*NY Times*, Nov 10), "My attitude is to be absolutely eclectic. I shall have no prejudice, no predisposition favoring singer's nationality". Contradicts "If two singers, say for example, an Italian and American, have equal ability, I shall give the preference to the American". Sheer pandering to clueless Americanos. Hireling Russell throws his net over the vocal school Nordica created, "I am determined to develop my idea of the new school of opera. America will control the opera of the world. I intend to have a big organization where we can educate, feed and clothe young singers from every part of the world". That is, he has a taste for naïve young cheap pliable he can control.

Seeks American singer—but not so fast: "To take young American singers alone would be fatal. I must search Southern Italy, Northern Russia, Sweden and Norway for fine-quality voices. These I intend to sow in America soil. In five years you will see what a bed of flowers I will have here in American [sic] grand opera". Hireling *non sequitur* flimflam.

Spinning his web, next he attacks stars. Why pay "huge salaries to induce foreign artists to come over to this country" such as, say, Constantino. Shareholders will cry fraud and rightly blame him for forcing away the starring talent they had invested. And he cares nothing of it.

Highly popular Nielsen; her NYC Met debut November 20 a big hit.

NY thrills: "We are out of the rut of old Mimi's...a popular success".

NY Telegraph (Nov 20) previews: "Alice Nielsen attains the wish of years this very night. It will be remembered that she stopped short in the midst of a career as a prima donna of comic opera that promised more than brilliantly. Her ambition was to be a star of grand opera...cheerfully she endured the years of struggle, of obscurity and of painful discipline to a new calling, as well as the forfeiture of all the reputation and profit naturally accruing to the heroines of long running 'fortune tellers' and the like. Tonight she will stand where every operatic singer wanted to stand— opposite the prompter of the Metropolitan Opera House. Well she has earned it".

Nov 20: Metropolitan Opera: *La Bohème*. Rodolfo: Alessandro Bonci; Schaunard: Adamo Didur; Benoit: Antonio Pini-Coral; Mimi: Alice Nielsen; Parpignoi: Giuseppe Tecchi; Marcello: Antonio Scotti; Colline: Andrea De Seguroloa; Colline: Andrea De Segurola; Meindoro: F. Gianoli-Galletti; Musetta: Bella Alten; Sergente: Edoardo Missiano; Doganiere: Guilio Pintosi; Conductor: Vittorio Podesti.

NY Evening Post, "Saturday night Alice Nielsen made her debut in the Metropolitan Opera House, and the large audience was delighted to receive the charming fresh voice and attractive personality of the new Mimi.

"Great pity if Miss Nielsen had stayed on the operetta stage. We need operatic voices more than ever. Hers is good sized and of a rich, warm quality, and she has studied so faithfully to reach the present heights that one feels she will have courage, perseverance and talents to go far beyond. She makes Mimi a sweetly shy, girlish, little creature for whom her audience feels real sympathy.

NY Herald: "In the first place there is a new Mimi. She was Alice Nielsen, well known here years ago in comic opera, where she charmed by grace of manner and good singing. Last night her singing of Mimi made the audience sit up and applaud, for she sang exceedingly well.... We are out of the old rut of Mimi's and may the bowers and Miss Nielsen be thanked!"

NY Sun: "*La Bohème* with a new Mimi. Former soprano of light opera makes a credible debut. It was a spirited presentation....there was a new Mimi in the person of Miss Alice Nielsen, who thus made her debut at the Metropolitan, and the four comrades of the garret studio were Messrs. Bonci, Scotti, Didur and de Segurola, a quartet of singing actors of first-rate effectiveness. Miss Nielsen's ambition to tread the coveted boards of the Metropolitan has not been hidded from public knowledge since she left the stage of light opera and made her serious studies abroad. Another period of her career has now been reached, however, for despite evidences of nervousness which may have been responsible for occasional failure to find the pitch in her attack.

"Miss Nielsen disclosed a voice of agreeable quality in the upper register and of acceptable sort throughout. She sang with sureness except for the lapses mentioned, and her management of her tones was sufficiently easy to allow the listeners to forget that the realms of serious opera have only recently become familiar to her. There was a pretty demureness in her acting and she showed good understanding of the character of Mimi. Miss Nielsen looked well in the costume of the period, and her impersonation was warmly received.

NY World: "Alice Nielsen, graduated from the ranks of musical comedy and operetta, made her NY debut in heavy opera at the Metropolitan....

What is more to the point, she made a popular success, singing with taste, discretion and effect".

NY Times: "Miss Nielsen was a most appealing Mimi. Her comic opera training has stood her in good stead in many ways. It undoubtedly saved her from the extreme nervousness to which most singers are accustomed on first nights. It has also made her an excellent actress. She sketched the brighter scenes with great skill in the last act. She was the pathetic figure which the libretto demands. Her voice is a clear light soprano, more powerful than had been expected, and last night she sang very well. She has much skill in modulating the quality of her tones and her voice is sympathetic".

NY Evening World: "Nielsen...acquitted herself exceedingly well. Her voice has considerable power and she controls it excellently. It suggests in a degree, Melba's as to tone and quality. Her acting was very good.

Town Topics: "Finely balanced cast sang *La Bohème*.... Miss Nielsen seems to have 'arrived' finally, for she scored a big success with the audience and did it legitimately. Her singing revealed all the refinements of careful schooling and intelligent application, and histrionically she has improved almost beyond recognition. Hers was a finished and deeply moving impersonation of Mimi. Miss Nielsen's voice has retained all its former purity and timbre and ease in emission.

NY Evening Globe, "Miss Nielsen as Mimi was in most respects delightful in appearance and acting. She has had no superior in this part, and her singing gave much pleasure".

NY Evening Mail, "Alice Nielsen's appearance aroused much curiosity, especially among those who knew her in a light opera career, and that some day her voice would fill the Metropolitan no one believed. It did however, and very acceptably did this talented and determined little woman achieve the aim of her life.

NY Tribune, "Miss Nielsen was Mimi last night, and if she effaced few memories she proved her ambition has not been in vain. That she possesses a voice that is clear and pleasing, that her stage presence is attractive was proved years ago", says the cringingly Melba man.

New York City, yes indeed Alice Nielsen has made quite an impression.

Back in Boston November 27, Nielsen and Antonio Pini-Corsi offer *Don Pasquale*. *Boston Globe*: "Miss Nielsen was in excellent voice. Her tones were of crystalline purity, always true to the pitch, admirable in the nuance and of a fine evenness in the florid phrases. The role of Norina well discloses her versatility. Here is exacting vocalization which demands beauty of voice and method, a facility in flortura and graceful embellishment. Here too, is a role which demands suppleness, lightness, wide divergence of mood and a native instinct for its clear interpretation. Miss Nielsen was successively convincing as the vivacious, mischievous girl ready for Muletest's plot upon the Don, as the demure and alluringly coy maiden who would whet his eager zest in wooing her, and the suddenly pert and saucy shrew when once the bond makes her his heir. Miss Nielsen's performance revealed her unfailing charm in the spontaneity, archness, grace and pretty, hoydenish humor with which she made her Norina work the disillusionment".

Pini-Corsi "foil of Miss Nielsen's admirably simulated moods... infused into the spirit of the play that spontaneity, zest and light fancy which mark him as an artist of rare distinction. This actor-singer invests his portrayal of Don Pasquale with a breadth and dignity which enhances its power as a comedy part". Pini-Corsi and Nielsen were "unquestionably considered the foremost exponents of their respective roles".

Boston America: "Alice Nielsen sang and played Norina to perfection. The resonance of her pure voice was so excellent that the most pianissimo notes were heard throughout the house, and the coloratura passages were delightful to hear; the delicacy and accuracy of the soft scales and arpeggio were exquisitely done.

Boston Herald: "Miss Nielsen when she comes to such a part as Norina in *Don Pasquale* may bless both her fortunes—the fortune that made her first a singing actress of operetta and the fortune that then schooled her in the art of song up to such music as Donizetti's. She sang it with a rare freshness of voice and light brightness of tone, with a nice sense of its flowing melodic line and quick regard of its rippling ornament. She could be delightfully delicate with it when she sang in half-voice, and then she would enrich it with what is now the bright, full timbre of her upper tones.

"While she thus sang the part to lively pleasure, she kept her song, except when the action pauses for vocal outflow and ornament and nothing else, a playful and characterizing speech. Whether she was Norina the pretending convent miss or Norina having her fling as a very fine and extravagant lady, or Norina amorous in the garden with the lover of her heart, she was a figure of light comedy, playful of gesture, glance and pose, as spontaneous and resourceful as an expert actress who happened to have the added advantage of songful speech, and Miss Nielsen appreciated this advantage, and Norina spoke in her tones no less than in her more strictly histrionic action".

Boston notes the gayety: "The gaiety of the whole impersonation animated it. Lightness of touch carried it equally on its vocal and histrionic side. The illusion was complete...capital foil to Mr. Bourillon's Ernesto".

Her acting matches her vocals, her artistic progress delights audiences.

After the two grand opera debuts, Nielsen brings her concert program to the Boston Opera stage. Her first Sunday afternoon concert attracts close critical interest.

Could she be a success unplugged from orchestra, story, chorus?

Her value-add to composers is again noted as a consistent theme.

November 28th *Boston Traveler*'s Mr. Bryant writes, "Tosti did not write his plaintively beautiful song *Good-bye* for Alice Nielsen in particular, but one might well imagine that he did. Tosti has heard her and he says no one can sing it better. He should know. Certainly her voice has just the quality to make it appeal. One can see the dying season, can feel hope fly, as she voices it. And Miss Nielsen sang it last night at the Boston Opera House...on a Sunday concert programme...sang it as only she can.

"Nielsen sang *Ah Fors' e lui*, Richard Strauss, Hann's *Si mes vero avaient des alles* and an aria from *Lucia*. She showed the power of her voice and its range without sacrificing any of its purity, any of its sweetness. Altogether she was the delight of the concert. For an encore she gave in contrast a merrily little song about a Dutch garden and the Gretchen in it. But it was not enough, so the audience got just what it showed by its preliminary applause with the opening bars that it wanted, *Swannee River*".

Boston Herald: "Miss Nielsen made her first appearance at these concerts ...encored with an enthusiasm that increased after she had sung. Her voice, with its distinctive quality of virginal freshness and charm and her use of that voice in opera, are familiar here, but she is not so well known as a singer of songs. She showed that she appreciated the wide difference between the requirements of the two arts. She not only sang, she interpreted with intelligence, and she was effective without the aid of tricks and manners to which a stage training often tempts. She was brilliant, without exaggeration and eloquent in *mezza voce*. She often sang so softly that a theatre of less good acoustic properties her tones would have been lost. Her interpretations had individual flavor. They were her own and not traditional. She was also in her subsequent numbers an adroit and accomplished singer of songs with thought of their subtler moods and of the quality of tone and the finesse of phrase that would best express not only their substance, but their spirit".

Boston American: "The phrase is somewhat stereotyped, and it is quite inadequate to describe the manner in which the entire house rose at the exquisite singing of Alice Nielsen. Miss Nielsen gave an admirable rendering of *Ah for e lui* from *La Traviata*. The limpid beauty of her voice and excellence of coloratura was never finer. The cadenza with its final trill and pianissimo note was perfect. For encore Miss Nielsen sang *A toi* [Hermann Bemberg 1859-1931] with charming grace and earnestness. Of the group of these songs I much preferred the interpretation of "*Si mes vers avant des ailes*" [Hahn]; the exquisite delicacy inherent in the composer's writing was well rendered..... As an encore she sang *Dutch Garden* [Loomis] with such excellent diction a second encore was obligatory". *Swannee River* "sung with beautiful expression, each word receiving a proper value, aroused enthusiastic applause from the audience, not to let the artist go".

Musical Courier awards its cover to "Alice Nielsen, Prima Donna Soprano, Boston Opera House" the week of December 9. Standing proudly in a plunging beaded concert gown with flowing train, she is more than lovely in a splendid full-length portrait by E. Chickering of Boston.

For her debut as Butterfly, Nielsen performs despite illness. Again.

December 8th, headlines *Boston Globe*, "Against physician's advice Miss Nielsen sings, and beautifully. Last night Alice Nielsen pluckily saved what was the first performance of Madam Butterfly both for herself and for the Boston opera company". At 5 o'clock yesterday afternoon, her physician "had found the condition of her voice so grave that he forbade her to sing last night on the peril of forfeiting future appearances.

"She bravely attempted the performance rather than disappoint her audience and gave a singularly convincing presentation of the role at this her first time in it on any stage. The evening was a remarkable demonstration of Miss Nielsen's excellent production of voice. The purity, carrying power and beauty of many of her upper notes would be praiseworthy in good voice and were extraordinary under such adverse conditions".

Critical praise admires Alice Nielsen's portrayal. Superior to other divas who attempt the role.

"So well did Miss Nielsen manage her mezzo voce that often its notes appeared to be delivered with a reserve calculated to deepen their impressive-ness rather than with the sacrifice imposed by a constriction of voice. At any rate, ill or well, this artist can sing and even had she been voiceless in the part there were moments when her pantomime would have held the attention quite oblivious to such lack of tone.

"This is not a role wherein merely a voice may satisfy of however exquisite a quality it may be possessed, or however perfect the condition it may be in. Butterfly's larger impressiveness lies in the appeal of the character itself, and in its gradual unfolding into a wider and more cruel knowledge of life. John Luther Long in his book and David Belasco in his derived drama have distilled tragedy into fatalism. They have cast it over the path of an innocent ...her simple, childlike trust is matured into a woman's passionate devotion. Then it reveals to her what to Pinkerton had been a tentative amusement... fate follows the opera like an encroaching terror. A less able actress would catch this bodement of doom...and would be lifted by it into too conscious an anticipation of what the composer would have the hearer know, but which must be revealed to the character only by the course of the action. Not so with Miss Nielsen. No role which she has assumed here demands so much of discretion, balance and finesse in the art of acting.

"This is a far cry from the more or less conventionally betokened grief of a Gilda or a Traviata. Indeed, Butterfly sings the music of Italian sentiment and passion, but in individuality of thought and action this wan little sprite of femininity, at first more child than woman, demands a new and alert understanding, of which no previous character in Puccini's operas has furnished a precedent. Here were the quaint modes, habits and touches of becoming personality to think out and acquire.

"Happily, Miss Nielsen did not adapt nor suggest the kittenish, mincing mannerism where often is the label of Japanese impersonation".

Only Alice Nielsen had spent a night with Yokohama geishas, drinking their tea, eating their supper, enjoying shared jokes. They had gathered in mutual play, exchanging clothes before Alice returns to her hotel singing their songs.

"At times her walk may have suggested that of a white woman more than the diminutive patter of feet of a geisha. If she did not continually demand the histrionic assistance of fan or parasol, this, too, was gratifying. These were details. The salient characteristics were present.

"Her Butterfly is a timid, affectionate nature, subordinated by her sex, steadfast in her love, deeply pathetic in the realization of her grief and quietly determined in her will to end it.

"In the last act Miss Nielsen acted with a just and clear realization of each detail, among them her eager childish joy at the news of her husband's return, which prevents Sharpless from coming to the cruel part of the letter; the patient vigil alone in watching for the ship which would bring him; the transport of joy when she supposes he has come, the pang of anguish at realizing the presence of the woman who already bears his name. Fussiness, bombast and exaggeration, all were lacking. It was the sincere and compelling portraiture of a great grief in a little life. It is Butterfly's opera. Otherwise the characters are incidental. Pinkerton is a banal abomination...."

In the cast: "Leiva sang the part with a lusty zeal. Mr. Fornari gave Sharpless ...dignity and becoming sympathy. Miss Freeman again adapted herself to detail of action with admirable insight and clear expression. Her voice was beautiful. Mr. Giocoone's conception of Goro...excellent". Miss Swartz managed Mrs. Pinkerton in good voice. "Players in other roles were capable". Conti "controlled his orchestra with better balance and discrimination than past readings have disclosed".

Loie Fuller's design: "The setting was elaborate and beautiful. The sun sank and evening enclosed a garden in the first act, enriched with flowers and shrubbery, lit anon by the twinkling of the cities below and of luminous stars above, which from their size had left their accustomed orbits to beam on Butterfly from closer vantage ground. Butterfly's house in the last two acts had an outlook through a garden bright with bloom out upon the city below and the distant bay. The lighting effects were admirable.

"What the performance...will be when Miss Nielsen's voice regains its wonted ease and sonority remains for future and pleasurable realization".

Phillip Hale: "There was a large and brilliant audience. Miss Nielsen took the part of Cho-Cho-San for the first time on any stage. It is a part that is eminently suited to her as actress and singer, for poor Mme. Butterfly is not a tragedy queen that struts and frets her hour upon the stage, indulging in heroics. Like Mimi, she is a humble sufferer, quietly pathetic, but none the less a heroine and a tragic figure.

"Soon evident that Miss Nielsen, although her intonation was refreshingly pure and her vocal skill abundantly in evidence, was not 'in voice', for the tones did not always go across the footlights, and certain tones which are usually clear and thrilling were clouded. Before the curtain of the second act it was explained that, a victim to the changes in the weather, Miss Nielsen was voiceless yesterday morning and in the afternoon her physician advised her not to sing; but sing she did, to save the performance.

"If it had not been for her courage there would have been no opera last evening. It was also evident that she had composed her impersonation with marked intelligence.

"Her Mme. Butterfly was something more than a prima donna wearing a Japanese costume as though at a masquerade; she was a loving woman, childlike in her simplicity and trustfulness, dazed by treachery, finding comfort in the distress that led to suicide by the of a future for her child.

"Miss Nielsen's impersonation was not episodic, now interesting, now dull; it was continuously engrossing and with a crescendo of emotion. It was artistic both in frank expression and in fine restraint. And although she was not able to use her voice as freely as she wished, though she was obliged to humor rebellious tones and could not always be effective either by volume or by use of color, she sang with true expression, and was often convincing or appealing by sheer strength or beauty of song. Indisposed as she was, her impersonation was the feature of the performance.

"These notes are with reference to a first performance".

Harry Parker: "If ever a singing-actress deserved her reward, Miss Nielsen does". Given Boston Opera as home "she has begun to gain the rewards—especially the reward of place and prestige—that she deserves. Her voice and her artistry—for she has it both on the vocal and the histrionic side—are near their maturity. Righteously and reasonably now she might devote herself—to herself. If Miss Nielsen's fortitude and loyalty thus had their unwisdom, they had also the reward that a kindly fate sometimes gives to them.

"The quality of her voice in the first act, especially in the long sweep of the duets with Pinkerton, first stirred to wonder, and then as the reason for it became clear, to lively sympathy. The opera proceeded, and as good fortune would have it, the singer's command of her tones increased and they regained something of their usual fineness of texture, brightness of body and variety of color. On she went through Puccini's unsparing music, relentless in its demand upon the higher range of a soprano's voice, asking now for sustained and impassioned cantilena and again for single phrases that shall be all poignant accent, and both against an orchestra that Puccini sometimes makes to count the voice as only one more of its instruments.

"The more familiar histrionic exactions of the play and the part are as severe. The stress of a task in which she could not falter once she had embarked upon it, the besetting anxiety as to the next the inevitable moment must have laid a grievous and a piteous burden upon Miss Nielsen. Old operatic hands feared for her fate....

Even so, "it was easy to see by her Cio-Cio-San an impersonation that, as soon as she is able to accomplish her ends, will stir alike to admiration of the singing-actress and to the emotions of the drama and of the music....

"Opera singers are a sensitive as well as a selfish folk, and the anxieties and the strain of the performance under all these circumstances must have keenly beset those that shared in it. None the less, they did for the most part what it was easy to expect of them".

In the cast: Leliva "neither the voice nor the manner", Fornari "walked the ways of rather wooden routine" as Sharpless. Miss Freeman "yet to learn that the more morose, stolid and watchful is Suzuke, the more do the woman's outbursts tell" and the "secondary and the minor parts went eagerly, but insecurely and with rough edges...." Conti "held the orchestra to an accompaniment, except when he could release his beloved brass, but the orchestra none the less should be, next to Butterfly, the soul and the voice of the whole drama and its music". Menotti followed the ways of the Opera-Comique "it was good to see" and not the text, "thrusting the child into the garden at the end and reducing the intolerable presence of Pinkerton's unspeakable...American wife". Insufficiently rehearsed, "conductor, the stage director, the orchestra and supporting players...did not have time to sharpen the fine details. It seemed very much a first performance".

During December, Loie Fuller and Nielsen begin joint concerts. Alice gives "the second and third acts of *Don Pasquale*" to precede "the first appearance of Loie Fuller and her muses".

On December 12, *NY Times*' "Romantic Stars Their Early Days" has a word on Nielsen, who "had offers and she needed money, she turned them down. She stuck to it and now she has reached the goal...."

December 13, regaining her health, Nielsen sings *Butterfly* Monday, *Faust* Wednesday, *Traviata* Thursday.

December 15, Philip Hale acclaims *Faust*: "Alice Nielsen and Florencio Constantino, in their first assumption in this city of the roles...of Marguerite and Faust, combined to fulfill what was the best performance of Gounod's opera Boston has known within recent memory. A sincere and just conception of the dramatic truth of the work permeated and inspired an interpretation which grew more convincing as the evening progressed.

"In no opera has there been such satisfactory excellence and balance of cast, so just an equilibrium between greater and lesser roles, and all things considered, so apt and eloquent an orchestra investiture and chorus here.... For this performance of so much that was beautiful and impressive, Miss Nielsen and M. Constantino were largely to be credited. Without a conception and portrayal of Marguerite which rings true, the opera is helplessly adrift".

"Last night Miss Nielsen again revealed how potent she is in the portraiture of life by other means than her tones alone. Perhaps not even with the exception of her singing, no one source of her power to impress was greater than that of the choices which gave clearness of meaning, telling emphasis often and at critical moments supreme conviction to her characterization last night.

"Marguerite is a role to be quietly suggested and not elaborately played. With possibly the exception of Miss Nielsen's action with the exploring of the treasure casket where one might have wished for still more of the arch and piquant as sings of the eagerness and freshness of new joy, here was a conscious study throughout the opera of what economy of purposeful detail will accomplish in projecting ideas.... This Marguerite pinned her faith to simplicity and a quiet intensity which gave the more convincingly because it withheld the more wisely. At her entrance in the scene before the city gate her cognizance of the courtly cavalier was more as obeisance to a superior being than to one whom she might hope to know. Simplicity again marked her entrance to the garden".

She carries flax without using the wheel, "the omission did not lessen but rather intensified the illusion. Throughout this act Miss Nielsen's performance suggested only the innocent trusting girl who has given herself to this handsome stranger with an affection as unquestioning and sincere as it is simply expressed. With the third act, this very economy of means declares, deepens and intensifies the poignancy of her grief.

"On the steps of the church it was not restless pacing of many steps, but often merely the swaying of a body numb with grief. Marguerite's action at Valentine's death confirms or belies a singer's histrionism.

"Admirable indeed was the device of slowly leaving the center of the stage just before Valentine fell, as though crushed by his curse. By no means could a keener suspense have been created. In her realization of his death, most admirable was the show of despair in a heart to dumb for outcry, save during the last few seconds of the scene, which bring relief in hysterical laughter. The closing act deepened the pathos by the same sincerity".

"Was a pleasure to hear Miss Nielsen's voice quite restored. The abandon which entered into many of her tones in the prison scene gave them surpassing beauty. The *Jewel Song* was done with clear regard for its ornament and foritura. Miss Nielsen's singing in the 'garden scene' to Faust, alone and with him, was remarkable for its purity, its serenity of outline and its simple loveliness".

"Constantino sang his aria of greeting to Marguerite's dwelling with much use of the light voice, but with discrimination and apt appreciation for the spirit of the scene. His voice blended with Miss Nielsen's to make the beauty of the duets memorable".

Hale corrects the tenor, clothes unchanged after he drank the elixir. And a showoff, "He sang as a distinguished tenor confident of applause to come, not as an impersonator of Faust, not as an intelligent phrases of Gounod's music". His address to Marguerite's cottage, chiefly for the audience "with now and then a shy glance at the dwelling. The entrance scene...is no time for Faust to caress his voice and throw appealing eyes to the ladies in the boxes...."

Follow Nielsen's example: "Her Marguerite of the garden scene was intelligently thought out and she sang and acted with marked skill. There were few, if any, traces of her recent indisposition. Her upper tones were clear and resonant and her middle and lower tones had a delightful quality. She sang with unusual appreciation of text and situation and her performance was full of delicate and effective nuances".

Other divas rush past *The King of Thule* to get to *Jewel Song* coloratura, "but the soul of the Marguerite of the opera is in this ballad, not in the florid air.... Miss Nielsen in the ballad, bared the soul of Marguerite, who was after all a simple maiden, impressionable, but not forward, given to reverie, but not melancholy".

Hale eggs the lone NYC critical holdout: Kreible's belief Marguerite a "grand dame" is "a curious view". She "is not a gawk; but she is far from being a grand dame, even in reduced circumstances".

Other divas—take Melba so admired by Kreible—distort *Jewel Song*, as though "a brilliant concert aria, they take all sorts of liberties both with the phrases and the rhythm, so that the air is often broken into little bits. Miss Nielsen's performance was not an exhibition of insolent bravura, as though on this one song she should be applauded or condemned, nor on the other hand did she check the musical continuity or rhythmic flow. Here and there she slackened the pace to gain legitimate effects by interpretation of the text; the characteristic figure recurred, the tempo was faithfully observed with due regard for the text, not with inexorable and aggressive metronomic rigidity.

"She sang the love-music of the duet with genuine emotion, and both in song and action there was a crescendo of passion, which found its climax in her confidences to the night; but this climax was not hysterical, nor did it become an amorous shriek". Even so, other portions of the duet and of the act "were at times too slow and the scene dragged in spite of Miss Nielsen".

Nielsen "sang and acted in the church scene with dramatic effect, and the effect would have greatly heightened had the scene been set properly and if Marguerite had been in the church with Mephistopheles behind a pillar. It is hard to see why the scene was thus set in defiance of all the traditions. A narrow front church scene would easily allow any preparation behind for the entrance of the troops and the consequent wait would be a very short one.

"All in all, the performance of Miss Nielsen was excellent, full of charm, emotion artistically controlled, and genuine distinction".

Musical Courier discusses this *Faust*. Nielsen's "conception was one to give rare pleasure by reason of its freshness and its legitimate unconventionality. For once, Marguerite was in truth sweet and unsophisticated. The character developed with fine logic and consistency. The *Jewel Song* was not a virtuoso piece, but the charming and naïve expression of the girl's innocent delight in her ornaments. When Faust bent over her shoulder he was the startled embodiment of her fancies at that moment. All this we know of Marguerite, but how seldom is such a delineation of the character, so simple, so unaffected, beheld upon the operatic stage! In the church scene and at the death of Valentine, Miss Nielsen was superbly dramatic.

"As Faust, Mr. Constantino sang in his accustomed manner. He is not a French but an Italian Faust. He has, first of all, regard for his passages as song. He relishes a high note, as did his audience".

December 16, Boston Opera gives a benefit performance of *Traviata* for the Boston Section of the Council of Jewish Women. Nine days later, Nielsen's kindly Bostonian mom Clara Barnabee dies.

Year ends with *Musical Courier* publishing "Alice Nielsen's Own Story", of her familiar pilgrim progress with new twists. She speaks more freely.

"Since Alice Nielsen has walked, she has sung. And since Miss Nielsen has acquired a flat in Boston town, her first flat by the way, she has evidenced an unaccustomed willingness to talk about herself. And when Miss Nielsen talks about herself, she is interesting to listen to, for she has personality that gets hold of you. Some artists have it not...."

Reflecting the simmering troubles backstage at Boston, the star singer finally backs off promoting her remora after eight years' overblown praise.

"Ask her how she has done it, and she tells you she began to sing in a child... had perhaps fewer lessons than any other of the well-known artists before the public, and for the rest, 'jest growed.'"

"You see, when I first appeared on the stage, no matter what the part was, I felt as if I were the whole show. I felt that the success of the failure of a performance depended mainly upon me, and I assure you that I didn't work a bit harder last summer when I was getting up *Madame Butterfly* than I did than I did when it felt good to be engaged by the Pike [Pyke] Opera Company at Kansas City, Mo". Only time she told this happened. Skips Burton Stanley. In these years her *Who's Who* entry mentions Pyke, later she skips Pyke and Stanley reappears.

"As for my roles, I like them all, I never want to take any part that I don't like, and from the time that I begin preparing a character I am living it. It seems to me that when a role is learned, the voice, like the action and the rest of it, has worked out its task too".

Of Italy, "That is the land for the voice. There is such warmth and beauty. The sea, the sun, the people conspire to make you sing".

Contradicts the remora-crafted *Prospectus*, "As for prejudice against Americans, as far as my experience goes, that is all nonsense. There I was, learning my roles in a language that was new to me. How easily the critics could have made everything hard! How friendly and profitable as a matter of fact was their advice and encouragement".

Now her sequence rings true. At Naples, "I sang first at the Teatro Bellini and then at the San Carlo... and the operas seemed gradually to become part of me with the atmosphere that I breathed.

"That means assimilation, and what you learn in that way stays by you for the rest of your life. In this country you either develop at top speed, or you fall behind. I don't think any musicians mature so quickly and learn so much in a given length of time as a gifted American. But nerves! Nerves! Only a few of us lead a normal existence here".

She reflects on what she has sparked since 1905: "What a tremendous musical development America has seen. Of course, people who live as I do really see the least of what is going on, but look what's happened in even the last two years".

She thrills: "Now I think that Boston, with her permanent company, holds the kernel of the operatic future in her hand. Think of the company we've got! Think of the house itself, and think of the staging!"

Artistic pride magnifies her family pride: "I am glad to be here, too. It feels like home for my mother's birthplace [childhood] was the historical mansion of General Warren in Roxbury.

"Boston often reminds me of London. I notice that the people here attend a great many instrumental concerts, choral performances, oratorios and all that sort of thing, as they do in London. And they certainly appreciate opera. Yes, I like London. I like to travel and I expect to see a lot of new places before I die. Now we're going on our Western tour. But when we get back it surely will be good to settle down again for a while".

Boston has become home for its founding star. Not the opera manager.

And this season, the Constantino Opera Company plays New Orleans billed as "the greatest lyric tenor and his own troupe of selected artists in grand opera".

After the usual problems with Hammerstein, Nielsen's co-star from Victor Herbert, alto Marguerite Sylva joins Boston Opera December 28 (*NY Times*). Sylva "who has not been singing for some weeks" was hired by Boston "to strengthen the cast" touring to Chicago where "Miss Sylva will be heard in *Carmen, Faust, Pagliacci* and *Cavalieria Rusticana*". As usual Hammerstein vindictively lies, "He had in no way broken his contract with Miss Sylva".

1909. Alice Nielsen has become forever a "prima donna of the Boston and Metropolitan grand opera companies".

Next year she flies in the new-fangled "aeroplane".

1910: GRAND OPERA & CONCERTS

Boston Opera departs on New Year's Day, heading west. For third year the Met judged inferior. January 1, 1910 (*NY Times*): The new Bostonians "to the number of 306 people, started in two special trains tonight for a five weeks' tour. The itinerary includes a week of grand opera in Pittsburg, two weeks in Chicago, a week in St. Louis, one day in Indianapolis, three days in Cincinnati, and a day in Springfield, Mass".

In the cast: The foggy details of Russian baritone Baklanoff, dismissed for "insubordination...back but only after forcing him to submit to terms which show...Russell is master at the opera house". Huge $10,000 fine plus "full apology" (*NY Times* Jan 4).

Hammerstein's second suit against a Boston star begins the 8th. Sylva left after he tries to downgrade her in *Griselidis* to "second soprano" and young Hammerstein Jr. mocks her red *Pagliacci* wig "Whatever happens, I shall never sing again at the Manhattan Opera House. Mr. Hammerstein has broken his contract with me by asking me to appear in a secondary role". Her attorney Nathan Burkan declares the Paris contract void "not signed by her husband" hence "invalid under French law".

In mid-January Boston Opera opens at Chicago.

"Miss Nielsen made her first appearance this season in Chicago as the singer of the music of Mimi. It is pleasant to be able to testify to the success of this achievement" said *Chicago Journal* (Jan 14).

"Miss Nielsen has strengthened her artistic position since she sang here last; she has acquired a firmer grasp of music that is in an interpretive sense more difficult to sing than the music in which she has specialized theretofore, and vocally her style has gained larger breadth and color".

Chicago admires her acting. "The reading given of this artist to the character and the music of Mimi differs in some respects from...other singers. Miss Nielsen makes the heroine of Puccini's opera a person of such gravity as one does not usually associate with the gay and careless existence of Bohemia. Yet one must believe that this reading is true to art and nature. For when Mimi stumbles into the lives of the students living up in the attic in the Latin quarter she has already learnt what are to be the wages of sin; what is to be the price that Bohemia asks of those who accept of its pleasure and how drink deeply of its joys. There was tragic pathos in Miss Nielsen's Third Act...the outward manifestations of consumptions were not insisted upon by the singer, who coughed less and sang better than many an interpreter of the part, who is loath to leave anything to the imagination".

Chicago Journal agrees: "Miss Nielsen is deserving of all praise. She sang gloriously and acted splendidly. It is no exaggeration to say that one seldom hears such a beautiful voice as she possess. It is rich, vibrant and absolutely true. In addition to its attractive natural qualities, she uses it in a highly artistic manner. She sings with the breadth and sweep of the true musician".

"Her acting was no less praiseworthy. Under her interpretation, the dainty little Japanese girl became a very appealing figure. The finale of the second act was a scene to be remembered. The patient figure of Butterfly standing at the sliding scene, looking out into the moonlight and waiting, made a picture which gripped the audience".

In the cast: "Enzo Leliva (Pinkerton) sing excellently and acted with considerable emotional force". Rodolfo Fornari, Sharpless. "Bettina Freeman was an excellent Suzuki. Ernesto Giaccone as Goro supplied an element of liveliness and humor which completed the picture. Elona Kirmen as Kate Pinkerton had little to do but look attractive, but she made a great success of that".

Conti's "orchestra played with all the dash and fire which the audience is accustomed to hear when that artist conducts. Not the least part of the success of this company is due to the orchestra. It is an organization of the first rank". *Chicago News* agrees, "The orchestra under the nervous baton of director Conti loosed all the glowing effects of mood values...the delicate voicings of the instrumental score were charmingly revealed".

"The cast in its entirety was the superior of any enlisted this season".

Nielsen's progress with new vocal teachers comes into view; in London with Blanche Marchesi and of course Tosti: "First came the surprise in the transformation of Alice Nielsen into the vocal stature of grand opera in the pathetic part of Mimi. Through some necromancy the sweet voice has been placed or displaced with remarkable broadening, particularly noticeable in the middle tones and gives the impress of fuller volume throughout in dramatic color. The change was so pronounced that it astonished her old audience. This seems to have been accomplished at some expense to the former bell-like charm of her soaring song but it widens her vocal horizon for operatic conquest.

"The clarity and truth of tone she established and the details of diction are well observed; barring some slight liberties in tempo which challenged...the orchestra, her singing gave the score tellingly. Her embodiment of Mimi was naïve and girlish, eminent...in its pathetic progression. The audience approved her work, recalls were frequent and flowers were not wanting".

Back in NYC the Met reorganizes. Clarence Mackay purchases stock of James Hyde, WK Vanderbilt the largest stockholder, then Otto Kahn. A merger with Hammerstein is discussed. Geraldine Farrar "delivered an ultimatum to the effect that she will sing no more new roles this season... unless some of her conditions are met with" (*NY Times* Jan 14). Farrar fears losing her monopoly prerequisites. "Farrar is said to be by no means pleased with the fact" that rival Destinn sang, she "considered the part her own.... Miss Farrar also wished to secure the copyright on *Tosca*".

Farrar is "on no very good terms with her impresarios. It is even rumored that she would like to forsake the Metropolitan for the larger returns of the concert stage". A string of affairs include Germany's Prince Wilhelm, Scotti, Toscanini and diverse. After Farrar's voice breaks during a 1913 performance she never regains strength. An early voice coach had been Nordica. Farrar will make several silent films, of course. Her political power exerted over the Met stage albeit temporary, solves the daffy Eaton puzzle of why Nielsen did not sing more frequently there. In 1915, Farrar pressures Toscanini too far, who resigns as conductor rather than divorce to marry her. Her last husband, Dutch silent star Lou Tellegrin, commits suicide 1923. Eaton knew but cannot speak freely. Nielsen simply sings.

January 17, Boston Opera performs *Carmen.*

Chicago News: "The Micaela of Alice Nielsen was one of the best pieces of work ever performed on the Auditorium stage. Her aria *Je dis* was a revelation, and was received enthusiastically.

In the cast: Carmen was "Madame Gay...vocally the singer was at her best.... Constantino was at his best. Baklanoff was above criticism, the Toreador song being given with originality, and as in all the roles in which the great Russian baritone has been heard, his success was overwhelming and well-deserved. The remainder of the cast was in good hands.

Chicago's "Miss Tinee" interviews Catalona's Maria Gay (1879-1943), "most attractive-looking woman, dark, with big eyes that laugh and talk by themselves and lovely white teeth. All of them show when she smiles and she smiles all the time". Gay's strong, coarse Carmen eats an orange and spits out the seeds before singing *Habanera.* She and tenor husband Giovanni Zenatollo settle in NYC, teach voice, manage Lily Pons. Gay had been imprisoned in Spain for singing patriotic Catalan songs. Speaking by interpreter, Gay "would rather sing in Chicago than any place else. In New York people go to the grand opera not to hear the singers but to look at each other. The women wish to see each other's gowns...and the jewels the same. Here the people come because they are lovers of music and can appreciate art. It is the joy of a lifetime...to sing in Chicago". Famed for the role, Gay "did not care for *Carmen*...she liked parts where there was more singing and less acting".

In the cast: Raymond Boulonge advocates suffrage, "Women are just as good as men and much smarter. The Masons [he is] "will see within the next three years that all women in France will have the power to vote" which will be delayed until 1944.

January 19: *Bohème* matinee, *Butterfly* night: Nielsen runs gauntlet.

Chicago News on *Mme. Butterfly*: "The Italian composer has been fortunate in having some wonderful interpreters of the part of Cho San but it is doubtful if there were ever one more sympathetic than Alice Nielsen.... Miss Nielsen has made the part one of the best in her extensive repertoire and offers a performance in which every detail has been considered. She is a remarkable actress as well as singer.

"The world of this American singer gives encouragement to other English-speaking singers. She has the true metal and should rise to great heights and absolutely delightful after"—only meat-packing Chicago critics dared say—"some of the corporeal and aged ladies who essay the ingénue".

Chicago's closing night, big disturbance. Nielsen and Constantino close Chicago with *Bohème. Green Book* tells all: "Pranks of a last night can be carried too far. for artistic purposes, yet even so the laughter may be no less hearty. All went smoothly until the last act, when some wag in the company loosened the slats in the bed on which Mimi dies. The...huge audience sat whisperless during the death-scene of Mimi, whose frail weight failed to overburden the bed. But when Constantino, the tenor lover, threw himself, in a paroxysm of grief, across the bed! Slam, bang, away they went, Alice Nielsen and Constantino, rolling over and over on the floor, while the curtain came down to a tumultuous roar of laughter from across the footlights".

In *St. Louis* January 26, Nielsen meets columnist "King Tootle". Harry King Tootle authored 1912's *Daughter of David Kerr*, "Women is queer creatures, Amos", says his character Judge Gilbert.

Nielsen begins with two words. "I've won. There isn't much to tell. I made my big success at the Metropolitan in *La Bohème* this season. Bonci sang with me. And it was the same in Boston. They welcomed me in *La Bohème* and after that it was all so easy".

NYC concert plans: "I had an engagement to sing [in concert] at the New Theatre in NYC but I was indisposed and had to cancel it. I shall sing there however after this tour ends. When I return East, I am to sing again with the Metropolitan and also in Boston. It may be I shall go on tour with the Metropolitan".

"But I want to tell you most about my own little home in Boston. It's really and truly mine. The deed's mine, the furniture's mine, the pictures are mine—it's all mine". In those days people never fail not to enjoy using negatives: "I don't live very far from the opera house..."

What does she do at night? "Go to the opera. Monday night I was just dying to go, but I didn't dare for fear of catching cold. My responsibilities are greater now than they were in the old days, and I have to exercise the greatest care. So Monday night I was afraid to go out. I moped around in my rooms awhile and finally said, 'Oh well, I suppose I might as well go to bed.' And to bed I went".

Of roles, "I don't know which of my roles I like best. I like them all. Mimi I love and Butterfly".

And says her phrases repeated of many towns, "I am glad that St. Louis is to hear me in these roles because I like them very much. Somehow, I feel at home here, and I want St. Louis to have my very best".

Tootle closes, "Wednesday night, St. Louis is to have the little American prima donna's 'very best.' And at the same time it will have the 'very best' of the great Spanish [Basque] tenor Constantino. And what is more, St. Louis will have...the 'very best' of Puccini in *La Bohème*".

As January ends, Nielsen makes her move into dramatic soprano roles. As announced on her arrival in NYC past fall, Wagner is on her schedule.

Musical Leader (Jan 27) has "upon good authority" Nielsen would sing Else in *Lohengrin* next season. She "is equipped splendidly for the role in the matter of voice and art, and her presentation...will also have the charm of originality, a quality which distinguishes all she does and gives value to each work in which she appears. Alice Nielsen can tackle any part in which a soprano has a right to appear and she does each one in such a manner as to make us believe that the particular one in which for the moment she is heard is the one best suited to her. She is an extraordinarily versatile artist and one who is rapidly gaining the height of her ambition. With equal facility" Nielsen sings French, German, Italian, and English and in *Bohème*, Mimi is "absolutely her own, and not once is there a suggestion of theatricalism or overdoing".

As the singing actor, "her voice is full, rich, beautifully produced, and she sings with a musical understanding and taste that many other opera singers would find it advisable to bring to their work. It is the singing of the artist who is also a finished recital singer".

Truth is in the world: Dallas, Cincinnati, LA, Chicago, Boston, NYC.

February 6th Constantino sued by Hammerstein for breach of contract over rejoining Boston and harassed with subpoenas. Is Russell's fault.

February 10 Philip Hale reviews *Don Pasquale* with Pini-Corsi. "Miss Nielsen sang delightfully, with a fluency that was never slovenly, with a purity of intonation that was refreshing in these evil days of song [that is, Geraldine Farrar]; with archness and with brilliance. She acted with grace and spirit".

February 14, *Boston Transcript's* Parker discourses on *Butterfly* of the 12th. As at any first of season their previous season's show had seemed half-prepared and Nielsen "with a voice that at any moment might have failed her, carried...a new and exciting part. Then the performance moved in jerks and gasps...."

Now "the singing-players bettered the performance". For example, "Mr. Hansen who has succeeded the departed and unregretted Leliva, has plausible presence as Pinkerton. At last too, Miss Nielsen undertook Butterfly with undiminished and dependable powers, and the part is relentlessly exacting. A few preliminaries done, she shares with the orchestra almost the whole burden of the drama. The music persists in the higher range of a soprano voice and Puccini's intervals are oftenest unsparing. Butterfly must sing in the vocally pitiless speech of modern music-drama and at the same time she must be the varying image of devoted happiness, devoted endurance and devoted disillusion".

Rarely will a Boston critic contrast sopranos. HTP considers Destinn, Farrar, and Nielsen: "The tones of Miss Destinn in the second act seek a tragic and a rather self-conscious intensity; Miss Farrar's are smoldering or flaming fire; Miss Nielsen is content to be wistful as a Butterfly who endures gropingly, who sees mistily, who wonders that life and fate are so hard. The less Butterfly does, beyond the bare necessities of speech and action, the better. Miss Nielsen was wisely simple and reticent, conscious of Butterfly and the moment, but unconscious of herself and the audience. Once more, her histrionic instinct and experience directed her well. Over-acted [Farrar], the end of Madama Butterfly would be intolerable. As it is, it needs the mists of sympathy—and of tears".

Alice's time with Duse and Hortense delivers results.

Boston Globe of *Bohème* (Feb 15): "Only two boxes were unoccupied last night for the opening of the second week...of the Boston opera company's season. Puccini's vivid opera is always as sure of a large attendance as *Carmen* even when it has been heard as many times as this season".

Globe pushes the star system people really want, "With Miss Nielsen and Constantino in the leading roles it becomes a stronger offering than ever. The production is now running smoothly, though it has not been speeded up to the tempo that other directors use. It gains much in three acts from this deliberation, for there are many delicate passages that are smothered in rapid time. But the second act suffers; even in the first act there are awkward pauses.

"Nielsen also sang with unusual clarity and with amazing sweetness of tone. Both of the singers showed the effects of the strain when the music passed into an upper register, but both had the restraint of true artistry and there was none of the yelling that has marred the performances of earlier days by other singers".

In the cast: Constantino "in good voice and sang the famous aria of the first act with exquisite feeling, winning a burst of applause that stopped the action for an appreciable time". Eugenia Bronskaja, Musetta, "splendid in the difficult moments of the last act and delicious in the little quarrel at the end of the third act". Raymond Boulogne, Marcello, "on his way to being a Boston favorite". Jose Mardones, Colline, "gave the impression of power and volume with utmost ease. Pulcini a fine Schaunard. Rest of the cast was thoroughly acceptable. The choruses...sung with plenty of fire".

And Hotel Lenox insults a Russian soprano. February 16 (*NY Times*) Lydia Lipkowska sues to stop Hotel Lenox using her name on menu for "Cup Lydia" and "Soufflé a la Lipkewska" claiming chef's compliment decreases earnings.

Romance follows any Nielsen project. This marriage has odd overtones.

After Lipkowska sues for the insult of soufflé, two Boston Opera people wed. Young soprano Marguerite Banks (1888-1974) marries manager Russell's secretary Frederick Toye (1887-1930) at St. Patrick's NYC. Circumstances strange. Both were abruptly fired by Russell mid-season. News foggy. Beautiful Banks, whose face would be famous as the Sun Maid Raisin girl, was hired personally by Russell then fled him.

"For some unknown reason she left the impresario [hireling] and came to NY with her mother" reports *NY Times*. And bridegroom Toye, a Harvard grad, had been "secretary to Henry Russell". Obvious why.

When an assistant's firing makes *NY Times*, this signals percolating trouble. How much does Jordan suspect? Toye's family tells the author that the Cleveland-born Marguerite had since 1907 studied voice in Italy before joining Boston. Lee Davis (*Bolton and Wodehouse and Kern* (1993) writes, "Long-limbed, willowy, fiery and blue-eyed", Marguerite had beauty and "fierce independence. Proud of her genius and protective of her honor" she refused Russell a pass, Davis speculates. Perhaps a kickback scheme.

When she complains to Toye about the abuse he confronts Russell who to stop word spreading to Jordan, summarily fires the couple. As he had swamped Loie Fuller. News gets out and about. No doubt Marguerite gave Alice the whole story. No doubt Alice would confront Russell. Not the first Boston fallout from Russell's foolish follies. Stories accumulate;

Very interestingly, the newlywed Toyes join Loie Fuller whose views of Russell's rackets are clear indeed. By 1911, Fred Toye would be Isadora Duncan's manager. As LA Symphony manager in 1913, Toye will hire Sylva, Nielsen, and other Boston stars. He manages his wife's career as Marguerite Namara until she drops him in 1917 for Guy Bolton.

Fred Toye could have saved Boston Opera if Russell had been fired.

Before March, Alice Nielsen makes aviation history. First New England woman to fly. Or try. Boston Aero Show at Mechanic's Hall, February 16-23, is the first American exhibition solely devoted to aircraft.

February 21st, *Boston Globe* proclaims, "Miss Nielsen Will Fly. The first aeroplane flight in Boston will be attempted Feb. 25 with a Page-Light biplane now on exhibition at the airship show. The flight will be made either from Boston Common or from Franklin field. Miss Alice Nielsen of the Boston opera company will be a passenger for a short flight and will be first woman in New England to make such a flight".

The biplane remains obscure. Rutherford Page of NYC built airplanes; the young Yale graduate dies 1912 at LA airshow, 114th aviation death, and Rev. FJ Emmett declines a mid-air wedding scheduled later that day.

The usual aviation history claims the first New England flight was February 28th, a Herring-Burgess biplane. Perhaps not! Eighteen prototype aeroplanes were shown at the Mechanic's Hall. The Boston airshow was in September; Wright Brothers and others gathered at Harvard-Boston field where, thanks to Alice's example no doubt, Harriet Quimby is inspired to become the first woman licensed to pilot; later dies in a crash.

Meanwhile at Met, Nielsen sings *Pasquale*. Milestone for her! Four years have passed since she faced that contrived disaster at Casino Theatre.

"Alice Nielsen...gives pleasure in her singing and her acting is arch and charming", captions *NY Times* (Fe 26). "Last night's performance served to introduce a new Norina ...who... appeared at the Metropolitan once during the Fall as Mimi in *La Bohème* and since then she has not been heard there until last evening. Miss Nielsen is really a member of the Boston Opera Company and it has been her continuous presence in that theatre which has prevented her appearing here.

"When this singer was heard in *La Bohème* it was remarked that she possessed a light voice of a delightful quality. It was also recorded that she was a charming actress. Norina is a role, perhaps, which suits her less well than Mimi, but nevertheless she was heard last night to advantage. Her voice lacks some of the flexibility and the brilliancy necessary to give some of the passages in this score their fullest effect. Her scale is not perfectly equalized with the result that her high voice is better than her lower voice. However, she can give much pleasure by her singing. Her acting last night was arch and charming".

In the cast: Bonci "always sings with art, but last night it seemed his tone was rounder and fuller than usual". Scotti and Pini-Corsi "repeated former brilliant performances. Mr. Tango conducted".

1910 seems to start as a peak year for both Nielsen sisters. Hortense and husband Charles Quintard establish the Nielsen Repertory Theatre in Los Angeles. They take a ten-year lease on Walker Theatre, Grand Avenue at 7th (*LA Times* Mar 3), "It requires courage to attempt what CA Quintard will do when he throws open the doors of the Nielsen Theatre, formerly the Walker, with a new stock company". After extensive expensive remodeling "starting today...it will be known in the future as the Nielsen Theatre". The repertory company is "headed by Miss Hortense Nielsen in First-Class Productions. First-class stock performances are promised...a number of high-class plays, notable among which are several Ibsen, Jones and Pinero plays, will be done at the remodeled theater. The company...will number several well-known players in its list, and rank and file will be of good sort".

They list an "IH Nielsen" as music director with eight musicians. Quite possibly the estimable pianist, sibling Erasmus.

And at last Alice Nielsen sings the composer Wagner. The Sunday concert at Boston Opera (*Boston Sunday Globe* Mar 6) features "many of the principal artists in arias from grand operas". Nielsen sings *Elsa's Dream* from *Lohengrin*. Continues with quintet from *Die Meistersinger von Neumberg* joined by Roberts, Hansen, Stroesceo and Baklanoff. Wallach Goodrich conducts, opening with *Overture to William Tell* and closing with *The Ride of the Valkyries*.

As expected, a crazy Polish soprano surfaces March 9 (*NY Times*). Mme. Sweike "found insane" near the Opera House giving "random replies... a subconscious feeling that she was bound to attend a rehearsal. Dr. Groves was called". The breakdown "due to overwork...need not necessarily result in hopeless insanity". Sent to Cambridge where the others nest.

Boston Opera reaches its second year. Initial stockholders get a changed deal. New stock at $100 is issued for $200,000, and stockholding subscribers are limited to guaranteed tickets for only one day per week so "the general public" can "obtain seats more easily" *NY Times* (Mar 8).

That wasn't all they would be surprised. A huge controversy erupts at the news that bankable Nielsen and Constantino were off the schedule.

Stockholders are dismayed, nay outraged, to discover the foreign hired manager Russell has ditched the stars Nielsen and Constantino which the Boston Opera stockholders have invested and subscribers paid to see.

Both stars found fault with him for cause. Challenged his contemptable dealings with others such as Loie Fuller and the Toyes. Difficult for Russell to see them around. They have influence. They have friends. He has secret plans to return rich to Europe. His Boston scheme is a temporary racket: pose, take, grab, go. Legacy be damned. Also from this point the hireling in hubris attempts to transfer to the Met, Chicago, or Philly. Abuses the press to pose; easily outmaneuvered by his betters. Word has spread. Nobody wants him. Astonishingly unaware what Nielsen alone had gifted him; a fog of corruptions blocks gratitude. His pal D'Annunzio had instilled a blindly hypnotic fascism within the suggestible sly hired hand ruling at Boston who rapidly removes every chance of sustainable success.

An actual albeit flawed manager, Perley had pointed out audiences will show up at first for any novelty; but loyalty needs the stars.

Against these schemes Boston press speaks out.

Russell's lobbying is revealed March 10th by *NY Times* (1910) when he unilaterally announces an "opera trust" [monopoly] linking Boston, NY, and Chicago "for mutual good...to control the operatic field. In order to get stars to sing in NY it is necessary to pay them for a great many more performances than can be given in one theatre. Road tours... necessitated doubling the chorus and orchestra so...the extra expense exceeded the returns". Stars rotate towns. Full tours eliminated. "Form a trust for the purpose of economy. The arrangement will work in other ways. The singers in foreign countries now have us at their mercy. If we control between us the operatic situation in America there is no reason why we should give foreign singers all they demand".

No gratitude in remora Russell with his three-year salary from Jordan.

This is Russell's first year at his first steady theatre job. Now he wants the Met, "I shall be very glad at any time to receive advice from Signor Gatti-Casazza in regard to opera matters about which he must know more than I do, and perhaps I can be of some small assistance to him because I speak English and am perhaps more familiar with American business methods" (*NY Times* Mar 12). To escalate things, he unwisely releases a telegram promoting himself as "co-director with Mr. Gatti-Casazza at the Metropolitan Opera House".

Badly overplays his hand. Response laughter. No, he cannot dip his fingers in the NYC till. Boston opera has a business manager, ain't him.

The Met's chief stockholder Vanderbilt supports director Gatti-Casazza with Andreas Dippel as "administrative manager". Gatti-Casazza "asked to have his position so clearly defined that he can have no further difficulties placed in his way". The Met board dismisses the Russell gambit. When Dippel leaves NY to run Chicago Opera, Russell appeals again to Kahn who rebuffs him. Without Nielsen as bait, no fish wish to invite the predator.

Alert Boston press observe these schemes with concern.

In March, Boston's board joined by Theodore Vail and Walter Baylies set the next season at twenty weeks, orchestra seats $5 (*NY Times* Mar 20). As April nears, the Met takes "seven day coaches and as many baggage cars" to Boston Opera for *Aida* (*NY Times* Mar 27). In show biz news, Victor Herbert lacks a dependable diva; Fritzi Scheff "obliged to suspend her tour" of *Mlle. Modiste* "several weeks ago" has rejoined in Pittsburgh "entirely recovered from her nervous breakdown" if she had one.

April 2, Nielsen Theatre in Los Angeles opens with Hortense in the drama *Carmen* by Olga Nethersole. Alice is in Chicago with the Met, so this possible drama-opera season by the sisters does not occur.

Nethersole (1871-1951), the British actress, dramatist and producer of Spanish descent, made a dozen plays 1894-1910. Charles Frohman star, her *Sapho* (Claude Fitch) shocked 1902 NY. In WWI, a Red Cross nurse.

In downtown LA, 900-seat Nielsen Theatre is "tastefully decorated in quiet tints in the art nouveau manner, with much ornamental staff in gules and rosettes". The color scheme "green and gold-brown, touched with gold", parquet and balcony fitted with opera chairs for reserved seating. Main lobby, brilliantly lit stretches sixty feet. Color scheme "different shades of restful greens... carried over to the pagoda-shaped box office directly in the center (*LA Times* Ap 2)".

Hortense is directed by husband Quintard.

Co-star is Mace Greenleaf, absent from stage "two years and a half" during his marriage to frivolous California heiress Lucy Banning who dumped him for a fling of many. Her pal Rebecca Dorsey meows of Banning, "She never heeded anyone's advice from the day she was born. Our very own Lucy Banning can share the stage with any two Lillian Russells. To phrase it delicately she was man-crazy".

Meanwhile Alice, praised by Hubbard for giving the "Boston Opera lesson to Chicago" (*Chicago Tribune* Jan 13), opens with the Met tour.

For *Rigoletto*, Glenn Dillard Gunn (*Chicago Tribune* Apr 6), "Nielsen a bright spot;" she makes the show. Cast: Nielsen, Campanari, Bonci, Didur.

Gunn is displeased by sloppiness: "The Metropolitan company lapsed into the carelessness and roughness that distinguished the organization in former years...stage management distinguished itself by the loud ringing of an electric bell during a duet between Miss Nielsen and Mr. Bonci in the second act, to the obvious embarrassment of the singers and the distraction of the player's attention".

Gunn apologizes to Alice for the Met, "It is a matter for sincere regret that Miss Nielsen made her first appearance in Chicago with The Metropolitan company under such unfavorable conditions.

Worse, "She found it impossible to remain true to the pitch in the songs with Bonci and Campanari, since they were almost constantly flat. But when she sang alone one realized that the voice had gained in warmth and in surety in the upper register even in the short time that has elapsed since she was heard here with the Boston company.

"Her last aria in the 2nd Act was remarkable for its tonal beauty as well as for its fine and sensitive regard for the melodic line. It was shaded and phrased with the same care that a capable violinist would have expended upon it, and it roused the house to demonstrative expressions of approval. Miss Nielsen found another grateful opportunity in the scene between the wronged daughter and the vengeful father" as she helps Bonci overcome "to some extent his tendency to disregard the pitch".

For the rest: "there remains little to record".

Chicago's attack on NYC continues, "Afternoon performance drags despite the work of Caruso and Miss Nielsen" in *Bohème*. This is their first performance together since Covent Garden.

Cast: Alice Nielsen, Mimi; Enrico Caruso, Rodolfo; Lenora Sparkes, Musetta; Giuseppe Campanari, Marcello; Adamo Didur, Schaunard; Giulio Rossi, Colline; Antino Pini-Corsi, Benoit. Vittorio Podest conducted.

Glenn Dillard Gunn reports, "Miss Nielsen and Caruso carried off honors at the matinee yesterday, and despite the fact that the great tenor had the misfortune to be vocally indisposed. The slight clouding of the voice noticed opening night had developed into an irritating cold. However, Caruso indisposed is usually to be preferred to any other tenor in good voice, and yesterday afternoon proved no exception to this.

"The combination of Caruso, Nielsen and Puccini should have won larger expression of public interest than was indicated by an audience that filled little more than half the seats". For the show's listlessness, "one is inclined to blame the stage management [director]". Without Toscanini, the Met productions are "executed clumsily. Nielsen and Caruso earned the largest portion of these expressions of favor and justly.

"Miss Nielsen... finds in Mimi a most sympathetic role. It not only permits her to display her admirable talents as an actress to fine advantage, but the music lies so well for her voice that her share in it is a source of delight. The temptation to dwell upon the beauty and purity of her upper register is not to be resisted. She soars to a high A or B flat with a freedom that seems to know no restraint. Only a slight harshness in her high C showed that the change from the lyric to the dramatic style has not yet been completely accomplished. For the rest one admired the warmth and sympathy of the voice in the middle and lower register and the interpretive taste and skill with which the signer varied the color of the tone to suit the passing moods of the text".

The Met loses $100,000 in Chicago (*Tribune* Apr 9), said to be half the losses of previous tours.

Back in NYC, tottering impresario Hammerstein produces more lawsuits than operas. Mary Garden "sailed away yesterday on the *Adriatic*" saying he "treated her like a chorus girl and that unless his attitude changed she would not return next season (*NY Times* Ap 10)". Hammerstein idiotically claims "by some oversight" Garden has been paid in dollars, not francs as contracted, "and he wanted his money back". Next, tenor Alfred Seligsberg sues for unpaid salary $33,800. Next, Marguerite Sylva wins her case, judge ruling that Hammerstein's claim she is unique is void since he scheduled other singers in Sylva's roles.

Jump cut. LA's Nielsen Theatre. Second week. "Hortense Nielsen, supported by Mace Greenleaf and a good sized company, is offering for her second week in the new Nielsen Theater...*Frou-Frou* [1870], the Augustin Daly [1838-1899] comedy. Especial attention has been paid to the mounting of the production. Mr. Greenleaf has the role of Sartoris, and the rest of the people are happily assigned. *Frou-Frou* will hold the boards for the remainder of the week" (*LA Times* April 13th).

Hammerstein quits (*NY Times* Apr 28). His son Arthur at Otto Kahn's place (8 East 68th St.) transfers buildings, rights, scenery, costumes, artist contracts and Philadelphia Opera House to the Met. Oscar cables son, "I'm glad and I'm sorry". Philadelphia financier Edward Stotesbury (1849-1938), JP Morgan partner, closed the deal in six weeks, "Hammerstein has decided to retire from the operatic field. I have purchased from him his Philadelphia Opera House".

Tragedy occurs for Hortense within a month. Almost makes a comic opera. Actor Mace Greenleaf bails out; the new leading man Jack Sheridan is fired, stopping the shows in mid-April. They have had two weeks in their new theatre. A replacement does not appear. Cash flow tight, despite the extensive remodeling and the big future plans, Hortense and husband Quintard prove unable to continue performances beyond April. All is lost.

So the plot thickens, *n'est pas*? Hapless Sheridan came to LA in vaudeville at Princess Theatre before hired by Hortense to replace Mace Greenleaf. Fired by the Nielsens, "thrown on his own resources and trouble resulted". Sheridan is charged with grand larceny by wealthy Mrs. SA Brooks who at fifty "devoted much time to philanthropy". She visiting a sick girl when "she met Sheridan, they became friends and the officers allege that Sheridan made life a burden for the woman by constantly asking that she give him $2,100" to start a moving-picture business. When Brooks consents and offers a check, he demands "nothing but cash". She gives. Sheridan "was leaving for Chicago with his wife when arrested". The "former leading man at the Nielsen Theatre and his wife, a vaudeville player...were locked up in the City Jail after they had resorted to every trick of the melodrama to induce the officers to turn them loose".

In May, Alice returns to Boston, her port of departure for scheduled European concerts. She provides celebrity endorsements for *NY Times* theatre ads. Praises a new Henry Miller play at the Garrick; calls comedy by AE Thomas, *Her Husband's Wife*, "absolutely delightful"; and the witty Chicago journalist George Ade has "A bully play". Shows with Nielsen connections onstage include Casino's *Chocolate Soldier* with libretto by Stanislaus Stange; and Marie Dressler stars in *Tillie's Nightmare*.

May 8, Alice Nielsen sails to London on White Star *Arabic* to perform again for Edgar Elgar "at Manchester and Birmingham, returning here in October to join the Metropolitan" (*NY Times* Ma 8). Son Benjamin Nielsen accompanies.

May 22 at London's Albert Hall, Nielsen joins Elgar, who made four conducting tours to America 1902-1914. Continuing to the continent, Alice sings several concerts, studies new operas in Milano (*Boston Globe* Se 26), then reaches Naples. She and son will travel extensively through Switzerland and Italy.

Back in LA, Hortense grimly survives two months before disaster. Her lovely remodeled theatre and ten-year lease are lost. And on July 2nd, "CA Quintard, a theatrical man arrested at San Diego, was brought back to the city today and arraigned before Justice Underwood on a charge of passing a bogus $50 check to a local grocer". Held by $1500 bond for a preliminary hearing, "Quintard is in bad physical shape and friends are trying to arrange a bond or to settle his indebtedness".

Specifics have not come to light. "On July 1st 1910 the local police of Los Angeles Cal apprehended CA Quintard for defrauding merchants with bogus checks drawn on a Los Angeles bank", writes *Banking Journal*, alas without a portrait. Making the jail sacrifice once again, he does not remain long in the hoosegow; Hortense springs him.

So it is. Within three months Hortense has lost everything. She goes from front page of the *LA Times'* Drama Section April 1st to a buried footnote July 1st. Turns practical. Within two weeks, July 17th *SF Call* reports "Hortense Nielsen ...who has gained much prominence in the east and middle west as an interpreter of Ibsen roles" had joined the LR Stockwell players. Next week (*SF Call* Ju. 24), Hortense at Princess Theatre plays Esther in *Mizpah* (1904), "story of Esther in dramatic form by Mrs. Ella Wheeler Wilcox and the late Luscombe Searelle".

Intriguing couple; Searelle is the British-born poet-composer raised in New Zealand who died at fifty-four in 1907 San Francisco. Wilcox (1850-1919), a Spiritualist poet, wrote famed *Solitude*: "Laugh and the world laughs with you, weep and you weep alone; For the sad old earth must borrow its mirth; But has trouble enough of its own". Interestingly, Ella Wilcox is among Marie Dressler's close friends along with Alice.

As July closes, Victor Talking Machines touts nine new records by Alice Nielsen and Constantino "of the San Carlo Opera Company [of SF etc]". The new set includes *Addio del passato* and *Mi chimano Mimi*.

In August, Balfe arrives at Boston Opera House without Alice. She skips flaunting her *Satanella*. Producers Milton and Sargeant Aborn run Balfe's *Bohemian Girl* two weeks Sept. 19 then tour "a strong cast, a chorus and ballet of 150" plus twenty horses onstage, none played by comic duos. Much later, the Aborns will briefly revive a version of Nielsen's Victor Herbert shows, also sans Alice.

September. Dippel now at Chicago Opera announces Nielsen slated as guest artist; also Constantino, Caruso, Scotti, Lipkowska, Farrar (*NY Times* Se 21).

From Naples, Alice and son reach Boston on White Star *Romantic* (*Boston Globe* Se 26). "Alice Nielsen the opera singer and her brother [*son*] Benjamin T. Nielsen were among the saloon passengers" arriving at Pier 43 Hoosac docks, Charlestown after brief quarantine for cholera at Azores.

Nielsen, "first returning American not to condemn the new customs duty on purchases abroad" says, "I think people rich enough to go abroad and purchase articles instead of purchasing them in this country should pay a duty". Also disembarking are Raffaele Vena and Boston Opera stage manager Theodore L. Stoddard of Cambridge. No relation to Nielsen's present pal and future husband the surgeon LeRoy Stoddard discovered.

As the company assembles, the salaryman Russell "before sailing from Boulogne" attacks the gayety: "encores would be prohibited this season" and "the German rule admitting none except those holding boxes to seats while the curtain is still up will also be enforced" (NY Times Oct 2).

Arrival and assembly of opera companies create impact. A shipping strike delays "costumes and properties of the singers of the Boston Opera House who arrived yesterday at Hoboken in the Holland-America liner Nieuw Amsterdam" (*NY Times* Nov 1).

In the cast: Lydia Lipkowska hides not child nor scandals. She lands proudly with young daughter Ariadne and chef Edmond Nowakowski who will make "sugared cakes, game pies and borscht, the national soup". Her husband had refused to sign her passport, the Tsar gave permission.

Fely Dereyne and sister Ida from Buenos Aires bring fluffy white kitten Pullucun "able to meow in Spanish and Russian". The usual "mob of vodka-crazed peasants" had delayed George Baklanoff when they "looted his estate at Kiev. Thirty arrested". Baklanoff, a lawyer, returns "to defend the peasants, asserting they were not responsible for their actions" and "all were set free". Elvira Leveroni, Carmen Mellis, Celina Bonheur, Janina Czaplinska, Leo Devaux, Lucette de Lievin, Leon Sibiriakoff stride down the gangplank. Leveroni and Bertha Wheeler were quarantined in Naples by a cholera scare. Constantino, delayed returning from South America, misses the first week.

Boston Opera opens its second season November 7 with *Mefistofele*, "a fine audience filled the Opera House...boundless enthusiasm prevailed". Critics grow "enthusiastic over the scenery, the ballet and the chorus, all of which show an advance even upon the high standard which was set last year".

Meanwhile back in LA, sad note November 10 (*LA Times*), "In Judge Willis's court...CA Quintard, charged with passing a bad check, was found guilty. He will be sentenced this morning". Details lost to us.

In Boston November 16th, Alice Nielsen sings the American premier and second world performance of Debussy's *L'Enfant prodigue*.

Boston Herald, "The opera proved a toothsome novelty, and is afforded effective contrast to the performance of *I Pagliacci* which followed. The staging was a wonderfully suggestive and artistic achievement". With nine segments "there is no plot, properly speaking. The production was excellent although Miss Nielsen and Mr. Blanchart were newer to the music than Mr. Lassalle".

November 30th, Nielsen in *Butterfly*. Her 1898 Yokohama kimonos had been integrated into the Josef Urban design.

Musical Courier: patroness Mrs. Gardner brings Nordica and Melba to the Boston performance as "interested spectators of Miss Nielsen's triumph". Melba will be working wiles on anyone with influence. Weakest link is old pal-on-demand Henry Russell who later describes their relations "on and off". And later, Melba in Australia will get the last laugh.

Last season, Nielsen sang "under the trying conditions of warding off a severe cold. But even then, she displayed the thoughtfully planned conception which, aided by the naturally plaintive timbre of her voice, absorbed and held the sympathetic attention of the audience.... Now, this conception has grown finer, larger, better developed, and Miss Nielsen makes the Geisha girl a figure foredoomed to suffer from the very inception. Without realizing it herself perhaps, Butterfly shows very little of the abandon, the coquetry of a young girl pursued in marriage by so handsome a suitor as Pinkerton. She is at once overwhelmed by a shy adoration of for this lover, which is combined with the foreboding engendered by the brutal curse of her kinsman at the conclusion of the marriage ceremony. This fear for her happiness already haunts the lovely duet filled with its delirious abandon at the close of the scene...when all is said and done Miss Nielsen has again created a conception which must add greatly to her artistic stature, both vocally and histrionically".

Boston Herald admires Nielsen's artistic growth, "her composition of the part is now more elaborate and in the second act she plays with more finesse and also with a greater intensity. She is now more effective in this act than the first".

Still, "before the marriage she takes herself too seriously; there is too little suggestion of coquetry; there is not the light and dainty touch. Perhaps Miss Nielsen thinks she is thus more in keeping with the true Japanese character and does not wish to be an operetta Madama Butterfly, for Miss Nielsen has her own ideas about the characters she impersonates; she works out her own theories. Miss Nielsen sang with appreciation of the significance of the text and the situations...."

Alice "sang in fine voice and was artistic in her interpretation, but emotionally she failed to make the part carry all its values. In her childishness she was not entirely naïve, and in her tragedy the heart did not break and the voice did not thrill with anguish. Miss Nielsen gave to the flower song its beauty and artistic sweep of color and emotion, the flowing, liquid quality of her voice being charmingly suited to it. She was in the part always dainty and appealing".

In the cast: "Blanchart as Sharpless did the most finished work of the evening" but these Italians merely masquerade in Japanese dress.

Nielsen without pause resumes far-flung concert tours. Local music clubs and groups sponsor her with financial guarantees, as had Bryn Mawr. She sings modern music mostly; her taste in song quite unlike the usual soprano recitals. Her mom's old favorites among Kansas City street songs make up the encores. Small American towns tell that side of the Alice Nielsen story best.

December 9, Hartford (CN). Alice sings American composer James Rogers as popularized by Nordica; plus Debussy, Arensky, Loomis, Max Stange's *Damon*; Greig's *Im Kahn*, Tosti's *Voi Dormite Signora*; and arias from *Butterfly*, *L'Enfant Prodigue*, and Bonocini's 1722's *Per La Gloria*.

Hartford Daily Current: at Parson's Theatre, Alice Nielsen "gave a song recital under auspices of the Musical Club and the fine audience...found much to enjoy in the singer's art" which "made most apparent her musical sense in abandoning a prosperous career in light opera.... The 'warhorses' of the usual soprano song recital program were conspicuous in their absence... German lieder appeared not at all and the old English songs too had no place...but there were plenty of modern songs in German, Italian and English, with a couple of Mozart numbers and one old Italian put in just to show the singer's range is not absolutely confined to the works of recent composers".

Her pianissimo skill prized: "Miss Nielsen has a voice of purity and strength and she possess especial skill in her management of quiet effects. There is power enough for the climaxes...but really her artistic strength was shown at its best in sustained tones of the half voice or even lighter".

Sensitive writers describe Nielsen's approach. Each note and word she carefully considers, notes preserved in pencil marks on her scores now stored at Kansas City Library.

Another masterpiece of performance insight arrives from *Harford Times* which with a subtle statement of great poetic truth delivers one of the best assessments of Alice Nielsen's approach to concerts.

"Miss Nielsen is a modern singer and a ballad singer par excellence. That is, she puts expression in the first pace and carries the audience somehow to the scene of the song. Then she makes them feel its intent, and so places the color and the passion, carried to the climax.

"There is a tenderness of expression which only becomes manifest when it touches the quick. And there is a passion and a feeling which find their way to the heart. In all these inward qualities one is apt to overlook the masterful performance, the beauty of tone, the more outward manifestation of singing. But all are there. Not the brilliancy and the sheen, not the mere splendor, of voice of power of artifice, it is the contents and the heart of the song which the modern audience prizes and the modern artist conveys".

Significantly, "the expression goes from mind to mind, from heart to heart—not simply that which goes from mouth to ear".

Nielsen observes audiences with keen interest. Boston critics say she sings better for any small attentive group than large disinterested ones.

"Fine looking ...of fair and open countenance, she came on stage with a free step and looked her audience in the face". After Debussy, she sings simple *Per la Gloria*. "With the third number *Do Not Delay*, the voice gained warmth and power and tenderness". For Roger's *Love Has Wings*, "this had to be repeated, the audience clamored for it. Especially did they want the concluding verse, in which Miss Nielsen exhibited all the art of the vocalist and all the romance of the ballad". And *A Little Dutch Garden* "had comedy and it had heart. The singer delivered it with a winsome, gay air and the audience responded gleefully". Liszt's *The Loreley* "sung in grand style. It was slow, dramatic and full of portent". Richard Strauss' *Serenade* had to be repeated by acclaim. And onward to the *Butterfly*'s *Un bel dì*".

Hartford has been home to South Carolina diva Louise Kellogg since 1887, an artist active in its cultural life until her 1915 death. The unsigned author captures the Alice Nielsen impact. "This evening... brought us modern ballads and a singer whose sterling worth in interpreting them is a revelation. One went home charged with the music, and the sentiment, and the poetry of these verses, indissolvably united".

Back in Boston as Loie Fuller warned, Russell keeps making trouble with many people. Cannot suppress every wicked thing. The press grows wary. He cleverly dodges scandal for a while, twisting arms of singers for kickbacks, expense-paid first class Europe junkets with entourage. These contribute to the rumor-mill. Thanks to Alice he got hired and emerges from the cloak of obscurity. Plight won; turns out he is stupidly talentless.

Absolute power tests a bad character absolutely.

All he needed do was let the stars shine and Boston Opera would live.

Russell gets away with much. Even so, curiously strange events continue to emerge. December the Russians revolt (*NY Times* Dec 13). Gracious Baklanoff is fired again "after a rather stormy disagreement" with Russell. Baklanoff declines to sing afternoon rehearsals of *La Habanera* after Russell puts him off *Otello* "a day or two ago" in favor of Sammarco.

"Baklanoff, who is very popular was much hurt. Mlle Lipkowska, who is also a Russian, may quit in sympathy with Baklanoff". Russell threatens them both with banishment from Boston, NY and Chicago! This leads to the exposure of his kickbacks and publicity payoffs laundered via a small Boston music magazine he controls with the press agent. Angers singers, creates gossip which steadily pressures journalists to tell the public.

Meanwhile, Alice Nielsen opens the new Montreal Opera. The fun town of her *Singing Girl* premier now finds her as *Butterfly*. Founded by Albert Clerk-Jeanotte, Frank Stephen Meighen, Charles Lamontagne, Montreal Opera eventually ends badly.

Nielsen's acting vies with praise for voice.

Le Canada (Dec 15, translated from French): "Last night our opera troupe gave a second performance of...*Madame Butterfly*, in Italian. The principal character was...Alice Nielsen, who was deeply emotional and charming to the large audience which filled the theatre. She acted like a great artist as the Geisha, who gives herself completely to the love of Pinkerton. The audience gave to the artist a true ovation, and at the end of every act, Miss Nielsen was called several times and flowers were presented her. At the end of the first and third acts, the reception given the artist was delirious".

La Presse: Nielsen "sang throughout with excellent effect...the second act ...was altogether charming. She sang...with splendid emotional force. There were numerous curtain calls".

Daily Star: "Alice Nielsen is no stranger to Montreal. Her return here recalls her triumphs in comic opera—not so many years ago—and her first essay in grand opera" as Mimi in *Bohème* she sang "at the Theatre Francais two years ago and since then her native land has claimed her. As an earnest and sincere artiste she is always assured of a warm welcome in this city, where she has many admirers". She creates "the Japanese aspect effectively...there is poetry in her gentle movements...expression, pose, gesture—these are admirable".

She sings with genuine feeling as gestures, Delsarte-like, tell the story.

"A good deal of the effectiveness of the second act was obtained through Miss Nielsen's delightful pianissimo singing" and acting: "Her sudden turn-about when she had identified Pinkerton's ship through the telescope, her whole body suggestive in pose and tenseness, of rapturous delight, her face lit up with joyous anticipation, was but one example of the work she can do".

Montreal Daily Herald: "Miss Nielsen is emphatically clever, she has excellent technique and a voice which is lyric...she was a coquettish and vivacious little Butterfly, and sang at all times pleasingly, and quite often brilliantly". Voice has "strength enough to carry it easily above an orchestra's fortissimo. Dramatically she was best in the parts with the 'bambino.'"

Back in Boston December 19th, Nielsen sings in *Carmen*. Excepting Gay and Nielsen, *Musical Courier* dislikes the cast. Board and Jordan must be noticing by now how the quality of singers drops under Russell's watch.

In the cast: "Gay's Carmen has been thoroughly discussed; Mr. Zenatello lacked artistic authority"; Mr. Rothier "distinct disappointment" with the bass singing a baritone role.

"Alice Nielsen, on the other hand, brought an arch freshness, a charmingly coquettish girlishness to bear upon the part of Micaela that lifted it from namby-pamby overly sweet creation of dull routine to a real live flash-and-blood woman. It is not to be supposed that Micaela can successfully combat the wiles of the gypsy, but she can be made more than a mere lay figure and Miss Nielsen carried that out splendidly in all way, her lovely voice with its fresh girlish timbre becoming a notable adjunct in her impersonation".

Three days later (Dec 22), Nielsen rushes to Pittsburg to join the composer Charles Wakefield Cadman, singing a new song learned in three days and polished on train. Favor for a friend. He plays as Nielsen sings.

Born 1881 in Johnstown, Pa., at fourteen Cadman became a church organist; at seventeen self-published *Carnegie Library March*, selling 6,000 copies door-to-door. He was fifteen when Herbert began conducting Pittsburgh Orchestra. Inspired by Bostonian's *Robin Hood*, he composed operettas. As organist at East Liberty Presbyterian Church, Cadman conducts Pittsburg Male Chorus; acts as music critic for *Pittsburg Dispatch* and *Musical Courier*; field-records tribal music for Smithsonian. In 1906 adapts American Indian tunes as art songs; 1908 moves to Santa Fe for tubercular plight. His Cherokee mezzo, Tsianni provides the plot for his opera *Shanewis*, performed at the Met. During the 1930s Cadmna lives in Virgin Islands, retires to California. This year singing with Nielsen he returned from Santa Fe to Pittsburgh for the town's gala in his honor.

Exiting her train two hours late due to snow, Alice says "I was so sorry when I first heard Mr. Cadman's health had given way. I was so glad when

I found out that Cadman himself is to accompany me on the piano when I sing his songs. It will help me do my best".

She adds, "It is too bad the Pittsburg Orchestra had to disband. I am at a loss to understand the failure to support an orchestra". After the star conductor, Victor Herbert left, orchestra unstrung itself. Warning Boston.

The concert reviews praise for quality, and give gratitude.

Pittsburg Dispatch: "The coming of Miss Nielsen, her great generosity... will go down in the musical history of the city as one of the most gracious things a famous singer has ever done. Pittsburgh's gratitude, Mr. Cadman's...the...committee's gratitude can scarcely be estimated. And how the wonderful little lady of the Boston company did sing!"

Cadman's new *Japanese Song Cycle* is the novelty. "Miss Nielsen, who has lived in Japan [a few weeks] and who is a student of Oriental folklore and ethnology, was enabled thereby to reveal the very essence of each phrase. It wasn't hard to see she had studied and analyzed every passage in the cycle. Then the beauty of tone, the poise and the finish of her singing, proclaimed her the great artist she is. The audience went wild at the conclusion of her work, and when she comes again—and it is hoped 'twill be soon—another royal welcome will undoubtedly be hers".

Pittsburg Sun: "Alice Nielsen was well deserving of the gloriously enthusiastic reception accorded her, as in a brief time for study she had thoroughly familiarized herself with the *Sayonara* song cycle and the *From The Land Of The Sky Blue Water*, singing them with a spirit and feeling which could not help please the most critical".

Pittsburg Dispatch: Nielsen's "singing of the beautiful Japanese song cycle *Sayonara* was something to be marveled at, considering that she had only a few hours a day for three days to learn it. Her mezzo voice was beautiful and in the more dramatic parts she was equally successful. So complete an understanding of the matter in hand and the wonderful interpretation of it made her work a genuine marvel".

Pittsburg Telegraph: "Nielsen's treat for the audience came near the end of the program. She sang the new Japanese suite...with the composer at the piano. Real Japanese themes are employed in this cycle and the perfect understanding and wonderful interpretation of the suite made her work marvelous. Both singer and composer were recalled many times".

Pittsburg Post: "Nielsen sang...with lovely vocal effect and sympathetic interpretation and Mr. Cadman's playing...was equally fine.

Returning to Boston, Alice Nielsen closes 1910 in a joint program with Anna Pavlova's Russian Ballet. Nielsen, Lassalle, Blanchart sing *L'Enfant Prodigue* conducted by Andre-Caplet. Pavlova and Mikail Mordkin follow with *Arabian Nights*, "supported by the Complete Imperial Russian Ballet".

Pavlova soon will shock Indianapolis, "one wonders what sort of woman will bare her body and exhibit it to public gaze. Art? One kind perhaps, but there are some people brought up with ideas of modest that will be willing to have this branch of their education underdeveloped" (quoted by Eaton 1965). Of course all the dance stars had these moments.

1911: BETRAYAL IN BOSTON

A new opera in English arose at Boston, Converse's *The Sacrifice*, dully set same era (or error) and place as *War-Time Wedding*. During the year, Herbert's grand opera *Natoma* debuts, same sad setting. Why a Mexican war fascinated librettists remains as obscure as the shows made of it. The Boston Opera *Titanic* speeds along, ignoring warnings of growlers ahead.

January 7, *Musical Courier*'s Gertrude Cowan sees Boston's *La Traviata* "dominated almost wholly by the splendidly artistic work of Miss Nielsen, ably aided by Mr. Constantino". The stars "crowded the opera house and called forth tremendous demonstrations of popular enthusiasm".

Boston's new opera house depends on this duo the hireling hates.

Cowan analyzes Nielsen's *bel canto*. "Alice Nielsen is one of those modestly unassuming artists who leaves her own personal ego absolutely behind her once she steps on the stage. With this, her art is so subtle, so refined and so perfectly finished, that unless one knows, and knowing, listens with intelligent mind and wide open ears, the perfection of the whole is apt to be taken as a matter of course....

"Different artists make differing appeals". Some bring glamour which fades to disillusion, others "work so quietly that with each appearance their hold grows stronger and stronger, so that with this legitimate growth naturally comes the artistic value to the community as a whole, and the reflex action from the box office as well. Such emphatically is...Miss Nielsen's success".

Cowan recognizes the style absorbed her art exudes. "Her Violetta was a distinct triumph of bel canto, of beautiful womanly appeal, and of the perfect 'art within art' to which a sincere artist rises only after years of the most rigorous work and self examination when all thought of the student lamp is so far behind.... Runs, trills, scales, all were round, even and lovely, each tone complete in its lower middle and upper vibrations, and tossed off with such ease, grace and lightness that all thought of the singer disappeared in the music. In the short phrase preceding *Ah fors' e lui*, the introductory turn, as well as the aria itself, was given with such incomparable beauty of tone that the audience fairly hung spellbound. But it is difficult to enumerate point by point when everything is so perfectly accomplished, even to the death scene".

Again appears the magic phrase: "always be recalled".

"Of necessity there were curtain calls galore for Mr. Constantino, whose impersonation had the exquisite vocal fervor that is his at all times, and Miss Nielsen whose performance has set a high water mark of perfection which will always be recalled by those fortunate enough to have been present".

This month among other performances, Nielsen and Constantino are busily preparing for the world premier of Converse's *Sacrifice*.

January 19th Nielsen crosses over to the Met to sing Mimi. She makes quite an impression. Draws large enthusiastic crowd as usual in NY. Why she is not scheduled more often.

Boston Globe (Ja 19): "Nielsen's appearance tonight at the Metropolitan opera house in the part of Mimi...drew one of the largest and most enthusiastic audiences of the present season. Miss Nielsen scored a veritable triumph both vocally and histrionically. She sang the famous aria of the first act brilliantly and was compelled to respond to many curtain calls after each act. She received several huge bouquets of flowers from her many admirers in this city".

Bouncing back to Boston, Constantino falls "pinned beneath a fallen horse in the premier of *The Girl of the Golden West*". They were just about to hang the tenor. Arms bound, Constantino rides with cowboy actor Fred Stone. His horse slips "riding over a four-foot-high bridge leading to the stage". They fall. As stagehands extricate them, "the orchestra, unaware of the accident in the wings, was thundering rhythmically along...." Bruised tenor "ran on the stage just in time to catch his first note" before being lynched.

Fascinating footnote in grand opera history, Fred Stone (1873-1959). Will Rodgers names a child after Stone, theatrical successor to Barnabee. Rising from circus, minstrelsy, vaudeville, and Broadway to films and this here grand opera, Stone played the scarecrow in that first musical *Wizard of Oz*. Appeared in Herbert's *Red Mill*. Made nineteen feature films. Stone is the "grand old man of show business" says *Time* (Mar 16 '59).

February, Alice Nielsen puts her name on a touring opera company and hits the regional road between Boston performances. Slight change of title from Herbert days: "Alice Nielsen Operatic Company".

February 7, Nielsen opens in Providence (RI) for the first annual concert of the Society for Organizing Charity. "Despite the ranging blizzard, Infantry Hall held an audience numbering close to two thousand persons". Sympathetic Boston Opera singers join her group and join the audience.

Gertrude Cowen (*Musical Courier*): "Participants were given an opportunity to appear in both the solo and ensemble numbers from their operatic repertory, while Miss Nielsen gave an example of the more intimate art of song interpretation for which she is now becoming widely celebrated and which will not soon be forgotten by those present on this occasion".

Program ends with *Lucia* sextet: Lassalle, Fornari, Mardones: Trio from *Faust, The Duel*. Mardones: Solo from *Samson and Dalila, Mon Coeur S'Ouvre a Ta Voix* and solo from *Le Cid* (Ambrose Thomas). Nielsen: Mozart, *Deh! Vieni Non Tardar, Non So Piu*. Lassalle: Solo from *Manon, Saint Sulpice*. Nielsen, Claessens, Lassalle, Fornari: Quartet from *Rigoletto*. Roberter, Fishers, Claessens, Giaccone, Devaux: Quartet, *Carmen*. Savage, Mm. Lassalle, Mardones: *Faust, Trio Final*. Claessens: Solo from *La Gioconda, Voce di Donna*. Lassalle: solo from *La Tosca, Lucevan Le Stelle*. Nielsen: *Lately In Dance* (Arensky), *Love Has Wings* (Rogers), *From The Land Of Sky-Blue Water* (Cadman), *Aria*, Second Act, *Madame Butterfly* (Puccini). Fornari: Solo from *Il Barbiere di Siviglia, Cavatina*. Nielsen, Savage, Lassalle, Fornari, Perini, Giaccone: Sextet, *Lucia*.

Cowen continues, "Most successful operatic singers are not as a rule equally successful on the concert platform. The reason too, is not hard to seek. When added to the boon of outward action there are stage accessories, costume and the glamour created by the orchestral 'story....' With all the paraphernalia omitted, however, the bare concert platform becomes an exceedingly severe test of a singer's capabilities. Again too, the personality and bearing of a singer usually play a prominent part in this....

"It is just this combination...which make Miss Nielsen one of the few ideal concert singers now before the public.

"As a result of the insistent demand for her recital services everywhere, a standard has been set which few countries may equal and none exceed.

"Beginning with her rendering of the Mozart aria, Miss Nielsen displayed a vocal purity, an evenness of scale and roundness of tone which gave her singing the deceptively simple quality of quiet perfection—so unassumingly was it all done that very few understood the real difficulty of the arias, even though the lovely timbre of the voice itself drew a spontaneous outburst of enthusiasm from her hearers, which did not cease until she sang Strauss' *Serenade* as encore. In her group of songs again, the singer differentiated the mood of each so subtly that the enthusiasm of the audience increased with every added selection, until Cadman's *Land Of The Sky-Blue Water* was so insistently re-demanded that it had to be repeated".

Nielsen "after the splendid culmination of Puccini's aria...was compelled to return so often that she at length conceded another encore, closing her performance with Tosti's *Good-Bye,* a special request for this number having been sent to her during the concert".

Accompanists, Ralph Lyford and the durable E. Romaine Simmons.

Boston Opera's program for a typical season week deserves detailing, and here the entire program February 5-11 of 1911.

February 5, Sunday: "Grand Operatic Concert" with chorus and orchestra; Mmes. Nielsen and Bonheur and MM. Constantino and Mardones, conducted by Conti, Goodrich and Andre-Caplet.

February 6, Monday: *The Girl Of The Golden West* with Mmes. Melis, Leveroni, MM. Constantino, Galeffi, Gilla, Gant-voort, Blanchart, Mardones, Fornari, Devaux, Perini, Pulcini, Stroesco, Giaccone, Montella, Tavecchia, Sandrini, Ghidini and Conti.

February 8, Wednesday: *L'Enfant Prodigue* with Mme. Nielsen with Mm. Lassalle, Blanchart and Andre-Caplet. This was followed by *Hansel Und Gretel* with Mmes. Mattfeld, Alten, Cales-sens, Wickham, Swartz, B. Fisher, M. Goritz and Goodrich conducting.

February 10, Friday: *Il Trovatore* with Mmes. Rappold, G. Fisher, Claes, Sens, Mm. Slezak, Amato, Perini, Giaccone and Moranzoni conducting.

February 11, Saturday matinee: *La Gioconda* with Mmes. Nordica, Claeseens, Leveroni, MM. Martin, Baklanoff, Mardones, Pulcini, Stroesco and Conti conducting.

Saturday evening: *Lucia Di Lammermoor* with Mme. Lipkowska, Savage, Mm. Constantino, Polese, Stroesco, Perini, Giacoone and the conductor Moranzoni.

Unlike Park Theatre, Nielsen sings only thrice. Behind her back, the heartless hireling plots to push her out from Boston Opera by concocting difficulties he denies. Loie Fuller proves right. Details clarify years after.

Other season highlights: Isadora Duncan with NY Symphony conducted by Walter Damrosch February 23, "an entirely new Bach-Wagner program"; March 9, Anna Pavlova, Mikail Mordkin and Imperial

Russian Ballet's *Giselle*, suite from *Coppellia* and *Divertissment*; March 11, Marguerite Sylva's *Carmen*, her only Boston appearance that season.

NY Times features a Sylva photo, again hailing that three women from Nielsen's Broadway cast have arrived at the Met.

February 20, Sylva and Nielsen in Philadelphia with the Met. At the matinee Sylva, *Tales of Hoffman*. That night Nielsen, *Butterfly*, "her voice was beautiful. The prima donna received enthusiastic applause and a most cordial reception, re-establishing herself with Philadelphia audiences", said *Musical Courier*.

Boston Globe visits Philadelphia: "Alice Nielsen...sang the title role of Puccini's *Madama Butterfly*. Her beauty of voice and splendid method of singing aroused the large audience to genuine enthusiasm. She received curtain calls after each act".

Philadelphia Inquirer: Nielsen's "voice has gained considerably in volume since it was last heard here and if it has lost something of its pristine freshness and sweetness, it is still sufficiently agreeable and sympathetic.... There was some suggestion of effort in the big climax of the first act and it was pretty evident that the singer had no reserve power left but the tone produced was for the most part adequate and its delivery smooth and well sustained.

"On its dramatic side, the impersonation was extremely satisfying and praiseworthy. Miss Nielsen did not, as some do, try to fit her conception to the absurd title which the opera bears. If the nature of Cio-Cio-San had been akin to that of the butterfly there could have been no second or third acts, and the tragic denouement would have been quite out of the question.

"In order to invest an already highly improbably story with any aspect of plausibility, it is necessary that its heroine should be portrayed as inspired with a deep and serious sentiment and so she was last evening. She did not simper and giggle and smile as in the orthodox Japanese manner, but by the tender sobriety of her demeanor indicated a realization of the gravity of the step she was taking and so prepared the way for the subsequent developments".

Nielsen, "a well-considered and intelligently executed piece of work".

February 25, in Boston Nielsen sang *La Bohème* with Constantino. The cast: Dereyne, Polese, Mardones, Pulcini, Mogan, Tavecchia, Huddy and Stroesco. Goodrich conducts. *Musical Courier* reports, "It would be difficult to imagine a more perfect Mimi than Miss Nielsen, who sings and acts the gentle little grisette with the naive simplicity and lovely lyric beauty of a voice that has not its counterpart anywhere".

Nielsen's connections within Boston grow closer. Harvard's Edda Club, (students of Scandinavian descent) feature Nielsen in a March 7 benefit. Nielsen "will sing; the Pierian Sodality, the Harvard orchestra, will play". Henry Elchheim, first violin for Boston Symphony is soloist, Swedish singing society Harmoni of Boston bring folksongs.

Meanwhile, Nielsen prepares to premier Converse's *The Sacrifice*. Converse oddly remarks he is not really pleased with his work, but could do no better: "I am not completely satisfied with my part of *The Sacrifice*, but I have done as good work as I can do now". Yet the production fine, "I am perfectly satisfied however, more than satisfied with the production. Matters are taking shape very well, and I am optimistic about Friday night. I may perhaps do better work in the future, but this is my best to date. I consider that it is an advance over *The Pipe Of Desire* and that it is destined to be more popular. Of course, there is more substance to this opera. This is a human real story, as the other is not".

As Chicago had feared, Boston runs to fairies. And of his imps, Converse confesses, "The appeal of symbolism is always to a limited few and does not reach the public at large". (*Boston Daily* Mar 2).

Converse (1871-1940), native of Newton, graduated Harvard, studied in Munich, teaches at Harvard and New England Conservatory. Boston Opera seems his creative peak. His first opera has pastoral Greek fairy themes, recall Disney's *Fantasia*'s Beethoven segment; *Pipes of Desire*, first American opera produced at Met. Symphonic poem *Magic Trumpeter*, taken from Walt Whitman's *Leaves of Grass* is his most popular effort.

"There is no earthly reason why we should not have American opera. There is an abundance of material for whoever seeks it", Converse continues. He wrote most of the text. His optimism eerily *Chanticleerian* given the ill-omened libretto setting. Perhaps he attended *War-Time Wedding* in Alice's Bostonian days. The memory persists in his mind.

Lyricist John Macy cynically complains, "Isn't it true that our American public would starve an American composer named Smith [librettist Harry Smith made fortunes]. But if he went to Munich and changed his name to Hofbrau and produced a successful opera, Mr. Zwinglejapper would bring it to New York and charge us $5 a seat for the privilege of hearing it".

Nice speech signifying nothing; apology for a dead imagination. Macy (1877-1932 Harvard 1899), publishes *Spirit of American Literature* (1913). In Boston he affects "a wide sombrero hat, and always troubled by an iron-gray forelock that droops over his brow". His wife is Anne Sullivan, teacher of Helen Keller. Macy advocates developing artistic strengths of a "dignified and self-respecting" regionalism, drawing on philosopher Josiah Royce's views for support and the inspiration he himself lacks. Never a deep thinker, his book omits opera. Reviewing hymns and poems, he claims, "Our poets desert the domestic landscape to write pseudo-Elizabethan dramas and sonnets... beside the shores of Lake Michigan they croon the love affairs of an Arab in the desert and his noble steed...the novelists are the worst offenders". Macy should know; writing about 1848 Mexico from remote Boston in an opera conspiracy with Converse who dabbles in dainty Greek fairies. Macy had spent too much time talking to undergrads.

To Boston press, Marcy clarifies his limited role, "I am not the author of the greater portion of the book. I merely wrote the words for two or three lyric passages, the music of which was already done. Converse made the book as well as the music. It was all but finished before I saw it".

Perhaps hinting at the backstage bothersome, Alice changes her mind.

She will promote "Opera in English" over a native-language libretto. Having learned Italian repertoire at a great cost, today she pitches Converse's English opera in strongest terms.

As Louise Kellogg suggests, a diva must be the best in chosen repertory. Shows that Herbert created for Nielsen for example. In the 1870s, Clara

Kellogg prospered with "opera in English. The subject of English opera—or, rather, foreign grand opera given in English—the giving of which was an undertaking on which I embarked in 1873. I became my own manager and, with CD Hess, organized an English Opera Company that, by its success, brought the best music to the comprehension of the intelligent masses. I believe that the enterprise did much for the advancement of musical art in this country; and it, besides, gave employment to a large number of young Americans, several of whom began their careers in the chorus of the company and soon advanced to higher places in the musical world". She toured three years. Boston's own Castle Square Company in 1897 celebrated its 500th performance of operas in English, expanding to NY, St. Louis, Chicago.

Glowing hopes for *Sacrifice* much resemble Kansas City's *Chanticleer.*

Nielsen glowingly chirps those overly-ripe last words: "Friday night, in my opinion, will be the most important date in American musical history. I am really unable to express all that *The Sacrifice* means". Her intent to pioneer American opera development is a goal she could achieve. "An opera by an American, with an American theme and setting, written in English and first produced on an American stage—it is the beginning of real American opera and means everything".

Cut short the progress by leaving Herbert.

"Of course, *The Girl* [*of the Golden West*] had an American stage and setting, but it was Italian none the less". Puccini's spaghetti western opera filtered through Belasco clichés without the genuine regional spirit which Los Angles critics demand should flower. Nielsen did her best possible promo pitch for the Converse piece. "But this, this is really American all through, and I believe it is going to be the first of a long line of American operas. American opera is destined to take rank with French or German or Italian opera".

And she knew the plot. Singing in war-time Mexico at a wedding. Droll as Lucia's dagger. Well done Alice, you gave your best.

Sacrifice is third premier of a Boston opera in English.

After Converse's *Pipe of Desire*, Damrosch's *The Scarlet Letter* (1895). *NY Times* reported (Ja 6 1895), "An interesting occasion. American composers of grand opera are scarce, and productions of their works are still scarcer. Here... we have an opera from a standard American novel on an American subject by an American literary man and set to music by an American composer". *Times* hates it. Libretto by George Lathrop, son-in-law of author Nathaniel Hawthorn, who ties lyrical knots: "*And so must flee, Whispering ever the hapless tidings?*"

Times suggests score monotonous. Probably was.

Ignoring omens, Nielsen gushes "I think that *The Sacrifice* is wonderful, no less: in theme, in music, in everything. Even without the music, the story would make it notable. The story is cumulative; the first act makes a strong impression, the second act intensifies it, the third is strongest of all. For my own part, if it had been written especially for me it could not have suited me better. In my own role I like especially the prayer in the second act and the duet with Bernal in the last act, but it is all so perfect that it is hard to choose".

She records her aria from *Sacrifice, Chonita's Prayer*.

Nielsen further pitches *Sacrifice* (she made the sacrifice), "Even without its importance as the first real American opera, I believe that *The Sacrifice* would be a very great opera and I look to see it become international and have a place in the repertoire of every big opera company as much as any opera of Verdi or Puccini". If only. Nielsen marks the moment as a great upwelling. "From this time on I believe we are going to have grand opera in English and that not only in this country and in England but on the continent as well. Of course, it will not be a matter of one year or two, but it is bound to come none the less".

If not now, when?

Her part had required six months practice. First premier since *Singing Girl*, once again "fussed over" by composer and conductor.

Alice claims "This is the first time that I have ever sung opera in English [forgetting *Martha* in Chicago, San Francisco's *Faust*, *Lucia*, and *Satanella* plus Herbert and other Tivoli repertoire], but I am sure it will not be the last. I had no little work in learning how to do it either, American as I am, and ever since last summer Mr. Converse and Mr. Goodrich have been teaching me my role.

"To sing English is going to mean the need of special study by American girls—perhaps even more by Americans than by those of other countries—just as now they give special study to singing French".

Praises cohorts: "I may say that it is really surprising how excellently Mssrs. Constantino and Blanchart and Mme. Claessens sing their roles with such perfect pronunciation. For them it was not only a new opera, but a new language to learn, especially from M. Constantino, who never attempted English singing before, and they have succeeded marvelously".

Predicts premier awesome: "I am sure that Friday will bring a very complete success and that it will be a very important date, the most important date in the history of American music".

Tenor agrees with soprano. Constantino comments, "*The Sacrifice* is a beautiful opera and that it will prove a great success in every respect. The story is a moving one full of spirit and vigor and of sweetness at the same time, and it appeals to me greatly. The music is exceptionally melodious. The two together make it a truly great opera".

Spent two weeks learning the words. "I am very glad to sing in it, and to sing in English. English is to me a wholly new language, and I have learned my role, the words of it at least, virtually in the last fifteen days. I have not found the task difficult however".

Constantino gladly advocates American opera. "English I find very well adapted to singing, more so than I had imagined it to be. In my opinion this will be the first of many American operas—you have no lack of subjects". Why frantic repeats of war-weary weddings in Mexico of yore?

"I do not believe however, that English opera…will ever become popular on the continent. None the less, this opera is truly great in itself and very important in what it represents. As I say, I am glad to sing in it, and I look for a great success. Every nation has its own opera. There is only really international language for opera and that is Italian".

Very wise man soon lost to Boston.

John Macy grabs Constantino's notion of regionalism for his next book *The Spirit of American Literature* without crediting the Basque originator of his stolen idea. Macy's thanks are implied just by taking up the notion: in a sense Macy does not plagiarize, he regionalizes Constantino's insight.

March 3, Boston turns out for the world premier of *The Sacrifice*. Story by Converse, verses by John Macy, story of Mexico 1846. Nielsen creates the role of Chonita and Constantino the Bernal.

Cast: Alice Nielsen, Florencio Constantino, Maria Claessens and Ramon Blanchart. C. Stroesco, Bernice Fisher, Grace Fisher, Anne Roberts, Carl Ganvoort, John Mogan, Howard White, Frederick Huddy and Pierre Letol. Stage director, Delfino Menotti; Wallace Goodrich conducts; O.P. Bernard, scenery.

The plot: Senora Chonita waits for sweetheart Bernal. Bandits appear, actually Yankee troops making the world safe for democracy. Lead bandit-Yankee falls in love with pretty girl, shoots boyfriend who doesn't dies really, he pulls dagger, "You wretched devil 'tis I she loves". Alike *Fortune Teller*, heroine (Chonita) runs between the men. Due to opera, stabbed. Yankees attack and die. "Love brings life and death", says Tomasa, gazing at the pile of bodies.

Same setting of *War-Time Wedding*; result same. Ends badly.

Some would much prefer the gayety of Alice Nielsen's *Satanella*.

March 4, *NY Times* covers Boston Opera's premier of the first three-act American grand opera by a Bostonian "with Alice Nielsen as heroine" who again declares "the part could not suit her better. Constantino, who has studied the English language in preparation, says he had no idea the tongue was so well suited to singing".

Musical Courier gives Nielsen her next cover March 6 posed as Chonita.

Reading reviews, compare what Converse achieves to what Herbert achieves. Herbert knows how to use the stage, the theatre. He scores opera in English. Herbert's stage scores tell a story. Converse's show is disliked for its use of the stage, for its the libretto, and theatricality not so hot.

Praise given Nielsen must not distract us from sensing just how discerning are these professional critics. Theatre is the biggest sport in the land. People have seen everything, and it all tours. The rawest audience in El Paso has seen the best, same as Chicago. Settings vary; halls vary; the shows are on the stage. If Nielsen is not great, they would tell. These men speak freely.

Converse has delivered a project they detest.

Cautiously, *Musical America* says *The Sacrifice* was "well-received at Boston premier" and a "decided advance dramatically [over Grecian-themed *Pipes of Desire*] although music has shortcomings". Switch focus: socially at least it was "one of the most important events of the second season. Nearly all those most prominent in musical and social circles were present".

Public enthusiasm high. "After each act the artists who had taken part were recalled repeatedly". After the second act, conductor Goodrich was called out "and finally, to cheers Mr. Converse made his appearance. He acknowledged several ovations...delighted with the manner in which his latest work had been presented", already convinced "his first act requires considerable alteration. Had he been a visiting celebrity from European shores there could not have been much more cordiality..." This last line eggs Russell with his fast talk and Euro-trash accent.

Constantino "with Miss Nielsen gave the finest vocal performance of the evening. He is a Mexican [Basque via Argentina] and it was therefore deemed particularly appropriate that he be cast for the role of Bernal for he looked the type and his temperament" alike. He "sang particularly well in the love-duets of the first and third acts".

Alice Nielsen "gave what was perhaps the most finished performance which she has yet given at Boston Opera House, and of course, the English tongue was familiar to her".

Courier pans the show: "Summing up all the merits and the defects of *The Sacrifice*, it must be said the opus misses fire signally and makes no revelation of any new Converse talents...." Not only bad, the composer must stop making opera: "He has not the operatic gift and in that respect is like several very celebrated composers who suffered no loss of esteem on that account".

Development discussion: bad story badly written and badly composed.

"Mr. Converse decided to write his own text after he had read seventy or eighty librettos by other authors. We cannot say what their books were like, but we feel no hesitation in declaring that they could not possibly have revealed less knowledge of stagecraft and the exigencies of dramatic construction than Mr. Converse displayed in *The Sacrifice*. Its action is petty...even the sacrifice itself...had no sense whatsoever".

Musically: "In orchestration Mr. Converse is equipped with technic rather than tact. To illustrate his text musically, Mr. Converse has recourse to several operatic styles for he mixes set numbers and the flowing music drama movement just as freely as he pleases. There are but few shifts and changes in his system of writing to meet the varying moods and movements of his text".

Performers made the show such as it was.

"Alice Nielsen was a prepossessing Chonita, who acted with rare grace and unfailing intelligence, rising with sure histrionic instinct to the few moments of real dramatic power which the text allowed her to portray. Miss Nielsen's voice sounded full, rich and vibrant in all its registers, and she sang her part with phrasing singularly smooth and musical, considering the unidiomatic Converse vocal writing for operatic uses.

"Florencio Constantino made a distinct impression in the ungrateful role of Bernal... taking his high tones in the most approved bravura manner and in all the registers giving fine examples of polished cantilena according to the best bel canto requirements".

These two stars were "painstaking and understandable in their English" if nobody else; and "stage management and scenic outfitting were first class".

Sacrifice plays three weeks.

Boston Opera's 1911 spring season ends before May. *Boston Sunday Globe* (Mar 12) remarks, "Considered an experiment last year to undertake a season of twenty weeks of $5 opera in Boston. The attendance...has been invariably good". Theatre was "practically filled" and "in the performances of particular interest the house has been entirely sold out".

Highlights Nielsen's drawing power, Boston Opera Board takes note.

During the season Alice is slated to return "as Norina in *Don Pasquale*, a part which she has played before with archness, piquancy and general charm". *Sacrifice* repeats "at the Saturday matinee and followed by the Russian Dancers. Pavlova and Mordkin will make their third appearance... in a varied program. Debussy's *The Prodigal Son* will precede them, in which Miss Ruby Savage is announced to sing Lia".

Alice Nielsen contributes to the cultural life of her new home town. Her wish to absorb the Wagnerian roles becomes clear. *Globe* reveals "at the Somerset next Tuesday afternoon, Kate Thecia Conley will give her lecture 'Phases of Wagner'" joined by Alice Nielsen and Boston Opera musicians under concertmaster Henrotte in *Lohengrin*.

"It is interesting to know that Miss Nielsen will add the role of Elsa to her repertoire next season. After her engagement here, she will go to Europe to study the Wagnerian operas".

Globe (Mar 15): "Kate Thecia Conley gave a Wagner lecture at the hotel Somerset yesterday, which was a brilliant artistic success. Several musicians from the orchestra of the Boston opera house, under the direction of Mr. Henrotte. A young woman harpist and Alice Nielsen gave the illustrative selections. For *Lohengrin*, "Mrs. Conley gave a dramatic conception of the story. The orchestra played the prelude to *Lohengrin* and *Elsa's Dream* was sung by Miss Nielsen". Patronesses listed are Mrs. John Corcoran, Mrs. Roger Wolcott and Mrs. Larz Anderson, two dozen others.

Anticipation for next season is about to get a shocking surprise.

THE STARS GO OUT

The third Boston Opera season opens to outrage of stockholders and the public with the manager's surprise announcement Alice Nielsen has been excluded. Press incredulous. Friends rally to her. She speaks vaguely of European engagements and concerts. The NYC music world makes its own grand gesture when the Met casts Nielsen with Caruso for its Boston tour.

Nielsen's banishment as Loie Fuller could predict, is masked at first.

Triggers strong press scrutiny of the Boston Opera manager.

Culminates as catalyst for a magnificent muckraking series by a new Boston music magazine whose editor quit his Boston Opera staff job to break the story. The *Titanic* controversy hints at disaster looming.

So everyone is blindsided when Jordan announces (*NY Times* Mar 20) the third Boston Opera season, and without Nielsen, has been "shortened from twenty to eighteen weeks". Singers exchanged between Boston, Chicago, and NY. Cost of producing Boston Opera is reported "as low, if not lower, than in NY", yet Boston sinks bankrupt, not NY.

Musical Courier's Gertrude Cowen is in Boston when the news breaks.

Public outcry demands official explanations which ring all-too-hollow, yet everyone knows the hireling, the foreign manager is behind it all. And as almost a travesty of himself, he plays the game Loie Fuller describes, pretending to say yes he acts no. Some staff resign. One begins to research Russell's claims, his past. The rest must align with Russell who demands "dignity" behind a wall of fog.

As he had used Hammerstein to lure Constantino into a trap, Russell uses Alice's current manager to push her out of town. Wrings his hands in public over her absence; denied her fee to cancel her appearance.

The released story is that the Chicago manager Charles Wagner has given Nielsen financial guarantees which Russell appears unable to match. In private, Russell has advised Wagner to do so since it suits his purpose to push Nielsen away from her stage. What Alice has been told by the backstabbing Russell could be another story entirely.

For Charles Wagner, she will join the week-long Redpath Chautauqua festival touring the West and South six months as highest paid performer, closing the week-long event at each town.

Alice Nielsen is at her career peak. Her lifetime stage sinks in a swamp.

When Nielsen goes, Constantino goes.

The powerful duo who moved many persons to never-forgotten raptures of acclaim across America have been removed from their home stage by malice. The Boston public and shareholders are the losers; and they know it. The great duo lost; their energy and art going elsewhere.

Does not bode best for Boston or Boston Opera.

For the season in progress Nielsen keeps singing of course.

March 21st *Musical Courier*: "Alice Nielsen, one of the most captivating Norinas on the operatic stage today, again sang the heroine's part in Donizetti's opera, and delighted the crowded auditorium as much by here inimitable and gaily coquettish humors as by her impeccable singing of a role that, with all its apparent simplicity, is still of tremendous difficulty". Courier points out that in 1910 Nielsen gave forty opera performances, "nineteen in the different opera houses and twenty-one here" plus the concerts and the charity gigs.

March 22, Nielsen's farewell Boston performance: *La Bohème*.

All Sold Out. *Musical Courier* (Mar 22): "A capacity house was there to greet her and the enthusiastic acclaim was such that she was made to realize more than ever strongly her vital hold on the Boston public both as artist and woman". *Courier* reconfirms the spark at Park.

Constantino shares her "triumph, since the splendid performance given this opera [at Park Theatre] by the San Carlo Opera Company [of SF, Nordica, Alice Nielsen etc.] about three years ago was the moving force in securing Boston Opera House for this city".

Good-bye Boston. "An operatic evening long to be remembered for its artistic perfection, its sympathetic atmosphere and the sentiment of loving good-fellowship pervading the whole".

Nielsen's departure by Russell's connivance is masked as a byproduct of her concert career. "Rumors of Alice Nielsen's great success in those concert engagements which she had time to fill betwixt and between her operatic appearances...came like a thunderclap to the ears of musical Boston...." Russell deceives the entire town.

As the Boston Opera press agent, shades of Perley, puts the break on Alice and masks the facts of things behind corporate double-speak, few or none are fooled.

"It was announced following the tempting guarantees given [by Charles Wagner] for a concert tour of three months' duration from coast to coast [deliberately during Boston Opera season], the popular prima donna decided to accept the terms offered [due antagonism by Russell] and sever her connection as a permanent member of the Boston Opera Company...."

People sniff. Why would the founding star in her prime surrender her rarest gift of an opera stage? Confirming confusion, *Boston Globe* (Mar 22) neatly gives a conflicting explanation, "Alice Nielsen's Farewell Tonight, Will Sing In Europe Next Season. With tonight's performance of *La Bohème* Alice Nielsen will practically bid a farewell to the stage of the Boston opera house". Plausible denial is smeared across press pages like hogwash.

"European engagements necessitating her appearance in opera in Berlin and Vienna, as well as concert engagements in this country, make it impossible for Miss Nielsen to become a permanent member of the Boston opera organization next season, and if she is to be heard at all it will be as a guest a few times during the eighteen weeks' period of opera".

Incredulous journalists remind readers of Nielsen's founder status. *Globe* gives credit due, "It is a strange coincidence that Miss Nielsen's farewell should take place in the same opera and with nearly the identical cast that served as the motive force in getting for Boston the great institution known as the Boston opera house".

Nielsen suffered Williams & Perley. Now Russell. She is very cautious speaking to the public. And after all, Boston held many friends and an adoring public. Her fans are in the house; her opera home.

For *Globe* she colors it thus: "Of course I am sorry to leave Boston but that is the life of an opera singer and contracts must be lived up to. Much as I look forward to my appearance in Berlin and Vienna, much as I am flattered by the eagerness shown by foreign managers in having me sing there, I do not hesitate in saying that the two seasons I spent with the Boston Opera Company were the happiest, both socially and artistically, in all my life. I expect to sing here in a few performances, and I hope that despite the fact of my not being a permanent member of the Boston opera organization, the Boston public will not look upon me as a stranger and that I will find in their hearts the same warm sympathy that they have lavished upon me so unstintedly for the past two seasons.

"I am going to sing abroad many of my old parts and I am to create several roles in new operas. I certainly will do my utmost to win success, not only for my own sake, but for the sake of my country.

"I am not saying goodby. This only *au revoir*".

By no coincidence Constantino immediately announces he is joining Buenos Aires Opera; he never sings in Boston again.

After two years, the two persons most responsible for inspiring Boston Opera are pushed out. Orchestrated by the deceiver up to no good.

So on March 23rd, Boston Opera stockholders are appalled to see the *Globe's* double disaster headline: "Constantino to sing in Buenos Aires" and "Alice Nielsen's farewell appearance with Boston Opera Company".

Public outcry is so great and so prolonged and so personal that Russell is soon forced to publish a long apologetic styled in that self-contradictory illogic today we call "waffling". This backfires badly. Putting his yes-no wordswamp into the public scrutiny undeceives the public.

Boston papers speculate on joint departure of these priceless assets the founding stars. Certainly if Jordan went wrong he had great power to fix things. He could not imagine the cost of hesitation. Within a year, of course, strong pressures bring Nielsen back. Irony of her using the Met's tour to retake the Boston Opera stage paired with comrade Caruso made its painful point with the Boston board of directors. Despite clear evidence of mismanagement, the Board shields the hired-hand foreign manager who hates developing Boston's lyric legacy. He doesn't live here.

Shareholders are outraged by the damage to their investment. Ticket sales plummet. Why endure the cheap foreign casts the manager curiously keeps hiring? Where are the stars we paid to build an opera house?

Boston complains. Many letters to editors. Outrage demands response.

The manager is forced to respond to protests blaming him for Nielsen's loss in *Boston Globe* (Mar 24), reprint by *Boston Herald* April 1. *Herald* slyly adds, that this "makes everything clear". Or imperfectly clear. His illlogic needs Loie Fuller's genius to analyze it properly. Alas here it is.

First he blames Nielsen; then blames the public for complaining.

He states: after "Miss Nielsen's resignation as a permanent member of the Boston Opera Company, I have received numerous letters of protest from the subscribers and the public". Many were angry and anonymous, yet "some of them bear signatures and therefore have a right to be answered".

He acknowledges, "This institution has rapidly become one of the most important factors in the artistic and social life of this city" in spite of himself. Then he personalizes the issues, seeks to circle the wagons around: him. He promises to "define in the clearest terms my attitude toward the public and the artistic policy I wish to pursue in the conduct of the Boston Opera House". Airily he dismisses any "suppositions which are not worthy of consideration, if regarded from a personal point of view".

If his comment implies his personal honor above reproach, no evidence supports he was. He wasn't. Daring people to question him is a coward's tactic. He is viciously unscrupulous, not simply unscrupulous. He acts secretly then speaks meaninglessly. As Loie Fuller pointed out.

Russell lists the suspicions against him: strong pressure against Nielsen brought to bear on him from high quarters [invented]; his prejudice against American singers [obvious]; his "personal preference for another prima donna [his personal preferences are the problem]"; clash between him and Nielsen [inevitable]; or, "she is the victim of the jealous intrigues of other singers [invented]".

Typically, first he denies everything. Nothing never his fault, you see.

Literally he claims "There is not the slightest truth in any of these statements". Certainly. The real complaints have a factual basis.

Next, Russell focuses aristocratically on his right to wield arbitrary power and leaving him alone to do so, no matter how wrong. He suggests pushing Nielsen out was a byproduct of his artistic policy; then denies it.

"A specific clause in my contract...gives me absolute freedom in all matters pertaining to the artistic policy of the house. At no times have they [the Board] interfered with me in the selection or rejection of singers or operas". Therefore he must not be questioned; almost could not be fired.

Public servant and dictator all at once. Aristocrat and democrat. Perhaps the Board needs act since the manager is clearly crazy. Loie Fuller perfectly deciphered the paradox of Russell illogic.

Lastly, he denies any influence over Nielsen's departure. "Far from any clash having arisen...she leaves our company by her own decision and with the best wishes of all concerned, and with the hope that she will be heard here as a visiting artist next season". He lies. As will be clear.

Reverses logic, takes credit for pushing her out. Indeed, her very resignation "serves as an excellent example of the policy which will be continued in the Opera House". Pushed Alice out a limb and sawed it off.

With sly deceit, he continues. Claims he could not afford Nielsen's salary; as he promised Wagner to tell her. Russell slyly suggests "the facts are simple. In the last two years Miss Nielsen's commercial value as a prima donna has increased over 100 per cent. Her offers from Europe and her concert negotiations in this country justify her in demanding a very high salary". Pretends flattery when denying her the stage she made.

"To procure artists of her caliber exclusively for our entire season makes it necessary to guarantee them from thirty to forty performances...."

Shifts focus to a gaslit fantasy of possible other singers while dismisses the rare talents of the dearly departed. "...consequently the public is deprived of hearing new singers who might please them as well and even more". Not much gratitude there. Crocodile tears shed.

Alice Nielsen must sing elsewhere, public deprived of her performances in the opera house she gave spark of life and filled to the rafters with fans.

While the scoundrel fattens on a salary, expenses, graft. Most ironic about Henry Russell is that he would be nothing without her.

After these canards he suggests the policy of cultivating stars has "proved so fatal to the artistic development of the Metropolitan Opera for years". For example, naming names, Madame Sembrich has been such a favorite "no soprano singing her roles could gain a hearing in that house".

Next denies it, and skips his many hiring promises to develop American artists of which Alice Nielsen the most salient. Suggests his arbitrary malice is only inevitable. Impossible "to bring new artists to America ...obligated to guarantee a large number of performances to the old ones".

Literally the two "old ones" refused to pay his graft. Busy twisting the knife. He had been in the job two years. Fast backstabber for a sidewinder.

Cutting compliments continue to slice the star who only serves "as an admirable illustration. Here is an artist who has been heard for two years in Boston and has proved an invaluable member of the company. In the words of Mr. Philip Hale, 'As a singer of sustained song she has been without a rival in the local company, and few of the visiting sopranos have equaled her.' By retiring as a permanent member of the company" she allows "public to hear new singers with other qualities and other standards". Dares suggest Nielsen made a public service—of the sort he would never—by sacrificing herself to depart the company she had established so that his graft and abuses could continue.

His advocacy of term limits does not apply to his salaried self. Wants expense accounts and first-class travel to Russia regular. Taking his own advice would serve a great benefit for Bostonian musical culture; if had packed saying goodbye Boston forever. Imagine Boston Opera with any person from Boston heading it from this point or the start; we need not imagine, it would be here today.

Piles it thick: twists things—as Fuller says. He suggests that Alice's popularity is bad because people like her. "Nothing would be more detrimental to the artistic interests of our house than that any one soprano, tenor or baritone should be allowed to obtain such a hold on the public as to exclude the entry of new ones...."

And asks for support to keep the star away so he could chisel the new hires: "and I look to the public to support me". Then shifts yet again. Slyly denies what he has just suggested, saying Nielsen, of course had never "endeavored to prevent any other singer from being heard in the Opera House. On the contrary, her amiability and generosity towards her comrades have endeared her to every member of the company".

Denies it is personal. "The fact is there is nothing personal in this matter...." Lards the language mighty fat: "But it is a question of precedent which will have an immense influence on the operatic development of America and in which I maintain that Boston should set the example, as it always has done in matters of high artist import".

And without her he is nothing. Takes both sides, paints himself humble "a public servant whose duty is to respect the public taste" yet a dictator in the Bolshevik manner. Sees himself a dictator of the people, "It is only right that the public should be guided by me, if I am worthy of retaining the position I have the honor to hold".

Boston isn't stupid. Some say off with his head. Savvy Puritans read his airhead treatise in false logic with rebellious eyes. Mutter of defenestration. Doubts about his presence flood the town like molasses.

Promises to push American singers and denies he will. Clear the stage for foreign singers "not yet heard" in America and never American "such as Anselmi, Storchio, Tita Ruffo, etc".

Closes assuring Beantown he has nothing: no schemes, no agenda, indeed no feelings, "I will take care that there are no preferences, no prejudices and no partisan feeling of any kind". That was what he said.

Ends the indigestible toxic wordswamp. Well now. Fair demonstration of a peculiar style of hypnotic which must reflect the narcissistic confusion within. As the *Herald* jokes, oh sure, he makes things perfectly clear.

Precisely what the Boston public objects. Proved right. He is regarded with extreme suspicion henceforth.

Loie Fuller never spoke out on this matter; she had long left.

Hireling Russell has maneuvered Constantino and Nielsen away. As a result, the two stars who precipitated a great grand opera awakening in America stop performing together. Their last appearance is Portland, March 17th, 1911. That year, they sang together thrice. Prolific performers both: during Constantino's 1909-10 peak he gave over a hundred shows. Nielsen more. Careers truncated by the loss of their Boston stage.

Saying farewell to Constantino we must salute him. Biographer Julio Goyen Aguado (1993) had missed the power Nordica and Nielsen played in his career; had not detected the faux impresario Russell's smallness and sabotage of the stars who made him. This oversight has been corrected by the excellent new Constantino biography by Konrado Mugertza where a few details on Russell's mischief come to light.

Similar to Loie Fuller's experience, when Constantino first bid goodbye to Boston in 1909, manipulated by Russell to cross to Hammerstein, he privately accused Russell of "diverse breaches in contracts" going back to the 1907 New Orleans contract for "F21,000 a month, plus extra for special performances", according to Aguado translated from Spanish by the author. Touring with so-called "San Carlo" Constantino is a hired voice.

Demonstrating a pattern of embezzlement, Russell takes Boston Opera money to pay his curious debt to the tenor. The debt seems to relate to some kick-back scheme where Russell withheld money due Constantino, attempting to keep it. According to Aguado, Russell reacts badly to the demand to repay. Revenge is to drive Constantino into Hammerstein's frying pan. The insult by Hammerstein coordinated with Russell, brings the angry tenor to accept the Boston too-low pay offer which was intended to discourage the tenor away from the town.

Instead of a celebrated man in Boston all his long life, Constantino leaves town and life all-too early. He ends badly. His recordings reveal his talent. Edison first recorded him "in London after the triumphs of the tenor in the theatres Waldorf and Covent Garden", says Aguado.

Eleven two-minute Edison cylinders were cut in August 1905; nothing by Nielsen in that London period has been discovered. Given his tragic ending after Boston fails him, now is time to honor him.

The wonderful biography *Florencio Constantino, 1869-1919, el hombre y el tenor*, by Julio Goyén Aquado (1993) appears only in Spanish. He was "born in Ortuella, Guipúzcua, Spanish Basque Country, in 1868. At twenty-one he decided to emigrate [abandon the Spanish navy] to Bragado in Argentina, where kin of his wife resided, occupied in agricultural tasks.

"Gifted of an extraordinary voice, he was heard singing in church by the Archbishop of Buenos Aires, who proposed him to be dedicated to lyrical song. Florencio accepted the challenge and left, first for Buenos Aires and then for Italy, to be perfected in the difficult discipline. A decade, 1895-1906, sufficed so the humble mechanic of Bilbao and singer of Bragado rose among the first figures of the lyric opera".

Constantino was conducted by Toscanini, Mancinelli, Messager, Conti, Mugnoni, Vitale, Mascagni. He "sang more than three-hundred operas in forty-seven theaters of thirteen countries, sang before the royal families of Portugal, England, Spain, Italy and the President of France. Composers Boito, Mascagni and Puccini declared him their favorite. He was 'an artist born for the world.'" Between 1906 and 1912, Constantino had "launched to conquest of America, he sang in Argentina, Brazil, Chile, Cuba and Uruguay. By 1912 he sang over eight-hundred operas and one hundred concerts in 103 cities of the world. He built Theater Constantino that year in Bragado. In 1917 he created the California Temple of Arts in Los Angeles. The leading exponent of the 'bel cantismo' died in Mexico in 1919 at the age of 51". This happens during the Mexican revolution; facts lost to us. He was found dead in the street.

Streets are named after Constantino in Mexico and Bilabo.

Showing Russell's spite, his memoirs "punished with silence the attitude of Florencio. His name as not mentioned a single time, even when speaking of the inaugural of Boston Opera" says Aguado. Of course, Russell scorns Nielsen, skips his own wives; yet praises his pal and travel roommate Grimthorpe.

Nielsen and Constantino were assets of greater value than the Boston Opera building itself. Small wonder Boston stockholders are outraged. As Loie Fuller described so well, demonstrated by his elaborate apologetics, weaving and bobbing, Russell has energy to talk people into things. His spew of phrases and bizarre illogic produces mental paralysis. Hypnotizing Jordan and cronies is a temporary shield. Others hate him now.

Jordan's error of trust squanders his greatest gift to the town he loves. Yet he seems not to suspect the obvious as it grows more so. To develop the Bostonian institution as Jordan intended was never in Russell's nature. Could not do the job Jordan gave. Jordan seems trapped; unable to react with decisive measures to defend this legacy. He made his gracious patron deed; he turns aside for the season to hunt at his Scotland estate. He put in power who could never be trusted; without safeguards. What if the hireling arty bureaucrat in possession of the regime is corrupt?

Nielsen and Constantino are "a gift from God" Boston loves.

Boston opera a dead man walking after Russell pushes out these star singers and begins in earnest his campaign to dominate the remaining pack for personal purposes of pelf. As Loie Fuller, Constantino and soon Nielsen discover: Russell lies.

Charles Wagner recalls his deal with Russell; Nielsen the pawn. Wagner has skill, he is a highly successful Chicago producer and manager. He handles Nielsen and the Irish tenor John McCormack, among others. Nielsen is one of his first clients. She then introduces him to the best talent in the business. She makes his career, too. But Wagner, unlike Russell, can stand success.

Tells the story in *Seeing Stars* (1940), "Miss Nielsen was the leading soprano of the Boston Opera...and had had considerable to do with persuading Jordan to back the enterprise and build the new Opera House, one of the finest and best equipped in the world. She had been for many years one of the most successful of light opera stars and her phenomenal success with the early Victor Herbert operas was the talk of the times".

Wagner knew Nielsen attract crowds, "The first time I ever saw the sign 'sRO' in front of a theatre announced 'standing Room Only' for this popular little star, whose beautiful voice, charming manner and winning face and figure had the public enthralled".

Wagner misspeaks, that after singing her Victor Herbert shows "a little later" she was with the Bostonians; he has reversed timing of that. He appears to award remora Russell credit for the 1905-6 Nordica-Nielsen's

"San Carlo Opera of SF etc". Then with a smirk suggests Russell reigned over Boston Opera "so many years". Droll joke for theatre insiders to enjoy.

Nobody knew better than Wagner what happened in Boston and how few years it took Russell to kill the community spirit which inspired Boston Opera before fleeing beyond arrest to Europe with the books, clutching his theft and fraud. Wagner also knew the artist who had sparked creation of that *Titanic* vessel sinking in a stupid disaster was great.

"Until Grace More appeared in recent years, Alice Nielsen was the only singer who made a genuine success in both light and grand opera". He appears mystified why she left Broadway. "As I see her now—"Alice sit-by-the-fire"—I wonder if it was really worthwhile".

Alice Sit-By-The-Fire, a popular James Barry (1860-1937) book made into a play (1919) like his *Peter Pan*, once upon a time also a musical project offered to Alice Nielsen. She herself, uncelebrated over her twilight years, uses the phrase during her last newspaper interview.

"Her early career...had made her supreme and placed her on the road to riches", Wagner recalls, obviously oblivious to the Williams & Perley thefts. "To me that was the greater of the two careers, for she sang to the masses, not merely to the jeweled lights of the gilded horseshoe". And made her manager, Wagner, much money. He will guide Nielsen into a huge concert fortune in the 1910s. He skips her powers to make grand opera popular which had filled Boston Opera to capacity.

When Alice finally faces facts about Russell's malignity at Boston she releases the conspiring Wagner as manager. She had made him great. He had started in St. Paul as a booking agent for NY's RE Johnson. In 1909 he relocated to NYC and readily signed Nielsen, John McCormack, and Rudolph Ganz, "They really constituted the first move in my career as a personal manager".

Seeking to sign the star, Wagner speaks secretly behind scenes to Russell who uses the chance to get her out of Boston by a foggy subterfuge.

Instead of facing facts, Wagner spins this: "As an operatic prima donna Miss Nielsen, testing her power, demanded many performances, which embarrassed both manager and backer though each agreed no other artist was doing better work". Absurd. Testing her power indeed. Consider the hijack underway by the hireling opera manager. Russell, as Loie Fuller pointed out, had many embarrassments.

Complete absurd to blame "backer" Eben Jordan. Nielsen made Boston Opera. The press, the backer, the audiences, and the shareholders knew; and when she returns by popular demand to the Boston Opera stage, Jordan himself brings her back. Forces the slick hireling to follow orders.

Wagner misrepresents things. Nielsen represents revenue so he grabs the malign suggestion. Best interests of star and Boston Opera never his concern. Charles Wagner doesn't mention speaking with Jordan. And he knows, as everybody knew, that Russell says whatever he wants people to believe yet, as Eaton and others, continues to push the story Russell, slippery critter, wanted told for a trick. Alice after all had promoted her remora for years saying almost anything that would generate coins for him.

Seeking to sign money-maker Nielsen, Wagner claims "this was the situation when I approached Russell in Boston on the matter of booking her". A secret backstage deal manipulates Nielsen's career and betrays her, Boston opera, the public and investors. Russell tells Wagner he wants Nielsen out of the way and Wagner conspires to help him.

Wagner spins this secret deal to manipulate Nielsen off her home stage as a pact between gentlemen. "In his blunt fashion he laid the cards on the table. 'Alice is damned difficult and as you know, I am helpless. Book her for a tour, keep her away as much as possible singing on the road, and in return you can have everything here that is not nailed down.'" Russell had played Constantino with Hammerstein the same way.

Of course Alice can be damned difficult dealing with Russell. She has facts he hates. Suits Wagner's purposes. Interaction between the hireling at Boston Opera and the star has become strained after a succession of scandals: near-loss of Constantino, abuse of the young soprano, of Loie Fuller, and others. As Perley had discovered, Nielsen could challenge. She demands fair play, cooperation, demands skillful decisions equal to the competent attention she gives her artwork. Assured Russell will not match the offer, he presents Nielsen a concert tour timed during next Boston Opera season. How Russell specifically denied her the Boston schedule we do not know. "It was a gentleman's agreement, sympathetic on both sides, and carried out to the letter", claims Wagner. Such scoundrels.

Alice Nielsen tossed into this artless scheme. Blocked from creating her Boston Opera legacy, she sings art songs in concert. Widely cherished.

Not her best work creating a sustained story onstage.

Wagner brags he kept Nielsen from Boston Opera almost a year. "So I took her out of Boston, arranging, besides recitals, an operatic novelty in the form of an abridged version of *The Barber of Seville*, played in costume to a two-piano accompaniment. This light, florid Rossini music lends itself better to piano than a large orchestra anyway.

"Alice sang Rosina and gave several extra arias in the Lesson Scene, and the supporting company was made up of artists from the Boston Company with the exception of the leading tenor—Riccardo Martin from the Metropolitan, then in the heyday of his popularity.

"Martin was a Kentuckian, a splendid musician with a fine social position and was given a chance at all the leading tenor roles at the Met. Most of this can be credited to his first wife, who bestowed constant care and sacrifice on him. I never saw anyone who could baby a tenor to better effect. Night after night she stood in the wings suggesting, prompting and encouraging. Miss Nielsen was most happy in this road work, sang many recitals and made numerous joint appearances with Martin, and our first touring season was a decided success". For profit of Charles Wagner.

So that is how the game went down against her in Boston Opera.

Alice Nielsen lost the second company meant for her. By corruption of men she had promoted. Without stars the cash crashes.

So it is. Boston Opera closes the second season, March 26 (*NY Times*). The twenty weeks offered hundred-and-one performances of twenty-six operas in five languages. Deficit of $137,000 "made up". Third season will be two two weeks shorter. Interestingly, "A special committee of experts conducted an investigation into the management of the opera company for the season and reported that opera had been produced here equal to any in the world and more economically than elsewhere".

The third season in the fall had no place for Alice Nielsen. And her oversight is absent. Risky Russell has unfettered arbitrary authority to charge the accounts. Lacking a scrupulous nature, he adopts the fog-fuzzy-fire technique. Same with Alice earlier. First, he proclaims he artily does not care about money: that is, of others. If a reliable business manager cuts the fog: fired. In short, he embezzles and takes kickbacks.

Ironically, Russell's motive for pushing Nielsen out, according to the Met's Eton, is his wish to promote a young soprano. No; Russell seeks young girls of course but is more about the money. Nielsen knows the gift of the legacy sabotaged by him. That is her scorn. To promote his pick of the week, Eton is all-too-correct, Russell will spend Boston Opera money under false pretenses. But Eton only hints at the financial shenanigans.

How many times had Alice Nielsen praised the remora's supposed lack of care for money (of others) during days when she had traded a series of lucrative management contracts for the guidance of Henry Russell Jr. who cheaply turned every possible trick pocketing the loot

Despite a brave public face, and mild words, Nielsen is shocked. In her plight and turmoil she turns to Nordica with trust. The two friends arrange for a singing trip to Carolina and make plans to perform in Berlin.

As the Boston season closes, Nielsen "appeared as the principal soloist at a sacred concert given in the Brookline town hall yesterday under the auspices of the Brookline education society. Fully a thousand people attended", says *Boston Globe* (Mar 27).

"Miss Nielsen contributed a group of songs, short selections all of them... she seemed especially pleased with the appreciation shown by the high school chorus of three-hundred voices and kissed her fingers in that direction when acknowledging the applause".

Students sing selections from Gounod's *St. Cecelia* mass and selections from Handel's *Messiah*. Hosea Starr Ballou, chairman, tells of "stimulating a general interest in good music and to get the people of the town together for a social intermingling". Edith Snow accompanist.

Musical Courier March 29 confirms Alice Nielsen had resigned as a permanent member of Boston Opera Company, no speculations why.

April 22nd, the Metropolitan Opera makes a fine statement about the situation by announcing Nielsen and Caruso will appear in Boston that fall. Alice is touring with the Met to Montreal at the time. Turns tables. So truth filters out. Disproving her face-saving gesture a few weeks earlier, Nielsen says re-arranging her European schedule to sing in Boston is simple: "As soon as I knew that Mr. Gatti-Casazza wished to engage me, I cabled to my European impresarios and the dates were arranged most satisfactorily" to change "Berlin and Vienna" engagements of *Bohème* and *Pasquale*. Her concert dates more so. Thereat "Miss Nielsen will appear several times in Boston as a visiting artist from the Metropolitan", not for Boston Opera, reports *NY Times* (Ap 22).

And Nordica takes Nielsen down to Carolina for a festival.

"Nordica...appears to be in more glorious voice than ever before", proclaims *Charlotte Observer* (Apr 5). April 25, the Nordica-Nielsen team arrive for the "7th Annual South Atlantic States Music Festival in Spartanburg, SC". Nielsen, Nordica, Scotti, "chorus of the Converse Choral Society numbering over two-hundred voices" are slated to join New York Symphony under Walter Damrosch".

For the week-long festival, Converse College crams "full of visitors... the great auditorium built for the purpose two years ago will be crowded for all concerts". Alas, Converse archives could find no details about its superb Music Festival started in 1895. With Alice Nielsen they celebrate the 1910 School of Music opening, Benjamin Wilson first president. The Music Festival continues annually through 1930.

After their Carolina week, the diva duo returned to Maine where both have property in small towns 60 miles (96km) apart outside Portland. Nordica was born in Farmington, Nielsen since 1901 has owned property in Harrison. Her big summer cottage, often called a pagoda, built at cost of $3,000, includes a soaring sixty-foot cathedral ceiling, huge stone fireplace, superb grand piano sited in a corner of the large living room. A cozy porch wraps around the back, facing a boat cottage on the lakefront.

The sunset view from that porch gorgeous. A singer's space, built on Naples road. Locals told the author an MIT engineer designed it, nobody knew his name. Harrison became a singer's colony after Nielsen arrived. Frederick 'Pa' Bristol "one of the best teachers of singing in America" had settled there from Cape Cod and NYC to create Bristol Music studio. His students bought homes on Long Lake, such as Swedish lyric soprano Marie Sundelius who sings at the Met (debut 1916), also on the Chautauqua circuit, and holds a summer singing school in Harrison. The splendid Deertrees theatre is a 1930s result built by Enrica Clay Dillon, helped by Helen Hays and Humphry Bogart. By 1939 Dillon joined forces with Bela Blau to rotate top Broadway talent to the stage. Nielsen would have enjoyed these performances, a summer resident through the 1940s.

May 2, Nielsen and Nordica sail from Portland, Maine, to Europe.

May 15th, Hortense is touring Ibsen across New England when husband "Charles A. Quintard, also known as Charles A. Arthur" again is arrested, now in Burlington, VT, over an unpaid hotel bill "for himself and company amounting to $175". Sheriff Allen very politely "after the evening performance by the company" in Middlebury arrested Quintard, "It is understood that the company will play in Bristol tonight". For "about a month...the piece was rehearsed on the roof garden of the hotel" Van Ness, and...Quintard told many stories about expecting a check for $500 and other sources of income from which he expected to settle for the company's board". Quintard "gave the hotel an order on the receipts of the Burlington performance...amounting to something like $63". Touring Ibsen was not a lucrative play. Charles has often resorted to the theatrical expedient of flipping his surname from Quintard to Arthur, which he will use in Chicago for answering the 1920 Census. It's a hard knock life.

BERLIN DEBUT; A NOVEL SALSOMAGGOIORE TRUFFLE

Pushed out of her rarest and greatest physical gift of an opera home at least for the moment by mutual connivance of a crooked former manager and a new ambitious one, Alice Nielsen spends a few weeks recuperating from the shock, joins business partner and co-star Nordica in Carolina and Maine. They sail for Europe as sister Hortense holds sway in New England, likely Alice's summer house as base. Of course, Alice Nielsen will not discover the exact nature of that dastardly private deal between Russell and Wagner for some years. Both do their worst to deceive her long as possible. Both gloat over the deception when they finally tell.

Before France, Nielsen visits London to sing at Albert Hall. When she arrives in Paris May 14 (*NY Times*), Duse's abusive D'Annunzio is in the news for losing his new girl to, by coincidence, a Boston Opera singer. The lusty playwright "whose enormous debts have driven him away from his native Italy, lives in quiet retirement" at Versailles...." Collaborates with Debussy in *Martyrdom of St. Sebastian* as Archbishop of Paris calls for a boycott. His gal Ida Rubinstein has been stolen away by Boston's feisty George Baklanoff. Press mock poet: "D'Annunzio said, 'Misfortune and exile are good, necessary and fertile—above all, the exile, for it remakes the soul.' But Paris, gossipy and amusement-seeking, laughs at his cool...and maintains it is fate's decree that D'Annunzio should suffer the tortures he once inflicted upon his famous countrywoman Eleanor Duse".

Nielsen continues over to Berlin May 21st to rehearse for her debut the 27th. Prewar Berlin is artistically fertile and a cultural center of civilization. The city "swarmed...with Broadway operatic and theatrical impresarios on a hunt for attractions, artists and ideas...American is coming more and more to draw upon the long-neglected fatherland" (*NY Times,* May 27).

Alice Nielsen's Berlin debut packed by producers and press.

Musical America: "A tempest of applause swept over the Komische Oper tonight for Alice Nielsen's singing of Mimi in Puccini's *La Bohème*. The American singer's performance was so brilliant that an ovation was inevitable and it was accorded in no uncertain manner. Rules were swept aside as though they did not exist and thirteen times, several after the third act, Miss Nielsen had to answer the enthusiasm".

Encores lost to Boston, as Bostonians realize with a burn.

NY Times: "Alice Nielsen of the NY Metropolitan and Boston Operas had a brilliant Berlin debut...." A large fashionable audience including the American Ambassador, Nordica, and "a number of American operatic and theatrical personalities...accorded the young American prima donna a rousing reception after the final curtain. M. Lafitte of the Paris Grand Opera shared the honors of the performance with Miss Nielsen".

Gatti-Casazza and Alfred Hertz attend. Whiten arrives "at the outset of his search for a cast for his English and American *Der Rosenkavalier* productions. His arrival synchronized with that of Alice Nielsen...at the Komische Oper. Mr. Whiten would like to engage Miss Nielsen to create the title role in the new Strauss opera, believing that she would be ideally cast for the part, but Miss Nielsen's concert engagements in the US will keep her busy until Christmas".

Posing in all directions as Loie Fuller noted, hireling Russell also attends, "while Miss Farrar ran in...for a couple of days' private visiting" flirty affairs upon German aristocrats.

Nielsen encores the show on the 28th due to popular demand.

May 30, Nordica sings *Tristan und Isolde* at Berlin's Royal Opera. She "had a packed house in spite of the sweltering heat". Some critics had a "decided preference that foreign singers remain away" yet even so, these two Americans are "exceptionally favored by the conductors" (*NY Times*).

German patriots defend Berlin from the American's pincer blitz. "Critics of Berlin have resented a new affront from the inroads of American singers. Alice Nielsen, as Mimi in *La Bohème*, recently made her first appearance at Berlin Opera Comique. The following evening Mme. Nordica, as Isolde, appeared at the Royal Opera for the first time".

Nordica's visit was arranged by Prince Henry of Prussia "who learned she had sung Isolde in French in Paris and insisted that she should sing it in German at Berlin" and made arrangements (*Boston Globe* (Jun 4).

Reaching Berlin together, "the dual shock was too much for the traditions and patriotism of the fatherland. The critics of Berlin refuse to admit any urgent need for the aid of American singers", quips *Boston Globe*, asking "Is there a native-born Mimi at the Comique better equipped for Puccini's *cantilena* than is Miss Nielsen? But *bel canto* is a superfluous and decadent art in the operatic inventory of the Teutons...."

Piquant loss of Nielsen to Boston Opera. These *Globe* remarks suggest the local lobby labors long and strong to bring her back. Shareholders wish their prime assets preserved, not squandered. The problem of Russell's arbitrary power seems ever more problematic; those in the know bide time hoping for best. And the hireling is under increasing scrutiny.

Proceeding to Dresden, Alice attends *Cavalier of the Rose* "wherein she has been offered the title role in the forthcoming English and American productions". Strauss and producer Fred Whiten offer Alice Nielsen the role of the *Rosenkavalier* page (*Musical Courier* Ma 24). *Courier* cleverly quotes *NY World* in a Chicago-flavored remark, "It is because of her voice, but it so happens that she is the only grand opera prima donna at present who has a sufficiently slender figure to fill the boy's role satisfactorily.' Will the other prima donnas ever forgive the *World* for that? Wait and see".

Leaving Teutonic territory toward Italy June 3, Nielsen returns to the spa resort Salsomaggiore, where salt-and-iodine-laced artesian waters are frequented by singers such as Caruso, and still in charming operation.

Nielsen spends the summer writing a novel.

Month later, *NY Times* (Jul 9) reports that Boston Opera has secured Louis Auberts' *Le Foret Bleue*. Bragging rights for bagging the production are entirely due Andre Caplet the intimate friend of Russell's wife she insisted bringing to Boston. Under Jordan's nose. Says *New Music Review*, "Thank Heaven, there are no Indians, either American or from the East; there are no sentimental miners, no cowboys, no Greasers. Furthermore, the chief theme is neither arson, murder, nor incest"; and very not an American's work in stark defiance of the chartered promises.

July delivers fascinating news about Nielsen's novel-in-progress. On her return from Salsomaggiore, she will bring "the manuscript of a novel to which she has devoted all her spare time during her present European sojourn". She's a fine writer, full of life. Writes as she speaks. She could tell what went on behind the scenes. Might just write what all she knew, she knew much. Yet the novel stays unpublished. Her manuscript lost.

Much went missing during the time she was lost to us. Letters not least.

In late July 1911, the rambling hired manager, after four months of first-class European travel and high living at expense of poor Boston Opera which cannot afford to pay its founding singers a good price, has provided contracts to seventy singers, "many of whom are new" so seventy kickbacks. Adds French and German choruses. Despite elaborate vows contrary to the stockholders, he ain't never spent no time in America seeking singers noways; again. So to speak.

Wagner in Boston is scheduled without Nielsen. They prepare *Pelleas et Melisande* by Maeterlinck and Debussy. The opera had premiered with Mary Garden, a snake-hipped Scots chosen by Debussy over Maeterlinck's wife who wishes to sing. Sensing opportunity, Boston offers the role to his wife if the reclusive man comes to Boston to meet the press. He agrees; interestingly, Hortense Nielsen will join his talks and speak his part.

Summer passes uneventfully until Alice Nielsen arrested.

September 3 the Italian police arrest Nielsen, reports *Boston Globe*. The report only true. You see, her maid's boyfriend's uncle Pietro Mora has been charged as a gangster in the anti-corruption Camorrist trial and tracing Mora's connections the cops hop over to Nielsen's villa in Rome to question the maid who "stoutly refused to answer...and Miss Nielsen, who speaks Italian perfectly, came to her defense". The police who "did not know who Miss Nielsen was, and presuming she was also an Italian" arrest her "for interfering". The singer now "thoroughly frightened...pleaded in vain. When she begged to be permitted to go to the American embassy, she was laughed at, as the shrewd commissary believed it...a ruse to escape. Only after numerous parleys" she is allowed to call the embassy. American officials take four hours to arrive, the waiting Nielsen "virtually a prisoner in her own home". After explanations, police seem satisfied "but Miss Nielsen is certain that she is...under surveillance".

The Camorra had served the Bourbon monarchy as police, army, and civil service until Naples united with the rest of Italy in 1861 under Garibaldi, when many of these swamp bureaucrats flee to America to join Mafia. Still centered in Naples to hawk fake-label clothing and distracting drugs. Less hierarchical than Mafia, they enjoy drive-by shootings, extortion and such instead of seeking the gayety of honest labor and trade. Code of silence stops them from speaking freely, as faithfully practiced by Nielsen's maid. And enforced by Jordan on one hapless Boston journalist; not to forget Tom Williams shooting *News Letter's* unarmed editor Mr. Marriott at home in the parlor before his wife.

After her visit with Italian police, Alice takes it on the lam. In Paris, she revisits Debussy, Maeterlinck, and other old friends. Apparently she continues speaking to the remora who flits on expense account by others than Alice. The singer is yet unaware of his complicity and conspiracy with her manager Wagner. As Loie Fuller warned, Russell very slick. Keeps on cordial terms with his victims to abuse longer. He plays while Boston pays.

From previous days, thanks to Nielsen, designer Josef Urban's sets will be shipped to Boston this fall for *Tales of Hoffman*. Nielsen's involvement with Urban (1872-1933) is much greater than suspected. Loie Fuller's influence on Urban is much greater than admitted. Charged with furbishing Boston Opera and finding creative theatre talent, Nielsen first encountered Urban's designs after the 1902 *Pelléas et Mélisande* premier at *Opera Comique* with Mary Garden. Alice of course had lived in Europe early 1901 through October 1905, and most summers thereafter.

When charged to get costumes, sets and properties for Boston Opera, she sought Urban's talent. Their hidden relation was only revealed by Urban's daughter Gretel, and that in an unpublished letter (Gretel Urban to Columbia University May 1988). The story becomes a kind of fairy tale.

To discover what Boston Opera would do with his sets, Gretel recalls, her father had stowed away on a freighter to reach America, he had no fare money. Magic happens; reaching Manhattan, he has someone place a collect call to "Alice Nielsen, opera star" in Boston. Nielsen wires back funds for his train ticket. Like the small-town Missouri pastor or as Arthur Pryor at *Eden Musee*, Nielsen put the itinerant Urban to work. He sends for his family, they spend their first American summer at Nielsen's place in Maine. The presence of Josef Urban and family in that artist colony designing for Boston Opera was fun: "Escorted by Buschi's faithful assistant, Benny Nielsen, we explored the surrounding countryside and went for a swim at his mother's cottage on the beach [on Long Lake]", recalls Gretl. "We went swimming off the cottage that belonged to Benny Nielsen's mother Alice, but it was Benny who lived there alone with a man servant and a groom who took care of his horses and ours".

Gretl seems oblivious to Nielsen's opera career.

To Gretl Urban, Alice Nielsen was "a well-to-do widow who had a nice country estate in the White Mountains in New Hampshire and spent her summers there". Gretel has confused Stoddard's place in NY with Marie Dressler's place in New Hampshire; Alice's other summer hangouts.

"Benny Nielsen, who was father's devoted assistant, worked for him at the Boston Opera as a sort of errand boy & Buschi [Urban] finally put him to work on models and discovered that he was rather clever about constructing the foundations of the models", Gretl recalls.

So Nielsen's son Ben became Josef Urban's "chief assistant" as a draftsman who built Urban's theatrical set models. Many of the models Bennie Nielsen crafted for Urban's Boston Opera gig are kept well-preserved at Columbia University. Urban began his designs with sketches, watercolors, then built the set models. At Columbia his small watercolor portrait of Alice Nielsen in *Faust* joins designs for *Madame Butterfly* which uses a palette of colors showcasing Nielsen's 1898 kimonos bought in Yokohama. Urban would create "over five hundred stage sets for more than 168 productions". Many he also directs.

Loie Fuller and Urban set the pattern for future stage designers. Following Fuller, Urban believes "music...should be accentuated on the stage by certain harmonious affects. The intimate concordance between color and sound, this modern art, as I have said, is limitless in its possibilities". Discovering that Urban and Fuller had combined in Boston certainly is one of the most intriguing artistic discoveries arising from Nielsen's career, right up there with the *Satanella* and Burton Stanley.

"The modern artist must paint with light", proclaims Josef Urban, taking the trail Loie Fuller blazed (*Boston Transcript* Oct 4, 1913).

Fuller the originator; Urban brings her insight into a manly world using his architectural and design skills to craft brilliant productions. Fuller wrestles with performing. Urban is a director who designs the stage as a story arc. As dancer, Loie Fuller had a motive to innovate her transforming designs, after all, she was in motion. To her theatrical lighting innovations famed in Paris, Urban applies his skills to her palette. For his biographer Cambridge (2006), "Urban's designs were simple in terms of line, but vibrant color created a sense of lushness and complexity. He achieved this by applying pointillist techniques—the juxtaposition of dots of color—to scene painting. This not only added new dimensions to painted scenery, but also allowed parts of the image to appear or disappear under different colored lights".

Urban's path to operatic theatre began by illustrating fairy tales and Poe's *Mask of Red Death*. A Vienna theatre manager saw the books and invited him to craft sets; Debussy, then Nielsen, next discover Urban. After Boston fails, Urban with Benjamin Nielsen move to NY where the Austrian architect with a Lithuanian name designs hundreds of Broadway shows and many movies. Becomes chief designer for the Met, *Ziegfeld Follies*, and the musical *Showboat* which Ziegfeld produced. Urban will architect the New School and the 1927 art deco Ziegfeld Theatre's 1600-seat egg-shaped auditorium. Charles Wagner said, Urban awakened "the somnambulant Met from its coma".

Alice Nielsen drags her age into modernity. Her best projects are artistic leading-edge. She and collaborators consciously create the new. And the women's contribution to Boston Opera became lost in fog of the avoidable. Her concerts showcase modernity, the composers she knows personally.

Urban has certain advantages at Boston. He can seize all the staging tasks and leave Russell to crime. "For in our opera republic, as Mr. Urban lately called the Boston Opera House, everyone is trying to give America not only a great opera, but also a modern stage" (*Boston Transcript* Sat 25, 1912). As a guy, Urban apparently got more republic than Nielsen or Fuller. In addition, he poses no moral restraint on Russell who hates to be distracted by design and staging when pockets can be picked. As also with Conti, Russell is quite *laissez-faire* with Josef.

Gretl Urban recalls, "Henry Russell had given him complete freedom to do as he pleased". Indeed, the hireling has distractions: he is no director, manager, designer, or conductor: gotta grub money and influence people.

With Fuller and Urban, the artists are onstage and backstage too.

Urban raises an artistic manifesto at Boston Opera: "The operatic stage is still laboring under an immense handicap in this country: dull, labored and uninspired. Realism in art is very different from realism in daily life". He advocates *Hagenbund's* motto, "We recognize tradition, we appreciate it and love it, but we do not cling to it".

With Nielsen, Urban shares eternal youthfulness, saying "We stand by youth and will remain young because of it. To youth—Eternity".

Without mentioning her dad owes Nielsen everything, Gretl recalls Alice being "always grateful to Buschi because he had taught Benny Nielsen how to work. She admitted that she had spoiled Benny because he was only ten years old when her husband and his father died...." Of course Sarah had raised the boy so mom could pose as his sister on voyages.

Boston binds three Nielsen generations; arrival port for Sarah and her parents. Bennie marries a Boston Opera ballet dancer. After Urban dies in 1933, Ben T. Nielsen brings his drafting skills back to Boston, joining the Corps of Engineers at Roxbury where he retires after designing dams, no more theatre sets for divas. His daughter Alice marries a Mitchell, recalling genial Julian Mitchell whose wife a ballerina, no link for that coincidence.

The Mitchells today recall Alice and Ben as sharing the trait of modesty. In later life, Ben skips telling grandchildren of his brilliant theatre days with Josef Urban; quite excited to design dams. Family reunions took place at the Nielsen-designed dams, not theatrical spaces.

Ben had lived with Sarah most of his young life. In 1910s, he threw light on daily life in a May 14 letter (no year) preserved at KC Museum. His message scrawled back of a letter from Alice's mom. Sarah had written Alice, "I received your letter and card and was pleased with both. I had company all day. I'm glad to know you are feeling better. Give my love to Aunt Hortense and Anna May, tell them I haven't forgotten them. I haven't seen the Nielsen family for three weeks. I can't write more this time. With best wishes and love write soon, Gram". Ben adds, "We are down at Gram's today. She is feeling fairly well, she's been trying to write this letter for two days, but a few words tire her very much. George has arrived and you've had a fine visit together. Give him our love. We are all wishing you the best of luck on your case and hope you lick tar out of them. Everyone sends love, we are going to Clayton's for dinner Sunday & haven't seen him since you were here, dearest love".

Another note jotted on another one from Sarah reveals his model-building skills had started early, "Yes mother I certainly enjoyed the book. Thanks so much for sending it. I really did not expect it so soon since I am working a model of a Clipper Ship at present".

Again, he heads "to Clayton's for dinner Sunday. We invited our selves. I suppose you are leaving for Glens Falls Sunday. Don't worry everything will be all right I know. After that I suppose you are off for Harrison. Is George Nance coming to Boston? If he does he would like to see him before he leaves for Texas. Give Aunt Hortense my love and also Auntie May. Well mother we all send love. See you soon. Fondest love always, your loving and devoted son, Bennie".

Glens Falls is the upstate NY family home of LeRoy Stoddard, NYC plastic surgeon who Nielsen marries 1917 after a decade dating. George Nance, Texas oilman, is less well known. The UT research ranch named after Nance knew of him not.

On business matters, nephew Tommy Nielsen helps organize her schedule for the Chautauqua tours. Referring to Alice, he says "I am not her manager", stating his powers are strictly limited. Yet Bennie's middle name is Tommy, creating confusion for this author chapters back. Perhaps the solution given is a fair guess. Seems so. Perhaps maybe. Sure.

Summer passes. Alice returns September 21st to Boston from Liverpool on White Star *Zeeland*. Liverpool, seaport her Irish family departed for

Boston before the American Civil War which fatally shortened her Danish dad's life.

1912-1919: BIG TIME POPULARITY

"If a line of airships crossing the ocean is ever established it will certainly get my business", Alice Nielsen tells *Boston Globe* (Se 21). During the passage she got seasick, seldom left her stateroom. Nielsen "greatly regretted that she would not be with the Boston Opera Company this season, for her home is here and she dearly loves Bostonians", records *Globe*. Gifts ready, she carries "a Chinese chow dog for her brother". She tells of being "much disappointed that the weather conditions prevented the steamer from making port here a day earlier".

Nielsen had enjoyed her first air flight and wants more. Speaking later that same day to *Boston Traveler*, "I shall be a passenger in the first transatlantic aeroplane. I've got tired of traveling in ships. I never did like them, and if the birdmen will give us an opportunity to cross the ocean with them, I'll try to help along the enterprise by promptly booking passage with them".

Traveler tells more about the puppy. "Miss Nielsen bought her brother, who lives here, a seven-weeks-old Chinese dog she has christened Chow. The dog is a lively, good-sized creature, with a handsome face and straight, seal-brown hair". Apparently Alice keeps Chow; or at least likes the name, she will be photographed for Boston papers in the 1920s with Chow or a doggy descendant.

To *Boston Herald*, Alice Nielsen is candid, "I just hate to leave Boston, it seems just like home to me. Perhaps one reason for this particular feeling is that this is the first place where I have really had a home of my own. Before coming here, I always lived in hotels".

Charles Wagner indeed keeps Alice Nielsen away from her mainstage at Boston Opera. He schedules the singer for Worcester Music Festival. Then she starts an eight weeks' concert tour with her own company, first of twenty-four concerts with tenor Riccardo Martin. Martin (1874-1952) from Kentucky, had finished voice training in Naples before joining Nielsen in New Orleans. He would sing at the Met 281 times 1907-1917; last show as Rodolfo of *La Bohème*. Tour ending, Alice rejoins the Met at Chicago

After her Boston Opera ambush—loss of her grand opera stage against all hopes which destroys plans for the continuous creation of new roles, Alice fled overseas to collect European successes as Boston yearns. Now back in Boston, she talks with press. We get a rare glimpse of home. *Herald* visits Nielsen's "attractive apartment", top floor of 114 Hemenway Street across from Fenway Park. Her lifestyle at home is described for the first time since London 1901. She continues kimonos.

"It was easy to understand her pleasure in the setting. Becomingly dressed in a teagown of palest pink, she sat at a dainty tea table, while the perfume of roses, red and white, arranged in tall vases was wafted through the room, and on the open piano stood large autographed portraits of faces, familiar figures in opera and drama, among others, Melba, Duse,

D'Annunzio, Paolo Tosti and Victor Maurel", her favorite portraits now preserved at Kansas City Museum. No news how Melba made the ranks.

Nielsen's summer? Oh same as any! "I spent two wonderful months of the summer motoring through Switzerland, Italy and the Pyrenees, and I don't think I ever enjoyed anything more. We seemed to go through sunshine all the time without a single rainy day, and we were fortunate enough not to suffer anywhere from heat. When we passed through Viterbo my chauffeur, a very patriotic Italian, insisted that I should stop over for a few hours to attend a session of the great trail of the Camorrists. It was most interesting. Poor Abbatemaggio the informer is very handsome, but he looked so funny sitting in his cage in the courtroom that I just couldn't help bursting out laughing. Then some man shouted, 'silence, or you'll have to go out!' So I thought I'd better keep very still. The accused men looked dreadfully unhappy, heavily handcuffed, as they were, and I really felt very sorry for them, poor things!

"I stayed out of Italy a good deal because I was afraid of cholera. In Rome the cholera scare was very much exaggerated, principally I think by certain people who wished to injure the success of the exposition. And they accomplished their object too, shameful as it was. I was told by a friend that many of those who had been largely interested in the exposition had practically become bankrupt". Yes, certain people hate success by others.

Regards artistry, "Last spring, soon after I sailed I sang at Albert Hall, and it spite of it being such a huge place, I found it very easy to sing in. Then in Berlin, I sang for the first time at the Komische Oper in *La Bohème*, and although it was not exactly instantaneous, I felt that I had a real success. For instance, I sang the aria in the first act *Mi Chiamano Mimi*, without a single hand of applause, but at the end of the act it was very different and at the end of the opera I got twenty-two calls. Everyone was very nice to me there. Although I did not see the doctor [Karl Muck], I saw Mrs. Muck, and she told me that both he and she want me to sing at the Royal Opera House". Muck conducts Berlin Opera; later Boston Orchestra.

The German rule is sing the language of the nation. "It seems a pity that the rule of having only opera in German at that opera house is so rigid. I can't imagine *Madam Butterfly* in German".

A hint to her deep trauma at losing Boston by betrayal: "Except for my engagements, I was glad to keep away from operas and theatres...."

Bounces back, her philosophy focused on singing. "One thing I did see in Vienna is the *Rosenkavalier*. In my humble opinion it is the best music Strauss has written. I was surprised to see what an elaborate and beautiful opera it really is, for I had expected something much lighter. But with four big prima donna roles and costly settings, it is a production that entails enormous expense". Set in 1740 Vienna, the comic opera has romantic chicanery, a silver rose, a drunken waltz.

"I do not know how it would be received over here. You know the libretto is very, very naughty and the scenes nothing if not realistic. When I went, I at first gasped and said, 'This is all right for Vienna, but how about NY or Boston?!'"

She gave a month "of hard study" learning two dozen songs by Shubert, Schumann, Brahms, and Hugo Wolf to include in concert tours. She also adds Wolf-Ferrari's *Il Segreto di Susanna* to repertoire, a piece "infinitely charming".

Alice discusses opera versus concert work. Concerts are splendid for increasing artistic abilities and a greater challenge to vocal quality. "If one is an opera singer as I am, it is so easy to get stale, and in concert nothing but the very best vocally will do. There is no chance of an orchestra coming in conveniently to cover up faults".

In Paris she looks at fashions but skips buying, partly due to the new custom duties adding expense—yet last year she had not objected.

Boston Opera steams ahead without her. The air gets chillier.

Its prospectus (*NY Times* Se 27) states the third season opens November 27 for eighteen weeks with opera in English, two German works *Tristan* and *Hansel und Gretel*, plus a long French and Italian list. Of these three, Puccini's *Manon Lescaut*, Boito's *Mefistofele* and Wolf-Ferrari's *Segreto di Susanna* are "not in the present Metropolitan repertoire". Weingartner will conduct *Tristan* with Nordica; 'Tis heralded that Mrs. Maeterlinck would appear in *Pelleas et Melisande*.

September 30th, Alice Nielsen sings the 54th annual Worchester Musical Festival at Mechanic's Hall.

October 8 (*NY Times*), the Boston Opera hireling apes Ziegfeld, faking a press report that Maeterlinck will visit Boston "incognito" and "not be interviewed". The manager sails on Lusitania, "Just before leaving Paris, Mr. Russell engaged Miss Eliza Amsden of Boston to sing the girl in *La Naciulla del West*".

October 30, a new Alice Nielsen Opera Company, with Riccardo Martin, performs in concert at Des Moines.

Meanwhile in Boston poignant reminders of Nielsen float across the town's papers. *Boston Sunday Globe* publishes "First Week Of Opera in Boston This Season" with photos of Nielsen, Emmy Destinn and Carmen Melis (Nov 12). Of course, Nielsen is slated to return only with the Met and Caruso. *Globe* pitches an egg at who they know did her wrong.

Boston Opera opens Monday Nov. 27, *Samson and Delilah* with Maria Gay and Zenatello; Nov 29 *Tosca* with Carmen Melis, Gaudenzi and Scotti; Dec 1 *Aida* with Destinn, Gay, Glovanni Zenatell, Polese and Edward Lankow. The theatrical style Nielsen set continues, "*Samson and Delilah*" will "both scenically and dramatically...form a wide departure from the established rules usually followed in the presentation of the Saint-Saens work. The scenic effects will surpass in beauty and effectiveness anything heretofore attempted on the stage of the Boston Opera House, while the costumes will prove a revelation in their barbaric splendor. The ballet will form a very important part of the production, as it usually does at the Scala Opera House in Milan".

November 19th, Nielsen appears in concert with "Russian Symphony Orchestra" at Hippodrome NYC. Mid-December she returns to Boston after ending her successful far-flung concert tour. "With Riccardo Martin and her own concert company, including Miss Swartz, Mr. Mardonnes, Mr. Fornari and Mr. Cilia of the Boston Opera Company, Miss Nielsen has just concluded a concert tour of six weeks, which extended as far west as

Alberta, Canada and included Winnipeg, Minneapolis, Chicago and other cities in the Middle West.

"At Nashville, Miss Nielsen's birthplace and formerly Mr. Martin's abiding place, there was great enthusiasm, as also at Kansas City. In addition to her appearances this season with the Metropolitan Opera Company, Miss Nielsen will be heard in Boston from time to time as guest (*Boston Herald* Dec 13)".

Asked to speak on what makes a woman attractive, Alice invites the *Boston Herald* reporter to tea. Fortunately she is quoted, not paraphrased. The story revealed quick-witted Nielsen jumping delightfully across many topics. As she speaks she feeds her new-kept puppy Chow lumps of sugar.

"Dear me, yes! I'll tell you what makes a woman attractive. That sounds tremendously conceited though, and I didn't mean it that way at all, but I'll tell you anyhow. She must be ingenuous. Yes indeed, and she must be tactful, and fresh—not in the slang sense, but as opposed to blasé.

"Ingenuousness is marvelously attractive. It doesn't depend on youth, either. Youth often isn't attractive at all. You may not think this is consistent with being ingenuous, but a woman should be conscious that she is attractive, yet not behave as if she were conscious of it. I'll admit that sounds terribly complex. A woman is more attractive when she feels that she is attractive. It's a consoling thought that every woman is attractive to somebody.

"Tact, freshness", Nielsen sat down her teacup and ticked the qualities off on her fingertips, "ingenuousness, spontaneity—that's an awful lot of things for one woman to possess, but if she possess even one of them!

"Beauty is tremendously powerful but not necessary, though it's every woman's duty to herself first and to her friends afterward, to make herself as good looking as she can. Magnetism and personality are the very essence of attractiveness. But what is magnetism? What is soul? Individuality of a pleasant kind, I suppose.

"Good dress covers a multitude of sins. Good dress doesn't mean buying the latest Paris modes. A woman should find her style and cling to it, changing it only slightly with the changing fashions.

"Do you know, I think a sense of humor will make almost any—yes I believe any—woman attractive? It's the leaven of life. Never mind how unprepossessing a woman may be, if she can make a joke or take a joke, you can't help feeling friendly toward her, and if you feel friendly toward her then you find her attractive. A sense of humor can be cultivated. I don't suppose it can be acquired outright if she hasn't the makings".

Spoken as any Marie Dressler friend, "Now I'm rather glad to say that I've got a sense of humor, such as it is. I got it from an Irish mother. My father as Danish and there's a good deal of the melancholy Dane in me, so I'm glad the melancholy is tempered by the Irish fun. Danish and Irish—it's just the proper combination, the fun-loving with the fray-loving. If I hadn't been a singer I'd have been a prize fighter.

"But I digress. Attractiveness, like art, has no age. Let me tell you though, that the combination of art with age isn't at all that bad. The most ungraceful thing in the world is an old woman trying to be young".

Speaking as an early facelift pioneer with fiancé grasping the scalpel, "But if a woman, especially a woman in public life, finds herself getting old she should doctor up. The best doctor for old age is the powder puff, aided and abetted by the dye-pot. Please don't mistake me, too much art is inartistic. But there are props which, judiciously used, are not only allowable but imperative".

Urges women to action. "If any woman, I don't care whiter she is old or young, finds that she looks better with her hair dyed blonde, let her dye it! If red hair is becoming let her get red hair! If she looks better in paint than without, let her put it on! Why shouldn't a woman massage to keep down a double chin? Why shouldn't she exercise to take lumps of fat off her shoulders? If her hair is getting gray and she doesn't like gray hair, why shouldn't she dye it black or brown or red or yellow or any shade that suits her complexion? When gray hairs start in my head, though thank the Lord, they haven't started yet—I shall doctor 'em". That this is her new promo for friend fiancé, could be.

Act and grow fit: "It's a shame for a woman with a good figure to let herself get fat. It's mere laziness. Let her keep well and strong—and thin—by hard work. Let her take an ice cold plunge every morning—but this isn't meant to be a beauty talk, just a talk on the attractive woman.

"Well then, although I'm an American I must admit—that American women lead the world in women who are attractive".

With Nielsen excluded from her stage, Mrs. Gardner makes a grand and telling gesture toward the Boston Opera boys—the male-only Board—by inviting Alice Nielsen to concert at her Fenway Court home December 13. Gardner's musicale becomes the biggest gala Boston ever gives Alice Nielsen. Friends among Boston Opera cast conspicuously attend, also the Boston press corps. This concert is covered as closely as her opera debut. Each Boston critic distinctly recommends Alice Nielsen to Boston Opera.

Boston unifies in support of Alice Nielsen and the gayety of nations.

The program divides six groups of songs among three soloists. Both Andre-Caplet and Wallace Goodrich accompany Nielsen. Edward Lankow starts with *Ombra mai fu—Xerxes* by Handel and *An die Musik* by Shubert. George Proctor follows with *Gavotte* by Bach and *Barcarolle* by Rubinstein. Nielsen sings four songs, Andre-Caplet playing piano, *Voi che sapete* by Mozart, *Fileuse* from *Gwendoline* by Chabrier, *Mandoline* by Debussy, *L'Heure Exquise* by R. Hahn.

Next set, Edward Lankow sings *Oh Isis* (*Magic Flute*) by Mozart and *Toper and the Devil* by Reissinger. George Proctor plays *Serennade dans Grenade* by Debussy, *Rigaudon* by MacDowell, and the *Waltz in F* from *Marionettes* by Tsherbatchett. Then Nielsen, Wallace Goodrich pianist, gives *Aria, Il Sergreto di Susanna* by Wolf-Ferrari, *Aria, Sacrifice* by Converse, *Sweetheart, Thy Lips Are Touched with Flame* by Chadwick, and *Down in the Forest* Landon Ronald.

Boston Journal: "Alice Nielsen was the star of a concert given at Fenway Court yesterday. Her voice retains its fresh and youthful tone and her art is riper than ever. The music room of Mrs. John Gardner's house was crowded with her friends and admirers".

Nielsen gives a master class to her company. "Many of the singers from Boston Opera House got up at the unconscionable early hour of 2PM to be on hand in time to hear her sing Mozart's *Voi che sapete*, the first of nearly a dozen numbers either down on the program or given as encores".

Boston Journal cannot resist, "And no prima donna heard here this season has sung any classic with purer tone or clearer diction or finer understanding.

"*Fileuse* from Chabrier's *Gwendoline*, the Debussy *Mandoline*, Hahn's *L'Heure Exquise* and *Si Mes Vers*, a charming aria from Wolf-Ferrari's new opera, *Il Segreto di Susanna...*, the flower song from Converse's *Sacrifice*, one of Chadwick's rippling love songs and Landon Ronald's *Down In The Forest*, sung with lark-like swiftness and sweetness, proved Miss Nielsen to be as delightful as ever".

Musical Courier goes to the point: "Though this recital was given jointly with George Proctor, pianist, and Edward Lankow, bass, as assisting soloist, Alice Nielsen was really the attraction which drew a capacity audience to Mrs. Gardner's beautiful palace, completely filling the artistic recital hall".

Courier cannot resist: "Indeed a pleasure exceeding all expectations to hear Miss Nielsen's clear, pure tones again.

"That she was in excellent voice and the best of spirits was evident at the very outset when Mozart's difficult aria, *Voi che sapete*, was given with the flawless perfections of phrasing and smoothly flowing vocal art, that left nothing to be desired. Nor was she less successful in the songs of Chabrier, Debussy and Hahn, which she gave with remarkable delicacy and charm. In the closing group, Miss Nielsen was particularly applauded for her exquisite diction in the English songs, of which Landon Ronald's *Down in the Forest* was particularly well received". Take note, Boston Opera board, "All in all, Miss Nielsen showed in herself the rare combination of a great operatic star and a concert singer.

"Mr. Lankow proved himself the possessor of a bass voice of unusual sonority and richness which he handled skillfully, while Mr. Proctor gave much pleasure by his piano solos".

Boston Record: "Absence of theatricalism in her concert appearances is commendable. The brilliancy and richness of her upper tones constantly improve. Chabrier's *Fileuse* was a fine example of her art. Debussy's familiar *Mandoline* and Chadwick's *Sweetheart, Thy Lips Are Touched With Flame*, showed her fine command of widely different schools of song and her mastery of the whole gamut of models and 'atmosphere.'

Boston Transcript: "Miss Nielsen came fresh-voiced and alert of spirit to an audience that had awaited her eagerly through Mr. Lankow's songs and Mr. Proctor's pianoforte pieces and that received her warmly. She sang first a group of lyric numbers...to Mr. Caplet's sensitive accompaniments. Her voice still keeps its charm, its evenness and its niceties of song and because she uses it with practiced and refined skill and discriminating sense of style. She sang these lyric pieces with such discernment and such poise, but when she passed later in the concert to operatic airs...she used her larger and more emphatic 'voice of the theatre' and her broader operatic style.

Boston Transcript cannot resist: "Her skill in song, her ear for quality abide. They are rare and to be desired in many an opera house".

Boston Herald: "In these days when few operatic celebrities can afford to submit themselves to the test of interpreting songs in a concert hall, it is a pleasure to hear a singer who, having made a reputation in opera, does not confound legato singing with spasmodic bursts and does not seek to turn lieder into themes for high-flown and incongruous declamation. Miss Nielsen's command of breath and maintenance of melodic lines was note-worthy. It was highly appreciated by the audience".

Boston Globe cannot resist: "It was a pleasure to hear Miss Nielsen sing again in Boston.

"Her voice, while broadening with time and study, retains that native charm and spontaneity which cannot be acquired by artifice. Her middle tones are warm and expressive; those above are brilliant and crystalline without shrillness, and the whole voice is used with equal freedom, in passages requiring fullness of power and in the support of a soft or vanishing phrase.

"Her ease in sustaining pure melodic lines was evidenced in the *Voi che sapete* from *Marriage of Figaro* and in the air from *The Secret Of Suzzanne*. It appears to have fallen to Miss Nielsen to be the first to introduce an excerpt here from this one-act opera by Wolf-Ferrari, which Mr. Dippel produced last year in NY, and which Mr. Russell has announced as a novelty for Boston.

"The aria has Italian characteristics, melody of graceful and flowing curve, grateful to the singer and inherently vocal and a dramatic accentuation of the thought, yet this promises something more than the sensuous style of Mr. Puccini. Beginning fancifully, the music broadens for voice and accompaniment, and affords a telling climax. It was well suited to Miss Nielsen's voice and one of her most effective numbers".

Globe cannot resist repeating: "It was a pleasure to see Miss Nielsen in such excellent spirit, and to listen again to the vocal beauty of her singing. Her voice has been ever welcome and a source of enjoyment in concert and in opera, and will be again when she returns to the Boston Opera House as guest this season".

Boston American cannot resist: "Her art has heightened since we last heard her. Miss Nielsen was a charming picture in her white gown, and her voice was just as clear and pure and sweet as ever. Seldom has the *Voi che sapete* of Mozart been sung in this city with such grace and loveliness. Her intelligence and vocal gifts enable her to make the *Mandoline* of Claude Debussy one of the most fascinating, fetching and wholly winning songs I have ever heard, and I am not so awfully fond of Debussy. Miss Nielsen's is a brilliant voice, but it is not without dramatic qualities, as was shown in an aria from *The Secret Of Susanne*, a new opera by Wolf-Ferrari, which by the way, is a very beautiful thing".

Reviewers beg to return Alice Nielsen onstage at Boston Opera. Popular pressure is intense to restore her. Will the Board act rightly? In addition, Russell's deficits and methods have attracted an investigative reporter who prepares a detailed exposé for publication that Spring.

Public scandal a-brewing.

During December, Maeterlinck stirs press on his American visit. After Debussy's opera collaboration, "I don't understand music. I consider it quite unnecessary noise" (*NY Times* De 19). Plays coy, "I will certainly pay a visit to America. Maybe I shall go via Montreal, maybe via Siberia, maybe some other way, maybe now, maybe later. I don't know myself, but in any case I object to being interviewed. Those who wish to know my thoughts and feelings have only to read my works. My visit to America will be strictly private and will not include any public speaking. My wife does all the talking and she is always right". Nevertheless, soon he goes public speaking on an American tour with the help of actress Hortense Nielsen.

Whatever Eben Jordan chooses to believe about his hireling foreign manager, Alice Nielsen's influence continues to change his life when his son Robert marries into theatre. Story foreshadows the new melodramatic age, headline "Rich Youth To Wed Actress", noting Robert at first denied it, "acting under pressure from his family". Nevertheless, Robert "son of Eben...with his father in the Jordan Marsh Company" has announced his engagement to Jane Malcom "a NY actress" in Frohman shows at Park Theatre. Robert, Harvard grad '07, "personally attends to the affairs of the Boston Opera House, of which his father was founder".

With art comes challenges. Nielsen's talk with Robert Jordan at Park Theatre led directly to creation of Boston Opera. Robert links her to Eben; Nielsen talent plus Eben Jordan resources equals Boston Opera House.

Now Eben has a new daughter-in-law from the stage.

1912: CHAUTAUQUA MOZART MONTREAL

1912 will be her most prosperous year as Alice Nielsen sings from the heart across the heartland. She re-enters pop culture in a big way. Ever since Jacob Dold's Kansas City birthday musicale with her first ride in a real carriage, Nielsen's concert programs consist of art songs, Celtic songs, and popular parlor songs dating from mom's mom. Nielsen has been singing to large, spirited audiences since 1890. 1912 enjoys the domestic tranquility of Jefferson's political ecology of spontaneous order without intrusions into the sovereign citizens' private finances for taxation, not long to last.

Alice has been famous across North America since 1896. Now she sings in concert four sets of songs in four languages followed by an aria, usually Puccini's *Un Bel Di*, plus the many encores of airs sung since childhood. Her pianist plays Chopin, or his own pieces between sets. She usually adds a virtuoso string player.

Reviews across the nation praise. Typical 1912 concert venue would be Wichita's New Crawford Theatre, "Artists expected to appear: John McCormack (Irish tenor); Alice Nielsen and the Grand Opera Concert Company (from Boston Opera Company); Wichita Forum Chorus; Rudolph Ganz (Swiss pianist); Kocian (Violinist); Sousa and his band".

Alice Nielsen performs at Carnegie Hall seven times between 1912 and 1916. Her usual accompanist at the big Baldwin grand piano becomes William Reddick. The famed Chautauqua tours are a nine-week summer season. She profits personally as Boston Opera sales decline.

Nielsen's new manager Charles Wagner recalls the summer tour: "1912 gave me an opportunity to take another crack at my old [managerial] opponent—the Circuit Chautauqua. Following my sale of [Wagner's circuit] Slayton to [Harry] Harrison of Redpath and his merger of the two Lyceum bureaus, he arranged what probably was the biggest Chautauqua program ever presented. I couldn't resist separating Circuit Chautauqua from nearly as much money for one artist as they normally paid for an entire six-day program, when I sold Alice Nielsen to Harrison for one-hundred recitals in one-hundred towns throughout the South and Mid-West—the only time I ever booked a long continuous summer tour for a great singer.

"Harrison sent her in a private car [per usual for Nielsen] and gave these towns the best musical treat they ever had. In some communities they still refer to it as 'Alice Nielsen Day.'" More than ever: true Americana.

Nielsen's 1912 *Who's Who in Music* entry by same, wrestles with the absurd and misleading company names. Now she refers to "Don Pasquale Opera Company 1906, San Carlo Opera Company [of SF, of NO] 1907-8, Boston Opera Company 1910-11, Metropolitan Opera House 1910".

Starting the New Year in Boston, Hortense and Alice greet Maeterlinck and colorful wife Georgette Leblanc, January 1 (*NY Times*). The couple's reception at Hotel Lenox brings out "some one-hundred-thirty of the elect of Boston society".

Mrs. Gardner sports diamonds and white silk. Alice Nielsen "a gown of white satin covered with a network of pearls and brilliants, and with a smart little Russian headdress with a black algrette, was one of the centers of attention". Leblanc appears "swathed in medieval veils, a diamond on her forehead, dressed in black velvet from the waist to the ankles. Her blouse is made of a Persian material in red tones. Her tawny yellow hair is drawn in braids".

Leblanc speaks freely, having "many ideas and she likes to talk about them", said *Times*. "She confesses frankly that it is her dream to sit with a person and be interrogated and then to tell only the truth".

In Paris, Leblanc was blocked by Debussy from *Pelleas and Melisande* to favor Mary Garden who recalls this was "a blow for the librettist Maeterlinck, as his mistress the soprano Georgette Leblanc desperately wanted the role. Stung into action by rage and jealousy, Leblanc began to exert her not inconsiderable influence over Maeterlinck to have the decision reversed".

Garden said Russell said, "Maeterlinck was furious when he heard that Georgette Leblanc would not have the part. The normally unemotional Belgian arrived at Debussy's attic home, burning with rage and armed with a walking stick. Madame Debussy opened the door and asked the poet what he wanted. Maeterlinck's reply was short and unusually direct. 'Madame, do you see this cane? I have brought it to thrash your husband because he refuses to allow Georgette to sing.'" To give Georgette the role, Maeterlinck came to Boston. Ever the manipulator behind a facade, afterwards Russell affects scorn, "I am compelled to say her singing was pitiable; the quality of her voice was harsh, her intonation defective and she knew nothing whatsoever about music". Interestingly, Garden's memoirs retell a Nielsen story, never attributing Alice by name.

Obviously the Nielsen sisters had a role with Maeterlinck's appearance.

January 5, Robert Jordan marries Jean Laurel. Among "few friends and relatives present" at Grace Church are his dad Eben Jordan and wife, John and Louise Drew, Ethel Barrymore and husband. Happy trails!

Busy buzz Alice raids Montreal again. Since 1900 Alice Nielsen has been welcomed. Opened *Singing Girl* with Quebec's famed basso Eugene Cowles. In 1910 for Montreal Opera she returns. And in Boston papers appear many pleas for her return. "Montreal Captured", proclaims January 6's *Boston Globe*. "The event of the opera season was the appearance tonight of Alice Nielsen as Rosina in Rossini's *Barber of Seville*. She received a veritable ovation after each act. At the end of the opera enthusiasm ran rampant. There were fully fifteen curtain calls before the audience stopped applauding and shouting bravos.

"In an interview, Miss Nielsen declared that if her engagements permit [Danish irony of diplomatic diva, no throw egg] she may appear later in the season at the Boston Opera House in the leading role of Wolf-Ferrari's opera *Il Segreto di Suzanne*, and she is to sing Mimi in *La Bohème* at the Metropolitan Opera House with Caruso on January 19". She implies Wagner controls access to Boston, of course his conspiracy with Russell yet unbeknownst.

Montreal Daily Witness: "Miss Nielsen is captivating and easy in style. Her naturalness is one of the great charms of her work. Her waltz song was so rapturously received that the audience would be satisfied with nothing less than an encore".

Conductor Jacchia opposes encores. Diva wants. Who wins? "The leader of the orchestra, is so strongly opposed to encores from an artistic point of view—and he is generally right—that even after Miss Nielsen had nodded her assent to the popular demand, he demurred".

Diva deals conductor: "Miss Nielsen quite calmly walked across the stage and sat on the edge of a table, until the orchestra was ready". When Jacchia surrenders she sings the encore "to everybody's great delight".

In Quebec, E. Stanley Gardner [not confirmed as *Perry Mason* author] writes: "It is indeed a pleasure to have Miss Nielsen with us once again. She is well known here and is justly popular on account of her charming personality and delightful art".

Gayety descends upon the Quebecois nation.

"Nothing more refreshing or interesting could be imagined than this performance of Rossini's opera comique. All the artists seemed to catch just the right spirit and the whole work bubbled and sparkled along...putting everybody in the best of spirits and coming as a welcome change from so much opera tragedy. Miss Nielsen was a captivating Rosina. She proved to be a comedienne of extreme cleverness and distinction, making her points with the greatest finesse and ease. Her voice is of exquisite quality and admirably suited to music of this kind; her coloratura is good and her intonation excellent.

"For the music lesson scene, she chose Arditi's *Il Bacio* waltz, and for once the 'no encore' rule had to be broken, so tremendous was the applause that followed her rendition of this number. The way she shaded the piece was quite remarkable. She obtained a pianissimo which was taken to the extreme limit of softness and yet was at all times of good carrying quality. It was most effective and quite unusual. It is to be hoped Miss Nielsen will be heard in Montreal again in the near future".

Montreal Herald: "Miss Nielsen as Rosina was in the happiest setting. Her voice and style are essentially applicable to comic opera and she coquetted through the scenes with a briskness and untiring enthusiasm which focused attention upon her. In appearance a charming and attractive Rosina, Miss Nielsen acted with an endless variety of business and irresistible gayety".

La Patrie: Mme. Alice Nielsen, de l'opéra de Boston, est une des meilleure chanteuses actueliment sur la scene americaine, et sa grand réputation n'est en rein surfaite. Si elle possede une voix tres pure, tres souple, tres fraiche et tres etendue, elle a aussi, en plus de su grace physique qui lui attire les sympathies, un remarquable talent de comedienne don't elle s'est servi sans menagements, pour nous camper une Rosine alerte, coquette, pimpante et bien vivante. Elle a ete accamee et converte de fleurs par l'auditoire nombreux et enthousiaste et a du meme bisser son grand air du troisieme acte, bien que ce ne solt pas la coutume de bisser. A l'opéra".

[*Alice Nielsen is one of best singers on the American scene, and her large reputation is not overrated. If she has a voice very pure, very flexible and very wide range, she also has the physical grace which attracts sympathies to her, a remarkably talented actress. She gave us a Rosine alert, vain and quite alive. She was acclaimed and given many flowers by the enthusiastic audience.*]

In Boston without Alice on her stage, the Debussy debut awaits.

The Maeterlincks are a social event. Belgian poet-philosopher famed; wife wears her "famous leopard-skin coat". She makes her clothes. And Leblanc speaks to *NY Times* (January 28), "I have talked with many women in Boston...and I have found them very much like other intellectual women I have known. They are mostly writers or artists or people who appreciate literature and art...." Leblanc notes "the extraordinary comprehension" of Americans. "I think the public should rise to art, and here I have recited and sung the most delicate and subtle verses of Maeterlinck. They have been understood and appreciated. And that makes me very happy".

American women are "much better off than the French girl. I love your liberty here. I approve of the idea that women can do what they want. Young girls here may go to theatres or dances; they know everything and know everything, and yet they are charming and simple. It is better to know; it is better to understand when one is young. French girls know nothing until after marriage, and after marriage is often too late".

Boston Opera conductor Andre Caplet "worked all of last summer in Paris with the composer and with the author to grasp every detail of their ideas in regard to the music-drama". The four-hour opera will be "given in entirety—for the first time".

Leblanc's singing "what little there was of it—was indication of a pure soprano of high range but of limited power. All her costumes were white. Her hair—a reddish gold—streamed down her back below the waist line. Her principal gesture was one of supplication. Her crying was natural...."

Maeterlinck's subsequent American lecture tour features Hortense Nielsen performing portions of his plays. Soon she gives his talk, his English proves poorly understood by audiences.

Leblanc finds American reporters pleasant, "I don't think that I am being interviewed at all. I am simply conversing. In France it is quite the opposite. It is there that the interviewers are stupid. They ask you want you eat and what you wear...." Leblanc, writing a childrens' book, wishes to meet painter Maxfield Parrish "whose work I admire".

Parrish of course had illustrated Frank Baum's best-selling Mother Goose a decade ago. Interestingly, Parrish created a strong blue background for many of his illustrations. Urban uses the same for theatre, ordered in large batches for the big Boston backdrops. Blue shade gets tagged not Parrish but "Urban blue". Urban carries the color to Ziegfeld Follies, Broadway, and Met designs.

Back in Boston without her, Urban's sets debut January 10 in *Pelleas et Melisande* as created in Paris for Debussy's 1902 premier. Despite a decade old, "Nothing like them has ever been seen in any opera on the American stage' says Henry Taylor Parker, *Evening Transcript*, quoted by Cynthia Barnes' "Urban Sensibilities" for Columbia's Rare Book and Manuscript Library (2006). Hybrid unity as a theatrical design concept seems a revelation to Americans, not French who have enjoyed the gayeties of Loie Fuller and Josef Urban a decade. This recalls the supposed hybrid horrors certain fellas had opined, scorning who can sing and dance.

An American in Paris, Loie Fuller inspires and reinvents Broadway with innovations. She choreographs lights and dancers in unity. To Boston Opera arrives Fuller then Urban. The pair changes theatre forever. Urban, directing and designing at Boston Opera with Robert Brunton as technical director, inherits and uses Fuller's lighting effects to "combine ballet with opera" marked by unity of scenic effects.

Nielsen's shows have been best designed, best directed, best sung. If Fuller's contributions are underplayed, so Nielsen.

Bohemian Church Bishop Jan "Comenius" Komensky had agreed with Epictetus that women "also are formed in the image of God... and endowed with equal sharpness of mind and capacity for knowledge, and they are able to attain the highest positions...to give sound advice... and other things which benefit the human race" so why "drive them away from books?" Declined invite to be Harvard's first president. Despite sage advice, boys on the Boston Board kept skilled women away. Pay dearly.

The New StageCraft (1913) excludes frustrated Fuller who leapt away from Boston Opera with a sharp warning, and promotes Urban. "For a little over a year a Viennese artist, Joseph Urban, has been revolutionizing the staging of opera in America. He has brought to the Boston Opera House and interpreted through his own fertile genius in color and life, the theories and practices which have transformed and reanimated the whole German theatre. His scenery, costumes and lights have given the productions of the opera-house a distinction which they could never have obtained through their singing and acting alone". Origins of the French style created by America's Broadway-grown Fuller are skipped in the rhetoric.

For *Pelléas et Melisande*, "Boston found among its conventional Italianate opera settings [selected by Nielsen, lit by Fuller, highly praised], a remarkable production...made of strange, shadowed and sun-flecked glimpses of wood and fountain, tower, grotto and castle, vivid in varied color, full of soft unworldliness of Debussy's music. This work is the first expression in America of a new but well-founded school in stage design", says *New Stage-Craft*. And the show's fourteen sets are copies of interiors at Maeterlinck's estate in Normandy, as Urban points out.

Urban also provides Boston "a jolly Hansel and Gretel, set being a blue-checkered, toy-box curtain; and a spacious Tristan and Isolde of beautiful solemnity". Continues to direct and design "with a unique staging of *Tales of Hoffman*. Then appears his new setting of Mozart's opera" sung by Alice Nielsen returning by demand to Boston Opera House. Picked to star, again.

Obviously, Nielsen goes to wild lengths to help her entourage. Urban could call her for money to reach Boston, she gives his family her Maine cottage and her son Bennie as guide who becomes Urban's chief assistant; she likely helped Urban achieve commissions in Palm Springs where she gives recitals. Value of her contacts to achieve practical results.

January 14, *NY Times* runs a picture of Alice as Mimi. Five days later at the Met she sings *Bohème*. In the cast: Dimitri Smirnoff, Rodolofo; Bella Alten, Musetta; Antonio Scotti, Marcello; Pini-Corsi, Alcindoro; and conductor Giuseppe Sturani. As in Chicago and Boston, NYC critics appreciate Nielsen's artistic progress. Demand soars for Nielsen. Yes, hers is quite an impression.

NY Times tells readers Nielsen should also play Butterfly at the Met: "Alice Nielsen, with voice fresh and appealing and histrionic ability remarkable developed since former opera appearances here, did a Mimi in *Bohème* which left practically no opening for criticism. Aside from the sincerity of her acting and her sympathetic appearance, Miss Nielsen's singing was one of the features of the evening and delighted critical listeners with its finish in phrasing, its adaptability to the merry as well as the melancholy moods of Puccini's measure, and its power and purity in the dramatic climaxes.

"She should be asked to a *Madam Butterfly* performance here".

Morning Telegraph: "Miss Alice Nielsen was warmly welcomed last night at the Metropolitan Opera House, but she brings to it the winsomeness of a pleasing presence, practiced acting and some excellent high notes of unusual and persuasive sweetness".

NY Express: With so captivating a rival in the cast it was difficult of course for Miss Nielsen to hold her own. Yet she succeeded in persuading a few persons in the theatre who were not dazzled by the tenor's performance that her Mimi was the best portrayal of that role presented so far this season.

NY Sun: "Miss Nielsen has sung Mimi at the Metropolitan before, and her impersonation had then some distinct merits which have increased. She has a pretty voice, which seemed last night to have gained in fullness of volume. She sang her music in a simple and unaffected style, in tune, with good phrasing and with excellent enunciation of the text".

NYC papers skip Alice's marriage proposal.

Boston Globe: "An offer of marriage pinned to a gorgeous bouquet of flowers was the unusual gift received by Alice Nielsen at her first appearance this season at the Metropolitan Opera House, where she sang tonight the role of Mimi in Puccini's *La Bohème*. The prima donna refused to give the name of the author of the epistle, but declared it was couched in a manner that made it one of the most touching tributes she has ever received during her artistic career". And she "was the recipient of enthusiastic applause after each act". Apparently pleased with proposal, marriage with LeRoy Stoddard is five years away.

And Alice Nielsen returns to Boston Opera only once, and on tour.

Springfield Daily Republican (Jan 23) cannot resist: "The great thing last night was, of course, Alice Nielsen's...Cio-cio San. It is preeminently her part; she does nothing quite so well, and no one does the part better. She has been heard here in a variety of roles, and always with success, but never did she impress her audience as last night. Her singing was never better, her acting was admirable, full of grace and pathetic dignity".

For *Springfield Union*, her Broadway skills bring a unique quality to her grand opera work. "Alice Nielsen sang the part of Butterfly with much dramatic force and pathetic appeal. She also was at her singing best, her voice being fuller and stronger of tone than we recall ever to have heard it before. Owing to her long experience in light opera, Miss Nielsen was able to give a piquant daintiness to her impersonation in the first act. Though she is not a tragedienne, yet she indicated with surprising dramatic power the suffering of the heartbroken woman. The tragic ending of the opera was acted with much feeling and there was much of sincerity in the outburst of grief over the child which precedes the tragic ending of the unfortunate Butterfly".

Significantly: "The opera last night was unusually well-cast".

Springfield Daily News: "Butterfly is peculiarly adapted to Miss Nielsen. It is practically certain that her entire repertoire contains nothing that displays the winsome artist to more distinct advantage, or that permits her to do more distinguished work. She plays and sings the role *con amore*, living the character of the hapless little Oriental bride while she is enacting it and injecting into it a simple pathos that reaches the heart.

"From first to last she remains in the picture. She is at the beginning the little geisha girl, *san souci*, supremely happy in the love of the American, Pinkerton. The maternal feeling is vividly shown the second act in her caressing of the child—now played with a large doll—and finally there is in the poignant tragedy of the last scene, the despair of Butterfly when she realizes that Pinkerton can no longer be anything to her but a memory and prepares to end an existence that for her has no more charm.

"It is a portrayal that is satisfying in every respect. Vocally the Puccini score demands nothing of Miss Nielsen that she cannot give. The opera is, of course, exacting on the prima donna, but Miss Nielsen meets every requirement admirably. She colors her tones beautifully and most expressively. Never has she sung more brilliantly here than last evening, her principal numbers being sung with feeling and power".

Alice's only Boston Opera Company appearance of the year.

Such a brave woman. Harvard helps.

Alice Nielsen again receives one of the great critical statements of her career when she appears at Sanders Theatre with professor WR Spalding (*Boston Transcript* Fe 10) who brilliantly reveals: "There is no opportunity of 'faking' in Mozart; every carelessness and shoddiness yells its sin to the world and requires equal portions of voice, natural talent, dramatic imagination, everyday common sense and tireless industry. These, but all of these and conscience, the every day variety of working conscience. Probably it is this conscience that makes Miss Alice Nielsen's singing of Mozart so thorough and so authoritative.

"No amount of original talent or artistic education could have done it alone. An aria like the *Voi che sapete*, from *Figaro*, demands too much of everything a singer has to be achieved by any esoteric or mystic quality. In the clear light of day, alike to the intellect and to the emotions, her singing stood the test. She had what every Mozart aria demands; first of all, pure voice; not so much natural voice or vocal bigness, but rather a high percentage of efficiency in the use of the voice one has. Then there was a clear realization of form, of mere decorative beauty. Next, a conception of this form as organic, with each part, down to the smallest grace-note, necessary and individual.

"Along with this an instinctive feeling for the drama and emotion of it.

"And finally, after, and not before these other qualities, all that makes any one of Mozart's arias distinct form every other one, and all the subtlety and finesse and personal charm which a singer can give to them—if she is rich enough. Perhaps it is the recognition of all these things what makes up the necessary conscience which etymologically means merely 'complete knowing.'

"Miss Nielsen certainly has all of them. She can make each aria Mozartian, individual and finally her own personal property. She has the disciplined taste that can retard a phrase just long enough to emphasize it but not so much as to disturb its organic relation. She has the fine sense that can prepare an ending so as to make the closing cadence enchanting in its sweetness and finality".

This Harvard tribute wonderfully summarizes Alice Nielsen's greatness of artistry at sustained song. Acclaim reveals the constant pressure on Boston Opera to make good and fix what people deeply miss. Nielsen's loss is seen a major deficit for Bostonian culture. Re-read the Harvard raptures.

Obvious to her many fans, absence of the founding star reveals something very vwrong in Boston Opera House. The misjudgment forces scrutiny. Pending is the savage muckraking report which publicizes the big mess the hireling had hopes to hide a big longer feathering his nest. People realize he has a story doesn't stick to any of them.

After Nielsen presents Mozart to Harvard, Boston Opera lamely offers discounts to Harvard students due to "great interest which members of Harvard University have lately shown in establishing closer relations between Harvard and the opera" and present *Pagliacci* in Sanders Theatre "at greatly reduced prices".

During January and February recordings are produced for Columbia (*SJ Mercury News* Jan 17), Alice Nielsen "recently of the Boston Opera Company is now one of the leading sopranos in the Metropolitan…an artist whose name has been known in every American household. The last few months she has devoted largely to making gramophone recordings for the Columbia Phonograph Company. It is natural to find Miss Nielsen rising within the space of a few years from the position of American's foremost light opera prima donna to the enviable place in grand opera she occupies today; and to find that each year her progress has so remarkably eclipsed her best of previous years".

Columbia's press release quotes the star, "The records you have sent me of my voice excel in perfection of tone my most sanguine expectations. There is a complete absence of the defects which have hitherto been associated with phonograph reproduction". Columbia has "the most perfect of any talking machine in the world...incomparably superior to any machine yet invented...." Buy this new miracle of technology in San Jose at Madsen Furniture.

Alice Nielsen returns to the White House on February 17th to sing a "lengthy list of selections ...at a small musicale" for President and Mrs. Taft. Her White House recitals span twenty-five years.

Fatally for Boston Opera, two days later the manager Russell's contract would be extended three more years (NY Times Fe 19). A board member gloats, "In the brief space of three years we find the Boston Opera House in the front rank of art institutions". For the first year it was. Thanks to Alice Nielsen and Constantino now tossed out by the iffy foreign manager.

Board should walk plank, failed to pierce fog. The public, the press, and the shareholders are undeceived. Costs rising, mission abandoned in America to scour Russia, the latest greatest Boston lyric institution used as mere steppingstone for its ill-chosen director of bad character and foggy past inexperience. As a pattern. Captain of vessel kept at the helm racing full speed ahead, off course and a hijacked agenda. At his reappointment, praised are new works, incessant engagement of unknown singers from afar, and with utter incoherence, "adherence to the art ideals which has characterized the Boston Opera House since its opening". This causes a certain amount of laughter around town.

Worse, after the increasingly controversial manager is rewarded with a raise, Jordan and Board immediately seek bailouts from taxpayers by latching onto the property tax. Proves immediately very unpopular and attracts considerable scrutiny of its operations and policies. Provokes many complaints about the loss of the stars who founded the place and brought the investors to invest. Still the era when a small flat tariff fuels the nation and pubic projects like Boston Opera are truly that: financed by voluntary subscription.

Controversy rapidly focuses on the wide gap between promises and reality at Boston Opera. What about sticking with the original prospectus goals and focus here on Boston and America? People want an opera success. Where are the stars Nielsen and Constantino? How about a Bostonian manager working here full time, here in the hometown of Castle Square Company, of Harvard, of New England Conservatory, of Boston Symphony? The turmoil begins to boil.

Meanwhile back in diva realms, dipping into the choir-to-stage potboiler, *NY Times* (Fe 25) has a piece about choir singers who went professional, including Alice Nielsen.

On Leap Day, Alice leaps for the ailing Lillian Nordica, and sings at York Oratorio Society in Pennsylvania.

Financial pressures on Jordan mount without her. In March, political lobbying by Jordan to establish an early version of a non-profit status for Boston Opera and to acquire a subsidy fail. Russell's reputation among rumors of the town are not helping Jordan. Gossamer gossip floats far.

March 7 (*NY Times*), Boston Mayor Fitzgerald's bill "that the city pay 5 cents of the city tax rate to the Boston Opera House as a subsidy to perpetuate Grand Opera" is killed by a House committee which rejects any policy "to exempt any private institution from taxation, and...the bill would indirectly exempt the Opera House from taxation". The Boston Opera proposal would establish a non-profit corporation, in today's biz jibe.

Yes, the corporation provides a public service. No, it stays in private, unelected hands. Therefore no tax exemption is deserved. Definitely no city taxes. Because if subsidized, the organization's operators benefit: those who dictate policy.

As for providing a public benefit, well, so does any business in a free market. And if Boston's Irish mayor really wants this gift why has the Company's founding Irish diva been sent into exile. Legislature rejects.

March 17, Alice Nielsen sings Puccini and Irish songs for People's Symphony Society, founded by Franz Arens "to educate the masses in the appreciation of classical music".

April 7, Alice celebrates Ireland when she unites with Gaelic Society NYC to sing at its 34th annual Easter concert. The previous year's guest, Victor Herbert. Nielsen sings *Black Bird, Harp in the Air, Last Rose of Summer* and others, her Gaelic learned from mom suffices.

To close the third season, and after the Maeterlincks leave, Russsell undercuts his erstwhile pals by bringing Mary Garden from Chicago for *Pelleas and Melisande*.

Boston Opera financials show "a loss slightly above" the previous year. Jordan realizes his deficit of $140,000 (about $3.1 million today) is in part due to Nielsen's absence. She sells tickets. The quality drop, the ragged overseas casting, prospect of further deficits, and collapse of the scheme to leech public funds by coercing the citizens, has him worried. The opera enterprise is at risk due to deficit-driven management.Findings do not flatter Russell.

Now the Met tosses an egg. NYC's Metropolitan arrives for eight weeks at the Boston Opera building. Headliners include Alice Nielsen and Enrico Caruso in *Pagliacci*. Also-rans include Humperdinck's *King's Children*, Farrar rightly Goosegirl. Savvy Metropolitan managers slap at conniving competitor's manager who had schemed for their jobs by profitably returning Nielsen to her Boston stage. And with Caruso.

Stars on the stage. Boston headlines are simplicity.

"Alice Nielsen's Return", *Boston Globe* (Apr 1). "After an absence of one year Miss Alice Nielsen will appear again on the stage of the Boston Opera House but this time as a member of the Metropolitan Opera Company of

NY, for the popular prima donna..." to debut as Nedda to Caruso's Canio in *Pagliacci* on Wednesday afternoon, April 17. And Boston also casts a longing glance toward Constantino, never to be forgotten.

April 6 and 11, the Met gives to Boston *Pagliacci*.

Cast: Alice Nielsen, Nedda; Canio, Enrico Caruso; Tonio, Pasqual Amato; Albert Reiss, Beppe; Dinh Gilly, Silvio. Sturani conducts.

"Who shall compute the magic of an eminent tenor's name?" says *Boston Daily Globe* (Apr 18). "Mr. Caruso was heartily enjoyed. It matters not whether the voice retained its magic color...and alas it does not—yet the 'lament' of the poor strolling player was again poignant and stirring. There was also pleasure at the pervading good humor and comic business....

"It is but fair to Miss Nielsen to say she took the part of Nedda for the first time in this country, or—it is said—in any other. Particularly her upper voice had marked purity and freshness in the bird song, and she played the first part of the last act with the true soubrette spirit".

In the cast: Amato a "particular success...in his plentitude of resonant voice and his superb dramatic style". The chorus women were the same as the local group, "but the men...might be the envy of any opera house".

Throughout April, Nielsen's cross-dressing chaperone over to Oakland, the long-lived funnyman Burton Stanley surfaces briefly at scattered shows of his own. His thoughts on Alice's grand opera life would make gay reading; alas these seem lost to us.

April 12, the Met announces Nielsen re-engaged.

April 17, she sang in *Pagliacci*, conductor Guiseppe Sturani.

Two weeks later, Alice's beloved mother Sarah passes age seventy-six May 1st in her home at 531 East Parkway near Erasmus Street, Brooklyn. Funeral at St. Thomas Church. Three daughters: Julia, Hortense, Alice, and the son Erasmus survive. Mary or Maria has fallen away.

Alice returns to Europe. Brings boy Bennie along as she works her usual busy concert schedule. Then Italy to master the new material she has selected to sing. Covent books her for *Bohème* with Caruso.

SUMMER IN EUROPE

July 28 (*Boston Globe*), WJ Hubbard, press agent at Boston Opera, reports from Paris, "Unlike the operagoer, the opera singer finds no rest during the Summer months". European managers who "will not or cannot pay" high American salaries must "put forward his most brilliant casts during the late Spring and Summer" aligned with London-Paris fashion season.

Covent Garden's season extends from mid-April till late July. In London this summer are Boston Opera's Alice Nielsen, Carmel Melis, Alice's friend Elvira Leveroni. And Marie Lousie Edvina, aristocrat revealed, "in private life the sister-in-law of Baron Kensington".

At Covent, "Miss Alice Nielsen had the honor of sharing with Caruso the festivities which attended the opening of the Italian season. She sang the part of the Countess Gill in the *Secret of Suzanne*, which was the companion piece to *Pagliacci* in the bill of the evening. Mr. Scotti assumed the role of the jealous husband, and so Londoners heard the cast which had introduced the Wolf-Ferrari gem to Bostonians a few weeks before".

Her Butterfly at Covent is the coincidence of Destinn's sudden illness: "A short time after...Miss Nielsen was called upon to sing the title role in *Madame Butterfly*. No one but the great Bohemian soprano had ever sung the part in London previously and Mme. Destinn is such a favorite and her portrayal is held in such high esteem by the Britishers that Miss Nielsen made her debut in the part under unusual circumstances to say the least". Alice makes quite an impression: "However, the very large audience made certain of its approval of all that the American prima donna did".

In the cast: Suzuki, "Elvira Leveroni, the young Boston contralto... shared in the evening's honors".

And Alice resumes "Melba" roles: "Afterward, Miss Nielsen sang Mimi to the Rodolofo of Signor Caruso in *La Bohème* and before the season closes will appear as Marguerite in *Mefistofele* and Zerlina in *Don Giovanni*". Hijacks Melba's turf. The older, fatter soprano had returned to Australia.

Mary Garden cannot cope, "Following the breakdown which came soon after her return to Paris" spends "summer quietly in the country...." Lacking Nielsen's technique, Garden "sang more frequently than ever before...and the result was that the prima donna was forced to cancel all her engagements...." Whilst Mary Garden suffers the vapors, Nielsen sings.

Constantino, busy creating a new opera house in his adopted home Argentina, is sued for $100,000 in a breach-of-promise suit August 22 (*NY Times*). Before sailing "for Buenos Aires Tuesday on the Lamport & Holt liner Vasari, taking with him the orchestra chairs, draperies for the boxes and new drop curtains for his new theatre at Bragado" attorney Max Schenkmann had served summons at Hotel Victoria on behalf of Marcelle Hontabat, "young French girl living in NY who is said to be very beautiful".

Constantino had arrived in Bragado 1889, heart full of Basque folk songs, to begin his pilgrim progress toward grand opera. He responds with focus on art, "I shall sing six performances free for charity in my new theatre, and after seeing that it is running smoothly I shall sail back to NY, arriving in November, and after a few concerts I will depart for Mexico".

Sadly for Boston's longing glance, Boston Opera is not his schedule.

Teatro Constantino still stands; serves opera, drama and comedy. He opened September with *Rigoletto*; November 25 with *Bohème*. His lovely theatre of 2000 capacity is sited in heart of the fertile Pampas at Bragado, a town of 30,000 210km from Buenos Aires.

The cultural transition from live to duplicated is well underway, parallel the auto and airplane era. Music beforehand, you or present company must make happen. On the marketing side of life with that new-fangled electric music, the push to sell—cylinders and disks—continues as Columbia advertises in *Life* (Se 19), "Just Two Ways of Hearing Alice Nielsen". Buy tickets and attend or "buy her Columbia Double-Disk Records and hear her—and invite your friends to hear her—in your own home any evening, and as many evenings as you please".

"Here is a prima donna—a Grand Opera Star—who can sing *Way Down Upon The Swannee River* and *Bonnie Sweet Bessie* without leaving out any of the human-ness". Columbia pushes Nielsen "as a singer of the old ballads...in these, the real songs of the people, Alice Nielsen is supreme. Hear her sing the *Last Rose Of Summer, Kathleen Mavourneen, The Old Folks At Home*; hear her sing of *Annie Laurie* and *Bonnie Sweet Bessie* and you will realize that here is an opera star who with all her fame is woman enough still to sing the old ballads as our grandmothers would have liked to hear them sung.

"All these records will play on your talking machine—no matter what the make, so long as it will play disk records". Your nearest Columbia dealer will "play some of the Nielsen records to you on the Columbia Grafonola 'Favorite', $50 instrument...standard instrument of the world". So says Columbia Phonograph Co. located in the Tribune Building, NYC.

BACK AT BOSTON OPERA HOUSE

After a year, the Boston manager she brought to the job, shamelessly and without statement, has been forced to return Nielsen to her stage. Details of pressures put upon him are not directly revealed. The entire press corps has united with shareholders and ticket buyers to demand her back. The tragedy of absence cost Boston Opera a year without the founding talents Nielsen and Constantino—only to appease the costly whims of a corrupt would-be impresario whose faults honest Loie Fuller had warned Jordan. Always a sham front, the hireling hiding in the wings. Redundancy of puff with empty pockets.

Of course, Alice's return is avidly heralded. Sails back into Boston by mid-September. First, sailing across the opera ocean since 1901, Alice Nielsen departs for another transcontinental tour.

September 22nd *Boston Globe*: "Nielsen soon begins season". A photo by Chicago's Matzene features her posed for *Secret Of Suzanne*. "The coming of the grand opera songster...presages Autumn. The first of the noted ones to reach Boston will be Miss Alice Nielsen, who sailed last week on the Franconia and should land here next Wednesday morning". She starts "a season of activity unusual even for her—and she never has been remarkable for professional idleness".

Globe cannot resist: "That she will be prominent again at the opera house this winter will be welcome news for the numerous admirers of her and her art.... Miss Nielsen will return to Boston however, in time for the opening of the opera season and will be heard in the course of the first week—probably in *Mme. Butterfly*" plus new roles: Suzanne in Wolf Ferrari's *Secret of Suzanne*, Zerlina in "the elaborate revival of Mozart's *Don Giovanni*" and "the important characters in *Jewels of the Madonna* and *The Blue Forest*".

Her concert tour is extensive. Charles Wagner and RE Johnson have booked Nielsen's company into $45,000 of guaranteed dates, relates *Musical Courier* (Se 25). Nielsen brings five singers (alto friend Jeska Swartz, tenor Alfredo Rameli, bassos Jose Mardones and Luigi Taverccia, baritone Rudolfo Fornari), starting in Toronto across the length of the

Pacific coast to "all the prominent musical centers...in the Middle West and North". Obviously this doesn't intrude on her Boston Opera schedule.

Wednesday, the World Series pits NY against Boston as the United Irish League tries to raise $175,000 to help "home rule" and *Boston Globe* confirms Nielsen has landed with a cry, The diva is coming!

Charles Henry Meltzer of *NY Mail* had sailed from Europe along with Nielsen on Cunarder *Franconia.* "On the way over I had several pleasant meetings with the American prima donna. She has spent the last five months chiefly in Italy and Germany. Before sailing, she heard Mary Garden's *Tosca* at the Opera Comique in Paris and thought it was wonderful". About opera in English, Alice speaks strongly for it, joining the new "Society for Opera in English".

Now, she contradicts her erstwhile remora readily. Implies the irony of putting any foreign national atop an American project is just unpatriotic.

"I am a firm and warm believer in the beauty of the English tongue, it seems to me that it is now high time we heard at least part of our operas in English. Our national pride, if nothing else, should make us anxious to encourage the new movement for the promotion of grand opera in our vernacular. I cannot understand why all our singers to not try to help that plan. They and the public would soon make it possible.

"I know that many Italian artists, among whom are Zenatello and Maria Gay, would be delighted to sing English in this country. Do we not sing in foreign tongues abroad? Then why should not our foreign friends be equally courteous when they appear here in grand opera?"

Alice strengthens logic with example: "They don't all see the question from my standpoint though, in Europe. Some years ago for instance, when I was engaged for one of the Puccini operas in German, I met Lili Lehmann. She asked me in what language I would sing my part. I told her, in Italian. On that she grew indignant and informed me that in Germany I ought only to sing German. I had a very deep respect for Lilli Lehmann. But this annoyed me. 'You Europeans don't sing English in New York' said I. 'Why should we have to learn your language in Europe?'

"I feel quite sure that before long we shall have foreign operas—some at all events—performed in our own language here. If I did not, do you suppose I would have committed myself, as I have done today, by joining the society, which has been founded in NY and other cities, to promote the idea?" She'd be useful on, say, the Board of an Opera Company.

Nielsen rehearses *Suzanna* two weeks then starts her tour.

Alice Nielsen's 1912 North American tour: Toronto (2 dates); Canton, Ohio; Indianapolis, Ind.' Grinnell, Iowa; Wichita and Topeka, Kansas; Des Moines and Iowa City, Iowa; Duluth, Minn.; La Crosse, Milwaukee, Oshkosh and Appleton, Wisconsin; Winnipeg (2 dates), Saskatoon, Calgary and Edmonton, Canada; Steers & Company in Portland, Oregon (4 dates); San Francisco (3 dates), Oakland and LE Behymer in Los Angeles (4 dates), California; Denver, Colorado; Kansas City and St. Louis, Missouri; Danville KY, closing December 12th to open Boston Opera season. As could have been done last season.

Popular response strong. Typical of public demand, Canton Ohio contacts Charles Wagner to ask, "Should we desire to sell fifty or seventy seats on the side of our large stage, would it interfere with Miss Nielsen's program? Every seat in the house is sold and there is a demand for more. Miss Nielsen will have at least 4,200 people in the house".

Musical Courier closes the report (Oct 2), "This is a return engagement and therefore very gratifying to Mr. Wagner".

October 7, Nielsen opens in Toronto, pal Marie Dressler present; giving a small glance into a friendship ongoing well until it ends a bit awkwardly.

"One of the Nielsen dates", Wagner recalls, "was the celebrated Music Festival of Toronto which had been inspired by grand old James Dalton, husband of the immortal comedienne Marie Dressler. Dressler was at the height of her stage career, starring in *Tillie's Nightmare*. She always had been very musical, but her cherished ambition to become a prima donna had been completely overshadowed by her superlative clowning ability.

"Dalton persuaded Lawrence Solman, owner of the Toronto baseball club and manager of the town's theatre, to back a week's festival of music. They did it up brown, engaging Nathan Franko and the Metropolitan Opera Orchestra with a grand array of big soloists, besides my Alice, the great Johanna Gadski. Two of the stars were on the Johnson [Wagner-derived] list—Rosa Olitzka the contralto, and Albert Spalding the violinist. So I had a triple reason to be present. The magnificent Marie Dressler was much in evidence during the week of this grand affair".

Wagner skips the long friendship of Dressler and Nielsen, both guided through backstage swamps by Lillian Russell (no relation to Henry). Dressler's summer place is a frequent haunt for Alice.

Dressler "sat with Miss Nielsen in a stage box on Gadski night dressed 'fit to kill' and plied her lorgnette on the star and the audience, playing the grande dame all too self-consciously. But she was the Saturday night popular star who closed the festival hilariously with her imitation of a coloratura soprano. This portrayal convulsed and shocked the staid Canadians...." While Dressler mocks, *la* Nielsen tours. On the road again.

October 12, *Musical America* prints photo of Alice with towering WJ Hubbard, a Boston Opera press agent who un-Puritanically promotes baritone Vanni Marcoux who divorced in Paris to "marry the daughter of an American millionaire who is an art patron and herself an artist of no mean ability". Marcoux, people say, "has been paying marked attention to the American heiress during her stay in Paris" (*NY Times* Oct 20).

October 22, Minnesota records an iconic moment of a magnetic charm (*NY Times*). Alice Nielsen makes dancing magic with friend Jeska Swartz in St. Paul. Makes national news. It is all so simple when magic happens.

Headline: "Two divas delay transcontinental train traffic dancing on station platform the Turkey trot, Gaby Glide, Grizzly Bear". You see, St. Paul back then was a busy bottleneck for transcontinental trains. Signaling by hand. When the conductor needs to clear the track, he gives a "go". Hand raised to signal, Nielsen and Swartz begin dancing among the luggage on the platform. Mesmerize the conductor. Staring, he freezes train traffic five minutes "even the US Mail" until he remembers to drop his raised signal arm and let "go".

Makes all the papers.

As Alice tours ahead, on November 3rd, Irish tenor John McCormack arrives in Boston where he will sing Mozart with Alice Nielsen (*NY Times*). Wife and two kids in tow, he is due back in London's Covent Garden by May. States he is "looking forward to the performance of *Don Giovanni*...a wonderful production with Weingartner conducting".

When Irish eyes are smiling; McCormack (1884-1945) had debuted Victor Herbert's 1911 *Natoma* with Mary Garden and toured with malicious Melba in Australia. Trained in 1905 Italy, famed for breath control and sustained song, he began recording 1904, Covent debut 1907. Only Caruso sold more recordings. McCormack's wealth soared. In the 1930s sound musical *Song O' My Heart* he would play a retired Irish tenor.

Imagine him, Herbert, Nielsen in a project of their own.

November 25th (*NY Times*) Boston Opera opens with Josef Urban's design and direction for *Tales of Hoffman*: "The house was filled with the critical, literary and musical, and with society in all its gayety...the setting has probably never been equaled for magnificence and historic accuracy...an usually lavish color scheme which emphasized the symbolical character of the plot". In the cast: Louise Edvina, Antonia; Edmond Clement, Hoffman; Debussy protégé Andre-Caplet conducts.

November, *la* Nielsen reaches Los Angeles. She meets Otheman Stevens (*LA Times* Nov 26) at her hotel for a quick word-portrait of the singer's daily life. No discussion of Hortense or Nielsen Theatre. Alice "surrounded by managers, photographers and reporters who came and went constantly, but through it all she was reposeful and serene for she had arrived; not that her fight is over, for success means no less than a prolonged fight; but she has earned the right by battle and that is the victory of work".

Nielsen: "Work is a joy. Do you remember that last time you talked to me? It was in Henry Russell's car at the Southern Pacific depot when I came here with the San Carlos company [of SF etc], and Constantino and I sang an aria from *La Bohème* for you. That was a beautiful season—after we got out of that skating rink down Main Street—and I remember that you said then that I would arrive and I have, for I am now with the Metropolitan, which is the same as the Chicago and the Philadelphia companies, and I hope this season to create Suzanne in NY".

Skips Boston and the opera-rustling Russell, still an agony to her.

Stevens: "And does the work pay? Do you think the work was worth the candle?" Nielsen's philosophy arises. Reveals her secret for joy and health by work. Her philosophy, very like the values of her dad's Dane dad.

Nielsen: "Of course it pays as any effort pays; labor is a joy; the secret of happiness is health, and health comes with hard work".

Tells Stevens how her company reached Boston. "It was not all smooth sailing with the San Carlo company [of SF, of NO etc] after we left here".

Poor Ullman the turfman went nuts, for one thing.

She speaks of the Boston Park Theatre miracle. "Finally we arrived in Boston. Nordica left the company. The [Park] manager told me one day that if they could get some singer that could spell me—sing the nights I was off—the theatre there in Boston would stand a show to make a little money.

"Well there was no one they could get. So I said that if I lived through it, I would sing at every performance; there were to be eleven of them in the eight days. I did it; I was all in at the end".

Now the bitter blade of Irish irony: "But a man had come to see our *Bohème*; he knew a great artist when he saw one...." How she stabs and twists the blade. "And he saw that Henry Russell was just that great artist".

Continues in that wit, "The result was that this man has built for Mr. Russell the most beautiful grand opera house in the whole country, and it is to be opened tonight. How I wish I could be there and see that curtain go up, and see the fruition of Mr. Russell's hopes for he has been living all this time in the hope of doing something big and beautiful, and now he can". If he could. Alice knows Boston is failing without her.

Ultimatum by Jordan and the Board has forced Russell to schedule her return. Pressured by united power of the press, the shareholders, the public. She knows the inside story. Sly egg.

Perhaps not until two decades, when Russell lies his brags, the cruel extent of his deceits emerges. As Loie Fuller observed, the remora a skilled deceiver cloaked in the artsy fogspeak of scorn for loot. Flattery fog fades away in time; people become undeceived; truth. Her many friends would keep her informed: before Boston Opera sinks: full speed ahead.

Nielsen, unlike London versus Perley, is doing well financially. She could afford to be gracious. Floated him since 1901, puffed his solicitations for a bit of spare change from singing kids, lofted him to his present job she knows he might not keep much longer. Where he sold her out.

Soon Alice will publish the antidote, *I Owe What I Am to Women*. Does not mention the backstabber by name.

Yet after all, Russell runs the joint over there in Boston where she sings this season. He is not on the stage. She be arch the diplomat. One last time she puffs the charade "gave me my chance. I had taken *Fortune Teller* over to Europe and was singing and dancing what voice I had, to ruin". Stress from Williams & Perley—now well exposed—untold in her story.

"From the first, I had determined to go into the big thing—real opera, and there I began to feel that I could never accomplish that end, but would always have to peg away at little comic operas. People heard me and seemed to like me; Russell [Tosti, Higgins, Bevignani] was then the greatest authority on singing in London [oh please], and he said, 'If you go to Italy and study five years and then you can get engagements and make your investment back with interest. Your voice will win out for you.'"

Speaking to Stevens she reveals her plight. When she stopped the show in early July, the company returned to America. How this saga maps to the fast-paced progress she made, is not apparent. Yet, "I went for as long as I could and then I went broke. I could not pay my hotel bill; my trunks were seized". Alice says this only once, here. Timing would have to be fall, July 1901. And we know things happened fast for her: concerts, recitals, well-paid gigs. She does not mention her travels with Yznaga that season or aid from Laurence Irving who could open doors for every opportunity.

Alice suggests, "I had to tell Russell that I was at the end and would have to go back to *The Fortune Teller* and to dancing an accompaniment to my singing". Yet Yznaga produced Florence Phillips.

Her patron appears. "But—there always seems to be a saying, But if you try hard—a wealthy Australian [sic] woman heard of me, became interested in my fight, and she financed me".

Alice skips the name. The possibilities are only two. By mental slip, Nielsen confuses Florence Phillips' South African accent with Australia. Or Melba, who did claim to support an unnamed "lazy" American singer until viciously cutting off funds and leaving her stranded. Perhaps in, say, Spain. The singer could not be identified by Melba's archivist in Australia, who scorned the notion Melba would assist any soprano. Nielsen skips speaking of Gladys Grey—closely connected to Melba—after that first London year. Alice often and consistently credits the Afrikander, Florence Phillips, as giving the funds to keep hopes alive. The Phillips archive could not verify this generosity. Nielsen's story of patron Phillips has been seconded by Russell. In LA a decade after, Nielsen speaks of weekly payments set to NYC. Her patron, surely Phillips, "sent my mother every week the money I had to send to her, and she paid my lessons and my living bills". Perhaps while in Italy and Spain. Alice in London was active with parlor paydays and concerts. How much money was taken by her cunning remora she does not disclose.

Sketches her pilgrim progress. "I did work, and instead of five years I made it in three and Russell [no, Bevignani] said I was ready. You know the rest as well as I do". Enrico Bevignani arranged her Napoli debut. And not three years, one. Debut at Covent by three years. Covent was Higgins, entirely. Instead of three years she did it in one; back to Covent by three.

"And is the hard work over?" Stevens asks.

"Over? Why for a singer the work is never over. I work harder now than ever. There are new operas coming out all the time, new singers springing up, and if one does not keep right along with the others, the public, the dear darling but changeable public, forgets you and takes up the next one and that ends you".

Backstage with a three-years salary, the cruel hireling at Boston Opera knew these fears and crows about new singers, scouring Europe and Russia to backstab "old" stars. Alice Nielsen scolded him for abusing advances toward her young friend who fled for a NYC marriage. Her workload increased after losing the security of her Boston stage. She lost the comfort of a single opera season within walking distance of home.

"No; life is more arduous to me than ever, but it makes me happy; and thanks to heaven I am well and strong and the work comes as easily to me as tattling does to some women. There is not much reward save the satisfaction of doing what you aimed to do when you began life; there is no ease to my life, no luxury, and decidedly no foolishness".

She describes her days: happy. "An automobile ride in the afternoon when I am not singing; meeting a few friends after the performance, and that cut short by the imperative necessity of getting enough sleep; about two months' vacation a year, and that spent among musical people talking music and really studying; that is my reward, and it is a beautiful, entirely satisfactory price to pay".

Wonderful Alice Nielsen: "I am happy, perfectly happy because I have done what I wanted to do and that is the best part of life".

Art keeps calling for her. Only she has had the experience of singing to all her shows to all her audiences. Only she stood on all those stages. Few people in the world have had experience of performing so much; today's pop stars sing to fifty-thousand in stadiums amplified, or broadcasted to many more. How many people will ever sing to sell-out theatres the seven Herbert shows a week; or the eleven grand operas in eight days?

Stevens praises her depth and variety.

After the "vocal slavery" in Italy, "today Alice Nielsen stands as one of the best Mimis in the world, as probably the best Countess Gil, and as about the only woman who can do *Don Pasquale* and *The Barber of Seville* in all the perfection of their lightsome intricacy. And next season if you happen to be in New York, you will pay anywhere from five to twelve dollars for a seat in which to listen to her" at the Met.

Nielsen feature stories dot her LA stay. Secret of her youthfulness is revealed by Hector Alliot (*LA Times* Nov 26). Photo shows Nielsen in full-length concert gown carrying roses, "the California songbird... won her first recognition in this State and is always seen at her best here because she feels at home".

Alliot continues "Actors, especially singers, dislike to rise early, but 'The Lark' waits not on day. So it happened that Alice Nielsen, sipping on a cup of English breakfast tea, was deposited at the Alexandria at an early hour this morning to meet a formidable company of interviewers and photographers. Nothing could demonstrate the celebrated good disposition of this artist better than the easy and smiling manner of her answers to a hundred questions, most of them singularly personal.

"Miss Nielsen not only is young, but looks young, because most people do not know that she began as a star at the age of five, even before, according to her mother's expert opinion".

Alliot had first met Nielsen in San Francisco, "Since an evening 18 years ago which was the most important event in her artistic career, I had not had until today the privilege of meeting her again at close quarters. To meet her again, off the train before breakfast, in the garish light of morning and being photographed, was certainly a test for beauty. Notwith-standing the terrible strain of several years of stage life, and constant study, Alice Nielsen retains the same youthful figure and face, with a delightful magnetism of personality".

He retells her pilgrim progress briefly a colorful way. New version of her Bostonian meeting. Now, Barnabee discovers her. Alliot knows San Francisco; perhaps he has a point. "She has not been spoiled by success; she is the same sweet and wholesome little lady who yet in her teens sang *Lucia* at the old Tivoli, in San Francisco. On that evening of long ago, the Sheriff of Nottingham [Barnabee] sat in a box, he heard the youthful Lucia, who very bravely sang her part, in a very creditable manner.

"After the second act dear old Barnaby requested to meet the white-gowned chorus girl who had been recently promoted. That eventful yet accidental meeting of two great people was the beginning of the gifted artist's career, and the beauty of it all is that the Metropolitan prima donna has always retained for her operatic godfather the keenest affection, and Henry Clay Barnaby, one of our greatest comedians and keen manager of light operas, still watches with parental interest the climbing of his young protégé, though long retired from the stage and three score and twenty".

Passing disputes had long vanished into the shadows.

"Alice Nielsen, born in Tennessee, is a Californian, as she was trained from infancy in San Francisco", Alliot believes. Quotes conflicted praise from Russell, "this artist had but one equal...possibly Mary Garden". As a simple London voice coach offering massage, he had told Mary Garden to skip grand opera. Stay a singing actress. If she had "made the fatal mistake of dedicating her studies and her voice to the operas of Mozart, Rossini, Bellini, Donizetti, etc, she would probably have achieved only a mediocre reputation; whereas by an intelligent appreciate of her own limitations, she directed her energy more towards the histrionic and interpretive side of her art and treated her voice rather as a medium of expression than an instrument on which to play".

Told Alice Nielsen the reverse. And destroys her home stage. She could sing what Garden could not. And Nielsen innovates, creates artistic alliances and financial partnerships; aye, many invest the golden goose.

Continues Alliot, both singers have "worked their way upwards through natural talents combined with constant and intelligent application".

Nielsen began "most humbly at the Wigwam, the first vaudeville house on the Coast. She entered the professional operatic ranks with the admirable organization the Tivoli, that first gave a stock opera company to California. Discovered by Barnabee, she joined the Bostonians, the greatest traveling opera company...and finally graduated as one of the best prima donnas of the Boston Opera house and the Metropolitan".

Alliot acknowledges Nielsen rose strictly by merit. Does not say Garden. "For a young woman handsome, clever and possessed of an excellent voice, there is nothing pyrotechnical about her rise, to be sure. It is only one of the rare American instances of that long and arduous training, slow advance of the great European artists".

Nielsen's hobby now: "English opera or operas given in English". Egg to the agenda of her erstwhile remora. Fails to link Victor Herbert to the program. "She will talk enthusiastically about it.... As a matter of fact...it is a little ridiculous not to understand one word and to follow the action with a translation in hand and miss half the performance".

Alliot focuses on "a rare operatic treat, certain to brush away the blues", her *Secret of Suzanne*, "a delightful operatic comedy. Alice Nielsen is quite sufficient for an evening", plus Jeska Swartz, Alfredo Ramella, Rodolfo Fornari, Luigi Tavechia, Jose Mardones and "large orchestra" with Cesare Clandestini as suddenly-drafted Boston Opera conductor: "the evening will be worthwhile. I learned all this while Miss Nielsen was wafting for breakfast, answering with the same good-natured smile all kinds of questions and I acquired also special knowledge in the gentle art of dermatology. How you keep your admirable complexion?"

Nielsen: "Cold cream and a rub with as big a chunk of ice as I can hold in my hand, morning and night, is the only complexion preservative I use".

"Your figure, how do you preserve it so well? Singers... Tetrazzini..." since fat ladies sang mostly, as Chicago observed constantly.

Nielsen: "Oh, I lead a quiet and simple life, eat well and wholesome food and work; that is all my secret".

Who was Barnaby? "He was the greatest comedian, the biggest man, the wisest manager of yesterday". And Alice closes the interview. The comradeship and mutual generosity of the Bostonians at their best makes a painful memory of contrast to the bitter Russell at Boston.

Next day, Alliot tells of the farewell matinee gala (*LA Times* Dec 1).

"Brilliant trio by Ramella, Fornari and Mardones opened the programme...celebrated trio of *Faust*. Miss Swartz sang the aria of *Carmen*...with an insidious charm of voice and gentleness that recalled her several times; she finally consented to give *Lullaby* as an encore. Ramella gave the tenor aria of *La Tosca* and *Santa Lucia*.

"Miss Nielsen, whose *Mme. Butterfly* has been much admired, sang the great aria of her role with rare excellence and after several curtain calls, gave the *Last Rose* and *Coming Thro' the Rye* to the enthusiastic satisfaction of the audience.

"Senor Mardones, setting aside Italian, showed himself under his true national colors and gave Spanish songs unknown here, which reflect the character of the Iberian, the land he lives in and the ruggedness of his inner sentiments. After several calls Don Jose sang by request *La Paloma*, the old yet always-popular song".

Second half: *Barber Of Seville* arranged for ensemble; perhaps size.

"As Rosina, Miss Nielsen was a great success; the best criticism...is to repeat Mme. Schumann-Heinck's own opinion, 'Mein Gott, Alice, but you don't resemble a prima donna! You look like a little girl!'"

Alliot notes Nielsen as "very unfortunate in having her musical director die recently...being compelled to select his successor somewhat hastily, as Signor Pablo Rimini is very young". More obscure than Alice's 1905 oboist.

The ensemble continues across North America. During December in Denver Nielsen draws another of the top critical statements on her career. The poetic piece is inspired by the writer's focus on the awed audience.

"There is more to singing than the voice and the methods of producing faultless high notes. There is soul and sentiment, a quality that grips your heart.... Sentiment—we are filled with it. Only fools deny its prevalence and its power" reports *Denver Post* December 4th.

"When last night Nielsen's melting voice rose in *Oh Haunting Memory!* in that house of fashion and 'music lovers', there was an instant response, a curious change in the very attitude of the people.

"The critical 'I-am-here-to-proclaim-my-culture' air was swept aside in a breath, and as the last flutelike note soared out above us and floated away, an old man near me who had been leaning forward with parted lips and strained attention, breathed a long, deep sigh and murmured, 'Ravishing, ravishing!' while a storm of applause confirmed his judgment".

Denver describes the Nielsen effect wonderfully.

In old New York, James Huneker had searched his imagination to express magnetic singerly magic; Harvard's Josiah Royce succeeded within his poetic philosophic masterpieces. This unsigned Denver critic reacts to Nielsen's sway over her audience. Carries poetry to profound. He explains what had motivated Boston Opera's construction, how Nielsen gives her audiences a gift past price.

Nielsen has "found that intangible something which defies analysis, but before which your emotions are as a leaf in a storm—helpless and at her mercy ...such a voice as hers, such perfection of tone, such delicacy of expression, such purity of sentiment, should be heard by the people...who would love her if they could hear her sing *Down In The Forest* and catch that last perfect line—'It was only the note of a bird'—they don't know what they were missing; they thought, mayhap, that it was something they could not understand.

"That is the folly of this everlasting pose about beautiful voices—perfect singing—perfect culture. It doesn't take a 'high brow' to enjoy such music. Everybody, almost, is a music lover in their hearts. And if you give them such music as we were permitted to hear last night, at concerts within their reach, no building in Denver would hold the people who would want to hear them".

Denver Post tells what the Jordans had sensed: to love music, "All the people need is an opportunity to hear Miss Nielsen and her company".

And to push her off her stage is to hate music and hate people.

For Alice Nielsen Concert Company with violinist Louis Persinger, "a large audience gave evidence of enthusiastic enjoyment". Jeska Swartz's "rich contralto and personal beauty won immediate favor, a superb-looking young woman with the carriage of a queen"; as did hearty, rich-toned basso Mardones. Tenor Ramella "stricken upon his arrival in this high altitude...was barely able to sing his part falsetto in the opera excerpt". Louis Persinger (1887-1966), accompanied here by Samuel Chotzinoff, is the violinist and pianist who would teach Yehudi Menuhin.

Boston Opera without Nielsen continues. Calamity avoided December 10th when baritone Bernardo Olkansky saves a hundred lives. His "family hotel" at 286 Huntington caught fire (*NY Times*). Waking in his smoke-filled room, he "ran from door to door ringing bells and calmly telling people to get up". Saves Evelyn Scotney, "young Australia", tenor Sachettie, "French conductor Charles Stroney and others".

As a passing gay delight appear tales of oddly reappearing tenor-tailor Enrico Aresoni who "vanished between Acts of *Aida* in Montreal" (*NY Times* De 15 and De 24). "Aresoni, born Henry Arenson" rose from Yiddish weddings to concert tenor. Hired by the Boston Opera manager (all-so-interestingly) two years earlier, he fled *Trovatore*, his voice "strong, but his legs weak". The men reconcile in Paris where he is rehired as "Enrico Aresoni". Their close relations remain in the all-so curious realm of broad hints. Why this baffle reaches the *NY Times* is a hint to the hints.

December's *Musical Courier* discusses Nielsen's Omaha program.

"Miss Nielsen's brilliant vocalism, her vivacity and her earnest wish to please caused much enthusiasm. Miss Nielsen appeared here under the management [guarantees] of Evelyn Hopper. The artist was in splendid form and sang with a richness of vocal equipment and a mastery of tone and shading which thoroughly justified the extravagant notices that preceded her coming". Evelyn Hopper, Midwest cultural luminary, teaches voice at Bellevue College, hit by 1908 tornado which in 1919 squelches the gayety by going military after Presbyterians stop funding.

Alice's program: *Two Japanese Songs*, Cadman; *Lullaby*, Cyril Scott; *Will o' the Wisp*, Spross; aria *Mia Piccinella* from Salvator Rosa, Gomez; *Pouquoi*, Saint-Saens; *Mandoline*, Debussy; *Tu Nous Souriais*, Andre Caplet; *A Toi*, Bamberg; *Down In The Forest*, Ronald; *But Lately In Dance*, Arensky; *Oh! Haunting Memory*, Bond; *Love Has Wings*, Rogers; *Botschaft and Vergehliches Standchen*, Brahms; *Solvejgs Leid* and *Ein Traum*, Grieg; aria, *La Tosca*, Puccini. Fabio Rimini, music director and pianist.

December 16, Alice Nielsen in Danville Kentucky closes her tour. She begins a new project immediately at Montreal Opera December 23. "From that time until May 31" when closing at the North Shore Festival in Evanston, Illinois, "she will be kept constantly engaged in operatic and concert work" (*Musical Courier* De 18). She has made lots and lots and lots of money this year. Without the intrusion, as Jefferson called it abolishing same, of taxes.

"Manager Charles L. Wagner may surely be congratulated at the successful outcome of the tremendous tour just being completed by Alice Nielsen and her operatic concert company, as well as for the brilliant booking ability which has kept the entire tour intact for the aggregation of artists, and which is now bringing to Miss Nielsen herself the financial reward of her great artistic ability".

Nielsen finds time in NYC for the Annual American Christmas Fund Benefit at the Hippodrome. Sousa leads orchestra, Nathan Franko accompanies at piano. Hans Kronold presents two cello solos.

Nielsen's popularity meets Montréal enthusiastic for her *Butterfly*.

"Alice Nielsen was responsible very largely for the crowded house on Friday, as she is a great favorite in Montreal, tells *Musical Courier* (De 27). She sang with such beauty of tone and possesses a personality of such charming grace that everyone was enraptured. Her voice is of glorious quality throughout its entire range, and is handled with consummate skill. The delicacy of her pianissimos and purity of her top notes stirred the audience to wild enthusiasm, so much so that at the close of the aria *Un bel di*, a few overzealous spectator attempted to interrupt the performance by applauding vigorously".

The fad to suppress encores is now well-established. "This however, it is pleasing to note, called forth a chorus of hisses from all parts of the theatre and the abominable practice was promptly squelched".

In the cast: Polese, Courso, Gaudenzi, Stroesco, Goddard.

After Montreal Opera, Nielsen continues concerts. As Nielsen had told us during her 1898 Japan visit, a "necessary evil" for a star is a business manager. Wagner has indeed kept her away from Boston as much as possible to her profit. Not sustained roles of grand opera. His collusion with Russell gave a measure of public plausibility to Henry's spin, and materially contributes to the *Titanic* disaster looming. Wagner was a quality manager when his interests align with the talent.

Nielsen had two years at Boston Opera. Melba sang three decades at Covent Garden; Farrar had a long stay at the Met (a period Wagner terms the Met's "coma") before crashing into silent films. Unlike Lady Gradys de

Grey, savior of Covent Garden, Isabella Stewart Gardner was blocked from participation at Boston Opera.

By a perverse irony, despite fatal flaws, Russell seems to sense vocal beauty: "In reality there is perhaps no kind of musical career which is so extraordinarily complicated as that of the singer, and especially that of the operatic singer. The human vocal organs...are, I believe, more complex than any other instrument and infinitely superior and more beautiful than any made by man". For that single passing moment his memoirs express honest emotion. Or is it only the pitch to lure a payee with spare change.

Charles Wagner could cut deals. Made big money for Alice Nielsen. That was his talent. Didn't care about onstage. Cared about box office. Frank Perley, the PT Barnum protégé, also made things happen to a point.

"I was too trusting", Nielsen explains her lost wealth and faded fame.

Unlike other stars she could not preserve her legacy. Fades to shadows as the brilliant Cleveland critic foretold. Now our experience grows.

1913: PHILIP KAHN's BOSTON OPERA MUCKRAKE

To fulfill promises to stockholders and the public, Boston Opera must showcase the founding stars. And have a prudent manager. This has not happened. Ever-increasing deficits force Jordan to supply more-and-more cash. His hireling manager is sheer expense. Alice creates profits. Her passion and quality inspire. Nielsen builds community; Boston now home. Her absence cost: quality, cash, momentum.

The hireling manager lacks loyalty to Boston; his paycheck is a purgatory. Longs for Paris, Italy: anywhere but America's Boston. Nielsen out, deficits in. Jordan needs Mayor Fitzgerald's help to subsidize the foreign manager who brags of discarding the town's favorite Irish diva.

"Rural members of the Legislature may not see their way to clear to help Boston pay for its operatic diversion..." (*NY Times* Ja 1). To limit losses, hope for a full house. Nielsen and Constantino guaranteed a full house. Yet the man who fired them got the raise. And Nielsen his ticket.

NY Times sees Boston's plight: "In spite of all the chatter about American opera and opera in English, the fact remains that opera...must be imported at great expense and tenderly nourished. On the whole we hope the Boston Opera House will get its subsidy, and...no local politician will be in a position to demand a revival of *The Bohemian Girl*" by Irish composer Balfe. The NY jab pricks at Eben Jordan who now pays more for less, and whose dissatisfaction doesn't get his money back.

With *la Nielsen* banned from Boston Opera she entertains His Majesty's Theatre at Montreal. Few hours by train from Copley Square.

Barber of Seville January 2 (*Musical Courier*), Standing Room Only.

"As Rosina, she has a part which is admirably suited to her voice and style and perhaps in no other role has she scored such a signal success here. Her singing of Arditi's famous waltz song, *Il Bacio*, which she gave during the lesson scene, brought forth a torrent of applause which refused to be quieted until Miss Nielsen consented to repeat it. It was a wonderful piece of vocal work and showed her glorious voice in its best possible light".

In the cast: Fornair, Ramella, Cervi, Huberty and Buck "inspired by the prima donna's performance and put forth their best efforts".

Returning to Washington January 16th, Nielsen warbles for a new president, Woodrow Wilson, a childhood friend of her Broadway designer Josef Physioc in Columbia SC days. Has sung for every president since Grover Cleveland.

Her program, sent the author by Lew Gould, consists of eleven songs from her concert series, E. Romayne Simmons pianist. Part 1: *Voi che sapete*, Mozart; *Im Kahne*, Grieg; *Du bist wie eine blume*, Shumann; *Solvejgs Lied*, Grieg; *Far off I hear a lover's flute*, Cadman; *Love has wings*, Rogers; *Down in the forest*, Ronald. After Simmons plays Chopin's *Polonaise*, Part 2: *Mandoline*, Debussy; *Fileuse "Gwendoline"*, Chabrier; *Si mes vers avaient des ailes*, Hahn; *Vissi d'arte "Tosca"*, Puccini. Usual encores of familiar airs.

Wilson she will in future recall as "the most musical president".

January 19th, joint concert at Carnegie Hall offers Alice Nielsen with John McCormack. Beyond Standing Room Only, they are All Sold Out.

Wittily the two Irish stars trade their famed concert songs. McCormack sings *The Spirit Flower* instead of Nielsen who performs a set of Cadman songs with Cadman at piano. She and McCormack trade sets of five songs, at the close combining for duet from *Butterfly*.

Encores follow. A great show unforgettable.

And romances! At Boston, January 30th, conductor Felix Weingartner (1863-1942) weds Lucille Marcell (1877-1921), American dramatic soprano and third wife. Bride wears brown chinchilla over black silk. Mrs. Nina Russell (wife of Henry in passing) is the witness. Weingartner had conducted at Berlin, Vienna, now Boston; he believes in objective interpretations. Born in Zara, Dalmatia now Yugoslavia, father died when he was five. Wife Marcell could now "sing Desdemona, Aida, Marguerite, La Tosca and other roles". Weingartner had promoted her steadily in Germany till "charged with favoritism" and she "finally resigned the position". In the passing Boston regime, Weingartner gets his way.

February 4 (*Musical America*), Nielsen's company visits Detroit, guests of Detroit Philharmonic under James DeVoe. Concert songs, arias, and a scene from Act II of *Il Barbiere di Siviglia* "in costume without scenery".

Same day, *Boston Globe* cannot resist proclaiming "Alice Nielsen, busiest of divas" and publishes her complete touring schedule.

Next day Alice writes Robinson Locke, the Toledo OH editor who collects massive scrapbooks on all performers including Hortense, "You 'hit it' in your article surely, and I appreciate very much your interest in me". The short note reveals her usual process. She reads press clips, and responds. "I hope to be in Toledo while making my next years' tour and hope to show the people that this city is nice that appreciates other than musical comedy because I know it is filled with musical people who love music for music's sake. My most cordial greetings to you and your charming wife.... Yours sincerely, Alice Nielsen".

Nielsen returns to Montreal Opera early February.

Then the celebrated singer resumes her Boston stage for *Don Giovanni* with McCormack. Seems the perfect possible casting, and same agent.

Frank Bertwall meets her during a rehearsal break. "On a snowy afternoon, to be sent to interview Miss Alice Nielsen, the prima donna! It makes one think of a cozy apartment, perhaps an open fire, an imperious diva relaxed for the moment, charmed to charm one person at a time—a pleasant prospect, with nothing in the way of regret except that one's shoes are going to be shocking and one's coat wet. Wasted regret; that isn't the way an interview with Alice Nielsen works out...she is the hardest working diva in the operatic Olympus. Word came back the best time of catching Miss Nielsen is before, during or after the rehearsal in the Opera House. She is very busy".

She just arrived from Quebec where she "sang Saturday night at 8pm.

"Sunday...she was at the Boston Opera House and her first rehearsal with Maestro Weingartner for *Don Giovanni* was underway. It lasted as long as strength permitted. And yesterday afternoon began again....

And even "now they rehearse...." Bertwall waits outside, "Easy to pick out Miss Nielsen's voice; it was still easier to hear and observe that she has never been in better voice. One marveled at its freshness and purity, its ease and timbre. The publicity man who sat by, explained that not only was all this true but it was the greater wonder, seeing that Miss Nielsen has been all the season working hard and traveling. At this point, the rehearsal beyond the wall becomes silent, and two or three singers drift out to smoke a brief cigarette".

Bertwall is summoned. "One is beckoned in and sits beside a rosy, plump little lady with very business-like eyes. Warned that rehearsal will recommence in just three minutes, singer and reporter utterly lose the power of finding a subject to talk about...and at that moment the flash strikes".

Constrained by diva diplomacy as Bertwall is by media mildness, we find Nielsen foreshadows the future. Yes, she has made cash and given much human happiness in concerts. But is her best purpose?

Nielsen: "I feel as if it were coming home. And that is more than being happy to get back to Boston. It is coming here to the Opera House: the sentiment I feel for it goes deeper than happiness; it makes one almost sorrowful".

Bertwall: "No doubting the simple honesty of this; it is just a burst of the feeling which makes one's eyes fill with the happiness is too great".

As Boston press uncover Boston Opera's errors, they restate Alice Nielsen's value, which of course duplicitous Russell slyly glad to lip-service. After all, the singer excluded by dirty deeds of conspiracy. Until Wagner publishes the truth decades later, who really knew how Russell dunnit: "And to any person who has heard Mr. Russell declare that Miss Nielsen's aid was one of the great helps which brought him to the point where the Boston Opera House became a possibility, her declaration has a deeper significance". Loie Fuller warned her daughter, Russell agrees, denies; says yes, does no. Or reverse. Words mean nothing to him.

"In Mr. Russell's own statement, Miss Nielsen is entitled to rank as one of the very few who helped to found the Opera House, and it is her home in the double sense that she belongs there and she—as much as any person owns his home—owns the Opera House".

Bertwall meditates on conflicted mysteries.

Weingartner calls rehearsal to resume. "Wasn't much of an interview but it was a rare pleasure to see Miss Nielsen as astonishingly well and in such marvelous voice after such campaigning".

Bertwall delivers one of those insightful assessments marking Alice Nielsen's career: "It was inspiring to meet a woman whose love for her art is higher than her care for her comfort or her insistence on her importance; and it was easy to understand even in three minutes' chat, how Miss Nielsen has won her hundreds of enthusiastic admirers in Boston".

February 7, Boston Opera stages *Giovanni*. Nielsen and McCormack have been equally famed singing Mozart. Their agent Charles Wagner makes millions promoting McCormack, wealthy from concerts and recordings: "McCormack's recital achievements were so outstanding the public has forgotten that in some operas and on certain occasions his operatic performances also were of high caliber". Of Wagner's showbiz career, his peak is producing the "greatest Boston opera successes" which "presented John in Don Giovanni with Nielsen, Emmy Destinn and others". Conductor Weingartner "told me it not only was the finest Giovanni he had conducted, but the first time he ever had heard the tenor role really sung". This performance is for eternity.

In the cast: Alice Nielsen, Zerlina; John McCormack, Don Ottavio; Vanni Marcoux, Don Giovanni; Jose Mardones, Il Commendatore; Emma Destinn, Donna Anna; Elizabeth Amsden, Donna Elvira; Adomo Didur, Leporello; Luigi Tavecchia, Masetto; plus *corps de ballet*. Conductor, Felix Weingartner.

Musical Courier (Feb 7): "Mr. McCormack is indeed fortunate in possessing a voice that is not only perfectly produced but of an exquisitely lovely and liquid quality as well. His singing of the two arias allotted the tenor in this opera was a perfect vocal and artistic joy, and fulfilled every requirement of Mozart's music, which is indeed high praise.

"Miss Nielsen too sang with the beauty and simplicity of phrasing, purity of tone, freedom of vocal emission and artistic finish distinctive of this charming prima donna's art, and was indeed a welcome visitor to the Boston operatic stage after her two season's absence. Her acting...was delightfully winsome and spontaneous, with just the right touch of rustic coquetry in her scene with Don Giovanni and of penitent tenderness in the following scene with Masetto".

Phillip Hale: "The music in *Don Giovanni* sufficiently characterizes the personages and embodies the action of the play. They have their being and illusion in it; in it the drama, such as it is, runs its clear course. The more fully the singing-players enter into their song, the more completely do they 'act' the play. Miss Destinn, Miss Nielsen and Mr. McCormack—and Miss Nielsen especially, gained this impersonation and illusion by the revealing virtues of their song.

"Miss Nielsen's singing was good to hear as so much music in the narrower sense of the word; but in her coloring and her accent went constant suggestion of a Zerlina who was quick to tease and quick to sympathize, who had her little vanities, her naïve curiosities, who was selfish and solicitous by turns, who could play the innocent minx one minute with Don Giovanni and the next be Masetto's affectionate little wife.

"Mr. McCormack neither overdid nor underdid poor Don Ottavio. In pure and sustained song, Mr. McCormack, Miss Nielsen and Miss Destinn succeeded best. Mr. McCormack surprised by his mastery of Mozartean suavity of phrase, by the adroit leading of the returns of his melodies, and by light elegance of tone and accent".

Paired with Nielsen, "Never within long recollection has he seemed so intelligent a singer". She "was apt in these suavities too; and she had clear sense besides, of the varied flow and the exquisite modulations of Zerlina's airs. She sustained them unfailingly; but she kept them also supple and glinting. Above all the rest she mingled song and action, the voice and the music and the voice of the personage at the moment in the play".

And there you have it.

February 12, Henry Higgins of Covent Garden announces he attended Nielsen's *Barber of Seville* in Montreal, inviting her to Covent in June.

Alice Nielsen made quite an impression. Just takes...a fair hearing.

At Chicago (*Chicago Press Herald* Fe 16), Nielsen sang her program at Orchestra Hall. Reviewer held "grievous sorrow" that Nielsen "once upon a time was connected with the comic opera stage.... "For who could be able to forget...the interpreter of Brahms...warbled in *Robin Hood*?"

1913 momentous socially, also arts. February 25 the American income tax amendment passes, pushed across Congress by plantation politician Senator Furnifold Simmons (D-NC) as a quid pro quo for JP Morgan and Jacob Schiff and cronies, the gang Senator Pettigrew (1922) would say ran the government via lawyers in office. The money from that and the new private central bank trust will make a bailout for Wall Street's foreign war profiteers; Secretary of State WJ Bryan had resigned in protest when the foreign war loans were allowed. Bronze historic markers on Jekyll Island, Georgia, tell part of the story. Accountants protest that the intrusive plan erodes privacy, lacks limits, promotes lying. Jefferson's Second Inaugural Address spells out the competent polical ecology, as a reform contrast.

Competent state constitutions ban political debt, steadily reduce living costs. 1900s reformers establish a coop bank in North Dakota to protect politics from corporations; Montana bans corporations from politics. The Anti-Imperialism League sought to keep politics focused on citizens, stop pushing plantation regimes overseas. Empire poisons domestic tranquility and kills the gayety of nations. General Smedley Butler famously authors *War is a Racket* on this theme, detailing decades as head of Marine Corps. Senator Pettigrew of South Dakota authors *American Empire*. Gustavus Meyers authors *Great American Fortunes*, and *History of Supreme Court*. Congressman Lindbergh tries for President to protect independence.

Reform still had hopes in these bright days of opera delight.

Against that risky-business backdrop, ecological pioneer Nielsen goes for the electric car; *LA Times* runs an Alice photo March 2nd "in her Baker Electric Broughham... this charming actress has decided in favor of the electric and the Baker is her choice. She enjoys her afternoon shopping trips and boulevard spins in the car". At least one Baker Electric just like hers still runs for Jay Leno in LA.

February Boston gets the news. Muckrake hits the street. Exposé of Henry Russell. Philip L. Kahn speaks out. His new national publication is *Music Magazine and Musical Stage Review*. Editor Kahn's first issue contains a three-part exposé on the Boston Opera manager.

Backstage whispers get a spotlight. Yes, an Italian newspaper in town first covered the scandals, albeit in Italian.

February 15th a premier issue of Boston-based *Music Magazine and Musical Stage Review* hits the stands. On the cover, Henry Russell in a 1909 Chickering photo as man in three-piece suit sitting in a chair holding a letter, hair slickly parted in middle. He is not being praised. Three years of deficits at Boston Opera, the attempts to seek public funds, plus Russell's announcement his salary was raised to $25,000 [about $500,000 today] motivates Kahn's critique. Kahn is a whistle-blower who worked at Boston Opera. And knows the right solution. Kahn is a reformer.

Unsung Boston hero. Well, martyr.

His high-quality premier issue includes a piece by William Gardner, founder of the "National Society for the Promotion of Grand Opera in English". The music-world news section tells us, intriguingly, that Fritzi Scheff "has changed managers quite as frequently of late as De Wolf Hopper, Lillian Russell and a few other matrimonial record-holders have changed marital partners, and finally it became a matter of common gossip that she was without and would remain without, a manager for the rest of the season.... She solved the problem ...by becoming her own manager...". Editor Kahn interviews composer Franz Lehar who wonderfully says: "Do not be mechanically clever. Remember—what comes from your heart will reach your hearers' hearts".

Prime focus of the magazine is a multi-issue Henry Russell muckrake titled *The Dr. Cook of Modern Grand Opera*. Kahn's witty title, perhaps obscure today, is based on the plight of explorer Dr. Frederick Cook, whose claim to reach the North Pole 1908 was infamously discredited when his navigational records are found to be taken from Jules Verne's novel *The English at the North Pole* (1864). Grandiose puffery published back when Boston Opera had opened receive a highly public and critical focus. And the opera hireling doesn't sustain scrutiny. Nor could he stand success.

Kahn spent a year at Boston Opera before founding the new magazine. Saw the evidence with his own eyes. Conclusions match Loie Fuller. Has facts. Knows people. Kahn has piercing questions, genuine concerns. He has connected the dots. His motive is to fix and preserve Boston Opera.

Kahn prefaces a disclaimer: "We have no personal quarrel with Mr. Jordan". He wishes to bring honesty to Boston Opera, a worthy project he hopes continues well into the future if managed competently.

"We are going after the shysters and the fakes of the musical world, regardless of their position. We will endeavor to hunt out the parasites that have fastened to Art and who fatten on the financial support that the music-loving public gives to musical expression". Henry Russell.

"Many an artist had his hopes shattered, his resources drained, and his future ruined by these vampires".

Prophesizes: "Many a musical enterprise of artistic and educational value was forced to go under because of them".

Defends Jordan. "Mr. Jordan's sanction of Russell's methods... most of his mistakes were simply errors of judgment. He was badly advised in a business of which he knew but little.

"He was imposed upon by a man who is a past master of the art of using the faith, generosity and ambitions of others to his own best advantage—a man who brags of being a 'cultured diplomat' and who is particularly proud of what he terms 'my hypnotic influence.'"

Kahn who has been on the Boston staff, has no hypnotic illusions.

As Thomas Paine, Phillip Kahn holds up truth to our ears.

"We believe that when the smoke of battle rolls away, Mr. Jordan will call us his friends. We believe that a frank discussion of Henry Russell and his 'policies' will show the real reasons for the non-success of Grand Opera in Boston. We believe that by showing that gentleman for what he really is, we will help the Boston Opera House [BOH] and add to the artistic and civic status of our city.

Attempts had been made by Russell and minions to suppress Kahn's report: "Best proof, perhaps, of the importance and truth of what we are about to reveal is shown by the efforts that were made to prevent the publication of *Music Magazine*. We are proud to say that we survived all the hardships, all slurs, and all threats, and it is needless to add that we absolutely refused to deal with the man who, when fearing exposure, made offers of the patronage at his disposal".

Kahn firmly believes he does Boston a civic favor as good citizen and will be appreciated as a truth-teller should. There has been, Kahn says, reasonable cause to doubt Russell's quality and question his honesty.

Kahn has done the research, interviewed the people. Now he publishes the facts, conclusions, and obvious solution.

Suggests that Jordan fire Russell and get someone better.

The gist of Kahn's research is that Russell was recklessly unqualified, never really interested in Boston, spends too freely, skims and makes side deals, demands kick-backs from talent, creates conflicts destroying quality, and has grievously misrepresented his past. It is only true.

Kahn's analysis will suggest that the Boston Opera deficits resulting in the recent appeals for public tax funding have been caused only by the manager's spendthrift ways. He has uncovered that Russell, who even now plans to leave Boston and build his own opera house in Europe at end of his second contract term, is corrupt. He holds proof.

Phillip Kahn has cause for concern. And out of an enormous affection for the gayety of nations, he offers truth and solutions. He is pained that the Boston Opera quality suffers so egregiously by the Russell abuses.

Jordan does not take this in the spirit offered. Nor do the Board. A vast silence spreads across the Boston newspapers. None speak freely.

In revenge Henry Russell demands a lynching. In his reaction, begs the Boston elite boys—how does he coax them—to attack who attacks one the annointed their own. As a result, the Kahn exposé is hated for its truth, and not appreciated for bringing much-needed clarity and helpful wisdom.

Crazily, Boston lads back the wrong horse. Kahn has underestimated Russell's hold over his hypnotized associates. Now exposed as fools.

Russell demands the Boston establishment act to protect their appointed, vaunted manager's lies and abuses by railroading Kahn to jail for libel. Few hints of the subsequent magazine suppression will hit the Boston papers owned by the Boston establishment. Few facts find the light of day elsewhere. Even so, Kahn has only told what people know around.

Word gets around.

So the job is done and Kahn after all, speaks from the evidence. Prints four issues of his magazine before he is speedily found guilty by a crony judge for "libeling criminally Henry Russell, director of the Boston Opera House" and instantly sentenced "to imprisonment in the House of Corrections for a year" (*NY Times* Jan 26 '14).

Kahn's publication vanishes, journalist successfully suppressed. The conspiracy to kill the truth-teller succeeds. Shamefully wicked. Jordan and the board have leveraged the old back-bay-boy network. Maliciously, Boston elite rallied to protect protégé Russell against uppity Kahn. Truth is burned at the stake. The richboys' club could suppress the Boston press if they chose to do so. They have power to railroad a journalist to jail. Their pals are the judges, lawyers. Jordan's worst hour is this, when he protects his vulnerable hireling from the truth. He might have listened to Phillip Kahn and profited to protect his legacy.

Phillip Kahn attempted to save Boston Opera. As he lost, they lost.

Jordan fails to heed the well-meant words of honest concern. Jordan maight have sensed the situation from complaints of Loie Fuller, Constantino, or others. Perhaps these had never fully surfaced to his ears.

Quiet conspiracy of secrets: Boston does as Boston does, as town still says today. Whispers never reached the great patron. Who had in other Boston music projects received the best cooperation from the best talents.

Pitching Russell as a man who can never be questioned, how stupid.

Hints of this disaster flit across the future, as the shooting of an editor in San Francisco by Thomas Williams colors press reporting rest of his life.

Phillip Hale's later comment that he could never speak freely about Boston Opera must be viewed in the light of Philip Kahn's persecution.

Kahn, after all, had been jammed into prison for speaking out. Hale is no fool. Decade later he dares not mention Kahn's name or plight in print. Journalists rallied in California when Williams shot the editor Marriott and rigged the trial. Not so in Boston for Kahn's legal lynching. Contemptible.

Phillip Kahn sought the truth of things. Examined the Opera Company *Prospectus* and financial statements. Finding flaws, Henry Russell's character was researched then on the evidence attacked or—as Loie Fuller, Constantino and others best might say—exposed.

What makes the sad Kahn trial peculiarly fascinating: Kahn's defense wase entirely suppressed by the Boston judge; and Russell never takes the stand under oath. "At the trial, counsel for Kahn tried to introduce evidence to support these charges [apply truth defense against Russell], but Judge Brown would not allow this. The defense then refused to contest the case, and Judge Brown directed the jury to return a verdict of guilty".

That's how fast Phillip Kahn crushed.

Without defense or witnesses, Kahn is instantly hustled over to the jailblock strictly on the unproved assertions of Russell's complaint. The Phillip Kahn witch-hunt presages the Comstock censorship suppressions.

Kahn's musical inquiry: banned in Boston; lynch the messenger.

Here is what Phillip Kahn reported. Recent efforts to gain public funds had drawn his attention. "While the BOH was...used for the strictly private purposes of its patron", there was no right to criticize. Now "at the end of last season...hue and cry went up that the Opera House was a sort of civic institution, and it devolved upon Bostonians to shoulder the financial burden of its upkeep. A fund of $150,000 was demanded; over $100,000 was pledged; bills were introduced in the Massachusetts Legislature" to exempt it from property tax. Its doings therefore have become "a matter for public knowledge".

Facing deficits and seeking public funds, Russell's already large salary has been raised: "While the public was being hypnotized" with fog about finances, "director Russell made the announcement that his salary was being raised to $25,000 a year [just under $600,000 today]. So do faithful public servants get their immediate reward!" Truly a fortune in those days.

Without singing a note, Russell has trumped the revenues of the stars whose fortunes he steadily exploited then viciously undermines.

Kahn asks, And why is that man running the Boston opera enterprise?

Russell "proudly points to his only great achievement—the restoring of Eleonora Duse's voice. But the famous tragedienne, for some reason, refuses to recognize the existence of one Henry Russell". Duse never praises Russell after Waldorf when he, as we know, must flee London.

Kahn, no Alice Nielsen friend, demonstrates Russell's fogginess: "He claims another achievement to his credit—the snatching of a singer from comic opera ranks and hoisting her upon an operatic pedestal. This singer is now no longer in her prime and fame has as yet eluded her".

As investigative journalist Kahn had merits. Not as music critic. But by holding great scorn for Russell, although certainly on the right track, Kahn blames Nielsen for bringing the bad manager to town and pushing him into the job by promoting him so absurdly to Eben Jordan, who Kahn likes.

Kahn has plenty to say of merit, without really penetrating the situation. Russell's malicious abuses have greatly harmed Constantino, Nielsen, Fuller, and other artists. Kahn does not focus on those relations.

Kahn simply wants Boston Opera to somehow survive Russell's cheats and exploitation.

"Why such enormous deficits?" The cast had grown increasingly cheap.

"Surely singers of the stamp heard in Boston...in which Zina Brozia and Jean Riddez were the principals, could not have eaten up all the money received. And this money was well over $500,000!

"Director Russell replies with a characteristic sigh that there are other singers who demand extraordinary prices. And some of these, who strangely enough can boast of no European engagements do receive, comparatively speaking, large sums for their services. Why?"

Russell takes kickbacks: "Why do these singers receive their cachets in cash and not by check—cash carried to them by the faithful alter ego of Henry Russell—Randolfo Barocchi? Why does Barocchi, Russell's private secretary, collect agents' commissions...? Find the answer to the last two queries and the riddle is solved".

To Philip Kahn, as any reasonable person, the Opera manager is not only expendable but a clear and present danger. Putting him in "absolute charge" of the institution was utter folly. Boston Opera would survive far better without him.

"To be brutally frank" Boston could get along fine without "Russell's quasi-artistic attempts. But...it is well to look into the matter and learn what is at present hidden behind a curtain of deep mystery, namely, what kind of a man is he to whom is entrusted the yearly expenditure of vast sums of money and who is in absolute charge of a publicly-subsidized Art institution".

Sadly for Russell, Kahn has studied the inflated foggy autobiographical statements. "That modest (?) account of his own achievements printed in the *Sunday Globe*, December 14, 1912, makes easy our task of presenting him in his true colors". Promises to help Henry Russell recall the facts to correct the lies. "His story was very incomplete and we will refresh Mr. Russell's memory to an amazing extent. We will help him recollect events as they really happened and will remind him of old associates whom he has chosen to forget".

Running Boston Opera, Kahn perceives Russell hires cheap and takes kickbacks. As we met him doing for Alice's calamitous opening at Casino NYC. The last three Boston seasons boasted "but a few" singers worth the price of tickets. Russell was "so fond of speaking" of ensemble while "boosting...singers not much above the chorus class as great artists".

Kahn also objects to "tremendous publicity given to Urban, the Vienna exile regarding whose acclaim as a great (?) stage manager [director] by the Boston press we shall have more to say later...."

Kahn praises conductor Weingartner, if the man "a passing event" rarely in town; calls Conti "a routinier"; calls Caplet "young man without any experience...may develop into a good, or even a great, chef d'orchestre, but is not $5 too large a sum to pay when the only compensation is the realization of a charitable deed in having helped in the education of a musical student?" Caplet, says Kahn, had a special status due to his cordial relations with Mr. and Mrs. Henry Russell, noting the pair keep separate their households.

"What are Henry Russell's qualifications as an opera director? A London attempt to produce grand opera which ended not only in a fizzle but in a hasty departure from Britain's capital.... Musical education? Mr. Russell has hardly any. True he plays the piano fairly well by ear and he also sings in falsetto voice. General education? Very little, as on his own admission he was forced to earn his living at sixteen. Did he study scenic art? Is he acquainted with the works of great composers, not by hearsay but by serious application? Not he".

And those were Henry Russell's good points. Now the bad.

"As a business man he is a notorious failure". Kahn reveals that the Conservatory's trusted business manager, Flanders, had been rapidly pushed out by Russell. Tragic organizational flaw, Flanders had reported only to Russell, not the Board. In that wild scheme, Russell simply did whatever he wanted for whim. Instead of obeying wrong orders beyond reason and become a co-conspirator, Flanders returns to NE Conservancy where he could be true. Yet Flanders did not act to expose Russell.

As Kahn warns of icebergs and fog his fears seem starkly prophetic. "The business methods inaugurated by Henry Russell, after Mr. Flanders' inglorious exit as general manager of the Opera House, made the non-success of that institution logical and inevitable".

Kahn predicts possible failure well in time to avoid any collisions. All Boston Opera needs is a prudent captain and competent navigation.

Russell "as a man...bears an unenviable reputation. Around the Opera House, mechanics swap stories of petty acts that would shame a $15-a-week clerk. Among the artists—but this is a story by itself".

So. Kahn knows what Loie Fuller knew.

And Russell had vowed to leave Boston rich within three years. "Rumor has it that Henry Russell has become, from the beggar of three years ago, a wealthy man today. He himself says that in three years more he will bid good-bye to America and build an opera house of his own in Europe.

Russell takes kickbacks and payoffs, Kahn has diverse proofs.

"'I can offer Russell no artists——he wants too much', the head of one of the largest European agencies is alleged to have said recently. Whoever wants may solve this enigmatic saying", Kahn reports as a start.

Kahn exposes the suppression of recent scandals: "Last year *Il Gazetta del Massachusetts*, an Italian newspaper published in Boston, made a series of revelations about the doings at the BOH. Russell spent several uncomfortable days for fear the matter get into the English press. But luckily for him the storm blew over...his press department got busy pacifying the editor".

Kahn reveals the Boston Opera House business managers MacDonald and Flanders have strongly complained of Russell's methods and expenses. MacDonald quoted, "It's no use trying to act the part of a business manager. Henceforth, I shall do just as I am told to do by Mr. Russell, for I am nothing but a clerk to him. But if the bills he renders could speak!"

Kahn paints Russell's spending as extravagant. He "travels with a suite of two secretaries, stenographer, valet and the latter's wife who is in charge of his household, for Mr. Russell and Mrs. Russell maintain separate establishments. Nothing but trains de luxe for him and his, for it is the Boston Opera Company that foots the bills...."

Boston's ethics are at stake: "Boston's pride is the moral status of the city and its society. If it be true...then to Henry Russell belongs the dubious honor of having brought into it an entirely new element".

Unfree press has been a problem in Boston. People fear to report freely.

"Were it not for the mantle of protection thrown around his shoulders because of the silence of the press, the question of tolerating him as a force in Boston's art life would have been brought to a head long ago".

Grand opera has not led a moral life in Boston. "While it is fairly questionable whether or not the BOH added to Boston's renown as an art center, it is undeniable that it has caused more scandalous gossip than any other art institution even with a ten-fold longer existence".

Obviously, says Kahn, Russell will end badly, drag Boston Opera down.

"Boston's fame as a cultured city can hardly gain from the fact that Henry Russell is one of its cultural leaders...."

By mid-February, the Boston Opera lawyers had been ordered to stop Kahn's publication of the Russell exposé with a criminal, not civil, libel case is filed in Russell's name.

"In a proceeding in the superior court, Managing Director Henry Russell of the Boston Opera Co. seeks to have PL Kahn of the Music Magazine Co. at 7 Water St., restrained from printing false statements about him, his management of the opera company, or his employees.

"Russell claims that in a pamphlet called *The Music Magazine, and Musical Stage Review* dated Feb 15, Kahn caused to be published defamatory statements about him, tending to hold him up to public ridicule and that on Feb 15 the pamphlet was offered for sale in front of the Opera House, thereby becoming a nuisance.

"Russell claims that the pamphlet contains reflections not only on himself, but upon others at the opera house, and that it is part of a scheme of coercion, to frighten and prevent persons from entering the employ of the opera company. Kahn, he alleges, was employed by the company from Dec 1911 to March 1912, and while there had access to information which is now being used. Russell asks the court to restrain Kahn from publishing any false statements about him, or about any of the employees, and from intimidating any of the latter".

Boston journalists watch the lynching with great interest. They do not take up the Kahn story. The big chill works. Word spreads around anyway.

Two decades later, when Boston bans James Cabell's novel *Jurgen*, the editor HL Mencken sells copies of *American Mercury* on Copley Square 1926 just to force a court hearing. Wins.

Despite the lawsuit, Kahn's magazine continues until the editor is locked away; tragedy strikes.

Feb 22 issue #2, Kahn discusses Russell's various methods of using Boston Opera to line his pockets. One method: taking control of his assistant Theodore Bauer's *Music* publication and charging Boston artists for publicity. Russell, if "childlike in his knowledge, or rather ignorance, of ordinary business methods and customs, has a peculiar talent for getting on the trail of loose change".

Kahn quotes Russell's secretary Barocchi saying Russell was "signing up the artists now for the next season and they understand they will have to pay *Music* for their portraits. When I get their orders I take the money out of their salaries". And a series of other Russell extortion methods are detailed by Kahn.

Finances are given a detailed analysis.

"Why a budget of over $750,000? Why such tremendous deficits?"

Pressure on Kahn mounts quickly, painfully. Suppression of the story begins to find success with the March 1st Issue #3: "Owing to the fact that the criminal libel proceedings", Kahn postpones the next installment on advice of his lawyer: "We beg our readers' indulgence".

Kahn appeals in the March 8th Issue #4 "to the public for fair play" and to the court for a speedy hearing. "Our business is being hurt by Russell's allegations. We are entitled to know for what we are being prosecuted. We are ready to go on with the hearing…the public fully expects Henry Russell to take the stand on March 10th and attempt to show cause for his allegations of libel".

Kahn repeats his kindly statement of good intentions. He supports the opera project while demanding reasonable accountability and consistency.

Phillip Kahn is "heart and soul" with Jordan to establish "permanent Grand Opera in this city. But merely as a matter of good faith it should be shown to the public that the $500,000 or more that the people of Boston paid to the Opera House last season is insufficient support for the kind of opera produced by Director Russell, and that the deficit of $300,000 was not due to 'improper management".

Of course, this is just the question Russell hates most.

"The general sentiment in Boston is strongly against the continuation of the present Opera House regime. The public is ready for a change. A little house-cleaning by Mr. Jordan will mean a tremendous operatic boom". Fire Russell. Make things honest with a competent manager: "the instituting of able, sane and scrupulous methods of management will effect the savings of great sums of money each season".

Return the stars, raise standards. "With all due respect to Mr. Russell's opinions, a raising of individual artistic standards is not only desirable but could be easily accomplished. Substantial methods of artistic and business direction will make permanent Grand Opera in Boston a real possibility, and perhaps and accomplished fact".

Truther Kahn is under savage attack: "All the resources and influence of millions are centered on the task of crushing the *Music Magazine*".

Russell cronies request a gag order. "Why be panic-stricken, Mr. Russell? The Boston press is friendly to you. Why did you not, first of all, ask the newspapers for space and defend your methods of managing grand opera? The public has more interest in that, than in anything else that you may say or do. The question is not whether we are rascals but whether Russell is the proper person to head a publicly-subsidized institution.

"Now is a good time to offer proof of his fitness for that post. Distorted newspaper reports of court affairs, threats and bravado are not proper demonstrations of it".

Phillip Kahn could say no more. Mighty Phillip has struck out.

That's why Phillip Hale feared to speak freely of Boston Opera. He stood back to watch without protest as Kahn was railroaded into prison by Jordan and clique to benefit the arty-robber Henry Russell, a crime only slightly less blatant than Tom Williams shooting an unarmed editor.

Jailed or free: Phillip Kahn is exactly right. Eben Jordan wrong. The tragedy of Phillip Kahn the prophet, hated by bringing truth to Boston. Yes, Kahn has put things in the plain air and now everybody knows.

Reform has ended badly. Mighty Phillip Kahn struck out.

Unheeded by those who most need him.

Alice Nielsen, no doubt aware of this tragedy, keeps singing.

March 9, *Boston Sunday Globe* discusses Nielsen's upcoming part in Wolf-Ferrari's "one-act comic operetta, *Secret Of Suzanne*…a sparkling and exquisite comedy, contrived and written in the spirit of a school that long added luster to Italian operatic art. The plot is tenuous but diverting and exquisite, since it holds up to graceful scorn and derision the too-zealous suspicions of a jealous husband, than which, what spectacle in the whole world is more pitiable and fatuous? Miss Nielsen...should find in its arch and sparkling comedy a particularly grateful part" as Suzanne.

Romances continue; Boston's Edith Barnes "most promising lyric soprano" marries Norman Mason of Chicago. Couple skips to Buenos Aires where Mason works in advertising.

After two Zerlina performances, Nielsen goes away from Boston for a month, returning for *Martha*. Quaintance Eaton said of *Martha*, "it could be understood anyway only from the lips of that expert trained in operetta, Alice Nielsen".

The *Martha* antique went on display March 25 (*Boston Globe*); Nielsen as Lady Harriet. Maria Gay, Nancy; Rodolfo Fornari, Sir Tristam; Lionel, Max Lipmann; Pluskett, Edward Lankow; The Sheriff, Bernard Olshansky.

Globe seems displeased by opera in English that isn't.

"The audience was a large one" with "a delegation of 1,000 from the Knights of Columbus...." Production panned. "First performance of *Martha* by this company and it was said to be in English. How fond the recollections of past *Marthas* in this town, and there have been some of them unutterably dreary. But the opera, like *Il Trovatore*, is hardy. Its characters are old friends. If it were essential that the Boston Opera Company should produce one opera in English, it is unfortunate that certain preliminary steps were overlooked".

One overlooked step would be a translation "which preserved the thought of the text with some degree of force and dignity...which would have served alike all the members of the cast".

Next overlooked step would be a cast with clear diction. "The cause of opera in English need claim no particular discussion at this time for the simple reason that the English language appeared for the greater part in disguise. There were words and phrases which were heard and understood, and the audience plainly showed its joy".

The point of "giving the opera with this cast, nominally in English, rather than in Italian is not clear".

In the cast: Lippman "hardly in place here. Mr. Fornari gave as little idea of the part as of the text. Mr. Lankow...is to be given credit for some intelligible lines.... Mme. Gay is an intelligent singer. The chorus sang lustily". Conductor Moranzoni "deserves credit for holding the performance together...unfortunately...unmistakable signs of scant rehearsal".

This *Martha* undercut Alice: "Be a pleasure to hear and see Miss Nielsen in this role surrounded by a cast of singers who possess some native fitness for the parts they undertake. Her voice, light, flexible, graceful and possessing lyric charm, is well adapted to this music. Last night Miss Nielsen made an effect and gave pleasure in the old ballad, *The Last Rose Of Summer* which Berlioz said shed a redeeming fragrance upon the rest of the opera. Her voice was telling and welcome in the quartets and in the finale, but Miss Nielsen's responsibility was a grave one and it sat heavily upon her".

Sadly alike NYC Casino, Nielsen again appears in a poor production whilst a fake friend manages things.

Yet Alice has the momentum.

March 31st, well-attended concert at Boston Opera House (*Boston Globe*) links Nielsen with Michael J. Dwyer "the ballad singer" and pianist Emiliano Renaud. A large audience was present. Miss Nielsen was in excellent voice. Her choice of songs was not wholly confined to the printed program, but her numbers included *The Lass With The Delicate Air*, *The Leaves And The Wind* by Leoni..., Landon Ronald's *Down In The Forest* and *When Love Is Kind* and *Comin' Thro' The Rye* as encores. There was a group of French songs by Hahn, Debussy, Chabrier and Bemberg and a final group of Irish songs including *Last Rose Of Sumer*".

Dwyer "said to have a cold...gave his audience pleasure by his singing of various old ballads, *Believe Me, If All These Endearing Young Charms*, *Drink To Me Only With Thine Eyes* and others". Renaud plays List, Godard and his own *Berceuse*. Charles Strony accompanies for Nielsen, Frank Waller for Dwyer. The concert closes with themes from *Tales Of Hoffman*.

March 14 (*NY Times*), Boston's free-speech advocate Philip Kahn jailed for publishing articles critical of Henry Russell. Magazine suppressed. Last episode of the reformer's series lost. Trial is conducted strangely.

Liberty takes a beating in Boston,

"Those who crowded Judge Brown's courtroom today hoping to hear sensational testimony...were disappointed. The trial ended abruptly. The defense offered no evidence and the court instructed the jury to return a verdict of guilty".

Philip Kahn's attorney Jesse Grove "was making his opening address when Thomas Lavelle, Assistant District Attorney, interrupted him, saying that Grove should confine his remarks to the specifications of the bill of particulars. The court sustained the prosecutor and Mr. Grove announced, that in view of the court's ruling, he would offer no defense at all".

No defense made. No evidence presented. Russell does not testify under oath. Jury responds as directed with guilty. Kahn railroaded to jail for speaking freely. Power has corrupted the court.

Lynchhing Kahn a sad episode in Boston Opera; shame on Boston; shame on Jordan. Facts stay unchanged. Jordan does not avail himself of Philip Kahn's good advice. Kahn's imprisonment begins, he becomes lost to us. Boston Opera steams ahead in the icy fog. Jordan will discover Kahn's honest advice wiser than the Russell lies.

And what about Burton Stanley? The sweet transvestite reappears in California theatre news. Just keeps going. *SJ Mercury News* (April 11) reports: WJ Sanlan as Ralph Rackstraw had a "fine tenor voice...heard to advantage in *Farewell My Own*, one of the gems from that comic opera. 'Josephine' was sung by female impersonator Burton Stanley".

April 27, Gatti-Casazzi announces Nielsen "of the Boston Opera" would be re-engaged by the Met next year, a slap at Henry Russell. At least Gatti-Casazzi doesn't warrant magazine features about his corruption.

Nielsen returns Europe summer as usual; soon sings at Covent.

As 1913 passes with tumult for theatre-people. "Revolt of the Actors" will challenge abuses of power by, well, Lee Shubert and cronies. Time for fairness. Nielsen's friends Lillian Russell, Ethyl Barrymore and Marie Dressler establish Equity, aided by Francis Wilson. Ironically, a Victor Herbert musical precipitates things.

Enchantress ran 112 Broadway shows before April 1912 then tours. Trouble hit the tour. Set in Royal Palace of Zergovia (and Vivien's Villa on the Danube), it sings: *If You Can't Be As Happy As You Like Be As Happy As You Can* and Nielsen spoof *Art Is Calling For Me (I Want To Be A Prima Donna)*. *Prima Donna* is a clever egg tossed by Herbert and Henry Blossom.

To the diva, art is calling: "*To sing on the stage that's the one life for me, My figure's just like Tetrazzini, I know I'd win fame if I sang in Bohème, That opera by Signor Puccini, I've roulades and the trills, That would send the cold chills, Down the backs of all hearers of my vocal frills. And Melba I'd oust if I once sang in Faust, That opera so charming by Gounod, Girls would be on the brink, Of hysterics, I think, Even strong men would have to go out for a drink.* Verses close: "*I long to be a prima donna, donna, donna; I long to shine upon the stage, With my avoirdupois, And my tra la la la la, I would be the chief sensation of the age, I long to hear them shouting: 'Viva' to the Diva...Art is calling for me*".

Enchantress tours to San Francisco where producer Joseph Gaites tells the cast that salaries could not be met. Hoping for best, the players troop to LA. Star Kitty Gordon collapses onstage and lawyers for librettist Fred de Gresac attach box office receipts for unpaid royalties. Fred is a pseudonym for Frederique playing Fred's widow. Show never re-opens. Cast of sixty-seven very popular players everybody on Broadway likes is stranded 3,000 miles from NYC and their next job.

Equity Actors Union is organized a month later. Challenged, Florenz Ziegfeld gets a first injunction against Equity. David Belasco, militant against the union, has a change of heart: "Abhorring each other, how can we think we are going to succeed? We cannot. Ours is a profession of intense and sympathetic temperamentality, less tangible than a dream; highly strung and emotional, the dearest and best and most bohemian people in the world, all of whom would give his or her life blood to any just cause...we are artists, first last and always". In tense negotiations Equity is represented by Lillian Russell who gets the final agreement with producers. September 5th, strike ends and Nielsen's erstwhile basso Eugene Cowles resumes *Chu Chin Chow* at Century.

Relations between playwrights, performers, stagehands and producers have remained warmly cordial festivals of mutual appreciation ever since.

With the onset of practical reforms for well-known problems, pressure on Boston Opera escalates. Public, press, cast, stockholders, and board are aware of the manager's poor choices and character flaws. Boston Opera is not what it should be. Not what it promised. Nielsen was removed.

According to Met's 1970s gossip Eaton, Farrar tried to keep Caruso away from Boston. Warns Caruso "airily that Boston audiences weren't very big, but made up in coldness for their sparse numbers". Farrar "had old scores to settle with Russell and never lost an opportunity" claims Eaton, skipping fears of being upstaged by Nielsen.

Russell made life difficult for many artists. As he admitted to Charles Wagner, with Alice he cannot cope. Alice can tell him off.

Frivolous Eaton dismisses Nielsen's practical concerns and objections, skips the fatal flaws. Exploits Nielsen financially—Eaton stupidly suggests opposite. Much blarney by Alice to promote her remora misled superficial Eaton's *Boston Opera* book co-written by Russell's daughter.

Even so, Eaton describes Russell targeting a young soprano at one of his vainity auditions for spare change. Here is Russell on the Boston payroll after firing Nielsen. Tells young Donna Shinn, "Little girl, I am going to do everything for you!" With other people's money. Cunning next steps curious to behold. Arranges for wife Nina to take Shinn to Europe, putting the girl's parents out of picture. No private island, but you get the picture. Misusing Boston Opera funds, he "contrived an ingenious if costly way to give his new singer experience: he built an opera company around her. Ostensibly to try out several singers he had tentatively engaged for Boston, he hired the theatre in a little North Italy town near Como" actually Varese, 55 km north of Milano. Shinn appears as Suzanne in Wolf-Ferrari's opera. For the Boston budget the folly "proved an expensive audition indeed", Eaton says. Continuing the Eaton gossip, Russell's wife Nina, bonking Andre Caplet, was glad to chaperone husband's next new girlfriend since "Henry was serious about the girl". Whatever. Russell and Nina divorce; marries Shinn. Nina returns to stage, acts with John Barrymore; dies 1941. Russell and Shinn divide time between Monte Carlo (where he has stashed cash) and nearby village La Turbie until ditches her for a fresh young wife met during an Australia tour with Melba who strands Russell just for fun of revenge after his predictable backstab.

At the end Eaton has a moment of clarity. Russell "said to have shown little need of the casual gratification of sex impulses that appears to be usual for a man of his métier". The salaryman was no Ziegfeld, Shubert, or Otto Kahn. Yet he had "the masculine possessiveness that dovetails with the other characteristics of so self-centered a man". Eaton grows so very very subtle: "It is possible to believe that his 'casting couch' was less occupied than gossip would have it". Preferntial whims for petite Italian poets, tailor-tenors, and the odd impresionable young girls.

Legal lynching of Philip Kahn was an outrageous abuse by Jordan's clique who railroad a journalist to prison for speaking freely of varmint Russell. Irony of Jordan's commercial empire based on quality and trust; a respected Boston businessman in value-add retail. His manager grew up in aristocratic circles where favors and flattery count most. Lacks business sense, wisdom, and Loie Fuller said: integrity. Details how he misused money will be difficult to determine when he disappears with the Boston Opera books. But the bills keep washing ashore like tea in Boston harbor.

Backstage backstabber kills the golden geese onstage.

MAY: COVENT GARDEN REVISITED

Nielsen has left for London with her son Benjamin Thomas. She appears at Covent for *Secret of Suzanne*, then *Butterfly*. During this season, Eben Jordan is invited to join Covent's board, and would meet Higgins of quality competence.

May 20 at Covent Garden, *Il Segreto di Susanna*: Nielsen, Susanna; Sammarco, Gil; Ambrosiny, Santé (*London Times* Ma 21). On a double bill with *Pagliacci* with Caruso and Carmen Melis: "Large part of the audience too showed that it was for Caruso...by dropping in casually while *Il Segreto di Susanna* was being sung and acted with delicious froth and freshness by Signor Sammarco and Miss Nielsen. The later, by the way, was also making a return to the stage of Covent Garden after a considerable interval of time and save for a certain amount of vibrato her whole performance was charming".

Pall Mall says "the Countess was taken by Miss Alice Nielsen cleverly though rather fussily"; *Yorkshire Post*, Susanna was impersonated last night by Alice Nielsen who acted with charm and vivacity, and used her pleasing light soprano voice with a skill that bore witness to culture".

May 21 and June 2, Nielsen gives *Madama Butterfly* with John McCormack, Elvira Leveroni and Dinh Gilly. Nielsen uses her usual style; great shock to *London Times* after Melba had bellowed the part for ages.

"Alice Nielsen, who sang the part of Madama Butterfly, seldom produced anything but a small tone. At times it sounded as though she were only trying over the part for her own amusement, and the tune she ought to burst into when she rushes to the window at the sound of the cannon was almost inaudible. On the other hand, there was delicacy and youthfulness in her treatment of the part, if there were not many signs of dramatic instinct, and her tone, insufficient though it was, sounded fresh and agreeable.

McCormack "tempered his voice with discretion in the duets, and did not try to make up for it by putting additional warmth into his acting. Gilly gave distinction to the rather thankless part of Sharpless, and as Suzuki Mlle. Leveroni was sympathetic and efficient".

Pall Mall adds, "the title role was taken with much skill and sympathy by Miss Alice Nielsen. It is a trying part for any singer, and she successfully avoided any danger...."

Globe confirms, "Last night brought a large audience to Covent Garden, and the performance had a double interest in that it enabled Miss Alice Nielsen to add to her successes, and to play a part in which she has not been seen for a long time at Royal Opera".

Yes, the Irish upstarts had success that London season.

August 24, back in Boston, recycling Jules Grau's 1890s approach to young affordable casts, Milton Aborn forms Century Opera Company "without stars. We shall not call them stars. This will be a company of artists—of real artists...." Aborn takes the opposite approach of Frohman and others. As if young casts were not cheaper than stars. In future, Aborn with try a Nielsen-Herbert revival.

September 2, romance continues as Nielsen's alto co-star and train station dancing partner Jeska Swartz marries Julius Morse of Boston in a ceremony by Rabbi Schlesinger.

In Britain, Alice Nielsen seeks to develop a new show bespoke for her. Desires a project by Puccini or Wolf-Ferrari to utilize story by JM Barrie, who she knew from the 1901 days with Laurence Irving. Setting these things in motion, Alice divides time between Paris and London as war clouds are connived to obscure the gaiety of the nations.

Her career in London in effect ends. Her name reappears in four years with marriage to Stoddard, another in four years with his plastic surgery practice, when she revisits 1921, and as 1922 tale retold by *Graphic* about the singer shushing King Edward VII as Tosti plays piano at a party hosted by Duchess of Manchester. That's Alice's last London mention.

OCTOBER: AMERICAN SEASON

Fall gives America a new opera in English. Victor Herbert's *Madeleine* opens at the Met without Alice Nielsen with six performances. Frances Alda sings the one-act show, paired with *Pagliacci, Pasquale,* or *L'amore medico.* In the cast: erstwhile Nielsen co-stars Segurola and Pini-Corsi. Plot, French play set in, well, France 1760s. Revolves around chef—no that was Louis in KC—yes, diva frantic to find a dining buddy for New Year's Day. Reflects *NY Times,* "not a notable landmark in the progress of native art".

October 10, Nielsen anchored in fog outside Boston. On this image we hang our story. Among 2,400 passengers on the steamer *Laconia* are Rev. William Van Allen, MIT president Richard MacLaurin, violinist Robert Pollack, French conductor Charles Strong, and Mr. and Mrs. Starling Burgess. Importantly, Eben Jordan and wife. Alice has joined them for many chats. Disembarks restored to Boston Opera Company.

Alice Nielsen "operatic star, and her brother [son] Benjamin Nielsen" are among those stuck in "heavy fog which shrouded the Atlantic from 1500 miles" for three days, anchored off the lightship until docking at East Boston.

The Jordans traveled widely, yet "spent the last two months at Castle Drummond, Scotland, where Mr. Jordan has a shooting preserve". Jordan is now "honorary director of the Covent Garden Syndicate. He said it was not so much a personal compliment to him as it was a recognition of the splendid productions the Boston Opera Company has furnished, and it also means a working agreement between the two companies".

Jordan feels the pinch, "If the public wants this sort of opera it is up to them to subscribe more liberally toward its support". The no-star policy proves unpopular with public. Despite the obvious, Jordan chides the public who skip starless nights: "Buying tickets on nights when some great star is to sing is not supporting the opera".

Waste your money, people. Jordan pinpoints what the removal of Constantino and Nielsen cost: "Vacant seats aggregating $250,00 was the result of insufficient support last year".

Did Jordan see the Philip Kahn pieces? Kahn rots in jail while Jordan slaughters Scottish pheasants in the halcyon days before WWI.

Dialogs between Jordan and Nielsen during the passage are lost to us. After she arrives the results clear. The gregarious diva with keen business savvy reveals plans to sing at Boston Opera often. Voyage had been more than coincidental. Eben Jordan knows why he built that opera house.

The "native language libretto" rule now is contradicted. Alice provokes the subject by asking "if the movement for grand opera in English had received any impetus in this country". Told it has not, she replies "It was simply ridiculous that American audiences should be compelled to listen to one opera in French, another in German, and another in Italian, and not one in ten comprehend a word. Such conditions would not be tolerated in any country in Europe".

Manon has joined her repertoire. After London she had traveled "to Paris for rest and recreation; after a concert tour she will return to Boston to sing with the Boston Opera Company. She will appear here in February when she sings the part of Manon for the first time".

October 18th when the Boston Opera's *Prospectus* arrives, Alice Nielsen has been fully restored: "among its members vocalists and world-wide eminence and many nationalities.... French and the Italian sections... strengthened and the singers required for...German have been engaged".

In the cast: sopranos: Alice Nielsen, Mary Garden, Emmy Destinn, Lina Cavalleri, Nellie Melba, Luisa Tetrazzini among twenty-four. Mezzo-sopranos: Elvira Leveroni, Maria Gay, Jeska Swartz among nine. Tenors: Gaetano Pini-Corsi, Ernesto Gaiccone, Edmond Celement among sixteen. Baritones: Rodolfo Fornari, Ramon Blanchart, Vanni Marcoux among ten. Basses: Joe Mardones among eight. Conductors: André-Caplet, Roberto Moranzoni, Felix Weingartner.

Three "most important" new names are soprano Rachel Frease-Green, mezzo-soprano Margherita Dalvares and tenor Giuseppe Opezzo. Dalvares and Opezzo sang for Russell "during the recent season given at Varese, Italy". Future wife he was promoting strangely remains unmentioned.

Boston will offer the world premier of Zandonai's *Francesco da Rimini,* American premier of Fuvrier's *Monna Vanna.* Last year's "*Djamileh, Le Foret Bleue, Pelleas et Melisande, Martha* "shelved for a time". Wagner's *Die Meistersinger* added, plus Ponchielli's *La Gioconda,* Massenet's *Manon,* and Puccini's *Manon Lescaut.* "Successful novelties of last year, including *Don Giovanni, The Jewels of the Madonna, The Secret of Suzanne, Tales of Hoffman,* and *Louise* will be retained".

Talent again gathers in Boston. Italian chorus "due to sail shortly, and from now until the middle of November, almost every liner will bring its quota to the Boston Opera". Assistant chorus-master Lyford daily rehearses the American chorus "and each morning the members of the ballet are put through their paces by Mme. Paporello. Every department is a hive of activity these days, including the subscription office".

October 12, publicity begins for Herbert's new show *Sweethearts.*

Crossing America by train, Alice Nielsen sings in San Jose's Victory Theatre with pianist Homer Samuels. *SJ Mercury News* reports only a "few people who appreciate high-class singing. The beautiful singing of Miss Nielsen charmed the auditors last evening and they felt like apologizing to her for the meager attendance". Her pilgrim progress repeats. She "received many recalls in the rendition of her excellent program last evening and responded gracefully. She sang *Last Rose Of Summer* as it has never been sung before on the stage of the Victory".

During this period, hireling Russell attempts to charm tycoons Otto Kahn of NY and ET Stotesbury of Philadelphia for "straightening out of the grand opera situation in the three cities" (*NY Times* Nov 2). "Kahn and Gatti-Casazza have been hearing a good deal...as to the difficulties of the Boston Opera Company....

Disconnected from diva who put him in his place, his hubris falls flat.

Otto Kahn keeps quiet, "I cannot discuss the matter at all at this time".

Unpopular casting choices, low quality, bottom line bad. People were talking. Philip Kahn jailed for saying what everybody knows—the few unaware are now wised. Scandal of putting Kahn away hurt Boston Opera.

Power used unwisely reveals the fool.

Scorning Boston, Russell made funny-business overseas. When he cries "short-term opera" cannot succeed, the *Times* cannot resist: as "proved in the case of Russell in Boston, whose backer Eben Jordan has had to face enormous deficits".

Jordan becomes the new scapegoat, who cannot allow "the proper long-term contracts... and a possible chance of making both ends meet financially". Turning to his next possible racket, Russell seeks to con two other opera tycoons whereby they pay to "supply Boston and Philadelphia with opera, engaging singers in conjunction with the Metropolitan and relegating Chicago" to Western tour. This windfall for himself "would make the proposed change a welcome one both to NY and Boston, if not to Philadelphia and Chicago". Intriguingly, said *Times*, Russell and Otto Kahn have been "more or less in touch with each other for six years".

Kahn, bankster associated with Schiff and Warburg (yes, musical name Warbucks), regards opera a hobby with perks and purpose when moving money overseas for terrorism.

Nielsen sings as her erstwhile remora makes frantic schemes.

December 7 (*NY Times*) Alice has NY concert of *Figaro* at Carnegie Hall. Despite bronchitis. Next week, sings Christmas benefit at Ritz.

Terrible news. Nordica has been making a world tour. December 24th her Dutch steamer *Tasman* shipwrecks on Bramble Cay in Gulf of Papua. Her tragedy prelude to America's greatest musical tragedy: the Boston Opera *Titanic*. Nordica's resources could refloat Boston, if she had lived.

1914: BOSTON SINKS, NIELSEN SOARS

1914 begins with notice by Gatti-Casazzi that Nielsen is re-engaged at the Met. Her presence the year before, "occasional".

January 18 (*NY Times*), cello virtuoso Jean Gerardy and Alice Nielsen engage Carnegie Hall. Gerardy plays Boellman's *Variations Symphonique*, Max Bruch's arrangement of synagogue song *Kol Nidrei*, two movements from a Baccherini suite plus Bach, Shumann, and Davidoff. "His big, noble, manly tone, his perfectly finished technical mastery and the self-effacing artistic spirit in which he approached the music" made "a masterly performance that rejoiced the musically minded".

Nielsen offers "two arias of an elder spirit", Handel's *Care Seive* and *Deh vieni* from Mozart's *Marriage of Figaro*, plus songs by German,

Scandinavian, French, and American composers. Still reeling from respiratory illness, Nielsen seems off-pitch and short of breath. Voice "agreeable... but its unsteadiness and the shortness of her phrasing mitigate against the artistic beauty of what she does; nor is she always fully in agreement with the pitch. But she was generously applauded, even more than Mr. Gerardy...."

Boston Opera makes its last and worst mistake.

Despite pressure to fix things in Boston, Russell wishes to be back in Paris and cooks a scheme. In blithe hubris he coaxes Jordan to make it so. Boston Opera Company will tour to Paris for Spring 1914. Leaving the gorgeous opera house created for it empty.

January 25, *NY Times* reveals that Boston Opera opens a May season at *Theatre de Champs Elysees*. Interlocking boards of Met, Covent, and Boston make possible the escapade. Covent's Henry Higgins will be "completing the arrangements abroad", *Times* wrongly suggests ever-puffing Russell holds "a similar position with the London organization".

Boston Opera singers, Covent Garden sets. Boston women's chorus.

Jordan's architect initiated the connections whilst working on *Theatre de Champs Elysees*, "one of the handsomest theatres in Europe..., built by Americans, the late JP Morgan furnishing part of the cash...." Morgan Sr. had died March 31 1913 in Rome. Theatres and houses of worship built by war profiteers bespeak the cruelest irony. The theatre had been closed a year since March 1913. Gabriel Astrue failed to compete with "subsidized Paris Opera Company". As had Hammerstein.

Despite omens, Jordan's cohorts include Baron d'Erlanger "millionaire composer of *Aphrodite* which was to have been the opening bill of Oscar Hammerstein's proposed season here, and several Americans who live in London or Paris". Same D'Erlanger Nielsen had observed getting boos. They will offer an American-German opera season in Paris with "Felix Weingartner the German conductor".

Meanwhile at Boston Opera, Alice Nielsen returns with Constantino.

February 4 (*Boston Globe*), Boston Opera gives *Barber of Seville* with Nielsen, Leveroni, Constantino, Ancons and Marcoux.

Friday, "only time this season": *La Gioconda* with Destinn, Leveroni, Constantino, Mardones. Saturday matinee *Die Meistersinger Von Nurnberg* with Frieda Hempel. Saturday night *Lucia* with Scotney, Tanlongo, Fornari.

Monday, "first time in Boston the sensational operatic novelty of the season *The Love of the Three Kings* (*L'Amore del Tre Re* 1913) with Lucrezia Boria, Ferrari-Fontana, and Amato. Composer Montemezzi born in Verona made a story medieval with blind king and sexy daughter-in-law. Urban "prepared the scenic production, which arouses pleasurable anticipation, and Mr. Moranzoni has been given the opportunity he deserves as conductor".

February 9 (*Boston Globe*), Nielsen sings "Sunday night concert of the Opera House". Rodolfo Fornari, Cara Sapin, Alfredo Ramelia and Tadeo Wronsky assist. Nielsen gives *Goodnight* quartet from *Martha*, Arditi's "*Kiss Waltz*", one group each of French and German songs plus four old-fashions: "*Annie Laurie, The Suwannee River, The Low-Backed Car* and

Believe Me If All Those Endearing Young Charms. On Friday Nielsen and Scotti play *Secret Of Suzanne*, followed by *Pagliacci* with Nielsen and Ferrari-Fontana.

Two days later Boston's invasion plan for 1914 Paris finalizes. The Met joins; English opera allies unite for the assault. They offer ten weeks of grand opera to Paris. *NY Times* (Fe 11) tells us: "A syndicate was formed by Kahn, Ernest Cassel, Lord Rothschild, Baron Grimthorpe, Baron Erlanger, Henry Higgins, Eben Jordan and others to lease *Theatre des Champs-Elysees* for five years". Capital outlay is $300,000 (about $6.5-million today). Gabriel Astruc had commissioned it for modern works and lost it by financial mismanagement. *Theatre des Champs-Elysees* still stands. Featured in films, this was the site of Ballet Russes notorious *Rite of Spring* debut with Nijinsky, a classical music riot.

Practically speaking, Russell has now abandoned Boston Opera for the Paris theatre. He will "show the Parisians what real grand opera was and if it proved successful, create in Paris a permanent operatic organization".

As if Paris has not created its own. "Spring, there are a great many Americans and English folk in Paris, and it is believed that the plan to give them opera with many of their favorite singers in the case will prove attractive to them". Operas will be sung in the libretto's original language, a challenge to the French regional autonomy. "Wealthy music lovers here and abroad are interested in this undertaking which is international in scope. We are going to give Parisians an opportunity to hear the very best of opera, sung by singers with international reputations".

In the cast: Alda, Barrientos, Cavalleri, Destinn, Edvina, Garden, Hempel, Tetrazzini, Matzenauer, and yes, Nielsen. Tenors: Ferrari-Fontana, Martinelli "and possibly Caruso". Baritones and bassos: Amato, Marcoux, Scotti. Back to stars, Russell nimbly reverses course because told to do so.

MIT Tech (Fe 28) reveals the company's ten-week season starts April 20th or 27th. Singers go. French musicians' union bans "importation of foreign orchestras". French operas dropped. Repertory "confined to German and Italian operas" of conductors three: Weingartner, Roberto Moranzoni, Arthur Nikisch. This Paris theatre, eight-hundred fewer seats than Boston. Prices for debuts and premiers $10 "American money", otherwise $5 as Boston.

In best *Chanticleer* tradition, optimism fills pre-opening press.

Skipping Covent sets, Urban wishes to ship Boston scenery he developed a decade ago for Paris, now said to offer the capital "something of a revelation, and if present plans do not miscarry...a season will result which will give great prestige to the Boston Opera Company, but to the city of Boston as well".

Stars were decided by the no-nonsense board. The Met had created "a short season at the Chatelet Theatre a few years ago"; last time "such a constellation of operatic stars has been gathered together in Paris...." Melba and Tetrazzini were known but heard "rarely of late" so "a royal welcome can be assured them".

For the Paris plan, Boston is slighted. Spring season "shortened from 18 weeks to twelve, and instead of reopening in November as in former years" date delayed to January 4, 1914.

Any pretense vanishes. Russell has apparently achieved his ambition to get paid in Paris and will forego any Boston focus.

Back in backwater Bean Town, Mary Garden ill, Melba cancels. "For three successive Saturdays the audiences have been disappointed, twice... Mary Garden was ill". Today "Melba would sing, and the diva arrived... and declared that though suffering from a cold she would try to sing *La Bohème*. She began to prepare for the matinee, but when she started to tune up no sound came. In alarm she called upon the doctor, who forbade her to sing if she wished to have her voice (*NY Times* Mar 7)".

Melba addresses audience, "My dear public, I am very very sorry to disappoint you by not singing this afternoon. I have been suffering from a cold three or four days. This morning my vocal cords were all right and I fully expected to sing but I am not able and am sorry, but will do so very soon".

Into the opportunity: "An even more extraordinary situation was the thrusting of young and untried Myrna Sharlow [of St. Louis] at a few minutes notice into the breach, while Melba herself remained in the wings to encourage and applaud her substitute. The performance was notable for the brilliant singing of Miss Sharlow who has youth, beauty, voice and intelligence in her favor" and a "great number of people" remain for the performance. Sharlow's understudy triumph, the stuff movies made of, propels her to Chicago Opera.

That March, the Weaver upright piano "used in concert work by Miss Alice Nielsen" and other fine artists is announced available at Almon J. Fairbanks, 521 Washington St., Boston: "In a class of its own".

March 19th a light alights on Russell's racket against Constantino (*NY Times*). Tenor tells press that Hammerstein's deliberate snub caused him to break the contract. The suit $25,000. Dated November 23, 1908, the contract gave the tenor ten shows at $500 each the first season, and $600 the second. Stipulates Constantino "advertised conspicuously", his name "lead all the rest". The contract's forfeit fee is the issue at law. Price makes an interesting calculus for Boston. One-hundred $5 tickets in big Boston Opera paid the tenor. House packs for him. Hollow rings Russell's foggy protestations about paying stars. Worst losers the shareholders and soon.

LA Times March 26th publishes "*Heart Songs*, the superb 20th Century song book with 400 of the sweetest songs in the world" with "full page halftone portraits of the sixteen greatest singers in the world". Each biographic sketch lists their favorite encore. Alice Nielsen joins Sembrich, Mary Garden, Emma Eames, Melba, Nordica, Adelina Patti, Jessie Bartlett Davis, Shumann Heink, Louise Homer, Johanna Gadski, Jenny Lind, Emma Abbott, Geraldine Farrar, Maria Gay, and Tetrazzini.

Nielsen blurb: "There is something of the winsome southern belle in the charming personality of Alice Nielsen, born at Nashville, Tenn., who studied music in San Francisco and made her first appearance on the operatic stage as Yum Yum in Gilbert's *Mikado* in 1893".

Favorite encore: "There is always a ripple of approval in an audience when Alice Nielsen responds with an encore in singing *Bonny Eloise*. *Bonny Eloise* with bonny Alice Nielsen singing it has set many a southern audience on fire. Men have cheered, women have wept, while its hallowed strains brought back wartime memories to the sons and daughters of the Lost Cause".

In fact, Celtic *Kathleen Mavourneen* vies with Georgia's *Swannee River*, Italy's *Goodbye Summer,* and Long Island's *Home Sweet Home* as her most popular encores. Not only did dad die on the anti-slavery side, her insistence on equality denies support for the long-lost slavery cause. Yet as Tennessee Congressman revealed during that conflict, the Confederacy was a secret racket by a few insiders who vamoosed to England. Of course, any ancient days must be recalled with cheers and tears. Regional pride at play. Tragic many boys lost to life so without building a better world.

Begins Boston Opera's departure (*Boston Post* Mar 30). Day had started with a brass band leading "a procession 400-strong" of civic groups from Boston City Club. Waiting is Red Star's *Lapland,* a two-stack steamer built in 1908 Belfast. "More than 5,000 people" crowd the pier to wave goodbye.

It ends poorly. People get unruly. Thieves roam the crowd. "Marred by extreme disorder, nearly all the members of the company were injured in the crush and some of them lost their hand baggage". Several women faint. Bruised are Myrna Sharlow, Beriza, Henri, Mrs. Danges; "Mme. Laffitte's handbag and tickets were wrenched away...and the manager WC McDonald was so injured about the stomach" he had to be carried aboard. "The company was angry over the episode".

Order restored, City Club's Frederick Fish and ex-Mayor Fitzgerald make speeches. The stand-in star "Miss Sharlow sang Star-Spangled Banner, some of her fellow-artists assisting, lines were cast off and the Lapland moved downstream, to shouting and the tooting of whistles".

So it was.

Arriving in Paris, "When the chorus first arrived they all went to the boarding house near the theatre, but now they have gained confidence in speaking the language, many have taken apartments". For chorus, Melba gives "a reception at her home in the Avenue Henri Martin".

Back in Boston May 2 (*NY Times*), Louise Converse, daughter of composer, gets engaged to Harvard's Junius Morgan, son of financier JP Morgan Jr. fast inflating an arms race into WWI with JM Keynes the bankster groupie.

Boston Opera opens Paris May 3 with opera not in French.

NY Times (May 3) says the start "exceeded all expectations". Boston gave the original language libretti with Urban's stage direction and set stylings first seen in Paris with Debussy thirteen years earlier. Debussy was no Converse of course.

Very alike the tone Russell used to poke himself the Boston opera job, rhetoric scorns the region: "Despite the competition of the [French] Opera and the *Opera Comique,* the Paris public is showing sincere appreciation of the effort to give it something new and different—opera in the original language of the libretti—with far better artists than are usually heard in Paris, and with scenery and stage management that are a revelation, for although the French acting standard is extremely high, the scenery and stage methods at best may be characterized as sloppy. The American chorus has already aroused great admiration, for the chorus is another item where the French" seem cheap.

And the tragedy closes for Nordica's distant shipwreck. Recovering from pneumonia and seeking to reunite with her husband in Genoa, Nordica leaves Thursday Island "against the advice of physicians". Relapses, dies in Batavia, Java. Her world tour began a year ago, April.

Alice's friend, costar, business partner is gone. A tragic loss to the gayety of nations. And to Alice Nielsen. Hearing of Nordica's death, their remora crazily claims "he had first introduced her to America with Alice Nielsen in the San Carlo Opera Company [of SF etc]".

Boston in Paris spring. Ticket sales for German operas are "heavy and there is every prospect of a splendid success", "wisely timed...concurrent with the Russian ballet at the Paris opera. *Parsifal* continues to be the greatest drawing card" says *Boston Globe*. The gayety of high culture truly unites the earth.

June 7, Boston Opera gives first "premiere of *Parsifal*" in German at Paris. Weingartner had mastered the score at 1882 Bayreuth. "Urban's production was of extraordinary beauty, and the choral effects were exceptional, the singers being aided by the boys' choir from the Church of Holy Trinity" known as American Cathedral, Episcopal confection for enduring edification (*NY Times*).

In June, the Paris-relocated Boston manager complains of competition in the third person as if Geraldine Farrar. French National Opera has counter-attacked. "The premiere of the new opera *Scemo*" now conflicts with Boston's *Otello*, and *Parsifal* June 15 had met with notice "the same opera will be sung on the same night at the National Opera".

Culprit is André-Charles Messanger (1853-1929), a man as familiar to Paris as Frederick Converse to Boston. The Boston hireling, buoyed by his recent success sending an American journalist off to jail on trumped-up charges of libel before a prejudiced judge, regards Messanger as spiteful. In response, Messanger declines to have an elitist goon squad drag Russell off to a mock court and imprisoned for libel. Coincidently, Boston's suppressed magazine editor Phillip Kahn begins appeals to Massachusetts Supreme Court on "numerous questions of law" (*Boston Globe* Jun 10).

Paris season of dislocated Boston Opera continues. Two weeks after Phillip Kahn files an appeal for justice, June 28th in Sarajevo a Yugoslavian Gavrilo Princip kills Franz Ferdinand, the Austro-Hungarian throne heir. Murderer Princip demands independence, never a bad thing. The incident organized by those who 1930s authors term "merchants of death".

Hapsburgs of Austria (remember murdered Ferdinand?) had pushed repeated crusades against Czechs until the 1614 White Mountain defeat lost the hijacked nationan its freedom of conscience; Treaty of Westphelia. Bohemians of Prague flee to Paris to inspire 19th Century poets, authors and opera where Alice Nielsen performs Mimi, who dies.

Rascal Russell rosily prattles plans for next summer's Paris season. Aping Nielsen's method of marshalling Bryn Mawr, ticket sales will be "organized by a committee of the most prominent women of Paris, who will guarantee a subscription sale of all the boxes for the season". Prominent are Duchesse d'Aosta, Princess Murat, De Polignac, and Mrs. Louise Stern. Over winter the theatre has been slated for newfangled "moving pictures".

July 28, month after Ferdinand murdered by Princip, Austria-Hungary declares war on Serbia for act of one man. Culture on the skids. Violence spreads fast and stalls for longer slaughters and the profits. Entire opera companies die. Composers, singers, conductors gone. Armenian genocide by Turks. European genocide by Europe and America. Nine million people die directly. The war racket creates in America alone, "eighteen-thousand millionaires and billionaires", reports Maj. General Smedley Butler in *War Is A Racket* (1935). Congressman Lindbergh in *Why Is Your Country at War* (1917) report details of coup which threw America into the war extending the slaughter two years. Conflict destroys Tsar, the hijacking Bolsheviks financed by Jacob Schiff and Otto Kahn who operate opera companies and launder funds to Trotsky until about 1920 when they can use banking transactions and stop opera pretense. JP Morgan will be shot twice in his parlor in front of his wife by a war protestor after packing munitions and celebs into cruise ships triggering the *Lusitania* tragedy later used as a propaganda excuse to bring the bailout which stops the British from suing for peace and defaulting the loan, says JM Keynes witness.

Largest conflict since Napoleon's wars makes Europe a battlefield until 1918, Russia 1924. Economies seized by war profiteers who command politics. In the encore, Stalin takes Russia, launches Hitler. Both financed by such as Jacob Schiff, Otto Kahn, JP Morgan of the Bankers Club atop 120 Broadway NYC. By 1917, Bernard Baruch commands the US economy from Washington, President Wilson sidelined by strokes, perhaps poison. As Trotsky the puppet Lenin. Keynes, who marries a Russian ballet dancer mysteriously quick-divorced from Henry Russell's assistant at Boston Opera, tells us instead of Britain suing for peace, paying Germany their reparations, defaulting the Schiff-Morgan loan, returning Constantinople to Tsar and Orthodox Christianity, they prolong the war to bailout the loan; then give the world a next war, Communism and Hitler. And Fritz Haber, chemist, personally debuts poison gas creating seventy-thousand battle casualties; returns home finding his PhD wife Clara Immerwahr in their garden dead by suicide of protest; does not prevent Haber receiving 1917 Nobel Prize. Covent Garden's Royal Opera House becomes a furniture warehouse until 1919, reopening ironically *La Bohème*, not *Daughter of the Regiment*. Song dies by mustard gas and machine guns.

Gayety of nations murdered by connivers. All so obvious.

Boston Opera's dislocation to Paris dissolves in chaos.

August 4th *NY Times*: "War Holds Stage Folk Needed Here. Frohman postpones three plays as Gillette, Sheldon and Miss Hedman cannot sail. Josef Urban Missing". Urban, feared seized by Austria's draft, is "anxiously sought. He has been engaged this Summer in designing the spectacular production the Liebler Company will make in the Park Theatre of *The Garden Of Paradise*". Producer George Tyler reaches Boston from Paris, tells press "Urban was on his way to Italy to join Sapelli, the costumer" and visit "great museum at Naples to study details of old costumes" before sailing for NY. Tyler could "get no trace of the man on whom so much of the success of this forthcoming production depends. Some of his sketches for scenery and costumes have been sent to NY, but the whereabouts of the artist remain a mystery...The firm is inclined to think that Mr. Urban has responded to the Austrian order of mobilization and is making the best efforts it can" to build the show from Urban's sketches. Of course, Urban's chief assistant Bennie Nielsen is key to doing so.

Boston Opera will be ne'er more.

August 27 from Scotland, Jordan cancels the Boston season, "War will deprive Boston of opera, Many artists scattered in various armies", reports *Boston Globe*. Jordan cabled, "Will not attempt to give a season of opera next Winter. This decision was made when it was learned definitely that fourteen singers and players at the Opera House have joined the armies and that many more will do so in the next few days".

The arts world recoils in horror as those great talents, "singers, musicians, painters and builders who came from all countries of Europe to the Boston Opera House to unite in producing a single work have now gone back to their countries to fight each other. The majority, however, have joined the Allies. Of the more prominent workers only Josef Urban, who introduced the new scenic art in America and Herr Adler...are fighting with the Austrians. There were practically no Germans employed" by Boston Opera as "German staff was borrowed from the Met...."

Joining French ranks are Andre Caplet, Marcoux five weeks' wed.

Deveaux and Deru join the Belgian Army.

"The drain...has not been greater because Italy has not yet been actively drawn into the encounter". If Italy goes into war "the entire male contingent of the chorus would be called...opera would be practically impossible".

At the first hint of hostilities Russell fled Paris for Italy. Fred Haley "a NY man" who, interestingly, is said to know Henry Russell "personally very well" arrives from Genoa on *Pincipie di Udine* August 29, telling *Boston Globe* that the Boston manager, "very low-spirited, asked him to tell the Boston newspapers...he is stranded in Genoa with fourteen of his business staff and without a dollar, and that they are living a hotel purely by sufferance of the proprietor". The group "left Paris in a great hurry when a declaration of war seemed inevitable...." Russell "failed to get any of his money which was tied up in the bank" of his friend and travel buddy.

As Russell hovels and Europe huddles, Alice Nielsen tours America adding to the gayety of the nation.

She returns to Kansas City October 23. *KC Journal*'s Frank Marshall tells us she receives a well-considered tribute as he describes home-town warmth, "It will be many a long day before Kansas City will tire of such a delightful woman and so satisfying an artist. Utterly unspoiled by the success which she has secured, a success resulting entirely from her own unceasing efforts, Alice Nielsen holds first place in the hearts of all Kansas Cityans, and she is welcome as the day is long, so often as she may have the opportunity of delighting her friends and charming her admirers here by 'singing for them.'

"That is perhaps the chief charm of Alice Nielsen's art, so far as Kansas City knows her. What she does in other cities and for other audiences, the people who love and admire her here have no means of knowing. But when she sings in Kansas City, she sings for and not merely to, those who come to hear her. There is a vast difference between the two methods. She is 'our Alice' and in that capacity she always dominates a Kansas City audience, even while achieving her most distinct artistic successes.

"The hundreds who applauded her to the very echo yesterday were thoroughly *en rapport* with her from the first note to the last, and she herself seemed to reciprocate the feeling, for she entered into every number with zest. Her art is steadily growing, ripening to the harvest....

"Long years of achievement may be confidently predicted for her as an artist pure and simple, and in these triumphs her friends in Kansas City will sincerely share".

"Typical Alice Nielsen programme, and of course, she sang *Comin' Thru The Rye*". She performs French, German, and English songs "in the best of spirits and superb voice. The warmth of her welcome seemed to please her immensely, and the bond of admiring friendliness which was a foregone conclusion before the concert began was strengthened with each succeeding number". She follows with Brahms, then *Un bel di*. Pianist Rudolph Ganz performs Chopin, Bach, and Hayden between vocal sets.

Whilst golden goose sings, November 27 (*NY Times*), Russell returns from Europe on Cunard liner Lusitania and visits Boston. Ambitions crushed, "He said he could not go into business matters relating to the opera company until he had consulted with the Directors". One director is the Met's Otto Kahn, and Kahn well knows the big money is in the war-making. That's why war was.

Returned manager bemoans corruption by others: "Paris...would have been a big success all Summer if the war had not intervened". Fallback hopes faded too, "It was a pity the Boston and Chicago opera companies had been taken off this season and there might be trouble with some of the artists". Points a finger at the Met bringing Nielsen back to Boston, "the tour of the Metropolitan Opera Company was one of the difficulties in the way of making a successful season..."

The star is on the stage.

December 13th Alice sings at a Ritz charity benefit for the New York Christmas fund. Same day, *Philadelphia Inquirer* oddly claims "the persistent rumor" Russell slides to Philly had "gained credence last night when ET Stotesbury, chief patron of opera in this city and a member of the Metropolitan Opera House Company of Philadelphia, refused to either deny or affirm the report". Stotesbury is far more alert and suspicious than Jordan who was dazzled by Alice Nielsen's performances at Park Theatre.

Stotesbury expresses "total ignorance of the alleged plan", prefers his own staff Celofonte Campanini and Bernard Ulrich. Trial balloon pierced: "The rumor came as a complete surprise to those interested in the Philadelphia-Chicago Opera Company. Its stars are regarded as being of a higher grade than the stars of the Boston Company. It was added that Philadelphia had received the very best in opera during the past seasons.... The rumor, emanating from Boston, came from Henry Russell".

Stotesbury continues knowingly, "Boston season was too long and the deficit large" so Russell seeks "patronage of Mr. Stotesbury".

Without stars, Russell is nothing. Boston Opera on hiatus.

Kahn spoke freely the truth people needed to hear. Whatever fate held the martyred journalist, he lost his magazine, his fate lost to us.

If Nordica had returned from her world tour, she could have saved it.

The Boston Opera Compay disbands. Building for rent. Furnishings for sale. Henry Russell caused Boston Opera's demise.

America's worst music tragedy. Boston's Hale a decade after: "If there is one great pity in the musical record of the United States that is remarked upon more than another, it is that the Boston Opera Company in 1914 had to go under [sic. Hale knows better]. What great things the company accomplished in the five years of its existence, what influence some of the reforms is started have had—especially in the line of scenic decoration—and what it might have done in holding American standards high, had it continued, are subjects that people interested in the cause of the theatre of song constantly review".

Boston Opera's great legacy is the creative community. Came to town of singers, conductors, chorus Italian and French, Loie Fuller's dancers, Russian ballet, Pavlova, Duncan. Gayety in the nation with Nielsen at the bat. Constantino. The Irish diva with Danish dad joining a Basque tenor inspired its creation.

Recalls Charles Wagner, Boston Opera "kept to a standard of production that lent to the five Boston years their peculiar artistic ambiance, never forgotten and never surpassed in the memories of those who experienced them". We could imagine Boston Opera operated by this talented manager Wagner. Andreas deSegurola recalls Wagner "good-looking and very sociable young man, who liked to talk to me about opera, singers and singing.... In a short time that man Wagner made history in the musical development of America. Charles Wagner became the most important artists' manager in the country. Mary Garden, Galli-Curci, John McCormack, John Charles Thomas, Fritz Kreisler, and other celebrities were soon under management contract to him. At this time, Charlie, as he became known all over the Americas, is national dean of concert agents and managers".

Boston Opera collapses. The entire contents of Boston Opera House slide to Rabinoff when son Robert sells the priceless legacy for a song. Rabinoff begins a National Opera Company of Canada; the "US impresario of Russian origin" after 1915 will produce a "Boston National Opera".

Christian Science Monitor (1914) cites Max Rabinoff, "head of the American Institute of Operatic Art at Stony Point, NY", that the Boston Opera budget had been $49,000 per week. Rabinoff, preparing to rent the Boston Opera building and remove its treasure-trove of properties, sets, costumes, hints at massive wrongdoing: "Without doubt, persons versed in theatrical management can determine...whether or not the money of the Boston Opera Company was carefully used. Just as those who directed opera in Boston were popularly supposed to spend extravagantly, those who handle matters in NY are commonly declared to spend penuriously and to devote their energies to making opera pay what amounts to dividends to stockholders".

So it is ended.

Boston is not the only opera company to close that winter. March 1914 diva Marie Rappold will rescue the touring Montreal Opera, abandoned in Denver. Its managers Mr. Hawkins, Mr. Baker, and interestingly Theodore Bauer one of Russell's cohorts at Boston, obtained advance bookings of $18,000. Skip town, stranding the players. Angel Rappold hires a special train to return the cast home to allow Montreal Opera disband with honor. Poignantly she says, "I've just been through such trouble... suffering not for myself alone, but from great anxiety over the plight of the chorus, the orchestra, and the lesser-paid singers ...the question whether they could get their salaries was one of life and death".

Officials graciously offer freely the Denver Auditorium for a fundraising concert. Despite a blizzard, townspeople pack the show. Rappold gives the difference, receiving honorary Denver citizenship.

Where there's fog, there's fire. None step up when Jordan needs Boston to protect his cherished lyric project. Had sidelined Isabel Gardner; Nordica lost at sea. Appalling scandal of continuous bad management left things all quiet on the lyric front. *NY Times* and Boston press tell the American public, Russell had vanished without a trace into war-swept Europe. Untrue. Boston board member Otto Kahn paid Russell's way to Monte Carlo where Alice Nielsen's friend Maxine Elliot, who had dated JP Morgan, had relocated. Elliot hosted Rothschild pal Winston Churchill between political jobs.

Interestingly, Russell's private secretary and bagman Randolfo Barocchi had married Boston Opera's Russian ballerina Lydia Lopokova (1892-1981). Before Boston she had danced with Diaghilev. When Russell skips Boston, Barrocchi works with Russell in Europe until he jumps over to London to run *La Boutique Fantasque* (1919) starring his wife in "a raucous performance with Leonide Massine in the Can-Can". In 1919 Lopokova quick-divorces if at all Barocchi to marry John M. Keynes, the British chief of war finance who had employed JP Morgan on commission to finance the Great War profitably. The new couple have Lopokova's marriage to Barocchi annulled on grounds of bigamy. Lopokova developed the habit of disappearing for months into Russia. She wed the mastermind of war finance inflation who ushered a generation of his nation into horrible death, a founder of World Bank. Now things get interesting, again. Keynes' diaries list sexual activity with men often banksters. Tall, gay of lads long before Lopokova, Keynes was fond of ballet. No children, he fond of boys bred by others. At the wedding he held hands throughout the ceremony with best boyfriend Lytton Strachey. Keynes is at the center of what Major General Smedley Butler calls racket war. Financial crimes against humanity. Keynes tells us Schiff and Morgan hijack US into WWI two weeks from British bankruptcy and default on loan. Suing for peace means sending reparations to Germany and handing Constantinople to the Tsar of Russia. Instead, he says, America's entry stops peace and continues the slaughter two years. America's mistake, said Churchill. Keynes' damage to the gayety of nations makes Russell's petty, but Russell was. They liked the same alike.

So it is.

After Boston fails, Russell does not vanish as *NY Times* misinforms the public. Paid agents of Boston Board member Otto Kahn, Russell and Barocchi handle Diaghilev's Ballet Russes and such groups laundering cash to hijack Russia. Barocchi manages the tours, Russell acts as Kahn's financial liaison with full financial powers. For example, Russell in Monte Carlo wires Kahn in NY: "Cable Diaghilev's January payment instantly or authorize me advance him money" December 15th, 1916. Payments for Nijinsky "duly relayed through Henry Russell" by Met business manager John Brown. Russell coaxes the Met to honor promissory notes he "apparently guaranteed" reports Lynn Garafola (*Diaghilev's Ballets Russes* 1998). Garafola skips Kahn's full usage of Russell. If a spy novel by Ian Fleming we'd know more. Facts make good fiction.

In any case, Boston Opera tottering, Otto Kahn slips Russell "several thousand dollars for his living expenses" according to the Met's Eaton, helping him abscond to do a few petty projects for Kahn. Instead of scraping scraps off Nielsen's petticoats or Jordan's largess, Russell takes the Kahn money and helps runs a racket. Dies as the poseur. Absconds, takes Boston Opera account books with him.

Alice's son Bennie waits out the war zone disappearance of Josef Urban and continues collaboration in NYC until the designer dies.

Recall that great glorious cultural gift known as Boston Opera?

Boston Opera is dark when its glorious developer dies. Eben Jordan Jr. called away the next year, 1915. Eben's youngest daughter has moved to England after marrying Queen Victoria's chaplain (*NY Times* Jun 11 1993). Rest of family relocate to NYC. Curiously, not trusty business manager Charles Taylor, but son Robert Jordan takes the reigns of Boston Opera House. 0Jordan family abandons ship. Building is leased eventually to the Shubert group. In 1970s after long disuse, demolished by fraud in the night against the wishes of many. Dreary brick dorm for Northeastern University now stands at Opera Place.

Where Alice Nielsen dazzled Boston into inspired gayety.

1915: TOURING SUCCESSES

Bittersweet concert career; profits peak as the tragic Boston Opera *Titanic* sinks to the bottom of time. Rarest gift of a home stage for sustained song: wantonly destroyed. Founding star Alice Nielsen sings only on other, less prestigious stages. Corrupt lyric murderer absconded to *Côte d'Azur* among the liars elite who make wars for cash. Betrayal of stars, the opera house, shareholders, Boston, American lyric culture. Shock and trauma.

Recall the hopes. Recall the genuine purpose of its founders. Alice's professional life will slowly turn obscure. Within seven years, activity wanes. Attractive becomes marriage to Stoddard and semi-retirement.

January 3rd, Nielsen joins a benefit in NYC. She immediately starts a concert tour to the West Coast. Her next Chautauqua tour, an annual cultural fair week eagerly awaited by the host communities she visits, has been put into the management hands of nephew Tommy.

As goes Boston Opera, so goes Charles Wagner. Kept her away from that stage in conspiracy with Russell; a cheat. Yet Wagner's contempt for Russell is everybody's contempt.

By 1915 Alice has comfortably settled into a star's suite at the Met building, in those days sited at 24th St. & 8th Ave. Nephew Thomas, sharing her Met suite, files bankruptcy January 16th. His plight appears related to the Boston Opera bankruptcy and disruption of cultural events from Europe due to the connived conflict. Crush his hopes and of many.

Thomas manages his aunt's schedule.

January 20, he writes Harry Harrison at Redpath Chautauqua, "Miss Nielsen will return from the Pacific Coast about February 23rd. She has about six dates in the east to fill after that time, leaving her free to do the Redpath dates from March 4th on". Alice limits her concerts: "She is desirous of filling all the dates postponed and will if necessary sing any other dates you may contract for, not exceeding sixteen in number, nor will she sing more than four concerts a week".

April 8 (*Boston Globe*), Alice gives a Boston concert "assisted by" baritone Rodolfo Fornari with pianist Emiliano Renaud, and William Reddick who becomes Nielsen's accompanist a decade. Imagine seeing Boston Opera House dark and foreseeing this magnificent opera house ever destroyed. At her Tremont Temple concert the grieving Boston music community of join her.

"There was a large audience, including many friends of Miss Nielsen during her association with the Boston Opera House". Skipping the usual German songs due to conflict over there, Alice presents "two groups of English songs, one of French, an aria from Mme. Butterfly.

"Known as a singer of beautiful voice, of archness and charm of personality, of a clearness and point of enunciation that made her singing of English songs and ballads a thing of intelligibility and delight to those who heard her, Miss Nielsen afforded enjoyment last night to an audience which proved that her popularity is not diminishing. Her voice retains body and intensity. Her singing of *Goodbye Summer* shows her in a colloquial style that has its attractiveness. With Mr. Fornari as a partner she impersonated Rosina in the scene from *Barber* with arch coquetry".

Reddick attracts praise, "Miss Nielsen was fortunate in her choice of an accompanist. Mr. Fornari, the ubiquitous baritone formerly of the Opera House, delivered Figaro's air with vivacity and variety that commended him and played up to Miss Nielsen in the scene from the opera. Mr. Renaud, an accomplished and sincere pianist, added to the program".

April 10 (*NY Times*) Alice Nielsen sings for the New York Mozart Society at West End Presbyterian still located at 105th Street.

April 22, Nielsen and Japanese spaniel "Li Hung Chang III" take the cover of weekly *Musical Courier* to celebrate start of her upcoming Chautauqua tour. Once again the highest-paid performer on that circuit, a popular annual thrill, a week-long performing-arts variety show taking place under a circus tent. Many performers, such as Arthur Pryor's Band, provide the variety. The cultural festival closes with Alice Nielsen. Singing six nights a week in six different towns, she travels in a luxury private train car, making the short hops from town to town. Nothing new for her, the car gets big publicity. Same transport she has used since 1896.

Starts April 22 in Jacksonville, Florida, closes September in Illinois.

May 1915. Alice Nielsen pockets a fortune from Chautauqua, Columbia Records gives her extensive promotions, Boston Opera goes bankrupt.

Instead of sustained operatic arts at Boston Opera House, Nielsen sings art songs *en plein air* under a tent with pianist and violinist Karel Havlick. Her program described in Charles Wagner's display ad in *Musical America* as "Song Recitals, Five months Chautauqua tour of South and West".

Typical Chautauqua town is, say, Darlington, SC: Standing Room Only.

"Darlington's first Chautauqua week came to a close Thursday evening with a musical programme by the Metropolitan Opera star Alice Nielsen", says the *Columbia State* (SC May 2). "The pavilion was filled to its utmost capacity, and many stood around on the outside eager to hear Miss Nielsen. In response to the burst of applause that broke out from the audience at the conclusion of almost every selection on the program, the great singer responded very graciously to their demands and came back time and time again. The contribution of these artists was a fitting climax to the week of entertainment.

"The Chautauqua is already a permanent thing here. Even those who were lukewarm in the beginning have become outspoken in their praise and demand that the town shall have a return of the festival in 1916.

"The Alice Nielsen private car will reach Columbia May 19 and leave the following morning for Augusta.

"Alice Nielsen Day will close the Chautauqua. With Miss Nielsen will be a pianist and a violinist and her program will consist of English selections for the most part. Also she has consented to sing a number of familiar Southern melodies", closes *Columbia State* (Ma 6).

May 11, Boston Opera formally files bankruptcy. Patron Eben Jordan does not speak to his pain. Financial experts examines things carefully. Flaws found. Becomes an operetta plot. Erstwhile mismanager vamooses to Europe, preferring to brave war wrath over Boston's. Grabs record-books and contracts before hightailing out the door. His theft makes the audit difficult, all-too-long, and all-too-frequently very surprising. In tragic plight, Boston's big-hearted music lover Eben Jordan passes away.

Preliminary audit states "Liabilities of $215,570.77 and assets of only $78,900 were disclosed...when Boston Opera Company, a Massachusetts corporation, filed through its treasurer Charles Hayden, a voluntary petition of bankruptcy in the US District Court. No creditors are secured except for taxes or on duties on imported scenery still in bond. Eben D. Jordan is the principal creditor of the company, chief item on his accounts being $30,780, a loan advanced in open account. Jordan is also a creditor for $11,162 as assignee for sundry claims for labor and merchandise".

Other creditors: Amos Albee auditing service, advertisers, publishers, insurance, coal supplier, lawyers, and performers. The Met is due about $1,000 for rentals and artists. Artist contracts, $6,019. Additional creditors include Society Anglo-Americaine d'Opera ($17,139) and Anglo-Austrian Bank ($4,638) for "costumes and scenery". About "sixty claims, aggregating about $75,000 for services rendered during the Spring and

Summer of 1914 by members of the orchestra" appear which Jordan suggests should be reduced to "services during the contract period" December 14, 1914 to March 26, 1915. Boston Opera "sets forth that it entered into contracts for services of singers, musicians and mechanics for the production of opera" valued in excess of $170,000, declaring "each of these contracts is terminated in accordance with its terms".

Absconder shamelessly claims $13,677 as "disbursements on his trip to Europe in 1914" or about $270,000 in today's terms. Seems high 'twas. People are outraged. Belatedly Jordan joins Philip Kahn—not prison of course—to dispute the absconder's integrity: "The petitioning company states...doubt as to the validity and amount of this claim".

Most ominous: "all the contracts and data relating thereto are in the hands of Henry Russell, now said to be in Europe and inaccessible owing to the existing war" states *NY Times*.

Certainly in Europe, hardly inaccessible. Of course a war hides many financial sins. Send angry Boston posse a wrong direction. Boston board member Otto Kahn at the Met knows the Jordans well. Has a fiduciary responsibility to reveal Russell's hideout. Kahn, as had Jacob Schill and JP Morgan when looting Equity Insurance, evades justice. From Monte Carlo, Russell serves as Kahn's courier for money laundering via showbiz tours. Mass murder and vast theft added.

Nielsen has claim to fame. Russell infamy. 1970-era gossip Quaintance Eaton would hire Russell's daughter Dorothy to assist making articles. Eaton confides, "Russell cared little for children". She knew Dorothy's side of things. Eaton's feelings could be trusted; her facts not so much. Never penetrates surfaces. Yet conflicted, confused Quaintance Eaton brands Russell with epitaph doubtless true, doubtless lifted from somebody: "Pretentious, snobbish, vain, of slighter stature than even the many tiny tenors he engaged, he fitted exactly the average man's idea of an impresario—a term incidentally, which he loathed, preferring to call himself an 'artistic director.'"

Even Eaton's epitaph veers wrong. Average man's idea of an impresario is magnificent Maurice Grau, true and honest who loved people. And Grau family: Jules let audiences cast votes to determine the week's repertoire.

Grau: popular quality art: the average man's impresario.

Eaton's purloined quote continues: "Lacking the business genius and capacity for self-effacement of a Gatti-Casazza, he possessed Maurice Grau's ability to handle [abuse] stars yet only a degree of that bygone impresario's tact. Lavish as Henry E. Abbey, cocksure as Heinrich Conried, Russell revealed innate taste akin to Oscar Hammerstein's but missed that great entrepreneur's flair for the real *beau geste*". Eaton missed that flair for the real *bon mot*.

Despite Eaton's plagiarism and errors—well, as Socrates advised, "In the old days people believed the sayings of rocks and trees, if only what they said was true". Eaton closes: "This wily yet winning man arrived in Boston with relatively little experience as absolute boss of an opera company. He had fallen into to the job as many before and after him".

Hardly. Of course, Eaton receives space here only because hers was the only reference on Boston Opera when this writer began, her falsehoods widely replicated. Press agent puffery by a hirling of the absconder. Entirely discredited by Philip Kahn. Worse, Eaton chose to spin the rising arguments between star and scoundrel away from the facts: abuse of young singers, financial abuse of Constantino and Nielsen, and other ongoing corruptions which Philip Kahn reported.

Loie Fuller's facts remained hid in unpublished letter far too long.

Kahn's suppressed magazine buried in Boston archives. Difficult to discover; jailing of honest editor Kahn even the famed Hale feared to discuss decades after.

Worst possible fate: not a new Boston manager, but total loss.

May 11th Eben Jordan's son Robert and William MacDonald handle the Boston Opera bankruptcy. No practical help for the predicament appears. Robert Jordan, "stung by one more evidence of his opera management's slipshod [criminal] way of doing business...paid and paid" Eaton closes it.

Back in Boston, the Met's John Brown sifts the contracts and properties of Boston Opera. Facts in everyone's face, Nielsen ends Charles Wagner's reign. John Brown becomes next manager; perhaps educated Alice on Boston corrupt realities of erstwhile remora. Parroted praise henceforth ceases. Ever-reliable Brown later manages Carnegie Hall.

August 1915, *Bookman* reveals Arlita Doge, author of *Cabaret Dancer*, a Maine native and Boston University graduate, had been Russell's secretary at Boston Opera. Doge dodges telling the story she must know.

The remora? Grabs young soprano Shinn to Europe. Later by odd oddity, ever-meddling Melba brings him as entourage to Australia where he and Shinn take "under their wing the stage-struck daughter of Lord Dufferin" who he marries June 4, 1926 divorcing Shinn. Melba kicked him off her tour when he tried the predicable pigheaded brags of domination she knew he would.

So it is. Boston Opera's *Titanic* cultural legacy gets lost in the wind or under the rug. Edwin Bacon's *Book of Boston* pushes the accepted cover-up: "Opening of the great European War in 1914 had a crushing effect upon this enterprise, and the performances were abandoned, temporarily, as first supposed. At length, however, in January, 1916, Mr. Jordan [no, Robert] sold the Opera House".

Despite tragic demise, Boston Opera had a deep impact.

Nordica, Nielsen, and Constantino gave brilliant seasons. Of course, the true heights of possibility were only pending for this ensemble. Inspired talent tried to make this Boston showcase the world's best lyric theatre.

Many people took inspiration from Boston Opera. And Alice Nielsen.

Boston Opera's influence is hinted by three people inspired.

Jimmy McHugh (1894-1969) wrote music for Dorothy Fields' *I'm In the Mood For Love*. Born in Boston "where as a young man he worked as a rehearsal accompanist for the Boston Opera Company". Inspired.

Motion picture pioneer Louis Mayer credited his love of musicals to Boston Opera's tour of *Madame Butterfly*. Alice Nielsen sang. At twenty-three he began operating 600-seat Orpheum in Haverhill, MA, leveraging into a regional chain, starting NY booking agency. Starts a Los Angeles film production company now called MGM. Mayer created the super-successful MGM star system: "more stars than in the heavens". He liked quality wholesome entertainment. Seeks to make popular art pay, as Alice Nielsen onstage. At MGM Mayer produced: *Wizard of Oz, Babes in Arms, Girl Crazy, Meet Me in Saint Louis, The Pirate, Easter Parade, The Band Wagon, Gigi, On the Town, An American in Paris, Singin' in the Rain.*

Just one more. Young composer Virgil Thompson saw Boston Opera on tour in Kansas City. During Gluck's *Orpheus and Eurydice*, the singers combined with Pavlova's ballet to dance and mime the story. Thomson admired the effect so much he applies that vision to 1927's *Four Saints*, libretto by Gertrude Stein.

Alice Nielsen made quite an impression. Inspiration.

Seeded a rising generation of artists by her example, giving the experience of a compelling, audience-intriguing art melded to a powerful aesthetic vision. People never forgot her; the great voice as she said, is unforgettable. Alice keeps singing.

Chautauqua's 1915 brochure describes her progress.

Jacksonville, Florida, brings out society "in full evening dress—an innovation at Chautauquas". Guest at Jacksonville Country Club. At Savannah GA, guest of honor for the Savannah and Columbia "base-ball" teams of South Atlantic League. The two teams are her guests at Chautauqua. And as everywhere, the ladies of Monroe NC bank the stage "beautifully and elaborately" with flowers.

Standing Room Only. Art songs in four languages.

As many as three-thousand people attend each Nielsen recital—although the tent seats only two-thousand. Chautauqua estimates Nielsen sang to 100,000 people during each tour. She travels in the Pullman "used by Presidents Taft and Roosevelt, Lillian Russell and Sarah Bernhardt. Nielsen's tour was the longest time the car was used by a single person".

What a festival; the moveable Woodstock. Chautauqua's outdoor camp meetings started as a cultural revival in upstate New York. Spread into Midwest and South. The name percolates across the nation for such events, such as the Chautauqua Park in the Black Hills of South Dakota at Hot Springs. The tour skips brick-and-mortar theatres controlled by monopolies. Music the big attraction. Alice Nielsen, biggest attraction. Her arrival to any town signifies "Alice Nielsen Day".

True Americana is the Chautauqua. Women's clubs sponsor the festival events. Garden Club of Newberry SC knew what it meant to have Alice Nielsen appear, just as Bryn Mawr's Chicago alumnae association knew. Neither Bryn Mawr nor Newberry have kept the splendid memory alive. Newberry, near Shealy's BBQ in Batesburg-Leesville, continues to operate a splendid 1881 Opera House by CL Norman.

Gay MacLaren tells his Chautauqua experience in *Morally We Roll Along* (1938): "Most pretentious of all the chains was the Redpath de Luxe Circuit managed by Harry P. Harrison...first organized in 1912. This circuit set up its first tent in Jacksonville, Florida, in April and the last one on the shores of Lake Michigan in Chicago the second week in September.

"In 1915 Redpath took Alice Nielsen...over the circuit in a private [rail] car. This was an innovation for Chautauqua [not Nielsen] and it was a question which made the biggest hit, the singer or the car [weak humor]. It was found that a private car switched onto a siding at the village depot [as usual] created a furor among the small-town inhabitants, so the idea was repeated the following summer with Julia Claussen of the Chicago Grand Opera Company".

Response each place was what we expect.

Montgomery Advertiser AL: "Miss Nielsen, surrounded on all sides by the floral tokens of regard of her many admirers, sang her way into the hearts of her hearers and added another triumph to her already large store. The restless audience quieted and all noise subsided into silence on her entrance, only to be broken by volumes of applause at the close of each number of an appealing and delightful program".

Augusta Chronical GA: "Alice Nielsen's voice is too well-known and her position in the musical world too secure to need any comment or criticism here. Her voice is not a heavy soprano, but is extremely sweet and wonderfully clear and flexible, her high notes sounding like a bird's sweetest note. Her mastery of voice placement and tone was marvelous.... Possibly no higher tribute will ever be paid Miss Nielsen than the fact that the big audience remained in their seats after two hours and a half of music and insisted on one more song. Possibly to many the last, *Home, Sweet Home*, was the most beautiful of all".

South Bend Tribune IN: the singer arrived Tuesday morning July 27 "in a special car which Pullman company has named 'The Alice Nielsen Car.' A party of seven people travel with her". Photos has son Benjamin T. beside his mother. "She will spend the morning in the car and in the afternoon she takes a 40-or-so-mile automobile ride". She keeps silence before singing, "she never enters in a conversation with anybody in the car", reports Alfred Arvold, who revamps her pilgrim progress via Louis Strang, "Her father was a Dane. He tried to make a living by playing violin, but failed. He loved art more than money". Alice "never lost her youth, she loves her work and retains good health". Her "concert programs are always varied. She is ever-mindful of her audience. She is very particular about her health and especially her voice. She loves flowers. She enjoys her Chautauqua work very much, having already appeared on eighty programs since the middle of April".

Danville Register IL: "Miss Nielsen's first appearance in this city, but there is little hazard in the prophecy that it will not be her last if the ovation accorded her last night may be accepted as any criterion or basis for prophecy. Her winsome personality, and her rare powers as a vocalist evoked enthusiasm and assured her a place in the kindly and cordial remembrance of those who heard her sing and made her acquaintance in this public way.

Battle Creek Enquirer MI: "Alice Nielsen sings as the birds sing, without effort, clearly, sweetly, every note perfect. She sang—but why try to tell how she sang in words? She is wonderful and her voice, if possible, is more wonderful even than she is". "Everybody in her audience loved her, and were terribly proud because she is an American...." She was grrrrrr-reat.

Port Huron Times-Herald MI: "Miss Nielsen's gracious manner and sweet girlish appearance immediately won for her a warm place in the hearts of the great audience which had gathered to hear her sing. And sing she did, in a rich beautiful voice, not only some of the operatic airs but some of the sweet old-fashioned tunes that have lived through years of usefulness and will live on through the years yet to come".

Saginaw Courier-Herald MI: "Gracious and charming, Miss Nielsen delighted her hundreds of auditors last night, not alone with her superb singing but also with her pleasing personality. Hers is a lyric soprano voice that has no equal in America. Clear and sweet and strong, her vocal ability seems to have no limitations. Although she has been singing night after night in the open for several months, her voice has not been affected, and she has established a record for great singers. Her enunciation is clear and distinct and her tones are beautiful...."

And that shall suffice for impact.

Chautauqua was very competently organized in best theatre style to give a year's supply of culture in a week, a performing arts "revival", a friendly, familial cultural circus wildly popular at popular prices. Here is the process: "As the Chautauqua season approached, a great army of advance men armed with placards, banners, and bills and 'one-sheet' swooped down on the circuit towns to announce the coming of the great week of culture", said MacLaren. From the middle of June (or April on the Southern circuits) straight through until September, preparations for Chautauqua Week were going on all over the United States. Housecleaning, canning and sewing were speeded up and disposed of so that the women of the farms and villages would be free for the 'feast of good things' to be set before them.

"Music was provided Chautauqua patrons in every conceivable form from banjo trios to 40-piece bands, from ladies' quartettes to Madame Schumann-Heink and Alice Nielsen. Groups of dusky Hawaiians, Filipinos and Serbians with native dress and instruments were always popular, and every summer the tents and auditoriums echoed with the Ooo-lea-eee-hooo of the Swiss yodelers".

The Circuit played about 120 towns. Redpath required a $2,100 guarantee from townspeople who pledged to sell 700 season tickets at three dollars. Cost of bringing Chautauqua to town $2,500, short of the actual expenses. Redpath gambled on adding the single admissions to make it pay.

"The most modern equipment was carried in this circuit. The tents, with a seating capacity of about two thousand, were what was known as square-end tents. Especially-designed folding chairs were used, which were a far cry from the old backless plank benches of early Chautauqua days. The stage was forty-feet wide and twenty-feet deep, with special drops to be used for the dramatic and opera companies and a good lighting system. There were dressing rooms on each side of the tent and a pup tent in the rear for the crew. The cost of operating the Redpath de Luxe Circuit was in excess of $16,000 a week [about $341,000 today—twice expense of *Fortune Teller*]".

"When it was time for the Chautauqua to open, the talent, musical, stage and educational directors, general and circuit managers, superintendents, advance men, junior works and crew boys left on a private train—the Redpath Special—going straight to Jacksonville. Seven Pullmans were required to carry the 'Redpath family' and eight seventy-foot steel baggage cars to transport a half million pounds of tents, stages, chairs and electrical equipment. On the way back to Chicago, the regular trains were used".

Alice Nielsen's preferred publicity pattern: in each town, her secretary visits the newspaper, sometimes with the star.

Elyria Ohio's *Telegram* writes, "Miss Nielsen and her private secretary Mrs. Stickle were callers at *The Telegram* office yesterday" joking that Nielsen had heard of the editor's fine voice and beseeched him to sing her a song.

During this year's tour, she gave Cadman and Nelle Eberhart the idea for a song based on her dad's story about meeting his father on the moon. Old friend Arthur Pryor and band were on the circuit. And Hortense plays venues such as Strand Theatre in Manchester NH with Bernard Shaw's *Arms and the Man* as Raina, giving "a beautiful performance, glowing with vitality, immensely skillful, and at times richly comic" with Wilbur Braun, Edwin Dudley, Jeanett Cass, and others. Scenery by French; settings by Newman; Costumes by Evens".

As Nielsen tours, she hits top of the charts (*Chicago Tribune* Jun 13) with recordings of "*Love's Old Sweet Song* and *Bendemeer's Stream*".

Chautauqua's Frank Clure (*Independent* Jul 21) in "Under The Big Tent" recalls: "The five months' Chautauqua tour of so noted a star as Miss Alice Nielsen, prima donna soprano of the Metropolitan and Boston Opera Companies, has caused wide comment in musical circles as an innovation which will open new and broader fields to the greatest musical talent. Miss Nielsen is at present in the South, where she is being greeted by great crowds". To help acoustics, "prior to her recital, which is on the last night of each Chautauqua, a special preparation is applied to the tent which makes a sounding board of the roof". And he discusses logistics at length.

Today Chautauqua's impact is lost to us; a lost gayety of the nation.

Back in 1915, however, Frank Clure asked the Minnesota governor Adolph Eberhardt to speak on it: "If I had the choice of being the founder of any great movement the world has ever known, I would chose the Chautauqua Movement" because it is "a constructive, a community-building and a business force". Chautauqua makes people think better of themselves.

As Alice tours the appreciative hinterlands with her private luxury train car, back in Boston the great opera building stands grimly unoccupied.

Alice-and-Hortense selected costumes, Josef Urban sets, stage equipment intact. Robert Jordan and the Board fail to appoint a new manager and rebuild. Music-lovers are stunned—Boston Opera shareholders outraged—when the Board who had given huge raises to the failed manager, abandon ship.

Frederick Johns makes an impassioned plea. Perhaps he tought of Oliver Wendell Holmes, poet-lawyer-judge who saved "Old Ironsides" with: *Aye, tear her tattered ensign down! Long has it waved on high, And many an eye has danced to see That banner in the sky. Nail to the mast her holy flag, Set every thread-bare sail, And give her to the god of storms,—The lightning and the gale!*

Johns speaks freely: "Shame on the wealthy people of Boston who are permitting $250,000 worth of the finest operatic scenery in the world to be peddled away piecemeal for a tithe of its value. Isn't there in the whole town a single millionaire who will step into the breach and save this marvelous Boston Opera House equipment for a future opera company? Isn't there the slightest public spirit among the wealthy denizens of Beacon Street, Commonwealth Avenue and Brookline who attended the opera for five years and heard some of the finest performances there that have ever been given in the world?"

"Boston is the richest city per capita in America. There are more millionaires here in proportion to the population of the city than anywhere else in America. Can't any of them be found to take up the burden that Eben Jordan laid down?

"Mr. Jordan invested the best part of two million dollars in opera in Boston. He supported it single-handed for five years. During this time I heard much conversation from society people in the opera house lobbies to the effect that the opera should be supported by a coterie of the choicest people rather than the burden of one man. Where is that coterie...?"

Johns raises the banner of public interest: "The public of Boston supported the opera much better than the public of Chicago or Philadelphia. The season in Boston averaged twenty weeks. In Chicago they were compelled to cut it to eleven and in Philadelphia they cut it to six weeks. Yet the wealthy people of Chicago have come together and reorganized their opera company so that they can have a stronger company and better season than ever this year".

Johns is intensely practical. Boston Opera stood in receivership of Joseph Conry with liabilities $250,000. Scenery and costumes easily worth that. The standing offer is from "Max Rabinoff, who is organizing a combination opera and ballet company", the former piano salesman based in Chicago.

Johns reasonably recommends a proven Boston manager: "The logical man to reorganize and manage the Boston Opera Company is Charles Ellis, manager of the Symphony Orchestra. Mr. Ellis is a business man, and if assured of the proper backing would probably undertake the task". Ellis had profitably managed the Met's recent three-week Boston season.

Ellis would "undoubtedly reawaken interest in opera so that the formation of a local company will not be difficult if the scenery and costumes are ready and waiting". Johns speaks of urgency: "The present need is to see that they do not leave Boston". Second crucial time, Boston ignores a wise journalist. Nobody responds to Johns' impassioned plea.

August 15th, *Boston Globe* sadly reports: "Stage At Opera Is Left Bare, Scenery, Costumes and Appliances Carted away". Boston Opera House had been stripped "of all its movable equipment down to the very electric bulbs". The outlook wasn't brilliant for the Boston chaps that day. Oh, somewhere in this favored land the sun was shining bright; the band was playing some-where, and somewhere hearts were light, And somewhere men were laughing, and somewhere children shout; But there was no joy in Musicland —the mighty Boston had struck out. Glory gone. Rabinoff scavenges scenery, costumes and props. He plans to give opera and ballet starring Anna Pavlova next season. The ballerina has been offered a lucrative starring film role which will help finance.

Boston Opera, meant to stand forever: "The costumes and settings had been put together with a similar intent. The richness of velvets and laces for many of the costumes which clothed singers in minor parts and members of the chorus would have been welcomed by the wealthy...for the latest gowns".

For seven weeks, fifty workmen labor to ship Boston's costumes and sets to Rabinoff's storage facility outside NYC, "working all day and long into the night". He obtains for "a song...properties of forty-seven operas, properties which it took five years and $500,000 to construct".

Rabinoff hires erstwhile Boston department heads: Josef Urban, electrician Brunton, conductor Roberto Moranzoni, "even Martha Pellgrini and Armondo Finzi, in charge of costumes". Pellgrini "herself sewed on the lace and other material that went to making of so many of the gorgeous costumes seen on the Boston Opera Stage". Picking a page from "San Carlo" ruse, Rabinoff rudely tours as "Boston Opera Company" in 1916, revising the name a year later at Salt Lake to "Boston-National Opera Company" with "Boston Grand Opera Company orchestra". Many original Boston Opera cast carry over. Not Nielsen.

Rabinoff (1878-1966) in 1922 will pitch an "American School for Operatic Arts" at Stony Brook-on-the-Hudson. Partners include Otto Kahn. The use of opera to launder funds has been noted. When Russia falls to Trotsky and Stalin this and other operatic fronts vanish because the banksters can directly deal.

For all practical purposes Boston Opera permanently vanishes August 15th. The stripped building is leased by the Shuberts for touring musicals.

So it is. That is how Boston Opera House became lost to us.

Alice spends summer singing six days weekly outdoors under a tent on the popular Chautauqua circuit. Returns to NYC in glory with piles of gold.

September 19, she returns from Chautauqua after singing "3,000 songs in 118 days", reports *NY Tribune*. Alice Nielsen sang 150 concerts on a six-per-week basis. Paid $50,000 in gold dollars ($1.1-million today).

The next-most expensive act was Giuseppe Creatore's brass band who had played Kansas City about 1890 with Arthur Pryor and brothers in the group. Dawn of radio, silent movies. Sound recordings. Microphones arise with the talkies.

Silent films will employ many musicians and talkies will fire them. The golden age of live performance is over. No longer must stars sing in person.

Marking this change, October 10th *Boston Sunday Globe* tells of Victor Herbert's score for a photoplay by DW Griffith, *Birth of a Nation*, playing at the same Majestic theatre where Nielsen sang a 2nd Boston season.

Disparaging film, stage star Wolf De Hopper speaks: "There is plenty to be said of the movies as an institution, an art and an influence on modern life, and plenty are saying it. I confine myself to personal grievances. First, the art does not appeal to me as an actor. The appeal of acting to those who practice it lies in the enkindling of the emotions of an audience and the reward of applause, laughter and tears then and there. This is the actor's daily bread, and the movies offer him a stone. One cheer in the hand, as far as I am concerned, is worth ten thousand in the bush. I would not swap the audible applause of the couple in the last row upstairs for all the fan mail in the post-office. So both the movies and I are satisfied".

Hopper believes the radio craze will pass like the 1880s' roller skate fad, and theatre owners someday drop films to return to live theatre. A few theatres have, Atlanta's Fox.

Boston Opera: April dark; May bankrupt; September empty. Decades later demolished, almost inevitably, by a next act of sly corruption.

Another weighty page of Nielsen's life turns 7th November. Thomas Williams dies at fifty-six (*LA Times*). His only fame, says the obit, was backing Alice Nielsen Opera Company. Also operated Bay View Race Track with twenty-five years at California Jockey Club. His crimes and assaults go strangely unmentioned. Shot *News-Letter*'s editor Marriott three times in cold blood; conspired to defraud and cheat Alice Nielsen. Surviving him, crazed shouter Beatrice Steele and two kids perhaps his own. Nielsen will later list Tom Williams among her closest men friends.

And she keeps performing. Pointless European wars keep murdering.

After her Chautauqua marathon, Nielsen joins the Humanitarian Cult concerts. Founded by baritone Mischa Appelbaum to protest capital punishment. Now vanished, the group had 4,000 members in 1916. Plays and movies supported its views.

November 14th, plans are announced for Nielsen to join Chicago Opera and in Los Angeles with a "La Scala Opera Company" in January.

LA Times heralds her return (Nov 14). The "popular prima donna... guest artist with the La Scala Opera Company to be heard here in January at Clune's Auditorium. She has been secured for a limited number of guest performances after her season with the Chicago Grand Opera Company". The company "assembled in Italy...will number 134" plus orchestra fifty.

LA Times adds a wishful canard: "And it is said that she has been prevailed upon to sing in a revival of *The Bohemian Girl* or *The Serenade* in English, just which has not been decided". This does not happen.

November 25th, reports suggest a Broadwa return in a musical adaptation of JM Barrie's *Little Minister*. Nielsen mentions Wolf-Ferrari as composer. This suggestion develops into something else before reaching the stage with Alice.

In November, Alice Nielsen awaits her Chautauqua scrapbook. She has never hesitated to make demands on management. After all, she is on the stage. November 25, she writes Chautauqua manager Harry Harrison, "When will I get the scrapbook & you know I did not all of the notices of my tour as I depended on you for a book. It was very kind of you to send the large photographs and I appreciate it very much". Harrison loses no time meeting her demand, sending the clipping book by messenger.

November 26, as she joins NY's Sunday Hippodrome concert with John Phillip Sousa, scrapbook arrives: "Thank you a thousand times for the beautiful scrapbook. How kind of you to have it so beautifully done for me. & will you kindly thank the one that put it together so beautifully. When do you expect to be in New York? I shall treasure the book as a souvenir of a wonderful tour & a most courteous and kind friend. Greetings to you and your family, Yours sincerely, Alice Nielsen".

She postpones full payment but charges interest: December 4th, keenly aware of financials, Alice writes Harrison: "I want to do everything in my power to help you, and at great inconvenience to myself I have arranged my affairs so that I can do with $500 Monday instead of the $1500 I had counted on getting. I wired you today that I can arrange to do this. The note was deposited with my bank (State Street Trust Company) some weeks ago. Undoubtedly the bank has forwarded the December 6 note to Chicago for collection. As soon as I have received your answer to my telegram, I will communicate with the bank and have them recall this note.

"You see Mr. Harrison, I had either spent, or planned the spending, of this money, and it is very difficult for me to suddenly change my plans. As I have said, I want to do everything I can to meet your wishes, and I have thought out the following arrangement". Charges 6% interest. Tells him to send her first, the check for three months' interest ($48.75), then eight notes for $343.75. "Insomuch as I am willing to make this arrangement solely because of you personally, I am sure you will be glad to put your personal endorsement on these notes". Returns his $1,500 note.

December's *Theatre Magazine* interviews her for January as *Alice Nielsen, The American Patti*. Doubtful she likes the label. Photos in costume as Butterfly, Marguerite, Zerlina, Norina, Mimi are featured, plus a day dress profile of the singer in an exquisite white fur hat, coat and shawl. "Miss Nielsen made a brief stay in NY recently to celebrate Christmas with her small niece and nephew and while here she chatted with" the perceptively sensitive writer Elsie Lathrop.

Nielsen recalls a time with Baron Rothschild at Park Lane, London. With Landon Ronald [Henry Russell brother] at piano, she sang *Il Bacio* and *Last Rose of Summer*. In Nielsenian theory, *Il Bacio* was only for Patti to sing. In fact Melba, Nordica, and many others sang it at Rothschild's. Whatever the case, Alfred Rothschild has delight: "You are a duck! I do not mean that you sing like a duck, but you are one all the same". He impulsively gives her a diamond-studded gold horseshoe. Tells Lathrop this was her first party after *Fortune Teller* closed, so the timing is early July 1901. Consuelo Yznaga, New Orleans' own Duchess of Manchester had arranged the party. Henceforth, "Miss Nielsen was engaged for many concerts in London, both private and public". Obviously, such money appeared instantly upon abandoning Shaftesbury Theatre.

After Nielsen sings for Chicago Opera, her publicity blurb proclaims her as prima donna for the Met, Boston, Chicago, Montreal companies. Her stint with anything labeled "San Carlo" goes out the fenestration.

December 4 *Musical America* reports, "Alice Nielsen, who has just completed a short concert tour of Kansas and Missouri...has been engaged for *Don Giovanni* with Chicago Opera...on January 3".

LA Times (Dec 12) announces La Scala Opera Company would open January 17th, "interest is growing rapidly in the season of grand opera...at Clune's Auditorium...particularly as the company promises to be the best heard in repertoire here in several seasons. Besides Alice Nielsen, always a favorite star" will arrive Rosing Zotti, Giuseppe Vogliotti, Ernesto Giacone and Claude Albight. Conductor Guerreri "has directed more operas in this city than anyone else.... He has always been a great favorite here on account of his superb control and beautiful interpretation..."

Christmas day brings Nielsen's last Met appearance; accidental. Subs for Hempfil as Rosina in *Barbiere* with 1-day's notice at Brooklyn. Figaro: Giuseppe De Luca; conductor Gaetano Bavagnoli. Only one performance 1913, two last Met operas 1915. Interestingly, Nielsen's complete schedule at the Metropolitan grew heaviest just before joining Charles Wagner's the heavy touring schedule. Sings at Met fourteen times, three in NYC. Press very clear about her NYC popularity; famed since 1896.

Alice Nielsen with the Met:

1909 Nov. 16 Philadelphia: *La Bohème*; 1909 Nov 20 NYC *Bohème*.

1910 February 16, Baltimore: *Rigoletto*; February 25: NYC: *Don Pasquale*; April 5: Chicago: *La Bohème*; April 9: Chicago: *Martha*; April 20: Chicago: *Il Maestro di Cappella, Don Pasquale*; April 21: Chicago: *La Bohème*; April 23: Chicago: *Martha*.

1911: January 18: NYC: *La Bohème*; January 31: Brooklyn: *La Bohème*.

1912: January 19: NYC: *La Bohème*.

1913: April 10: Boston: *Cavalleria Rusticana, Pagliacci*.

1915: December 25: Brooklyn: *Il Barbiere di Siviglia*.

New Orleans, Chicago, San Francisco, Los Angeles, Montreal, and Boston will remain Nielsen's most frequent American performance venues. Her tours reach every major city in North America and many minor ones.

She stands willing to give Broadway a last try.

1916: ALL FINE & HOPE FOR A BIG HOUSE

Nielsen's schedule as guest artist and touring stays heavy until she leaves for another European summer, despite war raging. For fall, Nielsen returns sailing from Copenhagen. Touring will taper down within a couple years.

Another milestone: Barnabee of the Bostonians publishes his wonderful witty *Reminiscences*. He speaks very well of her. Also this year, Eugene Cowles sings his famed *Armorer's Song* of *Robin Hood* by telephone from NY's Waldorf-Astoria to the Metal Trades Association in San Francisco. Cowles tours his Eugene Cowles Quartet, composes popular songs; big hit ballad *Forgotten*.

During 1916, Alice Nielsen's *Home, Sweet Home* climbs to number twenty-nine in worldwide record sales as her biggest hit.

Opera work continues in Chicago and LA. January 3rd, Nielsen gives *Don Giovanni* in Chicago with a familiar cast: Destinn, John McCormack, Scotti, Renaud, and Gilibert. *Chicago Daily Tribune*'s Eric Delamater (Ja 20) tells us the rare talent McCormack is "one of the few tenors of the day who are not dismayed entirely by the Mozart text".

January 17th Alice Nielsen, misspelled "Neilsen" by *LA Times* feature, is in LA's Clune's Auditorium with La Scala Grand Opera conducted by Fulgenzio Guerrieri. *Rigoletto* Tuesday, *La Bohème* Thursday and Saturday matinee, "*Il Trovatore* or *Lucia*" on Saturday night. And January 27, *Secret Of Suzanne*. *LA Times* remarks *Bohème* occurred in 1830 "some 85 years before Europe was seeped in blood".

Floods delay Nielsen's arrival so Rosini Zotti substitutes as Mimi. From her stalled train, "Golden State, Chicago-St. Louis-Kansas City-California", Nielsen writes Chautauqua's manager Harrison, "Here I am stuck in this place and missed closing the season in Los Angeles".

Most concerning for Alice, as always, is arrival in San Francisco: "Poor Mr. Behmer he is almost crazy, but not more so than I by my anxiety now is whether I can reach SF for the Monday opening that will indeed be a calamity if I can't. The floods here have been something terrible and all trains have been delayed. Should you be in San Francisco while I'm there, I should be delighted to see you. I shall stop at the St. Francis [Hotel built 1904, rebuilt 1907, still located on Union Square]. "With all good wishes to you and your family, believe me, Yours sincerely, Alice Nielsen".

January 30th in *LA Times*, Nielsen endorses yet another player piano, "The Art-Apollo is wonderful. In listening to its duplication of human playing, I find it difficult to realize that the pianist is not actually seated at the keyboard. Everything that characterizes the individuality of the artist is faithfully reproduced. On hearing this instrument, I think every musician will appreciate its influence as a factor in the musical education of all classes. Yours truly, Alice Nielsen". Frank Hart's Southern California Music Company will grab "your silent piano" in part-payment to deliver a brand new Art-Apollo.

Whatever understanding held between Nielsen and Charles Wagner, as we have alluded, after Boston Opera sinks he does not last long into 1916. She has cut Wagner by January. During their collaboration, Alice Nielsen helped him meet people in her usual supportive style. She connected Wagner to Caruso and other stars in her circle to give him opportunity for success. The Nielsen-Wagner separation never airs in public. She is determined to proceed without his help. Perhaps realizes her absence allowed the destruction of Boston Opera.

Alice installs nephew Thomas as assistant at her Met suite. Her choice puzzles the planning staff of Redpath Chautauqua. February 1st, Redpath staffer L.P. Crotty writes Thomas Nielsen at 1425 Broadway (Alice's suite at the Met), "We have heard from both you and Mr. Wagner and we hardly know just how to treat this matter since Mr. Harrison is on the Pacific coast and we are not informed as to which one we should give the information to. I shall be indeed glad to hear from you as to which one is going to handle the dates as we want the matter straight in order that we may correspond with the proper party and avoid any kind of mix-up".

Planned shows include Indianapolis, Racine, Lexington KY and Battle Creek the week of April 3; Springfield IL and Quincy the week of April 10. Rapidly Thomas Nielsen responds on his letterhead "Telephone 1274 Bryant, Thomas Nielsen, 1425 Broadway, New York" to Crotty in Evanston, Ill.: "beg to advise you that Miss Nielsen informed Mr. Harrison when he was in NY last, that I would act as her exclusive representative until she announced her new managers, so please consider me as such until further notice".

She is "determined to give 15 to 20 concerts between March sixth and week of April 10th" so "...I think you had better advise me what can be done for the other time". Tantalizingly, Thomas reveals Alice has movie offers.

"Trusting that you will communicate with me immediately as there are opera and movies to be considered". Specific film offers were not disclosed. Before 1920, the likely possibility would be Alice joining Lois Weber with Pavlova and remnants of Boston Opera Company. Not only Pavlova from Boston Opera, but several close colleagues adopt Hollywood: Marguerite Sylva marries and has a boy before launching her 1920-1940s film career; iconic Marie Dressler stars in thirty films 1914-1933 (big hit with Chaplin); Joe Cawthorn gains fifty-five film credits 1927-1942. Alice's son Bennie assists designer Josef Urban who will design twenty-five films for Marion Davis and others before 1933.

Alice Nielsen returns to opera-shocked Boston in February, warmly greeted for her gayety. Sings the 15th "before a large audience", joined by contralto Cara Sapin, cellist Ralph Smalley, and her usual accompanist William Reddick. John O'shea accompanies Sapin and Smalley, "prefacing the concert with a medley of patriotic airs" (*Boston Globe*). Sadly performs "indisposed...notwithstanding the handicap, which she succeeded to a great extent in overcoming, she gave her hearers evident pleasure throughout the rendition of her varied numbers".

Five days later, Eben Jordan's daughter Dorothy marries Teddy Roosevelt's nephew in Boston at Trinity. Bride wears white satin with court train and 18th-century Venetian lace; does not carry bouquet. Nielsen's subversion of Jordan's propriety is proved by his kids. Robert would marry an actress; Dorothy "won celebrity in society for her dancing", makes a debut in 1911's *Secret of Myrto*, dances in vaudevilles, joins "Vincent Sewing Circle".

Thomas Nielsen has his own projects beyond coordinating Aunt Alice. February 21, he pitches Harrison a lecture tour for "Dr. Karl Graves, the secret agent employed by the German Government" now in NY "producing a play dealing with his experiences...working for the Kaiser". Graves' *Secrets of the German Secret Service* is a best-seller. "Employed by the emperor for twelve years and was apprehended in England, and I am sure that you heard of his sensational trial in Scotland. Publicity has been enormous and I have it from a good authentic source that his publicity can be backed by the Hearst papers, why not get the Dr. to give some lectures?"

Alice Nielsen's peripatetic have-song-will-travel life continues with another Pacific Coast concert tour interspersed with a month of opera in San Francisco and Los Angeles. Performs *Rigoletto* and *Bohème* in San Francisco with "Beymer & Berry's La Scala Grand Opera Company" at Cort Theatre on February 26 to start two-city season. "She sings...with a specially engaged company to support her. Among other roles she will sing Antonia and Olympia in *The Tales of Hoffman*" (*Musical America*). Resuming concerts, Nielsen rails "far South as Texas, finally concluding the tour with a recital in Boston".

Cordial relations with Harvard are continuous yet after ads appear that Nielsen expected with Harvard Glee Club in NYC March 3, ill she stays home. March 4, nephew Thomas Nielsen writes to Harrison about bookings and adds a personal note, "We all motored to Far Rockaway yesterday and saw Miss Nielsen's brother [Erasmus]. He is getting along quite well. It is good of you to inquire regarding him".

Alice Nielsen is a fan of her audiences. Her loyalty to the people who like her grows clear when she forces Redpath to switch Indianapolis to the 12th or 16th so she may return to clamoring Boston.

March 11th, Thomas writes LB Crotty at Redpath, "Miss Nielsen... booked herself a return date in Boston where she had a tremendous success, for April 6". Alice has always created her success. Seasoned trouper. Thomas continues, "Regarding Miss Nielsen's appearance in Kansas City April 14...she will accept the $600 and pay her rails from Quincy, but she has made a condition...that you fill the date in Muskogee OK. on the same terms [to] make it a bit worthwhile and...mileage from KC to Muskogee is less than 250".

Family humor appears as Thomas reveals: "Miss Nielsen has added to her repertoire 'the mumps.' Of course it is against her will and she is disgusted. As she herself expresses it, 'I've had everything this winter but a baby.'"

Alice Nielsen continues to set the ticket prices low. March 13, Thomas Nielsen writes Harrison on stationary of NY Athletic Club, "Just a line to remind you that in Indianapolis, Kansas City etc., Miss Nielsen wishes that her prices prevail top at $1.50". And a promise a promise: "As you promised Miss Nielsen personally to attend to this matter, she is resting assured that it will be as she desires". Lastly, Thomas thanks for contacts to use promoting his German spy, "for your leads re: Graves. I will take up the matter immediately".

Mid-March NYC, Alice sings Puccini and Irish songs for People's Symphony Society. March 20, nephew Thomas writes Harrison to clarify a Missouri concert with Alice's old pal conductor Karl Busch, "Miss Nielsen would like to know what she is to sing besides the solo from *Sabat Mater* in Kansas City".

Redpath does not want Alice to change their Indianapolis booking. Despite Redpath, Thomas cannot oblige, "In my letter of the 13th, I did not mention that Indianapolis was OK. I am very sorry about this business of Indianapolis, but Miss Nielsen insists upon doing Boston the 6th, April".

Direct appeals to diva futile. She has decided for Boston. Thomas confirms his powerlessness to Crotty four days later, "I have fired my last gun. Miss Nielsen insists upon doing Boston in place of Indianapolis. Please arrange accordingly. Sorry about this but the Lady insists and I am not her manager". Same day sends Alice's concert program for publication.

During Chautauqua that year, Alice Nielsen selects six sets of songs.

Set one: *Deh Vieni-non tardar* from *Nozze di Figaro* (Mozart). Set two: in English with *A Spirit Flower* (Campbell Tipton), *Down In The Forest* (Ronald), *But Lately In Dance* (Arensky), *A Burst Of Melody* (Seiler). Set three: in French with *Si mes vers avient des ailes* (Hahn), *Mandolin* (Debussy), *Extase* (Duparc), *Ouvre tes yeux bleus* (Massenet). Set four: Italian, Aria: *Un Bel Di, Madam Butterfly* (Puccini). Set five: in German: *Zueignung* (Strauss), *Vergebliches Standchen* (Brahms), *Wiegenlied* (Brahms), *Kom lass Uns Spielen* (Bleichmann). Set six: in English, *My Lover*

He Comes On The Skee (Clough Leighter), *The Day Is Done* (Spross), *The Weathercock* (Lehmann) and *The Open Secret* (Woodman).

In practice *Un Bel Di* is placed last; afterwards encores, the "songs of the Kansas City streets" sung since child for people of town, sung at Dold Mansion, sung at the White House, sung at palaces, opera houses.

Again puts William Reddick on the massive Baldwin touring piano.

On March 5, Nielsen praises her audiences. "In my extensive travels through the country, I have been surprised to find that even in the smaller cities and towns the appreciation of the best in music has reached a point that places America in the foremost rank of the musical countries in the world". Returns to Boston April 6, her unwavering wish.

Program a joint concert with tenor Arthur Hackett and violinist Hildegard Nash. "Miss Nielsen will sing a group of songs in English and selections by Wolf, Liszt and Grieg. Mr. Hackett will contribute two groups of English songs and Miss Nash will play compositions by Svend, Cui, Borowski, Tor Aulin and Brahms-Joachim". Her songs detail as the familiar "group of songs in English by Parker, Leoni, Arensky, Clough-Leighter, *My Old Kentucky Home* by Foster, *In The Gloaming*, Harrison, *Bonnie Sweet Bessie*, Gilbert, *Annie Laurie*, Scott and selections by Liszt, Grieg and Hugo Wolf, closing with Arditi's *Il Bacio*" (*Boston Globe* Mar 26).

When Nielsen arrives to Kansas City to celebrate Karl Busch on April 15th, he conducts Kansas City Symphony, "More than seven thousand of Alice Nielsen's Kansas City admirers sat before her and listened and cheered". The Symphony and chorus of four-hundred entertain an hour before Nielsen appears onstage. She "threw both arms around Conductor Busch and kissed him smack on the cheek. This was a signal for more and greater applause".

Out go the lights.

"The hall, at first brilliantly lighted... began to dim. Finally the lights went out altogether". Busch decides to keep Alice dancing in the dark. They find a lantern for her pianist and put six candles around Alice Nielsen. She sings in darkness twenty-five minutes. Ronald's *Down in the Forest* and five other songs, then *Swannee River*. The place goes wild: "After this old great favorite...the hall shook with a demonstration, and she ended her set with *Last Rose of Summer*. By that lantern light, Alice made her way to the dressing room and sat down almost exhausted. To save one of the queerest situations she had sung eight songs straight". When the lights return, she completes the set.

Questioned, "'How do you feel?' 'Don't ask me how I feel', the singer said, laughing like a school girl. 'All during that ordeal there was only one thought crossing constantly through my mind. You ought to be able to guess. I was wondering where Moses was when the lights went out.'"

Hallelujah Chorus closes the evening.

Continues touring with "everything fine and hope for a big house".

April 16th Alice writes Harry Harrison on stationary of Claypool Hotel in Indianapolis. Confirms receipt of payment, checks sent to her hotels as she travels, a chancy arrangement: "I have received a check of $600 from you on the first two concerts & $600 from Mr. Homer for KC. I only remind you of this as last year some of the checks were not delivered to me & were sent back to you. Please let me know if any others were sent. Everything fine and hope for a big house tomorrow night. Look forward to seeing you in the near future & with cordial greetings believe me, Yours sincerely, Alice Nielsen".

April 22ⁿᵈ now in Louisville KY she gives the "concluding concert of the Redpath". Voice "as pure and lovely as ever, carried surprisingly in the vast building. Particularly this was true of her high pianissimo tones, which seemed to float like thistledown over the heads of the audience. She responded to numerous encores and the audience was enthusiastic in its expressions of pleasure". Pianist Reddick, the local reviewer continues, deserves "more than passing mention for the delightful and artistic support given the vocalist".

Two days later, hard-traveling Alice Nielsen hits NYC to sing a benefit for Russian war refugees: "Notable Russian Gathering to Take Place At The Waldorf" (*NY Times* Ap 24). Then she joins Syracuse Spring Festival, where reporters note the shared impact of her fashions, humor and voice.

Syracuse Herald, "Miss Nielsen leaves us crowned with the greatest success made by a singer at this festival, and perhaps with higher favor than any other artists repeatedly engaged by the directors has ever enjoyed. The smartly-gowned and fascinating Alice was the cynosure of all eyes. She has something besides a voice, she has a sense of humor. Also she has ten gowns in her trunk. Syracuse loves its Nielsen".

Sentiment flows at Optimists' Club lunch as Nielsen sings *Swannee River:* "tears were in the eyes of everyone as the final tones floated over the room". Everybody "expected Alice Nielsen to sing beautifully, and to smile, and flirt, and charm, and to look a vision of loveliness, and she came up to all expectations". In this elegant era, "even the women took their gloves off to applaud".

In June, Nielsen acquires "personal management" of John Brown, "formerly Business Comptroller Metropolitan Opera Co". His address is the Met building of yore at 1425 Broadway. Brown would be informative: made the closing audit at Boston Opera. And Alice's financial savvy is obviously strong. Wagner does not discuss Nielsen's move away. Nielsen skips any memoir mention of Wagner, Perley, or Brown.

June 2 when Alice Nielsen sings Mozart in Evanston IL, she draws many Chicago critics into a sixty-mile roundtrip. Five Chicago reporters:

James Whittaker (*Examiner*): "Sang Mozart perfectly. Not in a long time have we heard Mozart sung in such pure style and by so lovely a voice".

Edward Moore (*Daily News Journal*): "Were there a demand for a Mozart specialist in this country, Miss Nielsen would be the logical one for the position".

Herman Devires (*Evening American*): "One of America's favored and favorite soprano singers, contributed two Mozart arias to the pleasure of the audience. The *Deh Vieni* from *Marriage of Figaro* was exquisitely delivered and appreciated by a generous outburst of applause. It was transposed by Miss Nielsen an entire tone higher, from F to G. Miss Nielsen's voice gives great delight. It is even and pure and of a silvery, clean-cut quality ingratiating to the ear".

Karleton Hacket (*Evening Post*): She sang "two Mozart arias with delightfully fresh tone, finely poised and perfectly sustained. The tone was lovely, pure, in perfect tune and sustained with ease. She has just the voice to sing Mozart".

Sixth, consider if you will the local report by Walter Stults of *Evanston News-Index* at more length to highlight that era's very evenly-distributed quality of audiences nation-wide and their critical representatives:

"Let those pessimists who are wont to give voice to the cry that the art of *Bel Canto* is dead, and the day of good singing no more, sit up and take notice! That singing of such caliber as Miss Nielsen vouchsafed is all too rare we will admit, but since it is the function of festivals to bring to our hearing the best that the world of art affords, we desire publicly to express our sense of gratitude to a management that made possible the hearing of two Mozart arias sung in a manner that was perfection itself. Here is tone production at which one may not cavil, coupled with a highly developed interpretative instinct projected through the medium of a personality that is unaffectedly pleasing. The world of song affords no more difficult and exacting medium than that of Mozart wherewith to test the powers of the vocalist, and the triumphant manner in which Miss Nielsen last night met these exacting requirements speaks eloquently of the merit of her art".

Her summer, despite raging foreign war, includes passage on the liner *Baltic* for Liverpool July 26 for the familiar schedule of recitals.

By September 21 she has returned to NYC.

Musical Courier publishes George Whitehead's colorful if belated feature on her Chautauqua tour last summer. Visited singer at her 1901-built cottage in Harrison, Maine: "At her Japanese villa in the forests of Maine, Alice Nielsen is 'home again' from a nine weeks' season on the Redpath Chautauqua circuit. She has reveled in the unusual experiences of singing six nights a week, under canvas". She had lived in an "historic" private train car "Elysian". Nightly they rode about fifty miles to the next town. Weekly papers in fifty small towns of Ohio, West Virginia, and Kentucky said the appearance of such an artist was "an epoch to be recorded in the archives and talked of for years to come".

Whitehead describes the Baldwin touring piano as "immense... frequently occasioned train delays in the loading, and through profanity provocations often set back the provoked personages two or three revival meetings".

Her mood cheerful: "I certainly swallowed a gnat. Did you notice that when I was singing *The Weathercock* I simply had to stop and begin all over again? Well it was that gnat! The lights always attract every variety of flying bug, and it is a fight with my fan from the moment the show starts until it stops. But this is the closest acquaintance I have achieved. I shall remember him. Ugh!"

Nielsen's entourage included private secretary Mrs. CP Stickle, accompanist William Reddick, virtuoso cellist Karl Kirk-Smith (who had just joined NY Philharmonic); her son Bennie went without mention.

December, Alice revisits Wilson's White House. His daughter wishes to sing, yet as Goethe's Mephistopheles avowed, "the ambition great, the talent so-so".

Upcoming Carnegie Hall concert on Christmas Eve is widely promoted by Columbia Records; she is joined by People's Symphony.

Broadway reappears. For the first time since 1901, Alice Nielsen begins preparing for a musical. Everything in the world has changed; also about the project she first announced in London a few years back. Now the text is a David Belasco play, not JM Barrie. Instead of Puccini or Wolf-Ferrari, Bohemian composer Firml has the score.

This year Nielsen and Herbert give the world separate Irish projects. Nielsen essays a Belasco show; Herbert composes *Eileen*. Both projects set in their grandparents' 19th century. Plot: outwit British of course. What a pair these two great Irish artists made who never collaborated after 1901 despite three smash hits soaring over box office records.

Herbert would prove right, not just about money. They could indeed have made so much happen with the power of mutual success: new art, new theatre, new music, new methods, new styles: new shows. It was only the beginning.

1917: A BROADWAY BELASCO VERY BRIEFLY

January 29th Alice Nielsen joins a star-studded Biltmore Hotel with Caruso and other opera people of her set. Fancy-dress, frolic from the prank-loving child of Naples. Gayety holds full sway.

February 14th (*NY Times*), Nielsen headlines a Mozart society concert at Hotel Astor ballroom, Mrs. McConnell, president: "I consider Mrs. McConnell an interesting woman", Nielsen remarks. So does poet Sarah Lawman Roebling, whose honor Adelaide McConnell: "Our well loved President of Mozart..., Surely Super Woman—as all can see, Her fame will go down to posterity".

Alice sings a song created for her by Rudolph Ganz (1877-1972), *The Angels Are Stooping*, words from Yeats' *A Cradle Song*. She sings: "*The angels are stooping Above your bed; They weary of trooping With the whimpering dead. God's laughing in Heaven To see you so good; The Sailing Seven Are gay with His mood. I sigh that kiss you, for I must own That I shall miss you When you have grown*".

Under the weather, "Miss Nielsen was not in best voice, as she was victim of a cold, but her art triumphed", relates *NY Times*.

March 29 *Musical Courier* meets Nielsen at her suite in the Met to speak about voice. Boston Opera dead, remora vamoosed, now her facts clarify. Stops absurdly promoting the untrustworthy. Now speaks sincerely about the helpful influences on her career.

What follows is one of her best life statements. She lives simply for her complex art. Absorbs music and gives: herself. Her personal charm delights the reporter: "Alice Nielsen's secretary ushered the writer into the intimate, homelike, living room of the singer's suite...up there in the top floor of the Metropolitan Opera House Building, far above the hubbub of Old Broadway. And in a few moments...found herself engaged in a cozy chat with this famous singer. It was a delight to find Alice Nielsen when 'just herself' at home, the same winsome personality that music lovers the world over have learned to love and admire as an operatic prima donna, a favorite of operetta and concert singing. Miss Nielsen confessed directly to one hobby—her voice".

"I just hate cooking" Nielsen "interpolated with conviction".

"You always sing as if you just couldn't help it".

"I do not always feel like singing, though it may not appear so. But I have learned how to sing when not in the mood".

Courier: "Just what wizardry this songstress, who has sung since she was eight years of age, employs for this, Miss Nielsen neglected to divulge".

Asked of "the freshness of her voice after long exacting tours".

"I live as any human being should live, as simply as possible. I regulate my eating. As a matter of fact, I am only five pounds heavier than when in light opera. I must be up and around before a performance. One must be up and stirring. I prepare for a matinee as for evening performances. I don't like morning musicales".

Alice Nielsen, who habitually calls reporters over to release a message, now emphasizes the part women have played in her career: "My career has been built up to a great extent through the help of women. Lady Phillips was among the first; another was Mrs. Victor Herbert. I was singing in *The Wartime Wedding* when Mrs. Herbert heard me. As a result I became the lead singer in *The Serenade*".

Interviewer paraphrases, "Both *The Fortune Teller* and *The Singing Girl* were written for Alice Nielsen. When the soprano was singing these in London, Lady Phillips heard her and at once became interested, and as a result she began her study for an operatic career. Miss Nielsen's debut was made in Naples as Marguerite in *Faust*. Miss Nielsen is justly proud of the fact too, that after Melba she was the first to sing in *Bohème*, with Caruso at Covent Garden.As a result a friendship sprang up between Miss Nielsen and the famous tenor, and as a souvenir an autographed photograph is given a conspicuous place on the walls of her living room, among those of many other famous musicians, including Tosti.

"Miss Nielsen emphasized the necessity for patience and persistence on the part of the vocal student who expects to attain a place in the artistic world". *Musical Courier* closes with gratitude for "the long and fortunate career of that much-loved soprano Alice Nielsen".

By April, almost-astonishing news of her return to Broadway as Alice occupies the April 5 *Musical Courier* cover, the "weekly review of the world's music". Large round hat, fur-trimmed concert dress shows trim ankles. *Courier* recalls Nielsen's "success with the Boston Opera Company and later at the head of her own organization in the *Secret of Suzanne*. It also is a well-known fact...she was the undisputed queen of comic opera in the country.

"Miss Nielsen has been beguiled into returning to her first love and last week signed a contract" for a new musical from David Belasco based on his popular play *Kitty Darlin'*. "Most of the comic-opera prima donnas of the past decade or two were dancers and soubrettes, rather than vocalists and actresses. With her beautiful voice, histrionic gifts, charming personality and well-trained musicianship, Miss Nielsen will bring to comic opera a luster which perhaps it has not known since the days when she first abandoned it...." Such hopes.

Describing her help from women, the powerful opera partnership made with Nordica mysteriously slips out of sight. Perhaps painful.

Next day April 6th, America descends into the foreign war President Wilson swore not to enter. To bailout the banksters' foreign loan WH Bryan warned against allowing before he resigned as Secretary of State in protest.

May 1st, *KC Times* (May 1) interviews feisty Nielsen at Coates Opera House. "Why, I would shoulder a rifle, I would fight, and I shall fight, if we women are ever needed, or even given a chance", Nielsen says. She offers her Maine cottage "with its accompanying grounds including ten acres now planted with potatoes, to the government to use as an aviation field.

"The President may have all that I have, if it is needed for this great cause. Once I felt that I could give all but my boy to the cause. But now I feel, as every good American mother feels, that when his country needs him he has my consent to go".

Dwells on her town: "I came a little ahead of time, earlier than was necessary. But I never wait until it is necessary for me to be in Kansas City before I get here. I go there just as soon as I possibly could, and I am going to stay just as long as I can. This is home, and I have a great many friends here, friends of my younger days, and these I want to see". Repeats her familiar mantra for anytown anywhere: "Then too, my reaching here ahead of time will give me an opportunity to rest for my singing. I want to do my best singing for" anywhere and today, "Kansas City".

Of course, she is ready for Broadway. "Since I had left light opera I had been offered about every light opera that was written. I had refused. But I had heard that Mr. Belasco's *Kitty Darlin'* was to be put to music, and I casually expressed my interest to a friend".

Does not name the friend; Belasco is a friend. "It was less than two hours after I had done this that Mr. [Morris] Gest [Belasco's co-producer son-in-law] came to me and asked if I would not take the leading part. Within twenty minutes we had completed all arrangements for signing of the contract. Since signing the contract, I have had no reason to alter my predictions that a light musical play would be produced that would possess all the merit, from both a dramatic and musical standpoint, to meet all of my wishes".

Generous, given the switch from her original wishes.

Irish-flavored music arrives from Rudolph Friml, "a Hungarian" [Czech]. Nielsen plays "an Irish girl and in her speech must use a soft Irish dialect". Definitely "opera in English". Perhaps out of kindness nobody mentions the dismal record of any Belasco musical. Tries one a decade. All fail fast. But why not enjoy the prelude. And a digression.

Enters an unfortunate chapter in the friendship of Marie Dressler and Alice Nielsen, unable to resolve a lingering financial dispute. Nielsen, who sang for pennies as a girl is careful with money. She earned hers. For a time, as Marie herself admits, Dressler had badly advised friends on investments. Now Nielsen and others sue for fraud. In *My Own Story* (1934) Marie Dressler apologizes: "Almost beside myself with distress, I did what I could to straighten things out. This experience was one of the most humiliating of my life but it taught me a valuable lesson: hindsight, no matter how clear, cannot take the place of foresight".

Both women have had triumphs and difficulty. Dressler, blacklisted by producers in retaliation for founding Equity, sold pals some Florida swamp land and shady California mining shares. Unable to settle, Nielsen "sued in the Supreme Court to recover $4,500 which she says Marie Dressler and the latter's husband, James Dalton, persuaded her to invest in 9000 shares of the Ulida Consolidated Copper Company of California", reports *Boston Globe* (Ma 23). Nielsen wins. Does not collect until Dressler dies.

Rest of summer stays undocumented. Since 1909, she spent summers in Europe, or Caribbean, Maine or Stoddard's place in Glen Falls NY. Alice had also enjoyed Dressler's place in the White Mountains.

August 19, *Philadelphia Inquirer* reports Alice's mentor Burton Stanley soon appears as comic with Dumont's Minstrels.

August 24 *Washington Post* asks of her favorite song. Nielsen's choice is of words and meaning, *Old Black Joe* her favorite, "Because it is full of tenderness and it says something that means something to us. We know what it is all about and we understand its every throw. Because, best of all, it is American".

Stephen Foster's (1826-1864) *Old Black Joe* was published 1860. Born in Pennsylvania, Forster penned *Oh! Suzanna, Swannee River, Nelly Bly My Old Kentucky Home, Camptown Races* and *Jeannie with the Light-Brown Hair*; EP Christie minstrels monopolized the songs. Bob January (bobjanuary.com) says, "Stephen Foster's ability for the honest expression of real emotion is the life blood of art, no matter what its form". Foster was a child singer in local theatre. Only visit South beyond Kentucky was 1852 riverboat to New Orleans. He met black culture as boy attending "camp meetings" (outdoor worship) with the maid. The song Nielsen likes best is about being called away. *Swannee River's* original title "Pedee River", both names selected off a map.

Nielsen sang: *Gone are the days when my heart was young and gay/Gone are my friends from the cotton fields away/Gone from the earth to a better land I know/I hear their gentle voices calling Old Black Joe.*

Why do I weep, when my heart should feel no pain/Why do I sigh that my friends come not again?/Grieving for forms now departed long ago/I hear their gentle voices calling Old Black Joe. Where are the hearts once so happy and so free?/The children so dear that I held upon my knee?/Gone to the shore where my soul has longed to go/I hear their gentle voices calling Old Black Joe.

Chorus: I'm coming, I'm coming, for my head is bending low, I hear their gentle voices calling Old Black Joe. A song of passing and survival.

After sixteen years Alice Nielsen is about to re-open on Broadway in a bespoke if derivitive musical fashioned from a hit Belasco drama. Not the new-fashioned Herbert pieces; and at start of an agonizing war.

Ads for Nielsen's show, slated to open November 7th, first appear in *NY Times* October 28th. Out-of-town trials bring intense re-writes. First writers fired. The fix-it does not really help. Nielsen tries; probably does not care. Of everything she could have done; well, she did this show. Her stage presence is a flirty 19th-century Irish lass; almost a cartoon Alice.

From the delectable project she had first proposed in London, the actual musical is something completely different. Libretto switched from JM Barrie's *Little Minister* to a Belasco play based on a novel from siblings Agnes and Egerton Castle, *The Bath Comedy* set in 1793 of course Bath, England. A show very alike it is sharply satirized in MGM's 1952 *Singing in the Rain* Technicolor masterpiece of gayety which gave a few silly songs meaning only because the stars wonderfully act and dance.

Basis of Kitty, Belasco's hit play *Sweet Kitty Bellairs* had opened December 1903 for 203 performances. Sweet Kitty is an Irish girl at the center of attention for two regiments: the English 51st versus Irish Iniskillings. PG Wodehouse of *Jeeves* fame promised witty lyrics, Guy Bolton the book; prized team for twenty-one Broadway shows and not this.

Bolton, interestingly, will marry erstwhile Boston Opera soprano Marguarite Namara erstwhile wife of Frederick Toye; the very same odd couple oddly fired by the Boston's loathsome manager among all-too-peculiar circumstances.

Nielsen's composer of choice had been Wolf-Ferrari or Puccini. Despite Puccini's successes working from Belasco to make *Madama Butterfly* and *Girl of the Golden West*, and despite Wolf-Ferrari's success with *Secret of Suzanne*, Belasco hires Rudolf Firml to create the *Kitty* score.

Seven songs Act 1; four Act 2; five Act 3. Firml grew up Czech, a Dvorak-trained composer and concert pianist. Worked as *répétiteur* for Met rehearsals before composing 1912 hit *Firefly* after Victor Herbert abandoned its intended star Emma Trintini when she refused singing a *Naughty Marietta* encore. Firml soothed Trintini by starting an affair which precipitated his divorce. February 1917 Firml and Harbach also collaborated on *You're In Love* with sundry lyrical gems such as rhyming "meet you" with "greet you". Their sleepwalking heroine Marie Flynn gave 167 NYC performances.

Kitty sports historic uniforms, gowns, drawing rooms, wit and manners. Bedroom scene has a concealed person. Rainstorm pours down. Such Belasco effects were crowd-pleasers. Produces plays until he dies in 1931. Musicals not so much. Belasco produced a musical a decade. Never last long, hardly last at all. *Kitty* proves no exception. Associate producers are William Elliot, F. Ray Comstock, and Morris Gest. Gest, who will bring Duse to 1923 America for her last tour.

Nielsen does not regroup her famed Broadway creative team who have been very active. Julian Mitchell's *Hitchy-Koo* revue runs 220 times after opening June, his *Rivera Girl* seventy-eight. His last show would be 1926.

Kitty's director Edward Royce (1870-1964) had a string of Broadway shows including Alice-friend Fritz Kreisler's 1919 *Apple Blossoms* starring Adele and Fred Astaire, designed by Josef Urban with 256 performances. Edward Royce had been birthed in Bath, England. *Kitty's* music director is William Act, scene design by Theodore Reisig, costumes by Harry Collins and Mme. Julie.

In the cast: Frank Bradley as Mallo, George Callahan as Colonel Kimby McFinteon, Eleanor Daniels as Lydie, Sidonie Espero as Lady Bab Flyte, Worthe Faulkner as Captain Dennis O'Hara, Juanita Fletcher as Lady Julia Sandish, Patricia Frewen as Lady Beaufort, Glen Hall as Lieutenant

Lord Verney, Jackson Hines as Sir Jasper Standish, Alice Nielsen as Kitty Bellairs "a young widow", H. Jess Smith as Gandy, Edwin Stevens as Colonel Henry Villiers and Frank Westerton as Captain Spicer. Those the characters with names.

In the chorus: Edith Appleton, Rose Benedict, Peggy Brandon, Josephine Bryan, NP Bryan, Jane Buchana, Helen Christie, Molly Christie, Bert Clark, H. Clark, Mary Comerfod, S. Critcheson, Grace Dean, RG Elliott, C Enisman, Doris Faithful, Grace Dean, RG Elliott, C Enisman, Florence Haynes, Gertrude Hogan, William Hovel, Fayette Howard, Anton Ingaroa, Clare King, Olive Kingston, Louis LaVie, Charlotte Lenox, Shirley Love, Margaret May, Yetla Nicol, Albert Noome, Ann Page, Walter Palm, Benjamin Rogers, Muril Smither, Frank Sparling, Jeanne Sparry, R St John, Ema Steinway, Mary Lee Stevens, Ruby Thomas, B. Tieman, Peggy Troland and Ed Watson.

Before NYC, Boston. October 29 *Kitty Darlin'* first appears a week at Boston's Majestic. She looks into the house: "*When she gives him a rose or a lily, She but gives him a flower's perfume, But believe me, she gives all the heart of her, When she gives him a Shamrock bloom*".

Difficult today to appreciate the plodding plot; same difficult as 1917 saw it. Let Boston tell us.

Boston Globe (Oct 30): "Popular prima donna has a dashing role in *Kitty Darlin'* at Majestic. Alice Nielsen who lost several fortunes, thus opined the sagacious press agents in the Boston Opera days, by abandoning light opera has returned to it again. Long have the managers besought her.

"Acknowledging proudly a strain of Irish in her own blood, it is not strange that she was tempted by David Belasco's *Sweet Kitty Belairs*, the gay, roguish, witty, merrily bewitching belle of Bath, who romped away with the officers' hearts, whether they were English or Irish, and found her own being enough to defend another woman's name at the cost of her own.

"It does not greatly matter how closely here is followed the detail of Mr. Belasco's play. The form of the story told in light opera at the Majestic Theatre last evening keeps the principal incidents. Sir Jasper Standish, to avenge a fancied insult offered his namby-pamby wife by Lieut. Lord Verney, challenges the latter to a duel with pistols at dawn, the traditionally correct time for all well-conducted duels.

"In the second act, the adventurous Kitty, who, piqued at his lordships indifference to her blandishments, has wagered his speedy conquest" and so on as more stuff happens, until "at last Lord Varney announces that Kitty has consented to marry him and at the hall in the third acts appears suddenly and helps her face the women gossips of waspish tongues, sharpened by the jealous malice of Lady Bab".

Detects drastic rewrites: "*Kitty Darlin'* is said to be no exception to the plays which are rewritten during rehearsals and first performances". Boston may have trouble speaking freely, but never fears to bite. *Globe* has problems only with the show's direction, text and music.

"The first act shows in various ensembles, especially at Miss Nielsen's entrance, in which the music is neither well-written nor well-suited to her, that considerable sifting if not entire change has been going on. Not until the *Shamrock* song has Miss Nielsen a chance worthy of her, for the scene wherein she plays tailor to the lackyrmose Lady Julia moves heavily and keeps her too-long submerged". Firml seems better at creating "jingling" songs than Herbert-style musicals with a complete meaningful score.

"In the second act, by reason of her experience and skill as an actress, Miss Nielsen gave point and commanding emphasis to the dramatic situation, which fortunately has not been combined with music. Picking up the narrative in his score, Mr. Friml does not show the skill in setting dramatic action which he does as the familiar writing of tunes, bright in rhythm and catchy in melody, the kind that bring the supreme reward of being whistled". Herbert hated that kind of thing. Herbert prefers complex melody and subtle changes.

"It is likely that he has several of these in the *Swing Song* for Lady Bab, Spicer and Jasper, and in *I'd Do The Same*...which as done by Miss Daniels and Mr. Bradley, was among the cleverest things in the show".

Styles were changing with the war stupidity. Herbert created unified scores with dramatic music of many shifts. That's why the words could be lost. The post-Herbert style sprinkled "tunes" over the plot. *Chicago* (1975) or *Momma Mia!* (1999) or *Black Crook* (1866) wend the extravaganza way. Dancing cow helps, so *Momma Mia* (2008) the acting cows.

Nielsen delights: "In the situation in Verney's apartments, it is not easy to imagine another American singer in light opera better equipped to play the scene with the sense equally of its power as of its charm and lightness of touch, and to sing the closing duet with Mr. Hall with the voice and art which the light opera stage has not been able to offer. Miss Nielsen's reception was a cordial one, particularly after this act when she was recalled many times. The supporting company and the investiture all point to the lavish scale on which the star has been surrounded.

In the cast: Miss Espero "comely young woman of good voice, taste, presence and apparently of instinctive sense of mood and picture. Mr. Hines was a commanding and agreeable figure. He played with style, even with distinction. His voice would have been welcome in more telling music. As an actor, Mr. Hall struggles with a heroic part. His voice still can remind of his concert singing and the pleasure it gave. Edwin Stevens, by turns ponderous and drooling in the drunken scene, was occasionally funny. The colonel's sober moments were the more believable. Mr. Callahan gave a consistent characterization without horseplay or exaggeration. The chorus contains attractive, some of them beautiful young women who sing as well as pose and dance. The men's voices are unusual and the entire chorus which is large, does credit to the ensemble numbers which in most instances are wholly beyond the ordinary in comic opera. The settings and costumes are gorgeous in color and in excellent taste, the final scene a brilliant one. The audience was large and applauded warmly, demanding many encores".

Tragedy strikes or disaster looms. Take your pick. PG Wodehouse gets fired in Buffalo. Otto Harbach arrives to fix script. Re-writes extensive. Nielsen's opening songs get new words. Wodehouse was left three, including *Dear Old Dublin.* Wodehouse skips *Kitty Darlin'* in his memoirs with the remark he did not relish spending time with its problems. Does not share details or discuss development.

Perhaps Wodehouse was stretched thin: that year he and Bolton would create six musicals. *Oh Boy* ran 463 performances jumping from the 300-seat Princess on 39th Street to the 875-seat Casino.

For *Kitty*, Harbach (1873-1963) the script doctor, musical comedy career began with 1908's *Three Twins*. 1916 he generates book and lyrics for three musicals. *Two In Love*, set in sunny Southern California runs 167 shows at Casino; his *Pair Of Queens* closes after fifteen. His 1917 *Going Up* will run 351 times. He will create book and lyrics for about fifty musicals. His best-known show is 1925's *No, No, Nanette*. Harbach's best-known lyricsl, *Smoke Gets In Your Eyes*. Interestingly, his parents were Danish in Utah. His folks reach the Mormon colony a decade after the Nielsens. To Alice Nielsen, his culture will be familiar; playful Danes gave the world Victor Borge.

Modern settings are popular, antiques not so much.

For antique *Kitty Darlin'* despite drastic re-writes the producers keep a hard-charging schedule for NYC. At Syracuse Alice is unwell; her substitute Sidonie Espero at twenty-three is thrilled when Alice came up hoarse, "It happened this way. Alice Nielsen is our prima donna. She found herself completely hoarse a few minutes the curtain rose on *Kitty Darlin'*. The manager was crazy, everyone was frantic. There was a packed and hundreds of dollars to be refunded. That is where I came in...."

Raise the NYC curtain on a half-baked project. Curtains for Kitty.

November 7 at the Casino, Alice Nielsen opens *Kitty Darlin'*. Seems not in best voice. Five songs: *Love's Own Call, You'll See, When She Gives a Shamrock Bloom, Just We Two*, and *'Twas Pretense*. Same as any Belasco musical, *Kitty* closes in ten days. After twelve years Belasco tries again, adopting his play *Polly With a Past* to a musical in 1929. Runs a day longer than *Kitty*.

So it is. Nielsen's only flop runs two weeks the Belasco average.

NY Times: "Pleasant tunes and gay costumes with a very indifferent book...serves to bring Alice Nielsen again before the footlights. The production...has three specious scenes, striking military costumes of Irish green and British red and gay gowns of the heyday of fashionable Bath. Miss Nielsen sang pleasantly with excellent taste and was warmly greeted by the audience. It cannot be said that she has yet regained her former vigor and richness of coloring, and it must be added that she is not happy in rendering the sprightly whims and tempestuous ardors of *Sweet Kitty*".

Columnist DH: "A decade ago *Sweet Kitty Bellairs* charmed NY, and now *Kitty Darlin'* which is the same comedy dressed up with music, is repeating the achievement at the Casino. It is sung and acted well by Alice Nielsen, and she is a distinct contribution to the singers of the present. Time was when she was our leading light opera prima donna, and...quite as charming and talented as she was in her earlier prime. For one thing Miss Nielsen can sing. And if there be those who doubt the charm of her acting, a visit will dispel all doubts".

Evening Mail: "We can imagine few harder tasks than that which Alice Nielsen set herself last night when she made her first local reappearance in light opera at the Casino. She knew that one-half of her audience did not remember her and that the other half did. And it must have been a serious question with her as to which was the harder to face".

Two decades ago "she was something of a beautiful legend, a mystical charmer who once upon a time progressed from conquest to conquest.... And to those who did remember she had a promise to redeem that she knew she was incapable of meeting. For twenty [16] years are twenty [16] years, and may not be denied. But thanks to the quality of both music and setting in *Kitty Darlin'*, Miss Nielsen met the test gracefully".

Alice Nielsen's usual stage fright: "Because she was a pretty badly frightened prima donna, her performance lacked a spontaneity and authority that it doubtless will later acquire. She was not just sure of herself, and therefore hesitant and formal, dignified and operatic rather than being gaily irresponsible and the bit of a rogue Sweet Kitty was.... Her voice of course met all the demands she put on it. She sang as timidly as she acted, but the applause she won was friendly and sincere".

Regards story of a Dublin coquette "who set out to charm the most diffident Lieut. Lord Varney who had never been properly kissed is frail enough..." Act 1 seems "a bit conventional" and the rest "isn't much".

Mantel notes muddle, "Who prepared the book of this operatic version, no one seems to be quite certain. The indefatigable duo—Guy Bolton and PG Wodehouse—began it but later withdrew. And now the programme credits both book and lyrics to Otto Harbach. Whoever did the lyrics is entitled to a measure of praise for them at any rate, and though the comedy is not particularly stirring, it is mannerly and in good taste". That is, if it isn't funny it isn't rude.

"Much of the music by Rudolph Friml is really charming".

In the cast: Edwin Stevens had the same role with Belasco, Sidonie Espero, "eager and pretty young woman who sings well" was catty Lady Bab, Juanita Fletcher the weeping Lady Julia. Glen Hall sang Lord Verney, "looks it and occasionally acts it. Frank Westerton is a bold villain, Jackson Hines the suspicious Sir Jasper and Frank Bradley a comely valet".

NY World: "Miss Nielsen sang the role of Kitty with all the vocal fluency and charm which she in her other light opera days so easily controlled. She would have been a more effective Irish belle however, if she had been able to act with greater buoyancy and vivacity. Possibly it was due to her new surroundings, but this subdued, almost demure...Kitty's devilishness had to be largely taken for granted. It was when Miss Nielsen was singing the melodious measures which Mr. Firml had composed for her that she weaved her most potent spell over the audience. Vocally, Sidonie Espero was inferior to Miss Nielsen, but as the dethroned belle of the regiment she injected...much-needed sparkle and life.

NY Globe: Louis Sherman hates operetta. "This is a gallant attempt... because making the customers swallow Ibsen is an easy job [Hortense Nielsen] compared to the task of giving them operetta". The show lacks "the excitement, the gayety, the color, the general Dionysiac effects that make *Chu Chin Chow* and the big extravaganzas....fun. To be at all tolerable an operetta today must have wonderful music and be at least reasonably well sung.

"*Kitty Darlin'* on the other hand depends for its popularity on the fact that it is a musical version of David Belasco's *Sweet Kitty Belairs*. Of course, a great many people who liked the original play will be interested in the operetta.

"Most of the amusing ingredients of Mr. Belasco's comedy are there—especially the big four-poster bed with Kitty and Juli in it. The rainstorm [the most famed special effect of the play] is lacking.... It is quite obvious that no expense has been spared to make a pretty operetta...the scenery and costumes are even better than the original...the male chorus [thanks to Firml] is the best I have heard since *Iolanthe*...in the same theatre.

"For the rest—would it were silence! Rudolf Firml's music, except for the song *Sure 'Tis The Style Of Her*, is quite commonplace.

"As for Miss Nielsen, I suppose that if I had heard her in her prime, sentimentality or something might induce me to tell a few polite and pleasant lies about her. But the simple truth is that her vocalization last night was positively painful, except during the song she sang pianissimo. Her tone was wabbly and her roulades pitiful". This whippersnapper adds an absurdity, "there is only one reason for this and that is that Miss Nielsen's method is bad; in fact, it must have been bad from the beginning of her career...."

Evening Journal highlights the journalist generation gap, *Journal* is pleased with show and star. "NY had the opportunity of welcoming another prize favorite of other days in the person of winsome little Alice Nielsen—and the ovation she received at the conclusion of the premier on *Kitty Darlin'* must have caused her to...turn her head away to hide her happy emotions.

"Miss Nielsen's 'come-back' was...convincing. Although it is a far cry from *The Fortune Teller* and *The Singing Girl* to Rudolf Friml's newest musical composition, the Nielsen voice was more than equal to the effort and seems not to have lost a whit of its acknowledged sweetness with the passing of the years.

"Moreover, the Nielsen face and figure are no less easy to gaze upon than they were in days gone by" of sixteen years ago. To be sure, Miss Nielsen departure from the light opera stage was not in the nature of a retirement but a graduation".

Kitty Darlin' "a splendid vehicle for Miss Nielsen and the capable company.... The picturesqueness of Irish green as arrayed in opposition to British red cannot be denied. Nor will the charm of tales spun around the various romantic periods in Old England fail to allure as long as pretty girls and dashing youths continue to adopt the stage as a career".

In the cast: Glen Hall, "scored a personal triumph as Lieutenant Verney, Edwin Stevens" as Colonel Villers was worth mention. Chorus showed "careful selection" and "conscientious training".

Evening World: "Is there no way of escaping Belasco? Rudolf Firml has written very pretty music...the play is a thing of simple tricks that might have been performed by Becky Sharp when she was cutting her first tooth. It leaves us to grow old, musically". Clever reference mixes 19th-century novels and 1900s theatre. *Becky Sharp* was a 1900s play performed by

Mrs. Fiske based on character Rebecca Sharp in William Thackeray's 1847 *Vanity Fair: A Novel Without A Hero.*

"With more flesh and less voice than she possessed in earlier years, Alice Nielsen won her audience first of all with the song, *When She Gives Him A Shamrock Bloom.* But Miss Nielsen, unfortunately, left the shamrock to die on her lips by forgetting from time to time the Irish brogue necessary to Kitty. She lacked, too, the sparkle.... As a matter of fact, Miss Nielsen never got on speaking terms with her role, though she sang pleasingly when the musicians were kept down by their discreet leader".

In the cast: "Sidonie Espero carried off singing honors, Glen Hall "sang in the weak tones of a hopeless tenor". Chorus was "the best singing chorus that has been heard this season...and I leave you to find satisfaction in music that is old-fashioned but melodious".

NY Tribune: Ralph Block saw them old dramatic bones walking again same way Nielsen revive an antique at her last Casino gig: 1905's *Pasquale.*

"Vapors and red coats, swords at sunrise and curtsies and knee breeches, all the adornments of romance—somehow they've been driven far back into the shadowy hinterland. But Alice Nielsen...appears to keep them all still blooming with her, able to make them live once more. And now there's scarcely an odd'sblood to be found anywhere....

"The past is a dangerous thing to meddle with. I doubt whether anybody but Alice Nielsen, the Maid Marian of *Robin Hood* and the Irma of *The Fortune Teller* could have attempted the meddling with so many chances in her favor.... She brings many delicacies to the part of Kitty, and a voice that is still sweet and light and pliable and full of fine qualities in its upper tones, however curtailed the range might sometimes appear".

Block sees merit in her acting; surrounded by clichéd players. "She acts with an unfortunately faithful understanding of romance, because it puts to shame so much of the awkwardness in those who surround her".

For *NY Journal of Commerce*, Kitty Darlin' is "called a 'musical romance' but the musical part of it far outshines the romance. Mr. Friml and not Miss Nielsen is the star. His music is melodious and charming. It is a pity that it is not sung better. Mr. Harbach's book is not up to the music. One misses the dash, the spirit, the brilliancy of the old play. The librettist has adhered closely to the plot, but he has fallen down on the lines". These characters "do not shine with their old-time radiance".

Mentioning "keen interest" in Nielsen, "there were many in the audience who had pleasant memories of her in *The Serenade* and *The Fortune Teller.* But these two delightful operas were produced many years ago. Miss Nielsen was good to look at and at times sang well, but it was due more to the skill of the trained vocalist..." than real feeling. The show ran two weeks same as any Belasco musical; no fix for that.

Day after *Kitty* closes pundits nationwide ponder import of the "flop".

Boston Globe (Nov 18): "Alice Nielsen's return to the light opera stage has not met with the reception hoped-for and her brief season with *Kitty Darlin'* has been brought to an end".

Burns Mantle's "NY Letter" in *Chicago Daily Tribune* says "two idols toppled in the NY theatres last week. And one of them fell. Old Father Time was responsible in the one instance and a poor play in the other. The idols were Alice Nielsen and Laurette Taylor".

Laurette Taylor (1885-1946) starred in *Peg O' My Heart* on 1912 Broadway for 603 performances before making the King Vidor film. Noel Coward would write *Hay Fever* (1925) about her. Taylor makes a comeback as Amanda Wingfield in Tennessee Williams' 1945 *Glass Menagerie*.

Mantle suggests Alice Nielsen "sought to revive the spell of long ago, which was the spell of her youth.... Of Miss Nielsen's future we are not so hopeful. She has evidently waited too long to return gracefully to the light opera repertoire which was once so easy for her and with which she reigned supreme. The formality of the grand opera school has left its mark upon her. And the present generation of playgoers, knowing her not at all or only as the heroine of a pretty legend, told in the glowing enthusiasm of those who do remember, refuse to accept the substitute".

Ironically, after it closes, *Life* columnist Metcalf (Nov 22) promotes the show: "*Kitty Darlin'* brings back to the comic-opera stage Alice Nielsen, who can both sing and act such a coquettish heroine as the Kitty Belairs, taken from well-known book and play. With a well-defined plot, excellently realized costume possibilities, a most agreeable score by Mr. Rudolf Friml and a good singing company, *Kitty Darlin'* has sturdier claims to liking than most of the musical pieces we get. The comedy side is not neglected, Mr. Edwin Stevens legitimately distinguishing himself on that side of the bill. *Kitty Darlin'* brings the Casino back to something like its old estate".

Of all opportunities, Alice selects this.

Milking the dead fish, *Kitty* becomes a 1930 Warner musical with Claudia Dell, Ernest Torrence and Walter Pidgeon, director Alfred Green without any reuse of the 1917 project.

More than Broadway on her mind. December 21, month after closing, she weds LeRoy Stoddard (*NY Times*): "Alice Nielsen, one of the most celebrated of American operatic singers, and Dr. Leroy R. Stoddard, an prominent physician and clubman of New York, were married...." Sibling Erasmus and wife, joined by Stoddard's "best friend Charles White", attend the unannounced marriage ceremony conducted by Rev. Frank Carson at Greenwich Presbyterian, Conn. Reports of marriage carry across the country, including the *Bayfield Blade* LA.

Second for both. Stoddard had divorced Carolyn Williams of Detroit after meeting Alice Nielsen in his office. Nielsen has taken a married man; the couple sail for Cuba, a Havana honeymoon "to avoid both gifts and advice". On return Nielsen "will resume her professional career".

Speaking of Stoddard, she glows with obvious affection.

By our wending way, Alexander McDannald in *American Annual* speaks of a marriage by Alice Nielsen to JF Leffler by error; JF Leffler married Christiana Nielsen, no relation Alice. The error spreads; repeated in Alice's *NY Times* obit but not by any accurate honest papers.

According to Stan Malecki at Chapman Historical Museum in Glenn Falls, LeRoy lived at the Stoddard family home on 36 Elm Street until his high school graduation, when he went to NYU. Graduated 1896, got his NY Medical College degree 1900. Became house physician for Saks and Co. NYC. Married singer Carolyn Williams on March 14, 1906. Stoddard has a literary New York family connected to photographer Seneca Ray Stoddard (1843-1917). Prominent plastic surgeon, in Europe his patients were war casualties but in the USA "rich women and female stars". Along with reconstructive surgery on veterans at Bedford's Santorium Montefiore and Northern Westchester Hospital, by 1920 Stoddard has a large stage-and-screen cosmetic surgery practice. Member of "Manhattan, Aero, Automobile and Columbia Yacht clubs and Delta Phi, hw is active in society and theatre groups.

Stoddard and Nielsen buy a large historic house near Alice's 1898 co-star Marguerite Sylva in Bedford NY. Forty miles NW of NYC, fifteen miles from Greenwich CN. Bedford is by 1917 a commuter village for Manhattan connected by rail. Sylva, Nielsen, and other Broadway and grand opera stars, find in Bedford a "simple little home in the country amid the restful green fields". Two diva pals enter the cultural life of the village.

1918: ART SONGS ON THE REDPATH

Again this spring, Alice Nielsen takes her familiar Redpath Chautauqua circuit, sharing the stage with violinist Karel Havlicek and pianist William Reddick. Jacksonville FL, start of the tour, season's program:

1. *The Spirit Flower* (Campbell-Tipton), *Will O' The Wisp* (Spross), *I Came With A Song* (La Forge), *Love Has Wings* (Rogers).

2. *Symphonic Espanole* (Lalo) played by Havlicek.

3. *Si Mes Vers Avaient Des Ailes* (Hahn), *Vergebliches Standehen* (Brahms), *L'Heure Exquise* (Hahn), *Komm Lass Une Spiclen* (Bleichmann).

4. *Mediation* (from *Thais* by Massenet), *Wiegenlied* (Shubert) and *Dance Of The Goblins* (Popper) played by Havlicek.

5. *Love's Old Sweet Song* (Malloy), *The Low-back'd Car* (Lover), *But Lately In Dance* (Arensky), *The Year's At The Spring* (Beach).

6. Souvenir de Moscow (Wieniawsky) played by Havlicek.

7. Aria: *Vissi d'arte* (from *Tosca* by Puccini) sung by Nielsen with violin obbligato by Havlicek.

The program lists Nielsen's select 1918 encores: "*The Captain, Kathleen Mavourneen, Coming Thro' the Rye, The Waters of Minnetonka and other Indian Songs, Sky-Blue Water, Old Black Joe, My Old Kentucky Home, Swannee River, Last Rose Of Summer, Massa's In The Cold Cold Ground, Dixie, Genevieve, Home Sweet Home, An Explanation, Good-Bye, Believe Me If All Those Endearing Young Charms, Laddie, Bonnie Sweet Bessie, The Next Market Day, Robin Adair*".

Interestingly, *Un bel di* is missing by error; soon restored to print.

No hint Alice has sung anything of Victor Herbert since July in London.

After marriage, touring schedules taper.

March 28 (*KC Journal*), she revisits Kansas City. Gladly touring, gladly married: "Alice Nielsen, Kansas City's own prima donna, chatted pleasantly...at the Coates House last night. Perennially youthful, Miss Nielsen was radiantly happy and there was a smile with every word".

Alice says, "The latest news about me is the best. It is that I was married on December 21 to Dr. LeRoy Ray Stoddard of NY". She will curtail tours, yet carefully adds "my marriage will not interfere with my career. I cannot think of myself as not singing, any more than I can think of myself as not walking or eating. I am on my way to Topeka to sing tonight. I have come West for a brief tour of only eight engagements. All my tours hereafter will be short ones—I have somebody else to think about now, you see".

Home and husband in Bedford spark a first complaint of touring: "I shall do opera and concert work in the East next season, though under just what management I have not yet decided. But I shall undertake no more Chautauqua engagements or other long, tiresome trips".

Promotes Red Cross. "I am deeply interested in war work. It seems there is so much that desperately needs to be done and I want to do my full share. I want especially to help the Red Cross. I cannot sew or knit, but I can sing and my services are to be had for the asking any time I can help. And I shall be especially pleased to sing here in Kansas City, to help along the war work anytime it is arranged for me. And I want to do this not only for patriotic reasons but because this is my town, the old home town that has been so wonderfully good to me". Alice sang a Red Cross benefit in her husband's hometown of Glen Falls NY, raising "more than $1,000".

KC Journal states "Dr. Stoddard is a son of the late Henry L. Stoddard, widely-known American poet". Glen Falls in the Adirondacks is an artists' colony. Henry Stoddard (1825-1903) was blacksmith, writer, editor, librarian, clerk, editor, customs inspector: famed poet in 1852 married novelist Elizabeth Drew (1823-1902). Drew's best-known novel, *The Morgesons* (1862). Henry's *NY Times* obit failed to mentioned a son LeRoy.

Drew writes: "Fortunate or not, we were poor. It was not strange that I should marry; but that I should follow that old idyll; and accept the destiny of a garret and a crust with a poet, was incredible! Therefore, being apart from the diversions of society, I had many idle hours. One day..." she begins writing. A fan will be Nathaniel Hawthorne, who says "Pray pardon my frankness, for what is the use of saying anything unless we say what we think? There are very few books...of which I could retain any memory so long after reading them as I do of *The Morgesons*".

Skipping to May, *Musical Courier* reports Nielsen had "one of the busiest times of her long career this spring. She had scarcely returned from a long concert tour through the Southwest...before she was called away to a patriotic music festival at Charlotte, NC" where Nielsen represents America; Lucien Muratore, France; and Frances Alda, England. They sell autographs to raise money for Red Cross, visit the Army training camp for a group photo, sing at a Knights of Columbus hut, cheered "by the soldier boys".

Charlotte Observer covers the "Entente Allies' Music Festival" April 26 and 27". Alice Nielsen is "so well-known to the people of Piedmont Carolina that it is not necessary to say she a prima donna soprano of the Metropolitan Opera House. She might rightly be termed the most talented and versatile artist appearing in America. Whether it is on the concert platform or on the operatic stage, the result is always a perfectly finished performance that creates a truly enjoyable and lasting impression upon her audience". If reads like a press release, it was: hers.

Summer passes. Nielsen and Stoddard travel. Nielsen has said, there are a lot places to see before she dies. She has Stoddard, they go places: Caribbean, Europe, across the Americas.

In fall, Alice Nielsen resumes promoting artistic women. She knows what it takes. In Chicago September 6, she changes her concert set to bring composer Mrs. Lulu Jones-Downing to the stage. Louis Elson's *Modern Music* (1918) lists Jones-Downing "of this growing group of American woman composers...." She has been "musically active in Richmond, Indiana" and now "established in Chicago as a teacher and composer". She scores music to poems such as *Violets* by James Whedon, "*My heart is thine, Love, Now and always*".

In Nielsen's show Havelick plays his usual set and introduces *Menuett* by Beethoven and *Mazurka* by Zarzycki.

Set 1: *Spirit Flower* (Campbell-Tipton), *The Weathercock* (Liza Lehman), *Down In The Forest* (Landon Ronald), *My Lover He Comes On The Skee* (Clough Leighter).

Set 2: *La Papillon* (Fourdrain), *Vergebliches Standchen* (Brahms), *Zueignung* (Strauss), *Komm lass uns Spielen* (Bleichmann).

Set 3: *Burst Of Melody* (Seiler), *Mystery* (Irene Hale), *When Love Is Kind* (Old English Melody arranged by A.L.), *An Open Secret* (Woodman).

Set 4: *I Love My Jean*, and *June* by Jones-Downing who takes the stage to accompany on piano. Downing had scored poet Robert Burns' *Jean* in 1912.

Nielsen sang: "*I see her in the dewy flowers, I see her sweet and fair; I hear her in the tunefu' birds, I hear her charm the air. There's not a bonnie flower that springs, By fountain, shaw or green; There's not a bonnie bird that sings, But minds me o' my Jean*".

Nielsen's finale *Un bel di*; usual encores.

Ditching managers Wagner, then Brown, leaving Chautauqua, Nielsen loses powerful publicity engines. Relies on her own network for bookings. Besides performing, she travels with husband whose medical work carries him to Europe and California to aid mutilated American boys. If she has brought gayety to nations; he restores the wounded.

After 1918, Alice Nielsen's grand opera roles vanish. Lost her home stage, literally lost and gone forever. Fame fades with audience memories.

The unforgettable has become frozen in amber.

1919: TOURS LESS, BEDFORD MARRIAGE MORE

New Nielsen manager appears. Annie Friedberg handles opera stars and other concert artists competently from her offices at the Met. In a brilliant move, Friedberg creates publicity features about her artists at home for summer, and at tiller of her motorboat, Alice smiles within a *Musical America* photo collage showing the interior and exterior of her cottage. Friedberg, managing artists since 1911, lives in White Plains.

January 24, 1919, Nielsen returns to Kansas City Convention Hall with the baritone Reinald Werrenrath and "much admired violinist from Hutchinson, Kansas, Mrs. Laura Reed Yaggy". Benefit for Garrett's signal corps "now in Germany". Yaggy breaks a string; Werrenrath sings an aria from *Faust* and Irish songs. He is highly praised. Both deserve a glance.

Reed-Yaggy, as Laura prefers being called (1887-1984), the reigning concert violin prodigy from Kansas City, performed Mendelssohn Concerto with Karl Busch and KC Symphony in 1900 age thirteen, owns a rare Sanctus Serafine violin. Ardent suffragist. Married at eighteen, leapt out of home "retirement" for tours at twenty-five, always returning to husband and two kids in rural Reno County KS. Often plays pieces by Alice's virtuoso pal Kreisler.

Werrenrath, (1883-1953), Brooklyn baritone with tenor Danish dad, has had a grand opera and recording career since 1907. Records solo, or with Orpheus or Victor quartettes. His WEAF radio career begins 1930; joins NBC's music staff and Peabody Conservatory, Baltimore. Slates 3,000 concerts before retiring to Chazy Lake, NY.

Three hometown virtuosos, two with Danish roots.

KC Times critic MKP knew Nielsen since her youth, "Our Alice...proved even more than usually charming and youthful, as limpid and luscious of voice as when she made her debut in *The Fortune Teller*—probably more so, since her art has never served her so well as it does today. She might have been a debutant, judging from her appearance, but no debutant could have sung Mozart as she did nor have brought to the Indian lyrics by Cadman in imagination developed by rich experience. Her voice was at its best in the French group, all modern songs, full of subtleties.

Three months later Nielsen returns home again to Kansas City; March 27 chatting with *KC Star* "In her apartment at Coates House, she talked for a time of happy school days spent at St. Teresa's Academy in Kansas City. But the subject of the war was on her mind...." Red Cross is Nielsen's charity. "The British are still holding the line? That's splendid. The British are wonderful... such reserves of strength under their quiet exterior. Sometimes I wish I could be in the midst of the struggle, but I can do more by giving part of the proceeds of my concerts to the Red Cross".

Should art be "side-tracked" for the war? Stop the gayety of nations?

Nielsen grows gorgeously poetic. Supreme exponent of the gayety of nations faces war. Knows what her voice gives many many people. When the world is sane and beautiful once more:

"Most certainly not. We must keep the flame of beauty burning through these dreadful times. Music is the most appealing of the arts, and the human voice is the most exquisite music we know.

"Think of the pleasure that a beautiful voice can give. Who would wish to silence it until peace comes again? When the world is sane and beautiful once more, we will look back and realize how much music helped us to live through these abnormal times".

Interestingly, Nielsen states she has joined "one of the big opera companies to be organized this season in NY, though she cannot say at present what the opera will be". Hope does not materialize.

Alice sports a French decoration presented by Marshal Joffe, a gift for her Red Cross help. Stoddard is soon expected to join her, "she is so proud of him that she is very happy he is to be with her in her home city. Indeed, no bride was ever more enthusiastic over her husband than KC's operatic star is over Doctor Stoddard".

For nine months the newlyweds enjoy private life. Alice works with vocal coach Daniel Sullivan at 35 East 38th Street. Despite marriage 1919-20 are touring years. Skips concerts the spring and summer, Nielsen revisits the West in company with Stoddard's medical tours.

Because Alice cannot visit California without endorsing a piano, August 6th she blesses "Style 'X' Apollo player piano" sold by Wiley Allen Company, "She found it hard to realize that the pianist was not actually seated at the keyboard".

Before Christmas, *Musical America* reports Alice Nielsen has acquired rank of "honorary Lieutenant of the Woman's Police Reserve of NYC".

In June Hortense arrives in Asheville NC to perform Ibsen's *Ghosts* for the literary club. July and August she is Rosalind in *As You Like It* "assisted by 50 Asheville High Students". They tour; *French Broad Hustler* display ad calls it "Midsummer Shakespeare Festival for the People" with "enlarged" ukulele orchestra and tenor Alva Lowe at Hendersonville Opera House three days.

Alice travels as Mrs. Stoddard to accompany husband on surgery rounds. December 27, *LA Times* reports "Alice Nielsen, popular and beloved operatic star who has been at the Alexandria Hotel for several days, will leave this evening for British Columbia, where she will continue her concert tour begun several weeks ago, when she bid a temporary farewell to her home in NY.

"She will not sing in California this season unless at San Francisco for an orchestral engagement, but she will return to Los Angeles next year when she will appear in recital. Dr. LeRoy R. Stoddard…is with her, having come West to perform corrective operations on maimed soldiers in San Francisco and Santa Barbara. Dr. Stoddard has accomplished wonders in his humane profession and last evening showed many of his films at the Hampton studios, which give evidence of the transformations he has wrought in maimed countenances.

"Alice Nielsen is charming and vivacious as usual. Of her voice she says, 'I am singing better every day', and of her appearance, 'I have nothing to fear from the advance of time. Old age has no terrors for me. I have seen too much of what can be done to rejuvenate faces. When I am old I shall retire to the country for a week and at the end of that time will read my birth certificate in the paper. I shall be ready then for any part, and shall not hesitate to play 'Little Eva' [of *Uncle Tom's Cabin*].

"Although now on a recital tour, Alice Nielsen is loyal to opera. In fact loyalty is an outstanding characteristic of the singer. In speaking of her voice specialist, of Eleonora Duse, whom the singer knows and loves well, and even of the pet chow dog, which she has left with Maxine Elliot, Miss Nielsen has only the warmest tenderness". Never gave that puppy to her brother after all.

Maxine Elliot as a dog sitter; their talks would fascinate.

Elliot (1868-1940) is a wonder. Regarded one of world's most beautiful women, violet eyes with passion. Born Maine, marries young, leaves him for the stage. Begins Broadway 1894, joins Augustin Daly 1895, tours San

Francisco then Australia with comic Nat Goodwin who she marries. Joins Charles Frohman for a NYC hit Her Own Way, tours London 1905, divorces Goodwin 1908. Connects with JP Morgan Sr. in his 70s, makes a fortune investing, only woman owning a Broadway theatre, the Maxine Elliot on 39th. One wishes she had given Hortense the stage.

Elliot, known for her comedy, drama, and romances, acts or produces until retiring with pets to *Château de l'Horizon* in 1920 Cannes. This party place, a hangout for Winston Churchill and the ritzy set has a waterslide into the sea. Interestingly, Elliot made three 1913 films before returning to Brittan and a young tennis star beau soon killed by the Jacob-Schiff, JP Morgan war. In 1917 she made *Fighting Odds*. This fine Los Angeles year of 1919 Alice's friend and dogsitter Maxine Elliot completes her last film, *The Eternal Magdalene*, at MGM.

Alice Nielsen knew the top women filmmakers of her era, frequently visited Los Angeles, made no films.

Nielsen laughingly relates a poet's pass rejected: "D'Annunzio, poet and patriot, is the only person for whom Miss Nielsen expressed distaste", relates *LA Times*. Almost a legend now, D'Annunzio, Alice confides to wide-eyed reporter, "resided in a beautiful villa forty miles from Rome when I was there, living in the same spot [with Duse], and he is the most conceited man in the world. He thinks every woman, especially every American girl, is in love with him". She retells the garden story, "He asked me one moonlight evening if I had ever been in love, and I said 'Oh Lord yes', in a way which dampened his ardor".

In LA land Nielsen skips her chances: "She will not go in for the cinema. She would rather sing, and she doubts it is possible to do both". That egg-in-a-poke targets Farrar, well-publicized for DeMille's *Joan The Woman* released this year.

Cecile DeMille admires Alice Nielsen who inspires: she makes no films. If opportunity arose she does not elaborate. She has declined the offers; she has disliked the scripts; we get no insight to these tales.

1920s: TENDING BEDFORD's GARDEN

Leaving the tall tales of an independent Los Angeles making its own stories without dictation from New York, we now follow Alice Nielsen's recital tour into the smaller towns. Arrivals are arranged by local musical groups.

December 30th Alice hits Klamath Falls, sponsored by its Musical Study Club, "At her best and carried her audience with her. Her voice from the full low notes to the high pure quality of her high notes displayed remarkable range, power and ease. Nothing can surpass the beauty of phrasing, delicacy of touch, clearness of diction and pianissimo effects, sustained and marvelous".

January 5th she sings Portland for the first time in five years, sponsored by the Portland Oratorio Society. "Her voice is clear and sure, yet retaining on its upper register all the sweetness of the middle. She sings without apparent effort, and her diction is perfect".

January 9th she warbles for "the public of Wenatchee and vicinity" at "magnificent new Liberty Theatre. Never before has a Wenatchee audience shown such heartfelt appreciation of any artist's work as was evidenced last evening". Wenatchee, as you know, is "home of the world's best apples".

The night of January 16th, Nielsen in Lewiston's Temple Theatre joined by pianist Armin Doerner of Josef d'Harvard's Lewiston Conservatory.

Reaching Salt Lake her welcome will be as warm as usual. Salt Lake this year produces another of the greatest Nielsen tributes. Mormon Tabernacle Choir sponsors her visit.

January 22nd (*Salt Lake Tribune*), Nielsen sings at the Tabernacle, which "reinforced her preeminence in the hearts of her former admirers and added a host of new ones to the long list".

Utah presents Alice Nielsen a poetic appreciation ranking among her very best reviews: Los Angeles, Dallas, Chicago, Boston. Only another singer could create this sort of insight.

"Twenty songs, representing as many composers and a half dozen different types of music, running the gamut of human emotions in almost its entire range, this was the contribution of Miss Nielsen in her 'Evening Of Song.'"

She "entered into the soul of the song with an illuminated personality that went straight to the heart. Miss Nielsen's range of voice was unusually great. For purity and sheer beauty of tone she ranks with any soloist...while her lower register holds a vibrant richness reminiscent of a great contralto, and she exhibits a carrying power in sustained pianissimo that makes one thrill in wonder that amounts to awe".

Debussy's *Mandolin* "she was forced to repeat, so strong was its appeal". Sang *The Sea Hath Its Pearls*, a composition by her pianist Griselle, "a love song of high rank that deserves to live".

Salt Lake gives pianist Thomas Griselle his due: "Far more than a good accompanist, he was intelligently sympathetic with the singer throughout her part of the program and in his solo work demonstrated both skill and breadth, playing his own *Minuet* and *Bouree* with great effectiveness, and likewise in his interpretation of the Chopin numbers, *Impromptu in A Flat* and *Etude in C Major*, evidencing clear understanding of the composer's moods".

First encore: *Old Folks At Home*, then *Comin' Thru The Rye*, *Annie Laurie*, and the rest of her childhood songs from singing in the streets.

Danish cousins in Utah, Irish cousins in Boston. "At the conclusion of the concert which was under Tabernacle Choir auspices, Miss Nielsen held an informal reception and was cordially greeted and congratulated by many old and new friends".

Traveling onward by rail proceeds.

January 26th in Missoula, Montana, Dr. William Bateman reviews her concert. He knew her in Bostonian days, credits Alice with raising the group from decline. Bringing "youth, beauty, charm and a splendid voice to the aid of the famous Bostonians, she had lifted that wonderful organization from a temporary setback to a plane which enshrined it in the hearts of all hearers".

Bateman vividly recalls *Robin Hood* and *Serenade*, "the delectable vision presented by Alice Nielsen, the ringing bell-like voice, the charm which filled audiences with enthusiasm". He continues in the present: "rarely can a famous prima donna look so girlish; almost as seldom can one make an audience part and parcel of her song. In voice Miss Nielsen has found much; the beautiful quality is still there, enhanced by technical skill and experience.

"The program is well arranged and most generous. Among so many beauties it is hard to picture some as better than the others. The group of modern French songs however, was especially delightful, as was *The Weather Cock* and *Fairy Pipers*". Bateman also responds strongly to her sustained acting, "Miss Nielsen has an unusual ability to make 'atmosphere' for each mood, as was strikingly shown in *But Lately In Dance*". And then, "she sang *Swanee River*".

Ends the tour.

February 28th *Musical America* carries a double-page spread of her reviews with nothing but an oversized signature "Alice Nielsen" as the illustration. She returns home, sweet home. Bedford gives Nielsen a place to tend her garden, mostly flowers. Since 1900s the village attracts actors: Francis Wilson, Bessie Tyree, Marguerite Sylva and others settle down. Three residents, Nielsen, Sylva, and Wilson, have starred in Victor Herbert shows. Bedford, short commute to NYC by train or motorcar. Dr. Walton Carpenter built 1878's North Westchester Hospital there. Alice had first visited Stoddard's practice at 33 West 42nd Street.

The Stoddards enjoy their home, 379 Cantitoe Road named after Chief Katanah's favorite wife of several simultaneous in that traditional conservative American fashion Mormons rightly admire. Katanah had sold the land to twenty-two men from Stamford, Connecticut who began Bedford in 1680.

Nielsen's 1810 McCord-Tharp House has forty acres "situated behind a huge copper beech and several ancient maples". Bedford Historical

Association reveals the Stoddards purchased the property May 1st 1920 from Martha Tharp, widow of the village florist. Hence the greenhouses. House still is beautiful.

Parker Kuhn recalls Alice Nielsen removed the extensive greenhouses to grow more flowers. Bedford Riding Lanes Association was established soon after Nielsen arrived. Promises "to preserve, protect and maintain a system of country lanes and trails on private property for the convenience of equestrians".

Spring 1920 Alice Nielsen resumes concerts, revisits Boston. April 30th she sings at NYC's Aeolian recital then jumps back to Boston at—bittersweet—Symphony Hall. Feelings at rounding the corner to regard the Boston Opera House stripped and hijacked into a Shubert hall, we may try to imagine. Her Hemenway home overlooking Fenway only a short walk from the opera.

Orchestra manager LH Mudgett produces the May 2nd joint concert with Alice Nielsen and cellist Jean Bedettl. William Reddick plays piano for Nielsen, Alfred De Voto for Bedettl. Program has six sections; Nielsen and Bedettl trading. Alice starts with Mozart's *Deh vieni non tardar* from *Nozze di Figaro*, then Bedettl plays *Suite Ancienne* by SB Breval. Next set, Nielsen six French songs, *Chere Nuit* by Bachelet, *Mandolin* by Debussy, *Extase* by Dupare, *Papillon* by Fourdrain, *Ariette* by Vidal, and finishes with Mozart's *Batti, Batti*. Bedettl performs a set of Bruck, Glazounov, Shumann and Popper. Nielsen closes with *Lullaby* by Scott, *Under the Greenwood Tree* by Buzzi-Peccia, *The Weathercock* by Lehmann, *But Lately in The Dance* by Arensky and *An Open Secret* by Woodman.

Reviews mention the large glad audience assembled for the gayety.

Boston Globe (May 3): "After an absence of several seasons, Alice Nielsen, well-remembered soprano of the early days of the late Boston Opera Company" gave "a song recital of her own last evening in Symphony Hall where a large and enthusiastic audience welcomed her in a manner which must have shown her that she still holds a warm place in the hearts of Boston music-lovers.

"Charmingly gowned, as always, Miss Nielsen's appearance is still amazingly youthful in view of the years which have passed since she first achieved popular favor here with the Bostonians. No less striking is the manner in which her voice, a soprano of delicate quality and remarkable charm, has been preserved". Her Mozart is "in the style of music in which the soprano has always excelled".

She makes material more interesting than it really is; as *Fortune Teller*.

"She was at her best in a number of the dainty little songs with which her program was chiefly composed, trifles to which her voice and manner lend a charm and grace which raises them far above their normal plan. Foudrain's *Papillon*, Scott's *Lullaby* and *But Lately In The Dance*, by Arensky, were especially delightful. The singers was obliged to respond to many encores". Bedetti "particularly notable" in Breval's *Suite Ancienne*, Popper's *Tarantelle*.

Returning home to 1920s Bedford NY, Alice Nielsen and neighbors open a memorial to the fallen World War soldiers. Bedford Community House, a true gathering place, still stands. At street level is a small theatre with raised stage. Underneath, recreation room and kitchen. Main hall accommodates 350 people. When Alice sings, place packed. Newspaper clippings in Bedford's Historian Office shed light on that lively scene.

Homelife in the 1920s. How appropriate that one of her greatest tributes is from no place but home.

Bedford has a fine writer, unsigned, who feels the moment and knows the situation and setting. Writes in *North Westchester Times* of the Bedford Community House, "Built by the community and for the community and the whole community is behind it". To "commemorate those who served in the great war" and "make Bedford Hills a better place to live in".

All talent in town helps.

September 24 (*North Westchester Times*), Francis Wilson, Bessie Tyree, and Marguerite Sylva open Bedford Community House. Wilson and Tyree perform scenes from *School For Scandal*, "The polished voices, the supreme mastery of technique, the restrained forcefulness of gesture, the costumes, the setting, all combined to create a wish that the whole of the play could have followed". Sylva follows with "song after song, all delightful, sad, stirring and merry and showing that one who has mastered all the secrets of her art has not lost the pleasure of giving enjoyment to others". Nielsen several times yearly sings benefits at the village Community Center.

October 23, *Musical America* publishes Alice's portrait in furs and hat. Caption: "A great success is the result not only of a talent but of contact with life".

Her facelift receives news, the magazine discusses Stoddard's expertise to look young and promote the fad, and so promotes him. Once again lends her success to aid associates. Story reaches into the heartland of her home town, and Christmas Day, *KC Star* has a short feature: "Secret of the perennial youth of Alice Nielsen, Kansas City's prima donna, and the right of her husband, Dr. LeRoy Stoddard, to distinction of his own rather than being the consort of a famous singer, were revealed simultaneously recently by a story in *Musical America*. Dr. Stoddard is an expert in plastic surgery, part of the function of which is the removal of wrinkles and flabby flesh from faces".

Alice Nielsen has blazed another trail. "When asked if he ever had performed any of his operations on his wife, Dr. Stoddard said, 'I will answer by saying that critics recently have said that Miss Nielsen not only has regained her striking beauty, but has conquered youth itself, singing better than she ever did, and looking more beautiful than ever.'"

Stoddard reconstructs "soldiers' faces, cut by shell fragments. He also treats mental and nervous diseases, such as of persons who worry over a facial disfigurement". Inevitably with Alice, "Dr. Stoddard has a large practice among stage and screen folk and believes that, before long, plastic surgery generally will be resorted to".

Thanks 1920 US Census for whereabouts of Alice siblings: Erasmus and wife Julia live near NYC in Far Rockaway with two kids, Mary A. age 10 and Benjamin 8, plus Julia's Irish-born sister Mary Brennen. Alice's brother is listed born on "March 2, 1873". They live at 1336 Eggert Place, mile from St. Mary's Star of the Sea where Erasmus is organist, plus music director for town theatre. Hortense, husband, and two children have settled in Chicago.

1921: BOSTON SYMPHONY, BEDFORD, DUSE RETURNS

In March, Nielsen sings at Symphony Hall with Boston Orchestra conducted by Pierre Monteux. Same month in Boston, Kreisler plays violin, Toscanini makes a farewell appearance with La Scala orchestra, Rachmaninoff plays piano, Anna Pavlova back then spelled "Pavlowa" dances with Ballet Russe or some spinoff. At the newfangled movie house, Pola Negri "world's greatest 'vamp'" can be seen in photoplay *Passion,* "world's greatest romance of love and hatred" featuring a live orchestra until advent of sound recordings kill that gig within seven years.

Friday afternoon March 4th and Saturday evening, Boston Orchestra gives Mendelssohn's "Scotch" and Mozart's overture *Die Entfuhrung aus dem Serail,* and Alice sings *Deh vieni non tardar* from *Marriage of Figaro.*

Nielsen (from Italian): *"O come, don't be late my beautiful joy. Come where love calls you to enjoyment. Until night's torches no longer shine in the sky. As long as the air is still dark. And the world quiet. Come, come! I want to crown you with roses".*

They follow with *Don Giovanni, Batti, batti.*

Nielsen (from Italian): *"Strike, strike, dear Masseto, your poor Zerlina! I will stand like a little lamb and await your blows. I will let you pull me by the hair; I will let you pluck out my eyes, and even then will I gladly kiss your dear hands. Let us make up, my sweetheart! And afterwards we will spend the nights and days in contentment and mirth".*

Her Cadman songs, then Henry Gilbert's *Indian Sketches.* Boston's Gilbert had collected songs on recording cylinders for Edward Curtis's North American Indian project which he orchestrated and adapted.

Olin Downes recognizes Alice's constant artistic progress. Had the rare, "lost and gone" gift of attending Boston Opera when it was. Caught the artist Alice distancing herself from this audience of stiffs.

Downes (*Boston Post*): "Miss Nielsen sang the introductory measures of recitative of the air from "Figaro's Wedding" with exemplary musicianship and fineness of nuance. She has become each year, a most thoughtful interpreter.

"Add to this her inborn qualifications for the interpretation of Mozart. A singer who interprets, for example, the character of Zerlina, with her song of pleading to the discomforted and sorely tried Masseto, must have in her own artistic nature a certain naiveté and youthfulness, a spontaneity and innocence of sentiment, which are either felt or present or else absent, for they cannot be manufactured.

"In her phrasing and in her sentiment Miss Nielsen was very fortunate. She was, it is true, less spontaneous, less carefree in her vocalization than she ordinarily is. Why do singers betray such accursed caution every time they rise before a Boston Symphony audience?

"The reservation about Miss Nielsen's singing is this comparative lack of ease of and of contagious enthusiasm which is one of the gratifying and distinguishing characteristics of her art. In all probability these things will be in evidence this evening, after the first sight of a motionless audience and the plaster casts frowning down from the niches in Symphony Hall".

Downes connects beautifully. Subtly recalls collapse of Boston Opera; her present setting, after all, is just Symphony Hall: "That is not opera. That is not the stage for which Miss Nielsen is born, but on the other hand she is one of the few opera singers whose performances in the concert room sustain careful and critical examinations...."

Despite the cold starting out, things warm up, "the audience recalled her repeatedly yesterday afternoon".

Alice Nielsen rejoins Boston Symphony, same program March 8th Providence and March 24th Cambridge.

Returns to star at a Symphony Hall benefit to raise $2-million for Boston College (*Globe* Ap 21). *Boston Globe*: "Tonight at Symphony Hall Alice Nielsen, formerly of the Boston Grand Opera Company, will appear at a concert, the proceeds...donated to the Boston College fund".

Two Boston Opera alumnae anchor the benefit, Nielsen and Mrs. Alvan Fuller, formerly Viola Davenport, husband now Lieutenant Governor. The two singers join pianist Marjorie Church and a Boston Symphony ensemble directed by Augusto Vannini. The ten-day fund drive has been hosted by F. Loring Young, Speaker of the House.

Boston College owes everything to women. Committee-in-charge includes Kathryn McCathy, Elizabeth Sheridan. Fund-raising is led by women from "five of the big women's colleges" with Rev. William Murphy, faculty member of Boston College and former newspaperman. Meetings held at League of Catholic Women, 1 Arlington St., Back Bay; its members include Tina Lee, Marie Whall, and Eleanor O'Connor. Deeds done in Boston, ten days later Nielsen continues to a Chicago concert.

Alice receives word Duse will emerge from retirement and tour America, publishing "Eleonora Duse As Alice Nielsen Knows Her", syndicated by *Kansas City Star* (May 31). Rehashes time shared, almost unchanged when retold a decade later. Alice's Duse tale appears in *Drama* magazine.

DUSE RETURNS TO THE STAGE by ALICE NIELSEN

The great Italian tragedienne once more to tread the boards after many years of inexplicable retirement.

A cable dispatch from Rome the other day stated that Eleonora Duse, the great Italian tragedienne, is about to return to the stage. This news will bring joy to many thousands of her admirers the world over. For years, there has been much speculation as to the reason Duse no longer appeared before the public why she had hidden herself so completely as though she had vanished off the face of the earth. Illness, it was said, was depriving the world of her genius, but that was only partly true. Physically, the lovely Italian was well, but her brilliant mind had become benumbed as though from a blow. Her beautiful soul was ill. And the one who dealt the blow was Gabriele D'Annunzio, the celebrated poet and now military dictator of Fiume.

Whatever hypothetical reasons may have been given for Duse's retirement the truth is that it was simply due to the fact that D'Annunzio, through his power of suggestion, made her feel that she was old, when she was just upon the threshold of her prime. Blinded by the glamour of his genius, she thought she had met a soul as big as her own, and when she realized her mistake it almost killed her. I know, for I was with her all during that dark and bitter period of disillusionment. My meeting with Duse is an example of the child-like directness which is typical of her.

Some time before this, a mutual friend had arranged for me to meet the tragedienne, but she disappointed us by not appearing. A week later, a tea-party was arranged, and I was assured that the actress would come, but again I was doomed to disappointment.

Finally, I made up my mind I would meet her or die in the attempt. I learned that she was taking a train for Rome the next day. Ascertaining the time, I bought my ticket and boarded the train just in time to see the actress enter her compartment. When we started I presented myself. She smiled. The spell was broken and we began to converse. She laughed heartily when I told her the only reason I took the train was to get a chance to speak to her, and she made me get off at the next station and go home, with the exhilarating promise that she would write me upon her return.

Soon afterwards I received an invitation to attend a private musicale she was giving at her villa, the Palazzo Borghesi at Porto d'Anzio, forty-three miles from Rome.

It was a memorable evening. D'Annunzio was present, reciting some of his poetry, the beauty of his voice as well as the brilliance of his verse casting an indescribable romantic glamour upon his listeners. What thrilled me more, however, was the presence of Duse herself in that beautiful room, full of lovely antique things. She was sitting upon an ottoman, rather detached from the general company, in the background. Her elbows were upon her knees, and her face, upon which the lightning expressions flitted ceaselessly, was cupped in her beautiful hands.

Very adequately had D'Annunzio named her "*La donna delle belle mani*", the woman of the beautiful hands. At this time, I had not yet seen her in the Italian poet's *La Gioconda*" the play whose motive springs from a pair of hands, but I could easily imagine that Signora Duse's hands, as well as her face could express more than those of any other human being.

After D'Annunzio had finished, the tragedienne rose, and pushing me gently by the shoulders toward the center of the room, said: "Now, *La Piccola* (she always called me 'little one'), let me hear you sing". Motioning the accompanist to the clavischord, she went back to her corner upon the ottoman. I sang selections from some of the operas and a few of the old classics. During this performance, her intent gaze never left my face, and she only spoke at the end of each song to ask for "more".

At the end, she kissed me on both cheeks, thanking me for "my beautiful gift of song" as she expressed it, making me promise to come and sing for her often. Thus began a friendship which to me has been the most precious that the gods have bestowed.

Duse was often silent and aloof, but not consciously so ever, simply because her mind and soul dwelt upon a plane unknown to most of us poor mortals. This unconscious attitude is expressed in something she once said to me. We were on a train travelling together through Italy, and at the moment were passing the Alps. "If you had your choice", I asked, "where would you choose to live?" I had in mind the marvelously beautiful country through which we were passing. Without hesitation she pointed to the very highest peak of the mountains in the distance and answered simply, like a child: "At the top of that mountain!" I shivered in mock horror. "Oh", I replied, "I like the fields and the flowers and the warm brown earth much too well to leave them for a chilly mountain peak".

But I knew then, as I do now, that the things of the earth hold very little for her if the soul and the sublimated mind are found wanting. In such a way had she been disappointed in her poet.

Yet I knew Duse in her gay moods too. Although the world regards her as a tragic figure, I hold that she, a thing of beauty, was intended to be a joyous spirit ever. Instead, she was made a thing of sorrow by a mere man. In her merry moods, she seemed to be joy incarnate.

When I first knew her she would go into paroxysms of laughter over the funny little Scotch clothes she took upon herself to make for D'Annunzio's little daughter, who was then about eight years old. "See, is this not quaintly adorable and funny?" she would exclaim, holding the tiny pleated skirt in both hands.

She was in one of her most charming and playful moods, when, every morning, she fed her pack of wonderful greyhounds, of which many legends are told throughout Italy, regarding their precociousness and beauty. Duse made a lovely picture as, dressed in her long, grey nun-like robe, she made the graceful creatures jump high into the air for their food.

To me she seemed most fascinating and superbly beautiful, when, after the night's performance at the theatre, she would don a soft gown, which, like all her dresses indoors, fell in a simple graceful line from her shoulders to the ground, and wrap her lovely head round and round with yards of the finest, sheerest chiffon. Taking her place at the head of the long cloister-like table (something of the cloister was always suggestive about the surroundings of the great tragedienne), she looked like some oldtime saint, for I do not exaggerate when I say that a luminous, unearthly sort of light emanated from her face and seemed to form a halo round her turbaned head.

Upon these after-theatre supper occasions, it was my custom to take my place at the foot of the table, facing Duse. Invariably this hour before retiring we spent in unbroken silence, the servants, moving about noiselessly, serving the simple repast in earthenware dishes, another of Signora's hobbies.

One evening, after she had arrived from the theatre, I slipped away to my room. She sent a servant to summon me at once. "Why are you not at your place?" she asked. Remembering that for two evenings past, she had practically ignored me, I replied: "But Signora, it occurred to me you might prefer to be alone". "No, I do not prefer that when you are in the house. I love to look at your young and pretty face across the table. Never again fail to present yourself for supper!" And patting my cheek with her indescribably soft and satin-smooth hand, she smilingly pushed me toward my chair. Often, after that, she would look searchingly into my face and sigh: "Ah, you do not know how fortunate you are, to be so young and fair!"

Her child-like wonder and heartrending grief at the thought that things of beauty must perish and genius must die, never left her. She was the possessor of one of the five death-masks made of Richard Wagner. One day she came into the music room with this mask on a black velvet cushion, and showed it to me. I started to touch it but she raised her finger forbiddingly. Her own hand caressed the air above the face of the dead composer lovingly, as though it were too precious to touch. "Oh, dear, wonderful *maestro*, gone!" she murmured, while tears rolled down her cheeks.

Although she never mentioned it, I knew that the canker of the suggestion that she was growing old was eating into the very marrow of her being. A great soul, she could not rise above her disappointment in the man who had said it. She would not permit a word said against him, however. "Do not forget, he is Italy's greatest man!" was her answer. Her adoration of his genius is expressed in the following: "We must bow before the poet, even when it seems to us he does wrong. He is a poet; he has seen something; he has seen it in that way; we must accept his vision, because it is a vision".

There was a report at one time that Duse did not like America. The only reason she did not like this country, was because our public would not accept D'Annunzio's plays. The last time she toured America she started by presenting only his plays. Duse's managers had asked her not to act in these plays, but she insisted, and a great deal of money was lost. At one performance in Baltimore, after she had especially been requested not to give D'Annunzio, and she still persisted, there was not even one paid admission. After that she complied with the wishes of her managers, and in a two weeks' capacity run of *Cavalieria Rusticana* and *Camille* all losses were regained.

One day after a week's visit with Duse, on my way to Milan, D'Annunzio drove me to the station. "Why you study with Signora Duse?" he asked in his bad English. "She can teach you nothing; she too old!" And that beautiful soul, intended to be eternally young, was only forty-two at the time! [D'Annunzio, thirty-seven]

It was at this time that her friends began to notice a really great change in Duse. Her gay, merry moods grew fewer and farther apart, and finally she succumbed to a sort of trance of abysmal gloom. She would sit for hours, her eyes staring unblinkingly into space, with the hot scalding tears running down her cheeks.

The Flame of Life, the book in which D'Annunzio, the soul-hunter, carefully exposed portraits of "a celebrated Italian actress" and himself, set wagging the tongues of the curious, Duse herself seemed utterly unconscious of it all.

One of her friends, a little piqued at this indifference, asked her what she thought of the book. "I do not know, I am sure", she answered simply. "I have not read it".

She has the greatest brain of any person I have ever known. I was on the verge of saying she has a man's brain, but I check myself, remembering Mrs. Emmeline Pankhurst's retort when some kind friend complimented her in a similar fashion. "Show me the man!" she retorted. So say I about Eleanora Duse. She knew everything the topics of the day, politics, economics, art, ancient and modern history, literature; and she could read the soul of a man or women with uncanny intuition.

Far from being jealous of any rivals, she always seemed to be searching for talent and beauty in others. I remember when I was rehearsing *Traviata* for her. She taught me to stand perfectly still during the delivery of the aria in the scene with the father, letting my voice and face express all the emotion. As I sang, she crept toward me quietly, stealthily, never taking her eyes from my face.

When the song was finished she was so close to me, her cheek almost touched mine. Peering searchingly into my face, she straightened herself and joyously exclaimed, "Yes, you are pale, you have emotional talent, you will succeed in opera". If only she had known, it was fright at her extraordinary approach that made me lose color.

When I accompanied Duse upon her last provincial theatrical tour through Italy, I would stand, fascinated, in the wings and watch her. It was during a performance of *Monna Vanna*, in the scene where she rushes offstage to kill herself, that she frightened me. Her acting was so intense, her expression so fierce, that when she came face to face with me backstage, momentarily I had the feeling that she would kill me. In every role she played she hypnotized herself into believing she *was* the heroine she portrayed. She lived her roles and at the end of every performance she was absolutely exhausted.

Alice quotes Arthur Symons and a nameless writer—discovered as *Theatre* magazine's Gertrude Norman—at length about Duse before closing: "One of my dearest hopes was that this heaven-sent gift should again enrich the world. Now that we are told this wonder-woman has consented to resume her work before the public all theatre lovers will rejoice. Her genius, I know, must be undiminished, and her great soul, dwelling on the heights, will uplift and hearten the multitudes".

Intriguingly, Alice quotes Gertrude Norman (1843-1943) who jumped into films with David Belasco's 1915 silent film of his play *May Blossom*; ne'er any Nielsen in Belasco films. Norman appears in *Birth of a Nation*.

1922, Alice's schedule has been greatly reduced. She admits to singing only twenty times; her husband's wish.

April 30th for May Day, Alice sings at the Aeolian recital in NYC.

Meanwhile in Los Angeles May 1st, Bedford neighbor and co-star Marguerite Sylva stars as *Carmen* at Hollywood Bowl "with a chorus of 250, ballet of 100, orchestra of seventy-five". General manager Henry Hall hails Sylva as "greatest Carmen on the stage today". Artistic director Alexander Bevani, "former opera impresario and now vocal teacher who lives in San Francisco". After the event, Sylva departs Bedford for Hollywood. Two years earlier she had joined the movies, starring in 1920's silent film *The Honey Bee*. Among Sylva's last films as a character actress: *Gay Senorita* (1945), Bogart's *To Have and to Have Not* (1945). 1950s episode of *This Is Your Life* television show features Sylva.

October 2nd, 1922, Nielsen sings her second annual benefit for Bedford Hills Community House.

1923, March 27th Alice Nielsen sings her last concert with Boston Symphony, rendering *Batti, batti* and *Vedrai Cariuo* in Lowell, Mass.

July 30th, Duse's American return is celebrated by the cover of *Time Magazine*. Sponsors are Katherine Onslow, Barshiba Askowith, manager Morris Gest. Direct contact with Alice is unknown.

Back home in Bedford, she helps make a frolic. 1923's Bedford House annual *Follies* starts with "living pictures". Socialite Mrs. Stuyvesant Fish poses as a painting in 1492 costume while Rev. Arthur Ketchum reads poetry over soft music from Miss Byrnes' *Orchestra of NY*. Wait, there's more. Follows ballet; parody with "original and clever verses"; plus auctions of Paris hat. And puppy. After supper of salad, sandwiches, sausages, and cake: everybody dances.

Nielsen participates in the life of her village. She attends Community House events and gives her own. She sings by spontaneous surprise at the fall *Bedford Follies* of 1923: "The announcement by Canon Prichard that the unexpected arrival of an accompanist made this possible was heartily greeted by the audience. Miss Nielsen has sung at the Community House on many occasions and always her name on the program means a treat beyond description".

The local paper notes "in private life she is Mrs. LeRoy Stoddard and has a summer home in Bedford. With characteristic generosity she has offered her services in the interest of the community in which she lives part of the year".

Her annual Bedford Community House benefit is eagerly anticipated by the village. *North Westchester Times* urges universal attendance. This elegant local reporter proves a poet among wordsmiths.

"Once in a lifetime, a great singer, out of goodness of heart, out of sweet neighborliness, comes to sing for us without money and without price. Alice Nielsen, the lovely Mimi in *La Bohème*, the Gilda in *Rigoletto*, the great coloratura soprano of *Traviata*, night on night has held spell-bound and happy that tremendous audience that crowds the Metropolitan Opera House in the height of the NY season. For three years the *prima donna* of the Boston Opera Company cast her brilliance on the name.

"As a soloist with the finest of all our American orchestras, the Boston Symphony, she has delighted the country—and she lives right here in Bedford Village, to all appearance just like anybody else.

"Only between her and anybody else there are three outstanding differences. First, she sings like an angel from the heavenly choir. Second, she looks it. Third, she is as kind. Who else do you think would come and give us what she gives, simply for love?

"The whole performance is a benefit for Bedford Hills Community House to reduce its debt. And it would appear that if Madame Nielsen, a newcomer amongst us, can find it in her heart to make to this our local cause so great and so beautiful a gift, we should turn out, putting everything else aside, man, woman and child, to show our appreciation and do her honor".

The Bedford village paper summarizes for eternity her lifetime contribution to the gayety of nations: "Hundreds of thousands all over the land are happier because of...Alice Nielsen's voice and art".

Nielsen brings her all-star team to Bedford. Thomas Griselle, "composer and distinguished interpreter of Chopin, will accompany the star and will also give piano numbers". Beyond Alice Nielsen, Grisselle will also work with Artie Shaw and Rudy Vallée. Albert Verchamp, "young violinist...rapidly rising to country-wide fame will ...play some of the most charming things in his repertoire".

Tickets $2.50 or $1 available at Bedford Hills Garage. In those days, Met tickets are $7 "plus the war tax".

Bedford Community House overflows. And this unsigned Bedford journalist gives one of the greatest concert reviews ever penned for Alice Nielsen. For the 1923 concert, Miss Nielsen selects "a beautiful gown of crystal-beaded net. She stood against a background of old Flemish tapestry, the loan of one of the patronesses, and the stage was handsomely framed in banked hydrangeas, pink and blue". The night starts with scorching solos by young violinist Verchamp, *Gypsy Serenade* by Valdez and *Zapateado* by Sarasate.

Alice Nielsen sings her first group of five songs. "Responding to prolonged applause, and after the presentation of a large bouquet of pink roses, Mme. Nielsen sang with much feeling" *Swannee River.*

Westchester Times tells us of the concert with poet's heart and novelist's eye.

"Miss Nielsen, with her radiant face and winsome figure, was a pleasure to the eye. Her 'stage presence' is charming. Her graceful ease is entirely free from mannerisms, and when she emphasizes a point, that gesture is chosen with a delicacy and executed with a dainty gaiety that is like a child's presentation of a flower".

Griselle played two of his own compositions, *Minuet* and *Bourree*, and Chopin *Etude*, "the sincerity and simplicity of this true artist gave...a very rare delight. For an encore he gave an unusual piece, which seemed to be built on Debussy intervals and syncopated, to that the effect was that of an American rag".

Nielsen then sings her French group, proving "her art as a singer as well as her perfect enunciation so noticeable in her rendering of English; for an encore she sang *Annie Laurie* and brought down the house".

Vertchamp plays his second group of violin solos, *Romance Andaluza* by Sarasate, *Song of India*, and Levy's *Ghost Dance*. His encore *Ava Marie* as Mrs. Vertchamp plays piano. Nielsen's closing songs are Arensky's *But Lately In The Dance*, and *Un Bel di.*

The Bedford writer has a flashback to Boston Opera, "the singer's gifts of a beautiful legato, perfect breath control and dramatic intensity appeared at their best in poor Cio-Cio-San's aria and brought to the minds of those familiar with the singer's career the days when she created the part of 'Butterfly' while a member of the Boston Opera Company. "At this, the applause got beyond the power of hands and even feet to express. 'Brava! Brava! Brava!' rang from the house". She closed the show with Tosti's *Goodbye, Summer* "with all the feeling with which that well-known dramatic song can be invested".

Nielsen's intense emotional rapport with her audience is told when the reporter recognizes a famed NYC critic: "And here it may be told that a great professional critic had come from the city that night to sit in judgment on Alice Nielsen's voice. Through the previous numbers he had listened in growing approval, mathematically compiling her points—until the *Goodbye, Summer*. Then—brava, Nielsen brava!—all his own art left him. Suddenly the critic was no long a critic at all, but just a man like the rest—a man with his heart in his throat—a man who did not even know that the hot tears were raining down his cheeks. "Many old New Yorkers present left the building like people walking in a dream, saying 'It doesn't seem possible!' they repeated. 'This, in a country village—music like this! It doesn't seem possible! Not possible!'"

Forever vivid memories of all present. As we have heard many critics and reporters say many times of Alice Nielsen shows. Wherever Nielsen lives, she gives concerts. As in London, Naples, NY: so in Kansas City, Bedford, and Harrison, Maine where she will sing at the town church middle of each summer.

"People packed in to hear her", a Harrison woman told the author. "Miss Nielsen, that's what everyone always called her. She spoke to everyone she met", said a rare surviving witness to Nielsen's gregarious heart.

April 30th, sings for Duchess Richelieu at Hotel Ambassador. In this time she begins to focus on legacy. September 12th she starts an "Alice Nielsen Scholarship" for the first recipient, Boston's 19-year-old Nance O'Donnell. The gift consists of "three lessons weekly with Dr. and Mrs. Daniel Sullivan of NY" (*Westchester Times*).

During peaceful days Bedford's reporter meets Alice Nielsen "at her very attractive home directly across from St. Matthew's church" to ask about the scholarship. "Miss Nielsen, wearing a lovely large blue hat, came in from her garden where she delights to work", telling him "all her memories are those of music and because of this passion for her art she has established this scholarship in the hope of finding the future great American voice".

Winner of the Nielsen award sang in public for the first time "last Sunday night at nine o'clock from [radio] station WBZ, Springfield, Mass". She had been "selected from 24 students of musical ability at the Convent of New Rochelle".

For her next Bedford benefit, Alice invites Madame Leveroni, her mezzo friend from Boston Opera. Tickets are sold by Mrs. Bruce Smart, Adams' store, the tax office, Father Scanlan, and Miss Grace Smith at the Lighting Co. Nielsen's October 8th Bedford Community House gala is organized by Mrs. EK Trowbridge, Miss MM Newell, Mrs. Nelson Williams, Mrs. Magnus Rosberg, EG Amos, George Rogers, Rev. Martin A. Scanlan, and Rev. Arthur Ketchum.

North Westchester Times visits Nielsen "at her Bedford Center home across from St. Matthew's church". The singer again arrives from her garden, now with Elvira Leveroni. Two opera veterans are enjoying their visit "as they became staunch friends during the many appearances together" at Boston Opera, he does not add Covent Garden. Recounts how they created *Madame Butterfly* at Boston, Nielsen as title, Leveroni as Suzuki.

At Bedford, the duo recreate scenes from *Butterfly* with Nielsen's costumes, a show designed by Josef Urban "specially brought from Austria". Story of how Urban had stowed away, she skips when son Bennie is working for the designer.

Duo divas enjoy "motoring, always wonderful at this radiant season in the hills of Westchester...a source of delight to Madame Leveroni—but, if we may betray a confidence—she already has Doctor Stoddard classified as a speed demon".

For the concert, Nielsen, Leveroni, and Grisselle are joined by the Russian violinist Bernard Levitow, conductor of NYC's popular Hotel Commodore Dance Orchestra, whose big hit *Take In The Sun, Hang Out The Moon* had just been released by Edison cylinders and available in stores. Hotel Commodore, beside Grand Central Station, sports NYC's largest ballroom. Trump remodels it later.

That night Bedford Community House stage quality "equaled that of many a more ambitious theatre". *Butterfly* duets from the second and third acts closed their show, the two singers wearing the "original costumes". The child Piccolo Gioia is played by "little Barbara Rice"; stage direction by Mrs. EK Trowbridge "greatly assisted in her task by the kindness of Mr. Clarence Whybrow and Yamanaka & Co".

Nielsen's encores include the wonderful *Barney O'Hea* by Victor Herbert granddad Samuel Lover, also one of her early recordings.

About October 1923, a journalist appears whose interest in Nielsen will later produce the last feature on the singer. Zoë Beckley publishes "New Faces For Old" in *McClure's Magazine*, focused on surgeries of LeRoy Stoddard. Beckley befriends Alice. Beckley, author of *A Chance To Live* (1918) has previously interviewed Helen Keller, Calvin Coolidge, and other famed persons. "Zoë Beckley had spunk. She was a woman making her way in the journalism racket at a time when it was a boys' club", Nick Tosches told *Vanity Fair* (1905). Beckley authors a daily column for McNaught Syndicate. When she brings Queen Marie of Rumania to town, *New Yorker* (1925), calls her "a newspaper sob sister". She lives nearby in Connecticut, likes to garden, works in NYC. Likely that Beckley helps Nielsen place her memoirs, perhaps edits and adds a bit of the old melodrama. Alice has authored; lively style.

Beckley promotes disarmament. Appreciates Alice Nielsen's career. Ther 1923 story on Stoddard discusses in details the plastic surgery standards in England, Europe, and America. It was in Paris, "watching the wonders of Doctor Bourguet's clinic, I met a very distinguished plastic surgeon, LeRoy Stoddard of NY, who had come from America to England and Paris to see some of Major Gillies' and Doctor Bourguet's operations. He...began to specialize in facial surgery before the war. Indeed, his decision to become a plastic surgeon and his vow to be a successful one were arrived at in a dramatic way.

"As a youth he had adopted the profession of law, although his heart was not entirely in it. One day a client came to him, a woman whose looks had been utterly ruined by a jet of vitriol thrown into her face by a jealous rival. The young lawyer suffered at the sight of her. 'How much better if I could give back her beauty than win money damages!' he thought. And so completely did the idea of restoring wrecked beauty obsess him that he left the law to study medicine and surgery. Some success had come to him even before the war; but when that great catastrophe fell upon the world, Doctor Stoddard gave up all surgical work except for soldiers. Some of his operations were magnificent, especially those for the cure of hideous scars left by explosive wounds....

"Since 1920, however, there are few disfigured American soldiers left; and Doctor Stoddard...is free for civilian work. I saw three of his operations which he had been asked by a fellow surgeon to perform in Paris. One was for the flattening of a child's ears...one was for rejuvenating an elderly face that had sagged into double chins and let wrinkles flow into the neck; and the thirds was...for removing puffiness around the eyes. Using cocaine for anesthetic, the work was one in less than an hour.

Stoddard says, "There is no trick or mystery about this 'transformation scene', as you call it. Any good surgeon can perform these operations; but he must have constant practice in facial work to gain the requisite skill. In the hands of a competent surgeon there is no more need to fear a facial operation than a visit to a clever dentist. Nor can there be any danger of evil consequences".

Through surgery "came the romance of his life. The famous singer Miss Alice Nielsen had on one cheek a black mole which she disliked, although her public admired it. In every role it was to her a bugbear. Hearing of Doctor Stoddard from enthusiastic friends, she consulted him about it. The surgeon studied the mole and promised to remove it without a trace. He must have studied the rest of her face also, for the next operation was getting of a marriage license". The surgery probably was in 1909 before Stoddard proposed with a bouquet of flowers during Nielsen's Met debut.

Returning 1923. Alice after travels with Stoddard, returns on November 23rd to honor her longtime family friend, composer and conductor Carl Busch at Convention Hall in Kansas City. Attended by five-thousand people. Aviation pioneer Alice Nielsen flies as a passenger from NY.

Her flight becomes news. US Air Corps had just begun to require parachutes for its flyers; first non-stop flight across America; Charles Lindbergh, son of Congressman Lindbergh, buys his first surplus biplane to teach himself to fly! Typical commercial airplane of the day, such as the Stout Air Sedan, carries three passengers plus pilot and copilot. Monoplane with 90-horsepower motor is a forerunner of the Ford Trimotor. Safely landing, she prepares to sing.

Alice brings gayety to the Carl Busch gala. Austin Latchaw (*KC Star*): "They held a reunion today—Alice Nielsen, Kansas City's internationally known soprano and one of its favorite daughters, and Carl Busch who was the cause of Alice Nielsen's coming all the way from New York to sing here Sunday. The program consisted of Busch compositions and a group of songs by Miss Nielsen. This, too, was a great occasion, honoring two figures of the musical world whose gifts and attainments have reflected enduring credit on the city".

Alice stays at Hotel Muehlebach near Gayety Theatre, where Latchaw finds her and Busch on a first-name basis: "A person who never had met Alice Nielsen and knew her only by her operatic reputation, hardly could believe that this blue-eyed, vivacious person who was meeting friends at the Hotel Muehlebach was Miss Nielsen herself. But wasn't that Carl Busch with her and wasn't he calling her 'Alice' and wasn't she answering him 'Carl'?"

Nielsen says, "You would think it's remarkable that I'd make a flying trip from New York to sing at one concert here? This is a Carl Busch recognition concert and in my own home town. I'd come from Paris to Kansas City to sing at it and I'd be angry if they didn't invite me".

She reveals a schedule of twenty concerts, number chosen because "friend husband doesn't like for me to be away from home more". Return to NY Tuesday; she and Stoddard leave December 1st for San Francisco "by the water route, NY to New Orleans to Panama to the Golden Gate".

That Sunday, Nielsen sings at the Busch cantata premier *The Kansas City Spirit*. Text from Miss Clara Virginia Townsend, "who won *The Star's* poetry contest this spring", says Busch, "I had Alice in mind every time I wrote a note for the soprano part. I can't imagine having listened to anyone else sing it at the premiere"

Star foggily recounts saga of long friendship: "Before either the soprano or the maestro had won fame. Sallie Smith, a pretty girl, lived at the Nielsen home, 601 East 13th Street, and Carl Busch fell in love with her. He was a Dane, as was Mrs. Nielsen's husband Erasmus Nielsen, and that kindled a feeling of friendship of the Nielsen family toward the young man. Mrs. Nielsen decided that Mr. Busch was too nice a boy to be thrown on the mercies of the boarding house keepers in town, so they took him in to live with them. After a time Sallie Smith became Mrs. Carl Busch, but Mr. and Mrs. Busch and Mr. and Mrs. Nielsen and Alice and Erasmus Nielsen, the two children, lived together".

Star skips how Mr. Nielsen died in Warrensburg before his family reached town. Of course Nentwig had lived there, sad results.

"Carl was immensely fond of apple dumpling", Nielsen relates, "but he couldn't quite understand the pronunciation of the world. He used to make my mother laugh until she cried by saying, 'Mrs. Nielsen, may I have some more apple "don-key" please?'" Busch pleads guilty. He looks at his watch, "Alice, what do you say that we go out and get some apple donkey?" That ends the interview. The couple seek dessert, two famed master musicians very devoted to their adopted hometown, genial geniuses at creating the gayety of nations.

Busch was a well-honored man. Members of Carl Busch Recognition Society included Edvard Grieg, Jean Sibelius, Henri Rabaud, Walter Damrosch, Victor Herbert, Percy Grainger, George Chadwick, Fritz Reiner and Rudolph Ganz.

Before the concert, Busch receives a radiograph, "On this day of your great honor, the Danish Composers' Society sends you warm and heartfelt greetings ...thanking you for all you have done for music in Denmark and in the USA", signed by Peter Gram, Godtfred Skjerne, Einar Forchammer, Gunna Storm, Vilhel Paulsen. And Dr. Max Henius of Chicago sends, "Congratulations to a genius of music in memory of the Århus festival".

Star explains, "Århus is the city where Mr. Busch's cantata *The Brown Heather* was performed under his direction at the opening of a Danish national park some time ago". Busch has been knighted by the Danish king; the national park *Den Bamle By*, or *Århus Dryehave*.

Attending the Sunday concert are Governor Arthur Hyde; Constantin Brun, Danish ambassador; H. Bryn, Norwegian ambassador; Jean Juserand, French ambassador; Danish consul general George Beck. The program uses a mixed chorus of four-hundred and chorus of a thousand children, plus Alice Nielsen soprano and Tandy Mackenzie lyric tenor.

Busch conducts. The size recalls the marvelous Peace festivals by Patrick Gilmore when Alice was a kid.

Start with *Cantata The American Flag* by Busch: tenor solo, mixed chorus with orchestra. Nielsen sings *Papillon* (Fourdrain), *But Lately In Dance* (Arensky), *Wiegenlied* (Brahms), *Ouvre tes vaux bieux* (Massenet), *Canata Bobolinka* (Busch). Follows Busch cantata *Bobolinka* for children's solo voices, chorus and orchestra. Tenor Mackenzie (1892-1968) "by special request" gives "two songs in the Hawaiian language", *Mauna Loa* (King), *Na lei o Hawaii* (King), and then *At Night* (Rachmaninoff) and *Clelo e mar* from *La Gioconda* (Ponchielli).

His grandmother Hawaiian, Mackenzie was discovered in Kamehamha Glee Club by Alice's co-star John McCormack. He hit Broadway about 1912 touring *Bird Of Paradise*'s Hawaiian music. 1898 Alice had sung for Hawai's queen.

Premier of Busch's *The Kansas City Spirit* with Nielsen as soloist, plus mixed chorus and orchestra, closes the show.

1924: ALICE NIELSEN COMPANY REUNITES

April 21st there is national morning. Duse dies in Pittsburg near the end of her tour. She collapsed taking bows, never recovers. Alice's poet friend associated with Cadman, Nelle Eberhart: *To Duse Dead In Pittsburg*, *"Regret not that you came to die, In what might seem an alien place. Your wise soul led your long, last quest, To choose this fitting spot for rest"*.

Duse's body is moved to New York for a service and then to Italy. Two weeks later more deadly news arrives as a public shock. And personal shock to Alice Nielsen.

May 16, 1924 (*NY Times*) Victor Herbert dies, reports *NY Times*. Actually he dies on the stairway leaving offices of Dr. Emanual Baruch who lies to the press. Herbert was composing an overture for silent film *Janice Meredith* and composing music for the next Ziegfeld's *Follies*, where he assisted at rehearsals.

"His health apparently had been of the best" until lunch at Lambs' Club. That afternoon he was to meet Samuel Kingston who for Ziegfeld had handled Alice Nielsen's troubled 1905 NYC operatic return.

Herbert skips Kingston "and drove himself to the doctor's office. Weighing over 250 pounds" walking up the stairs to the medical office caused his collapse, as Dr. Baruch lies to *Times*.

Herbert's obit describes him composing "in his famous sound-proof room...perched on his high stool wearing a green jacket, a green vest and green necktie. He was a President of the Friendly Sons Of St. Patrick and of various other Irish societies. Herbert, an agitator, orator, writer and liberal contributor, in 1916...abandoned music" to author "long articles intended to enlist aid for Ireland...." Left his cello to the Manhattan School of Music, piano to ASCAP. Loyal member of Sons of St. Patrick, his address at the time was West 108th St. With Father Duffy, Herbert founded the Irish Musical Society.

Arrived in 1886 America, citizen in 1903 several years after composing Alice Nielsen's shows. Rights to his songs are sold by daughter to MGM whose guiding lights use copyright powers to prevent Nielsen from singing on radio the Herbert songs created for her.

Within a year, Alice Nielsen Opera Company will regroup for the only time, joining together to sing Herbert's memorial for NYC and WEAF.

1925: I OWE WHAT I AM TO WOMEN

De Wolf Hopper has insight into the shift in the gayety of nations when the days of direct encounters fade away. When Alice arose a star, plays started in New York because the publicity made money "in the hinterlands. The Broadway engagement frequently was played to a loss, but what of it? Six months' losses in New York could be retrieved usually in three months on the road.... A twelve weeks' run on Broadway once was phenomenal, but whatever the run, the production went on tour as a matter of course. Now [1925] a play may run a year on the Great White Way without finding anyone willing to gamble on it as a road venture".

Road was king "until labor and transportation costs and the movies virtually destroyed the legitimate stage in all save a handful of the greater cities". Alice and Hortense Nielsen prolonged the quality of this essential human gift as they toured into the 1920s.

Hopper continues, "The play of to-day is designed for Broadway and must make its money there or not at all ; certainly not one in fifteen New York productions is seen any more on the road other than in stock or repertory shows, and that one...will confine itself largely to cities of one hundred fifty thousand or more. Cincinnati and Kansas City see fewer good plays now than Zanesville, Ohio, and Springfield, Missouri, did twenty years since.

"Booth, at his zenith, played such towns as Bowling Green, Kentucky, and Saginaw, Michigan. I was about to say that one-night stands were history except for repertory shows, Tom shows, medicine shows, and the like, which play under canvas and still wheedle a living out of the towns of five hundred to ten thousand, when I happened to glance at the route list in the Billboard. There, in the second week of July, 1925, I found Miss Blanche Bates in *Mrs. Partridge Presents*, a moderate Broadway success of last season, listed as playing Pueblo and Grand Junction, Colorado, Price and Logan, Utah, and Pocatello and Idaho Falls, Idaho, all within seven days.

"Here are one-night stands as actors knew them before Hollywood. Pueblo may continue to see infrequent number-two and number-three road companies in new plays, but it is a safe hazard that Price, Logan, Grand Junction, Pocatello and Idaho Falls have not watched another Broadway cast headed by a star in a recent success in at least ten years. Many larger towns between Maine and Oregon have not been so favored in more years than that, their opera houses abandoned, torn down, burned or given over to films, occasional minstrels and political rallies.

"In one week in middle August, again, I found that splendid all-star revival company of *The Rivals*, headed by Mrs. Fiske, playing Everett,

Tacoma, Yakima, Walla Walla and Spokane, Washington, and Missoula and Helena, Montana. I'll wager that there were young men and women of voting and marrying age in the Yakima, Walla Walla, Missoula and Helena audiences who never had seen a stage play before. A teacher of elocution and dramatic coach in a town of twenty-two thousand in the Middle West canvassed the graduating class last spring and learned that only ten of its members had seen a play other than amateur in their lives. Perhaps the country is hungry again for the sound of the human voice in its drama. I hope so, but until there is more evidence of it, Miss Bates and the all-star revival of Sheridan's old comedy will have to be classed as missionary enterprises".

So it is. The fading of the gayety of nations.

April 26, 1925, a timid Philip Hale recalls Boston Opera, generating gossip but never salient facts. Fears to speak freely. Knows very well what happened to the journalist who spoke freely, Philip Kahn. Hale's journalistic brother got caged. Facts proved Philip Kahn a mighty prophet telling Boston a right cure.

Of course, old news by now. So this marks Hale as far more a cowardly lion of critics. Boston Opera "added to the gayety of the time", Hale says. "On November 8, 1910, in the second season of Henry Russell's reign at the Boston Opera House, Leon Sibiriakoff appeared on the stage as *Mephistopheles* in Boito's opera. He was a tall, stalwart person with a voice known to the Germans as a 'beer-bass.' He roared lustily at the unseen angels above", sang a month "Mephistopheles in Gounod's opera and as Don Basilio in *The Barber Of Seville*.

"After December 9, he was seen no more. It was whispered at the time that he had been grossly impertinent to the wife of the manager [Russell]; but many rumors about the members of the opera company were flying about. They added to the gayety of the time and broadened the social horizon". Russell and wife had separate quarters which accomidate petite tenors and young sopranos.

Oh Hale tell us, why Sibiriakoff? "Because *Le Semaine Musicale* of Paris" announced "April 15, Leon Sibiriakoff bass...would give a recital in Paris.... Fifteen years after he was in Boston, Mr. Sirbiriakoff turns up in Paris. What has he been doing in the meantime? Was he forced to leave Russia by the soviet government?" Hale could or would not say.

Hale speculates at the lost legacy of that great vanished artistic community. "What has become of those who sung here in opera?

"Robert Lassalle, a tenor and a poor one, went back to Paris and held a leading position at the Paris opera. Giaccone, we understand, is dead. Mr. Stroesco has given recitals in London with marked success. Mme. Alda is still with the Metropolitan. Mme. Carmen Melis, the beautiful Carmen Melis, sings and is applauded in Italy. Mme. Claessens was here yesterday, singing with unquenched fervor.

"Arnoldo Conti, the conductor who worked indefatigably, is dead. Alice Nielsen, happily married, retired [!] from the stage and so did Jeska Swartz, now Mrs. Morse, a charming Siebel when Mr. Sibiriakoff shooed her from the village dance....

"Constantino the useful tenor, is dead. He used to accuse the manager of not sufficiently interesting the critics in him. He really thought they were under pay to boom this or that singer. Poor misguided Constantino! Whenever he came upon the stage he cast an appealing, propitiatory glance at the top gallery".

"George Baklanoff has matured greatly in his art, which was fully appreciated here when he appeared recently as Escamillo, Golaud and in the *Love of the Three Kings*. Is Marie Mattfeld still living? She was alive a few years ago. She has had a long life on the stage, for she was touring with the Damrosch company in 1898. Herman Jadlowekr, the last we heard of him, was singing in Berlin. What became of Frederick Huddy?

"Lydia Lipkowska, unforgettable as Lakme, married to a French officer who rescued her and her daughter at Odessa, has been singing in Japan, China and India. Anne Roberts...married and left the stage. Mr. Fornari, voluble and chatty as Figaro ...is still with us; but where is the joyous Attillo Pulcini? We see him now in *La Bohème* wearing those astonishing trousers and throwing stage money right and left. And there was the excellent buffo Tavecchia. Pierre Letol, is he still on earth?"

And the culprit who Hale knew killed it all? "As for Henry Russell, he is writing articles about music for the Rivera edition of the *Chicago Tribune*, articles abounding in moral reflections, inveighing against 'snobisme' in music". In fact the Chicago paper has no mention of Russell after July 23, 1911 until his obituary October 12th, 1937, tags him as "former director" at Boston".

Too-timid Hale dares not celebrate Philip Kahn nor mention the martyred man. "Ah, if only one had the courage to write the aesthetic and social history of the Boston Opera Company from the beginning to the end! What an entertaining little book it would be! But the edition would necessarily be limited and privately printed, sold like Mr. Herkimer Johnson's colossal work, only to subscribers". With heartless irony, "Even then the writer might be obliged to leave Boston, sporting false whiskers and between trains". After a decade, Hale stays suppressed. He knew all; knew what happened to the hapless editor dragooned to jail for correctly prophesying doom, whose free advice could have saved everything if the Boston board had acted competently.

Hale (1854-1934) has the truth, knows his town, knew Philip Kahn. He cheats posterity when he does not speak freely. Might have done. Safely mocks the talents on the stage and fogs the realities of life. Hale is a cowardly ass.

With Nielsen and Constantino gone, things got dull: Russell's mad desire to destroy star power, fill his pockets, was, as most everybody knew at the time, a bad choice. Plus Russell hated Boston.

Lamely, "Would Boston Opera Company have continued performances if the war had not come in 1914? "The last performance was on March 28 of that year. The bill was comprised of *Il Segreto di Susanna* with Sharlow, Fornari and Tavecchia, the *Lucia* 'Mad' scene with Evelyn Scotney, the second act of *Faust* (Beriza, Swartz-Morse, Leveroni and Jou-Jerville and Ludikar) and the ballet "Dance Of The Hours" from *La Gioconda*. The season did not end in a blaze of glory", Hale suggests with a worldly sigh of resignation.

Hale dodges his duty to speak freely: "It would be an unprofitable task to give reasons why the company was disbanded. Mr. Jordan was discouraged; he had every reason to be, for he had maintained the existence of the opera at a great cost and others were not willing to assist in large measure, much less relieve him wholly of the burden".

Grows coy: "He had other reasons for discouragement, reasons that are known to all those who are intimately acquainted with the story of the undertaking from the modest beginning to the pretentious and extravagant ending". Almost idiotically Hale suggests a modest budget.

"Can Boston support opera for…more than two weeks? Would the supporters be contented with singers of moderate ability, with simple stage settings and a comparatively small orchestra? The sanguine say 'Yes.'

Evading the entire tragedy, the betrayed Boston Opera goals, the investors grossly cheated, and the widespread support dashed, Hale ends fatally, "The more experienced say 'No.' After all, opera even when it is given in only fairly satisfactory manner is a luxury. The moving pictures and the radio are enough for the great majority".

Thus the evasive Philip Hale leaves us foggy propaganda. Cravenly, Hale scuttles the gayety of nations. Worse, Philip Hale abandons the honest whistleblower Philip Kahn.

Consider the true story of Boston's *Titanic* opera disaster. The town which built Harvard, nurtured Mother Goose, Symphony Hall, Alice Nielsen, and New England Conservatory would kick down its own opera house? Hale makes a very wicked failure-by-design seem inevitable. Let us leave Boston as a lyric backwater lying about stuff, and segue to NY where finances and theatre of the nation are consolidating due to war profiteers.

Alice Nielsen Opera Company reunites for first time in twenty-two years to sing Victor Herbert's music Sunday afternoon May 24 this 1925. NYC hosts a big Victor Herbert party. He had given gayety to the world all his life. John Phillip Sousa conducts this ASCAP memorial Herbert concert, assisted by Arthur Pryor and many many stars. Broadcast and distributed nationally by WEAF radio, no recording found.

For the last time, Nielsen, Cowles, Sylva, and other Broadway greats gather together to sing songs Herbert created for their voices. Apparently just too early by a few fleeting months for radio recording technology to capture the event.

"One of the greatest musical features ever presented in this or any other country, the Victor Herbert memorial program, with a galaxy of world-famous artists…will be transmitted today by WCAE…in cooperation with WEAF, New York", relates *Pittsburgh Press*. *Daily Iowan* adds, "A feature of the program will be the Victor Herbert orchestra of 100 pieces, which will broadcast several of the late Victor Herbert's compositions under the direction of such famous conductors as Henry Hadley, John Phillip Sousa, Hugo Riesenfield, Nahan Franko, Armand Vecsay, and Max Bendix". Wish we could be there. And that's all there is. There ain't no more.

September 24th, Alice Nielsen broadcasts at 8:30pm on Radio WLWL, NY 288. During the show Cardinal Hayes speaks; the music is provided by

Paulist Choristers, Alice Nielsen, Carl Schlegal, Margaret Keys, Rinaldo Schione, Maria Montani, Kitty McLaughlin, John Valentine and William Stahl.

Again Alice's contribution is not recorded. By year's end recording grows common; a McCormack radio concert is recorded Jan. 1st 1926.

This year the opera rustler Henry Russell publishes his pathetic piles of insult to injury *The Passing Show*: need we say, a farce from beginning to end. Skips his bankster lackey life. Fond of men he mentions. Skips kids and wives. Never mentions by name the stars he cheated of a home stage. That kind of book from that kind of person. Loie Fuller saw Russell clearly for what he was.

Apparently Nielsen reads and grows wiser. Responds with September's *Alice Nielsen: I Owe What I Am To Women* in *Delineator*. She is promoted as national treasure. Remember the Alamo, the Nielsen, the Boston Opera!

"Alice Nielsen might have lived in noble estate if she had accepted the offer of adoption from a duchess. She might have continued a butterfly existence in the court circles of Europe, the colorful center of royal intrigues", says the *Delineator* introducing her article. "But something forever American and independent spurred her on—to drop light opera at the height of her success, to plunge into hard work and study, and so to become one of the highest stars of grand opera. Crowded with brilliant personalities and exciting events, her life is a fascinating story".

Nielsen begins, "In the crucial moments of my life some woman has always played an important part. Never was a singer so fortunate than I in having the helping hand of women". She thanks her late mother, "whose hand directed my destiny" by raising Bennie. She retells the impossible tale of playing Nanki-Poo, adroitly blending timescales.

Sarah "used to scold and spank me with the proud faith that thus she was preserving my morality. It was a good thing that her child of eight should have her control to lean on, for I was very independent from my very first rehearsal, when as Nanki-Poo I ordered certain scenery shifted that I might be better seen from the front. *Enfant terrible* though I must have been, I made enough during my tour in *The Mikado* to support my family for three years". Do you say.

Marvelous adventure seeking California now a sudden calling, as if a casting call: "Suddenly I was called to Oakland, California to sing the role of Yum Yum in *The Mikado*". Yes, salute to the gayety of Burton Stanley, the first profession theatreperson to put her into headlines as star. Suggests an impossible calendar. Unless she had dressed as a boy since age thirteen. And she went to Washington with a dress having a big bow. In any case, the dramatic part works. She expands life at Wigwam, "For seven years [*sic!*] I sang nothing but boys' parts and my first appearance as a girl gave me real stage fright.

"Yum Yum represented for me a change from trousers to skirts, and it was difficult for me to manage the latter. Right after" not seven, maybe two, trouser years she "went to the famous Tivoli in San Francisco, singing all the Gilbert and Sullivan operas" and skips the glory of *Satanella*.

"One day in San Francisco, in a theatre opposite the Tivoli, the famous Bostonians flung their banners on the outer walls. I decided to myself that

I was going to be one of the Bostonians..." And so forth. Into London years then return to America. She shifts focus to "many appearances at the White House", and reveals her glimpses of three Presidents.

"What a contrast the afternoon with Mrs. McKinley knitting socks for the Soldiers' Home, with the splendor of the days at the Duchess of Manchester's, the Rothschilds' and Mrs. Lionel Phillips". Yes indeed, the one nation promoting sovereign citizens' happiness versus two warlord families and an heiress.

"I went to the piano and played for this simple first lady of the land, and she asked me for such melodies as *Annie Laurie* and *The Last Rose of Summer*. A kindly, benevolent gentleman slipped into the room, 'Bravo', he exclaimed, 'Who is the little singer with the big voice?' It was in this unobtrusive manner I met the President of the United States.

"Shall I tell a story on President Taft? Will he forgive me, now that he is a Chief Justice? I was taken to an official reception given by Mrs. Taft. An imposing gold-laced officer led me to the small platform to sing. The President was detained by important business and was not there when I began, but presently one of the doors opened and I was the unmistakable expansiveness of the chief executive. He sat down on one of those ridiculously small gilt chairs, completely hiding it. My sense of humor imagined him suspended in mid-air. Suddenly there came to me while I sang the sounds of snoring. There could be no mistake—they beat above the piano notes. The President had fallen asleep. The kid glove applause awakened him and he clapped vociferously.

"The next time I sang at the White House no aide handed me up to the platform. President Wilson himself took my by the hand and led me out with that unforgettable courtesy he always showed me. I have many delightful letters from him". Let the record show they did exchange three courtesy notes.

On September 5, *Washington Post* partially reprints the *Delineator* piece as "Alice Nielsen, My friendship with Duse".

Librettist bites the dust. November 7 (*NY Times*), Harry Smith dies. Born Buffalo NY 1861, he had worked as critic for Chicago's *Daily News*. When Smith and Herbert made their first show *Wizard of the Nile* for comedian Frank Daniels, Herbert still was a Met cellist, whose music composed for an extravaganza titled *America* had been abandoned by the producer. During the next forty years, Smith creates about 300 'books' for comic operas; none really his. Originally. We may only imagine the lively improvisation onstage making the Nielsen *Fortune Teller* so very enjoyable.

November 19, Nielsen appears at Catholic Writers' Guild memorial for Joyce Kilmer (1886-1918). Author of poem *Trees* killed in a foreign war's battle for Marne not meaning much. Memorial St. Patrick's on 5th Avenue.

1927: DIVORCE AND RETURN TO MANHATTAN

1927 passes without much notice of Alice Nielsen.

January 11th her son "Benjamin T. Nielsen of Boston" sends $100 to the Warrensburg MO cemetery fund, "She visited her father's grave when she was here a few years ago. She has been spending the winter in the West Indies".

February, her Stoddard marriage is over. Divorce takes two years to complete; the stalling surgeon uses his legal training to harass his wife. Their sad finish seems an operetta plot. Alice Nielsen and pals had dashed to a NY hotel to discover the surgeon with a woman. They had separated in March.

Press has grown tabloid-y by those days.

Decade married; Alice builds his career. Things deteriorated by April culminating with "a raid on the doctor's apartment... at 11 o'clock the night of April 2, last. The former heroine of Metropolitan Opera and many Victor Herbert operettas led a little band of friends and private detectives to an apartment at 138 W 58th St., where Stoddard had resumed his single life following their separation a month before. There, they charged they found a woman identified only as "A.H". in a lavender nightie, and Dr. Stoddard, clothed in his undies, hiding in the bathroom. The diva planned an immediate divorce action and retained Edwin Phillips Kohl of 27 Cedar St to draw up the papers. The celebrated beauty-clinic romance that once startled the music and society world ended in grief with a divorce and a $40,000 cash settlement to the wife in Supreme Court, Manhattan".

Alice Nielsen is described as "now retired". She had moved to NYC, selecting the Osborne on 205 57th Street, exquisite 1883 residential building built cattycorner from Carnegie Hall only two blocks from Central Park South. With façade of dark reddish-brown stone, the interior lobby is "a luminous Byzantine dream of gilded tiles with contributions by Augustus St. Gaudens, muralist John La Farge, Tiffany Studios and Jacob Holzer. No other apartment building can boast as sumptuous and dazzling lobby", saith manager. Osborne has 111 apartments on twelve floors.

The complexity of her divorce sadly also grew operetta-like. "The action was delayed, however, when Henry Starr, detective, was sued by his wife for a separation. She claimed that the sleuth had hugged Miss Nielsen in the elevator as they descended to the street after the raid. Then Starr went to court to collect a $600 fee he claimed the songbird refused to pay him for engineering the raid.

"Both Miss Nielsen, a grandmother now, and Starr finally convinced his wife that the hugging match was merely a display of tempera-mental exuberance on the diva's part over having gotten the goods on the doctor, and the matter of the $600 fee also was settled".

Knowing Alice's financial plight, after breaking trust, after stopping or slowing her tours, LeRoy Stoddard undercuts his ex-wife all he can.

Stoddard becomes Alice's fourth male betrayer.

During 1928, the Nielsen in theatrical news is actress Hortense who has steadily worked. November 9 in Crookston, Minnesota Hortense "appeared in recital at Northwest School..... During the day, Miss Nielsen gave unstintingly of her talent by appearing before the advanced English classes during the forenoon, in addition to a special recital of Ibsen's play, *A Doll's House* in the afternoon, and Drinkwater's *Abraham Lincoln* in the evening. While at the Northwest School, Miss Nielsen added several hundred new friends to a list that includes thousands of students and faculty members from the leading educational institutions of America". And this suggests her market in the '20s; her Washington DC performances had been advertised as "Dramatic Recitals" at First Congregational Church at 10th & G. Sts. NW over a Monday and Tuesday in 1925 swapping the two shows between matinee to evening next day. Far cry from her own "Nielsen Theatre" in Los Angeles as a cherished legacy.

Another Alice nemesis percolating on a remote and tedious level in 1928 surfaces, ironically faced with an Equity appeal by Jeanne Eagels regarding *Her Cardboard Lover*. Actress claims that Perley mistreated her so badly she had to leave the show.

1929, February 13 (*NY Times*), Alice Nielsen is spotted in a Met Opera box for the debut of Polish soprano Ganna Walska.

By March, Nielsen's divorce is final, $40,000 settlement (about $650,000 today) with $325 monthly alimony (about $5,200 today). Justice Alfred Frankenthaler makes the award. Quickly April 6th, Stoddard sells their Bedford house and seven acres to an unnamed New Yorker with Frances Waters the broker. Alice must fight for years to hold Stoddard to his bargain. Alice Nielsen never remarries. Puts focus on friends and family. Later the scoundrel Stoddard marries his purple-nighty tramp "AH" as third wife, Mrs. Vine Booth Hubbell.

In May, Alice's costar Marguerite Sylva also files for divorce and relocates to Hollywood for film roles and to teach voice.

November 3rd, Nielsen attends a *Fortune Teller* revival at Jolson Theatre, where reporter Margaret Hess shows interest in the aging star. "When Tessa Kosta appeared on Monday evening in the revival of *The Fortune Teller*, Victor Herbert's popular operetta, Alice Nielsen, the first and original Musette, sat in a box and enjoyed herself heartily".

Hess visits Nielsen. "'I was surprised that I could watch the piece and yet feel so entirely detached', the former toast of Broadway confessed yesterday as she sat in her apartment on West 57th Street. 'My heart probably beat a little bit faster than anybody else's in the auditorium, but I was happy, not sad. Maybe that's against all old established tradition, but it's true. I had no longing to be there on the stage. I was perfectly happy to be where I was and to listen.'"

Hess notes, "Miss Nielsen does not look old enough to lay claim to the twelve-year-old grandchild of whom she is so proud. Small, slender, with lively sea-blue eyes and light brown bobbed hair, she looked extremely attractive. Clad in a black velvet dress with matching turban and a string of pearls as the sole ornament, she spoke well for the kindness with which the stage treated her during a career of more than a quarter of a century".

Nielsen asserts herself. Her help came "chiefly through women—and not through men". Only true.

"You know, Mrs. Victor Herbert was the one who really discovered me. She was singing in opera at that time and she was the power behind the throne for me. I was singing with the Bostonians, the greatest comic opera company that this country ever had, when she saw me over the footlights. I appeared in Victor Herbert's pieces[,] in Covent Garden in London and at the San Carlos in Naples.

"Both *Fortune Teller* and *Singing Girl* were written especially for me. I sang them before many, many presidents. Who was the most musical? They all seem to have been musical Presidents, but I believe Woodrow Wilson appreciated music the most of them all. Who was the least? Teddy Roosevelt. Well that's telling, and anyway that's another story".

Hess remarks, "With exceptional talent as dancer, singer, actress-- especially as comedienne—and endowed with unusual beauty, she had the world before her and a myriad of careers from which to choose. Although, when she deserted the world of comic opera for its more glamorous cousin, every outraged music critic literally 'spanked' her in print.

"Sponsored by the wife of a wealthy London businessman, in 1901 she sang in Covent Garden, opening the season in Mozart's *Don Giovanni*, [and that fall returning with genuine San Carlo to sing] in [not] the same cast with Caruso".

Nielsen recalls Caruso: "Great joy to work with him. It was a great happiness because he was so good and kind and considerate. He didn't seem to realize his own greatness. He never had 'the tenor complex', but was always a man o' a' that. It's a great memory to have because he was a very warm friend of mine". She plucks Caruso's picture from wall, points to the inscription, "To my very devoted friend" in Italian. That means so much to me, because it was given to me as a true friend and it's not merely a stereotyped autograph for any admirer".

Hess sees "host of others, all of whom were warm personal friends...on the photograph-plastered walls of the small sitting room: Melba, Calvé, Nordica, Duse, Scotti, D'Annunzio. On a table in a special place of honor is a large picture of Woodrow Wilson, one whose memory she most admires".

Nielsen describes *Pasquale* as "old-fashioned opera", adding "my last [major] appearance to date was in a concert with the Boston Symphony Orchestra as a soloist". She had apparently contemplated taking her old part in *The Fortune Teller* that season but "thought better of it since her husband feared it might be too strenuous". And now, no husband.

"I haven't retired yet. I sing all the time and play the piano. You never can tell if I'll sing in public again. I study voice with a very fine maestro and we go over all my old songs and programs to refresh my memory".

She would not teach, "I'd never have the patience to do any teaching. I'm afraid that if I did, there'd be a scene". Now she helped by audience, "I still love music as much as ever and go to all the symphony concerts and the opera and to musical comedies and reviews as well".

Empathetic Hess waxes philosophical, Why had Alice come to rest in a small place on 57th Street?

Singer replies typically, with pensive sincerity. "Because I lived in a world of my own imagining. I thought I would be always young and happy and a favorite of the gods. I spent with both hands. I gave without thought or stint. I never looked ahead".

Significantly, "I believed in everyone, trusted every one's integrity.

"From the time I sang in the streets of Kansas City as a child, for sheer love of life, I was hypnotized by my own joy and glamour. Tell young girls for me, to remember reality. Dreams are beautiful and romance is sweet.

When success comes easily, as it did with me, one doesn't think about failure. The sun won't always shine, tell them".

She speaks of love and money lasting: only if cared for. "Love won't always last—or money either, unless you take care of it. I was too carefree, my eyes always laughing up into the blue sky, never watching for pitfalls. Well—I can still laugh, still enjoy things, still hope, still believe, still remember and—" off she trills one of her Herbert arias.

Thirty years after Alice Nielsen Company, Nielsen at last gives her best candid assessment in this look-back: "Of course, Victor Herbert's operas when beautifully done are monuments to the genius of the man and to the musical world and will live forever, as all works of genius do. This composer—he was born in Ireland, you know—was the greatest, greater than Gilbert and Sullivan".

Alice passes on the jazz fad: "Today the public is a jazz public, because it always hears jazz. I like jazz occasionally, but jazz all the time is like too much stormy weather. It's too much of a good thing. But beautiful music you can hear all the time without ever getting tired of it. When I turn on the radio, though, I hear jazz all the time".

Recalling Duse's Chicago comment decades ago, Nielsen foretells beautiful music will return: "A great American voice will someday appear in musical comedy and then it will come into its own. It won't be long before that happens".

Tosses a wreath at Shubert organization, "I'd like to see the Shuberts discover the singer, because they would know what piece to choose for that person. Their interest in the Victor Herbert revivals shows that they appreciate fine things". Indeed, the revivals are notoriously cheap.

Hess observes Nielsen's joy as being "due to her nature". Proud mother, and grandmother: "With more pride than she had shown when exhibiting pictures of world-famous personages, she brought a photograph of her son—'his mother's boy' she called him—and daughter-in-law, and of her twelve-year-old granddaughter Alice Nielsen at the age of two. Pointing to the image of the baby, she admitted it was the image of grandmother and had blue eyes like her own".

"I'm happy, so happy" Nielsen smiles.

Hess agrees, "Her laugh and smile confirmed her words".

Nielsen: "You see, I always prefer doing the thing I'm doing at the moment, because I put the best effort into it. I always loved the opera that I did and I loved the song I was singing. I always sang the songs that I myself loved, regardless of whether they were the audience's favorites or not. That made me sing and feel much better.

Lastly, "I've always loved my public and its reactions. And, you know, the public always appreciates anything that's really good".

1930s-40s: STIRRING FADING

Alice Nielsen would never appears in films, silent or sound; very rarely heard on radio and these moments never preserved. Makes many Los Angeles trips, a celebrity celebrated in LA since 1896. Talk movies had begun by 1927 with her stage friends, as we have seen. In the 1930s Alice revisits Hollywood trek as MGM films its popular yet peculiar brand of Victor Herbert musicals. Score made stiff, voicings changed, roles dropped, storyline lost, comics gone serious: stylistically foolish. Even so, Jeanette McDonald with Nelson Eddy make superb chemistry. In their 1935 *Naughty Marietta*, original Alice co-star Joe Cawthorn plays Herr Shuman, Marietta's Parisian singing coach. MGM's copyright prevents Alice Nielson from singing on radio the songs Herbert had composed for her, his daughter to thank. That pleasure may be lost to us.

September 1930, *KC Times* tells of plans for a Hollywood trip: "Alice Maud Nielsen, whom Kansas City in the '90s called its own prima donna, is returning to the operatic stage again—through the talking motion pictures. She is leaving Boston soon for Hollywood to prepare for her new roles". This continues, that she "never seemed to grow old. She was still singing in this century when those with whom she had been cast in the '90s had perished. She sang with Caruso in his early years of opera; she sang with him in his prime. And now she is to sing again. She probably will make her first picture in January". The story ends strangely, "She probably will appear in a Chinese or Indian role. She can better hide her years in oriental costumes". Adding, "Already she is dieting to increase her weight". The paper suggests Alice "may be remembered by a few old-timers as a KC school girl in the '80s". Escaping Nentwig "her great fame came".

Did Alice Nielsen come to fame, or fame to her?

She does not gain a movie role.

Divorce drags out due to Stoddard. Finalizes November 19th (*LA Times*): "That famous romance in a beauty clinic wherein Alice Nielsen, internationally noted prima donna, became the bride of Dr. Leroy Stoddard, society plastic surgeon, came to grief today with a divorce and a $40,000 cash settlement granted her in Manhattan...."

1931 passes without notice of Alice Nielsen. May 14th, pal Belasco dies.

1932 Alice's 3-issue Colliers' memoir appears. Quoted in full across this biography. Alice could bring vivid detail, or playful fog. Her ironic silences told much; when we are in the know. Her letters have proved sparse among archives. She had time to complete her 1910s novel; never published; manuscript seems lost to us. In recollections at that point, Alice focuses on her arts and audiences, never betrayals. She has an admirably serene sustained outlook. In this decade her greatest focus is her family. She has seen many thousands of ovations.

In this year Josef Urban dies. Alice's son Bennie moves back to Boston area, where he leaves theatre designs for Corps of Engineers dam designs.

1933, Alice Nielsen returns to radio very briefly. September 18, Palmolive sponsors a three-minute interview during a radio broadcast of *Fortune Teller*, apparently unrecorded as unlisted in radio archives.

1934, Alice reveals she is not well-off: "This feeling of insecurity is a load on my chest. My friends have been responsible for my staying alive. They have stayed by me". Ex-husband Stoddard withholds alimony and challenges the divorce settlement in expensive litigations to delay his day of reckoning.

May 11, Mrs. Robinson-Duff, fifty years "teacher of singing in NY, Chicago and Paris" dies in NY. Born in Maine, studied singing under Mme. Marchesi. She taught fourteen-year-old Mary Garden. During two decades in Paris she coached Nielsen, Jessie Davis, Olive Fremstad, Frieda Hempel. "Breath and brains are the qualifications most necessary for a singer", Robinson-Duff wrote in *Simple Truths Used By Great Singers* (1919).

July 28th erstwhile friend Marie Dressler dies. No evidence they reconciled. Nielsen and two other women file claims against Dressler's estate. Alice seeks $4,500 "paid...Dressler under asserted fraudulent representations". Lucy Drage seeks $6,300 "invested with the actress for promotion of a motion picture". Claire Du Brey seeks $25,000 "secretarial and nursing" services. They each win a judgement to repay.

1935 Lewis Strang passes, author of *Famous Prima Donnas*, national critic who first named Nielsen best. After 1906 he had worked closely with Mary Baker Eddy who authorized him to teach Christian Science metaphysics. In 1924 he authored *Freedom Through Right Thinking*. Several of Nielsen's best appreciators had Christian Science affinities.

1936, Zoe Buckley, who a decade earlier had met Nielsen via surgeon Stoddard, publishes Alice's last interview in the *NY Evening Post* (Mar 13).

About radio, Alice remarks "Isn't it a pity that even if I had my big chance on radio, I wouldn't be allowed to sing the songs Victor Herbert wrote for me, note by note, as I sat beside him on the music-bench?"

Buckley writes, "Bright star also of NY's Metropolitan Opera Company, of the shining San Carlo in Naples; of distinguishing Covent Garden in London, and of the far-famed Bostonians (*Oh Promise Me* and *Brown October Ale*—remember?) besides heading the Alice Nielsen Opera Company her very own, in which she toured like a princess, coast-to-coast through the United States and Canada, private car, maids, secretary, retinue, dog and all".

Blocked from radio, Alice "sings them to herself though; nobody can stop that; and to old friends who drop in, begging a bar of *Cupid and I* or a bit from *The Serenade*, *The Fortune Teller* or *The Singing Girl*, which were written for her by Victor Herbert—hand made, cut, fitted, tailored and finished to her measure by the maestro's practiced hand".

Buckley describes Nielsen, alone in a "somber two-room apartment in West 57th Street whose only luster comes from the signed photographs of fellow celebrities that line its walls. Little Alice Nielsen, gay hearted despite her grievously altered environment, struck a few notes, hummed a few lines for me, then wheeled and just spoke the words that head this story".

Nielsen quips, "Now I'm Alice sit-by-the-fire", title of the Barrie play Charles Frohman had produced, Ethel and John Barrymore in the leads.

Buckley sees letters and papers lost to this biographer, the "enormous press clipping books, her old programs, her piled-up desk, her toppling mountains of old letters, photographs, souvenirs of every description that cram that old apartment I feel a little choky in the throat, a little moist of eye, a little sad".

Alice Nielsen has "the precious gift of philosophy. The outlook from her windows may be merely brick walls, but she sees through them to a pleasant world in which anything can happen. Her kitchenette cupboard may be unstocked, her rooms dark, her purse light, but she shrugs and makes a joke of it".

And Alice has just broken her wrist. "'But it's mending well', she grins, holding up the prettiest hand that ever held a bunch of stage-door-Johnny roses. 'Lucky I didn't break my fool neck.'"

"Was it luck that brought you and Victor Herbert together?"

"Sure! I was singing in *War-Time Wedding* at the old Murray Hill Theatre near where the Grand Central Station is now. Mrs. Herbert, a great prima donna in her day, was in the audience and told Victor she had found the typical girl to play 'Yvonne' in *The Serenade* which he was working on".

Buckley: "The master pounced upon the small, sweet singer with the glory voice and shaped the piece for her, adding a few extra high notes and cadenzas".

Closes the last press piece on Alice Nielsen.

1936, June 1st she loses a wonderful brother, Erasmus at 63, "organist of St. Mary Star of the Sea Roman Catholic Church of Far Rockaway for the last 30 years". He "died Monday at his home 4 East Ninth Road, Broad Channel, of a heart attack". Born Missouri, he had accompanied Alice "on many of her tours here and abroad". His widow Julia, son, daughter Mrs. Mary Tagen, and two sisters survive.

1937, January 2nd, Alice Nielsen sues Stoddard over alimony payments and the divorce settlement, eight years after they had parted ways. Alice versus the Stoddards, LeRoy and his sister Ella. Nielsen asks for $15,000 balance he owes her, plus court order "he resume paying her in addition $325 a month pursuant to the 1930 agreement". Stoddard attempts to void his part of the agreement by hilariously suggesting this was "made under a mutual mistake or procured by her through fraud" and "asks for $5,000 back plus all the alimony... he asked that his wife's suit be dismissed". In yellow-press phrases, "the blonde toast of kings and first-nighters at the turn of the century charged in a suit...that Dr. LeRoy Stoddard whom she wed in 1917 had welched on an agreement to provide for her". May 21, Nielsen wins. She immediately forecloses the $20,000 mortgage on the Glens Falls property given her by Stoddard as part of the property settlement. Stoddard's historic homestead is sold to repay her.

And the erstwhile remora Russell dies, obscure lad who Alice Nielsen dragged behind the limelight realms as entourage so he could cheat her. Rumors say when he died a chorus is heard singing (As flames appear in all directions, the earth trembles. From below, in hollow voices) *Torments eternal wait thee Burning in endless night.*

Or mayhaps be Mozart. Either or both.

1938, Alice advertises her Maine house for summer rental: "unique 15 acres, heavily wooded, 600 feet lakefront rustic camp; 12 rooms, furnished, all modern conveniences; season's bargain at $750, Butterfield 8-1281 or Miss Alice Nielsen, 245 East 72nd.

In NYC, Alice reappears in the news visiting Radio City Music Hall for *The Adventures Of Robin Hood* film starring Errol Flynn and Olivia de Havilland, "she started her career playing the part which the screen star, Olivia de Havilland, now assumes".

1939, Alice advises the press, "One would not combat the inroads of jazz, ragtime, turkey trot and grizzly bear with a revival of the type of show they had superseded, but with a new operetta, more modern, with new and younger stars". The shows she and Herbert would have created next.

1940s: FAREWELL HOME SWEET HOME

By summer 1940, Nielsen's beautifully-sited wood-frame lake house in Maine stands "for sale or rent". Ever gregarious, on July 4th 1940 Alice Nielsen writes to a Mrs. Seymour: "I do hope I shall see you here at my house with your young daughter for a chat and cup of tea, it will have to be some day early next week as I am going to Maine for the remained for the summer, of course this will have to suit your convenience as I know how busy you are". She is letting things go, "I am deeply sorry about the misunderstanding about the Duse fan, it was entirely my fault as I have confused the Marie Antoinette fan with the Duse one, so I hope you will forgive any inconvenience I may have caused you".

Health suffers, "Have not been well enough to write you before. Am writing Mr. Meadow tomorrow. Looking forward to seeing you and your daughter if not next week when you return in the fall. I'm looking up some old pictures for you. Cordially, Sincerely, Alice Nielsen".

For her hometown, Alice packs a trunk of costumes from Bostonians, Herbert, and Boston Opera. Gives away the beloved photographs from her walls, her published scores and music books. Apparently few or no letters. Perhaps these have been scavenged for the autographs of her famed friends. She has strength to make one last visit to Missouri. Her last visit to Kansas City is a celebration. Kansas City Museum is a new organization, future uncertain. Even so, the fading diva contacts its organizers to offer some of her costumes. Others stay in NY or go to Boston.

First announcement of her return is September, 1940. "Alice Nielsen, the one-time operatic star, is going to revisit Kansas City, her old home town", said *Kansas City Star* (Se 27 1940). "Miss Nielsen has not been in Kansas City in more than twenty years. She is bringing with her selected costumes, musical scores and other trophies of a glamorous professional life and making them a gift to the Kansas City Museum. The collection, which has been joyfully accepted by the Museum board, not only will represent the distinguished home-town daughter, but also a wonderful period of both comic opera and grand opera on the American stage. The presentation will be made in person...."

Her last gifts go out, almost inevitably, by Nielsen's own initiative.

"Correspondence with respect to the gift was initiated by Miss Nielsen, who has long desired to do something for the city of her girlhood and at the same time have the collection serve to keep her in memory. For several months the singer has been having the collection selected and prepared in her NY apartment...." Her reception is planned by Mrs. Clyde H. Porter chairman, and the museum's "costumes committee", Mrs. Fred Woosley chairman, with cooperation of the Kansas City Music Club.

October 3, *KC Star* recalls Alice as "pupil at St. Teresa's Academy, then at 12th and Washington streets. Sisters at the school recall that Miss Nielsen was the first woman to sing in the old Convention hall, and the former Miss Mary Rose Barrons, also at St. Teresa girl and now Mrs. Harold Furstenau, Ludington MI, was last to sing before the hall closed".

October 15th Nielsen arrives at Hotel Muehlebach: "I never expected to see Kansas City again, but here I am. And am I happy? I haven't been so happy for many a year; I am overjoyed. So far it all seems very real, but nevertheless, it is hard to believe".

As in that concert stop at Columbia SC long long ago, her Kansas City reservations were left unmade: "Helps a lot to be at the Muehlebach, where I used to stop, and to meet Manager Whitmore who always was the kindest of men and now has outdone himself. You see, there was some misunderstanding about the reservation and you know how crowded the hotels are now. Well, somehow Mr. Whitmore found a room for us. I only hope he did not throw out any bishops to accommodate us".

Kansas City Museum accepts "costumes, photographs, music scores and other trophies of her operatic career" at a 2:30pm ceremony Friday. She is "accompanied by Mrs. Frank Murphy of Little Rock, Arkansas, who also was a resident of Kansas City for many years. Mrs. Murphy was Mame Crowley, daughter of William Crowley, a pioneer identified with the Chouteau, Guinotte, and other pioneer families. Mrs. Murphy has assisted Miss Nielsen in preparing her collection for exhibition".

Alice vividly recalls the Bostonians: "One of the great satisfactions of my life is that after leaving Kansas City as a girl with just the beginnings of a musical training, I was able to return as a featured member of the great Bostonian company". Audience went wild. "It was wonderful the way I was received, and the reception seemed to brace me for the whole of my future. I felt secure, and I continued to feel that way, and when the time came to venture into grand opera I did not hesitate for lack of confidence.

"It has been a great satisfaction to have my collection accepted by the Kansas City Museum. I hope it will give my friends and the general public as much pleasure as it has given me to present it. I also shall have several pieces in the Boston museum for I was intimately associated with Boston too, especially in my grand opera years". Does not mention New York.

With typical candor she continues, "It makes me happy, even at times a little sad, to look back to the busy years of my career. My reflections are intensified as I come back to the scenes of my childhood and girlhood. I did have aspirations which I was very young, but I did not think they were rational. I know I did not dream of such good times, such splendid associations as came to be my lot later".

Nielsen, *Star* confides, "has not been well for several months, but has improved much lately. The trip to Kansas City was made with intervals of rest, but she was tired at its completion. Mrs. Murphy, who is a kind of devoted boss for her, says Miss Nielsen must rest for a day or so before she sees much of her friends, for she tires easily".

During the ceremony, local debutants don Alice's stage costumes for a group photo with the diva and sing her songs. For a while, the costumes will be used in local theatre shows. At some point they return to the trunk, forgotten. As an aside, you may be given to know that your author rediscovered Alice after a Manhattan chat with Victor Herbert's agent who recited a request to create a new libretto for the *Fortune Teller* show. Taking the challenge meant discovering why the show had existed. This led to finding Alice; and setting things right.

Here we are. Alice's last return to the sidewalks of Kansas City is portentous, Austin Latchaw notes: "On this homecoming Miss Nielsen will be welcomed by devotees of opera who enjoyed her singing, her triumphs in the old days, and by a generation which knows her only by reputation". She represents the era gone by, a freer time when the best talent created the gayety of nations directly with their audiences. Unreplicated, unrecorded and 'without a net'.

"It will not be the same for her of course, but it will be happy experience and it will give happiness to others. The tangible tokens of her career, with which she honors her city, will represent her to generations to come, and it is to be hoped the possessive 'Our Alice' will not disappear from the future allusions to her". Fine words for fine hopes.

October 15th *KC Star* prints a feature on her career for the new generation of the town. The unsigned article's author has known her since *Chanticleer*. "This time 'Our Alice' does not come by special train, chartered to carry a numerous company and the settings and costumes for an extensive repertoire, as she did when she was prima donna of the Bostonians, the best and most notable light opera organization that ever toured the country.

"She comes as one long retired.... In her apartment in NY there are whole ranks of scrapbooks piled high and a collection of programs, which are almost literally monumental evidence of the fullness of this woman's wonderful career. For the last two years Miss Nielsen with the aid of a few intimate friends, has been delving into these records and old letters to develop the story of Alice Nielsen's life, which it is the singer's hope to have published in the near future".

Seemingly these "whole ranks" of "old letters" vanished.

Her life "included a remarkable career in comic opera, subsequent years in grand opera and a distinctive and impressive career on the concert stage alone. This life brought acclaim to the Kansas City artist in every city, every large town and a great number of one-night stands throughout the country. Miss Nielsen always has held a deep sentimental interest in Kansas City. It was here she spent her childhood. It was here she earned her first little income as a singer. It was here she became ambitious to make a career. It was from here she went out undaunted to challenge the operatic world".

Star assesses her lifetime achievements: "Alice Nielsen's success was earned in the fullest. This singer didn't just happen. She was gifted, and she knew it, gifted in voice, gifted in personality, in dramatic instinct....

"The first time I saw her was when she and a Mrs. Carhart, contralto, came to my office in the old *Times* building, Ninth and Main streets. Alice, I think, was about sixteen. They asked an announcement of a new opera to be given soon for the first time on any stage, in which both were to appear. It was called *Chanticleer*, music by Mr. Cramer, organist of St. Mary's Episcopal church, and libretto by Mr. Paddock. Mrs. Carhart I knew as a church choir singer, 'but', I asked, 'who is to sing the leading soprano role?'

"'I am', said the light-haired youngster, and she said it with all the assurance of a seasoned trouper. She did sing the part and with unexpected credit to herself, but the opera was never heard of again.

"Before that, Nielsen had sung at the Music Hall on Broadway in *Beggar Student*, put on by Max Desci, then a popular and successful teacher and coach. She also sung a part in *Pinafore* and briefly joined a comic opera company doing small towns in Missouri and Kansas, as I remember it".

So at last, a small confirmation of her earliest pro gig.

Of course he retraces her career. Loss to America seemed incalculable when Nielsen skipped over to Italy; none could compare with the gayety she had brought the nation. "Even now, while the wisdom and inevitability of her advent in grand opera are recognized, there are thousands who bitterly lament the loss to operetta of a star whose like will not be seen again. Other gifted singers will appear. Audiences will applaud, and critics lavish praise. But others will recall the incomparable freshness and charm of the voice, the simplicity, archness, humor, the sentiment which never degenerated into foolishness or pathos, and they will say, 'But I heard Alice Nielsen in that part.'"

He notes Caruso who also debuted at Bellini, was paid 16 francs "less than the impetuous young American from Nashville, Tennessee".

In Italy, "she became the subject of a perfect furor of enthusiasm of the kind which only Italians can bestow on artists whom they adore. A sister of Henry Higgins told her brother, and Nielsen was cast for her London debut in *Don Giovanni*. The *Court Journal* said 'her undoubted triumph was the more acceptable because she is an English artist.' In the first Fall season of opera Covent Garden ever had, Miss Nielsen sang the part of Micaela for the first time with Enrico Caruso, who then made his first appearance of Jose in *Carmen*. She was the Mimi for his Rodolfo. Of her Nedda in *Pagliacci*, the *London Daily Graphic*, in a later season [July 21, 1913] said, "Miss Alice Nielsen was perhaps the best Nedda Convent Garden has seen".

Her Nordica association, rightly confirms *Star*, had formed the Boston Opera house. And he closes: "Miss Nielsen thus stands today, an artist with all the magnetism and enthusiasm of her beginnings, and with the reopened authority and individuality of one who has felt, reflected and embodied in her expression the knowledge of life richly lived", he closes.

Such a career so well described. If ever an artist appreciated at home, sweet home: Alice Nielsen. Over decades faded; lost to us. Rediscovered by this author who tracked the costume trunk down from its storage, sixty years or so later in 2005, Alice Nielsen's parting gift of her costumes has been inventoried by Kansas City Museum. Includes pieces from all companies of her career: the Bostonian's *Serenade,* Nielsen Company's *Fortune Teller* and *Singing Girl*, and opera costumes from *Don Pasquale, Madame Butterfly, La Bohème, Figaro, Faust, L'Amico Fritz and Carmen.*

Her *Fortune Teller* costume has "red wool jacket with white rabbit fur trim, the jacket is open down center front...fur around collar, cuffs, front opening and hem. The jacket is decorated with gold braid trim down sleeves, both sides of front opening and down center back", lined with white polished cotton. This goes with "red knit tights made of a silk and wool blend" and "thigh-high red kid-leather boots with 1-5/8 inch, covered, knock-on heels". Her stage sword brandished at Eugene Cowles was already an antique about forty years when the show opened. No prop, she held a real sword.

And gorgeous kimonos for *Madame Butterfly*. One, of "beige silk, brocaded with floral pattern, embroidered with roosters and butterflies" and lined with red silk appears in 1898 photographs of Alice Nielsen in Yokohama. Josef Urban used these to as palette for set designs at Boston.

Alice Nielsen returns to Manhattan after presenting her stage wardrobe to the ceremonial appreciation of Kansas City. Slowly fades. Leaves the Osborn for two quiet years at a private nursing home 65 E. 96th supported by friends and family. Legal guardian, entertainment attorney Georges Baptiste.

On March 8, 1943, Alice Nielsen would be called away.

A Spirit Flower (Martin Stanton, Campbell-Tipton)
AS SUNG BY ALICE NIELSEN

My heart was frozen, even as the earth
That covered thee forever from my sight.
All thoughts of happiness expired at birth;
Within me naught but black and starless night.
Down through the winter sunshine snowflakes came,
All shimm'ring, like to silver butterflies:
They seemed to whisper softly thy dear name;
They melted with the teardrops from mine eyes.
But suddenly there bloomed, within that hour,
In my poor heart, so seeming dead, a flower!
Whose fragrance in my life shall ever be
The tender, sacred memory of thee.

AFTER

Alice Nielsen's funeral is held at St. Paul's Church, near today's Lincoln Center, her Mass led by Rev. Joseph Malloy "who visited Miss Nielsen in her home at 201 W 57th Street in the early days of her illness. The actress was a member of the parish of St. Paul the Apostle". Choir sings *Oh Paradise*, organist plays *Lead, Kindly Light*.

"That the singer belonged to another era was evident when one hundred persons gathered for the services. Among those scattered through the large church yesterday were actors and actresses of Miss Nielsen's day", reports *NY Times*. Present are actress Nellie Brunton, actor Charles Payton, critic Will Gentz, and Nielsen's longtime secretary Mrs. CP Stickle. Her son Benjamin, his wife, and sister-in-law, attend from Boston. Friends who cared for Miss Nielsen during her illness include Mrs. Tyra Louden, Mrs. Helen Spencer, Mrs. Zoe Buckely the features writer, and Mrs. Irene Buchell, "Mrs. Nielsen's negro maid for twenty-five years".

Her funeral holds a mystery. As Mass closes, a man unknown to family or friends approaches coffin, genuflects, places red carnation and leaves.

Alice Nielsen is buried in her brother's cemetery at St. Mary's Star of The Sea of Far Rockaway, the plot a few miles north in Lawrence.

Her passing is noted by every region of the nation.

Kansas City Times: "Alice Nielsen meant a great deal to American music. She was a heart's delight to the devotees of operatic music, especially when she was a light opera prima donna. Her story, her voice, her joyous spirit have lingered in the memories of many, many thousands who shared unforgettable happiness with her".

NY Times: Of her work as Mimi and Butterfly, "Puccini was said to have been so impressed with her performance that he asked her opinion on the score. Later he made revisions in the score...."

Washington Post: "Alice Nielsen...former soprano star of the Metropolitan Opera who sang with the late Enrico Caruso...was a native of Nashville, Tenn. Miss Nielsen achieved about every triumph to which a popular singer could aspire. So important as a singer was she that Victor Herbert announced that he had written *Fortune Teller* and two other operettas especially for her. The others were *Serenade* and *Singing Girl*, the latter a score he said was ideal for her temperament". Even forty years after the terrible text takes a beating: "The author however placed the story and music in a German setting although there was nothing Germanic about Miss Nielsen's temperament. The singer repeated her triumph in *The Fortune Teller* in 1901 in London, where she was received with acclaim and Herbert's score was highly praised by the critics.

"Miss Nielsen began her public career as a street singer in Kansas City when she was only 7 years old. When she advanced from the sidewalks to the stage, she achieved one triumph after another. She made her London debut with Caruso in *Don Giovanni* and she was a triumph there, and all through the capitals of Europe, including the opera centers of Italy. In Rome she became a protégé of the immortal Duse...after many successful engagements in grand opera in England and Italy she returned to NY and made her debut at the Metropolitan Opera as Mimi in *La Bohème* in 1909".

Curiously, within two weeks of Alice's funeral LeRoy Stoddard is found dead at Baltimore's Emerson Hotel. A medical friend, EG Miller was summoned and "attributed death to natural causes". Stoddard's obit paragraph in *NY Times* mentions only his surgical repair of vets and a 13-year marriage to Nielsen.

1944, the wonderful Maine cottage sold by her estate. Ida Velerga dies.

1945, Hortense Nielsen passes away during a trip to Providence RI.

1946, October 26th. Plaza Art Gallery at 59th Street NYC sells the estate goods of Alice Nielsen: oriental rugs, silver, jewelry, furniture, and artwork.

1948, Nielsen's co-star Eugene Cowles dies September 23 in Boston.

1974, Alice Nielsen's son Bennie dies, July 6 in Needham MA. No mention of his long collaboration with theatre designer Josef Urban. April Asquith at the Needham Free Library supplied the *Daily Transcript* obit: "Benjamin Nielsen [misspelled Neilsen], retired draftsman. Funeral services will be held on Saturday for Benjamin T. Nielsen 84.... Born in Kansas City MO, he was a Needham resident for 51 years. He was a retired draftsman for the US Corps of Engineers".

Today the Mitchells' family resemblance to Alice Nielsen is unmistakable. The author had a glad moment meeting her grandson, hearing stories, seeing him hold up that 1898 *Telegraph* front page featuring only Alice Nielsen.

Intriguing trail. Your author rediscovered the singer when working in Reykjavik to create new words to Victor Herbert's "favorite score" composed for her company. Herbert's surviving agent passed along Herbert's requirements for the new show, now based on return of 1898 Alice Nielsen Company to Wallack's Theatre opening night when Alice told us she was possessed by music. After Alice's passing she became lost to us. Divas may be difficult taskmasters; none more than they hold themselves. Rediscovery of Alice Nielsen has added greatly to the gayety of the author, delighted to spend time with the unforgettable diva. Live theatre was the biggest nighttime sport and among the biggest industries. Touring stars brought the best talent into every theatre town. Acquiring cumulative experience, audiences grew seasoned and savvy. Music was an integral part of community life. Parlors and porches were a place to sing and play together. Before broadcasts, we had to make all the music.

Alice Nielsen's saga is art versus evil.

Boston Opera sinks in corruption writ large. Over in Bethlehem, Pennsylvania, a bronze tablet tells the story: after the arms bubble, the war. Most small American towns have a sad stone memorial to list the foreign war (loan) dead. How does a diva face the horrors of losing her beloved audiences who cheer and applaud? Popular hit song was, *I Didn't Raise My Boy To Be A Soldier*. It didn't have to be.

Alice's friend and patron Florence Phillips' speaks wisely in her brilliant 1913 *A Friendly Germany, Why Not?* Demands "new trains of thought and to put a new point of view" to counter "alarmist reports...war between Great Britain and Germany is inevitable and impending.... For the sake of Western civilization in particular and of the world in general, it is desirable that the two countries should be united by a close bond of friendship, and essential that they should not be parted by an artificial agitation...." Phillips warns against being "hypnotized by some morning paper". No "foreign situation... makes it inevitable that we and the Germans should put back the work of civilization by centuries" to "destroy one another on British or Continental soil".

As with Boston Opera, wisest of women were excluded. Speaking from the last year of peace, Phillips tells us, "I feel deeply the wickedness of what is being prepared".

American suffragettes believed women would stop war, given a vote.

Margaret Mitchell in *Gone With The Wind* has Scarlett say, "Most of the misery of the world has been caused by wars".

The gayety of nations aligns with Epictetus: Speak freely, enslave none, and enjoy the great festival of life with all. And with Bohemian church bishop Jan Komensky: let things spontaneously flow, without violence. So it is. Treasure the traditions of virtuoso fun.

HORTENSE & ALICE NIELSEN

ACKNOWLEDGEMENTS

For this 2023 Edition, Anna Jelen. This edition corrects, clarifies and condenses the earlier text. Wish the book had always been this one. And the shorter text allows redesign for better readability.

My grandfather, conductor, singer and master musician in Moravian Winston-Salem and Raleigh, introduced me to Victor Herbert's music. Herbert's agent Jacoby, also handling Charlie Chaplin and Eugene O'Neil, suggested the mission to "throw away all the words" to Herbert's 1898 score. My project became a new musical based on a fascinating original cast who had improvised their way to a success whose exact content is lost to us. Creating the libretto in Reykjavik, I received 1900s Alice Nielsen Company deluxe program from Michigan's John Guidinger. Nielsen's biography arose from my discovery that this great woman had been lost in an icy fog of lies. She was supremely popular as an icon of artistic integrity and talent. Story untold. Only I would try. Do what only you can do, said Boston's Josiah Royce; brilliant fan of magnetic melody as a singer sings.

Pulling Alice Nielsen from shadows took energy and original research.

As a result of my research, three costar biographies have been created. Most significant has been Konrado Mugertza's new biography of Constantino. Contact from Svein Henrik Nyhus resulted in correcting and expanding the Hortense Nielsen saga.

The author thanks NYC's Library of Performing Arts, NYC Public Library, *Mu Phi Epsilon*, NY City Museum Theatre Collection, Harvard Theatre Library, Boston Public Library, Bedford Historical Assoc., Kansas City Museum, Kansas City Public Library, Harrison ME Historical Society, Metropolitan Opera, New Orleans Opera Association, University of Texas—Austin, University of California—Berkley, British Museum, University of Iowa Chautauqua collection, NYU's Irish House, Library of Congress, Museum of Performance and Design in San Francisco, and Ringling Museum, among others. Internet literary services gave access to vintage books, newspapers and magazines.

My previous 1900s-era readings helped cope with the elaborate and innovative literary styles of a freer age of sovereign citizens who pursued happiness by cooperation. Huntington Cairns and others familiar with the 1900s cultural mind helped me appreciate this era long before I knew Nielsen existed. Grandfather would have heard her perform on tour; and started the classical concert series in his town which still operates. He was a professional singer and conductor with a radio show.

Children and grandchildren of Nielsen-era stars helped. I enjoy exchanges with, say, Stefanie Walzinger, granddaughter of Nielsen co-star Bertha Walzinger; Bud Toye; David Lepitre from Eugene Cowles' hometown of Stanstead-Derby Line in Quebec and Vermont. Alice's family in this generation, David Mitchell and father graciously gave time to talk. Spike Jones' grandson and countless people across the globe responded to queries. Others did not. For Danish translations, thanks Jonna Knudsen, for Italian, Bergamo's Paolo Sergi. Author translated Spanish, French, German. Lastly, NYC Lambs Club and The Players Club resonate with 1890s theatre and the author enjoys both.

Restoration of Alice Nielsen's historical recordings 1898-1928 was funded by author from original disks or cylinders. These and other projects are available online.

Coffee shops have replaced the tavern as a writer's studio. NYC's Think Coffee tolerated many hours. In Reykjavik, Mokka, Café Paris. In Barcelona, Café Opera. In Venice, Florian. In Paris, anyplace. In Raleigh, Cup-A-Joe, Raleigh Times, Second Place. In Atlanta, Press and Grind. In Black Mtn, the Dripolator. In Saint Augustine, Kookaburra. In Sioux Falls, Josiah's. In Sundance Wyoming, Wild West Expresso. In Spearfish SD, Blackbird Expresso and Leones' Creamery. In Yankton SD, Muddy Mo's. For regional ice cream suggestions contact the author.

This biography grew iteratively. Style suits the time told of. This is a practical piece to enlighten not any mere academic exercise. The author's accuracy and discovery revised Grove and other standard music histories.

As a result the effort is self-financed. A commercial publisher wished about one-quarter the length. The story seemed too obscure to capture in a few words at that time. My multi-media presentation of course is only about forty minutes jam-packed with images and musical selections.

Support for this project is welcome. PayPal: dallwilson@yahoo.com

This story should be available in schools, libraries, and archives as an important piece of musical culture. And as a lesson worth learning.

Youtube channel https://youtube.com/@dallwilson has the playlist *Alice Nielsen and the Gayety of Nations* with many recordings and other pieces by Alice, costars, talented friends, composers she knew and sang.

IMAGES

Alice Nielsen opening in *The Fortune Teller* 1898

LeRoy Stoddard and Alice Nielsen in the 1920s. Nielsen in 1917 as Kitty.

Clara and Henry Barnabee 1890s

Constantino 1910s

Henry Russell 1910s

Laurence Irving 1900s

Victor Herbert 1890s

Eugene Cowles 1900

Joseph Cawthorn 1900

Paul Steindorff 1890s

FINAL ACT FROM "THE SINGING GIRL."

Boston Opera House: Alice Nielsen in Converse's *The Sacrifice* 1910

Boston Opera House: Alice Nielsen in *Don Pasquale* 1909

Alice Nielsen Company: L to R, Joe Cawthorn, Eugene Cowles,
Marguarite Sylve, Alice Nielsen

The Fortune Teller

Alice Nielsen family in Harrison ME cottage 1930s.

Alice's Grandson 2009

Alice in Boston 1920s

Son Benjamin and Alice in 1910 and 1940

Alice Nielsen 1890s   John McCormack and Nielsen in *Punch*

The Famous Original Bostonians

From Photo by Prince.

THE BOSTONIANS.

1. HENRY CLAY BARNABEE. 4. EUGENE COWLES   8. JOSEPHINE BARTLETT. 12. T. KELLEY COLE.   16. HARRY BROWN.
2. JESSIE BARTLETT DAVIS. 5. GEORGE FROTHINGHAM. 9. WILLIAM E. PHILP.   13. G. E. LAUDIE.   17. HARRY C. DIXON.
3. W. H. MACDONALD,   6. HILDA CLARK.   10. CHARLES R. HAWLEY. 14. GRACIE QUIVE.   18. L. R. MERRILL.
                          7. ALICE NEILSEN.   11. R. H. BURNSIDE.   15. MARIE VON DRESSER.

Alice Nielsen and Eugene Cowles

Marguerite Sylva and Alice Nielsen

Alice Nielsen onstage

Alice Nielsen as Drogan in Geneviève de Brabant

Nielsen and Geraldina White 1890s

Arthur Pryor and Alice Nielsen in the 1900s

L-R: Ethyl Barrymore, Nielsen, Nordica,
Lillian Russell, Marie Dressler (2x), Duse

Alice Nielsen *The Fortune Teller 1898*   *1896 The Serenade*

Alice Nielsen

Hortense Nielsen

Loie Fuller

690

Alice Nielsen and Nordica in San Francisco 1907

Alice Nielsen 1900

Burton Stanley 1880s

Miss Ida Valerga, Who May Join Colonel Mapleson's Company.

Consuelo Yznaga   Christina Nilsson   Ida Valerga

Addison Dashiell Madeira   Alice Nielsen   Hortense Nielsen

Bevignani   Tosti   Florence Phillips

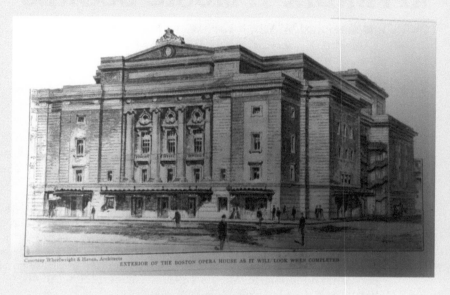

Courtesy Wheelwright & Haven, Architects
EXTERIOR OF THE BOSTON OPERA HOUSE AS IT WILL LOOK WHEN COMPLETED

The Boston Opera House

APPENDIX 1. MUSIC SCORES

Owned and annotated by Alice Nielsen at the Kansas City Library:

- *Il Maestro Di Cappella*, parole di Sofia Gay, Music Ferdinando Paer, published in Milano 1896. Features Barnaba (basso comico), Benetto (tenore), Geltrude (Soprano).
- Guiseppe Verdi (1813-1901). *Don Carlo*, opera. Opera completa per canto e pianoforte. By G. Riordi & company, Italy. Agent (Boosey & Co. 9 East 17th St NY. Elisabetta di Valois.
- Max Bruch (1838-1920) *Frithoif*, Scenes from Esaias Tegner's Frithoif-Saga. Schirmer, NY.
- Alexander Mackenzie Campbell 1847-1935, *The Dream Of Jubal* Op 41. (Jubal is 'father of all who handle the harp and pipe.' The father of music. A chorus of praise, a song of comfort, a patriotic march, a harvest song, a funeral march, a duet of lovers.
- Claude Debussy 1862-1918. *L'enfant prodigue*; scene lyrique de E. 1908. Has "Alice Nielsen created Lia at Boston Opera House" in Alice's handwriting.
- Ferdinando Paer (1771-1839). *Il maestro di cappela*; comic opera in un. *Parole di Sofia Gay*, musica di Ferdinando Paer. Riduzione per Canto e Pianoforte. Milano 1896. E. Ascherbert & Co. 46, Berners St.
- Ermanno Wolf-Ferrari (1876-1948). *The new life*, a cantata based on Dante's text c1902. Alice Nielsen 1904 (signed). English version by Percy Pinkerton. Printed 1902 D. Rahter, Leipzig.
- Alexander von Fielitz (1860-1930) *Eliland* : ein Sang om Chiemsee c1896. Breitkopf & Hartel Leipzig-London-NY. English & German text.
- Pauline Viardot-Garcia (1821-1910) *An hour of study*; exercises for the medium of the voice. Adopted by the Paris National Conservatory of Music. Signed "Alice Nielsen, New York -1899". NY G. Schirmer 1897.
- *Les Contes D'Hoffmann*, words Jules Barbier, Musique de J. Offenbach. Partition Chant et Piano. Paris. C Houdens 1907.
- *Don Carlo*, words Mery e Camillo Du Locle, musica di Giuseppe Verdi. Opera completa per canto e pianoforte. G Ricordi & C. agents Boosey & Co. 9 E 17th St, NY
- Wolfgang Amadeus Mozart 1756-1791, *Don Giovanni*. G Schirmer NY. Libretto by Lorenzo Da Ponte, Music by Mozart. Vocal score including recitatives. English y Natalie Macfarren. With essay on opera by HE Krehbiel. C1900.
- Jules Massenet 1842-1912. *Manon*. Opera comique. First edition 1895. In Paris A Durand & Fils. 4 Pl de la Madeleine.
- Daniel Francois Esprit, *Fra Diavolo*, opera in 3 acts 1871. Boosey & Co. 295 Regent St London W and 9 E 17th St NY. Edited by Arthur Sullivan and J. Pittman.

APPENDIX 2. DISCOGRAPHY

"From the opening of *The Fortune Teller* in 1898 right through her many successes in grand opera, Nielsen's work was marked by great sincerity and an outstanding ability for sustained song". Performing with the Boston Opera orchestra for the Columbia Recordings, Alice Nielsen recorded as many as nine records I a day. Her big hits: "Home Sweet Home" and "Un bel di".

BERLINER 1898
78/3138 LP-628 *Always Do What People Say You Should* (Herbert)

EDISON RECORDINGS
Song of Sorrow (Herbert)

VICTROLA RED SEAL 1907-1908
64068 Traviata: Addio del passato.
64091 Romeo: Ne fuis pas (w. Constantino)
74062 Bohème: Mi chiamano Mimi.
74063 Rigoletto: E il sol (w. Constantino)
74064 Lucia: Verranno a te (w. Consantino)
74074 Barber of Seville: Una voce poco fa.
74075 Traviata: Pargi o cara (w. Constantino)　(8035)
74076 Faust: Dammi ancor (w. Constantino)　(8035)
74087 Don Pasquale: Quel guardo
74107 Il Bacio (Arditi)　(6228)
74108 Romeo: Ange adorable (w. Constantino)
74117 Daughter of the Regiment: Convie partir
74121 Martha: Last Rose Of Summer　(6228)

COLUMBIA RECORDS 1911-1915
19734 Sweet Adeline (Armstrong)	(A1143)	(54M)
19735 Darline Nelly Gray (Hanby)	(A1143)	(54M)
30579 Martha: Last Rose of Summer	(A5283)	
30580 Old Folks At Home (Foster)	(A5299)	
30581 Marriage of Figaro: voi che sapete	(H1085)	
30582 Bonnie Sweet Bessie (Gilbert)	(A5299)	
30583 Don Giovanni (Batti, Batti)	(A5249)	
30585 My Laddie (Thayer)	(A5401)	
30586 Marriage of Figaro: Deh vieni	(A5249)	
30587 Faust: Le Roi de Thule	(A5247)	
30588 Annie Laurie (Scott)	(A5245)	(A6201)
30589 Kathleen Mavourneen (Crouch)	(A5245)	(A6201)
From the Land of the Sky-Blue Water(Cadman)	(A5298)	
The Sacrifice: Chonita's Prayer	(A5298)	
30591 Homes, Sweet Home (Bishop)	(A5283)	
30592 Il Bacio (Arditi)	(A5246)	
30593 Mme. Butterfly: Ancora un passo.	(A5248)	
30594 Mme. Butterfly: Piccolo Iddio.	(A5300)	
30595 Mme. Butterfly: Un bel di.	(A5250)	

30596 Bohème: Addio   (A5246)
30597 Mefistofele: L'altra notte.   (A5248)
30598 Tosca: Vissi d'arte.   (A5248)
30599 Carmen: Je dis que rien.   (A5247)
30728 Mme. Butterfly: Ieri son salita   (A5300)
30729 Good Bye (Tosti)   (A5401)
30737 Rigoletto: Si vendetta (w. Blanchart)   (A5301)
30738 Rigoletto: Tutte le feste (w. Blanchart)   (A5301)
30924 Faust: Tardi si fa (w. Zenatello)   (H1073)
30927 Sweet Genevieve (Cooper)   (A5425)
30941 In the Gloaming (Harrison)   (A5425)
37172 Oh, I'm not Myself (Lover)   (A5669)
37173 Believe Me If All Those
             Endearing Young Charms   (A5678)
37174 Love's Old Sweet Song (Molloy)   (A5670)
37178 Bendemeer's Stream (Gatty)   (A5670)
37179 Day Is Done (Spross)   (A5717)
37180 Spirit Flower (Tipton)   (A5717)
37184 Old Black Joe (Foster)   (A5678)
37202 Low Back'd Car (Lover)   (A5669)
37203 Killarney (Balfe)   (A5711)
37206 Barney O'Hea (Lover)   (A5711)
39874 By the Waters of Minnetonka (Lieurance) (A1732)
39875 From the Land of the Sky-Blue Water
             (Cadman)   A1732)

COLUMBIA RECORDS 1924
81648 A Little Coon's Prayer (Hope) (w. Qt)   (30007D)
81649 Nebber Min' Mah Honey (Riker) (w. Qt)   (30007D)